DAY BY DAY

The Thirties

Rodney P. Carlisle, Ph.D.

General Editor

Facts On File, Inc.

Day by Day: The Thirties

Facts On File, Inc.
An imprint of Infobase Publishing
132 West 31st Street
New York, NY 10001

Library of Congress Cataloging-in-Publication Data

Day by day : the 1930s / Rodney P. Carlisle, general editor.
    p. cm.
 Includes bibliographical references and index.
 ISBN 0-8160-6664-7 (alk. paper)
 1. Nineteen thirties-Chronology. I. Carlisle, Rodney P. II. Title: 1930s.
 D723.D39 2006
 909.82'30202-dc22

                        2006017697

Facts On File books are available at special discounts when purchased in bulk quantities for businesses, associations, institutions, or sales promotions. Please call our Special Sales Department in New York at (212) 967-8800 or (800) 322-8755.

You can find Facts On File on the World Wide Web at http://www.factsonfile.com

Golson Books, Ltd.

President and Editor	J. Geoffrey Golson
General Editor, The 1930s	Rodney P. Carlisle
Authors, The 1930s	John Barnhill, Joseph Geringer, Kevin G. Golson, Vickey Kalambakal, Pat McCarthy, Luca Prono, Kelly Boyer Sagert
Design Director	Mary Jo Scibetta
Layout Production	Kenneth W. Heller
Copy Editor	Jennifer L. Wallace
Proofreader	Barbara Paris
Indexer	Gail Liss

Photo Credits
Library of Congress: 1930 pages 4–5; 1931 pages 120–121; 1932 pages 232–233: 1933 pages 310–311; 1936 pages 568–569. National Archives and Records Administration: 1934 pages 384–385; 1937 pages 678–679: 1938; pages 814–815; 1939 pages 914–915. National Oceanic and Atmospheric Administration: 1935 pages 486–487.

Printed in the United States of America

10 9 8 7 6 5 4 3 2 1

This book is printed on acid-free paper.

CONTENTS

DAY BY DAY

The Thirties

VOLUME 1
1930 - 1935

INTRODUCTION

The decade of the 1930s was one of crises for the United States and the world. Day by day throughout the decade, headlines screamed forth not only with the usual round of crime, catastrophe, and celebrity misdeeds, but also revealed deeper and more troubling developments. Beginning with the stock market crash of October 1929, the nation's economy and that of nearly the whole world spiraled into the Great Depression, with tens of millions unemployed, factories closed, farm surpluses driving down food prices, and personal fortunes destroyed. In the world of international affairs, the long, drawn-out consequences of the Versailles Treaty that had marked the end of World War I (1914–18) resulted in bitter border and territorial conflicts and deep hostilities that seemed to lead the march toward another world war.

The Soviet Union, which had emerged from the Bolshevik Revolution in Russia during World War I, adopted a policy of spreading its doctrine through control and influence over Communist parties abroad. Fascist regimes in Europe imposed totalitarian one-party control, first in Italy, then in Germany, Portugal, and Spain. These states differed from the Soviet state in that they left most businesses and corporations in private hands, but regulated and controlled those enterprises in the interest of a militaristic, nationalistic state. Using demagogic appeals, the fascist states appealed to domestic conservatives, claiming that their policies represented a bulwark against the expansion of Communism and the threat of expropriation of private property. The broader masses followed fascistic leaders because of their appeals to national pride, racial chauvinism, or uglier emotions of revenge, hatred, or prejudice.

These three driving forces: economic crisis, revisionism or "revanchism" regarding the Versailles Treaty, and the strident appeals of Communist and fascist dogmas shaped the events of the decade. The interaction of these driving forces lay behind many of the day-to-day headlines, weaving through the decade in twisted strands.

In the United States and in some of the democracies of Europe, the principle of emergency state control of the economy to offset the effects of the Great Depression held great appeal. In the United States, a variety of methods to address the economic crisis were attempted by President Herbert Hoover in the period 1930–32, including regulating the bank lending rate through the operation of the Federal Reserve system and through a limited program of public works. More aggressive policies came during the development of the New Deal, headed by President Franklin Roosevelt after his inauguration in March 1933. At first, his administration devoted its efforts to relief and recovery. In 1935, he attempted to turn the policies toward economic regulation, reform, social security, and more lasting approaches to managing the economy. Some New Deal measures struck extreme conservatives as leaning toward socialism. That reaction was viewed by many defenders of the New Deal as itself a reactionary dalliance with fascism. The debate in the United States soon took on an ideological flavor, with the terms "left" and "right" characterizing the language and discourse in ways that had not come up in prior decades. Not surprisingly, the ideological tone and language was applied to regimes elsewhere in the world. In Latin America, Getúlio Vargas in Brazil was called fascistic by his opponents; in Mexico, Lázaro Cárdenas was called a "Communist" or a "Red" by his enemies. Although the policies of each had echoes of the distant ideological conflict in Europe, the terms were more in the nature of political slander than accurate analyses of the leaders' positions.

In Europe, Germany and Italy were both dissatisfied, for very different reasons, with the boundary and reparations settlements reached at Versailles. Germany believed the reparations that had to be paid to the British and French were excessive. Furthermore, the payment of reparations implied that all the guilt of World War I should be placed on the shoulders of the German people. Another grievance derived from the issue of self-determination. Although the right of self-determination on ethnic grounds had been one of Woodrow Wilson's Fourteen Points, and supposedly the basis for redrawing the map of Europe in 1919, certain limitations in the Treaty of Versailles appeared to deny that principle or right to German-speaking peoples. Under the treaty, German-speaking Austria, formerly at the core of the Austro-Hungarian Empire, was not allowed to unite with Germany. German majorities in the cities of Danzig and Memel on the Baltic Sea were placed under foreign jurisdictions, with German Danzigers in a free city associated with Poland, and Memel under Lithuanian jurisdiction. The German Rhineland was to be occupied by France into the mid-1930s, and if the region voted to rejoin Germany, it was not to be militarized. With these territorial grievances, coupled with economic woes that could, rightly or wrongly, be attributed to the policies of the victorious Allies in World War I, conditions were ripe for a demagogic, nationalistic appeal by Adolf Hitler and his National Socialist (Nazi) Party.

Italy was distressed for very different reasons. In order to win over Italy as an ally in World War I, Britain had promised to support Italian claims, not only to the Italian-speaking regions of the Tyrol, but to the port of Fiume and to other territories in what became Yugoslavia. At the same time, Serbia had been promised support in establishing the South Slav state. Italians believed that they had been betrayed at Versailles, both by Woodrow Wilson and by David Lloyd George, the British representative. Furthermore, while both France and Britain expanded their control over territories in Africa with the seizure of German colonies to be administered as League of Nations mandates, Italy was given no such compensation for its participation. From these vexations, Benito Mussolini, in the mid-1920s, had secured control of the Italian state under his Fascist Party. In the 1930s, he sought to address these grievances by seizing land from the one remaining independent African country in eastern Africa, Abyssinia (or as it came to be called, Ethiopia). Italy's policy of autarky, or aspiration to economic self-sufficiency, and its adoption of a policy of forced cooperation between labor and management under state control also characterized the Fascist policies.

In the Far East, another ally of Britain and France in World War I, Japan, had reason to be distressed at the resolution of boundaries and reparations at Versailles. Japan had expected to acquire German holdings in the Far East as the price of participating with the Allies. Instead, Japan was allowed only a temporary hold on the Shantung Peninsula where Germany had held a long lease, and Japan received a mandate over German islands north of the equator in the Pacific, with a prohibition against arming or otherwise developing the islands as military resources. As Japan interpreted self-determination, Asian peoples should be governed by Asians, not Europeans, and militaristic Japanese leaders expected that their nation should replace Europeans in controlling spheres of influence in China and the colonies held by Europeans in Southeast Asia, which included French Indo-China, British Malaya, Hong Kong and Sarawak, the Dutch East Indies, and possibly other foreign holdings including the U.S.-controlled Philippines and some of the

Pacific and Indonesian archipelagoes held by Australia. Evidence of Japanese ambitions surfaced as early as 1930, when Japan attended a London disarmament conference focusing on warship construction and demanded a greater degree of parity with European powers.

Inevitably, the three militaristic, revanchist powers gravitated toward each other, all opposing the British and French dominance of the colonial world and their influence in Europe. However, Britain, France, and the United States, although they shared some geopolitical interests and hoped to maintain the status quo established after Versailles, could not readily stand together. France was more concerned with a German threat, the United States remained isolationist, and Britain hoped to keep the peace by admitting to some of the validity of the revanchist grievances and by offering compromises to appease the discontented powers. Russia stood aside, consolidating its own totalitarian state under Josef Stalin and hoping to build worldwide support through its control of the international Communist Party.

In the Spanish civil war that broke out in 1936, Russia and Mexico supported the democratic and socialist regime; Italy and Germany supported the fascist/military regime. Britain, France, other European powers, and the United States took a course of neutrality toward the conflict in Spain. At the time, with the use of aircraft and some tanks in the first major European conflict since the early 1920s, the Spanish civil war was viewed as a kind of dress rehearsal for a possible World War II. Meanwhile, Italy expanded its holdings in Africa and eventually in Albania, and Germany extended its control in the Rhineland, Memel, Danzig, Austria, and Czechoslovakia. Japan expanded in Manchuria and then north China, and after 1937 into central China. Furthermore, in defiance of the League of Nations, Japan fortified its mandated islands. Clearly, Japan eyed the colonies still held by Europe. By the summer of 1939, it was clear that

the world was on the verge of World War II, which indeed began in Europe on September 1, 1939, when Germany invaded Poland.

While these international crises brewed through the decade of the 1930s, American domestic politics reflected the crosscurrents of financial crisis and ideological conflict that swept the rest of the world. As the day-by-day events within America unfolded in these years, many of them carried echoes, some clear, some distorted by distance and culture, of the world developments.

In 1930, with the effects of the stock market crash the previous October still being interpreted, the administration of Herbert Hoover moved quietly, quite in accord with the pro-business, hands-off policies of his two predecessors, Warren Harding and Calvin Coolidge. The worsening economic conditions were rightly viewed as the consequence of almost inevitable economic cycles. However, several factors tended to accentuate the effects of the crash and depression. First, the United States had been through a period of stock market and real estate inflation that brought a disproportionate prosperity to the wealthiest classes. While productivity climbed with new capital investment in equipment, real wages for industrial workers increased by a much lower percentage. Then, on the international scene, Germany had been unable to make its scheduled reparations payments to Britain and France, and those two countries had indicated that they would be unable to make their own scheduled payments on international loans from the United States that had been incurred during World War I unless Germany continued to make its payments. The solution to that impasse had come with a reduced reparations payment schedule and with heavy American investment in the German economy. In effect, American investors sent capital into Germany in the late 1920s, Germany stabilized and was able to make reparations payments, and the British and French made their loan payments. However, by 1930–31, there were signs that this circular arrangement would break down, especially since the stock market crash had reduced the capital available from American investors. With the payment cycle cut off at its origin, Germany stopped reparations payments, and soon the Allied nations owing war debts announced that they would need a moratorium or forgiveness on their payments to the United States.

With the drying up of capital in the United States along with unemployed consumers cutting back on purchases, the cycle of deflation, unemployment, and business closure accelerated. Herbert Hoover had few tools at his disposal to deal with the emergency. The Federal Reserve system reduced its interest rates, hoping to stimulate the economy, as did central banks in Europe. However, the conditions were too severe to be addressed by such tweaking of available credit rates. The Reconstruction Finance Corporation (RFC), established under the Hoover administration on February 2, 1932, began to provide direct loans to businesses and lending institutions from a $2.5 billion fund in order to increase production. Hoover also expanded federal construction projects that would employ workers on power and reclamation projects. However, Hoover and his supporters believed that such measures had to be taken with a balanced federal budget. For the federal government to go into debt at a time of crisis seemed particularly unwise. Despite the advice of economists like John Maynard Keynes, who suggested that increased deficit spending could help the whole economy expand and soon take up the slack created by the Great Depression, Republicans and Democrats alike continued to believe that a balanced budget and even reduced budgets were the best medicine for the nation's woes. In the eyes of Keynes and others, it seemed obvious that such policies were counter-productive. Although government leaders expected that a hands-off attitude toward business was the best policy, recovery seemed increasingly far away through 1931, 1932, and 1933.

Despite Hoover's best efforts, many of his actions and responses provided fuel for his opponents. A crisis developed in July 1932, when World War I veterans marched to Washington in a "Bonus Army." They sought payment of a promised bonus for veterans that took the form of adjusted compensation certificates, which were not scheduled to mature and be redeemable for several more years. When the Bonus Expeditionary Force received no satisfaction, some 17,000 camped on open ground along the Anacostia River in Washington. Frustrated at the continuing presence of the protesters, and amid rumors that Communists had infiltrated their ranks, Hoover ordered the Army to disperse them. On July 28, 1932, infantry, cavalry, and tanks, under the command of General Douglas MacArthur, rolled over the tent city and dispersed the demonstrators. The sight of U.S. troops marching on U.S. veterans did little for the reputations of either Hoover or MacArthur.

Under such conditions, it seemed apparent that popular discontent would turn against a second term for Hoover in the elections of 1932, and that the Democrats would easily take the White House and perhaps both houses of Congress. For this reason, the nominating convention held that summer in Chicago for the Democratic Party was particularly contentious. Al Smith, a Catholic and a former governor of New York as well as the losing presidential candidate in the 1928 election, hoped to win the nomination again. Franklin Roosevelt, who had run as a Democratic Party nominee for the vice presidency in 1920, had been stricken with polio in the early 1920s. Despite his handicap, which he and his advisers were careful to conceal from photographers and newsmen, Roosevelt had won the governorship of New York and had served in that post since 1928. Popular, likable, and genteel, and with the support of the reform wing of the Democratic Party, he had widespread support. John Nance Garner, a favorite-son nominee from Texas, had won the endorsement of newspaper magnate William Randolph

Hearst, and with Hearst's support, Garner entered the convention with delegates not only from Texas, but from California as well. After deadlocks on the first two ballots, Garner released his delegates to support Roosevelt, who won the nomination on the fourth ballot taken June 30, 1932. Hearst refused to deny rumors that he had helped arrange the deal, which included Roosevelt choosing Garner as his vice presidential candidate. Roosevelt won the election in November 1932, and Democrats took control of both houses of Congress as predicted.

With Hoover defeated but still in office from November 1932 through early March 1933, the government and economy drifted. In vain, Hoover sought to work out a transition plan with Roosevelt that would avert a crisis as banks began to fail that winter. Roosevelt, not wanting to be associated with any of the failures of the Hoover administration, refused, and Hoover resented the failure to cooperate for the rest of his life. On the eve of Roosevelt's inauguration, several states had declared "bank holidays" to prevent depositors from conducting runs on the banks to withdraw their accounts. Since banks tended to operate on a cash reserve that was a low proportion of total recorded deposits, such runs and panicky withdrawals simply destroyed banks. Without confidence in the system, the system was inoperative. Thus, on his inauguration, Roosevelt faced an immediate crisis. His reaction was to declare a federal bank holiday, and then, slowly, declare individual banks solvent and reopen them after bank examiners had determined that they were solvent. The method, based on slowly rebuilding confidence, was only the first of a series of measures taken in the first "Hundred Days" of the Roosevelt administration designed to build spirits and to provide some relief. Meanwhile, the Democratic administration continued to use the RFC established under Hoover to channel funds to the private sector to stimulate new businesses.

Through the first two years of his term Roosevelt established what came to be known as the First New Deal, with an emphasis on relief and recovery. Among other relief agencies established was the Civilian Conservation Corps (CCC), which directly employed young men to work in national forests and national parks. The CCC was at first authorized to hire 250,000 men between 18 and 25 years old. The young men received $30 per month, which was often sent home. The CCC continued to grow, and by 1935, there were up to 500,000 employed in the camps. When the program finally closed in 1941, the CCC had employed over 2 million youths.

The key new program of the period was the National Industrial Recovery Act signed on June 16, 1933, which established, under two titles, the National Recovery Administration or NRA (Title I), and the Public Works Administration or PWA (Title II). The NRA was a somewhat unique experiment in government involvement in the economy. Based on methods employed over the prior decade of the federal government working through industrial associations, the plan gave the associations official representation on "code authorities." These code authorities, which also had representatives from labor unions and from the general public, were empowered to set codes for each industry in a consultative procedure. The codes would specify product standards, employment conditions and pay, and prices.

In effect, the NRA's code authorities allowed businesses extraordinary power to become involved in noncompetitive price setting, with unions, government, and the public looking on. The public representatives were often academics or other specialists not associated either with labor or with ownership. After the codes were set, they were reviewed by NRA Administrator Hugh Johnson, who was appointed the same day the law was signed. After review of the codes, Johnson put them into effect, with some legal force. Those industries that conformed to the codes were given government endorsement in the form of the right to display the NRA blue eagle symbol. The implication was that the public would boycott those industries that did not display the symbol out of a sense of national support for the process. This system bore a striking resemblance to the syndicalist system established in Mussolini's Italy, and the NRA was immediately controversial.

Some businesses attacked the NRA system because it seemed to limit free enterprise in ways that violated existing anti-trust laws. Others found the provisions of the codes that required that labor disputes be submitted to a national labor board, established on August 5, 1933, highly objectionable. The right to unionize was guaranteed under Section 14a of all the codes. Thus the press and the public soon came to focus on 14a as a debating point in the period 1933–34.

In San Francisco in mid-July 1934, longshoremen went on strike, demanding union control of hiring halls. The San Francisco central labor council voted to support the strike with a citywide walkout of all organized workers. Although common in Europe and Latin America, the tactic of a general strike had been very rarely employed in the United States. Local papers reminded nonstrikers that a general strike in Britain in 1926 had been broken by volunteers and government action, and appeared to call for a vigilante response. Hugh Johnson flew to the city to attempt to offer his services as an arbitrator of the strike, but after conferences with local conservative leaders, including some from the newspaper publishers, Johnson condemned the strike as revolution. Within days, mobs attacked union offices, and some observers attributed the mob actions to incitement by the newspapers. Although the general strike was short-lived, it appeared to some that labor conflict in the United States had begun to verge on class war. Meanwhile, union organizers continued to attempt to build membership and gain bargaining recognition under the guarantees of Section 14a.

The operation of the NRA's code system was struck down by a Supreme Court case in 1935, growing out of a dispute by a chicken-raising firm on Long Island, New York. In this case, known to the press and the public as the Schechter Sick Chicken case, (295 U.S. 495) the NRA was overturned, although the PWA, the second title of the National Industrial Recovery Act, remained in force. To make up for the loss of the provisions protecting the right of labor to organize, Congress soon approved the Wagner Act signed into law on July 5, 1935. The Wagner Act established the National Labor Relations Board and institutionalized the right to organize, requiring supervised union elections in workplaces above a certain size. Together 14a of the NRA and the Wagner Act gave a great boost to labor organizing.

The American Federation of Labor (AFL) was organized along trade lines when it was founded in 1886, with each separate trade within a large company represented by a different local. In the burst of organizing under 14a, the AFL established new teams of organizers. The Committee of Industrial Organizations (CIO) sought to form unions on industrywide bases, with members from different trades represented in the local within a particular company. The CIO was far more active and radical in its methods than the traditional AFL. On December 31, 1936, workers at several General Motors plants in Flint, Michigan, staged a sit-down strike, in which they occupied the plant and defended it against attempts by management to reclaim it. The sit-down strike lasted a month and a half, and involved some 40,000 in occupying the plants and over 100,000 participating less directly. The sit-down method spread to the rubber and steel industries, shipbuilding yards, and oil refineries, eventually engaging over 500,000 strikers. Later declared illegal, the sit-down tactic was effective for several years, forcing employers either to resort to physical force to evict the strikers or to negotiate a settlement.

On May 30, 1937, a sit-down strike at Republic Steel in South Chicago resulted in bloodshed. Throughout the spring of 1937, the Steel Workers' Organizing Committee (SWOC) had secured representation as the official bargaining agent at U.S. Steel. SWOC was able to win a wage increase of 10 percent and recognition of a 40-hour week, with overtime paid at time and a half. Other steel corporations fought the constitutionality of the Wagner Act, finally upheld by the Supreme Court later that year in *NLRB v. Jones and Laughlin Steel Corporation* (301 U.S. 1). Several smaller steel companies, headed by Republic Steel, resisted the strikes. Police fired on strikers at the South Chicago plant, killing 4 and injuring over 80. It would be several years before all the steel companies would sign contracts with the CIO.

In May 1938, the AFL expelled John L. Lewis, who headed the industrial union United Mine Workers. Lewis, together with Sidney Hillman of the Amalgamated Clothing Workers, endorsed a much more aggressive unionization drive. In 1938, the CIO officially broke away from its parent organization and reformed as the Congress of Industrial Organizations, so named in order to preserve the acronym. The CIO continued to organize oil workers, steel workers, automobile plant workers, and electrical workers who had never been tapped by the AFL. Conservatives viewed the CIO with alarm, not only for its adoption of the sit-down strike method, but because of the fiery rhetoric of John L. Lewis and because of rumors of Communist Party infiltration of SWOC and other organizing groups.

While conservatives condemned the labor strife as near-revolution, progressives and liberals rallied to labor's cause. Senator Robert La Follette, Jr., headed a subcommittee to investigate anti-labor methods adopted by management. In December 1937, his committee issued its report detailing the use of blacklists, labor spies, and paid vigilante groups to break up unions and harass organizers. Regular strikebreaking services, paid armed units, and complete private arsenals held by some of the steel companies were detailed in the report. Furthermore, the use of terrorism in specific locales, including in Harlan County, Kentucky, where gun-toting vigilantes attacked striking miners in 1931, showed that labor violence could be attributed as much to management and conservative press agitation of vigilantes as to the organizers and strikers themselves.

Through 1935 and 1936, Roosevelt began to urge Congress to enact more far-reaching reform and regulatory legislation, in what came to be known as the Second New Deal. With the pro-labor policies incorporated in both the NRA and later in the Wagner Act, the Democratic Party solidified its position as a pro-labor party. To supporters, it seemed that the Democrats had come to resemble social-democratic and labor parties of Europe; to opponents, it seemed the Democrats had been infected with radical ideas. The ideological flavor of the debate continued.

Meanwhile, in Europe, Africa, and the Far East, the revanchist nations of Germany, Italy, and Japan continued their expansion. In Germany, Adolf Hitler was selected as chancellor and replaced the aging Hindenburg a few months before Roosevelt's inauguration in 1933, and was selected as head of state in 1934, establishing and expanding his totalitarian control of the nation. In 1935, Japanese troops began moving into provinces of China from their base in the independent puppet state of Manchukuo (formerly the province of Manchuria) formed under Japanese military control. In the same year, Italy, with the quiet assent of Britain and France, began its aggression against Ethiopia. Soon the news of Japanese, German, and Italian expansion would dominate the international pages, raising concerns in the United States about a possible war that could once again involve the country.

In Mexico, Lázaro Cárdenas moved the ruling PRI to the left, particularly with the takeover of oil properties. To maintain good relations and his Good Neighbor policy, Roosevelt did not support U.S. oil companies in their efforts to fight the expropriation. Together with ongoing suppression of religion in Mexico, state subsidies to leftist muralists, and the support that Cárdenas offered to the Loyalist regime in Spain, many observers gained the impression that Mexico was drifting further to the left. For the most part, however, Latin American regimes remained under the control of the local military.

The ideological flavor of international and domestic disagreements in the decade was no accident. After disputes with Leon Trotsky in the late 1920s, Josef Stalin had insisted on strict adherence to a single-party line, with deviation either to the left or right of his own positions simply regarded as incorrect. In the period 1928–34, the Third International or Comintern, financed and controlled out of Moscow, insisted that other groups on the left hoping to tap into the discontent of socially deprived or depressed classes should be shunned. Labor leaders in the United States and elsewhere hoping to appeal to mass discontent were labeled "social fascists" if they did not cooperate with official, Comintern-dominated leadership. However, beginning in 1934 and 1935, the Comintern officially adopted a more tolerant position that came to be known as the Popular Front policy. In "Popular Front from above" tactics, Communist parties around the world supported by Soviet funding were ordered to cooperate with other socialist and left parties to attempt to form anti-fascist coalitions. In "Popular Front from below" tactics, Communist cadres were expected to work through other organizations, or front groups, such as local labor movements, CIO-organizing teams such as SWOC, rent-strike organizations, civil rights advocacy organizations, and others. Where possible, Communist cadres would take positions of leadership in such organizations and use them to magnify their influence. Within the United States, such influence was exerted through organizations such as the League Against War and Fascism, devoted to international peace and disarmament, or to legal defense funds for particular individuals, such as the Scottsboro Legal Defense Fund, set up to prevent the legal lynching of several young black men accused of raping two white women in 1934.

In the late 1930s, the purges of Communist leaders within the Soviet Union and then, in 1939, the reversal of official Communist Party line when the Soviet Union formed an alliance with Nazi Germany in the Ribbentrop-Malenkov (or Hitler-Stalin) Pact, led to the disillusionment of many who had joined the party or front organizations out of opposition to fascism. In the United States and Britain, many individuals temporarily joined the local Communist Party, but soon became disillusioned after a few months or years when they realized that the party was no harbor for free-thinkers, but instead expected strict adherence to official policy as set by the Moscow-based Third International. Later, many individuals with liberal or progressive sympathy for such causes as minority rights, labor unions, international peace, or anti-fascism, who had temporarily joined the Communist Party, were embarrassed when such affiliations were publicly recalled in judicial or congressional investigations.

In Spain between 1936 and 1938, the Popular Front methods soon led to crises. The Communist Party there funneled military aid from the Soviet Union only to officers and units that adhered to official party doctrine. As a consequence, dissident groups such as Trotskyite or anarchist units received little support. The result was at least two minor civil wars within the larger civil war, in Barcelona and in Madrid, with loyalists of different factions fighting each other. News of such conflicts was distorted and only sorted out later by observers such as George Orwell, who authored a memoir, *Homage to Catalonia*, describing the problems in Barcelona. Ernest Hemingway wrote a short play, *The Fifth Column*, based on rumors of pro-fascist supporters operating inside Madrid.

In the United States, the Communist Party efforts to enlist the discontented masses had little success. Instead, a wide variety of homegrown demagogues and maverick politicians emerged during Roosevelt's first term and many continued to be active throughout the decade. Former governor of Louisiana, Huey Long, ran for and was elected to the U.S. Senate in 1930. Long had built a successful political machine in Louisiana by dispensing patronage to his supporters and by denouncing his opponents in flamboyant language. Long criticized Roosevelt for not doing enough to ease the suffering of the unemployed and it appeared he would challenge Roosevelt in 1936, either within the Democratic Party or with a third-party campaign based on his Share Our Wealth concept. Known by its acronym SOW, Long was making a slyly sarcastic commentary on the proliferation of "alphabet soup" agencies created under the New Deal. Under SOW, those earning over $5,000 per year would be subject to a heavy income tax; those earning less would receive a government check to help bring up their income toward the median level. The math did not work, but the idea had appeal.

Assassinated in 1935, Long was no longer a threat to Roosevelt, but his organization and alliances continued to attract support. Among those was the "Radio Priest," Father Charles Coughlin, based in Royal Oak, Michigan. Coughlin gave impassioned speeches denouncing international bankers, Jews, and others as disloyal. A dentist, Dr. Francis Townsend, came up with a plan to provide old-age pensions, while newspaper magnate William Randolph Hearst broke with Roosevelt over his labor and tax policies in 1935. While their critics called such leaders and spokesmen "fascists," they represented a wide variety of populist appeals. Some of the new demagogues, whether arguing from the left or the right, attacked the Roosevelt regime for not doing enough, while others, like Hearst, criticized Roosevelt for doing too much.

In Europe, fascism took different forms, with the most notable successes in Germany, Italy, Spain, and Portugal. During the Spanish civil war from 1936–39, the fascist parties of these four nations were allied in practice on the battlefield, with Portuguese, Italian, and German volunteers and official units serving alongside the Falangist and army forces of Francisco Franco to oppose the militias and peoples' armies supported by the elected government. However, in each of these four fascist-dominated countries, fascist policies took different pathways. In Germany, the Nazi party developed a cult of personality around Hitler, supported by a host of security organizations. Hitler based his popular appeal on revising the borders to unify the German people. His even more notorious and disastrous doctrines called for "strengthening the race" by elimination of Jews, Gypsies, homosexuals, and the handicapped, and stimulating childbearing by ethnically pure Germans. These drastic concepts were administered through euthanasia, sterilization, and eugenics at first, and later, more famously, through outright extermination camps into which Jews, Gypsies, homosexuals, and political dissidents were herded.

Elements of this story, but not all of it, circulated outside Germany through the later years of the decade. In Italy, Mussolini concentrated the Fascist Party focus on suppressing the left and political dissent, and on building national unity through a syndicalist structure of control of industry. The war against Ethiopia in Africa was followed by plans to extend Italy's power in the nearby Adriatic, with control of Albania and threats against Yugoslavia. The Spanish Falangist Party suppressed political dissent, and thousands of military and political prisoners simply vanished inside prison camps. Portugal, under Dr. Antonio de Oliveira Salazar from 1932, concentrated on building a corporative economic system similar to Italy's and suppressing dissent. His National Union party remained the only legal party in the nation until 1945. Hungary, Yugoslavia, and Poland all had dictatorial regimes through the period that incorporated elements of fascist doctrine.

With the increasing world awareness of the Nazi policy of harassing Jews, emigration of those Jews who could afford to leave began to attract attention through the late 1930s. Caught between its promise in the Balfour Declaration of 1916 to support the establishment of a homeland for Jews in Palestine and its commitment to support Arab independence in the region, Britain walked a difficult line. The solution to the dilemma was to limit immigration of Jews to Palestine. Meanwhile, Jews with resources emigrated to Latin American countries and in limited numbers to the United States. Zionists in Palestine and abroad continued to argue for the creation of a true Jewish nation, but British policy discouraged such talk through the 1930s.

With the effort of Communist Party leaders to build a base of support in the United States, and with many of the reforms of the New Deal departing from the tradition of free enterprise, some conservatives in the United States began to criticize Roosevelt and the Democratic Party as Communist-influenced. This attempt to revive the so-called "Red Scare" of 1919, and to use such charges as a means of marshalling support against Roosevelt, had little success. Although the 28 Hearst newspapers endorsed the campaign, and a small group of self-proclaimed experts attempted to convince the public and Congress that the threat of a leftist revolution was imminent, the movement was far less successful in the 1930s than it would become in the late 1940s and early 1950s. The revival of the Red Scare did make the news through the period 1936–39, even though it was of limited extent.

Congress continued its suspicion of foreign entanglements and regarded the rise of militarist states in Europe and the Far East as dangerous. A committee set up on April 12, 1934, under Senator Gerald P. Nye of North Dakota, examined the causes of U.S. entry into World War I, and the Nye Committee report tended to influence neutrality legislation through the period. The Neutrality Law was passed and amended repeatedly through the decade, adding refinements, many of them based on the lessons learned from the World War I experience. For example, the new Neutrality Law of 1935 prevented the sale of arms to belligerents and warned U.S. citizens against traveling on ships of belligerents. The 1936 Neutrality Law (passed on February 29, 1936) forbade the granting of loans to belligerents. It was assumed that because the United States had loaned money to Britain and France that Americans developed a financial interest in seeing those countries victorious in World War I. That was an idea originally suggested by Woodrow Wilson's Secretary of State, William Jennings Bryan, who had discouraged such loans for the period 1914–15 in hope of preventing the development of a vested interest in one side or the other. The Nye Committee had noted that loans, U.S. citizens aboard belligerent (mostly British) ships, and arms trade had all disposed the United States to waver from a neutral course and to support the Allies in World War I. Remembering the *Lusitania* and the loss of American lives aboard other ships registered to Britain and France was thus taken into account in the Neutrality Law. Furthermore, the laws established embargoes on weapons and ammunition to combatants (although traditional neutrality allowed such trade). In World War I, Britain and France had provided most of their own weapons, although both had purchased vast quantities of smokeless powder and other explosives from plants in the United States.

After the outbreak of the Spanish civil war on July 16, 1936, the Neutrality Act was modified once again to extend coverage to both of the opposing forces in Spain, in an act passed on January 6, 1937. Roosevelt complied and embargoed shipments to both sides, which tended to work against the loyalists. Franco's forces were well-supplied from Italy and Germany. Britain and France also embargoed shipments to both sides in a League of Nations-sponsored nonintervention agreement.

Examining the effect of the Neutrality Laws, Congress modified them again in 1937. The new law, adopted May 1, 1937, authorized the President to list commodities other than weapons that could be sold to belligerents, and the law simply prohibited U.S. citizens from traveling on belligerent ships rather than warning them to travel at their own risk. However, the President retained the power to invoke the laws by his ability to decide what sort of conflict constituted a war, except in the case of Spain which had been specifically mentioned in the January 1937 law.

Franklin Roosevelt did not favor these neutrality policies as they tended to place limits on the constitutional presidential power to set foreign policy. Roosevelt pointed out, as did other critics of the policies, that by placing an embargo on weapons to both sides in a conflict, the policy could actually encourage aggression by more powerful and well-armed states against those lacking weapons or possessing more primitive arms. Exactly that situation prevailed in the Italian-Ethiopian War, because Italy had no need for weapons from the United States, but could import petroleum because it was not covered by the neutrality legislation, nor could it be embargoed under the 1935 law. For these reasons, Roosevelt did not recognize the Japanese attacks after 1935 in China as a state of war but as a series of incidents, and the United States could continue to sell arms to the Chinese. Even so, on September 14, 1937, in the spirit of the law, Roosevelt forbade the transport of U.S. munitions to either Japan or China aboard ships of the U.S. government, and informed shipown-

ers that they transported such goods at their own risk. Since Japan had a large merchant fleet compared to that of China, critics charged that even this application of a neutrality policy tended to favor the aggressor, Japan.

On the domestic front in the late 1930s, the Second New Deal began to seriously alter the political makeup of the nation. The Democratic Party's political base became well-established under Roosevelt and set a pattern that would continue well into the late 20th century. With the Second New Deal's fundamental reforms in banking, regulation of the economy, labor relations, and social security, the Democratic Party's strength among urban residents and the rural poor was solidified. Meanwhile, government policies of direct employment in public works continued, as did programs with more radical reputations such as the Works Progress Administration (WPA) established April 8, 1935 (which also took over the existing CCC); the Resettlement Administration (RA) set up on May 1, 1935, under Rexford Tugwell; the Rural Electrification Administration (REA), established on May 11, 1935; the Tennessee Valley Administration (TVA) on May 18, 1935; and the National Youth Administration (NYA) set up June 25, 1935. The Social Security Act was signed into law August 14, 1935.

In some cases, the notoriety of specific agency administrators added to controversy, as with Harold Ickes at PWA, Hugh Johnson at the NRA, and later with Rexford Tugwell at RA, David Lilienthal at TVA, and Harry Hopkins at WPA. Admired by supporters and castigated by detractors as radicals, brains-trusters, parlor-pinks, or covert socialists, these administrators were never shy about press coverage, and their dramatic announcements and rulings kept their agencies in the news. To critics, the support of consumer cooperatives by the REA, the establishment of planned communities by the RA, and the takeover of power and rural development by the TVA seemed harbingers of a socialist state. The fact that Roosevelt's picture was prominently displayed in every CCC camp dining hall reminded his opponents of the huge posters of Mussolini or Hitler displayed in their European dictatorships. Despite such misgivings among conservatives, the New Deal coalition became firmly entrenched with urban and ethnic voters, rural poor, northern black voters, intellectuals, and union members. By not challenging segregation in the south, Roosevelt was able to win support from Democratic members of Congress from that region for his social policies. The internal contradiction between winning votes among northern blacks and appeasing southern white supremacists would come back to haunt the Democratic Party in later decades.

Many young African Americans grew impatient with the gradualist approach to improvement of race relations advocated by the National Association for the Advancement of Colored People (NAACP), founded by W.E.B. Du Bois with assistance from sympathetic white supporters in 1911. Du Bois had used the association's periodical, *Crisis*, as both an outlet for black writers and as a voice for racial equality, but few tangible actions or gains had resulted. The first executive secretary of the organization, James Weldon Johnson, had agreed with Du Bois's concept that publicity and education should be the primary tools of the movement. However, in 1930, the organization worked with labor unions to oppose the nomination of Judge John Parker of North Carolina to the Supreme Court. Parker had long opposed participation of African Americans in the political process and had been a member of the Klu Klux Klan (KKK). The NAACP and union opposition, with the direct threat of votes to be cast against Senators who voted for Parker, was widely regarded as a successful application of political clout and a lesson on how the vote could win progress.

The indirect tactic of marshalling votes against the most openly racist appointees, however, had little direct affect on economic or social conditions. In 1932, a self-proclaimed mystic and street agitator, Sufi Abdul Hamid, moved from Chicago to New York where he attempted to use a boycott method to force businesses to hire African-American employees in black neighborhoods. At first, his effort was opposed by local black leaders like Reverend Adam Clayton Powell of the Abyssinian Baptist Church. Soon, however, Sufi Hamid's method spread. He was instrumental in forming the Negro Industrial and Clerical Alliance that began picketing stores in Harlem. The NAACP and local churches joined in forming a competing Harlem Citizen's League for Fair Play that negotiated settlements with stores. The Alliance and the Citizen's League rivaled each other for leadership of the protests, but the more conservative black leaders found themselves pushed into adopting direct action tactics that soon began to generate some local gains.

Meanwhile, Du Bois began to advocate a policy that would accept some segregation in government programs in order to guarantee that black citizens would receive at least a share of the federal expenditures. Within the NAACP, a leadership crisis developed, with one faction accusing Du Bois of giving up on the organization's long-term goal of integration and the elimination of racial barriers. He resigned his position as editor of *Crisis* in 1934. The executive director of the NAACP, Walter White, together with the board of the organization, turned their attention and efforts to using the courts to attack segregation. Meanwhile, A. Philip Randolph, who had organized the Sleeping Car Porters' Union, an all-black organization, began to emerge as an influential black labor leader, whose voice was respected in the emerging CIO. Thus through the 1930s, black leadership began to experiment with new tactics that would eventually become part of the toolkit of the civil rights movement: boycotts, demonstrations, voting campaigns, and court cases.

Other black leaders, some of them heading sects or religious groups through the 1930s, also attracted popular followings based on a combination of religion, charismatic religious leadership, and communitarian living. One was George Baker, alias Father Divine. Through the 1920s, Divine had organized an interracial communal settlement in Sayville, Long Island, but in 1931, his organization fell afoul of the law. When neighbors complained of late-night noises from his community, he was arrested. A hostile judge sentenced Divine to a year in jail. Four days after the sentence, the judge, who was young and apparently in good health, died of a heart attack. The press caught the story and called it Divine Retribution. Father Divine was released from jail on a technicality, and with the attendant publicity, his organization immediately grew. Between 1933 and 1937, his organization leased 9 houses, 3 apartment houses, and 25 restaurants. In addition, he opened groceries and barber shops, and his organization operated a fleet of street-vending wagons. Soon, he had extensions of his operation in New Jersey, Connecticut, and Maryland. Known as the Peace Mission Movement, Father Divine's organization provided a haven for poor urban blacks and whites who sought a new religious identification, employment, and housing. A similar and competing movement was led by Daddy Grace, a black minister who developed a large following in the United House of Prayer which he set up, with establishments in many cities along the East Coast through the mid-1930s.

When Roosevelt ran for reelection in 1936, he faced critics both on the left and the right. Although Huey Long was dead, Father Coughlin and Gerald L.K. Smith organized the remnants of Long's organization and nominated a Republican Congressman from North Dakota, William Lemke, as the candidate of the Union for Social Justice. Dr. Townsend threw his support to the same organization. The Republicans nominated the governor of Kansas, Alfred M. Landon. Both Lemke and Landon condemned the New Deal

and accused Roosevelt of usurpation of power. Some conservative Democrats, including Al Smith and others, active in the Liberty League, gave their support to Landon. The Democratic Convention nominated Roosevelt and Garner to run again. The convention was noteworthy for abolishing the two-thirds rule, which had required two-thirds of the delegates to support a candidate. The rule had been in place in the party since 1836, and had caused numerous crises in the nominating process, including a long, drawn-out deadlock in 1924. Roosevelt campaigned with a strong attack on unnamed representatives of capital, whom he dubbed "economic royalists." Roosevelt was endorsed by several labor groups. The Communist Party nominated Earl Browder for president, and an African American, James W. Ford, for the vice presidency.

Prior to the election, the magazine *Literary Digest*, which collected opinions and news items from newspapers around the nation, predicted a win for Alf Landon. A little-known polling organization operated by Gallup predicted Roosevelt would win. The popular vote was overwhelmingly in favor of Roosevelt with some 27 million votes, compared to Landon's 16 million. Lemke garnered less than a million, while Browder got some 80,000 votes. *Literary Digest* soon went out of business, and politicians and the public began to seriously consider the value of the polling methods adopted by the Gallup organization. Democrats took strong majorities in both houses of Congress, with 77 Democrats to 19 Republicans in the Senate, and 328 to 107 in the House. With such an endorsement, it seemed Roosevelt would be invincible in developing and expanding the New Deal. However, early in 1937, new developments revealed cracks in his political support.

One branch of the government opposed some of Roosevelt's New Deal programs. The Supreme Court disallowed a number of pieces of legislation besides the NRA, including the Agricultural Adjustment Act. Viewing the Court as a barrier to reform, Roosevelt had a bill introduced on February 5, 1937, that would allow the appointment of more justices to the Court. His proposal called for an increase in the Court from 9 to a maximum of 15 judges, if judges over age 70 refused to retire. Furthermore, he asked for the addition of up to 50 new judges of all ranks to the federal courts, and for a provision that all appeals from a lower federal court on constitutional grounds be routed directly to the Supreme Court. The law Roosevelt proposed would also prohibit a lower court from issuing injunctions against any Congressionally passed law on constitutional grounds before a government attorney presented arguments.

This "court packing" scheme caused a rebellion within his own party as well as public outrage. Roosevelt was accused of attempting to undermine the Constitution and of trying to destroy the independence of the judiciary. Even members of his own party thought the aspects of the plan with merit should be incorporated in a constitutional amendment, rather than simple legislation. Senator Burton Wheeler of Montana, formerly a close supporter of Roosevelt, took the lead in the campaign to defeat the plan. Chief Justice Charles Evans Hughes sent a letter to Congress saying that the Court was not overwhelmed with work and needed no expansion of judges to keep up. At first Roosevelt tried to conduct a personal speaking campaign to win over support for the plan. Faced with the political backlash from this effort in his second term, Roosevelt backed down and accepted a compromise measure that allowed for voluntary retirement of judges at age 70. Roosevelt was further heartened when the Supreme Court sustained several New Deal measures, including both the Social Security Act and the Wagner Act.

Even though Roosevelt achieved some of his goals in his attack on the Court, the battle revealed a serious break with-

in Democratic ranks and strengthened the morale of conservatives opposing the New Deal. Conservative Democrats sided with Republicans to block several pieces of administration-sponsored legislation through 1937 and 1938, including an Executive Reorganization Bill. Roosevelt called a special session of Congress to meet in November and December of 1937, but the conservative coalition blocked efforts to pass wage and hour standards, a new agricultural bill, and bills related to conservation and development of natural resources.

Through the decade, isolationist and neutralist doctrines dominated public opinion, making it difficult to support a program of expansion of the War Department budgets. However, the build-up of the navy's fleet got underway, at first through funding from the Public Works programs on the grounds that naval construction provided employment. The ships launched through the 1930s would see action in World War II, many of them with up-to-date electrical and weapons systems. With increasing evidence of a looming conflict in Europe, Roosevelt asked Congress in 1938 for a tripling of the authorized naval construction fund and for millions devoted to special defense technological development, including anti-aircraft weapons and defense-industry tools. Evidence that the population and Congress still feared an administration would lure the country into war surfaced in early 1938 during the fight over the Ludlow Resolution, introduced by Indiana Congressman Louis Ludlow. This bill would require a national referendum for any declaration of war, except if the United States were invaded or attacked. The Ludlow Resolution was first introduced in 1935 and reintroduced in 1937 and 1938. Although it never passed Congress, polls indicated overwhelming popular support for the resolution. Furthermore, votes in Congress on the resolution demonstrated deep support for the bill in the west and midwest, with opposition concentrated in the south and northeast, regardless of party. Roosevelt was well aware of these divisions, and his own neutrality policy would be shaped by the fact that widespread support for a declaration of war would only come if the United States were directly attacked.

In 1938, Congress approved a massive expansion of the Navy, with over $1 billion authorized to build up a two-ocean Navy over a period of 10 years. The Vinson Naval Act was passed May 17, 1938, and the bill authorized new cruisers and aircraft carriers. Together with a new generation of destroyers, the U.S. fleet began to catch up with developments abroad, especially those in Japan. Nevertheless, aircraft development lagged behind.

Unnoticed by much of the press and the public, science made numerous advances in the decade, most notably in the field of nuclear physics. The United States became something of a haven for Jewish scientists escaping from Germany, Austria, and Hungary. As they settled in teaching and research positions at Columbia, University of Chicago, and University of California, they enriched the community of American-born scientists. Albert Einstein, who arrived in 1933, was followed by other prominent physicists including Leo Szilard in 1938. Other scientists arriving from Europe included George Gamow, who came from Russia in 1934; Hans Bethe from Germany in 1935; and Enrico Fermi, who left Italy with his Jewish wife in 1938. Such scientists closely followed and built upon work on the nucleus of the atom being conducted in Europe.

One Jewish scientist, Lise Meitner, left Austria in 1938 after Germany took control of the country. She emigrated first to the Netherlands, then Denmark, and finally settled in Stockholm, Sweden. In 1939, Lise Meitner and her nephew, O.R. Frisch, published a paper describing the process of nuclear fission, after working out the principle in a famous long-distance telephone call between Copenhagen and Stockholm. Reading the work of Meitner and Frisch,

"Disintegration of Uranium by Neutrons: A New Type of Nuclear Reaction," Leo Szilard and Albert Einstein recognized that nuclear fission could produce energy releases powerful enough to be incorporated in an extraordinarily powerful weapon, and wrote a confidential letter to Roosevelt in July 1939 outlining the concept of such a weapon. Roosevelt endorsed the letter with an instruction to his staff to follow up, an action that eventually led to the formation of the Manhattan Engineering District that built the atom bomb during World War II.

Other less earth-shattering technical developments through the 1930s abounded. Some, however, would shape the future world. In 1932, a researcher at Bell Labs, Karl Jansky, identified radio waves coming from outer space, forming the basis for the development of radio telescopes. Wallace Corothers, a Du Pont researcher, produced the first nylon thread on February 28, 1935. In 1937, John Atanosoff, at Iowa State University, developed a first-generation digital computer using vacuum tubes. In 1938, two Hungarian brothers resident in Argentina, Ladislao Biro and Georg Biro, invented the ballpoint pen. In the same year, Chester Carlson, an American inventor and physicist, developed a copy machine employing electrostatic charges and dry powdered ink in a process later known as Xerography. Also in 1938, Roy Plunkett at Du Pont developed the plastic later known as Teflon. In 1939, a Swiss chemist, Paul Hermann Muller, discovered that the chemical DDT, first synthesized in 1874, could be used as a very effective insecticide, inducing paralysis in insects. At the World Fair of 1939–40 held in New York, General Electric introduced to the market the first fluorescent lamps. In Germany, Hans von Ohain built the first jet-propelled aircraft, the Heinkel He-178, in 1939. The development and production of some of these materials and devices would have to wait until after World War II, although some, like the jet engine and DDT, proved crucial as the war unfolded.

Relations between Japan and the United States in the Pacific deteriorated through the 1930s. The United States approved a plan of self-government for the Philippines, with the selection of a local legislature and governor and a plan for eventual independence. Nevertheless, Japan saw the Philippines as an American colony. As Japan coupled its aggression in China with fortification of the islands mandated under the League, Roosevelt sought to exercise diplomatic pressure to limit Japanese policies. At the same time, the U.S. policy of building up bases in the Philippines, Hawaii, and Midway irritated the Japanese, who complained through diplomatic channels. By 1939, the Japanese government perceived the United States as a major barrier to their ambitions to supplant European control of the Far East with Asian, that is to say, Japanese, control.

The economic and international crises through the 1930s were reflected in the literature of the period. The social-problem novel was revived by such writers as James T. Farrell, whose trilogy, *Studs Lonigan*, published in 1932–35, portrayed the life of the Irish in the Chicago slums. Erskine Caldwell captured poverty in the South in his *Tobacco Road* (1932). John Dos Passos adopted a documentary style, with elements of newsreel and "camera eye" presentations in the *U.S.A.* trilogy, published in 1930, 1932, and 1936. His focus was on graft and corruption. John Steinbeck captured life among the migrants who escaped the conditions of the dust storms and dust bowl of the mid-1930s in *The Grapes of Wrath*, published in 1939. Steinbeck's other novels of the period, set around Monterey and Salinas, California, included *Tortilla Flat* (1935) and *Of Mice and Men* (1937). William Faulkner extended south his presentation of the decadence of the plantation, which he had begun in the 1920s in *The Sound and the Fury* (1929), with *As I Lay Dying* (1930), *Sanctuary* (1931), and *Light in August* (1932). Ernest Hemingway had established his reputation in the 1920s with *The Sun Also Rises* (1926) and *A Farewell to Arms* (1929). Some, but not all, of Hemingway's work in the

1930s was set against military conflict, although his examination of the lives of men performing under stress sometimes included other kinds of life-and-death situations. His work during the decade included *To Have and Have Not* (1937). His play, *The Fifth Column*, was published in 1938 in a volume that also included numerous short stories. Among the short stories Hemingway produced in the era were *Death in the Afternoon* (1932), which described bullfighting, and *Green Hills of Africa* (1935), based on big-game hunting. His classic, *For Whom the Bell Tolls*, published in 1940, described the adventures of an American volunteer fighting with the loyalists in Spain during the civil war.

With the introduction of Technicolor, a color film process developed by a team of researchers at the Massachusetts Institute of Technology in 1933, movie films began to attract huge audiences escaping from the constant round of depressing economic news and international crises. Margaret Mitchell's romantic novel of the Civil War and Reconstruction period, *Gone With The Wind*, was published in 1936 and the film version premiered in 1939. The first full-length Disney cartoon in Technicolor, *Snow White and the Seven Dwarfs*, was released in 1938. Black and white escape films included a series of musicals, including Busby Berkeley's *Gold Diggers of 1935*. Realistic films drew audiences as well, including such hits as *The Thin Man* (1934) and Fritz Lang's *Fury* (1936).

In the pictorial arts, the genre or style of social realism reached new heights, especially under the sponsorship of WPA arts projects. Some of the mural projects pitted idealized working classes against those with privilege and capital. A few were so controversial that they were either painted over or covered with partitions, such as the famous rotunda lobby of Telegraph Tower on Telegraph Hill in San Francisco. Reacting against both abstraction and social realism, several Midwestern painters, including Grant Wood, John Steuart Curry, and Thomas Hart Benton, depicted rural life realistically but with a tone of reverence. The most well-known and reproduced of these works may have been Grant Wood's *American Gothic*. The Public Works Administration and the Resettlement Administration sponsored architects to design projects and planned communities that were sometimes criticized for emphasis on standardization, including the Carl Mackley houses in Philadelphia, Lakeview Terrace in Cleveland, and the whole community of Greenbelt, Maryland. The WPA sponsored a Federal Music Project to provide employment for musicians. Some 225,000 performances employed about 15,000 musicians. Under the direction of Nikolai Sokoloff, the WPA set up the Composers' Forum-Laboratory in 1935 to help develop contemporary American composers. In the field of popular music, Irving Berlin left the memorable *Easter Parade* (1933) and *God Bless America* (1939). Regular broadcasts of opera, symphonies, as well as popular music over the radio provided free and high-quality entertainment for the masses through the decade.

In 1938–39, many international developments would come together in what later generations could see in retrospect as gathering war clouds. However, as day-by-day events unfolded, no one knew what the future would hold. Would Italy, Germany, and Japan achieve their revisionist, revanchist goals? How long would it take for the United States to emerge from the debilitating effects of the Great Depression? Would Roosevelt run for an unprecedented third term? Would the Democratic coalition forged in the New Deal survive his administration and the debates over the court-packing scheme? Would the Communist Party be able to retain its adherents, despite Comintern orders to reverse course and support Hitler's invasion of Poland? Would Russia remain allied with the Axis powers of Germany, Italy, and Japan? As 1939 drew to an end, all such questions remained open and unanswered.

Rodney Carlisle, Ph.D.
General Editor

YEARLY SUMMARIES

	World Affairs	Europe	Africa & The Middle East	The Americas	Asia & The Pacific
1930	The London Naval Conference leads to a limitation agreement on capital ships between the United States, Great Britain, and Japan.	Allied forces complete their military evacuation of the Rhineland. The region becomes a demilitarized buffer zone between Germany and France.	Ras Tafari becomes Emperor Haile Selassie in Ethiopia. . . . Iraq gains full independence.	The Chaco War between Bolivia and Paraguay begins. . . . Getulio Vargas emerges as leader of Brazil.	In India, British authorities arrest Mohandas Gandhi.
1931	A moratorium on the payment of international debts is proposed by the United States and goes into effect for one year.	A republican government is established in Spain, replacing the monarchy.		An earthquake in Managua, Nicaragua, kills 2,000.	The Japanese army invades Manchuria. . . . Mao Tse-Dong establishes a Communist government in the Chinese province of Kiangsi.
1932	The Lytton Report to the League of Nations condemns Japanese actions in Manchuria.	The Nazi party wins a majority in the German legislature. . . . António Salazar is elected president of Portugal.	The Kingdom of the Hejaz and Nejd officially changes its name to Saudi Arabia.	After a year of relative quiet, the Chaco War between Bolivia and Paraguay reerupts.	The Japanese establish the puppet state of Manchukuo.
1933	The London Economic Conference is held but breaks up in July.	Adolf Hitler becomes chancellor of Germany.	After protests from the Arab community, Britain imposes limitations on the immigration of Jews to Palestine.	President Roosevelt announces a "Good Neighbor Policy." At the Montevideo Conference, the United States and Latin American countries renounce the right to intervene in each others' affairs. . . . A revolution in Cuba removes President Gerardo Machado; Sgt. Fulgencio Batista assumes control.	Japan announces it will withdraw from the League of Nations. . . . The United States approves a plan for Philippine independence.
1934	The League of Nations admits the Soviet Union and grants it a position on the Security Council.	Germany abolishes labor unions. In the Night of the Long Knives, the Nazis murder 77 Brown Shirt members.	Saudi Arabia briefly invades Yemen.	The Chaco War intensifies.	Japan crowns Chinese heir Henry Pu-Yi as emperor of Manchukuo.
1935	The Communist Third International announces its "popular front" tactic, instructing Communist parties throughout the world to cooperate with socialist and democratic parties to oppose fascism.	The Saarland is restored to Germany.	After border clashes, Italy invades Ethiopia.	The Chaco War ends between Paraguay and Bolivia.	Japan completes its withdrawal from the League of Nations.
1936	Germany agrees to suspend use of the Nazi salute during the Olympics.	The Spanish civil war begins with a revolt by army officers stationed in Spanish Morocco.	Addis Ababa falls to Italian troops. Emperor Haile Selassie goes into exile.	At the Buenos Aires Conference, President Roosevelt warns countries not to interfere in the Western Hemisphere.	Japanese-Russian relations worsen over incidents in Manchukuo and Mongolia.
1937	The League of Nations condemns Japanese aggression in China, but is powerless to take action against it.	Rev. Martin Niemoeller, who opposes Nazi influence in religious affairs, is arrested in Germany.	The French suppress a Kurdish uprising in Syria.	Bolivia expropriates holdings of Standard Oil.	Fighting between the Chinese and Japanese escalates. . . . Japanese planes attack the U.S. gunboat *Panay* in the Yangtze River. . . . Japanese troops ravage the civilian population of Nanking, China.
1938		Germany takes over Austria in the *Anschluss*. . . . At the Munich Conference, France and Britain agree to the transfer of the Sudetenland section of Czechoslovakia to Germany.	Jewish-Arab tensions in Palestine continue; the British admit they have no plan for a solution.	Under President Lázaro Cárdenas, Mexico expropriates U.S. oil company holdings and other foreign properties. . . . Brazil suppresses a pro-fascist uprising of *Integralistas*.	The Japanese launch a major offensive in southern China, taking several major cities from the Chinese.
1939	Pope Pius XI dies; his successor takes the name Pius XII.	Franco's forces win a complete victory over the loyalist regime in Spain. . . . German armed forces invade Poland, launching World War II.	King Ghazi of Iraq dies in an automobile accident in Baghdad.	Thirty thousand are killed in an earthquake in Chile. . . . Three British cruisers attack the German pocket battleship *Graf Spee* and force the German warship into Uruguayan waters (La Plata Battle).	After brief clashes on the Mongolian-Manchurian border, Russia and Japan agree to a truce. They remain at peace with each other until August 1945.

A	B	C	D	E
Includes developments that affect more than one world region, international organizations, and important meetings of world leaders.	*Includes all domestic and regional developments in Europe, including the Soviet Union.*	*Includes all domestic and regional developments in Africa and the Middle East.*	*Includes all domestic and regional developments in Latin America, the Caribbean, and Canada.*	*Includes all domestic and regional developments in Asian and Pacific nations (and colonies).*

U.S. Politics & Social Issues	U.S. Foreign Policy & Defense	Economics & Great Depression	Science, Technology & Nature	Culture, Leisure & Lifestyle	
The Veterans Administration is established. . . . Republicans lose their majority in the Senate. . . . Huey Long is elected Senator from Louisiana.	U.S membership in the World Court is blocked in the Senate.	President Hoover requests an appropriation of up to $150 million for public works to provide employment.	Clyde Tombaugh discovers the planet Pluto.	Sinclair Lewis wins the Nobel Prize for Literature for his 1922 novel, *Babbitt*.	1930
In Alabama, nine African-American youths are arrested for rape; the trial of these "Scottsboro Boys" is held.	President Hoover proposes a one-year moratorium on international debt payments.	President Hoover vetoes the Veterans' Bonus Bill; it is passed over his veto.	Miles Laboratories start the production of Alka Seltzer.	The comic strip *Dick Tracy* begins.	1931
Al Capone goes to prison for tax evasion. . . . Franklin Roosevelt is elected president and Democrats win control of both houses of Congress.	A "Bonus Army" of veterans encamps in Washington; they are dispersed by federal troops.	The Reconstruction Finance Corporation is established.		Radio City Music Hall opens in New York City.	1932
Congress passes the Twenty-first Amendment to the Constitution, which repeals Prohibition, and sends it to the states for ratification. . . . Franklin Roosevelt is inaugurated president.	The United States recognizes the Soviet Union. . . . The United States abrogates the Platt Amendment with Cuba, giving up its right to intervene there.	President Roosevelt announces the New Deal. This package of legislation presented in the first 100 days of his administration establishes bank reform, the Civilian Conservation Corps, and the National Recovery Administration.	Karl Jansky reports the detection of radio waves from the center of the Milky Way galaxy. It is regarded as the beginning of radio astronomy.	*Newsweek* begins publication. Raymond Moley, a former member of the Roosevelt "brain trust" becomes editor. . . . *King Kong* premiers in New York. The film saves RKO from bankruptcy.	1933
Congressional elections give Democrats a gain in both houses of Congress.	Congress approves the Reciprocal Trade Act that empowers the president to negotiate individual tariff rates with different countries.	A general strike shuts down San Francisco; it is broken by business and government leaders.	Enrico Fermi artificially creates a new element: Neptunium (93).	Donald Duck debuts as a Disney character.	1934
Huey Long is assassinated in Louisiana.	Congress empowers the president to embargo arms shipments to countries at war.	Roosevelt announces the Second New Deal. . . . The Resettlement Administration is established. . . . The Supreme Court invalidates the NRA in the Schechter case.	Technicolor, developed at the Massachusetts Institute of Technology, is introduced in motion picture films.	Will Rogers dies in an airplane crash. . . . *Porgy and Bess* opens on Broadway.	1935
President Roosevelt is reelected by a 62 percent majority. . . . Democrats retain solid majorities in both houses of Congress.	The 1936 Neutrality Act forbids the extension of credit or loans to belligerents.	The Supreme Court invalidates the first Agricultural Adjustment Act. . . . Congress passes the Rural Electrification Act.	Johnstown, Pa., suffers a disastrous flood.	The winter and summer Olympic Games are held in Germany.	1936
President Roosevelt announces his plan to expand the number of judges on the Supreme Court.	Congress extends the Neutrality Act to cover the Spanish Civil War. . . . President Roosevelt embargoes arms to both Japan and China.		Wallace Corothers, who invented nylon in 1935, commits suicide.	Margaret Mitchell wins the Pulitzer Prize for her novel *Gone with the Wind*.	1937
The House Committee on Un-American Activities is established.	In spite of pressure from oil companies, the Roosevelt administration maintains its Good Neighbor Policy toward Mexico.	Congress passes the Second Agricultural Adjustment Act, which helps stabilize farm commodity prices.	Enrico Fermi receives the Nobel Prize for his discovery of artificial elements.	Orson Welles produces the play *War of the Worlds* on the radio, spurring widespread panic among listeners who believe the Earth is being invaded by Martians.	1938
The Daughters of the America Revolution forbid African-American contralto Marion Anderson from singing at Constitution Hall because of her race. First Lady Eleanor Roosevelt resigns her membership.	After declaring neutrality, the United States amends its neutrality laws to allow "Cash and Carry," which will permit Allies to buy arms in the United States and transport them on non-U.S. ships.		Ernest O. Lawrence is awarded the Nobel Prize for Physics for his work on the cyclotron.	*Mr. Smith Goes to Washington*, by Frank Capra, opens in Washington.	1939

F	**G**	**H**	**I**	**J**
Includes elections, federal-state relations, civil rights and liberties, crime, the judiciary, education, healthcare, poverty, urban affairs, and population.	*Includes formation and debate of U.S. foreign and defense policies, veterans affairs, and defense spending. (Relations with specific foreign countries are usually found under the region concerned.)*	*Includes business, labor, agriculture, taxation, transportation, consumer affairs, monetary and fiscal policy, natural resources, pollution, and accidents.*	*Includes worldwide scientific, medical, and technological developments, natural phenomena, U.S. weather, and natural disasters.*	*Includes the arts, religion, scholarship, communications media, sports, entertainment, fashions, fads, and social life.*

1930

Settling back in their rocking chairs, a farm family listens to the wonders of radio broadcasting in 1930.

	World Affairs	Europe	Africa & The Middle East	The Americas	Asia & The Pacific
Jan.	The second reparation conference in the Hague negotiates a new reparations payment plan for Germany.... The London Naval Conference begins. It will result in a naval disarmament treaty between Britain, Japan, and the United States and in the allocation of tonnage limitations for certain categories of warships.	Humbert of Savoy, Prince of Piedmont and heir to the Italian throne, marries Princess Maria José, the only daughter of the King and Queen of Belgium.		The Bolivian and Paraguayan governments start a war over the disputed Chaco region, territory claimed by both states.... Mexico severs diplomatic relations with Soviet Russia.	At the conference of the Indian National Congress, the more radical faction asking for complete independence from Britain gains the majority of the party.... Extraterritoriality rights are abolished in China.
Feb.	The League of Nations hosts an international conference in Geneva to reduce high tariff barriers and promote international trade.... Pope Pius XI protests against Russian persecutions of Christians.	Italy and Austria sign a Treaty of Friendship through which Italian Premier Benito Mussolini will try to support the fascist elements in Austria.	The Nejd and Iraqi governments sign a Treaty of Friendship to improve future relations.	Two hours after taking his oath as Mexican president, Pascual Ortiz Rubio is wounded by a gunman.... Brazilian Vice President Fernando Mello Vianna is shot while campaigning for the next presidential election.	A serious revolt against the French breaks out in Tonkin in French Indo China, led by the Vietnamese Nationalists (VNQDD). The French crush the revolt with strong military action.
Mar.	Negotiations between the British and Egyptian governments break down because of disagreements over the status of Sudan.	British novelist D.H. Lawrence dies of tuberculosis in Vance, France.... The names of the Turkish cities of Constantinople and Angora are changed to Istanbul and Ankara.... Heinrich Brüening is appointed German chancellor.	The Ethiopian Negus grants a dam construction concession to the American J.G. White Corporation with the support of the British and Egyptian governments.... The Persian government adopts the gold standard as the basis for the national currency.... The report of the Shaw commission on Palestine investigates Arab attacks against Jews.		Mohandas K. Gandhi begins the second civilian disobedience campaign against the British government. The campaign includes a march to the sea to protest against the British tax on salt.
Apr.	The London Naval Conference ends. The United States, Britain, and Japan sign the London Naval Treaty, which regulates submarine warfare and limits shipbuilding. Italy and France do not sign the main treaty.	The long-standing dispute between Romania, Czechoslovakia, and Hungary regarding the settlement of Hungarian landowners' claims for compensation is settled by the Brocchi Plan.... After its failure to obtain naval parity with France, the Italian government launches major air and naval programs to establish its superiority in the Mediterranean.	Ras Tafari becomes the new Emperor of Abyssinia under the name Haile Selassie.	The Bolivian and Paraguayan governments reach a temporary agreement on the Chaco dispute.	
May	A total of 17 countries negotiate refinancing agreements regarding their war debts owed to the U.S. government.	The German government begins reparation payments according to the Young Plan of June 1930.... Italian Premier Benito Mussolini calls for a revision of the Versailles Treaty.	The British government announces the restriction of Jewish immigration to Palestine, provoking widespread Jewish protests.... A new constitution for Syria is approved under which it becomes a republic with a representative government.... An earthquake in Iran kills 4,000 people.	Resenting the high tariff rates imposed by the United States on Canadian goods, Canada revises its own tariffs. It raises duties on American goods while providing preferential treatment to British goods.	British authorities arrest Gandhi, an act which provokes unrest in India.... The Japanese government signs a tariff agreement with the Chinese government at Nanking.
Jun.	The International Labor Organization holds its 14th session in Geneva.... The Permanent Court of International Justice holds its 18th session in The Hague.	Kurdish nationalists revolt against Turkish rule in the Mount Ararat region.... Allied forces complete their military evacuation of the Rhineland. The region becomes a demilitarized buffer zone between Germany and France.	The Wafd Party protests against the decision of the Egyptian King to resume negotiations with Britain. The party starts a campaign of noncooperation with the government and urges citizens not to pay taxes.... Iraq is recognized by Britain as an independent state.		The Simon report outlines the future of India, recommending administrative reforms but denying a fully responsible government.
Jul.	The League of Nations hosts a conference on child welfare and health in Lima.	British mystery writer and Sherlock Holmes creator Sir Arthur Conan Doyle dies.... An earthquake in Italy kills 1,500 people.		The Canadian Conservative Party wins a stable majority in parliament.	
Aug.	The League of Nations holds its second conference on syphilis to try to find a cure for the disease.	The Bulgarian government arrests the leader of the Macedonian Revolutionary Organization (IMRO), Ivan Mihailov.... Princess Margaret Rose, sister to Elizabeth, is born to King George VI and Queen Elizabeth at Glamis Castle, Scotland.	A League of Nations report on Palestine heavily condemns British authorities for their inability to protect Jewish citizens.	Richard Bedford Bennett becomes Canada's 11th prime minister.... A military junta stages a coup in Peru.	
Sept.	The League of Nations meets for its 11th session under the presidency of Romania.	German political elections reward radical political parties, while moderates suffer serious setbacks. The National Socialist Party, led by Adolf Hitler, becomes a major party.... The Dutch, Danish, Norwegian, and Swedish governments sign an economic agreement, designed to coordinate tariff policies and promote trade.	The Johnson-Christy Commission issues a report that finds that slavery still exists in Liberia.... Kurdish nationalists under Sheikh Mahmud rebel against the Iraqi government.	Latin American delegates meet in Washington for the first Pan-American Conference on Agriculture.... José Félix Uriburu stages a successful military coup, overthrowing Hipolito Yrigoyen, president of Argentina.... A violent hurricane causes damages and death in the Dominican Republic.	
Oct.	Delegates from the British Commonwealth meet in London to define relationships between Britain and its imperial dominions.... The Permanent Court of International Justice holds its 19th session in The Hague.	Princess Giovanna of Italy, daughter of King Victor Emmanuel III of Italy, marries King Boris of Bulgaria. The marriage strengthens Italian influence in the Balkans.... Greece and Turkey sign the Treaty of Ankara, which settles outstanding disputes between the two countries.	The British government releases the Passfield White Paper on the Arab attacks on Jews in Palestine. The paper stresses that Jewish immigration into Palestine should be contained as long as Arabs suffer from the lack of land and jobs.	In Brazil, Getulio Donelles Vargas leads the Revolution of 1930.... Widespread disorder breaks out in Cuba.	After bitter debate, the Japanese government ratifies the London Naval Treaty in spite of the inferior status of the Japanese fleet compared to the U.S. warships.... The British government restores the treaty port of Weihaiwei to Chinese rule in accordance with the Washington Naval Conference of 1922.

A	B	C	D	E
Includes developments that affect more than one world region, international organizations, and important meetings of world leaders.	Includes all domestic and regional developments in Europe, including the Soviet Union.	Includes all domestic and regional developments in Africa and the Middle East.	Includes all domestic and regional developments in Latin America, the Caribbean, and Canada.	Includes all domestic and regional developments in Asian and Pacific nations (and colonies).

U.S. Politics & Social Issues	U.S. Foreign Policy & Defense	Economics & Great Depression	Science, Technology & Nature	Culture, Leisure & Lifestyle	
The Commission on Law Observance and Enforcement describes the U.S. law enforcement system as a failure. . . . The 10th anniversary of Prohibition stirs debate on the Eighteenth Amendment in Congress.	President Hoover urges the U.S. delegates to the London Naval Conference to have a conciliatory spirit. He stresses the main aim of the United States is the reduction of military fleets.		The discovery of a sugar substance generated by tuberculosis germs generates new hope for the treatment of the disease. . . . Admiral Richard Byrd heads an expedition that charts a vast area of Antarctica.	Amelia Earhart sets an aviation record for women at 171 miles per hour in a Lockheed Vega. . . . Charles Lindbergh arrives in New York, setting a cross-country flying record of 14.75 hours.	Jan.
President Hoover appoints Charles Evans Hughes as Chief Justice of the Supreme Court after William Howard Taft resigns for ill health.	President Hoover appoints a commission to study a plan to end U.S. military presence in Haiti.		Pluto, the ninth planet of our solar system, is discovered by Clyde Tombaugh.	A Loening Air Yacht of Air Ferries makes its first passenger run between San Francisco and Oakland, Calif. . . . The Maltese Falcon by Dashiell Hammett is published.	Feb.
A federal grand jury indicts George Noel Keyston, president of the San Francisco Stock Exchange, for an alleged conspiracy to embezzle funds from the Post and Fillmore branch of the Bank of Italy in 1929. . . . William Howard Taft, former U.S. president and chief justice, dies in Washington.	The Hoover administration announces a new interpretation of the Monroe Doctrine, which is primarily directed against European interference in the Americas. . . . The Nautilus, the first streamlined submarine of the U.S. Navy, is launched.	Thousands of people throughout the United States demonstrate on Red Thursday (March 5) against unemployment. . . . The Senate passes a bill increasing tariffs.	Clarence Birdseye develops a method for quick-freezing food.	Flying High opens at the Apollo Theatre in New York. It will run for 45 weeks. . . . The Motion Picture Production Code is instituted. It provides strict guidelines for the treatment of sex, violence, religion, and crime in films.	Mar.
Henry H. Curran, president of the Association Against the Prohibition Amendment, announces that his organization will fund the Congressional campaigns of those candidates in favor of repealing the Eighteenth Amendment. . . . The Senate Judiciary Committee votes against the appointment of John J. Parker as an associate judge of the Supreme Court.	U.S. officials estimate that the U.S. occupation of Haiti has cost $23 million. Both U.S. soldiers and civilians wish to leave Haiti soon. . . . President Hoover praises the result of the London Naval Conference.	The stock exchange reaches its highest trading level since the beginning of the year. . . . President Hoover predicts a deficit of $20,000,000 in the next fiscal year.	The first synthetic rubber is produced.	Charles and Anne Lindbergh set a transcontinental speed record flying from Los Angeles to New York in 14 hours and 45 minutes. . . . The film All Quiet on the Western Front by Lewis Milestone and based on the book by Erich Maria Remarque has its premiere. . . . The first night game in the history of professional baseball takes place in Independence, Kans.	Apr.
The Supreme Court rules that buying liquor does not violate the U.S. Constitution.			The first planetarium in the United States opens in Chicago.	Marc Connelly is awarded the Pulitzer Prize. . . . Ellen Church becomes the first airline stewardess. . . . Soviet director Sergei Eisenstein arrives in Hollywood to work for Paramount.	May
The U.S. Coast Guard cutter Tingard captures the trawler 5048, also known as the Dora, and confiscates 400 cases of imported whiskey in California. . . . Chicago Tribune journalist Alfred Liddle is killed in Chicago. His links to organized crime will be uncovered during the murder investigation.	The Veterans of the First World War organization demonstrates in front of the Senate to obtain several benefits.	Despite the protests of economists, President Hoover signs the Smoot-Hawley Tariff Bill. It increases duties on raw materials from 50 to 100 percent over the 1922 schedules. Many countries retaliate against American goods.		William Beebe of the New York Zoological Society dives to a record-setting depth of 1,426 feet off the coast of Bermuda in a diving chamber called a bathysphere.	Jun.
A natural gas explosion in the Mitchell ravine tunnel of the Hetch Hetchy water project in California kills 12 men.	Congress creates the U.S. Veterans Administration.	President Hoover calls Congress for a special session to ratify the London Naval Treaty.	The construction of the Boulder Dam (now known as the Hoover Dam) begins on the Colorado River.	Uruguay wins the first football World Cup.	Jul.
Joseph Force Crater disappears in New York City. He had been recently appointed by Governor Franklin Roosevelt to the New York Supreme Court.				Betty Boop first appears in the animated film Dizzy Dishes.	Aug.
Louisiana Governor Huey P. Long wins the Democratic Senatorial nomination.	Former Secretary of State Frank B. Kellogg says he is ready to represent the United States on the World Court bench. . . . The United States expresses hope for better cooperation with new Argentine president José Félix Uriburu.	President Hoover asks for a ban on foreign immigration as a relief measure against unemployment.	Johann Ostermeyer patents the flashbulb. . . . 3M begins marketing Scotch tape.	The first nonstop airplane flight from Europe to the United States takes place as Captains Dieudonne Coste and Maurice Bellonte of France arrive in Valley Stream, N.Y. . . . Baseball player Lou Gehrig's errorless streak ends at 885 consecutive games.	Sept.
				Laura Ingalls becomes the first woman to fly across the United States as she completes a nine-stop journey from Roosevelt Field in New York to Glendale, Calif. . . . Singer Ethel Merman holds a high C for 16 bars while singing "I Got Rhythm" during her Broadway debut in Gershwin's Girl Crazy.	Oct.

F	G	H	I	J
Includes elections, federal-state relations, civil rights and liberties, crime, the judiciary, education, healthcare, poverty, urban affairs, and population.	Includes formation and debate of U.S. foreign and defense policies, veterans affairs, and defense spending. (Relations with specific foreign countries are usually found under the region concerned.)	Includes business, labor, agriculture, taxation, transportation, consumer affairs, monetary and fiscal policy, natural resources, pollution, and accidents.	Includes worldwide scientific, medical, and technological developments, natural phenomena, U.S. weather, and natural disasters.	Includes the arts, religion, scholarship, communications media, sports, entertainment, fashions, fads, and social life.

	World Affairs	Europe	Africa & The Middle East	The Americas	Asia & The Pacific
Nov.	The Preparatory Commission for the Disarmament Conference of 1932 starts its session. . . . The League of Nations hosts the Second International Conference on Concerted Economic Action to counter the global depression.	A bitter debate in the British parliament follows the publication of the Passfield White Paper on Palestine. Although the government denies it wants to change policy in Palestine, Jewish confidence in the government is seriously undermined. . . . General strikes and riots paralyze Madrid.	The Anglo-Iraqi Treaty confirms Iraq's complete independence and provides for the country's entry to the League of Nations.		The British government organizes the first roundtable conference with Indian representatives who are willing to cooperate with the British government. Delegates call for the establishment of a federation and of responsible government. . . . An earthquake kills 187 in Shizouka, Japan.
Dec.	The Preparatory Commission for the Disarmament Conference of 1932 approves a draft convention to serve as a basis for negotiations. Germany and Russia refuse to sign it. . . . Allied Forces complete the evacuation of the Saarland.	The governments of the Netherlands and Scandinavia sign the Oslo economic agreements, promising not to raise tariffs against each other. . . . A Dervish uprising takes place in Turkey and leads the government to execute 28 Dervish leaders. . . . The Spanish revolution begins.			

A	B	C	D	E
Includes developments that affect more than one world region, international organizations, and important meetings of world leaders.	*Includes all domestic and regional developments in Europe, including the Soviet Union.*	*Includes all domestic and regional developments in Africa and the Middle East.*	*Includes all domestic and regional developments in Latin America, the Caribbean, and Canada.*	*Includes all domestic and regional developments in Asian and Pacific nations (and colonies).*

U.S. Politics & Social Issues	U.S. Foreign Policy & Defense	Economics & Great Depression	Science, Technology & Nature	Culture, Leisure & Lifestyle	
Elijah Muhammad forms the Nation of Islam in Detroit.		The U.S. government takes a critical stance against the developments at the International Preparatory Commission for the Disarmament Conference of 1932.		Sinclair Lewis is the first American to win the Nobel Prize for Literature for his 1922 novel *Babbit.* . . . Two important musicals, *Sweet and Low* and *Smiles*, premiere in New York.	Nov.
Brewery heir Adolphus Busch, age 13, is kidnapped in a St. Louis suburb.	Senator William Borah blocks Senate approval of the World Court Protocol, which President Hoover had introduced for ratification.	President Hoover asks Congress for a $150 million public works program to stimulate the economy and provide employment.		Fred P. Newton swims for the longest distance ever (1,826 miles), when he swims the Mississippi River from Ford Dam, Minn., to New Orleans, La.	Dec.

F	G	H	I	J
Includes elections, federal-state relations, civil rights and liberties, crime, the judiciary, education, healthcare, poverty, urban affairs, and population.	*Includes formation and debate of U.S. foreign and defense policies, veterans affairs, and defense spending. (Relations with specific foreign countries are usually found under the region concerned.)*	*Includes business, labor, agriculture, taxation, transportation, consumer affairs, monetary and fiscal policy, natural resources, pollution, and accidents.*	*Includes worldwide scientific, medical, and technological developments, natural phenomena, U.S. weather, and natural disasters.*	*Includes the arts, religion, scholarship, communications media, sports, entertainment, fashions, fads, and social life.*

	World Affairs	Europe	Africa & The Middle East	The Americas	Asia & The Pacific
Jan. 1	Heavily in debt, Austria seeks an international loan worth $100 million, which leading financiers say will reinvigorate a declining Central Europe. . . . The U.S. Olympic Committee invites an unprecedented 52 nations to compete in the 1932 Winter Olympic Games in Lake Placid, N.Y.	British Chancellor of the Duchy of Lancaster Oswald Mosley, who would later go on to found the British Union of Fascists, releases the "Mosley Memorandum," recommending that in order to quell British unemployment, the state must take full control of both banking and national exports. . . . The name of the Norwegian city of Trondheim is officially changed to the original founders' name of "Nidaros." . . . Facing serious health problems and losing support from his military, Spanish dictator Primo de Rivera announces his resignation. Installed in 1923 via a military coup, Rivera's term of seven years is the longest of any leader of Spain since the 18th century.	Following the resignation of his cabinet, King Fuad of Egypt requests that Mustapha Nahas Pasha, whose party sealed victory in the general elections a few days prior, form a cabinet of Wafdists.		
Jan. 2	A delegation of Arab leaders lead by Emir Adel Arslan arrives in the United States to convince wealthy Arab Americans to return to Palestine to boost the region's fledgling economy. . . . British military presence in India stabilizes at 165,000 troops, of which 45,000 are English and 120,000 Indian.	Spain announces its automobile production has increased by 28 percent in the past year.		In an interview during a flight across the continental United States, famed aviator Charles Lindbergh praises the recent developments of radio technology in aviation and announces his intention to plan a flight to South America.	
Jan. 3	The United States gains ownership of the Turtle Islands, an archipelago in Southeast Asia with a population of 200, from Great Britain. . . . International diplomats meet in the Hague to discuss adopting the Young Plan, a comprehensive restructuring of Germany's war reparations.	The British Special Claims Commission demands $100 million from Mexico in reparations for revolutionary activities in 1910 and 1920, when Mexican revolutionaries damaged the Interoceanic Railway.			British-owned Indian newspaper *The Daily Herald* calls on Nationalist leader Mohandas Gandhi to cease his civil disobedience campaign, writing that nothing could be achieved with a simple "we will not play" approach.
Jan. 4	The second day of The Hague Conference begins. British officials remark publicly that Germany's loan demand would cost upwards of $65 million in treasury bills.	In a refugee camp in Hammerstein, Germany, for Russian immigrants of German descent, 52 children die of pneumonia. Major Fuchs, commander of the refugee camp, blames the outbreak on the children's having undergone undernourishment while residing in Russia.			
Jan. 5	French Minister of Commerce Pierre Flandin issues a formal complaint concerning the United States' trade policy, noting that while the French purchase over 5 billion francs per year in American goods, Americans purchase only 200 million francs worth of French goods.				
Jan. 6		*The Bankers Magazine* publishes a year-end review of Great Britain's economy, noting that in January 1929 Britain's Stock Exchange index was 129.1. By November, the figure had fallen to a two-year low of 120.9. . . . *The Economist* newspaper reports that British wholesale prices fell by over 7 percent in 1929.			China's main currency unit falls to 38 cents gold, resulting in the closing of five banks in the city of Peking.

A	B	C	D	E
Includes developments that affect more than one world region, international organizations, and important meetings of world leaders.	Includes all domestic and regional developments in Europe, including the Soviet Union.	Includes all domestic and regional developments in Africa and the Middle East.	Includes all domestic and regional developments in Latin America, the Caribbean, and Canada.	Includes all domestic and regional developments in Asian and Pacific nations (and colonies).

U.S. Politics & Social Issues	U.S. Foreign Policy & Defense	Economics & Great Depression	Science, Technology & Nature	Culture, Leisure & Lifestyle	
In a Manhattan New Year's Eve raid, 150 prohibition agents under the direction of Major Maurice Campbell simultaneously arrest 33 people charged with "conspiracy to violate the Prohibition Laws." In all, 17 speakeasies and nightclubs in Manhattan are raided, with seizures ranging from 1 to 150 bottles of illegal liquor. . . . The American Association for Labor Legislation submits its year-in-review, noting that 400 new labor laws involving "workmen's compensation . . . pensions, [and] employment of women" were passed in the previous year. California enacted the most, 36, while South Carolina enacted the least, one.		The United States Neediest Fund, a private donation program providing financial relief for 446 poverty-stricken families, reaches $309,554. This falls short of the previous year's $338,000 total contribution. The contributions themselves are exempt from federal and state income taxes. . . . The General Motors Corporation announces its number of stockholders increased from 71,185 to 198,600 in one year.	Prof. Hugo Junkers of Germany is awarded the Siemens ring by Von Siemens for his thermal research in aviation. He is only the fifth scientist to receive the award.	The University of Iowa is banned from athletic competition in the Western Conference following allegations that the university illegally funded prospective athletes. With the Hawkeyes' exclusion, the Western Conference, known as the Big Ten, now becomes the Big Nine. . . . National Collegiate Athletic Association president Palmer E. Pierce, who headed the association for most of its existence, resigns.	Jan. 1
U.S. Assistant Secretary of Commerce Clarence M. Young predicts substantial progress in commercial aviation in the coming year, basing his claims on a reported 62.5 percent increase in total commercial air miles flown in the past year. . . . Following a speech by New York Democratic Governor Franklin Roosevelt, in which he laid out plans to curb a declining U.S. economy, Republican Senate leaders respond by saying Roosevelt's proposals are "wholly familiar and obvious."		Tobacco prices in Knoxville, Tenn., rise by 7 percent in one month. . . . U.S. Labor Department employment director Francis I. Jones admits that in the previous autumn's stock market crash, the "fulcrum of business was . . . shaken," but he predicts that "1930 will measure in volume of business with the preceding year."		The first edition of *Astounding Stories* is published.	Jan. 2
Deputy Commissioner of Public Safety William A. Brennan of White Plains, N.Y., reports that his city's residential construction has dropped from $12,633,281 in 1928 to $7,184,967 in 1929, a loss of nearly 50 percent.		The American Cigar Co. omits its dividend to its stockholders. Company president George W. Hill claims the $12 million must be used to fund business expenditures. . . . The Federal Reserve Bank of New York announces that stock-brokers' loans have increased nearly $100 million in the past week, currently totaling $3,328,000,000.			Jan. 3
In an interview with *The Chicago Tribune's* Arthur Sears Henning, former president Calvin Coolidge states that he has considered running in the 1932 presidential election. . . . Congress receives a report stating the financial status of the Republican and Democratic National Committees. The RNC lists a surplus of $136,363. The DNC, a deficit of $449,686.		Testifying before a committee on subway labor in New York, representatives of four major contractors admit that they paid carpenters only half of the $1.50 per hour they were promised by the carpenters' union. . . . Representatives of major steel companies report to U.S. President Herbert Hoover that they expect steel production to rise above that of 1929's total. . . . Due to budget constraints, the city of Chicago is forced to dismiss 1,100 city employees.	In Bemidji, Minn., temperatures drop below 20°F after a period of unseasonable statewide warmth.	Jose Capablanca of Cuba clinches first place in the Hastings Tourney chess competition after defeating England's E.G. Seargent in the semi-final round.	Jan. 4
The U.S. Motor Vehicle Bureau reports a record year in 1929 for new licenses; over 2 million were issued. . . . Following comments by District of Columbia Municipal Court Judge Nathan Cayton that "the Jews of America have produced far more than their share of criminals," members of the American Jewish Committee demand a retraction, noting that in "New York City, where the Jews comprise 27 percent of the population, only 19 percent" of the prison population is Jewish.		Public utility officials report a record gross of $5.5 million in 1929, an increase of 27 percent over five years. . . . The U.S. Bureau of Public Roads estimates that $2.4 billion will be spent on new road construction in the coming year.	Former British Chief of Wireless Research Dr. James Robinson invents a new radio transmitter which "will receive radio stations on a band of less than 100 cycles in width." Standard technology permits only 10,000 cycles.	New York Governor Franklin Roosevelt orders that the traditional Puerto Rican gift-giving holiday, The Three Kings' Day, be recognized as a statewide holiday.	Jan. 5
Facing criticism for an aggressive approach in dealing with prohibition violators, U.S. Coast Guard Commandant Rear Admiral Frederick C. Billard gives a radio speech defending the use of force against unidentified sea vessels.		Chicago's wheat sales in 1929 are tallied; 221,758,000 bushels were sold, slightly less than half the total of 1928.	The first trip of a four-cylinder diesel-engine automobile is completed.	Jean Borotra and Andre Glasser of France win the men's doubles title in the French Open tennis tournament after defeating Luis and Domingo Toralva of Chile.	Jan. 6

F	G	H	I	J
Includes elections, federal-state relations, civil rights and liberties, crime, the judiciary, education, healthcare, poverty, urban affairs, and population.	Includes formation and debate of U.S. foreign and defense policies, veterans affairs, and defense spending. (Relations with specific foreign countries are usually found under the region concerned.)	Includes business, labor, agriculture, taxation, transportation, consumer affairs, monetary and fiscal policy, natural resources, pollution, and accidents.	Includes worldwide scientific, medical, and technological developments, natural phenomena, U.S. weather, and natural disasters.	Includes the arts, religion, scholarship, communications media, sports, entertainment, fashions, fads, and social life.

	World Affairs	Europe	Africa & The Middle East	The Americas	Asia & The Pacific
Jan. 7	On trial in Berlin for counterfeiting Russian rubles, a defendant claims the fraudulent bank notes were used to finance a revolution in Soviet Georgia. When further pressed, he refuses to name the co-conspirators.	The Council of Leitrim County in Dublin, Ireland, rejects a $4,750 gift given to them by the Carnegie Foundation for the purpose of building a library, saying "the fund might better be used to aid the poor."			
Jan. 8	U.S. Senator Hiram Bingham proposes a half-Filipino, half-American commission to study the feasibility of granting independence to the Philippines.	Northern Albanian tribes stage a revolt in the Albanian capital of Tirana against monarch King Zog. However, the government issues an official denial, declaring that "the whole country is perfectly peaceful."		The government of Argentina receives a $25 million loan from private London bankers.	
Jan. 9	Nearly 100 U.S. delegates depart from Hoboken, N.J., to attend the London Naval Conference.	The number of unemployed people living in Germany reaches 2 million. Of those, 85 percent receive financial relief. . . . Germany's Reichstag Finance Committee approves a naval budget of 590 million marks ($141,600,000).			
Jan. 10	Mexico is allowed limited participation in the League of Nations.	British Minister of Employment J.H. Thomas concludes an agreement with British financial institutions to extend liberal loans for the purpose of alleviating the nation's 1.5 million unemployed persons.	Former King of Afghanistan Amanullah Khan decides to permanently remain in exile in Italy.		
Jan. 11	At the preliminary proceedings of the London Naval Conference, Great Britain agrees to reduce the number of its cruiser ships to 50, altering its earlier agreement of 70. . . . The British Admiralty Intelligence Department publishes its annual report detailing major powers' naval strength. Japan, according to the report, is the world's foremost naval power. . . . On the occasion of the 10th anniversary of the founding of the League of Nations, Smith College president William Allen Neilson addresses his students, saying "there is no question . . . about the permanence of the League. . ."	The Detroit architectural firm Albert Kahn, Inc. enters into a five-year program with the Soviet Union to consult with the Communist nation on $1.9 billion in new buildings.			Japan lifts its embargo on the export of gold, in place since 1917.
Jan. 12	At the London Naval Conference, The League of Nations Union of Great Britain proposes a 10,000-ton limit on battleships, less than the originally proposed 35,000-ton limit.	Albert V. Alexander, British First Lord of the Admiralty, faces charges from critics at home who say Alexander's recommendation of a limit of 50 British cruiser ships will leave the island nation vulnerable to attack.			The Nanking Government of China announces it will allow foreigners to become citizens, contingent upon a rigorous examination.
Jan. 13		The British Board of Trade's Index of Industrial Output shows that production in the fall of 1929 was significantly higher than earlier in the year.	Palestine faces a political crisis as many members of its top executive branch resign, including the Chairman, Vice Chairman, and Secretary.		
Jan. 14					

A	B	C	D	E
Includes developments that affect more than one world region, international organizations, and important meetings of world leaders.	Includes all domestic and regional developments in Europe, including the Soviet Union.	Includes all domestic and regional developments in Africa and the Middle East.	Includes all domestic and regional developments in Latin America, the Caribbean, and Canada.	Includes all domestic and regional developments in Asian and Pacific nations (and colonies).

U.S. Politics & Social Issues	U.S. Foreign Policy & Defense	Economics & Great Depression	Science, Technology & Nature	Culture, Leisure & Lifestyle	
Hundreds gather at Young's Cemetery in Oyster Bay, N.Y., to pay tribute to former president Theodore Roosevelt on the 11th anniversary of his death. . . . Chief Justice of the Supreme Court William Howard Taft goes on temporary hiatus, checking in to Garfield Hospital in Washington, D.C. for "a recurrence of a bladder trouble."		In a report issued by the American Railway Association, President R.H. Aishton estimates that 1929's total railway income amounted to $1.2 billion, a yearly increase of over $100 million. However, November experienced a 31 percent decrease in income compared to the month prior.	Zenith Radio Corporation vice president Paul B. Klugh states during an industry luncheon that the year of 1929 was "the most prosperous" in radio's history.		Jan. 7
Associated Organizations executive secretary A.F. Anderson announces plans to organize simultaneous protest marches across the United States against the Eighteenth Amendment, a.k.a. the Prohibition Amendment, setting a goal of 30 million marchers. . . . The New York State Aviation Commission proposes a law that would prohibit low-flying over cities, classifying it as a misdemeanor.	In a farewell breakfast ceremony for delegates of the London Naval Conference, U.S. President Herbert Hoover urges conciliatory actions in the hope that they will drastically reduce naval building programs. World peace, he says, "rests . . . on the shoulders of the five delegations."	During an annual gathering of more than 1,400 automobile executives at the National Automobile Chamber of Commerce, Willys-Overland vice president G.M. Graham, delivering the evening's keynote address, warns about the dangers of overproduction. He accuses his colleagues of "hiding behind a barrage of exaggerated and often unconvincing optimism."		Authors of the British biographical publication *Who's Who?* commit a gaffe when they list famed aviator Col. Charles Lindbergh as "U.S. Ambassador to Mexico," a position his father-in-law holds.	Jan. 8
The U.S. Supreme Court denies Rhode Island's attempt to try a prohibition agent for entering a residence without a search warrant.	A consortium of American ship experts report that ship construction costs for the Navy are significantly higher than that of equally able foreign navies.	The French government considers raising the tariff on imported automobiles, estimating a 45–90 percent increase. . . . The National City Company publishes a report naming New York as the world's richest city with an assessed realty value of over $18 billion.	Dr. Lee De Forest, inventor of the triode vacuum tube, is elected president of the Institute of Radio Engineers.		Jan. 9
In a speech given before the Board of Directors of the New York Life Insurance Company, former president Calvin Coolidge estimates the number of the nation's insured to be 67 million at a cost of $133 billion per year. . . . Yale professor of theology Dr. Douglas Clyde is denied citizenship by the U.S. District Court for failure to "take the oath to bear arms." Clyde responds by saying warfare conflicts with his religious beliefs.	Prior to his departure for the London Naval Conference, Navy Secretary Charles Francis Adams appoints Assistant Secretary Jahncke as chairman of a committee to oversee development of a new navy building. . . . The U.S. Navy decommissions the destroyer ship USS *Humphreys*. The ship will now be used in training courses.	*The New York Times* reports a record high in 1929 for New York City's bank exchanges. Nearly three-quarters of a trillion dollars was traded, despite an 18.6 percent decrease in December compared to the prior month.		Philanthropist Edward W. Bok dies at his estate in Mountain Lake, Fla.	Jan. 10
Dr. Hagner, chief caretaker for Chief Justice William Howard Taft during his recuperation following his brother's death, reports that Taft "is getting along satisfactorily."	Col. Hunter B. Nelson, retired Army officer, dies at his home in Los Angeles, Calif.	The price of wheat in the United States falls to a year-low of $1.29.	After receiving an offer by an airline company to take a flight over his winter retreat in Fort Myers, Fla., 84-year-old inventor Thomas Edison responds by saying he is "too busy" to fly.	New Zealander M.J.C. Allom sets a record in international cricket competition, capturing the wickets of four batsmen with five balls.	Jan. 11
	New York Congressional Rep. Hamilton Fish proposes a bill authorizing appropriations of $1.5 million for a 10,000-acre expansion of West Point Military Academy.	French economic experts estimate that the newly created tariff on imported automobiles will result in a loss of 290 million francs annually.			Jan. 12
	Keystone Aircraft Corp. of Bristol, Pa., is awarded one of the largest army contracts since the end of World War I. At $2 million, the contract calls for 70 war planes to be built.	New York State Industrial Commissioner Frances Perkins reports that the state's factories saw an employment drop of 4 percent during December 1929. . . . Officials of the Reichsbank in Germany meet to discuss reducing the bank's discount from 7 percent to 6.5 percent.		Psychoanalyst Sigmund Freud publishes "The Discomfort of Civilization."	Jan. 13
Eight men detained in a Jackson, Ky., jailhouse for the Christmas Day lynching of Chester Fugate are released on a $10,000 bond. . . . Rep. William Williamson of South Dakota introduces a bill that would transfer prohibition enforcement from the Treasury Department to the Justice Department.		The U.S. Department of Commerce announces automobile exports totaled $537,153,119 in 1929, an increase of $15,055,145 from the previous year. . . . Coffee prices in the United States drop to a 20-year low.		In an annual report, New York State Secretary Edward J. Flynn states that boxing and wrestling netted the state $262,690 in tax collections. . . . W.H. Bowlus claims a new American gliding record when he stays aloft in the air for 6 hours, 19 minutes, and 3 seconds.	Jan. 14

F	G	H	I	J
Includes elections, federal-state relations, civil rights and liberties, crime, the judiciary, education, healthcare, poverty, urban affairs, and population.	Includes formation and debate of U.S. foreign and defense policies, veterans affairs, and defense spending. (Relations with specific foreign countries are usually found under the region concerned.)	Includes business, labor, agriculture, taxation, transportation, consumer affairs, monetary and fiscal policy, natural resources, pollution, and accidents.	Includes worldwide scientific, medical, and technological developments, natural phenomena, U.S. weather, and natural disasters.	Includes the arts, religion, scholarship, communications media, sports, entertainment, fashions, fads, and social life.

	World Affairs	Europe	Africa & The Middle East	The Americas	Asia & The Pacific
Jan. 15	The Afghan government pledges to Germany that it will reimburse them for all the expenditures taken by now-deposed King Amanullah Khan during his visit to Berlin two years prior. . . . Mexican National Highway Association president Octavio Dubois praises American aviation, saying "thanks to the splendid work of Dwight W. Morrow and Colonel [Charles] Lindbergh, there is a genuine feeling of friendliness in Mexico toward the United States."				Australia enacts $150 million in funds to modernize its railway system.
Jan. 16		Germany amasses 14,000 policemen to quell Communist uprisings.	The Roman Catholic Church purchases the Palestinian village of Rameh from Muslim Supreme Council member Ameen Abdul Hadi, the third such purchase in as many months.	Panama opts not to seek U.S. intervention in its territorial dispute with Costa Rica over the Coto section on Panama's northern border.	The value of the Mexican silver dollar in China drops to 35 cents from 49 cents one year prior. . . . Communist forces seize the Chinese city of Hoihow. American destroyer ships are dispatched to protect 15 American nationals.
Jan. 17	In a new treatise entitled "The Way to Peace," author H.G. Wells criticizes the concept of military conscription, saying children should be taught that "the attainment of human health and happiness are far finer ends than . . . tearing up one flag for the purpose of hoisting another." . . . British Prime Minister Ramsay MacDonald calls for a complete abolition of the most destructive of naval vessels, the battleship. . . . At the Council of the League of Nations, Italy proposes complete destruction of its naval fleet, contingent upon the other four major powers following suit.			The Canadian Newsprint Service Bureau reports an international record for newsprint production. In 1929, Canada produced 2,728,827 tons of newsprint.	
Jan. 18	U.S. navy officers express doubt that British Prime Minister Ramsay MacDonald's battleship abolition proposal will be considered at the London Naval Conference. . . . U.S. delegates at the London Naval Conference pressure Great Britain to transfer funds from battleship construction to public works projects for the unemployed.	Chinese railroad workers in the Soviet Union declare a strike following the previous week's dismissal of 280 Chinese employees.			Western diplomats estimate that nearly half of China's population lives on what the Western Hemisphere would consider a starvation diet.
Jan. 19	U.S. Secretary of State Henry Stimson visits 10 Downing Street, London, to meet with British Prime Minister Ramsay MacDonald for the purpose of naval negotiations. . . . In a speech before the International Diplomatic Academy, Prof. Vespasian Pella of Romania deduces that "war is a normal state for humanity," estimating that in the 3,400 years of humanity's history, only 248 have been peaceful.	France begins to broadcast crop prices over its national radio service. . . . After being excluded from the five-power naval talks, Russia reminds the world of its naval prowess by sending two warships through the Black Sea in clear view of surrounding nations.		Governor Franklin Roosevelt of New York formally visits the Caribbean territory of Puerto Rico, where, after delivering a speech, throngs of gatherers begin to shout, "viva el gobernador!"	
Jan. 20		The Air League of the British Empire issues a report detailing the amount of air defense machines by country: France, 4,730; United States, 1,813; Italy, 1,641; Great Britain, 1,292; Japan, 572.		Argentina's Minister of Finance reports that exports decreased by 9 percent in 1929 as compared to previous year.	Chinese military forces launch an offensive against rebel forces, amassing a large amount of troops to the city of Pengpu, the home of rebel leader General Shih Yu-shan.
Jan. 21	King George of Great Britain officially commences the London Naval Conference in a speech in the Royal Gallery of the House of Lords.			The Bolivian Foreign Office issues a statement blaming Paraguayan revolutionaries for the recent clashes on the Bolivian-Paraguayan border.	

A	B	C	D	E
Includes developments that affect more than one world region, international organizations, and important meetings of world leaders.	Includes all domestic and regional developments in Europe, including the Soviet Union.	Includes all domestic and regional developments in Africa and the Middle East.	Includes all domestic and regional developments in Latin America, the Caribbean, and Canada.	Includes all domestic and regional developments in Asian and Pacific nations (and colonies).

U.S. Politics & Social Issues	U.S. Foreign Policy & Defense	Economics & Great Depression	Science, Technology & Nature	Culture, Leisure & Lifestyle	
The National Safety Council reports that 31,500 deaths were attributable to automobile accidents in 1929, 13 percent more than in 1928.	At the London Naval Conference, the United States agrees to reduce its total number of battleships from 18 to 15 by 1936, contingent upon a similar reduction by Great Britain.	The Bureau of Aeronautics of the U.S. Department of Commerce announces plans in the coming year to spend $75 million to build 1,361 airports.			Jan. 15
The case of Mary Ware Dennett, who in 1918 authored a pamphlet entitled, "The Sex Side of Life and Explanation for Young People," and was arrested soon thereafter, is appealed in federal court in Brooklyn, N.Y. . . . Industrial Relations of the National Urban League director T. Arnold Hill insists that the American Federation of Labor begin to admit African-American workers.		The New York State Old Age Security Commission creates a pension system for "penniless citizens over 70" at a cost of $15 million a year.			Jan. 16
		The Federal Reserve Bank of New York reports that stockbrokers' loans recently exceeded $3.5 billion, with an increase of $37 million in the past two weeks. . . . After filing for bankruptcy with losses of $3 million, the Bankers' Capital Corporation is indicted for fraud for concocting false financial reports.			Jan. 17
U.S. Assistant Secretary of Commerce for Aeronautics reports that 1929 saw a marked increase in aviation safety, with only one fatal accident occurring for every 442,530 miles flown.			Norman Smith of Australia sets the world record for amount of time taken to ride 10 miles in an automobile, accomplishing the feat in four minutes, two seconds at a rate of 148.637 miles per hour.	Englishman Jack "Kid" Berg wins the world lightweight championship when he defeats the former champion, Tony Canzoneri, at Madison Square Garden.	Jan. 18
U.S. Prohibition Bureau Commissioner James M. Doran announces the establishment of new training courses designed to teach prohibition agents proper legal procedures. . . . The annual convention of the Anti-Saloon League of America, a prominent pro-prohibition organization, is held in Detroit, Mich.			The Western Air Express Airport in Alhambra, Calif., introduces a color-coordinated air traffic control system, the first of its kind.	The film version of Erich Remarque's German World War I novel, *All Quiet on the Western Front*, is released.	Jan. 19
Surgeon General Hugh S. Cumming publishes his report detailing America's health status for 1928, noting that, compared to the previous year, the death rate increased, but total births decreased.	The American Bureau of Shipping reports that naval construction reached 344,461 tons in 1929, placing the United States near the top of the list of major naval powers. . . . The U.S. Navy decommissions the destroyer ship USS *Paul Hamilton*.		The temperature in New York City reaches its lowest point of the winter, 10°F.		Jan. 20
Forty-seven oil companies including The Standard Oil Companies of New Jersey and Indiana are convicted of violating the Sherman Antitrust Law through a process known as "oil-cracking." . . . Chicago coroner Dr. Herman N. Bundeson reports that deaths relating to alcoholism in Chicago increased from 20 in 1920 to 300 in 1929.	Rep. Burton L. French of Idaho, chairman of the naval expenditures subcommittee, advocates complete abolition of all battleships for all nations "in the interest of the reduction of the cost of armaments."				Jan. 21

F	G	H	I	J
Includes elections, federal-state relations, civil rights and liberties, crime, the judiciary, education, healthcare, poverty, urban affairs, and population.	*Includes formation and debate of U.S. foreign and defense policies, veterans affairs, and defense spending. (Relations with specific foreign countries are usually found under the region concerned.)*	*Includes business, labor, agriculture, taxation, transportation, consumer affairs, monetary and fiscal policy, natural resources, pollution, and accidents.*	*Includes worldwide scientific, medical, and technological developments, natural phenomena, U.S. weather, and natural disasters.*	*Includes the arts, religion, scholarship, communications media, sports, entertainment, fashions, fads, and social life.*

	World Affairs	Europe	Africa & The Middle East	The Americas	Asia & The Pacific
Jan. 22	British Prime Minister Ramsay MacDonald, the opening speaker at the London Naval Conference, states that unless the five participating nations exercise mutual cooperation, the world will experience "the same sort of armament race which brought disaster in 1914."		The Palestinian Arab Executive selects a delegation of six to travel to London to request abolition of the Balfour Declaration.		
Jan. 23	Journalists in Berlin, Germany, hail U.S. Secretary of State Henry Stimson's London Naval Conference speech as "the only speech of importance . . . [which] means that the Americans will claim leadership."	The London Times reports that funds gained from a reduction of naval expenditures will be used for social services, not lowering taxes, as had been widely assumed.			
Jan. 24	Polish journalists covering the London Naval Conference call for a complete abolition of navies from Poland's bordering body of water, the Baltic Sea.	Fear of environmental disruption prompts Austria to ban all imports on parrots and other exotic birds. . . . Great Britain reports that its birth rate for 1929 dropped to a record low of 16.3 births per 1,000 people.	Upon the acquittal of 12 Palestinian Arabs who were accused of murdering a small Jewish family, throngs of Arabs gather outside the courthouse shouting, "Long live the Palestine Government!"		
Jan. 25	English and French delegates to the London Naval Conference argue over whether naval reduction should be categorized as reduction by total tonnage or by tonnage by category.	Representatives in the British House of Commons debate a law that would end the criminality of blasphemy.	The Portuguese colony of Angola reports three cases of bubonic plague among its citizens		
Jan. 26		In a creative attempt to boost Austria's economy, officials urge men to grow beards and moustaches, so that the nation's barbers may benefit. Austrian journalists doubt the idea will work, writing, "Austrian women will have something to say about it."		Army officials award Brazil with four anti-aircraft batteries at a cost of $1.8 million.	
Jan. 27		The average stock price in Berlin levels off at 111.2, up 6 percent from the end of 1929. . . . A court in Berlin decides that the term "butcher of workingmen" is slanderous, after the Communist newspaper Rote Fahgne (Red Flag) uses it to describe the Berlin Chief of Police. . . . Small, sporadic demonstrations by the Hungarian unemployed occur in the country's capital, Budapest.		Bolivia and Paraguay approach the brink of war following border clashes. The League of Nations considers military intervention.	Following anti-Filipino riots in California, Police Chief C.E. Pitts of Manila, the capital of the Philippines, assures Americans living there that they "[are] in no danger."
Jan. 28	Peter A. Bogdanov, former chief of the Soviet Economic Council, is elected chairman of the Amtorg Trading Corp. of New York.	The British government announces the decommissioning of four naval cruisers.	A 20-foot-high wall is unearthed by archaeologists in the ancient city of Jericho. Archaeologists say the wall dates back to 2000 B.C.E.		
Jan. 29	President Herbert Hoover appoints former ambassador to Portugal Fred Morris Dearing to the post of Ambassador to Peru, succeeding Alexander Moore, who becomes the Ambassador to Poland.		Two hundred Egyptian workmen participating in Egypt's first excavation expedition unearth 12 tombs near the Giza Pyramids.		

A	B	C	D	E
Includes developments that affect more than one world region, international organizations, and important meetings of world leaders.	Includes all domestic and regional developments in Europe, including the Soviet Union.	Includes all domestic and regional developments in Africa and the Middle East.	Includes all domestic and regional developments in Latin America, the Caribbean, and Canada.	Includes all domestic and regional developments in Asian and Pacific nations (and colonies).

U.S. Politics & Social Issues	U.S. Foreign Policy & Defense	Economics & Great Depression	Science, Technology & Nature	Culture, Leisure & Lifestyle	
The House of Representatives unanimously passes a bill authorizing $300 million in federal aid to the states for highway construction.		Police in Berlin, Germany, unearth a counterfeiting ring manufacturing fraudulent U.S. $100 bills. They believe thousands of the bills are already in circulation in America and Europe.	American radio engineers employ the world's most far-reaching radio system to broadcast King George of Britain's opening speech at the London Naval Conference.	The U.S. Postmaster General bans a device advertised as an "electric cure-all machine" from being distributed through the mail.	Jan. 22
		Colonial Trust Company treasurer T.J. Norman is sentenced to 3–5 years in prison for "misapplication of the bank's funds."	U.S. Admiral Richard Byrd embarks on a sailing expedition to newly found Discovery Inlet in Antarctica. . . . General Electric begins construction on the world's largest hydroelectric generator. The generator will be used exclusively in the Soviet Union.		Jan. 23
	Addressing a group of businessmen, Rear Admiral W.S. Crosley warns against naval reduction, saying any decrease in size would be "harmfully intemperate" to both the economy and national security.	The American banking firm of Dillon, Read & Co. agrees to extend a $25 million loan to the German banking firm of Siemens & Halske, repayable within 100 years. . . . The Conference for Progressive Labor Action calls Hoover's building construction projections for 1930 "a gigantic publicity stunt." . . . The stock price of the Fox Film Corporation rises 54 percent in a period of a few hours.	Aviation designer G.M. Bellanca begins construction on a 12-passenger single-motored transport designed to significantly reduce the cost of flying.	New Yorker Edwin A. Hodgson becomes the first deaf person to lend his voice to a radio broadcast.	Jan. 24
	Delegates to the London Naval Conference insist that cruisers, submarines, and destroyers be limited before limitation of battleships is addressed.			The newly appointed head of the American Episcopal Church, Rev. Charles Palmerston Anderson, suffers a heart attack.	Jan. 25
Immigration Committee chairman Rep. Albert Johnson of Washington introduces a bill recommending compulsory annual registration of all aliens living in the United States, noting during his remarks on the House floor that a "surreptitious influx" of illegal aliens has greatly contributed to the nation's unemployment rate. . . . Rep. L.C. Dyer of Missouri calls for a repeal of the federal automobile theft law, saying, "we are convicting too many young men . . . to federal penitentiaries . . . for mere joy rides across state lines."		The New York Stock Exchange reports that 1929 saw both a five-year-low and a five-year-high in stock market prices.		Engineers estimate that the radio audience for the London Naval Conference exceeds 100 million listeners. . . . J.S. Haldane publishes "The Sciences and Philosophy."	Jan. 26
	Capt. Albert W. Stevens is awarded the Mackay trophy by the U.S. War Department for his skill in reconnaissance.				Jan. 27
The New York State Industrial Commission reports that doctors in unsanitary health clinics have been bribing local officials with liquor prescriptions. . . . Congress urges governmental regulation of the American Telephone & Telegraph Company.		The price of crude petroleum was consistently at $1.575 per barrel during the previous week, according to The Oil, Paint and Drug Reporter.		Presiding Bishop of the Episcopal Church Rev. Charles Anderson's condition is downgraded to "very critical" after a week of recuperation from cardiac arrest.	Jan. 28
The last surviving founder of the American Bar Association, Francis Rawle, dies in his home in Philadelphia, Pa.		The U.S. Steel Corporation discloses in its annual report that its net earnings for 1929 amounted to $258,659,889, the most since the years of World War I. . . . The U.S. Department of Labor reports that in the week ending on January 13, employment rose 3.3 percent as compared to the week prior. . . . Reports indicate that U.S. grain exports for the week ending on January 25 dropped 18 percent.	The American Museum of Natural History announces the discovery of a 20,000-year-old petrified human skeleton in Florida. The finding contradicts earlier scientific studies which purported man did not inhabit North America until 5,000 years ago.	During a town hall meeting, a Danish official criticizes American-made films, which account for 90 percent of all films shown in Denmark, as being "tommyrot," adding that the films "[take] the bread out of Danish artists' mouths."	Jan. 29

F	G	H	I	J
Includes elections, federal-state relations, civil rights and liberties, crime, the judiciary, education, healthcare, poverty, urban affairs, and population.	Includes formation and debate of U.S. foreign and defense policies, veterans affairs, and defense spending. (Relations with specific foreign countries are usually found under the region concerned.)	Includes business, labor, agriculture, taxation, transportation, consumer affairs, monetary and fiscal policy, natural resources, pollution, and accidents.	Includes worldwide scientific, medical, and technological developments, natural phenomena, U.S. weather, and natural disasters.	Includes the arts, religion, scholarship, communications media, sports, entertainment, fashions, fads, and social life.

	World Affairs	Europe	Africa & The Middle East	The Americas	Asia & The Pacific
Jan. 30	In a speech before the London Royal Society of Arts, metallurgist Sir Thomas Holland proposes the prohibition of the export of raw minerals to be used in warfare. Prohibition, he says, would greatly increase world peace.	An ancient penalty of the Napoleonic Code is invoked when a French murderess accused of matricide is forced to walk to the guillotine barefoot.		The Legislative Assembly of Haiti forwards a request to U.S. President Herbert Hoover, asking for assistance militarily and otherwise in conducting a popular election.	
Jan. 31		The 67-year-old Queen of Sweden is admitted to a hospital after falling "seriously ill" from a bronchial infection.		Cuban officials encounter charges of racism after denying the admission of Marcus Garvey, president of the Universal Negro Improvement Association and African Communities League.	
Feb. 1	U.S. Navy Secretary Charles Francis Adams expresses agreement with Great Britain's proposal of naval limitation by category. The proposal is in sharp contrast with France, which seeks to limit navies by total tonnage.	The French Department of Commerce reports on the expansion of the Bank of France. With over 500 branches and offices, the Bank holds an estimated 300 million francs in reserves. . . . The Bank of Poland reduces its discount rate by one half percent, from 8.5 percent to 8 percent. . . . French Foreign Minister Aristide Briand returns to France following the London Naval Conference.			
Feb. 2		French citizens describe Premier Andre Tardieu's performance at the London Naval Conference as "strong [and] intelligent," a French newspaper reports.			
Feb. 3		Claiming it is defeatist, officials in Prague, Czechoslovakia, remove an anti-war memorial that reads: "Remember what the World War meant and think what a future world war would mean." . . . In its forecast for the coming fiscal quarter, The Federation of British Industries reports that "there appears to be no reason for not anticipating a general setback in British trade."			The government of Australia borrows $53 million from private loaners.
Feb. 4					Chinese President Chiang Kai-shek announces he will leave the capital of Shanghai the following week to investigate the rebel-controlled area of Canton. . . . The president of the Philippine-American Chamber of Commerce, Charles D. Orth, appears before the U.S. Senate Committee on Territories and Insular Possessions to warn against a withdrawal of U.S. troops from the Philippines. The Filipinos, he says, should be given a period of 20 years to ensure complete independence.

A	B	C	D	E
Includes developments that affect more than one world region, international organizations, and important meetings of world leaders.	Includes all domestic and regional developments in Europe, including the Soviet Union.	Includes all domestic and regional developments in Africa and the Middle East.	Includes all domestic and regional developments in Latin America, the Caribbean, and Canada.	Includes all domestic and regional developments in Asian and Pacific nations (and colonies).

U.S. Politics & Social Issues	U.S. Foreign Policy & Defense	Economics & Great Depression	Science, Technology & Nature	Culture, Leisure & Lifestyle	
Twenty-two officials and residents of Pottawatomie County, Okla., plead guilty to charges of conspiracy to violate the national prohibition act. . . . The New York State Legislature estimates the cost to construct Attica State Prison to be $12,050,000.					Jan. 30
Liquor racketeers in Seattle, Wash., kidnap a federal prohibition agent after a failed undercover arrest.		The Federation of British Industries blames the U.S. stock market crash on luxurious decadence, saying, "the general standard of living in America [was] at a level much above . . . the actual earnings of American citizens."		Funeral services are held for the Presiding Bishop of the American Episcopalian Church, Rev. Charles Anderson.	Jan. 31
House Judiciary Committee Chairman Rep. George S. Graham, a Prohibition opponent, notes in a speech to the Federal Bar Association of New York that half of those in federal prisons are there as a result of Prohibition violations.		With its country's automobile industry dwindling, the Belgian publication Vingtieme Siecle (Twentieth Century) calls for a quota on American-imported automobiles. . . . The New York Stock Exchange reports that total listings for the previous month aggregated $2,113,141,303, as compared with the previous January's total of $1,428,097,780.			Feb. 1
The New York Times reports that membership in the American Communist Party has dropped to about 5,000 people from 25,000 seven years ago. . . . The bankrupted U.S. city of Chicago borrows $300 million from loaners at an interest rate of $18 million a year. . . . The first lynching in Georgia in three years occurs when 500 men storm the jailhouse of tiny Ocilla, Ga., and kidnap Jimmy Levine, a black man accused of slaying a 14-year-old white girl. . . . Board of Education President George J. Ryan reports that a new school building was built every 13 days in the last decade. . . . A federal survey reveals women make up over 87 percent of public school teachers.		Twelve former employees of the U.S. Union Industrial Bank are sentenced to a combined 240 years in prison for embezzling the company of $3,693,996. . . . The Neediest Cases fund of New York increases to $339,090.55.	Earl O. Hanson unveils his newest invention, a set of special cables designed to allow airplane pilots to better travel through darkness and fog.	Parisian Dr. Alexander Alekhine clinches the championship in the San Remo chess tourney by defeating his opponent in 28 moves.	Feb. 2
The New York State Legislature appropriates $18.3 million for 6,000 additional beds in the state's insane asylums. . . . A professor of Howard University, an all-black college, insists that the American Federation of Labor admit black members. . . . Chief Justice of the Supreme Court William Howard Taft resigns due to ill health.		The international average commodity price stands at 93.3, down from 100 one year ago, according to economics expert Prof. Irving Fisher.		William A. Leonard of Cleveland, Ohio, is named the new American Episcopalian Church Presiding Bishop.	Feb. 3
The United Hospital Fund amasses a record amount of donations, $702,825.	Admiral William Howard, a member of the 1885 naval expedition that helped grant statehood to Alaska, dies at the age of 70 in his home in Newport, R.I.	The New York Times reports that in 1929, the Panama Canal saw its greatest amount of trade in terms of tonnage.			Feb. 4

F	G	H	I	J
Includes elections, federal-state relations, civil rights and liberties, crime, the judiciary, education, healthcare, poverty, urban affairs, and population.	Includes formation and debate of U.S. foreign and defense policies, veterans affairs, and defense spending. (Relations with specific foreign countries are usually found under the region concerned.)	Includes business, labor, agriculture, taxation, transportation, consumer affairs, monetary and fiscal policy, natural resources, pollution, and accidents.	Includes worldwide scientific, medical, and technological developments, natural phenomena, U.S. weather, and natural disasters.	Includes the arts, religion, scholarship, communications media, sports, entertainment, fashions, fads, and social life.

	World Affairs	Europe	Africa & The Middle East	The Americas	Asia & The Pacific
Feb. 5	Charles Evans Hughes leaves the League of Nations' Permanent Court of International Justice in The Hague, Netherlands, to become U.S. Chief Justice of the Supreme Court.	Premier Benito Mussolini of Italy orders the disbandment of all Italian fascist organizations operating outside Italy. . . . General Primo de Rivera, who recently seized power in Spain, declares a general amnesty for all political prisoners.		Boy Scouts founder Sir Robert Baden-Powell travels to Panama to view the Panamanian Boy Scout organization. . . . The U.S. War Department issues a report detailing use of the Panama Canal. During the month of January, 531 commercial vessels passed through it, paying tolls of $2,360,211.24. . . . The Mexican state of Morelos reports that 600 citizens have died of smallpox in the previous two weeks.	
Feb. 6	Delegates to the London Naval Conference express frustration with the slow progress of the conference, blaming it on the U.S. delegates' scrutiny over every proposal. The United States responds by saying its democratic system of government prevents it from acting swiftly.	By a vote of 241–129, the British House of Commons approves a new trade agreement with the Soviet Union, whereby the communist nation is expected to purchase $1.2 billion in British goods over the next three years. . . . The French Chamber of Deputies appropriates a $120 million budget for the Air Ministry.		The newly instated President of Mexico, Pascual Ortiz Rubio, is wounded by an assassin's bullet shortly after reciting the oath of office.	
Feb. 7			Afghan officials of the deposed regime of King Amanullah say they expect Western reforms to continue to be implemented under the new leadership.		The Nanking government of China cancels its aviation contract with the U.S. company China Airways Federal, Inc., prompting company officials to level accusations of a breach of contract.
Feb. 8	Support of Great Britain's battleship abolition proposal begins to dwindle among foreign delegates at the London Naval Conference. British delegates respond by saying they hope the measure is accepted in time for the next naval conference.	Austrian Chancellor Johann Schober meets with Italian Premier Benito Mussolini at his residence in Rome to sign a "treaty of understanding." . . . Two hundred people gather outside the Mexican Consulate in Hamburg, Germany, to protest the recent imprisonment of Mexican communist revolutionaries.			
Feb. 9		Two Georgians indicted for counterfeiting Russian rubles for the purpose of leading a revolution in Soviet Georgia are acquitted in Berlin, Germany, after the judge declares their case applies to the general political prisoner amnesty law of 1928. . . . The publication Moscow Emes states that 400,000 Russian Jews are in need of immediate financial relief.			In a recorded message, Gen. Emilio Aguinaldo of the Philippines formally apologizes for leading an insurrection campaign against U.S. colonial rule 20 years prior. A "mistaken comprehension of mutual objectives," he says, was the only reason for the conflict.
Feb. 10	The half-brother of the deposed King of Afghanistan is arrested in India for planning an uprising against the new Afghan regime.	Frankfurter Zeitung reports the index of the German Exchange has increased by 6 percent since the end of 1929.			
Feb. 11	The 14,000-mile air tour of Latin America by America's finest doctors is completed. They visited 11 countries in 17 days.		Excavations begin in Cairo at the presumed tomb of the 1st century King of Macedon, Alexander the Great.		
	A Includes developments that affect more than one world region, international organizations, and important meetings of world leaders.	**B** Includes all domestic and regional developments in Europe, including the Soviet Union.	**C** Includes all domestic and regional developments in Africa and the Middle East.	**D** Includes all domestic and regional developments in Latin America, the Caribbean, and Canada.	**E** Includes all domestic and regional developments in Asian and Pacific nations (and colonies).

U.S. Politics & Social Issues	U.S. Foreign Policy & Defense	Economics & Great Depression	Science, Technology & Nature	Culture, Leisure & Lifestyle	
Charles Evans Hughes is named as the frontrunner to succeed William Howard Taft as Chief Justice of the Supreme Court. . . . Approximately 25,000 dressmakers go on strike in the city of New York. Governor Franklin Roosevelt authors a letter inviting both the workers and the employers to meet with him at his Executive Mansion to discuss an outcome.		The U.S. Department of Commerce reports that automobile exports have increased 588 percent over an 8-year period.	The New York City Board of Aldermen introduces a bill that would regulate the use of radio loudspeakers. . . . Dr. Jules Auclair of Paris discovers that birds are immune to human tuberculosis. Subsequently, he extracts the substance he believes causes the immunity and concocts a serum with it. . . . Using a device that detects smoke and dust in the air, the New York City Meteorology Observatory discovers that for every million cubic yards in the city, there exists 1.35 pounds of impurities.	Sir Alfred Knox of the British House of Commons calls for a ban on American-made talking films "to protect the English language."	Feb. 5
Three thousand additional dressmakers strike, joining the 25,000 who walked out the previous day.					Feb. 6
Merrill Lynch & Co. reports that chain store sales in January showed an increase of 6.49 percent as compared to January of 1929.		The Annalist reports that the average wholesale commodity price in the United States has dropped to a five-year low of $138.4.		Home-run record holder George Herman "Babe" Ruth tells reporters during his 36th birthday celebration that he will be demanding a three-year, $255,000 contract from the New York Yankees.	Feb. 7
A federal grand jury in Montgomery, Ala., indicts 250 people on charges of violating Prohibition laws. . . . In remarks on the House floor before a crowded gallery, Rep. James M. Beck of Pennsylvania calls for a repeal of the Prohibition Amendment to "end the system of tyranny and hypocrisy." . . . A federal Prohibition agent sues a building owner for $25,000 after collapsing through a stairwell and breaking his leg during a liquor raid. . . . The American Banker reports that the total number of banks in the United States was reduced by 1,100 last year.	Secretary of State Henry L. Stimson's naval reduction proposals that originated from talks at the London Naval Conference are met with divisiveness in the Senate. The plan calls for a decrease in cruisers from 21 to 18, or a decrease in cruiser tonnage from 327,500 to 300,500.	New York Governor Franklin Roosevelt expresses optimism in finding an outcome for the dressmakers' strike, saying he believes at least a portion of the state's 30,000 striking dressmakers will be able to return to work the following week.			Feb. 8
A group of oilmen led by American Independent Petroleum Association president Wirt Franklin requests that Congress impose a tariff of $1 per barrel of imported crude petroleum. . . . The Metropolitan Life Insurance Company estimates that 31,400 people in the United States died the previous year as a result of automobile accidents.	Rep. Burton L. French, chairman of the naval subcommittee of the Naval Appropriations Committee, praises Secretary of State Henry Stimson's naval reduction proposals.	The League of Nations publishes a report stating that American tourists spent $300 million in foreign countries in 1927. . . . A report by the League of Nations detailing each country's trade increase in the period of 1926–28 is released. Germany had the highest trade increase, followed by the United States and Canada.	Physician Dr. Ralph Arthur Reynolds of San Francisco completes his two-month study of inmates at the San Quentin Prison. He concludes that all crime is attributable to physical abnormalities.	The Belgian army defeats the British army 4–2 in the first round of the international army soccer tournament.	Feb. 9
Police in Chicago arrest 917 gang members over a 24-hour period.	Naval expert Commander Holloway H. Frost issues a report stating that following the London Naval Conference, Great Britain's total naval tonnage amounts to 607,950 tons; the United States, 523,400 tons.	The Economist reports British wholesale prices have dropped 8 percent in one year.			Feb. 10
Three officials of the Glenwood Distilling Company are indicted on charges of embezzling 115,000 gallons of alcohol for private sale. . . . Americans across the nation celebrate the 121st birthday of former president Abraham Lincoln. . . . In a speech before 50 Brooklyn clergymen, New York Prohibition administrator Maurice Campbell asserts that New Yorkers consume more alcohol than they did before federal Prohibition.					Feb. 11

F	G	H	I	J
Includes elections, federal-state relations, civil rights and liberties, crime, the judiciary, education, healthcare, poverty, urban affairs, and population.	*Includes formation and debate of U.S. foreign and defense policies, veterans affairs, and defense spending. (Relations with specific foreign countries are usually found under the region concerned.)*	*Includes business, labor, agriculture, taxation, transportation, consumer affairs, monetary and fiscal policy, natural resources, pollution, and accidents.*	*Includes worldwide scientific, medical, and technological developments, natural phenomena, U.S. weather, and natural disasters.*	*Includes the arts, religion, scholarship, communications media, sports, entertainment, fashions, fads, and social life.*

	World Affairs	Europe	Africa & The Middle East	The Americas	Asia & The Pacific
Feb. 12	At a press conference, British Prime Minister Ramsay MacDonald compares his efforts at the London Naval Conference to that of Stonewall Jackson, a southern general who continuously outmaneuvered the north in the American Civil War. European journalists are confused by the reference.	Three thousand anti-Communist demonstrators stage a mini-riot outside the Soviet Embassy in Paris, France.			
Feb. 13	Dr. Cosmo Gordon Lang, the Archbishop of Canterbury, strongly condemns religious persecution in atheist Soviet Russia.	The number of unemployed in Great Britain in January was 130,215 more than January of the previous year, according to a report by the British Board of Trade.		In Haiti, a memorial service is held honoring Haitians who were killed in a clash with U.S. marines on December 6.	
Feb. 14	Japan's demand to retain its current submarine fleet is met with disagreement from British and U.S. delegates, who fear an acceptance will allow Japan to obtain naval superiority.		South Africa, the richest nation on the continent of Africa, passes a new immigration quota bill allowing only 50 immigrants annually, except those from the United States, Britain, and 12 Nordic countries.		China's abolition of extraterritoriality comes into effect as an American is tried in a Shanghai court for the alleged running over of a Chinese cyclist.
Feb. 15	The League of Nations reports that the United States signed 20 of the 34 treaties passed in 1929, the most of any nation.		Egypt enacts an 8-cent tariff on oranges. Bordering Palestine is expected to be adversely affected.	The Fourth District Court of Mexico denies Mexican police the ability to arrest Medellion Ostos, suspected shooter of newly elected President Ortiz Rubio.	
Feb. 16					Lawlessness pervades China as bandits pillage the city of Liyang. Numbering 3,000, the gang kills 350 people and causes damages of $10 million while in the process of looting goods worth $3 million.
Feb. 17	As the fifth week of the London Naval Conference opens, U.S. delegates state their goal is to reduce Japan's submarine fleet by 50 percent.	French industrialists report that total industry rose about one-half of a percent during the past six months. . . . The German Finance Minister approves a budget appropriating 9 million marks ($2.5 million) for construction of a navy cruiser named the Ersatz Preussen (Replacement Prussia).		The Bank of Argentina reports a profit of 3,074,000 pesos ($2,674,380) for the year of 1929.	
Feb. 18		Lord Beaverbrook of Great Britain launches the United Empire Party. Committed to free trade, the party has an initial membership of 200,000.			
Feb. 19	U.S. automobile manufacturers attend a hearing of the French Chamber of Deputies to protest a "prohibitive" tariff imposed on American-made automobiles.	Ending months of speculation, France submits its naval goal for 1936, the year of the next naval conference, at 725,000 tons.		Cuban Ambassador to the United States Dr. Orestes Ferrera urges more trade between the two countries, noting that American investments in Cuba total only $1.5 million.	China teeters on the brink of civil war as President Chiang Kai-shek rejects rebel leader Yen His-shan's proposal for their joint resignations.

A	B	C	D	E
Includes developments that affect more than one world region, international organizations, and important meetings of world leaders.	Includes all domestic and regional developments in Europe, including the Soviet Union.	Includes all domestic and regional developments in Africa and the Middle East.	Includes all domestic and regional developments in Latin America, the Caribbean, and Canada.	Includes all domestic and regional developments in Asian and Pacific nations (and colonies).

U.S. Politics & Social Issues	U.S. Foreign Policy & Defense	Economics & Great Depression	Science, Technology & Nature	Culture, Leisure & Lifestyle	
The number of arrests of Chicago-area gang members totals 2,181 in a three-day period.		A report by the British Imperial Economic Committee states that Great Britain's trade accounts for 27.75 percent of all the world's exports and imports.	Inventor Thomas A. Edison turns 83. Celebrating at his home in Fort Myers, Fla., he urges Americans to "pay more attention to engineers than to politicians," and comments that Prohibition will continue.		**Feb. 12**
Joseph Patrick Carley becomes the first man arrested in Washington, D.C., on Prohibition charges. . . . William J. Granfield becomes the first Democrat elected to represent the Second Congressional District of Massachusetts. Republicans had held the post since its organization in 1893.	Former senator Frederic Mosley Sackett assumes the position of U.S. Ambassador to Germany, succeeding Dr. Jacob Gould Schurman. . . . U.S. naval officials estimate it will cost $500 million over five years to accomplish naval equality with Great Britain.	*Automotive Industries* reports American automotive exports reached a record high in 1929 at $772,660,331. . . . U.S. Currency Controller John W. Pole announces the total resources of the 7,408 national banks in the United States amount to $28,882,483,000.		Tickets for the annual Army-Notre Dame football game sell out within hours of going on sale.	**Feb. 13**
New York State Senator Seabury C. Mastick of Westchester accuses Governor Franklin Roosevelt of "hysteria" for his proposals to dramatically increase state programs.	The entire task of protecting America's coasts is transferred from naval authority to army authority.				**Feb. 14**
Senator Samuel Bratton of New Mexico assails the Commerce Department for their refusal to release aviation crash records.			Army pilots Will White and Clement McMullen set the record for time taken to fly from Newark, N.J., to Miami, Fla., beating the previous record by three hours.		**Feb. 15**
Aviator Bert Acosta, who three years prior had flown across the Atlantic Ocean, is sentenced to six months in jail in New York for failure to pay alimony. . . . Senators debate over the Prohibition Amendment. Pro-Prohibitionists seek to limit beverages to no more than one-half of a percent of alcohol, while Anti-Prohibitionists argue the percent should be raised to 2.75. . . . Charles Evans Hughes is appointed Chief Justice of the Supreme Court. The appointment follows the resignation of former Chief Justice and President William Howard Taft due to ill health.		The American Bankers Association publishes a report showing for the first time in 20 years a decrease in personal savings. The period of 1928 to 1929 showed a record increase of $2.3 billion, but 1929 to 1930 saw a decrease of $195 million.	The second annual New York Aviation Show is attended by 200,000 people.		**Feb. 16**
		The U.S. Department of Commerce reports that the United States traded approximately $400 million in 1928 at the Hamburg Port, Germany's main trading post. The figure is the most of any nation.	The second annual International Aircraft Expedition is held in St. Louis, Mo. . . . Barney Zimmerly of Marshall, Mo., sets the world altitude record for light planes, achieving a height of 27,350 feet.		**Feb. 17**
New York legislators consider a bill that would abolish daylight savings time for the state. . . . Polish Ambassador Alexander P. Moore of Pittsburgh dies at California Hospital from a throat infection. . . . The Department of Commerce announces 1929 was a record year in terms of automotive exports. Estimates stand at 354 planes worth $5,574,480, an increase of over 200 percent.		By 41–39, the U.S. Senate passes a law lowering the tariff on aluminum from 5 cents to 2 cents.		Trustees of the Metropolitan Museum of Art in New York report an $883,384.25 deficit of administration expenses.	**Feb. 18**
		With Chicago suffering from a mounting burden of debt, 50 of the city's biggest taxpayers, known as the Strawn group, are formally asked to contribute about $74 million to the city's budget.		Al Brown of Panama claims the world bantamweight title by defeating American Johnny Canzoneri in 10 rounds.	**Feb. 19**

F	**G**	**H**	**I**	**J**
Includes elections, federal-state relations, civil rights and liberties, crime, the judiciary, education, healthcare, poverty, urban affairs, and population.	*Includes formation and debate of U.S. foreign and defense policies, veterans affairs, and defense spending. (Relations with specific foreign countries are usually found under the region concerned.)*	*Includes business, labor, agriculture, taxation, transportation, consumer affairs, monetary and fiscal policy, natural resources, pollution, and accidents.*	*Includes worldwide scientific, medical, and technological developments, natural phenomena, U.S. weather, and natural disasters.*	*Includes the arts, religion, scholarship, communications media, sports, entertainment, fashions, fads, and social life.*

	World Affairs	Europe	Africa & The Middle East	The Americas	Asia & The Pacific
Feb. 20		The Bank of Budapest reports a profit of 1,967,837 pengos ($344,175) for 1929. . . . Lord Beaverbrook of Great Britain publishes a two-page manifesto in popular British newspapers outlining the goals of his newly formed United Empire Party. The manifesto reaches approximately 6 million people. . . . In Bulgaria, the National Credit Bank, the Bulgarika Bank, and the Franco-Bulgarian Bank unite to form the Bulgarian National Bank.		Mexican military authorities announce that the trial and investigation of Daniel Flores, who attempted to assassinate President Ortiz Rubio on his inauguration day, will be handled by civilian authorities.	
Feb. 21	34,950,915 automobiles were registered throughout the world in 1929, according to an annual report by *Automotive Industries.* Of the total, 26,634,210 registrations occurred within the United States.			Arriving in Buenos Aires via airplane, U.S. Lts. Will White and Clement McMullen visit with the Argentine chief of aviation, who urges scientific cooperation between the two nations.	
Feb. 22		British Foreign Secretary Sir Austin Chamberlain condemns the formation of the United Empire Party, saying the party's goal of free trade is achievable at the present time.		Major Van Slobbe is elected Governor of the Carribean Dutch colony of Curacao.	
Feb. 23	One of the two senior U.S. naval advisers present at the London Naval Conference, Admiral Henry Jones, falls ill and is forced to sail to a hospital in the United States. Naval Secretary Adams announces Jones will return to London the following day.		The Ford Motor Company opens an auto manufacturing plant in the Turkish city of Constantinople.	Canadian statisticians report American tourists spent approximately $150 million in Canada in 1929. The figure could be doubled, one statistician predicts, if American tourism were more encouraged.	
Feb. 24	Newly elected French Premier Camille Chautemps asserts at the London Naval Conference that his naval policies will not differ significantly from those of his predecessor.	The British Ministry of Labor reports that the cost of living in Great Britain decreased by about 2 percent in the past year.	Deposed Afghan King Amanullah travels to Turkey to meet with President Mustapha Kemal.		In Shanghai, China, protests occur outside theaters showing the American comedy film *Welcome Danger,* the locale of which is the Chinese section of San Francisco.
Feb. 25	Pessimism is the prevailing attitude at the London Naval Conference, with U.S. and French delegates deadlocked over a proposal on tonnage. . . . In a press release, Lord Beaverbrook, head of the United Empire Party, calls the month-long London Naval Conference a "failure."	At a luncheon for the British Poetry Society, Parliament member Carlyon Bellairs proposes a joint U.S.-British commission to create a unified English language.	In an interview in Turkey, former King of Afghanistan Amanullah blames his deposition on his citizens' lack of support for Westernization. . . . An alliance is signed between King Faisal, ruler of Iraq, and King Ibn Saud, ruler of Mecca.		The third session of the Philippine Independence Congress is held in Manila. Proposals include a call for a reduction of tariffs on American-imported goods, and to make Tagalog the country's official language.
Feb. 26		The French Chautemps Cabinet falls. Lasting only four days, it is the shortest duration for a French government since World War I.			Journalists in Shanghai, China, write that "large scale civil war is inevitable."
Feb. 27	At the London Naval Conference, U.S. and French delegates continue to disagree over whether to negotiate a five-power or three-power treaty. . . . Speaking at a meeting of the British Navy League, former Chancellor of the Exchequer Winston Churchill criticizes Britain's stance at the London Naval Conference. British delegates make Britain appear to be, according to Churchill, "a passive nation upon which the policies of the other naval nations will imprint themselves."	The British Chancellor of the Exchequer reports a projected budget deficit of $50 million for 1930. . . . In order to repay a loan of $5 million, officials in Berlin, Germany, sell off the city's power companies stock.			
	A Includes developments that affect more than one world region, international organizations, and important meetings of world leaders.	**B** Includes all domestic and regional developments in Europe, including the Soviet Union.	**C** Includes all domestic and regional developments in Africa and the Middle East.	**D** Includes all domestic and regional developments in Latin America, the Caribbean, and Canada.	**E** Includes all domestic and regional developments in Asian and Pacific nations (and colonies).

U.S. Politics & Social Issues	U.S. Foreign Policy & Defense	Economics & Great Depression	Science, Technology & Nature	Culture, Leisure & Lifestyle	
A lawsuit is brought against New York public school principal William J. Hoffman for his refusal to accept applications of Catholic teachers. . . . Senators debate on President Herbert Hoover's nomination for Interstate Commerce Commissioner, Hugh M. Tate. . . . Assistant Deputy Commissioner of Prohibition William C. Blanchard testifies before a federal grand jury that he was instructed by his superior, Prohibition Deputy Commissioner L.G. Nutt, to "pad" monthly narcotic reports being sent to Washington.			Lts. Will White and Clement McMullen break the record for time taken to fly 7,000 miles, achieving the feat in 52 hours and 15 minutes. . . . The ship *City of New York* departs from the Bay of Whales in Antarctica, thus completing its Antarctic expedition.	A record 1,760 canines compete in the 18th annual Eastern Dog Club competition.	Feb. 20
	Army deputy chief of staff Gen. Briant H. Wells is reassigned to command the Army's First Division. He is succeeded as deputy chief of staff by Gen. Preston Brown.	Standard Oil of New Jersey reports its number of stockholders increased 32 percent over a two-month period in 1929.	Herbert Hoover, Jr., son of the U.S. president, addresses a meeting of the Aeronautical Chamber of Commerce, predicting a law will be passed requiring commercial airliners to install radios in their cockpits.		Feb. 21
As Prohibition arrests continue to increase at an alarming rate, legal experts testify before the House Judiciary Committee. One attorney, Frederic R. Goudert of New York, predicts that if Prohibition were fully enforced, nearly half of the country's citizens would be imprisoned.	Rep. Fred A. Britten of Illinois decries that Great Britain is "scheming" the United States at the London Naval Conference for the purpose of obtaining naval superiority.				Feb. 22
			Returning to New York, Admiral Byrd estimates that his Antarctic expedition charted upwards of 150,000 square miles.	*Happy Days*, the world's first wide-lens feature film, debuts at the Roxy Theatre in New York.	Feb. 23
		The Reichsbank of Germany considers reducing its discount rate to 5.5 percent. . . . *The Guaranty Survey* publishes a report detailing U.S. economic conditions in January. While steel and automotive production rose, retail sales dropped sharply, and the average level of employment was the lowest since 1922.			Feb. 24
Deaths attributable to automobile mishaps rose 11 percent in 1929 as compared to the previous year, according to a report issued by the Travelers Insurance Company.		Former British prime minister Stanley Baldwin comments on his country's newly formed United Empire Party, saying the party's goal of free trade is "a great ideal, but unattainable." . . . The U.S. steel companies Republic Steel Company, Gulf States Steel Company, Woodward Iron Company, and Sloss Sheffield Iron Company merge in a $500 million deal.		Frank Boucher of the New York Rangers sets a National Hockey League assist record with 33.	Feb. 25
Fred A. Victor is elected superintendent of the New York Anti-Saloon League, a prominent anti-Prohibition organization. . . . The New York State Assembly passes a resolution forcing the Army and Navy football programs to compete against one another. The storied rivalry had been discontinued in years prior due to disagreements over eligibility rules.		The Association of National Advertisers reports that the 1930s advertising budget for all major companies exceeds last year's budget by 9.7 percent.		Bat Battalino retains the title of world boxing featherweight champion by defeating Ignacio Hernandez in 10 rounds before an audience of 10,000 in Hartford, Conn. . . . The world's oldest living man, Capt. James Smith, who fought in four wars, dies at his home in Philadelphia at the age of 124.	Feb. 26
	Former New York governor Nathan L. Miller issues an appeal calling for humanitarian aid to Puerto Rico. "Nearly two-thirds of the country's children," he claims, "are undernourished."	The Soviet Union's Commissariat of Agriculture reports that as of February 20, 50 percent of Russia's farms have been "socialized." . . . The U.S. city of Chicago raises $23,630,400 in one day, making the relief fund needed to avoid bankruptcy $7 million away from the desired $50 million.			Feb. 27

F	**G**	**H**	**I**	**J**
Includes elections, federal-state relations, civil rights and liberties, crime, the judiciary, education, healthcare, poverty, urban affairs, and population.	*Includes formation and debate of U.S. foreign and defense policies, veterans affairs, and defense spending. (Relations with specific foreign countries are usually found under the region concerned.)*	*Includes business, labor, agriculture, taxation, transportation, consumer affairs, monetary and fiscal policy, natural resources, pollution, and accidents.*	*Includes worldwide scientific, medical, and technological developments, natural phenomena, U.S. weather, and natural disasters.*	*Includes the arts, religion, scholarship, communications media, sports, entertainment, fashions, fads, and social life.*

	World Affairs	Europe	Africa & The Middle East	The Americas	Asia & The Pacific
Feb. 28		Editors of the British publication *Saturday Review* resign in protest following the purchase of the publication by Lord Beaverbrook, head of the United Empire Party. . . . Officials in Russia blame the nation's food shortage on lack of transportation infrastructure.	Seventeen-year-old Abdul Ghani, who assassinated the Jewish Attorney General of Palestine the previous year, is sentenced to 15 years in prison. . . . Eight thousand men are mobilized by the Palestine Department of Agriculture to destroy the eggs of locusts over an area 500 square miles.		
Mar. 1	The Union of Orthodox Jewish Congregations of America calls for an end to religious persecution in the atheist Soviet Union.	Fearing a backlash from the Soviet Union, Great Britain bans prayer by Russian-born Britons serving in the British army.		Brazil holds its presidential election. Conservative candidate Dr. Julio Prestes is considered the frontrunner.	
Mar. 2	Argentine Foreign Affairs Minister Horacio Oyahanarte appears before the U.S. Senate to detail how his country plans to appropriate a U.S. loan of 100 million pesos.			The South American nation of Uruguay celebrates its 100th anniversary of becoming a republic.	
Mar. 3	In a radio speech, U.S. Navy Secretary Charles Francis Adams voices optimism as the London Naval Conference nears its seventh week of negotiations. "Japanese and American delegates," he says, "are coming nearer to an understanding."	The British Shipping Board reports its total commerce in terms of tonnage increased threefold during the past decade.	The Prince of Wales is stricken with malaria during a hunting trip in the East African British colony of Kenya.		
Mar. 4	At the London Naval Conference, Japanese delegates announce they will not reduce their navy to anything less than 70 percent of the American fleet.	Explosions rock the Bulgarian city of Nish. Responsibility is claimed by Macedonian revolutionary Komitadjus, who seek to end friendly relations between Bulgaria and Yugoslavia. . . . Seeking to increase its country's export revenue, the British government creates two new commercial trading posts in Montreal, Canada, and Durban, South Africa.			
Mar. 5	An amendment is debated at the League of Nations that would allow any nation threatened with war to become a temporary member. . . . At the London Naval Conference, French delegates state that their country will only participate in naval reductions if a non-aggression pact is signed between countries bordering the Mediterranean Sea.	The province of Catalonia, located in the northeastern section of Spain with a population of 5 million, requests independence from Spanish rule.		The production output of sugar, one of Cuba's main exports, is considerably lower than at the same time last year, according to figures published by the Cuba Sugar Club. . . . With a vote of 94–6, the Cuban House of Representatives approves an $80 million U.S. loan.	
Mar. 6		Seven thousand policemen are dispatched to Berlin, Germany, to oversee a Communist demonstration. The demonstration had been declared banned by the chief of police earlier in the week.		Fearing a corrupt election process, citizens of Haiti call on the United States to militarily oversee their upcoming presidential election on April 14.	Calling on the United Nations for humanitarian aid, Chinese diplomats note that in some of the poorer provinces of their country the infant mortality rate is 20 percent, or one out of every five births.
Mar. 7	Upon his return to the London Naval Conference, French Foreign Minister Aristide Briand meets with British Prime Minister Ramsay MacDonald.	Pandeli Evangeli succeeds Kostaq Kotta as Premier of Albania. . . . Great Britain reduces its annual naval budget by $20 million, from $270 million the previous year to $250 million currently.		Returns from the March 1 Brazilian presidential election indicate that Conservative candidate Dr. Julio Prestes is the victor over Liberal candidate Dr. Getuilio Vargas by 153,000 votes.	

A	B	C	D	E
Includes developments that affect more than one world region, international organizations, and important meetings of world leaders.	Includes all domestic and regional developments in Europe, including the Soviet Union.	Includes all domestic and regional developments in Africa and the Middle East.	Includes all domestic and regional developments in Latin America, the Caribbean, and Canada.	Includes all domestic and regional developments in Asian and Pacific nations (and colonies).

U.S. Politics & Social Issues	U.S. Foreign Policy & Defense	Economics & Great Depression	Science, Technology & Nature	Culture, Leisure & Lifestyle	
Chicago exceeds its budget crisis fund goal of $50 million by $4 million.	Indian Commissioner of the Interior Department Charles J. Roads requests of Congress an additional $600,000 in foreign aid to India.				Feb. 28
In an effort to boost New York State's fledgling economy, a bill is introduced in the State Senate that would relax antitrust laws.		American journalists express doubt over the new issue of the American Labor Legislative Review, in which U.S. Secretary of Labor James Davis asserts unemployment will drop sharply in the coming month. . . . The U.S. Interstate Commerce Commission approves the Baltimore and Ohio Railroad Company's acquisition of Buffalo and Susquehanna Railroad. . . . Bond trading for the week ending March 1 was nearly 300 percent greater than the amount traded at the same time the previous year, according to the New York Stock Exchange.	Americans C.M. Drayton and F.O. Willy discover a previously unknown 80-foot-high Aztec pyramid while hunting in Matamaros, Mexico.	Alfred Banuet of the United States wins the international handball championship.	Mar. 1
Immigration officials in Newark, N.J., arrest approximately 250 suspected illegal aliens over a 24-hour period in one of the largest immigration crackdowns in U.S. history.				Home-run king George Herman "Babe" Ruth makes an appearance at the New York Yankees spring training complex, but refuses to don pinstripes until his contract dispute is settled.	Mar. 2
	Senator Burton K. Wheeler of Montana authors a bill that would restrict U.S. military personnel from assisting Latin American countries.	American economist Dr. O.M.W. Sprague is appointed to the position of Economic Adviser for the Bank of England.			Mar. 3
Secretary of Labor James Davis announces his intention to run for the Republican Senate seat in Florida.	A State Department memorandum prepared by Undersecretary of State J. Reuben Clark declares that the Roosevelt Corollary, which calls for expanding U.S. commercial interests into Latin America, does not apply to the Monroe Doctrine.	The U.S. Department of Commerce releases a report stating that New York City's property taxes have increased by 126 percent over the past decade. . . . The Niagara Fire Insurance Company issues a report estimating that in the past 10 years, Americans have discarded 15 million defunct automobiles for which they paid $12 billion.		George Herman "Babe" Ruth participates in his first spring training practice with the New York Yankees despite still being unsigned. . . . Tickets for the opening game of the Major League Baseball season sell out only days after being put on sale. . . . English novelist D.H. Lawrence, author of Sons and Lovers, dies at the age of 46 in the Ad Astra Sanitarium in Vence, France. Among those by his bedside was noted author and fellow countryman Aldous Huxley.	Mar. 4
New York state legislators appropriate $2 million to restore the Croton Aqueduct. . . . Bostonians celebrate the 300th anniversary of their city's founding. . . . In Phoenix, Ariz., 15,000 people attend the opening of the Coolidge Dam. Designed to provide water for people living within an area of 1 million acres, it is named after former president Calvin Coolidge.		Communist "unemployment" demonstrations organized by Soviet Russia occur all throughout the world. Soviet officials hope the demonstrations will spark Communist revolutions, but prominent Russian socialist Raphael Abramovitch disagrees, remarking in newspaper editorials that "all Communist ambitions for establishment of a Communist dictatorship outside Russia are now mere dreams and illusions."	U.S. Congressmen debate a bill that would ban the hunting of America's national animal, the bald eagle, in the state of Alaska, where the reward of 50 cents is paid to each hunter who captures one.	Dissatisfied with "talkie" films, silent film legend Charlie Chaplin announces plans to spend $10 million per year exclusively on silent movie projects.	Mar. 5
Authorities in the city of Chicago deny the local Communist Party's request to hold a demonstration, fearing that the paraders will be armed with knives and blackjacks to attack the police. . . . In New York City, Communist Party officials predict that the "unemployment" demonstration in Union Square will include 60,000 people.		The price of cotton in the United States falls to its lowest point since April 1927. . . . In the United States, the East Orange Trust Company bank is robbed of $1,000 after the teller on duty claims he was "hypnotized" out of the money by a "gypsy woman." . . . The Bank of Trust Company of New York lends 2.5 million pesos to the government of Colombia.		The yacht Enterprise is chosen as the ship to represent the United States in the upcoming sailing competition, the America's Cup.	Mar. 6
Appearing before the House Judiciary Committee, supporters of the Eighteenth Amendment cite statistics that show that "the eleven years of Prohibition have saved 26,400 lives."		The Annalist Weekly reports an all-time low in U.S. wholesale commodity prices.		During opening day at Yankee Stadium, George Herman "Babe" Ruth sustains an injury while sliding into third base. His contentious 3-year, $85,000 contract request had been met with an offer of 2 years at $75,000 per year.	Mar. 7

F	G	H	I	J
Includes elections, federal-state relations, civil rights and liberties, crime, the judiciary, education, healthcare, poverty, urban affairs, and population.	Includes formation and debate of U.S. foreign and defense policies, veterans affairs, and defense spending. (Relations with specific foreign countries are usually found under the region concerned.)	Includes business, labor, agriculture, taxation, transportation, consumer affairs, monetary and fiscal policy, natural resources, pollution, and accidents.	Includes worldwide scientific, medical, and technological developments, natural phenomena, U.S. weather, and natural disasters.	Includes the arts, religion, scholarship, communications media, sports, entertainment, fashions, fads, and social life.

	World Affairs	Europe	Africa & The Middle East	The Americas	Asia & The Pacific
Mar. 8		Lord Beaverbrook, founder of the three-week-old British United Empire Party, resigns as party head, ceding control to co-founder Viscount Rothermore. . . . In Great Brtiain, planning begins for the upcoming festival celebrating the 20th anniversary of the reign of King George V.		Newspapers in Brazil differ over the outcome of the March 1 presidential election. Some place Prestes ahead of Getuilio Vargas by a wide margin, while others report a close victory for Vargas. . . . The Haitian Catholic Church aligns itself with the movement for Haitian independence from American rule.	
Mar. 9	A border dispute occurs between the United States and Canada over a million-acre tract of land near the Minnesota national border known as Hunter's Island.	As deposed King of Afghanistan Amanullah Khan visits the Vatican, newspapers report the Muslim king is considering a conversion to Catholicism.			
Mar. 10		Floods in France kill an estimated 400 people and cause damages totaling $5 million.			
Mar. 11	At the London Naval Conference, French Foreign Minister Aristide Briand says his country will only participate in naval reduction if a political pact of "goodwill" is signed between the five naval powers.			Two Cuban trade unions, The Workers Federation of Havana and The National Federation of Workers of Cuba, are declared illegal by Interior Secretary Manuel Delgado, who says the organizations are influenced by Soviet Communists in Moscow.	Belgium cedes ownership of a concession in the East Asian province of Tientsin to China.
Mar. 12	Statesmen at the League of Nations express their condolences over the death of former U.S. president William Howard Taft, who had a role in the organization's inception in 1919.		The Prince of Wales announces plans for a hunting expedition to the Belgian Congo.		China enters into a trade agreement with Cuba, whereby $125 million worth of Cuban sugar will be imported annually. . . . China formally requests advice and assistance from the League of Nations in the creation of its public health service. The request, according to health committee chairman Dr. T. Madsen, is "a long step further toward establishing the position of the League as a world-wide and not merely European association of the States."
Mar. 13	With the failure of his security "goodwill" pact looming, French Foreign Minister Aristide Briand predicts that the London Naval Conference will reach an unscheduled sour conclusion within two weeks.	The British Board of Trade reports that February's export revenue was the lowest monthly total since December 1926. . . . Great Britain lowers its annual army budget by $3,025,000. . . . Djfer Vila, the Albanian minister to Yugoslavia, is appointed as the new Albanian Foreign Minister.		A special commission organized by Herbert Hoover arrives in Haiti to report on the feasibility of granting independence to the Caribbean protectorate.	Fear of imperialism prompts China to extend conciliatory gestures to Japan, including a liberal loan to Tokyo worth $100 million.
Mar. 14	British Prime Minister Ramsay MacDonald offers his country's final proposal at the London Naval Conference: a 15-15-9 naval ratio for the United States, Great Britain, and Japan respectively. . . . Japanese delegates to the London Naval Conference insist they must maintain a navy that is at least 70 percent as effective as those of the United States and Great Britain.	British newspapers publish editorials blaming the French delegation for the failure of the six-week-old London Naval Conference, saying it is French Foreign Minister Aristide Briand's proposal of a security pact that has forced the conference into a deadlock. The popular French newspaper *Le Temps* rebukes the claim by commenting, "This responsibility for failure falls upon those who refuse to accord all nations real guarantees of security." . . . The Bank of France reports a record number of banknotes circulated for the previous week. . . . By a vote of 42–5, the German Reichsrat (Federal Council) ratifies the Young Plan. Created by Owen D. Young, the plan calls for a total payment of $26.35 billion over a period of 58 years. German nationalists condemn the ratification.		The Peruvian Navy visits Chilean seaports as part of a ceremony celebrating the end of long-standing border disputes between the two South American countries. . . . A law requiring all employers to guarantee eight-hour workdays to their employees comes into effect in Argentina.	Mohandas Gandhi, along with his 80 followers, begins his civil disobedience campaign for Indian independence from British rule in the west Indian village of Aslali. . . . Sen Gupta, mayor of the Indian city of Calcutta, is arrested following a speech in which he praises revolutionary Mohandas Gandhi for his independence efforts. Refusing bail, he is set to stand trial the following day. . . . Five thousand Filipino and Chinese laborers lose their homes as fires rip through the Singalong district in the Philippine capital of Manila. It is the second major fire in as many years.
	A Includes developments that affect more than one world region, international organizations, and important meetings of world leaders.	**B** Includes all domestic and regional developments in Europe, including the Soviet Union.	**C** Includes all domestic and regional developments in Africa and the Middle East.	**D** Includes all domestic and regional developments in Latin America, the Caribbean, and Canada.	**E** Includes all domestic and regional developments in Asian and Pacific nations (and colonies).

U.S. Politics & Social Issues	U.S. Foreign Policy & Defense	Economics & Great Depression	Science, Technology & Nature	Culture, Leisure & Lifestyle	
Appealing for greater enforcement of narcotics laws, Rep. William Sirovich of New York recommends diverting some of the state's $36 million in Prohibition enforcement funds to narcotics enforcement. As a chilling example, he states that 200 tons of opium are imported to the United States annually. . . . William Howard Taft, the only person to serve as both U.S. president and Chief Justice of the Supreme Court, dies of cerebro-arteriosclerosis at Garfield Hospital in Washington, D.C, at age 72.		By a vote of 45–37, the U.S. Senate passes a bill raising the tariff on cement to 6 cents per 100 pounds. . . . In a speech in North Carolina, U.S. Secretary of Labor James J. Davis estimates the state's number of unemployed to be 250,000 or 8.3 percent of the population.		New York Yankees owner Colonel Ruppert offers George Herman "Babe" Ruth a one-year salary of $85,000, which would be the largest in baseball history. . . . S.S. Curran is reelected as head of the Grand National Curling Club of America.	Mar. 8
		U.S. President Herbert Hoover personally asks of Congress $100 million in addition to the $500 million already reserved for farm relief.	The radio station WGY of New York debuts its 200-kilowatt broadcaster, the most powerful of its kind.	Set construction begins for the biopic *Abraham Lincoln*, one of the final films by legendary director D.W. Griffith.	Mar. 9
Twenty-five thousand people gather for the funeral of Carl Mackley, an unemployed hosiery worker who was killed by employees of the H.C. Aberle Company as he was protesting labor conditions. Representatives of the American Federation of Labor tell the crowd that Mackley is a "martyr to the cause of labor." . . . The New York Chamber of Commerce forms a committee of businessmen to combat Communist subversion. The committee will deport "shiploads" of Communist illegal immigrants, as well as "induce employers to discharge all employees with radical tendencies."	Military officials estimate the U.S. Navy is 60 percent as effective as Great Britain's.	The U.S. National Unemployment League suggests legislation greatly increasing public works projects for the purpose of alleviating the nation's estimated 5 million unemployed persons. . . . The Bethlehem Steel Corporation and the Youngstown Sheet and Tube Company merge in a $1 billion deal. . . . Foreign loans by Great Britain over the previous year nearly matched those by the United States, according to statistics published by the U.S. Department of Commerce.	French aviator Dieudonne Costes, who holds the world record for longest distance flown in a straight line, is awarded the annual international trophy by the International League of Aviators.		Mar. 10
Funeral services for former president and Chief Justice William Howard Taft are held in his hometown of New Haven, Conn.		New York State Industrial Commissioner Frances Perkins reports that February's unemployment was the lowest of any February since 1914.		*Who's Who In Theatre*, a book containing 3,000 biographical blurbs of people in theater and entertainment, is published. . . . Columbia University clinches the title in the Intercollegiate Basketball League by defeating Dartmouth College by a score of 56–28.	Mar. 11
The Standard Oil Company of Maine is forced to change its name following accusations of copyright infringement by the Standard Oil Company of New York.	The U.S. delegation to the London Naval Conference says it will not participate in French Foreign Minister Briand's proposal for a five-power pact of "goodwill."		The Society of Arts and Sciences awards its annual gold medal to California chemistry professor Dr. Gilbert N. Lewis and psychology author Dr. J. McKeen Cattell.		Mar. 12
Postmaster General Walter F. Brown announces the expansion of air-mail service for the south. A thrice-daily trip will be made between New York and Atlanta, he reports.	Congress appropriates $300,000 for the rebuilding and restoration of the USS *Constitution*, a historic frigate commissioned by the U.S. Navy in 1797.	According to a survey conducted by The Salvation Army, the largest relief aid organization in the United States, unemployment is 30–50 percent higher than it was a year ago.	Princeton physicist Dr. Karl T. Compton succeeds Samuel W. Stratton as the president of the Massachusetts Institute of Technology.	Eddie Benson retains the title of National Guard heavyweight champion by knocking out George Giacchino in the ninth round.	Mar. 13
Members of the Ladies' Garment Workers Union, a subsidiary of the American Federation of Labor, strike in Boston with the participation of 2,500 members. Demands include the establishment of a 40-hour workweek and an unemployment insurance fund.		The American Tobacco Company reports a record year in earnings for 1929. Earnings amounted to $30,231,348, an increase of $5,165,048 from 1929. . . . Seeking a boost of capital, the Bank of Poland reduces its discount rate from 8 to 7 percent and its interest security rate from 9 to 8 percent. . . . The Cooperative Exports Agency of Cuba finalizes a sales deal whereby Cuba will deliver 125,000 tons of crude sugar to three American sugar refineries.	Clyde Tombaugh, researcher at the Lowell Observatory in Arizona, telegraphs news to Harvard College Observatory announcing the discovery of a new planet, "Planet X." Of all the discovered planets, according to Tombaugh, Planet X appears to be the farthest from the Earth's sun. Scientists await statistical data to determine the physical characteristics of the planet, later dubbed Pluto.	Penn State and Cornell battle for the title of intercollegiate wrestling champion.	Mar. 14

F	G	H	I	J
Includes elections, federal-state relations, civil rights and liberties, crime, the judiciary, education, healthcare, poverty, urban affairs, and population.	Includes formation and debate of U.S. foreign and defense policies, veterans affairs, and defense spending. (Relations with specific foreign countries are usually found under the region concerned.)	Includes business, labor, agriculture, taxation, transportation, consumer affairs, monetary and fiscal policy, natural resources, pollution, and accidents.	Includes worldwide scientific, medical, and technological developments, natural phenomena, U.S. weather, and natural disasters.	Includes the arts, religion, scholarship, communications media, sports, entertainment, fashions, fads, and social life.

	World Affairs	Europe	Africa & The Middle East	The Americas	Asia & The Pacific
Mar. 15	At the London Naval Conference, U.S. delegates broker a compromise between Great Britain's 60 percent Japanese-U.S. naval ratio and Japan's 70 percent ratio proposal. The new ratio will be put at 67 percent.	Despite setbacks in the London Naval Conference, French Foreign Minister Aristide Briand maintains a level of optimism, noting to reporters, "The nations represented here possess 85 percent of all the navies and have the power to guarantee world peace permanently."		Roy Taskoe Davis is appointed as the new U.S. Ambassador to Panama.... Charles C. Eberhardt is appointed as the new U.S. Ambassador to Costa Rica.	
Mar. 16		In Budapest, Hungary, 150,000 people attend the funeral of celebrated violinist Bela Radics. Known as "the king of gypsies," Radics is credited with popularizing gypsy music.		Guyana, a British colony located along the northern coastline of South America, sends a resolution to the British Labor Party in England calling for legislators to extend women's suffrage to the colony. Under the resolution, women will be allowed to vote for members of the colony's Assembly.	Chinese revolutionaries attack five American and two Chinese steamers in the Yangtse River in China, near Shanghai. No Americans are harmed, and the number of Chinese casualties is uncertain.
Mar. 17	The League of Nations commissions a group of crime experts to study the effects and capabilities of international liquor smuggling.	The British Board of Trade reports the index number of wholesale prices has fallen to 127.8. It is the lowest number since the index's inception in 1920.	In Jerusalem, Arabs show their disdain for Jews by beating drums and making other loud distractions while Jewish prayer services are held at the Wailing Wall.	Argentina's commerce suffers as railway workers purposely arrive at destinations from one to five hours late. The reason, according to railway representatives who deny that there is a strike taking place, is to improve hourly wages.	
Mar. 18	The League of Nations hears testimony from Russian refugees who fled the country as a result of the collective farm movement. The refugees request that Congress provide relief funds to Russia's bordering nations, where many of the refugees have settled.			With the help of the United States, Paraguay and Uruguay settle a territorial dispute. Under the agreement, Paraguay will rebuild the war-torn Fort Vanguardia and return it to Uruguayan rule.... Alvarez de Toledo, former Argentinean Ambassador to France, is named as Argentina's new Foreign Minister.	
Mar. 19	The League of Nations sets a limit on territorial water control. The limit was set at three miles beyond a country's coastline, with some specific exceptions for which the limit was extended up to 12 miles.	Great Britain releases its estimated air force budget for the coming year. $89.25 million will be spent, an increase of $4.45 million from the previous year. Former Air Minister Samuel Hoarse applauds the increase, saying, "In the years to come, the most urgent questions will have reference to fighting planes."		President Ortiz Rubio of Mexico tells a consortium of newspapermen in the country's capital that Communist uprising has all but ceased. Rubio was nearly killed by a Communist revolutionary on his inauguration day earlier in the year.	National government offices in the southern Chinese city of Peking are taken over by rebels acting under the orders of General Yen Hsi-Shan, who controls the northern part of China.... Organized bandits overrun the town of Fuan in the Chinese province of Kiangsi, massacring 2,000 people. . . . Crown Prince Frederick of Denmark arrives in Tokyo. The purpose of the trip is to discuss the ongoing London Naval Conference with Japanese Foreign Affairs Minister Baron Kujio Shidehara.
Mar. 20		Arthur Balfour, Prime Minister of Great Britain from 1902–05, dies at the age of 82 from natural causes at his home in Surrey, England.			
Mar. 21			Following a month-long trial, five Arabs are sentenced to death for the murder of four Jews during the Arab-Jewish riots in the Palestinian city of Hebron the previous summer.		

A	B	C	D	E
Includes developments that affect more than one world region, international organizations, and important meetings of world leaders.	Includes all domestic and regional developments in Europe, including the Soviet Union.	Includes all domestic and regional developments in Africa and the Middle East.	Includes all domestic and regional developments in Latin America, the Caribbean, and Canada.	Includes all domestic and regional developments in Asian and Pacific nations (and colonies).

U.S. Politics & Social Issues	U.S. Foreign Policy & Defense	Economics & Great Depression	Science, Technology & Nature	Culture, Leisure & Lifestyle	
Postmaster James F. Martin of Santa Claus, Ind., requests Congressional funds to hire employees to sort through the literally thousands of children's letters addressed to the town's patron saint.		The New York Stock Exchange reports that the week ending March 13 was the second most prosperous of the year in terms of new bond offerings.	Prof. John Q. Stewart of the Princeton astronomy department estimates that the global temperature of the newly discovered Planet X is minus 350°F. Stewart says the extremely low temperature is a result of Planet X's distance from the sun.	Jack Dempsey, the 35-year-old former heavyweight champion, announces plans for a comeback, despite not having boxed in over three years. . . . J. Tishel of Cleveland, Ohio, sets a record in the American Bowling Congress Tournament, scoring 277 points in one game.	Mar. 15
			Italy announces that "an aerial circuit race" will commence at the country's Littori Airport in August. All nations are welcome, say Italian representatives.	The second annual Central American Olympic Games begin in Havana, Cuba, with 800 athletes representing nine nations.	Mar. 16
Invoking America's 15 percent divorce rate, Rev. Father John Carter Smith declares that "America is fast becoming a land of Mormons. The laws of the country forbid continuous polygamy, but we have substituted it for consecutive polygamy." . . . Basing his findings on a 1920 census, Interior Secretary Ray Lyman Wilbur estimates that 5 million people, or 4 percent of the population, are unable to either read or write. . . . An anti-religion demonstration is attended by 12,000 people in New York. Hosted by the Friends of the Soviet Union, a Communist organization, it is intended to counter American protests of religious persecution in Russia. . . . Chicago gang leader Al Capone is released from the Philadelphia Eastern Penitentiary following a ten-month incarceration for gun possession. While Capone's sentence was originally one year, prison officials shaved off two months for good behavior.					Mar. 17
		Horaco Oyhanarte, Foreign Minister of Argentina, travels to the United States to negotiate a $100 million loan.			Mar. 18
The Senate adopts a resolution giving U.S. district courts, not customs officials, the final say when determining whether foreign media material should be censored.		The American gasoline companies United, Magnolia, and Louisiana merge in a $220 million deal. . . . The Salvation Army requests public support to continue to be able to serve 1,000 free meals per day to unemployed workers. . . . The Dutch Farmers' Cooperative Buying Association announces a boycott on all Russian products, due to the atheist nation's religious persecution. As a result, Russia is forced to divert ships carrying some 30,000 tons of goods to Great Britain.	Clyde Tambaugh, discoverer of the new Planet X, humorously suggests to newspaper reporters that the official name of the planet should be "Bacchus," the Roman god of wine and celebration.	Sherlock Holmes author Arthur Conan Doyle, 71, quits as a prominent member of the Society for Psychical Research. In an indignant letter to Sir Lawrence Jones, chairman of the Psychic Research Council, Doyle writes that the society "has done no constructive work for a generation," and is "an evil influence." . . . Judge J.R. Rutherford, President of the International Bible Students Association, puts his $75,000 house in San Diego, Calif., on a perpetual trust for the "ancient kings and prophets of Palestine," who, if they divinely appear on Earth, will be able to claim ownership of Rutherford's home.	Mar. 19
	President Herbert Hoover appears at the commemoration of a memorial built near the American Red Cross in Washington, D.C., to honor the sacrifices and services of American women in World War I.	American automobile manufacturers report an increase of 50,792 cars produced in February as compared to January. The figure is still 142,456 below the total of February 1929, however.			Mar. 20
Secretary of Commerce Robert Patterson Lamont announces in a radio address via the Columbia Broadcasting System that "homemaking" will be listed as an official occupation on U.S. Census surveys. Among other new additions to the Census, Lamont says, is the measurement of unemployment.	The Army Air Corps awards the Keystone Aircraft Corporation with a $2,208,137 contract for 73 bombardment planes.	The Bank of England reduces its rediscount rate to 3.5 percent, the lowest rate since 1922. It is the sixth bank rate reduction since the U.S. stock market crash the previous autumn.	Edward Arthur Milne, professor of mathematics at Oxford University, expresses doubt over Clyde Tambaugh's discovery of a new planet, suggesting it may only be a comet. In response, Harvard Observatory issues a statement independently confirming the discovery. . . . Paleontologists of Rutgers University discover dinosaur footprints that are over 85 million years old in Woodbridge, N.J.	Australian swimmer Bonnie Mealing sets the record for the 150-yard backstroke, beating the previous record by one-fifth of a second.	Mar. 21
F	G	H	I	J	
Includes elections, federal-state relations, civil rights and liberties, crime, the judiciary, education, healthcare, poverty, urban affairs, and population.	*Includes formation and debate of U.S. foreign and defense policies, veterans affairs, and defense spending. (Relations with specific foreign countries are usually found under the region concerned.)*	*Includes business, labor, agriculture, taxation, transportation, consumer affairs, monetary and fiscal policy, natural resources, pollution, and accidents.*	*Includes worldwide scientific, medical, and technological developments, natural phenomena, U.S. weather, and natural disasters.*	*Includes the arts, religion, scholarship, communications media, sports, entertainment, fashions, fads, and social life.*	

	World Affairs	Europe	Africa & The Middle East	The Americas	Asia & The Pacific
Mar. 22	Newspapers in France blame the failure of the London Naval Conference squarely on their bordering neighbor, Italy. "Italy's insistence on parity with France and refusal to state what she deems to be her needs in figures of tonnage render the chances of reaching an agreement practically nil," reads an editorial in a popular French newspaper.	French economic officials estimate an increase of $100 million in taxes for U.S., British, and Swedish companies engaging in business in France. In response, the U.S. Embassy assembles a commission comprised of officials from the Treasury and Commerce Departments to state their case against the taxation.		Unemployment riots in Medellin, Colombia, cause scores of deaths and injuries, as well as the damage of over 200 structures. The riots come a day after the Assembly enacted $6 million in foreign loans for public work projects.	As China's internal strife threatens to plunge the country into civil war, Chang Hsueh-liang, Governor of Manchuria, attempts to mediate a peace agreement between the two warring factions of President Chiang Kai-shek's Northern Army and General Yen Shi-shan's Southern Army.
Mar. 23	The international Administrative Committee of the Jewish Agency meets in London, England, to discuss Arab uprisings in Jerusalem and Palestine. . . . Japanese delegates to the London Naval Conference balk at the Anglo-American proposal of a 2 to 1 Japanese-U.S. naval tonnage ratio.			Catholics across the United States call for humanitarian aid for poverty-stricken residents of the American protectorate of Puerto Rico, of whom many are Catholic. . . . Panama issues its annual report on commercial traffic through the Panama Canal. According to statistics, a total of 31,450,493 tons passed through the canal in fiscal year 1929, a record for a 12-month period.	
Mar. 24	Japan's request of increased cruiser tonnage for its navy causes a further delay of three weeks at the London Naval Conference.				
Mar. 25	Rear Admiral Richard E. Byrd announces he will claim for the United States the land he discovered while on his Antarctic expedition, repudiating an earlier interview that falsely quoted Byrd as saying he had no intentions of claiming any land. . . . Delegates at the League of Nations debate a resolution allowing nations to grant citizenship to naturalized, foreign-born citizens. . . . With a deadlock looming at the London Naval Conference, Dino Grandi, head of the Italian delegation, requests an adjournment of six months to settle any parity disputes.	Lloyd George of the British House of Commons presents figures during a debate showing that British unemployment has risen 27 percent in the past 10 months, from 1.1 million to 1.54 million. . . . Great Britain names Henry Getty Chilton, former British Ambassador to the Vatican, as its first Ambassador to Chile. . . . Reports that renowned socialist Leon Trotsky's health is nearing critical condition are labeled erroneous by his friends and family. While he suffers from rheumatism, it is not life threatening.			Authorities in Shanghai, China, lift the ban on the American newspaper *The Shanghai Evening Post*, in place since November 6, 1929.
Mar. 26		The British National Unemployed Workers' Movement announces the organization of a protest march against Prime Minister Ramsay MacDonald's unemployment policies, to be held later this spring. More than 1,000 people are expected to participate.		Chile announces the creation of its first Ministry of Aviation, appointing Commandant Merino Benitez as its first secretary. . . . Chile updates its military conscription laws, requiring only 30 percent of the population over 20 years of age to serve in the armed forces. Formerly, all men over the age of 20 were required to serve.	
Mar. 27	Prime Minister Nahas Pasha of Egypt arrives in London along with three of his Cabinet members to request complete independence from British rule. Great Britain had granted Egypt partial independence eight years ago.			President Ibanez of Chile releases figures showing the country has a budget surplus of 77 million pesos, or $9.24 million. Ibanez says he plans to spend the surplus to help stimulate Chile's fledgling agriculture industry.	Northern China acquires new military technologies from Germany to combat Communist uprisings in southern China. Among the new technologies are modern trench systems, machine gun nests, electrified barbed wire, liquid fire, and modern airplanes. . . . British imperial officials in Surat, India, announce they will likely employ military measures to disrupt Mohandas Gandhi's civil disobedience marches.

A	B	C	D	E
Includes developments that affect more than one world region, international organizations, and important meetings of world leaders.	Includes all domestic and regional developments in Europe, including the Soviet Union.	Includes all domestic and regional developments in Africa and the Middle East.	Includes all domestic and regional developments in Latin America, the Caribbean, and Canada.	Includes all domestic and regional developments in Asian and Pacific nations (and colonies).

U.S. Politics & Social Issues	U.S. Foreign Policy & Defense	Economics & Great Depression	Science, Technology & Nature	Culture, Leisure & Lifestyle	
President Herbert Hoover nominates John J. Parker, federal judge of the Fourth Circuit Court, to succeed Edward T. Sanford as Associate Justice of the Supreme Court. Parker receives the support of most Senators. . . . President Hoover appoints Benjamin M. Day to the post of Commissioner of Immigration at the Port of New York. Day had previously held the position of Ellis Island Immigration Commissioner. . . . Chicago Mafia leader Al Capone, newly released from prison, is instructed by Police Commissioner John Stege to leave the Chicago area or face additional jail time. . . . The Presbyterian Board of Christian Education publishes a survey detailing teenagers' use of illegal liquor. Of 1,000 high school students polled, only 21.3 percent admitted occasional drinking, and none reported frequent drinking.		Emulating other national banks who have recently cut their rates as a means of increasing capital, the Austrian National Bank reduces its rate to 6 percent from 6.5 percent. . . . U.S. bank clearings for the week ending March 20 amounted to 18.4 percent less than the same period a year before, according to statistics published by the Department of Commerce. . . . Due to investors' credit restraints, the amount of trading on the New York Stock Exchange falls by 21 percent in one day.	In a speech at the American Museum of Natural History, Dr. Albert Wigand tells a group of sociologists that unless eugenics is implemented in America, the present government will not outlast the century. "Morons," he says, "are multiplying much faster than college professors, businessmen, or skilled workmen."	The horse Playfellow Dreams breaks the track record at St. Johns Park in St. Augustine, Fla., by four-fifths of a second.	Mar. 22
Judge Thomas D. Thacher is unanimously confirmed by the Senate to assume the post of Solicitor General. The appointment follows the resignation of former Solicitor General Charles Evans Hughes, Jr., who left after his father was chosen to succeed William Howard Taft as Chief Justice of the Supreme Court. . . . Officials in Newark, N.J., announce the creation of a 1,000-man committee to crack down on organized crime.		The Chase National Bank, The Equitable Trust Company, and the Interstate Trust Company merge to form the world's largest bank with resources totaling more than $2 billion. . . . The volume of bond issues in the United States for the month of March fell comparatively below the March total of the previous year, from $78 million to $11 million or a decrease of 85 percent, according to officials from the Department of Commerce.	In San Francisco, Calif., one of the first "air ferries" created completes its first month of operation, with an estimated 11,000 passengers.	French author H. Dubreuil publishes *Robots or Men?*, a critique of American mass production.	Mar. 23
Reports issued by New York education officials indicate that 5–10 percent of the city's schoolchildren suffer from hearing disabilities. As a solution, officials suggest implementing sign language and lip reading education.		The Jewish Agricultural Society releases a report stating that there are now 90,000 Jewish farmers in the United States. It is an increase of 9,000 percent over the past three decades.	A group of scientists embarks off the port of Miami in the yacht *Nourhamal* for a month-long cruise in the Galapagos Islands. The purpose of the trip is to discover new plant and animal life, of which the Galapagos Islands have many.		Mar. 24
In a private session with the Senate Judiciary Committee, George W. Wickersham, head of President Hoover's law enforcement commission, advocates harsher penalties for Prohibition violators. "Prohibition could be measurably enforced," he says, "although human appetite is widespread." . . . The 66-year-old auto magnate Henry Ford voices his opinions on Prohibition in an interview in *The Ladies' Home Journal*. "Our present industrial system," he says, "simply cannot work with liquor. We must choose between drink and poverty or prohibition and prosperity. There is no middle ground."		A delegation of U.S. economic experts is sent to France to negotiate the abolishment of excessive taxation of U.S. goods and services. . . . The U.S. Justice Department declares the proposed merger between the Vacuum Oil Company and the Standard Oil Company of New York to be illegal, claiming it will result in a monopoly. The Justice Department cites an earlier court case that had a similar ruling.	A group of British mountain climbers leaves London to embark on an expedition to Nepal, where they will climb Mt. Kanchenjunga. At 28,146 feet, it is the third highest mountain in the world, behind K2 and Mount Everest.	Rev. Thomas F. Gailor, Bishop of Tennessee, is named as the frontrunner to replace Charles P. Anderson, who died on January 30, as Presiding Bishop of the Episcopal Church.	Mar. 25
Dr. Colt Bloodgood, head of cancer research at Johns Hopkins University, testifies before the Senate Commerce Committee, calling for an appropriation of $100,000 for a national survey to correctly identify the severity of cancer in the United States. Based on loose statistics, Bloodgood estimates the number of cancer deaths has risen by 12.5 percent in one year.	In accordance with the Young Plan, the U.S. House Ways and Means Committee approves a bill under which the United States will receive $273 million from Germany for military expenditures during World War I.	The United States exports 6 million pounds of copper in one day, the highest total for one day in six months. Domestic buying, however, remains stagnant.	Dr. Walter Levinthal discovers a virus called psittacosis, which, according to him, is primarily found in South American parrots but is transferable to humans.		Mar. 26
				James De Wolf Perry is elected head of the Protestant Episcopal Church, replacing the late Charles Palmerston Anderson, who died a few months before.	Mar. 27

F	G	H	I	J
Includes elections, federal-state relations, civil rights and liberties, crime, the judiciary, education, healthcare, poverty, urban affairs, and population.	Includes formation and debate of U.S. foreign and defense policies, veterans affairs, and defense spending. (Relations with specific foreign countries are usually found under the region concerned.)	Includes business, labor, agriculture, taxation, transportation, consumer affairs, monetary and fiscal policy, natural resources, pollution, and accidents.	Includes worldwide scientific, medical, and technological developments, natural phenomena, U.S. weather, and natural disasters.	Includes the arts, religion, scholarship, communications media, sports, entertainment, fashions, fads, and social life.

	World Affairs	Europe	Africa & The Middle East	The Americas	Asia & The Pacific
Mar. 28	U.S. Secretary of State Henry L. Stimson suggests a consultative peace pact to help further along negotiations at the London Naval Conference.	The British National Council for the Prevention of War issues a memorandum to Prime Minister Ramsay MacDonald, urging him to be more forthcoming and cooperative with his international counterparts at the London Naval Conference.		Carlos Alfredo Tornquist, president of the Buenos Aires Tornquist Bank, travels to New York to lend his hand in negotiations for a large U.S. foreign loan. If negotiations succeed, local newspapers speculate, Tornquist is expected to be promoted to the position of Argentinian Government Financial Agent to the United States.	
Mar. 29	The Australian city of Sydney accepts a $5 million floating bond at a rate of 5.5 percent from the U.S. banking firms of Banc-America Blair Corporation, E.H. Rollins & Sons, and Halsey, Stuart & Co., Inc.	In the French city of Calais, 20,000 people engage in a protest march after word is broken that the U.S. Senate has raised the tariff on imported lace, one of France's leading exports. The tariff increase is reported to be 150–300 percent, depending on the quality. . . . King Boris of Bulgaria receives the new American Ambassador to Bulgaria, Colonel Henry W. Shoemaker, in an official ceremony in the Bulgarian capital of Sofia.		The Argentine National Mortgage releases its annual report showing a net profit of 15,843,000 pesos, or $1,901,160, for 1929. Argentina's total reserve fund now stands at 196,661,000 pesos, or $23,599,320. . . . Canada's total number of liquor exports to the United States in February is reported as 150,997, as compared with 282,985 for February 1929. The figure is the result of tighter border regulations.	
Mar. 30	Sir Ronald Lindsay, who succeeded Sir Esme Howard as British Ambassador to the United States, arrives in Washington on his first official visit.		Officials of the poverty-stricken nation of Turkey report that in the past year, approximately 5,000 Turks, mostly from the eastern region, migrated to Syria.		
Mar. 31					
Apr. 1		The British Labor Government, headed by Prime Minister Ramsay MacDonald, announces an ambitious bill to be debated in the House of Commons that would eliminate England's slums in the next 40 years. With a goal of rehousing 100,000 poverty-stricken Britons every year, the proposal is expected to cost $1.25 million annually. . . . Hungary falls victim to an April Fools' joke when local newspapers receive reports from Egypt stating that Count Albert Apponyi had died. Apponyi, alive and well, issues a statement saying the reports originated from Egyptian diplomats.	A group of Ubangi natives from French Equatorial Africa arrive in New York to participate in the Barnum & Bailey Circus. Besides the initial attraction of a primitive yet fascinating culture, the natives feature a large, wooden disk attached to their lips, which, when left in since childhood, can produce a duck-billed effect.	The Mexican Ambassador to Argentina is recalled from the Argentinean capital of Buenos Aires following diplomatic failures. Local newspapers place the blame on Argentine President Juan Hipolito Irigoyen's diplomatic isolationism. . . . Noted Chilean author Raul Simon arrives in his homeland from the United States by way of the steamship *Santa Barbara*. During a speech, he arouses optimism in Chileans stating, "Chile is the only country in South America which has no unemployment problem."	China continues to suffer from internal strife as bandit raids escalate in intensity and frequency. In the city of Soochow, near the Taihu Lake, bandits captured 57 wealthy Chinese and demanded ransom, else the prisoners be killed. Eight thousand bandits in northern Kiangsi region issue threats to overrun the city of Nanchang.
Apr. 2	Following press leaks to influential American business organizations, the U.S. delegation to the London Naval Conference announces it will restrict daily press conferences to qualified newspapermen.	Sir Douglas Mawson returns to Great Britain following the nine-month-long Discovery expedition along the coast of the Antarctic continent. Over 300 miles of coastland were discovered and claimed as British territory. . . . Prisons in the Bulgarian capital of Sofia overflow as wholesale arrests of Macedonian revolutionaries occur. Those who cannot fit into the prisons are accommodated at the lavish Hotel Rome.			The newly formed Labor Administration of Australia proposes to British imperial authorities the appointment of an Australian-born man to succeed Lord Stonehaven as Governor General of Australia. It would be the first time an Australian had held the post.
Apr. 3	The National Association of Women Lawyers requests President Herbert Hoover to influence the League of Nations to impose sanctions on any nation that does not include equal civil and political rights for women.	U.S. Secretary of State Henry Stimson voices unparalleled optimism at the London Naval Conference when he calls the prospects of a five-power naval treaty between Great Britain, the United States, France, Italy, and Japan "bright."		The trial of Daniel Flores, who attempted to assassinate Mexican President Ortiz Rubio on his inauguration day last winter, is set to begin in the coming weeks. The maximum penalty Flores can endure, authorities say, is 20 years in prison.	

A	B	C	D	E
Includes developments that affect more than one world region, international organizations, and important meetings of world leaders.	*Includes all domestic and regional developments in Europe, including the Soviet Union.*	*Includes all domestic and regional developments in Africa and the Middle East.*	*Includes all domestic and regional developments in Latin America, the Caribbean, and Canada.*	*Includes all domestic and regional developments in Asian and Pacific nations (and colonies).*

U.S. Politics & Social Issues	U.S. Foreign Policy & Defense	Economics & Great Depression	Science, Technology & Nature	Culture, Leisure & Lifestyle	
The American Civil Liberties Union files an injunction against three New York City police officers for their "unnecessary violence" in the Communist demonstration on March 6 in Union Square. . . . Col. Robert R. McCormick, president of *The Chicago Tribune*, expresses outrage at a law in Minnesota that allows district court judges to suppress any "malicious, scandalous, or defamatory" newspaper. Enacted in 1925, the law had not been fully enforced until recently. . . . The Protestant Episcopal Church of America passes a resolution condemning Soviet religious persecution and calling on all Episcopalians to launch a nationwide protest.	Rep. Louis T. McFadden of Pennsylvania warns in a radio address that America's involvement in the Young Plan, a World War I reparations settlement plan, will lead to unnecessary foreign entanglements. He specifically fingers American financial organization J.P. Morgan & Co., the main contributor to the Bank of International Settlements, which organized the Young Plan.	Former U.S. senator Clayton Lusk favors creation of a federal Industrial Aid Bureau to combat unemployment and economic stagnation. . . . As the export market for coffee in Brazil faces a crisis, government officials announce a "wheat week," during which local farmers will be forcibly encouraged to switch to wheat production. Enmeshed in a tropical terrain, Brazil is currently unable to produce enough wheat to feed its domestic population.		The National Collegiate Athletic Association releases the collegiate lacrosse schedule for the coming spring season. Army will play Springfield College in the opener on April 5. . . . Displaying his contempt for Hollywood's misrepresentation of German author Erich Remarque's World War I novel *All Quiet on the Western Front*, Dr. Wolfram Sievers of the Reich Foreign Office suggests in testimony to the Reichstag that a new law be created to restrict misrepresentative foreign film adaptations from being shown in Germany.	Mar. 28
The House of Representatives debates a resolution that would bestow the name of "Taft Bridge" upon the Rock Creek Park Bridge, which the late Supreme Court Justice walked over nearly every day according to his friends and family. . . . Officials in Rapid City, S.Dak., author a letter to recently released Chicagoland gangster "Scarface Al" Capone, inviting him to take up his residence in the small city. However, Governor W.J. Bulow says he will bar Capone from living there.		U.S. bank clearings for this week are 16.7 percent lower than the comparable period a year ago, according to figures released by U.S. economic officials. Despite this, seven of the banks listed on the New York Stock Exchange experience record highs for the year. . . . The U.S. Commerce Department releases figures showing that February's manufactured exports decreased by $34,454,000 as compared to the previous February.		Sculptor Gutzon Borglum announces that the 60-foot sculpture of George Washington's head on Mount Rushmore in Keystone, S.Dak., is nearly complete. The sculpture will be unveiled on Independence Day this year, according to Borglum. . . . Sixteen American polo players are invited to compete in an international polo tournament against Great Britain on September 6.	Mar. 29
					Mar. 30
		In a forum on African-American employment in New York, Fritz Kaufman, chief of the Bureau of Employment of the New York State Department, places the blame for the unemployment situation on "technological changes in industry and mergers."			Mar. 31
The Motion Picture Producers and Distributors Association of America convenes in New York to add a new set of rules to its code of ethics. Among them, "every effort shall be made to reflect in drama and entertainment the better standards of life," "law, natural or human, shall not be ridiculed," and "sympathy shall not be created for the violation of the law."			Dr. Henry Benjamin discovers that by injecting hormones into male patients, the aesthetic ravages of aging can all but be eliminated. However, the procedure does not technically prolong life, according to Benjamin. . . . The experimental flight from Germany to the Canary Islands of the Dornier-Wal, one of the first flying ships or "sea planes" created, was a success, according to officials in Berlin.	On trial for "indecent performance," a group of New York City acrobats perform a routine for a stone-faced judge and jury in order to prove the innocent nature of their craft. . . . At the halfway point of the annual Masters golf tournament in Augusta, Ga., renowned golfer Bobby Jones leads by three strokes with a score of 144, or even par.	Apr. 1
		The New York Industrial Bureau issues a statement saying unemployment is the worst in the state since 1914. . . . Major U.S. auto manufacturers issue a collective report showing that automobile production for March was virtually the same as for February.	Speaking before the U.S. Radio Commission, radio engineer Joseph A. Burch predicts that baseball and football will be able to be televised within the year.		Apr. 2
Former secretary of the interior Albert B. Fall is convicted of accepting a bribe worth $610,000 from Pan-American Petroleum and Transport Company president Edward L. Doheny. In exchange for the bribe, Doheny was given a lease to the oil fields in Elk Hills, Calif. . . . The Autostrop Safety Razor Company announces it is suing the Gillette Razor Company for infringement of Autostrop's patented Probak blade and holder. . . . Recording of the 15th U.S. census begins in New York with 2,347 enumerators responsible for 6,930,000 people.		*Dun's Review* publishes its monthly index of U.S. commodity prices, showing that average prices declined by 1 percent in March, a total loss of 6.5 percent in the past year.	Dr. William C. Geer announces the invention of "overshoes," 100-pound sheets of vulcanized rubber that fit over planes' wings to combat debilitating ice.	Frankie Anslem retains his title of U.S. National Guard bantamweight champion by defeating Willie Rose, the former titleholder.	Apr. 3

F	G	H	I	J
Includes elections, federal-state relations, civil rights and liberties, crime, the judiciary, education, healthcare, poverty, urban affairs, and population.	*Includes formation and debate of U.S. foreign and defense policies, veterans affairs, and defense spending. (Relations with specific foreign countries are usually found under the region concerned.)*	*Includes business, labor, agriculture, taxation, transportation, consumer affairs, monetary and fiscal policy, natural resources, pollution, and accidents.*	*Includes worldwide scientific, medical, and technological developments, natural phenomena, U.S. weather, and natural disasters.*	*Includes the arts, religion, scholarship, communications media, sports, entertainment, fashions, fads, and social life.*

	World Affairs	Europe	Africa & The Middle East	The Americas	Asia & The Pacific
Apr. 4				Mexican officials in the state of Jalisco file an injunction against the American mining company Cinco Minas, requiring them to overturn the decision to dismiss 2,000 workers on March 22. Spokesmen for the company state declining silver markets made it necessary for the mass dismissal.	The Japanese Finance Ministry releases a report stating that the savings from the naval reductions proposed at the London Naval Conference will result in an accumulation of $331.5 million in five years. . . . The Australian Commonwealth Parliament updates its tariff law, affixing an additional 50 percent surcharge to most imported commodities, including tobacco, spirits, and preserves.
Apr. 5	German delegates to the League of Nations suggest an amendment to Article XVII, which grants non-member nations the right to become temporary members if threatened with military invasion from foreign powers.	Former British prime minister Stanley Baldwin, head of the Tory Party, announces that if his party returns to power in the coming general election, he will enact strict tariffs to protect Great Britain's economy.		Canadian officials announce $25 million will be spent in the coming year to modernize Canada's railroad system.	Imperial British police in Bombay, India, fire upon a crowd of 2,000 striking railway workers, injuring 30 of them.
Apr. 6	A meeting between British Prime Minister Ramsay MacDonald and French Foreign Minister Aristide Briand results in a newfound hope for a five-power naval reduction treaty, which seemed nearly impossible earlier this year.	Italian delegates to the London Naval Conference object to the French delegation's proposal of a large reduction of Italy's navy. It is unnecessary, write Italian newspapers, because France has "the most powerful army and the largest air force in the world."			
Apr. 7		To combat sinking tourism, France appoints Gaston Gerard to the newly created position of High Commissioner of Tourism. . . . Officials of the British cabinet say it is unlikely they will accept the British Admiralty's proposal of an average of 52,700 tons for submarines.	King Ras Tafari Makonnen (Haile Selassie) of Abyssinia, crowned in 1928, declares himself Emperor following the defeat of the opposing rebel army and the death of the Empress Zaudita.	American bankers and officials from the U.S. Department of Commerce arrive in Buenos Aires, Argentina, to study the country's economic problems. Many agree that while the economic situation seems dire, it does not appear that it can get any worse.	
Apr. 8	The French Colonial Institute requests that the French government break off relations with the Soviet Union, which has been inciting Communist rebellion in the French colonies. "It will be futile to appropriate billions for the development of our colonies if this expansion is to be compromised by insurrection," reads a statement.	Former British prime minister Stanley Baldwin offers an explanation for the recent dramatic tariff increases in Europe. "Europe is afraid of the United States," he says, elaborating that many European nations fear economic exploitation. He adds, "There is jealousy in Europe of that great country." . . . In accordance with a report issued by the Royal Commission of Inquiry, wage reductions occur for workers in the wool industry, which has seen a downward trend in recent months. Workers' unions respond by requesting the reductions be cut in half.			
Apr. 9	Sixty-year-old American oil baron J.E. Bristow, who was captured by Mexican bandits on March 10, is released following the acceptance of ransom money by the bandits.	Germany's Reichstag parliament agrees to follow the suggestions of Minister of Agriculture Martin Schiele and dramatically increase tariffs on imported foodstuffs.		Bolivia's Secretary of State announces the country is postponing its presidential election due to economic distress caused by a depressed mining industry. . . . Former Colombian finance minister Francisco de Perez publishes a letter in local newspapers addressed to President Miguel Abadia Mendez, predicting that unless drastic action is taken by the U.S. Congress, the deficit in Colombia will reach 25 million pesos ($24,187,500) by the end of the year.	Inspecting his country's army, President Chiang Kai-shek of China announces he will wait to begin combat operations against rebels in the northern part of China. He hopes to rely on disunity in the rebel groups to diminish their strength.
Apr. 10		Count Bethlen, Premier of Hungary, leaves from his country's capital of Budapest to travel to Rome, Italy, where he will meet with Italian Premier Benito Mussolini to extend the already friendly scope of Italo-Hungarian relations. . . . Funeral services for Victoria of Baden, Queen of Sweden, are held in the German Evangelical Church in Rome, Italy. Queen since her father-in-law's death in 1907, Victoria died at the age of 62.			The U.S. State Department warns Americans living in the Chinese cities of Shiuchow and Linchow to be wary of encroaching Communist bandit forces. Especially in danger are American missionaries, whose beliefs stand in sharp contrast with Communist atheism. . . . Philippine Director of Labor Hermenegildo Cruz authors a letter to Henry Ford, asking the auto magnate to build an automobile technicians' school to help boost the Philippines' tiny automobile manufacturing industry.
	A Includes developments that affect more than one world region, international organizations, and important meetings of world leaders.	**B** Includes all domestic and regional developments in Europe, including the Soviet Union.	**C** Includes all domestic and regional developments in Africa and the Middle East.	**D** Includes all domestic and regional developments in Latin America, the Caribbean, and Canada.	**E** Includes all domestic and regional developments in Asian and Pacific nations (and colonies).

U.S. Politics & Social Issues	U.S. Foreign Policy & Defense	Economics & Great Depression	Science, Technology & Nature	Culture, Leisure & Lifestyle	
		The Little Church Around the Corner in New York City hands out a record number of meal tickets for one day, 1,960, bringing the church's three-week total to 31,742. The tickets are redeemable for a meal worth 20 cents. . . . The National Automobile Chamber of Commerce releases its monthly automobile production report. Production increased by 18 percent in March as compared to February, while it decreased by 36 percent as compared to March 1929.		In *Collier's Magazine*, Hall of Fame baseball player Honus Wagner selects a team of the greatest ballplayers and personnel in major league baseball history. Notables include Babe Ruth and Ty Cobb. Modestly, Wagner leaves himself off the list. . . . The International Tennis Federation votes on whether to allow amateurs to compete in tournaments. Of the 22 nations that voted, only Great Britain and the United States voted positively. . . . Tom Blankenburg wins the National AAU indoor 220-yard breast stroke swimming championship.	Apr. 4
By a vote of 285–17, the House of Representatives passes a bill extending pension plans for government employees at a cost of $16 million annually. . . . New York State Commissioner of Education Dr. Frank P. Graves announces that April 25, May 2, and May 9 will be chosen as the dates that various sections of New York will observe Arbor Day. . . . New York state legislators consider lowering the minimum age required to receive retirement pensions to 65, rather than 70.	U.S. delegates to the London Naval Conference oppose the Japanese delegation's request to modernize its existing submarine and destroyer fleet. Americans say the modernization will result in a lack of parity.	Economic officials in Australia announce the absolute ban on 80 imported commodities, most of which are foods including cheese, lemons, oranges, peanut butter, and pork. With unparalleled high tariffs, Australia already has a very restrictive trading system.		Alabama University wins the Southern Conference collegiate basketball title, defeating Duke University by a score of 31–24. Alabama was the only team to finish the regular season undefeated.	Apr. 5
The National Forest Preserve Commission purchases 36,428 acres of forest in Louisiana. The purchased acres will henceforth be known as the Kisatchie National Forest.	The Army Air Corps awards a $1,450,570.72 contract to the Pratt & Whitney Company for construction of 252 engines for bombardment planes.	The Alaska Game Commission reports that fur exports for 1929 totaled $4,513,863.76. Compared to last year, it is an increase of $215,226.63, despite 38,629 fewer furs having been sold. . . . U.S. economic officials state that 1929's export total to Australia of $32 million is expected to be drastically reduced for 1930 because of Australia's new high tariffs, which some officials call "the highest tariff barrier in the world."	The Radcliffe Observatory, one of Great Britain's first and largest astronomical observatories, announces it will move its entire operation to South Africa, where the flat terrain makes it easier for observations to take place. . . . Canadian officials announce the creation of the world's fastest long-distance train. The train will be able to complete a route from Montreal to Chicago in 18 hours.		Apr. 6
New York City hospital officials estimate over 16 percent of the total patients being treated are there as a result of alcoholic intoxication.		*The Economist* releases its monthly index of wholesale prices. The index of British prices for March was 83.1 percent, down by 1.2 percent since February. The figure pales in comparison to last year's March index of 96.1.		An estimated 100,000 people arrive in Washington, D.C., to admire the blooming cherry blossoms, given to the United States as a gift from Japan on March 27, 1912. Police in Washington say the visitors have caused "the greatest congestion in the history of Washington."	Apr. 7
	One of the largest warfare simulations occurs in the military airport Crissly Field in San Francisco, with over 100 planes simulating an air force attack. Results of the simulation indicate holes in Crissly Field's air defenses.	The U.S. Federal Reserve Board releases figures showing that while this week saw an increase of $35 million in Federal Reserve borrowings, government deposits declined by $21 million.	The U.S. Radio Commission officially modifies the frequencies of 17 broadcast stations, making the average separation between radio stations 1,117 miles. Formerly, the average separation was 522 miles.		Apr. 8
	Seeking to increase the United States' aviation exports, former army flier James H. Doolittle leaves New York for northern and central Europe to demonstrate four new types of American planes.	The Argentine government accepts a loan of $50 million from a U.S. banking group headed by Chatham Phenix Corporation of New York.	German engineer Ernest Bexel arrives in Brazil to oversee the completion of the construction of the airship *Graf Zeppelin*, which in later years would become the most traveled airship in history.		Apr. 9
	The Army Air Corps awards a contract to the Curtiss Aeroplane and Motor Company, Inc., worth $660,280 for 100 D-12-E engines, which are to be installed in the model A-3B attack airplane. . . . British naval officials tell American newspaper reporters in London that it will cost an estimated $1 billion over the next five years to achieve naval parity with Great Britain.	In a speech before 350 prominent heads of business, industry, and finance, National Business Survey Conference chairman Julius Barnes blames the unemployment situation in the United States on "idleness" caused by improvements in machinery and technology.			Apr. 10

F	G	H	I	J
Includes elections, federal-state relations, civil rights and liberties, crime, the judiciary, education, healthcare, poverty, urban affairs, and population.	Includes formation and debate of U.S. foreign and defense policies, veterans affairs, and defense spending. (Relations with specific foreign countries are usually found under the region concerned.)	Includes business, labor, agriculture, taxation, transportation, consumer affairs, monetary and fiscal policy, natural resources, pollution, and accidents.	Includes worldwide scientific, medical, and technological developments, natural phenomena, U.S. weather, and natural disasters.	Includes the arts, religion, scholarship, communications media, sports, entertainment, fashions, fads, and social life.

	World Affairs	Europe	Africa & The Middle East	The Americas	Asia & The Pacific
Apr. 11	The draft of a new Anglo-Soviet trade treaty is sent from London to Moscow for approval by Soviet officials. If approved, trade between the two countries will resume.	The Grand Mufti of Jerusalem, along with his followers, addresses the British Parliament, calling for greater power for Arabs serving in the British-controlled Palestinian government. "Arabs have been submitted to a policy of oppression which has deprived them of anything in the way of self government," he says, adding, "we have had taxation without representation."	In Amman, Palestine, one-third of the city's population is commissioned by local government officials to help quell plagues of locusts. Already, huge numbers of locusts have been destroyed.	Argentina's Minister of Finance publishes a report showing that exports for the first two months of 1930 declined by 29 percent as compared to the first two months of 1929.	
Apr. 12	Japanese, U.S., and British delegates to the London Naval Conference finally agree upon total tonnage for their navies. In the next five years, the United States will be allowed to produce ships with a total weight of 526,200 tons. The British are allotted 541,700 tons, while the Japanese are allotted 367,050 tons. First Lord of the British Admiralty A.V. Alexander estimates total savings from the naval reductions to be between £60–70 million.	Newspapers in Great Britain express the British people's frustration over the lack of a five-power treaty at the conclusion of the London Naval Conference, despite the success of the three-power treaty.			Employees of two Japanese cotton mills in the cities of Osaka and Kobe go on strike following word that workers' wages were to be reduced by 25 percent.
Apr. 13		American citizen Antonio Pizzucco is released by Italian authorities after mistakenly being conscripted into the Fascist Italian Army. Local authorities blame their mistake on Pizzucco's Italian lineage.			
Apr. 14		France sets a record for itself in terms of banknote circulation. According to published reports, 71,576,000,000 were in circulation this week.		The Argentine newspaper La Nacion publishes a report showing that in the past 10 years, Argentina's national budget has increased by 73 percent, despite an increase in the country's total wealth of only 25 percent. . . . Following the resignations of his entire Cabinet, President Abadia Mendez of Colombia signs a decree appointing a new Cabinet comprised of four Conservatives and four Liberals, who will resume the duties of the resigned Cabinet members the following day.	
Apr. 15	Two American tourists are arrested in Constanza, Hungary, while taking photographs of the city's harbor. Suspected of being spies on behalf of Soviet Russia, the tourists are taken into custody to have their passports scrutinized to ascertain the authenticity of their claim to U.S. citizenship.	The National Socialist Minister of Education of the German city of Thuringia, Dr. Fricke, bans all "negro culture," mainly African-American jazz musicians. "The suppression of this decay is in the interest of the German national character," Fricke says.	Two Arabs in Palestine are acquitted of having committed the murder of railway worker Abraham Motel during the Arab-Jew riots the previous autumn.	Despite a loan of $50 million by U.S. bankers one week prior, the price of the Argentine peso continues to fall, declining by 45 cents in one day.	
Apr. 16		The French Parliament approves the government budget for 1930, originally slated to be passed last December 31, by a vote of 405–191. Total expenditures for the budget total 50 billion francs, or $2 billion.			Bishop J.W. Robinson of India arrives in the United States to attend the conference of Bishops of the Methodist Church. He notes that in India over the past 40 years, the number of Christians has increased from 28,000 to 500,000. He cites this as the reason that Mohandas Gandhi's nonviolent resistance campaign will eventually fail.
Apr. 17	British Foreign Secretary Arthur Henderson and Soviet Ambassador to Great Britain Grigori Sokoinikoff sign a commercial trade agreement establishing "most favored nation" status between the two countries. . . . French Foreign Minister Aristide Briand sends a questionnaire to 27 European nations, asking for their input on the concept of a federated Europe.	By a vote of 194–50, the British House of Commons overturns an earlier House of Lords ruling that reinstated the army's death penalty for cowardice and desertion among British soldiers. . . . Despite their country's economy approaching a crisis, legislators in the British House of Commons devote their time to debating whether or not the "inhumane" practice of boiling lobsters alive should be outlawed.	Egyptian Premier Nahas Pasha and British Foreign Secretary Arthur Henderson agree to terms on a treaty that would grant Egypt virtual independence from British rule.		The Australian government reduces its military budget by approximately $2.5 million for the year 1930.
	A Includes developments that affect more than one world region, international organizations, and important meetings of world leaders.	**B** Includes all domestic and regional developments in Europe, including the Soviet Union.	**C** Includes all domestic and regional developments in Africa and the Middle East.	**D** Includes all domestic and regional developments in Latin America, the Caribbean, and Canada.	**E** Includes all domestic and regional developments in Asian and Pacific nations (and colonies).

U.S. Politics & Social Issues	U.S. Foreign Policy & Defense	Economics & Great Depression	Science, Technology & Nature	Culture, Leisure & Lifestyle	
The New York State Assembly passes a resolution, by a vote of 82–61, calling on the U.S. Congress to hold a constitutional convention to repeal the Prohibition Amendment.	The launch of the 10,000-ton USS *Chicago* at the Mare Island Naval Shipyard in Solano County, Calif., is attended by 20,000. One of the first of the U.S. Navy's 10,000-ton cruisers, the U.S.S. *Chicago* would eventually be sunk by the Japanese in the Battle of Rennell Island on January 30, 1943.	Representatives from the U.S. Bureau of Mines report that over 40 percent of the world's tin production is consumed in the United States, with nearly all of it imported.			Apr. 11
The House of Representatives unanimously passes a bill granting Carlsbad Caverns, designated as a national monument, the title of national park.		New bond offerings on the New York Stock Exchange for the week totaled $192,530,000, according to U.S. economic officials. The total is the highest this year since the week of January 17. . . . The British Board of Trade publishes reports showing that the total amount of imports and exports for the country in March declined by £7 million as compared to March of last year.	The governments of the United States and Canada enter into an agreement whereby they will "interlock" their radio aircraft communication systems.		Apr. 12
At the quarterly meeting of the American Psychological Association, speakers urge psychologists to help ease the pain of older, unemployed workers in the United States. . . . New York University physical education director Jay B. Nash cites homework as the number one reason for both the lack of the city's park and playground use and growing childhood delinquency. "Homework," he says, "amounts to legalized criminality." . . . Three Chicago movie theaters, under pressure from the Chicago League of the Hard of Hearing, agree to install electrical hearing devices to allow the city's 300,000 deaf people to hear "talkies."		The American Automobile Association publishes a report showing the number of gallons of gasoline taxed last year by state. California consumed the most gasoline with 1,139,738,244 gallons, while Nevada consumed the least with 16,307,535 gallons. . . . A consortium of U.S. economic experts reports that the average yearly wage for workers in the United States is $1,300. . . . In an address, Chase National Bank economist Dr. Benjamin Anderson warns against borrowing from federal reserves to solve the nation's financial crisis. "If the dose is large enough," he says, "a very substantial temporary effect can be brought about, but headaches will follow. It is not the sound way to do it."		The state-owned Commercial Press of China publishes a 2,000-volume "complete library," which contains most of history's great literary works translated into Chinese.	Apr. 13
The National Unemployment League requests of President Herbert Hoover that April 27 be designated as "Unemployment Day," the purpose of which is to set aside time to organize a federal public works project. . . . President Herbert Hoover officially nominates John J. Parker of North Carolina to fill the vacancy on the U.S. Supreme Court.		The American Paper Co. ships a record amount of paper to the economically struggling South American continent. This allows 250,000 pounds of high quality stationery to be sold at prices lower than European competitors. . . . Steel production in the United States in March fell at a rate of 2.7 percent as compared to February, reports from economic officials indicate.		Chinese officials condemn the American film *Murder Will Out*, which depicts Chinese men as opiate distributors and murderers.	Apr. 14
Regional Planning Federation aviation commission chairman Major Samuel B. Eckert announces the creation of 30 new airports to be built in the tri-state area of Pennsylvania, New Jersey, and Delaware. The new airports will cover an area of 4,000 square miles.	The U.S. Navy withdraws the sale of the former presidential yacht, the *Mayflower*, after the highest bid of $60,000 is deemed inadequate.	The American Express Co., a subsidiary of Chase National Bank, opens its first bank in New York City with a starting capital of $15 million. . . . Reports from the British Chancellor of the Exchequer indicate the United States and Great Britain attain the same annual tax revenue, approximately $4 billion.	The Lamartine Field airport in Lamartine, Pa., is quarantined by U.S. federal authorities following reports of an outbreak of smallpox.		Apr. 15
The number of Catholics in the United States is 20,078,202, or approximately 16 percent of the total U.S. population, according to statistics in the newly published Catholic Directory. . . . Construction on the United States' tallest skyscraper, the Chrysler Building, is completed in New York City. The Chrysler Building will remain the tallest building in the United States until the Empire State Building is built the following year.	Lloyd's Register of Shipping issues its quarterly report, showing that the United States is now third in the world in terms of shipbuilding, with 222,974 tons of ships under construction.	The price of copper in Great Britain falls to £62 per ton, a day after closing at £67 per ton. It is the lowest price since 1928. . . . The American Railway Association announces that car loadings in the United States totaled 907,928 cars for this week, a reduction of 50,297 cars from the corresponding week of 1929.		The Commonwealth Film Censorship Board of Australia reports that last year more than 79 percent of imported films to Australia were American made, while only 11 percent were made in Great Britain.	Apr. 16
			A bejeweled white and gold town car, said to be the costliest ever built, completes construction. The car was designed exclusively for Reza Khan, Shah of Iran.		Apr. 17

F	G	H	I	J
Includes elections, federal-state relations, civil rights and liberties, crime, the judiciary, education, healthcare, poverty, urban affairs, and population.	*Includes formation and debate of U.S. foreign and defense policies, veterans affairs, and defense spending. (Relations with specific foreign countries are usually found under the region concerned.)*	*Includes business, labor, agriculture, taxation, transportation, consumer affairs, monetary and fiscal policy, natural resources, pollution, and accidents.*	*Includes worldwide scientific, medical, and technological developments, natural phenomena, U.S. weather, and natural disasters.*	*Includes the arts, religion, scholarship, communications media, sports, entertainment, fashions, fads, and social life.*

	World Affairs	Europe	Africa & The Middle East	The Americas	Asia & The Pacific
Apr. 18		In conjunction with Easter, King Boris of Bulgaria grants a general amnesty, completely exonerating over 100 political prisoners as well as reducing the sentences of 250 political prisoners.	In retaliation for the U.S. tariff on imported cotton, the Egyptian Chamber of Deputies considers a 60 percent tariff raise on all U.S. goods entering Egypt.		
Apr. 19	French Foreign Minister Aristide Briand leaves Paris to return to London, where he will conclude the London Naval Conference by writing his signature alongside his international counterparts'.	The French Finance Committee agrees on a proposal that would cut taxes in the country by 1.9 billion francs ($76 million) by the year 1931. . . . In the small town of Gaesti, Hungary, 144 Christian churchgoers celebrating Good Friday burn to death.		Dr. Enrique Olaya Herrera, president-elect of Colombia, arrives in New York to be welcomed by diplomatic communities.	Premier Scullin of Australia estimates that improving unemployment conditions in his country will cost $24 million to $29 million annually. . . . Fires rip through the Northern Occidental Negros Province of the Philippines, destroying the homes of 5,000 people and causing damages of $2.5 million.
Apr. 20	70-year-old Danish Ambassador to the United States Constantin Brun, who has held the post for 31 years, announces his retirement, effective in October.	Adolf Hitler, leader of the National Socialist German Workers' (Nazi) Party, celebrates his 41st birthday. . . . German Minister of Finance Dr. Paul Moldenhauer announces the imposition of a 75 percent increase in tax on beer, which many Germans substitute for water as their daily beverage.		Canadian economic officials announce that the total amount of wheat exports for the country has fallen by 64 percent in one year.	
Apr. 21	The Italian Ambassador to China formally demands $500,000 from Kwangtung authorities for the recent slaying of two Italian missionaries by Chinese bandits. Officials respond by saying the Nationalist government in Nanking is responsible for the reparations. . . . Copies of the text of the final agreement at the London Naval Conference are distributed to international delegates, but are yet to be made public. The text is said to contain over 5,000 words.	According to estimates by the Ministry of Labor, the cost of living in Great Britain has risen 57 percent in the past 25 years.			
Apr. 22					
Apr.23	British Ambassador to the United States Sir Ronald Lindsay travels to New York, where he will speak before the British Empire Chamber of Commerce in the United States.			In Brazil, former British army officer Capt. H. Holland is arrested by Rio de Janeiro police following accusations that he took aerial photographs of strategic military installations. Holland had been working with a private aerial photography company for the past year. . . . Mexican bandits in Guadalajara kidnap American dentist Dr. George Edward Purnell, 64, demanding a ransom of $6,000 for his release. Purnell is the third kidnapping victim in Mexico in as many weeks.	
Apr.24	The newly created Bank for International Settlements names Pierre Quesnay as its first managing director. Newspapers in Germany express frustration that a German, who would be more likely to solve Germany's debt problems, was not chosen.			In a speech before the Colombian-American Chamber of Commerce, President-elect Dr. Enrique Olaya Herrera urges greater economic cooperation between the two countries. "As long as I am president," Herrera says, "I assure all American capital fair treatment."	

A	B	C	D	E
Includes developments that affect more than one world region, international organizations, and important meetings of world leaders.	Includes all domestic and regional developments in Europe, including the Soviet Union.	Includes all domestic and regional developments in Africa and the Middle East.	Includes all domestic and regional developments in Latin America, the Caribbean, and Canada.	Includes all domestic and regional developments in Asian and Pacific nations (and colonies).

U.S. Politics & Social Issues	U.S. Foreign Policy & Defense	Economics & Great Depression	Science, Technology & Nature	Culture, Leisure & Lifestyle	
The U.S. Food and Drug Administration bans the use of "artificial yellow colors" in mayonnaise and salad dressings. The reason, according to spokesmen, is that the artificial color makes food appear to be higher in egg content than it actually is.	The War Department announces the creation of a new gas mask developed by the Chemical Warfare Service. The masks will primarily be used on transport horses. . . . Tests occur in San Francisco to demonstrate the usefulness of "autopilot," a new technology allowing planes to travel to destinations without the aid of human hands.	*The Annalist* Weekly releases its weekly list of average international wholesale commodity prices. The average international price stands at 133.4, a decline of 1.6 points from a week ago and 11.9 points from the comparable period a year ago.		Acadia University wins the Eastern Canada basketball championship, defeating Windsor Academy by a score of 26–24. . . . Arthur Hammerstein, son of legendary playwright Oscar Hammerstein, announces his retirement from theater producing following the productions of *The Bird of Paradise* and *Madeline.*	Apr. 18
Rep. R.Q. Lee of Texas dies at the Emergency Hospital in Washington, D.C., following five weeks of recovery from a stroke he sustained on Capitol Hill. Out of respect for Lee, members of the House of Representatives announce they will adjourn for three days.		Former Czech minister of agriculture Dr. Milan Hodza urges all European nations to raise tariffs on U.S. and Canadian imported goods, so that Europe may rely less on foreign imports. He also suggests uniform European tariffs. . . . The Canadian Department of Finance reports that it currently holds $65,889,439 worth of gold. . . . The U.S. Department of Commerce announces that check payments dropped by approximately 5 percent in this week as compared to last.	Italy sets a record for speed for big ships when its light cruiser *Nicoloso da Recco* travels around the Mediterranean at just over 36 knots, bettering the record held by the French destroyer *Byson* at 35.8 knots.		Apr. 19
The Senate Judiciary Committee approves the Williamson Bill, a resolution transferring anti-Prohibition activities from the Treasury Department to the Justice Department. The bill also allows the Attorney General, head of the Justice Department, to veto any industrial alcohol permit.	A new sea vessel combining boat and airplane completes construction at Quincy Point, Mass. The vessel cost $25,000 to construct.	According to published reports, citizens of Great Britain and the United States pay an approximately equal amount of income tax. In Great Britain in 1930, citizens paid a total of $1.47 billion in income tax; in the United States, the figure is slightly lower, at $1.1 billion.			Apr. 20
Federal census supervisors announce that those willfully refusing to answer questions posed by census workers will be prosecuted in federal courts. . . . Former president Calvin Coolidge praises Dwight W. Morrow, U.S. Ambassador to Mexico and father-in-law of famed aviator Charles Lindbergh, in a 1,500-word foreword to a biography written by Hewitt H. Howland.		The Bank of England receives £1 million worth of gold from the government of Australia. . . . The U.S. Federal Reserve Board reports that bank loan rates reached their lowest point since 1924 in March.		Kent Cooper, general manager of the Associated Press, estimates that over 300,000 words of news are printed daily by the Associated Press.	Apr. 21
In remarks on the Senate floor, Senator Smith Wildman Brookhart blames the growing movement in the United States to repeal the Prohibition Amendment on Wall Street interests.	Speaking before the American Society of Newspaper Editors, Andre Gerard, editor of the French newspaper *The Echo de Paris*, decries U.S. foreign policy. "The European problem cannot be solved as long as the attitude of America remains an unknown," he says. In response, Foreign Relations Committee chairman Senator William Edgar Borah of Idaho calls the editor's comments "absurd."	The U.S. Department of Labor reports that April estimates for new building expenditures increased by 50.6 percent as compared to March. . . . An injunction is filed in the U.S. Supreme Court to halt the merger between General Theatres Equipment, Inc. and the Fox Film Company.		Noted pro golfer Alex Smith, who won the national open championship in 1906 and 1910, dies at the age of 58 at a hospital in Baltimore, Md. Funeral services are held the next day at St. Mary's Cemetery in Glen Cove, N.Y. . . . Diplomats from 44 countries arrive in the United States' capital of Washington, D.C., to witness a historic concert: for the first time, the bands of all three armed forces services (Army, Navy, and Marines) will perform at the same event.	Apr. 22
A petition is introduced in the Miami Circuit Court to bar the estate of Al "Scarface" Capone, whose release from prison last month sparked a wave of crime in Florida. Capone's estate is declared "a harbor for all classes of criminals." . . . New York City Health Commissioner Dr. Shirley Wynne reports that the birth rate for last week was the lowest of any point in the year. Wynne cites an outbreak of measles as a contributing factor to the low birth rate.		The American Petroleum Institute reports that crude oil production in California for the month of March averaged 635,493 barrels per day. It is a decrease of 110,433 barrels per day as compared to February.	New York City experiences its coldest April 23 on record as temperatures fall two degrees below the freezing point. The average for the day was 36°F, or 16 degrees below the city's normal average.		Apr. 23
A *Reader's Digest* poll conducted in Boston indicates Bostonians favor repealing the Eighteenth Amendment by a 2 to 1 margin. Over 50,000 people were polled. . . . Harry W. Bennett, chief of the Ford Motor Company's private police force, announces that the company will fire any employee who "reports for work with the odor of liquor on his breath." Exceptions will be made to those whose families are extremely poor, Bennett says.		The Italian Ministry of Finance announces that the Bank of Italy will be reducing its discount rate from 6.5 percent to 6 percent.			Apr. 24

F	**G**	**H**	**I**	**J**
Includes elections, federal-state relations, civil rights and liberties, crime, the judiciary, education, healthcare, poverty, urban affairs, and population.	*Includes formation and debate of U.S. foreign and defense policies, veterans affairs, and defense spending. (Relations with specific foreign countries are usually found under the region concerned.)*	*Includes business, labor, agriculture, taxation, transportation, consumer affairs, monetary and fiscal policy, natural resources, pollution, and accidents.*	*Includes worldwide scientific, medical, and technological developments, natural phenomena, U.S. weather, and natural disasters.*	*Includes the arts, religion, scholarship, communications media, sports, entertainment, fashions, fads, and social life.*

	World Affairs	Europe	Africa & The Middle East	The Americas	Asia & The Pacific
Apr. 25		Archduke Leopold of Austria is put on trial after accusations surface that he played a part in the illegal sale of a $400,000 Napoleonic era diamond necklace on February 1. He is released after paying $7,500 bail.	In Egypt, local practitioner Dr. Fakhry, who was born Muslim but recently converted to Christianity, is arrested by Egyptian authorities after statements he made led to charges of "defamatory language against the established religion." Dr. Fakhry is purported to have said that Islam does not promote an egalitarian society.		
Apr. 26	A group of American tax experts departs from New York to travel to Paris, where they will meet with their French counterparts to discuss commercial disagreements between the two countries.				British women and children in the Indian city of Peshawar are evacuated by the Imperial Police after rioters kill at least 13 people. An order is also issued prohibiting any British soldiers from leaving the country.
Apr. 27		Reports by German sociologists indicate an influx of 80,000 immigrants settled in the capital of Berlin last year, making the city's population of 5 million among the highest of major European cities.			
Apr. 28					With Communist agitation mounting in the Chinese city of Shanghai, local officials ban public meetings and announce that marshal law will be instituted throughout the city beginning May 1. The announcement follows a weekend during which over 250 suspected agitators were arrested.
Apr. 29		Following a meeting between German Zeppelin commander Dr. Hugo Eckener and representatives of the British Air Ministry, the two countries sign an "airship truce," promoting a free exchange of technological information. . . . Austria enters into an agreement with France whereby 15,000 of Austria's workers will be employed in industries in France. Austria's only stipulation is that the workers cannot be used to build military installations aimed at Germany, of which Austria is a close ally.		A report issued by Canadian Defense Minister J.L. Raston shows that Canada has a standing army of approximately 3,500 men, making it one of the world's smallest armed forces.	Chinese bandits invade the northern city of Kingsuchen, slaughtering all of the city's officials along with 1,000 other helpless villagers. Kinguschen is 100 miles from the capital of Nanking, which the bandits seek to invade.
Apr. 30	U.S. delegates to the London Naval Conference, along with U.S. Secretary of State Henry Stimson, arrive in New York Harbor, officially marking the end of the Conference. While the terms may be agreed upon, Stimson says, the real challenge now is ratification.		In an interview with the Jewish Telegraphic Agency, Emir Arslan, head of an Arab delegation to the United States, says that peace between Arabs and Jews in Palestine can only be achieved through the abolition of the 1917 Balfour Declaration, which established a Jewish "national home" in Palestine. "We cannot recognize any foreign political power in our country," he says, "and we consider the Zionists (Jews) such a power."	The inexplicable appointment of professional boxer Justo Suarez to the post of Chancellor of the Argentine Consulate General at New York draws condemnations from Argentine newspapers, who request that the post be filled by a professional diplomat. Another Argentine boxer, Hector Mendez, already presides over the Consulate in Baltimore. . . . The Canadian House of Commons reports that since January 1, 1922, 48 civilian Canadian ships have been seized by U.S. Prohibition enforcement officers for smuggling alcohol into the United States. However, no Canadians have been harmed in the seizures.	
May 1		Seeking to boost its country's capital, the National Bank of Belgium reduces its discount rate from 3.5 to 3 percent. The rate of interest on advances is also reduced, from 5 to 4 percent.			

A	B	C	D	E
Includes developments that affect more than one world region, international organizations, and important meetings of world leaders.	Includes all domestic and regional developments in Europe, including the Soviet Union.	Includes all domestic and regional developments in Africa and the Middle East.	Includes all domestic and regional developments in Latin America, the Caribbean, and Canada.	Includes all domestic and regional developments in Asian and Pacific nations (and colonies).

U.S. Politics & Social Issues	U.S. Foreign Policy & Defense	Economics & Great Depression	Science, Technology & Nature	Culture, Leisure & Lifestyle	
President Herbert Hoover nominates Robert P. Patterson, former chairman of the *Harvard Law Review*, to succeed Thomas Day Thacher, who recently became New York's solicitor general, as judge for the Southern District of New York. . . . By a vote of 37–36, the Senate rejects the repeal of the Immigration Act of 1924, which limits the number of legal European immigrants to 150,000 per year.		*The Annalist* Weekly index of wholesale commodity prices shows a decline of 0.2 points from the previous week. The figure stands at 133.1, compared with 145.2 on the corresponding date last year.		Dr. C.H. Townsend of the New York Aquarium returns from the Galapagos Islands with specimens of new species of reptiles, fish, and other sea animals. The Galapagos Islands were made famous in Charles Darwin's 1859 book, *The Origin of Species*.	Apr. 25
New York Commission on Old Age Security secretary Dr. Luther Gulick announces that beginning January 1, 50,000 senior citizens in New York City will begin to receive pensions.		According to reports by R.G. Dun & Co., U.S. bank clearings for this week stood at $9,381,577,000, 13 percent less than the corresponding period a year ago. Economic officials blame the decline on the Christian fasting holiday Good Friday.		For the second consecutive year, the New Westminster Adanacs win the Canadian basketball championship, defeating Acadia College in the title game by a score of 34–19.	Apr. 26
New York City Welfare Commissioner Christopher J. Dunn estimates that it will cost the city $10 million annually to pay for old age pensions. . . . The welfare department of Massachusetts estimates old age pensions will cover 8,115 senior citizens at a cost of $3.3 million annually.			With the completion of his latest intercontinental flight, Charles Lindbergh becomes the most traveled aviator in history, with approximately 350,000 miles flown over a three-year period.	Before a crowd of 100,000 at Wembley Stadium in London, the Arsenal Football Club defeats Huddersfield Town by a score of 2–0 to win the English Association Cup final. . . . American Dan Beattie establishes the world shot put record by throwing it 68 feet. Beattie eclipsed the old record, set by Ralph Rose in 1907, by 4.5 inches.	Apr. 27
Richard C. Patterson, New York corrections commissioner, releases figures detailing the city's growing prison population. Among the most alarming statistics, the female prison population has more than doubled in the past decade, from 1,150 female inmates in 1920 to 2,391 currently. Patterson says the Women's Suffrage Act of 1919 at least partly contributes to this problem. Overall, the total prison population has increased by 39 percent in the past six years, from 3,820 inmates in 1923 to 5,304 in 1929.		Speaking before the 18th session of the U.S. Chamber of Commerce, Julius H. Barnes, chairman, says that despite poor economic conditions, construction and building in the United States appears to be on pace to meet last December's projections.	For the second straight week, a record number of cars pass through New York's Holland Tunnel, which connects the island of Manhattan with mainland America. A total of 55,400 automobiles passed through it, exceeding the previous week's record by approximately 700 cars.		Apr. 28
Filibusters begin in the Senate over the nomination of conservative judge John J. Parker for the vacant slot on the Supreme Court. Senator William Edgar Borah, who helped to sponsor the bill that created the Department of Labor in 1913, took nearly two hours to essentially state that the confirmation of Parker would be an "inhuman" decision against organized labor, on the grounds of his former membership in the KKK.					Apr. 29
The national death rate has increased by 13 percent in one year, from 23.3 per 1,000 people to 26.4, according to published reports.		The U.S. House of Representatives agrees on a bill imposing a tariff of 2.2 cents per pound on imported raw Cuban sugar.			Apr. 30
President Herbert Hoover chooses former Consul General at Mexico City William Dawson to replace Gerhard A. Bading as U.S. Ambassador to Ecuador. . . . The Metropolitan Life Insurance Company releases a report estimating that the death rate of blue collar workers for March was 9.4 per 1,000 people. The figure indicates the best health conditions for low-income workers for any comparable period in any year.	The Shipping Board sells six obsolete sea vessels for a sum of $68,460 to the Boston Iron and Metal Company of Baltimore. . . . The destroyer ships USS *Osborne*, USS *Worden*, USS *Toucey*, USS *Billingsley*, and USS *Lamson* are decommissioned by the U.S. Navy.	Retail prices of coal in New York City are reduced by $1 per ton, in order to stimulate early buying of coal needed for the next winter. The reduction is in effect until July 1. . . . Corporate dividends in the United States for April increased by 18 percent as compared to April of last year, published reports show.	The Duchess of Bedford sets the record for least amount of time taken to fly from England to South Africa and back, accomplishing the feat in 21 days. The record for amount of flight hours, however, is still attributed to Sir Alan Cobham, who flew the same route in 25 less hours than the Duchess.		May 1
F Includes elections, federal-state relations, civil rights and liberties, crime, the judiciary, education, healthcare, poverty, urban affairs, and population.	**G** Includes formation and debate of U.S. foreign and defense policies, veterans affairs, and defense spending. (Relations with specific foreign countries are usually found under the region concerned.)	**H** Includes business, labor, agriculture, taxation, transportation, consumer affairs, monetary and fiscal policy, natural resources, pollution, and accidents.	**I** Includes worldwide scientific, medical, and technological developments, natural phenomena, U.S. weather, and natural disasters.	**J** Includes the arts, religion, scholarship, communications media, sports, entertainment, fashions, fads, and social life.	

	World Affairs	Europe	Africa & The Middle East	The Americas	Asia & The Pacific
May 2				Two people are killed and scores of others are injured as Communist demonstrations take place in the Cuban city of Regla. Labor leaders call on President Gerardo Machado to either sternly deal with the demonstrators so as to prevent a larger riot, or improve labor conditions.	Former Japanese foreign affairs secretary Etsuijiro Uyehara leads a *seiyukai* (opposition) against the newly completed London Naval Treaty during a session of the Japanese House of Representatives, saying that allowing the United States to increase its naval capacity "jeopardizes Japan's defense scheme." Uyehara places blame squarely on current foreign minister Baron Shidehara, who led the Japanese delegation at the London Naval Conference.
May 3	Terms of Germany's $300 million loan, the largest of its kind since World War I, are agreed upon by international financiers representing nine different nations in Brussels, Belgium. France and the United States will be responsible for more than half of the total loan, while the seven other countries will be responsible for the remaining $150 million.	Austrian Chancellor Johann Schober arrives in London to begin a three-day visit with Prime Minister Ramsay MacDonald. It is the first time an Austrian Chancellor has visited Great Britain since the end of World War I.			American Territorial Governor of Hawaii Lawrence M. Judd requests from Interior Secretary Ray Lyman Wilbur funds to study the ongoing problem of leprosy in Hawaii.
May 4					
May 5		Austrian economic officials report on foreign trade for their country in March. Among the statistics, imports decreased by 60 million schillings as compared to the corresponding period in 1929.			Mohandas Gandhi, leader of the civil disobedience program in India, is arrested by authorities in the city of Surat. No charge is given, except that Gandhi was in violation of "Ordinance 25 of the year 1827." News of the arrest prompts the closing of many Indian schools and the observance of a day of mourning.
May 6		Throngs of cheering gatherers appear outside Buckingham Palace in London to celebrate the 20th anniversary of the ascension of King George V to the British throne.			
May 7	U.S. Ambassador to Japan William R. Castle announces his retirement, effective May 27, when he will return to Washington to assume the duties of Assistant Secretary of State. Castle's tenure is the shortest of any U.S. Ambassador to Japan in 17 years. He would eventually be replaced by W. Cameron Forbes, who would hold the post from the fall of 1930 to the spring of 1932.	In the small Mediterranean island nation of Malta, the presiding Catholic Archbishop bans two local newspapers, *The Daily Malta Chronicle* and *Ix Xemex (The Sun)*, both of which are protected under the country's constitution. The Archbishop says his motives "must be evident to anybody who has the least Christian sentiment." . . . Twenty-two demonstrators of the Communist organization League of Redfront Fighters are arrested in Berlin, Germany, on the one-year anniversary of the organization's outlawing.		Col. Harry Burgess, governor of the Panama Canal, issues a report to the U.S. War Department detailing the canal's commercial traffic in April. The canal was used by 489 commercial vessels during the month, paying tolls of $2,232,763. This compares with 540 vessels and tolls of $2,261,087.27 in April 1929.	
	A *Includes developments that affect more than one world region, international organizations, and important meetings of world leaders.*	**B** *Includes all domestic and regional developments in Europe, including the Soviet Union.*	**C** *Includes all domestic and regional developments in Africa and the Middle East.*	**D** *Includes all domestic and regional developments in Latin America, the Caribbean, and Canada.*	**E** *Includes all domestic and regional developments in Asian and Pacific nations (and colonies).*

U.S. Politics & Social Issues	U.S. Foreign Policy & Defense	Economics & Great Depression	Science, Technology & Nature	Culture, Leisure & Lifestyle	
Representatives of the American Amalgamated Taxi Association appear before the Supreme Court to argue New York City Police Commissioner Whalen's decision to ban low-rate taxicabs. . . . According to reports by the Catholic Archdiocese of New York, 45,938 people were given free healthcare last year by Catholic hospitals at a cost of more than $3 million. . . . The New York City public school board unanimously approves a resolution allowing elective Hebrew courses to be taught in two public high schools. Over 25 percent of New York City's population is Jewish. . . . Communist demonstrations in New York City result in the arrests of 50 people, most of whom were distributing Communist leaflets.		The Annalist Weekly's report on wholesale commodity prices in the United States is issued, showing that the average figure stands at 132.3, a decline of 0.7 points from the previous week.		Dr. David Bryson Delavan is dubbed "the dean of American laryngology" by the New York Academy of Medicine on the occasion of Bryson's 80th birthday.	May 2
	Secretary of the Navy Charles Francis Adams announces that former chief naval adviser to the London Naval Conference Admiral William V. Pratt will succeed the post of Chief of Naval Operations from Admiral Charles F. Hughes, who plans to retire in October.	The Socialist Women's Kitchen of New York reports that a near majority of those to whom they give aid are "white collar" workers. . . . The National Bank of Denmark lowers its discount rate from 4.5 to 4 percent.			May 3
Aviation officials estimate the total amount of miles flown per day in the United States is 83,000, the largest of any country.		U.S. economic officials fear economic deflation as reports are published showing that the average sale in retail stores has decreased by 10 cents in the past six months. . . . Salvation Army head Col. Winchell announces that breadlines in New York City will close following a decrease in men and women aided. The previous week saw a decrease from 600 to 300 people in three days.	In a radio speech in Rome broadcast to the entire world, Guglielmo Marconi, credited with inventing the radio, says wireless technology will be a large factor in promoting world peace. Radio, he says, "will promote a mutual understanding of our respective feelings, habits, and ideals."	In accordance with the seventh annual National Music Week, a nationwide poll in the United States is conducted to determine whether music making is decreasing or increasing across the country. The poll results show that 86 percent of the respondents said it is increasing in their region. . . . The film adaptation of German author Erich Remarque's All Quiet on the Western Front premiers in New York to rave reviews. "Few books have been adapted to the screen with such success," writes one reviewer. The film will eventually go on to be selected as the 54th greatest film of the 20th century by the American Film Institute.	May 4
New York City establishes the Bureau of Municipal Investigation to help curb corruption among the city's elected public officials. . . . In an interview with Eugenics Magazine, Prof. Roland M. Harper of the University of Georgia says America's rising crime and divorce rates are directly attributable to coffee, tobacco, and automobiles. "Our present crime wave and high and rapidly increasing divorce rates are probably due in large measure to too much pleasure seeking," he says.		The Economist's monthly index of British wholesale prices is released. The average stands at 81.6, a decrease from 83.1 a month prior and 94 one year ago. It is the lowest figure of the year. . . . The American Economic Association authors a letter to U.S. President Herbert Hoover, urging him to veto the Smoot-Hawley Tariff Act, which would raise tariffs on over 20,000 dutiable items, if it is passed by Congress. They argue that increased tariffs would significantly raise the cost of living for "the majority of our citizens."	A ninth magnitude comet is discovered by Drs. Arnold Schwassman and Arno Arthur Wachmann at the Hamburg Observatory in Hamburg, Germany. Further computations are needed, the scientists say, to determine whether the comet will ever reach magnitude 1, the magnitude needed to observe the comet by naked eye.		May 5
The Association of National Advertisers, a group comprised of 300 men and women, meets in New York to conduct its semiannual meeting. Among the topics discussed: automobiles, drug products, and food products. . . . Secretary of State Henry L. Stimson addresses rumors of a possible New York gubernatorial run on the Republican ticket this year. While he is slightly interested, he says, Governor Franklin Roosevelt is too likely to be reelected.		Construction is completed on the Bank of Manhattan Building in New York City. Completed in just one year, it exceeds the world record for skyscraper construction by at least one year. At a height of 927 feet, it is also one of the world's tallest skyscrapers, second only to the city's newly constructed Chrysler Building. It will be rechristened in 1996 as the Trump Building, named after an American business executive who purchased the building.	Lt. Col. Roscoe Turner departs from New York en route to Los Angeles, saying before he takes off that he will either break Charles Lindbergh's record or his own neck in the attempt.		May 6
Representatives of the Checker Cab Sales Corporation appeal to New York City Mayor James J. Walker to establish the city's taxicab companies as public utilities.		The Bank of France lowers its discount rate from 3 percent to 2.5 percent.			May 7

F	G	H	I	J
Includes elections, federal-state relations, civil rights and liberties, crime, the judiciary, education, healthcare, poverty, urban affairs, and population.	Includes formation and debate of U.S. foreign and defense policies, veterans affairs, and defense spending. (Relations with specific foreign countries are usually found under the region concerned.)	Includes business, labor, agriculture, taxation, transportation, consumer affairs, monetary and fiscal policy, natural resources, pollution, and accidents.	Includes worldwide scientific, medical, and technological developments, natural phenomena, U.S. weather, and natural disasters.	Includes the arts, religion, scholarship, communications media, sports, entertainment, fashions, fads, and social life.

	World Affairs	Europe	Africa & The Middle East	The Americas	Asia & The Pacific
May 8		The German Reichstag Parliament debates a bill that would allow ambassadorship to the South American nations of Argentina, Brazil, and Chile. . . . The Soviet Commissariat for Home Affairs issues a decree prohibiting the sale of alcoholic beverages on workers' paydays and revolutionary holidays. . . . The Society of Indians in Central Europe holds a rally in Berlin, Germany, to protest the recent arrest in India of nonviolent revolutionary Mohandas Gandhi. . . . Unemployment in England reaches 1.7 million people, or 4.6 percent of the total population.		The death rate in Chile has dropped by 10 percent in the past 25 years, according to census reports.	
May 9	U.S. President Herbert Hoover signs a debt repayment agreement with Foreign Minister Prochnik of Austria. Under the agreement, Austria will pay to the United States a total of $24,614,885 over a period of 40 years.	Gen. Martinez Anido is detained by party officials in Spain for suspicion of leading a coup against the government. . . . Sir William Peel is appointed by British authorities to the post of Governor of Hong Kong, succeeding Sir Cecil Clementi, who resigned in March. Peel would serve for five years until May 1935.			Clashes between supporters of Mohandas Gandhi and the British Imperial Police result in the deaths of 25 people in the Indian city of Sholapur, population 120,000. It is the largest explosion of violence since Gandhi's civil disobedience campaign began. . . . Civil war erupts in China as 5,000 Nanking soldiers are wounded in the city of Suchow by soldiers of the Northern army. . . .15,000 Chinese rebel forces sack the city of Yungyang, slaughtering 4,000 people and kidnapping 500 wealthy residents for the purposes of ransom. It is the latest in a series of bandit raids that Chinese officials attribute to "cold, famine, and Communism."
May 10				The Argentine Finance Ministry releases its monthly report, showing a steep decline in the country's exports. $188,135,645 worth of goods was exported in the first quarter of this year, as compared with $280,382,919 in the first quarter of 1929, a decline of 32.9 percent.	
May 11	French Foreign Minister Aristide Briand submits a document outlining a proposal for a United States of Europe to 26 European governments. The proposal is expected to receive sharp criticism.			Costa Rican economic officials report that in 1929, banana exports for the country fell by nearly 50 percent.	Chinese warlord Sun Liang-chang, who up until recently was a supporter of the Nationalist government in Nanking, officially sides with the Northern rebel army, adding his squadron of 60,000 men to the front lines.
May 12		Gold deposits in the Bank of England for last week totaled £1.35 million, despite withdrawals of £4,302,633, most of which was for French economic relief. . . . Steel output in France rose at a rate of 6 percent over the past year, according to French industrialists. . . . The German budget for the year of 1930 is compiled by the Reichstag, showing a deficit of 1.65 billion marks, or $393,794,749. . . . Germany decides to abolish the 10 percent "capital yield tax," which is deducted from interest obtained from foreign loans.	French President Gaston Doumergue visits the North African colony of Algeria, where local winemakers decry the tariff imposed on them by their mother country, noting that all French imports enter Algeria duty free.		
May 13	Members of the Palestinian Arab delegation that had come to London to convince British authorities to grant greater political freedom to Arabs in Palestine leave dissatisfied. "The Arab case in Palestine will not be justly solved by the British Government, with whom the Zionists have great influence," a statement reads.			President Ortiz Rubio of Mexico declares a national day of mourning for aviators Pablo Sidar and Carlos Rivirosa, who disappeared while attempting to fly non-stop from Mexico to Buenos Aires, Argentina. As a consolation, the United States offers Mexico two reconnaissance planes to assist in finding the bodies.	Military officials of Japan announce they will send 25 educators to China to serve as military training instructors in the Nationalist capital of Nanking, where battles between Nationalist forces and Northern Communist rebel armies continue to rage on.
	A Includes developments that affect more than one world region, international organizations, and important meetings of world leaders.	**B** Includes all domestic and regional developments in Europe, including the Soviet Union.	**C** Includes all domestic and regional developments in Africa and the Middle East.	**D** Includes all domestic and regional developments in Latin America, the Caribbean, and Canada.	**E** Includes all domestic and regional developments in Asian and Pacific nations (and colonies).

U.S. Politics & Social Issues	U.S. Foreign Policy & Defense	Economics & Great Depression	Science, Technology & Nature	Culture, Leisure & Lifestyle	
Census officials in Los Angeles, Calif., conclude that Beverly Hills has experienced the greatest population growth of any U.S. city, with an increase of 2,485.6 percent in the past 10 years.	Congressmen approve the construction of a new $4.5 million "metal clad airship," with an estimated hauling capacity of 100 tons. The ship is expected to operate at 100 miles per hour, 25 miles faster than the *Graf Zeppelin*, the world's largest airship.	*The Iron Age* estimates in its new issue that the United States' iron production for April was the smallest of any April since 1922.	Forest fires erupt on the border between New York and Massachusetts, eradicating over 25,000 acres. Only heavy rain says Conservation Commissioner William Bazeley, can quell the fires.		May 8
Louis D. Brandeis, the first Jew to hold the office of Supreme Court Justice, donates $15,000 to Histadruth, the Jewish Labor Federation of Palestine. . . . *Reader's Digest* publishes a nationwide poll showing that over 40 percent of the U.S. population favors repeal of the Eighteenth Amendment.		*The Annalist's* weekly index of wholesale U.S. commodity prices is released. At 131.9, the figure is the lowest since World War I. Economic officials place the blame on sharp declines in metals and textiles.	Dr. Franz Alexander of the Psychoanalytic Institute of Berlin presents his development of the Freudian theory of dream interpretation to members of the American Psychoanalytic Association in Washington, D.C. According to Alexander, "bad dreams" are the result of a guilty conscience. . . . Earthquakes in Burma kill an estimated 3,000 people.	Billy Burke equals the record set at the Yale University golf course with a score of 68.	May 9
Estate Planning Commission president Clinton Davidson formally objects to a proposed bill greatly increasing taxation on imported goods. Davidson says the bill will adversely affect American corporations operating abroad. . . . The Travelers Insurance Company reports that the state of Idaho has experienced a 300 percent gain in deaths attributable to automobiles in the past year. . . . Sixteen residents of New York City are subpoenaed by a federal grand jury after refusing to answer questions posed by census workers.	House Naval Committee chairman Rep. Frederick Britten introduces a bill appropriating $936,995,000 for naval construction over the next 10 years. Fellow Naval Committee member Rep. French objects in response, noting that since World War I, the United States naval budget has not exceeded $50 million annually. Britten says the budget is necessary to achieve naval parity with Great Britain.	Check clearings in the United States aggregated $51,674,915,292 for the month of April, less than 1 percent of the previous month, according to published reports.			May 10
W.L. Powlison, head librarian at the National Automobile Chamber of Commerce, estimates that of all the patents applied for in the United States, over 25 percent pertain to the automotive industry. . . . Census officials report that cities with a population over 10,000 have seen an average growth of 21.3 percent over the past 10 years.		U.S. economic officials report that chain store sales have increased by 3.9 percent in the past year. . . . Prominent bankers in the Untied States say the record low commodity prices are due to "overproduction." The only solution, they say, is forcibly lowering prices, which would hurt the producers of the commodities.	Chrysler Motors announces the introduction of a new line of Plymouth cars, the average price of which is $600.	*Assorted Articles,* the first posthumous work of late English author D.H. Lawrence, who died early last month, is published. . . . With its local theater industry plummeting, Austria places a ban on all American-made "talkies." In a statement, local theater owners claim, "The cinema public has been misled by mighty propaganda conducted by the American electrical industry."	May 11
People's Lobby president John Dewey calls on President Herbert Hoover to appropriate $250 million for a federal unemployment insurance program to aid the country's estimated 3–5 million unemployed persons, approximately 4 percent of the population.		U.S. Commerce Department officials estimate that the new tariffs in Canada will result in a $225 million decrease in annual trade between the United States and Canada. Canada is already the United States' biggest export market, with $800 million bought annually.			May 12
At a meeting of the Dental Society of New York State, more than 3,000 dentists conclude that over 80 percent of the U.S. population suffers from poor dental hygiene.		The British Board of Trade reports that British exports for the month of April fell below the total of April 1929 by £13,384,405, or 13.75 percent.	Norwegian explorer Fridtjof Nanse, who was awarded the Nobel Peace Prize in 1922 for his work as High Commissioner of the League of Nations, dies from heart paralysis at the age of 68 at a hospital in the Norwegian capital of Oslo.	Alabama University is crowned the Southern Conference baseball champion, finishing the season with an .833 winning percentage.	May 13

F	G	H	I	J
Includes elections, federal-state relations, civil rights and liberties, crime, the judiciary, education, healthcare, poverty, urban affairs, and population.	*Includes formation and debate of U.S. foreign and defense policies, veterans affairs, and defense spending. (Relations with specific foreign countries are usually found under the region concerned.)*	*Includes business, labor, agriculture, taxation, transportation, consumer affairs, monetary and fiscal policy, natural resources, pollution, and accidents.*	*Includes worldwide scientific, medical, and technological developments, natural phenomena, U.S. weather, and natural disasters.*	*Includes the arts, religion, scholarship, communications media, sports, entertainment, fashions, fads, and social life.*

	World Affairs	Europe	Africa & The Middle East	The Americas	Asia & The Pacific
May 14			Egypt announces it is lifting the ban on excavations headed by German scientists, following the return of an ancient Egyptian sculpture from the Berlin Museum to Egypt. A dispute over the rightful owner of the sculpture had been the source of the ban.	Citizens of Brazil celebrate the country's anniversary of the emancipation of slaves. It was 42 years ago in 1888 that Princess Isabel issued a proclamation freeing the slaves. . . . Following an outbreak of psittacosis, or "parrot disease," in British Columbia, the Canadian Department of Agriculture bans the importation into Canada of "parrots, parakeets, cockatoos, macaws," and other small birds.	
May 15	During the world conference of the Methodist Episcopal Bishops, Bishop Frederick B. Fisher of Calcutta urges Great Britain to grant Dominion status to India.			Prominent banker Louis Eugene Roy is selected by American High Commissioner to Haiti John H. Russell to succeed Louis Borno, who resigned earlier this month, as president of Haiti.	
May 16		The Soviet publication *Izvestia* releases figures indicating 110 million acres of land have been sown with grain this spring, with over half sown by "collective," or socialist, farms.	The Egyptian Finance Ministry announces it is hiring an American tobacco-growing expert to assist in improving Egypt's near non existent tobacco industry. Approximately $60,000 will be appropriated for this use.		
May 17	Dwight W. Morrow, U.S. Ambassador to Mexico and father-in-law of famed aviator Charles Lindbergh, urges greater understanding between the United States and Mexico in a speech to the New Jersey Bankers' Association in Atlantic City, N.J.	French Prime Minister Andre Tardieu announces he is withdrawing the remaining French troops from the Rhineland, the area in Germany that is officially demilitarized as stipulated by the Treaty of Versailles, reached in 1919 after World War I.	Two Arabs charged with murdering 24 Jews in a Palestinian synagogue last August are sentenced to death by a court in Jerusalem, Israel.		
May 18	British diplomats reject French Foreign Minister Aristide Briand's proposal of a United States of Europe, saying that Great Britain's commitment to its Atlantic partner, the United States, is too great to allow its inclusion.	Romania decrees an order prohibiting the Soviet Union from sending its warships into the Black Sea, which Romania borders. The decree follows an incident last winter in which three Russian cruisers were sent to the Black Sea for experimental purposes.			
May 19		Newspapers in Berlin, Germany, react to French Foreign Minister Aristide Briand's United Europe proposal. Most agree the proposal grants too much privilege to France or, as one leading newspaper puts it, "Too much France."		President Hernando Siles Reyes of Bolivia officially appoints a new Cabinet to succeed the short-lived Cabinet that resigned on May 16.	
May 20	U.S. missionaries in the Chinese city of Chiaying, where hostilities between Northern and Southern armies are escalating, are instructed by the U.S. State Department to go immediately to the city of Swatow, where violence is less destabilizing. . . . U.S. Secretary of State Henry L. Stimson says French Foreign Minister Aristide Briand has assured him his proposal of a United States of Europe will not adversely affect the United States of America.				After refusing to vacate the premises of the Wadala salt depot, 72 Gandhi supporters are arrested by Bombay police. Now 500 prisoners, mostly Gandhi followers, are encamped behind barbed wire at the Worli detention center.

A	B	C	D	E
Includes developments that affect more than one world region, international organizations, and important meetings of world leaders.	Includes all domestic and regional developments in Europe, including the Soviet Union.	Includes all domestic and regional developments in Africa and the Middle East.	Includes all domestic and regional developments in Latin America, the Caribbean, and Canada.	Includes all domestic and regional developments in Asian and Pacific nations (and colonies).

U.S. Politics & Social Issues	U.S. Foreign Policy & Defense	Economics & Great Depression	Science, Technology & Nature	Culture, Leisure & Lifestyle	
Organized crime boss Al Capone, who was released from prison two months prior after a 10-month incarceration for gun possession, is arrested again in Miami by Police Chief Guy C. Reeve on a charge of "investigation." He is released the next day due to lack of evidence.		The 6,000 members of the Chicago Typographical Union vote to institute a five-hour workday as a means of reducing unemployment. Presently, members of Chicago Typographical Union work five and one-half days per week, the remaining one-half day reserved for unemployed workers.	Dr. E.S. Sundstroem of the University of California announces he has discovered a method to cure cancer in rats. By subjecting them to a low oxygen environment, nearly 83 percent of the rats were cured. Sundstroem admits he doubts the method will work on humans, however.	Attorney Charles E. Murphy is elected president of the New York Advertising Club, succeeding James Wright Brown, whose term expired.	**May 14**
The Senate approves a bill transferring Prohibition enforcement authority from the Treasury Department to the Justice Department.	Argentina buys 18 two-passenger training planes from the U.S. government. It is by far the largest order for U.S. planes by Argentina.	The government of Australia announces it is lifting the ban on imported ale, spirits, tobacco, and matches, but that the items will still be subject to extraordinarily high tariffs.	Admiral Richard Byrd, who began his journey home two months prior after his Antarctic expedition, arrives in the Panama Canal to throngs of cheers from U.S. Navy men and canal workers.		**May 15**
Census officials report that California has experienced a 57 percent population increase in the past 10 years. . . . Insurance executives of New York City conclude that taxi drivers who own their own cab are four times less likely to cause accidents than those who work on a commission basis. . . . An income statement released by the American Anti-Saloon League illustrates the population's waning support for Prohibition. When the Eighteenth Amendment was first being implemented in 1919, the Anti-Saloon League received donations of $919,984.65. By 1929, however, donations totaled $265,237.93, a decrease of 70 percent.	American Federation of Labor secretary Frank Morrison calls on U.S. President Herbert Hoover to curb unemployment in the country's naval yards by beginning modernization of naval vessels.	In its new issue, *The Annalist* reports that zinc production in the United States has fallen to its lowest level since June 1922. . . . Chinese economic officials report that the country's silver currency exchange rate has fallen to its lowest point in recent years. . . . A report of Germany's foreign trade indicates 1930 has seen a trade surplus for the first time in four years. So far, 976,653 marks worth of goods have been exported, with 888,178 marks worth of goods imported. Previous years have seen a trade imbalance of 150,000 marks.			**May 16**
Census officials say California's population increase of 2 million people since the last census was taken in 1920 is a record for population growth in the United States, exceeded only by New York's increase of 1,845,000 people in the period between 1900 and 1910.	Admiral Mark L. Bristol, chairman of the Navy General Board testifying before the Senate Foreign Relations Committee, objects to the London Naval Treaty, saying Japan is ahead of the United States in several naval categories including submarines and destroyers.	The American Bureau of Metal Statistics releases its figures detailing the world's copper production in April. A decrease of 3 percent is noted, with 143,798 short tons produced as compared to 148,005 in March. . . . U.S. bank clearings for this week totaled $10.1 billion, a decrease of 17 percent from the comparable period a year ago, according to reports. . . . The U.S. Department of Commerce reports check payments for the week ended May 10 were 13 percent higher than the week ended May 3, and 1 percent higher than the comparable period a year ago.		The United States wins the biennial Walker Cup international golf tournament, winning 10 of the tournament's 12 matches in Sandwich, England. Great Britain has never won the tournament.	**May 17**
New York City Police Commissioner Grover Whalen releases a set of figures detailing the city's traffic problems. Over 1 million motor vehicles travel through the city's 5,043 miles of road each day. The city has the country's greatest traffic enforcement force, with approximately 4,500 more traffic enforcement officers than the second city, Chicago.		The U.S. Federal Reserve Board reports that debits to individual accounts for the week ended May 14 aggregated $14.6 billion, 20 percent below the week ending May 7 and 22 percent below the corresponding period last year.		English author Aldous Huxley publishes his third compilation of short stories, entitled *Brief Candles*. It is his last work before writing *A Brave New World*, considered his masterpiece. . . . Frank Crowley sets the record for the national interscholastic one-mile run, with a time of 4 minutes, 21.25 seconds.	**May 18**
Calling Prohibition "a hypocritical farce," pastor Charles J. Finnegan calls for a repeal of the Eighteenth Amendment, noting that Christ Himself partook in libations. "Those hypocrites who shout against Prohibition are like those who scoffed at Christ when He took compassion on Mary Magdalene," he says. . . . Democratic Senator Kenneth Douglas McKellar of Tennessee assails the proposed Hawley-Smoot tariff bill, which would dramatically increase tariffs on over 20,000 dutiable items. Calling it a "monstrosity," he predicts further economic stagnation if the bill is passed.		The U.S. Federal Reserve Board reports that banks' loans to stock brokers totaled $2.9 billion for the month of April, nearing the national record. . . . Unemployment in Great Britain has reached 1,720,000 people, an increase of 13,614 from the previous week and 579,295 from a year ago, according to British economic officials. The figure is the largest since Great Britain's trade depression of 1921, when 2.5 million people were out of work.		At the Churchill Downs in Louisville, Ky., 60,000 people witness the 3-year-old horse Gallant Fox win the Kentucky Derby by a sizable margin. Gallant Fox's owner, William Woodward, receives $60,725 in prize money, to be split between the horse's jockey and trainer. $582,384 was placed in bets, of which $207,706 was placed on Gallant Fox.	**May 19**
The Senate passes a bill authorizing the presentation of medals to Admiral Richard E. Byrd and other members of his ship *City of New York*, which just returned to New York Harbor following a two-year Antarctic expedition.	Sixty-five naval vessels, headed by the flagship *Texas*, embark off New York Harbor, traveling to the Virginia Capes for inspection by President Herbert Hoover. The New York Bible Society contributed 28,606 Bibles to be put on board the vessels.	The U.S. Federal Reserve Board reports that borrowings from the Federal Reserve Bank have declined by $29 million as compared to last week.		American golfer Bobby Jones wins the *Golf Illustrated* gold vase tournament in Sunningdale, England, with rounds of 75 and 68 respectively. His 68 is also a round record for the Sunningdale golf course. Jones would go on later this year to consecutively win all four major golf championships, a feat unparalleled until Tiger Woods accomplished it in 2001.	**May 20**
F *Includes elections, federal-state relations, civil rights and liberties, crime, the judiciary, education, healthcare, poverty, urban affairs, and population.*	**G** *Includes formation and debate of U.S. foreign and defense policies, veterans affairs, and defense spending. (Relations with specific foreign countries are usually found under the region concerned.)*	**H** *Includes business, labor, agriculture, taxation, transportation, consumer affairs, monetary and fiscal policy, natural resources, pollution, and accidents.*	**I** *Includes worldwide scientific, medical, and technological developments, natural phenomena, U.S. weather, and natural disasters.*	**J** *Includes the arts, religion, scholarship, communications media, sports, entertainment, fashions, fads, and social life.*	

	World Affairs	Europe	Africa & The Middle East	The Americas	Asia & The Pacific
May 21				Air show demonstrations by both the Cuban and U.S. air forces occur as Cuba celebrates its 28th anniversary of independence from U.S. colonial rule and the founding of its republic.	
May 22	U.S. Consul General to Berlin G.B.B. Ravndal announces his retirement after 32 years in the U.S. Foreign Service.	Anti-Semitic riots occur in the Romanian capital of Bucharest following the appointment of an anti-Semitic leader, Prof. Alexander Cuza, to the country's Parliament. Most of the riots have been led by the newly formed civilian "Iron Guard." . . . First Lord of the British Admiralty Albert V. Alexander announces the construction of six new naval vessels, including one six-inch cruiser, two destroyers, one 1,800-ton submarine, and two 650-ton submarines.			
May 23	Paul Claudel, chosen as French envoy to Washington, D.C., in 1927, makes his first visit to the United States' capital to speak at a dinner held in his honor by the American Club.	The Banco di Napoli Trust Company of New York obtains exclusive privilege from Italian authorities to be the sole bank responsible for foreign Italian money orders.	After the vessel catches fire in the port of Sudan in northern Africa, 100 immigrants aboard the French steamer *Asia* are killed.		
May 24		The 26-year-old British aviator, Amy Johnson, lands in Darwin, Australia, becoming the first woman pilot to fly from England to Australia. The 11,000-mile trip took her 19.5 days to complete. Popular newspapers give her $50,000 as a token of appreciation. British authorities consider bestowing on Johnson the title Dame of the British Empire, or, because of her young age, Lady of the British Empire.	The newly elected King of Afghanistan, Nadir Shah, warns his tribal warriors not to interfere with the increasingly debilitating political situation in India, fearing that conflicts with British soldiers in India could lead to a war with Great Britain.	Members of the Argentinean Confederation of Commerce, Industry, and Production send a cablegram to U.S. President Herbert Hoover protesting the proposed Smoot-Hawley Tariff Act.	
May 25		In a speech before the Hungarian Parliament, Count Albert Apponyi, Hungary's League of Nations representative, requests that his country implement a secret ballot box for upcoming elections, as opposed to the current open ballot elections. Hungary is the only European nation besides Russia to not have secret ballots. . . . Poland reacts to French Foreign Minister Aristide Briand's United Europe proposal, saying that although the idea is appealing, only an extension of peace treaties and security guarantees could make a United States of Europe a reality.			Chinese citizens in the towns of Hankow, Wuchang, and Hanyang fear invasion as Communist bandits swarm the adjacent Yangtse River.
May 26					Former Japanese envoy to Washington, D.C., Hanihara meets with U.S. Ambassador to Japan William Castle to discuss updating the U.S. Immigration Act of 1924, which severely limited the number of Japanese immigrants permitted to enter the country annually. In response, House Immigration Committee Chairman Johnson introduces a bill allowing 200 Japanese immigrants per year.
May 27		Prince Mircea Cantacuzene of Hungary dies from injuries sustained while distributing nationalist leaflets aboard a doomed airplane. . . . Former Archduke of Austria Karl Rainer dies from automobile accident injuries in a hospital in Vienna, Austria. He was 35.	The Egyptian Chamber and Senate unanimously pass a resolution granting "most favored nation" status to the United States.	The Aeronautics Trade Division of the U.S. Commerce Department releases a survey showing that Latin America's airways total 44,000 miles, a threefold increase since December 1928.	Clashes between Hindus and Muslims in the Indian city of Dacca result in the deaths of six people and scores of injuries and arrests.

A	B	C	D	E
Includes developments that affect more than one world region, international organizations, and important meetings of world leaders.	*Includes all domestic and regional developments in Europe, including the Soviet Union.*	*Includes all domestic and regional developments in Africa and the Middle East.*	*Includes all domestic and regional developments in Latin America, the Caribbean, and Canada.*	*Includes all domestic and regional developments in Asian and Pacific nations (and colonies).*

U.S. Politics & Social Issues	U.S. Foreign Policy & Defense	Economics & Great Depression	Science, Technology & Nature	Culture, Leisure & Lifestyle	
		Speakers at the annual meeting of the American Advertising Federation strike a cheery chord into the hearts of U.S. citizens when they say the Depression is "all but over." . . . U.S. President Herbert Hoover signs a bill appropriating $155,397,770 for agricultural subsidies.		Walter Emery of New York receives a fine of $10 for disorderly conduct after he parks his car on train tracks and then boards when the train makes an unscheduled emergency stop to avoid hitting the parked car.	May 21
		The U.S. Commerce Department reports automobile production for April totaled 442,630 motor cars, the highest total for any April in history except for last year, when auto production reached 621,910 cars. . . . The American Bankers Association releases a report blaming the lack of economic prosperity on "over issuance of securities, overproduction and uncertainty caused by prolonged delay in tariff legislation."		The American Bible Association releases its annual report detailing Bible distribution in the United States. Over 11,102,664 Bibles in 179 different languages and dialects were produced in 1929, the highest of any year in the organization's 114-year history. Since 1816, the year of the organization's founding, 216,198,915 total Bibles have been produced, more than double the population of the United States.	May 22
John D. Rockefeller, Jr., the only son of the founder of Standard Oil who carries the same name, is awarded honorary membership of the American Institute of Architects at their annual convention in Washington, D.C. . . . The New York City Board of Education requests an appropriation of $14,832,770 for new school construction. Education officials say the new schools will help improve the United States' 4.3 percent illiteracy rate.		*The Annalist* publishes its weekly index of commodity prices, which stands at 132.1, a decline of 8 percent from the corresponding date last year, but still ahead of the post-World War I low point of 131.9 set earlier this month.		The International Boxing Union in Berlin, Germany, announces its list of world champions by weight class, all of whom are American. The winners include Frankie Genaro, flyweight; Battling Battalino, featherweight; Sammy Mendell, lightweight; and Jack Thompson, welterweight. The titles of bantam, middle, light heavy and heavyweight were declared vacant. . . . Seeking to increase the United States' 96 percent literacy rate, publishing houses across the country announce a 50 percent price reduction rate on most, if not all, books.	May 23
	Army officials in West Point, N.Y., commission a group of major league baseball players to conduct an experiment to ascertain the speed at which balls are thrown. After several demonstrations, Philadelphia Athletics pitcher Robert Moses Grove is declared the fastest pitcher in baseball, with the ability to throw a ball 175 feet per second, or 121 miles per hour. . . . The destroyer ship USS *William Jones* is decommissioned by the U.S. Navy.		An avalanche engulfs the expedition party attempting to climb the unconquered Kanchenjunga Mountain in Nepal. One porter is killed and two others are injured.	Robert D. Kohn, president of the New York Building Congress and the Society for Ethical Culture, is elected president of the American Architectural Institute, succeeding C. Herrick Hammond of Chicago.	May 24
The National Conference on Street and Highway Safety reports that fatalities attributable to automobile accidents totaled 33,060 for 1929, or one fatality every 16 minutes. Fatalities increased by 8.2 percent over 1928. Economic damage resulting from the fatalities was estimated to be at $850 million.		Economic officials in Canada report that April's steel production of 102,681 tons was the lowest of any month so far in 1930.	Herbert Owbridge of Oakland, Calif., age 18, claims the world record for most flight time sustained by a model airplane with a time of 8 minutes, 49 seconds, eclipsing the previous record by 16 seconds.	J. Griffith Boardman is crowned the Atlantic Coast golf champion after defeating J. Winston Kindt by one point in match play.	May 25
The National Conference on Street and Highway Safety reports over 15 percent of all auto fatalities in the United States occur as a result of "defects" in automobiles. The conference recommends legislation requiring periodic inspection of auto manufacturing plants.					May 26
		German economic officials estimate the number of unemployed Germans to be approximately 2.5 million. . . . British economic officials predict that come winter, unemployment in the country will have risen from approximately 1.5 million persons to 2 million, an increase of 25 percent.		Sales of the German language edition of Erich Remarque's World War I novel *All Quiet on the Western Front* reach 1 million copies, establishing a new record. Despite being published only 15 months ago, 2 million copies of foreign language editions have also been sold.	May 27

F	G	H	I	J
Includes elections, federal-state relations, civil rights and liberties, crime, the judiciary, education, healthcare, poverty, urban affairs, and population.	Includes formation and debate of U.S. foreign and defense policies, veterans affairs, and defense spending. (Relations with specific foreign countries are usually found under the region concerned.)	Includes business, labor, agriculture, taxation, transportation, consumer affairs, monetary and fiscal policy, natural resources, pollution, and accidents.	Includes worldwide scientific, medical, and technological developments, natural phenomena, U.S. weather, and natural disasters.	Includes the arts, religion, scholarship, communications media, sports, entertainment, fashions, fads, and social life.

	World Affairs	Europe	Africa & The Middle East	The Americas	Asia & The Pacific
May 28	By a vote of 20–19, the German Olympic Committee in Berlin adopts a resolution tightening eligibility requirements for the upcoming 1936 Summer Olympic Games. Among the changes, no athlete will be allowed to compete in a sport "for which he is a professional."	George William Forbes is chosen to succeed 74-year-old Joseph Ward, who suffers from severe heart conditions, as president of New Zealand. Ward would eventually succumb to his illness on July 8, while Forbes would serve as president until the national elections of 1935.			
May 29		Winston Churchill publicly questions the motives of the MacDonald government during a session of the British House of Commons, objecting to a recent export of British tanks to the Soviet Union. "[They are] definitely adopting a position of making profits by the sale of armaments to countries that may be involved in war with its neighbors."		President Fernando Siles of Bolivia formally resigns, ceding power to his newly appointed Cabinet. The reason for his resignation, according to the Cabinet, was "grave reasons of State."	
May 30		Seeking to compete with the dominant U.S. automobile manufacturing industry, a group of British automobile manufacturers announce they will be moving their operations to Canada, where it will be easier to export to the United States.		Bolivia and Spain sign a military pact allowing nationals of both countries to serve in each other's armies.	
May 31		Belgian Ambassador to the United States Prince Albert de Ligne arrives in Washington, D.C., for an official state visit.		Canada bans the exportation of rum following complaints from the U.S. border patrol.	
June 1		Great Britain officially opens its first publicly owned airport in the city of Bristol. Along with national service, the airport allows access to and from France, Germany, Holland, Belgium, and Italy.	Twenty-two Arab men who were sentenced to death for instigating anti-Jewish riots in Palestine last year have their sentences commuted to life in prison by High Commissioner John Chancellor.	Canada's liquor export ban comes into effect with the closing of 10 export docks. . . . Canadian officials estimate nearly 5,000 cases of Canadian liquor were smuggled over the U.S. border the previous week in anticipation of the newly imposed liquor export ban.	
June 2		A bill is debated in the English Parliament that would replace 500,000 low-income homes with better dwellings, causing the relocation of approximately 2.5 million people. . . . The British newspapers *Daily Chronicle* and *Daily News* merge to become the *Daily News Chronicle*. Circulation is expected to reach 1.6 million people, or approximately 3 percent of the British population. The merger results in the dismissal of 1,800 workers.	Turkey bans the use of the Arabic language in all official government institutions. Failure to comply will result in a charge of misdemeanor, say Turkish officials.	The Buenos Aires City Council of Argentina considers a bill that would increase taxes by 200 percent on theaters exclusively showing foreign films, effectively banning them.	China and Japan mobilize troops to quell Korean Communist uprisings.
June 3		Yugoslavian Minister of War General Hadzic is named the new Ambassador to Hungary. . . . Austria holds its first state funeral in 12 years with the burial of Archduke Karl Rainer.		Georges Parent is appointed by Canadian Prime Minister William Lyon Mackenzie King to succeed Louis Lavergne as representative of Quebec in the Canadian Senate. Parent would occupy the post until his death on December 14, 1942.	Returning from India aboard the French liner *Rochambeau*, noted writer Gopal Mukerji, author of *Caste and Outcaste*, says Indian civil war is inevitable. "No statesmanship," he says, "[is] great enough to prevent it." . . . In defiance of an ordinance that had banned picketing, 5,000 women picket various clothing shops in the Indian city of Bombay.
June 4		Carl Gustaf Elkman, a liberal, is chosen as the new Swedish prime minister by King Gustav, following the resignation of Arvid Lindman, a conservative. Elkman had previously served as prime minister from 1926–28.			Bombay Bishop Brenton Badley, in a statement released to the U.S. media, denies that there is a "general uprising" taking place in India, and that widespread "misinformation" has caused Americans to believe so. . . . Great Britain amasses 42 bombardment planes to attack rebel forces in the Indian city of Shabkadar.

A	B	C	D	E
Includes developments that affect more than one world region, international organizations, and important meetings of world leaders.	Includes all domestic and regional developments in Europe, including the Soviet Union.	Includes all domestic and regional developments in Africa and the Middle East.	Includes all domestic and regional developments in Latin America, the Caribbean, and Canada.	Includes all domestic and regional developments in Asian and Pacific nations (and colonies).

U.S. Politics & Social Issues	U.S. Foreign Policy & Defense	Economics & Great Depression	Science, Technology & Nature	Culture, Leisure & Lifestyle	
Rep. Emanuel Celler of New York introduces a bill to the House of Representatives that would raise the salary of federal judges by an average of $5,000. . . . The Chrysler Building, New York City's tallest structure, officially opens.		The U.S. Commerce Department reports wheat production for April totaled 3,050,000 bushels, a decrease of 25 percent from production in April 1929. . . . The American Petroleum Institute reports that daily average crude oil production for the week ended May 24 was 2,579,000 barrels, as compared to 2,607,900 barrels the previous week, a decrease of 28,400 barrels.			May 28
Former House Banking Committee head Henry M. Dawes warns that the growing bank mergers in the United States will result in a monopoly if action is not taken. . . . The newly elected Archbishop of Dubuque, Iowa, Francis Bechman, takes a unique approach to objecting to Prohibition in a sermon to his townspeople, saying, "Prohibition has killed sociability and has made real conversation a lost art."		Argentina's Minister of Finance releases a report showing Argentine exports for the first four months of 1930 were $120,882,102, less than the first four months of 1929 at a decrease of 37 percent.		Legendary Russian filmmaker Sergei Eisenstein arrives in Hollywood, Calif., to begin work with Paramount Pictures.	May 29
Ten prominent Chicago politicians are indicted on charges of conspiring to defraud the Chicago Sanitary District of $5 million.		General Motors President Alfred P. Sloan releases a statement objecting to the proposed Smoot-Hawley tariff act, saying it will certainly increase the U.S. unemployment rate.		Japan wins the Far Eastern Olympic baseball championship, defeating China by a score of 17–10.	May 30
Herbert Hosking of New Jersey, who killed the father of New Jersey Police Superintendent Norman Schwarzkopf in an automobile accident, is arraigned on charges of manslaughter.		New bond offerings on the New York Stock Exchange for the week ending on May 30 aggregated $49,428,000, the lowest total of any week this year except for January 10.	The Burma Ruby Mines Company announces the discovery of a sapphire gem weighing 30 pounds, believed to be the heaviest on record, exceeding those in the New York Natural History Museum.		May 31
	Following two years of modernization, the battleship USS Oklahoma is sent to the West Coast for fleet operations.		The New York City Weather Bureau announces that yesterday was the coldest May 31 on record, with temperatures dropping below the previous record of 46°F set in 1884. Tourism was severely affected, with a 50 percent decrease in daily Holland Tunnel traffic.	The American Orchestral Society officially disbands following an announcement the previous week of the resignations of its conductor, Chalmers Clifton, and founder, E.H. Harriman. . . . The Northern Baptist Convention calls on government officials to place the motion picture industry under "government control," noting that 90 percent of weekend film audiences are children. . . . American golfer Bobby Jones wins the British Open at St. Andrews golf course in Scotland, defeating Roger Wethered by seven shots. It is the first of his record four major championships won in a single year.	June 1
Owen Josephus Roberts is chosen to replace Edward Terry Stanford, who died on March 8, as Associate Justice of the Supreme Court.	The U.S. Navy decommissions the destroyer ship USS Sloat. . . . The U.S. Navy recalls the destroyer ship USS Trever to active duty, following seven years of being decommissioned.	Gold withdrawals at the Bank of England for this week totaled £653,362, against £11,360 deposited, netting a deficit of £642,002.	Roosevelt Memorial Association president James Garfield announces the annual Roosevelt medal will be given to Antarctic explorer Richard Byrd, American Federation of Labor president William Green, and penologist Hastings Hart. . . . Automotive pioneer Andrew Lawrence Riker, whose 1899 speed record for electric cars lasted 10 years, dies at the age of 62 at his home in Fairfield, Conn.	Carl Thompson wins the Metropolitan Archery Association's annual tournament for the second consecutive year.	June 2
The House and Senate overturn President Herbert Hoover's veto of a bill increasing pensions for veterans of the Spanish-American War. Only 32 of the 391 votes cast agreed with the veto. It is only the 50th time in U.S. history that a presidential veto has been overturned.		A record $84 million in taxes was collected by New York City on May 31, according to Controller Berry.	The American Academy of Pediatrics is founded.	The International Amateur Swimming Federation officially recognizes the 800-meter swim as an event for which world records are accepted.	June 3
The New York City Board of Education estimates there are 3,446 unemployed elementary school teachers in the city. . . . Census taking in New York City is completed. The city has a population of 6,395,063, an increase of 775,015 over the last 10 years. . . . New York City Health Commissioner Dr. Shirley Wynne reports that last week's death total of 1,416 is a record low for the year.		Representatives of the B&O Railroad announce the company is reducing its standard workweek from 44 hours to 40 hours, affecting some 7,000 workers. Budget restraints prompted the decision, according to the representatives.	Lt. Apollo Soucek sets a new world record for altitude in a seaplane, flying at a height of 43,166 feet.		June 4

F	G	H	I	J
Includes elections, federal-state relations, civil rights and liberties, crime, the judiciary, education, healthcare, poverty, urban affairs, and population.	Includes formation and debate of U.S. foreign and defense policies, veterans affairs, and defense spending. (Relations with specific foreign countries are usually found under the region concerned.)	Includes business, labor, agriculture, taxation, transportation, consumer affairs, monetary and fiscal policy, natural resources, pollution, and accidents.	Includes worldwide scientific, medical, and technological developments, natural phenomena, U.S. weather, and natural disasters.	Includes the arts, religion, scholarship, communications media, sports, entertainment, fashions, fads, and social life.

	World Affairs	Europe	Africa & The Middle East	The Americas	Asia & The Pacific
June 5		Pope Pius, head of the Catholic Church, announces that new Cardinals will be chosen on July 3.			Although the purpose of the march is unknown, 1,200 Afghan tribesmen march on Fort Bara near the city of Peshawar.
June 6		In the Hungarian capital of Budapest, 100 suspected Communist agitators, operating out of ostensible grocery stores, are arrested.		The Canadian Department of Finance reports savings deposits in the country have decreased by $14,169,871 in the past month. . . . Seeking to alleviate his nation's budget crisis, President Gerardo Machado of Cuba voluntarily reduces his salary by 50 percent, from $25,000 per year to $12,000, saving the country $13,000 annually.	Dissidents in India celebrate "Gandhi Day," marking the first month of the civil disobedience leader's prison term. . . . Court proceedings end for 140 Indian salt marchers, 115 of whom received three months of imprisonment. The remaining 25, who are minors, received one-day sentences. . . . Chinese military officials report that Tsinan, the capital of the Shandong province, is close to being captured by Northern rebel troops.
June 7		Carol, son of former Romanian King Ferdinand I, arrives in Romania following a brief period of exile. Proclaiming himself King, his reign would last until September 6, 1942, when he would be forced to resign under pressure from foreign influence.		John Ewen Sinclair is chosen by Canadian Prime Minister William Lyon Mackenize King to represent Prince Edward Island in the Canadian Senate. Sinclair would occupy the post until his death on December 23, 1949.	In the war-torn Chinese city of Tsinan, 110 Americans are urged to evacuate by U.S. Consul Edwin F. Stanton.
June 8		National Peasants' Party head Gheorghe Mironescu is named as the new Romanian prime minister following the resignation of Iuliu Maniu.		Published statistics show that the Argentine city of Buenos Aires is growing at a rate of 4,500 people per month.	Chinese bandits demand a ransom of arms and ammunition for the release of Rev. Clifford King, who was kidnapped in a Catholic missionary in the city of Sinyangchow a week ago.
June 9		*The Economist* releases its weekly index of wholesale British commodity prices. At 80.6, the figure is 12 percent less than at the corresponding period a year ago. . . . German industrialists report the monthly average of machinery exports for 1930 is 63,500 tons, compared with an average of 32,700 tons five years ago.			Indian medical professionals unanimously approve a resolution at their semiannual meeting banning the sale of all British-made medicine. . . . Feng Yu-hsiang, leader of the Northern Chinese rebel forces, telegraphs a message to Chinese President Chiang Kai-shek, saying he will stop his invasion if Chiang resigns.
June 10	League of Nations economic intelligence chief A. Loveday blames economic instability on increased workers' pay, saying wealth decreases the need for essential manufactured products.	The Indian Statutory Commission, undergoing a two-year study of the feasibility of granting India independence from British rule, releases its report. Members of the Commission unanimously agree that granting India independence must be a slow process.			In China, 15,000 Cantonese rebels occupy the city of Chenchow. . . . The Australian Commonwealth Loan Council announces it will be seeking a $50 million loan from Australian citizens, redeemable in eight years at an interest rate of 6 percent.
June 11	The U.S. government rebukes a proposed League of Nations treaty that would codify international smuggling.				Admiral Kanji Kato, head of the Japanese Navy General Staff, resigns amidst internal clashes over proposed disarmament provisions of the London Naval Treaty.

A	B	C	D	E
Includes developments that affect more than one world region, international organizations, and important meetings of world leaders.	*Includes all domestic and regional developments in Europe, including the Soviet Union.*	*Includes all domestic and regional developments in Africa and the Middle East.*	*Includes all domestic and regional developments in Latin America, the Caribbean, and Canada.*	*Includes all domestic and regional developments in Asian and Pacific nations (and colonies).*

U.S. Politics & Social Issues	U.S. Foreign Policy & Defense	Economics & Great Depression	Science, Technology & Nature	Culture, Leisure & Lifestyle	
Indian National Congress of America president Sailendra Nath Ghose attacks British Prime Minister Ramsay MacDonald's Indian policy at a protest rally in New York City. . . . Queens is named by census officials as New York City's fastest growing borough, with an estimated growth of 130 percent in the past 10 years.	The Shipping Board sells 15 obsolete naval vessels to the Union Shipbuilding Company of Baltimore for a sum of $237,950. The vessels weigh a total of 133,683 tons.		In a speech before the annual convention of the Radio Manufacturers' Association of America, Federal Radio Commission president Maj. Gen. Charles Saltzman suggests the appointment of a federal "director of broadcasting" to oversee broadcast applications.	The horse Bienheim, an 18 to 1 underdog, wins the English Derby, completing the 1.5-mile course in 2 minutes, 38 and one-fifth seconds. Approximately 500,000 people attended the Derby.	June 5
Electric power production in the United States has fallen by approximately 8 percent in the past year, according to published reports.		*The Annalist* releases its weekly index of U.S. wholesale commodity prices. At 135.2, it is an increase of 0.3 points from the previous week, and a decline of 10.4 points from the corresponding date last year. . . . The Federal Reserve Bank of New York cuts its bank rate to the lowest in six years.			June 6
Prohibition officials discover that a six-story warehouse that burned to the ground was actually an illegal distillery. Agent H.J. Simmons describes it as one of the largest distilleries ever discovered in the East. . . . Census officials report Boston has fallen from seventh to ninth place in the ranking of largest U.S. cities in terms of population.	Naval Secretary Charles Francis Adams officially assigns names to four new light cruisers, all of which are named after U.S. cities, including New Orleans, Astoria, Minneapolis, and Portland.	The National Automobile Chamber of Commerce reports automobile production in the first five months of 1930 was 31 percent lower than the first five months of 1929. . . . U.S. economic officials report bank clearings for the country are down 13 percent from the corresponding period a year ago. . . . The Federal Reserve Board of Ohio announces it is lowering the bank rate from 4 to 3.5 percent.		With a 72-hole score of 289, golfer Charles Whitcombe wins the Irish Open golf championship.	June 7
Harvey Raab, assistant chief of the fire department in Allenhurst, N.J., is arrested on charges of arson after he admitted to setting afire a lumberyard shed. . . . Census statistics of Chicago are published, showing the city's population to be 3.35 million, making it one of the world's largest cities. The city has experienced a population increase of 650,000 since the last census was taken in 1920.				Bill Agee sets a District of Columbia record for the 15-mile run, completing it in 1 hour and 26 minutes. . . . Noted French author Jacques Chardonne publishes *Eva, ou le Journal Interrompu*, considered by critics to be the best of his works. . . . The Institute of Social and Religious Research estimates there are 212 different denominations of religion in the United States, with 232,000 churches or temples comprised of 44,380,000 members. Based on these numbers, 36 percent of the country are regular churchgoers.	June 8
		British economic officials report that gold deposits this week at the Bank of England totaled only £70,000, against £839,912 withdrawn.			June 9
President Herbert Hoover signs a bill increasing total pensions by $12 million for veterans and widows of the Civil War. The bill will affect approximately 50,000 veterans and 27,000 widows, who will receive $75 a month. The age limit for pensions is also lowered from 75 to 70 years. . . . The New York City Health Department reports 2,768 babies were born this week, making it the highest birth rate for the city for any week of 1930 thus far.		American Federation of Labor president William Green estimates 2,000 naval yard workers have been fired since last November.			June 10
Assistant Postmaster General Clover reports that air-mail poundage for May amounted to 687,053, compared with 671,391 pounds for April, an increase of 2 percent.	$74,243,000 is given out in compensation by war claims arbiter James W. Remick for those who had their ships seized during World War I. Among them is Kaiser Wilhelm II of Germany, whose award of $522.28 will be deducted from Germany's World War I reparations.	American Society of Mechanical Engineers vice president Ralph E. Flanders admits in his organization's semiannual meeting that the creation of new industrial machines has contributed to the present unemployment crisis. "In the long run, however," he says, "the overhauling, upkeep, and repairs of machinery give employment to large numbers of men."		Boxer Benny Bass of Philadelphia retains the title of American junior lightweight champion by knocking out Eddie Anderson of Chicago in the third round of a scheduled 10-round bout.	June 11

F	G	H	I	J
Includes elections, federal-state relations, civil rights and liberties, crime, the judiciary, education, healthcare, poverty, urban affairs, and population.	Includes formation and debate of U.S. foreign and defense policies, veterans affairs, and defense spending. (Relations with specific foreign countries are usually found under the region concerned.)	Includes business, labor, agriculture, taxation, transportation, consumer affairs, monetary and fiscal policy, natural resources, pollution, and accidents.	Includes worldwide scientific, medical, and technological developments, natural phenomena, U.S. weather, and natural disasters.	Includes the arts, religion, scholarship, communications media, sports, entertainment, fashions, fads, and social life.

	World Affairs	Europe	Africa & The Middle East	The Americas	Asia & The Pacific
June 12		King Infante Don Jaime of Spain hosts U.S. Ambassador to Spain Irwin Boyle Laughlin at a formal state dinner at the U.S. Embassy in Madrid.		The Bank of Argentina loses $1 million from swindlers operating within Argentine financial institutions.	
June 13		The German Interior Ministry officially forbids the wearing of uniforms, emblems, or other apparel indicating membership in the National Socialist (Nazi) Party. Police chiefs are instructed to arrest any person wearing such apparel. . . . The Bank of France reports its gold reserves now total $43,816,000, the highest in the history of the bank.		The Uruguayan Finance Ministry reports the country has a present trade surplus of $17,889,000. . . . The Canadian Minister of Agriculture announces it will be sending a bacteria expert to Jamaica to help curb the country's ravaging banana disease.	In Bombay, 3,000 Indian *satyagrahists* (civil disobedience volunteers) defy British imperial orders by holding a procession celebrating the one-month anniversary of the Sholapur riots, a turning point in the Indian independence movement.
June 14	Ralph H. Booth is chosen as the new U.S. Ambassador to Denmark. . . . Brazilian President-elect Dr. Julio Prestes travels to Washington, D.C., for an official state visit.	British economic officials report exports for May were approximately 25 percent less than the corresponding period last year, with imports decreasing 12.5 percent.			The British government of Bombay announces it is amassing 500 soldiers from the city of Poona to quell rapidly increasing independence demonstrations.
June 15	A treaty is signed between Great Britain and the Middle Eastern country of Iraq, allowing Great Britain access to air bases in the cities of Basra and Al Habbaniyah, as well as the ability to move British troops across the country.			Former Venezuelan minister of the Interior Dr. Pedro M. Arcaya, who served as Minister to the United States from 1922–26, is appointed Venezuelan Minister in Washington, D.C.	
June 16		The British Navy completes the "refitting" of the World War I-era HMS *Hood*. . . . More than 3,000 members of the Finnish anti-Communist Lapua Movement arrive in the city of Oulu to destroy the offices of the Communist newspaper *Pohjan Voima*. . . . The government of the small Mediterranean island nation of Malta officially prohibits public political meetings, allowing no more than three people to simultaneously converse on the streets at any given time. . . . Austrian economic officials estimate unemployment in the capital city of Vienna has increased by 20 percent in one year.			
June 17	Ralph H. Wootan, military attaché of the Chilean U.S. Embassy, leaves the capital of Santiago, boarding a search plane to ascertain the whereabouts of a French pilot who disappeared over the Andes Mountains.	In Berlin, Germany, Prof. Albert Einstein explains his theory of relativity in a speech to 4,000 delegates of the World Power Conference.		The exchange rate of the Argentine peso falls to its lowest since March, with one U.S. dollar equaling 118.35 pesos. Argentine economic officials blame the decline on unseasonable rains, which have hurt crop deliveries.	Civil war in China causes the exchange rate for the Chinese tael to drop. One tael is now worth four U.S. dollars.
June 18	Belgian Ambassador in Washington Prince de Ligne sends a letter to the U.S. government formally protesting the newly passed Smoot-Hawley Tariff Act.				

A	B	C	D	E
Includes developments that affect more than one world region, international organizations, and important meetings of world leaders.	Includes all domestic and regional developments in Europe, including the Soviet Union.	Includes all domestic and regional developments in Africa and the Middle East.	Includes all domestic and regional developments in Latin America, the Caribbean, and Canada.	Includes all domestic and regional developments in Asian and Pacific nations (and colonies).

U.S. Politics & Social Issues	U.S. Foreign Policy & Defense	Economics & Great Depression	Science, Technology & Nature	Culture, Leisure & Lifestyle	
Representatives from 13 national women's organizations meet with President Herbert Hoover, requesting legislation to increase maternity welfare.		The Department of Commerce reports auto exports for the month of April were $37,443,661, a decrease of $2,521,307, or 6.3 percent, from the total for March.		U.S. heavyweight boxing champion Jack Sharkey squares off against German contender Max Schmeling for the title of world heavyweight champion. In the fourth round of the bout, Sharkey is disqualified for delivering a punch to his opponent below the belt, and Schmeling is declared the winner by default. It remains the only occasion in boxing history where a heavyweight champion has been crowned through disqualification. Sales of the fight netted $800,000.	June 12
Chicago Tribune reporter Alfred Lingle, whose murder by a supposed gangster sparked a crackdown on organized crime, is buried with a military salute in Our Lady of Sorrows Church.		The Annalist releases its weekly index of U.S. wholesale commodity prices. At 129.7, it is a decrease of 2.5 points from the previous week, and a 14.9 point decrease from the corresponding 1929 date. . . . The Annalist reports business activity has reached a new low point for the year, mainly due to a sharp decline in cotton consumption.			June 13
New York City Board of Estimates budget director Charles Kohler announces salary increases for 200 city officials amounting to $519,000.		New bond issues on the New York Stock Exchange for this week amounted to $233,673,200, the second highest total of the year. . . . Due to the decline in wheat sales, prices on the American Cotton Exchange drop to their lowest point of the year. Crop deliveries also fell to the lowest point since 1927.		Americans across the country celebrate Flag Day, created in 1917 to celebrate the anniversary of the creation of the American flag. . . . Earl D. Marks is found guilty of violating the "indecent literature law" by selling a copy of erotic novelist Pierre Louys's Aphrodite.	June 14
W.K. Kellogg donates $66 million in Kellogg Company stock to help found the W.K. Kellogg Child Welfare Foundation. . . . The Chrysler Building, the world's tallest structure, leases 65 percent of its space after being opened only for a few months. . . . Pittsburgh attorney William N. McNair reports that his 1928 senatorial campaign, for which he received 1,029,055 votes, cost him only $182 in campaign funds. McNair's budget is the lowest reported of any U.S. senatorial campaign that garnered substantial votes.		U.S. agriculture officials estimate there are now 558,000 farms with electrical power, an increase of 300 percent in the past six years. Based on these figures, officials predict there will be 1 million electrified farms within five years.	German scientists introduce the Enigma I, a typewriter-like machine used to encrypt and decode military messages, which would be used before and during World War II. . . . Eight people die as summer storms ravage southern Chile. . . . Upon returning from the tiny South Pacific Easter Island, where the mystery of ancient giant statues has baffled scientists for decades, New Zealand University professor J. Macmillan Brown presents a theory that the island was once the center of a great empire, and that the statues are memorials of past leaders.	England defeats the United States in the Wightman Cup, the most prestigious of women's tennis tournaments. The United States and Great Britain now stand at four wins apiece in the history of the tournament.	June 15
Amidst charges of negligence for the murder of Chicago Tribune reporter Alfred Lingle, Chicago Police Commissioner William F. Russell and Deputy Commissioner in charge of detectives John P. Stege announce their resignations.		The Sinclair Reporter reports that in the last six months, an average of 3,013,674 barrels of oil was produced daily, as compared to an average of 3,427,674 barrels produced in the two-year peak period of August 1929. . . . The Frankfurter Zeitung's index of German Stock Exchange prices stands at 109.7, a decrease of 33 percent since May 1927.			June 16
Approximately 1,000 veterans of World War I assemble on the steps of the U.S. Capitol to await word of legislation that would grant them benefits. . . . Edwin J. Cooley, former head of the Prohibition Bureau, is tried before the Supreme Court on charges of questionable accounting.	The U.S. Navy commissions the heavy cruiser ship USS Houston for active duty. Nicknamed the "Galloping Ghost of the Java Coast," the USS Houston would be sunk during World War II on February 28, 1942.	President Herbert Hoover signs the Smoot-Hawley Tariff Act into law. . . . U.S. economic officials report the price of wheat in July was the lowest since 1914, and the price of rye was the lowest since 1900. . . . National Manufacturers' Association president John E. Edgerton releases a statement responding to the signing of the Smoot-Hawley act into law. According to Edgerton, the act will bring "a breath of relief to all industry and business."		The United States Football Association, the official governing body of soccer, appoints James Armstrong to succeed co-founder Thomas W. Cahill as the organization's head. . . . Primo Carnera, who would become the largest heavyweight boxing champion in history, is conscripted into the French army.	June 17
Architect William Van Alen, designer of the world's tallest structure, the Chrysler Building, sues the W.P. Chrysler Building Corporation for $725,000 in unpaid architectural fees. . . . The American Railway Association reports the index of car loadings for the week ended June 7 was 89.1, a decrease of 12 percent from the comparable period a year ago.	The State Department vetoes the $2 million sale of 20 Glenn L. Martin Company bombing planes to Soviet Russia, effectively placing an embargo on armament exportation to the Communist nation. The State Department will still allow the exportation of commercial planes, a statement reads.	The price of bar silver in New York falls to 34 cents per troy ounce, causing a crisis in Mexico, the world's largest silver producer with 100,000 ounces produced annually. Many Mexican mines are indefinitely shut down.	Admiral Richard E. Byrd and his ship City of New York return to the United States following a two-year Antarctic expedition. . . . Aviators Edward Schlee and William Brock set a record for the 2,112-mile route between Florida and California, completing it in 13 hours, 55 minutes and 30 seconds.		June 18

F	G	H	I	J
Includes elections, federal-state relations, civil rights and liberties, crime, the judiciary, education, healthcare, poverty, urban affairs, and population.	Includes formation and debate of U.S. foreign and defense policies, veterans affairs, and defense spending. (Relations with specific foreign countries are usually found under the region concerned.)	Includes business, labor, agriculture, taxation, transportation, consumer affairs, monetary and fiscal policy, natural resources, pollution, and accidents.	Includes worldwide scientific, medical, and technological developments, natural phenomena, U.S. weather, and natural disasters.	Includes the arts, religion, scholarship, communications media, sports, entertainment, fashions, fads, and social life.

	World Affairs	Europe	Africa & The Middle East	The Americas	Asia & The Pacific
June 19				New Brunswick holds its 37th general election for members of the Legislative Assembly. The Conservative Party captures 31 of the 48 legislative seats. . . . In elections for the Legislative Assembly in Alberta, the United Farmers Party captures 39 of the 63 legislative seats. . . . A group of Bolivian exile rebels living in Argentina enter southern Bolivia and capture the city of Villezon. . . . Over 100 delegates of the Union of Pan-American Architects meet in the Brazilian capital of Rio de Janeiro to conduct the Union's fourth Congress.	Chinese military forces of the capital of Nanking recapture the city of Changsha, capital of the Hunan Province, from Kwangsi rebels. Western rebels destroy the Tsinan-Pukow Railway.
June 20	Representatives of both the U.S. and German film industries meet in Paris, France, to discuss lifting the German embargo on American-made "talkies" that has lasted for over one year.	In an interview with newspapermen, recently crowned King Carol of Bulgaria says he will tolerate full freedom of the press, as well as allow any public political demonstrations.	Prime Minister of Egypt Mustafa Nahhas Pasha resigns, ceding control to Ittehadist (King) Party head Ismael Sedki Pasha. Mustafa Pasha would later serve four more terms as prime minister, the last of which would end on January 27, 1952. . . . Great Britain announces the creation of High Commissioner posts for the colonies of Uganda, Kenya, and the mandate of Tanganyika.		In order to combat growing resistance movements, the British government in Bombay distributes leaflets calling the boycott campaign against British goods impractical.
June 21		Peacetime conscription is implemented in France as each male citizen is required to serve at least one year in the French army. . . . The Reichsbank of Germany lowers its rediscount rate from 4.5 to 4 percent.		A Bolivian rebel group lead by Roberto Hinajosa, which had overrun the Bolivian frontier city of Villazon, is driven out of the city by Bolivian soldiers. . . . The Canadian Dominion Statistics Bureau reports pig iron production has increased by 11 percent in one month.	
June 22	German Foreign Minister Dr. Julius Curtius pledges peaceful cooperation between the United States and Germany in a speech in English broadcast across the American continent. "Germany needs and desires peace," he says, adding, "A peace that is honorable for everybody."		Col. Bento Roma, Governor General of Portuguese West Africa, officially resigns following the shooting of Deputy High Commissioner Lt. Moraes Sarmento by rebels.	The U.S. Department of Agriculture announces the creation of a field office in the capital of Panama to ascertain the best route for an inter-American highway system.	
June 23	Italian Fascist Party secretary Augusto Turati makes the first public response by an Italian official on the recently passed U.S. Smoot-Hawley Tariff Act. He accuses the United States of "taking us by the throat economically in order to make us slaves."			Argentine economic officials report grain exports for May were 3,400,063 tons less than the corresponding period last year.	
June 24					Four trainloads of grain reach Shensi, China, sent by the United States to address the severe famine crisis.
June 25		Italian Ambassador to Great Britain Count Manzoni forwards a message to French Foreign Minister Aristide Briand, apologizing for the recent anti-French demonstrations in the Italian city of Bari. . . . Fierce rioting in the Spanish city of Seville results in 250 injuries and the arrests of more than 300 suspected agitators.			
	A Includes developments that affect more than one world region, international organizations, and important meetings of world leaders.	**B** Includes all domestic and regional developments in Europe, including the Soviet Union.	**C** Includes all domestic and regional developments in Africa and the Middle East.	**D** Includes all domestic and regional developments in Latin America, the Caribbean, and Canada.	**E** Includes all domestic and regional developments in Asian and Pacific nations (and colonies).

U.S. Politics & Social Issues	U.S. Foreign Policy & Defense	Economics & Great Depression	Science, Technology & Nature	Culture, Leisure & Lifestyle	
Col. Edward C. Carrington announces his intention to seek the New York Republican gubernatorial nomination on a platform of repealing the Eighteenth Amendment. . . . Census officials report states west of the Mississippi River are experiencing a greater population growth than states east of the Mississippi.			South African astronomers H.E. Wood and Cyril V. Jackson of the Johannesburg Union Observatory discover the "1595 Tanga" asteroid. . . . Harvard professor P.W. Bridgman achieves the greatest pressure compression known to man, compressing gases equal to 580,000 pounds per square inch. . . . Dr. Charles F. Geshickter announces the discovery of a new "stain," which, when placed on human skin, can rapidly detect cancer cells.		June 19
President Herbert Hoover presents the National Geographic gold medal to Antarctic explorer Richard E. Byrd. . . . Richard E. Byrd receives an honorary degree from New York University.		Members of the Federal Reserve Bank of New York vote to reduce the rediscount rate to 2.5 percent, making it the lowest rediscount rate of any Federal Reserve Bank in history.		Future Hall of Fame ballplayer Grover Cleveland Alexander, whose current earned run average is 300 percent higher than the career earned run average, is signed by the independent Texas League for a record salary of $1,500 per month.	June 20
		The Annalist releases its weekly index of U.S. wholesale commodity prices. At 127.4, it is a new record low for the post–World War I period and 12.1 percent lower than the comparable period a year ago. . . . New bond offerings on the New York Stock Exchange this week totaled $143,212,500, a decrease of 39 percent from last week's total of $233,673,200. . . . The U.S. Commerce Department announces business check payments have increased by 6 percent as compared to the previous week, but are still 10 percent below the same period a year ago. . . . The Federal Reserve Bank of Chicago lowers its rediscount rate from 4 percent to 3.5 percent, making it the third U.S. city along with Cleveland and Boston to have a 3.5 percent rediscount rate.	Inventor Thomas Edison receives a gold medal in recognition of his contributions to electrical science from the Argentine Association of Electro-Technicians.	American golfer Bobby Jones of Atlanta, Ga., wins the British Open golf championship, the second of his record four consecutive major championship victories.	June 21
Charles Augustus Lindbergh, Jr., son of famed aviator Charles Lindbergh and author Anne Lindbergh, is born. Dubbed "The Eaglet" by the media, Charles Jr. would enjoy celebrity status as the son of arguably America's most famous person until his abduction on March 1, 1932, at the age of 20 months. . . . The United States Bureau of Fisheries announces that last year saw the planting of more than 7 million fish and fish eggs, a record for a 12-month period.		Two thousand of the 14,000 mine-workers of the Pittson Company of Pennsylvania go on strike to improve wages.	John Q. Stewart, Associate Professor of Astronomical Physics at Princeton University, prophesizes that a manned mission to the Earth's moon will take place in the year 2050.	Lord Chamberlain of Great Britain refuses to grant a production license to the American Pulitzer Prize-winning play "The Green Pastures" by Marc Connelly on the grounds that it is "blasphemous." . . . Yale University wins the intercollegiate polo championship, defeating Princeton University by a score of 11–0.	June 22
J. Sheehy, warden of Sing Sing Prison, announces that there are currently 2,250 inmates incarcerated, an unprecedented number in the prison's 105-year existence. Of all the prisoners, 16 are sentenced to death row. . . . Representatives of major U.S. steel companies report production of steel has fallen to only 65 percent of its total capacity, and, with declining commodity prices, is expected to fall to 60 percent in the coming months.	The U.S. Navy sells the obsolete submarine USS S-51 to the Borough Metal Company of New York.	The exchange value of the Argentine peso falls to a new year low, with one U.S. dollar equaling 119.55 pesos. . . . In the annual analysis of balance of international payments, U.S. Commerce Secretary Robert Lamont writes that a very significant cause of the Great Depression was "the reduction of $561,000,000 in our net capital export." . . . The American Banker prepares an analysis showing New York City bank stocks have declined by $2 million from this year's peak point.		Chicago Cubs ballplayer Hack Wilson becomes one of only dozens of players in Major League history to hit a single, a double, a triple, and a home run in a single game.	June 23
					June 24
The U.S. Commerce Department announces births for 1929 totaled 2,142,124, as compared with 2,220,187 for 1928, a decrease of 3.6 percent.				The American Council of Learned Societies publishes the fifth volume of The Dictionary of American Biography.	June 25

F	G	H	I	J
Includes elections, federal-state relations, civil rights and liberties, crime, the judiciary, education, healthcare, poverty, urban affairs, and population.	Includes formation and debate of U.S. foreign and defense policies, veterans affairs, and defense spending. (Relations with specific foreign countries are usually found under the region concerned.)	Includes business, labor, agriculture, taxation, transportation, consumer affairs, monetary and fiscal policy, natural resources, pollution, and accidents.	Includes worldwide scientific, medical, and technological developments, natural phenomena, U.S. weather, and natural disasters.	Includes the arts, religion, scholarship, communications media, sports, entertainment, fashions, fads, and social life.

	World Affairs	Europe	Africa & The Middle East	The Americas	Asia & The Pacific
June 26		French Census officials report births for the first three months of 1930 outweighed deaths by 10,797 people, making it the first time in more than a decade that France has seen a positive birth rate. . . . Great Britain announces its naval construction program for 1930. Three cruisers, nine destroyers, and three submarines, along with numerous small vessels, will be built at an estimated cost of $45 million.		Theodore Roosevelt, Jr., governor of Puerto Rico, appeals to U.S. legislators to appropriate $7.3 million for medical relief to the children of Puerto Rico. . . . Police in Bolivia kill an estimated 34 people during a violent demonstration by university students and low-income workers.	
June 27				Canadian Prime Minister William Lyon Mackenzie King chooses Ian Alistair Mackenzie to succeed Charles Stewart as Interior Minister. . . . After a month of campaigning, Dwight W. Morrow, U.S. Ambassador to Mexico and father-in-law of famed aviator Charles Lindbergh, returns to Mexico to resume diplomatic duties.	Chiang Kai-shek, president of the Chinese Nanking government, amasses 100,000 troops to capture the Northern rebel-controlled city of Kaifeng, capital of the Hunan province.
June 28	Iceland, Denmark, Sweden, Norway, and Finland sign a treaty pledging to settle all disputes in the international court in The Hague, Netherlands.	The British Trades Union Congress releases a report asking the government to implement family allowances to help feed undernourished children. Under the plan, families will receive $1.25 weekly for each child born.		Less than a month after the unexpected resignation of Hernando Siles Reyes, the Bolivian cabinet chooses Carlos Blanco Galindo as the new prime minister.	
June 29		Seeking to decrease their country's debt, members of the German Reichstag vote to severely increase taxes on unwed Germans. Officials estimate the increased taxes will net approximately $25 million annually.			Construction begins in Madras, India, on a 1.85 million cubic yard masonry dam, said to be the world's largest.
June 30		The withdrawal of French troops from the Rhineland, the area in Germany demilitarized by the 1919 Versailles Treaty, is completed well ahead of schedule.	Bedros Effendi, former Turkish minister of public works, is stripped of his citizenship.	On the heels of the Argentine peso falling to its lowest exchange rate in five years, the price of wheat falls to 91 cents per barrel, the lowest in 20 years.	
July 1	Portugal agrees to enter into the Geneva Protocol, an international treaty banning chemical weapons that was first signed in 1925.				
July 2		Lord Earl Beatty, one of the leaders of the British Grand Fleet during World War I, assails the London Naval Treaty in a speech before the House of Commons. "Britain, the only nation to which sea power means existence, is the only power to make any disarmament to such an extent as to render her impotent."		The U.S. Department of the Interior reports that the territory of Alaska produced $16,066,000 worth of minerals in 1929, as compared to $14,061,000 in 1928, an increase of 12.5 percent. Over a 50-year period, Alaska has produced $615,501,000 worth of minerals.	

A	B	C	D	E
Includes developments that affect more than one world region, international organizations, and important meetings of world leaders.	Includes all domestic and regional developments in Europe, including the Soviet Union.	Includes all domestic and regional developments in Africa and the Middle East.	Includes all domestic and regional developments in Latin America, the Caribbean, and Canada.	Includes all domestic and regional developments in Asian and Pacific nations (and colonies).

U.S. Politics & Social Issues	U.S. Foreign Policy & Defense	Economics & Great Depression	Science, Technology & Nature	Culture, Leisure & Lifestyle	
Census officials report the capital of Washington has experienced a 10 percent population growth in the last decade, and now has approximately 500,000 residents.		German Minister of Economics Hermann Dietrich is chosen by Chancellor Heinrich Bruning to succeed Paul Moldenhauer as Finance Minister.		Hollywood film producer Howard Hughes purchases Multi Color Films, Inc., for a sum of $500,000.	June 26
With falling commodity prices, the Tin Producers Association announces it will cut production by an estimated 20 percent. . . . The federal government's index of electrical power production falls to an all-time low of 92.2, compared with 102.5 for June 1929, a decrease of 10 percent.		The Annalist releases its weekly index of U.S. wholesale commodity prices. At 124.6, it is a decline of 2.2 points from the post-World War I record low established the previous week. . . . The Federal Reserve Bank of New York reports brokers' loans have dropped by $371 million in one week. . . . The U.S. Commerce Secretary releases census figures showing the country's unemployed to be 2,298,588 persons, or 1.87 percent of the total population, a figure much smaller than previous estimates. American Federation of Labor president William Green criticizes the figure, saying the amount of Americans jobless is actually closer to 3.5 million.	American mining engineer William Boyce Thompson dies at his home in Yonkers, N.Y., at the age of 61.		June 27
The Swedish Engineering Society places the birthplace of famed aviator Charles Lindbergh on the real estate market. . . . Maurice Campbell, Prohibition administrator for New York City, announces his resignation.	Secretary of State Henry L. Stimson signs a treaty of arbitration with Chinese Foreign Minister Dr. C.C. Wu.	Amidst an outbreak of the apple fruit fly, Great Britain places an embargo on certain grades of U.S. apples, requiring the U.S. Agriculture Department to accurately label each apple imported to Canada with its grade. . . . Indian supporters of Mohandas Gandhi celebrate the news of Great Britain's latest trade report, which shows that cloth imports to India have fallen by 23 percent in one year, an indication the boycott of British goods is working.			June 28
The largest merger of industrial alcohol companies occurs as the American Solvents and Chemical Company of New York acquires the General Industrial Alcohol Corporation and the Rossville Commercial Alcohol Corporation.		National Business Survey Conference chairman Julius H. Barnes releases figures showing construction contracts for the first five months of 1930 total $554 million, against $1,045,000 for the comparable period a year ago, a decrease of 47 percent.	Architect Frank Lloyd Wright announces his intentions to build a "glass tower" in New York City.	The American Federal Office of Education estimates there are more than 500 radio broadcasting stations currently being operated.	June 29
Former Assistant Prohibition Commissioner Harry J. Anslinger is appointed as the first commissioner of the newly created Federal Bureau of Narcotics. . . . Republican National Committee chairman Claudius Huston, whose testimony to the Senate Lobby Committee indicates criminality, refuses President Herbert Hoover's request to resign.		The U.S. Chamber of Commerce reports export revenue for the first quarter of 1930 totaled $1.129 billion, a decrease of 4 percent from the average of similar periods from 1924–28.			June 30
United Hospital Fund general director Homer Wickenden sends a letter to New York City Police Commissioner Edward Mulrooney, requesting greater enforcement of firecracker ordinances during the upcoming Fourth of July celebrations, fearing his patients may be alarmed.	The U.S. Navy commissions the submarine USS Nautilus, with Lt. Cmdr. Thomas J. Doyle in command.	The Annalist's weekly index of U.S. wholesale commodity prices is released, showing a rise of 0.6 points, or 4 percent, from the previous week.			July 1
The U.S. Treasury Department estimates that despite the introduction in July 1929 of new, smaller-sized dollar bills, of which $3,759,649,324 worth was circulated, there still exists today approximately $1,060,795,609 in old, large bills.		R.G. Dun & Co. reports there were 2,026 bankruptcies in the United States in June, an increase of 15 percent from the comparable month a year ago. . . . Reporting the biggest loss the Exchange has reported since October 1929, 240 companies on the New York Stock Exchange experience a cumulative depreciation of $6,684,266,644 for June.		Carl Reynolds of the Chicago White Sox becomes only the third player in major league baseball history to hit three home runs over the span of two innings.	July 2

F	G	H	I	J
Includes elections, federal-state relations, civil rights and liberties, crime, the judiciary, education, healthcare, poverty, urban affairs, and population.	Includes formation and debate of U.S. foreign and defense policies, veterans affairs, and defense spending. (Relations with specific foreign countries are usually found under the region concerned.)	Includes business, labor, agriculture, taxation, transportation, consumer affairs, monetary and fiscal policy, natural resources, pollution, and accidents.	Includes worldwide scientific, medical, and technological developments, natural phenomena, U.S. weather, and natural disasters.	Includes the arts, religion, scholarship, communications media, sports, entertainment, fashions, fads, and social life.

	World Affairs	Europe	Africa & The Middle East	The Americas	Asia & The Pacific
July 3		Anti-Semitic riots occur in Romania. In the city of Campulung, 3,000 local farmers forcibly close all Jewish-owned shops and homes.... British First Lord of the Admiralty A.V. Alexander appears before the House of Commons to present new naval building estimates. In the coming year, according to Alexander, the United States will construct 140,000 tons in ships; the United Kingdom, 115,000 tons.			The Northern rebel army in China is driven back 46 miles by the Chinese government's army. In the city of Lanfeng, 5,000 rebels, along with their ammunition, are seized by government forces.
July 4		The Bank of France announces it currently holds 44 billion francs worth of gold, the highest total ever in the history of the bank.... The German government announces it is forbidding all civil servants and officials from becoming members of either the National Socialist (Nazi) Party or the Communist Party. "Both parties can be regarded only as organizations whose aim is the forceful overthrow of the existing order," a statement reads.	In Beersheba, Palestine, representatives of warring Arab tribes agree upon a settlement whereby 40 camels will be given for each life lost in past conflicts.		
July 5	Members of the British Labor Party send a message to Colonial Secretary Sidney James Webb, requesting that he lift the order prohibiting Jewish immigration into Palestine.	An estimated 25,000 coal miners in the Belgian city of Brussels go on strike to protest unfair old age pensions.		The Argentine dairy industry authors a letter to the Argentine Foreign Minister, complaining of the newly imposed U.S. tariffs on imported goods. They note that while dairy exports to the United States account for over 50 percent of Argentina's total exports, they only make up 0.8 percent of the United States' total dairy consumption.	By a vote of 15–1, the Australian Senate rejects a bill that would partially nationalize the country's wheat industry.
July 6			Scientists discover what they say is the first known instance of alphabetic writing in the Sinai Peninsula, Egypt. The discovery lays to rest the question of whether the modern European alphabet originated in Babylon, Crete, Cyprus, or Egypt.		British imperial officials in India ban the publication *Young Men of the Frontier,* saying its Communist viewpoints have contributed to the ever increasing civil disobedience movement.
July 7	The French publication *Aeronautique* publishes figures showing that for each mile flown by commercial air transport planes, French citizens pay a tax of $1.09. The Germans pay a tax of 90 cents; the Italians, 77 cents; the Americans, 70 cents.	In Helsinki, 12,000 members of the Finnish anti-Communist Lapua Movement demonstrate in a "Peasant March." In response, the government outlaws Communist newspapers under the Protection of the Republic Act.... French Premier Andre Tardieu officially opens a museum in the village of Bierancourt, commemorating the cooperation between the French and Americans in rebuilding districts ravaged by World War I.			
July 8	In a London radio address broadcast to the United States, Edward Albert Windsor, Prince of Wales, calls U.S. oil magnate John D. Rockefeller a "model philanthropist" in an appeal for £30,000 to construct a National Union of Students building.	The German Democratic Party merges with the People's National Reich Association to form the liberal German State Party.... In Sciacca, Sicily, 241 alleged members of the Italian mafia are put on trial before the Court of Assizes. The members are represented by a group of highly paid attorneys, including one former Italian senator. All but 60 of the defendants plead guilty.	The Roman Catholic Church purchases from the Palestinian Muslims the Nebi Daoud mosque, the site in Christian teachings of Jesus's Last Supper.		Joseph Ward, who resigned as prime minister of New Zealand on May 28, dies of heart failure.
July 9			Two Palestinian policemen in the city of Haifa are ambushed and one is killed by a group of Jewish assailants.	Argentineans celebrate their country's 114th anniversary of the declaration of independence from Spanish colonial rule.	Waziri tribesmen in the Indian city of Peshawar attack two British colonial posts, burning one of them to the ground.

A	B	C	D	E
Includes developments that affect more than one world region, international organizations, and important meetings of world leaders.	Includes all domestic and regional developments in Europe, including the Soviet Union.	Includes all domestic and regional developments in Africa and the Middle East.	Includes all domestic and regional developments in Latin America, the Caribbean, and Canada.	Includes all domestic and regional developments in Asian and Pacific nations (and colonies).

U.S. Politics & Social Issues	U.S. Foreign Policy & Defense	Economics & Great Depression	Science, Technology & Nature	Culture, Leisure & Lifestyle	
Prohibition agents in Elizabeth, N.J., seize 500 gallons of liquor in one of the largest liquor busts on record. . . . New York City Health Commissioner Shirley Wynne reports that there were 2,450 births last week as compared with 1,378 deaths.	Members of the Chamber of Commerce call on the Senate to ratify the provisions of the London Naval Treaty.	*Bradstreet's* reports total U.S. bank clearings for the month of June amounted to $49,910,305,000, the lowest sum since 1927.		In Buffalo, N.Y., 12,000 spectators witness the first professional night baseball game on the East Coast, as the Bisons defeat Montreal 5–4. . . . Charles Collins claims the world's low-parachute drop record, making a successful descent from an altitude of 800 feet.	July 3
Americans across the country celebrate the 154th anniversary of the drafting of the Declaration of Independence. . . . In accordance with the Fourth of July, Mayor J. Allen Couch of Atlanta, Ga., declares a general amnesty for more than 200 prisoners.	Rear Admiral Henry H. Hough is appointed Commandant of the Fifteenth Naval District in the Panama Canal.	The U.S. Department of Commerce reports automobile exports for the month of May amounted to $31,618,407, as compared with April's total of $37,443,601, a decrease of 15 percent.	The colossal statue of the head of former president George Washington, under construction since 1927, is unveiled at Mount Rushmore in Keystone, S.Dak.		July 4
Good Words Magazine reports that the Atlanta Federal Penitentiary currently exceeds its maximum capacity by over 60 percent. . . . In Harlem, 2,500 people assemble to witness the funeral service of Mexican Communist Gonzalo Gonzales, who was shot to death by a policeman during a political rally. Speakers at the funeral describe Gonzales as a "martyr" to the cause of Communism.		U.S. economic officials report bond offerings for this week totaled $75,564,000, an increase of 84 percent from the comparable period a year ago.			July 5
Aviation officials report the city of Chicago has increased threefold its sale of airline passenger tickets in one year.		The Studebaker Corporation announces that of its 28,356 stockholders, at least one resides in every U.S. state.	*The Architectural Record* announces the construction of the world's first all-metal apartment house, to be built in Chicago, Ill.		July 6
Appropriations for construction of the Hoover Dam are set. Named after President Herbert Hoover, the project is expected to cost a total of $165 million over five years and, when finished, will provide over 1,000 megawatts of electricity. It will be designated as a National Historic Landmark in 1985. . . . Two African Americans who were accused of killing two white men during the Fourth of July are lynched in Emelle, Ala.	Major General Commandant of the Marine Corps Wendell C. Neville dies. Neville occupied the post of head of the Marine Corps for more than a year.	*The Economist* releases its monthly index of British wholesale commodity prices. At 113.2, the figure is a 2 percent decline from May, and a 14 percent decrease from June 1929.	Bob Buck of Elizabeth, N.J., age 16, sets the world's junior light plane altitude record, flying at a height of 15,000 feet. The senior altitude record of 24,070 feet is credited to Barney Zimmerly of St. Louis, Mo.	Author Arthur Conan Doyle, who created the popular detective character Sherlock Holmes in his 1887 book *A Study in Scarlet*, dies at the age of 71. . . . The Swedish boat *Bissbi* wins the international "One-Ton Cup" international sailing tournament.	July 7
Citizens of Massachusetts celebrate the 300th anniversary of the founding of the Massachusetts Bay Colony by Puritan settlers.	The U.S. Navy strikes the destroyer ship USS *Zeilin* for scrap sale. . . . General Ben Hebard Fuller is chosen to replace the late Wendell C. Neville as Major General Commandant of the Marine Corps.	U.S. automobile manufacturers report automobile production has fallen to its lowest level since December 1929.		Americans Wilmer Allison and John Van Ryn win the Wimbledon men's doubles titles for the second consecutive year, defeating George Lott and John Deog in three sets, 6–3, 6–3, and 6–2. British newspapers attribute the American victory to the "far nobler fighting qualities and more robust physique" of Allison and Ryn.	July 8
The New York City Board of Aldermen approves $5 million for construction of a bridge connecting Manhattan to the Bronx and Queens. . . . A federal grand jury in San Francisco, Calif., releases a statement describing Prohibition enforcement methods as "stupid" and "laughable." . . . Chicago mobster Al Capone is indicted on two charges of perjury in Miami, Fla. . . . Census taking in New York City is officially completed. According to officials, the city's current population is 6,960,000, an increase of 1,355,036, or 23 percent, in 10 years.			Gilbert G. Budwig, director of the aeronautics branch of the U.S. Department of Commerce, officially denies a request to sanction an experimental flight where two crews will switch planes while in midair. In a statement, Budwig says the stunt has no practical benefit to aviation.		July 9

F	G	H	I	J
Includes elections, federal-state relations, civil rights and liberties, crime, the judiciary, education, healthcare, poverty, urban affairs, and population.	*Includes formation and debate of U.S. foreign and defense policies, veterans affairs, and defense spending. (Relations with specific foreign countries are usually found under the region concerned.)*	*Includes business, labor, agriculture, taxation, transportation, consumer affairs, monetary and fiscal policy, natural resources, pollution, and accidents.*	*Includes worldwide scientific, medical, and technological developments, natural phenomena, U.S. weather, and natural disasters.*	*Includes the arts, religion, scholarship, communications media, sports, entertainment, fashions, fads, and social life.*

	World Affairs	Europe	Africa & The Middle East	The Americas	Asia & The Pacific
July 10	The International Advertising Congress, with over 200 delegates representing 14 nations, concludes its annual meeting in Brussels, Belgium.	The British Board of Trade releases its June export figures, showing a $40,835,000 decrease from May and a $35,240,000 decline from the comparable period last year.		Canadian Pacific Railway president E.W. Beatty blames the ever increasing Canadian unemployment rate on U.S. immigration.	With a budget deficit of $68 million, Australia votes to drastically increase its taxation, which government officials say will increase the weekly standard of living by $5 per person.
July 11	The Mandates Commission of the League of Nations releases a report blaming the ever increasing violence in Palestine on the limited amount of British troops serving in the region.	The Bank of England releases figures showing its gold reserves to be £164,502,394, the highest total of the year to date.		Cuban Interior Secretary General Delgado announces the discovery of a Communist subversion plot that would have instigated major riots in late summer. Four men in connection with the plot were deported. . . . President Carlos Blanco Galindo of Bolivia announces national elections will take place in November, when a constitutional government will replace the current military government.	The Hong Kong-based Chinese Industrial and Commercial Bank declares bankruptcy with estimated losses of $600,000 gold.
July 12	U.S. Secretary of State Henry L. Stimson officially requests that Great Britain modify its embargo on U.S. apples, saying that the fruit fly disease which caused the embargo has only been found in apples originating from east of the Mississippi River.	In the Romanian city of Szuchzawa, 1,000 farmers participate in an anti-Semitic rally that injures several Jews. . . . Archduke Leopold of Austria is imprisoned for his role in the unauthorized sale of a $400,000 Napoleon-era diamond necklace on February 1.			
July 13		Austria and Portugal send a message to French Foreign Minister Aristide Briand, generally agreeing with his proposal to create a United States of Europe. Both countries stipulate, however, that the federation should be closely connected with the League of Nations.		The first FIFA World Cup soccer tournament begins in Montevideo, Uruguay, with two opening matches: France defeats Mexico by a score of 4–1, and the United States defeats Belgium by a score of 3–0.	
July 14		Citizens in France celebrate the 151st Bastille Day, a national holiday commemorating the destruction of a political prison during the Revolution of 1789.	British High Commissioner of Egypt Sir Percy Lorraine suspends the ongoing parliamentary session by way of royal decree, saying that the Wafdists, Egypt's number one political party, are inciting the populace to revolt against colonial rule.		
July 15	Great Britain requests of Panama $5,000 in compensation for the death of a British seaman who was beaten to death unlawfully by Panamanian police a year ago.	Anti-Semitic riots continue in Romania. In the city of Cioburgiu, 200 houses are burned to the ground and over three-fourth's of the city's population is left homeless.	Dr. Frick, education minister of the German state of Thuringia, introduces a bill in the German Reichstag parliament that would grant German citizenship to Austrian-born National Socialist (Nazi) leader Adolf Hitler.		
July 16		The 16th Congress of the Communist Party of the Soviet Union is completed in Moscow. . . . The number of unemployed in Great Britain increases by 42,000 in one week, bringing the total to 1,933,500, or approximately 5 percent of the population. It is the highest total since the national coal strike of 1921, when unemployment reached over 2 million people.	Emperor Haile Selassie of Ethiopia signs his country's first constitution into law.		Foreign military observers remark to journalists that the present civil war in China is fast approaching a "stalemate."

A	B	C	D	E
Includes developments that affect more than one world region, international organizations, and important meetings of world leaders.	Includes all domestic and regional developments in Europe, including the Soviet Union.	Includes all domestic and regional developments in Africa and the Middle East.	Includes all domestic and regional developments in Latin America, the Caribbean, and Canada.	Includes all domestic and regional developments in Asian and Pacific nations (and colonies).

U.S. Politics & Social Issues	U.S. Foreign Policy & Defense	Economics & Great Depression	Science, Technology & Nature	Culture, Leisure & Lifestyle	
		The National Automobile Chamber of Commerce reports passenger car and truck production for June was 39 percent below the corresponding period a year ago.	The American Scantic liner *Argosy* sets the record time taken to sail between New York City and Copenhagen, Denmark, completing the trip in 10 days, 7 hours and 50 minutes at an average speed of approximately 14.5 knots.	The Dreyfus collection, the greatest private collection of Italian Renaissance art in the world, is sold to the Duveen brothers, art dealers, for a sum of $5 million. It is believed to be the largest single art transaction ever.	**July 10**
The Treasury Department reports that in the year ended June 30, the day before Prohibition duties were transferred from the Treasury to the Justice Department, 68,186 Prohibition violators were arrested, an increase of 1,308 from the year before.		*The Annalist* releases its weekly index of U.S. wholesale commodity prices, showing a decrease of 1.2 points from the previous week, and a 16 percent decline from the corresponding period the previous year. . . . The U.S. Federal Reserve Bank reports a $16 million decline for this week in brokers' loans. The decline brings the total amount of loans to $3.2 billion, the lowest reported total since August 31, 1927.			**July 11**
		Austria announces it will reimburse Italy for its food relief efforts during the winter of 1919. Austria will pay a sum of $2,430,000 over a period of 30 years. . . . *Dun's Review* reports that because of the shortened business week, U.S. bank clearings experienced an unusual drop of 38.4 percent from the corresponding week a year ago.		The popular radio program "Amos n' Andy" goes on hiatus for the first time since being broadcast in 1928, as the two title performers embark for Hollywood to create their first movie, called *Check and Double Check*. . . . More than 10,000 spectators witness the opening of the U.S. Open golf tournament.	**July 12**
Charles S. Johnson publishes *The Negro in American Civilization*, a sociological study of America's second most populous race. Among the figures presented: there is only 1 hospital bed for every 1,941 African Americans in the United States, compared with one for every 139 white persons. Despite this, the mortality rate and illiteracy rate have declined by approximately 50 percent in 50 years.	The Advanced Flying School of the Army Air Corps officially adds the art of "blind flying," or piloting an aircraft without manual control, to its curriculum.	Prof. Paul H. Douglas publishes *Real Wages in the United States, 1890-1926*, a book detailing employment conditions over a 30-year period as based on statistics by the U.S. Bureau of Labor. In it, he concludes that "in 1926 the workers enjoyed an income which was approximately 55 percent higher than during the 1890s."	Aboard the ship *Miss England II*, Sir Henry Segrave of Great Britain breaks the world's water speed record with a speed of 98.76 miles per hour. Segrave would later suffer fatal injuries while trying to improve upon the record. . . . Hershel C. Parker announces a new patented process by which to extract gold from the Pacific Ocean. The process is expected to allow miners to obtain a 75 percent profit on every 2 cents gold mined.		**July 13**
Aviator Bert Acosta, who flew from Long Island, N.Y., to France in 1927 and who is known as the "Bad Boy of the Air" due to his heavy drinking and multiple divorces, is released from the Mineola County, Long Island, prison after serving 5 months of a six-month sentence for failure to pay alimony and child support. Acosta regained his pilot's license upon being released.		The Bank of England reports its gold intake for this week was £760,137, against £937,722 withdrawn, a difference of £177,585.	One of the first live television broadcasts occurs as Italian playwright Luigi Pirandello's play *The Man With The Flower In His Mouth* is broadcast in England. While the technology only permitted one actor on screen at a time, the experiment is dubbed a success. . . . Four schoolboys in Hackensack, N.J., complete a 168-hour nonstop bike ride, besting the previous record of 120 hours set last year.	By a score of 2–1, Yugoslavia defeats Brazil in the first round of the FIFA World Cup. . . . Romania beats Peru by a score of 3–1.	**July 14**
The American Civil Liberties Union responds to former Secretary of War Elihu Root's proposal of a federal police department to combat Communist subversion, saying it "is based upon obvious ignorance of the existing law."		U.S. automobile manufacturers release their weekly index of automobile production. At 83.3, the figure is an 18 percent increase from last week's index of 67.9. . . . French Counsel General Maxime Mongrende estimates his country's unemployed to be approximately 1,000 people, or a mere 0.0025 percent of the total population.		Argentina defeats France by a score of 1– 0 in the first round of the FIFA World Cup.	**July 15**
Lawyer Robert Szold is elected by the Zionist Organization of America as head of its administrative committee.		The American Bankers Association estimates U.S. wheat consumption has fallen by 20 percent in the years following World War I. . . . Car loadings in the United States fell by approximately 2 percent last week, according to economic officials. . . . The U.S. Census Bureau reports cotton consumption totaled 405,181 bales for June, a drop of 14 percent from May's total of 473,917 bales.	The American Austin, the smallest car ever built in the United States, is exhibited for the first time at the headquarters of the car's manufacturer, the American Austin Car Company. The Austin has an estimated sale price of $499.	The second International Tourist Plane Contest begins in Berlin, Germany. . . . Chile defeats Mexico by a score of 3–0 in the first round of the FIFA World Cup. . . . World featherweight champion Bat Battalino squares off against Ignacio Fernandez of the Philippines in the first featherweight title bout since Battalino obtained the crown last September. The fight is attended by 9,000 spectators, who witness Battalino knock out Fernandez in the fifth round. Sales of the fight netted $20,000.	**July 16**

F	**G**	**H**	**I**	**J**
Includes elections, federal-state relations, civil rights and liberties, crime, the judiciary, education, healthcare, poverty, urban affairs, and population.	Includes formation and debate of U.S. foreign and defense policies, veterans affairs, and defense spending. (Relations with specific foreign countries are usually found under the region concerned.)	Includes business, labor, agriculture, taxation, transportation, consumer affairs, monetary and fiscal policy, natural resources, pollution, and accidents.	Includes worldwide scientific, medical, and technological developments, natural phenomena, U.S. weather, and natural disasters.	Includes the arts, religion, scholarship, communications media, sports, entertainment, fashions, fads, and social life.

	World Affairs	Europe	Africa & The Middle East	The Americas	Asia & The Pacific
July 17	British Prime Minister Ramsay MacDonald announces the dispatch of the battleships *Queen Elizabeth* and *Ramillies* to Egypt, the purpose of which is to protect foreigners, mainly Britons, from ongoing civil disturbances. . . . The American Bureau of Metal Statistics reports copper production for the entire world in June amounted to 145,556 short tons, nearly identical to the total for May.	Germany releases a statement responding to French Foreign Minister Aristide Briand's United Europe proposal. "All attempts at an improvement of the political situation of Europe will be dependent upon . . . complete equality and equal security for all.". . . Great Britain issues an indifferent, yet conciliatory, response to French Foreign Minister Aristide Briand's United Europe proposal. . . . Czechoslovakia responds to the United Europe proposal, recommending that a commission be created in Geneva in the autumn to further study the proposal.			
July 18	An international delegation in London known as the Inter-parliamentary Union passes a resolution favoring public registration of trusts and cartels. U.S. delegates abstain from voting, saying the resolution allows too lenient treatment of trusts. . . . The British government calls the terms of French Foreign Minister Aristide Briand's United Europe proposal "unacceptable," but says the concept should be further discussed when the League of Nations reconvenes in September.	After an unpopular finance reform bill is vetoed by the German Reichstag parliament for the second occasion, Chancellor Heinrich Bruning issues an emergency decree dissolving the Reichstag. . . . Romanian Interior Minister Alexander Vayda-Voevod lays blame for the recent anti-Semitic riots on police negligence, noting however that recently enacted financial measures impacting farmers have aroused public bitterness.		Bolivia officially transfers the Fort Boqueron military facility, under Bolivian control for more than a decade of war, to Paraguay in accordance with a proposal established in Washington last September. An army officer from Uruguay, the country that borders both Paraguay and Bolivia, oversaw the transfer.	
July 19			A five-hour meeting between Arab and Jewish members of the Wailing Wall Commission in Jerusalem results in the Arab members refusing to recognize the Wailing Wall as a place of Jewish worship, preferring instead to label it as a place of historical artifact.		Australian economic officials estimate the newly enacted automobile tariffs will result in an average price increase for Australian motorists of $85 to $500.
July 20	The New York Trust Company reports on Latin American economic development over the past two decades in *The Index*, showing that in 1913 British investments to Latin America totaled $5 billion, while U.S. investments totaled only $1.24 billion. By 1928, however, Great Britain's investments had increased to only $5.89 billion, while U.S. investments had increased over 350 percent to reach near equality with Great Britain at $5.59 billion.				
July 21		Romanian Foreign Minister Alexander Vayda-Voevod announces the arrests of two orthodox Christian priests, along with 29 others, in connection with the recent anti-Semitic riots.			
July 22		Viennese District Attorney Crain informs an imprisoned Archduke Leopold of Austria that his trial for the alleged theft of a $400,000 Napoleon-era diamond necklace will commence no earlier than October 1.		Officials of the Panama Canal report that in the fiscal year ended May 31, U.S. ships accounted for 14,499,233 tons, or 47 percent, of the total cargo. It is an increase of 423,502 tons from the previous fiscal year. . . . Andres Ortiz of the National Revolutionary Party is elected governor of the Mexican state of Chihuahua.	
July 23	King George of Great Britain hosts King Faisal of Iraq at Buckingham Palace.	A devastating Irish railway strike is averted as an emergency meeting is called by the Ministry of Industry and Commerce, during which an agreement is successfully brokered.		U.S. Ambassador to Argentina Robert Woods arrives in the capital of Buenos Aires for an official state visit.	

A	B	C	D	E
Includes developments that affect more than one world region, international organizations, and important meetings of world leaders.	*Includes all domestic and regional developments in Europe, including the Soviet Union.*	*Includes all domestic and regional developments in Africa and the Middle East.*	*Includes all domestic and regional developments in Latin America, the Caribbean, and Canada.*	*Includes all domestic and regional developments in Asian and Pacific nations (and colonies).*

U.S. Politics & Social Issues	U.S. Foreign Policy & Defense	Economics & Great Depression	Science, Technology & Nature	Culture, Leisure & Lifestyle	
	Approximately 400 members of the United States Army Ambulance Corps assemble in Atlantic City, N.J., for their annual meeting.	*The Annalist* reports business activity has fallen to its lowest level since July 1924.	The Chrysler Corporation announces the creation of two new cars, the Chrysler Eight and the Imperial Eight, both of which are the first eight-cylinder cars Chrysler has produced.	In the first round of the FIFA World Cup, Yugoslavia triumphs 4–0 over Bolivia to clinch a spot in the tournament's semifinal. . . . The United States beats Paraguay 3–0 to advance to the FIFA World Cup semifinals.	July 17
Senator John Blaine of Wisconsin introduces a resolution that would officially recognize Indian independence from British colonial rule. . . . The Federal Reserve Bank of New York announces stockbrokers' loans increased by $40 million this week, ending a continuous decline that began on June 4. Total loans now stand at $3.243 billion, a decrease of 44 percent from the comparable period a year ago.		*The Annalist's* weekly index of U.S. wholesale commodity prices is released. At 123, the figure is 18 percent lower than the corresponding period last year, when the figure stood at 150.1. . . . French Finance Minister Paul Reynaud criticizes the United States, among other countries, for the recently constructed "tariff walls," which seriously impact international commerce. He says, "Raising the tariff wall amounts only to forcing your neighbors to climb over it and establish themselves in your own country," noting the recent construction of an Italian automobile manufacturing plant by Henry Ford.		Uruguay defeats Peru 1–0 in the first round of the FIFA World Cup.	July 18
	United States Army Ambulance Corps national commander Glenn M. Coulter estimates his organization's membership to be 1,430 persons, with an increase of 10 percent during the past year. At the organization's annual meeting, members vote to force Congress to publish all World War I records.	R.G. Dun & Co. announces bank clearings for this week totaled $10.1 billion, a decline of 20.4 percent from the comparable period a year ago.		Chile defeats France by a score of 1–0 in the first round of the FIFA World Cup. . . . Argentina defeats Mexico by a score of 6–3. . . . In Paris, France, 3,000 spectators witness the opening of the Davis Cup international tennis tournament as American Willmer Allison defeats Giorgio de Stefani of Italy in five sets. The scores were 4–6, 7–9, 6–4, 8–6, and 10–8.	July 19
A Congressional hearing on Communist activities reveals the Amtorg Trading Corporation contributes hundreds of thousands of dollars per year to Soviet causes.		Senator Arthur Capper of Kansas blames ever decreasing U.S. commodity prices on overproduction, speculation, and a declining rural population. . . . A study entitled, "Wages in the United States, 1914–1929" is completed by the National Industrial Conference Board. According to the study, the average hourly wage of manufacturing workers for 1929 was 58 cents, compared with 57 cents for the previous year.		Brazil beats Bolivia 4–0 in the first round of the FIFA World Cup. . . . Paraguay defeats Belgium 1–0.	July 20
People's Lobby president Prof. John Dewey calls on U.S. President Herbert Hoover to appropriate $1 billion, or 2 percent of the country's aggregate income, on a special federal unemployment insurance program. . . . Census officials report that California's large population growth in the last 10 years will result in the addition of 9 Californians to the U.S. House of Representatives.		George Eder, chief of the Latin American section of the U.S. Bureau of Foreign and Domestic Commerce, reports that U.S. trade with Latin America has increased by 27 percent in the last decade.	Duke University Medical Center, one of the top 10 health care organizations in the United States, officially opens its doors to patients.	Uruguay clinches a spot in the FIFA World Cup semifinal by defeating Romania 4–0.	July 21
	The U.S. Navy strikes the destroyer ships USS *Shirk*, USS *Henshaw*, USS *Farragut*, and USS *Wood* from the Naval Vessel Register.	Argentine oil officials report their country produced approximately 1,645,358 tons of crude oil in the past year, 775,000 tons of which were consumed by Argentineans alone. . . . The U.S. Department of Commerce reports automobile production fell by 19 percent in June, with 335,475 total cars produced.	Grigory Nikolaevich Neujmin announces the discovery of a new asteroid named 1306 Scythia. . . . During an attempt to break the world's flight endurance record of 553 hours, Tex Anding becomes violently ill and is forced to land at Roosevelt Field.	Argentina clinches a spot in the FIFA World Cup semifinal, defeating Chile by a score of 3–1.	July 22
Peter A. Bogdanov, head of the Soviet owned Amtorg Trading Company, testifies before the House Committee on Communist Activities. Rep. Hamilton Fish, chairman of the committee, questions the legality of Bogdanov's alien status, citing immigration laws which state that foreign citizens of nations without commercial treaties cannot reside in the United States.		Argentina's Ministry of Finance reports exports for the first five months of 1930 totaled 300,526,000 pesos, a decrease of 33 percent from the first five months of 1929.			July 23

F	**G**	**H**	**I**	**J**
Includes elections, federal-state relations, civil rights and liberties, crime, the judiciary, education, healthcare, poverty, urban affairs, and population.	*Includes formation and debate of U.S. foreign and defense policies, veterans affairs, and defense spending. (Relations with specific foreign countries are usually found under the region concerned.)*	*Includes business, labor, agriculture, taxation, transportation, consumer affairs, monetary and fiscal policy, natural resources, pollution, and accidents.*	*Includes worldwide scientific, medical, and technological developments, natural phenomena, U.S. weather, and natural disasters.*	*Includes the arts, religion, scholarship, communications media, sports, entertainment, fashions, fads, and social life.*

	World Affairs	Europe	Africa & The Middle East	The Americas	Asia & The Pacific
July 24		By way of royal decree, Spain dramatically increases tariffs on imported automobiles. European manufacturers will be charged a duty of 1,440 pesetas on each car imported, while U.S. manufacturers will be charged 2,400 pesetas.		The Bond and Shareholders Association announces Argentina currently has a budget deficit of 4.16 billion pesos, despite the trading of 721 million pesos on the New York Stock Exchange in the year ended June 30.	
July 25		The Bank of England reports its gold holdings decreased by £1,338,000 this week.		American Mark Lullinsky is detained by Mexican officials for suspicion of being a Communist propagandist in league with the Amtorg Trading Company.	
July 26		The German Taxicab Owners' and Drivers' Association recommends to the police that the city of Berlin's 9,000 taxicab drivers be forced to work four-day weeks as a means of reducing traffic congestion. . . . By a 38 percent majority, the British House of Commons passes a $4 billion finance reform bill. Conservative L. Worthington-Evans opposed the heavy taxation clauses of the bill, saying, "It is more important today to increase employment than to increase the sinking fund."		Mexico settles its national railway debt of $500 million, agreeing to pay an annual sum of $15 million to international bankers over a period of 30 years.	
July 27		King Victor Emmanuel of Italy officially surveys the damage caused by an earthquake that forced the evacuation of 14,000 people and caused the death of 2,142 others.	A Syro-Palestine delegation of Arabs sends a request to the League of Nations to nullify the 1917 Balfour Declaration, which created a Jewish national home in Palestine.		Australia announces its wheat harvest for the year ended July 25 was 126,477,000 bushels.
July 28	Albert Einstein visits the League of Nations in Geneva, Switzerland, commenting that the League "could do no greater work than to help make the elementary schools throughout the world better."	Austrian bank officials report their country's gold holdings currently total 870 million schillings, the highest ever recorded. Austria's current reserve cover ratio of 81 percent is also a record, officials say.			
July 29		British aeronautical officials complete the first test run of the airship HM R.100. . . . French economic officials report exports for their country in June totaled 3.352 billion francs, compared with 3.733 billion francs in May, a decrease of 10 percent.	British aviator Amy Johnson, the first woman to fly from Great Britain to Australia, flies to Cairo, Egypt, where she is greeted by throngs of cheering supporters. . . . Appearing before the British Arab Executive, a Palestinian Arab delegation says that Palestine "will use every legal means in its power to defend itself against" the 1917 Balfour Declaration.		
July 30				In a press conference, President Ortiz Rubio of Mexico announces the closing of gambling houses on the Mexico-U.S. border, and says his country will have a budget surplus of 15 million pesos ($7.5 million) by the end of the year.	Approximately 10,000 Chinese Communists seize the city of Changsha, burning all government offices, and announce the intention to destroy the British Consulate near Changsha. Officials say the attacks were instigated by Soviet agitators based in Moscow.
July 31	Seeking to boost international trade, Great Britain sends a group of economic representatives representing the cotton, steel, and wool industries to China and Japan. . . . Auto magnate Henry Ford is interviewed on his 67th birthday. When asked what industry he believes has the potential for great growth, Ford says, "There is a great field in the manufacture and distribution of some kind of pure water which everyone would like." Bottled water would become a $22 billion industry by 2005.				The Indian National Congress opens session with Vallabhai Patel presiding. With 21 of its 31 members imprisoned, the remaining 10 members vote to boycott upcoming parliamentary elections.

A	B	C	D	E
Includes developments that affect more than one world region, international organizations, and important meetings of world leaders.	Includes all domestic and regional developments in Europe, including the Soviet Union.	Includes all domestic and regional developments in Africa and the Middle East.	Includes all domestic and regional developments in Latin America, the Caribbean, and Canada.	Includes all domestic and regional developments in Asian and Pacific nations (and colonies).

U.S. Politics & Social Issues	U.S. Foreign Policy & Defense	Economics & Great Depression	Science, Technology & Nature	Culture, Leisure & Lifestyle	
The American Institute of New York City votes to merge with the New York Electrical Society. . . . Speaking before the House of Representatives, Peter A. Bogdanov, chairman of the Soviet-owned but American-based Amtorg Trading Company, threatens to halt all Russian trade with the United States unless Congressional inquiries cease.		U.S. steel representatives release their weekly steel production index. At 82.3, the figure is a decline of 3 percent from last week's index of 85.2. . . . General Motors president Alfred P. Sloan reports his company's net earnings for the first six months of 1930 amounted to $98,355,355, compared with $151,860,310 for the first six months of 1929, a decline of 35 percent.			July 24
	Rear Admiral Harry Rousseau, director of the navy petroleum reserves, suffers a fatal stroke aboard the Panama Canal-bound steamship *Cristobal*.	The Washington Mutual Savings Bank acquires the Continental Mutual Savings Bank. . . . The Federal Reserve Bank of New York reports brokers' loans declined by $17 million this week, bringing the current total to $3.226 billion.		Noted thespian Laurence Olivier marries British actress Jill Esmond. . . . Congo Pictures is sued by a group of mammologists for the documentary *Ingagi*, on the grounds that the gorillas filmed in the documentary were "faked."	July 25
Republican Senator Simeon D. Fess of Ohio is chosen as the new Republican National Committee chairman, replacing Claudius Huston, who resigned.		R.G. Dun & Co. reports bank clearings for this week totaled $8,836,423,000, a decrease of 27.2 percent from the corresponding period a year ago.	Antarctic explorer Richard E. Byrd is named an honorary member of the Brazilian Aero Society in Rio de Janeiro.	Argentina defeats the United States by a score of 6–1 to advance to the FIFA World Cup championship.	July 26
	The Army Air Corps awards $460,550 to the Fokker Aircraft Corporation to build 20 single-engine cargo airplanes.			Uruguay defeats Yugoslavia by a score of 6–1 to advance to the FIFA World Cup championship. . . . With a time of 126 hours, 25 minutes and 23 seconds, Andre Leducq of France obtains the lead in the 28th annual Tour de France cycling competition.	July 27
		U.S. Assistant Secretary of Commerce Dr. Julius Klein announces in a radio address that U.S. citizens are the most indebted of any nationality. . . . Germany releases its weekly index of wholesale commodity prices. At 125.5, the figure is a rise of 0.7 points, or 0.1 percent, from the previous week's index of 124.8. . . . The Boerse, Germany's stock exchange, experiences the largest three-day slump since the "Black Friday" period of May 1927.		Poland, led by Akiba Rubenstein, wins the International Chess Federation championship, defeating Finland in the 17th and final round.	July 28
Demanding a shorter workday and three paid holidays, 2,000 members of the International Barbers' Union in New York City go on strike.	The U.S. Navy strikes the submarine USS *O-12* from the Naval Vessel Register.	American Tobacco Company president George W. Hill announces during a stockholder meeting that, based on projected earnings, 1930 will mark the company's greatest profit year since 1911.		A hearing is held by the U.S. Labor Department Board of Review to determine the legality of Italian boxer Primo Carnera's alien status.	July 29
President Herbert Hoover instructs the Justice Department to thoroughly investigate business bankruptcy, which he says results in losses of $750 million annually to U.S. businessmen.	In accordance with the treaty at the London Naval Conference, the U.S. Navy scraps the submarines USS *O-14* and USS *O-15*.	The American Petroleum Institute estimates that for the week ended July 26, crude oil production averaged 1,877,800 barrels per day, compared with an average of 1,885,200 barrels for last week, a decline of 7,400 barrels, or 0.3 percent.	Eddie August Schneider, an 18 year-old, announces he will fly across the Pacific and back this August.	Uruguay wins its first and only FIFA World Cup soccer championship, defeating Argentina by a score of 4–2 in the final match. Approximately 500,000 people witnessed the tournament. Guillermo Stabile of Argentina, who scored eight goals in five games, is declared the most valuable player.	July 30
The Interstate Commerce Commission files a brief against the Pennsylvania Railroad Company, alleging that the 1927 acquisitions of the Lehigh Valley and Wabash railroads violated the 1917 Clayton Anti-Trust Act.		With temperatures in the Deep South reaching 110 degrees, the price of cotton falls to 13 cents, the lowest price since December 1926. . . . American Federation of Labor president William Green reports slight unemployment growth for trade unions in June, with only a 1 percent increase from May.	The Department of Agriculture reports that West Virginia experienced only 66 percent of its normal rainfall from December through June, the driest spring and summer since 1901.	The first broadcast of the mystery radio program "The Shadow" is heard. . . . One of Walt Disney's first cartoons, *Night*, is released. . . . Leo Deigel defeats Tommy Armour in a 36-hole playoff match to win the Canadian Open golf championship.	July 31

F	G	H	I	J
Includes elections, federal-state relations, civil rights and liberties, crime, the judiciary, education, healthcare, poverty, urban affairs, and population.	*Includes formation and debate of U.S. foreign and defense policies, veterans affairs, and defense spending. (Relations with specific foreign countries are usually found under the region concerned.)*	*Includes business, labor, agriculture, taxation, transportation, consumer affairs, monetary and fiscal policy, natural resources, pollution, and accidents.*	*Includes worldwide scientific, medical, and technological developments, natural phenomena, U.S. weather, and natural disasters.*	*Includes the arts, religion, scholarship, communications media, sports, entertainment, fashions, fads, and social life.*

	World Affairs	Europe	Africa & The Middle East	The Americas	Asia & The Pacific
Aug. 1		Poland test flies its newest fighter aircraft, the *PZL P.6*, which would win the American National Air Races in 1931 and take part in the 1939 German invasion of Poland. . . . Polish dictator Jozef Pilsudski, who took power in 1926, proclaims himself prime minister. . . . German Labor Minister Dr. Adam Stegerwald announces his government will no longer award contracts to companies that have an "unsocial" attitude toward the current unemployment crisis.	Several hundred rebels are killed and 3,000 more are taken into custody as a revolt against King Nadir Shah of Afghanistan is successfully quelled.	Canada's Dominion Bureau of Statistics releases the results of its census, showing Canada's total population to be 9,934,500, with an increase of 137,700 in the past year.	
Aug. 2		During a session of the British Parliament, King George V of the United Kingdom, through a statement read by First Viscount John Sankey, expresses "profound satisfaction" with both the London Naval Conference and the evacuation of the demilitarized Rhineland by British soldiers.			In India, the ongoing nationalist boycott against British cloth causes the shutdown of six more cotton mills, increasing the nation's jobless by 15,000 people. . . . Changha, the capital of the Chinese Hunan province, is burned and looted by Communist agitators, forcing hundreds of foreigners to flee to warships bound for their native lands. As Communist hordes encroach the capital of Nanking, military officials declare martial law and institute a midnight curfew throughout the nation.
Aug. 3			Aviator Amy Johnson of Great Britain, who this spring became the first woman to successfully fly from Great Britain to Australia, is awarded by King Fuad of Egypt the "gold medal for merit." Johnson is the first woman to receive the award.		
Aug. 4	The British Imperial Government appropriates $1.6 million for road construction, water supplies, and health facilities for the British West Indies.	British economic officials report the Bank of England deposited £872,241 worth of gold last week, against £2,065,956 withdrawn, leaving a weekly deficit of £1,193,715.		Former president Adolfo Diaz of Nicaragua, during interviews with the local press, expresses confidence in the fairness of the upcoming national elections that will be overseen by U.S.-Nicaraguan National Board of Elections head Alfred W. Johnson, who was appointed by U.S. President Herbert Hoover.	
Aug. 5		Aviator Amy Johnson returns to England following an international tour. She is greeted by 50,000 Britons. . . . Former president Edouard Herriot of France submits a proposal to create a Chair of Peace at the University of Lyons. "The study of peace and its organization is one which should be taken up by all universities," he says. . . . Artillery shells are fired and church bells are rung in Brussels, Belgium, to commemorate the 16th anniversary of the failed invasion attempt by Germany during World War I. Similar remembrances are held throughout Europe, including a bank holiday in Great Britain.			
Aug. 6				Bolivia celebrates the 105th anniversary of the founding of its first republic and the gaining of independence from Spanish colonial rule.	Twelve people are killed and 150 more are injured after police fire into a crowd of hostile demonstrators in the northwestern Indian city of Sukkur.
Aug. 7				Edmond Baird Ryckman is chosen to replace William Daum Euler as the Canadian Minister of National Revenue. . . . Hugh Guthrie is chosen to succeed Esioff-Leon Patenaude as the Canadian Minister of Justice. . . . Thomas Gerow is chosen to replace Ian Alistair Mackenzie as the Canadian Minister of the Interior. . . . Charles Hazlitt Cahan is chosen to replace Fernand Rinfret as the Canadian Secretary of State.	Chinese military officials announce they are withdrawing troops from the city of Kanchow, where Communist insurgents have transformed it into an uninhabitable war zone.

A	B	C	D	E
Includes developments that affect more than one world region, international organizations, and important meetings of world leaders.	*Includes all domestic and regional developments in Europe, including the Soviet Union.*	*Includes all domestic and regional developments in Africa and the Middle East.*	*Includes all domestic and regional developments in Latin America, the Caribbean, and Canada.*	*Includes all domestic and regional developments in Asian and Pacific nations (and colonies).*

U.S. Politics & Social Issues	U.S. Foreign Policy & Defense	Economics & Great Depression	Science, Technology & Nature	Culture, Leisure & Lifestyle	
		The Bank of Belgium reduces its discount rate from 3 percent to 2.5 percent. . . . The Federal Reserve Bank of New York reports brokers' loans increased by $2 million as compared to last week, the smallest net increase or decline of any week of the year. The total amount of loans now stands at $3.2 billion, a decline of 45 percent from the total of August 1929. . . . Representatives of Germany's metal industry announce they will be dismissing 10 percent of their office workers as a means of increasing profit.			Aug. 1
	The Shipping Board receives bids of $193,774 and $139,055 from the Union Shipbuilding Company and the Iron and Metal Company of Baltimore respectively, for 18 obsolete steel cargo steamers.	*The Annalist* releases its weekly index of U.S. wholesale commodity prices. At 120.9, the index is 1.1 points lower than the previous week and shows a decline of 20 percent from the comparable week a year ago. . . . Traders on the New York Stock Exchange report new bond offerings for this week totaled $123,460,440, against $76,846,000 last week, an increase of 37 percent.			Aug. 2
Seven men in Atlanta, Ga., are charged with voluntary manslaughter and sentenced to 12–15 years for the murder of African-American college student Dennis Hubert.			Assistant Postmaster General W. Irving Glover announces that two new air mail routes will begin operation on August 22. The two routes will run from New York to Los Angeles and from Atlanta to Los Angeles respectively.	U.S. tourism officials report this summer was the highest on record for tourist travel, with approximately 3 million Americans visiting their country's national parks and an estimated 500,000 traveling to foreign countries.	Aug. 3
Six men are arrested in Atlanta, Ga., on charges of "insurrection" for distributing Communist literature. Sixty-two prominent members of the Atlanta community condemn the arrests in a statement, saying, "We believe the Communists should be protected in their Constitutional rights of free speech and free assemblage."		Prof. Irving Fisher's index of international commodity prices is released, showing a decrease of 0.4 points, from 83.3 a week ago to 82.9 currently.		Emilio Azcarraga Vidaurreta founds the radio station XEW in Mexico City, Mexico.	Aug. 4
		The U.S. Department of Commerce's weekly index of U.S. automobile production rises 1.5 points, from 37.9 last week to 39.4. Despite the rise, the index of 37.9 is still 67 percent below the corresponding index last year. . . . The New York Stock Exchange reports brokers' loans for the month of July totaled $3,689,482,287, the smallest amount for any month in three years. Blame for the decline is laid to a newly imposed harsh call money rate.		Eight-year-old Barbara Tompkins becomes the youngest known person to swim the entire length of the Bosporus, the 1.25-mile body of water that separates Europe from Asia.	Aug. 5
Upon his return from a West Coast aviation inspection tour, Assistant Commerce Secretary for Aeronautics Clarence H. Young pessimistically declares 1930 to be the world's worst year in commercial aviation history.		The American Railway Association's weekly index of U.S. freight car holdings falls to 85.1, a record all-time low. It is also a decline of 17 percent from the corresponding period in 1929. . . . *Dun's Review* publishes its monthly index of U.S. wholesale commodity prices, showing an average decline of 1.3 percent for each category of commodities listed.			Aug. 6
African Americans Abram Smith and Thomas Shipp, who were accused of murdering a white factory worker, are lynched in Marion, Ind. The incident led to the passage of an anti-lynching law by the Indiana state legislature.	The Navy Department formally considers eliminating expensive government-owned automobiles for admirals as a means of reducing the Navy's budget deficit.	The Mexican Federation of Transports and Communications recommends to President Ortiz Rubio that in order to improve the country's railroad system, pay cuts must me made for railroad executives, rather than laborers, as had been previously suggested. "Enormous sums of money, unwarranted and unearned, go to the directors of our national railways," a statement reads. "These are spent to the detriment of the loyal workers, whose wages are not sufficient to support even the most modest homes."	The U.S. Department of Commerce reports that in the first six months of 1930, 1,684 airplanes were produced, of which 1,325 were civilian planes, 359 were conscripted by the Army and Navy, and the rest were used exclusively in export trade.		Aug. 7

F	G	H	I	J
Includes elections, federal-state relations, civil rights and liberties, crime, the judiciary, education, healthcare, poverty, urban affairs, and population.	Includes formation and debate of U.S. foreign and defense policies, veterans affairs, and defense spending. (Relations with specific foreign countries are usually found under the region concerned.)	Includes business, labor, agriculture, taxation, transportation, consumer affairs, monetary and fiscal policy, natural resources, pollution, and accidents.	Includes worldwide scientific, medical, and technological developments, natural phenomena, U.S. weather, and natural disasters.	Includes the arts, religion, scholarship, communications media, sports, entertainment, fashions, fads, and social life.

	World Affairs	Europe	Africa & The Middle East	The Americas	Asia & The Pacific
Aug. 8			The British Royal Air Force bombs a makeshift military encampment housing 10,000 hostile Afghan tribesmen in the Indian city of Peshawar.	Liberal candidate Enrique Olaya Herrera is elected president of Colombia, ending a 20-year reign of Conservative rule.	The Australian Federal Loan Council, a group consisting of the top Australian banks, votes to pool its collective resources of $180 million together and deposit it in the Bank of England. . . . Australian officials estimate a reduction of $85 million to $120 million will be needed to balance the federal budget.
Aug. 9	French tourism officials report the amount spent by Americans visiting France in 1929 totaled $130 million, a decrease of 20 percent from the previous year. In spite of this, they say, American tourism in Great Britain, Germany, Italy, and Austria has increased.	Carrying the headline, "We Will Not Allow the Ways of the Bourgeois American in the U.S.S.R," the Russian newspaper *Trood* reports that "a reactionary group among the 300 American engineers and mechanics employed in the tractor plant beat up a Negro and threw him out of the common mess hall for the unique reason that he is a Negro." Tractor workers at the plant hold a mass meeting and adopt a resolution "to remind those of our comrades who do not understand that the U.S.S.R. is the fatherland of all workers, including negroes."		Conservative Party leader Richard Bedford Bennett is elected prime minister of Canada, receiving 47.79 percent of the popular vote. Bennett succeeds William Lyon Mackenzie King, whose first term as president began on December 29, 1921.	Legislators of the Southeast Asian country of Burma announce the creation of an army, navy, and air force to be instituted following the separation of Burma from India. Officials say the army will "gladly fight on Britain's side."
Aug. 10		In order to stimulate industry, Great Britain creates two new offices, the Securities Management Trust and the Bankers' Industrial Development Company, whose job it will be to "assist manufacturing firms with advice and guidance." Both of these companies will start with approximately £5 million worth of capital.		The military junta led by General Carlos Blanco Galindo that overtook Bolivia earlier this summer announces the first step toward a return to a constitutional government. According to the announcement, a presidential election will be held on January 5, 1931, with a congressional election scheduled for the next day.	
Aug. 11	A U.S. banking group headed by A.G. Becker & Co. extends a loan to the German Building and Land Bank worth 25 million reichsmarks. The loan will be used in Germany's housing improvement program for 1931.	The All-Union Society of Militant Atheists announces the construction of an anti-religious university to be built in the worldwide Communist capital of Moscow. The university is expected to provide facilities for over 400 students.		The United States Commercial Attaché in Argentina reports exports to the United States for June amounted to $4,109,000, less than 50 percent of the total for June 1929.	Six troops of the British Imperial Army are killed in a raid against a group of hostile Afghan militiamen situated on the India-Afghanistan border.
Aug. 12					
Aug. 13				The city of Princeza, which for the past six months has been a stronghold of rebel activity, is attacked and seized by 1,500 Brazilian federal troops. Casualties are reported to be small.	

A	B	C	D	E
Includes developments that affect more than one world region, international organizations, and important meetings of world leaders.	*Includes all domestic and regional developments in Europe, including the Soviet Union.*	*Includes all domestic and regional developments in Africa and the Middle East.*	*Includes all domestic and regional developments in Latin America, the Caribbean, and Canada.*	*Includes all domestic and regional developments in Asian and Pacific nations (and colonies).*

U.S. Politics & Social Issues	U.S. Foreign Policy & Defense	Economics & Great Depression	Science, Technology & Nature	Culture, Leisure & Lifestyle	
The aeronautics branch of the Department of Commerce releases a survey showing that there are currently 13,041 licensed pilots operating 9,773 aircraft in the United States, along with 8,842 registered mechanics. Only 2 percent of the total pilots surveyed were women.		*The Annalist* index of weekly U.S. wholesale commodity prices is released. At 122.2, the figure is a rise of 1.4 points from the previous week.... General Motors president Alfred P. Sloan reports that his company's assets currently total $1,324,889,764, an all-time high.... The San Francisco Federal Reserve Bank lowers its rediscount rate from 4 percent to 3.5 percent. It is the first reduction in six months.			Aug. 8
			According to statistics published by the Metropolitan Life Insurance Company, deaths related to appendicitis have increased by approximately 15 percent since 1925, with a near 100 percent increase for children under five. Medical officials say the cause for the increase is "abuse of laxatives and mineral oils."	At the international shooting competition in Antwerp, Belgium, the U.S. team breaks the world's rifle competition record by scoring 1,910 points. The previous record, set by another U.S. team in Rheims, France, in 1924, was 1,906 points.	Aug. 9
			Fritz Morzik wins the International Tourist Aircraft Contest in Berlin, Germany.	The Bank of United States baseball team wins the 1930 Bankers Athletic League championship by defeating the Chatham Phenix team 12–5. The team finished the regular season with 25 wins and only 2 losses.	Aug. 10
Baptist ministers in the United States call for the deportation of Communists, whose ideological beliefs of atheism contrast with Christianity.				Betty Boop, the first famous female cartoon character, premiers in the animated motion picture *Dizzy Dishes*.	Aug. 11
Assistant Postmaster General W. Irving Glover announces that total air mail for July amounted to 695,627 pounds, an increase of 12,067 pounds from June. Glover says there are 24 air routes currently being operated within the United States.	The War and Navy departments formally disagree over which department should have aerial defense control of the Panama Canal Zone and the Pearl Harbor military base in Hawaii. President Herbert Hoover is called upon to personally resolve the matter.... The Navy Department places the steamship *American Farmer* on drydock in Southampton, England, following an incident yesterday in which the *American Farmer* collided with the German *Liechtenstein* steamship in the English Channel.	Due to the resumption of production at the Ford Motor Company, the U.S. Department of Commerce's weekly index of U.S. automobile production increases sharply to 73.0 from 39.4 last week, a rise of 46 percent, the largest of the year. Despite the increase, the current index is still 42 percent below the corresponding week the year prior.... U.S. economic officials report their country's total export trade to Argentina for June amounted to $12,066,000, nearly 50 percent less than the corresponding period a year ago.			Aug. 12
Assistant Postmaster General W. Irving Glover announces the implantation of fireproof mailbags, which he says will eliminate the Post Office's 0.0063 fire loss rate.	Attorney General William Mitchell authors a letter to Navy Secretary Francis Adams, in which a recommendation is made to settle the Army-Navy dispute over control of coastal aerial defense. "Hereafter the Army Air Service shall control all aerial operations from land bases, and Navy aviation shall control all aerial operations attached to a fleet," Mitchell recommends. Adams responds by saying the proposal is unconstitutional, as it limits the president's power as commander-in-chief.... President Herbert Hoover commissions the Efficiency Bureau to settle the Army-Navy dispute over aerial defense control.	The American Railway Association's weekly index of U.S. freight car loadings falls to 84.2, 0.9 points behind the record low of 85.1 established the week prior.			Aug. 13

F
Includes elections, federal-state relations, civil rights and liberties, crime, the judiciary, education, healthcare, poverty, urban affairs, and population.

G
Includes formation and debate of U.S. foreign and defense policies, veterans affairs, and defense spending. (Relations with specific foreign countries are usually found under the region concerned.)

H
Includes business, labor, agriculture, taxation, transportation, consumer affairs, monetary and fiscal policy, natural resources, pollution, and accidents.

I
Includes worldwide scientific, medical, and technological developments, natural phenomena, U.S. weather, and natural disasters.

J
Includes the arts, religion, scholarship, communications media, sports, entertainment, fashions, fads, and social life.

	World Affairs	Europe	Africa & The Middle East	The Americas	Asia & The Pacific
Aug. 14		The Permanent Court of International Justice in Geneva, Switzerland, releases a list of 15 potential nominees to replace Charles Evans Hughes, who became Chief Justice of the U.S. Supreme Court following his resignation as the judge of the Court of Arbitration.	Turkey sends thousands of troops to Iran to help quell Kurdish insurgencies.		
Aug. 15		In Budapest, Romania, anti-Semitic leader Celea Cordreanu is acquitted of leading a militant group to assassinate Secretary of State Constantin Angelescu. . . . Newspapers in Budapest, Romania, speculate on the mysterious location of Premier Count Bethelen, whose failure to appear before Congress earlier this week sparked a wave of confusion, with newspapers printing headlines reading, "Europe's disappearing Premier."			
Aug. 16		In Germany, Berlin Sturm Abteilung (Storm Trooper Department) commander Walter Stennes calls for a general strike against the Nazi Party; Stennes fears that the Nazi Party is attempting to take over the organization.	In Jerusalem, the extremist Arabic newspaper *Al Hayat* is indefinitely suspended following the publication of a speech by Arab leader Zaki Pasha in which he states that Arab murderers of Jews were heroes "before whom the Arabs should bow down."	Dominican Republic dictator Rafael Trujillo Molina, who seized power in March, proclaims himself president.. . . . Abelardo Pachecho, editor of the Cuban nationalist, anti-government newspaper *Voice of the People*, is killed by 10 assassin's bullets while walking the streets of Havana. Pachecho's newspaper had been extremely critical of President Gerardo Machado in recent weeks, branding him El Gallo (The Rooster.)	
Aug. 17		Emile Vandervelde, leader of the Second International socialist movement, arrives in Soviet Russia for a "personal visit." . . . The fifth congress of the Profintern, or the Revolutionary International Union of Workers, which claims membership of more than 17 million people, is held in Moscow, Russia.	Turkish military officials report there are currently 50,000 soldiers amassed along the Turko-Persia border to quell invading Kurdish troops. . . . The British Postal Workers' Union votes to bar women from working as telephone operators. In response, Postmaster General Hastings Bertrand Lees-Smith releases a study showing that women operate telephone switchboards approximately 5 seconds faster than men.		Chinese military officials report the confiscation of 30,000 rifles from Northern rebels operating in the city of Tsinan, which was recaptured from the rebels earlier this week. The officials also announce the Shantung provincial government will be moved from Tsing-tao to Tsinan.
Aug. 18	League of Nations officials discuss the possible reinstatement of Costa Rica, which was admitted as a member in 1920 but expelled from the League in 1927 for failure to pay annual dues.	With Germany still reeling from the Lufthansa seaplane incident two months ago, in which five people were killed, the Minister of Transportation officially recommends that a special maritime aviation court be created.	President Mustapha Kemal of Turkey announces a penalty will be imposed on printers who publish their documents in the standard 482-letter Turkish Arabic alphabet, instead of the newly created 29-letter Latin alphabet, which was created to help promote easier reading in a country with an approximately 75 percent illiteracy rate. . . . British military officials report that after weeks of heavy bombing, the invading Afghan tribesmen on the border between Afghanistan and India are now in full retreat.	In an interview with the Associated Press, President Gerardo Machado of Cuba asks for U.S. intervention in the ongoing Cuban political crisis. In response, the Nationalist Union of Cuba issues a proclamation denying the need for the United States to intervene.	
Aug. 19		The Czechoslovak Land Reform Office purchases 323,770 acres of arable land from the Prince of Lichtenstein for a sum of approximately $50 million.			Six American missionaries in China face grave peril as Communist hordes seize their respective cities.

A	B	C	D	E
Includes developments that affect more than one world region, international organizations, and important meetings of world leaders.	Includes all domestic and regional developments in Europe, including the Soviet Union.	Includes all domestic and regional developments in Africa and the Middle East.	Includes all domestic and regional developments in Latin America, the Caribbean, and Canada.	Includes all domestic and regional developments in Asian and Pacific nations (and colonies).

U.S. Politics & Social Issues	U.S. Foreign Policy & Defense	Economics & Great Depression	Science, Technology & Nature	Culture, Leisure & Lifestyle	
New York City Fire Department commissioner Dorman releases a report showing that there were 29,723 fires in the city in 1929, an increase of 13 percent from the previous year. Dorman says the figures indicate 1929 was the worst year on record for New York City in terms of fires. . . . The National Conference of Commissioners on Uniform State Laws recommends to various state legislatures the updating of child labor laws to prohibit children under 14 from being employed unless school requirements are upheld.					Aug. 14
Governor Fred Green of Michigan asks Governor Franklin Roosevelt of New York to extradite Theodore Pizzino, who gunned down pro-Prohibition radio commentator Jerry Buckley in Detroit, Mich., on July 23. Police say Buckley's murder is undoubtedly crime related. . . . The New York City Board of Education votes to increase its budget to $141,296,636 for 1931, the largest school budget in the history of the city.	Gen. Colden L.H. Ruggles, aassistant chief of ordinance in the War Department, announces his retirement effective August 23.	The Annalist lists its weekly index of U.S. wholesale commodity prices at 121.6, a decline of 0.6 points from the previous week and 18 percent from the corresponding week the previous year. . . . A coal mine in the Soviet city of Ural reports that in the first five days of August, there were 3,000 instances of "improper absences from work, mostly owing to drunkenness." The mine's total work force is 5,000 men.		The Right Hon. R.G. Sharman-Crawford is chosen as Great Britain's representative in the upcoming America's Cup international sailing competition.	Aug. 15
U.S. immigration officials begin proceedings on a woman who claims to be Grand Duchess Anastasia Tchaikovsky of Russia, the surviving daughter of the deposed Czar Nicolas II. Officials say she must prove she resided in the country since 1928 to obtain legal residence. The woman would later be exposed as a fraud after failing to convince handwriting experts and refusing to submit to a blood test. However, upon her death, many newspapers would print obituaries authenticating her claim.		The Statistics Bureau of the Argentine Ministry of Finance reports export revenue for the first seven months of this year totaled 393,046,000 gold pesos, 35 percent less than the first seven months of 1929.	Capt. Frank M. Hawks breaks the world's transcontinental aerial speed record by flying over 2,500 miles in 12 hours, 25 minutes, and 3 seconds. The record was previously held by Charles Lindbergh, who flew the same course in 14 hours and 45 minutes.		Aug. 16
		British economic officials report total exports have declined by 16.3 percent and imports by 10.2 percent in the first seven months of 1930. . . . Dun's Review reports bank clearings for this week totaled $8,286,650,000, less than 34 percent of the corresponding week of 1929. . . . Representatives of the New York Stock Exchange report new bond offerings for this week amounted to $33,514,000, less than half of last week's sum and the smallest weekly total of the year to date. . . . The New York Stock Exchange reports there are currently 1,661 branch offices operated by Exchange members, a new high record.		The British Empire Games commence in Hamilton, Ontario. There are 350 athletes registered, representing England, Scotland, Ireland, Newfoundland, Bermuda, British Guiana, New Zealand, South Africa, Australia, and Canada.	Aug. 17
A survey of U.S. tobacco manufacturers indicates U.S. tobacco sales will exceed last year's record-breaking total of 127.4 billion total cigarettes sold. The survey also shows the profit of major U.S. tobacco companies has nearly doubled over the past two years. . . . The Women's Christian Temperance Union releases a statement estimating 105 of the United States' 148 alcoholic detoxification hospitals have been forced to close their doors due to Prohibition laws.		British economists report the Bank of England's gold deposits amounted to £1,185,038 this week, against £115,667 in withdrawals, a surplus of £1,069,371. . . . British economic officials report exports for July fell 23.7 percent below the total for July 1929. Imports decreased 7.9 percent. . . . Prof. Fisher releases his index of international commodity prices. At 83.8, the figure is an increase of 0.7 points from last week's index, but still 7 percent below the highest total of the year.		Ub Iwerks finishes production on the first color sound cartoon ever created, called Fiddlesticks.	Aug. 18
The Baltimore & Ohio Railroad Company announces it is temporarily suspending without pay approximately 5,000 workers until September 2 as a means of improving company capital.		The U.S. Department of Commerce's weekly index of U.S. automobile production shows an increase of 5 points, from 73.0 to 78.0, during the week. The current index is still 47 points below the week last year . . . The price of cotton in the United States decreases by half a cent in both domestic and foreign markets.	The Atlantic Broadcasting Corporation seeks a permit to construct a 50,000-watt transmitting station in Wayne, N.J. In hearings, Assistant Attorney General Duane Minard tells company representatives that the people of New Jersey "want to hear their own stations, without your invasion." Emerson Richards, counsel for Atlantic Broadcasting Company, calls Minard's language "ridiculous."	Gooose Goslin of the St. Louis Browns becomes only the fourth player in Major League Baseball history to hit three home runs over two consecutive innings.	Aug. 19

F
Includes elections, federal-state relations, civil rights and liberties, crime, the judiciary, education, healthcare, poverty, urban affairs, and population.

G
Includes formation and debate of U.S. foreign and defense policies, veterans affairs, and defense spending. (Relations with specific foreign countries are usually found under the region concerned.)

H
Includes business, labor, agriculture, taxation, transportation, consumer affairs, monetary and fiscal policy, natural resources, pollution, and accidents.

I
Includes worldwide scientific, medical, and technological developments, natural phenomena, U.S. weather, and natural disasters.

J
Includes the arts, religion, scholarship, communications media, sports, entertainment, fashions, fads, and social life.

	World Affairs	Europe	Africa & The Middle East	The Americas	Asia & The Pacific
Aug. 20			An expedition headed by Jewish archaeologist Isaac Benzvi discovers the remains of a 1,400-year-old hospice in Upper Galilee, Jerusalem.	The Canadian federal government in Ottowa, Ontario, debates banning the importation of all cars produced outside Canada. American auto manufacturers estimate the proposed ban will result in the loss of $40 million annually.	
Aug. 21	In an interview, Yugoslav Foreign Minister M. Marinkovitch threatens that unless action is taken by the League of Nations against Macedonian terrorists in bordering Bulgaria, military troops will be committed.	Amidst heavy internal criticism, Premier Heinrich Held of Bavaria officially resigns following an incident in which opponents say he abused his power. After a cattle slaughtering tax bill was defeated in the Bavarian parliament, Held invoked an article in his country's constitution allowing a head of state to overturn a parliamentary veto.		President Jose Maria Moncada Tapia of Nicaragua declares a general amnesty for all those who committed "political" offenses on or after January 1. While the number of political prisoners is few, the move is seen as a reaffirmation of President Tapia's desire to hold a free and fair election.	
Aug. 22	The United States nominates former Secretary of State Frank B. Kellogg to fill the vacancy on the Permanent Court of International Justice. Kellogg is noted as a peaceful negotiator, having successfully brokered a political alliance with France during his term as Secretary of State in 1928.			The Bank of Chile raises its rediscount rate by 1 percent, from 6 to 7 percent. . . . The exchange rate of the Argentine milreis falls to its lowest value in nearly seven years, approximately 10 percent as valuable as one U.S. dollar. President Washington Luis calls a conference with his Finance Secretary and the president of the national bank.	An emergency session of Australia's federal financial authorities concludes a reduction of $150 million must be made from the federal budget to solve an ongoing financial crisis.
Aug. 23				U.S. Treasury Secretary Andrew Mellon announces an agreement has been reached with Cuban cigar manufacturers, allowing them to prepay the customs duty through a special representative in Florida. . . . The military junta controlling Bolivia announces the nomination of an unopposed presidential ticket for the upcoming national elections. The nominated president, Daniel Salamanca Urey, will eventually be deposed in a coup in 1934.	
Aug. 24				The Canadian Dominion Treasury estimates it is costing Canada approximately $12 million annually to cut off illegal liquor exports to the United States. . . . The U.S. Bureau of Statistics reports that since the construction of the Panama Canal in 1914, over 60,133 commercial vessels have passed through it, providing 279,338,333 long tons of cargo. Over the 16 years, $250,660,068 in tolls has been collected.	
Aug. 25					Experiencing bronchial trouble, President James Scullin of Australia says he doubts he will be able to attend tomorrow's Imperial Conference. . . . President Chiang Kai-shek of China announces rewards worth up to $1 million will be made to militant citizens who recapture the northern cities of Kiafeng, Chenchow, or Honanfu from Communist rebels.
Aug. 26	The report of the League of Nations Mandates Committee is released. In it, the committee places blame for the Wailing Wall riots last August, which killed several people, on an inadequate number of British police and military forces in Palestine.	A meeting of farmers in Finland passes a resolution barring all Communist agricultural laborers. The resolution has yet to receive official backing from the Finnish government. . . . British naval officials announce the destroyer ships *Crusader* and *Comet*, as well as the mining ship *Nightingale*, will be "laid down" on September 12 at the dockyard in Portsmouth, England.		The Brazilian Federal Congress in Rio de Janeiro passes a resolution charging President Washington Luis with violating states' rights for the sending of troops to the state of Paraíba last month to quell local disturbances.	The Hong Kong government in China purchases 15 million ounces of pure silver from the Indian government. International economic experts say the purchase will adversely affect the price of silver around the globe.

A	B	C	D	E
Includes developments that affect more than one world region, international organizations, and important meetings of world leaders.	Includes all domestic and regional developments in Europe, including the Soviet Union.	Includes all domestic and regional developments in Africa and the Middle East.	Includes all domestic and regional developments in Latin America, the Caribbean, and Canada.	Includes all domestic and regional developments in Asian and Pacific nations (and colonies).

U.S. Politics & Social Issues	U.S. Foreign Policy & Defense	Economics & Great Depression	Science, Technology & Nature	Culture, Leisure & Lifestyle	
The Actuarial Society of America releases the results of a study conducted from January 1927 to March 1930. The study found that the death rate for air passengers was 1 in 5,000, and that this death rate decreases by 63 percent when the passengers' pilot has had 400 or more hours of experience. Additionally, it was discovered that travel by railroad is 200 times safer than travel by air.		The American Railway Association's index of U.S. freight car loadings continues to fall despite record lows established in two consecutive weeks. At 83.8, the index is a decline of 0.4 points from the previous week and 17 percent from the corresponding 1929 period. . . . Assistant Secretary of Commerce for Aeronautics Clarence M. Young reports that professional air pilots receive an average monthly salary of $550.	The U.S. Census Bureau reports that the total value of aircraft production for 1929 amounted to $61,973,079, an increase of 129 percent from the total of 1927, the last year the census was taken. Additionally, there were 5,130 airplanes produced in 1929.	Noted French poet and playwright Andre Rivoire dies in his home in Paris, France, at the age of 58. His last play, Pardon, Madame, was produced in Paris earlier this spring.	Aug. 20
Pittsburgh Airways, United States Airways, Southwest Air Fast Express, and the Ohio Transport Company merge in a $4 million deal to form the United Aviation Company. . . . New York City legislators announce a bill will be put forth to the state legislature this winter that would institute a city-wide annual minimum wage of $2,500.		British railway officials estimate that by the end of the year, total railroad earnings will be approximately $25 million less than the previous year.		In Prague, Czechoslovakia, 15,000 spectators witness the first appearance of professional U.S. soccer players in Europe, as the Fall River, Mass., team draws with the Prague Slavia team, 2–2.	Aug. 21
Pan American Airways purchases the New York, Rio, and Buenos Aires Airlines for a sum of $4 million. The purchase makes Pan American the world's largest airline, with an estimated 100,000 miles flown weekly between the United States and every nation in Central and South America.		According to The Annalist Weekly, U.S. wholesale commodity prices increased this week, with an increase of 1.3 points in the publication's weekly index. . . . The U.S. Census Bureau reports the cotton spinning industry operated at only 67.4 percent of its capacity during the month of July, compared with 100.2 percent capacity in July 1929, a decrease of 33 percent.			Aug. 22
Police in Boston, Mass., raid a public meeting of the International Labor Defense Committee, arresting three officials and dispersing a crowd of 5,000 people. The meeting was held to memorialize anarchists Nicola Sacco and Bartolomeo Vanzetti, who were executed in Boston three years ago.				The SS Morro Castle, one of the largest luxury cruise ships ever built, embarks on its maiden voyage. . . . Australia wins the international cricket championship, defeating Great Britain in the last of a series of five matches.	Aug. 23
The Standard Oil Company of Indiana, along with 45 other oil companies, files an appeal in the Supreme Court for a case which found them guilty of violating the Sherman Anti-Trust Act. . . . The New York City Department of Water Supply, Gas, and Electricity reports that in 1929, residents consumed a record 319 billion gallons of water, an average of nearly 100 million gallons per day. New Yorkers consumed more than 17 billion gallons over the previous year.		In sessions of the Canadian House of Commons, legislators suggest barring the importation of Russian coal produced by convict labor, the low price of which has been hurting Canada's domestic coal industry.	Construction begins on the world's longest natural gas pipeline, a 1,000-mile-long system between Texas and Chicago that will cost $100 million. The pipeline is estimated to weigh approximately 210,000 tons.		Aug. 24
Republican National Congressional Committee chairman Will R. Wood releases a statement accusing Democratic National Committee Chairman John J. Raskob of hiring a professional journalist "at a large salary to develop misrepresentations of the President in an attempt to systematically undermine his influence to do service."		During the present week, the Bank of England's gold reserves increased by £544,877, with £599,855 in deposits and only £54,978 in withdrawals.	Eddie August Schneider, age 18, sets the world's transcontinental air speed record for pilots younger than 21, completing the trip from Westfield, N.J., to Los Angeles, Calif., in 27 hours and 19 minutes.	Philosopher Addison Webster Moore, who was former president of the American Philosophical Assocation, dies at the age of 64. . . . Officials of the Chicago Cubs baseball team report that the recently completed series against the New York Giants was seen by 178,000 people, the largest audience for a four-game series in major league baseball history. . . . C.S. Jones wins the 50-mile cabin plane race at the National Air Races in Chicago, Ill.	Aug. 25
		The U.S. Department of Commerce's weekly index of U.S. automobile production remains relatively unchanged from the previous week, from 77.5 to 78 currently.		Gladys O'Donnell wins the women's Class A Pacific Air Derby by completing the designated course in 15 hours, 13 minutes, and 16 seconds.	Aug. 26

F	G	H	I	J
Includes elections, federal-state relations, civil rights and liberties, crime, the judiciary, education, healthcare, poverty, urban affairs, and population.	Includes formation and debate of U.S. foreign and defense policies, veterans affairs, and defense spending. (Relations with specific foreign countries are usually found under the region concerned.)	Includes business, labor, agriculture, taxation, transportation, consumer affairs, monetary and fiscal policy, natural resources, pollution, and accidents.	Includes worldwide scientific, medical, and technological developments, natural phenomena, U.S. weather, and natural disasters.	Includes the arts, religion, scholarship, communications media, sports, entertainment, fashions, fads, and social life.

	World Affairs	Europe	Africa & The Middle East	The Americas	Asia & The Pacific
Aug. 27			An expedition headed by Dr. Melvin Grove Kyle of the American School of Jerusalem Oriental Research unearths a 3,000-year-old statue of a lion in the Tell Belt Mirsim. Kyle says the statue will be put on display at the Palestine Museum.	In Cuba, Mario Reyes and Salustiano Sarrillo are arrested after agents discover letters in their possession written by leaders in Moscow instructing them on how to conduct propaganda operations. The letters indicate the Communist international leadership seeks to dominate foreign government departments.	Communist hordes seize the Chinese city of Yuayang, razing 9,500 houses to the ground and massacring over 15,000 inhabitants. . . . Northern Chinese forces celebrate the recapturing of the city of Taianfu from Communist rebels.
Aug. 28		In the tiny Scottish island of St. Kilda, where the infant mortality rate is estimated at 80 percent, 36 inhabitants flee to the Scottish mainland, leaving the island virtually uninhabited. . . . Police in Budapest, Hungary, ban the upcoming Socialist unemployment protest on September 1, after the newspaper *Nepszava* recommends violent agitation for the protest's participants.			
Aug. 29	Ireland agrees to enter into the Geneva Protocol, an international treaty banning the use of "asphyxiating gas, or any other kind of gas, liquids, substances or similar materials" that was first signed in 1925.	The Spanish Ambassador to Argentina informs the Argentine government that Spain is lifting its embargo on imported corn produced in Argentina as a means of improving commercial relations between the two countries. The maneuver is expected to undoubtedly improve Argentina's corn export revenue, which is currently 21 percent below the level of 1929.		In Peru, Luis Miguel Sanchez Cerro is chosen as the new president following a coup that ousted the dictator Augusto B. Leguia, who had reigned for 11 years. . . . The Argentine Ministry of Agriculture announces that 34,504,550 acres of grain were sown this spring, an increase of 1,363,150, or 4 percent, from the spring of 1929.	
Aug. 30	U.S. Ambassador to Peru Fred M. Dearing travels to Peru to meet with President Luis Miguel Sanchez Cerro, who recently overthrew the 11-year dictatorship of Augusto B. Leguia. . . . Representatives of the League of Nations express doubt over French Foreign Minister Aristide Briand's United Europe proposal, which will be publicly presented when the League of Nations convenes on September 10.			In Brazil, the newspaper *Correio da Manha* publishes an article blaming the present currency crisis on capitalists. "The exchange rate crisis has been precipitated by a group of capitalists of Sao Paulo, who are selling short and already have made approximately $200,000."	
Aug. 31		Berlin police officials announce that beginning soon, taxi-cab operators will be forced to take an exam in order to receive their license. Also, taxi-cab drivers are advised to "keep smiling" to help promote tourism. . . The Portuguese government bans sidewalk cafes.		Martha Louis Lane Morlote is arrested in Havana, Cuba, on charges of spying and conspiracy. Authorities claim Morlote is guilty of attempting to sell to the United States the secret code of the Cuban Flying Corps. While imprisoned, Morlote steadfastly maintains her innocence.	
Sept. 1	Chancellor Heinrich Bruening of Germany assures his citizenry in a campaign speech that their government's foreign policy will remain peaceful. "No responsible German statesman would dream of involving the German people in a foreign adventure of any sort." Bruening's remarks come after Gottfried Treviranus, minister for occupied areas, publicly recommended a military campaign to the Polish Corridor.	In Germany, Magda Behrend, future wife to Nazi Propaganda Minister Joseph Goebbels, officially joins the National Socialist German Workers' Party. . . . Kurt Meyer, who would become the youngest divisional commander in World War II and a recipient of the highest military honor of the Third Reich, officially joins the National Socialist German Workers' Party. . . . Police in Warsaw, Poland, conduct raids on the homes of 16 suspected Communists, seizing large amounts of propaganda.			Thousands of followers of Mohandas Gandhi in Maidan Esplanade, India, witness Congress War Council presidential nominee Kamdar hoist the Indian national flag in a demonstration against British imperialism. The British chief magistrate warns that if the demonstration is held near infantry regiments, troops will most likely be forced to engage.
	A Includes developments that affect more than one world region, international organizations, and important meetings of world leaders.	**B** Includes all domestic and regional developments in Europe, including the Soviet Union.	**C** Includes all domestic and regional developments in Africa and the Middle East.	**D** Includes all domestic and regional developments in Latin America, the Caribbean, and Canada.	**E** Includes all domestic and regional developments in Asian and Pacific nations (and colonies).

U.S. Politics & Social Issues	U.S. Foreign Policy & Defense	Economics & Great Depression	Science, Technology & Nature	Culture, Leisure & Lifestyle	
The Federal Farm Board announces it will furnish cash for needy farmers affected by the summer's dry spell. . . . Senator Cole L. Blease wins the South Carolina senatorial democratic primary, garnering 10,000 more votes than his contender, Congressional Representative James F. Byrnes. . . . Officials of Sing Sing Prison in Ossining, N.Y., estimate that 55 percent of all parole nominees are granted parole every month.		The American Railway Association's weekly index of U.S. freight car loadings finally experiences an upswing of 0.3 points, from 83.8 to 84.1, after three consecutive weeks of record lows. . . . The New York Stock Exchange announces the Pure Oil Company and the Lago Oil and Transport Corporation have been stricken from the trading. Additionally, the General Italian Edison Electric Corporation and the American and Foreign Power Company are both officially admitted to the Exchange.			Aug. 27
Englishman Lewis Levin files a suit in the Supreme Court against the Fox Film Corporation, who he alleges failed to pay $100,765 in performed services when Levin was the company's English manager. . . . New York City Police Commissioner Edward Mulrooney requests $4.5 million in addition to the $60 million already reserved for next year's city police budget. Mulrooney says the money will be used to open five new station houses and to hire 1,000 more employees.				The 39th annual national baby parade in Asbury Park, N.J., attracts 200,000 spectators, who witness 6-year-old Gloria Matthews of Lakewood, N.J., being crowned for the third time as "Little Miss America." The prize of the title is $500.	Aug. 28
		The Annalist releases its weekly index of U.S. wholesale commodity prices. Due to sharp rises in the price of livestock meats and foodstuffs, the index saw an upturn of 1.5 points, from 122.9 to 124.6. Despite this, the current index is still 16 lower than the corresponding week last year. . . . The U.S. Tariff Commission debates whether seven commodities are able to be taxed. These commodities include wood furniture, bells, laces, hides and skins, sugar candy, matches, and refined sugar. . . . The Amalgamated Silk Corporation files for bankruptcy with an estimated debt of $5 million.	Norwegian whalers discover the remains of Solomon August Andree, a Swedish engineer who in 1897 attempted to reach the North Pole in a hot air hydrogen balloon.		Aug. 29
Roy D. Young announces his resignation from the post of chairman of the Federal Reserve Board.	The cruiser USS *West Virginia*, struck from the Naval Vessel Register since March 12, is sold in accordance with the London Naval Treaty.	Argentina pays back $1 million of its recently negotiated New York loan of $90 million. . . . American economic officials report bank clearings this week totaled $7,208,603,000, less than 36.4 percent of the comparable period a year ago. . . . New bond offerings on the New York Stock Exchange this week totaled $72,552,000, twice more than last week's total, $31,680,500, which was the smallest for any week of the year to date.		Tollien Schuurman of the Netherlands sets the women's world record for the 100-meter dash, beating the previous record by 0.1 seconds. . . . Representatives of U.S. motion picture corporations agree to cease selling American-made films to New Zealand, who recently imposed a 25 percent tax on all imported films.	Aug. 30
A small, privately owned biplane is stolen from the Roosevelt Airfield in New York. It is the first time a plane has been stolen from the location.		The U.S. Department of Commerce releases its weekly index of U.S. business activity. At 88.0 the figure is a rise of 0.4 points from the previous week and a decline of 16 percent from the corresponding period of last year's index of 105.4. . . . New securities on the New York Stock Exchange for the month of August totaled $236,250,000, the smallest total for any month of 1930 so far, according to economic experts. The figure is also 57 percent lower than the new securities total for August 1929.			Aug. 31
In Malines, Belgium, 200,000 people attend the National Belgian Eucharistic Congress.	The Puget Sound Naval Shipyard in Bremerton, Wash., completes construction of the heavy cruisers *Astoria* and *Louisville*. The *Astoria* will eventually be sunk by the Japanese during World War II on August 19, 1942.	The U.S. Department of Commerce reports that retail sales declined by 6.7 percent in the first six months of 1930 as compared to the first six months of 1929. . . . British economic officials report the Bank of England experienced a deficit in deposits of £177,038 during the week ended August 30.		Dr. Christian Schreiber is installed as Bishop of Germany. Schreiber is the first Catholic Bishop to occupy the post since Mathias van Jagow in 1544.	Sept. 1

F	G	H	I	J
Includes elections, federal-state relations, civil rights and liberties, crime, the judiciary, education, healthcare, poverty, urban affairs, and population.	Includes formation and debate of U.S. foreign and defense policies, veterans affairs, and defense spending. (Relations with specific foreign countries are usually found under the region concerned.)	Includes business, labor, agriculture, taxation, transportation, consumer affairs, monetary and fiscal policy, natural resources, pollution, and accidents.	Includes worldwide scientific, medical, and technological developments, natural phenomena, U.S. weather, and natural disasters.	Includes the arts, religion, scholarship, communications media, sports, entertainment, fashions, fads, and social life.

	World Affairs	Europe	Africa & The Middle East	The Americas	Asia & The Pacific
Sept. 2				Delegates of the Panamanian National Assembly convene for the opening session. For the first time in history, the opening message is spoken by the President himself.	
Sept. 3				Conservative Senator Pierre Édouard Blondin becomes the new Speaker of the Canadian Senate. Blondin replaces liberal Senator Arthur Charles Hardy, whose party lost its majority in this year's national elections. . . . U.S. Ambassador to Europe E.V. Morgan embarks from Brazil en route to Europe. Morgan will return in time for the presidential inauguration in November. . . . The military junta of President Sanchez Cerro of Peru issues a decree officially banning gambling. Gambling in Peru had been prohibited since 1920, except in 1929 when now deposed President Leguia lifted the ban.	
Sept. 4	Alfredo Lopez Pietro, Argentine Consul General to Turkey, dies from a self-inflicted gunshot wound.			Martha Lane Morlote, who on August 31 was arrested by Cuban authorities for suspicion of leaking secret codes of the Cuban Flying Corps, is released from prison. Cuban army private Luis Marti had confessed to the crime, which cleared Morlote of any wrongdoing.	President Chiang Kai-shek of China announces that an army consisting of approximately 500,000 men will attack the Northern rebel stronghold in the city of Tientsin.
Sept. 5	Andre Bouzet, French Consul to New York City for the past eight years, dies of pneumonia at the age of 57. . . . The League of Nations Assembly debates the solution to the problem of 40,000 Armenian refugees situated in Greece. One proposal is to evacuate all the Armenians to an isolated location, possibly residences in the Caucasus Mountains.			In Argentina, two die and 30 are injured as the police clash with over 2,000 student protestors.	
Sept. 6	Fred M. Dearing, U.S. Ambassador to Peru, arrives in the capital of Lima for an official state visit. . . . Representing 26 different nations, 400 delegates arrive in Budapest, Hungary, to participate in the opening of the International Congress of Architects.			A military coup occurs in Argentina as second-term president Juan Hipolito Yrigoyen is overthrown. General Jose Felix Uriburu, son of former Argentine president Jose Evaristo Uriburu, proclaims himself president. Uriburu chooses Enrique Santamarina as his new vice president.	
Sept. 7		Albert Axel Marie Gustave, who would reign as King of Belgium from 1951 until his death in 1993, is born in Kasteel Stuyvenberg, Laeken, Belgium as the eldest son of King Leopold III. . . . The cabinet of the French government officially approves Foreign Minister Aristide Briand's proposal to creature a United European federation. Briand will present the proposal to delegates at the League of Nations in the coming week.		Olegario Dias Maciel is chosen as the new governor of Minas Gerais, the second-most populous state of the Brazilian federation. . . . The 245 members of the Canadian House of Commons and 96 Senators meet in Ottawa for the opening session of the 17th Canadian Parliament. The session is held primarily to formulate anti-poverty policies. Conservative leader and newly elected prime minister R.B. Bennett presides.	

A	B	C	D	E
Includes developments that affect more than one world region, international organizations, and important meetings of world leaders.	Includes all domestic and regional developments in Europe, including the Soviet Union.	Includes all domestic and regional developments in Africa and the Middle East.	Includes all domestic and regional developments in Latin America, the Caribbean, and Canada.	Includes all domestic and regional developments in Asian and Pacific nations (and colonies).

U.S. Politics & Social Issues	U.S. Foreign Policy & Defense	Economics & Great Depression	Science, Technology & Nature	Culture, Leisure & Lifestyle	
Police in Chicago, Ill., arrest Israel Alderman, suspected assassin of *Chicago Tribune* reporter Alfred J. Lingle, who was gunned down on June 9. . . . A Ku Klux Klan meeting consisting of over 10,000 people is held in Peekskill, N.Y. . . . The annual convention of the International Law Association is held in New York City. Delegates discuss the implementation of an international code to regulate air traffic.	The U.S. Navy decommissions the cruiser USS *Galveston*.	American Federation of Labor president William Green proclaims during a speech that an annual wage system is needed to correct unemployment problems. . . . The British Trade Union Conference is held in Nottingham, England. During a speech, president John Beard is booed when he defends Labor Party President Ramsay MacDonald's policies. Beard claims the current unemployment figure of 2 million is acceptable.	U.S. aviation officials report that 225 total passengers flew between New York, Philadelphia, and Washington on September 1, a record for any one-day period.	Billy Arnold of Chicago, Ill., wins the annual 200-mile Labor Day auto race in Altoona, Pa. Arnold's victory guarantees him the 1930 American Automobile Association racing championship, according to Ted Allen, secretary of the association.	Sept. 2
More than 500 retired people in New York City apply for the city's old-age relief pension program, which will take effect in January. . . . A federal grand jury begins investigating the American Fascist Association. Charges against the association include inducing employers in rural Georgia to dismiss black workers and replace them with whites.		The U.S. Department of Commerce releases figures showing that machinery exports for the first seven months of 1930 totaled $149,483,812, nearly identical to last year's seven-month total of $148,134,032. . . . Argentine economic officials report that during August, there were 12,658,516 pesos in commercial failures, less than 5 million pesos than the total in July.	Dieudonne Costes and Maurice Bellonte arrive in New York City after a nonstop flight that originated in Paris. The pair is one of only a handful of aviators to complete the feat. Costes and Bellonte's feat is remarkable due to the fact that the pair used only a single engine during their flight. . . . Over 100 astronomers attend the 44th annual meeting of the American Astronomical Society in Chicago, Ill.		Sept. 3
	Gen. Henry T. Allen, commander of the American Army of Occupation in Germany, is buried in Arlington National Cemetery with full military honors.	Argentine economic officials report that during August there were 2.6 billion pesos in bank clearings. The figure is 14 percent less than August 1929, when there were 3.2 billion in bank clearings during the month. . . . *The Iron Age* reports iron production in the United States for August amounted to 2,526,500 tons, less than 32 percent of the August 1928 total of 3,136,570 tons.			Sept. 4
Serial killer Carl Panzram, who confessed to the murders of more than 20 people, is executed by hanging in Indianapolis, Ind. . . . New York City health commissioner Shirley Wynne reports that last week there were 2,448 births and 1,198 deaths. . . . Thousands of people are forced to evacuate their homes as fires rip through Staten Island, N.Y. Damages from the fire are estimated to be approximately $1 million. . . . Prohibition Director Amos Woodcock officially bans the practice of recruiting small boys to spy on suspected Prohibition violators. When Woodcock was appointed, he pledged to carry out Prohibition enforcement with the most legal methods possible.		Despite sharp declines in wheat, grains, and cotton, *The Annalist's* weekly index of U.S. wholesale commodity prices rises one-tenth of a point to 124.6. . . . The Federal Reserve Bank of New York reports broker loans' for this week totaled $3.11 billion, an increase of $8 million from the previous week's total.			Sept. 5
		U.S. economic officials report bank clearings for the month of August amounted to $38,910,243,713, a reduction of 34 percent from the corresponding period of 1929. It is the smallest total since February 1926. . . . Officials of the New York Stock Exchange report new bond offerings for this week totaled $53,889,000, a 25 percent reduction from a week ago and a 79 percent increase from the comparable period a year ago.	Leon Goodrich of New York climbs and descends the Matterhorn, one of the highest mountains of the Swiss Alps, in 3 hours and 15 minutes. The feat is a new record. Normally, it takes a climber five to six hours to climb the Matterhorn.	Home run king Babe Ruth opens his first memorabilia shop, Babe Ruth's Shop for Men, Inc. in New York City. A crowd of nearly 1,000 eagerly await Ruth's arrival.	Sept. 6
	The Army test flies its new "flight tutor" device. Upon successful testing, the Army will require each candidate of the Army Air Corps to pass the simulation in order to enter the Corps.	*The Iron Age* reports American steel plants are currently operating at only 55 percent of their total production capability.	The National Aeronautic Association informs 17-year-old Alexander Garafolo that his ascent of 19,246 feet in an airplane on August 10 was a record for small planes. . . . Representatives of the U.S. Federal Radio Commission tell reporters that this coming autumn's number of pending applications, 350, is the highest in the history of the Commission.		Sept. 7

F	G	H	I	J
Includes elections, federal-state relations, civil rights and liberties, crime, the judiciary, education, healthcare, poverty, urban affairs, and population.	*Includes formation and debate of U.S. foreign and defense policies, veterans affairs, and defense spending. (Relations with specific foreign countries are usually found under the region concerned.)*	*Includes business, labor, agriculture, taxation, transportation, consumer affairs, monetary and fiscal policy, natural resources, pollution, and accidents.*	*Includes worldwide scientific, medical, and technological developments, natural phenomena, U.S. weather, and natural disasters.*	*Includes the arts, religion, scholarship, communications media, sports, entertainment, fashions, fads, and social life.*

	World Affairs	Europe	Africa & The Middle East	The Americas	Asia & The Pacific
Sept. 8	The Johnson-Christy Commission, a committee with members from both the United States and the League of Nations, concludes its six-month study of labor conditions. The committee found that while the government has officially banned forced labor, slavery is still widespread throughout many nations. . . . The 60th session of the League of Nations Council commences in Geneva, Switzerland. Delegates discuss French Foreign Minister Aristide Briand's United Europe proposal, the final settlements for World War I reparations, and the military evacuation of the Rhineland.			Brazilians celebrate their country's 108th anniversary of independence from Portuguese colonial rule. The day's festivities include a military parade and a Miss Universe pageant. . . . Anita Villa, daughter of Mexican revolutionary Pancho Villa, is detained by U.S. immigration authorities in Corpus Christi, Tex., and deported back to Mexico on charges of being an "undesirable character."	
Sept. 9		The price of rubber in London falls to the lowest price ever in the history of rubber production record keeping. Economists say the decline is due to the lifting of restrictions on rubber produced in India. Rubber manufacturing investors have already lost an estimated $600 million.		A counter-revolt occurs in Argentina as the remnants of the deposed regime of President Hipolito Irigoyen agitate civil disturbances that result in injuries to more than 200 people. . . . The death count for the devastating hurricane that hit the Dominican Republic last week reaches 4,000 people. U.S. and Dominican soldiers are dispatched to quell looting and rioting.	
Sept. 10	The seventh annual session of the League of Nations Assembly begins in Geneva, Switzerland. Nicolas Titulesco of Romania is named as president of the Assembly.	The British navy commissions the battleship HMS *Nelson*, named after Napoleonic War-era Admiral Horatio Nelson.		President Jose Uriburu of Argentina is swiftly evacuated to the battleship *Belgrano* as increasingly escalating riots in the capital city of Buenos Aires rage on.	
Sept. 11		In Great Britain, Herbert Richmond Palmer is chosen to replace Edward Brandis Denham as the colonial head of the small African colony of Gambia.	Led by Sheikh Mahmud, Kurdish nationalists in Iraq revolt against Prime Minister Nuri al-Said. The fighting will continue until the rebellion is quelled in early 1931.		
Sept. 12	The 60th session of the League of Nations Council ends in Geneva, Switzerland.				

A	B	C	D	E
Includes developments that affect more than one world region, international organizations, and important meetings of world leaders.	Includes all domestic and regional developments in Europe, including the Soviet Union.	Includes all domestic and regional developments in Africa and the Middle East.	Includes all domestic and regional developments in Latin America, the Caribbean, and Canada.	Includes all domestic and regional developments in Asian and Pacific nations (and colonies).

U.S. Politics & Social Issues	U.S. Foreign Policy & Defense	Economics & Great Depression	Science, Technology & Nature	Culture, Leisure & Lifestyle	
Heywood Broun, Socialist candidate for New York's 17th Congressional District, recommends increased taxes for the wealthy and greatly lessening the military budget as a means of remedying the "tragic national crisis" of unemployment. . . . The Census Bureau reports there are currently 129,532 farms in the state of Nebraska, an increase of 5.4 percent over the past 10 years.		In an effort to increase its country's fledgling industries, the Canadian Parliament holds a special session that results in the raising of tariffs on over 125 classes of tradable goods, including agricultural equipment, cast-iron pipe, electrical equipment, fertilizers, jewelry, meats, paper, shoes, and textiles. . . . General Evaristo Uriburu, head of the military junta controlling Argentina, assures British statesmen that despite change in leadership, existing trade treaties between the two countries will remain intact. . . . The Canadian Bank of Commerce estimates that this year's wheat crop for grain-rich western Canada will amount to approximately 350 million bushels, an increase of 20 percent from the 1929 crop estimate.	The company 3M announces the beginning of marketing of Scotch transparent tape. . . . French aviators Dieudonne Coste, and Maurice Bellonte arrive in New York City to be received by President Herbert Hoover.		Sept. 8
The Department of Agriculture reports that recent droughts in the southeast have only slightly affected crop outputs, with a reduction of only 22,000 bales from this month's crop estimate.		The U.S. Department of Commerce releases its weekly index of U.S. automobile production. At 63.9, the index is 10 percent less than last week and a reduction of nearly 50 percent from the corresponding week a year ago. . . . The Treasury Department reports the amount of gold earmarked for foreign banks decreased by $62,981,630 last month.			Sept. 9
The New York City Department of Public Welfare reports that in one week, a total of 3,252 people over 70 years of age have registered for old-age relief pensions. . . . The American Federation of Labor releases a statement saying the legalization of beverages with an alcoholic content of 2.75 percent will result in the lowering of the U.S. unemployment figures by 100,000 men.		The Austrian National Bank reports it is lowering its rediscount rate by 0.5 percent, from 5.5 percent to 5 percent. It is the third such reduction in the period of one year. . . . The New York News Bureau Association releases a survey of over a dozen automobile company presidents' outlook on the auto industry. All of them agreed production output will exceed 4 million units for 1931.	Scientists conclude that Solomon Andree's unsuccessful expedition to the North Pole in 1897 ended with Andree's crew marooned on an island of ice in the uncharted areas of Antarctica. . . . Belgian Transport Minister Maurice Lippens opens the annual international air transport conference, sponsored by the International Air Transport Association.		Sept. 10
American Federation of Labor president William Green sends a message to President Herbert Hoover, thanking him for his efforts in tightening immigration. Green says illegal immigrants hurt employment opportunities for American workers. . . . New York City police commissioner Edward Mulrooney considers banning Communist demonstrations and meetings in the city after receiving dozens of complaints. . . . The radio station WHEC in Rochester, N.Y., officially bans the support of Prohibition reform by its radio commentators, for fear of having its license revoked.	The U.S. submarine Narwhal is transferred to its place of origin, the Portsmouth Navy Yard, for repairs and training.	A group of U.S. and British bankers extend to the Argentine Government a loan worth 100,000 pesos ($36,810,000) at an interest rate of 5 percent.	U.S. Assistant Secretary of Commerce for Aeronautics Clarence Young announces that for the upcoming America's Cup sailing competition on September 13, civilian planes flying overheard will not be allowed to fly lower than an altitude of 1,000 feet.	Frank Shields, age 18, defeats second-seeded American Willmer Allison in five sets, 7–9, 6–4, 6–1, 2–6, 8–6, to advance to the U.S. Open national tennis championship quarterfinal in Forest Hills, N.Y. . . . The annual National Baptist Convention of America is held in New York City. Delegates to the Convention debate whether to reelect standing president Dr. John W. Hurse.	Sept. 11
Senator Pat Harrison of Kentucky accuses "President Hoover and his cheerleaders" of giving the American people a false view of present economic conditions. "Never in the history of this country has the confidence of the public in those who direct the affairs of the government been so shaken and our whole economic machinery so thrown out of gear," he said. . . . The American Bankers Association Journal reports on business conditions for over 150 major companies. The companies experienced an average inventory reduction of 7 percent during the past two months.		The Annalist releases its weekly index of U.S. wholesale commodity prices. At 124.9, the figure is a 0.3 point increase from the previous week, one of the smallest changes of the year. . . . National Automobile Chamber of Commerce general manager Alfred Reeves estimates that U.S. citizens pay $800 million each year in automobile taxes. Reeves added that the government should use the funds exclusively for the improvement of the United States' highway system. . . . The International Brotherhood of Bookbinders' Union reaches an agreement with several publishers in New York City, reducing the workweek of the city's 1,800 bookbinders by an average of 7 hours.		Wilfred Rhodes, considered by many to be the greatest cricket player of the 20th century, plays in his final match against the Australian national squad, hitting an excellent 5 of 95 wickets. . . . The quarterfinals of the Professional Golfers' Association's annual championship conclude at the Fresh Meadow Country Club in New York. The only American remaining in the tournament is Gene Sarazen, who won the event in 1922 and again in 1923.	Sept. 12

F	G	H	I	J
Includes elections, federal-state relations, civil rights and liberties, crime, the judiciary, education, healthcare, poverty, urban affairs, and population.	*Includes formation and debate of U.S. foreign and defense policies, veterans affairs, and defense spending. (Relations with specific foreign countries are usually found under the region concerned.)*	*Includes business, labor, agriculture, taxation, transportation, consumer affairs, monetary and fiscal policy, natural resources, pollution, and accidents.*	*Includes worldwide scientific, medical, and technological developments, natural phenomena, U.S. weather, and natural disasters.*	*Includes the arts, religion, scholarship, communications media, sports, entertainment, fashions, fads, and social life.*

	World Affairs	Europe	Africa & The Middle East	The Americas	Asia & The Pacific
Sept. 13					
Sept. 14	Members of the Permanent Court of International Justice in Geneva, Switzerland, announce a vote will be held in two days to select a successor to Charles Evans Hughes, whose death left a vacancy in the Court. Former U.S. Secretary of State Frank B. Kellogg is considered the frontrunner.	Parliamentary elections are held in Germany. The National Socialist German Workers' (Nazi) Party, headed by convicted felon and best-selling author Adolf Hitler, garners 18.3 percent of the total vote and increases its representation in the Reichstag from 12 to 107 members, making it Germany's second-largest political party, behind the Social Democratic Party.			
Sept. 15	The League of Nations holds its third conference on the eradication of syphilis, which kills an estimated 100,000 people each year, in Copenhagen, Denmark.	British economic officials report the Bank of England took in £878,142 in gold during this week, against £92,849 in gold in withdrawals, a surplus of £785,293.		The First Pan-American Conference on Agriculture is held in Washington, D.C. Delegates seek to establish a continent-wide policy to protect a fledgling agricultural industry.	Police in Lahore, India, discover 14 explosive devices near the Ravi River. Police say the bombs are part of a widespread conspiracy designed to induce British authorities to release political prisoners. Twenty arrests have been made so far. . . . A mob of 3,000 people in Bombay, India, stone a group of 14 patrolling policemen, prompting authorities to forcibly disperse the crowd.
Sept. 16		Leading European bankers express no concern with results of the Reichstag elections in Germany, where the fascist National Socialist Party nearly tripled its parliamentary representation. One banker, however, sees corruption in the Party's economic doctrine: "While it bears the term 'socialist,' it has really nothing to do with socialism, for in fact its aims are diametrically opposed to socialism's principles."		A large hurricane hits the mainland of the Caribbean nation of the Dominican Republic, killing thousands and leaving the country's capital, Santo Domingo, nearly eradicated.	The British Royal Air Force begins bombing operations on a group of Chamkanni tribesmen encamped near the Afghanistan-India border.
Sept. 17	The League of Nations Council holds its 61st session in Geneva, Switzerland. . . . The Daily Herald newspaper in Great Britain reports that the "new Argentine government, formed after the overthrow of President Irigoyen, is to be recognized immediately by Great Britain." Five other nations, the Vatican, Germany, Italy, Sweden, and Paraguay, had expressed formal recognition earlier in the week. The United States is expected to follow suit in the coming days.	The Metropolitan Life Insurance Company issues infant mortality rates for all major nations. Russia is the highest with 20 percent; New Zealand, the lowest with 3.6 percent. The United States has an infant mortality rate of 6.7 percent. Additionally, the worldwide infant mortality rate has improved by 33 percent since 1915.			A bomb is hurled into the police headquarters in Karachi, India, causing significant structural damage. Police earlier in the week had seized a large weapons cache near the Ravi River. . . . On the Yangtse River in China, approximately 200 miles near Hanchow, the U.S. gunboat Oahu exchanges fire of small arms with small Communist bandit crafts. Similar incidents were reported with French, Japanese, and British vessels.
Sept. 18		A trial date is set for 68 Hungarians accused of instigating anti-Semitic riots in the capital city of Budapest.		Canadian agricultural officials estimate this year's wheat crop to be between 365 million and 375 million bushels, considerably higher than last year's wheat production.	

A	B	C	D	E
Includes developments that affect more than one world region, international organizations, and important meetings of world leaders.	Includes all domestic and regional developments in Europe, including the Soviet Union.	Includes all domestic and regional developments in Africa and the Middle East.	Includes all domestic and regional developments in Latin America, the Caribbean, and Canada.	Includes all domestic and regional developments in Asian and Pacific nations (and colonies).

U.S. Politics & Social Issues	U.S. Foreign Policy & Defense	Economics & Great Depression	Science, Technology & Nature	Culture, Leisure & Lifestyle	
William J. Hughes, deputy treasurer for New York City, admits to a committee investigating alleged tax crimes that he defrauded the city of $25,000. Hughes is immediately arrested and subsequently released on a bond of $10,000. Hughes's boss, Treasurer John McCabe, escaped implication in the crime by pleading full ignorance, saying he left "details" up to his staff. . . . The Travelers Insurance Company reports automobile fatalities in the United States for the first eight months of 1930 amounted to approximately 19,700 people, an increase of 7 percent from the total of the first eight months of 1929 of 18,500 people.	The U.S. Navy transfers the decommissioned ship USS *Hunt* to Coast Guard control, for the purpose of Prohibition enforcement.	The price of wheat in Liverpool, England, and Chicago, Ill., falls to season lows. Blame for the decline is placed on sellers who feared recent droughts would impact wheat production. . . . U.S. economic officials report bank clearings for this week totaled $8.1 billion, less than 38.7 percent of the total of the corresponding period in 1929.		The America's Cup international sailing competition begins in Newport, R.I. The favorite contender for the title is Sir Thomas Lipton, whose yacht, *Shamrock*, has competed in the Cup four separate times since 1899. Thomas Lipton would go on to found Lipton Tea, the largest tea brand in the world with items sold in over 110 countries.	Sept. 13
Owners of the radio station WHEC in Rochester, N.Y., lift the ban on anti-Prohibition commentary by its radio commentators, in place since September 11. Representatives of the station say the decision was a "serious mistake."		British economic officials report total steel output for August was 451,300 tons, a decrease of 27 percent from July and a decline of 40 percent from August 1929. . . . Representatives of the Royal Dutch air mail service announce an agreement that will end the service's strike. A committee comprised of one pilot, one director, and one government representative will officially draft the new contract.		The final round of the Professional Golfers' Association annual championship concludes at Fresh Meadow Country Club in Great Neck, N.Y. British golfer Tommy Armour is declared the winner after defeating two-time winner Gene Sarazan by one stroke.	Sept. 14
Speakers at a meeting of the American Federation of Full-Fashioned Hosiery Workers say there will be a "trade catastrophe" unless wages for hosiery workers are raised.		The French publication *Statistique Generale* releases its monthly index of French wholesale commodity prices. At 544, the figure is a decline of 0.7 percent from last month's index of 548. . . . The British publication *The Economist* reports British wholesale commodity prices have declined by an average of 18 percent during the past year.			Sept. 15
Millionaire Eugene Meyer is appointed by President Herbert Hoover to serve as Federal Reserve Board Chairman. Meyer replaces Roy D. Young, who retired on August 31. . . . Police in Louisville, Ky., arrest Ted Geisking in connection with the murder of *Chicago Tribune* reporter Alfred Lingle, who was killed on June 9.		The U.S. Department of Commerce releases its weekly index of U.S. automobile production. At 62.5, the index is a 2 percent decline from last week and a reduction of 47 percent from the corresponding week in 1929. . . . British steel exports for the month of August totaled 218,828 gross tons, less than 84,616 tons from the previous month's total, according to official financial reports.		Fritz Gross defeats Donald Grant by a score of 2–1 to win the Austrian amateur golf championship. . . . The yacht *Enterprise* defeats the *Shamrock V* to win the annual America's Cup sailing competition.	Sept. 16
Construction of the Hoover Dam officially begins.	Former Naval War College president William V. Pratt is chosen as the new Chief of Naval Operations, replacing Admiral Charles Hughes, whose term expired.			Detective writer Agatha Christie marries museum archaeologist Max Mallowan.	Sept. 17
Aviator Bert Acosta, who in April 1927 set a flight endurance record of 51 hours, 11 minutes, and 25 seconds, is arrested in Bridgeport, Conn., on charges of flying a plane with a suspended pilot's license. Acosta was suspended in January of last year for stunt flying over the Connecticut countryside, for which he received a fine of $500. . . . Congressional primaries are held in several states. The results indicate the American public favors reform of the Prohibition law, if not its complete removal.		The Brazilian Finance Ministry releases a report estimating that the 1931 total federal revenue will be $152 million. Expenditures are estimated at $150 million, leaving a small surplus of $2 million.		Citizens of Boston, Mass., celebrate the 300th anniversary of the founding of the Massachusetts Bay Colony. Approximately 40,000 marchers, 200 floats, and 100 bands marched through the city streets in a lavish parade. . . . Italian boxer Primo Carnera records his 23rd knockout since immigrating to the United States, delivering a crushing blow to Jack Gross of Philadelphia in the fourth round of a 10-round bout. . . . The Philadelphia Athletics clinch the American League pennant for the second consecutive year, defeating the Chicago White Sox by a score of 14–10.	Sept. 18

F	G	H	I	J
Includes elections, federal-state relations, civil rights and liberties, crime, the judiciary, education, healthcare, poverty, urban affairs, and population.	*Includes formation and debate of U.S. foreign and defense policies, veterans affairs, and defense spending. (Relations with specific foreign countries are usually found under the region concerned.)*	*Includes business, labor, agriculture, taxation, transportation, consumer affairs, monetary and fiscal policy, natural resources, pollution, and accidents.*	*Includes worldwide scientific, medical, and technological developments, natural phenomena, U.S. weather, and natural disasters.*	*Includes the arts, religion, scholarship, communications media, sports, entertainment, fashions, fads, and social life.*

	World Affairs	Europe	Africa & The Middle East	The Americas	Asia & The Pacific
Sept. 19		Sir Neville Reginald Howse, who in 1900 became the first Australian to receive the highest British military award, the Victoria Cross, dies from cancer in London, England.			
Sept. 20	Rep. Hamilton Fish of New York urges Secretary of State Henry Stimson to investigate the claims of Antonio Ascolese, who says he was beaten on the Italian steamship Roma by sailors for refusing to cheer for Italian Premier Benito Mussolini.				
Sept. 21				Canada announces it will undertake its first census next June, the main purpose of which is to study the causes of seasonal and unseasonal employment. The project is expected to require over 15,000 enumerators.	
Sept. 22					In China, T.V. Soong replaces Tan Yankai as head of the Executive Yuan, China's executive branch. Soong would later serve as Chinese Foreign Minister during World War II.
Sept. 23					
Sept. 24	Emperor Haile Selassie (Ras Tafari) of Ethiopia confers the Grand Cordon of Solomon, Ethiopia's highest honor for a foreigner, on Premier Benito Mussolini of Italy.	Great Britain's Ministry of Labor releases unemployment figures, showing there to be 2,103,413 people out of work, 618,511 of whom are only temporarily unemployed. The figure is 36,158 less people than last week, but an increase of 55 percent over the past year. . . . Germany's total number of unemployed rises to 2,983,000, approximately 5 percent of the population.			
Sept. 25		Karl Vaugoin, Austrian vice chancellor and head of the Christian Socialist Party, announces his resignation. Vaugoin's decision comes as a result of his failed appointment of Fascist party member Dr. Strasella to the post of general manager of the Austrian State Railways.		U.S. immigration officials report that during August, only 406 Mexicans entered the United States legally, compared with a normal amount of 6,000. The downturn is a result of strict anti-immigration laws passed by the United States 18 months ago.	

A	B	C	D	E
Includes developments that affect more than one world region, international organizations, and important meetings of world leaders.	Includes all domestic and regional developments in Europe, including the Soviet Union.	Includes all domestic and regional developments in Africa and the Middle East.	Includes all domestic and regional developments in Latin America, the Caribbean, and Canada.	Includes all domestic and regional developments in Asian and Pacific nations (and colonies).

U.S. Politics & Social Issues	U.S. Foreign Policy & Defense	Economics & Great Depression	Science, Technology & Nature	Culture, Leisure & Lifestyle	
The Justice Department reports that each year, over $3 billion is exchanged through the illegal liquor trade.	The U.S. Navy strikes the submarines *T-1*, *T-2* and *T-3* from the Naval Vessel Register. . . . Representatives of the War and Navy departments announce budget cuts for their respective departments will be made for the current fiscal year. The War Department's budget will be reduced by approximately $20 million, while the Navy's budget will be reduced by approximately $29 million.	Argentine economic officials report exports for the first eight months of 1930 totaled 438,902,213 gold pesos, less than 37 percent of the total for the first eight months of 1929, 698,845,030.	The British National Radio Exhibition opens in London, England. Speakers say that despite the worldwide economic depression, Great Britain's radio industry has survived. Radio manufacturer representatives announce the construction of six new major factories that will cover a land space of 200,000 square feet.	The Philadelphia Athletics baseball team defeats the Chicago White Sox by a score of 14–10 to clinch the American League pennant and a berth in the World Series. The Athletics will be looking to repeat their World Series success last year, when they beat the Chicago Cubs in five games. Manager Connie Mack will be seeking his fifth World Series title.	Sept. 19
The American Telephone and Telegraph Company purchases the Teletype Corporation of Chicago in an estimated $15 million deal. Company executives release a statement, reading, "It seemed desirable to acquire Teletype in order to realize the maximum of progress and economy."	The U.S. Navy sells the Eagle class patrol craft *PE-49* for scrap.	*The Annalist's* index of weekly U.S. wholesale commodity prices falls to 124.3, a decrease of 0.5 points, after two consecutive weeks of positive gains. . . . *Dun's Review* reports bank clearings in the United States this week amounted to $9,224,654,000, less than 34 percent of the total clearings from the corresponding week a year ago. In New York City, the decline is 37 percent. . . . According to published reports, new bond offerings on U.S. stock exchanges this week totaled $80,771,000, a decrease of 43 percent from the previous week but an increase of 41 percent from the corresponding week in 1929. . . . The Province of Buenos Aires, the City of Cordoba, and the American Tobacco Company are all stricken from the list of tradable companies on the New York Stock Exchange. The Union Oil Company of California is admitted to the list.			Sept. 20
The Michigan Democratic State Convention unanimously adopts a resolution calling for a national referendum on the Prohibition Amendment. The resolution also assails the Smoot-Hawley Tariff Act, criticizing it as an "unconscionable crime against the American people in favor of special interests."		U.S. Chamber of Commerce chairman Julius H. Barnes estimates that there are currently 42 million employed workers in the United States, against 31 million employed workers in 1921. Marsh recommends that President Herbert Hoover call a special session of Congress to appropriate $500 million for unemployment insurance and public works.			Sept. 21
		New York City insurance superintendent Thomas Behan announces that at the end of 1929, the total assets of life insurance companies operating within New York State amounted to $15,015,941,517, an increase of $1.25 billion over the preceding year. . . . Democratic political operatives remark to reporters that they intend to make the Smoot-Hawley Tariff Act, which they say costs the American people $1 billion annually, the central theme of the upcoming fall elections.			Sept. 22
Rep. Loring Black of New York calls on President Herbert Hoover to call a special session of Congress to amend the Prohibition Act. "Immediate modification of the act would restore 250,000 men to work in the breweries," he says.		New York State Superintendent of Public Works Colonel Greene reports to Governor Franklin Roosevelt that in one year, the amount of men employed in state public works projects has increased by 39 percent, from 4,575 men employed in August 1929, to 7,550 men currently. Roosevelt had earlier asked Greene to expedite state projects as a means of increasing employment.			Sept. 23
The Census Bureau reports that cotton production for the first eight months of 1930 amounted to 3,729,683 bales, the highest eight-month total for any year since 1925. . . . Republican National Committee Chairman Simeon D. Fess remarks to reporters that he "will simply not stand for" any religious debate during the Ohio congressional campaign currently under way.		U.S. Senator Tasker Oddie of Nevada proposes a bill that would impose restrictive embargoes on Russian manganese, coal, lumber, woodpulp, gelatin, glue, and wheat. Russia has been accused recently of short selling its tradable resources. In the past year, 1.188 billion pounds of barley and 224 million pounds of wheat have been shipped from the Soviet Union.			Sept. 24
		The price of copper in the United States falls to 10.25 cents per pound, approximately 43 percent less than the price at the corresponding period last year of 18 cents per pound. Leading economists say the price is quite possibly the lowest in over 30 years.		The Beverly Country Club in Chicago, Ill., is chosen as the site for the 1931 national amateur golf championship.	Sept. 25

F	G	H	I	J
Includes elections, federal-state relations, civil rights and liberties, crime, the judiciary, education, healthcare, poverty, urban affairs, and population.	Includes formation and debate of U.S. foreign and defense policies, veterans affairs, and defense spending. (Relations with specific foreign countries are usually found under the region concerned.)	Includes business, labor, agriculture, taxation, transportation, consumer affairs, monetary and fiscal policy, natural resources, pollution, and accidents.	Includes worldwide scientific, medical, and technological developments, natural phenomena, U.S. weather, and natural disasters.	Includes the arts, religion, scholarship, communications media, sports, entertainment, fashions, fads, and social life.

	World Affairs	Europe	Africa & The Middle East	The Americas	Asia & The Pacific
Sept. 26		Fernando de Rosa, who attempted to assassinate Prince Humbert of Italy on October 24 of last year, is put on trial in Brussels, Belgium. Court documents reveal Rosa's motivation for the assassination stemmed from his anti-Fascist beliefs. . . . Anti-German demonstrations occur in Prague, Czechoslovakia, as Czech nationalists smash the windows of German- and Jewish-owned establishments. . . . During a speech to the Reich Supreme Court in Leipzig, Germany, National Socialist party leader Adolf Hitler insists that if given power, he will strike Germany's signature from the 1919 Treaty of Versailles reparation plan.			
Sept. 27				Argentina's Minister of Agriculture contacts the United States in the hope of enticing them to waive the customs duty on corn. The Minister hope to sign an agreement allowing a minimum of 500,000 tons of corn to be shipped to the United States annually. Argentina's corn exports currently make up only 1–2 percent of the United States's total grain consumption.	
Sept. 28		Prince Leopold of Bavaria, who received Germany's highest military order, the Pour le Merite, for his services in World War I, dies in Munich, Germany. . . . As a result of an outbreak of tuberculosis on British sea vessels, the British Board of Trade officially limits the workday for seamen to 12 hours, so as to hinder the possibility of infection. Previously, seamen had been working at least 16 hours per day.		Statistics compiled in Canada show that 600,000 more people voted in this year's national election than in the national election of 1926. An estimated 60 percent of the new voters picked Conservative candidates.	
Sept. 29		Leading bankers in Germany express concern over the parliamentary elections held last week, where the National Socialist party nearly tripled its representation. The Boerse, Germany's stock exchange, fell by 2 and one-half points as a result of the speculation. Despite this, leading bankers tell reporters that if right-wing extremists were to gain power, they are assured they would act "responsibly." . . . French Foreign Minister Aristide Briand meets with German Foreign Minister Julius Curtus to discuss the results of the German Parliamentary election.		Ecuadorian Interior Minister Julio Moreno announces his resignation. Moreno was earlier accused by opponents of intervening in local elections.	
Sept. 30		Richard Schmitz is chosen to replace Carl Vaugoin as Vice Chancellor of Austria.	The Afghan National Council votes to deny former King Amanullah's request for the return of his property. The Council also votes to demand the return of state jewels that Amanullah smuggled upon leaving office.	Argentina's Finance Ministry releases a report showing there to be currently $357,709,623 in the country's Gold Exchange Office.	

A	B	C	D	E
Includes developments that affect more than one world region, international organizations, and important meetings of world leaders.	Includes all domestic and regional developments in Europe, including the Soviet Union.	Includes all domestic and regional developments in Africa and the Middle East.	Includes all domestic and regional developments in Latin America, the Caribbean, and Canada.	Includes all domestic and regional developments in Asian and Pacific nations (and colonies).

U.S. Politics & Social Issues	U.S. Foreign Policy & Defense	Economics & Great Depression	Science, Technology & Nature	Culture, Leisure & Lifestyle	
		The *Annalist's* index of weekly U.S. wholesale commodity prices falls 1.3 points to 123.0, the lowest index in one month. . . . The Bank of France releases its weekly statement, showing an increase of 129 million francs worth of gold. The Bank of France now has a gold reserve of 47.7 billion francs, the largest total ever reported in the history of the bank.	Alanson B. Houghton is elected president of the American Academy of Political Science. Houghton replaces Samuel Lindsay, who retired after two decades of serving as Academy head. . . . American aviator Amelia Earhart suffers a head wound as her plane nearly crashes on the runway at Roads Naval Air Station in Norfolk, Va.		**Sept. 26**
Alabama state agricultural statistician F.W. Grist estimates in a statement that the droughts in Alabama this summer will result in poverty for 130,000 people. . . . New York City police commissioner Edward Mulrooney announces that henceforth, court summons will be given out to motorists who "blow their automobile horns unnecessarily."		*Dun's Review* reports that bank clearings in the United States for this week totaled $8.6 billion, less than 37 percent from the corresponding period a year ago. . . . New bond offerings on the New York Stock Exchange this week amounted to $133,346,307, a rise of 39 percent from last week, and an increase of 80 percent from the corresponding period a year ago, according to published reports. . . . Representatives of the New York Stock Exchange add the Wabash Railway Company to the list of tradable companies. The Union Oil Company of California is stricken from the list.		The St. Louis Cardinals baseball team defeats the Pittsburgh Pirates by a score of 10–5 to win the 1930 National League pennant. The victory marks an impressive turnaround from a fourth place position at the start of the last month of the season. St. Louis will host its third World Series contest in five seasons.	**Sept. 27**
The Master Barbers of America formally asks the Census Bureau to classify their occupation as "professional service," rather than the current classification of "domestic and personal service." Barbers insist the change should be made because they had to learn different forms of bacteriology, anatomy, and histology in order to obtain a barber's license. Census officials deny the request, saying a barber's work is equal to a manicurist's.		Canadian National Railways passenger traffic manager C.W. Johnston estimates that the amount of foreign tourists in Canada has doubled over the past five years. Last year's tourist revenue aggregated $300 million.			**Sept. 28**
Arriving from across the country, 6,000 delegates assemble at the annual convention of the American Bankers Association. The question of "branch banking" will be the highlight of the association's discussion. President Herbert Hoover is expected to address the convention on October 2.	The U.S. Navy sells the armored cruiser *Montana*, struck from the Naval Vessel Register since July, to John Irwin, Jr.	According to published reports, Argentina's wheat exports for this week amounted to 435,210 bushels. The total wheat exports for the year to date are 69,656,205 bushels, less than 66 percent of the total from the corresponding period a year ago of 204,380,758 bushels.		Famous Russian painter Ilya Yefimovich Repin dies in Kuokkala, Finland, at the age of 86. . . . Cornelius Shields pilots his yacht *Aileen* to victory in the final round of the Bermuda Trophy national sailing competition. Shields won by only 16 seconds.	**Sept. 29**
The Department of Commerce releases its weekly index of U.S. automobile production, showing the index to be currently 53.4, approximately 50 percent less than the corresponding period a year ago.		The governments of the Netherlands, Denmark, Norway, and Sweden sign an economic agreement. The agreement calls for the coordinating of tariff policies in order to better promote trade between the four countries. The agreement would be expanded in December to include Belgium and Luxembourg. . . . According to published reports, the revenue total for all Class 1 railroads operating in the United States for August was $96,750,000, less than 31 percent of August of last year's total. . . . U.S. economists report total cotton exports for the month of August amounted to $27,484,805, 14 percent greater than the total of August 1929.		Local officials of Philadelphia, Pa., report that the recently completed national amateur golf championship netted $55,670 in ticket revenue, the highest in the history of the championship. Over 20,000 total tickets were sold throughout the six-day event. . . . Representatives of the French and German film industries enter into an agreement whereby an unlimited amount of films will be allowed to be distributed between the two countries.	**Sept. 30**

F	**G**	**H**	**I**	**J**
Includes elections, federal-state relations, civil rights and liberties, crime, the judiciary, education, healthcare, poverty, urban affairs, and population.	*Includes formation and debate of U.S. foreign and defense policies, veterans affairs, and defense spending. (Relations with specific foreign countries are usually found under the region concerned.)*	*Includes business, labor, agriculture, taxation, transportation, consumer affairs, monetary and fiscal policy, natural resources, pollution, and accidents.*	*Includes worldwide scientific, medical, and technological developments, natural phenomena, U.S. weather, and natural disasters.*	*Includes the arts, religion, scholarship, communications media, sports, entertainment, fashions, fads, and social life.*

	World Affairs	Europe	Africa & The Middle East	The Americas	Asia & The Pacific
Oct. 1	French Foreign Minister Aristide Briand appeals to German Foreign Minister Julius Curtius to prevent "Adolf Hitler and his hotheads" from undermining peace with France. Hitler's party nearly tripled its parliamentary representation in the national elections held last month.	The Soviet Union completes construction of a stone mausoleum designed to display the body of Vladimir Lenin, the first premier of the Soviet Union. Previously, Lenin had been on display in a mausoleum made of wood, which officials said did not properly preserve Lenin's body. . . . Great Britain announces it will begin conducting its census on April 24 of next year. The census is taken once every 10 years.	Trial proceedings begin in Haifa, Palestine, for Rashid Hadj Ibrahim and Ramsi Omar, who are accused of murdering Christian newspaper editor Jameel Bakhry. Police were forced to disperse a group of rioting Arab sympathizers outside the trial's courthouse.	Police in Sao Paulo, Brazil, arrest a group of Communistic revolutionaries who intended to assassinate President Washington Luis. The group is lead by former Brazilian army captain Luis Carlos Prestes, who was exiled to Uruguay in 1925. The group was questioned and subsequently released. . . . Chilean journalists publish an article stating that the Bolivian national revolution which took place in June was financed by the American Standard Oil Company. The Bolivian government subsequently releases a statement calling the accusations "perfectly absurd."	
Oct. 2				President Jose Felix Uriburu of Argentina, who recently gained power via a military coup, declares that he will implement constitutional and electoral reforms before calling a presidential election to take place.	
Oct. 3	Jules-Gaston Henri Carde replaces Pierre-Louis Bordes as French colonial head of Algeria.				
Oct. 4		The British airship *R101*, the largest flying aircraft ever built, departs from London en route to India for its first trial flight. There are 54 passengers aboard the ship for its maiden voyage, including Air State Secretary Christopher Thompson and Director of Civil Aviation Sefton Brancker.		Amidst internal political struggle, the Cuban Congress votes to grant President Gerardo Machado's request to temporarily suspend constitutional freedoms until general elections are held on November 1. Cubans will have no freedoms of the press, assembly, speech, or the right to vote.	In order to cut federal expenditures, Australian lawmakers agree to reduce ministerial salaries by 15 percent and parliamentary salaries by 15 percent. The changes are expected to reduce Australia's federal budget by approximately $20 million annually.
Oct. 5		British lawmakers consider a bill that would make it a crime to demolish buildings deemed historically significant. The bill is designed to counter the American practice of purchasing British historical buildings and reconstructing them abroad. . . . The 36-year-old King Boris Xaver III of Bulgaria announces his marital engagement to Princess Giovanna of Italy. The marriage is expected to greatly strengthen ties between the two monarchs' respective nations.			
Oct. 6		The British publication *The Economist* reports that British wholesale prices have fallen approximately 20 percent during the past year.		Thousands of workers under the direction of the Economic Vigilance Committee in Montevideo, Uruguay, go on strike to protest minimum wages and old-age pensions.	
Oct. 7		Approximately 50 sailors aboard the British ship *Revenge of the Mediterranean* are arrested for reportedly "hissing" at a superior officer and complaining about the ship's food. Great Britain had earlier passed a law lowering the Navy's meat supply by approximately $1 million annually. . . . The annual British Imperial Conference is held in London, England. Delegates discuss whether citizens of British dominions should be granted full citizenship.			
	A Includes developments that affect more than one world region, international organizations, and important meetings of world leaders.	**B** Includes all domestic and regional developments in Europe, including the Soviet Union.	**C** Includes all domestic and regional developments in Africa and the Middle East.	**D** Includes all domestic and regional developments in Latin America, the Caribbean, and Canada.	**E** Includes all domestic and regional developments in Asian and Pacific nations (and colonies).

U.S. Politics & Social Issues	U.S. Foreign Policy & Defense	Economics & Great Depression	Science, Technology & Nature	Culture, Leisure & Lifestyle	
The National Electrics Product Corporation reduces its price of copper metal by one-half cent to 10 cents per pound, the lowest copper price of any manufacturer since 1896.	The U.S. Navy transfers ownership of the destroyer *Welborn C. Wood* to the Coast Guard and strikes it from the Naval Vessel Register.	Bond trading on the New York Stock Exchange aggregates in one day $14,326,000, the largest daily total since April 16 of this year. . . . British economists report that in the first half of the current financial year, total tax revenue amounted to $1,477,404,555, against $1,768,498,885, in total budgetary expenditures, leaving a deficit of approximately $250 million. . . . The American Railway Association estimates that total freight car revenue in 1930 will be 7.3 percent below the total of 1929. . . . The New York Stock Exchange removes the Alleghany Corporation and the Conley Tin Foil Corporation from its list of tradable companies. International Carriers, Ltd., and Youngstown Sheet and Tube Co. were added to the list.	The first test flight of the Polish fighter jet *PZL P.7*, which would take part in the 1939 German invasion of Poland, is completed.	Sports bookies across the country estimate odds that the Philadelphia Athletics baseball team will repeat as world champion are approximately 7 to 10. Home run king Babe Ruth tells reporters that the Athletics will win in four straight games. . . . An estimated 32,000 people, including U.S. President Herbert Hoover, witness the Philadelphia Athletics defeat the St. Louis Cardinals by a score of 5–2 to win the first game of the World Series.	Oct. 1
	The U.S. Navy sells the armored cruiser USS *Colorado* for scrap.			The Philadelphia Athletics defeat the St. Louis Cardinals by a score of 6–1 to take a 2 to 0 game lead in the World Series. George Earnshaw of the Athletics pitches a complete game, surrendering one run and six hits over nine innings.	Oct. 2
		The Annalist's index of weekly U.S. wholesale commodity prices is released. At 121.0, the index is, with one exception, the lowest since December 1915.			Oct. 3
		Australian federal authorities place an embargo on all imported steel from any country. The decision comes as many Australian steel plants declare bankruptcy due to an inability to compete with the prices of foreign imports. The embargo is expected to most severely affect the British steel industry.	Robert Buck of New Jersey, age 16, sets the world's transcontinental air speed record for pilots under 21 years of age with a time of 23 hours and 47 minutes. The previous record was established by Eddie August Schneider on August 25 of this year.	The St. Louis Cardinals win Game 3 of the World Series, defeating the Philadelphia Athletics by a score of 5–0. Bill Hallahan of the Cardinals throws a complete game, a seven-hit shutout. The Athletics now lead the series 2 to 1.	Oct. 4
In Atlantic City, N.J., 5,000 delegates attend the 12th annual convention of the American Gas Association. Speakers include Consolidated Gas Company president Clifford E. Paige. . . . During a speech, National Association of Real Estate Boards president Leonard Reaume calls for national real estate tax revision, noting that in most major U.S. cities, more than 75 percent of the total tax revenue is gained through real estate taxes. . . . The District Court of Appeals of California declares the unconstitutionality of a law that suspends one's driver's license for failure to pay damages. "Such legislation," a statement reads, "is unfair discrimination against the driver who has not the finances to meet the judgment."		Swiss economists estimate that since the U.S. Smoot-Hawley Tariff Act was passed this summer, Swiss exports to the United States have been reduced by approximately 30–45 percent.	The British airship *R101* encounters heavy winds over the French countryside during its first trial run, forcing the ship's pilot to reduce traveling speed to 13 mph. The change is made in vain, though, as the *R101* eventually crashes into a hillside in Beauvais, a small city north of Paris. Of the 54 passengers, 46 are killed instantly and 2 later die of injuries. It marks one of the worst aviation disasters in history and the end of Great Britain's attempt to produce a usable airship.	The St. Louis Cardinals defeat the Philadelphia Athletics by a score of 3–1 to win Game 4 of the World Series. Cardinals' pitcher Jesse Haines throws a complete game, giving up one run and four hits over nine innings. The series is now tied at 2 games apiece.	Oct. 5
President Herbert Hoover selects former State Department special counsel Joshua Clark to succeed Dwight W. Morrow as U.S. Ambassador to Mexico. Morrow, whose son-in-law is famed aviator Charles Lindbergh, resigned to run for the vacant senate seat in New Jersey.		British economists report the Bank of England took in £1,070,125 worth of gold this week, against £251,001 in withdrawals, most of which were reserved for France. . . . Financial fear stemming from the recent parliamentary elections engulfs Germany. During this week, 978 million reichsmarks were given out as credit loans by the Reichsbank, 80 percent more than the corresponding period of 1929. Bank officials attribute this not to political nervousness, but to low German interest rates.	U.S. aeronautics experts place blame for the British airship *R101*'s crash on a hydrogen explosion, adding that if helium were used, a crash would most likely not have happened.	The Philadelphia Athletics defeat the St. Louis Cardinals in Game 5 of the World Series by a score of 2–0. George Earnshaw pitches eight shutout innings, vacating the mound in the ninth inning for future Hall of Fame inductee Lefty Grove to complete the game. The Athletics now lead the series 3 games to 2.	Oct. 6
		The Bank of Japan lowers its discount rate by 0.37 percent, from 5.48 percent to 5.11 percent. . . . Merrill Lynch Co. reports that U.S. chain store sales in September amounted to approximately $133,562,677, compared with a total of $144,776,318 for September 1929, a decrease of 7.7 percent.	American airship experts insist that despite the crashing of the British *R101*, airships are still an effective and safe means of travel, noting that in the previous 11 transatlantic crossings, no incidents have occurred. "The rigid airship is undoubtedly the ideal medium for fast and comfortable intercontinental travel," says Alexander Klemin, head of the New York University School of Aeronautics.	Canadian Dominion Football Association secretary Sam Davidson announces Canada will be represented by a soccer team in the upcoming 1932 Summer Olympic Games in Los Angeles, Calif.	Oct. 7
F	G	H	I	J	
Includes elections, federal-state relations, civil rights and liberties, crime, the judiciary, education, healthcare, poverty, urban affairs, and population.	*Includes formation and debate of U.S. foreign and defense policies, veterans affairs, and defense spending. (Relations with specific foreign countries are usually found under the region concerned.)*	*Includes business, labor, agriculture, taxation, transportation, consumer affairs, monetary and fiscal policy, natural resources, pollution, and accidents.*	*Includes worldwide scientific, medical, and technological developments, natural phenomena, U.S. weather, and natural disasters.*	*Includes the arts, religion, scholarship, communications media, sports, entertainment, fashions, fads, and social life.*	

	World Affairs	Europe	Africa & The Middle East	The Americas	Asia & The Pacific
Oct. 8		The British newspaper *The Daily Express* reports that British film censors have officially banned the Fox Film Corporation's talkies *Liliom* and *The Sea Wolf*, on the grounds that the films contain undesirable content.		President Gerardo Machado commits his first dictatorial act since being given broad authoritative powers by the Cuban Congress last week. The weekly newspapers *La Semana* and *Karikato* are officially banned, prompting riots in the streets that kill several newsboys. Dr. Cosme de la Torriente, former president of the League of Nations and now opposition leader, estimates that 70–80 percent of the Cuban population is against Machado's policies.	
Oct. 9		Mayor Gustav Boess of Berlin, Germany officially retires "for reasons of health." Boess will receive a pension of approximately $7,500 annually. His administration had come under scrutiny recently after accusations of business "favoritism" surfaced. . . . British Agriculture Minister Dr. Christopher Addison announces that as a means of reducing unemployment, the government will purchase farmland and turn it over to unemployed workers. "We shall equip the men with the best of material and stocks for a time until they get established."		President-General Jose Uriburu of Argentina appoints former ambassador to the Netherlands Felipe A. Epsil to the post of Minister to Norway and Denmark.	
Oct. 10	During a speech to the Canadian Chamber of Commerce, U.S. Chamber of Commerce chairman Julius Barnes lays blame to the ongoing business depression on governmental regulations. "The major continuous force in social stability lies in the field of economics of business rather than in the field of politics of government," he says.	Russian geographers establish the Khakassia subdivision, located in southern Siberia. . . . Memorial proceedings are held in St. Paul's Cathedral in London, England, for those aboard the British airship *R-101*, which crashed into the French countryside during its maiden voyage last week. The 48 coffins lie in state as thousands of Britons pay their condolences. Air Ministers from France, Italy, and the Netherlands are present.		Brazilian army officials announce that the city of Mineas Geraes, which was captured by rebel forces last week, is close to being recaptured.	
Oct. 11	The British Admiralty announces the British cruiser ships *Delhi* and *Dauntess* have been ordered to sail to Brazil in order to protect British interests.			As Brazil's infrastructure continues to be severely damaged from internal military conflicts, economic officials decide to temporarily suspend import duties on rice, lard, meat, potatoes, beans, condensed milk, butter, corn, and stock feed. The suspension will last no more than one month, according to U.S. Commercial Attache Carlton Jackson, who is situated in Rio de Janeiro.	
Oct. 12		British aeronautics officials say that due to the *R-101* airship disaster, Great Britain will produce no more flying airships. Instead, the lone remaining airship *R-100* will be flown cautiously, if at all. They add that helium will likely be substituted for hydrogen as the airship's fuel.	Health officials in Melilla, Morocco, report a small outbreak of the bubonic plague. Only a handful of infections have been discovered, but officials have taken the precautionary measure of instructing port authorities to keep a watchful eye.		
Oct. 13		Testimonies from leading British agriculturists on the floor of the House of Commons indicate the present farm crisis in Great Britain is the worst in over 50 years. Liberal lawmakers wish to solve the crisis by implementing a marketing board, while conservatives hope to establish a wheat quota.		Argentina finishes construction on its first airplane produced entirely within its borders. The small monoplane will undergo testing at the Cordoba airfield next week. The tests will be overseen by War Minister Medina.	

A	B	C	D	E
Includes developments that affect more than one world region, international organizations, and important meetings of world leaders.	*Includes all domestic and regional developments in Europe, including the Soviet Union.*	*Includes all domestic and regional developments in Africa and the Middle East.*	*Includes all domestic and regional developments in Latin America, the Caribbean, and Canada.*	*Includes all domestic and regional developments in Asian and Pacific nations (and colonies).*

U.S. Politics & Social Issues	U.S. Foreign Policy & Defense	Economics & Great Depression	Science, Technology & Nature	Culture, Leisure & Lifestyle	
The American Paper and Pulp Association reports that U.S. paper output in August was 15 percent lower than the total of August 1929.				The Philadelphia Athletics defeat the St. Louis Cardinals by a score of 7–1 to win the Major League Baseball World Series for the second consecutive year. George Earnshaw, who surrendered one run and five hits over nine innings, is declared the series' Most Valuable Player. Earnshaw garnered two wins and an earned run average of 0.72.	Oct. 8
The United Textile Workers of America requests $360,000 from the American Federation of Labor to enable 4,000 workers to strike at a textile plant in Danville, Va.		The U.S. Department of Commerce reports that during September, the U.S. shipped approximately 15,000 bales of cotton to Great Britain, less than 50 percent of the total from August 1929.	British aeronautical authorities notify the Airship Guarantee Company, Ltd. that due to the crash of the airship R-101, the government-owned company will most likely be disbanded.		Oct. 9
The National Broadcasting Company purchases the radio station WTAM in Cleveland, Ohio.		The Annalist releases it's weekly index of U.S. wholesale commodity prices. Sharp upturns of livestock and food products caused the index to rise 1.3 points from last week. Despite this, the current index is still 16 percent below the corresponding period in 1929. . . . R.G. Dun & Co. reports that in three months ended on September 30, there were a total of 102 bank failures, compared with 82 bank failures for the corresponding period of 1929. . . . The Federal Reserve Bank of New York reports that total brokers' loans in the U.S. for this week amounted to $2.9 billion, a decline of $158 million from last week and the lowest total seen since April 27, 1927.			Oct. 10
A group of prominent economists reports to New York Governor Franklin Roosevelt on ways to reduce his state's unemployment rate. Among them are the establishment of employment clearing houses, the appropriation of $175 million for public works projects, and the repeal of Prohibition to revive the alcohol industry and to provide jobs.		Dun's Review reports U.S. bank clearings for this week amounted to $9,654,927,000, 31 percent less than the total from the corresponding period one year ago. . . . U.S. economists report U.S. brokers' loans for this week amounted to $135,295,000, 45 percent less than last week. The change is mainly attributed to the decline of foreign loans. . . . Chile raises tariffs on both wool and radio sets. Wool will now have a duty of 40 pesos per gross kilogram; radio sets, 7 pesos per gross kilogram.			Oct. 11
		The British Board of Trade reports that during September, Great Britain exported approximately £78,650,000 worth of goods, less than 13 percent of the September 1929 total. Great Britain also imported approximately £42,740,000 worth of goods.		In Altoona, Pa., Billy Arnold defeats Deacon Litz in the Tiptown Bowl to clinch the title of national automobile racing champion.	Oct. 12
The American Federation of Labor denies a request to recognize a splinter group of the United Mine Workers of America as an official union. Explaining the decision, American Federation of Labor president William Green says his organization's official policy is to forbid "dual unionism." . . . In New York City 1,565,939 people register to vote in the upcoming gubernatorial election. There were 463,679 more registered voters for the 1928 presidential election, when former New York City governor Alfred Smith ran against Herbert Hoover.		The Commercial Attaché of the U.S. Embassy in Argentina reports that exports to the United States for the month of August totaled $3,341,000, against a total of $7,791,000 for August 1929, a decrease of 57 percent. Imports to the United States also fell by 47 percent as compared to August 1929.	Dr. D.W. Bronk of the University of Pennsylvania demonstrates a method whereby the electrical impulses generated through muscle contractions can be converted into audible sound via a radio amplifier. The method will be used to research nervous system diseases such as epilepsy.	Argentina clinches the annual South American tennis championship, defeating the Chilean squad in three straight sets, 7–5, 6–4, 6–4.	Oct. 13
F Includes elections, federal-state relations, civil rights and liberties, crime, the judiciary, education, healthcare, poverty, urban affairs, and population.	**G** Includes formation and debate of U.S. foreign and defense policies, veterans affairs, and defense spending. (Relations with specific foreign countries are usually found under the region concerned.)	**H** Includes business, labor, agriculture, taxation, transportation, consumer affairs, monetary and fiscal policy, natural resources, pollution, and accidents.	**I** Includes worldwide scientific, medical, and technological developments, natural phenomena, U.S. weather, and natural disasters.	**J** Includes the arts, religion, scholarship, communications media, sports, entertainment, fashions, fads, and social life.	

	World Affairs	Europe	Africa & The Middle East	The Americas	Asia & The Pacific
Oct. 14		First Baron Amulree William Warrender MacKenzie is appointed British Secretary of State for Air. MacKenzie replaces Christopher Birdwood Thompson, who perished in the airship *R-101* disaster on October 5. The position is the effective head of the Royal Air Force, and was first occupied by future prime minister Winston Churchill in 1919. . . . The German Trade Union Council releases a statement attributing the Versailles Treaty war reparations to be the cause of not only the current German business depression, but the worldwide depression as well. The council calls on the German government to "rid the world of this disturbing influence."			
Oct. 15	A five-day festival celebrating the independence of Belgium from colonial rule begins in New York City at Wanamaker Auditorium. Among the speakers at the festival is Prince Albert de Ligne, Belgian Ambassador to the United States.			The Brazilian government purchases 10 bombing planes from the American-owned Curtiss-Wright Export Corporation for use in ongoing internal military conflicts. . . . U.S. Secretary of State Henry Stimson meets with Brazilian Ambassador to the United States S. Gurgel de Amaral to discuss placing an embargo on war supplies to Brazilian revolutionists.	
Oct. 16	Warrington Dawson, former Special Attaché of the American Embassy in France, is awarded the ceremonial title of Commander of the Legion of Honor by French military authorities. French Foreign Minister Aristide Briand calls Dawson "an outstanding writer, historian and thinker."			Five university students in Havana, Cuba, are arrested during a demonstration to honor the death of Rafael Trejo, a student who was killed by police during a riot on September 30.	
Oct. 17		The trial of Archduke Leopold is set for November 7 by Judge Koenig in the French General Sessions. Leopold is accused of the unauthorized sale of a $400,000 Napoleonic-era diamond necklace. He was released earlier on a bail of $7,500.		The Canadian Ministry of Finance reports its gold reserve increased by $39,437,020 this week as compared to last.	In the city of Bombay, 200 Indian nationalists are arrested by imperial authorities, bringing the total to 350 people arrested since raids began on organizations of the All India Congress yesterday. Many of those arrested are "revolutionary singers."
Oct. 18				Argentine officials report automobile imports to the country in September are as follows: American, 3,191 automobiles and 156 trucks; Italian, 22 automobiles; British, 22 automobiles and 11 trucks; French, 4 automobiles; German, 3 automobiles; Belgian, 1 automobile and 1 truck; Swiss, 2 trucks. . . . The Mexican newspaper *Excelsior* reports that armed bandits lead by Leocadio Velasco have taken control of the village of Comitan.	Wholesale arrests of members of the All India National Congress by imperial authorities continue. Among those arrested include the secretary of the boycott committee, the president of the Youth League, and the editor of the Congress *Bulletin*.
Oct. 19	Police in New York City ban an upcoming demonstration at the British Consul General that would have protested the death sentences passed by British imperial authorities upon three Indian nationalists. Communist leader Bert Miller denounces the decision, saying, "the police exist for beating the unemployed and for the protection of British and American imperialism."	Former British Schneider Cup champion O.F. Worsley, one of the most famous aviators in Great Britain, experiences a head-on automobile collision and is pronounced dead upon his arrival at the local hospital.			

A	B	C	D	E
Includes developments that affect more than one world region, international organizations, and important meetings of world leaders.	*Includes all domestic and regional developments in Europe, including the Soviet Union.*	*Includes all domestic and regional developments in Africa and the Middle East.*	*Includes all domestic and regional developments in Latin America, the Caribbean, and Canada.*	*Includes all domestic and regional developments in Asian and Pacific nations (and colonies).*

U.S. Politics & Social Issues	U.S. Foreign Policy & Defense	Economics & Great Depression	Science, Technology & Nature	Culture, Leisure & Lifestyle	
Sessions of the National Conference of Jewish Farmers conclude in New York City. Delegates numbering 200 elect a committee of nine people to coordinate various Jewish farm organizations into a national body. . . . The Supreme Court grants the state of Arizona the right to file suit against owners of the Hoover Dam. Arizonans claim the dam deprives their state of valuable water and electrical rights.		The U.S. Department of Commerce releases its weekly index of U.S. automobile production. At 112.7, the figure is a reduction of 56 percent from the corresponding period a year ago. . . . By governmental decree, The Bank of Peru and London, the oldest bank in the history of Peru, is permitted to suspend tax payments to the government for one week. Economic officials fear the bank is approaching insolvency. . . . Metal workers in Berlin, Germany, vote to reject an arbitration that called for 7 percent wage cuts. Trade union representatives say at least 40,000 metal workers will go on strike tomorrow in response.			Oct. 14
At a meeting of the Conference for Progressive Labor Action in the New York City Free Employment Bureau, Executive Secretary Louis Budenz calls for a mass march on Washington to persuade President Herbert Hoover to appropriate $100 million for unemployment insurance.					Oct. 15
In a campaign speech, New York State Republican gubernatorial candidate Charles Tuttle assails the Democrats for their supposed delay in authorizing public works projects, adding, "The Democratic administration is hoping that the condition of depression may continue long enough in order that they might capitalize on it." . . . Former New York City police commissioner Grover Whalen reports that in the first nine months of 1930, 899 persons were killed and 40,762 more were injured in automobile-related accidents. Nearly a quarter of these people were children. Whalen adds that approximately 3,000 people in the United States die each year from automobile accidents.		Executives of the American Trust Company and the Bank of Manhattan Trust Company agree to merge their companies together. The combined financial resources of the two newly merged companies will be $461 million.			Oct. 16
The American Austin Car Company raises the listed price of its Austin coupe by $20 to $465. The Austin is the smallest car ever built inside the United States.		The monthly index of U.S. business activity as reported by *The Annalist* falls to a new low level of 78.6, 22 percent less than the corresponding index in 1929. . . . The National Electric Light Association reports that electric power output has fallen by 13 percent in one year. . . . The U.S. Federal Reserve Bank reports brokers' loans for this week amounted to $2.8 billion, a decline of $153 million from last week and the lowest total since February 16, 1927, when the figure was $2,718,634,000.	German astronomer Karl Wilhelm Reinmuth discovers the asteroids 1172 Aneas, 1173 Anchises, 1174 Marmara, and 1175 Margo at the Konigstuhl Observatory in Heidelburg, Germany.	The Association of National Advertisers extends an invitation to President Herbert Hoover to speak at their convention in Washington, D.C., on November 10. Hoover responds by saying he will take the request under consideration.	Oct. 17
The Navy awards a contract of $19 million to the Newport News Shipbuilding and Drydock Company to construct the country's first aircraft carrier since the Washington Naval Treaty of 1922. The vessel is temporarily known as *No. 4*.	In accordance with the London Naval Treaty, the U.S. Navy sells the destroyer USS *Corry* for scrap. . . . Construction of the yacht USS *Carnelian* is completed at Bath Iron Works in Maine. The ship would participate in Caribbean reconnaissance missions during World War II. . . . The U.S. Navy sends the 10,000-ton cruiser *Pensacola* to Brazil in order to protect U.S. nationals situated in the war-torn country.	*Dun's Review* reports bank clearings in the United States this week amounted to $9 billion, 36 percent less than the corresponding period a year ago.			Oct. 18
President Herbert Hoover and Interior Secretary Ray Wilbur approve a manual written by Dean William Gray of the College of Education of Chicago University that will instruct America's teachers on how to combat illiteracy among the nation's schoolchildren. The manual will be heavily distributed across the country.		Canada's Minister of Trade and Commerce begins an advertising campaign called "Prosperity Week" designed to inspire consumer confidence in the Canadian economy. Additionally, $20 million has been appropriated for unemployment insurance. The funds will be evenly distributed among Canada's various provinces. . . . The U.S. Department of Labor announces it is limiting the number of immigrant Canadian lumberjacks as a means of reducing national unemployment.			Oct. 19

F	G	H	I	J
Includes elections, federal-state relations, civil rights and liberties, crime, the judiciary, education, healthcare, poverty, urban affairs, and population.	Includes formation and debate of U.S. foreign and defense policies, veterans affairs, and defense spending. (Relations with specific foreign countries are usually found under the region concerned.)	Includes business, labor, agriculture, taxation, transportation, consumer affairs, monetary and fiscal policy, natural resources, pollution, and accidents.	Includes worldwide scientific, medical, and technological developments, natural phenomena, U.S. weather, and natural disasters.	Includes the arts, religion, scholarship, communications media, sports, entertainment, fashions, fads, and social life.

	World Affairs	Europe	Africa & The Middle East	The Americas	Asia & The Pacific
Oct. 20	The World Union of Zionist Revisionists assails a recent policy change by the British government that effectively negates the 1917 Balfour Declaration. "It is a considered and planned attack on all the bases upon which Jewish effort and achievement in Palestine have hitherto been rested," a statement reads.	British economists report the Bank of England took in approximately £1,750,666 worth of gold this week, against £479,477 withdrawn, a gold surplus of £479,477. . . . French Foreign Minister Aristide Briand faces internal criticism from those who believe he is partly responsible for the recent German elections in which fascist extremist parties gained significant representation. . . . Unemployment in Great Britain reaches 2,176,191 men, an increase of 14,502 men from the previous week and 768,966 men in 12 months, according to published reports. It is the highest total since 1921, except for the general business strike of 1926.		Vice President Enrique Santamarina of Argentina resigns. The office of vice president will remain vacant until the death of dictator Jose Felix Uriburu in 1932.	
Oct. 21		Police in Bucharest, Romania, uncover a Soviet spy ring numbering 140 people. Gustave Metha is identified as the organization's leader.			
Oct. 22		Seymour Parker Gilbert, agent general for reparations under the Dawes Plan, comments on the recent German Reichstag elections, calling Adolf Hitler "a stick of dynamite in the European situation."		President Washington Luis of Brazil signs a decree extending Brazil's bank holiday until November 30. The bank holiday has been in effect since the beginning of October. . . . Brazilian rebel forces announce the capture of the states of Matto Grosso and Goyaz.	
Oct. 23				Canadian economists report their country's gambling revenue has fallen by 15 percent in one year.	
Oct. 24	Leading British financial experts predict that the recent revolution in Argentina will have an adverse effect of $40 million on British railway trade.	Austria makes public a failed putsch attempt headed by General Ellison that would have taken place on October 25. The putsch was foiled when Interior Minister Prince von Starhemberg became aware of the plot. . . . The Zionist Pioneer Youth Organization smashes the windows of the British Consulate building in Warsaw, Poland, in a protest against Great Britain's policy towards Palestine.		Amidst decreasing coffee prices and internal political turmoil, President Washington Luis Pereira de Sousa of Brazil resigns peacefully in order to avoid military conflict. He is succeeded by his former Treasury Secretary Getulio Vargas, who resigned earlier this year to run for president. Vargas's term would last 15 years, unprecedented in Brazilian presidential history.	
Oct. 25	U.S. government officials express surprise over the Brazilian revolution. The official policy of the U.S. government had been to support loyalist forces. Economists fear trade with Brazil, which has increased by nearly 100 percent since World War I, may be adversely affected if the newly installed Brazilian government decides to declare international debts invalid.				British imperial officers say the recent border intrusions by Afghan Afridi tribesmen were probably financed by members of the revolutionary All India National Congress.

A	B	C	D	E
Includes developments that affect more than one world region, international organizations, and important meetings of world leaders.	*Includes all domestic and regional developments in Europe, including the Soviet Union.*	*Includes all domestic and regional developments in Africa and the Middle East.*	*Includes all domestic and regional developments in Latin America, the Caribbean, and Canada.*	*Includes all domestic and regional developments in Asian and Pacific nations (and colonies).*

U.S. Politics & Social Issues	U.S. Foreign Policy & Defense	Economics & Great Depression	Science, Technology & Nature	Culture, Leisure & Lifestyle	
		Rev. R.W. Sockman of the Madison Avenue Methodist Church calls the worldwide depression "basically a thing of the mind's creation" in his weekly sermon. "The trouble with our world is not that it has lost money, but that it has lost confidence," he says. . . . British economists report that during the month of September, Great Britain's steel output totaled 580,600 tons, 30 percent less than the corresponding period a year ago, when the total output was 847,900 tons.			Oct. 20
The city of Boston appropriates $3 million for unemployment relief. "Something must be done to insure protection and happiness this coming winter. The only solution is money," says City Councilor John F. Dowd in remarks to the press.		The Bank of Italy and the Bank of America of California merge to form the America National Trust and Savings Association. The combined resources of the two companies will be $1.25 billion. Bank of Italy president Arnold J. Mount will become the company's new president.		President E.S. Barnard of baseball's American League calls for an end to the sacrifice fly, which was instituted as a rule two years ago. "The sacrifice fly is one of the most absurd rules in baseball," he declares.	Oct. 21
Gang leader George "Bugs" Moran, a longtime rival of Al Capone, is arrested in Chicago, Ill., on charges of vagrancy. Many of Moran's associates were killed in the famous St. Valentine's Day Massacre of 1929. . . . The New York Stock Exchange announces the Houston Oil Company of Texas; the Cleveland & Pittsburgh Railroad Co.; the Pittsburgh, Cincinnati, Chicago, and St. Louis Railroad Co.; and the Republic of Cuba Co. have all been admitted to the exchange's list of tradable companies.	The U.S. Navy strikes the destroyers Osborne, Charles Ausburn, Toucey, and Flusser from the Naval Vessel Register.	Leading U.S. economists report that the recent revolution in Argentina has had a beneficial effect on U.S. trade to the South American country, as the new regime is friendlier toward U.S. business interests. . . . The American Railway Association reports U.S. car loadings for this week totaled 954,874 cars, less than 16 percent of the corresponding period a year ago.			Oct. 22
Spectator publishes a report made by the Prudential Life Insurance Company which shows that the current alcoholic death rate is 0.004 percent, 300 percent greater than the first year of Prohibition, when the alcoholic death rate was 0.001 percent.	Battery C of the Sixth Field Artillery in Fort Myer, Va., fires a ceremonial shot at 6:05 a.m. to commemorate the first shot fired by U.S. armed forces during World War I in 1917. The shot also marks the opening of the 12th reunion of the Society of the First Division. . . . The Navy General Board completes its 15-year naval construction outline which adheres to the terms set forth by the London Naval Treaty. $100 million is expected to be the average annual construction cost.	During a meeting of the Berlin Municipal Council, Mayor Reinhold Scholz announces the city's budget deficit is currently $20 million. Scholz says the deficit has been caused by unemployment expenditures, and that it will likely increase during the winter months. City treasurer Dr. Lange calls for an emergency appropriation of $5 million to pay city employees' salaries.			Oct. 23
Gang leader Joe Aiello, rival of Al "Scarface" Capone and partner of George "Bugs" Moran, is riddled with assassins' bullets and killed in a residential district of Chicago, Ill. . . .The Department of Commerce publishes statistics showing that U.S. infant mortality and birth rates for 1929 were the lowest of any year since 1915, with one exception. The infant mortality rate for 1929 was 6.8 percent, while the birth rate was 1.9 percent. The state of New Mexico had the highest infant mortality rate, 14.5 percent, and also the highest birth rate, 2.7 percent.		The Annalist releases its weekly index of U.S. wholesale commodity prices. At 121.2, the figure is a drop of 0.4 points from last week's index and a reduction of 17 percent from the corresponding period a year ago. . . . British economists report the Bank of England took in £1,104,000 worth of gold this week. . . . The U.S. Federal Reserve Bank reports brokers' loans for this week totaled $2,.6 billion, $139 million less than last week and the lowest figure since November 24, 1926, when the total was $2,608,283,000.			Oct. 24
Transcontinental and Western Airways begins operating the first regular passenger flights between New York and Los Angeles.		The trustees of the Philippine Sugar Association adopt a resolution curbing sugar output as a means of improving the price of sugar. . . . Dun's Review reports U.S. bank clearings for this week totaled $9,375,558,000, 36 percent less than the corresponding period a year ago. . . . U.S. economists report new bond offerings on the New York Stock Exchange this week totaled $99,698,598, 19 percent greater than last week's total of $80,106,000.			Oct. 25

F	G	H	I	J
Includes elections, federal-state relations, civil rights and liberties, crime, the judiciary, education, healthcare, poverty, urban affairs, and population.	Includes formation and debate of U.S. foreign and defense policies, veterans affairs, and defense spending. (Relations with specific foreign countries are usually found under the region concerned.)	Includes business, labor, agriculture, taxation, transportation, consumer affairs, monetary and fiscal policy, natural resources, pollution, and accidents.	Includes worldwide scientific, medical, and technological developments, natural phenomena, U.S. weather, and natural disasters.	Includes the arts, religion, scholarship, communications media, sports, entertainment, fashions, fads, and social life.

	World Affairs	Europe	Africa & The Middle East	The Americas	Asia & The Pacific
Oct. 26					
Oct. 27	The Belgian government officially bans the Soviet importation of Russian grains, flours, and wines. The Antwerp Chamber of Commerce releases a statement denouncing the decision. The government also stipulates that henceforth all ships entering Belgian territory must provide a label identifying the ship's nationality. In response, the Russian government diverts 20 ships en route to the major industrial city of Antwerp.	British economists report the Bank of England took in approximately £1,250,854 of gold last week, against £267,423 in gold withdrawn, a gold surplus of £983,431. . . . Germany's financial market reacts favorably to news of possible renegotiations of the World War I reparations. Fascist leader Adolf Hitler has officially denounced the reparations.			
Oct. 28		Newspapers in Albania report on the grave condition of King Ahmet Zogu, who is suffering from throat cancer. Three Italian medical specialists are overseeing the King's recuperation.			
Oct. 29	Emperor Haile Selassie of Ethiopia officially welcomes the Duke of Gloucester, son of King George V, in the city of Addis Ababa. A makeshift throne room was constructed to make the monarch feel at home.	King George V of the United Kingdom delivers a speech opening the official session of Parliament.			
Oct. 30	Adolphe Deitte replaces Georghes Prouteaux as French Lieutenant-Governor of Upper Oubangui, later known as the Central African Republic.				
Oct. 31	The Netherlands agrees to enter into the Geneva Protocol, an international treaty banning chemical weapons that was first signed in 1925.				
Nov. 1		The Communist Party of Iceland is formed. Soviet officials immediately make the party a member of the Comintern, the predominant international Communist organization. The party will dissolve in 1938.			

A	B	C	D	E
Includes developments that affect more than one world region, international organizations, and important meetings of world leaders.	*Includes all domestic and regional developments in Europe, including the Soviet Union.*	*Includes all domestic and regional developments in Africa and the Middle East.*	*Includes all domestic and regional developments in Latin America, the Caribbean, and Canada.*	*Includes all domestic and regional developments in Asian and Pacific nations (and colonies).*

U.S. Politics & Social Issues	U.S. Foreign Policy & Defense	Economics & Great Depression	Science, Technology & Nature	Culture, Leisure & Lifestyle	
Mayor Jimmy Walker of New York City orders the display of the American flag on all public buildings in commemoration of Navy Day. Navy Secretary Charles Francis Adams chose October 26 as Navy Day because it is the birthday of former president Theodore Roosevelt, who was also Assistant Secretary of the Navy and the first American to win the Nobel Prize.		The Baltimore & Ohio Railroad purchases 75,000 tons of rail worth approximately $4.8 million. . . . Panama Canal officials report that during the month of September, 2,432,783 tons of cargo passed through the canal, 100,000 tons less than the previous month and 15 percent less than the corresponding period a year ago. . . . The U.S. Department of Commerce reduces the export price of copper by 0.5 cents, from 10.3 to 9.8 cents a pound. The change was made to reflect the price reductions of private copper smelters. As a result, 800,000 pounds of copper are sold for export the next morning.		The American Amateur Athletic Union appoints a group of 600 sportsmen to select this year's recipient of the James E. Sullivan Memorial Medal. . . . Fred Paisley publishes *Al Capone: The Biography of a Self-Made Man.*	Oct. 26
The Department of Commerce reports that 29,531 people died in automobile accidents during the year of 1929, a rise of 3,000 deaths over the previous year. The report also adds that the automobile death rate for 1929 was 0.25 percent.		The Italian Bank, the International Bank of Peru, the Popular Bank of Peru, the German Transatlantic Bank, the National City Bank, the Anglo-South American Bank, and the Royal Bank of Canada collectively pool resources worth $2 million to help the Bank of Peru and London pay off its savings depositors.			Oct. 27
Police in Pittsburgh, Pa., officially forbid James H. Maurer, Socialist gubernatorial candidate, from holding public demonstrations and campaign rallies. Police Superintendent Walsh says the meetings are a traffic nuisance.	In a speech marking the celebration of Navy Day, naval operations chief Admiral William Pratt declares that "economy, pacifism, international brotherhood, and what not" are destroying the U.S. Navy. . . . The Wisconsin Council of the American Legion recommends to Washington that they allow unemployed men to enlist in the army as means of reducing national unemployment. The plan is a suitable alternative to a "dole" system, says Wisconsin State Adjutant Austin Peterson.			National Academy of Design associate Albert Sterner assails French art in a speech marking the opening of one his exhibitions. "The adulation by the so-called intellectual group in America of the work of French modernists has caused a psychological state of mind in every young artist which forces him to imitate the foreigners in order to be thought a good artist at all," he says.	Oct. 28
	Congress passes a resolution creating an anti-war board, whose purpose is to eliminate war profiteering and maintain peaceful international relations. Among the members of the board are War Secretary Patrick Hurley, Navy Secretary Charles Francis Adams, Agriculture Secretary Arthur Hyde, Commerce Secretary Robert Lamont, Labor Secretary James Davis, and Attorney General DeWitt Mitchell.				Oct. 29
					Oct. 30
	In accordance with the London Naval Treaty, the U.S. Navy sells the destroyer *Kidder* for scrap. . . . The U.S. Navy transfers the destroyer *James K. Paulding* to the Philadelphia Navy Yard for decommissioning.				Oct. 31
	The U.S. Navy strikes the light cruiser *Galveston* from the list of the Naval Vessel Register. Constructed by the William R. Trigg Company of Virginia in 1901, the USS *Galveston* was responsible for convoy escort duties in both Europe and Southeast Asia over a period of 30 years.	*Dun's Review* reports U.S. bank clearings for this week totaled $7,996,946,000, 14 percent less than the preceding week's total of $9,375,558,000 and a decline of 65 percent from the corresponding period a year ago. . . . The New York Stock Exchange reports that new bond offerings this week amounted to $24,228,000, compared with $99,698,598 in the preceding week. It is the lowest amount since the week of December 27, 1929, when on the heels of the stock market crash, bond offerings amounted to only $9,010,000.			Nov. 1

F	**G**	**H**	**I**	**J**
Includes elections, federal-state relations, civil rights and liberties, crime, the judiciary, education, healthcare, poverty, urban affairs, and population.	*Includes formation and debate of U.S. foreign and defense policies, veterans affairs, and defense spending. (Relations with specific foreign countries are usually found under the region concerned.)*	*Includes business, labor, agriculture, taxation, transportation, consumer affairs, monetary and fiscal policy, natural resources, pollution, and accidents.*	*Includes worldwide scientific, medical, and technological developments, natural phenomena, U.S. weather, and natural disasters.*	*Includes the arts, religion, scholarship, communications media, sports, entertainment, fashions, fads, and social life.*

	World Affairs	Europe	Africa & The Middle East	The Americas	Asia & The Pacific
Nov. 2					
Nov. 3	A jury in Egypt awards 15 American tourists financial compensation for losses sustained during a fire aboard the Egyptian tourist train *Khedival* in March 1928. The Egyptian government subsequently issues an appeal of the decision.		King Tafari Makonnen of Ethiopia is officially crowned emperor and changes his name to Haile Selassie, the baptismal name given to him during his christening as an infant. Selassie succeeds Empress Zauditu, who died from complications arising from diabetes six months prior. Selassie will implement Ethiopia's first written constitution and bicameral legislature. He will endure a brief period of exile after the invasion of his country by fascist Italy in 1935, during which time he will win *Time* magazine's Man of the Year award. He will return after Italy's defeat by the Allied forces in 1941 and rule as emperor until his death in 1975.	Panamanians celebrate their country's 27th anniversary of independence from Colombian rule. It was in 1903 that a separatist junta led by Dr. Manuel Amador Guerrero defeated the Colombian army. U.S. troops were dispatched by then president Theodore Roosevelt to protect the newly installed government. Because of the military assistance, the United States was granted in 1914 exclusive construction and administration rights of the Panama Canal.	
Nov. 4	French Deputy Foreign Minister Henry Bouillon criticizes Foreign Minister Aristide Briand's peaceful appeasement policy on German rearmament in a speech to the French Radical Independent Party. "If Germany wishes to change their eastern or western boundaries and revise the Treaty of Versailles, it means only one thing, and that is war. There is only one way to avoid war, and that is for all Frenchmen to unite and declare firmly that we have a military alliance with Poland and whoever touches Poland touches France." He predicts, "When we begin talking in that manner the danger will vanish."				
Nov. 5		Rauof Fitzo, Albanian minister of foreign and interior affairs, officially announces his resignation. Deputy Interior Minister Musa Juka is nominated as his successor. . . . Police in Vienna, Austria, conduct a raid on the headquarters of the Socialist Party. Newspapers including *Allgemeine Zeitung* and stores supportive of socialism are also raided. Viennese police confiscate over 4,000 rifles and 20 machine guns. Socialist leaders urge their followers to remain passive against the government, as they fear a backlash will lead to a postponement of the upcoming elections.			In Kowloon, Hong Kong, construction begins on the La Salle College, a seven-story secondary school capable of housing over 1,800 students. Hong Kong Governor William Peel oversees the construction. La Salle College would teach such notable alumni as actor Bruce Lee and television producer James Wong.
Nov. 6				Veteran American aviator Orton Hoover is arrested in Sao Paulo, Brazil, by the newly installed Brazilian government on charges of spying for the U.S. government. Hoover had conducted bombing raids against rebel forces during the recent revolution.	

A	B	C	D	E
Includes developments that affect more than one world region, international organizations, and important meetings of world leaders.	Includes all domestic and regional developments in Europe, including the Soviet Union.	Includes all domestic and regional developments in Africa and the Middle East.	Includes all domestic and regional developments in Latin America, the Caribbean, and Canada.	Includes all domestic and regional developments in Asian and Pacific nations (and colonies).

U.S. Politics & Social Issues	U.S. Foreign Policy & Defense	Economics & Great Depression	Science, Technology & Nature	Culture, Leisure & Lifestyle	
		The Annalist releases its weekly index of U.S. business activity. At 82.5, the figure is a drop of 0.5 points from the preceding week and a decline of 17 percent from the corresponding week a year ago. Economists say the decline was caused by sharp declines in electric power production and steel mill activity. . . . The New York Stock Exchange adds the Columbia Carbon Company to its list of tradable companies.	Noted American paleontologist Oliver Perry Hay dies. Hay was a research associate of the Carnegie Institute. His writings are archived by the Smithsonian Institute.		**Nov. 2**
	The U.S. Navy strikes the destroyer *Moody*, named after Supreme Court Justice William Henry Moody, from the list of the Naval Vessel Register. She will eventually be sold in 1933 to executives of the Metro-Goldwyn-Mayer film studio, who detonated the ship and filmed it for use in the movie *Hell Below*.	German economics officials raise the Berlin financial money rate from 6 percent to 7 percent.		The play *The Private Lives of Elizabeth and Essex* premieres in New York City. The play would be adapted into a film version in 1939.	**Nov. 3**
The Census Bureau reports that in 1929 there were 4,339 deaths attributable to alcohol poisoning, compared with 4,627 deaths in 1928, a decrease of 6 percent.					**Nov. 4**
Mafia kingpin Alfred "Al Mineo" Manfredi, leader of one of the five major crime families in New York City, is shot to death in the Bronx, New York, by armed men associated with mob rival Salvatore Maranzano. . . . The American Bureau of Shipping reports 22 U.S. shipyards are currently constructing 408,155 tons of ships.	The U.S. Navy strikes the destroyer *Abel P. Upshur*, named after the Naval Secretary of the same name, from the list of the Naval Vessel Register. The USS *Abel P. Upshur* will be sold to Great Britain in 1940 and renamed the HMS *Clare* as part of an agreement whereby the United States exchanged 50 obsolete destroyers for military bases in British colonial territory.	The American Railway Association reports U.S. freight car loadings for this week totaled 931,085 cars, against 959,335 cars from the preceding week, a decline of 3 percent. It is also a decline of 15 percent from the corresponding week a year ago.		The Third Academy Awards of Arts and Sciences is held in the Ambassador Hotel in Los Angeles, Calif. Universal Pictures' *All Quiet on the Western Front*, based on the novel by Erich Remarque, is awarded Best Picture and Best Director. Norma Shearer and George Arliss win Best Actress and Best Actor, respectively. The 83-year-old inventor Thomas Edison is made an honorary Academy member.	**Nov. 5**
	In accordance with the London Naval Treaty, the U.S. Navy sells the hospital ship *Solace* to the Boston Metal Co. for scrap. Purchased from France in 1898, the USS *Solace's* main activity was transporting wounded U.S. servicemen out of Spain during the Spanish-American War of 1899.	U.S. economists report the price of rye has fallen to its lowest point since 1898. . . . Canadian Labor Minister Gideon D. Robertson reports that a bill providing $37 million for public works projects has received final approval from the Canadian Senate. Most of the funds will be reserved for the Canadian National Railways, which economic officials hope will improve the country's infrastructure.			**Nov. 6**

F	G	H	I	J
Includes elections, federal-state relations, civil rights and liberties, crime, the judiciary, education, healthcare, poverty, urban affairs, and population.	*Includes formation and debate of U.S. foreign and defense policies, veterans affairs, and defense spending. (Relations with specific foreign countries are usually found under the region concerned.)*	*Includes business, labor, agriculture, taxation, transportation, consumer affairs, monetary and fiscal policy, natural resources, pollution, and accidents.*	*Includes worldwide scientific, medical, and technological developments, natural phenomena, U.S. weather, and natural disasters.*	*Includes the arts, religion, scholarship, communications media, sports, entertainment, fashions, fads, and social life.*

	World Affairs	Europe	Africa & The Middle East	The Americas	Asia & The Pacific
Nov. 7	Sessions of the Preparatory Disarmament Commission resume in Geneva, Switzerland. Delegates from over a dozen nations are present. Chairman Jonkheer Loudon of the Netherlands comments that a failure to reach an agreement "would be in the highest degree prejudicial to the cause of peace, which more than ever in the present disturbed state of affairs requires to be strengthened."				
Nov. 8	At the Preparatory Disarmament Commission in Geneva, Switzerland, representatives from Great Britain, the United States, and Japan tentatively agree on a proposal that would strictly limit the amount of personnel able to serve in each country's navy.			Judge Eleodoro Fierro is arrested by Argentine authorities in the city of Buenos Aires. Fierro, a former president of the Argentine Federal Court of Appeals, was stripped of his title for refusing to recognize the legitimacy of the military junta which overran President Hipolito Yrigoyen's government in September.	Jack Lang begins his second term as premier of New South Wales. Lang was elected in October in a landslide over conservative incumbent Thomas Bavin of the Nationalist Party, who had worsened economic conditions by cutting public works programs. Lang implemented several measures to stimulate the economy, including the cancellation of interest payments by Australian banks and the abolition of the gold standard. The measures backfired, however, and by 1932 Australia's unemployment rate had skyrocketed to 28 percent of the working male population.
Nov. 9					
Nov. 10					
Nov. 11	Armistice Day is celebrated by nations across the world. The day marks the official end of World War I on November 11, 1918. After World War II, the United States changed it to Veterans' Day and Great Britain changed it to Remembrance Day.		Ethiopian Emperor Haile Selassie announces the construction of a $1 million palace. Under Ethiopian law, the Emperor does not receive a salary, so the palace's construction funds will be largely based on "voluntary contributions" from the Ethiopian people.	In Argentina, the Independent Socialist Party merges with the National Democratic Federation.	
Nov. 12				Dr. Don Manuel E. Malbran is appointed Argentine Ambassador to the United States. Malbran had earlier occupied the position, but resigned in late 1928 in a protest against President Hipolito Irigoyen's policies toward the United States. He now resumes the post under General Jose Felix Uriburu's newly installed military regime.	
Nov. 13	British lawmakers draft a proposal on the importation, exportation, and production of cocaine and other various narcotic drugs. The proposal will be submitted to the League of Nations' Opium Advisory Committee when sessions convene in January.	Anti-Semitic demonstrations occur in the Hungarian city of Szeged. University students attempt to overrun the offices of a liberal, Jewish newspaper, but police successfully quell them with force. Szeged is the second largest city in Hungary, behind the capital of Budapest.		The Colombian Senate introduces a bill that would for the first time regulate cocaine traffic in the South American country. The newly created Office of Public Hygiene would assume a government monopoly of the drug, while penalties would include confiscation, fines, and imprisonment.	

A	B	C	D	E
Includes developments that affect more than one world region, international organizations, and important meetings of world leaders.	Includes all domestic and regional developments in Europe, including the Soviet Union.	Includes all domestic and regional developments in Africa and the Middle East.	Includes all domestic and regional developments in Latin America, the Caribbean, and Canada.	Includes all domestic and regional developments in Asian and Pacific nations (and colonies).

U.S. Politics & Social Issues	U.S. Foreign Policy & Defense	Economics & Great Depression	Science, Technology & Nature	Culture, Leisure & Lifestyle	
The Chamber of Commerce of New York State calls on President Herbert Hoover to place a ban on Soviet immigration, which the Chamber says has seriously undermined U.S. economic interests.	Major General Guy Henry reports the Army's cavalry currently totals 7,974 men, a reduction of 60 percent from 1920, when 20,000 enlisted men were a part of the cavalry.	*The Annalist* releases its weekly index of U.S. wholesale commodity prices. At 120.3, the figure is a reduction of 1.6 points from the preceding week and is 16 percent less than the corresponding period of last year. It is also the lowest index since January 1916. Blame for the decline is placed on sharp price drops in grains, livestock, and cotton. . . . The National Electric Light Association releases its weekly index of U.S. electric power production. At 88.7, the figure is nearly identical to last week's index of 88.8. Economists say the stabilization was caused by an increase in East Coast power production, offset by a decrease in west coast power production.			Nov. 7
		Dun's Review reports U.S. bank clearings for this week totaled $8,208,958,000, 3 percent greater than the preceding week's total of $7,996,946,000 but a decline of 50 percent from the corresponding period a year ago. . . . U.S. economists report new bond offerings of the New York Stock Exchange this week amounted to $41.3 million, an increase of approximately $17 million from the previous week.	Aviator Alicia Patterson lands at Curtiss Airport in Long Island, N.Y., after completing a trip from Cleveland, Ohio, in 2 hours and 49 minutes. Patterson's time is a U.S. record for women.		Nov. 8
	Tasker Howard Bliss dies in Washington, D.C., and is buried at Arlington National Cemetery. Bliss served as Army Chief of Staff from 1917–18 and was a recipient of the Distinguished Service Medal and the Legion of Honor.	*The Annalist* releases its weekly index of U.S. business activity. At 83, the figure is exactly identical to the preceding week and a decline of 17 percent from the corresponding week a year ago. Economists say the stabilization was caused by sharp declines in steel mill production, offset by an increase in freight car loadings.			Nov. 9
	The U.S. Navy transfers the destroyer *Sands* to Philadelphia to begin the process of deactivation. The USS *Sands* was constructed at the New York Shipbuilding Corporation and would conduct coastal escort missions both before and during World War II.				Nov. 10
Albert Einstein, largely considered the greatest scientist of the 20th century, is awarded U.S. Patent No. 1,781,541 for his invention of a thermodynamic refrigeration cycle.					Nov. 11
		The American Railway Association reports U.S. freight car loadings for this week totaled 934,640 cars, against 959,335 cars from the preceding week, a decline of 2.5 percent. It is also a decline of 13 percent from the corresponding week a year ago. . . . The U.S. Federal Reserve Board reports that during the month of October, bank debits in 141 leading financial institutions amounted to $54 billion, nearly 50 percent less than the total of the corresponding month a year ago, $95,527,155,000. . . . The New York Stock Exchange strikes the Hershey Chocolate Corporation and the Buffalo and Susquehanna Railroad Company from its list of tradable companies.			Nov. 12
New York City Police Commissioner Edward Mulrooney, anticipating the popularity of the city's newly constructed West Side Highway, sets a speed limit of 35 miles per hour and temporarily bans trucks. The highway will be completely rebuilt after collapsing in 1973, and renamed the Joe DiMaggio Expressway to honor the late baseball player in 1999.			New York City's West Side Highway, one of the first urban freeways ever built, is officially opened for traffic after 18 months of construction and nearly $15 million in funds spent. It spans from 57th Street to 72nd Street in the heart of Manhattan. The idea for the highway was initially conceived by former police commissioner Richard Enright, who claimed traffic congestion had created blockages for fire engines.		Nov. 13

F	G	H	I	J
Includes elections, federal-state relations, civil rights and liberties, crime, the judiciary, education, healthcare, poverty, urban affairs, and population.	Includes formation and debate of U.S. foreign and defense policies, veterans affairs, and defense spending. (Relations with specific foreign countries are usually found under the region concerned.)	Includes business, labor, agriculture, taxation, transportation, consumer affairs, monetary and fiscal policy, natural resources, pollution, and accidents.	Includes worldwide scientific, medical, and technological developments, natural phenomena, U.S. weather, and natural disasters.	Includes the arts, religion, scholarship, communications media, sports, entertainment, fashions, fads, and social life.

	World Affairs	Europe	Africa & The Middle East	The Americas	Asia & The Pacific
Nov. 14	Major international copper manufacturers meet in New York City to discuss falling prices, and agree on a proposal that would limit copper production by 20,000 tons per month. Manufacturers hope the reduction will make supply fall in line with demand. The price of copper has fallen from a record high of 24 cents a pound in early 1929 to approximately 10 cents currently, the lowest price at which copper has been traded in over 30 years.			President Gerardo Machado of Cuba temporarily suspends his country's constitution as severe riots between students and police result in the deaths of seven people and property damages of $100,000. The suspension will reportedly last for 25 days. Police conduct wholesale arrests on students and newspaper vendors.	
Nov. 15				The provisional military government controlling Argentina announces that elections will likely take place in either March or April of next year. . . . Dr. Landaburu of Argentina is administered the oath of office and becomes the governor of the Argentine province of San Luis. . . . Holcroft Watson and Ermyntrude Harvey of Great Britain win the Argentine women's tennis doubles championship, defeating Lilli de Alvarez and Inez Anderson in straight sets, 6–3, 6–3, and 6–2.	
Nov. 16					The annual anti-opium week is held in China under the control of the National Anti-Opium Association. Post offices are required to distribute anti-opium literature, and movie houses are to show anti-opium films. Airplanes are used to drop pamphlets in locations outside China's major industrial centers, where opium use is the most prevalent.
Nov. 17		Henry Cheron is chosen as the new French Minister of Justice, a position he would hold until 1931. Cheron's predecessor was Raoul Peret.			
Nov. 18	U.S. leaders in Washington express casual indifference over the election of Stenio Vincent as president of Haiti. Vincent's anti-Americanism, they allege, is the Haitian norm, as years of U.S. occupation have created a culture of anti-imperialism. . . . Former U.S. Undersecretary of State Reuben Clark leaves from Washington, D.C., en route to Mexico to assume his duties as Ambassador to Mexico. Clark had earlier officially replaced Dwight W. Morrow, who resigned to run for the New Jersey Senate on the Republican ticket.			Stenio Vincent is chosen by the Haitian National Assembly to assume the duties of the country's presidency. Vincent had gained a reputation in Haiti's national legislature as a staunch anti-American who detested his country's occupation by U.S. military forces. He replaces Louis Eugene Roy, who was chosen as the interim president of Haiti following the resignation of Louis Borno. Vincent will be forced to resign as president in 1941, when critics allege he chose a tepid response to the murder of 15,000 Haitian migrant workers in the Dominican Republic.	
Nov. 19				Charles Dalton replaces Frank Richard Heartz as Lieutenant Governor of the Canadian province of Prince Edward Island. Dalton would occupy the post until his death in 1933.	

A	B	C	D	E
Includes developments that affect more than one world region, international organizations, and important meetings of world leaders.	Includes all domestic and regional developments in Europe, including the Soviet Union.	Includes all domestic and regional developments in Africa and the Middle East.	Includes all domestic and regional developments in Latin America, the Caribbean, and Canada.	Includes all domestic and regional developments in Asian and Pacific nations (and colonies).

U.S. Politics & Social Issues	U.S. Foreign Policy & Defense	Economics & Great Depression	Science, Technology & Nature	Culture, Leisure & Lifestyle	
	The U.S. Navy strikes the destroyer *Henshaw*, named after Naval Secretary David Henshaw, from the list of the Naval Vessel Register. A product of the Bethlehem Shipbuilding Corporation, the ship will provide training exercises for naval recruits in the Pacific coast for 10 years. . . . The destroyer *Wood* is sold for scrap by the U.S. Navy. After being constructed by the Bethlehem Shipbuilding Corporation in 1919, the USS *Wood* would conduct training exercises in the Pacific.	The National Electric Light Association releases its weekly index of U.S. electric power production. At 87.2, the figure is a decrease of 1.5 points from the preceding week and a decline of 13 percent from the corresponding period of last year. Industrialists say the decline was only seasonal, as it was caused by the Election Day national holiday.	Great Britain test flies its newest aircraft, the *H.P.42*, a four-engine biplane that was designed and built by Imperial Airways, later known as British Airways. The *H.P.42* would be used for commercial and tourist transport until becoming obsolete in 1940 at the outset of World War II.	The Army and Navy football teams agree to compete in the 40th annual contest on December 13.	Nov. 14
The advertising agencies H.K. McCann Company and Erickson Company merge to form McCann-Erickson, Inc. . . . Gangster Al "Scarface" Capone opens a soup kitchen on 935 South State Street in Chicago, Ill. The kitchen is designed to feed 3,000 hungry men and women daily. . . . Filming is completed on Universal Pictures' *Dracula*. The film's budget is $355,000, or approximately $40 million if adjusted for modern inflation. An adaptation of a novel by Bram Stoker, *Dracula* would be remade over a dozen times. In 2000, the American National Film Preservation Board deemed the film "culturally significant."	The U.S. Navy recommissions the destroyer *Lamberton* for the purposes of providing training exercises for navy recruits. The USS *Lamberton* had earlier conducted Atlantic Fleet reconnaissance missions. In 1940, the ship will be reclassified as a "minesweeper" and will conduct sweeping operations until being sold for scrap in 1947 at the end of World War I. . . . The U.S. Navy decommissions the destroyer *Hazelwood*, named after naval officer John Hazelwood. Constructed by the Union Iron Works Company in 1917, the USS *Hazelwood's* primary purpose was to conduct Mediterranean and Caribbean escort missions.	*The Annalist* releases its weekly index of U.S. wholesale commodity prices. At 188.6, the figure is a reduction of 1.7 points from the preceding week and is 16 percent less than the corresponding period of last year. It is also the lowest index in nearly 20 years. Blame for the decline is placed on sharp price drops in wheat, cotton, and hogs. . . . *Dun's Review* reports U.S. bank clearings for this week totaled $8,554,562,000, 4 percent greater than the preceding week's total of $8,208,958,000 but a decline of 41 percent from the corresponding period a year ago. . . . Recently released economic documents indicate new bond offerings on the New York Stock Exchange this week totaled $24,464,000.		The multi-million dollar war movie *Hell's Angels* is released throughout the United States. The film is the directorial debut of aviator and businessman Howard Hughes, who would go on to direct only one more motion picture, *The Outlaw*, in 1943. With such an expensive budget, the film failed to turn a profit and was considered a financial failure. However, *Hell's Angels* would be nominated for the 1931 Academy Award for Best Cinematography.	Nov. 15
New York state budget directors report that income taxes account for over 69 percent of the state's total tax revenue.		*The Annalist* releases its weekly index of U.S. business activity. At 81.2, the figure is a drop of 1.8 points from the preceding week and a decline of 17 percent from the corresponding week a year ago. Economists say the drop was caused by sharp declines in steel mill production, freight car loadings, and electric power production.	Rev. Dr. Fulton Sheen of Catholic University assails an article in *The New York Times* that was written by Albert Einstein, in which he espouses his atheist theory of a "cosmical" origin of mankind. "Because Einstein knows a great deal about mathematical physics does not mean that he knows about religion," Sheen says. He humorously adds that Einstein's theory should be "comical" instead of "cosmical."		Nov. 16
		The American Exchange Trust Company of Little Rock, Ark., announces the "suspension of payments to depositors." Officials say the action was taken after an excessive amount of $4 million was withdrawn by bank patrons over a period of five days. The suspension is expected to last for 10 days. The American Exchange Trust Company is one of the oldest banks in Arkansas, having been established in the year 1870.		The National Hockey League opens its season at Madison Square Garden in front of a crowd of 15,000 people. The West Point Military Academy marching band dons skates to perform the opening ceremony program. Only one goal was scored in the contest, as the New York Americans defeated the Montreal Maroons by a score of 1–0.	Nov. 17
Clarence D. Clark, the first Congressional representative from the state of Wyoming, dies at his home in Evanston, Wyo. . . . The New York Stock Exchange strikes the Houston Oil Company of Texas and the Utah Power and Light Company from its list of tradable companies.	The U.S. Navy strikes the destroyer *Sumner* from the list of the Naval Vessel Register. The USS *Sumner's* only naval activity outside of patrolling was its dispatch to Mexico in 1921 to protect Americans from violent revolutionaries. . . . The U.S. Navy decommissions the destroyer *Downes*. A product of the New York Shipbuilding Company, the ship served as a convoy escort for British port-bound vessels, as well as a member of the U.S. Rum Patrol. . . . The U.S. Navy strikes the USS *Ludlow* from the list of the Naval Vessel Register. Named after naval officer Augustus Ludlow, it was constructed by the Union Iron Works Company in 1918 and conducted training missions for more than 10 years.	The American Acceptance Council reports bankers' bills for the month of October amounted to $1,508,243,726, an increase of $141,509,569 from the month of September. . . . More than 50 banks in the southern United States are forced to temporarily suspend business. One bank president, James Brown of the National Bank of Kentucky, attributes the closings to "withdrawals in the past week and constantly increasing rumors on the streets," adding, "it was advisable to close the banks, at least temporarily, for the best interests of the depositors and all concerned." U.S law stipulates that banks may suspend payments to depositors for a maximum of five days. Police have been contacted to control rioting crowds in front of several banks.			Nov. 18
The American Bar Association releases the results of a survey on the repeal of the Prohibition Amendment for which 20,000 members of the association were polled. Of these, 13,779 voted yes for Prohibition repeal. Representatives say the American Bar Association will likely draft a resolution reflecting the study's statistics.		The American Railway Association reports U.S. freight car loadings for this week totaled 881,401 cars, against 934,640 cars from the preceding week, a decline of 5 percent. It is also a decline of 16 percent from the corresponding week a year ago. Economists claim the decline was caused by sharp decreases in coal, ore, and grains.		The play *Should Ladies Behave* premiers in New York City. It will be adapted into a film version in 1933.	Nov. 19
F Includes elections, federal-state relations, civil rights and liberties, crime, the judiciary, education, healthcare, poverty, urban affairs, and population.	**G** Includes formation and debate of U.S. foreign policies, veterans affairs, and defense spending. (Relations with specific foreign countries are usually found under the region concerned.)	**H** Includes business, labor, agriculture, taxation, transportation, consumer affairs, monetary and fiscal policy, natural resources, pollution, and accidents.	**I** Includes worldwide scientific, medical, and technological developments, natural phenomena, U.S. weather, and natural disasters.	**J** Includes the arts, religion, scholarship, communications media, sports, entertainment, fashions, fads, and social life.	

	World Affairs	Europe	Africa & The Middle East	The Americas	Asia & The Pacific
Nov. 20	During sessions of the League of Nations in Geneva, Switzerland, Romanian Commerce Minister M. Manoilescu asks Western European nations to exercise preferential treatment toward Polish agriculture exports. Manoilescu claims the trade relationship between the United States and Western Europe has created unbalanced commerce. The countries Manoilescu asks for preferential treatment include Germany, France, Great Britain, Holland, Italy, Austria, Czechoslovakia, Belgium, Norway, Sweden, Finland, and Switzerland.				
Nov. 21					
Nov. 22			Approximately 500 hostile Afridi tribesmen situate themselves on the Afghan-Indian border. The tribesmen threaten to invade unless the region known as Khyber Pass is remapped into Afghan territory.	A specially selected Bolivian financial commission departs from the capital of La Paz en route to New York City. Once there, the commission will attempt to renegotiate their country's foreign debt. Bolivia's federal tax revenue has decreased by nearly 30 percent in one year, which commission members say is the reason for the visit.	
Nov. 23					
Nov. 24	A group of 151 prominent U.S. citizens, including clergymen, college presidents, state governors, judges, bankers, businessmen, and former government officials sends a letter to U.S. President Herbert Hoover urging him to assist in drafting an international law making war illegal. Fears of growing fascist movements in Europe and elsewhere prompted the letter. A poetic passage of the letter reads, "The next great war will be the end of civilization. To save civilization we must destroy war, or it will destroy us."	French economists report their country's exports for the month of October were 75 million francs less than October 1929. Imports also decreased by 884 million francs as compared with the same month of last year.			
Nov. 25	Speaking before members of the Economic Club of New York, former Reichsbank president Dr. Hjalmar Schacht declares that the United States and Great Britain are "extorting" Germany with unfair reparation payments and war debts. "It seems absurd," he says, "to keep the whole world in unrest and in political and economic disorder just for extorting another $10 billion out of one member of the international civilized community."				A major earthquake in the Izu Peninsula of Japan kills an estimated 223 people and causes the destruction of 650 buildings. Tens of millions of dollars in damages are reported. It is the greatest Japanese natural disaster since the Great Kanto Earthquake of 1923, during which over 100,000 people were killed and 2 million more left homeless, a billion dollars in damages was caused, and the port city of Yokohama became completely destroyed.
	A *Includes developments that affect more than one world region, international organizations, and important meetings of world leaders.*	**B** *Includes all domestic and regional developments in Europe, including the Soviet Union.*	**C** *Includes all domestic and regional developments in Africa and the Middle East.*	**D** *Includes all domestic and regional developments in Latin America, the Caribbean, and Canada.*	**E** *Includes all domestic and regional developments in Asian and Pacific nations (and colonies).*

U.S. Politics & Social Issues	U.S. Foreign Policy & Defense	Economics & Great Depression	Science, Technology & Nature	Culture, Leisure & Lifestyle	
	The U.S. Navy sells the submarine *T-2* for scrap in accordance with the London Naval Treaty. The *T-2* was active for only 18 months, conducting reconnaissance missions on the Atlantic coast. . . . The U.S. Navy sells the submarine *T-3* for scrap in accordance with the London Naval Treaty. Originally constructed at the Fore River Shipbuilding Company, the *T-3* conducted Atlantic Fleet reconnaissance missions from 1920–27. . . . The U.S. Navy sells the submarine *T-1* for scrap. The ship was constructed by the Fore River Shipbuilding Company in 1916 and spent her years conducting training exercises off the Atlantic coast.				Nov. 20
		The National Electric Light Association releases its weekly index of U.S. electric power production. At 85.6, the figure is a drop of 1.6 points from the previous week and a decline of approximately 15 percent from the corresponding week a year ago. Industrialists say the decline was caused by sharp decreases in the Midwest.			Nov. 21
The American Association of State Highway Officials calls on President Herbert Hoover to appropriate $375 million for construction of new interstate highways. AASHO representatives say the highways will give a much needed boost to the nation's economy. . . . Marking an increase of 75 percent from the corresponding period a year ago, $109,230,000 in new bond offerings was marketed on the New York Stock Exchange this week.	The destroyer *Sinclair* is renamed *Light Target* by the U.S. Navy. Constructed by the Bethlehem Shipbuilding Corporation in 1919, the USS *Sinclair* will participate in training exercises in the Caribbean and Pacific coast until it is struck from the Naval Vessel Register list in 1935.	The New York Stock Exchange announces it is striking Orpheum Circuit, Inc. from its list of tradable companies. . . . *The Annalist* releases its weekly index of U.S. wholesale commodity prices. At 117.6, the figure is a reduction of 1 point from the preceding week and is 16 percent less than the corresponding period of last year. It is also the lowest index in nearly 20 years. Blame for the decline is placed on sharp price drops in corn, hogs, steers, and lambs. . . . *Dun's Review* reports U.S. bank clearings for this week totaled $8,405,634,000, a mere 1 percent less than the preceding week's total of $8,554,562,000 and a decline of 44 percent from the corresponding period a year ago.		A two-week art show displaying the talents of Francis Bacon is completed in London, England.	Nov. 22
Officials of the Sing Sing Prison in Ossining, N.Y., report there are currently 2,272 inmates jailed, 38 percent of whom were arrested for burglary. Sing Sing Prison is the largest of New York's four state prisons.		*The Annalist* releases its weekly index of U.S. business activity. At 80.1, the figure is a drop of 0.8 points from the preceding week and a decline of 17 percent from the corresponding week a year ago. It is also the lowest index in recorded history. Economists say the decline was caused by sharp declines in steel mill production, freight car loadings, and electric power production.		The London-based football club Arsenal defeats the Middlesborough football club by a score of 5–3. . . . The Everton football club defeats the Stoke City football club by a score of 5–0 to climb to the top of the English Second Division leader board. . . . The Notts County football club draws with the Northampton Town Football Club to remain undefeated.	Nov. 23
The Kellogg Company cereal manufacturer announces it is implementing a six-hour workday to replace the current eight-hour workday. The company will also raise its minimum wage rate by 12.5 percent to $4 per day. The decisions will allow the company to employ approximately 25 percent more workers.					Nov. 24
		The New York Stock Exchange adds the J.I. Case Company to its list of tradable companies. . . . In a speech before the Bond Club of New York, International Settlements Bank vice chairman Charles Addis calls the current business depression "the worst in 100 years. The future is no doubt gloomy and the prospects dark. There is very little to see a turn of the tide." He offers a solution of minimal price stabilization as a means of improving conditions.			Nov. 25

F	G	H	I	J
Includes elections, federal-state relations, civil rights and liberties, crime, the judiciary, education, healthcare, poverty, urban affairs, and population.	*Includes formation and debate of U.S. foreign and defense policies, veterans affairs, and defense spending. (Relations with specific foreign countries are usually found under the region concerned.)*	*Includes business, labor, agriculture, taxation, transportation, consumer affairs, monetary and fiscal policy, natural resources, pollution, and accidents.*	*Includes worldwide scientific, medical, and technological developments, natural phenomena, U.S. weather, and natural disasters.*	*Includes the arts, religion, scholarship, communications media, sports, entertainment, fashions, fads, and social life.*

	World Affairs	Europe	Africa & The Middle East	The Americas	Asia & The Pacific
Nov. 26				Maj. Gen. Preston Brown officially bans alcohol consumption by U.S. soldiers serving in the Panama Canal zone. "Not a single drop of liquor is to be brought into any of the posts," he sternly warns.	
Nov. 27					A Communist army numbering 20,000 men captures the Chinese city of Kwanghchan, located in the southern Hunan Province.
Nov. 28					
Nov. 29					
Nov. 30					
Dec. 1		British economists report the Bank of England took in £372,859 worth of gold last week, against £2,073,040 withdrawn, a net loss of £1,700,881. £350,000 was deposited from the country of South Africa, and £1,976,805 was withdrawn from the country of France.		Argentine political leaders announce their country will begin implementing daylight savings time for the first time ever on March 31 of next year. All clocks will be set ahead one hour. Officials say the implementation was made to combat the Argentine people's "lack of social discipline."	
Dec. 2		Prime Minister Andre Tardieu of France faces internal political turmoil over the failure of the Oustric Bank, with which he and several members of his Cabinet had close connections. Tardieu's Minister of Justice, among others, has already resigned due to the alleged scandal. However, upon questioning, Tardieu officially denies the prospect of his own resignation. . . . Archduke Leopold Salvator of Austria is injured in a car crash in Vienna, Austria. While Salvator sustains serious injuries, his condition is not critical.			
Dec. 3		By a vote of 433–139, the French Chamber of Deputies votes to appropriate an additional $24 million in military expenses. War Minister Andre Maginot says the funds will mainly be used to defend his country's southeastern frontier. . . . The price of metal in Great Britain rises by 1.5 cents to $20.44 per ounce, the highest price since 1925, when Great Britain reimplemented the gold standard. British economists fear the price rise could lead to a worldwide gold famine. Bank of England governor Montagu Norman meets with Federal Reserve Bank of New York governor George Harrison to discuss the matter.			

A	B	C	D	E
Includes developments that affect more than one world region, international organizations, and important meetings of world leaders.	Includes all domestic and regional developments in Europe, including the Soviet Union.	Includes all domestic and regional developments in Africa and the Middle East.	Includes all domestic and regional developments in Latin America, the Caribbean, and Canada.	Includes all domestic and regional developments in Asian and Pacific nations (and colonies).

U.S. Politics & Social Issues	U.S. Foreign Policy & Defense	Economics & Great Depression	Science, Technology & Nature	Culture, Leisure & Lifestyle	
The strike of the International Garment Workers' Union enters its ninth week in New York City.	Former Army chief of staff Charles Summerall declares the current standing army of the United States to be "entirely inadequate" in a report to the Secretary of War. Since 1920, he reports, the amount of men serving in the Army has decreased from 280,000 to 118,750, a reduction of 57 percent.	The American Railway Association reports U.S. freight car loadings for this week totaled 829,251 cars, against 881,401 cars from the preceding week, a decline of 5 percent. It is also a decline of 16 percent from the corresponding week a year ago. Economists blame the decline on sharp drops in the cargo of coal, forest products, and ore.			Nov. 26
					Nov. 27
		The National Electric Light Association releases its weekly index of U.S. electric power production. At 85.6, the figure is a rise of 0.2 points from last week, but a decrease of 6 percent from the corresponding week a year ago.			Nov. 28
Catholic Archbishop Austin Dowling of Minneapolis, Minn., dies of old age at his home. Dowling had served as Archbishop since January 31, 1919.		*Dun's Review* reports U.S. bank clearings for this week totaled $6,219,952,000, 26 percent less than the preceding week's total of $8,405,634,000 and a decline of 40 percent from the corresponding period a year ago. . . . The New York Stock Exchange strikes the Norwegian Hydro-Electric Nitrogen Corporation, the Western Dairy Products Co., and the Moon Motor Car Co. from its list of tradable companies. The Sterling Securities Co., the Kansas Gas and Electric Co., the City of Sydney Co., and the California Packing Corporation are all admitted to the list.			Nov. 29
		The Annalist releases its weekly index of U.S. business activity. At 78.8, the figure is a drop of 1 full point from the preceding week and a decline of 16 percent from the corresponding week a year ago. It marks the 15th consecutive week that the index experienced a decline. Economists say the decline was caused by sharp drops in steel mill production and freight car loadings.	Antarctic explorer Richard E. Byrd returns from his South Pole expedition. Byrd had flown in his airplane *Floyd Bennet* from New York City to the South Pole and back in a span of only 18 hours and 41 minutes.		Nov. 30
The City Affairs Committee of New York City calls on lawmakers to build low-cost housing as a means of reducing homelessness. Paul Bianshard, director of the committee, says the rent on the new housing could be as low as $7 per month.	The U.S. Navy transfers the submarine *S-44* from San Diego, Calif., to Pearl Harbor. The ship was constructed by the Bethlehem Shipbuilding Corporation in 1921. . . . The submarine *S-26* is transferred from San Diego, Calif., to Pearl Harbor by the U.S. Navy.	Prof. Irving Fisher of Yale University releases his weekly index of international commodity prices. The figure is 80.6, a decline of 0.2 points from the preceding week and 14 percent from the corresponding week a year ago. Fisher, a world renowned economist, famously commented a few days before the 1929 stock market crash that "stock prices have reached what appears to be a permanently high plateau."		Irish tenor John McCormack performs at the Royal Albert Hall in London, England, before a crowd of over 6,000 people.	Dec. 1
					Dec. 2
		The American Railway Association reports U.S. freight car loadings for this week totaled 779,757 cars, against 829,251 cars from the preceding week and 949,716 cars from the corresponding week a year ago. The report adds that the change was caused by sharp declines in coal, ore, and livestock.		At a screening of the surrealist film *L'Age d'or* in Paris, France, the fascist League of Patriots hurls purple ink at the theater screen in a sign of protest. The film is soon withdrawn from circulation. . . . Filming completes on Gerhard Lamprecht's adaptation of his book, *Zweierlei Moral*.	Dec. 3

F	**G**	**H**	**I**	**J**
Includes elections, federal-state relations, civil rights and liberties, crime, the judiciary, education, healthcare, poverty, urban affairs, and population.	*Includes formation and debate of U.S. foreign and defense policies, veterans affairs, and defense spending. (Relations with specific foreign countries are usually found under the region concerned.)*	*Includes business, labor, agriculture, taxation, transportation, consumer affairs, monetary and fiscal policy, natural resources, pollution, and accidents.*	*Includes worldwide scientific, medical, and technological developments, natural phenomena, U.S. weather, and natural disasters.*	*Includes the arts, religion, scholarship, communications media, sports, entertainment, fashions, fads, and social life.*

	World Affairs	Europe	Africa & The Middle East	The Americas	Asia & The Pacific
Dec. 4		Prime Minister Andre Tardieu of France is voted out of office by the French Senate in an extremely close vote, 147–139. His entire Cabinet resigns along with him. As the votes are being cast and word of the Senate's decision reaches him, he humorously remarks to a colleague, "Well, at least I can sleep until 10 o'clock tomorrow morning." Tardieu had taken office on March 2 following the resignation of Radical Party Prime Minister Camille Chautemps.	King Ibn Saud of Saudi Arabia writes a personal letter to King Fuad I of Egypt in the hope of improving relations between the two leaders' respective countries. In the letter, Saud praises Egypt as "the foremost country of the Orient." Egypt and Saudi Arabia's relations have been strained ever since the former refused to recognize the legitimacy of King Ibn Saud's government.		Chiang Kai-shek replaces T.V. Soong as the premier of China.
Dec. 5	Preparatory Disarmament Commission Chairman Jonkheer Loudon announces a worldwide conference will be held in 1932 to set limits for land, air, and sea defense. Senator Louis de Brouckhere of Belgium is considered the likely candidate for head of the conference. Loudon estimates that 3,000 delegates will attend the conference. The Soviet delegation to the Preparatory Disarmament Commission derides the upcoming conference as "practically worthless."			Wheat harvesting begins in the Argentine provinces of Cordoba and Santa Fe. Economists predict the harvest will provide jobs to hundreds of unemployed, despite the fact that a slump in cereals will significantly reduce pay.	
Dec. 6	The American Red Cross announces it is appropriating approximately $1,000 to aid victims of the recent earthquake in Albania, which killed an estimated 30 people. The funds will be handed over to the director of the Albanian Trade School. . . . Seventy-five foreign aliens who had planned to spend New Year's Eve in the United States are turned away at New York Harbor by immigration officials who claim the aliens do not have the proper identification provided by the U.S. Department of Immigration.				
Dec. 7		Former French prime minister Louis Barthou is chosen to succeed Andre Tardieu, who resigned along with his Cabinet after being voted out by the Senate last Thursday. The position was earlier offered to 70-year-old former prime minister Raymond Poincare, who politely declined because of his advanced age. Barthou served as French prime minister for nine months, from March 22, 1913, to December 9 of the same year. He will now begin the process of selecting his cabinet members.	Police in Jerusalem ban the American-made film *White Shadow*, as they claim the film depicts Israelites as being exploited by European slave traders. It marks the first time an American film has been banned in Jerusalem. *White Shadow* was produced by the Metro-Goldwyn-Mayer film company in 1923.		
Dec. 8	Sixty-two Italian immigrants who had earlier been barred from entering Australia call on Italian Premier Benito Mussolini to correct the matter. The immigrants were forbidden to enter because of the growing Australian unemployment crisis.	British economists report the Bank of England took in £600,187 worth of gold last week, against £2,943,661 withdrawn, a net loss of £2,343,474. Approximately £500,000 was deposited from the country of South Africa, and £1,700,000 was withdrawn from the country of France.			
Dec. 9				Bolivian economists estimate their country's foreign debt to be approximately $21,428,571. A commission of bankers leaves the capital of La Paz en route to New York City to discuss the alleviation of debt with wealthy creditors.	

A	B	C	D	E
Includes developments that affect more than one world region, international organizations, and important meetings of world leaders.	Includes all domestic and regional developments in Europe, including the Soviet Union.	Includes all domestic and regional developments in Africa and the Middle East.	Includes all domestic and regional developments in Latin America, the Caribbean, and Canada.	Includes all domestic and regional developments in Asian and Pacific nations (and colonies).

U.S. Politics & Social Issues	U.S. Foreign Policy & Defense	Economics & Great Depression	Science, Technology & Nature	Culture, Leisure & Lifestyle	
Economist Dr. B.M. Anderson of the Chase National Bank lays blame to the current business depression on "pessimism." By analyzing economic figures, he says, one can logically conclude that current economic conditions are no worse than the recession of 1921. He adds, however, that the Smoot-Hawley Tariff Act passed earlier this year has severely inhibited global trade.		The Iron Age releases its weekly index of U.S. steel production. At 55.9, the figure is a decline of 1.4 points from the previous week and 33 percent less than the corresponding period a year ago. Economists say the decline last week was caused by a sharp decline in pig iron output, which some claim has fallen to its lowest level since February 1922.		The film adaptation of German author Erich Remarque's World War I novel All Quiet on the Western Front is released in Germany. The film was the recipient of two Academy Awards.	**Dec. 4**
The Department of Commerce reports U.S. automobile production for the month of November amounted to 146,185 cars, compared with the November 1929 total of 226,997 cars, a decrease of 35 percent.	Trubee Davison, assistant secretary of war for aeronautics, announces that come next May, 500 planes will assemble in New York City to conduct aerial maneuvers. It will be the highest concentration of military planes ever in peacetime. Davison says the maneuvers will last for over two weeks.	The Annalist releases its weekly index of U.S. wholesale commodity prices. At 118.9, the figure is a rise of 0.5 points from the previous week and a decline of 17 percent from the corresponding week a year ago. Economists say the increase in the index was caused by rises in the prices of grains, hogs, meats, copper, and rubber. . . . The National Electric Light Association releases its weekly index of U.S. electric power output. The index stands at 85.7, a decline of 0.1 points from the previous week and 12 percent less than the corresponding week a year ago. The total output amounted to 1.7 billion kilowatt hours.			**Dec. 5**
	The U.S. Navy transfers the destroyer Evans to New York City to conduct naval training operations. Named after Admiral Robley Evans, she was constructed by the Bath Iron Works Co. in 1918. In 1940, the United States sold the ship to Great Britain, who renamed it the HMS Mansfield. . . . Charles Francis Adams, secretary of the Navy, honors the 100th anniversary of the founding of the Hydographic Office of the U.S. Navy in a speech broadcast over the nationwide Washington-based radio network WJZ.	Dun's Review reports U.S. bank clearings for this week totaled $9.7 billion, 24 percent less than the corresponding week of last year. . . . The U.S. Department of Commerce releases its weekly index of U.S. bank debits. At 99.1, the figure is a decline of over 20 points from the previous week and a fall of 23 percent from the corresponding week a year ago.		Film critics in Germany respond to the U.S. film adaptation of Erich Remarque's World War I novel All Quiet on the Western Front, which was released in Germany a week ago. Most politically conservative critics agree that it is fiercely anti-German, prompting the Defense Ministry to call for a ban on the film. Protests are held outside movie theaters, with shouts of "Out with the Jews!" echoing throughout the streets. The demonstrations are led by future Nazi propaganda minster Joseph Goebbels.	**Dec. 6**
	The U.S. Navy transfers the submarine S-19 to Pearl Harbor to conduct training operations. The S-19 would remain at Pearl Harbor until being decommissioned three years later. . . . Frank Anslem of the 369th Infantry wins the National Guard bantamweight boxing title, defeating Tommy Adoba of the 102nd Medical Regiment in a twelve-round bout.	The Annalist releases its weekly index of U.S. business activity. At 79.8, the figure is a rise of 1.6 points from the previous week and a decline of 15 percent from the corresponding week last year. Economists say the rise was caused by increases in electric power production and automobile output.			**Dec. 7**
The New York City Transit Commission urges Governor Franklin Roosevelt to appropriate $31 million for the purpose of updating the city's railroad system. . . . Senator David Walsh of Massachusetts introduces a bill in the Senate that would limit government employees to a five-day workweek. The remaining two days will give employment opportunities to idle workers.		Prof. Irving Fisher of Yale University releases his weekly index of international commodity prices. The index currently stands at 80.7, a rise of 0.1 points from the preceding week and 13 percent from the corresponding week a year ago.		Edgar T. Appleby retains the title of national amateur billiard champion by defeating challenger Ray Fessenden 900–491.	**Dec. 8**
Rep. John Cable of the 4th district of Ohio introduces a bill in the House of Representatives that would make "any right enjoyed by one sex equally available to the other."		The U.S. Department of Commerce releases its weekly index of U.S. automobile production. At 100.5, the figure is a decline of 8.7 points from the previous week, but a sharp rise of nearly 20 points from the corresponding week a year ago. Economists say the decline last week was caused by a curtailment in production by the Ford Motor Company. . . . The U.S. Department of Commerce reports that in the first nine months of 1930, $6,783,123 in aircraft equipment was exported out of the United States, 5 percent less than last year's record nine-month total of $7,130,916.			**Dec. 9**

F	G	H	I	J
Includes elections, federal-state relations, civil rights and liberties, crime, the judiciary, education, healthcare, poverty, urban affairs, and population.	Includes formation and debate of U.S. foreign and defense policies, veterans affairs, and defense spending. (Relations with specific foreign countries are usually found under the region concerned.)	Includes business, labor, agriculture, taxation, transportation, consumer affairs, monetary and fiscal policy, natural resources, pollution, and accidents.	Includes worldwide scientific, medical, and technological developments, natural phenomena, U.S. weather, and natural disasters.	Includes the arts, religion, scholarship, communications media, sports, entertainment, fashions, fads, and social life.

	World Affairs	Europe	Africa & The Middle East	The Americas	Asia & The Pacific
Dec. 10	The Preparatory Disarmament Commission concludes its sessions in Geneva, Switzerland. The delegates had agreed to host a worldwide conference on military defense limitation in 1932. Delegate Count von Bernstorff of Germany warns the commission that there will exist "grave dangers" if disarmament is not accomplished.	Archduke Leopold Hapsburg of Austria, who was accused of stealing a $400,000 Napoleon-era diamond necklace last February, is cleared of all charges. Court documents indicate there was little, if any, evidence needed to convict the nobleman.			
Dec. 11		The Irish Free Senate approves the provisions of the London Naval Treaty, and recommends to the executive branch to immediately take steps toward ratification.		South Americans across the continent observe the 100th anniversary of the death of "libertador" Simon Bolivar, who is credited with leading revolutions in the countries of Venezuela, Colombia, Ecuador, Peru, Panama, and Bolivia.	The Australian Literature Society presents its annual gold medal for best book to Henry Handel Richardson, whose novel *Ultima Thule* drew lavish praise from literary critics.
Dec. 12		The German Supreme Film Censorship Board officially bans the American-made film adaptation of Erich Remarque's *All Quiet on the Western Front*. In a statement, the commission says the film "is intentionally calculated to increase the psychic pressure under which the nation is suffering and also to quicken further existing political and economic conflicts, thereby making it a distinct menace to public order and safety." Liberal newspapers denounce the decision, charging that the ban will fan the flames of public disorder, rather than extinguish them.			
Dec. 13		Former prime minister Camille Chautemps replaces Pierre Marraud as French Minister of Education. Marraud left the post after the resignation of Prime Minister Andre Tardieu. . . . Louis Barthou replaces Andre Maginot as the French Minister of War. Maginot left the post after the resignation of Prime Minister Andre Tardieu.			As the third anniversary of the Communist uprising that killed thousands of people in Canton, China, approaches, police forces declare martial law to protect citizens from possible violent demonstrations. Troops patrol the streets as well as theaters and restaurants.
Dec. 14					
Dec. 15		British economists report the Bank of England took in £487,557 worth of gold last week, against £3,153,050 withdrawn, a net loss of £2,665,493. It marks a total loss of £9 million in a period of five weeks. No foreign country deposited any money into the bank, but over £3 million was withdrawn from the countries of France and Germany.		The U.S. Commercial Attaché to Argentina reports that during the first 10 months of this year, Argentina's imports to the United States amounted to $112,173,000, compared with $181,143,000 from last year, a decrease of 39 percent. Additionally, exports to the United States have declined by over 30 percent. Argentine newspapers claim the decline is a direct result of the recently passed Smoot-Hawley Tariff Act.	
Dec. 16				The Canadian publication *National Revenue Review* reports Canada's total import and export revenue for the month of November amounted to $150,975,835, 33 percent less than the November 1929 total of $221,979,663.	

A	B	C	D	E
Includes developments that affect more than one world region, international organizations, and important meetings of world leaders.	Includes all domestic and regional developments in Europe, including the Soviet Union.	Includes all domestic and regional developments in Africa and the Middle East.	Includes all domestic and regional developments in Latin America, the Caribbean, and Canada.	Includes all domestic and regional developments in Asian and Pacific nations (and colonies).

U.S. Politics & Social Issues	U.S. Foreign Policy & Defense	Economics & Great Depression	Science, Technology & Nature	Culture, Leisure & Lifestyle	
A California farmer named Arthur G. Phelps discovers while rummaging through his attic one of the original 55 copies of the 1776 Declaration of Independence. Antiquity experts say the copy is a priceless artifact, but could be sold for over $25,000.		The American Railway Association reports U.S. freight car loadings for this week totaled 702,085 cars, against 779,757 cars from the preceding week and 836,310 cars from the corresponding week a year ago. The report adds that the change was caused by declines in forest products, ore, grain, and livestock.		The Walt Disney animated film *Pioneer Days* is released across the United States.	**Dec. 10**
The McGraw-Hill Construction Daily reports there is $51,872,000 in public works projects currently under way in the United States, compared with $62,224,000 in the previous week and $66,588,000 from the corresponding week a year ago.	The U.S. Navy transfers the destroyer *Rizal* from Manila, the Philippines, to the West Coast of the United States to begin the process of deactivation. . . . The U.S. Navy decommissions the ship *Grampus*.	*The Iron Age* releases its weekly index of U.S. steel production. At 52.4, the figure is a decline of 3.5 points from the previous week and 29 percent from the corresponding week a year ago. It is also the lowest recorded index in almost three years. . . . The price of butter on the Chicago Mercantile Exchange falls to a new recorded low of 27.75 cents a pound.			**Dec. 11**
The Baltimore & Ohio Railroad Company acquires the Chicago & Alton Railroad Company for a sum of $73 million. . . . In New York City, the Bank of the United States, a nonfederal institution, officially closes its doors, placing control in the hands of the New York State Banking Department. In a statement, bank officials express hope for an early reopening. Customers will receive 50 percent of their total deposits. The Bank had approximately $160 million in deposits upon closing.	The U.S. Navy transfers the submarine *R-20* from Pearl Harbor to Philadelphia to begin the process of deactivation. She was constructed by the Union Iron Works Company in 1918 and would defend San Francisco's harbor for over 10 years. . . . The U.S. Navy transfers the submarine *R-14* from the Pearl Harbor military base to the Atlantic Coast to help in instructing students of the Navy's Submarine School. . . . . The U.S. Navy transfers the submarine *R-12* from Hawaii to New London, Conn., to conduct training exercises with the Destroyer Squadrons of the Scouting Force. . . . The submarine *R-16* is transferred from the Panama Canal to Philadelphia by the U.S. Navy.	*The Annalist* releases its weekly index of U.S. wholesale commodity prices. At 117.8, the figure is a decrease of 1.1 points from the previous week and a decline of 16 percent from the corresponding week a year ago. It is the lowest index recorded since January 1916. Economists say the decrease in the index was caused by increases in livestock, offset by sharp declines in barley, oats, corn, cotton, meat, butter, oranges, and lard. . . . The Electric Light and Power Association's index of U.S. electric power output falls to a new year low of 85.2. It is also a decline of more than 10 percent from the corresponding period a year ago. The total output of electric power was 1,729,341,000 kilowatt hours.			**Dec. 12**
The U.S. Department of Commerce releases its weekly index of U.S. bank debits. At 107.1, the figure is a rise of 8 points from the previous week and a fall of 17 percent from the corresponding week a year ago.		The Great Atlantic and Pacific Tea Company, later known as simply A&P, reports that 1930 sales have exceeded $1 billion. . . . *Dun's Review* reports U.S. bank clearings for this week totaled $7.6 billion, 35 percent less than the corresponding week of last year's total of $11,832,046. It is also the lowest total in over three months. . . . Officials of the New York Stock Exchange report new bond offerings this week amounted to $21,412,000, a decline of 75 percent from the previous week and 80 percent from the corresponding week a year ago. The decline was caused by sharp decreases in public utility and railroad bonds.			**Dec. 13**
		The Annalist releases its weekly index of U.S. business activity. At 79.8, the figure is a decline of 0.5 points from the previous week and a decline of 16 percent from the corresponding week last year. Economists say the decline was caused by an increase in freight car loadings, offset by decreases in steel mill activity, automobile output, and electric power production.		Several Austrian lawmakers introduce a bill that would ban the showing of the film adaptation of Erich Remarque's *All Quiet on the Western Front*. Earlier, Germany had officially banned the film.	**Dec. 14**
A report on the attendance of U.S. universities is released by *School and Society*, showing that attendance has increased by 3.5 percent from the school year of 1929–30. "The explanation probably lies in the continued faith of the American people in higher education and likewise in present economic conditions," writes Dr. Raymond Walters, author of the report.		Prof. Irving Fisher of Yale University releases his weekly index of international commodity prices. The index currently stands at 79.8, a decline of 0.9 points from the preceding week and 15 percent from the corresponding week a year ago. It is also the lowest recorded index of the year.			**Dec. 15**
A court in Cincinnati, Ohio, sentences bankers Frank and Clarence Dorger to 10 years in prison along with $5,000 in fines for their role in the misusing of funds from the Cosmopolitan Bank and Trust Company.		The U.S. Department of Commerce releases its weekly index of U.S. automobile production. At 90.3, the figure is a decline of 10.5 points from the previous week and nearly 20 points from the corresponding week a year ago.	The New York Academy of Sciences awards its annual first prize of $750 to Prof. H. von Zeipel of the Astronomical Observatory of Uppsala, Sweden, for his essay on the origin of solar energy.		**Dec. 16**

F	G	H	I	J
Includes elections, federal-state relations, civil rights and liberties, crime, the judiciary, education, healthcare, poverty, urban affairs, and population.	*Includes formation and debate of U.S. foreign and defense policies, veterans affairs, and defense spending. (Relations with specific foreign countries are usually found under the region concerned.)*	*Includes business, labor, agriculture, taxation, transportation, consumer affairs, monetary and fiscal policy, natural resources, pollution, and accidents.*	*Includes worldwide scientific, medical, and technological developments, natural phenomena, U.S. weather, and natural disasters.*	*Includes the arts, religion, scholarship, communications media, sports, entertainment, fashions, fads, and social life.*

	World Affairs	Europe	Africa & The Middle East	The Americas	Asia & The Pacific
Dec. 17					
Dec. 18	Argentina accepts a loan of £5,000,000 from the British government. . . . In an interview with the Associated Press, President Gerardo Machado of Cuba expresses a desire to be fully cooperative with U.S. journalists. The president states that "not a single outgoing line or word given to any American newspaper has been withheld or censored in any way."		British imperial police are dispatched to an area south of Palestine to settle clashes between Arabs and Jewish settlers who purchased a tract of land in the predominantly Arab Herzlia colony.	An inquiry into the December 1 collision between the liners *Benovorlick* and *Willboro* in the Panama Canal is completed. The inquiry finds the sea pilot aboard the *Willboro* to be guilty, and requires him to pay $70,000 in damages.	
Dec. 19	The British *Who's Who* publication of international figures is released. Among the Americans added are tennis star Paul Robeson and Governor Franklin Roosevelt of New York.	French economists report the Bank of France currently possesses a total of 5,278,900,000 francs, against 4,124,800,000 francs from the corresponding week a year ago, an increase of 22 percent. . . . The German Reichstag adopts a resolution calling for formal League of Nations questioning of German disarmament. Specifically, the resolution questions the safety of a demilitarized Germany, as well as calling for universal worldwide demilitarization. . . . The British government appropriates over $662 million to provide public works projects for the unemployed. The funds are expected to give employment to over 500,000 men and women.			
Dec. 20	The U.S. Department of Commerce reports that during the first nine months of this year, over 130,000 American tourists visited the United Kingdom, an increase of 3,000 tourists from 1929. It is the highest tourist total on record. . . . Several transatlantic liner companies including the United States Line and the French Line agree to cut travel rates from 10–50 percent as a means of improving transatlantic commerce and tourism.	The royal physician of Prince Edward Windsor of Wales reports on his patient's current medical condition, saying the Prince is making "satisfactory" progress recovering from what he describes as a "slight chill."		An oil bill is presented before the Colombian Congress. If passed, the bill would make it more difficult for foreign oil companies to benefit from Colombian petroleum reserves.	
Dec. 21	The military junta controlling Bolivia selects a commission to send to London to request the curtailing of the production of tin, which is one of the leading commodities of Bolivia. The commission includes Antenor Patino, the son of a tin magnate.	Sir Harry Armstrong, British General Consul to New York City, officially announces his retirement. Armstrong has held the position for nearly 40 years. So successful was Armstrong at diplomacy that a special provision was created to allow him to work past the mandatory retirement age of 60. Reflecting on his many years spent in New York, he comments, "the city has changed from a metropolis to a cosmopolis."		The Argentine provisional government led by General Jose Felix Uriburu issues a decree reducing its duty on imported silk by approximately 50 percent. The change comes as a result of years of illegal smuggling of silk goods into the country. . . . Argentina's Bureau of Rural Statistics estimates that this year's wheat harvest will be approximately 100 million bushels greater than the previous year's crop estimate.	
Dec. 22		British economists report the Bank of England took in £1,120,076 worth of gold last week, against £2,262,819 withdrawn, a net loss of £1,142,743. From Brazil, £920,000 was deposited, and over £2 million was withdrawn from the country of France. . . . French economists report on their country's foreign trade for the first 11 months of 1930. Imports decreased by 5.2 billion francs from 1929, and exports decreased by 6 billion francs.		The Colombian newspaper *El Tiempo* reports that the Venezuelan border town of Lobatera was raided by approximately 300 revolutionists, who murdered the town's mayor. Federal troops forced the armed men to scatter to nearby mountains. Venezuelan officials claim the revolutionists were only intent on simply looting, and not taking over, the town.	

A	B	C	D	E
Includes developments that affect more than one world region, international organizations, and important meetings of world leaders.	*Includes all domestic and regional developments in Europe, including the Soviet Union.*	*Includes all domestic and regional developments in Africa and the Middle East.*	*Includes all domestic and regional developments in Latin America, the Caribbean, and Canada.*	*Includes all domestic and regional developments in Asian and Pacific nations (and colonies).*

U.S. Politics & Social Issues	U.S. Foreign Policy & Defense	Economics & Great Depression	Science, Technology & Nature	Culture, Leisure & Lifestyle	
Members of the House of Representatives introduce a Department of Agriculture bill worth $213,043,702. It is an increase of $50 million from the funds already appropriated for 1931. Most of the new funds will go toward construction of federal highways. . . . In an interview with reporters, former president Calvin "Silent Cal" Coolidge says he has no desire to run for the presidency in 1932, but rather believes that Herbert Hoover will be nominated and reelected to a second term.		The American Railway Association reports U.S. freight car loadings for this week totaled 787,173 cars, against 702,085 cars from the preceding week and 933,306 cars from the corresponding week a year ago. The report adds that the change was caused by sharp gains in coal, grain, and livestock. . . . The U.S. Department of Commerce issues a report showing that during the whole of this year, automobile production in the United States totaled $3,415,636,810 worth of motor vehicles, an increase of 35 percent from the total from 1927, when statistics were last recorded.		Col. Frank Knox resigns from his position as general manager of Hearst newspapers. In a statement, Knox says that he and owner William Randolph Hearst had reached "a difference of opinion" over the style of management. When reached for comment, multimillionaire Hearst expresses disappointment over Knox's departure.	Dec. 17
	The U.S. Navy strikes the submarine K-7 from the list of the Naval Vessel Register. Constructed in 1914 by the Union Iron Works Company, the ship spent most of her years cruising the waters of the South Pacific. . . . The U.S. Navy strikes the submarine USN-1 from the list of the Naval Vessel Register. The ship was constructed by the Seattle Construction and Drydock Company in 1916. . . . The U.S. Navy strikes the ship Grampus and the submarines H-3, K-6, N-2, N-3, and K-6 from the list of the Naval Vessel Register.	The Iron Age releases its weekly index of U.S. steel production. At 52.4, the figure is a decline of 0.4 points from the previous week and 32 percent from the corresponding week a year ago.			Dec. 18
		The Annalist releases its weekly index of U.S. wholesale commodity prices. At 115.4, the figure is a decline of 2.3 points from the previous week and a decline of 18 percent from the corresponding week a year ago, the lowest index recorded since December 1915. Economists say the decrease in the index was caused by declines in all categories of commodities except fuel. . . . The Electric Light and Power Association's index of U.S. electric power production falls to an all-time low of 84.5, against 85.2 from the previous week. Total electric output, as reported by the association, was 1,748,063,000 kilowatt hours,			Dec. 19
In New York City, 1,300 Christmas trees are given out by the mother of Governor Franklin Roosevelt to the city's poor and needy families. . . . The U.S. Department of Commerce releases its weekly index of U.S. bank debits. At 97.9, the figure is a decline of 9.2 points from the previous week and a fall of 22 percent from the corresponding week a year ago.	The U.S. Navy sells the destroyer Farenholt for scrap. Named after Civil War-era officer Oscar Farenholt, the USS Farenholt was constructed by the Bethlehem Shipbuilding Corporation in 1921 and would spend most of her years conducting training exercises in the Panama Canal Zone.	Dun's Review reports U.S. bank clearings for this week totaled $10 billion, 14 percent less than the corresponding week of last year's total of $11,693,344. . . . Officials of the New York Stock Exchange report new bond offerings this week amounted to $30,167,000, an increase of 33 percent from the previous week, but a decline of 87 percent from the corresponding week a year ago. The increase from last week was caused by a sharp increase in public utility bonds.			Dec. 20
The New York City Employment Bureau reports that during the past week, a record number of 2,285 people were provided employment in the city's public sector.		The Annalist releases its weekly index of U.S. business activity. At 77.8, the figure is a decline of 1.6 points from the previous week and a decline of 16 percent from the corresponding week last year. Economists say the decline is a result of sharp decreases in automobile production and freight car loadings.			Dec. 21
		Prof. Irving Fisher of Yale University releases his weekly index of international commodity prices. The index currently stands at 79.4, a decline of 0.4 points from the preceding week and approximately 15 percent from the corresponding week a year ago.		The film adaptation of Kathleen Norris's novel The Passion Flower premiers in New York City. . . . Birth of a Nation, one of the last films produced by legendary film director D.W. Griffith, is re-released at the George M. Cohan Theatre in New York City.	Dec. 22

F	G	H	I	J
Includes elections, federal-state relations, civil rights and liberties, crime, the judiciary, education, healthcare, poverty, urban affairs, and population.	Includes formation and debate of U.S. foreign and defense policies, veterans affairs, and defense spending. (Relations with specific foreign countries are usually found under the region concerned.)	Includes business, labor, agriculture, taxation, transportation, consumer affairs, monetary and fiscal policy, natural resources, pollution, and accidents.	Includes worldwide scientific, medical, and technological developments, natural phenomena, U.S. weather, and natural disasters.	Includes the arts, religion, scholarship, communications media, sports, entertainment, fashions, fads, and social life.

	World Affairs	Europe	Africa & The Middle East	The Americas	Asia & The Pacific
Dec. 23	British Foreign Office naval expert Robert Craigie travels to Rome, Italy, to negotiate with his counterparts the terms of the London Naval Treaty, which Italy has yet to agree upon.	Belgians across the country celebrate the 21st anniversary of the ascension of Albert Meinrad as the King of Belgium. The son of the Count of Flanders, Meinrad took the throne after the death of his uncle, King Leopold II. He was instrumental in the defeat of Germany during World War I.			
Dec. 24		Leon Borgers succeeds Oscar Defawe as the Belgian colonial head of Burundi.			Upon leaving Punjab University, Governor Geoffrey de Montmorency of Punjab, India, is shot at by an assassin standing 15 feet away. He suffers wounds in his left arm and back, but is declared healthy a few hours later after arriving at a local hospital. The assassin is identified as Hari Kishen, a Hindu medical student sympathetic toward the Indian independence movement. Punjab Association president Sardar Hardit Singh denounces the act as a "cowardly attack." . . . An outbreak occurs in the Burmese district of Tharrawaddy as a mob of several hundred people attacks two villages, murdering local officials and stealing several firearms.
Dec. 25					
Dec. 26				The trial of Aldo Baroni, a Cuban newspaper editor charged with sedition, begins in the capital of Havana. The editor of the satirical paper *Karikato*, Baroni was arrested after writing an editorial addressed to newly installed President Gerardo Machado entitled "Get Out." . . . Mayor Domingo Azcuy of the Cuban town Consolacion del Norte is released from prison after serving 10 days on charges of sedition. Interior Secretary Vivanos ordered his release due to a lack of evidence.	
Dec. 27					
Dec. 28					

A	B	C	D	E
Includes developments that affect more than one world region, international organizations, and important meetings of world leaders.	Includes all domestic and regional developments in Europe, including the Soviet Union.	Includes all domestic and regional developments in Africa and the Middle East.	Includes all domestic and regional developments in Latin America, the Caribbean, and Canada.	Includes all domestic and regional developments in Asian and Pacific nations (and colonies).

U.S. Politics & Social Issues	U.S. Foreign Policy & Defense	Economics & Great Depression	Science, Technology & Nature	Culture, Leisure & Lifestyle	
	The U.S. Navy places the destroyer *Bainbridge* out of commission. The ship spent most of her years as a member of the Special Service Squadron, patrolling the waters of Nicaragua to protect U.S. nationals from civil disturbances.	The U.S. Department of Commerce releases its weekly index of U.S. automobile production. At 98.3, the figure is a rise of 8 points from the previous week and nearly 40 points from the corresponding week a year ago.	Physicians of Queen Elizabeth of Belgium report their patient is suffering from influenza contracted during a recent trip to Paris, France. The Queen will have to remain secluded for several days in order to fully recover. Despite her illness, she participated in a national ceremony commemorating the ascension of Albert Meinrad to the throne of Belgium.		Dec. 23
The Michigan Steel Corporation purchases the National Steel Corporation.		The American Railway Association reports U.S. freight car loadings for this week totaled 744,443 cars, against 787,173 cars from the preceding week and 922,861 cars from the corresponding week a year ago. The report adds that the change was caused by a sharp decline in livestock. . . . The Federal Reserve Bank of New York reduces its rediscount rate by 0.5 percent to 2 percent. It is the lowest rate in the history of the U.S. Federal Reserve System, and the lowest of any central bank in the world at the present time. It is also the fifth such reduction in one year. The decision was made, according to Federal Reserve officials, to "open the doors wide" of business and commerce, especially toward areas like the Midwest that are most suffering from business conditions.			Dec. 24
In the spirit of Christmas, over 30,000 needy families in New York City are given free food and toys by dozens of charitable organizations including The Salvation Army, The Volunteers of America, The Rescue Society, St. Vincent's Hospital, and St. Mary's Mission.	The U.S. Navy transfers the light cruiser *Denver* from Florida to Philadelphia to begin the process of decommissioning. The ship sent most of her years patrolling the coasts of Mexico and Nicaragua. The ship was the first to be named after the capital city of the state of Colorado.	*The Iron Age* releases its weekly index of U.S. steel mill activity. At 49.2, the figure is a drop of 3.6 points from the previous week and 28 percent from the corresponding week one year ago. Economists say the decline was caused by a lack of workers due to the holiday season.		The American adventure film *The Mysterious Island* is released in Finland. . . . The Young Communist League holds an "anti-religious dance" at the New Harlem Casino in New York City.	Dec. 25
The New Jersey legislature introduces a bill that would ban the sport of cockfighting. . . . The New York Central Lines places an order for 11,380 tons of rail from the Carnegie Steel Company. The order is expected to provide employment for thousands of idle workers.		*The Annalist* releases its weekly index of U.S. wholesale commodity prices. At 115.7, the figure is a rise of 0.3 points from the previous week and a decline of 18 percent from the corresponding week a year ago. Despite the rise, the index is still the lowest in over 15 years. Economists say the increase in the index was caused by rises in the prices of copper, tin, and zinc.			Dec. 26
In an ironic twist of fate, New Jersey Traffic Superintendent Edmund B. Loughran is killed in an automobile accident while driving to celebrate the holidays with his family in North Carolina. . . . The U.S. Department of Commerce releases its weekly index of U.S. bank debits. At 119.3, the figure is a rise of 21.4 points from the previous week and a decline of 17 percent from the corresponding week a year ago.		*Dun's Review* reports U.S. bank clearings for this week totaled $7,390,619,000, 15 percent less than the corresponding week of last year's total of $8,672,302. . . . Officials of the New York Stock Exchange report new bond offerings this week amounted to $10,357,000, a decline of 67 percent from the previous week, but an increase of 10 percent from the corresponding week a year ago. The decline from last week was caused by the Christmas holiday.			Dec. 27
The Census Bureau reports that during the month of November, 129,437 motor vehicles were produced in the United States, 14 percent less than last month and 31 percent less than the total from November 1929. . . . New York District Attorney Crane initiates a grand jury investigation into the closing of the Bank of the United States. Crane will seek charges of fraud and illegal fundraising. "We believe the closing of this institution will uncover the worst banking scandal in the history of this country," says New York State Supreme Court Justice Goldstein.	The U.S. Navy converts the submarine *O-1* to an experimental vessel. The ship was constructed shortly before the end of World War I in 1918 by the Portsmouth Navy Yard.	*The Annalist* releases its weekly index of U.S. business activity. At 77.8, the figure is nearly identical to the previous week but a decline of 16 percent from the corresponding week last year. Economists say the stabilization is a result of a decline in steel mill activity, offset by a rise in automobile production.		Anton Reiser publishes *Albert Einstein*, a biography of the 51-year-old scientist whom many consider to be the greatest mind of the 20th century. The book presents an interesting perspective on Einstein's personality and sense of humor.	Dec. 28

F	G	H	I	J
Includes elections, federal-state relations, civil rights and liberties, crime, the judiciary, education, healthcare, poverty, urban affairs, and population.	Includes formation and debate of U.S. foreign and defense policies, veterans affairs, and defense spending. (Relations with specific foreign countries are usually found under the region concerned.)	Includes business, labor, agriculture, taxation, transportation, consumer affairs, monetary and fiscal policy, natural resources, pollution, and accidents.	Includes worldwide scientific, medical, and technological developments, natural phenomena, U.S. weather, and natural disasters.	Includes the arts, religion, scholarship, communications media, sports, entertainment, fashions, fads, and social life.

	World Affairs	Europe	Africa & The Middle East	The Americas	Asia & The Pacific
Dec. 29		British economists report the Bank of England took in only £200,000 worth of gold last week, against £1,416,581 withdrawn, a net loss of £1,216,581. Over £100,000 was deposited from the country of South Africa, and over £500,000 was withdrawn from the country of France.			
Dec. 30					
Dec. 31					

A	B	C	D	E
Includes developments that affect more than one world region, international organizations, and important meetings of world leaders.	Includes all domestic and regional developments in Europe, including the Soviet Union.	Includes all domestic and regional developments in Africa and the Middle East.	Includes all domestic and regional developments in Latin America, the Caribbean, and Canada.	Includes all domestic and regional developments in Asian and Pacific nations (and colonies).

U.S. Politics & Social Issues	U.S. Foreign Policy & Defense	Economics & Great Depression	Science, Technology & Nature	Culture, Leisure & Lifestyle	
					Dec. 29
		The U.S. Department of Commerce releases its weekly index of U.S. automobile production. At 67.1, the figure is a decline of nearly 30 points from the previous week and 16 points from the corresponding week a year ago. The heavy decline was caused by low automobile factory attendance due to the Christmas holiday.			Dec. 30
	The U.S. Navy decommissions the destroyer *Kane*. Constructed by the New York Shipbuilding Corporation in 1918, the ship would spend 10 years cruising the waters of the Mediterranean, the Pacific, and the Caribbean.	The American Railway Association reports U.S. freight car loadings for this week totaled 713,810 cars, against 744,443 cars from the preceding week and 842,775 cars from the corresponding week a year ago. The report adds that the change was caused by sharp declines in forest products, grain, and livestock.			Dec. 31

F	G	H	I	J
Includes elections, federal-state relations, civil rights and liberties, crime, the judiciary, education, healthcare, poverty, urban affairs, and population.	*Includes formation and debate of U.S. foreign and defense policies, veterans affairs, and defense spending. (Relations with specific foreign countries are usually found under the region concerned.)*	*Includes business, labor, agriculture, taxation, transportation, consumer affairs, monetary and fiscal policy, natural resources, pollution, and accidents.*	*Includes worldwide scientific, medical, and technological developments, natural phenomena, U.S. weather, and natural disasters.*	*Includes the arts, religion, scholarship, communications media, sports, entertainment, fashions, fads, and social life.*

Mid-New York

1931

The world's tallest building to date in 1931, the Empire State Building (left) has 102 floors and rises to a height of 1,250 feet.

Skyline

	World Affairs	Europe	Africa & The Middle East	The Americas	Asia & The Pacific
Jan.	The Allied Military Control Committee, which oversaw the demobilization of German military forces after World War I, is dissolved. . . . The Permanent Court of International Justice holds its 20th session in The Hague.	New border incidents take place between Greece and Bulgaria. . . . Poland is officially rebuked by the League of Nations for its treatment of the German minority in Upper Silesia. . . . Winston Churchill resigns as aide of Conservative leader Stanley Baldwin. . . . Pierre Laval becomes prime minister of France.	The Persian government passes a law forbidding foreigners to buy agricultural land in the region.		Gandhi is released from prison. British Viceroy Lord Irwin begins negotiations on the country's future. . . . Isaac Isaacs is the first Australian-born Australian Governor General.
Feb.	The League of Nations hosts a second conference on the unification of laws pertaining to bills of exchange, promissory notes, and checks in an attempt to restore international trade. . . . The League of Nations holds a conference in Paris to study ways to limit agricultural surpluses, thus raising grain prices.	Sir Oswald Mosley leaves the British Labor Party and launches the New Party. He plans to field candidates in all constituencies at the next general election. . . . Pehr Evind Svinhufvud is elected president of Finland.	The Persian government imposes more rigid control on all foreign trade and seizes control of the Persian lines of the Indo-European Telegraph Company.	Peruvian revolutionaries hijack a Ford trimotor plane and drop propaganda leaflets all over Lima, the capital city.	New Delhi becomes the capital of India. . . . A violent earthquake destroys much of the city of Napier in New Zealand.
Mar.	The League of Nations holds an international conference in Geneva for police officials to determine a common practice against currency counterfeiting. . . . A second Conference of Concerted Economic Action is held in Geneva to revive the world's economy.	The Soviet and Turkish governments sign a naval agreement to halt the enlargement of their Black Sea fleets. . . . The German and Austrian governments propose an Austro-German customs union. Other European countries react negatively to the proposal. . . . The Soviet Union bans the sale or importation of Bibles.	The Trans-Jordanian and Iraqi governments sign a Treaty of Friendship, which marks an important step toward pan-Arab unity.	An earthquake destroys Managua, Nicaragua, killing more than 2,000 people.	Gandhi and Lord Irwin sign the Delhi Pact. Gandhi promises to attend future roundtable conferences and end civil disturbances. In exchange, the British will free all political prisoners who are not guilty of violent acts.
Apr.	The Permanent Court of International Justice holds its 21st session in The Hague.	The French and Swiss governments agree to a new round of negotiations on the status of free zones on their borders under the supervision of the Permanent Court of International Justice. . . . King Alfonso XIII of Spain leaves the country. . . . The Portuguese government declares martial law in Madeira and the Azores.	Sheikh Mahmud surrenders to Iraqi forces, ending the Kurdish Revolt that began in September 1930. . . . The Egyptian and Iraqi governments sign a Treaty of Friendship, marking the advent of Egyptian relations with other Arab states.	Canadian representatives meet in Ottawa to discuss relations with Britain in light of the Statute of Westminster on Anglo-Canadian relations. The representatives agree that laws passed by the British parliament would not apply to Canada unless the dominion approved them too. . . . Argentine anarchist Severino Digiovanni is executed.	Japanese pilot Seiji Yoshihara crashes his plane in the Pacific Ocean while trying to be the first to cross the ocean nonstop.
May	Pope Pius XI issues the encyclical Qaudragesimo Anno, which asks for a fairer redistribution of wealth but still condemns socialism and Communism. . . . The International Labor Organization holds its 15th session in Geneva. The main issue at the session is the working hours in coal mines.	The Soviet and Lithuanian governments renew the Treaty of 1926 for another five-year period. . . . The Austrian bank Kredit Anstalt fails, threatening the economic and political stability of central Europe. . . . Kemal Ataturk is reelected president of Turkey.			The New Zealand government ends compulsory military service and establishes a voluntary system.
Jun.	To reduce and eventually eliminate diphtheria and scarlet fever epidemics, the League of Nations hosts a conference of medical experts in London. . . . The Soviet and Afghan governments sign a treaty of neutrality.	The Italian government extends a major 10-year loan to Albania, thus imposing its influence on the Albanian economy. . . . The Soviet and Polish governments sign a Treaty of Friendship that includes the promotion of trade between the two countries.		To protect the national economy, the Canadian government revises the Tariff of 1930 in the attempt to cut off two-thirds of imports from the United States.	British authorities in China arrest Indo-Chinese Communist leader Ho Chi Minh.
Jul.	The Permanent Court of International Justice holds its 22nd session in The Hague.	The May Committee issues a report on the British economy, which advocates austere measures to reduce the anticipated deficit. . . . The Norwegian government annexes the east Greenland coastal region, violating Denmark's claim to the region. . . . The banking crisis that began in Austria spreads to Germany as the Danatbank collapses.	The Benguella-Katanga Railway officially opens, connecting Lobito Bay in Angola with Katanga in the Belgian Congo. . . . Emperor Haile Selassie of Ethiopia signs the first constitution of Ethiopia.		Violent anti-Chinese rioting erupts in Korea in response to a false report regarding an incident at Wanpaoshan in Manchuria. . . . The Yellow River flood kills millions of people in China.
Aug.	Delegates meet in London to discuss implementation of President Hoover's debt moratorium plan. . . . An international committee of bankers meets in Basel, Switzerland, to review the international banking crisis. The committee issues the Layton-Wiggin Report, which calls for a six-month extension of foreign credit to Germany.	A plebiscite is held in Catalonia to determine the region's autonomous status. . . . The French government provides a major loan to Hungary.			Following the report that a Japanese officer was executed by the Chinese in western Manchuria, strong anti-Chinese sentiments erupt in Japan.
Sept.	The Vatican and the Italian government sign a supplementary treaty to the Lateran Pacts to allow the religious organization Azione Cattolica to operate in Italy, provided it refrains from political interventions.	In light of international opposition, Germany and Austria voluntarily renounce their proposal for a common customs union. . . . King Alexander I of Yugoslavia announces the end of the dictatorship and the introduction of a new democratic constitution. . . . The Bank of England withdraws from the gold standard.		After years of negotiations, the Mexican government decides to join the League of Nations.	The second roundtable conference on the future of India takes place in London. . . . The Japanese army starts the occupation of key cities in Manchuria after the Mukden Incident. The region will be eventually renamed Manchukuo.

A	B	C	D	E
Includes developments that affect more than one world region, international organizations, and important meetings of world leaders.	*Includes all domestic and regional developments in Europe, including the Soviet Union.*	*Includes all domestic and regional developments in Africa and the Middle East.*	*Includes all domestic and regional developments in Latin America, the Caribbean, and Canada.*	*Includes all domestic and regional developments in Asian and Pacific nations (and colonies).*

U.S. Politics & Social Issues	U.S. Foreign Policy & Defense	Economics & Great Depression	Science, Technology & Nature	Culture, Leisure & Lifestyle	
The Wickersham Committee issues a report asking for revisions of Prohibition, but not repeal.	The United States awards civil government to the Virgin Islands. . . . The American Legion gives its support to the principle of the immediate cash retirement of the adjusted compensation certificates for World War veterans.	More than 500 hungry farmers badly hit by drought storm the town of England, Ark., demanding food for their families. President Hoover pleads to the nation to aid the Red Cross, whose help in the drought area is needed.			**Jan.**
Congress allows California to build the San Francisco-Oakland Bay Bridge.		In his Lincoln Day address, President Hoover urges American citizens to resist the trend to centralize economic policies to counter the economic depression, saying state intervention destroys initiative.		The U.S. opera *Peter Ibbetson* by Deems Taylor premieres at the Metropolitan Opera House in New York City. . . . Amelia Earhart, aviatrix, marries George Palmer Putnam, divorced heir to a publishing empire, in Noank, Conn.	**Feb.**
President Hoover signs a bill making "The Star-Spangled Banner," written by Francis Scott Key, the national anthem of the United States. . . . The Scottsboro Boys, accused of raping a white woman, are arrested in Alabama.		Nevada legalizes gambling to stabilize the state's economy and raise tax revenues.	Schick, Inc., markets the first electric razor.	Cab Calloway and his orchestra record "Minnie the Moocher" on Brunswick Records. . . . Charlie Chaplin receives France's prestigious Legion of Honor.	**Mar.**
The first Scottsboro trial for nine African Americans accused of raping a white woman begins.				Jackie Mitchell becomes the first female professional baseball player when she signs with the Chattanooga Baseball Club.	**Apr.**
The Empire State Building opens in New York City. A 3,000-man construction crew completed the building in one year and 45 days.		In his Memorial Day address, President Hoover urges the American people to fight the economic depression by standing "steadfast in our great tradition through this time of stress."		Singer Kate Smith begins her long-running radio program on CBS.	**May**
Al Capone is indicted with 68 others for violation of Prohibition laws.	President Hoover proposes a one-year suspension of all intergovernmental debt to halt the international banking crisis.		Prof. Robert H. Goddard patents a rocket-fueled airplane.	Wiley Post and Harold Gatty fly in a single-engine plane, the Winnie Mae, from New York on a round-the-world flight. They return to New York in 8 days, 15 hours, and 51 minutes, a new world record.	**Jun.**
The trial of Constance May Flood Gavin, an alleged illegitimate daughter, begins in San Mateo, Calif., for a daughter's share in the James L. Flood estate. The trial will lead to a clash between Judge George Buck, who orders a directed verdict in favor of the Flood family, and 10 jurors who refuse to sign the verdict.	President Hoover announces that all of the important creditor governments have accepted the intergovernmental debt moratorium. Delays in applying the moratorium will still lead to the closure of many German banks.		Grasshoppers in Iowa, Nebraska, and South Dakota destroy thousands of acres of crops.	Clyde Panghorn and Hugh Herndon take off from Roosevelt Field, N.Y., in an attempt to set a round-the world speed record, but fail.	**Jul.**
African-American activist Roy Wilkins joins the National Association for the Advancement of Colored People.			Hubert Wilkins, Australian explorer, reaches within 550 miles of the North Pole in the submarine *Nautilus*.		**Aug.**
		The New York Stock Exchange is badly hit by the withdrawal of Britain from the gold standard and the consequent monetary crisis.			**Sept.**

F	**G**	**H**	**I**	**J**
Includes elections, federal-state relations, civil rights and liberties, crime, the judiciary, education, healthcare, poverty, urban affairs, and population.	*Includes formation and debate of U.S. foreign and defense policies, veterans affairs, and defense spending. (Relations with specific foreign countries are usually found under the region concerned.)*	*Includes business, labor, agriculture, taxation, transportation, consumer affairs, monetary and fiscal policy, natural resources, pollution, and accidents.*	*Includes worldwide scientific, medical, and technological developments, natural phenomena, U.S. weather, and natural disasters.*	*Includes the arts, religion, scholarship, communications media, sports, entertainment, fashions, fads, and social life.*

	World Affairs	Europe	Africa & The Middle East	The Americas	Asia & The Pacific
Oct.	The League of Nations Council holds the second meeting of its 65th session in Geneva.	The Irish government outlaws the Republican Army. . . . The Austrian National Assembly passes an austere economic program in an attempt to balance the country's budget. . . . The Turco-Soviet Alliance is renewed for five more years. . . . Universal female suffrage is established in Spain.	The League of Ulemas is founded in Constantine, Algeria. The league's goal is to advance Islamic reform.	The 98-foot statue of Christ the Redeemer is unveiled in Rio de Janeiro.	
Nov.	Focusing on the international financial crisis, a number of nations agree to a one-year truce on armaments expansion. . . . The Permanent Court of International Justice holds its 23rd session in The Hague.	A committee of the Spanish Assembly finds King Alfonso guilty of treason and exiles him.			The Japanese offensive in Manchuria leads the Chinese to boycott Japanese goods. A Chinese military counter-offensive fails because of Communist guerillas and heavy floods. . . . Mao Tse-Dong proclaims a Communist Republic in Jiangxi (Kiangsi) province.
Dec.	The League of Nations appoints the Lytton Commission to review the events that led to the Japanese intervention in Manchuria.	The British parliament passes the Statute of Westminster, which makes Britain and the Dominions autonomous communities within the British Empire. . . . The Constitutional Assembly gives a new constitution to Spain. Alcala Zamora becomes president of the country.	The Spanish republican government reorganizes the colonial government in Spanish Morocco.		The Japanese government withdraws from the gold standard.

A	B	C	D	E
Includes developments that affect more than one world region, international organizations, and important meetings of world leaders.	*Includes all domestic and regional developments in Europe, including the Soviet Union.*	*Includes all domestic and regional developments in Africa and the Middle East.*	*Includes all domestic and regional developments in Latin America, the Caribbean, and Canada.*	*Includes all domestic and regional developments in Asian and Pacific nations (and colonies).*

U.S. Politics & Social Issues	U.S. Foreign Policy & Defense	Economics & Great Depression	Science, Technology & Nature	Culture, Leisure & Lifestyle	
Anne LeRoi and Hedvig Samuelson are murdered, dismembered, and shipped in trunks to Los Angeles. Winnie Ruth Judd, subsequently known as the "Trunk Murderess," is responsible. . . . Al Capone is convicted for tax evasion and sentenced to 11 years in prison. . . . The George Washington Bridge, linking New York City and New Jersey, is completed.	President Hoover warns the Philippines that to gain effective independence, the islands should also be economically self-sufficient. . . . The Hoover administration accepts the invitation of the League of Nations and appoints Prentiss B. Gilbert to participate in discussions on the Manchurian crisis.		Inventor Thomas Edison dies at the age of 84.	The comic strip *Dick Tracy* appears for the first time in New York. . . . Eugene O'Neill's *Mourning Becomes Electra* premieres in New York City.	Oct.
	Secretary of State Henry Stimson announces that the United States will not participate in a League of Nations economic boycott against the Japanese for their invasion of Manchuria.		Col. Charles Lindbergh inaugurates Pan-American Airline's service from Cuba to South America.		Nov.
American reformer Jane Addams is the first American woman to receive the Nobel Prize for Peace.			Miles Laboratories starts the production of Alka Seltzer.	*Hansel und Gretel* by Engelbert Humperdinck is the first opera ever to be broadcast on the radio by New York's Metropolitan Opera.	Dec.

F	**G**	**H**	**I**	**J**
Includes elections, federal-state relations, civil rights and liberties, crime, the judiciary, education, healthcare, poverty, urban affairs, and population.	*Includes formation and debate of U.S. foreign and defense policies, veterans affairs, and defense spending. (Relations with specific foreign countries are usually found under the region concerned.)*	*Includes business, labor, agriculture, taxation, transportation, consumer affairs, monetary and fiscal policy, natural resources, pollution, and accidents.*	*Includes worldwide scientific, medical, and technological developments, natural phenomena, U.S. weather, and natural disasters.*	*Includes the arts, religion, scholarship, communications media, sports, entertainment, fashions, fads, and social life.*

	World Affairs	Europe	Africa & The Middle East	The Americas	Asia & The Pacific
Jan. 1	The Chatham Phenix National Bank and Trust Company of New York denies a request by the Argentine government to renew a loan worth $16 million. Certain stipulations in the signed contract that the Argentineans were not aware of allowed the bank to deny the request. Argentine officials say the Spanish version of the bank's English-language contract did not properly illustrate the matter. The Bank of Nations subsequently creates a gold conversion fund of $30 million to repay the loan.				Chinese military officials estimate there are currently around 2.5 million soldiers serving in the nation's army.
Jan. 2				In Managua, Nicaragua, eight U.S. Marines are killed and two more are wounded by a band of hostile rebels under the tutelage of revolutionary Augusto Sandino, who has formally protested U.S. military occupation. It marks the largest Nicaraguan attack against U.S. military personnel in terms of body count since New Year's Eve 1928, when five Marines were killed. In response to the attack, U.S. defense officials assemble a group of 50 Marines to hunt down and capture the rebels.	
Jan. 3		The newspaper *Ora* reports that Albania has formally sought a loan worth $10 million from the Italian government. Italy's response remains to be seen.		Uruguay denies the request of Argentina to extradite former Argentine Foreign Minister Horacio Oyhanarte, who fled his country as the regime of his superior, President Hipolito Irigoyen, began to unravel. Oyhanarte was then captured by Uruguayan border authorities. Uruguay denied the extradition request on the grounds that Oyhanarte is a "political offender," rather than a criminal one.	
Jan. 4		The British royal family releases a statement on the health status of Princess Royal, the eldest sister of King George. The Princess, who is 64-years-old, is said to be suffering from a heart condition, from which she has shown "increasing weakness" over the past few days. The condition has left the Princess bedridden for several months.		The Provisional Government of Brazil announces it will begin to curb immigration from other South American countries, effectively reversing decades of "open door" policy. Brazilian economists say the influx of immigrants has created extremely low wages for the country's manual laborers, especially in the coffee producing markets, where even the most skilled laborer can expect to earn nothing more than $50 per year.	
Jan. 5		British economists report the Bank of England took in £200,000 worth of gold last week, against £1,322,864 in withdrawals, netting a deficit of £1,122,864. Approximately £1,250,000 was withdrawn by the country of France.		The provisional government controlling Argentina announces it is considering abolishing the Gold Conversion Office and establishing a central bank with a new currency system. Financial experts claim the changes will give greater strength to the Argentine peso, which has recently fallen to new low exchange rates.	
Jan. 6					

A	B	C	D	E
Includes developments that affect more than one world region, international organizations, and important meetings of world leaders.	Includes all domestic and regional developments in Europe, including the Soviet Union.	Includes all domestic and regional developments in Africa and the Middle East.	Includes all domestic and regional developments in Latin America, the Caribbean, and Canada.	Includes all domestic and regional developments in Asian and Pacific nations (and colonies).

U.S. Politics & Social Issues	U.S. Foreign Policy & Defense	Economics & Great Depression	Science, Technology & Nature	Culture, Leisure & Lifestyle	
	In accordance with the London Naval Treaty, the Navy Department transfers the battleship USS *Wyoming* to Philadelphia to begin the process of conversion into a "training ship." . . . U.S. Minister to Berne, Switzerland, Hugh R. Wilson signs a document that ends the requirement of foreign military service for U.S. citizens with immigrant parents. The U.S. State Department had earlier received complaints from citizens who, when entering their parents' country of origin, were arrested by authorities for failure to perform military service.	The U.S. Department of Commerce releases its weekly index of U.S. steel production, showing a decline of 4.7 points from the previous week, and a drop of 25 percent from the corresponding week last year. Responsibility for the decline was placed on curtailed worker attendance stemming from the Christmas and New Year's holidays.		Australian Olympic participant Bonnie Mealing sets the world record for the 150-yard backstroke by swimming the distance in under 1 hour and 54.6 seconds.	Jan. 1
		The Bankus Corporation, The City Financial Corporation, the Delaware Bankus Corporation, and the Municipal Corporation simultaneously declare bankruptcy. Presiding over the bankruptcy hearings is federal Judge John M. Woolsey, who estimates to reporters that the liquid assets of the four companies amounts to no more than $100,000.		Arthur Hammerstein, uncle of famous playwright Oscar Hammerstein, announces his intention to retire from theatrical production, effective as soon as his musical comedy *Ballyhoo* ends its two-week engagement on the Broadway stage. Hammerstein notes that he has lost over $1 million in his last eight theatrical productions. He would remain a creative force in the United States following his retirement, writing a #1 romantic ballad, *Because of You*, for lounge singer Tony Bennett in 1951.	Jan. 2
George Akerson, personal secretary to President Herbert Hoover, announces his resignation. Akerson accepted an offer from the movie studio Paramount, and will receive an annual salary of $30,000, three times the amount under the President.		*The Annalist* releases its weekly list of U.S. wholesale commodity prices. At 115.3, the index is a drop of 0.4 points from the previous week and a decline of 18 percent from the corresponding week a year ago. Economists say the decline was caused by a sharp drop in the price of farm products. . . . The Argentine peso exchange rate falls to 141.2, or one U.S. dollar equaling 141.2 pesos.			Jan. 3
The New York City Free Employment Bureau announces that in one day, it received over 60,000 applications for work from unemployed men and women.		The weekly business index compiled by *The Annalist* is released, showing a decline of 0.3 points from the previous week and a drop of 15 percent from the corresponding period in 1930. Responsibility for the decline was attributed to declines in steel mill activity and automobile production.			Jan. 4
	The destroyer ship USS *Breese* is redesignated as a "minelayer" and has its name changed to *DM-18*. Naval officials say she will require a process of conversion at the Mare Island Navy Yard for approximately six months before becoming operational once again. . . . After almost eight years of inactivity, the destroyer ship USS *Montgomery* is reclassified by the Navy Department as a "minelayer." She will now undergo the process of conversion for approximately six months, say naval experts. . . . The USS *S-22* submarine is transferred from New London, Conn., to the naval base at Pearl Harbor, Hawaii, where she would stay until 1938. The submarine was constructed in 1920 by the Bethlehem Shipbuilding Corporation.	Prof. Irving Fisher of Yale University releases his weekly index of international commodity prices. The figure is 78.5, a reduction of 0.5 points from the preceding week and 16 percent below the corresponding week a year ago. Fisher, a world renowned economist, famously commented a few days before the 1929 stock market crash that, "Stock prices have reached what appears to be a permanently high plateau."	British aviator Amy Johnson, who last May became the first woman to fly from Great Britain to Australia, encounters heavy fog during a flight from London to China and is forced to make an emergency landing in the Polish village of Amelin.		Jan. 5
Members of the House of Representatives debate a bill that would decrease the War Department's current fiscal year budget by approximately $4 million. . . . *Motor Magazine* reports there are currently 26,661,596 cars and trucks in operation inside the United States, an increase of only 6 percent from a year ago. It is the smallest yearly increase since 1927. . . . Major U.S. literature publishers announce that the Christian Bible was the top-selling book in 1930.		The weekly index of U.S. automobile production as compiled by the Department of Commerce is released. The index stands at 55.9, a reduction of 11.2 points from the preceding week and a decline of 21 percent from the corresponding period one year ago. The drop from last week was attributed to the closings of several Ford Motor Company factories.		The Walt Disney animated short *The Birthday Party*, featuring one of the first appearances by the celebrated cartoon character Mickey Mouse, is released across the United States. . . . Boxer Benny Bass successfully defends his title of junior world lightweight champion, defeating Lew Massey in a 10-round bout. Bass and Massey each weigh 128 pounds.	Jan. 6
F Includes elections, federal-state relations, civil rights and liberties, crime, the judiciary, education, healthcare, poverty, urban affairs, and population.	**G** Includes formation and debate of U.S. foreign and defense policies, veterans affairs, and defense spending. (Relations with specific foreign countries are usually found under the region concerned.)	**H** Includes business, labor, agriculture, taxation, transportation, consumer affairs, monetary and fiscal policy, natural resources, pollution, and accidents.	**I** Includes worldwide scientific, medical, and technological developments, natural phenomena, U.S. weather, and natural disasters.	**J** Includes the arts, religion, scholarship, communications media, sports, entertainment, fashions, fads, and social life.	

	World Affairs	Europe	Africa & The Middle East	The Americas	Asia & The Pacific
Jan. 7	Prime Minister James Scullin returns to Australia following the British Imperial Conference in London, where British officials had formally expressed a preference for U.S. goods, rather than Australian goods. . . . The Czechoslovakian newspaper *Bohemia* reports that Czech Foreign Minister Eduard Benes is the leading candidate to assume the position of League of Nations Council President. Benes earlier occupied the post from 1927–28.				The Australian Federal Statistician releases a statement estimating the nation's unemployed to be approximately 200,000 people, half of whom are trade unionists. The situation is most dire in South Australia, where an estimated 25 percent of trade unionists are unemployed. "Our present financial position undoubtedly is leading to national bankruptcy," predicts Health Minister Frank Anstey. "Within two months the banks will close down on all governments. After that, chaos."
Jan. 8		Albert de Ligne, Belgian Ambassador to the United States, leaves the United States for the final time aboard the liner *Britannic*. Ligne had earlier announced his retirement. . . . Oil heir John D. Rockefeller, Jr., is awarded the title of Grand Officer of the Crown by the Belgian government for his philanthropic support of the University of Brussels. Rockefeller has committed hundreds of thousands of dollars to the cause of Belgian higher education.		The Banco de la Nacion of Argentina ships $5 million worth of gold to the U.S. banks Chase National, Guaranty Trust, and Irving Trust. The funds make up one-third of a $16 million loan given to Argentina that was due on January 1.	
Jan. 9					
Jan. 10	Polish Interior Minister General Felician Skladowski reveals that there are currently over 1,000 Ukrainians detained in Polish prisons in connection with the revolutionary disorders which occurred last fall. The revelation follows a formal protest filed on November 8 by the United National Ukrainian Association to the League of Nations.	King Alfonso XIII of Spain issues a decree suspending the country's air force for approximately one month. Following reorganization, the air force will become a branch of the army.			
Jan. 11		French Agriculture Minister Victor Boret announces that his government will be raising the duty on imported sugar, contingent upon a parliamentary vote. Boret says the increase is necessary to stimulate France's fledgling sugar beet industry. . . . The Belgian Labor Minister appeals to Parliament to appropriate $6 million in public works projects for the unemployed. Public Works Minister Caenagem estimates that idle workers are currently being paid 60 cents daily for living expenses. He recommends public works projects as a cheaper alternative.			
Jan. 12		British economists report the Bank of England took in £628,000 worth of gold last week, against £1,748,906 in withdrawals, netting a deficit of £1,120,906. Approximately £1.5 million was withdrawn by the country of France. Of the £628,000 deposited, £250,000 came from South Africa.	The Palestine Arab Executive publishes a letter sent to the British Colonial Office by a group of Arab nationalists. The letter calls for the abolition of the 1917 Balfour Declaration, which officially declared Palestine as the "Jewish national home." The letter also calls for the establishment of a representative Arab government, as well as the cessation of Jewish immigration into Palestine.		

A	B	C	D	E
Includes developments that affect more than one world region, international organizations, and important meetings of world leaders.	*Includes all domestic and regional developments in Europe, including the Soviet Union.*	*Includes all domestic and regional developments in Africa and the Middle East.*	*Includes all domestic and regional developments in Latin America, the Caribbean, and Canada.*	*Includes all domestic and regional developments in Asian and Pacific nations (and colonies).*

U.S. Politics & Social Issues	U.S. Foreign Policy & Defense	Economics & Great Depression	Science, Technology & Nature	Culture, Leisure & Lifestyle	
	The Navy Department strikes the battleship USS *North Dakota* from the list of the Naval Vessel Register. In operation for more than 20 years, she was built by Fore River Shipbuilding in 1908. . . . The battleship USS *North Dakota*, the first Navy ship named after the state of North Dakota, is struck from the list of the Naval Vessel Register, rendering the ship inactive. She was constructed by the Fore River Shipbuilding Company in 1910.	The American Railway Association estimates that U.S. freight car loadings in the past week amounted to 538,419 cars, a reduction of 175,391 cars from the preceding week. The weekly total is also 15 percent below the corresponding period last year. Economists say the decline is a result of reductions in coal, grain, and livestock, as well as the Christmas and New Year's holidays.			Jan. 7
New York State lawmakers introduce a bill that would make it a felony to spread "derogatory rumors" about the financial condition of state banks. . . . The U.S. Department of Commerce reports aircraft exports for the first 10 months of 1930 amounted to $7,288,014, 6 percent less than 1929's record 10-month total of $7,761.977.		The U.S. Department of Commerce releases its weekly index of U.S. steel production, showing a rise of 5.6 points from the previous week, but a decline of 29 percent from the corresponding week last year. Responsibility for the increase from last week is placed on steel mill workers who returned last week from their Christmas and New Year's holiday celebrations.			Jan. 8
The New York City Department of Welfare announces it has received 12,802 applications for old-age relief in four months, a record amount for the time period. Welfare Commissioner Frank J. Taylor says his staff has mailed over 10,000 checks since the new old-age relief state law came into effect on January 1.		*The Annalist* releases its weekly list of U.S. wholesale commodity prices. At 115.6, the index is a rise of 0.3 points from the previous week, but a drop of 18 percent from the corresponding week a year ago. Economists say the decline was caused by drops in every commodity category, excluding farm products.		*All Quiet on the Western Front*, Universal Studios' film adaptation of German author Erich Remarque's World War I novel, is released in Finland. The film was the recipient of two Motion Picture Academy Awards, including Best Picture. . . . First National Studios' crime drama film *Little Caesar* is released in New York City. As one of the first "gangster" movies ever made, the film will be archived for the enjoyment of future generations by the U.S. National Film Preservation Board in 2000. It will also be nominated for the Best Screenplay Academy Award in 1931.	Jan. 9
	The Navy Department transfers the heavy cruiser ship USS *Houston* from New York Harbor to the Pacific Coast.			Construction of the largest indoor skating rink in the United States is completed by the Army Athletic Association. The rink, with a skating area of 232 feet by 90 feet, has the capability to produce over eight tons of ice in one day.	Jan. 10
R.G. Dun & Co. announces that in 1930, there were 3,446 more commercial bank failures than 1929, a 15 percent increase. Total liabilities of the failed banks also increased by $185 million. Conclusively, it was a record year in the United States for both bank failures and liabilities, an unmistakable after-effect of the 1929 stock market crash.	The destroyer ship USS *Toucey* is sold for scrap by the Navy Department. Named after Naval Secretary Isaac Toucey, she was constructed by the Bethlehem Shipbuilding Corporation in 1919 and spent most of her operational years conducting reconnaissance missions in the Caribbean.	The weekly business index compiled by *The Annalist* is released, showing a drop of 0.3 points from the previous week and a decline of 15 percent from the corresponding period in 1930. Responsibility for the decline is attributed to drops in electric power and automobile production.			Jan. 11
The American Association Against the Prohibition Amendment president, Henry Curran, issues a statement showing that nearly half of the United States' 50 states support repeal of Prohibition. Curran predicts that the necessary votes needed to create national legislation will be garnered within two years. Curran's prediction ultimately proves correct, as Congress will pass the 21st Amendment, which declared the Prohibition Amendment unconstitutional, on February 20, 1933.	The destroyer ship USS *Breck* is sold for scrap by the Navy Department in accordance with the London Naval Treaty. The ship was constructed in 1919 by the Bethlehem Shipbuilding Corporation.	Prof. Irving Fisher of Yale University releases his weekly index of international commodity prices. The figure is 78.5, a decrease of 0.2 points from the preceding week and 16 percent from the corresponding week a year ago.			Jan. 12

F	**G**	**H**	**I**	**J**
Includes elections, federal-state relations, civil rights and liberties, crime, the judiciary, education, healthcare, poverty, urban affairs, and population.	*Includes formation and debate of U.S. foreign and defense policies, veterans affairs, and defense spending. (Relations with specific foreign countries are usually found under the region concerned.)*	*Includes business, labor, agriculture, taxation, transportation, consumer affairs, monetary and fiscal policy, natural resources, pollution, and accidents.*	*Includes worldwide scientific, medical, and technological developments, natural phenomena, U.S. weather, and natural disasters.*	*Includes the arts, religion, scholarship, communications media, sports, entertainment, fashions, fads, and social life.*

	World Affairs	Europe	Africa & The Middle East	The Americas	Asia & The Pacific
Jan. 13		Five leaders of the Romanian anti-Semitic organization Iron Guard are arrested by police authorities on charges of inducing public disorder, agitation against the state, and creating "secret military organizations" whose purpose is to violently overthrow the existing political order.			
Jan. 14			In New York City, 10,000 people attend the funeral of Jewish philanthropist Nathan Strauss, who for years was one of the leading financial contributors toward a Jewish national home in Palestine. Strauss made his fortune as one of the co-owners of the Macy's department store, and served as the New York city park commissioner from 1889–93.	The Argentine peso exchange rate falls to 148.52, or $1 equaling 148.52 Argentine pesos. It is the lowest level since 1921.	
Jan. 15				Argentina conscripts 25,600 men into its army and 11,000 men into the navy. The conscripts will serve one year. . . . Leading Argentine financial experts release a statement blaming the current slump of the Argentine peso on panicky U.S. businessmen, who they say have hurt the peso through excessive foreign investment.	
Jan. 16	Mexican court officials announce that the trial of Daniel Flores, who attempted to assassinate newly elected President Ortiz Rubio on February 5 of last year, will officially begin on February 12. If convicted, Flores will likely receive a sentence of 20 years in the Tres Marias Islands penal colony.			The Cuban National Association of Industrialists formally asks permission from President Gerardo Machado to extend liquor sales into waters extending three miles off the Cuban coast. Machado responds by saying an approval of the request will likely result in increased smuggling of liquor into the United States, which he and U.S. officials have signed a formal treaty to prevent.	
Jan. 17	The Brazilian provisional government formally considers purchasing 11 military planes from the Italian government. Each plane will cost approximately 600 contos, or $72,000. The agreement is contingent upon Brazil granting Italy greater access to the former's coffee markets.				
Jan. 18				The Argentine Bureau of National Statistics publishes figures showing the country's exports for 1930 totaled 612,550,000 pesos, against 953,744,000 pesos from 1929, a decline of 36 percent.	

A	B	C	D	E
Includes developments that affect more than one world region, international organizations, and important meetings of world leaders.	Includes all domestic and regional developments in Europe, including the Soviet Union.	Includes all domestic and regional developments in Africa and the Middle East.	Includes all domestic and regional developments in Latin America, the Caribbean, and Canada.	Includes all domestic and regional developments in Asian and Pacific nations (and colonies).

U.S. Politics & Social Issues	U.S. Foreign Policy & Defense	Economics & Great Depression	Science, Technology & Nature	Culture, Leisure & Lifestyle	
The 28th annual convention of the American Road Builders' Association commences in St. Louis, Mo. Thomas McDonald, head of the Agriculture Department's Bureau of Public Roads, predicts that road construction in 1931 will be 30–50 percent greater than the previous year, and will cost $2 billion. Association president W.A. Van Duzer says that if the funds were increased by $5 billion, the entire lot of the nation's unemployed could end their idleness. He criticizes the British alternative of a "dole" system. "That is charity in Sunday clothes," he says, adding, "Let's stick to the good old American system of a day's pay for a day's work."	The destroyer ship USS *Hatfield*, constructed by the New York Shipbuilding Corporation in 1919, is officially decommissioned by the Navy Department. . . . At the Philadelphia Navy Yard, the destroyer ship USS *Goff* is decommissioned by naval authorities. She is named after Nathan Goff, who served as Secretary of Navy for a brief period during 1881. The ship was built by the New York Shipbuilding Corporation in 1920. . . . The Navy Department sells the destroyer ship USS *Maury* for scrap. She was constructed by the Fore River Shipbuilding Company in 1918 and would spend more than 10 years as an experimental minelayer in the waters of the Atlantic.	The weekly index of U.S. automobile production as compiled by the Department of Commerce is released. The index stands at 70, a gain of 13.5 points from the preceding week but a decline of nearly 20 percent from the corresponding period one year ago. The increase from last week was attributed to resumption of production at several factories of the Ford Motor Company.			Jan. 13
Congress appropriates $528,700 for the promotion of economic partnerships with Latin American nations.	The Navy Department sells for scrap the USS *Osborne* destroyer ship. Constructed by the Bethlehem Shipbuilding Corporation in 1919, she would spend her years as a member of the Navy's Atlantic Fleet. . . . The USS *Charles Ausburn* destroyer ship is sold for scrap by the Navy Department. The ship was built in 1919 by the Bethlehem Shipbuilding Corporation.	The American Railway Association estimates that U.S. freight car loadings in the past week amounted to 615,382 cars, an increase of 26,963 cars from the preceding week. The weekly total is also 20 percent less than the corresponding period last year. Economists say the increase is a result of sharp gains in coal, grain, and livestock.		The romantic comedy film *One Heavenly Night* is released across the United States. The film is directed by George Fitzmaurice of France, who would be awarded a star on the Hollywood Walk of Fame.	Jan. 14
Admiral Thomas Hart, commander of the U.S. Fleet Control Force, is chosen by the Navy Department to succeed Admiral S.S. Robinson as Naval Academy Superintendent, effective when the latter officially retires on May 15. . . . The American Telephone and Telegraph Company announces its net earnings for 1930 amounted to approximately $150 million, a decline of 10 percent from last year's total of $166,189,758.	The Navy Department commissions the heavy cruiser ship USS *Louisville*, built by the Puget Sound Naval Yard in September of last year. During World War II, she would engage in various naval battles against Japan in the waters of the Pacific Ocean. . . . The destroyer ship USS *Billingsley* is sold for scrap by the Navy Department. A member of the Atlantic Fleet Destroyer Force for over 10 years, she was constructed in late 1919 by the Bethlehem Shipbuilding Corporation.	The U.S. Department of Commerce releases its weekly index of American steel production, showing a minimal gain of 0.1 points from the previous week, but a decline of 33 percent from the corresponding week last year. Responsibility for the minimal change from last week was placed on a curtailment of steel shipments.			Jan. 15
		The Annalist releases its weekly list of U.S. wholesale commodity prices. At 115.5, the index is nearly identical to the previous week's index of 115.6, but a decline of 18 percent from the corresponding week a year ago. Economists say the stabilization was caused by a drop in food products, offset by gains in farm products and building materials.	A worldwide conference of leprologists is held in Cebu, Philippines. Delegates agree to officially change the word "leper" to "case of leprosy," as the former is considered derogatory.	The British gangster film *The Man From Chicago*, loosely inspired by the life of Al "Scarface" Capone, is released in the United States.	Jan. 16
The Travelers Insurance Company reports that during the whole of 1930, there were 32,500 deaths attributable to automobile accidents, an increase of 4 percent from the previous year, despite a decrease of 10 percent in total motor vehicle mileage; $300 million was paid out to injured or deceased motorists by American insurance companies.	The Navy Department sells the obsolete naval vessel *DD-287* for scrap. The ship was constructed in 1919 by the Bethlehem Shipbuilding Corporation, and would spend most of her years conducting torpedo experimentation missions. . . . In accordance with the London Naval Treaty, the Navy Department sells the destroyer ship USS *Case* for scrap. Built by the Bethlehem Shipbuilding Corporation in 1919, she spent most of her years conducting goodwill missions in British and Mediterranean waters. . . . The destroyer ships USS *Worden*, USS *Converse*, and USS *Sharkey* are also sold for scrap by the Navy Department in accordance with the London Naval Treaty.	Argentina's Gold Conversion Office ships $5,182,000 to European markets as means of improving the exchange rate of the slumping peso. . . . The weekly business index compiled by *The Annalist* is released, showing a drop of 0.2 points from the previous week and a decline of 16 percent from the corresponding period in 1930. Responsibility for the drop was attributed to declines in freight car loadings and electric power production.		The crime caper film *The Gang Buster* is released across the United States. The film is directed by A. Edward Sutherland, who would command the production of nearly 50 feature films over the span of a 40-year career.	Jan. 17
	The Boston Iron and Metal Company purchases the cruiser USS *Galveston* from the Navy Department for a sum of $16,665. . . . The destroyers *Hull*, *J.F. Burnes*, *La Vallette*, *Farenholt*, *Robert Smith*, and *Thompson* are purchased by Moore Drydock for $36,000.			Comte Louis de Lichtervelde publishes *Leopold I, The Founder of Modern Belgium*, a biography of the current King of Belgium, who is credited with implementing his country's first democratic political system.	Jan. 18

F	G	H	I	J
Includes elections, federal-state relations, civil rights and liberties, crime, the judiciary, education, healthcare, poverty, urban affairs, and population.	Includes formation and debate of U.S. foreign and defense policies, veterans affairs, and defense spending. (Relations with specific foreign countries are usually found under the region concerned.)	Includes business, labor, agriculture, taxation, transportation, consumer affairs, monetary and fiscal policy, natural resources, pollution, and accidents.	Includes worldwide scientific, medical, and technological developments, natural phenomena, U.S. weather, and natural disasters.	Includes the arts, religion, scholarship, communications media, sports, entertainment, fashions, fads, and social life.

	World Affairs	Europe	Africa & The Middle East	The Americas	Asia & The Pacific
Jan. 19		British economists report the Bank of England took in £1.25 million worth of gold last week, against £2,306,563 in withdrawals, netting a deficit of £1,056,563. Approximately £2 million was withdrawn by the country of France. Of the £1.25 million deposited, £1 million came from Brazil.			
Jan. 20	The 62nd session of the League of Nations Council convenes in Geneva, Switzerland. Delegates debate the date for the upcoming international disarmament conference, as well as the solution for the settlement of the ongoing Polish-German minority dispute. Council representatives say the date debate will be settled no later than tomorrow. The Council also approves a proposal by the Central Opium Board that imposes harsher penalties for those convicted of illegal international narcotic trafficking. Members of the Board say the international narcotic trade is "vast and enormous."				
Jan. 21		In sessions of the French Parliament, Senate President Paul Doumer requests increasing the country's national defense bill as a way of ensuring European peace. "In the present condition of Europe," he says, "we cannot abandon the safety of our country to the hands of international justice. Peace can be guaranteed only if the nations declaring it are strong enough to enforce it."		Simultaneous railway station explosions occur in the Argentine capital of Buenos Aires. Three persons are killed and 13 more are injured. Interior Minister Sanchez Sorondo says the explosions were committed by mere angry laborers, and should be no cause for anxiety.	The trial of 25 members of the Indian National Congress who are accused of sedition begins in Bombay, India. Court prosecutors allege the members have created a "terrorist committee" designed to commit violent acts.
Jan. 22				Presidential elections are held in El Salvador. Returns indicate Arturo Araujo, who received 104,093 votes, will become the nation's next president, effective after the inauguration ceremony in March. Araujo's closest competitor, Gomez Zarate, garnered 64,097 votes. Araujo would serve as president until December 1931, when a palace coup led by Defense Minister Maximiliano Martinez forces him out of office.	
Jan. 23		A national holiday is observed in Russia to commemorate the seventh anniversary of the death of Vladimir Lenin, Communist revolutionary leader. Thousands in the capital of Moscow flock to Red Square, where the perfectly conditioned remains of the former Soviet Premier are housed. The four other national holidays in Russia all pay tribute to the 1917 revolution. Other holidays, such as Christmas, were banned last year after being determined to be detrimental to the five-year industrial plan.			
Jan. 24				President Jose Uriburu of Argentina issues a decree reducing the salary of government employees whose pay exceeds 100 pesos a month. An earlier proposal called for a flat 10 percent pay cut, but was abandoned in favor of a more progressive system which places the burden on high-ranking government officials.	

A	B	C	D	E
Includes developments that affect more than one world region, international organizations, and important meetings of world leaders.	Includes all domestic and regional developments in Europe, including the Soviet Union.	Includes all domestic and regional developments in Africa and the Middle East.	Includes all domestic and regional developments in Latin America, the Caribbean, and Canada.	Includes all domestic and regional developments in Asian and Pacific nations (and colonies).

U.S. Politics & Social Issues	U.S. Foreign Policy & Defense	Economics & Great Depression	Science, Technology & Nature	Culture, Leisure & Lifestyle	
	The Navy Department transfers the submarine USS *R-4* from the Panama Canal to New London, Conn.	Prof. Irving Fisher of Yale University releases his weekly index of international commodity prices. The figure is 77.9, a reduction of 0.4 points from the preceding week and 16 percent from the corresponding week a year ago.	American Airways, Inc., issues a report showing that in 1930, there were a total of 60,074 airline passengers, compared with 17,819 passengers for 1929, an increase of over 237 percent. There were also 1,221,757 more miles flown.	Alfred Hitchcock's thriller film *Blackmail*, based on the play written by Charles Bennett, is released in Finland. Considered by film historians to be the first "talkie" released in Great Britain, Hitchcock shot the film silently, but later added sound to the background as new technology became available.	Jan. 19
	The destroyer ship USS *Reuben James*, named after Revolutionary War era Boatswain's Mate Reuben James, is decommissioned by the Navy Department in Philadelphia, Pa. Recommissioned in 1932, the ship would eventually be sunk by the German submarine *U-552* while navigating the waters of Iceland on October 31, 1941.	The weekly index of U.S. automobile production as compiled by the Department of Commerce is released. The index stands at 69.4, a rise of 0.6 points from the preceding week but a decline of approximately 10 percent from the corresponding period one year ago. The increase from last week was attributed to continued Ford Motor Company factory reopenings.		The French romantic comedy film *Le Petit Café* premiers in New York City. It is based on the play by Tristan Bernard, who became something of a cultural status symbol after being interned by the Nazis during the military occupation of France. The Parisian theater-playhouse, Theatre Tristan Bernard, is named after him.	Jan. 20
		The American Railway Association estimates that U.S. freight car loadings in the past week amounted to 714,521 cars, an increase of nearly 100,000 cars from the preceding week. The weekly total is also 18 percent below the corresponding period last year. Economists say the gain from last week is a result of increases in coal, forest products, grain, and livestock.			Jan. 21
Rep. L.F. Stone of the Tennessee legislature introduces a bill that would require daily Bible readings in the state's public schools. Critics say the bill is a clear violation of the Constitutionally protected separation of church and state. Rep. Stone counters by saying the concept of states' rights should permit the readings.		The U.S. Department of Commerce releases its weekly index of American steel production, showing a reasonably large gain of 3.7 points from the previous week, but still a decrease of nearly 30 percent from the corresponding week last year. Responsibility for the gain from last week was placed on an increased demand for steel from automobile manufacturers.			Jan. 22
	The War Department chooses 248 pilots to participate in the Army Air Corps flying school class of 1931. Of these, 26 are currently enlisted men. Only a quarter of the 858 potential recruits were selected.	*The Annalist* releases its weekly list of U.S. wholesale commodity prices. At 114.6, the index is a decline of 0.9 points from the previous week and a drop of 18 percent from the corresponding week a year ago. Economists say the decline was caused by sharp drops in the prices of farm products, food products, and chemicals.			Jan. 23
	The USS *Hart* destroyer ship arrives in San Diego, Calif., to begin the process of deactivation. She was built in 1918, a product of the Union Iron Works Company.	American-Russian Chamber of Commerce of New York president Hugh Cooper urges the U.S. Treasury Department to remove the embargo on Russian imports. The regulations, he says, "have caused a substantial disruption of American-Russian trade."			Jan. 24

F	G	H	I	J
Includes elections, federal-state relations, civil rights and liberties, crime, the judiciary, education, healthcare, poverty, urban affairs, and population.	Includes formation and debate of U.S. foreign and defense policies, veterans affairs, and defense spending. (Relations with specific foreign countries are usually found under the region concerned.)	Includes business, labor, agriculture, taxation, transportation, consumer affairs, monetary and fiscal policy, natural resources, pollution, and accidents.	Includes worldwide scientific, medical, and technological developments, natural phenomena, U.S. weather, and natural disasters.	Includes the arts, religion, scholarship, communications media, sports, entertainment, fashions, fads, and social life.

	World Affairs	Europe	Africa & The Middle East	The Americas	Asia & The Pacific
Jan. 25					
Jan. 26	Former British chancellor of the exchequer Robert Horne comments in an op-ed piece in the *New York Times* that British World War I debts to the United States are not a "heavy burden" upon the British taxpayer. Horne says a significant amount of funds are derived from French and German war debts, which in turn are paid to the United States.			In the Cuban capital of Havana, 63 Chinese immigrants are arrested for operating an opium den situated directly next to a Chinese theater. Police confiscate a large amount of illegal narcotics.	
Jan. 27	The second branch of the German-American Chamber of Commerce convenes in Cologne, Germany. Among those in attendance is German Ambassador to the United States Fred Sackett, who is the principal speaker. . . . H.B. Butler, deputy director of the League of Nation's International Labor Office, authors a report stating that any unemployment relief efforts must be coordinated internationally. The report adds that rapid technological advances are the main contributing factor toward unemployment, although the destabilizing effects of new technology are only temporary.				
Jan. 28					Australian Trade Minister J.E. Fenton resigns in protest against the reinstatement of E.G. Theodore as federal treasurer. Theodore, who earlier occupied the post from 1929–30, was forced to resign after a Royal Commission concluded he illegally profited from the sale of a Queensland mine. The scandal came to be known as the Mungana Affair.
Jan. 29				According to a report made public by the Canadian Dominion Bureau of Statistics, 109,103 less automobiles were manufactured in Canada in 1930 than in 1929.	

A	B	C	D	E
Includes developments that affect more than one world region, international organizations, and important meetings of world leaders.	Includes all domestic and regional developments in Europe, including the Soviet Union.	Includes all domestic and regional developments in Africa and the Middle East.	Includes all domestic and regional developments in Latin America, the Caribbean, and Canada.	Includes all domestic and regional developments in Asian and Pacific nations (and colonies).

U.S. Politics & Social Issues	U.S. Foreign Policy & Defense	Economics & Great Depression	Science, Technology & Nature	Culture, Leisure & Lifestyle	
A rare 1918 24-cent airmail stamp is sold in Philadelphia, Pa., for a sum of $2,360, a new record for the sale of a stamp. Antiquity experts say an unintentional manufacturing error greatly increased the rarity of the stamp.		The weekly business index compiled by *The Annalist* is released, showing a rise of 0.7 points from the previous week but a decline of 16 percent from the corresponding period in 1930. Responsibility for the drop was attributed to declines in automobile production. . . . The New York Stock Exchange strikes the Berlin City Electric Co., the City of Bergen Co., the Cleveland and Pittsburgh Railroad Co., the United Biscuit Co., the White Sewing Machine Corporation, the Consolidated Agricultural Loan Co., and the Tri-Continental Corporation from its list of tradable companies.	U.S. Patent No. 1,788,553 is awarded to Adolf Thomas of New York for his invention of a long-lasting radio receiver, which, unlike regular radio receivers, does not "burn out" after excessive use.		Jan. 25
	The Army Air Corps purchases 30 Curtiss Falcon "service observation" planes from the Curtiss-Wright Corporation. The new planes are equipped with a new style of machine gun.	Prof. Irving Fisher of Yale University releases his weekly index of international commodity prices. The figure is 77.6, a drop of 0.3 points from the preceding week and 16 percent from the corresponding week a year ago.			Jan. 26
The Senate passes a bill authorizing the distribution of 20 million bushels of wheat to hungry families suffering from last year's drought. The estimate of the cost of the distribution is $15 million, which will be deducted from the Farm Board's annual budget.	At the Mare Island Naval Yard off the coast of California, the hulk of the USS *Shirk* destroyer ship is sold to industrialist P.J. Willett for an undisclosed sum.	The weekly index of U.S. automobile production as compiled by the Department of Commerce is released. The index stands at 78.1, a rise of 0.5 points from the preceding week but a decline of 16 percent from the corresponding period one year ago. The increase from last week was attributed to favorable news of increased U.S. automobile exports.			Jan. 27
New York City Police Commissioner Edward Mulrooney requests the Board of Aldermen to set a citywide curfew of 1 a.m., instead of the present 3 a.m. curfew. A disruptive gang brawl on Saturday that lasted until the wee hours of the morning prompted the request by Mulrooney. . . . In a speech before members of the National Boot and Shoe Manufacturers Association, U.S. Senator David Walsh criticizes U.S. tariffs on imported hides, which he says are a vital aspect of the nation's shoe industry. Walsh estimates that the tariffs cost U.S. taxpayers between 50 cents and $1 for every pair of shoes.		The American Railway Association estimates that U.S. freight car loadings in the past week amounted to 725,938 cars, an increase of 11.687 cars from the preceding week. The weekly total is also 15 percent below the corresponding period last year. Economists say the increase from last week is a result of gains in coal, forest products, and grain.			Jan. 28
The New York City Board of Education announces a record number of registrations have been filed for the upcoming 1931–32 school year. Harold Campbell, deputy high school superintendent, says that 150 new teaching positions will be needed to properly instruct the new students. . . . The Welfare Council of New York City publishes *Guide to Statistics of Social Welfare in New York City*, a 300-page study conducted over two years that details the history of dozens of cases of welfare recipients. The book is considered by sociologists to be the first of its kind.		The U.S. Department of Commerce releases its weekly index of American steel production, showing a small gain of 1.2 points from the previous week, but a decline of over 30 percent from the corresponding week last year. It marks the fourth consecutive week that the index has experienced a gain. Credit for the gain from last week was given to the implementation of swifter delivery systems by major steel manufacturers. . . . In a published report, the National Association of Mutual Savings Banks estimates that U.S. savings deposits in 1930 increased by approximately $1 billion as compared to 1929, with an increase of 500,000 total depositors. The Bowery Savings Bank of New York City is declared to be the country's largest savings bank with $400,249,663 in deposits.		The entire works of George Bernard Shaw are bound together in a single volume by the playwright's publisher. The price of the compilation is $3.	Jan. 29

F	G	H	I	J
Includes elections, federal-state relations, civil rights and liberties, crime, the judiciary, education, healthcare, poverty, urban affairs, and population.	*Includes formation and debate of U.S. foreign and defense policies, veterans affairs, and defense spending. (Relations with specific foreign countries are usually found under the region concerned.)*	*Includes business, labor, agriculture, taxation, transportation, consumer affairs, monetary and fiscal policy, natural resources, pollution, and accidents.*	*Includes worldwide scientific, medical, and technological developments, natural phenomena, U.S. weather, and natural disasters.*	*Includes the arts, religion, scholarship, communications media, sports, entertainment, fashions, fads, and social life.*

	World Affairs	Europe	Africa & The Middle East	The Americas	Asia & The Pacific
Jan. 30		The Soviet anti-religious organization Godless Internationale announces it will be moving its main headquarters from Moscow, Russia, to Berlin, Germany. Devout German Christians request the government to do everything in its power to prevent such a potentially damaging situation from taking place.	Iranian Premier Reza Shah Pahlavi selects Charles Carroll, an American, to oversee his country's construction of a state railway system. Carroll is a graduate of the Sheffield Scientific School of Yale University. . . . In Turkey, 78 people are given condemnation sentences for attempting to organize a revolt against President Mustapha Kemal Ataturk's regime. An additional 400 suspects currently imprisoned in Turkish political prisons are currently awaiting trial.		
Jan. 31	The Hope Engineering Oil Company acquires the Northern European Oil Corporation of Germany. . . . U.S. Gen. Smedley Butler formally apologizes to the Italian government for the spreading of a rumor that Premier Benito Mussolini once caused the death of a small child in a hit-and-run automobile accident. Butler's alleged source of the tale was Cornelius Vanderbilt III. "I never saw Cornelius Vanderbilt in my life," says Mussolini in remarks to the International News Agency. "And as for the story that I ran over a child, the only living thing I can remember ever having run over was one dog."	The U.S. government awards a contract to the Owen Engineering Corporation for 1,000 tons of machinery that will be used to produce weldless steel tubes. British economists estimate that 500 unemployed men will be put to work as a result of the contract.			The heavy cruiser ship USS *Houston* sails for the Chinese city of Shanghai. Once there, she will protect U.S. citizens endangered by the deteriorating relations between China and Japan.
Feb. 1	A team of psychoanalysts commissioned by the League of Nations tells members of the international governing body that the U.S. State Department suffers from what is known as a "big-power complex."	Major Belgian fruit manufacturers meet in the capital of Brussels to discuss ways to improve their country's domestic industry, which has been hurt in recent months by heavy importations from the United States. . . . Patrick J. O'Carroll, an advocate of the Northern Ireland separatist movement, is found dead near a roadside in the city of Belfast, an apparent victim of a bomb planted by Irish nationalists.		A replica of industrial London costing $2.5 million completes construction in Buenos Aires, Argentina. The replica's construction had the support of more than 800 separate corporations. It is expected to attract flocks of British tourists to the economically struggling South American nation.	
Feb. 2		British economists report the Bank of England took in £1,039,845 worth of gold during the past week, against £1,633,939 withdrawn, netting a deficit of £594,094.		Argentine agriculturalists report their country's grain exports declined by 245,800 tons this month as compared to last, a result of price drops in wheat. . . . Argentine anarchist Severino di Giovanni, whose international terrorist actions include the 1927 bombing of the First National Bank of Boston, is executed by firing squad in the Argentine National Penitentiary. Police investigators say the recent train station bombings that have unnerved the Argentine public in recent weeks are no longer a mystery, as Giovanni and his associates Paulino and Scarfo have formally confessed.	Communist bandits along the Yangtze River in Hankow, China, ambush the U.S. gunboat *Panay*, inciting an intense battle that results in the bandits' defeat. The crew aboard the *Panay* suffers no casualties.
Feb. 3	British poverty expert B. Seebohm Rowntree calls for an international unemployment parley to be hosted by Great Britain at the League of Nations.	King Alfonso XIII of Spain visits with Prime Minister Damaso Berenguer Fuste, who has been bedridden for several weeks with foot eczema. . . . By a vote of 15–11, the Reichstag Foreign Relations Committee rejects a bill submitted by the Nazi party that calls for immediate withdrawal from the League of Nations. In response, party leaders request President Paul von Hindenburg to officially dissolve the Reichstag and hold new elections. The proposed bill was technically illegal, as League rules stipulate a period of two years must elapse before withdrawal is universally accepted.		Argentina's bank clearings for the month of January amount to $1.2 billion, $216 million less than the total from January 1930, according to a published report by leading Argentine economists.	
Feb. 4		King Victor Emmanuel III of Italy officially transfers Clipperton Island over to French control. Located in the Pacific Ocean, Clipperton Island was seized by Italy in 1908.		The military junta controlling Bolivia announces a national budget of $11 million for 1931, approximately 35 percent less than last year.	

A
Includes developments that affect more than one world region, international organizations, and important meetings of world leaders.

B
Includes all domestic and regional developments in Europe, including the Soviet Union.

C
Includes all domestic and regional developments in Africa and the Middle East.

D
Includes all domestic and regional developments in Latin America, the Caribbean, and Canada.

E
Includes all domestic and regional developments in Asian and Pacific nations (and colonies).

U.S. Politics & Social Issues	U.S. Foreign Policy & Defense	Economics & Great Depression	Science, Technology & Nature	Culture, Leisure & Lifestyle	
	The destroyer ship USS *Sturtevant* is decommissioned at Philadelphia, Pa., by the Navy Department. Named after the naval officer of the same name, the ship will eventually be sunk by enemy mines in the Caribbean during World War II on April 26, 1942. She was constructed by the New York Shipbuilding Corporation in 1920.	*The Annalist* releases its weekly list of U.S. wholesale commodity prices. At 133.6, the index is a drop of 0.9 points from the previous week and a decline of 11 percent from the corresponding week a year ago. Economists say the decline was caused by price drops in farm products, food products, and chemicals.	Aviation expert Charles Lawrence is elected president of the U.S. Aeronautical Chamber of Commerce. Lawrence's predecessor is Frederick B. Renschler, who has served as president since 1929. In a statement to the Chamber's board of governors, Lawrence optimistically remarks, "I believe that aviation has passed through the severest part of its inevitable readjustment."	Charlie Chaplin's romantic comedy film *City Lights* is released for the first time in Los Angeles, Calif. Among those in attendance at the premiere is scientist Albert Einstein. The film is considered by some to be Chaplin's best work, and for this reason, the U.S. National Film Registry will deem it "culturally significant" in 1991 and archive it for the enjoyment of future generations.	Jan. 30
	The submarine USS *Narwhal* is transferred from the Panama Canal to San Diego, Calif. She will eventually become one of the five submarines attacked by Japan during the raid on Pearl Harbor on December 7, 1941. . . . The Navy Department decommissions the destroyer ship USS *Luce*, which has been in operation for less than one year.	The U.S. Department of Commerce reports that 3,354,870 automobiles were produced in the United States in 1930, against 5,358,420 produced in 1929, a decline of 38 percent. . . . *Dun's Review* reports U.S. bank clearings for the week ended January 29 totaled $7.5 billion, 21.7 percent below the corresponding week of 1930.			Jan. 31
	The U.S. Navy transfers the destroyer *Greer* to the Scouting Fleet. Constructed by the William Cramp & Sons Ship & Engine Building Co. in 1918, *Greer* became the first American naval vessel to fire upon a German ship in World War II.	The Merchants and Planters Bank of Arkansas reopens its doors after several months of being closed due to financial insolvency.			Feb. 1
Rep. John Cochran of Missouri introduces a bill on the House floor that would allow the sale of beer with an alcoholic content of 3.75 percent. Cochran proposed the bill as a suitable alternative to complete repeal of the Eighteenth Amendment.	At the Philadelphia Naval Yard, the destroyer *Fox* is decommissioned by the U.S. Navy. *Fox* will be recommissioned the next year and eventually sold for scrap at the end of World War II in 1945.	Prof. Irving Fisher of Yale University releases his weekly index of international stock exchanges. The figure is 99, a rise of 2 points from the preceding week but a decline of 28 percent from the corresponding week a year ago.	The annual Groundhog Day ceremony is held in Punxsutawney, Pa. Visitors from all across the United States flock to the town's square to witness the city's most reliable "weatherhog," Punxsutawney Phil, perform his annual ritual. Sleeping late, he finally emerged at 12:27 p.m., much to the delight of the onlooking crowd. But, his furry body cast a long, dark shadow, indicating another six weeks of bitterly cold winter.		Feb. 2
The United Parents' Association of Greater New York Schools requests Congress to overturn a decision by the New York City Board of Education to include mandatory "war drills" in the citywide curriculum. Members of the association express fear that the drills will ultimately lead to peacetime conscription.	The U.S. Navy transfers the destroyer *Wickes* to Tampa, Fla., to take part in the Florida State Fair festivities. The ship will provide an exciting attraction for visiting tourists, say Floridian officials. . . . The destroyer *Overton* is placed out of commission in reserve by the U.S. Navy. Named after Marine Corps officer Macon Overton, the ship would eventually be sold for scrap near the end of World War II on August 13, 1945.	The weekly index of U.S. automobile production as compiled by the Department of Commerce is released. The index currently stands at 61.7, a decrease of 3.0 points from the previous week, and a decline of 36 percent from the corresponding week one year ago. The drop from last week was caused by a decline in output of a medium-priced automobile manufacturer, say leading economists.			Feb. 3
Former Supreme Court Justice Alfred Rider Page dies in his home in Southampton, N.Y., at the age of 71. Page was instrumental in upholding the constitutionality of the 1917 Adamson Act, which required an eight-hour workday for most of the country's laborers.		Freight car loadings for the past week amounted to 715,690 cars, according to figures published by the American Railway Association. The total is 10,248 cars less than the previous week, and a decline of 17 percent from the corresponding week a year ago. The decline from last week was attributable to drops in coal and grain products.			Feb. 4

F	G	H	I	J
Includes elections, federal-state relations, civil rights and liberties, crime, the judiciary, education, healthcare, poverty, urban affairs, and population.	Includes formation and debate of U.S. foreign and defense policies, veterans affairs, and defense spending. (Relations with specific foreign countries are usually found under the region concerned.)	Includes business, labor, agriculture, taxation, transportation, consumer affairs, monetary and fiscal policy, natural resources, pollution, and accidents.	Includes worldwide scientific, medical, and technological developments, natural phenomena, U.S. weather, and natural disasters.	Includes the arts, religion, scholarship, communications media, sports, entertainment, fashions, fads, and social life.

	World Affairs	Europe	Africa & The Middle East	The Americas	Asia & The Pacific
Feb. 5	Carnegie Institute of Technology president Thomas Stockham Baker announces the third international coal conference will be held in Pittsburgh, Pa., from November 16 to November 21 of this year.			The Argentine Bank of the Nation ships $2,478,000 worth of gold to the United States as part of a repayment of a loan given by the Chase National Bank Company.... Heavy rains in the Bolivian capital of La Paz cause estimated damages of $500,000. Officials were forced to suspend service on the International Railroad to Argentina.	
Feb. 6	Great Britain updates its immigration policies in the Middle Eastern territory of Palestine, allowing a greater number of Jewish laborers to enter the territory, but limiting the amount of land they can own.	In Italy, Michele Shirru is arrested for the attempted assassination of Premier Benito Mussolini. Shirru was found in his apartment upon his arrest with two high-powered explosives.			
Feb. 7	The France-America Society holds a ceremony to honor the 153rd anniversary of the 1778 Treaty of Alliance, which gave the young United States a strategic edge over Great Britain during the Revolutionary War.	The Italian-born American citizen Michele Schirru, who was arrested one day earlier for the attempted assassination of Premier Benito Mussolini, confesses to Italian police investigators after a lengthy interrogation. Police say the source of Schirru's funds while living in Italy is a mystery.			
Feb. 8	Leaders of several Jewish aid organizations recommend the mountains of Peru as a suitable national home for eastern European Jews suffering from overcrowding in their native countries.	The Vienna City Council bans the presentation of a motion picture detailing the training of the Austrian army. The Council releases a statement saying, "warlike acts are injurious to youth for pedagogical reasons."		The Rio de Janeiro police department officially bans the consumption of alcoholic beverages during the upcoming four-day Mardi Gras holiday, an effort that police say was made to reduce excessive and potentially damaging celebration.	
Feb. 9		British economists report the Bank of England took in £342,711 worth of gold during the past week, against £102,768 withdrawn, netting a surplus of £239,943. Of the £102,768 withdrawn, approximately £100,000 was reserved for the country of France, and about £300,000 was deposited by South Africa.... The second son of Count Folke Bernadotte of Sweden is born in the American city of Pleasantville. The nephew of King Gustav V, Bernadotte will successfully negotiate the surrender of Nazi Germany during World War II as vice-president of the Swedish Red Cross.		The exchange rate of the Brazilian milreis falls to a new year low, with one milreis equaling 11 American gold dollars.	
Feb. 10	U.S. Secretary of State Henry Stimson draws international criticism for his endorsement of Aro Obargo revolutionists who oppose Mexican President Ortiz Rubio's regime. *The London Times* prints an editorial with the headline, "Stimson Backs the Wrong Horse."			The provisional military government controlling Bolivia announces it is suspending its debt repayment to international creditors until national elections are held on December 12.	The capital of India is officially moved to New Delhi. Laborers now begin the process of constructing a new capitol building, along with a presidential palace.

A	B	C	D	E
Includes developments that affect more than one world region, international organizations, and important meetings of world leaders.	*Includes all domestic and regional developments in Europe, including the Soviet Union.*	*Includes all domestic and regional developments in Africa and the Middle East.*	*Includes all domestic and regional developments in Latin America, the Caribbean, and Canada.*	*Includes all domestic and regional developments in Asian and Pacific nations (and colonies).*

U.S. Politics & Social Issues	U.S. Foreign Policy & Defense	Economics & Great Depression	Science, Technology & Nature	Culture, Leisure & Lifestyle	
	The U.S. Coast Guard commissions the destroyer *Hunt*, formerly a part of the U.S. Navy. The Coast Guard would utilize the destroyer as a key component of the Rum Patrol, the maritime government agency responsible for the enforcement of Prohibition. . . . Court-martial proceedings begin for Gen. Smedley Butler, who is accused of spreading a false rumor that Premier Benito Mussolini of Italy once killed a small child in hit-and-run incident.	*The Iron Age* releases its weekly index of U.S. steel mill activity. The index currently stands at 57.0, an increase of 0.9 points from the previous week, but a decline of 36 percent from the corresponding week one year ago. *The Iron Age* adds that the increase from the preceding week is attributable to gains in steel rail output. . . . As a result of ever-shrinking steel prices, the Pittsburgh Steel Products Company eliminates mill operations on weekends. The salaries of top executives are also reduced by 14.5 percent to account for the expected fall in revenue.			Feb. 5
Hundreds of people in New York City attend the funeral of former Supreme Court Justice Alfred Page. The pallbearers of Page's coffin include Supreme Court Justices Samuel Seabury and John Proctor Clarke.		*The Annalist* releases its weekly index of U.S. wholesale commodity prices. At 112.4, the figure is a drop of 1.2 points from the previous week, and a reduction of 19 percent from the corresponding period a year ago. Economists say the decline from last week was caused by drops in farm products and textile products.	The National Electric Light Association reports U.S. electric power output for the past week amounted to 1,686,749,000 kilowatt hours, 32,596,000 kilowatt hours less than the preceding week, and a decline of 6.3 percent from the corresponding period one year ago. The National Electric Light Association attributes the decline from last week to unseasonably warm weather.	Charlie Chaplin's award-winning romantic comedy *City Lights* is released in Great Britain. *City Lights* would be deemed in 1991 by the U.S. National Film Preservation Board as "culturally significant" and archived for the enjoyment of future generations. . . . Trial proceedings begin for world heavyweight boxing champion Max Schmeling, who is accused of hurling an 18-year-old busboy down a flight of stairs at the Hotel Commodore in New York City.	Feb. 6
Two young members of the Young Communists' League are found guilty of sedition by a jury in Philadelphia for distributing Communist literature to National Guardsmen on January 12 of last year. When asked by reporters to describe the defendants, Assistant Prosecutor Vincent Carroll labels them as "misguided children involved in Communism, the Red racket." The pair will receive sentences ranging from 10–20 years, including the possibility of permanent deportation.				While vacationing at his home in London, England, British novelist Arnold Bennett is stricken with a severe case of influenza, rendering the 63-year-old author of *The Old Wives' Tale* immobile. . . . Famed American aviatrix Amelia Earhart marries 44-year-old publisher George Palmer Putnam in the tiny village of Noank, Conn. Earhart became a household name in 1927 after becoming the first woman to fly solo across the Atlantic Ocean.	Feb. 7
		The Annalist releases its weekly index of U.S. business activity. At 77.5, the figure is a rise of 0.6 points from the previous week but a drop of 20 percent from the corresponding period last year. Economists say the rise from last was caused by increases in electric power production and automobile output.			Feb. 8
The U.S. Congress authorizes the construction of the San Francisco-Oakland Bay Bridge, a 4.35-mile structure that will connect two of the State of California's most populous cities.	The submarines *R-2* and *R-14* are transferred to New London, Conn., by the U.S. Navy. They will spend the next 10 years providing training exercises for the U.S. Submarine School. The Fore River Shipbuilding Company constructed both of the submarines in 1917 and 1918, respectively. . . . The submarines *R-3*, *R-7*, *R-13*, *R-18*, and *R-20* are transferred to New London, Conn.	Prof. Irving Fisher of Yale University releases his weekly index of international stock exchanges. The figure is 99, virtually unchanged from the preceding week but a decline of 33 percent from the corresponding week a year ago. . . . A consortium of Parisian banks offers a loan of $32 million to the German government.		Paramount Pictures begins production on *The Smiling Lieutenant*, an adaptation of the German operetta *Ein Walzertraum*. The film would be nominated for the 1932 Academy Award for Best Picture.	Feb. 9
The New York Chapter of the American Red Cross reaches its fundraising goal of $1.5 million, which will be used to provide unemployment relief to the city's poor.		The weekly index of U.S. automobile production as compiled by the Department of Commerce is released. The index currently stands at 63.1, an increase of 1.4 points from the previous week, but a reduction of 41 percent from the corresponding week one year ago. The rise from last week was caused by an increase in production schedules by the Ford Motor Company, say leading economists.		The 55th annual Westminster Kennel Club Dog Show begins in New York City's Madison Square Garden, where 2,513 dogs from 76 different breeds will be in contention for the title of Best in Show.	Feb. 10

F	G	H	I	J
Includes elections, federal-state relations, civil rights and liberties, crime, the judiciary, education, healthcare, poverty, urban affairs, and population.	Includes formation and debate of U.S. foreign and defense policies, veterans affairs, and defense spending. (Relations with specific foreign countries are usually found under the region concerned.)	Includes business, labor, agriculture, taxation, transportation, consumer affairs, monetary and fiscal policy, natural resources, pollution, and accidents.	Includes worldwide scientific, medical, and technological developments, natural phenomena, U.S. weather, and natural disasters.	Includes the arts, religion, scholarship, communications media, sports, entertainment, fashions, fads, and social life.

	World Affairs	Europe	Africa & The Middle East	The Americas	Asia & The Pacific
Feb. 11		The City Council of Madrid requests from Premier Damaso Berenguer Fuste a general amnesty for all political prisoners.		The Bolivian Interior Minister, Col. Oscar Mariaca Pando, reveals that a Communist plot that sought to overthrow the existing military junta was foiled days before it was to be executed. The Bolivian newspaper *La Republica* dismisses the revelation as a fabricated ploy by Minister Pando to suspend the transfer of power over to President-elect Daniel Salamanca.	
Feb. 12					Nearly 3,000 Chinese miners in the city of Muken are trapped underground as an explosion rips through the mine in which they were working. Rescue workers were only able to unearth a handful of the miners, and the rest, authorities say, have most likely perished in a black pit of despair.
Feb. 13				Election returns in El Salvador indicate that Arturo Araujo will become the nation's 43rd president. Araujo will be sworn in during the inauguration ceremony in the nation's capital of San Salvador on March 1.	
Feb. 14	During a luncheon of the Argentine-American Chamber of Commerce, Argentine envoy to Washington, D.C., Don Manuel Malbran complains about the lack of U.S. exportation to the economically struggling South American nation. He notes that while there exist 56 million cattle in the United States, Americans only consume 25 percent of them, leaving a large surplus that has yet to be exported.				Prime Minister James Scullin of Australia enacts several measures to stabilize his country's currently chaotic financial condition; among them, a heavy reduction of civil servant salaries, as well as a tax increase of approximately 10 percent on all public loans.
Feb. 15		Newspapers all across Europe accuse the Soviet Union of censoring from its citizens certain portions of Pope Pius XI's worldwide address on February 12. Soviet Union officials steadfastly deny the claim.			
Feb. 16	Police in Nuremberg, Germany, officially ban a conference of the Proletarian Freethinkers' Society, an anarchist organization alleged by police to be a propaganda arm of the Soviet Union.	Pehr Evind Svinhufvud is elected president of Finland, succeeding Lauri Kristan Relander, whose six-year term was marred by internal squabbling. Relander committed several dictatorial acts, including the expulsion of all Communist members from the Finnish parliament. . . . British economists report the Bank of England took in £250,860 worth of gold during the past week, against £111,467 withdrawn, netting a surplus of £139,393. Of the £111,467 withdrawn, approximately £100,000 was reserved for Great Britain itself, and £250,000 was deposited by South Africa.			
Feb. 17		In a radio address broadcast throughout the whole of England, Tory Party leader Stanley Baldwin recommends protective tariffs as a solution to the ever-increasing unemployment rate. "I am tired of seeing men in Britain thrown out of work owing to cheaper goods coming from abroad," he says, adding, "If present conditions are maintained, nothing can prevent lower wages unless the country prefers unemployment. Protection, therefore, is the answer."	The Muslim Supreme Council threatens to boycott the recent decision by the British government to allow increased numbers of Jewish laborers into Palestine. Famed scientist Albert Einstein officially supports the decision in a statement, saying the Zionist ideal of a Jewish homeland will "maintain the feeling of solidarity of the Jewish people in a time of stress."	Nicaraguan authorities report a band of revolutionists have overthrown the northeastern city of Gracias a Dios, laying waste a squadron of National Guardsmen detached to quell them.	

A	B	C	D	E
Includes developments that affect more than one world region, international organizations, and important meetings of world leaders.	*Includes all domestic and regional developments in Europe, including the Soviet Union.*	*Includes all domestic and regional developments in Africa and the Middle East.*	*Includes all domestic and regional developments in Latin America, the Caribbean, and Canada.*	*Includes all domestic and regional developments in Asian and Pacific nations (and colonies).*

U.S. Politics & Social Issues	U.S. Foreign Policy & Defense	Economics & Great Depression	Science, Technology & Nature	Culture, Leisure & Lifestyle	
President Herbert Hoover's former head secretary George Akerson assumes his duties as an executive of Paramount Pictures. Interviewed by reporters, he modestly admits that he has "everything to learn" about the process of producing motion pictures.		Freight car loadings for the past week amounted to 719,281 cars, according to figures published by the American Railway Association. The total is 3,591 cars more than the previous week, but a decline of 24 percent from the corresponding week a year ago. The rise from last week was attributable to rises in forest products, grain, and livestock.	The Royal Astronomical Society awards its annual Jackson-Gwilt medal to American astronomer Clyde Tambaugh, who last spring discovered the planet Pluto. Pluto is named after the Roman god of the underworld, otherwise known as Hades.		Feb. 11
In comments to reporters, New York State Industrial Commissioner Frances Perkins recommends that a primary focus of the state's unemployment relief efforts should be on "white collar girls." Perkins will become the first female Secretary of Labor in the nation's history under the Franklin Roosevelt administration.	The U.S. Navy Department opens bidding on the construction rights for a new light cruiser temporarily named No. 37. The contract stipulates that the vessel must be completely constructed in a period of 36 months. The Newport News Shipbuilding and Drydock Company of Newport News, Va., submits the highest bid of $11.3 million.	The Iron Age releases its weekly index of U.S. steel mill activity. The index currently stands at 58.8, a rise of 1.8 points from the previous week, but a decline of 36 percent from the corresponding week one year ago. The Iron Age adds that the gain from the preceding week is attributable to an increase in structural steel bookings.		The film adaptation of Bram Stoker's novel Dracula premiers in New York City. A staple of American cinema, Dracula will be deemed "culturally significant" by the U.S. National Film Preservation Board in 2000 and archived for the enjoyment of future generations.	Feb. 12
Americans celebrate the 121st anniversary of the birth of former president Abraham Lincoln, who many historians believe to be the greatest political leader in the history of the United States. New York City Assemblyman J.E. Stephens, an African American, comments to reporters on the progress of his people since the days of Reconstruction: "The American Negro alone stands today, as in 1860, as a challenge to American democracy. This nation either must live up to the ideals of democracy or Negroes will constitute an imponderable mass of rising discontent."	Naval Secretary Charles Francis Adams visits the U.S. Capitol to request support from House Speaker Nicolas Longworth to pass the proposed $100 million naval construction bill as soon as possible.		The National Electric Light Association reports U.S. electric power output for the past week amounted to 1,678,794,000 kilowatt hours, 7,955,000 kilowatt hours less than the preceding week, and a decline of 5.9 percent from the corresponding period one year ago. The National Electric Light Association attributes the decline from last week to an 8.6 percent drop in the industrial Midwest.	The fox terrier Pendley Calling, owned by John G. Bates of New Jersey, wins the annual Best in Show award at the Westminster Kennel Club Dog Show, beating out a field of over 2,500 different dogs. Ten thousand spectators seated in Madison Square Garden witnessed the coronation.	Feb. 13
	The light cruiser Denver is decommissioned by the U.S. Navy. The first ship to be named after the capital of the state of Colorado, Denver was built in 1902 by the Neafie and Levy Ship and Engine Building Company in Philadelphia, Pa.				Feb. 14
Lawmakers on Capitol Hill introduce a bill appropriating $27 million for the augmentation of foreign and domestic airmail service. If passed, the bill's funds will enable the creation of six new domestic airmail routes between Louisville and Forth Worth, Kansas City and Denver, Pittsburgh and Norfolk, St. Paul and Winnipeg, Richmond and Jacksonville, and Columbus and Augusta.	Gen. Smedley Butler's court-martial trial is cancelled, as U.S. leaders fear a public trial with intense media speculation will lead to international embarrassment. Butler was court-martialed after a speech in which he recanted a tale that Premier Benito Mussolini of Italy once killed a small boy in a hit-and-run accident.	The Annalist releases its weekly index of U.S. business activity. At 77.7, the figure is a rise of 0.2 points from the previous week but a decrease of 20 percent from the corresponding period last year. Economists say the increase from last week was caused by a rise in automobile production.			Feb. 15
Nearly 130 leading economists and labor leaders draft a letter to President Herbert Hoover urging him to support New York Senator Robert F. Wagner's unemployment bill, which upon passage would provide increased levels of federal aid to state and local programs.	The battleship Florida is decommissioned by the U.S. Navy. A highlight of Florida's career was the assistance toward the British Grand Fleet during World War I. The battleship was constructed in 1910 at the New York Navy Yard.	Prof. Irving Fisher of Yale University releases his weekly index of international stock exchanges. The figure is 104.1, an increase of 5.1 points from the preceding week but a decline of nearly 33 percent from the corresponding week a year ago. . . . Austria's trade deficit for 1930 amounted to 851 million schillings, 247 million schillings less than the previous year, according to published reports authored by leading economists.			Feb. 16
The House Immigration Committee approves a bill authored by Rep. Free of California reducing Filipino immigration into the continental United States to 500 persons annually.		The weekly index of U.S. automobile production as compiled by the Department of Commerce is released. The index currently stands at 59.4, a drop of 3.7 points from the previous week, and a decline of 39 percent from the corresponding week one year ago. The rise from last week was caused by a reduction in output by a manufacturer of low-priced automobiles, say leading economists.			Feb. 17

F	G	H	I	J
Includes elections, federal-state relations, civil rights and liberties, crime, the judiciary, education, healthcare, poverty, urban affairs, and population.	Includes formation and debate of U.S. foreign and defense policies, veterans affairs, and defense spending. (Relations with specific foreign countries are usually found under the region concerned.)	Includes business, labor, agriculture, taxation, transportation, consumer affairs, monetary and fiscal policy, natural resources, pollution, and accidents.	Includes worldwide scientific, medical, and technological developments, natural phenomena, U.S. weather, and natural disasters.	Includes the arts, religion, scholarship, communications media, sports, entertainment, fashions, fads, and social life.

	World Affairs	Europe	Africa & The Middle East	The Americas	Asia & The Pacific
Feb. 18	The 51-year-old American-born British Duchess of Mecklenburg-Schwerin dies from pneumonia in the U.S. city of San Francisco.	Juan Bautista Aznar Cabanas is chosen as the new premier of Spain, succeeding Damaso Berenguer Fuste, who seized power via a military coup last January from dictator Primo de Rivera.			
Feb. 19	A court in London, England, decides to award damages amounting to "millions of pounds sterling" to the American General Asphalt Company for a breach of contract committed by the Anglo-Saxon Petroleum Company. The contract called for the General Asphalt Company to assume a share of 9.3 percent on all oil produced in the Venezuelan Vigas oilfield, the output of which is estimated to be over 2,000 barrels of oil daily.				
Feb. 20		Governmental representatives of several eastern European powers fix the debt of the dissolved Austria-Hungary empirical monarchy, formally broken up in 1918 at the end of World War I, at 10 million kronen, or $2 million. Hungary, whose debt exceeds that of Yugoslavia and Romania, is expected to pay 1.4 billion kronen, or $300 million. . . . British Chancellor of the Exchequer Philip Snowden recommends increasing tax rates on foreign investments as a means of stimulating domestic industries.			
Feb. 21		During a speech, President Dimitrui of Moldavia formally protests the occupation of his country by Romanian military forces. "In the past 13 years, the Romanian occupation has changed Moldavia from a rich and prosperous region to a land of misery and horror," he says.			
Feb. 22					

A	B	C	D	E
Includes developments that affect more than one world region, international organizations, and important meetings of world leaders.	*Includes all domestic and regional developments in Europe, including the Soviet Union.*	*Includes all domestic and regional developments in Africa and the Middle East.*	*Includes all domestic and regional developments in Latin America, the Caribbean, and Canada.*	*Includes all domestic and regional developments in Asian and Pacific nations (and colonies).*

U.S. Politics & Social Issues	U.S. Foreign Policy & Defense	Economics & Great Depression	Science, Technology & Nature	Culture, Leisure & Lifestyle	
Senator Sam Bratton of New Mexico asks his colleagues in the Senate to support a bill requesting $15 million from the American Red Cross for the purposes of providing relief to southern drought victims who suffered from last summer's irregularly high temperatures. . . . Former president of Sperry Gyroscope, Inc., Thomas Morgan, is chosen to be president of North American Aviation, Inc.	U.S. Treasury Secretary Andrew Mellon estimates the cost to provide financial relief to U.S. veterans of foreign wars to be approximately $3 billion. As the federal budget is currently stretched to its limits, Mellon says higher taxes will be needed to make the funds available.	Freight car loadings for the past week amounted to 719,053 cars, according to figures published by the American Railway Association. The total is 228 cars less than the previous week, and a decline of 19 percent from the corresponding week a year ago. The microscopic decline from last week was attributable to drops in grain and livestock, offset by gains in forest products and coke.	Heavy snowstorms in the Hungarian capital of Budapest strand several citizens in neighboring villages, including Premier Istvan Bethlen, who left the capital earlier this week and has been unable to return since.		Feb. 18
Chicago gangster Al Capone defends himself against a speech made by Gen. Smedley Butler, in which the General suggests Capone should be immediately deported, as he is a detriment to the United States: "The General is ill-informed. The laws of this country prevent the deportation of anyone who was born in this country." As a testament to his societal contributions, Capone notes that he has "been feeding between 2,500 and 3,000 people daily in Chicago for the last six months."	The submarine V-6 is rechristened as Nautilus by the U.S. Navy. Immediately following the renaming, Nautilus is transferred to Pearl Harbor, where it becomes the flagship of SubDiv 12. The submarine was constructed in 1927 by the Mare Island Naval Shipyard in Vallejo, Calif. . . . The submarine V-5, the lead boat of its class, is renamed Narwhal by the U.S. Navy. Narwhal refers to an arctic whale. The submarine was constructed in 1927 by the Portsmouth Navy Yard.	The Iron Age releases its weekly index of U.S. steel mill activity. The index currently stands at 56.8, a drop of 2.0 points from the previous week, and a decline of 38 percent from the corresponding week one year ago. The Iron Age adds that the drop from the preceding week was attributable to a decrease in operations of the U.S. Steel Corporation.			Feb. 19
The Illinois Department of Labor announces that the number of laborers employed in the state's unemployment programs has declined by 2.3 percent in the past month, with an additional decrease of 3.4 percent of total administrative employees.		The Annalist releases its weekly index of U.S. wholesale commodity prices. At 111.0, the figure is a decline of 0.8 points from the previous week, and a reduction of 19 percent from the corresponding period a year ago. Economists say the drop from last week was caused by reductions in the prices of farm products, food products, and building materials.	As a solution to the destabilization of the U.S. domestic petroleum industry, alleged by economists to have been caused by overproduction, Prof. Leonard Logan of the University of Oklahoma recommends the creation of a national oil czar who would be given broad authoritative powers similar to those of the head of the Federal Narcotics Bureau, and whose duties would include the modification of tariffs to reflect changing oil prices. . . . The National Electric Light Association reports U.S. electric power output for the past week amounted to 1,676,452,000 kilowatt hours, 2,342,000 kilowatt hours less than the preceding week, and a decline of 1.9 percent from the corresponding period one year ago. The National Electric Light Association attributes the decline from last week to heavy rains over the Pacific Coast, which resulted in power outages.	Filming is completed on Iron Man. The film is directed by Tod Browning, who would command the production of over 50 feature films in the span of a 25-year career.	Feb. 20
A bill is introduced on the U.S. House floor that calls for the complete restriction of immigrant Communists entering the United States. The bill would also decrease the amount of time necessary to complete official deportation procedures. In response, the American Civil Liberties Union releases a statement of condemnation that reads in part, "the attempt to outlaw a political movement because of its principles violates the American tradition of civil liberty."		According to figures published by the Department of Commerce, U.S. aeronautical exports for the whole of 1930 amounted to $8.8 million, nearly equaling the record total established in 1929. Leighton Rogers, chief of the Aeronautics Trade Division, comments to reporters that the figures indicate a "gratifying trend."			Feb. 21
	The U.S. Navy transfers the heavy cruiser Houston to the Philippine capital of Manila. Upon arrival, Houston becomes the flagship of the U.S. Asiatic Fleet. Nicknamed the "Galloping Ghost of the Java Coast," the cruiser was constructed by the Newport News Shipbuilding in 1929.	The Annalist releases its weekly index of U.S. business activity. At 77.7, the figure is a rise of 0.1 points from the previous week but a decline of 20 percent from the corresponding period last year. Economists say the rise from last week was caused by increases in electric power production, cloth cotton output, and freight car loadings.		On Catalina Island off the coast of California, the Chicago Cubs baseball franchise begins its spring training exercises, the first major league baseball team to do so. The Cubs finished last year in second place with a record of 90–64, two games behind the St. Louis Cardinals, who lost the World Series to the Philadelphia Athletics in six games. . . . The Belgian Ministry of Sciences and Arts donates 50 volumes of Belgian literature to New York University's Bibliotheca Belgica, the only catalogue of literary works by Belgian authors in the continental United States.	Feb. 22

F	G	H	I	J
Includes elections, federal-state relations, civil rights and liberties, crime, the judiciary, education, healthcare, poverty, urban affairs, and population.	Includes formation and debate of U.S. foreign and defense policies, veterans affairs, and defense spending. (Relations with specific foreign countries are usually found under the region concerned.)	Includes business, labor, agriculture, taxation, transportation, consumer affairs, monetary and fiscal policy, natural resources, pollution, and accidents.	Includes worldwide scientific, medical, and technological developments, natural phenomena, U.S. weather, and natural disasters.	Includes the arts, religion, scholarship, communications media, sports, entertainment, fashions, fads, and social life.

	World Affairs	Europe	Africa & The Middle East	The Americas	Asia & The Pacific
Feb. 23		British economists report the Bank of England took in virtually no gold last week, but withdrawals were approximately £81,696.		In the Cuban capital of Havana, 13 small bombs, one of which was planted near police headquarters, explode, causing small damages. Searching for suspects, police raid a student council meeting of the National University, arresting 18 students believed to be connected to the bombings. . . . U.S. Senator Walter George of Georgia assails the Smoot-Hawley Tariff Act in a statement released through the Democratic National Committee, saying the tariffs have negatively affected trade relations with the United States' foremost trading partner, Canada. "We recklessly undertook to exclude Canadian imports by duties virtually prohibitive," part of his statement reads. "The Canadian Government is simply following a program of retaliation."	
Feb. 24				President Luis Miguel Sanchez Cerro of Peru announces he will not be a presidential candidate in the upcoming spring elections that will replace the existing military junta with a permanent democratic governing body. Cerro claims he made the decision to demonstrate a revolutionary pledge he made for a constitutional government. His pledge would be seen in the eyes of history as merely a ruse, as he ran for and was elected president in the winter of 1931. . . . Police in Buenos Aires, Argentina, announce that a coup attempt headed by Gen. Toranzo has been foiled, with the General now in hiding in a neighboring Latin American country after a hasty departure.	
Feb. 25		French War Minister Andre Maginot announces in the Chamber of Deputies that his department will appropriate $480 million this year for "security" purposes, including foreign intelligence gathering and the protection of French citizens against subversive threats. Maginot, in comments to reporters, estimates that France has reduced its military effectiveness by 50 percent since the end of World War I in 1918. . . . Great Britain's *Official Gazette* announces that by April 1, the British Admiralty will force the retirement of 1,044 naval officers, a decision naval officials say was made to lessen the Navy's excessively high budget deficit.		French Gen. Huntzinger arrives in Sao Paulo, Brazil, to instruct his Brazilian counterparts on how to better improve their country's army and navy.	
Feb. 26	China ships $1,159,000 worth of gold to the United States.	Italy and France seek an accord over naval reduction proposals. . . . Members of the British House of Commons consider passing a bill officially updating the lyrics of the British national anthem.		The military junta controlling Peru announces it will begin a major assault on a group of rebels who seized the city of Arequipa.	
Feb. 27			The Wailing Wall Commission, a specially appointed group whose purpose is to study the causes of tension between Arabs and Jews in Jerusalem, is rumored by Arab officials to be heavily biased toward Jewish interests.		Indian revolutionary leader Mohandas Gandhi meets with British Viceroy Lord Irwin.
Feb. 28	Canada officially places an embargo on imported Russian coal, wood pulp, pulpwood, lumber, and timber. Canadian spokesmen say the decision was made as evidence of Russia's slave-labor program surfaced.			As the international price of silver continues to decline, the Santa Maria de la Paz, the third largest mine in Mexico, dismisses 1,600 of its workers.	

A	B	C	D	E
Includes developments that affect more than one world region, international organizations, and important meetings of world leaders.	Includes all domestic and regional developments in Europe, including the Soviet Union.	Includes all domestic and regional developments in Africa and the Middle East.	Includes all domestic and regional developments in Latin America, the Caribbean, and Canada.	Includes all domestic and regional developments in Asian and Pacific nations (and colonies).

U.S. Politics & Social Issues	U.S. Foreign Policy & Defense	Economics & Great Depression	Science, Technology & Nature	Culture, Leisure & Lifestyle	
An estimated 1,295 people in New York City died as a result of alcoholic intoxication in 1930, according to an annual report issued by Chief Medical Examiner Dr. Charles Norris. He notes that many of those who died were consumers of industrial alcohol, into which the federal government inserted lethal toxins for the explicit purpose of frightening potential Prohibition violators.	The U.S. Navy transfers the submarine O-7 from New London, Conn., to Philadelphia, Pa., to begin the process of decommissioning. A product of the Fore River Shipbuilding Company, O-7 was constructed in 1917.	Prof. Irving Fisher of Yale University releases his weekly index of international stock exchanges. The figure is 106.2, a rise of 2.1 points from the preceding week but a decline of 28 percent from the corresponding week a year ago.		The New York Bible Society reports it distributed 876,983 free Bibles during the whole of 1930, according to general secretary Rev. Millard Robinson. The Society was founded in 1809 by devout Christians who sought to spread their beliefs.	Feb. 23
		The weekly index of U.S. automobile production as compiled by the Department of Commerce is released. The index currently stands at 55.9, a drop of 3.5 points from the previous week, and a decline of 35 percent from the corresponding week one year ago. The decline from last week was caused by decreased output by the Chevrolet Corporation, say leading economists.			Feb. 24
Rep. Samuel Kendall of Pennsylvania authors a bill that would place an embargo on all imported goods produced and distributed through slave labor. Several Senators voice opposition to the bill, including Pennsylvania Senator David Reed, who estimates that "50,000 men in cigar factories in Pennsylvania would be thrown out of work" as a result of the embargo. Senator King of Utah petulantly comments that "many people in my state want an embargo on everything. If this disposition prevails, we will have embargoes on all imported products."	Nine hundred employees of the New York Shipbuilding Company are rehired nearly a week after being dismissed due to a lack of company funds. The employees were rehired as the result of the signing of new government construction contracts for two 30,000-ton liners.	Freight car loadings for the past week amounted to 720,689 cars, according to figures published by the American Railway Association. The total is 1,636 cars more than the previous week, but a decline of 19 percent from the corresponding week a year ago. The increase from last week was attributable to gains in coal and livestock.			Feb. 25
	The U.S. Navy commissions the submarines H-6, H-5, H-4, H-8, and H-9, all of which were purchased from the Soviet Union on May 20, 1918. . . . In a statement, Antarctic explorer Richard E. Byrd urges immediate passage of the pending naval bill, saying those who oppose its passage are committing "a crime against common sense."	The Iron Age releases its weekly index of U.S. steel mill activity. The index currently stands at 57.8, an increase of 1.0 points from the previous week, but a decline of 36 percent from the corresponding week one year ago. The Iron Age adds that the increase from the preceding week is attributable to increased buying of tin plates. . . . Alaskan salmon producers officially reduce their output by approximately 25 percent.			Feb. 26
		The Annalist releases its weekly index of U.S. wholesale commodity prices. At 109.3, the figure is a reduction of 1.7 points from the previous week, and a decline of 19 percent from the corresponding period a year ago. Economists say the drop from last week was caused by declines in farm products, food products, and building materials.	The National Electric Light Association reports U.S. electric power output for the past week amounted to 1,679,534,000 kilowatt hours, 3,082,000 kilowatt hours less than the preceding week, and a decline of 3.6 percent from the corresponding period one year ago. The National Electric Light Association attributes the decline from last week to a decrease in power consumption in the industrial Midwest.		Feb. 27
Mayor Bill Thompson of Chicago criticizes President Herbert Hoover for his failure upon taking office to provide federal relief funds for those still suffering from the effects of the 1927 Mississippi flood.		U.S. economists report that U.S. bank clearings have declined by 22 percent since February 1930.			Feb. 28

F	G	H	I	J
Includes elections, federal-state relations, civil rights and liberties, crime, the judiciary, education, healthcare, poverty, urban affairs, and population.	Includes formation and debate of U.S. foreign and defense policies, veterans affairs, and defense spending. (Relations with specific foreign countries are usually found under the region concerned.)	Includes business, labor, agriculture, taxation, transportation, consumer affairs, monetary and fiscal policy, natural resources, pollution, and accidents.	Includes worldwide scientific, medical, and technological developments, natural phenomena, U.S. weather, and natural disasters.	Includes the arts, religion, scholarship, communications media, sports, entertainment, fashions, fads, and social life.

	World Affairs	Europe	Africa & The Middle East	The Americas	Asia & The Pacific
Mar. 1	Argentina sends $2,475,000 in gold to the New York City-based Central Hanover Bank and Trust Company. Representatives of the company say the funds will be used to stimulate the sagging Argentine peso in American markets.	A court in Yugoslavia sentences 43 bandits to extensive terms in the country's state prisons. Two of the bandits receive death sentences for organizing the group, while 10 others are given life sentences. The remaining 31 will be imprisoned for at least 10 years.		President Luis Miguel Sanchez Cerro of Peru resigns from office after being informed of a possible mutiny in the navy. In a statement, Cerro claims he has "no political ambitions" and only wishes "to save his country" from a violent revolution. His successor is chosen by the navy to be Chief Justice Ricardo Leoncio Elias Arias of the Peruvian Supreme Court.	
Mar. 2		British economists report the Bank of England took in £500,159 worth of gold during the past week, against £174,071 withdrawn, netting a surplus of £326,088. Of the £174,071 withdrawn, approximately £100,000 was reserved for France; £500,000 was deposited by South Africa. . . . Newspapers in Great Britain predict that Robert L. Craigie of the British Foreign Office will be knighted for his successful attempt to broker a naval disarmament agreement with Italy.		Cuban authorities arrest Raul Martin, former high-ranking official of the capital of Havana, for his complicity in the attempted bombing of the presidential palace last week. It marks the fourth such arrest that authorities have made in connection with the bombing.	
Mar. 3		A major flood occurs in Budapest, Hungary, completely destroying the city's communications infrastructure, including telephone and telegraph service.			
Mar. 4		British chemical companies reduce the price of gasoline to four cents per gallon. It is the lowest price in nearly 10 years. The Soviet Union announces it will follow suit to remain competitive in the international market.		Daniel Salamanca Urey is inaugurated as the 33rd president of Bolivia.	
Mar. 5		The Spanish government announces the lifting of censorship restrictions for foreign journalists, in place since the presidency of Juan Bautista Aznar Cabanas began on February 18.		The Prince of Wales travels to Mar Del Plata, Argentina, for an official state visit. . . . President-elect Daniel Salamanca is administered the oath of office at a ceremony in La Paz, Bolivia. Salamanca will now begin the process of selecting his Cabinet.	
Mar. 6				Cuba's Treasury Secretary announces an agreement with the Chase National Bank of New York, whereby the latter will grant a loan worth $20 million, repayable within a period of two years.	
Mar. 7					Empress Nagako of Japan gives birth to a baby girl. She is the fourth child of the Japanese royal family, all of whom have been female. The citizenry had hoped for the birth of a boy to succeed the royal throne of Emperor Hirohito.

A	B	C	D	E
Includes developments that affect more than one world region, international organizations, and important meetings of world leaders.	Includes all domestic and regional developments in Europe, including the Soviet Union.	Includes all domestic and regional developments in Africa and the Middle East.	Includes all domestic and regional developments in Latin America, the Caribbean, and Canada.	Includes all domestic and regional developments in Asian and Pacific nations (and colonies).

U.S. Politics & Social Issues	U.S. Foreign Policy & Defense	Economics & Great Depression	Science, Technology & Nature	Culture, Leisure & Lifestyle	
The Connecticut State Agricultural Experiment Station assembles a group of voluntary citizens to combat an estimated 15 million insect parasites that traditionally attack the state's peach crop at the outset of the summer.	The New York Navy Yard completes construction on the heavy cruiser USS *New Orleans*. The lead ship of its class, *New Orleans* will be commissioned by the U.S. Navy in 1934, and will be moored at Pearl Harbor during the Japanese bombing on December 7, 1941.	*The Annalist* releases its weekly index of U.S. business activity. At 76.9, the figure is a decrease of 0.9 points from the previous week and a decline of 19 percent from the corresponding period last year. Economists say the decline from last week was caused by decreases in freight car loadings and automobile production. . . . U.S. bank debits for the past week were 9 percent less than the preceding week, according to weekly figures published by the Department of Commerce.	The U.S. Federal Radio Commission submits a list of questions to various radio outlets to determine the educational merits of each broadcast. The questionnaire will ascertain the percentage of time reserved for high-quality programming such as classical music.	Production is completed on First National Pictures' war drama *Chances*, an adaptation of the novel written by A. Hamilton Gibbs. The film features the largest set ever constructed by First National Pictures.	Mar. 1
A bill is passed in the Senate that will enlarge New York's Adirondack Park by approximately 1,550,000 acres, making it the country's largest national park. Conservation Commissioner Henry Morgenthau, Jr., says that once the park's revisions are complete, it will encompass two entire counties.		Prof. Irving Fisher of Yale University releases his weekly index of international stock exchanges. The figure is 110.7, an increase of 4.5 points from the preceding week but a decline of 25 percent from the corresponding week a year ago. Fisher, a world renowned economist, famously commented a few days before the 1929 stock market crash that "stock prices have reached what appears to be a permanently high plateau."			Mar. 2
Representatives of the city of Atlanta, Ga., formally protest the accuracy of its population statistics as recorded by the U.S. Census. The census had recorded Atlanta's population as 270,366, but representatives insist the figure is incorrect by approximately 100,000 people. . . . Gangster Al "Scarface" Capone, who recently was sentenced to six months in prison for contempt of court, is released on $5,000 bond. . . . About 257 illegal immigrants residing in the United States are rounded up and taken to Ellis Island, where they will be deported to their respective countries of origin.		The weekly index of U.S. automobile production as compiled by the Department of Commerce is released. The index currently stands at 59.2, a rise of 3.2 points from the previous week, but a decline of 33 percent from the corresponding week one year ago.	The British Medical Council formally challenges the scientific findings of Prof. C.R. Stockard, who discovered that a daily administration of alcohol to guinea pigs led to the production of weak and defective offspring. The council conducted experiments over a period of nine years, and concluded that "alcohol by itself cannot produce the factors which contributed to the production of Professor Stockard's results."		Mar. 3
Former U.S. senator David Baird announces his candidacy for the upcoming New Jersey gubernatorial election. Baird will run on the Republican ticket.		Freight car loadings for the past week amounted to 713,938 cars, according to figures published by the American Railway Association. The total is 6,751 cars less than the previous week, and a reduction of 14 percent from the corresponding week a year ago. The decline from last week was attributable to drops in coal, coke, and forest products.	The 32nd annual International Aeronautical Conference commences in London, England. Delegates to the conference discuss such issues as the lighting of nighttime air routes. "Britain is anxious to cooperate with the rest of the world in everything that can be done to popularize aviation," says the British Undersecretary of State for Air, who chaired the conference.		Mar. 4
Chicago Judge Frank Padden sets the trial of gangster Al Capone for March 20. Capone was arrested earlier this year on charges of vagrancy.		*The Iron Age* releases its weekly index of U.S. steel mill activity. The index currently stands at 59.9, an increase of 2.1 points from the previous week, but a decline of 35 percent from the corresponding week one year ago. *The Iron Age* adds that the rise from the preceding week is attributable to increased public works projects spending.	The U.S. National Research Council, established in 1927 by Dr. Joseph Ames, releases a report estimating the earth's age to be approximately 1.8 billion years. The estimation was based on the study of the disintegration of radioactive elements.		Mar. 5
American Telephone and Telegraph Company president Walter Gifford announces that its subsidiary, Bell System, currently has assets in excess of $5 billion, the largest coffer of wealth of any American company in history. Bell System was founded by telephone inventor Alexander Graham Bell more than half a century ago. . . . Funeral services are held for Thomas Garland, Bishop of the Pennsylvania Protestant Episcopal diocese.		*The Annalist* releases its weekly index of U.S. wholesale commodity prices. At 109.6, the figure is an increase of 0.3 points from the previous week, but a decline of 19 percent from the corresponding period a year ago. Economists say the increase from last week was caused by rises in farm products, food products, and metals.	Aviatrix Ruth Nichols attains a height of 28,743 feet aboard a Lockheed Vega monoplane at Jersey City Airport, setting an international altitude record for women. The previous record was held by Elinor Smith, who achieved an altitude of 27,743 feet early last year. Nichols gained the record in a 225-mile flight from New York to Washington, D.C., that lasted 1 hour, 4 minutes, and 50 seconds.		Mar. 6
	The destroyer *Herndon* is commissioned by the U.S. Navy. *Herndon* was constructed by the Newport News Shipbuilding Corporation in 1919. In 1940, the destroyer was given to Great Britain in accordance with the Destroyers for Bases Agreement and renamed the HMS *Churchill*. . . . Admiral Noble E. Irwin is selected as the new Commandant of the 15th Naval District in Balboa, Panama.				Mar. 7

F	G	H	I	J
Includes elections, federal-state relations, civil rights and liberties, crime, the judiciary, education, healthcare, poverty, urban affairs, and population.	Includes formation and debate of U.S. foreign and defense policies, veterans affairs, and defense spending. (Relations with specific foreign countries are usually found under the region concerned.)	Includes business, labor, agriculture, taxation, transportation, consumer affairs, monetary and fiscal policy, natural resources, pollution, and accidents.	Includes worldwide scientific, medical, and technological developments, natural phenomena, U.S. weather, and natural disasters.	Includes the arts, religion, scholarship, communications media, sports, entertainment, fashions, fads, and social life.

	World Affairs	Europe	Africa & The Middle East	The Americas	Asia & The Pacific
Mar. 8		President Tomas Masaryk of Czechoslovakia appropriates 300,000 crowns for the study of lung cancer, a leading cause of death of many workers of the Joachimsthal state radium mine. In addition, a bill is introduced in the Czechoslovakian parliament that would require mine owners to provide adequate ventilation.			
Mar. 9		British economists report the Bank of England took in £495,132 worth of gold during the past week, against £312,969 withdrawn, netting a surplus of £182,163; £250,300 was deposited by South Africa.			
Mar. 10		Czechoslovakia drastically raises tariffs on imported automobiles. The move essentially bans U.S. automobiles from entering the country for sale. Foreign manufacturers are now required to pay a duty of $810 for every automobile imported. U.S. economists estimate the tariff will result in a loss of $2 million annually.	The first ever airmail plane to Africa by the British Imperial Airways arrives in Kampala, Uganda.		
Mar. 11				President Daniel Salamanca Urey of Bolivia, who seized power on March 5, announces the granting of a general amnesty to all political prisoners. He also announces the cutting of governmental salaries by more than 10 percent.	
Mar. 12					
Mar. 13				Colombian Public Works Minister Francisco Jose Chaux presents a bill in the House of Representatives that would create a national highway system totaling approximately 4,000 miles. If passed, the bill will require the approval of the National Council of Ways and Communications before being implemented.	
Mar. 14	The USS *Texas* arrives in Balboa, Panama. Among the ship's passengers is Naval Secretary Charles Francis Adams, who upon his arrival makes a brief visit to the presidential palace to meet with President Ricardo Joaquin Alfaro Jovane. . . . U.S. State Secretary Henry Stimson receives an invitation from Great Britain to join an international committee that will write the final draft of the Franco-Italian naval agreement. The committee will consist of delegates representing the world's five major naval powers.				

A	B	C	D	E
Includes developments that affect more than one world region, international organizations, and important meetings of world leaders.	Includes all domestic and regional developments in Europe, including the Soviet Union.	Includes all domestic and regional developments in Africa and the Middle East.	Includes all domestic and regional developments in Latin America, the Caribbean, and Canada.	Includes all domestic and regional developments in Asian and Pacific nations (and colonies).

U.S. Politics & Social Issues	U.S. Foreign Policy & Defense	Economics & Great Depression	Science, Technology & Nature	Culture, Leisure & Lifestyle	
		The Annalist releases its weekly index of U.S. business activity. At 76.6, the figure is a drop of 0.1 points from the previous week and a reduction of 20 percent from the corresponding period last year. Economists say the drop from last week was caused by a decrease in electric power production.		Ex-Plumber, a comedic short film directed by Roscoe "Fatty" Arbuckle, is released throughout the United States. It is one of the last films directed by the legendary silent-film-era comedian, who suffered an untimely death from a fatal heart attack in 1933 at the age of 46.	Mar. 8
The National Association of Building Owners and Managers reports that there are currently 1,935 vacant office buildings in the United States. The vacancy is a result of excessive construction in the midst of the economic boom of the 1920s, say association representatives. . . . U.S. Chief Justice Oliver Wendell Holmes turns 90 years old, making him the oldest person ever to serve on the nation's highest court.	The submarine V-2 is rechristened as Bass by the U.S. Navy. V-2 was constructed by the Portsmouth Navy Yard in 1924, and would spend its years as part of the Atlantic Fleet. . . . The heavy cruiser Chicago is commissioned by the U.S. Navy. A product of the Mare Island Navy Shipyard, Chicago will eventually be sunk by Japan during the Battle of Rennell Island in 1943.	Prof. Irving Fisher of Yale University releases his weekly index of international stock exchanges. The figure is 107.3, a decline of 3.4 points from the preceding week and a reduction of 29 percent from the corresponding week a year ago.		The World War I play Who Goes Next? by Reginald Simpson and James Wedgwood Drawbell premiers in London, England. Theater critics contend the play is a worthy successor to Journey's End, the most famous work of playwright Robert Cedric Sheriff.	Mar. 9
Herbert Hoover campaigner Alan Fox predicts the reelection of his employer in the upcoming 1932 presidential election. He adds that history will ultimately compare his presidency to that of such greats as George Washington and Abraham Lincoln.	In Philadelphia, Pa., the destroyer King is decommissioned by the U.S. Navy. A product of the New York Shipbuilding Corporation, King spent most of its years patrolling the waters of the Mediterranean. . . . The destroyer Ludlow is sold for scrap by the U.S. Navy. A product of the Union Iron Works Co., Ludlow spent most of its years conducting training exercises along the Pacific Coast.	The weekly index of U.S. automobile production as compiled by the Department of Commerce is released. The index currently stands at 61.1, a rise of 1.9 points from the previous week, but a decrease of 30 percent from the corresponding week one year ago. The rise from last week was caused by an increase in operations of Ford Motor Company manufacturing plants, say leading economists.		Georgia Tech freshman C.M. Witcher is awarded the title of top scholastic achiever, garnering better grades than any of the university's 2,355 students. Witcher accomplished the feat despite being blind since birth. He is also one of only five students to receive a grade of "A."	Mar. 10
The U.S. Federal Reserve Board reports bank debits for the whole of 1931 amounted to $38 billion, a decline of approximately 28 percent from last year's total of $52.6 billion. The greatest loss in debits was reported in the city of New York, where the difference from last year was $10 billion.	Admiral Louis R. de Steiguer announces his retirement from the position of Commandant of the New York Naval District, effective on April 1 when he reaches the required retirement age. Steiguer will be replaced by Admiral William Phelps, who is currently Commandant of the Portsmouth Navy Yard.	Freight car loadings for the past week amounted to 682,000 cars, according to figures published by the American Railway Association. The total is 31,938 cars less than the previous week, and a decline of 25 percent from the corresponding week a year ago. The decline from last week was attributable to drops in coal and livestock.			Mar. 11
The American Tobacco Company announces its net earnings for 1930 amounted to $43,345,370, the highest total in the history of the company. The total is also $13,116,165 more than 1929, and an increase of 43 percent. The American Tobacco Company currently produces 38 percent of the country's cigarettes. Economists say the record earnings are unfortunately a result of the public's growing apprehension over economic conditions.	Ten steel cargo ships are made available for sale by the Shipping Board. These include the North Pole, Polar Sea, South Pole, Conotton, Quitticas, Provincetown, Eastern Chief, George E. Weed, Lake Girth, and Luella.	The Iron Age releases its weekly index of U.S. steel mill activity. The index currently stands at 57.5, a decrease of 2.4 points from the previous week, and a drop of approximately 33 percent from the corresponding week one year ago. The Iron Age adds that the decline from the preceding week is attributable to a decrease in steel buying by U.S. Steel, the leading American steel manufacturer.	According to statistics published the U.S. National Automobile Chamber of Commerce, American automobile production in February amounted to 230,364 units, an increase of 29 percent over January. It marks the highest total in nearly six months.		Mar. 12
	The War Department allots $52.8 million for improvements to the country's rivers and harbors. The largest beneficiary of the funds is the state of Missouri, which will receive approximately $7,650,000 to renovate the Missouri River. A large portion of the funds will be reserved for defense barricades, especially in coastal regions where vulnerability to foreign invasions is most apparent.	The Annalist releases its weekly index of U.S. wholesale commodity prices. At 110.7, the figure is a rise of 0.8 points from the previous week, but a decline of 20 percent from the corresponding period a year ago. Economists say the increase from last week was caused by gains in farm products and food products.	Fifteen hundred villagers in Chatelard, France, flee their homes in anticipation of an impending 600,000-cubic-feet avalanche. Originating in the Monod Gorge, the avalanche is currently crashing down the French mountainside at a speed of 1.2 miles per day.		Mar. 13
Archbishop Michael Curley of the Protestant Episcopal Diocese of Maryland assails the decision of the Maryland state legislature to overturn a longstanding "blue law" that prohibited the showing of films on Sundays. Describing movies as "morally rotten," Curley says in a statement that "spiritual values are an asset to any city. The trend of current movies is to destroy these values. Educating our youth is costing us millions. Immoral movies tear down what our schools are trying to build up."		Acting on the recommendation of U.S. President Herbert Hoover, major American oil manufacturers agree to reduce importations in order to help improve the country's domestic oil industry. The United States currently imports approximately 100 million barrels of oil annually, most of which originate in South America and Mexico. Exports amount to 156 million barrels, and total consumption is estimated by Interior Secretary Ray Lyman Wilbur to be 900,000 barrels.		Edgar Selwyn's romance film Men Call It Love, based on the play written by Vincent Lawrence, is released throughout the United States. At the end of Selwyn's career in 1942, he had directed over 20 feature-film productions, all of which were play adaptations.	Mar. 14

F	G	H	I	J
Includes elections, federal-state relations, civil rights and liberties, crime, the judiciary, education, healthcare, poverty, urban affairs, and population.	Includes formation and debate of U.S. foreign and defense policies, veterans affairs, and defense spending. (Relations with specific foreign countries are usually found under the region concerned.)	Includes business, labor, agriculture, taxation, transportation, consumer affairs, monetary and fiscal policy, natural resources, pollution, and accidents.	Includes worldwide scientific, medical, and technological developments; natural phenomena, U.S. weather, and natural disasters.	Includes the arts, religion, scholarship, communications media, sports, entertainment, fashions, fads, and social life.

	World Affairs	Europe	Africa & The Middle East	The Americas	Asia & The Pacific
Mar. 15	Two Americans, carpenter John Raditch of Chicago and mechanic Anthony Koszuba of New York, are elected members of the Soviet Union.				
Mar. 16	The second session of the League of Nations Second International Conference on Concerted Economic Action commences in Geneva, Switzerland. . . . Also in Geneva, the League of Nations European Conference on Road Traffic is held. The purpose of the conference is to coordinate and unify European traffic laws, so as to promote commerce among European nations.	British economists report the Bank of England took in £250,087 worth of gold during the past week, against £71,747 withdrawn, netting a surplus of £178,940; £250,000 was deposited by South Africa.			
Mar. 17	Former British ambassador to Japan Charles Norton Elliot dies aboard the liner *Hakone Maru*. Elliot had been suffering from heart disease. He was 69 years of age. . . . Lord Viscount Cecil of Chelwood predicts disaster if delegates the upcoming 1932 international disarmament conference fail to reach an agreement. "The result of failure would be a demand from Germany to rearm," he says.	Police in Leipzig, Germany, officially bar an anti-religious demonstration led by the General Congress of the Proletarian Freethinkers' Society from taking place. A similar demonstration was prohibited from taking place in Berlin on March 14.			
Mar. 18	The second session of the League of Nations Second International Conference on Concerted Economic Action ends in Geneva, Switzerland.				
Mar. 19				Uruguayan Foreign Minister Juan Carlos Blanco travels to Argentina to meet with President Jose Uriburu, in the hope of improving strained relations between the two countries. Uruguay had earlier refused to extradite former high-ranking Argentine officials, who fled their country as the regime of President Hipolito Irigoyen began to crumble.	
Mar. 20			With the threat of extinction facing the South African lion, authorities place a ban on the hunting of the indigenous creature. Lion hunting is a popular pastime for vacationing Englishmen.		
Mar. 21					

A	B	C	D	E
Includes developments that affect more than one world region, international organizations, and important meetings of world leaders.	Includes all domestic and regional developments in Europe, including the Soviet Union.	Includes all domestic and regional developments in Africa and the Middle East.	Includes all domestic and regional developments in Latin America, the Caribbean, and Canada.	Includes all domestic and regional developments in Asian and Pacific nations (and colonies).

U.S. Politics & Social Issues	U.S. Foreign Policy & Defense	Economics & Great Depression	Science, Technology & Nature	Culture, Leisure & Lifestyle	
Plant Industry Bureau chief William Taylor recommends to the average American citizen to grow small vegetable gardens as a way to avoid the high cost of food.	The U.S. Navy reassigns the destroyer *Twiggs*, named after Marine Corps officer Levi Twiggs, to the Scouting Fleet. *Twiggs* was constructed in 1918 by the New York Shipbuilding Corporation. . . . Army Air Corps chief Gen. James Fechet announces that his organization will soon award contracts for 388 military airplanes.	*The Annalist* releases its weekly index of U.S. business activity. At 77.0, the figure is a rise of 0.2 points from the previous week but a reduction of 17 percent from the corresponding period last year. Economists say the increase from last week was caused by gains in freight car loadings, automobile production, and cotton cloth production.	A skeleton of the extinct dinosaur species diplodocus, weighing approximately 52,000 pounds and with an age of 170 million years, arrives in Washington, D.C., where it will be displayed at the city's National Museum.	Nearly the entire crew of the adventure film *The Viking* is killed as the ship they were shooting on, the *S.S. Viking*, explodes off the coast of Newfoundland, Canada. . . . The Italian comedic play *Money! Money!* premiers at the Royal Theatre in London, England. The play is written by Luigi Chiarelli.	Mar. 15
	The battleship *North Dakota* is sold for scrap by the U.S. Navy. *North Dakota* was constructed in 1907 by the Fore River Shipbuilding Company. Highlights of its career include the escort of the deceased Italian ambassador to American soil in 1919.	Prof. Irving Fisher of Yale University releases his weekly index of international stock exchanges. The figure is 106.6, a reduction of 0.7 points from the preceding week and a decline of 30 percent from the corresponding week a year ago.			Mar. 16
Theodore G. Joslin is chosen as the new head secretary of President Herbert Hoover. Joslin succeeds George Akerson, who left his post earlier this year to pursue a career in motion pictures.		U.S. President Herbert Hoover raises tariffs on imported cylinder wires, wool felt hats, and edible gelatin. The average increase of the tariffs is 55 percent. The changes will take effect in 30 days. . . . The American Telegraph and Cable Company is stricken from the New York Stock Exchange's list of tradable companies.			Mar. 17
Hawaiian territorial representatives announce a public hearing will be held on March 26 to determine the feasibility of granting statehood to the Pacific Ocean island. Hawaii officially became a United States territory in 1898 following the passage of the Newlands Resolution.		Freight car loadings for the past week amounted to 723,534 cars, according to figures published by the American Railway Association. The total is 41,534 cars greater than the previous week, but a decline of 17 percent from the corresponding week a year ago. The rise from last week was attributable to gains in coal and forest products.			Mar. 18
Senator Wesley Jones of Washington defends the 1930 Smoot-Hawley Tariff Act in remarks on the Senate floor, saying that a reversal of policy would adversely affect American workers. He describes the group of 1,500 economists who have criticized the act as "cloistered professors." "The Democratic party would substitute the foreign low wage for the American high wage, with a consequent collapse of American standards that have come to be the envy of the people of the world."	The U.S. Navy sells the destroyer *Coghlan* for scrap. *Coghlan* was constructed in 1920 by the Bethlehem Shipbuilding Corporation. Its naval career included serving as a guard plane during the Army's round-the-world flight in 1924. . . . The destroyer *Mullany* is sold for scrap by the U.S. Navy. . . . In accordance with the London Naval Treaty, the battleship *Kennedy* is sold for scrap by the U.S. Navy. A product of the Bethlehem Shipbuilding Corporation, its career mainly consisted of conducting training exercises in the Caribbean.	*The Iron Age* releases its weekly index of U.S. steel mill activity. The index currently stands at 58.1, an increase of 0.6 points from the previous week, but a decline of 31 percent from the corresponding week one year ago. *The Iron Age* adds that the increase from the preceding week is attributable to a traditional seasonal rise.		The Caddo Co.'s comedy film *The Front Page*, starring Hollywood Walk of Fame inductee Mary Brian, premiers in New York City. Directed by Lewis Milestone, who would go on to direct nearly 50 feature films over a 45-year career, the film would be nominated for three Academy Awards, including Best Picture and Best Director. . . . A record 6,100 persons attend the 15th annual exhibition of the Society of International Artists in New York City. Thirteen pictures have so far been sold, including works by such notable painters as Grant Wood.	Mar. 19
The Rhode Island Senate passes a resolution denouncing Prohibition, adding to a growing political movement that calls for the repeal of the Eighteenth Amendment. . . . The Justice Department reports there were 2,367 bank failures in the United States last month, with total liabilities amounting to $48,354,290. The largest amount of liabilities occurred in the state of Pennsylvania, with an estimated $9,214,287.		*The Annalist* releases its weekly index of U.S. wholesale commodity prices. At 109.3, the figure is a drop of 1.4 points from the previous week, and a decline of 17 percent from the corresponding period a year ago. Economists say the reduction from last week was caused by drops in farm products and fuels.	The National Electric Light Association reports U.S. electric power output for the past week amounted to 1,664,186,000 kilowatt hours, 13,150,000 kilowatt hours greater than the preceding week, but a decline of 3.4 percent from the corresponding period one year ago. The National Electric Light Association attributes the increase from last week to increased electricity demand in U.S. cities adjacent to the Pacific Ocean.	George Melford's Hungarian-language version of *Dracula*, based on the novel by Bram Stoker, is released in Spain. Melford will go on to command the production of over 100 feature films. Earlier, the American film company Universal Pictures had released an English-language version, which went on to be archived by the U.S. National Film Preservation Board in 2000.	Mar. 20
	Retired Admiral Joseph Ballard Murdock dies in Manchester, N.H., at the age of 80. . . . The War Department awards contracts worth $1.2 million to four separate companies for the construction of state-of-the-art airplanes and spare parts. The largest of the contracts is awarded to the Pratt & Whitney Aircraft Company of Hartford, who will receive $728,912.50 for the construction of 60 radial air-cooled engines.			Doctors of British novelist Arnold Bennett report that their patient's physical condition has been downgraded to critical. Bennett, whose best-known works include *Anna of the Five Towns* and *The Old Wives' Tale*, has been derided in the past by critics who allege he panders to the populace for financial gain. He is famously quoted as saying, "Am I to sit still and see other fellows pocketing two guineas apiece for stories which I can do better myself? If anyone imagines my sole aim is art for art's sake, they are cruelly deceived."	Mar. 21

F	G	H	I	J
Includes elections, federal-state relations, civil rights and liberties, crime, the judiciary, education, healthcare, poverty, urban affairs, and population.	*Includes formation and debate of U.S. foreign and defense policies, veterans affairs, and defense spending. (Relations with specific foreign countries are usually found under the region concerned.)*	*Includes business, labor, agriculture, taxation, transportation, consumer affairs, monetary and fiscal policy, natural resources, pollution, and accidents.*	*Includes worldwide scientific, medical, and technological developments, natural phenomena, U.S. weather, and natural disasters.*	*Includes the arts, religion, scholarship, communications media, sports, entertainment, fashions, fads, and social life.*

	World Affairs	Europe	Africa & The Middle East	The Americas	Asia & The Pacific
Mar. 22					
Mar. 23		British economists report the Bank of England took in £836,444 worth of gold during the past week, against £44,834 withdrawn, netting a surplus of £791,610. Of the £836,444 deposited, £830,000 came from South Africa.			
Mar. 24	James Sutherland Spore is chosen as the new governor of American Samoa. Spore succeeds Gatewood Sanders Lincoln, whose term expired. . . . The United States grants most-favored-nation status to Germany.	By a vote of 271–224, the British House of Commons ratifies a bill that will merge all of London's public transport systems into a government monopoly headed by five transportation experts to be named at a later date. The total amount of capital of London's private transport systems amounts to approximately $650 million. Conservative Parliament members who voted against the bill deride its ratification, saying it is one step closer to outright Communism.		U.S. Naval Secretary Charles Francis Adams and Naval Operations Chief William Pratt return from Panama, where they oversaw naval tactical maneuvers. Both officials comment upon their return that the U.S. Navy appears to be in good condition.	
Mar. 25	German Industry Federation president Carl Duisberg contends that only the United States can solve the world's financial crisis by eliminating World War I reparation debts. "By taking radical steps in order to break the political debt bonds now preventing the undisturbed functioning of the world's economies, the United States could not only overcome its own crisis but give the world a new period of prosperity," he says.			The Buenos Aires & Pacific Railroad Co. announces that it will forgo payment of dividends to its stockholders. A dividend of 3 percent was paid in the spring of 1930. . . . The Argentine Foreign Minister publishes a letter in newspapers recommending state control of Argentina's private wheat industry, similar to the Soviet Union's five-year industrial plans.	
Mar. 26	Argentina appoints Gregario Araoz Alfaro to represent his country at the Pan-American Public Health Conference, to be held in Washington, D.C. Alfaro is currently the Argentine Chief of the National Bureau of Hygiene.		King Faisal I of Iraq and King Abdullah I of Jordan sign a treaty of friendship in order to influence economic and cultural cooperation between the two leaders' respective countries.	In a crackdown on dissidents, hundreds of homes in the Cuban capital of Havana are searched by police, who arrest 60 people for possession of various firearms and ammunition. The search was prompted by the discovery of 12 large bombs near the home of Justice Secretary Octavio Averhoff.	
Mar. 27					
Mar. 28				Cuban Interior Secretary Clemente Vivancos lays blame for the recent bombings aimed at high-ranking officials on a Communist campaign designed to incite violent revolution. He says officials of his department will be conducting searches of every house in the capital of Havana to hopefully expose the perpetrators.	

A	B	C	D	E
Includes developments that affect more than one world region, international organizations, and important meetings of world leaders.	Includes all domestic and regional developments in Europe, including the Soviet Union.	Includes all domestic and regional developments in Africa and the Middle East.	Includes all domestic and regional developments in Latin America, the Caribbean, and Canada.	Includes all domestic and regional developments in Asian and Pacific nations (and colonies).

U.S. Politics & Social Issues	U.S. Foreign Policy & Defense	Economics & Great Depression	Science, Technology & Nature	Culture, Leisure & Lifestyle	
		The *Annalist* releases its weekly index of U.S. business activity. At 77.3, the figure is a gain of 0.6 points from the previous week but a decline of 17 percent from the corresponding period last year. Economists say the increase from last week was caused by increases in steel mill activity, electric power production, and cotton cloth production.		R.H. Tawney publishes the last of his seven non-fiction works, *Equality*, in which he espouses a theory of a socialist state. A passage from the book reads, "To desire equality is not to cherish the romantic illusion that men are equal in character and intelligence. It is to hold that it is the mark of a civilized society to aim at eliminating such inequalities."	Mar. 22
		Prof. Irving Fisher of Yale University releases his weekly index of international stock exchanges. The figure is 108.2, an increase of 1.6 points from the preceding week but a drop of 29 percent from the corresponding week a year ago.			Mar. 23
President Herbert Hoover's Emergency Committee for Employment appropriates $145 million for 371 public works projects, bringing the total amount of funds since December 1930 to over $1 billion. The largest public works projects will be in the state of New York, where a new post office building costing $10.4 million will be constructed.	The submarine *O-12*, decommissioned since 1924, is rechristened by the U.S. Navy as *Nautilus*. The submarine will take part in an Antarctic expedition later in 1931, but will be accidentally sunk off the Norwegian coast in November. . . . The destroyer *Lansdale*, named after naval officer Philip Lansdale, is decommissioned in Philadelphia, Pa., by the U.S. Navy. *Lansdale* was constructed in 1918 by the Fore River Shipbuilding Company.	The weekly index of U.S. automobile production as compiled by the Department of Commerce is released. The index currently stands at 60.2, a drop of 0.8 points from the previous week, and a decline of 31 percent from the corresponding week one year ago.			Mar. 24
		Freight car loadings for the past week amounted to 734,262 cars, according to figures published by the American Railway Association. The total is 10,728 cars more than the previous week, but a reduction of 16 percent from the corresponding week a year ago. The increase from last week was attributable to gains in coal, forest products, and livestock. . . . The exchange rate of the Argentine paper peso experiences a sharp rise, with one peso currently equaling 35 American cents, up from 32 cents on February 24.		Production begins on the German film *Zwischen Nacht und Morgen*, based on the play written by Wilhelm Braun.	Mar. 25
The New York Police Academy graduates 259 students.		The *Iron Age* releases its weekly index of U.S. steel mill activity. The index currently stands at 58.0, a drop of 0.1 points from the previous week, and a decline of 31 percent from the corresponding week one year ago. The *Iron Age* adds that the microscopic decrease from the preceding week is attributable to an increase in construction contracts.			Mar. 26
The average price of industrial alcohol inside the United States falls to 11 cents per gallon, a result of price wars between major competitors. . . . The Department of Agriculture estimates that this year's spring wheat crop will be approximately 25 percent lower than last year's. . . . U.S. immigration officials report that nearly 100,000 aliens have been barred from entering the country in the past five months. The United States currently admits 148,466 European immigrants per year. White House spokesman Walter Newton says the quotas are in place to "protect American working men from further competition."	Military officials report the attendance at various military training camps across the country exceeds the national recruitment total by about 5,000 recruits. Officials say the recruitment excess is unfortunately a result of depressed economic conditions.	The *Annalist* releases its weekly index of U.S. wholesale commodity prices. At 108.5, the figure is a reduction of 0.8 points from the previous week, and a decline of 19 percent from the corresponding period a year ago. Economists say the decline from last week was caused by drops in farm products, food products, and fuels.	Major American airline companies announce air service to Washington, D.C., will be expanded by 50 percent on April 1. . . . The National Electric Light Association reports U.S. electric power output for the past week amounted to 1,663,208,000 kilowatt hours, 978,000 kilowatt hours less than the preceding week, and a decline of 2.3 percent from the corresponding period one year ago. The National Electric Light Association attributes the decline from last week to increased electric power consumption in U.S. cities adjacent to the Pacific Ocean.	British novelist Arnold Bennett dies from typhoid disease at his home in London, England. He was 64 years of age.	Mar. 27
Attendance in New York City's public schools in February dropped by 1.5 percent as compared to last year, according to a report compiled by the city's Board of Education. The report lays blame for the drop in attendance on an outbreak of influenza.		During interviews with press in Cleveland, Ohio, General Motors president Alfred Sloan attributes low automobile sales to a lack of consumer confidence brought on by the ongoing worldwide financial crisis. He tentatively states that business conditions will improve in the coming years, however. "There is a better feeling throughout the country, and hope for a revival is brighter," he says.		Ernest S. Barnard, president of the American League baseball association, a division of the major league, suffers a fatal heart attack while preparing for the upcoming baseball season at his home in Rochester, Minn. Barnard was 56 years old.	Mar. 28

F	G	H	I	J
Includes elections, federal-state relations, civil rights and liberties, crime, the judiciary, education, healthcare, poverty, urban affairs, and population.	*Includes formation and debate of U.S. foreign and defense policies, veterans affairs, and defense spending. (Relations with specific foreign countries are usually found under the region concerned.)*	*Includes business, labor, agriculture, taxation, transportation, consumer affairs, monetary and fiscal policy, natural resources, pollution, and accidents.*	*Includes worldwide scientific, medical, and technological developments, natural phenomena, U.S. weather, and natural disasters.*	*Includes the arts, religion, scholarship, communications media, sports, entertainment, fashions, fads, and social life.*

	World Affairs	Europe	Africa & The Middle East	The Americas	Asia & The Pacific
Mar. 29					
Mar. 30					
Mar. 31					
Apr. 1		Austrian Foreign Minister Johann Schober announces the cancelling of most-favored-nation status with Yugoslavia and Hungary, a decision influenced by the treaty's restriction to allow Austria to expand its markets into other central European countries. Schober intimates, however, that new treaties with Hungary will be negotiated this summer. Until then, both Hungary and Yugoslavia will be subject to Austria's high tariffs on agricultural imports.		An earthquake that measures 6.0 on the Richter scale rocks the Nicaraguan city of Managua, killing 2,000 people and completely destroying the city's government district. Martial law is declared, and 40 percent of the citizenry is immediately evacuated to makeshift housing camps near the Mototombo seashore. Officials estimate the total property damage to be $30 million and say the earthquake is possibly the most devastating in Nicaraguan history.	
Apr. 2	The Danzig City Council votes to deny the right of the Polish federal government to store warships in the Danzig Harbor. Council members say the vote was influenced in part by certain provisions imposed by the League of Nations that stipulate the city of Danzig must remain free of offensive military units, as its proximity to the Baltic Sea constitutes a significant threat to bordering nations.	The Romanian Court of Appeals upholds an earlier court decision acquitting Zelea Codreanu and Nicolai Tutu of inciting major anti-Semitic riots.			
Apr. 3		In a display of compassion designed to stimulate public approval, King Alfonso XIII of Spain and his wife Queen Victoria ceremonially wash the feet of 12 poor commoners in the royal place in the capital of Madrid.		President Jose Uriburu of Argentina establishes a new holiday, Pan-American Day, to be held on April 14 of each year.	Australia raises tariffs on imported automobile parts, foodstuffs, and boots. The increases are expected to most negatively affect Great Britain and New Zealand.
Apr. 4		King George V of the United Kingdom is stricken with a debilitating lung illness, an ailment his personal doctors say was likely caused by the monarch's heavy smoking, and is bedridden in his London palace. King George is most noted for a royal decree issued during World War I that changed the name of the British Royal House from the more German-sounding House of Saxe-Coburg-Gotha to the House of Windsor, a propaganda act designed to increase British troop morale in battles against Germany.		Ninety-eight Americans situated in Managua, Nicaragua, at the time of the April 1 earthquake are transferred to the Pacific coastal city of Corinto.	

A	B	C	D	E
Includes developments that affect more than one world region, international organizations, and important meetings of world leaders.	*Includes all domestic and regional developments in Europe, including the Soviet Union.*	*Includes all domestic and regional developments in Africa and the Middle East.*	*Includes all domestic and regional developments in Latin America, the Caribbean, and Canada.*	*Includes all domestic and regional developments in Asian and Pacific nations (and colonies).*

U.S. Politics & Social Issues	U.S. Foreign Policy & Defense	Economics & Great Depression	Science, Technology & Nature	Culture, Leisure & Lifestyle	
		The Annalist releases its weekly index of U.S. business activity. At 77.8, the figure is an increase of 0.3 points from the previous week, but a decline of 17 percent from the corresponding period last year. Economists say the rise from last week was caused by a gain in electric power production.			Mar. 29
	The U.S. Navy transfers the battleship *Mississippi* to Norfolk Navy Yard to undergo a process of modernization. Named in honor of the 20th U.S. state, the main highlight of its 30-year career will be the bombing of the Japanese Marshall Islands during World War II.	Prof. Irving Fisher of Yale University releases his weekly index of international stock exchanges. The figure is 107.9, a drop of 0.3 points from the preceding week and a decline of 31 percent from the corresponding week a year ago.			Mar. 30
	The U.S. Navy strikes the submarine *S-50* from the list of the Naval Vessel Register. . . . The battleship *New Mexico* is transferred to Philadelphia, Pa., to undergo a process of modernization. Constructed at the New York Navy Yard in 1915, *New Mexico* will receive six battle stars for heroic bravery in World War II.				Mar. 31
A merger occurs between the New York City-based companies Hibernia Trust and Broadway Plaza and Trust. . . . Freight car loadings for the past week amounted to 741,942 cars, according to figures published by the American Railway Association. The total is 7,680 cars more than the previous week, but a decline of 15 percent from the corresponding week a year ago. The rise from last week was attributable to increases in grain and livestock.	U.S. military officials announce there were 2,500 personnel situated in Managua, Nicaragua, at the time the deadly hurricane hit.	The Labor Ministry of Great Britain announces unemployment has fallen by 59,515 persons in the past week, with a total of 2,580,118 now registered as unemployed, 1 million more than a year ago.		Legendary football coach Knute Rockne dies at the age of 43 as an airplane he was aboard crashes into the cornfields of Kansas. Regarded by many as the greatest football coach in history, Rockne won six national championships in 12 seasons as head coach of Notre Dame University, compiling a record-winning percentage of 88 percent. Rockne's destination on his ill-fated flight was supposed to have been Hollywood, where he was set to participate in the film *The Spirit of Notre Dame.*	Apr. 1
The allied Boston bricklayers' and carpenters' unions, representing approximately 10,000 laborers of their respective fields, negotiate an agreement with employers to reduce the standard workweek from 44 hours to 40 hours. Much to the disappointment of striking workers, however, the unions fail in their attempt to increase pay, and the average hourly wage of $1.25 remains intact. . . . At their annual meeting in New York City, prominent stockholders of the American Tobacco Company nearly unanimously agree to reinstall the company's board of directors by a vote of 2,603,525 to 24,428.	The Bethlehem Shipbuilding Company, one of the largest contractors of maritime defense modules, sues the U.S. Navy for $10 million in unpaid construction fees.	Representatives of the New York Stock Exchange report the total value of stocks for the month of March declined by $2,310,966,491, compared with a gain of $2,720,313,453 for the month of February. Economists say the decline is attributable to disillusionment caused by unfavorable economic figures. . . . *The Iron Age* releases its weekly index of U.S. steel mill activity. The index currently stands at 58.8, a rise of 0.8 points from the previous week, but a reduction of approximately 35 percent from the corresponding week one year ago. *The Iron Age* attributes the rise to an increase in production of independent steel manufacturers.	Heavy rains overflow the Argentine rivers of Parana, Salado, and Saladillo, causing residents of the nearby city of Santa Fe to fear a potential flood.		Apr. 2
		The Annalist releases its weekly index of U.S. wholesale commodity prices. At 108.1, the figure is a drop of 0.4 points from the previous week, and a reduction of 19 percent from the corresponding period a year ago. Economists say the decline from last week was caused by sharp drops in farm products, fuels, and textiles. . . . The National Automobile Chamber of Commerce reports production of the Ford Motor Company increased by 26 percent in March as compared to February.	The National Electric Light Association reports U.S. electric power output for the past week amounted to 1,680,841,000 kilowatt hours, 17,663,000 kilowatt hours more than the preceding week, but a decrease of 10 percent from the corresponding period one year ago. The National Electric Light Association attributes the rise from last week to increased power consumption from U.S. citizens residing in states bordering the Pacific Ocean.		Apr. 3
A minimum sentence of 14 years is imposed by a Chicago jury upon Leo Brothers, who earlier this week was found guilty of murdering *Chicago Tribune* reporter Alfred Lingle. . . . Judge Frank Padden of the Chicago Felony Court dismisses vagrancy charges against reputed gangster Al Capone, on the grounds that not enough police evidence exists to convict the 42-year-old Brooklyn-born man whose business cards identify him as a "used furniture salesman."		The U.S. Justice Department announces that an audit of the Bank of the United States, which declared insolvency and closed its doors earlier this winter, will be completed in two weeks. . . . The American Federation of Labor releases its monthly survey of business conditions, concluding that, while conditions may currently appear to be unstable, "in the fall we may look forward to the beginning of a more definite climb upward toward prosperity." . . . Leading U.S. economists report the country's bank clearings for the past week amounted to $9.5 billion, a reduction of 24 percent from the corresponding week in 1930.		St. Louis first baseman Lu Blue, a three-time Most Valuable Player finalist, is sold to the Chicago White Sox for an undisclosed amount.	Apr. 4
F *Includes elections, federal-state relations, civil rights and liberties, crime, the judiciary, education, healthcare, poverty, urban affairs, and population.*	**G** *Includes formation and debate of U.S. foreign and defense policies, veterans affairs, and defense spending. (Relations with specific foreign countries are usually found under the region concerned.)*	**H** *Includes business, labor, agriculture, taxation, transportation, consumer affairs, monetary and fiscal policy, natural resources, pollution, and accidents.*	**I** *Includes worldwide scientific, medical, and technological developments, natural phenomena, U.S. weather, and natural disasters.*	**J** *Includes the arts, religion, scholarship, communications media, sports, entertainment, fashions, fads, and social life.*	

	World Affairs	Europe	Africa & The Middle East	The Americas	Asia & The Pacific
Apr. 5	The U.S. State Department announces the creation of an international agency that will direct relief efforts for those afflicted by the recent earthquake in Nicaragua. The agency will be headed by American Ernest J. Swift, former emissary to the Red Cross. Nicaraguan President Jose Maria Moncada Topia is named an honorary member.	Spanish Reformist Party leader Melquiades Alvarez calls for a constitutional conference to update old, outdated, and monarchal sections of the country's constitution, which was first signed in 1812.		Argentine political officials report that so far 60,000 Argentineans have registered to vote in the country's upcoming congressional elections. It will be the first open election held since the regime of President Hipolito Irigoyen fell last September. The Argentine voter will be limited to three choices, the parties of the Radicals, the Conservatives, or the Socialists.	Australia's new immigration restrictions that were formulated on January 10 officially come into effect. Each alien is now required to receive special permission from the Department of External Affairs in order to enter the island nation.
Apr. 6		The personal physician of King George V of the United Kingdom, Nurse Davies, comments to reporters on her patient, saying the physical condition of the 66-year-old monarch has shown marked improvement.		According to reports published by Argentine commerce officials, the country's grain exports for the year to date total 3,464,286 tons, 986,934 tons greater than the comparable total from 1930. . . . Brazilian economists report their country's coffee exports fell by approximately 20 percent this month as compared to last.	
Apr. 7		A revolt occurs in the tiny Portuguese-controlled island of Madeira, as rebels led by Gen. Sousa Dias capture and imprison High Commissioner Silva Leal and establish a military junta comprised of nine men. Portugal directs its warship *Pedro Gomez*, along with 870 troops and Acting High Commissioner Fernando Borges, to the Madeiran coast to retake the island militarily.			
Apr. 8		Great Britain sends its cruiser *London* to the Madeiran capital of Funchal to protect any British citizens possibly in danger of attacks from revolutionists.		Congressional elections are completed in Argentina, with 463,847 people, or 77 percent of the population, having cast ballots. Election officials estimate that at least two weeks will be needed to correctly identify the winners. Members of both the Radical and Conservative parties have made speeches declaring victory.	The Chinese city of Hwangchow is invaded and looted by a group of 3,000 domestic Communist bandits. Bombing planes are immediately dispatched by the Chinese government.
Apr. 9				In the Panama Canal Zone, 1,500 laborers of the United Fruit Company go on strike, causing delays in the company's scheduled shipments of bananas. The Panamanian government subsequently threatens to deport the striking laborers, many of whom are of Nicaraguan and Costa Rican descent.	
Apr. 10				Congressional election returns in Argentina show the Radical Party with a lead of 3,196 votes over the Conservative Party and 25,777 votes over the Socialist Party. Over 75 percent of the Argentine electorate voted.	
Apr. 11	Representatives of the world's major sugar producers conclude their discussions in Paris, selecting The Hague as the location for the establishment of an International Sugar Council. The council will likely be headed by American businessman Francis Powel, who is chairman of the American Chamber of Commerce in London.				

A	B	C	D	E
Includes developments that affect more than one world region, international organizations, and important meetings of world leaders.	Includes all domestic and regional developments in Europe, including the Soviet Union.	Includes all domestic and regional developments in Africa and the Middle East.	Includes all domestic and regional developments in Latin America, the Caribbean, and Canada.	Includes all domestic and regional developments in Asian and Pacific nations (and colonies).

U.S. Politics & Social Issues	U.S. Foreign Policy & Defense	Economics & Great Depression	Science, Technology & Nature	Culture, Leisure & Lifestyle	
Leading industrial alcohol manufacturers announce the average price of alcohol has been raised by five cents to 24 cents a gallon.		The *Annalist* releases its weekly index of U.S. business activity. At 78.9, the figure is a gain of 0.7 points from the previous week but a decline of 16 percent from the corresponding period last year. Economists say the rise from last week was caused by increases in electric power production and cotton cloth production.			Apr. 5
	In New York City, 20 young adult organizations merge together to form the Youth Peace Federation. Members of the organization were inspired by a recent speech by scientist Albert Einstein, in which he stated that "if you can get 2 percent of the population to assert in times of peace that they will not fight, you can end war."	Prof. Irving Fisher of Yale University releases his weekly index of international commodity prices. The figure is 75.3, a decrease of 0.3 points from the preceding week and a decline of 9 percent from the corresponding week a year ago. Fisher, a world renowned economist, famously commented a few days before the 1929 stock market crash that "stock prices have reached what appears to be a permanently high plateau."			Apr. 6
A bill is introduced on the New York State Assembly floor by C.P. Miller requiring each plane operating within New York State to be equipped with one emergency parachute per passenger. The bill is a direct result of the death of legendary football coach Knute Rockne, who perished in an air crash on April 3.		Published reports by Argentine economists indicate there were bank failures totaling $15,169,699 during the month of March, the highest total for any March in the past 30 years. . . . The weekly index of U.S. automobile production as compiled by the Department of Commerce is released. The index currently stands at 69.5, a rise of 5.9 points from the previous week, but a decline of 26 percent from the corresponding week one year ago.		Manager Connie Mack of the World Series champion Philadelphia Athletics announces that beginning this season, his players will wear identification numbers on the back of their jerseys during road games.	Apr. 7
		Freight car loadings for the past week amounted to 740,079 cars, according to figures published by the American Railway Association. The total is 1,863 cars less than the previous week, and a decrease of 15 percent from the corresponding week a year ago. The decline from last week was attributable to drops in coke, grain, and livestock.	In Cleveland, Ohio, the Harmon trophy for aviation is awarded to Jimmy Doolittle, Shell Oil manager and future recipient of the Medal of Honor for his services as a lieutenant colonel in the U.S. air corps during World War II.	During the annual Easter egg roll ceremony held on the White House lawn, one of the participants, 10-year-old Samuel Jackson of Michigan, stumbles and breaks his arm. After receiving treatment at the local hospital, Samuel is extended an invitation by the First Lady to visit the White House. . . . New York State Athletic Commissioner James A. Farley comments to reporters that the license of banned Italian boxer Primo Carnera will likely be renewed. Carnera's license was revoked last year for his involvement in a match suspected of being fixed.	Apr. 8
In a speech broadcast throughout the country, Interior Secretary Ray Lyman Wilbur reports that the nation's illiteracy rate has been reduced by 12.6 percent in the past decade. "It is my belief that Americans will renew their energy in extending a helping hand to our millions of unfortunates who can neither read nor write," he says.		The *Iron Age* releases its weekly index of U.S. steel mill activity. The index currently stands at 56.6, a decrease of 2.0 points from the previous week, and a decline of approximately 35 percent from the corresponding week one year ago. The *Iron Age* adds that the drop from the preceding week is attributable to excessive stocking of steel by an unnamed major automobile manufacturer.	Harvard surgery professor Harvey Cushing announces the findings of his 17-year study on gastric ulcers. Cushing discovered that ulcers are triggered by electrical impulses generated from the diencephalon, the area of the brain that governs primitive emotions and essential functions such as breathing and heartbeat.	Okey Bevins claims the United States women's hang-gliding record, remaining suspended in the skies of New York's Mt. Peter for over 51 minutes.	Apr. 9
The U.S. State Department reports there are currently 386,272 American citizens living abroad in foreign countries, almost half of whom are situated in Canada and Newfoundland. The rest are scattered throughout Europe, the West Indies, and Asia.	Assistant Secretary of War F. Trubee Davison announces the purchase of 135 pursuit planes from the Boeing Airplane Company for a near record sum of $1,541,366.90.		The National Electric Light Association reports U.S. electric power output for the past week amounted to 1,672,405,000 kilowatt hours, approximately 8 million kilowatt hours less than the preceding week, and a decline of 1.5 percent from the corresponding period one year ago. The National Electric Light Association attributes the drop from last week to a sharp decline in power production in the industrial Midwest.	The University of Notre Dame announces the appointment of Heartley Anderson as the replacement for deceased head football coach Knute Rockne. Anderson played guard under Rockne for three years, earning all-star honors.	Apr. 10
	Admiral Frank H. Schofield is appointed next in line for the position of Commander in Chief of the U.S. Fleet, a post he will occupy when Admiral Jehu V. Chase retires in September.	The *Annalist* releases its weekly index of U.S. wholesale commodity prices. At 107.1, the figure is a drop of 0.4 points from the previous week, and a reduction of 20 percent from the corresponding period a year ago. Economists say the decline from last week was caused by drops in farm products and fuels.			Apr. 11

F	G	H	I	J
Includes elections, federal-state relations, civil rights and liberties, crime, the judiciary, education, healthcare, poverty, urban affairs, and population.	*Includes formation and debate of U.S. foreign and defense policies, veterans affairs, and defense spending. (Relations with specific foreign countries are usually found under the region concerned.)*	*Includes business, labor, agriculture, taxation, transportation, consumer affairs, monetary and fiscal policy, natural resources, pollution, and accidents.*	*Includes worldwide scientific, medical, and technological developments, natural phenomena, U.S. weather, and natural disasters.*	*Includes the arts, religion, scholarship, communications media, sports, entertainment, fashions, fads, and social life.*

	World Affairs	Europe	Africa & The Middle East	The Americas	Asia & The Pacific
Apr. 12					
Apr. 13					
Apr. 14		King Alfonso XIII of Spain abandons his throne, leaving the position of King vacant. His reign would be remembered as one of mediocrity, as he oversaw his country surrender its colonies in Cuba, Puerto Rico, and the Philippines.			
Apr. 15					
Apr. 16	The largest commercial trader between the United States and the Soviet Union, the Amtorg Trading Corporation, closes the doors of its Seattle, Wash., branch office as a result of what northwest representative Peter Belsky calls "the attitude toward the very limited volume of Soviet goods brought into this country." Amtorg, a corporation whose high-level executives reside in the Soviet Union, now begins the process of liquidating the Seattle branch's remaining assets.				
Apr. 17		The British Foreign Office publicly offers asylum to deposed King Alfonso XIII of Spain, who abandoned his throne without formal abdication on April 14.		The American Commercial Attaché of Buenos Aires releases figures showing that U.S. trade to Argentina has fallen by approximately 58 percent during the past year.	
Apr. 18		Deposed King Alfonso XIII of Spain, traveling under the name Duke of Toledo, tells reporters in Paris that he plans to sit atop his throne once again, just as soon as conditions are ripe for return.		Argentinean President Jose Uriburu completes the selection of his Cabinet, holding a swearing-in ceremony at the early hour of 5:30 a.m. The Cabinet positions include Minister of the Interior, Minister of Foreign Affairs, Minister of Finance, Minister of War, and Minister of Agriculture. All of the men in Uriburu's Cabinet had sworn undying allegiance to him before the coup that thrust him into power occurred.	

A	B	C	D	E
Includes developments that affect more than one world region, international organizations, and important meetings of world leaders.	Includes all domestic and regional developments in Europe, including the Soviet Union.	Includes all domestic and regional developments in Africa and the Middle East.	Includes all domestic and regional developments in Latin America, the Caribbean, and Canada.	Includes all domestic and regional developments in Asian and Pacific nations (and colonies).

U.S. Politics & Social Issues	U.S. Foreign Policy & Defense	Economics & Great Depression	Science, Technology & Nature	Culture, Leisure & Lifestyle	
		The Annalist releases its weekly index of U.S. business activity. At 80.6, the figure is a rise of 1.8 points from the previous week but a decline of 16 percent from the corresponding period last year. Economists say the rise from last week was caused by rises in freight car loadings, electric power production, and automobile production.			Apr. 12
		Prof. Irving Fisher of Yale University releases his weekly index of international commodity prices. The figure is 75.2, a drop of 0.1 points from the preceding week and a decline of 18 percent from the corresponding week a year ago.			Apr. 13
	Parades and demonstrations mark the celebration of the 14th annual Army Day, the anniversary commemorating the United States' official entry into World War I.	The weekly index of U.S. automobile production as compiled by the Department of Commerce is released. The index currently stands at 70.3, a rise of 0.8 points from the previous week, but a decline of 25 percent from the corresponding week one year ago. The increase from last week was caused by an increase in production of high-priced cars, say leading economists.			Apr. 14
		Freight car loadings for the past week amounted to 728,511 cars, according to figures published by the American Railway Association. The total is 11,568 cars less than the previous week, and a decline of 16 percent from the corresponding week a year ago. The drop from last week was attributable to reductions in coal and forest products.			Apr. 15
		The Iron Age releases its weekly index of U.S. steel mill activity. The index currently stands at 57.1, an increase of 0.5 points from the previous week, but a decline of approximately 35 percent from the corresponding week one year ago. *The Iron Age* adds that the increase from the preceding week is attributable to a rise in production from independent steel manufacturers.			Apr. 16
The Society for the Reformation of Juvenile Delinquents reports that there were 323 new patients committed last year to New York City's Randall's Island, the highest total since 1919.		*The Annalist* releases its weekly index of U.S. wholesale commodity prices. At 106.5, the figure is a drop of 1.1 points from the previous week, and a reduction of 20 percent from the corresponding period a year ago. Economists say the decline from last week was caused by drops in farm products and food products. . . . President Herbert Hoover meets with noted economist-statistician Roger Babsen, who reassures the embattled President that despite no evidence of a stock market revival, American business in general has "turned the corner" from the disastrous Wall Street crash of 1929.	The 39th annual convention of the National American Wholesale Lumber Association in Atlantic City, N.J., reaches its conclusion. Delegates drafted a formal resolution requesting Congress to place a ban on imported Russian lumber. Arthur E. Lane was reelected president of the Association. . . . The National Electric Light Association reports U.S. electric power output for the past week amounted to 1,638,691,000 kilowatt hours, approximately 35 million kilowatt hours less than the preceding week, and a decrease of 1.6 percent from the corresponding period one year ago.	The provisional government of Argentina issues a decree establishing a tax of 20 percent on all profits made by foreign film distributors.	Apr. 17
		Leading American economists report the country's bank clearings for the past week amounted to $8,422,537,000, a decline of 23 percent from the corresponding week in 1930. The largest loss occurred in the city of New York, where the difference from last year was approximately $2 billion.	The National Geographic Society releases a report showing the United States to be the world's largest commercial airline provider, with over 50,000 miles flown each year. France is a distant second, with 18,000 miles. The report adds that the international airport in Newark, N.J., is the world's busiest.		Apr. 18

F	**G**	**H**	**I**	**J**
Includes elections, federal-state relations, civil rights and liberties, crime, the judiciary, education, healthcare, poverty, urban affairs, and population.	*Includes formation and debate of U.S. foreign and defense policies, veterans affairs, and defense spending. (Relations with specific foreign countries are usually found under the region concerned.)*	*Includes business, labor, agriculture, taxation, transportation, consumer affairs, monetary and fiscal policy, natural resources, pollution, and accidents.*	*Includes worldwide scientific, medical, and technological developments, natural phenomena, U.S. weather, and natural disasters.*	*Includes the arts, religion, scholarship, communications media, sports, entertainment, fashions, fads, and social life.*

	World Affairs	Europe	Africa & The Middle East	The Americas	Asia & The Pacific
Apr. 19	King Prajadhipok of Siam arrives in the United States to undergo an eye operation, marking the first time an Asian monarch has visited the United States in more than a century. Prajadhipok's reign would last the shortest of any of the kings of the Chakri Dynasty, which took power in 1782.	France announces the opening of a new bureau, the Maison de France, which will provide valuable information to visiting tourists including the prices of over 7,000 hotels. The new bureau is under the auspices of the National Touring Bureau and the Ministry of Public Works.			
Apr. 20		Austria lifts its two-day-old embargo on Russian chicken eggs, a decision based on the Soviet Union's threat to cancel the importation of Austrian electrical accessories with an estimated value of $1.5 million.		The price of newsprint in Canada is reduced from $8 to $5. . . . Mexican bandits sack the small village of Juchitan, killing at least a dozen locals and laying waste the town's entire infrastructure. Military officials summon a squad of National Guardsmen, who after intense fighting capture and kill six of the bandits.	Governor Chang Hsuchliang of Manchuria is promoted to the position of Vice Commander in Chief of the Chinese Nationalist forces. Chang now beings the process of establishing his headquarters in the city of Peiping.
Apr. 21	Argentina sends $10 million worth of gold to the Chase National Bank, the Irving Trust Company, and the Guaranty Trust Company as part of the repayment of a loan issued to the South American nation early last year. . . . France, Italy, Switzerland, and Poland "agree in principle" on a League of Nations proposal to create an "international agricultural mortgage bank," which would provide loans of up to $550 million for the purpose of improving agricultural infrastructure. French National Economy Minister Andre Francois-Poncet comments to reporters that the agreement indicates "European solidarity."	A group of Icelandic students calling for independence from Dutch colonial rule demonstrate outside the Dutch Legation in the Danish capital of Copenhagen.			
Apr. 22	In a speech delivered during a dinner commemorating the 10th anniversary of the beginning of his reign, Hungarian Premier Stephen Bethlen severely criticizes the League of Nations, calling it "an organization of the victor States which can offer neither justice nor peace to the other group of nations which they conquered."	Deposed King Alfonso XIII of Spain visits the British capital of London, where shouts of "¡Viva el Rey!" ("Long live the king!") are heard echoing throughout the streets. . . . British Foreign Secretary Arthur Henderson announces that his government has officially recognized the new Spanish republic, established on April 14 of this year after the abdication of King Alfonso XIII.		The exchange rate of the Argentine peso falls to 33.39, or one peso equaling 33.39 U.S. cents.	
Apr. 23	Great Britain announces the appointment of Admiral Frederic C. Dreyer to represent his nation on the League of Nations Permanent Advisory Commission. Dreyer succeeds Admiral Murray Anderson, who resigned.	King Albert I of Belgium issues a royal decree requiring each foreign laborer to obtain a permit from the Industry, Labor, and Social Welfare Department before entering the country.		Three-fourths of the Cuban parliament votes to appoint a special committee to recommend changes to the country's constitution, first signed when independence was gained from Spain in 1902.	
Apr. 24		On the occasion of his 70th birthday, British Marshal Edmund Allenby prophetically predicts to reporters that "the next war will mean the complete end of civilization as we know it." During World War I, Allenby led the Egyptian Expeditionary Force, which captured the holy city of Jerusalem on December 11, 1917.			

A	B	C	D	E
Includes developments that affect more than one world region, international organizations, and important meetings of world leaders.	Includes all domestic and regional developments in Europe, including the Soviet Union.	Includes all domestic and regional developments in Africa and the Middle East.	Includes all domestic and regional developments in Latin America, the Caribbean, and Canada.	Includes all domestic and regional developments in Asian and Pacific nations (and colonies).

U.S. Politics & Social Issues	U.S. Foreign Policy & Defense	Economics & Great Depression	Science, Technology & Nature	Culture, Leisure & Lifestyle	
Famed Chicago gangster Fred Burke enters a plea of guilty for the December 14 slaying of Michigan policeman Charles Skelly, effectively placing himself behind bars for the remainder of his days. Lawyers for the condemned mob hit man say Burke entered a guilty plea to avoid a possible death sentence.		The Annalist releases its weekly index of U.S. business activity. At 79.5, the figure is a drop of 0.7 points from the previous week but a decrease of 16 percent from the corresponding period last year. Economists say the drop from last week was caused by decreases in freight car loadings and electric power production.		The London-based soccer club Arsenal clinches the English First Division championship with two games remaining in the regular season. Aston Villa, whose home stadium is in the city of Birmingham, is declared the runner-up.	Apr. 19
Americans all across the country celebrate Patriot's Day, the holiday commemorating the anniversary of the Battle of Lexington and Concord, generally considered by historians to be the beginning of the American Revolutionary War. . . . Internal Revenue Service employee William Duggan is elected chairman of the American Salvation Army's Federal Division.		Prof. Irving Fisher of Yale University releases his weekly index of international commodity prices. The figure is 74.6, a drop of 0.6 points from the preceding week and a reduction of 17 percent from the corresponding week a year ago.		James Henigan of Massachusetts wins the 35th annual Boston Marathon, completing the designated course in 2 hours, 46 minutes, and 45 seconds. Henigan triumphed over a field of 228 participants.	Apr. 20
The Young Men's Christian Association of Tulsa, Okla., draws condemnation from local Baptist ministers for allowing racially mixed dancing and swimming classes to be held.		New York State economists report the total assets of the state's 115 federal and national banks declined by approximately $1 billion during the past winter. This compares with a drop of $390 million in the previous winter. . . . The weekly index of U.S. automobile production as compiled by the Department of Commerce is released. The index currently stands at 72.1, a rise of 1.8 points from the previous week, but a decrease of 25 percent from the corresponding week one year ago. The increase from last week was caused by the official opening of a medium-priced car manufacturer, say leading economists.			Apr. 21
Governor Franklin Roosevelt of New York signs into law a bill raising the state's highway speed limit from 30 miles per hour to 40. The bill is expected to create a boost for intrastate commerce.	Admiral Rodney Ingersoll, age 83, who served in both the Civil War and World War I, dies from prolonged uremia at his home in LaPorte, Ind.	Freight car loadings for the past week amounted to 737,934 cars, according to figures published by the American Railway Association. The total is 9,423 cars greater than the previous week, but a reduction of 16 percent from the corresponding week a year ago. The increase from last week was attributable to rises in forest products and ore.			Apr. 22
Chevrolet Motor Company president W.S. Knudsen announces there are currently 34,000 workers on the company's payroll. . . . New York City Health Commissioner Shirley Wynne reports that there were 1,076 cases of diphtheria reported during the first quarter of 1931, a record-low figure for any three-month period in the city's history.		The Iron Age releases its weekly index of U.S. steel mill activity. The index currently stands at 54.9, a drop of 2.2 points from the previous week, and a decline of approximately 35 percent from the corresponding week one year ago. The Iron Age adds that the drop from the preceding week is attributable to unstable production caused by small, sporadic wage strikes.		An estimated 7,500 spectators witness the home opener of the St. Louis Cardinals, the 1930 National League champions. Governor Henry Caulfield of Missouri throws the ceremonial first pitch. The Cardinals defeat the visiting Cincinnati Reds 3–2 with a stellar pitching performance by Syl Johnson.	Apr. 23
Eight African Americans imprisoned in Birmingham, Ala., for the alleged murder of two Caucasian girls deny the legal assistance of International Labor Defense. A representative of the imprisoned tells reporters that he wishes "the Communists would lay off."		The Annalist releases its weekly index of U.S. wholesale commodity prices. At 105.6, the figure is a drop of 0.9 points from the previous week, and a reduction of 20 percent from the corresponding period a year ago. Economists say the decline from last week was caused by drops in farm products. . . . General Motors president Alfred Sloan announces that profits for the first quarter of 1931 were the lowest quarterly total since 1925. Sloan dismisses the figures as a mere reflection of current trends in the automobile industry. . . . The U.S. Department of Commerce reports that the total auto output of March was the highest monthly total since June 1930.	The National Electric Light Association reports U.S. electric power output for the past week amounted to 1,632,828,000 kilowatt hours, approximately 5,000,000 kilowatt hours less than the preceding week, and a drop of 10 percent from the corresponding period one year ago. The National Electric Light Association attributes the decline from last week to continuing decreases in power consumption in the Midwest.	World lightweight boxing champion Tony Canzoneri squares off against world welterweight champion Jack Berg in a match in Chicago, Ill. Canzoneri is declared the victor in the third round after delivering a knockout blow to Berg's jaw, and becomes the only player in boxing history to hold two world titles simultaneously.	Apr. 24

F	G	H	I	J
Includes elections, federal-state relations, civil rights and liberties, crime, the judiciary, education, healthcare, poverty, urban affairs, and population.	Includes formation and debate of U.S. foreign and defense policies, veterans affairs, and defense spending. (Relations with specific foreign countries are usually found under the region concerned.)	Includes business, labor, agriculture, taxation, transportation, consumer affairs, monetary and fiscal policy, natural resources, pollution, and accidents.	Includes worldwide scientific, medical, and technological developments, natural phenomena, U.S. weather, and natural disasters.	Includes the arts, religion, scholarship, communications media, sports, entertainment, fashions, fads, and social life.

	World Affairs	Europe	Africa & The Middle East	The Americas	Asia & The Pacific
Apr. 25	Argentina ships $10 million worth of gold to the United States, reducing its total gold reserves to $384,323,895.	The Belgian newspaper *Antwerp Neptune* prints an editorial expressing distress over the 275 million bushels of low-priced American grain expected to hit Belgian markets this summer. The paper speculates the influx of grain will severely impact small crop farmers. . . . Great Britain's Ministry of Labor reports that over half of the nation's shipbuilders are currently unemployed, largely a result of depressive economic conditions. The ministry's report recommends either a reduction in workers' salaries or raw material costs as a means to stabilize the industry.		Cuban Corp. Jose Heredia, who was court-martialed for gunning down 40 political prisoners during a prison riot earlier this year, is nearly mauled by a mob of 2,000 as he is being transferred by military guards to a Havana courthouse.	
Apr. 26	The average price of oil around the globe falls to its lowest price in nearly 40 years, according to Russell Brown, executive manager of the Independent Petroleum Association.	In a major speech given in the House of Commons, British Chancellor of the Exchequer Philip Snowden estimates that the federal government's budget for the fiscal year of 1931–32 may run as high as $4 billion. Snowden says that high industrial taxes have made the prospect of recovery from gloomy economic conditions look darker.		Panama Canal officials report a loss in traffic of 25 percent during the past year. . . . Former Argentine president Marcelo Alvear receives am uproarious welcome upon his arrival in the capital of Buenos Aires following two years of exile in France. Alvear peacefully transferred power over to now-deposed General Hipolito Irigoyen in 1928. . . . The Argentine Bureau of Rural Statistics estimates this year's crop production to be approximately 370,873,750 bushels of grain, a figure officials say could have been much higher had it not been for an unseasonably dry March.	
Apr. 27		President Alcala Zamora of the newly created Second Spanish Republic delivers his first speech before a crowd of 60,000 at Barcelona's national stadium.		Argentina defeats Chile to win the South American Davis Cup golf championship. The Argentineans will now play the as-of-yet undetermined winner of the North American championship.	
Apr. 28	The U.S. Treasury Department officially approves a shipment of Russian lumber into New York City, after an investigation confirmed the lumber was not produced by slave labor, as had been alleged by anti-Communist critics.	Former Spanish premier Damaso Berenguer is arrested by authorities for his alleged involvement in a revolt in the city of Jaca last December. Gen. Francisco Franco, who would serve as dictator of Spain from 1939 until his death in 1975, is appointed Berenguer's defense attorney. . . . The provisional government of the Second Spanish Republic chooses a red, yellow, and purple design as Spain's new national flag.			
Apr. 29			A group of chieftains representing over 10 million East Africans travels to London to plead for greater freedom from British colonialists. "I think of [Great Britain] as my father," says Chief Koinange of the Kikiyu tribe in his own native language, "but my mother is the land in which I was born."		
Apr. 30					

A	B	C	D	E
Includes developments that affect more than one world region, international organizations, and important meetings of world leaders.	Includes all domestic and regional developments in Europe, including the Soviet Union.	Includes all domestic and regional developments in Africa and the Middle East.	Includes all domestic and regional developments in Latin America, the Caribbean, and Canada.	Includes all domestic and regional developments in Asian and Pacific nations (and colonies).

U.S. Politics & Social Issues	U.S. Foreign Policy & Defense	Economics & Great Depression	Science, Technology & Nature	Culture, Leisure & Lifestyle	
		Leading U.S. economists report the country's bank clearings for the past week amounted to $8.1 billion, a decline of 12 percent from the corresponding week in 1930. The largest loss occurred in the city of New York, where the difference from last year was approximately $2 billion. . . . Only $18 million in new bonds was offered on the New York Stock Exchange during the past week, the smallest weekly total in more than two months, according to published reports.		The American Newspaper Publishers Association reelects *Los Angeles Times* publisher Harry Chandler as the association's president.	Apr. 25
Colorado becomes one of many states to ratify a proposed constitutional amendment that would create federal child labor legislation.		*The Annalist* releases its weekly index of U.S. business activity. At 79.8, the figure is a decrease of 0.3 points from the previous week and a decline of 16 percent from the corresponding period last year. Economists say the drop from last week was caused by declines in steel mill activity and electric power production.			Apr. 26
Attica State Prison in New York constructs a new wing to house 500 prisoners from Sing Sing Prison, which has been experiencing overcrowding due to a record number of inmates.		Prof. Irving Fisher of Yale University releases his weekly index of international commodity prices. The figure is 74, a drop of 0.6 points from the preceding week and a decline of 17 percent from the corresponding week a year ago. . . . U.S. Labor Secretary William Doak declares that a survey taken by the U.S. Employment Service indicates there has been "some improvement" in American industry during the month of March. . . . The American Bankers Association reports that U.S. bank failures have fallen by 77 percent during the past two months.		The Amateur Athletic Union national boxing championship begins at New York City's Madison Square Garden. A record 150 boxers have registered to participate.	Apr. 27
		The weekly index of U.S. automobile production as compiled by the Department of Commerce is released. The index currently stands at 68.1, a drop of 4.0 points from the previous week, and a decline of 25 percent from the corresponding week one year ago. The drop from last week was caused by a reduction in production by the Ford Motor Company, say leading economists. . . . Greyhound Bus Lines reports a reduction in earnings of nearly $1 million for 1930 as compared to 1929.		Boxing promoters announce a world heavyweight title bout between American Jack Sharkey and Italian Primo Carnera will be held on June 10 at Ebbets Field in New York City.	Apr. 28
		Freight car loadings for the past week amounted to 760,002 cars, according to figures published by the American Railway Association. The total is 22,068 cars more than the previous week, but a reduction of 16 percent from the corresponding week a year ago. The rise from last week was attributable to increases in forest products, grain, and livestock.		In an early season game against the St. Louis Browns, starring pitcher Wes Ferrell of the Cleveland Indians becomes only the 32nd player in major league baseball history to throw a no-hitter. A strong batsman as well, Ferrell also clubbed a double and a home run during the contest, leading many sportswriters to superlatively compare his talent to that of Babe Ruth.	Apr. 29
		The Iron Age releases its weekly index of U.S. steel mill activity. The index currently stands at 54.8, a drop of 0.1 points from the previous week, and a decline of approximately 35 percent from the corresponding week one year ago.			Apr. 30

F	G	H	I	J
Includes elections, federal-state relations, civil rights and liberties, crime, the judiciary, education, healthcare, poverty, urban affairs, and population.	*Includes formation and debate of U.S. foreign and defense policies, veterans affairs, and defense spending. (Relations with specific foreign countries are usually found under the region concerned.)*	*Includes business, labor, agriculture, taxation, transportation, consumer affairs, monetary and fiscal policy, natural resources, pollution, and accidents.*	*Includes worldwide scientific, medical, and technological developments, natural phenomena, U.S. weather, and natural disasters.*	*Includes the arts, religion, scholarship, communications media, sports, entertainment, fashions, fads, and social life.*

	World Affairs	Europe	Africa & The Middle East	The Americas	Asia & The Pacific
May 1	For the fifth time in the span of a decade, the British parliament votes down a proposed measure to grant women's suffrage to the small North Atlantic island nation of Bermuda. Only a third of those who voted for the measure supported it. After hearing the measure's outcome, a group calling itself the Suffrage Society holds a hostile demonstration outside the parliament building.	Six miners in Brussels, Belgium, are imprisoned beneath the earth as the underground tunnel in which they are working collapses. Rescue efforts begin immediately, and local officials cancel May Day celebrations to allow citizens to quietly grieve in peace.	A group of archaeologists excavating in Jordan announce they have discovered what appears to be the remains of the ancient Biblical city of Sodom. The excavation is led by Dr. John Oliver La Gorce, president of the National Geographic Society of Washington. According to Christian scripture, Sodom was smote by God during ancient times for its citizens' sinful behavior.		
May 2				Argentina accepts an invitation from the League of Nations to participate in the upcoming 15th annual labor conference to be held in Geneva, Switzerland, on May 28.	
May 3		German economists report the Reichsbank took in 20,899,000 reichsmarks during the past week from various depositors. . . . Construction is completed on Germany's tallest building to date, a skyscraper with an estimated floor space of 300,000 square feet.		Argentine economists report that bank failures in their country have nearly doubled this year as compared to last.	
May 4				The provisional government of Argentina restores government salaries to their pre-revolutionary levels. The decision arouses suspicion among certain circles in Argentina, as President Jose Uriburu had promised a populist revolution. Uriburu releases a statement to reassure his citizenry that the salary increases will not inhibit economic growth.	
May 5		Prime Minister Pierre Laval of France is accused by German nationalists of stirring up anti-German sentiment during a speech in which he derided Germany's growing fascist movement.	Portuguese military officials transfer the 56-year-old battleship *Vasco de Gama* to the coast of Portuguese Guinea to quell an ongoing rebellion led by Jose Soares, whose moniker is *malatesta*, or "bad head."	Representatives of the Canadian National Railways announce it currently has a debt of over $2 billion.	
May 6	The death toll of the severe earthquake that rocked the Armenian region of Nakhivhivan last week reaches 500 people with an additional 1,153 suffering from critical injuries, according to official estimates. The Armenian government has appropriated over 2 million rubles so far for rescue efforts, and Ukraine has donated 100,000 rubles. International newspapers in Moscow and Leningrad hold relief fundraising drives to aid the victims.	Hungarian Col. Paul Pronay is jailed in Vienna, Austria, on charges of leading a group of hostile agitators that recently created violent disturbances in Jewish neighborhoods.			Japan's standing army is reduced by 25,000 men to 200,000 men, effectively reducing the army's annual budget by more than 80,000,000 yen. Military officials say the savings will be put toward research on new weapons, instead of public works projects as was expected. Progressive local newspapers print editorials criticizing the government for engaging in military expansion at the expense of the Japanese commoner.
May 7		Celebrations are held in England to commemorate the 21st anniversary of George Ernest Albert's ascension to King of the United Kingdom.		The Argentine newspaper *Critica* is banned by authorities "for reasons of public order." *Critica* had earlier criticized the regime of President Jose Uriburu. . . . Bermuda announces that approximately 20,000 tourists have visited the North Atlantic island nation so far this year, a record total for any four-month period.	

A	B	C	D	E
Includes developments that affect more than one world region, international organizations, and important meetings of world leaders.	Includes all domestic and regional developments in Europe, including the Soviet Union.	Includes all domestic and regional developments in Africa and the Middle East.	Includes all domestic and regional developments in Latin America, the Caribbean, and Canada.	Includes all domestic and regional developments in Asian and Pacific nations (and colonies).

U.S. Politics & Social Issues	U.S. Foreign Policy & Defense	Economics & Great Depression	Science, Technology & Nature	Culture, Leisure & Lifestyle	
		Leading American economists report the total amount of brokers' loans during the past week, $1.73 billion, is near the record weekly low established on February 4, 1930.	Aviator Frank Hawks flies the 285 miles from London to Dublin in one hour and 40 minutes, breaking the world record by nearly one hour. When questioned by reporters about his successful journey, Hawks says that it was "doggone lonesome" soaring hundreds of miles above his family with only the clouds for companionship, despite being aloft in the air for less than two hours.		May 1
The Chevrolet Motor Company announces its April output of 108,096 cars is the highest monthly total of the year.	Assistant Secretary of War for Air F. Trubee Davison announces a contract has been awarded to the Keystone Aircraft Corporation of Bristol, Conn., for 64 bombardment planes at a cost of $1,920,510. The new contract brings the Army's total aircraft construction costs for 1931 to nearly $10 million. . . . The U.S. Navy announces the decommissioning of the coastal defense submarines *R-7* and *R-9*.	Representatives of the National Raw Silk Exchange report 34,150 bales of silk were traded during April, the highest monthly total since the exchange was established.			May 2
Police in Chicago, Ill., begin a citywide manhunt for reputed gangster Al Capone, who is suspected of masterminding the recent slaying of local racketeer Michael Heitler.		*The Annalist* releases its weekly index of U.S. business activity. At 79.4, the figure is a drop of 0.3 points from the previous week and a reduction of 16 percent from the corresponding period last year. Economists say the drop from last week was caused by decreases in freight car loadings and automobile production.		The 27th annual convention of the Advertising Federation of America begins in New York City.	May 3
		Prof. Irving Fisher of Yale University releases his weekly index of international commodity prices. At 73.1, the index is a decline of 17 percent from the corresponding week in 1930.	Seiji Yoshihara, known to the press as "the Lindbergh of Japan," embarks from Tokyo en route to San Francisco.	With more than two days remaining in the competition, Argentina clinches the seventh annual South American Athletic Championships, besting runner-up Chile by more than 50 points.	May 4
The U.S. Treasury Department reports that the country's budget deficit has grown by nearly $1 billion during the past year. Treasury Secretary Andrew Mellon had forecast a deficit of $180,076,000 in his annual report issued last December.		The weekly index of U.S. automobile production as compiled by the Department of Commerce is released. The index currently stands at 70.6, a rise of 2.5 points from the previous week, but a decline of 25 percent from the corresponding week one year ago. The rise from last week was caused by an increase in output by manufacturers of low-priced automobiles, say leading economists.	Ernest Laws and John Skinner file a patent application for an air compression device that, when attached to the wings of an airplane, will make flying much safer. A prototype of the device is expected to weigh approximately 100 pounds.	World junior lightweight boxing champion Benny Bass retains his title by knocking out Eddie Mack of Denver in the third round of a 10-round match. Ringside referees declared the fight over after a physician confirmed that Mack's jaw had been broken by a devastating punch to the chin.	May 5
The New York City Police Department places a ban on excessive automobile honking in the city's Broadway theater district, a decision resulting from declining tourism revenue. Violators will be warned and then, if excessive honking persists, arrested on misdemeanor charges of disturbing the peace.		Freight car loadings for the past week amounted to 759,272 cars, according to figures published by the American Railway Association. The total is 730 cars less than the previous week, and a decline of 16 percent from the corresponding week last year. The drop from last week was attributable to declines in coke and grain products.			May 6
U.S. immigration officials report that a total of 16,344 aliens were admitted into the United States during the month of March, with a total of 17,444 aliens permanently departing. The immigration deficit is no doubt a result of unfavorable economic conditions, say officials.		*The Iron Age* releases its weekly index of U.S. steel mill activity. The index currently stands at 54.1, a decrease of 0.7 points from the previous week, and a decline of approximately 40 percent from the corresponding week one year ago. . . . The Shell Union Oil Corporation announces a net loss of $5,095,574 for the fiscal year of 1930. . . . The National Automobile Chamber of Commerce estimates March's auto output to be 348,909 units, 21 percent greater than the total from February, but a decline of 25 percent from the corresponding month of 1930.			May 7

F	G	H	I	J
Includes elections, federal-state relations, civil rights and liberties, crime, the judiciary, education, healthcare, poverty, urban affairs, and population.	Includes formation and debate of U.S. foreign and defense policies, veterans affairs, and defense spending. (Relations with specific foreign countries are usually found under the region concerned.)	Includes business, labor, agriculture, taxation, transportation, consumer affairs, monetary and fiscal policy, natural resources, pollution, and accidents.	Includes worldwide scientific, medical, and technological developments, natural phenomena, U.S. weather, and natural disasters.	Includes the arts, religion, scholarship, communications media, sports, entertainment, fashions, fads, and social life.

	World Affairs	Europe	Africa & The Middle East	The Americas	Asia & The Pacific
May 8		French economists report the Bank of France took in $2 million worth of gold during the past week. . . . The Romanian government formally apologizes to a group of German diplomats who were mistakenly barred from entering Romania a week ago. The diplomats were attempting to enter Romania to sign a recently negotiated trade treaty.		The exchange rate of the Argentine paper peso falls by 0.75 cents, with one paper peso equaling 31 U.S. cents.	
May 9				President Jose Uriburu of Argentina orders a regiment of cavalrymen to the capital of Buenos Aires to quell ongoing student riots. The liberal newspaper *La Libertad* is officially banned as well. In response to critics who allege he is establishing a permanent totalitarian state, President Uriburu pledges to his people that congressional elections will be held no later than November 8, with presidential and vice presidential elections soon thereafter. . . . The Ecuadorian Superintendent of Banks suspends the operations of the Bank of Ecuador, pending an investigation into allegations of illegal accounting.	The Australian government announces the cancellation of embargoes on imported steel and iron, in place since October 1930.
May 10		In Paris, France, 15 university students are arrested for protesting outside the Chamber of Deputies against Foreign Minister Aristide Briand, who has recently been accused by critics of undermining peace with Germany.		The Brazilian coffee producers Theodor Willie & Co. and J. Aron & Compania merge to form Theodor Willie & Co., Ltd.	The Australian Federal Treasury reports the country currently has a trade deficit of nearly $100 million.
May 11		British economists report the Bank of England took in £1,451,080 worth of gold during the past week, over £1 million of which was deposited from South Africa.		Chilean Gen. Barcelo Lira is deported to Argentina following an investigation that revealed he was the ringleader of an attempted coup of President Carlos Ibanez del Campo that occurred last September. . . . The Bolivian Chamber of Deputies debates a pair of bills that would greatly lessen corporate and industrial taxes, a move economists say will provide a much-needed boost to Bolivian industry.	
May 12		The Austrian government advances a loan worth $23 million to the country's largest private bank, the Kreditanstalt, as rumors of a potential bank failure begin to circulate.		Argentine economists report the country currently has a federal budget deficit of nearly 100 million pesos. Local newspapers lay blame squarely on President Jose Uriburu, who geared the nation toward revolution last autumn with pledges of fiscal conservancy. His critics allege that his rampant spending has clearly indicated a reversal in policy.	Thirty thousand Chinese soldiers fighting in the eastern coastal city of Shanghai desert their commanding officers and join the ranks of the Communist rebels with whom they were earlier engaged in combat. The desertion reduces the Nationalists' forces by nearly 25 percent. Gen. Chiang Kai-shek offers $1 million to the rebel leadership for a temporary cease-fire.
May 13	The U.S. Shipping Board reports that American sea vessels traded 40 percent of the world's total commerce during the past fiscal year. . . . Argentine Ambassador to Great Britain Jose Evaristo Uriburu, who is also the cousin of President Jose Felix Uriburu, officially announces his retirement.	Italian War Minister Gen. Pietro Gazzera strongly recommends that the proposed measure to reduce the nation's required military conscription from 18 months to one year be struck down by the Chamber of Deputies. Gazzera says Italy must adequately defend itself against its neighbors, who he claims "have armed themselves to the teeth."		Supporters of Argentinean President Jose Uriburu request that he lift the ban on the liberal newspapers *Critica* and *La Libertad* as a gesture of his desire for democracy. Uriburu enacted the ban earlier this spring to preserve order as the country prepares for elections.	
May 14		A British welfare commission selected by Prime Minister Ramsay MacDonald concludes that the current dole system will drown Great Britain in debt unless drastic changes are made. The commission estimates that $30 million, or 10 percent of the total unemployment fund, is fraudulently obtained by various "poverty impostors" each year. . . . Irish economists predict that the federal budget deficit of Northern Ireland will reach $225,000 by the year's end.		Brazil raises its tax on matches from 35 reis per box to 90 reis. Brazilian newspapers print front-page editorials protesting the decision.	

A	B	C	D	E
Includes developments that affect more than one world region, international organizations, and important meetings of world leaders.	Includes all domestic and regional developments in Europe, including the Soviet Union.	Includes all domestic and regional developments in Africa and the Middle East.	Includes all domestic and regional developments in Latin America, the Caribbean, and Canada.	Includes all domestic and regional developments in Asian and Pacific nations (and colonies).

U.S. Politics & Social Issues	U.S. Foreign Policy & Defense	Economics & Great Depression	Science, Technology & Nature	Culture, Leisure & Lifestyle	
		The Annalist releases its weekly index of U.S. wholesale commodity prices. At 104.5, the figure is a reduction of 0.4 points from the previous week, and a decline of 19 percent from the corresponding period a year ago. Economists say the drop from last week was caused by decreases in farm products, food products, and metals.	The National Electric Light Association reports U.S. electric power output for the past week amounted to 1,622,146,000 kilowatt hours, 25 million kilowatt hours less than the preceding week, and a decline of 3.1 percent from the corresponding period one year ago. The National Electric Light Association attributes the decrease from last week to ever lessening power consumption on the Pacific Coast.	The League of Advertising Women elects Dorothy Crowne as the organization's president.	**May 8**
		The U.S. Federal Reserve Board reports total bank clearings for the month of April aggregated $39.9 billion, 21.2 percent less than the corresponding month of 1930. . . . Brazil reduces its budget for 1931 by 142,000 contos. Local newspapers hail the move as one that will provide a much-needed boost to Brazil's sagging economy. . . . During sessions of the International Chamber of Commerce, British economist Henry Bell describes the 1930 Smoot-Hawley Tariff Act as "a machine gun, a high explosive, a poison gas."		At the opening of the South American Athletic Championships, Juan Carlos Zabala of Argentina sets the South American 3,000-meter-dash record, besting the previous record time by less than two seconds. . . . Little, Brown & Co. publish The Road Back, a sequel to Erich Remarque's World War I novel All Quiet on the Western Front, which has sold over 3 million copies. Major American film studios have contacted Remarque with the hopes of repeating the Oscar-winning success of the film version of All Quiet on the Western Front.	**May 9**
Dr. W.H. Burton of the University of California releases the results of a nationwide survey that asked inner city schoolchildren to identify which aspects of "community life" are most familiar to them. The number one answer given was "bootlegging." Number two was "divorce." Responding to the survey, Commissioner William Cooper of the U.S. Office of Education says that America's public schools are able to either "stimulate growth or to plant the fungi of social decay."	George Washington Craig of Louisville, Ky., who is six feet, seven inches tall, is admitted into the Army, making him the United States' tallest soldier.	The Annalist releases its weekly index of U.S. business activity. At 79.3, the figure is a decrease of 0.1 points from the previous week and a decline of 15 percent from the corresponding period last year. Economists say the drop from last week was caused by reductions in steel mill activity and cotton cloth production.	Dr. Fred Allison of the Alabama Polytechnic Institute discovers the last of the unknown chemical elements, "Element 85," which he found small traces of in fluorite, potassium bromide, and sea water, among others. It is the third such discovery by an American scientist since 1926. Dr. Allison plans to name the element alabamine, after the state in which he resides.		**May 10**
The trial of Bank of the United States president Bernard K. Marcus enters its seventh week. Marcus was arrested earlier this year for questionable accounting practices.		The London Economist releases its monthly index of British wholesale prices. The index stands at 90.0, compared with 112.3 at the corresponding date last year, a decrease of approximately 20 percent. Blame for the decline is laid to sharp losses in the prices of cereals and meats, textiles, and minerals.		Silent film comedian Charlie Chaplin tells reporter Gordon Beckles of The Daily Express that he doubts he will make another film in Europe, as he fears growing nationalist movements will lead to another world war. "Patriotism is the greatest form of insanity the world ever suffered," he says.	**May 11**
Dwight L. Hoopingarman of the American Construction Council asks Congress for $250 million to renovate and rebuild America's inner-city slums. . . . Fifteen hundred barbers in New York City go on strike, protesting low wages and poor working conditions.		The weekly index of U.S. automobile production as compiled by the Department of Commerce is released. The index currently stands at 70.0, a drop of 0.6 points from the previous week, and a decline of 22 percent from the corresponding week one year ago. The drop from last week was caused by a reduction in the production schedules of the Chevrolet Motor Company, say leading economists.	Emperor Hirohito of Japan witnesses the opening of what Japanese scientists claim is the largest and most expensive aeronautical research facility in the world. The facility cost $1.9 million to construct and covers an area of 14 acres.		**May 12**
	The Navy Department awards a contract to the Shell Oil Company for 4,620,000 barrels of oil at a cost of $2,260,100.	Freight car loadings for the past week amounted to 775,291 cars, according to figures published by the American Railway Association. The total is 16,019 cars greater than the previous week, but a decline of 16 percent from the corresponding week last year. The increase from last week was attributable to gains in coal, forest products, ore, and coke.		The 1930 World Series champions, the Philadelphia Athletics, defeat the Chicago White Sox by a score of 5–2. The victory places the Athletics atop the American League standings for the first time this year.	**May 13**
The Travelers Insurance Company reports that automobile fatalities in the United States increased by 9 percent during the first quarter of 1931. . . . Americans all across the United States celebrate Jamestown Day, which commemorates the 1607 founding of Jamestown, the first permanent English settlement in North America.	Army Chief of Staff Douglas MacArthur tells members of the War Policy Commission that if the United States were to declare war today, 4 million troops would be ready to serve in combat. The commission is headed by War Secretary Patrick Hurley and includes Cabinet members and congressional representatives.	The Iron Age releases its weekly index of U.S. steel mill activity. The index currently stands at 54.0, a drop of 0.1 points from the previous week, and a decline of approximately 40 percent from the corresponding week one year ago. The Iron Age adds that the drop from the preceding week is attributable to a recession in steel mine operations. . . . The price of pig iron in Pennsylvania fell by 50 percent this week as compared to last, according to reports published by notable economists.			**May 14**
F Includes elections, federal-state relations, civil rights and liberties, crime, the judiciary, education, healthcare, poverty, urban affairs, and population.	**G** Includes formation and debate of U.S. foreign and defense policies, veterans affairs, and defense spending. (Relations with specific foreign countries are usually found under the region concerned.)	**H** Includes business, labor, agriculture, taxation, transportation, consumer affairs, monetary and fiscal policy, natural resources, pollution, and accidents.	**I** Includes worldwide scientific, medical, and technological developments, natural phenomena, U.S. weather, and natural disasters.	**J** Includes the arts, religion, scholarship, communications media, sports, entertainment, fashions, fads, and social life.	

	World Affairs	Europe	Africa & The Middle East	The Americas	Asia & The Pacific
May 15		King Gustav V of Sweden awards the ceremonial North Star title to American bankers Frederick Allen and Donald Durant. . . . British economists report the Bank of England took in £3,090,000 worth of gold during the past week.	Turkish Secretary of State C.H. Cahan announces that applications from Armenian citizens living in Canada for reparations for the 1915 Armenian Genocide have been denied on the grounds that the reparations are only available to those who currently reside in Armenia. Some 900,000 Armenians were systemically killed or deported by Turkey during World War I.	Brazil updates its automobile tariff policies to end ad valorem duties, or duties that are based on the assessed value of a product. The update comes as the result of an investigation that revealed automobile manufacturers were undervaluing their products to avoid paying the ad valorem duty.	
May 16	The International Olympic Committee announces that Germany has been chosen as the host for the upcoming 1936 Summer Olympics. Officials in the capital of Berlin now begin the process of renovating the city, including the expansion of the German Gymnastic Stadium by 44 percent to seat additional spectators.	The Bank of Netherlands reduces its interest rate from 2.5 percent to 2 percent.		Argentina rounds up 600 alleged petty criminals and deports them to Uruguay. Uruguayan newspapers complain that the deportations are causing the country to be infested with crime. Argentine officials claim the measure is in retaliation for Uruguay's refusal to hand over high-ranking officials of President Hipolito Irigoyen's now-deposed regime.	
May 17		Spanish railway workers in Barcelona discover an undetonated bomb planted on one of the city's most used trains. Officials say the bomb was likely planted by remnants of the regime of King Alfonso XIII, who was deposed a week earlier.			
May 18		The average of British wholesale prices has fallen by approximately 16 percent in one year, according to leading economists. . . . The Bank of England receives £900,000 worth of gold from South Africa. . . . British economists report that exports from Great Britain have declined by 30 percent during the past year and imports by 16 percent.	President Musa Kazem Pasha el Hussein of the Palestine Arab Executive lays to rest repeated rumors about his resignation, saying that despite his ill health he will continue his duties as long as the people's trust in him persists.	Argentine economists report their country's grain exports have increased by 15,000 tons this week as compared to last.	
May 19	Former U.S. president Calvin Coolidge offers an explanation for the worldwide steel depression to a group of visiting reporters. "Steel has been cheapened by the increased use of machinery in its production," he says.	French economists publish figures showing an adverse trade balance of 1 billion francs for the month of April.		A mob of unemployed tin miners in the Bolivian mining city of Oruro incite a series of sporadic riots, smashing store windows and causing panic for the city's estimated 100,000 residents. . . . At the annual Brazilian coffee conference, a group of liberal economists recommends the implementation of price fixing and five-year quotas as means of stabilizing Brazil's coffee industry. . . . The Argentine steamer Northern Prince arrives in New York City with $2,540,000, most of which will be invested in the New York Stock Exchange.	New Zealand announces the end of military conscription and the establishment of an all-volunteer army. Military officials say the move was made for economic reasons, as conscription has severely limited the number of laborers needed for New Zealand's industries to thrive.
May 20	In Geneva, Switzerland, the League of Nations Council votes to settle the matter of the disputed Austro-German customs union before the Permanent Court of International Justice at The Hague.	For the first time in more than 20 years, a death sentence for murder in Great Britain is overturned. William Herbert Wallace, a Liverpool insurance agent who was earlier convicted of murdering his wife, is found not guilty before the Criminal Court of Appeal.		The American Commercial Attaché in Buenos Aires releases figures detailing Argentine trade to the United States during the first three months of 1931. Exports totaled $8,711,000, 71 percent less than last year, while imports were 61 percent less than last year at $36,174,000.	
May 21	At the international wheat parley in London, the United States casts the only dissenting vote among 11 of the world's largest grain-exporting countries against Poland's proposal for an international governing body that would impose export quotas.	The German newspaper Deutsche Allgemeine Zeitung demands the resignation of Foreign Minister Julius Curtius for his failure to convince world leaders to accept the proposed Austro-German customs union. The paper also echoes earlier statements made by fascist leaders in calling for Germany's complete and immediate withdrawal from the League of Nations.			

A	B	C	D	E
Includes developments that affect more than one world region, international organizations, and important meetings of world leaders.	Includes all domestic and regional developments in Europe, including the Soviet Union.	Includes all domestic and regional developments in Africa and the Middle East.	Includes all domestic and regional developments in Latin America, the Caribbean, and Canada.	Includes all domestic and regional developments in Asian and Pacific nations (and colonies).

U.S. Politics & Social Issues	U.S. Foreign Policy & Defense	Economics & Great Depression	Science, Technology & Nature	Culture, Leisure & Lifestyle	
	The coastal defense submarine *R-19* is decommissioned at the Philadelphia Navy Yard, where it will remain inactive until being transferred over to British control during World War II as part of the Lend-Lease Agreement. . . . Maj. Gen. Preston Brown officially bars enlisted men from entering the Panamanian city of Colon, as the result of a recent conflict between the military and local police that drew a formal protest from Panamanian authorities.	*The Annalist* releases its weekly index of U.S. wholesale commodity prices. At 103.9 the figure is a drop of 0.6 points from the previous week, and a decline of 23 percent from the corresponding period a year ago. Economists say the drop from last week was caused by decreases in food products and building materials.	The National Electric Light Association reports U.S. electric power output for the past week amounted to 1,599,939,000 kilowatt hours, 25 million kilowatt hours less than the preceding week, and a decline of 2.4 percent from the corresponding period one year ago.	The American Bible Society holds its 115th annual meeting in New York City, where delegates reelect the entire board of managers.	May 15
		Before an audience of 10,000 labor representatives, Pope Pius XI delivers an address broadcast throughout the world in which he states that in spite of poor economic conditions, the world must refrain from entering into an age of socialism, as he fears it is a flawed system that will lead people of all religions down a path of destruction. Pope Pius delivered the address three consecutive times, each time in a different language.			May 16
Secretary William Wheeler of the Building Trades Employers' Association reports that injuries relating to construction mishaps have declined by approximately 25 percent during the past year.		*The Annalist* releases its weekly index of U.S. business activity. At 77.8, the figure is a reduction of 1.4 points from the previous week and a decline of 16 percent from the corresponding period last year. Economists say the drop from last week was caused by decreases in freight car loadings and electric power production.		Bill Agee of Baltimore is declared the 1931 sprinter champion of the National Amateur Athletic Union. Agee clinched the title after winning a recent marathon with a time of 2 hours, 32 minutes, and 38 seconds. . . . J. Griffith Boardmen defeats C. Bayard Mitchell in match play, 2–1, to retain the title of Atlantic Coast golf champion.	May 17
The New York City Community Council asks President Herbert Hoover to increase public works projects spending by $2 billion as a means of improving employment figures. "With private business still suffering under the weight of an economic depression," a statement reads, "the Council feels that every possible effort should be made to stimulate public enterprise."			A series of fires in the Japanese capital of Tokyo destroys nearly 1,500 homes and causes the deaths of more than 25 people.		May 18
Chevrolet Motor Company president W.S. Knudsen announces his company currently employs over 36,000 total workers, who on average work nearly 50 hours per week.	U.S. Ambassador to Cuba Frank Guggenheim meets with U.S. Secretary of State Henry Stimson to discuss the possibility of increasing American troop presence in the Caribbean island nation.	The weekly index of U.S. automobile production as compiled by the Department of Commerce is released. The index currently stands at 69.6, a drop of 0.4 points from the previous week, and a decline of 25 percent from the corresponding week one year ago. The drop from last week was caused by a decline in production from low-priced manufacturers, say leading economists. . . . The Coca-Cola Company announces profits of $2.9 million were made for the first four months of 1931. . . . American economists report that total exports for the month of April declined by 8 percent as compared to March.		The 1930 World Series champions, the Philadelphia Athletics, win their 10th consecutive game, defeating the Cleveland Indians by a score of 10–7.	May 19
	Former war secretary Newton Baker urges the United States to officially join the League of Nations, and not to remain what he calls "a bump on the international log."	Freight car loadings for the past week amounted to 747,449 cars, according to figures published by the American Railway Association. The total is 27,482 cars less than the previous week, and a decline of 20 percent from the corresponding week last year. The drop from last week was attributable to losses in coal, grain, and livestock. . . . The average price of cotton on the Cotton Exchange falls to 10 cents a pound, the lowest price in over 15 years.	In Copenhagen, Denmark, 137 delegates representing 33 nations assemble to take part in the 27th annual World Congress of Radio Technicians and Scientists.		May 20
The National Safety Council reports that during 1930, 99,000 Americans perished in accidental deaths, the highest yearly total on record. Property damage resulting from accidents totaled over $3 billion, according to the report's estimates.	War Secretary Pat Hurley announces the abandonment of 53 Army posts as a means of reducing the federal budget deficit. The total savings of the cuts is estimated to be $25 million.	*The Iron Age* releases its weekly index of U.S. steel mill activity. The index currently stands at 52.2, a reduction of 1.8 points from the previous week, and a decline of approximately 40 percent from the corresponding week one year ago. *The Iron Age* adds that the decline from the preceding week is attributable to lessening consumer steel demand.	Winter crop estimates in Texas, Oklahoma, Kansas, and Nebraska increase as the result of favorable weather reports indicating prolonged periods of unseasonably high temperatures.		May 21

F	G	H	I	J
Includes elections, federal-state relations, civil rights and liberties, crime, the judiciary, education, healthcare, poverty, urban affairs, and population.	*Includes formation and debate of U.S. foreign and defense policies, veterans affairs, and defense spending. (Relations with specific foreign countries are usually found under the region concerned.)*	*Includes business, labor, agriculture, taxation, transportation, consumer affairs, monetary and fiscal policy, natural resources, pollution, and accidents.*	*Includes worldwide scientific, medical, and technological developments, natural phenomena, U.S. weather, and natural disasters.*	*Includes the arts, religion, scholarship, communications media, sports, entertainment, fashions, fads, and social life.*

	World Affairs	Europe	Africa & The Middle East	The Americas	Asia & The Pacific
May 22		Spanish Finance Minister Idalecio Prieto, who was appointed following the abdication of King Alfonso XIII, releases a report estimating the entire fortune of the deposed monarch's royal family to be only 84,974,171 pesetas, or nearly $8.5 million. The report comes as a surprise to the Spanish public, who long had believed that the royal fortune far exceeded $20 million.			
May 23	The Unionist Party of Puerto Rico begins a publicity campaign designed to convince U.S. leaders to grant full independence to the Caribbean island nation.			The Cuban Supreme Court announces that Major Arsenio Ortiz will be court-martialed for the recent slaying of 40 political prisoners.	
May 24				Newspapers in Brazil publicly demand the return to constitutional government from provisional President Getulio Vargas, who seized power in a coup on October 24, 1930.	
May 25				Argentina celebrates the 121st anniversary of its declaration of independence from Spanish colonial rule.	
May 26	The International Skating Union officially approves a list of regulations submitted by American officials that will apply to all skating events at the upcoming Winter Olympic Games in Lake Placid, N.Y.			Argentina defeats Uruguay 5–3 to win the annual South American soccer championship.	
May 27		French Foreign Minister Aristide Briand reassures Premier Pierre Laval that he will not resign despite an ongoing domestic media campaign pressuring him to do so.		Federal troops in Honduras engage in open battle with a group of rebels seeking to establish a junta in the city of Tela, home to the headquarters of the United Fruit Company. Over 54 rebels and 12 federal troops are killed in a series of clashes that reportedly last nine hours.	
May 28	The 15th session of the International Labor Conference begins in Geneva, Switzerland. Delegates to the conference say the main priority will be the examination of working conditions of coal miners.	As the Austrian Credinstalt bank faces near collapse, the federal government pledges the granting of unlimited credit resources in the hope of keeping the bank afloat.		The Canadian House of Commons votes to ban all Russian imports, a decision based mainly on the Soviet Union's official policy of atheism.	
May 29		U.S. citizen Michele Schirru is executed by an Italian firing squad following three months of trial and imprisonment for an assassination attempt against Premier Benito Mussolini.			The Imperial Bank of India reduces its discount rate by 1 percent, from 7 to 6 percent.
May 30	Austrian delegate to the League of Nations Dr. Bruno Schulz urges his international counterparts in Geneva to follow the example set by the United States in 1925 and permanently outlaw the manufacture, distribution, and consumption of heroin.			A group of Cuban army officers gathers in the presidential palace to pledge firm loyalty to President Gerardo Machado amid rumors of a violent revolution.	

A	B	C	D	E
Includes developments that affect more than one world region, international organizations, and important meetings of world leaders.	*Includes all domestic and regional developments in Europe, including the Soviet Union.*	*Includes all domestic and regional developments in Africa and the Middle East.*	*Includes all domestic and regional developments in Latin America, the Caribbean, and Canada.*	*Includes all domestic and regional developments in Asian and Pacific nations (and colonies).*

U.S. Politics & Social Issues	U.S. Foreign Policy & Defense	Economics & Great Depression	Science, Technology & Nature	Culture, Leisure & Lifestyle	
	The destroyer *Downes* is transferred from Coast Guard to naval control and sails for Philadelphia, where in 1934 it will be sold for scrap in accordance with the London Naval Treaty. . . . The Navy regains custody of the *Ammen* destroyer after seven years of Coast Guard control.	*The Annalist* releases its weekly index of U.S. wholesale commodity prices. At 102.5 the figure is a decrease of 1.3 points from the previous week, and a decline of 25 percent from the corresponding period a year ago. Economists say the drop from last week was caused by decreases in farm products, food products, and building materials.	The National Electric Light Association reports U.S. electric power output for the past week amounted to 1,614,135,000 kilowatt hours, 15 million kilowatt hours more than the preceding week, but a decrease of 3.4 percent from the corresponding period one year ago. The increase is attributed to rising power consumption by Americans living in Atlantic coastal towns.		May 22
	The heavy cruiser *Augusta* is reassigned as the flagship of the Atlantic Scouting Force. *Augusta* and her crew would have the honor of transporting U.S. Presidents Franklin Roosevelt and Harry Truman during World War II. *Augusta* was constructed by the Newport News Shipbuilding Company in 1928.	Argentine economists report their country's foreign trade for the whole of 1930 was $362,717,800 less than the total from 1929.	Construction workers complete a $1 million renovation of the famous Atlantic City boardwalk that extends its length to more than two miles. It was originally constructed in 1870 to prevent sandal-clad tourists from tracking sand into beachfront hotels.	World featherweight boxing champion Christopher "Bat" Battalino retains his title by defeating favored fighter Fidel La Barba in 15 rounds before a crowd of 12,000 at New York City's Madison Square Garden.	May 23
The U.S. Potters' Association announces that based on an agreement between unions and employers, professional potters' salaries will be reduced by an average of 10 percent beginning on October 1, 1932.	The War Department awards contracts to seven separate aircraft companies for 56 military airplanes and 130 engines at a total cost of $1,961,001.67.	*The Annalist* releases its weekly index of U.S. business activity. At 77.4, the figure is a drop of 0.4 points from the previous week and a decline of 16 percent from the corresponding period last year. Economists say the drop from last week was caused by declines in steel mill activity and cotton cloth production.			May 24
The Emergency Committee for Employment reports that during April, 7,296 miles of road were constructed at a cost of nearly $100 million, more than double the total of April 1930.		The U.S. National Association of Manufacturers urges its members to cut retail prices in order "to provide greater employment for workers and dividend payments to thousands of investors."			May 25
		The weekly index of U.S. automobile production as compiled by the Department of Commerce is released. The index currently stands at 70.5, a rise of 0.9 points from the previous week, but a decline of 25 percent from the corresponding week one year ago.	Inventor Thomas Edison suffers acid burns while conducting an experiment at his laboratory in Fort Myers, Fla. His only explanation for the mishap: "Got hold of a bottle with the wrong label."	The world champion Philadelphia Athletics win their 17th consecutive game, only three games behind the Chicago Cubs' record of 20 consecutive games that was set in 1880.	May 26
		Freight car loadings for the past week amounted to 747,732 cars, according to figures published by the American Railway Association. The total is 283 cars higher than the previous week, but a decline of 20 percent from the corresponding week last year. The rise from last week was attributable to gains in forest products and ore.	John Parkinson sets the Canadian flight altitude record, attaining a height of 22,000 feet over the skies of Montreal in his small Curtiss-Reid biplane.	Major League Baseball's American League elects William Harridge as its president. Harridge succeeds Ernest Barnard, whose term as president was tragically cut short by his untimely death at the age of 57.	May 27
The Census Bureau reports that U.S. automobile production in April amounted to 335,708 vehicles, an increase of 15 percent from the previous month's total of 395,011 vehicles.		*The Iron Age* releases its weekly index of U.S. steel mill activity. The index currently stands at 51.1, a drop of 1.1 points from the previous week, and a decline of approximately 40 percent from the corresponding week one year ago. The decline from the preceding week is attributable to regular seasonal influences.			May 28
The newly created Commission for the Study of Unemployment Insurance holds its first meeting in New York City.		*The Annalist* releases its weekly index of U.S. wholesale commodity prices. At 101.0, the figure is a drop of 1.5 points from the previous week, and a decline of 25 percent from the corresponding period a year ago. Economists say the decline from last week was caused by drops in farm products and metals.	The National Electric Light Association reports U.S. electric power output for the past week amounted to 1,600,063,000 kilowatt hours, 15 million kilowatt hours less than the preceding week, and a decline of 15 percent from the corresponding period one year ago. The National Electric Light Association attributes the drop from last week to ever-lessening power consumption in the industrial Midwest.		May 29
The Justice Department releases figures showing there were 18 percent fewer murders committed nationwide in April than in March.		The U.S. Department of Commerce reports that 3,531,000 barrels of grain were exported out of the United States during April, more than twice the total from March.			May 30

F	**G**	**H**	**I**	**J**
Includes elections, federal-state relations, civil rights and liberties, crime, the judiciary, education, healthcare, poverty, urban affairs, and population.	*Includes formation and debate of U.S. foreign and defense policies, veterans affairs, and defense spending. (Relations with specific foreign countries are usually found under the region concerned.)*	*Includes business, labor, agriculture, taxation, transportation, consumer affairs, monetary and fiscal policy, natural resources, pollution, and accidents.*	*Includes worldwide scientific, medical, and technological developments, natural phenomena, U.S. weather, and natural disasters.*	*Includes the arts, religion, scholarship, communications media, sports, entertainment, fashions, fads, and social life.*

	World Affairs	Europe	Africa & The Middle East	The Americas	Asia & The Pacific
May 31		Legislation is introduced in Belgium that would make French the country's second official language along with Flemish, and would require all state officials to be proficient in both languages.		Argentine Finance Minister Enrique Uriburu reports that exports for the first four months of 1931 amounted to 220 million gold pesos, 12 percent less than the corresponding period in 1930.	
Jun. 1	Mayor James Curley of Boston, Mass., travels to Rome to meet with Pope Pius XI. Boston is home to the United States' largest concentration of Roman Catholics.	British economists report the Bank of England took in £435,019 worth of gold during the past week, against £10,000 withdrawn, netting a surplus of £425,019. Approximately £236,000 was deposited by South Africa. . . . French economic officials report total government revenue in April was 190 million francs below the corresponding total from last year.		Canadian economists estimate their country's federal budget deficit for the fiscal year ended March 31 to be nearly $100 million. Lawmakers anticipate a reduction in public works projects spending of $40 million, as well as a sales tax increase, will be needed to reduce the deficit.	Three hundred Filipino Communists are arrested on charges of sedition during what officials call the largest political crackdown in the history of the Pacific island nation.
Jun. 2	The Egyptian government sells 25,600 bales of cotton to the Soviet Union.			Fifteen thousand Mexicans march in the annual Dia Comercio (Commercial Day) parade. Many marchers carry banners with anti-Semitic slogans, including, "The Mexican People Will Never Be Enslaved By Voracious Jews.". . . Canadian Premier Paul Bennett announces in his annual budget speech to the House of Commons that his government will begin raising tariffs on over 200 dutiable items. The tariff raises are expected to most negatively affect American commerce.	
Jun. 3	President J.M. Moncada of Nicaragua awards medals of recognition to 19 U.S. servicemen for their service in providing relief for those suffering from a devastating earthquake that struck the capital of Managua earlier this year.			Brazil officially legalizes gambling, a decision criticized in local newspapers, but praised by government officials who say it will provide a tremendous source of revenue.	
Jun. 4	John Lawson, chief British delegate to the International Labor Conference, defends his country's unemployment system to his international counterparts in Geneva, Switzerland. He notes that personal savings accounts have increased, and public drunkenness and begging have lessened considerably.			Argentine economists report that the number of bank failures in May was more than double the total from May 1930.	
Jun. 5	U.S. Secretary of State Henry Stimson travels to Europe to discuss with his international counterparts the upcoming 1932 international disarmament conference.	The Socialist Broadcasting Society suspends its programming for 30 minutes in protest against a Dutch radio commission's decision to prohibit the broadcast of a "socialist play." . . . The National Bank of Bulgaria reduces its discount rate by 0.5 percent, from 9 percent to 8.5 percent. . . . A special commission appointed by Prime Minister Ramsay MacDonald recommends a reduction of $165 million in annual unemployment program funds.			
Jun. 6	Soviet work visas are denied to six American clergymen, in what officials describe as a cautious prevention against a possible religious subversion of the atheist Soviet Union. Many of those who were denied visas expressed admiration for the Soviet socialist system. . . . The Bank for International Settlements announces it currently has $408,841,505 in total assets.	Austrian Federal Railways general manager Dr. Strafella is forced out of office by President Wilhelm Miklas. Miklas says the decision was influenced in part by Strafella's pronounced devotion to fascist principles. . . . Presidential elections are held in Belgium. Jules Renkin is declared the victor over incumbent Henri Jaspar. . . . The Soviet Union purchases from Argentina 180,000 salted steer hides, one of the largest single orders of agricultural goods made by the Soviet Union since its inception.		By vote of 17–11, the Bermudan parliament votes to reject a bill that would have sharply increased cruise ship fares. The Mid-Ocean newspaper characterizes the vote as a victory for Bermuda's tourism industry.	

A	B	C	D	E
Includes developments that affect more than one world region, international organizations, and important meetings of world leaders.	Includes all domestic and regional developments in Europe, including the Soviet Union.	Includes all domestic and regional developments in Africa and the Middle East.	Includes all domestic and regional developments in Latin America, the Caribbean, and Canada.	Includes all domestic and regional developments in Asian and Pacific nations (and colonies).

U.S. Politics & Social Issues	U.S. Foreign Policy & Defense	Economics & Great Depression	Science, Technology & Nature	Culture, Leisure & Lifestyle	
The trial of the Bank of the United States enters its 10th week of proceedings.	War Secretary Patrick Hurley enthusiastically announces in a radio speech broadcast nationwide that "the army is better organized, better trained, better equipped, better housed and better officered than ever before in peace time."				May 31
	The U.S. Navy recommissions the destroyer *Breese* after nearly a decade of inactivity. *Breese* will be stationed at Pearl Harbor on December 7, 1941, and engage in open combat with attacking Japanese fighter planes, sustaining minimal damage.	The Argentine newspapers *La Nacion* and *La Prensa* echo recent statements made by the Argentine Ambassador to the United States in printed editorials criticizing the United States' tariff policies. . . . Prof. Irving Fisher's index of international commodity prices falls to 70.8, the lowest index of this year. Fisher, a world renowned economist, famously commented a few days before the 1929 stock market crash that "stock prices have reached what appears to be a permanently high plateau."		Archbishop Cardinal Raymond Rouleau of Quebec, the only Canadian Cardinal, succumbs to angina pectoris and dies at the age of 65.	Jun. 1
New York City Public Welfare Deputy Commissioner C.J. Dunn announces the Municipal Lodging House will discontinue providing free lunches to thousands of the city's unemployed residents.	Col. Robert Patterson is chosen to replace Gen. Merritte Ireland as Army Surgeon General. Ireland resigned earlier this month as he reached the Army's mandatory retirement age.	The weekly index of U.S. automobile production as compiled by the Department of Commerce is released. The index currently stands at 75.3, a gain of 4.8 points from the previous week, but a decline of 26 percent from the corresponding week one year ago. The rise from last week was caused by a decrease in worker attendance due to the Memorial Day holiday, offset by increases by the Chevrolet Motor Company, say leading economists.		Funeral services are held for Canadian Archbishop Cardinal Raymond Rouleau.	Jun. 2
A statue of Jefferson Davis, president of the Confederacy during the Civil War, is unveiled in Statuary Hall on Capitol Hill. The statue's sculptor was commissioned by Missouri, the second state to secede from the Union prior to the Civil War. . . . Democrats in Congress criticize the recent Canadian tariff increases, regarding them as a direct retaliation for the 1930 Smoot-Hawley Tariff Act.		The American Railway Association reports that freight car loadings for this week amounted to 755,071 cars, 7,339 cars above last week, but a reduction of 25 percent from the corresponding week last year. The gain from last week was attributable to rises in coal, ore, coke, and grain products.			Jun. 3
In a radio speech broadcast throughout the country, American newspaper mogul William Randolph Hearst tells listeners that a "$5 billion construction program" will be needed to alleviate America's unemployment crisis.	The *New York Times* describes American engineer John Calder, who is assisting the Soviet Union in the construction of large steel mills, as a "world-meddling troublemaker."	*The Iron Age* releases its weekly index of U.S. steel mill activity. The index currently stands at 49.0, a drop of 2.1 points from the previous week, and a decline of approximately 44 percent from the corresponding week one year ago. The drop from the preceding week is attributed to a sharp drop in pig iron production.	Ten thousand insects are shipped from South America to Louisiana, where they will be unleashed onto farm fields to eliminate parasites that each summer nearly devastate Louisiana's sugar crop.	Bishop James Cannon of the Washington, D.C., Methodist Episcopal Church files a libel suit against Rep. George Tinkham for his claims that Cannon accepted illegal campaign contributions during the 1928 congressional elections.	Jun. 4
The annual meeting of the National Automobile Chamber of Commerce is held on Madison Avenue in New York City. The meeting includes speeches from the heads of over a dozen major U.S. automobile manufacturers.		The U.S. National Automobile Chamber of Commerce reports that automobile production declined by 4 percent in May as compared to April.	The National Electric Light Association reports U.S. electric power output for the past week amounted to 1,564,576,000 kilowatt hours, 35 million kilowatt hours less than the preceding week, and a decline of 3.8 percent from the corresponding period one year ago. The National Electric Light Association attributes the drop from last week to the Memorial Day national holiday.	Retired American golfer Bobby Jones announces that after three months of attempting a film career in Hollywood, Calif., he has grown weary of the glitz and glamour, and will practice law in his hometown of Atlanta, Ga., as soon as his contract with Warner Bros. expires.	Jun. 5
Reputed gangster Al "Scarface" Capone is indicted by a Chicago federal grand jury on charges of evading income taxes totaling $215,080.48.		*The Annalist* releases its weekly index of U.S. wholesale commodity prices. At 100.4, the figure is a drop of 0.6 points from the previous week, and a reduction of 24 percent from the corresponding period a year ago. Economists say the drop from last week was caused by drops in farm products and metals.			Jun. 6

F	G	H	I	J
Includes elections, federal-state relations, civil rights and liberties, crime, the judiciary, education, healthcare, poverty, urban affairs, and population.	*Includes formation and debate of U.S. foreign and defense policies, veterans affairs, and defense spending. (Relations with specific foreign countries are usually found under the region concerned.)*	*Includes business, labor, agriculture, taxation, transportation, consumer affairs, monetary and fiscal policy, natural resources, pollution, and accidents.*	*Includes worldwide scientific, medical, and technological developments, natural phenomena, U.S. weather, and natural disasters.*	*Includes the arts, religion, scholarship, communications media, sports, entertainment, fashions, fads, and social life.*

	World Affairs	Europe	Africa & The Middle East	The Americas	Asia & The Pacific
Jun. 7	The Argentine Bank of the Nation ships $881,630 worth of gold aboard the *American Legion* liner to New York City. The shipment is expected to improve the exchange rate of the slumping Argentine peso.	The Austrian National Bank raises its discount rate from 5.5 percent to 6 percent. . . . British economists report the number of unemployed Britons has increased by nearly 1 million during the past year.		Colombian Finance Minister Francisco de Paula Perez reports that due to fiscal conservancy measures implemented by President Enrique Herrera, Colombia will enjoy a balanced federal budget for the first time in nearly 30 years.	
Jun. 8		British economists report the Bank of England took in £918,160 worth of gold during the past week, against £245,955 withdrawn, netting a surplus of £672,205. Of the £918,160 taken in, approximately £580,000 was deposited by South Africa.		The exchange rate of the Argentine peso falls to 144.85, with 100 U.S. dollars equaling 144.85 gold pesos.	
Jun. 9	During an interview with European press, British First Lord of the Admiralty A.V. Alexander expresses fear of an impending world war. "Unless we can remove the hate and fear of one another," he says, "we will go to the greatest war in history within a short time."	The Carnegie Endowment for International Peace president Nicholas Butler travels to the troubled region of central Europe. . . . Catholic officials in Vatican City undertake the first steps toward the canonization of Pope Pius X, who died in 1914 at the outbreak of World War I.			Chinese Communist rebels advance on the city of Foonchow, prompting officials to warn foreign nationals to leave the city immediately.
Jun. 10	A group of American excavators under the auspices of the American School of Archaeology uncover a 1,500-year-old irrigation system on the site of what once was ancient Athens.	Herr von Plessen of the German Foreign Office formally protests the inferiority of his country's navy as stipulated by the 1919 Versailles Treaty.			
Jun. 11	The Amateur Athletic Union reports that 3,500 athletes representing 40 nations have registered to compete in the upcoming 1932 Summer Olympic Games in Los Angeles, Calif.	France and Great Britain enter into a new trade pact, whereby they will reduce tariffs on each other's imported goods, so as to better promote commerce between the two European nations. . . . The British Board of Trade reports that Great Britain's exports in May fell by 34 percent as compared to May of last year. Imports fell by 23 percent.	France appoints Louis Jacques Fousset to the vacant post of colonial head of Mali.	Bolivian Foreign Minister Daniel Bustamante announces his resignation, citing health reasons.	
Jun. 12		Irish Civil Guards combing the mountains of Dublin discover what they believe to be the headquarters of the banned Irish Republican Army. A cache of weapons was uncovered, including 50 rifles and several high-powered explosives.		Cuba formally asks the United States to lower its tariff rates on imported Cuban sugar, as Cuba heavily relies on U.S. markets to promote economic growth.	After 54 hours of searching, rescue efforts are abandoned for 18 seamen trapped in the British submarine *Poseidon*, which sank off the coast of China following an accidental collision with the Chinese steamer *Yuta*.
Jun. 13	The British ship *Shuben Acadia* is sunk 50 miles off the U.S. Atlantic Coast after sustaining damage from an intentional collision by the U.S. Coast Guard destroyer *Davis*. Coast Guard officials claim the *Shuben Acadia* was used to smuggle rum.		A bill is passed in Turkey restricting foreign aliens from working in certain professions, including law, medicine, and public transportation.		A group of mountain climbers hailing from both Great Britain and Nepal begin an ascent of the Kamet Mountain in India. After a laborious journey, they will eventually accomplish the first successful ascent of the 25,000-foot-high mountain.
Jun. 14				President Juan Batista Perez of Venezuela announces his resignation in the midst of repeated threats of impeachment. Congress sets the date of a new presidential election for June 19. Foreign Affairs Minister Itriago Chacin is selected as the acting president. Perez only served two years of a seven-year term, having been elected in May 1929.	

A	B	C	D	E
Includes developments that affect more than one world region, international organizations, and important meetings of world leaders.	*Includes all domestic and regional developments in Europe, including the Soviet Union.*	*Includes all domestic and regional developments in Africa and the Middle East.*	*Includes all domestic and regional developments in Latin America, the Caribbean, and Canada.*	*Includes all domestic and regional developments in Asian and Pacific nations (and colonies).*

U.S. Politics & Social Issues	U.S. Foreign Policy & Defense	Economics & Great Depression	Science, Technology & Nature	Culture, Leisure & Lifestyle	
	Capt. Hayne Ellis replaces Capt. Harry Baldridge as Director of the Office of Naval Intelligence.	*The Annalist* releases its weekly index of U.S. business activity. At 76.7, the figure is a gain of 0.3 points from the previous week, but a decline of 18 percent from the corresponding period last year. . . . The average stock price on the New York Stock Exchange falls to the lowest point of 1931, or 46 percent below the corresponding period in 1930.			Jun. 7
The trial of Bank of the United States president Bernard Marcus enters its 11th week of proceedings		Prof. Irving Fisher of Yale University releases his weekly index of international commodity prices. The figure is 70.0, a drop of 0.3 points from the preceding week, and a decline of 19 percent from the corresponding week a year ago.		Babe Ruth is presented the Silver Slugger Award for the 1930 season by Baseball Writers' Association president Daniel M. Daniel.	Jun. 8
The Travelers Insurance Company reports that U.S. highway fatalities have increased by 5.47 percent this year as compared to last.		The weekly index of U.S. automobile production as compiled by the Department of Commerce is released. The index currently stands at 72.3, a drop of 3.0 points from the previous week, and a decline of 28 percent from the corresponding week one year ago. The drop from last week is attributed to a regular seasonal decline.		Dr. Earnest A. Hooton publishes *Up From the Ape*, in which he characterizes the theory of racial superiority as "a ridiculous boast." Proponents of the theory include French aristocrat Arthur de Gobineau, who wrote the 1855 *Essay on the Inequality of the Human Races*.	Jun. 9
In a sign of the desolate employment conditions plaguing the United States, 500 unemployed men in New York City form a line three blocks long behind the Sunshine Purity Ice Cream Company manufacturing plant, seeking to fill just four vacant truck driver positions. Plant superintendent Antonio Guardino mistakes the gathering crowd for an ensuing riot, and calls the police for protection.	The destroyer *Moody* is sold for $35,000 to the Metro-Goldwyn-Mayer film company. *Moody* would be altered to resemble a German submarine for use in the 1933 war epic *Hell Below*.	Freight car loadings for the past week amounted to 710,934 cars, according to figures published by the American Railway Association. The total is 44,137 cars less than the previous week, and a decline of 18 percent from the corresponding week last year. The drop from last week was attributable to losses in forest products, grain products, and livestock.	During a speech at the annual meeting of the American Psychiatric Association, Dr. A.A. Brill characterizes former U.S. president Abraham Lincoln as a "schizoid manic personality." In response, New York State Senator William Lathrop Love introduces legislation banning the practice of psychoanalysis, saying it is "akin to hypnotism," and has "an unhealthy effect on many persons, especially neurotic women."		Jun. 10
Six banks in Chicago with assets totaling $20 million close their doors, citing an excessive amount of withdrawals by depositors.	In accordance with the London Naval Treaty, the U.S. Navy scraps the destroyer *Hull*. . . . The U.S. Shipping Board approves a request by the U.S. Lines Co. to use the *Leviathan* as a tourist vessel.	*The Iron Age* releases its weekly index of U.S. steel mill activity. The index currently stands at 47.7, a drop of 1.3 points from the previous week, and a decline of approximately 45 percent from the corresponding week one year ago. *The Iron Age* adds that the drop from the preceding week is attributable to a regular seasonal decline.			Jun. 11
Chicago District Attorney E.C. Johnson announces that the arraignment for reputed gangster Al Capone, who was arrested earlier this month for income tax evasion, will be held in one week. . . . U.S. Education Commissioner William J. Cooper describes the Eighteenth Amendment as a menace to freedom in remarks to reporters.			The National Electric Light Association reports U.S. electric power output for the past week amounted to 1,561,810,000 kilowatt hours, 3 million kilowatt hours less than the preceding week, and a decline of 2.9 percent from the corresponding period one year ago. The National Electric Light Association attributes the drop from last week to decreased power consumption in the industrial Midwest.		Jun. 12
Seeking a method to keep the costs of old-age pensions under control, the Massachusetts state legislature passes a bill imposing a tax of $1 on all citizens of Massachusetts over 20 years of age. The so-called "age tax" is one of the first of its kind.		*The Annalist* releases its weekly index of U.S. wholesale commodity prices. At 100.5, the figure is nearly identical to the previous week, but a reduction of 25 percent from the corresponding period a year ago. Economists say the stabilization from last week was caused by drops in textile products and fuels, offset by gains in farm products and food products. . . . *Dun's Review* reports bank clearings for the past week totaled $7.9 billion, 22 percent below the corresponding week a year ago.			Jun. 13
Americans across the country celebrate Flag Day, commemorating the official adoption of the American flag by the Second Continental Congress in 1777. The holiday was created in 1916 by President Woodrow Wilson, who sought to improve his country's morale as America was preparing to enter World War I.		*The Annalist* releases its weekly index of U.S. business activity. At 75.3, the figure is a drop of 1.4 points from the previous week, and a decline of 19 percent from the corresponding period last year. Economists say the drop from last week was caused by reductions in freight car loadings, steel mill activity, electric power production, and automobile production.	International telephony experts report that Canadians are the world's most frequent telephone users, making approximately 10 percent more calls per capita than the United States, the nearest competitor.		Jun. 14

F	G	H	I	J
Includes elections, federal-state relations, civil rights and liberties, crime, the judiciary, education, healthcare, poverty, urban affairs, and population.	*Includes formation and debate of U.S. foreign and defense policies, veterans affairs, and defense spending. (Relations with specific foreign countries are usually found under the region concerned.)*	*Includes business, labor, agriculture, taxation, transportation, consumer affairs, monetary and fiscal policy, natural resources, pollution, and accidents.*	*Includes worldwide scientific, medical, and technological developments, natural phenomena, U.S. weather, and natural disasters.*	*Includes the arts, religion, scholarship, communications media, sports, entertainment, fashions, fads, and social life.*

	World Affairs	Europe	Africa & The Middle East	The Americas	Asia & The Pacific
Jun. 15	A record daily total of $42,000,000 is withdrawn from the Reichsbank's foreign exchange market.	British economists report the Bank of England took in £5,578,632 worth of gold during the past week, against £421,169 withdrawn, netting a surplus of £5,157,463. Of the £5,578,632 taken in, approximately £4,266,000 was deposited by Germany, and £1 million by South Africa.			The Chinese Nationalist government reports that 20,000 soldiers have been killed in recent battles with Communist rebels in the Hunan and Fukien provinces. Some 200,000 additional troops are dispatched to preserve order.
Jun. 16		The Hungarian National Bank raises its discount rate by 1.5 percent, from 5.5 percent to 7 percent. The Austrian National Bank raises its discount rate by 1.5 percent, from 6 to 7.5 percent. . . . Chancellor Heinrich Bruening of Germany issues an emergency decree greatly increasing tax rates. Bruening tells his citizens that the increases are necessary to meet World War I reparation obligations.		The entire Costa Rican Cabinet resigns in protest over Minister to Washington Manuel Quesada's failure to promote goodwill with the United States during his trip there earlier last week. The Cabinet members left their posts following a refusal by Quesada to resign.	
Jun. 17	Sir Donald Cameron replaces Sir Graeme Thomson as the British Governor-General of Nigeria.	Grand Duke Peter Nicolaievich of Russia, a direct descendant of Czar Nicholas I, dies at the age of 67 in France, where he had fled following the Russian Revolution of 1917. . . . The entire Austrian Cabinet quits amid internal tension over the failure of Austria's largest bank, the Creditanstalt. Newspapers speculate that a Cabinet with a Christian Social Party majority will be formed.	The Muslim Supreme Council begins drafting a memorandum of protest against what they perceive as unfair persecution against Muslims in Palestine. Upon completion, the letter will be distributed to the British government as well as to the League of Nations.		In China, future Vietnamese Communist leader Ho Chi Minh is arrested by British authorities.
Jun. 18			A group of Cameroonian natives sends a check worth $3.37 to the "starving in America." An article in the local *Bulu* newspaper that described poor conditions within the United States prompted the natives, most of whom live in abject poverty, to send the minuscule, yet generous, donation.	In an apparent act of violent demonstration against the government of President Gerardo Machado of Cuba, a bomb rocks one of Havana's largest churches, inspiring panic in dozens of solemn worshipers.	
Jun. 19	France appoints Gabriel Descemet to the vacant post of colonial head of Mauritania. . . . France appoints Louis Vingarassamy to the vacant post of colonial head of Gabon.	The British Labor Ministry asks Parliament to appropriate an additional $575 million in unemployment insurance funds.	British High Commissioner in Iraq Francis Humphreys tells members of the British Mandates Commission that after a decade of mandate status, Iraq "is now capable of self-government." Humphreys expects Iraq to join the League of Nations in late 1931.	A major flood in the Canadian province of Alberta forces the evacuation of hundreds of residents.	
Jun. 20	Seeking a way to prevent a potential banking meltdown in central Europe, President Herbert Hoover issues the Hoover Moratorium, urging Congress to suspend World War I reparation payments from Europe for at least one year. Influential congressional Democrats publicly state that Hoover's plan is an unnecessary conciliation.	In a single day, $14 million is withdrawn from the Reichsbank's foreign exchange market.	Spain selects Jorge Buenrostro to replace Francisco Jordana as the High Commissioner of Morocco.		U.S. Senator Harry Dawes of Missouri publicly advocates political independence for the Philippines, which was established as a U.S. territory in 1913 following a costly war. Filipino leaders invite Senator Dawes to speak before the Philippine legislature. . . . Chinese Communist rebel forces announce a cease-fire agreement has been reached with Generalissimo Chiang Kai-shek, commander of the Nation-alist army.
Jun. 21	Disillusioned Europeans express newfound hope over U.S. President Herbert Hoover's proposed moratorium of World War I debts. . . . At the International Coffee Conference in Sao Paulo, Brazil, delegates discuss the possibility of creating an "international coffee bureau."			Brazilian President Getulio Vargas, whose military junta seized power on October 24, 1930, announces the granting of a general amnesty to all political prisoners, effective July 5.	
Jun. 22	The German Reichstag passes a bill officially accepting the terms of U.S. President Herbert Hoover's proposed suspension of World War I reparation payments, also known as the Hoover Moratorium. . . . *The London-News Chronicle* declares in an editorial that the Hoover Moratorium is "the most important event that has occurred in Europe since the armistice."	British economists report the Bank of England took in £4,881,632 worth of gold during the past week, against £536,989 withdrawn, netting a surplus of £4,344,643. Approximately £3.8 million was deposited by Germany. . . . French President-elect Paul Doumer is inaugurated in Paris. . . . The Albanian Parliament fixes its country's federal budget for the fiscal year of 1931–32 at $6.3 million.		The Cuban city of Bayamo is placed by authorities under martial law following bloody clashes between National Guardsmen and hostile demonstrators. . . . Argentine economists report their country exported 484,366 tons of grain during the past week, a record total.	Chinese Communist rebel forces ambush a division of Generalissimo-President Chiang Kai-shek's Nationalist army, seizing 10,000 firearms.

A	B	C	D	E
Includes developments that affect more than one world region, international organizations, and important meetings of world leaders.	*Includes all domestic and regional developments in Europe, including the Soviet Union.*	*Includes all domestic and regional developments in Africa and the Middle East.*	*Includes all domestic and regional developments in Latin America, the Caribbean, and Canada.*	*Includes all domestic and regional developments in Asian and Pacific nations (and colonies).*

U.S. Politics & Social Issues	U.S. Foreign Policy & Defense	Economics & Great Depression	Science, Technology & Nature	Culture, Leisure & Lifestyle	
The 27th annual convention of the Advertising Federation of America commences in New York City with delegates numbering 1,500. A personal message written by President Herbert Hoover is delivered by Gilbert Hodges, president of the federation.		Prof. Irving Fisher of Yale University releases his weekly index of international commodity prices. The figure is 69.7, a drop of 0.3 points from the preceding week, and a decline of approximately 20 percent from the corresponding week a year ago.	The Wilkes-Barre Airways Co. announces that a daily air route from Pennsylvania to Buffalo will soon begin operation. It marks the first air route created providing daily service to Buffalo, an ideal Canadian tourist destination because of its close proximity to the Canadian border.	Monograms Pictures releases its feature film, a pirate action-adventure named *Ships of Hate*.	Jun. 15
U.S. State Undersecretary William Castle publicly states that if a financial disaster akin to the 1929 Wall Street crash were to occur in Germany, the United States would consider suspending or even eliminating World War I reparation payments.	An Army barracks in Honolulu, Hawaii, housing the 23rd Bombardment Squadron is engulfed in flames from an accidental fire and burns to the ground. Damages are estimated by Army officials to be $70,000.			World featherweight boxing champion Bat Battalino retains his title by defeating challenger Johnny Dotto in a fight held in Hartford, Conn.	Jun. 16
Hoping his pronounced guilt will garner sympathy and a lighter sentence, reputed gangster Al Capone pleads guilty in a Chicago courtroom to two felony counts of income tax evasion and one count of Prohibition violation. He faces a maximum sentence of 34 years imprisonment and a $90,000 fine. The presiding judge sets the sentencing to be held in two weeks.		Freight car loadings for the past week amounted to 760,890 cars, according to figures published by the American Railway Association. The total is 50,000 cars higher than the previous week, but a decline of 17 percent from the corresponding week last year. The rise from last week was attributable to gains in forest products, ore, and livestock.			Jun. 17
Prohibition officials announce that the number of agents assigned to investigate Prohibition violations will increase by 350 this summer, following a rigorous selection process and a subsequent two-week period of intense training.			The Harvard Archaeological Expedition discovers what they believe to be a 4,000-year-old inscription in a cave in the tiny Egyptian island of Uronarti.		Jun. 18
Salaries of Chicago's civil service employees are reduced by 10 percent in order to offset growing city budget deficits.		*The Annalist* releases its weekly index of U.S. wholesale commodity prices. At 100.8, the figure is a gain of 0.3 points from the previous week, but a decline of 21 percent from the corresponding period a year ago. Economists say the gain from last week was caused by rises in farm products and food products.		The Federation of German Motion Picture Theatre Owners calls on German legislators to ban the Howard Hughes-directed war epic *Hell's Angels*, contending that the film is "derogatory to the reputation of the German people." The film cost $3.8 million to produce, making it the most expensive movie to date.	Jun. 19
The American Gas Association reports that U.S. consumer gasoline sales have fallen by 3 percent during the past year.		*Dun's Review* reports U.S. bank clearings for the past week amounted to $8.8 billion, 29 percent less than the corresponding week in 1930.	The National Electric Light Association reports U.S. electric power output for the past week amounted to 1,581,220,000 kilowatt hours, 20 million kilowatt hours more than the preceding week, but a decline of 4.9 percent from the corresponding period one year ago. The National Electric Light Association attributes the rise from last week to a regular seasonal increase.		Jun. 20
Alabama residents express resentment over what they perceive as "outside interference" in the legal case of nine African Americans who are accused of raping two white women in the spring of 1931. The Supreme Court will later rule that the defendants were denied their constitutionally protected right to counsel. The case will come to be known as the Scottsboro Boys incident.		*The Annalist* releases its weekly index of U.S. business activity. At 74.4, the figure is a drop of 1.5 points from the previous week, and a decline of 19 percent from the corresponding period last year. Economists say the decline from last week was caused by reductions in freight car loadings and automobile production.	The German railcar *Schienzeppelin*, designed by engineer Franz Kruckenerg in 1929, sets the world land speed record for railed vehicles, traveling between Berlin and Hamburg at a speed of 230.2 kilometers per hour. A tremendous feat, the record will last for more than 20 years, finally being surpassed in 1954.	Legendary conductor Arturo Toscanini is released from an Italian prison following incarceration for his refusal to conduct a patriotic hymn penned by fascist authorities.	Jun. 21
		Four large New York City mutual savings banks simultaneously reduce their interest rates from 4 percent to 3.5 percent. . . . Prof. Irving Fisher of Yale University releases his weekly index of international commodity prices. The figure is 70, a rise of 0.3 points from the preceding week, but a decline of approximately 20 percent from the corresponding week a year ago.			Jun. 22

F	G	H	I	J
Includes elections, federal-state relations, civil rights and liberties, crime, the judiciary, education, healthcare, poverty, urban affairs, and population.	Includes formation and debate of U.S. foreign and defense policies, veterans affairs, and defense spending. (Relations with specific foreign countries are usually found under the region concerned.)	Includes business, labor, agriculture, taxation, transportation, consumer affairs, monetary and fiscal policy, natural resources, pollution, and accidents.	Includes worldwide scientific, medical, and technological developments, natural phenomena, U.S. weather, and natural disasters.	Includes the arts, religion, scholarship, communications media, sports, entertainment, fashions, fads, and social life.

	World Affairs	Europe	Africa & The Middle East	The Americas	Asia & The Pacific
Jun. 23	Great Britain announces the selection of its delegates for the upcoming session of the League of Nations Assembly. Among those present will be Foreign Secretary Arthur Henderson and Viscount Robert Cecil of Shelwood. . . . Netherlands Trading Company president Mynheer Van Aalst comments to the *New York Times* that the Hoover Moratorium "offers no real solution."	British Chancellor of the Exchequer Philip Snowden strongly recommends to Parliament a swift and complete acceptance of the Hoover Moratorium. Snowden's recommendation is met with uproarious applause from members of the House of Commons. . . . The stock exchanges of the Central European nations of Austria, Hungary, and Czechoslovakia experience a favorable reaction to the news of U.S. President Herbert Hoover's Moratorium.			
Jun. 24	Premier J.H. Scullin of Australia describes the Hoover Moratorium as "the first important step toward the solution of the world economic depression," and asks that it be extended to include Australia, whose debt to the United States amounts to approximately $15 million. . . . King Nadir Shah of Afghanistan signs a "treaty of neutrality" with the Soviet Union.				Famed aviator Charles Lindbergh announces he will make an "aerial tour" of the Far East sometime in the summer, pending approval by the Japanese government.
Jun. 25		The Belgian parliament approves a bill increasing Belgium's national defense budget by $6 million. . . . A rumor circulates in Romania that Magda Lupescu, mistress of King Carol II, recently overdosed on the barbiturate veronal.		The Canadian Board of Grain Commissioners reports that Canada's grain stock currently amounts to 116 million, 15 percent less than the total from the corresponding period in 1930.	
Jun. 26	During an address broadcast by the National Broadcasting Company, Puerto Rican Governor Theodore Roosevelt, Jr., urges the United States to establish the Caribbean island nation as a "laboratory" for the study of medicine and agriculture.	The Soviet-based Amtorg Trading Company requests approval from the United States to import a cargo of pulpwood. U.S. Treasury Secretary Andrew Mellon responds by saying Russia must offer proof the cargo is not a product of slave labor, as had earlier been the case.		The Chilean newspaper *Espectador* urges the nation of Colombia to accept the terms of Chile's proposed Latin-American customs union.	
Jun. 27	The American-made World War I epic *All Quiet on the Western Front* is permitted by the German Censor Board to be shown in movie houses owned by private German societies including "trade unions, veteran's associations, and peace leagues." The ruling reverses an earlier decision that enacted a complete and total ban of the film.	Five men in the Spanish capital of Madrid are arrested for the attempted assassination of Señor Gallarza, Spanish chief of police. . . . The Romanian Banca Generala temporarily closes its doors after failing to repay deposits totaling $5 million. Officials say the bank will be able to meet its obligations to its depositors within three years.		Relations between Bolivia and Paraguay worsen as quarrels over the disputed Chaco border region intensify.	
Jun. 28	The Argentine Ambassador to the United States, Manuel Malbran, is reassigned to the post of Ambassador to Great Britain following a speech in which he assailed the 1930 Smoot-Hawley Tariff Act. His replacement is Felipe Espil.	The Viennese newspaper *Arbeiter-Zeitung* reports that there were 80 labor strikes in 1930, compared to 202 in 1929, a decline of over 60 percent.		President Getulio Vargas of Brazil appoints a commission to create a new tariff scheme. The United States is expected to benefit most from the new scheme, as more than 50 percent of Brazil's total exports go to the U.S. market. . . . Canada's Bureau of Statistics reports gold production in April totaled 223,082 ounces, a record monthly total.	
Jun. 29	British economic officials predict a financial resurgence will occur after the passage of the Hoover Moratorium.	British economists report the Bank of England took in £1,117,653 worth of gold during the past week, against £299,984 withdrawn, netting a surplus of £817,669. Approximately £900,000 was deposited by South Africa. . . . Alexsandur Malinov of the Bulgarian Democratic Party is elected to his third term as president, succeeding incumbent Andrey Lyapchev, whose conservative economic policies did not bode well with poverty-stricken Bulgarian voters.		Argentina ships $12.5 million to London as part of a repayment of a loan issued late in 1930 by Barring Brothers & Morgan. . . . News of the Hoover Moratorium skyrockets prices on the Brazilian stock exchange.	

A	B	C	D	E
Includes developments that affect more than one world region, international organizations, and important meetings of world leaders.	Includes all domestic and regional developments in Europe, including the Soviet Union.	Includes all domestic and regional developments in Africa and the Middle East.	Includes all domestic and regional developments in Latin America, the Caribbean, and Canada.	Includes all domestic and regional developments in Asian and Pacific nations (and colonies).

U.S. Politics & Social Issues	U.S. Foreign Policy & Defense	Economics & Great Depression	Science, Technology & Nature	Culture, Leisure & Lifestyle	
		The weekly index of U.S. automobile production is released. The index stands at 64.2, a drop of 7.8 points from the previous week, and a decline of 31 percent from the corresponding week one year ago. The drop from last week is attributed to a rumor of massive downsizing by the Ford Motor Company. . . . The U.S. Treasury Department reports that the federal budget deficit has risen to $879,168,500, against a surplus of $199,978,000 in the corresponding week of 1930.	The British Royal Geographical Society awards its annual Patron's Medal to Antarctic expeditional Richard E. Byrd. . . . Temperatures in the U.S. town of Cedar Rapids reach 101°F, making it the hottest June 23 in the United States in more than 40 years. . . . Aviators Wiley Post and Harold Gatty establish a world record by flying around the world in a span of 8 days, 15 hours, and 51 minutes.		Jun. 23
Rep. Patrick H. Drewry of Virginia warns his fellow lawmakers that the passage of the Hoover Moratorium will have a debilitating effect on the U.S. economy. . . . The U.S. Federal Reserve Board reports there were 87 bank failures in May, compared with 64 in April, an increase of 26 percent.		Freight car loadings for the past week amounted to 732,453 cars, according to figures published by the American Railway Association. The total is 28,437 cars less than the previous week, and a decline of approximately 17 percent from the corresponding week last year. The decline from last week was attributable to losses in grain, forest products, and ore.			Jun. 24
Lawmakers consider placing a ban on gangster films following the accidental shooting death of a 12-year-old New Jersey boy during a playful yet fatal reenactment. . . . Four major American cigarette manufacturers simultaneously raise the wholesale price of cigarettes by 45 cents to $6.85. Tobacco shares on the New York Stock Exchange increase from 4.5 points to 11 points on the heels of the announcement.		The Iron Age releases its weekly index of U.S. steel mill activity. The index currently stands at 43.1, a sharp reduction of 4.6 points from the previous week, and a decline of approximately 50 percent from the corresponding week one year ago. The Iron Age adds that the drop from the preceding week is attributable to a decrease in steel purchases by major corporations.			Jun. 25
	The U.S. Navy transfers the armored cruiser Pennsylvania to Baltimore to begin the process of decommissioning.	The Annalist releases its weekly index of U.S. wholesale commodity prices. At 101.8, the figure is a rise of 1.1 points from the previous week, but a decline of 21 percent from the corresponding period a year ago. . . . The Federal Reserve Board reports brokers' loans on the New York Stock Exchange this week were $13 million less than the previous week, marking the 10th consecutive weekly decline.	An Arctic ascent record is claimed by members of the British Arctic Air Route Expedition, who attained a height of 10,880 feet while climbing the Arctic Mountains. The previous record was 9,660 feet.		Jun. 26
Rep. Leonard W. Schuetz, Democrat from Illinois, urges President Herbert Hoover to appropriate funds from the Federal Reserve Bank to provide relief for those affected by recent bank crashes. . . . The White House categorically denies repeated rumors of Prohibition repeal, which began circulating after Rep. Albert Johnson claimed President Herbert Hoover would soon make a "staggering announcement."	The Philadelphia Navy Yard completes construction of the heavy cruiser USS Minneapolis, one of many American ships that would be stationed at Pearl Harbor during the Japanese sneak attack on December 7, 1941.	New bond offerings on the New York Stock Exchange for the past week amounted to $188,141,000, the highest weekly total since April 10, 1931, according to published reports.	The National Electric Light Association reports U.S. electric power output for the past week amounted to 1,579,185,000 kilowatt hours, 2 million kilowatt hours less than the preceding week, and a decline of 11 percent from the corresponding period one year ago. The National Electric Light Association attributes the drop from last week to a decline in consumption by citizens residing near the Pacific coast.		Jun. 27
People's Lobby president John Dewey criticizes a recent speech made by President Herbert Hoover in which he stated "whatever the immediate [economic] difficulties may be, we know they are transitory in our lives and in the life of the nation."		The Annalist releases its weekly index of U.S. business activity. At 73.4, the figure is a reduction of 0.8 points from the previous week, and a decline of approximately 20 percent from the corresponding period last year. Economists say the drop from last week was caused by losses in steel mill activity, automobile production, and cotton cloth production.			Jun. 28
Four major Albany banks simultaneously reduce their interest dividend rates from 4.5 percent to 4 percent, a result of what officials say are "present economic conditions." . . . In a speech before members of the League for Industrial Democracy, Socialist Party presidential candidate Norman Thomas urges Congress to appropriate $5 billion for unemployment relief.		Prof. Irving Fisher releases his weekly index of international commodity prices. The figure is 70.3, a gain of 0.3 points from the preceding week, but a decline of approximately 20 percent from the corresponding week a year ago. . . . The price of U.S. cotton rises to $7.50 per bale on the heels of the announcement of the Hoover Moratorium.	Temperatures in Monticello, Fla., rise to 109°F, an all-time record for the state of Florida.		Jun. 29

F	G	H	I	J
Includes elections, federal-state relations, civil rights and liberties, crime, the judiciary, education, healthcare, poverty, urban affairs, and population.	Includes formation and debate of U.S. foreign and defense policies, veterans affairs, and defense spending. (Relations with specific foreign countries are usually found under the region concerned.)	Includes business, labor, agriculture, taxation, transportation, consumer affairs, monetary and fiscal policy, natural resources, pollution, and accidents.	Includes worldwide scientific, medical, and technological developments, natural phenomena, U.S. weather, and natural disasters.	Includes the arts, religion, scholarship, communications media, sports, entertainment, fashions, fads, and social life.

	World Affairs	Europe	Africa & The Middle East	The Americas	Asia & The Pacific
Jun. 30		Election returns in Hungary indicate that the Unity Party of Prime Minister Stephen Bethlen won over 90 percent of the total Hungarian parliamentary seats. Party opposition members claim the landslide is a result of voter fraud.		A group of nonunion newsboys in the Panamanian city of Balboa go on strike. . . . Unseasonable frosts in the Brazilian city of Sao Paulo reduce coffee crop estimates by 25 percent.	
Jul. 1	Rioting Communists in Berlin smash the windows of the U.S. Consulate building, in an apparent protest against the alleged unfair persecution of nine Alabamian African Americans accused of raping a white woman. Communist newspapers call on U.S. lawmakers to "save the victims of judicial murder."	Italy restores capital punishment after more than 40 years of abolishment. Convicted murderers previously faced a maximum penalty of life imprisonment.	Excavators in Jerusalem discover the remains of the 2,000-year-old "Wall of David."	Argentine economists report a favorable trade balance of 20 million gold pesos for the first five months of 1931.	Chinese Foreign Minister C.C. Wu announces his retirement.
Jul. 2	Belgium officially accepts the terms of the Hoover Moratorium.	A bomb explodes on a train stationed in the Yugoslavian city of Belgrade, the third such incident in Yugoslavia in as many weeks.		Peruvian officials report the entire southern area of Peru is under revolt. Troops are dispatched to engage in battles with hostile rebels and reinstall order. . . . Via a presidential decree, the Latin American nation of Costa Rica nationalizes its gasoline industry, echoing earlier decisions to nationalize its alcohol and insurance industries.	Chinese military officials estimate that recent lootings by Communist bandits have resulted in damages of $6 million. An estimated 200,000 troops are dispatched to engage in battles with the rebels, who are entrenched in the hills of Nanchang.
Jul. 3	U.S. diplomats report that after weeks of deadlock with France over the proposed Hoover Moratorium, they are now close to reaching an agreement that includes the granting of a $25 million credit loan. . . . Great Britain suggests an international parley to discuss France's objections to the Hoover Moratorium. . . . China refuses to allow the continuation of an American excavation in Mongolia, citing America's "arrogance."	British economists report the Bank of England's gold reserves increased by £408,000 this week as compared to last.		Argentine bankruptcies more than doubled in June 1931 as compared to June 1930, according to published reports. . . . Foreign Minister Mello Franco of Brazil formally rejects Chile's proposal of a Latin-American Financial Conference. . . . International human rights experts allege that Cuba unlawfully arrested citizens accused of organizing an assassination attempt against President Gerardo Machado.	Small-arms fire is exchanged along the Korean-Chinese border over an ownership dispute of water rights.
Jul. 4	Hungary receives a short-term credit loan of $20 million from the combined resources of the Federal Reserve Bank of New York, the Bank of England, the Bank of France, and the Bank for International Settlements.	By a vote of 277–24, the French Senate acts on War Minister Andre Maginot's recommendation to increase eastern frontier defense fortifications by $57 million.	Delighted by the news of the Hoover Moratorium, a couple in French Equatorial Africa name their newborn child "Hoover."	Bolivia announces the suspension of diplomatic relations with Paraguay, after weeks of heated debate over the disputed Chaco border region. All Bolivian diplomats situated in Paraguay are ordered to return to La Paz. . . . The Colombian Controller General estimates his country's federal budget deficit will rise to $34 million by the end of the year. . . . In what officials said was a demonstration against American colonial rule, the Philippine capital of Manila is shrouded in darkness for 30 minutes after bandits cut the wires of dozens of the city's electrical poles.	
Jul. 5	France officially accepts the terms of the proposed Hoover Moratorium. Passage of the moratorium still remains contingent upon U.S. congressional approval. . . . Albert Einstein personally condemns the public officials involved in the Scottsboro Boys rape case, involving African-American men accused of raping a white woman in Alabama.	The German Statistics Bureau reports that the population of the capital city of Berlin has increased from 1,888,000 to 4,297,000 since 1900.		Brazil's federal budget surplus rises to $4 million, according to figures published by Brazilian economic officials. . . . Bermuda celebrates Somers Day, commemorating the founding of its first settlement in 1515.	Australian economists report their country's exports have declined by 21 percent during the past year, from $455,130,000 to $580,855,000.
Jul. 6	The Automotive Division of the U.S. Department of Commerce reports that Americans own and operate nearly 75 percent of the world's total motor vehicles. The report adds that France is a distant second with ownership of 4 percent of the world's total vehicles.	British economists publish figures showing the Bank of England took in £1,584,985 worth of gold during the past week, £900,000 of which was deposited by South Africa.		Based on record shipments of grain and the announcement of the Hoover Moratorium, the exchange rate of the Argentine peso rises, with one peso equaling 32.28 American cents.	Following mob riots targeted at Chinese residents of Korea, 1,000 Chinese men and women are temporarily housed at the Chinese Consulate in Seoul to prevent further disturbances. Police arrest 100 Koreans said to be affiliated with the riots. . . . In China, American missionary Rev. Oscar Anderson is freed following three months of being held captive by Communist rebels. Gen. He Long demands a ransom of $75,000 for the release of a dozen other missionaries.

A	B	C	D	E
Includes developments that affect more than one world region, international organizations, and important meetings of world leaders.	Includes all domestic and regional developments in Europe, including the Soviet Union.	Includes all domestic and regional developments in Africa and the Middle East.	Includes all domestic and regional developments in Latin America, the Caribbean, and Canada.	Includes all domestic and regional developments in Asian and Pacific nations (and colonies).

U.S. Politics & Social Issues	U.S. Foreign Policy & Defense	Economics & Great Depression	Science, Technology & Nature	Culture, Leisure & Lifestyle	
	The destroyer USS *Stoddert* is reclassified as a miscellaneous auxiliary vessel and is renamed *AG-18*. . . . The U.S. Navy announces the cruiser *Olympia* has been reclassified as *IX-40*. It would become the only ship in the Spanish-American War to be preserved for museum use.	The U.S. Commerce Department's weekly index of U.S. automobile production is released. At 63.2, it is a decline of 1 point from the previous week, and a reduction of 29 percent from the corresponding week in 1930.	In Portland, Ore., temperatures rise to 102°F, establishing a record for the city.		Jun. 30
The New York City Public Welfare Department reports that $7 million will be needed to provide relief for the city's elderly in the upcoming fiscal year. . . . Senator Royal Copeland of New York criticizes President Herbert Hoover for his delay in providing debt relief to nations drowning in World War I reparations payments.		Freight car loadings for the past week amounted to 739,116 cars, according to figures published by the American Railway Association. The total is 6,663 cars less than the previous week, and a decline of 25 percent from the corresponding week last year. The drop from last week was attributable to losses in coke.	The AP reports that the death toll from the severe heat wave that swept across the United States last week has risen to 600 people.	New York City places a ban on fireworks celebrations for the Fourth of July holiday.	Jul. 1
The New York State Board of Education considers placing a ban on the reading of the Shakespeare play *Merchant of Venice*, contending it has stirred up anti-Semitic sentiment.		Uruguayan economists report their country net a trade balance of $2.5 million for the first six months of 1931. . . . The Standard Oil Company of New York reduces gasoline prices in what company officials say is a move to counteract ever decreasing consumer buying power. . . . *The Iron Age* releases its weekly index of U.S. steel mill activity. The index currently stands at 42.2, a decrease of 0.9 points from the previous week, and a decline of approximately 50 percent from the corresponding week one year ago.	The National Broadcasting Company applies to the Federal Radio Commission for an experimental 5,000-watt television station.	In a nontitle bout held in New Jersey, world featherweight champion Bat Battalino defeats Irish challenger Bobby Brady before a crowd of 7,000.	Jul. 2
	The Army announces that the entire disbanding of forces stationed in the Mitchel Airfield, near New York City, has been completed.	Stockholders of the Bethlehem Steel Corporation unanimously vote to cut company executives' salaries by nearly 10 percent. The reductions were first proposed by Chairman Charles M. Schwab, who sought to improve worker morale.	The annual International Congress of the History of Science and Technology is held in London, England. Delegates discuss designating biology as an independent science. . . . The National Electric Light Association reports U.S. electric power output for the past week amounted to 237,900,000 kilowatt hours, 1.7 million kilowatt hours more than the preceding week, but a decline of 4 percent from the corresponding period one year ago.		Jul. 3
The number of unemployed workers in the United States rises to 5.3 million. Despite this, the American Federation of Labor releases a survey showing consumer confidence to be improving as a result of the proposed Hoover Moratorium.		*The Annalist* releases its weekly index of U.S. wholesale commodity prices. At 102.2, the figure is a rise of 0.4 points from the previous week, but a decline of 18 percent from the corresponding period a year ago. Economists say the gain from last week was caused by rises in food products, textile products, fuels, and metals. . . . The U.S. Treasury Department announces the federal budget deficit has risen to $28,943,385.		Americans celebrate the 155th anniversary of the signing of the Declaration of Independence.	Jul. 4
Seeking to alleviate an increase in crime, the state of Michigan passes a bill requiring every owner of a firearm to have his or her fingerprints archived by police authorities.		A consortium of international economists announces that the Soviet Union's five-year plan, first conceived in 1928 with a primary focus on farming collectivization, is behind schedule. Soviet officials respond by saying the plan is near completion. . . . *The Annalist* releases its weekly index of U.S. business activity. At 73.7, the figure is a rise of 0.2 points from the previous week, but a decline of 20 percent from the corresponding period last year.	Germany loans the *LZ127 Graf Zeppelin* to Great Britain for use in a 24-hour tourist flight. Admission on the flight is expected to cost $150, say British aviation officials.	The third annual Conference of Anglo-American Historians is held in London, England, with 500 delegates representing both nations.	Jul. 5
The Association of Southern Women for Prevention of Lynching announces that lynchings within the continental United States have declined by over 83 percent during the past decade.		The Bank for International Settlements announces it currently has assets amounting to $342,388,288.	British aviatrix Amy Johnson, who in 1930 became the first woman to fly from England to Australia, announces plans for an upcoming flight from England to Japan across the Atlantic Ocean.		Jul. 6

F	G	H	I	J
Includes elections, federal-state relations, civil rights and liberties, crime, the judiciary, education, healthcare, poverty, urban affairs, and population.	Includes formation and debate of U.S. foreign and defense policies, veterans affairs, and defense spending. (Relations with specific foreign countries are usually found under the region concerned.)	Includes business, labor, agriculture, taxation, transportation, consumer affairs, monetary and fiscal policy, natural resources, pollution, and accidents.	Includes worldwide scientific, medical, and technological developments, natural phenomena, U.S. weather, and natural disasters.	Includes the arts, religion, scholarship, communications media, sports, entertainment, fashions, fads, and social life.

	World Affairs	Europe	Africa & The Middle East	The Americas	Asia & The Pacific
Jul. 7	German Foreign Minister Julius Curtius announces an accord has been reached with France over the terms of the proposed Hoover Moratorium after weeks of deadlocked debate. France had requested a guarantee from Germany that the funds derived from the moratorium would not be put toward remilitarization.	Members of the British House of Commons debate a bill that would reduce the workday of the nation's coal miners to 7.5 hours.	King Faisal I of Iraq arrives in the Turkish city of Angora for a three-day visit with President Mustapha Kemal.	A group of Nicaraguan rebels unsuccessfully attempts to capture the city of Limay.	
Jul. 8	Newspapers around the globe hail the Franco-German accord on the Hoover Moratorium as a step in the direction of international economic recovery.	Great Britain appoints former consul General to Los Angeles Richard Nosworthy to the vacant post of British Ambassador to Bolivia.		Newly appointed Argentine Ambassador to the United States Don Espil embarks on his first trip to the United States. . . . The Canadian Dominion Bureau of Statistics reports that this summer's wheat crop forecast is the lowest on record.	Philippine police authorities raid a private residence said to be the headquarters of a banned Communist organization. After days of exhaustively combing the premises, police uncover a cache of 200 weapons. . . . In a prelude to the Long March of 1934, Communist rebels in the Kiangsi province engage in a full retreat.
Jul. 9		Spanish lawmakers revise their constitution to grant full autonomy to the region of Catalonia. . . . Amid a strike of Spanish telephone industry workers, two undetonated bombs are found by police near newly erected telephone poles. Three men who police say are responsible for the attempted bombings are arrested.		Mexican Foreign Secretary Genaro Estrada alleges that U.S. authorities acted unlawfully in the fatal shooting of two Mexican students in Oklahoma on June 9, 1931.	
Jul. 10	International producers of lead agree to simultaneously curtail production by 5 percent so as to stabilize worldwide prices.	French economic officials announce that 12 billion francs worth of gold have been added to France's gold reserves during the past year. . . . Wages of over 200,000 British textile workers are reduced by 11.7 percent.		Argentina attempts to act as a mediator between Bolivia and Paraguay in the ongoing dispute over the Chaco border region. . . . A prison revolt in the Bulgarian city of Sofia results in the deaths of five inmates after soldiers are dispatched to reinstate order.	Secretary of State for India Wedgwood Benn describes Mohandas Gandhi as "a great force working for peace" during sessions of the British House of Commons.
Jul. 11	Via a decree issued by President Gerardo Machado, Cuba reduces its tariff on imported British whiskey by 20 cents, from $1 to 80 cents. The decision is regarded in international circles as a return of favor for Great Britain's tariff reductions on imported Cuban sugar and tobacco.	Leading German economists estimate Germany requires a long-term loan of approximately $474,600,000 in order to achieve financial stabilization.		Three Cuban university students in the capital of Havana are arrested for "terrorist" activities after a police raid uncovers a cache of bombs and small arms.	Australian Finance Minister Edward Theodore presents to members of the House of Representatives his budget forecast for the upcoming fiscal year. In it, he estimates a federal budget deficit of $86,078,310. . . . Chinese Finance Minister T.V. Soong reports in a budget forecast for the upcoming fiscal year that 87.5 percent of China's budget is reserved for military expenditures.
Jul. 12	Following a bipartisan meeting of high-ranking British officials who attempted to formulate a scheme for universal international disarmament, Field Marshal William Robertson declares that "the majority of the people in the world now think war hurts everybody and helps nobody—except the profiteers—and settles nothing."	The Social Democratic Party of Austria bans its members from visiting either Italy or the Soviet Union. . . . Physically disabled homeless men and women in Vienna, Austria, are given business cards by welfare officials identifying their occupation as "professional beggars." . . . A German man on trial in Potsdam for allegedly "disrespecting" the German national flag during a public ceremony claims his hoots and catcalls were merely the effect of him swallowing a lit cigarette.		Brazil suspends service on the Madeira-Mamore railroad route. . . . President Jose Guggiari of Paraguay commends Argentina's role in providing arbitration between Bolivia and Paraguay over the disputed Chaco border region.	
Jul. 13		Austrian economists report their country's foreign trade has declined by approximately 25 percent during the first five months of 1931 as compared to 1930. . . . British economists report the Bank of England took in £2,579,556 worth of gold during the past week, £793,000 of which was deposited by South Africa.	Belgian military officials dispatch 150 troops to quell a rebellion led by tribal warlords in the Belgian Congo.	President Carlos Ibanez of Chile appoints the task of selecting a new Cabinet to Pedro Blanquier after three days of total vacancy.	A parade in the Philippine capital of Manila originally intended to honor U.S. Senator Harry Hawes dissolves into a protest against American colonial rule, with shouts of "give us liberty or give us death" echoing throughout the streets.

A	B	C	D	E
Includes developments that affect more than one world region, international organizations, and important meetings of world leaders.	Includes all domestic and regional developments in Europe, including the Soviet Union.	Includes all domestic and regional developments in Africa and the Middle East.	Includes all domestic and regional developments in Latin America, the Caribbean, and Canada.	Includes all domestic and regional developments in Asian and Pacific nations (and colonies).

U.S. Politics & Social Issues	U.S. Foreign Policy & Defense	Economics & Great Depression	Science, Technology & Nature	Culture, Leisure & Lifestyle	
During a month-long strike of silk workers in Allentown, Pa., three silk mills are severely damaged by bombs that police say were planted to intimidate the striking workers. The explosions come on the eve of an arbitration meeting between mill owners and employees. . . . Construction begins in Cleveland, Ohio, on a $12 million sewer system that officials estimate will provide employment for approximately 500 idle workers.		The weekly index of U.S. automobile production as compiled by the Department of Commerce is released. The index currently stands at 64.6, an increase of 1.4 points from the previous week, but a decline of 5 percent from the corresponding week one year ago.	A raging inferno blazing through the Romanian city of Bucharest forces the evacuation of over 100 families.	The first annual International Wine Tasting Conference is held in London, England. Among those present at the festivities is noted British science-fiction writer H.G. Wells, author of the 1895 novel *The Time Machine*.	Jul. 7
In remarks to the press, Senator James Couzens of Michigan describes President Herbert Hoover's proposed moratorium as "dumb diplomacy." Despite this, Rep. John Tilson of Connecticut claims that Hoover has "sufficient support" from members of Congress, and predicts a speedy passage.		American economists report U.S. retail sales have declined by more than 2 percent during the past month. . . . *Lamborn & Co.* predicts the United States will have a sugar surplus of 658,000 tons by the end of 1931.	Monstrous floods in southern China cause the destruction of over 10,000 houses and the drowning deaths of 2,000 people.		Jul. 8
In a speech broadcast throughout the United States, Undersecretary of State William Castle says the Hoover Moratorium has "opened the gates to a return of prosperity." . . . The average price of cigarettes in the United States rises by 40 cents, following reports of record profits for the tobacco industry in the year ended July 1.		The U.S. Department of Commerce reports the U.S. received $17 billion in international reparation payments during 1930, a decrease of 15 percent from 1929. . . . The American Railway Association reports U.S. freight car loadings for the past week amounted to 759,290 cars, a decline of 21 percent from the corresponding week in 1930. . . . *The Iron Age* releases its weekly index of U.S. steel mill activity. The index currently stands at 41.2, a decrease of 1.0 points from the previous week, and a decline of approximately 50 percent from the corresponding week one year ago.	The U.S. Agriculture Department estimates 1931's cotton acreage to be 41.5 million acres, the lowest estimate since 1923. . . . In its annual report, the Actuarial Society of America announces that the number of U.S. deaths attributable to airplane crashes has declined by 325 percent since 1928.	New Jersey boxing officials announce Primo Carnera will challenge Max Schmeling for the title of world heavyweight champion this September in Jersey City.	Jul. 9
During a campaign speech, New Jersey gubernatorial candidate David Baird calls President Herbert Hoover "the world's savior."		*The Annalist* releases its weekly index of U.S. wholesale commodity prices. At 102.6, the figure is an increase of 0.3 points from the previous week, but a decline of 18 percent from the corresponding period a year ago. Economists say the rise from last week was caused by gains in farm products, food products, and fuels.		British golfer Percy Allis shoots a 67 in the second round of the Canadian Open golf championship, the lowest score for any round in the Open's history. . . . Germany officially bans the sale and distribution of German author Erich Remarque's World War I novel *All Quiet on the Western Front*. The decision echoes an earlier motion that prohibited the showing of the novel's film adaptation.	Jul. 10
Columbia University education professor Dr. Thomas Briggs urges Congress to adopt a national high school curriculum.		*Dun's Review* reports U.S. bank clearings have declined by approximately 15 percent over the past year.		In an op-ed piece in the *New York Times*, screen legend Will Rogers first writes a saying that would be repeated far beyond his passing: "Why play Wall Street and die young when you can play cowboy and never die," he philosophically opines.	Jul. 11
		The British Board of Trade reports Great Britain's exports for the month of June amounted to £29,430,000. . . . *The Annalist* releases its weekly index of U.S. business activity. At 74.3, the figure is a gain of 0.4 points from the previous week, but a decline of 17 percent from the corresponding period last year. Economists say the rise from last week was caused by increases in freight car loadings and automobile production.	The Ford Motor Company introduces the Model A convertible sedan "Sunshine Saloon," the price of which will range from $385 to $570, say company officials.	American Francis Brobell claims the world motorboat speed record by traversing the waters of Albany, New York, at a speed of 51.836 miles per hour.	Jul. 12
Twelve hundred railroad workers in Central Falls, R.I., go on strike, protesting low wages and poor working conditions.		Members of the Federal Reserve Bank of New York consider granting a loan worth $100 million to the German Reichsbank. . . . The assets of the B&O Railroad Company rise to $1.2 billion.		A historic baseball match is held in St. Louis between the Cardinals and the Chicago Cubs. A stadium record of 45,715 people witness the Cardinals establish a team record for doubles in a single game, with 23.	Jul. 13

F	G	H	I	J
Includes elections, federal-state relations, civil rights and liberties, crime, the judiciary, education, healthcare, poverty, urban affairs, and population.	Includes formation and debate of U.S. foreign and defense policies, veterans affairs, and defense spending. (Relations with specific foreign countries are usually found under the region concerned.)	Includes business, labor, agriculture, taxation, transportation, consumer affairs, monetary and fiscal policy, natural resources, pollution, and accidents.	Includes worldwide scientific, medical, and technological developments, natural phenomena, U.S. weather, and natural disasters.	Includes the arts, religion, scholarship, communications media, sports, entertainment, fashions, fads, and social life.

	World Affairs	Europe	Africa & The Middle East	The Americas	Asia & The Pacific
Jul. 14	The annual British and American Students' Conference commences in Ann Arbor, Mich., where delegates urge the United States to officially join the League of Nations. . . . Canada grants economic most-favored-nation status to Australia, contingent upon approval by the respective parliaments of each nation.		Belgian officials announce the administrative costs of the Belgian Congo are currently running at a $2 million deficit.	Provisional President Jose Uriburu of Argentina declares in a statement that he has no plans to hold presidential or congressional elections "within any given space of time." Earlier rumors claimed elections would be held on November 8. Uriburu accepts the resignation of Provisional Governor of the State Senhor Jualberto.	
Jul. 15	Greece notifies the Bank for International Settlements that it will not support the proposed Hoover Moratorium.	Spain begins the process of drafting a new constitution after nearly a half century of monarchist rule. . . . In a measure to prevent excessive withdrawals, the Hungarian Cabinet Council votes to suspend operations of all Hungarian banks for three days. . . . Rumors begin to circulate in Germany that former Reichsbank president Hjalmar Schacht is close to establishing a "financial dictatorship" that would invalidate the terms of the 1919 Treaty of Versailles.		Forty Argentine army officers accused of planning a revolt in January 1930 are transferred by authorities to the Ushuaia penal colony. . . . The 15th Regiment of the Peruvian army incites a hostile rebellion against the regime of President Luis Cerro. The rebellion ultimately fails, and regiment commander Col. Cabrera is court-martialed.	
Jul. 16	By a vote of 103–42, the World Zionist Organization elects Berl Locker as its New York representative.		An ancient city long-buried under the sands of Persia and estimated to be nearly 5,000 years old is discovered by Dr. Frederick R. Wulsin, American excavator.	Officials of the Panama Canal Zone begin experimental crop dusting over areas traditionally devastated each summer by thousands of parasitic mosquitoes. . . . Two German banks located in Brazil, the Banco Alleman Transatlantico and the Banco Germanico, experience heavy withdrawals following rumors of a potential collapse of the Reichsbank.	
Jul. 17		British economists report the Bank of England currently possesses £163,200,108 worth of gold, an increase of £10 million from the previous week, and the highest total of 1931 to date. . . . Belgian Foreign Minister Paul Hyams travels to London to discuss the Hoover Moratorium with his international counterparts.	Emperor Haile Selassie of Abyssinia signs into law his country's first ever constitution. Among the provisions of the document is the American model of a bicameral legislature. "In the future," he tells a group of visiting reporters, "everyone will be subject to the law."	Colombian lawmakers approve a federal budget of $41.5 million for the upcoming fiscal year, $2 million less than the previous year. Nearly 10 percent is allotted for military expenditures.	
Jul. 18	Delegates representing 24 nations at the International Convention for Limiting the Manufacture of Narcotic Drugs sign a cooperative agreement to curb the worldwide use of illegal drugs.	The Bank of Danzig, Poland, raises its discount rate by 1 percent, from 6 to 7 percent.		Bolivian Foreign Minister Ballon Mercado officially denies a Paraguayan press report that stated 5,000 Bolivian troops stationed along the border had received orders from military commanders to invade. "Bolivia once more affirms her pacific spirit and her to desire to solve the Chaco territorial dispute in a friendly way," he says.	
Jul. 19		Germany and Hungary sign a free-trade agreement after more than 15 years of economic disunity.	The Egyptian branch of the Deutsche Orient Bank closes its doors following a declaration of insolvency.	Health authorities in Mendoza, Argentina, close several public buildings after reports surface of an outbreak of pneumonia.	Senator Arthur Robinson of Indiana travels to the Philippines, where former Filipino president Emilio Aguinaldo urges him to convince his fellow Senators to grant independence to the Pacific island nation.
Jul. 20	The United States announces its official support of Harmadio Arias in his candidacy for the Panamanian presidency.	British military officials perform the first air raid defense simulation since 1928. . . . The T.F. Schroeder Banking Corporation of Germany closes its doors to its patrons for a week to undergo a period of "reorganization."	A bomb is detonated near the Egyptian Justice Ministry Building, shattering all of its windows. Lacking a suspect, Egyptian police speculate the bomb was planted by Wafdist members seeking an end to British military occupation.		
Jul. 21	Revolutionary leader Mohandas Gandhi is invited to serve as a member on a British committee that will attempt to formulate a new Indian constitution.	The trial of four French officials said to be connected with the Oustric Bank failure that occurred late in 1930 commences in Paris.		Juan Esteban Montero is appointed by Chilean authorities to the vacant post of interior minister. . . . The number of striking Brazilian textile workers rises to 70,000. Representatives say the workers demand a prohibition of child labor as well as an increase in wages.	In what is claimed as a prevention against potential Communist invasions, Chinese Vice Marshal Chang Hsueh-liang declares martial law in the cities of Peiping and Tientsin.

A	B	C	D	E
Includes developments that affect more than one world region, international organizations, and important meetings of world leaders.	*Includes all domestic and regional developments in Europe, including the Soviet Union.*	*Includes all domestic and regional developments in Africa and the Middle East.*	*Includes all domestic and regional developments in Latin America, the Caribbean, and Canada.*	*Includes all domestic and regional developments in Asian and Pacific nations (and colonies).*

U.S. Politics & Social Issues	U.S. Foreign Policy & Defense	Economics & Great Depression	Science, Technology & Nature	Culture, Leisure & Lifestyle	
For the first time in history, the Communist Party is listed on election ballots in Hudson County, N.J. . . . Based on the nationwide popularity of New York Governor Franklin D. Roosevelt, members of the Democratic National Committee consider holding the 1932 Democratic National Convention in California, considered a stronghold of President Herbert Hoover, who influential Republicans say is likely to receive his party's nomination for reelection.		Argentine Ambassador to the United States Don Espil requests the Brown Brothers & Co. banking firm to renew a $50 million loan granted to Argentina early in 1931. . . . The weekly index of U.S. automobile production as compiled by the Department of Commerce is released. The index currently stands at 69.2, a rise of 4.6 points from the previous week, but a decline of 17 percent from the corresponding week one year ago.	An airplane carrying eight Russian army officers crashes over the city of Alabino, instantly killing everyone aboard. Among those who perish in the fatal flight is the Russian Chief of Army Headquarters.		Jul. 14
William Edgar Borah, chairman of the Senate Foreign Relations Committee, comments on the Hoover Moratorium by saying, "there can be no permanent or durable peace that does not have its foundation in economic justice."		Colombian economists report a trade surplus of $35,228,181 for the first five months of 1931. . . . Freight car loadings for the past week amounted to 667,879 cars, according to figures published by the American Railway Association. The total is 91,411 cars less than the previous week, and a decline of 16 percent from the corresponding week last year. The drop from last week was attributable to reductions in forest products, coal, coke, and livestock.		Hawaiian youth Clarence Crabbe retains his title of AAU one-mile swimming champion during a match held in his native land.	Jul. 15
New York City Police Commissioner Edward Mulrooney begins a crackdown on fortune tellers, who he claims fraudulently obtain thousands of dollars each year from disillusioned poor people.	The battleship *Idaho* wins the Navy's annual battleship class gunnery competition.	*The Iron Age* releases its weekly index of U.S. steel mill activity. The index currently stands at 39.4, a drop of 1.8 points from the previous week, and a decline of approximately 50 percent from the corresponding week one year ago. . . . The Bethlehem Steel Corporation purchases the Farmers and Merchants Bank of Reedsville, Pa.	The Plattsburgh Broadcasting Corporation applies to the Federal Radio Commission for a new radio station. . . . An unseasonable heat wave on the East Coast claims the lives of dozens of people as temperatures rise to over 100°F.		Jul. 16
		The Annalist releases its weekly index of U.S. wholesale commodity prices. At 102.5, the figure is a drop of 0.1 points from the previous week, and a decline of 16 percent from the corresponding period a year ago. Economists say the drop from last week was caused by declines in farm products, textile products, and metals.	The National Electric Light Association reports U.S. electric power output for the past week amounted to 1,655,245,000 kilowatt hours, 75 million kilowatt hours more than the preceding week, and an increase of 8 percent from the corresponding period one year ago.	Great Britain wins the annual Lord Derby Cup international golf competition, besting the United States, which finished second, by a score of 11–5.	Jul. 17
Rep. Francis B. Condon of Rhode Island asks President Herbert Hoover to federally intervene in a strike of 2,500 textile workers.		*Dun's Review* reports U.S. bank clearings in the past week totaled $7,342,738,000, a decline of 27.3 percent from the corresponding week in 1930.		Governor Franklin Roosevelt of New York bans an upcoming simulated battle by the National Guard that was to be held in Albany, after receiving complaints from both Jewish and Christian clergymen that the battle violates Sabbath laws.	Jul. 18
		The Annalist releases its weekly index of U.S. business activity. At 73.5, the figure is a drop of 1.2 points from the previous week, and a decline of 18 percent from the corresponding period last year. Economists say the drop from last week was caused by losses in freight car loadings, steel mill activity, and cotton cloth production.		Eight Bishops in Germany officially protest the upcoming German Women's Sports Day, saying that "unnatural imitation of the gymnastics of men is in contradiction with the moral order."	Jul. 19
A seven-week strike of Alaskan fishermen ends after an independent arbiter successfully brokers an agreement between employers and workers.		Noted American economist Stuart Chase argues in a newly published essay that an "economic dictatorship" is the only realistic means to achieve financial stabilization.		The United States is eliminated by Great Britain in the annual Davis Cup international golf competition.	Jul. 20
Labor Department officials report the average price of food in the United States declined by 2 percent during the month of June.		The weekly index of U.S. automobile production as compiled by the Department of Commerce is released. The index currently stands at 69.5, a gain of 0.3 points from the previous week, and an increase of 38 percent from the corresponding week one year ago.			Jul. 21

F	G	H	I	J
Includes elections, federal-state relations, civil rights and liberties, crime, the judiciary, education, healthcare, poverty, urban affairs, and population.	Includes formation and debate of U.S. foreign and defense policies, veterans affairs, and defense spending. (Relations with specific foreign countries are usually found under the region concerned.)	Includes business, labor, agriculture, taxation, transportation, consumer affairs, monetary and fiscal policy, natural resources, pollution, and accidents.	Includes worldwide scientific, medical, and technological developments, natural phenomena, U.S. weather, and natural disasters.	Includes the arts, religion, scholarship, communications media, sports, entertainment, fashions, fads, and social life.

	World Affairs	Europe	Africa & The Middle East	The Americas	Asia & The Pacific
Jul. 22		British military officials say the recent air raid defense tests indicate that the city of London would be wholly unprepared to defend itself in the event of a surprise attack. . . . By a vote of 167–89, the British House of Commons rejects a bill that would have permitted sterilization of the mentally retarded.		A battle in the Argentine city of Corrientes between nationalist troops and hostile demonstrators results in the deaths of 100 soldiers.	
Jul. 23		The Austrian National Bank raises its bank rate by 2.5 percent, from 7.5 percent to 10 percent. . . . The Bank of England reports withdrawals totaling $16,911,700, the highest loss for a single day in the bank's history. . . . A strike of London wool combers ends as the combers accept an average wage reduction of 11.7 percent.		Argentine Col. Gregorio Pomar is given exile by Panamanian officials after fleeing from Argentina, following a failed revolt in the city of Corrientes that Pomar had masterminded. . . . Former president Plutarco Calles of Mexico is appointed president of the Banco de Mexico. . . . The Canadian Dominion Bureau of Statistics reports Canada's gold production in 1930 amounted to 2,012,068 ounces, a record yearly total.	
Jul. 24				President Jose Uriburu of Argentina orders the arrest of the editor of the socialist newspaper *Vanguardia*, following the appearance of an editorial that called for Uriburu's resignation.	Chinese military officials carry out bombing raids against Communist rebels stationed in the city of Shihchiachuang.
Jul. 25		A clash between Communist demonstrators and police in the Bulgarian city of Jamboli results in the deaths of two citizens.		The Argentine province of Entrerios is placed under martial law in what officials say is a move to prevent destructive civil disturbances. Nearly 1,000 suspected agitators are arrested. . . . Two students of the University of Chile are killed and 500 more are injured when a political demonstration on the streets of the Chilean capital of Santiago turns violent. President Carlos Ibanez del Campo calls an emergency conference to consider appropriate action.	
Jul. 26	A consortium of international economists releases figures showing that the American worker earns approximately 20–25 percent more than a worker from England. According to a report supplementing the figures, Americans earn higher wages "because the English employee produces proportionately less than the man in America."	A commercial plane carrying two Americans crashes over the Bulgarian city of Sofia, instantly killing everyone aboard.		Argentina ships $4 million worth of gold to the United States.	
Jul. 27		The German newspaper *Die Bank* assails the German government's hesitant stance on the proposed Hoover Moratorium.		Argentine economists report a favorable trade balance of $27,989,010 occurred in the first six months of 1931. . . . Brazilian economists report total coffee exports for the month of June were 20 percent below the same month of 1930.	
Jul. 28				The Argentine Bureau of Rural Statistics predicts in an official report that 1931's grain acreage will amount to 20 percent less than 1930's acreage.	
Jul. 29		King Alfonso XIII of Spain tells international reporters that "there is no truth whatsoever" to the repeated rumors of his upcoming abdication of the Spanish throne.			

A	B	C	D	E
Includes developments that affect more than one world region, international organizations, and important meetings of world leaders.	Includes all domestic and regional developments in Europe, including the Soviet Union.	Includes all domestic and regional developments in Africa and the Middle East.	Includes all domestic and regional developments in Latin America, the Caribbean, and Canada.	Includes all domestic and regional developments in Asian and Pacific nations (and colonies).

U.S. Politics & Social Issues	U.S. Foreign Policy & Defense	Economics & Great Depression	Science, Technology & Nature	Culture, Leisure & Lifestyle	
In an interview with reporters, former senator James Reed of Missouri describes the Hoover Moratorium as "sheer foolishness," saying that it would impose an unnecessary burden upon American taxpayers. . . . Polish native Edith Berkman is deported back to Poland by the Labor Department after an arrest for alleged "communist activities."			The National Electric Light Association reports U.S. electric power output for the past week amounted to 1,666,848,000 kilowatt hours, 11 million kilowatt hours more than the preceding week, but a decline of 29 percent from the corresponding period one year ago.	Commander in Chief C.A. Desaussure of the United Confederate Veterans declines an invitation to appear at an upcoming ceremony honoring former president Abraham Lincoln.	Jul. 22
The New York State capital of Albany celebrates the 245th anniversary of its founding.		Freight car loadings for the past week amounted to 763,581 cars, according to figures published by the American Railway Association. The total is 95,702 cars greater than the previous week, but a decline of 17 percent from the corresponding week last year. The rise from last week was attributable to gains in grain products, ore, coal, and livestock. . . . The Iron Age releases its weekly index of U.S. steel mill activity. The index currently stands at 41.8, an increase of 2.4 points from the previous week, but a decline of approximately 50 percent from the corresponding week one year ago.			Jul. 23
Rep. Allen Treadway of Massachusetts urges President Herbert Hoover to call a special session of Congress before it reconvenes in December in order to ensure speedy passage of the Hoover Moratorium.		The Annalist releases its weekly index of U.S. wholesale commodity prices. At 101.2, the figure is a drop of 1.3 points from the previous week, and a decline of 17 percent from the corresponding period a year ago. Economists say the drop from last week was caused by losses in farm products, food products, fuels, metals, and building materials.	After years of studious research, Prof. Martin Sprangling of Chicago University concludes that the alphabet was invented by the Semites, and not the Phoenicians as had been widely assumed.	The Philadelphia Athletics defeat the Cleveland Indians by a score of 5–2 to win their 10th consecutive game. . . . American boxer Bat Battalino retains the title of world featherweight champion by defeating challenger Freddy Miller in a 10-round title bout in Cincinnati, Ohio.	Jul. 24
	During a radio address broadcast throughout the United States, Governor Albert Richie of Maryland, a potential Democratic candidate for the 1932 presidential election, calls for an end to U.S. isolationism.	Bolivia reduces government employees' salaries by 15 percent in order to circumvent a further rise in federal budget deficits. . . . Upon returning from a visit to Brazil, British economist Otto Niemeyer recommends Brazilians create a central bank modeled after the U.S. Federal Reserve System.	The U.S. Commerce Department releases figures showing that the number of U.S. airfields increased by 206 during 1930. . . . A forest fire near Ocean City, N.J., results in the eradication of over 100 acres of "valuable" timber. . . . In a meeting between two of the 20th century's most influential figures, auto magnate Henry Ford visits inventor Thomas Edison in the latter's home in West Orange, N.J.		Jul. 25
		The Annalist releases its weekly index of U.S. business activity. At 74.8, the figure is a rise of 0.5 points from the previous week, but a decline of 13 percent from the corresponding period last year. Economists say the rise from last week was caused by increases in steel mill activity and electric power production.			Jul. 26
National Miners' Union of Pennsylvania relief secretary Alfred Wagenknecht is arrested for alleged Communistic activities. . . . Patrick Callahan of Louisville, Ky., is elected to the board of trustees of the National Child Labor Committee.		German trading activity is suspended following the declared insolvency of some of Germany's most widely used banks.			Jul. 27
In a statement issued to the press, Rep. Clarence Cannon of Missouri cites figures showing that 147,316 American farms have been abandoned by their owners in the past 10 years due to high tariffs. The statement adds that total farm income has decreased by approximately $2.5 billion.		The weekly index of U.S. automobile production as compiled by the Department of Commerce is released. The index currently stands at 63.1, a decline of 6.4 points from the previous week, but an increase of 39 percent from the corresponding week one year ago.	English aviatrix Amy Johnson, who in 1930 became the first woman to fly from England to Australia, completes the first stage of an unprecedented flight to Japan.		Jul. 28
Albany Public Works Commissioner James Lennon dies from a self-inflicted gunshot wound to the head.		Freight car loadings for the past week amounted to 757,755 cars, according to figures published by the American Railway Association. The total is 6,026 cars less than the previous week, and a decline of 17 percent from the corresponding week last year. The drop from last week was attributable to losses in coal and coke.	British aviatrix Amy Johnson lands in the Russian capital of Moscow after completing the first leg of her trip to Japan.		Jul. 29

F	G	H	I	J
Includes elections, federal-state relations, civil rights and liberties, crime, the judiciary, education, healthcare, poverty, urban affairs, and population.	Includes formation and debate of U.S. foreign and defense policies, veterans affairs, and defense spending. (Relations with specific foreign countries are usually found under the region concerned.)	Includes business, labor, agriculture, taxation, transportation, consumer affairs, monetary and fiscal policy, natural resources, pollution, and accidents.	Includes worldwide scientific, medical, and technological developments, natural phenomena, U.S. weather, and natural disasters.	Includes the arts, religion, scholarship, communications media, sports, entertainment, fashions, fads, and social life.

	World Affairs	Europe	Africa & The Middle East	The Americas	Asia & The Pacific
Jul. 30		A Russian man is arrested in the French city of Cannes for allegedly impersonating a member of the Romanov family, which ruled Russia from 1613–1917. . . . The Alpine Montangesellchaft, the largest Austrian steel company, closes its mines in the Erzberg Mountains, affecting nearly 1,000 workers.		Cuban police arrest a group of Communist organizers who planned to hold a demonstration in the capital city of Havana on August 1.	
Jul. 31		France and Italy begin talks to limit the growth of their respective navies. . . . Following a round of golf in the English capital of London, Prince Edward Windsor of Wales is injured in an accidental automobile collision.			
Aug. 1		In an editorial in the German National Socialist newspaper *Voelkischer Beobacher* (National Observer), future Nazi leader Adolf Hitler writes that "never in my life have I been in such high spirits." . . . Great Britain officially closes eight shipyards with a combined annual output of 276,000 tons.		A raid is conducted in Buenos Aires, Argentina, on an office building said to be the headquarters of a small Soviet commercial agency named Yuyantorg. Police arrest 100 employees on the grounds of engaging in communistic activity. . . . The Chilean National Savings Bank reopens its doors after four days of extensive reorganization.	
Aug. 2	In a statement released through the International Opponents of War Conference, acclaimed scientist Albert Einstein pleads with his colleagues not to apply their scientific minds to the creation of weapons. Ironically, in 1939 Einstein would write a letter to U.S. President Franklin Roosevelt advocating the study of nuclear fission, one of the common aspects of nuclear missile technology.	Spanish antiquity experts estimate the royal fortune of deposed King Alfonso XIII to be $8.5 million, placing him near the top of the list of the wealthiest deposed European monarchs.		Brazilian officials destroy 800,000 bags of coffee in an effort to balance supply and demand. . . . Canadian economists predict an increase in gold output of $6 million for the whole of 1931. . . . Brazil acts on Otto Niemeyer's centralized bank proposal and begins to introduce legislation that would create a system similar to the U.S. Federal Reserve Board.	The Chinese national government formally requests Japan to cease providing military and financial assistance to Communist rebels situated in the southern Chinese city of Canton.
Aug. 3		The Bank of England raises its bank rate by 1 percent, from 3.5 percent to 4.5 percent. . . . The British Royal Licensing Commission recommends to members of parliament to pass legislation to nationalize England's brewery industry. . . . Physicians of 68-year-old British Father of the House David Lloyd George comment to reporters that their patient is in stable condition after undergoing successful surgery.		A Communist parade on the streets of the Canadian city of Vancouver turns violent as several policemen and six hostile demonstrators are hospitalized.	Australian economists report their country's total exports during the past fiscal year declined by more than $115 million.
Aug. 4		King Carol II of Romania finalizes divorce proceedings against his wife, Queen Helen.		Brazil considers lowering tariffs on imported French goods as a gesture of goodwill to prevent a proposed French embargo of imported Brazilian coffee.	A riot in Bombay, India, turns chaotic as British loyalists clash with supporters of Mohandas Gandhi, resulting in approximately 30 serious injuries. . . . Dedicating a temple in the Indian city of Ahmedabad, revolutionary Mohandas Gandhi says, "I take a thousand times greater interest in my work as a reformer than in politics."
Aug. 5				The exchange rate of the Argentine peso falls, with 152 pesos equaling 100 U.S. dollars. . . . Chile announces its presidential elections will be held on October 14. . . . Chile reduces its discount rate by 1 percent, from 9.5 percent to 8.5 percent.	Chinese Marshal Chang Hsueh-liang categorically denies reports of his country's withdrawal from north China, where anger against economic and social inequality has festered over the years into an outright Communist rebellion.
Aug. 6	Senator Robert Wagner of New York denounces the growing nationalist movements in Europe as "saber rattling." . . . The Bank for International Settlements announces it currently possesses $313,826,714 in total assets.	In a first step toward forming the future Axis alliance of World War II, Germany proposes a "triple economic alliance" between itself, Italy, and Austria. . . . Premier Pierre Laval of France appoints diplomat Andre Francois Poncet to the post of French Ambassador to Germany.			

A	B	C	D	E
Includes developments that affect more than one world region, international organizations, and important meetings of world leaders.	*Includes all domestic and regional developments in Europe, including the Soviet Union.*	*Includes all domestic and regional developments in Africa and the Middle East.*	*Includes all domestic and regional developments in Latin America, the Caribbean, and Canada.*	*Includes all domestic and regional developments in Asian and Pacific nations (and colonies).*

U.S. Politics & Social Issues	U.S. Foreign Policy & Defense	Economics & Great Depression	Science, Technology & Nature	Culture, Leisure & Lifestyle	
Convicted gangster Al Capone reveals that he has rejected on moral grounds offers from film companies to make a motion picture based on his life, saying, "gangster films are doing nothing but harm to the younger element of this country."		*The Iron Age* releases its weekly index of U.S. steel mill activity. The index currently stands at 41.9, a rise of 0.1 points from the previous week, but a decline of approximately 50 percent from the corresponding week one year ago.			Jul. 30
		The Annalist releases its weekly index of U.S. wholesale commodity prices. At 101.3, the figure is a gain of 0.1 points from the previous week, but a decline of 16 percent from the corresponding period a year ago. Economists say the drop from last week was caused by losses in food products, metals, and building materials.	American aviators Russell Boardman and John Polando set the world's flight distance record by flying 5,014.5 miles. . . . The National Electric Light Association reports U.S. electric power output for the past week amounted to 1,680,358,000 kilowatt hours, 14 million kilowatt hours more than the preceding week, but a decline of 10 percent from the corresponding period one year ago.		Jul. 31
The Chicago Crime Commission adds 28 suspected gangsters to its list of "public enemies." . . . Presidential physician James Coupal tells reporters that his former patient, President Calvin Coolidge, is considering running for the 1932 presidential election on the Republican ticket.	Acting on the recommendation of President Herbert Hoover, Naval Secretary Charles Francis Adams announces significant naval budget reductions for the upcoming fiscal year of 1933. . . . The U.S. Navy transfers the battleship *Pennsylvania* to Guantanamo Bay, Cuba. . . . The heavy cruiser USS *Augusta* is renamed *CA-31*.	A British commission assigned to recommend changes in Great Britain's fiscal policy urges the House of Commons to pass legislation reducing government spending by $500 million through cuts in government salary rates and social services.	British aviatrix Amy Johnson encounters poor flying conditions during an attempted flight to Japan, and is forced to make an abrupt landing in the Siberian village of Diyazeinsk.	The Academy Award-nominated film *The Smiling Lieutenant* is released throughout the United States.	Aug. 1
Howard Withy is chosen to be head of the U.S. Consulate in Paris, France. . . . The American Motorists Association reports that the average price of a U.S. automobile has decreased by approximately $53 over the past year.		*The Annalist* releases its weekly index of U.S. business activity. At 74.3, the figure is a drop of 0.4 points from the previous week and a decline of 13 percent from the corresponding period last year. Economists say the loss from last week was caused by a sharp decline in automobile production.			Aug. 2
American Federation of Labor vice president Matthew Woll claims to reporters that wage cuts ultimately lead to "world bitterness, international dissension, chaos, and world ruination." He recommends stockholder dividend reductions as a suitable alternative.				A special Argentine delegation of cultural experts arrives in Hollywood, Calif., whereupon they conclude following a screening of blockbuster films that most of America's movies are "low in mental capacity, designed for infantile intellects, and poorly directed."	Aug. 3
A three-week strike by nearly 1,000 highway workmen in White Plains, N.Y., ends as employers cave in to the workers' demands of union recognition and an increase in wages. . . . The Anti-Saloon League calls on Prohibition Director Amos Woodcock to ban the sale of $2 apiece "wine concentrates."		The weekly index of U.S. automobile production as compiled by the Department of Commerce is released. The index currently stands at 59.9, a drop of 3.2 points from the previous week, but an increase of 34 percent from the corresponding week one year ago.	Thomas Edison's health condition improves, say his doctors, after weeks of taking a turn for the worse in his fight against several diseases. However, his request for a cigar is met by his doctors with a refusal.		Aug. 4
Senator James Couzens of Michigan urges his fellow lawmakers to hold a special session of Congress in October for the purpose of providing relief for those Americans in desperate need of food for this coming winter.		Chancellor Heinrich Bruening of Germany tells his citizenry in a nationwide radio broadcast that the delay of the Hoover Moratorium has "wrought great harm to the economic and political life of Germany." He continues, "The foreign withdrawals of billions of marks has meant a severe loss of blood in the economic life of our country."	British aviatrix Amy Johnson begins the last leg of her trip to the Japanese capital of Tokyo.	Great Britain places first in the annual international model yacht championship, garnering 114 points with the *Hermoine*. The American vessel *Bostonia IV* places second with 99 points.	Aug. 5
Ernest Cherrington, general secretary of the World League against Alcoholism, declares in a speech that the relatively high prevalence of automobile owners in the United States is directly attributable to Prohibition laws, contending that less consumption of alcohol has led to fewer automobile accidents, thus increasing auto ownership.	Gen. Smedley Butler, commander of forces at the Quantico Marine Base, officially announces his retirement. Butler became famous late in 1930 for spreading a rumor for which he was court-martialed that Italian Premier Benito Mussolini was once the perpetrator of a hit-and-run accident.	*The Iron Age* releases its weekly index of U.S. steel mill activity. The index currently stands at 42.0, a drop of 0.1 points from the previous week, and a decline of approximately 40 percent from the corresponding week one year ago.	James Goodwin Hall flies from Chicago to New York in four hours and three minutes, establishing a new record for time taken to fly between the two cities. Despite the feat, it is only two minutes faster than Frank Hawks's 1929 record.		Aug. 6

F	**G**	**H**	**I**	**J**
Includes elections, federal-state relations, civil rights and liberties, crime, the judiciary, education, healthcare, poverty, urban affairs, and population.	*Includes formation and debate of U.S. foreign and defense policies, veterans affairs, and defense spending. (Relations with specific foreign countries are usually found under the region concerned.)*	*Includes business, labor, agriculture, taxation, transportation, consumer affairs, monetary and fiscal policy, natural resources, pollution, and accidents.*	*Includes worldwide scientific, medical, and technological developments, natural phenomena, U.S. weather, and natural disasters.*	*Includes the arts, religion, scholarship, communications media, sports, entertainment, fashions, fads, and social life.*

	World Affairs	Europe	Africa & The Middle East	The Americas	Asia & The Pacific
Aug. 7	Hungarian officials invite New York City Mayor James Walker to visit their capital of Budapest.	French economists report the Bank of France currently possesses 58.4 billion francs worth of gold, the highest total since the bank's inception. . . . Prime Minister Pandeli Evangjeli of Albania bestows upon U.S. diplomat Telford Erickson the Order of Scanderbeg for his efforts to improve Albanian-American relations.		Mexican officials announce the shutdown of several Mexico City merchants accused of "price boosting." . . . Bolivia celebrates the 106th anniversary of the founding of its first republic.	
Aug. 8				President Jose Uriburu of Argentina orders the deportation of four politicians accused of inciting riots against his provisional regime. . . . Brazil deports suspected Soviet agitator Marcos Pandarsky. . . . Canada's federal budget deficit rises to $2,248,468,307.	New Zealand raises tariffs on imported tobacco, confectionary sugar, silk, and floor coverings. . . . As Communist uprisings threaten to uproot the socioeconomic order of China, the Industry Ministry estimates the number of unemployed Chinese to be 200 million, or nearly 50 percent of the country's total population of 432 million.
Aug. 9	In the United States, a temporary visa expires for a woman claiming to be Grand Duchess Anastasia of Russia, the sole surviving member of the family of deposed monarch Czar Nicholas II. DNA tests conducted late in the 20th century would prove the woman's claim to be fraudulent.	The British Board of Trade releases figures showing that during the whole of 1930, Great Britain imported 279.9 million rubles worth of Soviet goods, the most of any country. . . . Chancellor Heinrich Bruening of Germany travels to Vatican City to meet with Pope Pius XI, who urges the 46-year-old head of state to improve relations with Poland.		An additional nine Argentine politicians said to be involved in an uprising against President Jose Uriburu are deported.	
Aug. 10	The international Democratic Peace Conference concludes its sessions in Constance, Germany.	A Communist riot in the German capital of Berlin results in the deaths of over 100 people. . . . Gold reserves of the Bank of Netherlands increase to 57 million guilders. . . . A grenade explodes on a train en route to the German city of Jueeterbog, critically injuring 15 passengers. While combing the crime scene, police discover a copy of the newspaper *Der Angriff (The Attack)*, the organ of the National Socialist German Workers' Party.		Floods in Mexico force 6,000 residents to take refuge in hilltop villages.	In a speech delivered in the city of Bombay, revolutionary leader Mohandas Gandhi nearly bursts into tears as he urges Indian Muslims and Hindus to refrain from engaging in sectarian violence. With moist eyes, he asks, "How can we, torn from within, attain independence?"
Aug. 11	U.S. Ambassador to Cuba Harry Guggenheim reports to the U.S. State Department that the Caribbean island nation is teetering on the brink of revolution.	The Bank of Danzig lowers its discount rate by 3 percent, from 10 percent to 7 percent. . . . Germany celebrates Constitution Day, commemorating the signing of the Weimar constitution on August 11, 1919. Communist agitators interrupt the festivities by engaging in hostile clashes with Berlin police.		Striking Cuban streetcar workers hurl a bomb onto a passing streetcar in the capital of Havana. . . . Canadian economists report a favorable trade balance for the month of July. . . . Ecuador celebrates the 122nd anniversary of independence from Spanish colonial rule. . . . President Gerardo Machado of Cuba institutes martial law throughout the entire country and mobilizes a force of 900 troops to battle armed revolutionaries.	
Aug. 12	U.S. War Secretary Patrick Hurley embarks on a trip to the Philippines. Upon arrival, he tells reporters that the task of negotiating an "independence compromise" will prove a daunting and formidable task.				
Aug. 13		The British Board of Trade reports that Great Britain attained a favorable trade balance of £30,960,000 during the month of July.		Nicaraguan Finance Minister Jose Barbereno praises the U.S. military presence in his country as "highly beneficial." . . . Five Canadians are arrested as the Royal Mounted Police undertake a crackdown on Communistic activities. Among those taken into custody is former *Worker* editor Malcolm Bruce.	Heavy floods in the Philippine capital of Manila leave over 3,000 residents homeless.

A	B	C	D	E
Includes developments that affect more than one world region, international organizations, and important meetings of world leaders.	Includes all domestic and regional developments in Europe, including the Soviet Union.	Includes all domestic and regional developments in Africa and the Middle East.	Includes all domestic and regional developments in Latin America, the Caribbean, and Canada.	Includes all domestic and regional developments in Asian and Pacific nations (and colonies).

U.S. Politics & Social Issues	U.S. Foreign Policy & Defense	Economics & Great Depression	Science, Technology & Nature	Culture, Leisure & Lifestyle	
As the nation prepares for a hungry winter, a Chicago grain broker named Thomas Howell admits to having stored up to 8 million barrels of grain, thus indicating short selling.		Belgium officially fixes the price of domestically grown wheat at $27 per ton. . . . *The Annalist* releases its weekly index of U.S. wholesale commodity prices. At 101.7, the figure is a gain of 0.4 points from the previous week, but a decline of 12 percent from the corresponding period a year ago. Economists say the gain from last week was caused by increases in fuels.		The Will Rogers comedic vehicle *Young as You Feel* premieres. . . . Legendary filmmaker Frank Capra's *The Miracle Woman*, starring Oscar-nominated actress Barbara Stanwyck, is released throughout the United States.	Aug. 7
A team of thugs working for Al Capone collects $100,000 from various Chicago bookies in order to pay for the convicted gangster's legal defense fees. . . . The Chicago Industrial Club releases a report recommending the repeal of Prohibition as a means of reducing nationwide crime. "The essential part of crime's income comes from the illicit traffic in alcohol, the existence of which is traceable directly to the prohibition situation," the report reads.			Physicians of 84-year-old inventor Thomas Edison report their patient has partially recovered from a collapse that occurred at his home in West Orange, N.J., on August 1. . . . The *ZRS-4* airship, constructed in 1929 by the Goodyear-Zeppelin Corporation, is christened as the USS *Akron* by First Lady Lou Henry Hoover.	MGM's horseracing film *Sporting Blood*, starring legendary actor Clark Gable, is released. . . . Warner Bros., *Night Nurse* is released. The film stars Clark Gable and Barbara Stanwyck. . . . RKO Pictures, *The Woman Between*, directed by Hollywood Walk of Fame inductee Victor Schertzinger, is released throughout the United States.	Aug. 8
	The number of foreign-born soldiers serving in the U.S. Army rises to 14,000, with an additional 600 enlisted as officers.	At the Empire Sugar Conference in London, where nine countries are represented by 40 delegates, it is revealed that Australia consumes more sugar per capita than any other nation. . . . *The Annalist* releases its weekly index of U.S. business activity. At 73.9, the figure is a gain of 0.2 points from the previous week but a decline of 13 percent from the corresponding period last year. Economists say the rise from last week was caused by gains in freight car loadings and cotton cloth production.	Paleontologists in Ann Arbor, Mich., discover the skeletal remains of a 50-million-year-old prehistoric "phytosaur."		Aug. 9
In a published report, the American Federation of Labor recommends the repeal of Prohibition in order to generate much-needed tax revenue. . . . President Herbert Hoover celebrates his 57th birthday.		U.S. Senator David I. Walsh criticizes public works projects, saying they will place an unfair burden upon American taxpayers. Proposing fiscal conservatism, he says, "the government must do what the individual must do—reduce his expenditures to meet his income."	Due to extreme droughts, the tide level of the Mississippi River falls to the lowest level for August since 1864.		Aug. 10
Chairman Felix Hebert of the Senate Unemployment Insurance Committee declares that the creation of a national worker welfare system will lead the United States down the path of socialism.		The weekly index of U.S. automobile production as compiled by the Department of Commerce is released. The index currently stands at 53.6, a drop of 6.6 points from the previous week, and a decline of 27 percent from the corresponding week one year ago. . . . The Federal Reserve Bank of New York receives $580,000 from China.		In his newly published book *Modern Civilization on Trial*, Prof. C. Delisle Burns of Glasgow University writes, "If the danger of war in 1931 is as great as it was in 1909, we are five years from another great war."	Aug. 11
Fifty-two silk workers are arrested in Patterson, N.J., as a strike organized by the American Federation of Labor turns violent. . . . Reclamation Commissioner Elwood Mead predicts that a strike of Nevada tunnel workers that has halted the construction of the Hoover Dam will soon end. . . . Senator John Blaine calls on President Herbert Hoover to request a special session of Congress in September to appropriate relief funds for idle workers.		Australia abstains from signing the Hoover Moratorium, contending that the potential benefits from a suspension of World War I debts would only apply to European nations.	The U.S. National Institute of Health reports that after three years of research, they have failed to discover the cause or cure for infantile paralysis, or "polio" as the disease is more commonly known.		Aug. 12
New York City Health Commissioner Shirley Wynne announces that 1,570 polio cases were reported during the first seven months of 1931. Wynne says that pigeons may play a role in spreading the disease.		*The Iron Age* releases its weekly index of U.S. steel mill activity. The index currently stands at 42.7, a gain of 0.7 points from the previous week, but a decline of approximately 45 percent from the corresponding week one year ago. . . . The Texas legislature introduces a bill that would place oil production in the hands of the State Railroad Commission.	Aviator Frank Hawks establishes a record for time taken to fly between New York and Chicago, traversing the skies that separate the two cities in a span of four hours and six minutes.	In a letter to the *London Times*, world renowned playwright George Bernard Shaw praises the Soviet Union, writing, "Russia operates a system from which the disastrous frictions of private interest have been ruthlessly eliminated."	Aug. 13

F	G	H	I	J
Includes elections, federal-state relations, civil rights and liberties, crime, the judiciary, education, healthcare, poverty, urban affairs, and population.	Includes formation and debate of U.S. foreign and defense policies, veterans affairs, and defense spending. (Relations with specific foreign countries are usually found under the region concerned.)	Includes business, labor, agriculture, taxation, transportation, consumer affairs, monetary and fiscal policy, natural resources, pollution, and accidents.	Includes worldwide scientific, medical, and technological developments, natural phenomena, U.S. weather, and natural disasters.	Includes the arts, religion, scholarship, communications media, sports, entertainment, fashions, fads, and social life.

	World Affairs	Europe	Africa & The Middle East	The Americas	Asia & The Pacific
Aug. 14	U.S. Senator William Borah remarks during a press interview that recent increases in French military expenditures "can mean nothing less than the destruction of Germany." He adds, "France is in a position of greater security today than any European nation in the last 200 years."			The Cuban Congress suspends its sessions as the Caribbean island nation teeters on the brink of civil war. President Gerardo Machado offers a general amnesty to all rebel forces, contingent upon complete disarmament within 24 hours. . . . By a vote of 40–1, the Mexican Senate passes a bill requiring that 90 percent of the country's hired employees be Mexican citizens, effectively requiring all Mexican businesses to engage in discriminatory hiring practices.	
Aug. 15	Pope Pius XI sends $12,500 to China for flood relief.	Hungary receives a one-year loan of $25 million from France, Switzerland, the Netherlands, and Italy.	Newly appointed Egyptian Ambassador to the United States Sesostris Sidarouss Pasha embarks on his first trip to the United States.	Gen. Mario Menocal, Cuban revolt leader, is captured by loyalist forces in the Pinar del Rio province along with half a dozen of his followers.	Revolutionary leader Mohandas Gandhi tentatively refuses Great Britain's request to participate in an upcoming roundtable discussion on Indian independence. . . . The tide level of the Yangtze River rises to the highest level ever recorded. The Chinese government creates the National Flood Relief Commission to coordinate relief efforts for the estimated 1 million Chinese affected. Finance Minister T.V. Soong is appointed as chairman.
Aug. 16		The Housing Bureau of Berlin receives 40,000 "urgent" applications for immediate housing in a single day. . . . Great Britain's federal budget deficit rises to £120 million. Prime Minister Ramsay MacDonald calls a meeting of five of Great Britain's leading financial officials to solve the matter. . . . The number of unemployed British merchant marines rises to 1,048. . . . The German city of Hamburg cuts city employee salaries to alleviate an estimated $9 million budget deficit.		The provisional government of Brazil begins to formulate plans for upcoming presidential elections. . . . Brazil deports American William Barrett on the grounds of "undesirability."	Japan reports that its population has increased by 4,713,183 people, or 6.9 percent, since 1925.
Aug. 17		German economists report that German wholesale prices declined by approximately 5 percent during the past week. . . . The average price of British wholesale commodity prices falls to its lowest point of 1931. . . . British economic officials estimate Great Britain's federal budget deficit will rise to $500 million by the end of fiscal year 1932. Cuts in infrastructure construction and government salaries must be made in order to reduce the daunting figure, say the officials.		Cuban Ambassador to the United States Orestes Ferrara travels to New York to escape potential dangers brought on by violent uprisings.	The government of the Chinese province of Canton formally demands the resignation of Premier Chiang Kai-shek.
Aug. 18	Viennese psychiatrist Olga Knopf declares that it is women's "own fault" for their failure to achieve equality with men.		The Palestinian Arab Executive calls for a nationwide protest against what they perceive as the pro-Zionist policies of the British government.	U.S. military officials announce that there are no plans in place to militarily intervene in Cuba, yet "contingency plans are constantly being updated."	The Philippine legislature introduces a bill that would grant suffrage to women. . . . In a prelude to the Mukden Incident, a Japanese army officer, Captain Nakamura, is murdered while on a trip to the Chinese territory of Manchuria.
Aug. 19		Austria drastically cuts the salaries of its military personnel in order to generate much-needed stimulation for a fledgling economy. . . . The total number of idle English workers rises to 2,714,359, an increase of 620,438 from the corresponding period in 1930.		Ecuador and Colombia resume diplomatic relations following more than six years of inactivity. . . . Colombian newspaper editor Ismael Arciniegas is appointed to the post of Colombian Ambassador to Ecuador.	
Aug. 20		Romania enacts a ban on all imported Soviet goods, following repeated rumors of widespread slave labor in Russia. Customs authorities are instructed to carefully inspect all incoming packages. . . . New York City Mayor James Walker visits Czechoslovakia, where he is greeted by a "frenzy of cheering."		Amid heavy criticism of his regime for the failure to successfully negotiate a foreign loan, Premier Istvan Bethlen of Hungary announces his resignation, ending a 10-year rule. The Hungarian parliament selects conservative politician Gyula Karolyi as the replacement. Karolyi pledges to continue to implement the anti-Communist policies put forth by Bethlen.	Premier J.T. Lang of New South Wales gives $50 million to the New South Wales Savings Bank to prevent the institution from falling into bankruptcy.

A	B	C	D	E
Includes developments that affect more than one world region, international organizations, and important meetings of world leaders.	Includes all domestic and regional developments in Europe, including the Soviet Union.	Includes all domestic and regional developments in Africa and the Middle East.	Includes all domestic and regional developments in Latin America, the Caribbean, and Canada.	Includes all domestic and regional developments in Asian and Pacific nations (and colonies).

U.S. Politics & Social Issues	U.S. Foreign Policy & Defense	Economics & Great Depression	Science, Technology & Nature	Culture, Leisure & Lifestyle	
			The Sioux Native American tribe awards the title of Chief Flying Hawk to Frank Hawks for his record-breaking aviation feat. . . . Charles Lindbergh announces he will undertake a round-the-world flight sometime late in the summer. . . . The National Electric Light Association reports U.S. electric power output for the past week amounted to 1,642,858,000 kilowatt hours, 2 million kilowatt hours less than the preceding week, and a decrease of 3 percent from the corresponding period one year ago.	Russell Hoogerhyde wins the annual U.S. archery championship for the second consecutive year.	Aug. 14
The Prohibition Bureau reports that the number of convicted violators of Prohibition has increased by approximately 25 percent during the past year.		The U.S. Chamber of Commerce recommends to President Herbert Hoover the implementation of a guaranteed five-day workweek as a means of stabilizing industry.	New York City residents witness a dazzling spectacle of aurora borealis, otherwise known as the northern lights.	Boxer Steve Dimeter knocks out Paul Brackton to claim the title of U.S. Navy heavyweight champion. . . . Paramount Pictures' Huckleberry Finn, based on the Mark Twain novel of the same name, is released.	Aug. 15
		The Annalist releases its weekly index of U.S. business activity. At 72.5, the figure is a drop of 1.3 points from the previous week and a decline of 16 percent from the corresponding period last year.	In the Mexican village of San Pedro Jicayan, 100 children die of dysentery in a single day.	The 1930 American League Triple Crown winner Lefty Grove wins his 15th consecutive baseball victory of the year, surrendering three runs over nine innings.	Aug. 16
New York City education officials report that the city's illiteracy rate has declined by 1.72 percent since 1920.		The strike of silk workers in Patterson, N.J., enters its fourth week. Representatives of the Associated Silk Workers confer with the local mayor in an attempt to reach an equitable settlement.	Aviator Frank Hawks is fined $500 for performing an illegal landing onto Floyd Bennett Field in Burlington, Vt.		Aug. 17
The United Mine Workers of America calls on President Herbert Hoover to intervene in a strike of West Virginia coal miners. . . . In a speech before members of the American Legion, Assistant Secretary of the Navy Ernest Lee Jahncke says, "In the past 10 years, the working week has dropped from 6 days to 5.5, and will soon reach the five-day stage."		The weekly index of U.S. automobile production as compiled by the Department of Commerce is released. The index currently stands at 54.7, a rise of 1.1 points from the previous week, but a decline of 29 percent from the corresponding week one year ago.	The German airship Graf Zeppelin embarks from Germany on its first-ever flight to Great Britain.		Aug. 18
President Herbert Hoover's son, Herbert Hoover, Jr., announces he will become a member of the faculty of the California Institute of Technology beginning in the fall semester. . . . New York City Police Commissioner Edward Mulrooney reports that $500,000 is stolen each year from tourists who hand their bags over to thugs who claim to be "baggage handlers."			The National Electric Light Association reports U.S. electric power output for the past week amounted to 1,629,011,000 kilowatt hours, 13 million kilowatt hours less than the preceding week, and a decrease of 3 percent from the corresponding period one year ago.	During training for the Schneider Trophy European seaplane competition, British aviator Gerald Brinton, age 26, dies as his Supermarine S-6 plane crashes into the sea. . . . The American plane New York takes off from the German aircraft carrier Bremen and flies 700 miles to Boston, Mass., establishing a world distance record for flights originating from aircraft carriers.	Aug. 19
Mayor Anton Cermak of Chicago tells reporters that unless emergency funds are appropriated, Chicago's City Hall may be forced to close.	The U.S. Navy decommissions the destroyer Rizal, which was constructed in 1918 by the Union Iron Works Company. . . . The U.S. Navy recommissions the destroyer Montgomery.	The Iron Age releases its weekly index of U.S. steel mill activity. The index currently stands at 45.3, a gain of 2.6 points from the previous week, but a decline of approximately 44 percent from the corresponding week one year ago. . . . General Theatres Equipment, Inc., is added to the New York Stock Exchange's permanent list of tradable companies.	The body of British aviator Gerald Brinton is discovered one day after his fatal seaplane crash.	The fourth annual international Chocolate and Confectionary Exhibition opens in London, where it is revealed that America consumes the most candy out of all the world's nations.	Aug. 20

F	G	H	I	J
Includes elections, federal-state relations, civil rights and liberties, crime, the judiciary, education, healthcare, poverty, urban affairs, and population.	Includes formation and debate of U.S. foreign and defense policies, veterans affairs, and defense spending. (Relations with specific foreign countries are usually found under the region concerned.)	Includes business, labor, agriculture, taxation, transportation, consumer affairs, monetary and fiscal policy, natural resources, pollution, and accidents.	Includes worldwide scientific, medical, and technological developments, natural phenomena, U.S. weather, and natural disasters.	Includes the arts, religion, scholarship, communications media, sports, entertainment, fashions, fads, and social life.

	World Affairs	Europe	Africa & The Middle East	The Americas	Asia & The Pacific
Aug. 21	While vacationing in New York City, the daughter of the Dresden, Germany, police chief kills a 24-year-old Brooklyn native in an automobile accident, sparking a minor international incident.	Hungarian Premier Gyula Karolyi begins the process of selecting the members of his Cabinet.			The American Red Cross extends a gift of $100,000 to the Chinese government.
Aug. 22	The American Civil Liberties Union wires $500 to four Filipino Communists who were arrested on charges of sedition. . . . In an interview with the Associated Press, *London Daily Express* owner Lord Beaverbrook criticizes the League of Nations, calling it "a branch of the French Foreign Office."	Italy drastically raises duties on imported aluminum.		Bolivia accuses the Standard Oil Company of tax evasion of $700,000. . . . U.S. Ambassador to Cuba Harry Guggenheim reports to the State Department that the ongoing revolt in Cuba is near collapse.	Chinese Premier Chiang Kai-shek personally thanks U.S. President Herbert Hoover for his efforts in providing relief for those affected by heavy floods in Chinese regions adjacent to the Yangtze River.
Aug. 23	Former U.S. senator Henry Berenger says in an interview with *Financial World* that the key to economic recovery in Germany is "strong leadership."	A Belgian man who "conscientiously objected" to undergoing compulsory military service is sentenced to a three-month prison term. Socialist author H.G. Wells writes a letter to a Belgian newspaper demanding his immediate release.	Emperor Ras Tafari of Ethiopia issues a decree outlawing slavery in the west African nation. Those convicted of slave trading will likely be put to death, the decree states. Out of an estimated 4 million slaves worldwide, 2 million are Ethiopians.	Canadian farmers are issued arms by the government to protect their cattle from an overpopulation of bears.	
Aug. 24	The Soviet Union announces that 6,000 American skilled workers have been sent to Russia to offset a labor shortage caused by the Five-Year Plan.	British economists report the Bank of England took in £559,522 worth of gold during the past week, against £37,000 in withdrawals, netting a surplus of £522,522. . . . British Prime Minister Ramsay MacDonald resigns amid criticism over his economic policies. . . . In Brussels, 200,000 Belgians gather to participate in a ceremony honoring those who died during World War I.		Argentina announces budget cuts of 200 million pesos for the upcoming fiscal year. . . . President Isidro Ayora of Ecuador resigns along with his entire Cabinet as hostile chants of "Down with Ayora!" echo throughout the Ecuadorian capital. Col. Luis Alba is appointed as acting president.	Indian revolutionary leader Mohandas Gandhi travels to the city of Simla to confer with British colonial authorities.
Aug. 25		Eight people drown as a forceful gale hits the waters adjacent to the French city of Audierne. . . . France and the Soviet Union begin to negotiate a nonaggression treaty. The Polish newspaper *Gazeta Polska* praises the discussions.		The Canadian Dominion Bureau of Statistics reports Canada's birth rate has declined by 2 percent during the first seven months of 1931, a result of diminished food supply caused by the Great Depression.	
Aug. 26		German officials express an indifferent attitude toward the proposed nonaggression pact between France and the Soviet Union. Many doubt it will disrupt German-Russian relations.			The Communist rebel government controlling the Chinese province of Canton places a ban on all imported German goods, following the seizure of a German arms supply ship en route to the official capital of Nanking.
Aug. 27		Four Polish peasants attempting to cross the Polish-Russian border in search of work are killed by vigilante border guards.			The estimate of the number of Chinese men, women, and children left homeless by the flooding of the Yangtze River rises to 100 million.
Aug. 28		Greek wine growers request lawmakers to prohibit the manufacture and distribution of beer. . . . Spanish Interior Minister Miguel Marra announces that five cases of bubonic plague infection have been reported in the city of Hospitalet.			

A	B	C	D	E
Includes developments that affect more than one world region, international organizations, and important meetings of world leaders.	Includes all domestic and regional developments in Europe, including the Soviet Union.	Includes all domestic and regional developments in Africa and the Middle East.	Includes all domestic and regional developments in Latin America, the Caribbean, and Canada.	Includes all domestic and regional developments in Asian and Pacific nations (and colonies).

U.S. Politics & Social Issues	U.S. Foreign Policy & Defense	Economics & Great Depression	Science, Technology & Nature	Culture, Leisure & Lifestyle	
On the occasion of his 99th birthday, American Bar Association dean George Darlington, a practicing attorney for more than 75 years, tells friends and family that "One hundred years on this earth is something to be proud about, but 98 or 99 is nothing." . . . Illinois University dean Thomas Clark announces his retirement after more than 30 years of heading the prestigious institution. His explanation: "I just grew tired of waiting for students to think up new alibis for absences and excuses for cutting classes."		*The Annalist* releases its weekly index of U.S. wholesale commodity prices. At 102.3, the figure is a rise of 0.5 points from the previous week, but a loss of 13 percent from the corresponding period a year ago. . . . The New York City Public Welfare Department asks for $19,694,415 in addition to funds already appropriated for the upcoming fiscal year, the largest budget increase request in the department's history.		During a game against the St. Louis Browns, New York Yankees slugger George Herman "Babe" Ruth hits his 600th home run, further eclipsing by nearly 500 the career-home-run record of 138 established in 1897 by Roger Connor.	Aug. 21
A strike of Chicago motion picture theater workers ends as union representatives and owners reach a settlement.	President Herbert Hoover characterizes retired Gen. Smedley Butler, who was court-martialed earlier last year for spreading a false rumor about Italian Premier Benito Mussolini, as "a very distinguished and gallant officer."	Argentina's National Statistics Bureau reports a favorable trade balance of 50,110,000 gold pesos for the first seven months of 1931.		The German musical-comedy play *The Blond Nightingale* premiers in New York City. . . . Paramount Pictures' *An American Tragedy*, based on the novel by noted author Theodore Dreiser, is released throughout the United States. . . . The Oscar-nominated motion picture drama *The Star Witness* is released. . . . MGM's Oscar-nominated motion picture *Romance*, based on the play by Edward Sheldon, is released throughout the United States.	Aug. 22
		The U.S. Bureau of Mines reports the United States is the world's third largest producer of tin. . . . *The Annalist* releases its weekly index of U.S. business activity. At 72.5, the figure is an increase of 0.2 points from the previous week but a decline of 17 percent from the corresponding period last year.			Aug. 23
New York City begins a widespread crackdown on criminal elements. . . . The city of Detroit requests from the federal government $10 million for unemployment relief in the coming winter.		Figures are released showing that steel production in Great Britain has declined by 31 percent since the summer of 1930. . . . The New York State Board of Social Welfare writes in a published report that "very few cities have made any definite plans for work relief projects."		Universal Pictures begins production on the first-ever film adaptation of Mary Shelley's 1817 novel *Frankenstein*.	Aug. 24
		The weekly index of U.S. automobile production as compiled by the Department of Commerce is released. The index currently stands at 52.9, a drop of 1.8 points from the previous week, and a decline of 32 percent from the corresponding week one year ago.	An outbreak of infantile paralysis, or "polio" as it is more commonly known, in New York City threatens to delay the opening of the new school year. . . . The British Duke of Gloucester undergoes an operation for appendicitis.	World chess champion Alexander Alekhine assumes the lead in the International Chess Masters tournament by defeating S. Tartakower of Poland in the second round of play.	Aug. 25
		In an effort to reduce budget deficits, Great Britain lowers government employee salaries by an average of 10 percent.	Seventy-seven new cases of infantile paralysis, or "polio" as it is more commonly known, are reported in New York City in a single day.	In a 15-round bout, Panamanian boxer Al Brown defends his title as world bantamweight champion, defeating Norwegian challenger Pete Sanstol. . . . Oscar-nominated director King Vidor's *Street Scene*, based on the play by Elmer Rice, premiers in New York City.	Aug. 26
New York City police engage in open and unmerciful force against a group of Communists staging a demonstration on the steps of the state legislature building.		*The Iron Age* releases its weekly index of U.S. steel mill activity. The index currently stands at 44.6, a drop of 0.7 points from the previous week, and a decline of approximately 47 percent from the corresponding week one year ago.	Aviatrix Ruth Nichols, who in 1930 established the international women's transcontinental air speed record, resumes flying after more than six weeks of inactivity due to an injury sustained during a crash on the East Coast.		Aug. 27
New York City allots $70 million for subway construction in 1932, a decrease of $30 million from the previous year. . . . Harvard economics professor Dr. John Black is appointed to the position of chief economist of the Federal Farm Board. . . . Governor Franklin Delano Roosevelt of New York appropriates $500,000 to investigate allegations of corruption.		*The Annalist* releases its weekly index of U.S. wholesale commodity prices. At 101.3, the figure is a drop of 0.9 points from the previous week, and a decline of 20 percent from the corresponding period a year ago. Economists say the drop from last week was caused by losses in farm and food products. . . . China ships $2.5 million worth of gold to the United States.	Austrian schoolmaster Karl Naumestnik, age 38, becomes the first person to water ski across the English Channel.	Legendary filmmaker Frank Capra finishes production on his romantic comedy, *Platinum Blonde*.	Aug. 28

F	G	H	I	J
Includes elections, federal-state relations, civil rights and liberties, crime, the judiciary, education, healthcare, poverty, urban affairs, and population.	Includes formation and debate of U.S. foreign and defense policies, veterans affairs, and defense spending. (Relations with specific foreign countries are usually found under the region concerned.)	Includes business, labor, agriculture, taxation, transportation, consumer affairs, monetary and fiscal policy, natural resources, pollution, and accidents.	Includes worldwide scientific, medical, and technological developments, natural phenomena, U.S. weather, and natural disasters.	Includes the arts, religion, scholarship, communications media, sports, entertainment, fashions, fads, and social life.

	World Affairs	Europe	Africa & The Middle East	The Americas	Asia & The Pacific
Aug. 29	Argentina's Bank of the Nation ships $1,398,280 worth of gold to the United States as part of the repayment of a loan issued early in 1931.			The provisional government of Argentina issues a decree scheduling presidential and vice presidential elections for November 8. The decree also states that the elected president will serve a six-year term.	Famed aviator Charles Lindbergh arrives in the Japanese capital of Tokyo along with U.S. Ambassador to Japan Cameron Forbes. Japanese officials describe Lindbergh as "likeable."
Aug. 30		A consortium of railway experts releases statistics showing that Great Britain has the safest of all the world's railways.			
Aug. 31		British economists report the Bank of England took in £620,327 worth of gold during the past week, against £786,312 in withdrawals, netting a deficit of £165,985. Of the amount withdrawn, £550,000 was reserved for South Africa.		The eighth Canadian Baron de Longueuil dies in Pau, France, at the age of 73. The Baron de Longueuil is the only royal Canadian title. . . . Dr. Lisandro de la Torre is nominated by the Argentine Progressive Democratic Party as its candidate for the November presidential elections. Socialist leader Nicolas Repetto is chosen to be Torre's running mate.	
Sept. 1					Cantonese Communist rebels deny the Chinese nationalist government's offer of a cease-fire.
Sept. 2	Capitulating to American pressure, Brazil temporarily removes its embargo on imported wheat flour.	The French Weather Bureau reports that during August, Paris endured rainfall for 25 straight days, a record. . . . The Bank of Danzig reduces its interest rate by 1 percent, from 7 percent to 6 percent. . . . The English unemployment rate rises to 7.2 percent, an increase of 1.1 percent from September 1930.		President Getulio Vargas of Brazil signs a decree limiting the powers of provisional governors. Newspapers praise the move as a step in the direction of democratic reform. . . . Members of the Chilean navy stage a mutiny aboard a battleship in Coquimbo, demanding salary increases.	Chinese Foreign Minister C.T. Wang asks the United States to grant asylum to a group of Chinese nationals in Mexico who have undergone prejudicial persecution. U.S. State Department officials respond by saying that admitting the refugees would be in violation of the 1882 Chinese Exclusion Act.
Sept. 3				Charles Orr, Governor-General of the British territory of the Bahamas, retires after more than four years of service at age 61, citing poor health.	
Sept. 4		Following months of futile negotiations, Austria and Germany renounce their proposed customs union pact. . . . As the German Boerse reopens following seven weeks of inactivity, average stock prices fall by approximately 35 percent.		The Chase National Bank renews a loan to Cuba of $20 million for an additional 60 days.	China purchases 450,000 tons of wheat from the United States.

A	B	C	D	E
Includes developments that affect more than one world region, international organizations, and important meetings of world leaders.	Includes all domestic and regional developments in Europe, including the Soviet Union.	Includes all domestic and regional developments in Africa and the Middle East.	Includes all domestic and regional developments in Latin America, the Caribbean, and Canada.	Includes all domestic and regional developments in Asian and Pacific nations (and colonies).

U.S. Politics & Social Issues	U.S. Foreign Policy & Defense	Economics & Great Depression	Science, Technology & Nature	Culture, Leisure & Lifestyle	
	The War Department awards contracts totaling $2.6 million to a dozen aircraft companies for the construction of 71 airplanes and 92 airplane engines.		Fifty-three new cases of infantile paralysis, or "polio" as it is more commonly known, are reported in New York City in a single day, prompting Health Commissioner Shirley Wynne to recommend delaying the opening of the city's public schools "as an extra precaution.". . . The National Electric Light Association reports U.S. electric power output for the past week amounted to 1,643,011,000 kilowatt hours, 14 million kilowatt hours more than the preceding week, but a decrease of 4 percent from the corresponding period one year ago.	First National Pictures' dramatic film *The Last Flight* is released throughout the United States. . . . Five-time America's Cup runner-up Sir Thomas Lipton, who went on to create the Lipton tea brand, announces he will not compete in the annual sailing competition for the first time in 30 years. . . . The centerfielder of the world champion Philadelphia Athletics, George "Mule" Haas, suffers a season-ending injury.	Aug. 29
The National Industrial Conference Board reports that U.S. auto registrations have increased by 160 percent since 1921. . . . Customs officials discover a 10-acre field of marijuana in Philadelphia. Property owners are notified that the field will be burned down within a matter of days.		*The Annalist* releases its weekly index of U.S. business activity. At 72.3, the figure is a drop of 0.1 points from the previous week and a decline of 17 percent from the corresponding period last year. Economists say the drop from last week was caused by losses in steel mill activity and cotton cloth production.		Gallant Fox, a terrier, wins the title of Best in Show at the North Shore Kennel Club Dog Show.	Aug. 30
Twelve of the nation's leading book publishers report that despite depressive economic conditions, book sales within the United States have remained remarkably high.			The annual international Berne Hygiene Exposition begins in Geneva, Switzerland.	Noted film director Fritz Lang's *M*, considered to be one of the greatest films of the 20th century, is released in Sweden. . . . The U.S. National Amateur golf championship begins, with 142 contestants participating. . . . Lou Gehrig hits his 37th home run, tying his Yankee teammate George Herman "Babe" Ruth for the league lead.	Aug. 31
Crime experts report the number of prisoners in New York City's jails has increased by 20 percent since August 1931. . . . The Census Bureau releases figures showing that divorces within the United States have more than doubled since 1920. . . . New York Governor Franklin Roosevelt recommends to lawmakers the appropriation of $8,120,000 for bridge construction as a means of providing employment for idle workers.	The submarine *H-2* is sold for scrap by the U.S. Navy.	In the United States, construction is completed on a $100 million natural gas pipeline that spans 1,000 miles from Illinois to Texas.	Forty-four new cases of infantile paralysis, or "polio" as it is more commonly known, are reported in New York City in a single day. . . . New York City Health Commissioner Shirley Wynne announces that the opening of the city's public schools for the 1931–32 school year will be delayed eight days in an effort to prevent further spreading of polio. The decision affects over 1 million children.	Filming is completed on MGM's musical comedy *Flying High*. The film stars future Hollywood Walk of Fame recipients Pat O'Brien and Hedda Hopper.	Sept. 1
The city of Los Angeles places a ban on nude sunbathing.	The destroyer USS *McCawley* is sold for scrap after more than a year of being decommissioned. . . . The U.S. Navy sells the destroyer *Selfridge* for scrap to the Marine Salvage Company.		The New York, Philadelphia, and Washington Airway announces a record number of 66,289 passengers have flown without accident during the past year. . . . The 82nd annual convention of the American Chemical Society commences in Buffalo, N.Y., where Du Pont chemists Wallace Crothers and Julian Hill introduce a new "synthetic silk."	Metro-Goldwyn-Mayer begins production on the romance film *Possessed*, starring Oscar winners Joan Crawford and Clark Gable.	Sept. 2
The budget deficit of the U.S. Postal Department rises to $100 million. Postmaster General Walter Brown recommends a rate increase of 25 percent on all first-class mail. . . . The U.S. Labor Department announces that 3,174 immigrants were admitted into the United States in August 1931, compared with 7,428 immigrants who departed.	Construction of the cruiser USS *Tuscaloosa* is completed in Camden, N.J. It would become one of the four ships made famous for escorting U.S. President Franklin Roosevelt to the 1941 Atlantic Conference. . . . House Appropriations Committee chairman Will Wood recommends sweeping military reductions as a solution to ever-increasing federal budget deficits. "We are not at war, and we are by no means threatened by war," he says.	*The Iron Age* releases its weekly index of U.S. steel mill activity. The index currently stands at 43.3, a drop of 1.3 points from the previous week, and a reduction of approximately 48 percent from the corresponding week one year ago. . . . U.S. Treasury officials predict that at the present rate of economic diminishment, the federal budget deficit will soon rise to over $2 billion.	The Metropolitan Life Insurance Company reports that deaths attributable to cancer within the United States have increased by 8 percent since September 1930.	First National Pictures releases a film adaptation of the Philip Barry play *The Bargain*, starring Hollywood Walk of Fame recipients Lewis Stone, Charles Butterworth, and Una Merkel. . . . The team of Allison-Van Ryn, a perennial contender, wins the English national tennis doubles championship.	Sept. 3
The National Association for the Advancement of Colored People authors a letter to President Herbert Hoover protesting a recent decision to reduce African-American troop levels by 13 percent. The letter accuses Army officials of "abolishing the so-called colored regiments."	The liner *America* is transferred to Hoboken, N.J., where it begins the process of decommissioning.	*The Annalist* releases its weekly index of U.S. wholesale commodity prices. At 101.1, the figure is a drop of 0.2 points from the previous week, and a decline of 20 percent from the corresponding period a year ago. . . . The stock price of the U.S. Steel Corporation falls to its lowest point since 1922.	Statistician Dr. Frederick L. Hoffman reports that the U.S. appendicitis death rate is the highest among all of the Western industrialized nations. . . . The 82nd annual meeting of the American Chemical Society concludes in Buffalo, N.Y. . . . Fifty-three new cases of infantile paralysis, or "polio" as it is more commonly known, are reported in New York City in a single day.		Sept. 4

F	G	H	I	J
Includes elections, federal-state relations, civil rights and liberties, crime, the judiciary, education, healthcare, poverty, urban affairs, and population.	Includes formation and debate of U.S. foreign and defense policies, veterans affairs, and defense spending. (Relations with specific foreign countries are usually found under the region concerned.)	Includes business, labor, agriculture, taxation, transportation, consumer affairs, monetary and fiscal policy, natural resources, pollution, and accidents.	Includes worldwide scientific, medical, and technological developments, natural phenomena, U.S. weather, and natural disasters.	Includes the arts, religion, scholarship, communications media, sports, entertainment, fashions, fads, and social life.

	World Affairs	Europe	Africa & The Middle East	The Americas	Asia & The Pacific
Sept. 5	The Bank for International Settlements announces it currently possesses 1,631,899 Swiss francs, or $40,797,475 in total assets.			Mexican Foreign Secretary Genaro Estrada announces that his country will soon seek official membership to the League of Nations. Mexico was one of the few South American countries that was denied membership at the time of the League's creation in 1919, since Mexico's controlling power was then an internationally unrecognized military junta. . . . A strike of public transportation workers in the Chilean city of Valparaiso forces many commuters to walk to work.	
Sept. 6		As a deterrent to future strikes, a ban is placed by Spanish authorities on public Communist meetings. . . . New York City Mayor James Walker is made an honorary member of the Legion of Honor by the French government. . . . Parisian officials consider closing the July Column, an attraction honoring the fall of the Bastille Prison during the French Revolution, due to repeated reports of suicidal young men climbing the Column and leaping to their deaths.		Seven striking Mexicans are killed in clashes with the police in Mexico City. . . . The U.S. War Department reports that total traffic through the Panama Canal in August was the lowest total of any month of 1931.	
Sept. 7		Noted writer Aldous Huxley writes a letter to various British newspapers demanding a reduction of 25 percent in British military expenditures. . . . Police in Vienna, Austria, discover a document written by the Moscow Third International that contains instructions on how to incite violent demonstrations.		A protest against provisional President Jose Uriburu of Argentina is held. Shouts of "Down with the dictator!" are heard echoing throughout the streets. . . . Reports circulate in Bolivia that the entire Cabinet of President Daniel Salmanaca is close to resigning.	
Sept. 8	New York City Mayor James Walker meets with King Faisal I of Iraq in Cannes, France. The first question the mayor poses to the Iraqi monarch is: "Where is Iraq?"	Several U.S. diplomats dispute the Soviet Union's claims of full employment in Russia. The diplomats allege the unemployment figure is roughly 30 percent.		Brazilians celebrate the 109th anniversary of their gaining of independence from Portuguese colonial rule. Festivities are dampened by a tropical rainstorm. . . . A week-long mutiny aboard a ship stationed in the Chilean port of Coquimbo ends as the mutineers suffer huge losses from a massive aerial bombardment by the Chilean air force.	
Sept. 9	U.S. Secretary of State Henry Stimson returns to Washington, D.C., following a diplomatic tour of Europe. He comments to reporters that recent policy discussions between French and German statesmen are a "hopeful step" toward European economic stabilization.			Brazil establishes a trade treaty with several European powers including France, Germany, Holland, and Sweden. Under the terms of the treaty, Brazil will reduce tariffs on imported goods from the European countries, in exchange for "protection" of its coffee exports.	
Sept. 10	In Holland, 2.4 million people sign a petition calling for universal international disarmament. . . . Following a visit to troubled Germany, former U.S. senator Henry Allen writes to the *New York Times* that "Germany is not thinking in terms of revolution."	The number of British idle workers rises to 2,762,219, an increase of 701,775 from September 1930. . . . Prince August Wilhelm, son of deposed Kaiser Wilhelm II, is banned by German authorities from speaking at a rally of the National Socialist German Workers' Party. Officials express the belief that Wilhelm's presence might provoke violent disturbances.			Chinese Gen. Chiang Kai-shek mobilizes 70 war planes to engage in battle with southern Communist rebels.
Sept. 11	Argentina ships $10 million worth of gold to the United States as part of a repayment of a loan issued early in 1931. . . . The League of Nations releases a 337-page book entitled, "The Course and Phases of the World Economic Depression."	Great Britain reduces its unemployment insurance fund by $129 million for the upcoming fiscal year. Additionally, the total salaries of public officials are reduced by $22,670,000. . . . The discount rate of the Hungarian National Bank is reduced by 1 percent, from 9 percent to 8 percent.		One Paraguayan and five Bolivians are killed as small-arms fire is exchanged in the disputed Chaco border region. Bolivia subsequently releases a statement condemning Paraguay for "thwarting Bolivia's unalterable pacific spirit."	

A	B	C	D	E
Includes developments that affect more than one world region, international organizations, and important meetings of world leaders.	*Includes all domestic and regional developments in Europe, including the Soviet Union.*	*Includes all domestic and regional developments in Africa and the Middle East.*	*Includes all domestic and regional developments in Latin America, the Caribbean, and Canada.*	*Includes all domestic and regional developments in Asian and Pacific nations (and colonies).*

U.S. Politics & Social Issues	U.S. Foreign Policy & Defense	Economics & Great Depression	Science, Technology & Nature	Culture, Leisure & Lifestyle	
Following a visit to Hyde Park, New York State Social Welfare Board president Victor Riddler publicly expresses support for Governor Franklin Roosevelt's proposed $20 million unemployment relief fund. Riddler's comments stand in sharp contrast to the viewpoints of state Republican leaders. . . . Labor Day is celebrated throughout the United States.	The U.S. Navy reclassifies the destroyer *Boggs* as a "miscellaneous auxiliary" vessel.	Following repeated robberies, the Mercantile State Bank, one of Philadelphia's largest banking institutions with reported assets totaling $200,000, announces it is closing its doors indefinitely.	The National Electric Light Association reports U.S. electric power output for the past week amounted to 1,637,533,000 kilowatt hours, 6 million kilowatt hours less than the preceding week, and a decline of 3 percent from the corresponding period one year ago.	The film *Daughter of the Dragon*, based on a novel by Sax Rohmer and starring Hollywood Walk of Fame recipients Anna May Wong and Sessue Hayakawa, is released throughout the United States. . . . Future Hall of Fame baseball player Lefty Grove wins his 27th game of the 1931 season. . . . The U.S. Naval Academy ends its membership in the Intercollegiate Boxing Association.	Sept. 5
The American Bond and Mortgage Company, a multimillion-dollar enterprise, files for bankruptcy before a federal court in Chicago, Ill. . . . As the prospects of an economically harsh autumn loom, President Herbert Hoover vacations in Rapidan, 100 miles from Washington, D.C., where aides say he is "taking it easy and loafing."		*The Annalist* releases its weekly index of U.S. wholesale commodity prices. At 70.7, the figure is a drop of 1.2 points from the previous week, and a decline of 20 percent from the corresponding period a year ago. Economists say the drop from last week was caused by reductions in freight car loadings, steel mill activity, and automobile production.	The 46th annual meeting of the American Astronomical Society convenes in Delaware, Ohio.		Sept. 6
Many American economists express the belief that an economic recovery will not occur until the end of the coming winter.	The U.S. Navy transfers the destroyer *Idaho* to the East Coast.	Prof. Irving Fisher of Yale University reports that his index of the average price of international commodities has fallen to its lowest point of 1931. Fisher, a world renowned economist, famously commented a few days before the 1929 stock market crash that "stock prices have reached what appears to be a permanently high plateau."	A man in Middletown, N.Y., dies from what doctors call a "severe case of the hiccoughs."	Famed aviator Bert Acosta, who in April 1927 established the world flight endurance record, is arrested for driving while intoxicated in Long Island, N.Y. He is subsequently released on $200 bail. . . . UFA Studios begins production on the musical comedy film *Ronny*.	Sept. 7
A celebration is held in Tampa, Fla., to commemorate the 50th anniversary of the founding of the American Federation of Labor. . . . Former president James Garfield visits President Herbert Hoover at his vacation home in the city of Rapidan, where the pair informally discuss the growing American unemployment problem.			British aviatrix Amy Johnson lands in Koenisberg, Germany.		Sept. 8
	The Mare Island Navy Yard completes construction on the cruiser USS *San Francisco*. The *San Francisco* will be present at the Pearl Harbor naval base during the Japanese sneak attack on December 7, 1941, and will sustain minor damage.	General Motors reports that sales of its automobiles during August 1931 declined by 18 percent as compared to July 1931. . . . The U.S. Federal Farm Board officially rejects a proposed sale of 7.2 million bushels of wheat to Germany.	Benjamin Morowitz, age 12, drowns while attempting to break the world underwater endurance record. . . . The physician of Thomas Edison, Dr. Hubert Howe, reports that the 84-year-old inventor of the light bulb is "definitely failing in health."	Famed aviator Bert Acosta is found not guilty by a court in Long Island of driving under the influence of alcohol, for which he was arrested on September 7.	Sept. 9
Eighteen people accused of fixing milk prices are arrested in New York City.		*The Iron Age* releases its weekly index of U.S. steel mill activity. The index currently stands at 41.7, a decrease of 1.6 points from the previous week, and a decline of approximately 49 percent from the corresponding week one year ago. . . . The U.S. National Automobile Chamber of Commerce reports that U.S. automobile production has declined by 16 percent during the past year.	A Pittsburgh Airways plane flies from Pittsburgh to Newark in one hour and 31 minutes, establishing a record for time taken to fly between the two cities.	Blue Dan, an English setter, is declared Best in Show at the Canadian National Dog Show.	Sept. 10
A New York City librarian who was arrested for selling copies of D.H. Lawrence's *Lady Chatterly's Lover* through the mail is acquitted on charges of "distributing obscene material." . . . Census officials report that the U.S. public school attendance rate has increased by 5 percent since 1920.			A hurricane strikes the Caribbean island of Puerto Rico, causing considerable damage. . . . The National Electric Light Association reports U.S. electric power output for the past week amounted to 1,627,380,000 kilowatt hours, 10 million kilowatt hours less than the preceding week, and a decline of approximately 5 percent from the corresponding period one year ago.	In a bout at the Polo Grounds, world lightweight boxing champion Tony Canzoneri defends his title by defeating English challenger Jack Berg in 15 rounds.	Sept. 11

F
Includes elections, federal-state relations, civil rights and liberties, crime, the judiciary, education, healthcare, poverty, urban affairs, and population.

G
Includes formation and debate of U.S. foreign and defense policies, veterans affairs, and defense spending. (Relations with specific foreign countries are usually found under the region concerned.)

H
Includes business, labor, agriculture, taxation, transportation, consumer affairs, monetary and fiscal policy, natural resources, pollution, and accidents.

I
Includes worldwide scientific, medical, and technological developments, natural phenomena, U.S. weather, and natural disasters.

J
Includes the arts, religion, scholarship, communications media, sports, entertainment, fashions, fads, and social life.

	World Affairs	Europe	Africa & The Middle East	The Americas	Asia & The Pacific
Sept. 12	Speaking on behalf of his constituents at the League of Nations Assembly, French Foreign Minister Aristide Briand says, "We will not in any case, for any cause, or in any circumstances, allow war." . . . Argentina ships $4,255,000 in gold to the United States as part of a repayment of a loan issued early in 1931.	Admiral Walter Gladisch is appointed to the post of Commander in Chief of the German navy. Gladisch succeeds Admiral Ivan Oldekop, who retired. . . . The average salary of British army officers is reduced by 11 percent. . . . Hungarian officials forcibly close down the socialist newspaper *Nepsava*. Protests subsequently break out on the streets of the capital of Budapest.		Four American citizens are deported from Cuba for allegedly participating in illegal revolutionary activities.	In an interview with the *New York Times*, Indian revolutionary leader Mohandas Gandhi says he will not visit the United States, as he believes he is "not wanted." He adds that Americans would likely regard his native customs and attire as oddly peculiar.
Sept. 13		Prime Minister Ramsay MacDonald of Great Britain publicly rejects repeated demands for his resignation. . . . In an editorial in the popular French newspaper *Le Matin*, Jules Sauerwein writes, "France would like to cooperate with her neighbor Germany, even though we have disagreeable memories of the World War."	In Iraq, the death toll from an outbreak of cholera that began on August 1, 1931, rises to 415.		China formally apologizes to Japan for the murder of a Japanese army officer in the Chinese region of Manchuria on August 17, 1931. . . . A deadly typhoon hits the Taiwanese city of Tainan. Twenty-six are killed and 1,000 others are forced to evacuate their homes.
Sept. 14		In Austria, a putsch initiated by the political organization *Heimwehr* is quelled by Austrian national forces. Police say the putsch was led by Dr. Walter Pfriemer, who prior to ordering the seizure of various Austrian government offices had proclaimed himself dictator. . . . British economists report the Bank of England took in a net surplus of £1,337,609 during the past week. Approximately £300,000 was deposited by South Africa.			The first radio speech ever given by Indian revolutionary leader Mohandas Gandhi is broadcast throughout the world. In it, Gandhi expresses his belief of patient pacifism. "I personally would wait, if need be, for ages, rather than seek to obtain the freedom of my country through bloody means," he says.
Sept. 15	German Foreign Minister Julius Curtius declares in a speech to the League of Nations that "all Germans are determined to follow French Foreign Minister Aristide Briand as our leader to the promised land of peace." Nationalist German newspapers describe Curtius's words as unnecessarily conciliatory.	The School of Medicine at the University of Seville burns to the ground in what Spanish officials say is an apparent act of anarchistic arson. . . . Four people are killed as a violent storm drenches the Romanian city of Timisoars.		Puerto Rican Governor Theodore Roosevelt, Jr., arrives in Detroit, Mich., to attend sessions of the American Legion.	
Sept. 16	During a tour of England, New York City Mayor James Walker decides to explore the London nightlife rather than meet his obligation of a pre-arranged meeting with Indian revolutionary leader Mohandas Gandhi. Gandhi is left idly waiting in the lobby of the Kingsley Hall House for over an hour.			A monstrous hurricane hits the British colony of British Honduras of Belize. Russell Taggart, U.S. Consul to Belize, is killed.	Indian revolutionary leader Mohandas Gandhi tells reporters that the goal he wishes to attain through peaceful rebellion is "an India not held by force but by the silken cord of love."
Sept. 17	Dressed in his traditional loin cloth and sandals, Indian revolutionary leader Mohandas Gandhi visits the British House of Commons, where he admits to British reporters that the Indian independence movement faces "formidable difficulties."	Neville Chamberlain, chairman of the British Conservative Party, recommends raising tariffs on all imported goods by 33.3 percent.			
Sept. 18	Following a six-month visit to the United States, Robert Masson, head of France's largest private banking institution, tells members of the American Club in Paris that "America's misfortunes are made up to a great extent of relativity. The fact that they have no starvation and no disorders is an extraordinary achievement." . . . Brazil and Holland preliminarily sign an economic most-favored-nation status agreement.	Austria declares an amnesty for two low-level instigators of the failed putsch that occurred on September 14, 1931. The pair is Prince Rudiger Starhemberg and General Puchmayr. . . . The Berlin Police Department announces that the official newspaper of the German Communist Party, *Rote Fahne (Red Flag)*, will be forcibly shut down for one month.			The Manchurian incident occurs. A Japanese-owned railroad near the Sino-Japanese border is destroyed by a massive explosion. Japanese military officials immediately blame a group of Chinese dissidents for perpetrating the explosion, and order an invasion of Manchuria for the stated purpose of preventing further acts of violence. In later years, China would officially adopt the position that Japan deliberately planted the bombs in order to create a suitable rationale for the invasion of Manchuria.
Sept. 19	American philosopher John Dewey writes a letter to Mohandas Gandhi urging him to visit the United States following round-table independence discussions in England. Spokesmen for the Indian revolutionary leader respond by saying he will likely pay a visit in December 1931, if scheduling conflicts do not arise.			Fifteen hundred residents are reported killed in the hurricane that hit British Honduras. The American ship *Sacramento* is dispatched by U.S. naval authorities to provide reconstruction efforts. . . . Four Chilean seamen are sentenced to death via firing squad for participating in a mutiny aboard the cruiser *O'Higgins* early in August 1931.	A major battle between Chinese Communist rebel forces and nationalist troops in the city of Hengchow results in the rebels being forced to retreat southward.

A	B	C	D	E
Includes developments that affect more than one world region, international organizations, and important meetings of world leaders.	Includes all domestic and regional developments in Europe, including the Soviet Union.	Includes all domestic and regional developments in Africa and the Middle East.	Includes all domestic and regional developments in Latin America, the Caribbean, and Canada.	Includes all domestic and regional developments in Asian and Pacific nations (and colonies).

U.S. Politics & Social Issues	U.S. Foreign Policy & Defense	Economics & Great Depression	Science, Technology & Nature	Culture, Leisure & Lifestyle	
		The Annalist releases its weekly index of U.S. wholesale commodity prices. At 101.2, the figure is a gain of 0.1 points from the previous week, but a decline of 20 percent from the corresponding period a year ago. Economists say the increase from last week was caused by gains in farm products and fuels. . . . The Federal Farm Board sells 7.5 million bushels of wheat to Germany.		RKO Pictures' comedy *Smart Woman*, starring Hollywood Walk of Fame recipients Mary Astor and Edward Horton, is released throughout the United States.	Sept. 12
New York University observes the 100th anniversary of its founding.	Senator William Borah of Idaho proposes a five-year naval construction "holiday" for Great Britain, Japan, France, Italy, and the United States.	*The Annalist* releases its weekly index of U.S. business activity. At 69.8, the figure is a reduction of 1.2 points from the previous week, and a decline of 20 percent from the corresponding period a year ago.	Arctic explorer Admiral Richard Byrd announces that he will soon return to the icy landscape of the South Pole. . . . German biologist Erich Murr discovers that a cat's eyesight is approximately 40 times stronger than that of a human being.	Oscar winner Bing Crosby's musical-comedy short film *I Surrender Dear* is released throughout the United States.	Sept. 13
Encouraged by the widespread appeal within the United States for Senator William Borah's proposal for a five-year naval construction "holiday," members of the Republican National Committee consider nominating the Idaho statesman for the 1932 presidential election.	The submarine *H-3* is sold for scrap by the U.S. Navy.			The Society of American Magicians aids police in ridding New York City of fortune tellers and astrologers. . . . The German Ski League passes a resolution stating that it will not compete in the 1932 Winter Olympics Games in Lake Placid, N.Y. Members of the League tell reporters that a lack of funds due to depressive economic conditions greatly influenced the decision.	Sept. 14
Noted lawyer Clarence Darrow, who defended teacher John Scopes in the infamous Scopes Monkey Trial, is appointed by the National Association for the Advancement of Colored People to lead the legal appeal of eight African-American boys who were convicted early in 1931 of raping a white woman in Scottsboro, Ala.		The weekly index of U.S. automobile production as compiled by the Department of Commerce is released. The index currently stands at 45.3, a decrease of 1.4 points from the previous week, and a reduction of 29 percent from the corresponding week one year ago.	U.S. Assistant Commerce Secretary for Aeronautics Clarence Young reports that during the first six months of 1931, there were only nine deaths attributable to airline accidents.		Sept. 15
	U.S. Army Chief of Staff Gen. Douglas MacArthur is made an honorary member of the French Legion of Honor by War Minister Andre Maginot.	Former Hoven State Bank president Thomas O'Brien is convicted of embezzlement and sentenced to a four-year prison term. . . . Canada ships $1 million worth of gold to the United States.		The Philadelphia Athletics defeat the Cleveland Indians by a score of 14–3 to clinch their third consecutive American League pennant. Every member of the Athletics starting line-up garnered a hit in the victory.	Sept. 16
The 54th annual convention of the American Bar Association convenes in Atlantic City, N.J.	Retired Gen. Smedley Butler is urged by constituents of Philadelphia's Eighth Congressional District to run for office.	The average price of U.S. export copper falls to 7.5 cents, a record low. . . . The advertising agencies Kling-Gibson Company and Critchfield & Co. merge. . . . *The Iron Age* releases its weekly index of U.S. steel mill activity. The index currently stands at 43.5, an increase of 1.8 points from the previous week, but a decline of approximately 49 percent from the corresponding week one year ago.	Eight hundred delegates representing 34 nations converge in Paris to participate in the annual International Geographical Union Congress.	The world champion Philadelphia Athletics win their 100th game of the 1931 season. . . . The St. Louis Cardinals defeat the Philadelphia Phillies to clinch their second consecutive National League title. . . . Former U.S. Gen. John Clinnin is reelected as president of the National Boxing Association.	Sept. 17
The American Bar Association releases the results of a survey showing that 65 percent of its members favor repeal of Prohibition.			The Madison Square Garden Corp. announces construction plans for a boxing arena to be built in Jersey City, N.J., with a capacity of 70,000. . . . The National Electric Light Association reports U.S. electric power output for the past week amounted to 1,582,267,000 kilowatt hours, 50 million kilowatt hours less than the preceding week, and a decline of 8 percent from the corresponding period one year ago.		Sept. 18
The *New York Times* newspaper turns 80 years old. . . . The Census Bureau reports that the number of foreign-born whites residing in the United States increased by only 111,033 from 1920 to 1930.		Brazil drastically lowers tariffs on imported goods from the United States, effectively granting most-favored-nation status.		*Monkey Business*, considered to be one of the Marx brothers' greatest films, is released throughout the United States. . . . Athletics pitcher Lefty Grove defeats the Chicago White Sox 3–1, setting a record number of wins for left-handed pitchers at 30.	Sept. 19

F	G	H	I	J
Includes elections, federal-state relations, civil rights and liberties, crime, the judiciary, education, healthcare, poverty, urban affairs, and population.	*Includes formation and debate of U.S. foreign and defense policies, veterans affairs, and defense spending. (Relations with specific foreign countries are usually found under the region concerned.)*	*Includes business, labor, agriculture, taxation, transportation, consumer affairs, monetary and fiscal policy, natural resources, pollution, and accidents.*	*Includes worldwide scientific, medical, and technological developments, natural phenomena, U.S. weather, and natural disasters.*	*Includes the arts, religion, scholarship, communications media, sports, entertainment, fashions, fads, and social life.*

	World Affairs	Europe	Africa & The Middle East	The Americas	Asia & The Pacific
Sept. 20		Hungarian excavators in the city of Pecs discover the remains of what are believed to be artifacts from the ancient Celtic civilization. . . . Victoria Kent becomes the first Spanish woman to be appointed to the position of director of the country's state prisons. . . . An unnamed niece of future Nazi leader Adolf Hitler commits suicide in one of her uncle's homes in Berlin. German newspapers say her motive for suicide is undetermined.		Provisional President Jose Uriburu of Argentina signs a decree extending his nation's ban on imported Paraguayan oranges for 30 days. Argentine newspapers claim the decision will have economically detrimental consequences. . . . Panamanian Finance Minister Enrique Jimenez announces his resignation amid internal strife. . . . The Canadian unemployment rate rises to 5 percent.	
Sept. 21	The U.S. Census Bureau reports that Germany has the world's highest percentage of foreign-born residents. . . . Indian revolutionary leader Mohandas Gandhi writes a letter to the *New York Times* in which he states, "To me, truth and nonviolence are faces of the same coin. Wherever you are confronted with an opponent, conquer him with love."	German labor experts report that the number of registered unemployed Germans has decreased by nearly 1,000 since the winter of 1930–31. . . . British economists report the Bank of England took in £977,440 worth of gold during the past week, against £4,378,225 in withdrawals, netting a deficit of £3,400,785. Approximately £900,000 was deposited by South Africa.			Famed aviator Charles Lindbergh expresses a willingness to assist Chinese authorities in relieving those affected by a recent flooding of the Yangtze River. . . . A tremendous earthquake rocks the Japanese capital of Tokyo. Officials claim the earthquake's magnitude is the largest recorded in nearly 10 years. . . . Chinese Foreign Minister C.T. Wang invokes the 1927 Kellogg-Briand Pact, which declared war to be illegal, in protesting the Japanese invasion of Manchuria.
Sept. 22		British naval officials reduce the salaries of all naval officers by an average of 10 percent. . . . Austria allows future Nazi leader Adolf Hitler to attend his niece's funeral in Vienna, under the condition that he refrain from engaging in political activities.		The value of the Canadian dollar falls to its lowest point since July 1924.	Refusing offers of Japanese food aid, Chinese National Flood Relief Commission head T.V. Soong tells visiting Japanese diplomats that "you will doubtless understand that recent events in Manchuria prevent my commission from accepting the supplies."
Sept. 23	Indian revolutionary leader Mohandas Gandhi meets with American silent film comedian Charlie Chaplin. The meeting was arranged at Gandhi's request. . . . The League of Nations requests U.S. assistance in preventing war between China and Japan.	The British unemployment rate decreases for the first time since July 1931. . . . Five Spaniards are killed during a Communist riot in Toledo. . . . Following a meeting with the newly appointed French Ambassador to Germany, Andre Francois-Poncet, German President Paul von Hindenburg urges full cooperation with the French government in solving the worldwide financial crisis.	Two Egyptian stock exchanges located in the cities of Alexandria and Cairo close their doors as market conditions worsen.	Members of the Cuban House of Representatives consider passing a bill that would add human rights amendments to their country's constitution.	
Sept. 24	Prime Minister Pierre Laval of France announces he will pay a diplomatic visit to the United States in October.	Twenty-three German youths are sentenced to one-year prison terms for participating in a National Socialist riot during the most recent Jewish New Year.			Chinese leaders declare September 24 a "national humiliation day," and ask citizens to reflect on the Japanese invasion of Manchuria.
Sept. 25	During sessions of the League of Nations, French Finance Minister Pierre Flandin declares that the League's objective of solving the worldwide financial crisis is "impossible" without the assistance of the United States.	Fifty thousand people demonstrate in London, England, against a reduction in dole payments. Police are dispatched to preserve order. . . . The Soviet Union denies repeated rumors of the mobilization of troops along the Manchurian border. . . . Genevieve Tyler is made an honorary member of the Legion of Honor by the French government for her work with French soldiers blinded in World War I.		President Olaya Herrera of Colombia forbids the exportation of gold in an effort to improve the slumping Colombian peso.	Chinese leaders report that growing public sentiment favoring war with Japan has evolved into "almost unbearable tension." . . . China officially adopts a policy of nonresistance toward invading Japanese forces in Manchuria.
Sept. 26	In a statement, Japanese Viscount Kikujiro Ishii formally protests a proposed League of Nations committee that would be sent to Manchuria to investigate China's claims of direct Japanese perpetration in the Manchurian Incident. "The idea of sending such a mission," Ishii says, "can emanate only from suspicion of the accuracy of the solemn statement made by the Japanese government."	Prime Minister Pierre Laval of France and Foreign Minister Aristide Briand travel to Germany in an attempt to improve relations between the two countries. . . . Prime Minister Eleftherios Venizelos of Greece announces that the Greek Stock Exchange will remain closed until October 5. . . . Army Chief of Staff Douglas MacArthur arrives in Belgrade, Yugoslavia, to review and recommend changes to the Yugoslavian army.		Honduran lawmakers reduce their country's federal budget by $2 million.	The Bombay Stock Exchange reopens after nearly a week of inactivity.

A	B	C	D	E
Includes developments that affect more than one world region, international organizations, and important meetings of world leaders.	*Includes all domestic and regional developments in Europe, including the Soviet Union.*	*Includes all domestic and regional developments in Africa and the Middle East.*	*Includes all domestic and regional developments in Latin America, the Caribbean, and Canada.*	*Includes all domestic and regional developments in Asian and Pacific nations (and colonies).*

U.S. Politics & Social Issues	U.S. Foreign Policy & Defense	Economics & Great Depression	Science, Technology & Nature	Culture, Leisure & Lifestyle	
Chairman Simeon Fess of the Republican National Committee predicts an "overwhelming" landslide for President Herbert Hoover in the upcoming 1932 presidential elections. Laying blame for present economic conditions on the aftermath of World War I, he warns Americans to be wary of proposed "quack remedies" such as a national dole system.		The Annalist releases its weekly index of U.S. wholesale commodity prices. At 69.8, the figure is nearly identical to the previous week, but a decline of 19 percent from the corresponding period a year ago. Economists say the stabilization from last week was caused by increases in steel mill activity and electric power production, offset by losses in automobile production.		Wallace Fox's western Near the Trail's End is released throughout the United States. . . . Side Show, starring Hollywood Walk of Fame recipient Charles Butterworth, is released. . . . Future Hall of Fame baseball player Mel Ott is knocked unconscious in a game against the St. Louis Cardinals as a screeching fastball by pitcher Burleigh Grimes hits the back of his skull. He is rushed to the local hospital, where doctors confirm that he suffered a major concussion.	Sept. 20
White House spokesmen announce that President Herbert Hoover's federal public works fund currently amounts to $1.6 billion.				Alexandre Alekhine of France defeats a lowly challenger in 15 moves to remain undefeated in the annual International Chess Masters' tournament. . . . The 35th annual U.S. women's national golf championship commences in Williamsville, N.Y.	Sept. 21
		The weekly index of U.S. automobile production as compiled by the Department of Commerce is released. The index currently stands at 45.2, a drop of 0.1 points from the previous week, and a decline of 27 percent from the corresponding week one year ago.	Future Medal of Honor recipient James Doolittle establishes a record for time taken to fly between New York City and Memphis, Tenn., traversing the skies between the two cities in a span of four hours and 57 minutes.	The Philadelphia Athletics win their 105th game of the 1931 season, establishing a team record.	Sept. 22
Two thousand National Guard troops are dispatched into Iowa to enforce a newly passed unpopular law requiring all cows to undergo testing for tuberculosis.		The U.S. federal budget deficit rises to $363,089,200.	The U.S. airship Akron, christened by First Lady Lou Henry Hoover in early August, embarks on its maiden voyage, flying around the skies of Cleveland, Ohio. Among those aboard the vessel is Naval Secretary Charles Francis Adams.		Sept. 23
Governor Franklin Roosevelt of New York signs a bill creating a $20 million unemployment relief program. . . . Senator Burton Wheeler of Montana tells reporters that "the sentiment for Governor Franklin Roosevelt is so strong, that I have no hesitancy in predicting that he will be nominated on the first ballot of the 1932 Democratic presidential nomination."		The Iron Age releases its weekly index of U.S. steel mill activity. The index currently stands at 41.8, a drop of 1.7 points from the previous week, and a decline of approximately 51 percent from the corresponding week one year ago. . . . The American Legion requests President Herbert Hoover to declare a national state of emergency in order to solve the growing unemployment crisis.	News of only 22 new reported cases of infantile paralysis, or "polio" as it is more commonly known, in New York City prompt health officials to declare that "the disease is disappearing." . . . Aviator Frank Hawks eclipses James Doolittle's Memphis to New York flight record by seven minutes.		Sept. 24
		The Annalist releases its weekly index of U.S. wholesale commodity prices. At 100.0, the figure is a drop of 0.4 points from the previous week, and a decline of 18 percent from the corresponding period a year ago. Economists say the drop from last week was caused by losses in food products, metals, and building materials.	Personal physicians of Thomas Edison report that the 84-year-old inventor's health has taken a turn for the better.	RKO's Devotion, starring Hollywood Walk of Fame recipients Ann Harding and Leslie Howard, is released throughout the United States. . . . The film Call of the Wild, based on the Jack London novel of the same name, is released throughout Spain. . . . The New York Yankees host a special exhibition game to benefit New York City's idle workers. The ticket revenue of $50,000 is added to the city's unemployment relief fund.	Sept. 25
The People's Bank of Alliance, Ohio, suspends operations following excessive withdrawals.	The Newport News Shipbuilding Company completes construction on the aircraft carrier USS Ranger.		Aviator Frank Hawks sets a New York interstate speed record by flying from New York City to Schenectady in 39 minutes. . . . The National Electric Light Association reports U.S. electric power output for the past week amounted to 236,500,000 kilowatt hours, 1 million kilowatt hours less than the preceding week, and a decline of 11 percent from the corresponding period one year ago.	The Betty Boop animated short film Minding the Baby is released throughout the United States by Paramount Pictures.	Sept. 26

F	G	H	I	J
Includes elections, federal-state relations, civil rights and liberties, crime, the judiciary, education, healthcare, poverty, urban affairs, and population.	Includes formation and debate of U.S. foreign and defense policies, veterans affairs, and defense spending. (Relations with specific foreign countries are usually found under the region concerned.)	Includes business, labor, agriculture, taxation, transportation, consumer affairs, monetary and fiscal policy, natural resources, pollution, and accidents.	Includes worldwide scientific, medical, and technological developments, natural phenomena, U.S. weather, and natural disasters.	Includes the arts, religion, scholarship, communications media, sports, entertainment, fashions, fads, and social life.

	World Affairs	Europe	Africa & The Middle East	The Americas	Asia & The Pacific
Sept. 27				Uruguay proposes a commercial treaty to Cuba under which the former's chief export, jerked beef, would be exported into Cuba at a substantially low tariff rate in exchange for the importation into Uruguay of 50,000 tons of crude sugar annually. . . . The Canadian Dominion Bureau of Statistics reports a drop in the Canadian unemployment rate during the month of August 1931.	
Sept. 28		British economists report the Bank of England's gold reserves have risen to £135 million.			
Sept. 29	The German newspaper *Volkszeitung* (*The People's Paper*) announces that German Chancellor Heinrich Bruening will visit U.S. President Herbert Hoover in Washington, D.C., in December 1931.				American explorer Roy Chapman Andrews returns to the United States following his failed expedition to the Gobi Desert. Chapman claims that Chinese governmental objections prevented the expedition from continuing.
Sept. 30		The number of British idle workers rises to 2,811,615, an increase of 22,535 in one week. Economists attribute the figures to a sagging British automobile industry.			
Oct. 1		King Albert I of Belgium arrives in France along with Queen Elizabeth. The pair will confer with French lawmakers. . . . British economic officials release figures showing that their country's federal budget deficit has nearly doubled since September 1930, from £58,208,866 to £98,410,249.		In an effort to boost their country's agriculture, Peruvian lawmakers drastically reduce taxes on fertilizer.	
Oct. 2		The newly appointed Argentine Ambassador to Great Britain, Don Manuel Malbran, makes his first official visit to London, where he presents his credentials to King George V.		Argentine economists publish figures showing that losses from business bankruptcies in September 1931 amounted to 35,269,304 pesos.	
Oct. 3				A bomb explodes near a merry-go-round attraction in Havana, Cuba, severely injuring 10 small children. . . . Brazilians celebrate the one-year anniversary of the overthrow of President Washington Luis's regime.	
Oct. 4		French Foreign Minister Aristide Briand visits the gravesite of 1926 Nobel Peace Prize recipient Gustav Stresemann in Berlin, Germany. He encounters a group of saluting Nazi party members, who he assumes were expressing admiration for the French statesman's "peaceful" nature. . . . German Chancellor Heinrich Bruening issues a decree placing a cap on the salaries of high-ranking officials of private industrial corporations.			

A	B	C	D	E
Includes developments that affect more than one world region, international organizations, and important meetings of world leaders.	Includes all domestic and regional developments in Europe, including the Soviet Union.	Includes all domestic and regional developments in Africa and the Middle East.	Includes all domestic and regional developments in Latin America, the Caribbean, and Canada.	Includes all domestic and regional developments in Asian and Pacific nations (and colonies).

U.S. Politics & Social Issues	U.S. Foreign Policy & Defense	Economics & Great Depression	Science, Technology & Nature	Culture, Leisure & Lifestyle	
President Herbert Hoover announces he will recommend to Congress the cutting of governmental expenses as a means of reducing the national budget, instead of raising taxes as had been suggested by some lawmakers.		*The Annalist* releases its weekly index of U.S. wholesale commodity prices. At 68.9, the figure is a reduction of 1.1 points from the previous week, and a drop of 19 percent from the corresponding period a year ago. Economists say the reduction from last week was caused by drops in steel mill activity and cotton cloth production.		The mystery film *The Spider*, starring Hollywood Walk of Fame recipient Edmund Lowe, is released throughout the United States. . . . Heavy rainstorms in Philadelphia force the cancellation of the last two games of the Athletics' baseball season, denying them the chance to tie the American League win record of 110.	Sept. 27
Socialist Party national chairman Morris Hillquit declares in a statement that implementation of socialist economic policies is the only veritable means to offset what he calls "the grave emergency which is fast developing into a national calamity." He claims that "industry leaders prate about 'self-help' when the masses are helpless to cope with the monstrous industrial organizations that dominate their lives."				The animated short film *Fairyland Follies* is released throughout the United States. . . . Philadelphia Athletics outfielder Al Simmons is declared the American League batting champion. Simmons garnered 200 hits in 513 at-bats, netting a batting average of .390.	Sept. 28
In an article in the *Saturday Evening Post*, former president Calvin Coolidge, who served from 1923–29, advocates a second presidential term for his successor, Herbert Hoover. . . . In New York City, 1,800 candy factory workers go on strike, protesting low wages and long hours.		The weekly index of U.S. automobile production as compiled by the Department of Commerce is released. The index currently stands at 43.9, a decrease of 1.3 points from the previous week, and a decline of 19 percent from the corresponding week one year ago.		Maureen Orcutt wins the annual Canadian women's national golf championship. . . . St. Louis Cardinals leftfielder Chick Hafey is declared the National League batting champion. Hafey garnered 157 hits in 450 at-bats, netting a batting average of .349.	Sept. 29
Republicans in Washington, D.C., tell reporters that Calvin Coolidge's endorsement of President Herbert Hoover all but assures him the 1932 Republican nomination.		Chile and the United States enter into an economic most-favored-nation status agreement.	Equipped with a new patented fuel containing gasoline and wood alcohol, British aviator G.H. Stainforth sets the world airspeed record by flying around the skies of Calshot, England, at 408.8 miles per hour.	The Jeffrey Dell play *Payment Deferred* premiers in New York City.	Sept. 30
The Labor Department issues figures showing that nationwide employment in manufacturing industries has declined by 12 percent since September 1930. . . . A strike of nearly 2,000 New York City candy factory workers ends as union representatives and employers reach a compromise. . . . Arriving at his recuperative resort in Warm Springs, Ga., Governor Franklin Roosevelt of New York is told by members of the Georgia Democratic Party that the Democratic National Convention has "practically met and nominated" him for the 1932 presidential election.	At his retirement ceremony, Gen. Smedley Butler officially retires with the words, "You may haul down my flag, sir," and is officially placed on the U.S. Marines' list of retired generals. Butler gained national acclaim in 1930 when he spread a rumor that Italian Premier Benito Mussolini was once the perpetrator of a hit-and-run accident.	*The Iron Age* releases its weekly index of U.S. steel mill activity. The index currently stands at 39.4, a drop of 2.4 points from the previous week, and a decline of approximately 52 percent from the corresponding week one year ago. . . . California legislators vote to construct a $200 million aqueduct that officials say will provide employment for 10,000 Californians for six years.		Las Vegas bookies place odds of 7 to 10 that the Philadelphia Athletics will win their third straight World Series title. . . . The Philadelphia Athletics defeat the St. Louis Cardinals by a score of 6–2 in the first game of the 1931 World Series. Future Hall of Famer Lefty Grove surrenders only two runs over nine innings pitched.	Oct. 1
Retired Gen. Smedley Butler tells reporters that the main economic problem facing the United States is "that the bulk of the nation's wealth is concentrated in the hands of the few."		The U.S. Commerce Department reports that U.S. grain exports have declined by nearly 1 million bushels since September 1930.	The National Electric Light Association reports U.S. electric power output for the past week amounted to 1,660,204,000 kilowatt hours, 2 million kilowatt hours less than the preceding week, and a reduction of 3 percent from the corresponding period one year ago. . . . A devastating drought in Uruguay leaves citizens of the city of Melo without drinking water.	By a score of 2–0, the St. Louis Cardinals defeat the Philadelphia Athletics in the second game of the World Series. The series is tied at one game apiece. Cardinals pitcher Bill Hallahan shuts out the Athletics, surrendering only three hits over nine innings pitched.	Oct. 2
American Federation of Labor president William Green warns that depressive economic conditions may result in a nationwide "revolt" unless tax increases are levied upon high-income earners.	Naval Secretary Charles Francis Adams tells newspaper reporters that he is considering cutting the Navy's budget by 20 percent as a means of improving the nation's fledgling economy.	Anticipating future comments by Franklin Roosevelt that "the only thing we have to fear is fear itself," Prudential Insurance Company president Edward Duffield claims that psychological effects are the main cause for the Great Depression.	Inventor Thomas Edison, age 84, is stricken with indigestion, weakening his already anemic health. . . . Aviator Frank Hawks flies from New York City to Columbus, Ga., in four hours and 45 minutes, establishing a record for time taken to fly between the two cities.		Oct. 3
The New York City Uniformed Firemen's Association submits to the Board of Aldermen a petition asking for a universal eight-hour workday. The petition includes over 2 million signatures. . . . In an editorial in *The American Federationist*, American Federation of Labor president William Green writes, "50 cents added to the weekly wages of every wage-earner in the country would do more to start us toward prosperity than wage cuts or price cuts."	Senate Naval Affairs Committee chairman Frederick Hale tells reporters he will vigorously challenge Naval Secretary Charles Francis Adams's proposed naval budget reductions.	*The Annalist* releases its weekly index of U.S. business activity. At 68.0, the figure is a drop of 0.7 points from the previous week and a decline of 22 percent from the corresponding period last year. Economists say the drop from last week was caused by reductions in freight car loadings and steel mill activity.			Oct. 4

F	G	H	I	J
Includes elections, federal-state relations, civil rights and liberties, crime, the judiciary, education, healthcare, poverty, urban affairs, and population.	*Includes formation and debate of U.S. foreign and defense policies, veterans affairs, and defense spending. (Relations with specific foreign countries are usually found under the region concerned.)*	*Includes business, labor, agriculture, taxation, transportation, consumer affairs, monetary and fiscal policy, natural resources, pollution, and accidents.*	*Includes worldwide scientific, medical, and technological developments, natural phenomena, U.S. weather, and natural disasters.*	*Includes the arts, religion, scholarship, communications media, sports, entertainment, fashions, fads, and social life.*

	World Affairs	Europe	Africa & The Middle East	The Americas	Asia & The Pacific
Oct. 5		German economists report that nearly 63 percent of the country's construction workers are unemployed.		Presidential elections are held in Chile. Conservative candidate Juan Esteban Montero, a former professor at the University of Chile, is declared the victor, receiving over 60 percent of the popular vote. He pledges to establish "the sanest, most honest constitutional administration."	
Oct. 6	The Chinese government sends a letter to the State Department requesting that the United States formulate a special commission to investigate the Manchurian Incident. Washington insiders tell reporters that the United States will likely not act on China's request.	Austrian Finance Minister Joseph Redlich announces his resignation.		The entire Cabinet of Panamanian President Ricardo Jovane resigns.	Japanese military officials reverse an earlier decision to withdraw troops from Manchuria on October 14, claiming that violent disturbances require continued troop deployments.
Oct. 7		The number of jobless Britons rises to 2,825,722, an increase of 664,083 from October 1930. . . . German Foreign Minister Julius Curtius announces his resignation after reports surface of the failure of the proposed German-Austrian customs union. Curtius first took office upon the death of 1926 Nobel Peace Prize winner Gustav Stresseman.			Chinese officials express fear of an imminent Japanese invasion of Shanghai. . . . Continued anti-Japanese disturbances in southern China prompt Japanese military officials to dispatch an additional 300 troops to the region.
Oct. 8	American Federation of Labor president William Green urges the extension of the Hoover Moratorium for "several years."	Romanian officials report that the capital city of Bucharest has nearly doubled in population since 1912, from 341,000 to 632,000. . . . Forty thousand Italian youths march on Rome in celebration of the one-year anniversary of the founding of their fascist youth organization, *Giovine Fascisti*. Premier Benito Mussolini personally reviews the youngsters.			Famed aviator Charles Lindbergh leaves China after surveying the damage caused by the recent flooding of the Yangtze River.
Oct. 9	The Japanese aerial bombing of the Chinese city of Chinchow arouses concern in Washington, D.C. Chinese Chargé d'Affaires Yung Kwi holds a private conference with U.S. Secretary of State Henry Stimson. . . . Cuban Secretary of the Interior Octavio Zubizarreta orders the deportation of 16 Americans accused of spreading subversive propaganda and participating in labor disputes.	Yale University president James Angell is made an honorary officer of the French Legion of Honor by the French Ambassador to the United States, Paul Claudel.		President Getulio Vargas of Brazil declares a 60-day moratorium for all debts owed to the South American nation. . . . Four Chilean naval officers, including six captains and four commanders, are dismissed from their ranks for participating in a failed coup that occurred early in September 1931.	
Oct. 10	The American-Chinese Merchants' Association announces it will boycott all imported Japanese goods in retaliation for the Japanese invasion of Manchuria.	Irish officials announce that they have documents in their possession that establish a direct link between the Irish Republican Guard, a "terrorist organization," and the Soviet Union.		Argentine economists report that their country exported 382,000 metric tons of corn during the past week, a new weekly record. . . . President Gerardo Machado of Cuba calls on Cuban senators to pass legislation heavily raising taxes. . . . Former Ecuadorian president Isidro Ayora, who left office early in 1931, is accused of "misappropriating public funds" by the Ecuadorian Chamber of Deputies. The Chamber cites a lavish party thrown in honor of U.S. President Herbert Hoover as an example of Ayora's misdeeds.	
Oct. 11	Members of the League of Nations urge the United States to discontinue its isolationist stance toward the Japanese invasion of Manchuria.	The Yugoslavian government awards Helen Keller the ceremonial title of St. Sava for her work with the blind. . . . Chancellor Heinrich Bruening predicts in remarks to reporters that this winter the number of unemployed Germans will rise to 7 million. Bruening adds that an unemployment fund of nearly $1 billion will be needed to offset what he predicts will be the worst winter Europe has ever experienced. . . . A strike of Greek taxi workers forces many citizens of Athens to walk to work.			Mohandas Gandhi publishes *Gandhi at Work*, an autobiography of the 62-year-old Indian revolutionary leader's life and times.

A	B	C	D	E
Includes developments that affect more than one world region, international organizations, and important meetings of world leaders.	Includes all domestic and regional developments in Europe, including the Soviet Union.	Includes all domestic and regional developments in Africa and the Middle East.	Includes all domestic and regional developments in Latin America, the Caribbean, and Canada.	Includes all domestic and regional developments in Asian and Pacific nations (and colonies).

U.S. Politics & Social Issues	U.S. Foreign Policy & Defense	Economics & Great Depression	Science, Technology & Nature	Culture, Leisure & Lifestyle	
In New York City, Rev. Randolph Ray claims the chief cause of the Great Depression is Prohibition.		Yale economics professor James Rogers lays blame for the Great Depression on the 1930 Smoot-Hawley Tariff Act, which he says has forced many industries to flee abroad. . . . The U.S. Chamber of Commerce recommends the lifting of anti-trust laws as a means of stimulating business and industry.	During a speech in Berlin, Germany, Albert Einstein offers an explanation for his career choice: "When I was a boy, I planned to become an engineer, but I said to myself, 'So much has already been invented, why should I, too, devote myself to that sort of thing?'"	The St. Louis Cardinals defeat the Philadelphia Athletics by a score of 5–2 to take a 2 to 1 advantage in the World Series. Cardinals pitcher Burleigh Grimes tosses a complete game, surrendering two runs over nine innings pitched. President Herbert Hoover is among those in the stands.	Oct. 5
New Jersey Senator Dwight W. Morrow, father-in-law of famed aviator Charles Lindbergh, dies suddenly from a cerebral hemorrhage at his home in Englewood, N.J. President Herbert Hoover calls him "the sort of American who makes our country great." . . . Two thousand Communist demonstrators in Cleveland, Ohio, march on City Hall. Police are dispatched, leading to open fistfights.		Freight car loadings for the past week amounted to 739,029 cars, according to figures published by the American Railway Association. The total is 4,599 cars less than the previous week, and a decline of 21 percent from the corresponding week last year. The drop from last week was attributable to losses in grain products, forest products, and ore.		J. Roy Stockton is elected president of the Baseball Writers Association of America. . . . By a score of 3–0, the Philadelphia Athletics defeat the St. Louis Cardinals to tie the World Series at two games apiece. Athletics pitcher George Earnshaw, who was named the most valuable player of the 1930 World Series, throws a two-hit shutout.	Oct. 6
Rep. John McDuffie of Alabama calls on President Herbert Hoover to create a World Cotton Conference. . . . The Metropolitan Life Insurance Company reports that the U.S. death rate for the month of August was 0.74 percent, the lowest on record. . . . Funeral services are held for deceased senator Dwight Morrow.			The National Electric Light Association reports U.S. electric power output for the past week amounted to 1,645,587,000 kilowatt hours, 15 million kilowatt hours less than the preceding week, and a decline of 4 percent from the corresponding period one year ago.	The St. Louis Cardinals defeat the Philadelphia Athletics by a score of 5–1 to take the lead, 3 games to 2, in the World Series.	Oct. 7
Speaking from his retreat in Warm Springs, Ga., New York Governor Franklin Roosevelt expresses caution toward President Herbert Hoover's proposed $500 million credit corporation.		The Iron Age releases its weekly index of U.S. steel mill activity. The index currently stands at 40.8, a rise of 1.4 points from the previous week, but a decline of approximately 48 percent from the corresponding week one year ago.			Oct. 8
American farmers rejoice over the Department of Commerce's report that the U.S. cotton crop for the 1931–32 season will amount to 16,284,000 bales, the second largest crop total on record.		The Annalist releases its weekly index of U.S. wholesale commodity prices. At 99.9, the figure is nearly identical to the previous week, but a decline of 18 percent from the corresponding period a year ago. Economists say the stabilization from last week was caused by a rise in food products, offset by a decrease in building materials.		Philadelphia Athletics pitcher Lefty Grove pitches a complete game to help his team trounce the St. Louis Cardinals 8–1 and tie the World Series at three games apiece.	Oct. 9
	The War Department awards contracts totaling $1,931,954 for the construction of 53 new aircraft and 100 aircraft engines. . . . The Navy Department purchases 15 observation planes from the Chance Vought Corporation for a sum of $280,650.	The Brazilian National Coffee Council requests a loan of $109.6 million from various creditors, both domestic and international.		Game seven of the World Series is held in Sportsman's Park in St. Louis, Mo. The St. Louis Cardinals defeat the Philadelphia Athletics 4–2 with a stellar pitching performance by Burleigh Grimes to win their second World Series title. Cardinals rookie centerfielder Pepper Martin is declared the most valuable player. Martin batted 12 for 24 during the Series, netting an average of .500.	Oct. 10
The state of Michigan begins construction on a $10 million highway system that officials say will provide employment for over 30,000 idle workers.		The Annalist releases its weekly index of U.S. business activity. At 68.6, the figure is a rise of 0.7 points from the previous week but a decline of 18 percent from the corresponding period last year. Economists say the rise from last week was caused by increases in freight car loadings, steel mill activity, and cotton cloth production.	The New York state capital of Albany experiences a near-record low temperature for the month of October, 34°F.	The Recreation Congress of the United States announces the first annual World Recreation Congress will be held in Los Angeles, Calif., in July 1932.	Oct. 11

F	G	H	I	J
Includes elections, federal-state relations, civil rights and liberties, crime, the judiciary, education, healthcare, poverty, urban affairs, and population.	Includes formation and debate of U.S. foreign and defense policies, veterans affairs, and defense spending. (Relations with specific foreign countries are usually found under the region concerned.)	Includes business, labor, agriculture, taxation, transportation, consumer affairs, monetary and fiscal policy, natural resources, pollution, and accidents.	Includes worldwide scientific, medical, and technological developments, natural phenomena, U.S. weather, and natural disasters.	Includes the arts, religion, scholarship, communications media, sports, entertainment, fashions, fads, and social life.

	World Affairs	Europe	Africa & The Middle East	The Americas	Asia & The Pacific
Oct. 12	Descendants of opposing Revolutionary War generals Charles Cornwallis and George Washington meet in Philadelphia, Pa., to "patch up the ancient differences between Great Britain and the United States."	Attempts by statesmen to improve relations between France and Germany are marred by jingoist posturing by future Nazi leader Adolf Hitler. A headline in a popular nationalist German newspaper reads, "Hitler Declares War on France." Editorials express the belief that German Chancellor Heinrich Bruening will soon resign. France adopts a position of "watchful waiting" toward the tense political situation in Germany.		Uruguayan economists release figures showing that Argentina has officially surpassed the United States as the chief source of Uruguayan imports.	
Oct. 13	During a speech in London, England, Indian revolutionary leader Mohandas Gandhi expresses his views on martyrdom, saying, "I would consider it nothing if we had to pay a million lives for our liberty, but I am praying the future historian will say that India won her liberty without shedding human blood." . . . The League of Nations reports that China's army is nearly 10 times the size of Japan's. Officials say the inferiority of Japan's army prevents them from fully invading China.	Several of Germany's most powerful labor unions formulate plans to counter the Nationalist Socialist party's rumored ambitions of a fascist dictatorship. . . . France's gold reserves rise to $2.4 billion.		Approximately 100,000 Chinese residents of Cuba draft a petition protesting the Japanese invasion of Manchuria.	
Oct. 14	Boston Mayor James Curley sends a personal invitation to Indian revolutionary leader Mohandas Gandhi to visit his city.	The number of unemployed British workers drops to 2,791,520, a decrease of 33,525 from the week ended October 7. Officials hail the figures as a return to prosperity in Great Britain. . . . In a speech during sessions of the Reichstag, German Chancellor Heinrich Bruening threatens the expansion of executive power, declaring, "The present state of distress demands the concentration of all power of the State against subversive activities."			Prof. Grover Clark of the Chinese National University alleges in a radio broadcast that Japan planned well in advance the invasion of Manchuria: "Every unit evidently knew precisely what to do when the signal came."
Oct. 15	The United States announces that despite cooperation with the League of Nations in solving the Manchurian Incident, it will continue to refrain from officially becoming a member of the League. Japan announces it will only accept U.S. assistance in resolving the Manchurian Incident if the United States becomes a permanent member.			Four members of Mexican President Ortiz Rubio's Cabinet announce their resignations: the Minister of War, the Minister of Communications, the Minister of the Interior, and the Minister of Agriculture. Former president Plutarco Calles is called out of retirement to assume the post of War Minister.	China announces it will refuse to discuss peace talks with Japan unless Japanese forces are completely evacuated from Manchuria. Japan responds by saying continued deployments are necessary to protect the lives and property of Japanese citizens residing in the region.
Oct. 16	Indian revolutionary leader Mohandas Gandhi praises American Prohibition in a letter to the U.S. Anti-Saloon League: "It was a brave step, and it would be a shame if America returned to the drink evil."	A Communist demonstration in the German capital of Berlin on the eve of a "critical Reichstag session" results in scores of arrests and injuries. . . . The gold reserves of the Bank of France rise to 60.5 billion francs, the highest total on record. . . . The number of unemployed Italians rises to 747,000, an increase of 54,000 from September 1931, according to statistics compiled by Italian economic officials.		Fearing a revolt, Uruguayan Interior Minister Francisco Ghigliani temporarily bans all public demonstrations considered to be subversive.	
Oct. 17	French officials express opposition toward the invitation by the League of Nations for the United States to participate in Council deliberations over the Japanese invasion of Manchuria. . . . The League of Nations reports that Germany's armaments expenditures in 1930 amounted to $176,930,655.	By a vote of 83–65, Irish lawmakers pass a bill enabling the country's military courts to conduct their own trials against those accused of seditious activities.			Japanese military officials claim the 1928 Kellogg-Briand Pact, which declared war anywhere in the world to be illegal, does not apply to the invasion of Manchuria.
Oct. 18	British officials describe Japan's formal objection to the United States' participation in resolving the Manchurian Incident as "intolerable." . . . The 14th anniversary of the opening of armed hostilities between German and American troops in World War I is observed by German and American veterans' organizations.	In an incident mirroring a horror movie, a Romanian merchant named Vassile Schiller rises from his coffin during funeral processions, inspiring panic and fear among his friends and family. Schiller, who had merely been in a "trance," is given an apology by doctors for mistakenly identifying him as a dead man.		Canadian economic officials report a favorable trade balance of $3,619,334 for the month of September 1931. . . . Fifteen Chilean naval officers who were earlier condemned to death for participating in a failed mutiny have their sentences commuted to life imprisonment.	

A	B	C	D	E
Includes developments that affect more than one world region, international organizations, and important meetings of world leaders.	Includes all domestic and regional developments in Europe, including the Soviet Union.	Includes all domestic and regional developments in Africa and the Middle East.	Includes all domestic and regional developments in Latin America, the Caribbean, and Canada.	Includes all domestic and regional developments in Asian and Pacific nations (and colonies).

U.S. Politics & Social Issues	U.S. Foreign Policy & Defense	Economics & Great Depression	Science, Technology & Nature	Culture, Leisure & Lifestyle	
The United Mine Workers of America calls on Congress to pass legislation reclassifying coal as a public utility, and thus make it subject to the same regulatory standards as water or electricity. . . . Puerto Rican Governor Theodore Roosevelt, Jr., is urged by the Republican National Committee to be President Herbert Hoover's running mate in the 1932 presidential election. Repeated reports indicate that Vice President Charles Curtis will not join Hoover in seeking reelection.		Officials of British Columbia cut government employee salaries by an average of 5 percent.			Oct. 12
A two-week strike of 29,000 workers of the Glen Alden Coal Company ends.		U.S. economic officials report that U.S. automobile production has declined by more than 60 percent in the 20 months since February 1930.	Personal physicians of Thomas Edison report that the 84-year-old wizard of Menlo Park is "slowly slipping into a coma."	World featherweight boxing champion Bat Battalino is defeated by challenger Roger Bernard in a nontitle bout held in Philadelphia, Pa.	Oct. 13
The Lafayette College president lays blame for the Great Depression on Americans' persistence in "trying to keep up with the Joneses."		Freight car loadings for the past week amounted to 777,837 cars, according to figures published by the American Railway Association. The total is 39,808 cars greater than the previous week, but a decline of 21 percent from the corresponding week last year. The increase from last week was attributable to gains in ore, coal, coke, and livestock.	New York City health officials report that despite a serious scare in September 1931, incidences of infantile paralysis, or "polio" as it is more commonly known, have now returned to the "normal" rate.	Socialist author H.G. Wells travels to New York, where he pessimistically tells a gaggle of reporters that civilization itself faces "probable collapse."	Oct. 14
	The U.S. Congress considers passing a bill that would grant women's suffrage to the Philippines.	The Iron Age releases its weekly index of U.S. steel mill activity. The index currently stands at 40.7, a drop of 0.1 points from the previous week, and a decline of approximately 47 percent from the corresponding week one year ago.			Oct. 15
The 52nd annual convention of the American Federation of Labor is held in Vancouver, British Columbia. President William Green is reelected by a wide margin. Delegates vote to recommend to Congress the modification of the Volstead Act, as well as the continuation of the 1924 Immigration Act.		The U.S. federal budget deficit rises to $512,666,149, an increase of $484 million from October 1930.			Oct. 16
Elizabeth Cutter, widow of deceased New Jersey senator Dwight Morrow, rejects repeated requests by Republicans to fill the vacant senate seat left by her late husband.	Naval officials estimate that the 1932 naval budget will amount to $347,782,886.	The Annalist releases its weekly index of U.S. wholesale commodity prices. At 100.3, the figure is a rise of 0.4 points from the previous week, but a decline of 18 percent from the corresponding period a year ago. Economists say the rise from last week was caused by gains in farm products.	New Jersey health officials announce that $2 million will be spent in 1932 to combat the spread of tuberculosis. . . . The U.S. National Committee for Mental Hygiene holds sessions in New York City.	New York City Park Commissioner James Browne announces plans for the construction of Knute Rockne Memorial Field, a football stadium designed to seat 100,000 spectators.	Oct. 17
		The Annalist releases its weekly index of U.S. business activity. At 68.3, the figure is a reduction of 0.2 points from the previous week and a decline of approximately 25 percent from the corresponding period last year. Economists say the drop from last week was caused by losses in freight car loadings and steel mill activity.	Thomas Edison dies while in a coma at his home in West Orange, N.J., at age 84. New York Governor Franklin Roosevelt describes him as "a great inventor and a great citizen." Edison's inventions include the incandescent light bulb, the phonograph, and the dictaphone.		Oct. 18

F	G	H	I	J
Includes elections, federal-state relations, civil rights and liberties, crime, the judiciary, education, healthcare, poverty, urban affairs, and population.	Includes formation and debate of U.S. foreign and defense policies, veterans affairs, and defense spending. (Relations with specific foreign countries are usually found under the region concerned.)	Includes business, labor, agriculture, taxation, transportation, consumer affairs, monetary and fiscal policy, natural resources, pollution, and accidents.	Includes worldwide scientific, medical, and technological developments, natural phenomena, U.S. weather, and natural disasters.	Includes the arts, religion, scholarship, communications media, sports, entertainment, fashions, fads, and social life.

	World Affairs	Europe	Africa & The Middle East	The Americas	Asia & The Pacific
Oct. 19	British lawmakers tighten immigration restrictions as a means of reducing unemployment in England.... The League of Nations considers extending a moratorium to Hungary.... The U.S. Committee on Economic Sanctions, the purpose of which will be to study the feasibility of using economic sanctions as a means of preventing war, is formed.	France officially invokes the 1928 Kellogg-Briand Pact, which declared war anywhere in the world to be illegal, in protesting the actions of the Japanese military.... Thirty thousand members of the National Socialist German Workers' Party march on Berlin following a speech by Adolf Hitler in which he declared, "The great hour when the disgrace of 1918 will be wiped out will surely come." Future Propaganda Minister Joseph Goebbels tells reporters that the Nazis' main commitment is for worldwide military disarmament.			
Oct. 20	Indian revolutionary leader Mohandas Gandhi alleges that the British imperial police force routinely subjects poor Indian villagers to harsh physical violence.	An American rabbi returning from Poland describes the economic circumstances of Polish Jews as "tragically helpless."	Nuri al Said resigns as Prime Minister of Iraq. He informs King Faisal I that intense disagreements with Interior Minister Muzahim Pachachi forced his resignation.	A bomb explodes in the Cuban capital of Havana near the home of the principal of the Havana High School.	
Oct. 21	Great Britain denies repeated reports that China requested British military assistance following the Manchurian Incident.... Indian revolutionary leader Mohandas Gandhi expresses disgust with Great Britain's refusal to grant independence to India, saying that British diplomats have "exhibited a spirit of parasitic greediness."	The second annual Balkan Conference opens in Istanbul, Turkey, with 200 delegates present representing six nations.		The Cuban Butchers' Association files a formal complaint to the Interior Secretary alleging that a large "meat trust" has driven up the price of meat by nearly 33 percent since October 1930.	
Oct. 22	In a letter to the *New York Times*, Indian revolutionary leader Mohandas Gandhi writes that India could not possibly remain a dominion of Great Britain since Indians and Britons are wholly separated by a different language.	President Paul von Hindenburg of Germany appoints a special economic advisory board comprised of 25 industry leaders in the fields of agriculture, banking, and labor unions.		Presidential election returns in Ecuador indicate that independent candidate Neptali Bonfiaz will become the South American nation's newest president.... Capitulating to repeated protests by Mexican theater owners, President Ortiz Rubio of Mexico officially suspends a controversial tariff that all but excluded foreign motion pictures from being imported into the nation.	
Oct. 23	French Premier Pierre Laval arrives in Washington, D.C., where a crowd of cheering supporters welcomes him. He tells reporters he will discuss "things in general" with U.S. President Herbert Hoover, and describes accusations that France plans to militarily dominate Europe as "absurd." "Our only desire is peace," he says.... Rejecting invitations to visit the United States, Indian revolutionary leader Mohandas Gandhi tells reporters, "America is not ready to receive me."	The Bank of France deposits a gift of $8.5 million into the Austrian National Bank.... The number of unemployed Germans rises to 4,484,000, an increase of 129,000 since the beginning of the month.		Cuba enacts measures allowing police authorities to crack down on narcotics distributors as reports surface showing a rise in drug use in the Caribbean island nation.	
Oct. 24	French Premier Pierre Laval declares in a speech that "France will consent once more for the hundredth time to whatever new sacrifices are necessary to guarantee her certitude that she will not again be invaded."	Spanish lawmakers bring up charges of treason against King Alfonso XIII, who was deposed on April 14, 1931. ... French Finance Minister Pierre Flandin submits a $120 million public works project fund to the Chamber of Deputies.		Cuban naval commander Capt. Juan Rivera is forced out of office after reports surface implicating him as a leader of a recent rebellion.	
Oct. 25		Romanian officials indefinitely suspend operations of the newspapers *Ordinea* and *Lupta* for publishing editorials that heaped heavy criticism upon National Bank governor M. Manoilescu.		Cuban economic officials report that total imports into the Caribbean island nation during the first six months of 1931 fell nearly 50 percent below the total from the comparable period of 1930.... Presidential election returns in Peru indicate that Luis Sanchez Cerro will become the South American nation's newest president.	

A	B	C	D	E
Includes developments that affect more than one world region, international organizations, and important meetings of world leaders.	Includes all domestic and regional developments in Europe, including the Soviet Union.	Includes all domestic and regional developments in Africa and the Middle East.	Includes all domestic and regional developments in Latin America, the Caribbean, and Canada.	Includes all domestic and regional developments in Asian and Pacific nations (and colonies).

U.S. Politics & Social Issues	U.S. Foreign Policy & Defense	Economics & Great Depression	Science, Technology & Nature	Culture, Leisure & Lifestyle	
President Herbert Hoover is awarded an honorary doctor of law degree from the College of William and Mary. . . . President Herbert Hoover makes a nationwide radio address, in which he states that the Great Depression is nothing more than a "passing incident in our national life." He stresses private charity and personal responsibility as a means to combat poverty and unemployment.			U.S. President Herbert Hoover announces he will attend the funeral of the late Thomas Edison, whom he describes as the greatest American inventor in history and "a precious asset to the whole world." . . . Guglielmo Marconi, considered to be the "father of radio," calls the late Thomas Edison "the world's greatest benefactor."		Oct. 19
New York State Superintendent of Banks Joseph Broderick is indicted on misdemeanor charges of bank fraud. Governor Franklin Roosevelt tells reporters he will not ask for Broderick's resignation, calling him a man of "integrity."		Canada prohibits the private export of gold. Those wishing to export gold will require a special permit issued by the Ministry of Finance, and violators will receive a prison term of three years.			Oct. 20
The National Council of American Shipbuilders reports that total U.S. shipping tonnage has declined by 18.75 percent since 1921, from 16,952,018 tons to 13,543,947 tons. The Council attributes the loss to the demobilization of merchant marine ships following the end of World War I.		Freight car loadings for the past week amounted to 763,864 cars, according to figures published by the American Railway Association. The total is 13,973 cars less than the previous week, and a decline of approximately 25 percent from the corresponding week last year. The drop from last week was attributable to losses in grain products, forest products, ore, and coal.		St. Louis Cardinals' second baseman and captain Frank Frisch is awarded the 1931 National League most valuable player award. Frisch garnered 161 hits in 518 at bats, netting an average of .311. . . . Major league baseball officials consider changing the official ball used in play to a more tightly wound ball that would likely result in increased offensive statistics.	Oct. 21
The Federal Reserve Board reports that there were a total of 298 bank failures with liabilities amounting to $271,299,000 during the month of September.	President Herbert Hoover denies reports that the Navy Department will soon scrap the historic frigate USS Constitution, known as Old Ironsides, as a means of reducing the federal budget deficit.	The Iron Age releases its weekly index of U.S. steel mill activity. The index currently stands at 39.9, a drop of 0.8 points from the previous week, and a reduction of approximately 48 percent from the corresponding week one year ago.	Funeral services are held for deceased inventor Thomas Edison. Among those in attendance at the service in West Orange, N.J., are financier Owen Young and steel mogul Charles M. Schwab. . . . Two thousand residents in Calcutta, India, are left homeless by massive floods. Ninety percent of the city's cattle are reported to be dead as a result of drowning.		Oct. 22
A consortium of automobile safety experts releases a report blaming ever-increasing U.S. automobile accidents on car manufacturers' advertisements that stress speed vehicles.	House Appropriations Committee chairman Will Wood alleges during remarks on Capitol Hill that a "big-navy clique" has been distributing propaganda to newspapers designed to "arouse public sentiment against the President's naval economy program."	The Annalist releases its weekly index of U.S. wholesale commodity prices. At 101.1, the figure is a rise of 0.8 points from the previous week, but a decline of 17 percent from the corresponding period a year ago. Economists say the rise from last week was caused by gains in farm products and fuels. . . . The U.S. Federal Reserve Board reports there were deposits totaling $51.8 billion in the 21,903 U.S. banks as of August 1, 1931.			Oct. 23
Senate Foreign Relations Committee chairman William Borah publicly advocates the cancellation of all German reparation payments to the United States. Borah also expresses displeasure toward a proposed "security pact" with France.			The National Electric Light Association reports U.S. electric power output for the past week amounted to 1,656,051,000 kilowatt hours, 3 million kilowatt hours more than the preceding week, but a decline of 4 percent from the corresponding period one year ago.	Arriving in New York following a trip to Europe, British author Bertrand Russell declares that Europe is teetering on the brink of a socialistic revolution.	Oct. 24
Convicted gangster Al Capone faces sentencing. Federal Judge James Wilkerson sentences Capone, who, during his reign as public enemy number one officially identified himself as an "antique furniture salesman," to an 11-year prison term in addition to a $50,000 fine.	A large protest is held in Boston, Mass., over Naval Secretary Charles Francis Adams's proposal to "abandon" the historic Charlestown Navy Yard. The Boston Chamber of Commerce submits a petition with 50,000 signatures to Washington in the hope of forcing Adams to reconsider.	The Annalist releases its weekly index of U.S. business activity. At 67.2, the figure is a drop of 0.8 points from the previous week and a decline of approximately 25 percent from the corresponding period last year. Economists say the drop from last week was caused by losses in freight car loadings, steel mill activity, electric power production, and automobile production.		British novelist Virginia Woolf publishes The Waves, considered to be the most experimental of her eight published novels. . . . Annoyed by an audience member's sneeze, famed conductor Leopold Stokowski abruptly ends a performance in Philadelphia, Pa.	Oct. 25

F	G	H	I	J
Includes elections, federal-state relations, civil rights and liberties, crime, the judiciary, education, healthcare, poverty, urban affairs, and population.	Includes formation and debate of U.S. foreign and defense policies, veterans affairs, and defense spending. (Relations with specific foreign countries are usually found under the region concerned.)	Includes business, labor, agriculture, taxation, transportation, consumer affairs, monetary and fiscal policy, natural resources, pollution, and accidents.	Includes worldwide scientific, medical, and technological developments, natural phenomena, U.S. weather, and natural disasters.	Includes the arts, religion, scholarship, communications media, sports, entertainment, fashions, fads, and social life.

	World Affairs	Europe	Africa & The Middle East	The Americas	Asia & The Pacific
Oct. 26	French Foreign Minister Aristide Briand expresses dissatisfaction with the failure of the League of Nations to resolve the conflict in Manchuria between China and Japan.	Italian Foreign Minister Dino Grandi arrives in Germany to meet with Chancellor Heinrich Bruening. "The world is in ferment," he tells reporters. . . . French economic officials report that total government revenue has increased by 203 million francs since September 1930.	Approximately 300 British troops aboard the cruiser *Colombo* are dispatched to the Mediterranean island of Cyprus to quell ongoing anti-British riots that officials say have been provoked by high taxation.		
Oct. 27	Polish Ambassador to the United States Tytus Filipowicz accuses Senator William Borah, who earlier advocated the appeasement of European fascist movements by recommending the cancellation of central European reparation payments and handing over the Polish Corridor to Germany, of "encouraging and stimulating the activities of the nationalistic element in Europe." Borah responds by admitting that his knowledge of European affairs is limited.	The Bulgarian Finance Minister escapes an assassination attempt in the capital city of Sofia. . . . German-Italian relations improve as Italian Foreign Minister Dino Grandi and German Chancellor Heinrich Bruening express agreement on a number of issues including disarmament and reparation payments.			Chinese officials estimate in a report that over 60,000 people have been left unemployed as a result of destruction caused by the Japanese invasion of Manchuria. Japanese military commander Gen. Honsho says that troops must remain in the region "in order to prevent anarchy."
Oct. 28	U.S. President Herbert Hoover releases a statement in which he declares that the economy of the Philippines must be improved "before political independence can be successful."	Italians celebrate the ninth anniversary of the March on Rome, the event during which 25,000 fascist supporters marched on the capital of Italy, leading to the ascent of Benito Mussolini to the position of premier. Mussolini orders that all periodicals be printed with the words "Anno X," meaning "10th year" in English.		Five Nicaraguan rebels are killed by a squad of National Guardsmen in the capital, Managua. . . . In the Cuban city of Matanzas, eight prominent citizens alleged to be involved in a plot against President Gerardo Machado's regime are arrested by military authorities.	
Oct. 29	The League of Nations sets a deadline of November 16, 1931, for all Japanese troops to evacuate from the war-torn region of Manchuria.	Parliamentary elections are held in Great Britain. The Laborites lose over 200 seats from the previous election, while the Tories nearly double their representation. The Tories assume the largest party majority in Great Britain in nearly 100 years. . . . Czechoslovakia celebrates the 13th anniversary of the founding of its first republic.			
Oct. 30		The number of idle British workers decreases by 86,950 in one week.			Australia announces it will monopolize radio broadcasts, similar to Great Britain's British Broadcasting Corporation, beginning June 30, 1932.
Oct. 31	1929 Nobel Peace Prize winner Frank Kellogg praises his co-author of the 1928 Paris Pact, French Foreign Minister Aristide Briand, for his efforts in attempting to alleviate tensions between China and Japan. . . . Portugal schedules its first importation of gold since 1914. Officials announce a shipment of $2 million worth of gold will arrive in Lisbon from New York City in early November.	The wages of Belgian miners are reduced by an average of 5 percent.		Warrants are issued for over 100 Cuban citizens alleged to be involved in a plot against President Gerardo Machado's regime that was discovered by authorities on October 28. . . . In an effort to reduce the usage of narcotics, Cuban Narcotics Department head Cesar Muxo announces that all cafes and nightclubs where drug use is apparent will be closed permanently. . . . The fourth attempted Brazilian revolt of 1931 is quelled.	
Nov. 1	Polish newspapers report that due to his comments favoring rearranging Poland's borders with Germany, U.S. Senator William Borah has become one of the most hated men in Poland.	The British Ministry of Transport reports that the number of licensed automobiles within the United Kingdom has declined by nearly 2,312 in a span of one year.			

A	B	C	D	E
Includes developments that affect more than one world region, international organizations, and important meetings of world leaders.	Includes all domestic and regional developments in Europe, including the Soviet Union.	Includes all domestic and regional developments in Africa and the Middle East.	Includes all domestic and regional developments in Latin America, the Caribbean, and Canada.	Includes all domestic and regional developments in Asian and Pacific nations (and colonies).

U.S. Politics & Social Issues	U.S. Foreign Policy & Defense	Economics & Great Depression	Science, Technology & Nature	Culture, Leisure & Lifestyle	
American Federation of Labor president William Green describes New Jersey Republican gubernatorial candidate David Baird as an "enemy of labor."		French automobile mogul Andre Citroen declares in a speech that despite the Great Depression, the United States remains "rich and well organized."	Albert Einstein announces the creation of a new "unified field theory" of physics. . . . The George Washington Bridge, the longest suspension bridge ever constructed at its time at over 3,500 feet, officially opens for traffic. The bridge connects the New York City borough of Manhattan with the state of New Jersey. Over 50,000 automobiles and 100,000 pedestrians cross the bridge on its first day of operation.		Oct. 26
	Upon returning from a trip to the Philippines, War Secretary Patrick Hurley expresses opposition to the Filipino independence movement, and requests the resignation of Governor-General Dwight Davis. Hurley recommends Theodore Roosevelt, Jr., governor of Puerto Rico, as the successor to Davis if he chooses to resign. . . . On the occasion of Navy Day, President Herbert Hoover declares that the maintenance of a strong navy is "the first necessity of government."				Oct. 27
The U.S. Court of Appeals grants an appeal hearing to be held in two months for convicted gangster Al Capone, who on October 25 was sentenced to 11 years in prison. . . . Theodore Roosevelt, Jr., publicly endorses War Secretary Patrick Hurley for the 1932 Republican vice presidential nomination.		Freight car loadings for the past week amounted to 761,719 cars, according to figures published by the American Railway Association. The total is 2,145 cars less than the previous week, and a reduction of 11 percent from the corresponding week last year. The drop from last week was attributable to losses in ore.		Japanese athlete Chuhei Nambu establishes the world running broad jump record at 26 feet and 2.5 inches, eclipsing the previous record by 2 inches.	Oct. 28
		The Iron Age releases its weekly index of U.S. steel mill activity. The index currently stands at 39.6, a drop of 0.3 points from the previous week, and a decline of approximately 44 percent from the corresponding week one year ago.		Philadelphia Athletics pitcher Lefty Grove is named the 1931 American League most valuable player. He is only the second pitcher to receive the award in the league's history. Grove won 31 games and lost 4, and netted an earned run average of 2.06.	Oct. 29
The Ford Motor Company decreases its daily minimum wage rate by $1, from $7 to $6. Despite the reduction, company spokesmen claim "Ford's wages remain the highest in the automotive industry." . . . American Federation of Labor president William Green predicts that there will be over 7 million unemployed members of his organization by January 1932.		The Annalist releases its weekly index of U.S. wholesale commodity prices. At 100.7, the figure is a drop of 0.4 points from the previous week, and a decline of 17 percent from the corresponding period a year ago. Economists say the drop from last week was caused by losses in textile products, metals, and building materials. . . . The average bond price on the New York Stock Exchange falls to its lowest point of the year.			Oct. 30
The National Association of Manufacturers holds an annual meeting in New York City. Delegates express fierce opposition to a proposed system of compulsory unemployment insurance.			Aniceto Martinez establishes a new South American parachute-drop record by jumping out of a plane suspended in the skies of Buenos Aires at 11,500 feet. . . . The National Electric Light Association reports U.S. electric power output for the past week amounted to 1,646,531,000 kilowatt hours, 10, million kilowatt hours less than the preceding week, and a reduction of 6 percent from the corresponding period one year ago.		Oct. 31
The American Association for Old Age Security commends Senator C.C. Dill for his announcement that he will soon introduce federal old-age pension legislation on the Senate floor. It will be nearly four years before the Social Security Act is passed under the administration of President Franklin Roosevelt. . . . The U.S. Chamber of Commerce passes a referendum recommending that aid to those afflicted by the Great Depression "be left to private charity and/or state and local governments."		The Annalist releases its weekly index of U.S. business activity. At 66.2, the figure is a reduction of 0.2 points from the previous week, and a decline of 20 percent from the corresponding period last year. Economists say the reduction from last week was caused by losses in steel mill activity, electric power production, and cotton cloth production.	Professors Jacob Papish and Eugene Wainer of Cornell University discover one of the two remaining unknown period elements. Known as "element 87," Papish and Wainer claim its properties are similar to caesium.	The American comedy crime film Pardon Us, starring Hollywood Walk of Fame recipients Stan Laurel and Oliver Hardy, is released in Finland. To accurately portray the two African-American main characters, Laurel and Hardy smeared their faces with grease and mud, known as "blackface." This technique would be deemed offensive in later eras. . . . The film Heute Nacht Eventual is released throughout Finland.	Nov. 1

F	G	H	I	J
Includes elections, federal-state relations, civil rights and liberties, crime, the judiciary, education, healthcare, poverty, urban affairs, and population.	Includes formation and debate of U.S. foreign and defense policies, veterans affairs, and defense spending. (Relations with specific foreign countries are usually found under the region concerned.)	Includes business, labor, agriculture, taxation, transportation, consumer affairs, monetary and fiscal policy, natural resources, pollution, and accidents.	Includes worldwide scientific, medical, and technological developments, natural phenomena, U.S. weather, and natural disasters.	Includes the arts, religion, scholarship, communications media, sports, entertainment, fashions, fads, and social life.

	World Affairs	Europe	Africa & The Middle East	The Americas	Asia & The Pacific
Nov. 2			A large group of Palestinian auto workers goes on strike, protesting a recent government decision to introduce harsh taxes on gasoline.	Brazilian economists report that October's coffee exports amounted to 980,000 sacks, the highest monthly total since March 1931.	
Nov. 3	Cuban Senator Viriato Gutierrez declares in a speech that the early 20th century U.S. military occupation of Cuba and the 1930 Smoot-Hawley Tariff Act are wholly responsible for poor economic conditions in Cuba. Cuban Popular Party president Celso Del Rio formally disagrees with Gutierrez's statement in remarks to reporters, saying, "Cubans themselves are the only ones responsible for present conditions in Cuba."	Municipal elections are held in Great Britain. The results largely mirror the October 1931 parliamentary elections, which saw the Conservatives assume the largest party majority in nearly a century. The Laborites lose a total of 201 Council seats, while the Tories gain 144.			
Nov. 4				The exchange rate of the Argentine paper peso increases by 2 percent over a period of three days.	American missionary W. Vinson is captured by Chinese bandits near the city of Haichow. The U.S. State Department demands that Chinese authorities take action to ensure Vinson's safety.
Nov. 5	South Africa becomes the 38th nation to pledge to adhere to the League of Nations proposed "one-year armament holiday." Poland refuses to sign the agreement unless all major military powers adopt it. Polish officials fear that "the vague provisions concerning the truce might easily be exploited."	Prominent politicians of Monaco urge Prince Louis II to reinstate the principality's constitution, which was indefinitely suspended in December 1930 following violent riots.	Emperor Haile Selassie of Ethiopia celebrates the first anniversary of the beginning of his reign . . . . Ethiopia's first written constitution comes into effect. Elections for the bicameral legislature that was created as the result of the constitution remain to be scheduled.		
Nov. 6		The Swiss comedy film *Falska Millionaran* (*The False Millionaire*) is released in France to generally mixed reviews.		The exchange rate of the Mexican silver peso falls to its lowest value in nearly a year.	
Nov. 7		Russians celebrate the 14th anniversary of the date in which Bolshevik leaders Vladimir Lenin and Leon Trotsky lead soldiers in overthrowing the Russian provisional government. . . . Former French premier Edouard Herriot is elected president of the French Radical Socialist Parliamentary Party. . . . Irish lawmakers impose a tax of 4 pence a gallon on gasoline.		For the first time since the autumn of 1930, President Jose Uriburu of Argentina repeals martial-law status and restores civil rights guaranteed by the country's constitution. The decision was made in observance of upcoming elections.	
Nov. 8	German newspapers accuse U.S. President Herbert Hoover of capitulating to France over the issue of World War I reparation payments.	In Germany, a group of Halle University students said to be heavily devoted to the National Socialist cause hold a protest to demand the resignation of theology professor Guenther Dehn, who has aroused anger for his lectures advocating pacifistic Communism. . . . Leading financial experts in France tell reporters that the worldwide depression has reached "its most acute stage."		President Gerardo Machado of Cuba considers granting amnesty to former president Mario Mennocal, who is accused of plotting to overthrow the present order. . . . The wages of approximately 12,000 Nova Scotian mine workers are reduced by an average of 25 percent.	

A	B	C	D	E
Includes developments that affect more than one world region, international organizations, and important meetings of world leaders.	Includes all domestic and regional developments in Europe, including the Soviet Union.	Includes all domestic and regional developments in Africa and the Middle East.	Includes all domestic and regional developments in Latin America, the Caribbean, and Canada.	Includes all domestic and regional developments in Asian and Pacific nations (and colonies).

U.S. Politics & Social Issues	U.S. Foreign Policy & Defense	Economics & Great Depression	Science, Technology & Nature	Culture, Leisure & Lifestyle	
Naval Secretary Charles Francis Adams expresses fierce opposition to President Herbert Hoover's proposed naval economy program. He notes that "although the United States' naval budget is greater than that of foreign powers, the ratio of the naval budget to national income is much less than that of other leading naval powers." . . . The Federal Public Health Service reports that automobile accidents are the leading cause of death among U.S. children ages 5–19.	The airship USS Akron departs on her maiden voyage. She was constructed in 1929 by the Goodyear-Zeppelin Corporation. Akron will eventually crash into the Atlantic Ocean along the New England coast as a result of inclement weather on April 3, 1933.	Freight car loadings for the past week amounted to 769,673 cars, according to figures published by the American Railway Association. The total is 7,954 cars greater than the previous week, and a decline of 21 percent from the corresponding week last year. The increase from last week is attributable to rises in grain products and coal.		The mystery film Convicted, starring Hollywood Walk of Fame recipient Aileen Pringle, is released throughout the United States. . . . Night Life in Reno is released throughout the United States. The film features a performance by Hollywood Walk of Fame recipient Virginia Valli. . . . East Lynne, directed by Academy Award-winning filmmaker Frank Lloyd and starring Hollywood Walk of Fame recipients Ann Harding and Conrad Nagel, is released in Finland.	Nov. 2
Workers of All America Cable, Inc., go on strike to protest a 10 percent reduction in wages. A spokesman for the workers says the company's decision is "unjustifiable."		The weekly index of U.S. automobile production as compiled by the Department of Commerce is released. The index currently stands at 24.3, a rise of 1.9 points from the previous week, but a decline of 52 percent from the corresponding week one year ago.		The German war film Die Nacht der Entsheidung (The Night of The Decision) is released in Finland. The film stars Olga Tschegowa and Trude Hesterberg, both of whom would become German Film Award nominees.	Nov. 3
Naval Secretary Charles Francis Adams refutes newspaper reports of his imminent resignation. Tension has grown in recent weeks between President Herbert Hoover and Adams over the President's proposed naval economy program. Adams tells reporters that he "had tears in his eyes" upon learning of the false reports. White House spokesmen call the reports wholly unfounded.		Dun's Review reports U.S. bank clearings for the past week amounted to $5.7 billion, 30 percent less than the corresponding week in 1930. . . . Prof. Irving Fisher of Yale University releases his weekly index of international commodity prices. The figure is 68.5, a rise of 0.3 points from the preceding week, but a decline of approximately 21 percent from the corresponding week a year ago.	The USS Akron establishes an airship passenger record, carrying 207 persons while cruising the skies of New Jersey and New York.	Children of the Pleasure, an American musical comedy, is released in Finland. The film is directed by Academy Award-nominated filmmaker Harry Beaumont.	Nov. 4
The U.S. Department of Commerce reports that the number of U.S. air passengers has declined by 10 percent since July 1931.		The Iron Age releases its weekly index of U.S. steel mill activity. The index currently stands at 41.3, a rise of 1.7 points from the previous week, but a decline of approximately 38 percent from the corresponding week one year ago.		The Betty Boop animated short Kitty from Kansas City is released throughout the United States.	Nov. 5
A consortium of notable economists including future U.S. Labor Secretary Frances Perkins releases a report recommending the creation of state-mandated unemployment insurance. The report says that "the haphazard and degradingly wasteful methods of private charity" are inadequate. . . . Nebraska Rep. Ashton Shallenberger announces he will seek reelection on a platform on reducing government employees' salaries, including that of the President, as a means of improving economic conditions.		The Annalist releases its weekly list of U.S. wholesale commodity prices. At 101.8, the index is a rise of 1.2 points from the previous week but a decline of 15 percent from the corresponding week a year ago. Economists say the increase from the previous week was caused by gains in farm products and fuels.	Robert J. Van de Graaff of Princeton University develops an inexpensive electric generator capable of generating 15 million to 20 million volts.	Zlatye Gory, a Russian-language film detailing the fictional story of a factory workers' strike on the eve of the 1917 Russian Revolution, is released throughout the Soviet Union. The film's star, Boris Poslavsky, would receive the title of Honored Artist of the Republic for his performance.	Nov. 6
Famed aviator Charles Lindbergh is appointed by President Herbert Hoover as a member of the National Advisory Committee on Aeronautics, based in Langley, Va.	The heavy cruiser USS Indianapolis, constructed in 1930 by the New York Shipbuilding Corporation, is launched. She would spend the years of World War II in the South Pacific, engaging in battles against Japan.		The National Electric Light Association reports U.S. electric power output for the past week amounted to 1,651,792,000 kilowatt hours, 5 million kilowatt hours more than the preceding week, but a decline of 12 percent from the corresponding period one year ago.	Academy Award-winning director Michael Curtiz's The Mad Genius is released throughout the United States. The film stars Hollywood Walk of Fame recipients John Barrymore, Charles Butterworth, and Carmel Myers.	Nov. 7
A group of schoolchildren in Denver, Colo., name famed aviator Charles Lindbergh as the quintessential American hero.		The Annalist releases its weekly index of U.S. business activity. At 65.4, the figure is a drop of 0.6 points from the previous week, and a decline of 19 percent from the corresponding period last year. Economists say the reduction from last week was caused by losses in freight car loadings, electric power production, and automobile production.		The Man Who Came Back, based on the play by Jules Goodman, is released throughout the United States. The film is directed by Raoul Walsh and stars Janet Gaynor and Charles Farrell, all of whom would become Hollywood Walk of Fame recipients.	Nov. 8

F	G	H	I	J
Includes elections, federal-state relations, civil rights and liberties, crime, the judiciary, education, healthcare, poverty, urban affairs, and population.	Includes formation and debate of U.S. foreign and defense policies, veterans affairs, and defense spending. (Relations with specific foreign countries are usually found under the region concerned.)	Includes business, labor, agriculture, taxation, transportation, consumer affairs, monetary and fiscal policy, natural resources, pollution, and accidents.	Includes worldwide scientific, medical, and technological developments, natural phenomena, U.S. weather, and natural disasters.	Includes the arts, religion, scholarship, communications media, sports, entertainment, fashions, fads, and social life.

	World Affairs	Europe	Africa & The Middle East	The Americas	Asia & The Pacific
Nov. 9		Leading financial experts in France tell reporters that the worldwide depression has reached "its most acute stage."		In Argentina, the first presidential election since the overthrow of Hipolito Irigoyen's regime in 1930 is held. Nearly 80 percent of registered voters in the capital of Buenos Aires cast ballots.	Two thousand Muslims donning red shirts are arrested by British imperial authorities following riots in the Indian region of Kashmir.
Nov. 10				Election returns in Argentina indicate that Gen. Agustin Rolon will become the nation's first elected president since the overthrow of Hipolito Irigoyen's regime in 1930. Rolon's term would be marred by accusations of corruption, yet he succeeded in instituting the Argentine Central Bank and the country's first nationwide income tax.	The American-owned Chinese newspaper *Shanghai Post-Mercury* prints a headline reading "Japanese Censors in Mukden Suppress and Change Reports," and accuses Japanese military officials of engaging in censorship "comparable only to that during the World War."
Nov. 11	The 13th annual Armistice Day, marking the end of hostilities between Western nations in World War I, is celebrated throughout all the world's nations with the exception of Germany. The main newspaper of the German National Socialist Party prints an editorial declaring that "the disgrace of 1918 will be atoned for and forever wiped out." The date would be declared a U.S. federal holiday and renamed Veterans' Day following World War II.	In the Polish capital of Warsaw, several secondary educational institutions, including the School of Dental Surgery and the Veterinary Institute, are closed in what officials say is a move to prevent further anti-Semitic student riots.		Argentine economists report that Argentina's exports have increased by 21 percent since October 1931.	
Nov. 12		In Naples, Italy, a bomb is detonated near the headquarters of the local Fascist Federation.		President Gerardo Machado of Cuba declares a general amnesty for all prisoners accused of participating in a failed coup attempt in August 1931. . . . The Cuban Justice Secretary reports that the number of Cuban residents has increased by over 25 percent since 1919, from 2.8 million to 3.8 million.	
Nov. 13	U.S. exports to Great Britain increased by 10 percent in October 1931, as compared to September 1931, say economic officials of both nations.	Finland officially ends prohibition of alcoholic beverages.			China reacts favorably to news of a proposed League of Nations patrol force that would potentially assist Japan in evacuating troops from the war-torn region of Manchuria.
Nov. 14	Acting at the behest of the Chinese Merchants' Association, millions of Chinese-American citizens begin to boycott Japanese-produced goods in a protest against the Manchurian Incident.	In a speech delivered to members of the Centrist Party, German Chancellor Heinrich Bruening predicts that an international accord over Germany's World War I reparation payments will soon reach summation. Addressing the rising popularity of National Socialist leader Adolf Hitler, Bruening declares that the 42-year-old author of *Mein Kampf* is "powerless to bring salvation to Germany."		Eight Canadians accused of being leaders of a large-scale Communist movement are given two-year prison terms. Police officials announce they will begin wholesale arrests of the movement's members.	The Uraga Dock Company completes construction on the Japanese destroyer *Ushio*. A member of the fleet that would attack Pearl Harbor on December 7, 1941, *Ushio* became one of the few ships of her class to survive all of the naval battles of World War II. *Ushio* was eventually scrapped in 1948 during the American military occupation.
Nov. 15	Italian Foreign Minister Dino Grandi arrives in Washington, D.C., to confer with President Herbert Hoover on matters of European political stability.	In an interview, noted German philosopher Oswald Spengler criticizes the League of Nations as an "anemic utopian idea" and predicts that "the age of the Caesars is distinctly approaching." Spengler would cast his ballot for the National Socialist party in the 1932 German parliamentary elections.			A group of Chinese refugees tells the League of Nations that they would prefer a Japanese puppet state over the regime of Premier Chiang Kai-shek.

A	B	C	D	E
Includes developments that affect more than one world region, international organizations, and important meetings of world leaders.	Includes all domestic and regional developments in Europe, including the Soviet Union.	Includes all domestic and regional developments in Africa and the Middle East.	Includes all domestic and regional developments in Latin America, the Caribbean, and Canada.	Includes all domestic and regional developments in Asian and Pacific nations (and colonies).

U.S. Politics & Social Issues	U.S. Foreign Policy & Defense	Economics & Great Depression	Science, Technology & Nature	Culture, Leisure & Lifestyle	
In an editorial in the *New York Times*, auto magnate Henry Ford offers his opinion on the Great Depression, writing, "To regard present conditions as permanent and then to legislate as if they were is a serious mistake." Ford became known for controversial comments in 1916, when he told the *Chicago Tribune* that "history is more or less bunk."		Freight car loadings for the past week amounted to 740,363 cars, according to figures published by the American Railway Association. The total is 29,310 cars less than the previous week, and a decline of 21 percent from the corresponding week last year. The drop from last week was attributable to losses in forest products, ore, coal, coke, and livestock.		Metro-Goldwyn-Mayer's *The Guardsman* is released throughout the United States. The film, directed by Hollywood Walk of Fame recipient Sidney Franklin, features Academy Award-nominated performances by Alfred Lunt and Lynn Fontanne.	Nov. 9
The Southern Commission on the Study of Lynching reports that nearly 10 percent of African Americans lynched during 1930 were wholly innocent of the crimes for which they suffered a homicidal fate at the hands of indignant mobs.		The weekly index of U.S. automobile production as compiled by the Department of Commerce is released. The index currently stands at 15.5, a drop of 8.9 points from the previous week, and a decline of 69 percent from the corresponding week one year ago. . . . Operations of the insolvent People's Bank of Maryland are handed over to the state's banking commission.		*Around the World in 80 Days*, a documentary profiling Academy Award-nominated actor Douglas Fairbanks, is released throughout the United States.	Nov. 10
	The destroyer USS *Rizal*, constructed by Union Iron Works in 1918, is struck from the list of the Naval Vessel Register. A member of the Pacific Fleet, *Rizal* spent its career cruising waters near China, Japan, and the Philippines. . . . The U.S. Navy strikes the destroyer *Hart* from the list of the Naval Vessel Register. Constructed in 1918 by Union Iron Works, *Hart* was wholly a peacetime vessel, operating off the waters of China and the Philippines.	*Dun's Review* reports U.S. bank clearings for the past week amounted to $5.2 billion, 38.8 percent less than the corresponding week in 1930. . . . Prof. Irving Fisher of Yale University releases his weekly index of international commodity prices. The figure is 68.3, a reduction of 0.2 points from the preceding week, and a decline of approximately 17 percent from the corresponding week a year ago.		*Heartbreak*, a World War I drama starring Hollywood Walk of Fame recipients Charles Farrell and Madge Evans, is released throughout the United States.	Nov. 11
Speaking before a meeting of the American Newspapers Publishers Association, President Herbert Hoover states that "recovery and stability can return only through a return of confidence." . . . C. Van Ness Leavitt, brother-in-law of President Herbert Hoover, is arrested on charges of liquor possession in Santa Monica, Calif. . . . Henry Ford tells reporters the he once considered a run for the U.S. presidency in 1924.		*The Iron Age* releases its weekly index of U.S. steel mill activity. The index currently stands at 45.1, a rise of 3.8 points from the previous week, but a decline of approximately 27 percent from the corresponding week one year ago.			Nov. 12
	The U.S. naval budget for 1933 is set at $343 million, $17 million less than the 1932 budget. President Herbert Hoover reassures the American people that despite the budget cuts, Navy personnel will not be reduced "by a single man."	*The Annalist* releases its weekly list of U.S. wholesale commodity prices. At 102.6, the index is a rise of 1.6 points from the previous week but a decline of 13 percent from the corresponding week a year ago. Economists say the rise from the previous week was caused by gains in farm products and fuels.	Automotive enthusiasts observe the 100th anniversary of the creation of John Bull, the first steam locomotive to carry American passengers.	Warner Brothers' crime film *Blonde Crazy* is released throughout the United States. The film's director, Roy Del Ruth, and its three stars, James Cagney, Joan Blondell, and Ray Milland, will all become Hollywood Walk of Fame recipients. . . . The 15th season of the National Hockey League begins.	Nov. 13
			The National Electric Light Association reports U.S. electric power output for the past week amounted to 1,628,147,000 kilowatt hours, 13 million kilowatt hours less than the preceding week, and a decline of 13 percent from the corresponding period one year ago.	Metro-Goldwyn-Mayer's musical comedy *Flying High*, starring Hollywood Walk of Fame recipients Pat O'Brien and Hedda Hopper, is released throughout the United States. It is the first film to feature a performance by Bert Lahr, who was made famous in 1939 for portraying the cowardly lion in *The Wizard of Oz*.	Nov. 14
		The Annalist releases its weekly index of U.S. business activity. At 65.3, the figure is a drop of 0.1 points from the previous week, and a decline of 19 percent from the corresponding period last year.	Great Britain completes construction on the prototype of a specially designed amphibious tank.	*The Cisco Kid*, a western starring Hollywood Walk of Fame recipients Warner Baxter and Edmund Lowe, is released throughout the United States.	Nov. 15

F	**G**	**H**	**I**	**J**
Includes elections, federal-state relations, civil rights and liberties, crime, the judiciary, education, healthcare, poverty, urban affairs, and population.	Includes formation and debate of U.S. foreign and defense policies, veterans affairs, and defense spending. (Relations with specific foreign countries are usually found under the region concerned.)	Includes business, labor, agriculture, taxation, transportation, consumer affairs, monetary and fiscal policy, natural resources, pollution, and accidents.	Includes worldwide scientific, medical, and technological developments, natural phenomena, U.S. weather, and natural disasters.	Includes the arts, religion, scholarship, communications media, sports, entertainment, fashions, fads, and social life.

	World Affairs	Europe	Africa & The Middle East	The Americas	Asia & The Pacific
Nov. 16	Argentine economists report that exports to the United States have declined by approximately 29 percent since September 1930.	A 31-year-old Austrian man named Anton Schweizer is arrested for posing as the Prince of Gradiska-Vedun. . . . Great Britain enacts high tariffs on imported cloths in an effort to improve British garment industries. . . . British economists report that steel output in Great Britain has increased by approximately 20 percent since August 1931.		Brazil reports its budget surplus currently amounts to $2.3 million.	
Nov. 17	As reports surface of a sharp decline in Soviet imports into the United States, Amtorg, the leading Soviet commercial trading agency in the United States, reduces its personnel by 50 percent.	The *New York Times* describes National Socialist leader Adolf Hitler as a "mischief maker." . . . The airship *R-100*, constructed at a cost of $2 million, is sold by Great Britain in an effort to reduce the Air Ministry's budget. . . . Finland begins legal proceedings on eight foreign citizens accused of conducting espionage for the Soviet Union.		Cuban tourism officials report that 130,000 travelers from all across the globe visited the Caribbean island nation in the summer of 1931.	
Nov. 18	The International Committee for Anti-Fascist Protest criticizes U.S. President Herbert Hoover's decision to meet with Italian Foreign Minister Dino Grandi. . . . Referring to proposals of worldwide arms reductions, Italian Foreign Minister Dino Grandi tells reporters that "the sky's the limit."	French Foreign Minister Aristide Briand falls victim to a "sudden attack of weakness" in the Chamber of Deputies in the capital of Paris.			Chinese diplomats express pessimism over the ability of the League of Nations to effectively oversee the evacuation of Japanese troops from the region of Manchuria.
Nov. 19	Chinese diplomats urge the League of Nations to "put an effective and immediate stop to Japan's aggressive activities."				A battle between Japanese and Chinese troops results in the deaths of 300 soldiers and 4,000 soldiers, respectively. . . . Gen. Chang Ching-hui is appointed chief of the Chinese Peace Maintenance Committee.
Nov. 20	New York City Police Commissioner Edward Mulrooney assembles a force of 2,000 men to protect visiting Italian Foreign Minister Dino Grandi against an assassination threat. . . . A letter written by Abraham Lincoln in 1853 that contains plans to establish Rome as the capital of a new United States of Europe is discovered in Italy.	Rumors circulate in France that Foreign Minister Aristide Briand is close to announcing his resignation.			The League of Nations forms a special inquiry board to travel to the Far East and formally investigate the Sino-Japanese Manchurian conflict.
Nov. 21	U.S. Senator William Borah, chairman of the Senate Foreign Relations Committee, calls the recommendation that the United States must intervene to solve the Manchurian crisis "incredible." Borah concedes, however, that he views the Japanese invasion of Manchuria as deplorable.	Spain officially exiles deposed King Alfonso XIII. . . . Austrian lawmakers consider monopolizing their country's gasoline industry.		Mexican citizens celebrate the 20th anniversary of the overthrow of dictator Porfirio Diaz's regime.	The British steamer *Hanyang* is seized and looted by a group of Chinese bandits.
Nov. 22	Great Britain enacts new tariffs expected to negatively affect U.S. commerce at a cost of approximately $275 million annually. . . . Indian revolutionary leader Mohandas Gandhi tells reporters that during a recent party at the home of the British Viscountess Astor, he was forced to avert his eyes in shame at the sight of scantily clad female guests. "Even in tropical India, women would never dream of appearing half dressed as they do in London. Western women are mad with their own vanity," he says.	Warsaw University reopens after being closed for two weeks following student anti-Semitic riots. An editorial in the *Gazeta Polska* claims that the university students achieved nothing with their "dejudaization" campaign.		President Getulio Vargas of Brazil orders the exile of *El Mundo* reporter Juan Vignale on the grounds of writing subversive editorials. The Buenos Aires Press Association formally protests the decision.	
Nov. 23	Italian newspapers report that a recently discovered letter written by Abraham Lincoln in 1853 that contained visions for establishing Rome as the capital of a new United States of Europe may have been forged by fascist propagandists.	Great Britain increases tariffs on imported steel and iron to 33.3 percent.			British imperial authorities appoint Sir John Anderson to the post of governor of the Indian region of Bengal.

A	B	C	D	E
Includes developments that affect more than one world region, international organizations, and important meetings of world leaders.	*Includes all domestic and regional developments in Europe, including the Soviet Union.*	*Includes all domestic and regional developments in Africa and the Middle East.*	*Includes all domestic and regional developments in Latin America, the Caribbean, and Canada.*	*Includes all domestic and regional developments in Asian and Pacific nations (and colonies).*

U.S. Politics & Social Issues	U.S. Foreign Policy & Defense	Economics & Great Depression	Science, Technology & Nature	Culture, Leisure & Lifestyle	
The Travelers Insurance Company reports that nearly 100 Americans died each day in automobile accidents during the first 10 months of 1931.		*Dun's Review* reports U.S. bank clearings for the past week amounted to $5.9 billion, 30 percent less than the corresponding week in 1930. . . . Prof. Irving Fisher of Yale University releases his weekly index of international commodity prices. The figure is 68.5, a rise of 0.2 points from the preceding week, but a reduction of approximately 17 percent from the corresponding week a year ago.		The RKO Pictures drama *Are These Our Children?*, starring Hollywood Walk of Fame recipients Eric Linden and Rochelle Hudson, is released throughout the United States.	Nov. 16
Democratic Party leaders begin a "militant" campaign to capture the presidency in the 1932 election.		The weekly index of U.S. automobile production as compiled by the Department of Commerce is released. The index currently stands at 14.6, a drop of 0.9 points from the previous week, and a decline of 74 percent from the corresponding week one year ago.	Temperatures in Chicago, Ill., rise to 72°F, the highest for the city on November 17 in over 50 years.	The dramatic film *Kameradschaft*, a story about cooperation and friendship between a group of German and French miners, is released throughout Germany. The film was written by Ladislaus Vajda, who collaborated with future Nazi propagandist Leni Riefenstahl on the 1929 film *Die Weisse Holle Vom Piz Palu*.	Nov. 17
A statue of Woodrow Wilson, the 28th president of the United States, is unveiled during a ceremony in Richmond, Va. . . . Henry Fletcher announces his resignation as chairman of the U.S. Tariff Commission, effective on November 30.		Freight car loadings for the past week amounted to 717,029 cars, according to figures published by the American Railway Association. The total is 23,334 cars less than the previous week, and a decline of 22 percent from the corresponding week last year. The drop from last week was attributable to losses in grain products, forest products, coal, and livestock.		The World War I drama *Suicide Fleet* is released throughout the United States. The film stars Hollywood Walk of Fame recipients William Boyd, James Gleason, and Ginger Rogers.	Nov. 18
The Federal Reserve Board reports that a record monthly total of 512 bank closings occurred in October 1931. The deposits of the 512 banks amounted to $567 million. . . . Daniel Willard is reelected president of the Baltimore & Ohio Railroad Co.		*The Iron Age* releases its weekly index of U.S. steel mill activity. The index currently stands at 44.8, a drop of 0.3 points from the previous week, and a decline of approximately 29 percent from the corresponding week one year ago. . . . The average price of copper in the U.S. domestic market falls to 6.25 cents, nearly the lowest on record.		Legendary director Jean Renoir's drama *La Chienne (The Bitch)* is released throughout France. The American Academy of Motion Picture Arts and Sciences would later refer to Renoir as a "genius."	Nov. 19
Criticizing his naval policy, Senator Hiram Johnson of California calls on President Herbert Hoover to refuse his party's nomination for the 1932 presidential election.	Naval Secretary Charles Francis Adams urges all enlisted men to donate three days' pay to unemployment relief funds.	*The Annalist* releases its weekly list of U.S. wholesale commodity prices. At 102.3, the index is a drop of 0.3 points from the previous week and a decline of 13 percent from the corresponding week a year ago. Economists say the drop from the previous week was caused by declines in fuels, metals, and building materials.		Academy Award-nominated director Clarence Brown's *Possessed* is released throughout the United States. The film stars Academy Award-winning actors Clark Gable and Joan Crawford.	Nov. 20
War Secretary Patrick Hurley defends the presidency of Herbert Hoover in an address before the U.S. Chamber of Commerce.			The National Electric Light Association reports U.S. electric power output for the past week amounted to 1,623,151,000 kilowatt hours, 5 million kilowatt hours less than the preceding week, and a decline of approximately 10 percent from the corresponding period one year ago.	At Madison Square Garden, 19,000 spectators witness world lightweight champion Tony Canzoneri retain his title by defeating Cuban challenger Kid Chocolate in a 15-round decision. . . . Universal Pictures releases *Frankenstein*, an adaptation of the 1818 novel by Mary Shelley, throughout the United States. . . . *His Woman*, starring multiple-Oscar-winner Gary Cooper, is released throughout the United States.	Nov. 21
		The Annalist releases its weekly index of U.S. business activity. At 64.8, the figure is a drop of 0.3 points from the previous week, and a decline of 19 percent from the corresponding period last year. Economists say the reduction from last week was caused by losses in freight car loadings, steel mill activity, and electric power production.		The mystery film *The Deceiver* is released throughout the United States.	Nov. 22
		Prof. Irving Fisher of Yale University releases his weekly index of international commodity prices. The figure is 68.6, a rise of 0.1 points from the preceding week, but a decline of approximately 15 percent from the corresponding week a year ago.		The Betty Boop animated short *Jack and the Beanstalk* is released throughout the United States. . . . An opera performance attended by Italian Foreign Minister Dino Grandi is interrupted by shouts of, "Down with Grandi! Long live liberty!"	Nov. 23

F	G	H	I	J
Includes elections, federal-state relations, civil rights and liberties, crime, the judiciary, education, healthcare, poverty, urban affairs, and population.	*Includes formation and debate of U.S. foreign and defense policies, veterans affairs, and defense spending. (Relations with specific foreign countries are usually found under the region concerned.)*	*Includes business, labor, agriculture, taxation, transportation, consumer affairs, monetary and fiscal policy, natural resources, pollution, and accidents.*	*Includes worldwide scientific, medical, and technological developments, natural phenomena, U.S. weather, and natural disasters.*	*Includes the arts, religion, scholarship, communications media, sports, entertainment, fashions, fads, and social life.*

	World Affairs	Europe	Africa & The Middle East	The Americas	Asia & The Pacific
Nov. 24	Retired British statesman Gareth Jones declares in a speech that a dictatorship in Germany "seems inevitable."	British economic officials report that total tax receipts have declined by more than 10 percent since November 1930.		Newly appointed Bolivian Ambassador to Uruguay Pinto Escalier makes his first trip to the Uruguayan capital of Montevideo. He will discuss with his counterparts the issue of the disputed Chaco border region.	In a written statement distributed to all interested parties, China demands that Japanese troops evacuate from the region of Manchuria within two weeks, and that the evacuation be supervised by "neutral observers."
Nov. 25		The Prussian Ministry of the Interior releases a report outlining plans for a potential future National Socialist government.	Palestinian census officials report that the population of Palestine has increased by 25 percent since 1922.	Martial law is declared in the Nicaraguan capital of Managua following an incident in which Honduran bandits seized and looted the village of Chichigalpa. . . . In an effort to regulate fledgling commerce, the Bank of Uruguay fixes the rate at which private banks may buy and sell the Uruguayan peso at 45 cents.	Anti-Japanese riots occur in the Chinese city of Shanghai. Thousands of university students take to the streets to protest the Japanese invasion of Manchuria, demanding that their government declare war on Japan.
Nov. 26		By a vote of 23–15, Holland passes a bill introducing stringent requirements for the issuance of corporate liquor licenses. . . . French officials discover a large arms cache near the Spanish border. Two young Spaniards residing in France confess that the cache is theirs, and that they planned to use it to incite a violent revolution to restore the Spanish monarchy.		Bolivian economic officials announce that the South American nation currently owes $62 million to foreign creditors. . . . Esteban Jaramillo is appointed as the new Colombian Minister of Finance. . . . Cuban citizens mournfully observe the 60th anniversary of the date on which eight young revolutionaries were slaughtered by Spanish imperial authorities.	Australian parliamentary elections are set for December 19.
Nov. 27	The League for Independent Political Action urges the United States to respond to Japanese invasion of Manchuria by ending diplomatic relations with the Pacific island nation.			Several small bombings occur in the Cuban capital of Havana in what officials describe as an elaborate protest perpetrated by university students angered by the government's decision to outlaw public ceremonies honoring the death of eight young revolutionaries in 1871.	Martial law is declared in the Chinese city of Canton by Admiral Chen Chak, commander in chief of the Cantonese navy.
Nov. 28	Former Canadian prime minister Vincent Massay accuses the League of Nations of aggravating tensions between Japan and China.	Upon leaving the United States following a two-week diplomatic visit, Italian Foreign Minister Dino Grandi describes U.S. journalists as "fair and understanding."			China imposes a 10 percent tax on all imported flood relief funds. . . . Indian revolutionary leader Mohandas Gandhi declares that "no army, no armored tanks, no airplanes, no machine guns can frighten" those seeking Indian independence.
Nov. 29		Seeking friendlier relations between one another, Great Britain and Germany announce plans for cultural exchange. An Anglo-German ball, nearly the first since the outbreak of World War I in 1914, will be held in London, England, in the autumn of 1931.			
Nov. 30	U.S. Ret. Gen. Smedley Butler is accused of painting unfair descriptions of several South American nations in articles written for the American magazine *Liberty*. Butler, the future author of *War is a Racket*, gained worldwide notoriety in 1930 when he spread a rumor that Italian Premier Benito Mussolini was once the perpetrator of a hit-and-run accident that resulted in the death of a small boy.			Former Argentine ambassador to the United States Harmodio Arias is nominated by the Doctrinal Liberty Party for the upcoming presidential election.	International newspapers report that Bonifacio Day, celebrated on November 30 in the Philippines to honor 19th-century revolutionary Andre Bonifacio, who led an unsuccessful revolution against Spanish colonial rule, was celebrated quietly, as many Filipinos were reminded of their continued subservience to colonial powers. . . . The Australian Department of Agriculture estimates that its wheat crop for 1931 will fall 25 percent below total wheat production in 1930.

A	B	C	D	E
Includes developments that affect more than one world region, international organizations, and important meetings of world leaders.	Includes all domestic and regional developments in Europe, including the Soviet Union.	Includes all domestic and regional developments in Africa and the Middle East.	Includes all domestic and regional developments in Latin America, the Caribbean, and Canada.	Includes all domestic and regional developments in Asian and Pacific nations (and colonies).

U.S. Politics & Social Issues	U.S. Foreign Policy & Defense	Economics & Great Depression	Science, Technology & Nature	Culture, Leisure & Lifestyle	
		The weekly index of U.S. automobile production as compiled by the Department of Commerce is released. The index currently stands at 16.5, a rise of 1.9 points from the previous week, but a decline of 79 percent from the corresponding week one year ago.		*Quick Trigger Lee*, directed by western luminary J.P. McGowan, is released throughout the United States.	**Nov. 24**
		Freight car loadings for the past week amounted to 690,366 cars, according to figures published by the American Railway Association. The total is 26,633 cars less than the previous week, and a decline of 18 percent from the corresponding week last year. The decrease from last week was attributable to losses in grain products, forest products, ore, coal, and coke.		The film *Her Majesty Love* is released in Finland. . . . British lawmakers consider a bill that would ban all actors from participating in British theater productions "except those of exceptional talent."	**Nov. 25**
		The Iron Age releases its weekly index of U.S. steel mill activity. The index currently stands at 36.1, a reduction of 5 points from the previous week, and a decline of approximately 44 percent from the corresponding week one year ago.		Academy Award–nominated screenwriter Joseph Than's *Der Draufganger* (*The Gears*) is released in Germany.	**Nov. 26**
The American Association for the Advancement of Atheism holds its first annual "blamegiving service" in New York City.		*The Annalist* releases its weekly list of U.S. wholesale commodity prices. At 101.2, the index is a drop of 1.0 points from the previous week and a decline of 14 percent from the corresponding week a year ago. Economists say the decline from the previous week was caused by drops in farm products, food products, textile products, fuels, metals, and building materials.	Governor Franklin Roosevelt of New York declares in a speech given in Warm Springs, Ga., that ending infantile paralysis, the disease from which he suffers, "is a task which fires the imagination."	The romantic comedy film *Hyppolit A Lakaj* (*Hippolyt the Lackey*) is released throughout Hungary. The film is considered by many critics to be one of the top 10 best Hungarian films ever made.	**Nov. 27**
A group of protestors march down Pennsylvania Avenue, the street on which the White House is located, carrying signs reading, "Mr. Hoover, We Demand Food and Lodging."			The National Electric Light Association reports U.S. electric power output for the past week amounted to 1,655,051,000 kilowatt hours, 32 million kilowatt hours more than the preceding week, but a decline of approximately 10 percent from the corresponding period one year ago.	The American dramatic film *Over the Hill* is released throughout the United States. The film stars Hollywood Walk of Fame recipients Mae Marsh and James Dunn.	**Nov. 28**
U.S. immigration authorities release figures showing a veritable indication of the effect of the Great Depression. According to an official report, 10,857 aliens permanently departed the United States during the month of October 1931, compared with a total of 3,913 who entered. . . . President Herbert Hoover begins to adopt a routine of arriving at the White House in the wee morning hours and indulging in a festive game of "Hoover ball," which he describes as a hybrid of volleyball and tennis. Among the President's playmates is Interior Secretary Ray Lyman Wilbur.	The destroyer USS *McDermut*, constructed in 1918 by the Bethlehem Shipbuilding Corporation, is struck from the list of the Naval Vessel Register.	*The Annalist* releases its weekly index of U.S. business activity. At 63.2, the figure is a drop of 1.4 points from the previous week, and a decline of 20 percent from the corresponding period last year. Economists say the drop from last week was caused by losses in freight car loadings and steel mill activity.		The American western film *The Conquering Horde* is released in Finland. The film features the performances of Hollywood Walk of Fame recipients Richard Arlen and Fay Wray.	**Nov. 29**
	The U.S. submarine *O-12* renamed the *Nautilus*, a submarine made famous for becoming one of the first underwater vessels to successfully operate underwater near the North Pole, is scuttled near the waters of Bergen, Norway. *Nautilus* was constructed in 1916 by the Lake Torpedo Boat Company.	*Dun's Review* reports U.S. bank clearings for the past week amounted to $4,306,690,000, 31 percent less than the corresponding week in 1930. . . . Prof. Irving Fisher of Yale University releases his weekly index of international commodity prices. The figure is 67.8, a decrease of 0.8 points from the preceding week, and a decline of approximately 20 percent from the corresponding week a year ago.		The American western *Billy the Kid* is released in Denmark. The film is directed by King Vidor and stars Johnny Mack Brown, Wallace Beery, and Karl Dane, all of whom would receive a star on the Hollywood Walk of Fame. . . . Metro-Goldwyn-Mayer's *West of Broadway* is released throughout the United States. The film stars Hollywood Walk of Fame recipients John Gilbert, Madge Evans, Ralph Bellamy, and Hedda Hopper. . . . Argentine sprinter Juan Pina ties the world 100-meter dash record of 10.4 seconds, held by Americans Charley Paddock and Eddie Tolan.	**Nov. 30**

F	**G**	**H**	**I**	**J**
Includes elections, federal-state relations, civil rights and liberties, crime, the judiciary, education, healthcare, poverty, urban affairs, and population.	*Includes formation and debate of U.S. foreign and defense policies, veterans affairs, and defense spending. (Relations with specific foreign countries are usually found under the region concerned.)*	*Includes business, labor, agriculture, taxation, transportation, consumer affairs, monetary and fiscal policy, natural resources, pollution, and accidents.*	*Includes worldwide scientific, medical, and technological developments, natural phenomena, U.S. weather, and natural disasters.*	*Includes the arts, religion, scholarship, communications media, sports, entertainment, fashions, fads, and social life.*

	World Affairs	Europe	Africa & The Middle East	The Americas	Asia & The Pacific
Dec. 1	League of Nations representatives tell U.S. President Herbert Hoover that "the situation in Manchuria is greatly confused by the uncertainty of the American policy," and urge him to uphold the 1928 Kellogg-Briand Pact.	German banking authorities consider merging the Dresdner Bank and the Danat Bank into one single banking institution in an effort to increase the country's lending power.	An American man vacationing in Jerusalem is accosted by a group of Arab thieves, who steal his passport and all of his cash. The incident attracts heavy local media attention. . . . Egyptian Ambassador to the United States Sesotris Pasha arrives in New York City to study the city's advanced drinking water system.		In the last session of the Indian round-table conference held in London, England, Mohandas Gandhi pledges that he will end his civil disobedience campaign: "I wish to give all my cooperation, if you will allow me."
Dec. 2	Germany requests that the upcoming international arms reduction parley, to be held in February 1932, be delayed until the summer of 1932. Officials cite the Manchurian conflict and French and American elections as reasons for its request.				
Dec. 3		French economic officials predict that France's federal budget deficit may rise to as high as 6 billion francs in the upcoming fiscal year of 1932.		The Canadian Board of Conciliation recommends to business leaders a reduction of 10 percent in the wages of Canadian railway workers.	Japan pledges its commitment not to enter the demilitarized region of Chinchow, contingent upon the withdrawal of Chinese general Chang Hsueh-liang.
Dec. 4	French National Deputy Henry Franklin-Bouillon recommends the creation of "a commercial alliance" between France, Great Britain, and the United States to force Germany to pay its World War I reparation debts.	British economists report the Bank of England's reserve ratio currently stands at 28.44 percent, a decrease of 7 percent from the previous week, and a decline of 17 percent from the corresponding week one year ago. The bank's gold holdings currently amount to £121,598,967, a decrease of £35 million from the previous week, and a decline of £30 million from the corresponding week one year ago.	Turkish lawmakers consider a bill that would completely ban all importations of coffee. Turkey's annual coffee output is among the lowest in the world.	Representatives of the central banks of Chile, Peru, Colombia, Ecuador, and Bolivia meet in the Peruvian capital of Lima to discuss ways to improve their respective countries finances.	
Dec. 5	Deposed Spanish King Alfonso XIII announces his intentions to visit the United States.	Rumors circulated across the globe that Germany would officially default on its World War I reparation payments forces German bonds on the New York Stock Exchange to decline sharply. . . . King Carol of Romania dismisses Michael Manoilescu from the post of governor of the Romanian National Bank. The news comes as a shock to many Romanians, who had considered Manoilescu a personal friend of King Carol.			Australian economists report that the total amount of imports into Australia during the autumn of 1931 fell 48 percent below the comparable total from 1930.
Dec. 6		Rumors of a mutiny among generals circulate in Spain, leaving many common Spaniards to express the belief that the young Second Spanish Republic, established after the abdication of King Alfonso XIII on April 14, 1931, will soon fall victim to a military coup.		Canadian census officials report that Canada's population has increased by 1,565,829 people since 1921, from 8,787,949 to 10,353,778.	
Dec. 7		International newspapers print speculative articles predicting that German National Socialist head Adolf Hitler is close to seizing power as the leader of Germany.		A prominent Uruguayan newspaper calls for the South American country to resign from the League of Nations, saying the international peace organization has "abjectly surrendered" to the Roosevelt Corollary, which states that the United States has the right to intervene in South American affairs.	Three Filipinos are arrested for inciting a Communist "outbreak."

A	B	C	D	E
Includes developments that affect more than one world region, international organizations, and important meetings of world leaders.	*Includes all domestic and regional developments in Europe, including the Soviet Union.*	*Includes all domestic and regional developments in Africa and the Middle East.*	*Includes all domestic and regional developments in Latin America, the Caribbean, and Canada.*	*Includes all domestic and regional developments in Asian and Pacific nations (and colonies).*

U.S. Politics & Social Issues	U.S. Foreign Policy & Defense	Economics & Great Depression	Science, Technology & Nature	Culture, Leisure & Lifestyle	
		The weekly index of U.S. automobile production as compiled by the Department of Commerce is released. The index currently stands at 21.4, a rise of 3.6 points from the previous week, but a decline of 80 percent from the corresponding week one year ago. . . . *Dun's Review* releases its weekly index of U.S. bond prices. At 92.8, the figure is a drop of 2.2 points from the previous week, and a decline of 13.7 points from the corresponding week one year ago.		The John Wayne western *Range Feud* is released throughout the United States. Wayne's co-star is 42-year-old western legend Buck Jones, whose star on the Hollywood Walk of Fame is displayed prominently.	Dec. 1
Senate Foreign Relations Committee chairman William Borah declares that he will fiercely oppose a proposed bill that would officially enter the United States into the World Court. Borah's views stand in sharp contrast to President Herbert Hoover, who says he is "anxious" for the United States to join the international institution.		Freight car loadings for the past week amounted to 653,503 cars, according to figures published by the American Railway Association. The total is 36,863 cars less than the previous week, and a decline of 16 percent from the corresponding week last year. The drop from last week was attributable to losses in grain products, forest products, ore, and coal.	Lowell Bayles establishes the world land plane speed record by attaining a speed of 284.7 miles per hour on the runways of the Wayne County Airport in Detroit, Mich.	The German adventure film *Emil und dies Detektive* (Emil and the Detectives) premiers in the German capital of Berlin. The film's director, Gerhard Lamprecht, its writer, Erich Kastner, and its two stars, Kathe Haack and Fritz Rasp, all are recipients of the German Film Awards.	Dec. 2
		The Iron Age releases its weekly index of U.S. steel mill activity. The index currently stands at 37.4, a rise of 1.3 points from the previous week, but a decline of approximately 36 percent from the corresponding week one year ago. . . . *Dun's Review* releases its weekly index of the U.S. federal reserve ratio. At 83.9, the figure is a rise of 1.2 points from the previous week, but a decline of 21 points from the corresponding week one year ago.		Academy Award-winning director George Cukor's *Tarnished Lady*, starring Hollywood Walk of Fame recipient Tallulah Bankhead, is released in Finland. . . . The U.S. National Academy of Design vigorously protests a proposed congressional measure to heavily tax artistic works.	Dec. 3
		The Annalist releases its weekly list of U.S. wholesale commodity prices. At 100.0, the index is a drop of 1.2 points from the previous week and a decline of 15 percent from the corresponding week a year ago. Economists say the drop from the previous week was caused by losses in food products, textile products, fuels, metals, and building materials. . . . *Dun's Review* releases its weekly index of U.S. business failures. At 120.9, the figure is a drop of 25 points from the previous week, but an increase of 7 points from the corresponding week one year ago.	The U.S. Department of Commerce releases a report showing that the number of U.S. air passengers has increased by 3 percent since December 1930.	Academy Award-winning director William Wyler's *A House Divided*, starring Hollywood Walk of Fame recipient Walter Huston, is released throughout the United States.	Dec. 4
		The U.S. Department of Commerce reports that bank clearings for the past week amounted to $6,327,677,000, a rise of $2 billion from the past week, but a decline of $3 billion from the corresponding week one year ago. . . . *Dun's Review* releases its weekly index of U.S. bank debits. At 74.9, the figure is a drop of 16 points from the previous week, and a decline of 25 points from the corresponding week one year ago.		The German musical comedy *Der Kongress tanzt* (The Congress Dances), is released in Denmark. The film stars German Film Award winners Lilian Harvey, Willy Fritsch, Carl-Heinz Schroth, and Lil Dagover, and is directed by German Film Award winner Erik Charell. . . . The American comedy short *The Kickoff* is released throughout the United States.	Dec. 5
Approximately 1,360 policemen in Washington, D.C., are dispatched to Pennsylvania Avenue to prevent a massive demonstration of "hunger marchers" from dissolving into chaos.		*The Annalist* releases its weekly index of U.S. business activity. At 63.6, the figure is a rise of 0.4 points from the previous week, but a decline of 22 percent from the corresponding period last year. Economists say the rise from last week was caused by gains in steel mill activity, electric power production, automobile production, and cotton cloth production.	The National Electric Light Association reports U.S. electric power output for the past week amounted to 1,599,900,000 kilowatt hours, 50 million kilowatt hours less than the preceding week, and a decline of 4 percent from the corresponding period one year ago.	The French musical comedy *Le Capitaine Craddock* (Captain Craddock) is released throughout France. The film is based on the novel by Fritz Reck-Malleczewen.	Dec. 6
The National Child Labor Committee reports that the number of U.S. children not attending any school has decreased by 11.1 percent since 1905, from 29.6 percent to 18.5 percent.		Prof. Irving Fisher of Yale University releases his weekly index of international commodity prices. The figure is 67.6, a decline of 0.2 points from the preceding week, and a reduction of approximately 16 percent from the corresponding week a year ago.		Academy Award-winning director John Ford's *Arrowsmith*, based on the novel by Sinclair Lewis, is released throughout the United States. The film is written by Sidney Howard and stars Ronald Colman and Helen Hayes, all of whom received at least one Oscar statuette during their careers. *Arrowsmith* received multiple Academy Award nominations in 1932, including Best Art Direction, Best Cinematography, Best Writing, and Best Picture.	Dec. 7

F	G	H	I	J
Includes elections, federal-state relations, civil rights and liberties, crime, the judiciary, education, healthcare, poverty, urban affairs, and population.	*Includes formation and debate of U.S. foreign and defense policies, veterans affairs, and defense spending. (Relations with specific foreign countries are usually found under the region concerned.)*	*Includes business, labor, agriculture, taxation, transportation, consumer affairs, monetary and fiscal policy, natural resources, pollution, and accidents.*	*Includes worldwide scientific, medical, and technological developments, natural phenomena, U.S. weather, and natural disasters.*	*Includes the arts, religion, scholarship, communications media, sports, entertainment, fashions, fads, and social life.*

	World Affairs	Europe	Africa & The Middle East	The Americas	Asia & The Pacific
Dec. 8		German Chancellor Heinrich Bruening calls a state of emergency, granting him wide economic powers, including the setting of interest rates, salaries, and wages.		Thirteen Peruvians die in clashes with local police in the capital of Lima.	
Dec. 9		In a radio address broadcast throughout Germany, German Chancellor Heinrich Bruening warns his people not to give in to the demagogic nature of the National Socialist party. "The tendency to regard politics from the emotional viewpoint must never get the upper hand, or there will be an end of Germany," he says. He threatens a "state of siege" if conditions deem it necessary.			
Dec. 10		British economists report an unfavorable trade balance of £46,410,000 for the month of November.			Japan conducts bombing raids on a Chinese village near the city of Peiping. A total of 21 bombs were dropped. . . . A group of Chinese bandits numbering 1,000 begin their march toward the Japanese-occupied region of Manchuria. Japanese military officials say their forces will be wholly prepared for the bandits' advance.
Dec. 11		British economists report the Bank of England's reserve ratio currently stands at 30.28 percent, a rise of 2 percent from the previous week, and a decline of 15 percent from the corresponding week one year ago. The bank's gold holdings currently amount to £121,516,967, a drop of £31 million from the previous week, and a decline of £32 million from the corresponding week one year ago.			Newspapers around the globe speculate that a "national emergency government" in Japan will soon be established. The intention of the new government would be to increase Japan's military capabilities.
Dec. 12	Future British Prime Minister Winston Churchill declares in a speech that "wherever the pathway may lead, we shall travel more securely if the United States and Great Britain do it together like good companions." He says that "the leading men of all countries do not seem to have a clear idea" of the present world situation.				The Japanese Ambassador to the United States travels to Washington, D.C., to discuss with U.S. Secretary of State Henry Stimson Japan's troubling political situation, as well as the Manchurian Incident.
Dec. 13	In a speech before the U.S. Intercollegiate Conference on World Peace in Oberlin, Ohio, former U.S. war secretary Newton Baker declares that "what happens in Germany in the next few months will determine what kind of world our children shall live in."				
Dec. 14		The Soviet Union announces plans for construction of a 370-foot-high bronze statue of Communist revolutionary Vladimir Lenin. Construction costs are expected to exceed $1,250,000.		Argentine grain prices fall to near record lows. Pessimism is cited as a cause for the swift decline. . . . Remnants of the regime of deposed Argentine premier Hipolito Irigoyen personally thank Uruguay for granting exile to more than 3,000 of its party members.	

A	B	C	D	E
Includes developments that affect more than one world region, international organizations, and important meetings of world leaders.	Includes all domestic and regional developments in Europe, including the Soviet Union.	Includes all domestic and regional developments in Africa and the Middle East.	Includes all domestic and regional developments in Latin America, the Caribbean, and Canada.	Includes all domestic and regional developments in Asian and Pacific nations (and colonies).

U.S. Politics & Social Issues	U.S. Foreign Policy & Defense	Economics & Great Depression	Science, Technology & Nature	Culture, Leisure & Lifestyle	
The New York City Emergency Unemployment Relief Fund urges all city residents to contribute $1 each to the fund. . . . Officials of Sing Sing Prison, one of America's oldest correctional facilities, request New York state legislators to pass legislation to racially segregate the prison. The request comes as reports are released of increased prison murders owing to racial hatred.	Gen. Lytle Brown, chief of the army engineers, urges Congress to appropriate $60 million for the construction of harbors.			*Private Lives*, based on the play by Noel Coward, is released throughout the United States. The film features a host of Oscar-winning talent, including its director, Sidney Franklin, and its four stars, Norma Shearer, Robert Montgomery, Jean Hersholt, and Una Merkel.	Dec. 8
The Buffalo, New York, Board of Education bans the William Shakespeare play *Merchant of Venice*, following complaints by local Rabbis of the play's anti-Semitic content.		Freight car loadings for the past week amounted to 558,807 cars, according to figures published by the American Railway Association. The total is 94,696 cars less than the previous week, and a decline of 21 percent from the corresponding week last year. The drop from last week was attributable to losses in grain products, forest products, coal, and livestock. . . . *Dun's Review* releases its weekly index of U.S. bond prices. At 90, the figure is a drop of 2.8 points from the previous week, and a decline of 16 points from the corresponding week one year ago.	The American Institute of Chemical Engineers holds its annual meeting in Atlantic City, N.J.		Dec. 9
	Admiral Frank Upham tells Naval Secretary Charles Francis Adams that reducing the Navy's fleet will result in "grave consequences."	*The Iron Age* releases its weekly index of U.S. steel mill activity. The index currently stands at 34.7, a decline of 2.7 points from the previous week, and a decline of approximately 36 percent from the corresponding week one year ago. . . . The weekly index of U.S. automobile production as compiled by the Department of Commerce is released. The index currently stands at 20.0, a drop of 1.4 points from the previous week, and a decline of 80 percent from the corresponding week one year ago.		One of the early films of suspense luminary Alfred Hitchcock, *Rich and Strange*, premiers in London, England. The film stars German Film Awards recipient Elsie Randolph.	Dec. 10
The U.S. Immigration Department reports that a total of 97,139 immigrants were granted permanent residence in the United States during the year ended June 30, a sharp decline of 60 percent from the previous year.	Isolationist Senators express fierce opposition to proposals to further extend the Hoover Moratorium.	*The Annalist* releases its weekly list of U.S. wholesale commodity prices. At 98.9, the index is a drop of 0.8 points from the previous week and a decline of 15 percent from the corresponding week a year ago. . . . *Dun's Review* releases its weekly index of U.S. bank debits. At 79.1, the figure is a rise of 4.9 points from the previous week, but a decline of 27 points from the corresponding week one year ago.		*Men in Her Life*, a short film, is released throughout the United States. The film is one of the first directed by Hollywood Walk of Fame recipient William Beaudine, who made over 250 short films over the span of a 50-year career.	Dec. 11
Governor Joseph B. Ely of Massachusetts officially endorses former New York governor Al Smith for the 1932 presidential election.		The U.S. Department of Commerce reports that bank clearings for the past week amounted to $5,090,306,000, a loss of $1.3 billion from the past week, and a decline of $2.5 billion from the corresponding week one year ago. . . . *Dun's Review* releases its weekly index of the U.S. federal reserve ratio. At 84.6, the figure is a rise of 0.7 points from the previous week, but a decline of 18 points from the corresponding week one year ago.		Stan Laurel and Oliver Hardy's musical comedy short *Beau Hunks* is released throughout the United States. The film is said to be the personal favorite of two-time Oscar-winning director Hal Roach.	Dec. 12
		The Annalist releases its weekly index of U.S. business activity. At 63.8, the figure is a rise of 0.1 points from the previous week, but a decline of 21 percent from the corresponding period last year. Economists say the rise from last week was caused by gains in freight car loadings. . . . *Dun's Review* releases its weekly index of U.S. bond prices. At 87.9, the figure is a drop of 2.1 points from the previous week, and a decline of 18 points from the corresponding week one year ago.	The 1931 Nobel Peace Prize winners are announced. For the 11th time in the history of the award, two people are declared co-winners. Those are Jane Addams, international president of the Women's International League for Peace and Freedom, and Nicholas Murray Butler, president of the Carnegie Endowment for International Peace.	The crime drama film *X Marks the Spot*, starring Hollywood Walk of Fame recipient Wallace Ford, is released throughout the United States. The film is written by legendary screenwriter F. Hugh Hubert.	Dec. 13
Ninety-eight criminals in Newark, N.J., are rounded up in an effort by police authorities to reduce criminal activity on the eve of the holiday buying season.		Prof. Irving Fisher of Yale University releases his weekly index of international commodity prices. The figure is 67.1, a drop of 0.5 points from the preceding week, and a decline of approximately 16 percent from the corresponding week a year ago.		The romantic comedy *Good Sport*, starring Hollywood Walk of Fame recipients John Boles and Hedda Hopper, is released throughout the United States.	Dec. 14

F	G	H	I	J
Includes elections, federal-state relations, civil rights and liberties, crime, the judiciary, education, healthcare, poverty, urban affairs, and population.	*Includes formation and debate of U.S. foreign and defense policies, veterans affairs, and defense spending. (Relations with specific foreign countries are usually found under the region concerned.)*	*Includes business, labor, agriculture, taxation, transportation, consumer affairs, monetary and fiscal policy, natural resources, pollution, and accidents.*	*Includes worldwide scientific, medical, and technological developments, natural phenomena, U.S. weather, and natural disasters.*	*Includes the arts, religion, scholarship, communications media, sports, entertainment, fashions, fads, and social life.*

	World Affairs	Europe	Africa & The Middle East	The Americas	Asia & The Pacific
Dec. 15	In his first interview given to the American press, Chinese Premier Cheng Minshu describes the United States as "a young lady with an enormous diamond necklace. It's all show; pure luxury." . . . A postal worker in Philadelphia, Pa., discovers several packages shipped from Germany containing a bottle of cognac alcohol obscured inside a loaf of rye bread. The evidence is turned over to police authorities.				Cheng Minshu becomes the new premier of China. Cheng replaces Chiang Kai-shek, who was described by his opponents as "too weak to lead and too strong to overthrow." He would resume power again in 1935.
Dec. 16			Followers of Mohandas Gandhi cable a message to Egyptian authorities requesting 10 bottles of goat's milk and an array of fruits and vegetables for the Indian revolutionary leader upon his scheduled visit.		Burmese rebel leader Aung San and four of his followers are arrested by police authorities of the southeast Asian nation. . . . A massive fire in the Siamese city of Bangkok results in over 500 buildings being burned to the ground. Two thousand residents are left homeless. Damages are estimated at $2 million.
Dec. 17		Denmark Transportation Minister Friis Skotte announces plans for the longest bridge ever constructed in Europe: a 10,725-foot railway bridge that will span the Storstrommen. Construction costs are expected to run as high as $7.7 million.			Chinese Marshal Chang Hsueh-liang resigns as commander of the Chinese forces stationed in Manchuria, ceding power to Chang Tso-hsiang.
Dec. 18		British economists report the Bank of England's reserve ratio currently stands at 26.62 percent, a decline of 3.5 percent from the previous week, and a reduction of 11 percent from the corresponding week one year ago. The bank's gold holdings currently amount to £121,428,344, a decrease of £30 million from the previous week, and a reduction of £31 million from the corresponding week one year ago.			
Dec. 19		Residents in Amsterdam hold a demonstration to protest against a City Council decision to increase the requirements for idle workers to receive relief funds.		Cuba officially bans the showing of the musical comedy film *Cuban Love Song*, contending it paints an unfair portrait of the Caribbean island nation as a backward, uncivilized country.	Australian lawmakers appropriate 500,000 British pounds to assist needy farmers during the winter of 1931–32.
Dec. 20	Nazi leader Adolf Hitler is interviewed by the *New York Times*. When asked how his party intends to solve the worldwide dispute over the 1918 Versailles Treaty, he replies, "We hope by the application of reason. Of course we want peace with every country."			By way of presidential decree, members of the Costa Rican Communist Party and the Costa Rican army are forbidden to participate in the country's upcoming elections.	
Dec. 21		French economists report that total French exports have fallen by nearly 150 million francs since December 1930.			Parliamentary elections are held in Australia. The United Australia Party becomes Australia's largest party, increasing its seat representation from the last election by 12, from 23 to 35.

A	B	C	D	E
Includes developments that affect more than one world region, international organizations, and important meetings of world leaders.	Includes all domestic and regional developments in Europe, including the Soviet Union.	Includes all domestic and regional developments in Africa and the Middle East.	Includes all domestic and regional developments in Latin America, the Caribbean, and Canada.	Includes all domestic and regional developments in Asian and Pacific nations (and colonies).

U.S. Politics & Social Issues	U.S. Foreign Policy & Defense	Economics & Great Depression	Science, Technology & Nature	Culture, Leisure & Lifestyle	
		Prof. Irving Fisher of Yale University releases his weekly index of international stock prices. The figure is 54.4, a reduction of 3.3 points from the preceding week, and a decline of approximately 45 percent from the corresponding week a year ago.		Legendary director Richard Thorpe's mystery motion picture *The Devil Plays* is released throughout the United States.	Dec. 15
During Congressional testimony, Treasury Undersecretary Ogden Mills declares that "it would be to the everlasting disgrace of the Congress if it refused to ratify" the Hoover Moratorium.		Freight car loadings for the past week amounted to 636,366 cars, according to figures published by the American Railway Association. The total is 77,559 cars more than the previous week, but a decline of 19 percent from the corresponding week last year. The rise from last week was attributable to gains in grain products, coal, coke, and livestock.			Dec. 16
		Dun's Review releases its weekly index of U.S. business failures. At 141.3, the figure is a rise of 6 points from the previous week, and an increase of 3 points from the corresponding week one year ago. . . . *The Iron Age* releases its weekly index of U.S. steel mill activity. The index currently stands at 32.2, a drop of 2.5 points from the previous week, and a decline of approximately 41 percent from the corresponding week one year ago. . . . The weekly index of U.S. automobile production as compiled by the Department of Commerce is released. The index currently stands at 27, a rise of 7 points from the previous week, but a decline of 78 percent from the corresponding week one year ago.		The U.S. Supreme Court officially bans the sale and distribution of "*Strange Career of Mr. Hoover—Under Two Flags*," on the grounds that the book's author plagiarized most of its contents.	Dec. 17
		The Annalist releases its weekly list of U.S. wholesale commodity prices. At 97.2, the index is a drop of 1.4 points from the previous week but a decline of 16 percent from the corresponding week a year ago. . . . *Dun's Review* releases its weekly index of the U.S. federal reserve ratio. At 83.9, the figure is a drop of 0.7 points from the previous week, and a decline of 19 points from the corresponding week one year ago.		The John Wayne motion picture *Maker of Men* is released throughout the United States. The film is directed by Edward Sedgwick, and stars Jack Holt and Richard Cromwell, all of whom are recipients of the Hollywood Walk of Fame.	Dec. 18
	The destroyer *Boggs* is recommissioned by the U.S. Navy after nearly a decade of inactivity. Now known as the miscellaneous auxiliary vehicle *AG-19*, the ship will spend the rest of its career stationed off the West Coast.	Prof. Irving Fisher of Yale University releases his weekly index of international stock prices. The figure is 49.2, a decline of 5.2 points from the preceding week, and a reduction of approximately 55 percent from the corresponding week a year ago.	The National Electric Light Association reports U.S. electric power output for the past week amounted to 1,671,717,000 kilowatt hours, 25,000 kilowatt hours greater than the preceding week, but a decline of 4 percent from the corresponding period one year ago.	The comedic short *Taxi Tangle*, starring legendary comedian Jack Benny, is released throughout the United States.	Dec. 19
In an editorial published in the *New York Times*, Agriculture Secretary Arthur Hyde urges the nation's farmers, who comprise more than 20 percent of the total population of the United States, to remain patient.		*The Annalist* releases its weekly index of U.S. business activity. At 63.2, the figure is a drop of 0.5 points from the previous week, and a decline of 21 percent from the corresponding period last year. Economists say the drop from last week was caused by losses in steel mill activity, electric power production, and cotton cloth production.		*Skippy*, directed by Academy Award–winner Normon Taurog, is released in Finland. The film would be nominated for four Academy Awards, including Best Director, Best Actor, Best Picture, and Best Screenplay.	Dec. 20
	The U.S. Navy sells the armored cruiser *Pennsylvania* for scrap in accordance with the London Naval Treaty. Constructed in 1901 by William Cramp and Sons Co., *Pennsylvania* became the lead ship of its class, and spent the main portion of its career cruising the waters of the Pacific.	Prof. Irving Fisher of Yale University releases his weekly index of international commodity prices. The figure is 67, a drop of 0.1 points from the preceding week, and a decline of approximately 16 percent from the corresponding week a year ago.			Dec. 21

F	G	H	I	J
Includes elections, federal-state relations, civil rights and liberties, crime, the judiciary, education, healthcare, poverty, urban affairs, and population.	*Includes formation and debate of U.S. foreign and defense policies, veterans affairs, and defense spending. (Relations with specific foreign countries are usually found under the region concerned.)*	*Includes business, labor, agriculture, taxation, transportation, consumer affairs, monetary and fiscal policy, natural resources, pollution, and accidents.*	*Includes worldwide scientific, medical, and technological developments, natural phenomena, U.S. weather, and natural disasters.*	*Includes the arts, religion, scholarship, communications media, sports, entertainment, fashions, fads, and social life.*

	World Affairs	Europe	Africa & The Middle East	The Americas	Asia & The Pacific
Dec. 22	Chinese diplomats tell the League of Nations that the Chinese army "will be compelled in self-defense to resist" any attempted advance by Japanese troops into Chinese territory.	Arnaldo Mussolini, the brother of Italian Premier Benito Mussolini, dies suddenly from injuries sustained in a car crash.		Mexican lawmakers introduce a bill that would limit the number of priests allowed to serve in the capital of Mexico City to one per 100,000 residents.	
Dec. 23		The number of British idle workers falls to 2,572,602, according to official estimates. The figure is a decrease of 54,722 workers from the preceding week.		Colombia sets its federal budget for the year of 1932 at $37,150,000, $6 million below the budget for 1931.	
Dec. 24	The League of Nations receives word that despite the League's insistence that Japan militarily evacuate from the disputed region of Manchuria, "she is still contemplating extending her military occupation."		Socialist author George Bernard Shaw announces his intentions to visit the economically desolate African continent.		Japan announces it will return to China the 600 miles of railroad it seized during its invasion of Manchuria.
Dec. 25		British economists report the Bank of England's reserve ratio currently stands at 20.94 percent, a decrease of 6 percent from the previous week, and a decline of 9 percent from the corresponding week one year ago. The bank's gold holdings currently amount to £121,353,240, a decrease of £30 million from the previous week, and a decline of £31 million from the corresponding week one year ago.		Representatives of Cuba's sugar mills meet in the capital of Havana to discuss ways to alleviate ever declining international sugar prices.	
Dec. 26	In a speech before members of the American Chamber of Commerce, the U.S. Ambassador to Germany, Frederic Sackett, urges all of the world's national central banks to cooperate fully in solving worldwide depressive economic conditions.				A group of Chinese Communist rebel leaders tell reporters that they anticipate a complete collapse of the Chinese government during the spring of 1932. . . . Citizens of the Dutch East Indies hear the first radio broadcast ever given by Queen Wilhelmina of the Nether-lands.
Dec. 27		French military officials announce that essential improvements will be added to defense fortifications along the French-Italian border in the coming year.		Canadian Manufacturers Association president W.H. Miner tells local reporters that he believes the Great Depression will soon be at an end, basing his prediction on previous historical parallels: "History has shown that after a three-year period of hard times, things get better."	
Dec. 28	China criticizes the League of Nations for what it perceives as "its dismal failure" in solving the Manchurian Incident.		In Damascus, Syria, four people are killed amid riots contesting recent parliamentary elections.		Premier Ki Inukai of Japan declares that his country cannot afford "the expense of maintaining" the occupation of the region of Manchuria.

A	B	C	D	E
Includes developments that affect more than one world region, international organizations, and important meetings of world leaders.	Includes all domestic and regional developments in Europe, including the Soviet Union.	Includes all domestic and regional developments in Africa and the Middle East.	Includes all domestic and regional developments in Latin America, the Caribbean, and Canada.	Includes all domestic and regional developments in Asian and Pacific nations (and colonies).

U.S. Politics & Social Issues	U.S. Foreign Policy & Defense	Economics & Great Depression	Science, Technology & Nature	Culture, Leisure & Lifestyle	
Newly elected Senator Warren Barbour of New Jersey urges his colleagues to pass legislation allowing the entry of the United States into the League of Nations Permanent Court of International Justice.		The Iron Age releases its weekly index of U.S. steel mill activity. The index currently stands at 30.7, a drop of 1.5 points from the previous week, and a decline of approximately 40 percent from the corresponding week one year ago. . . . The weekly index of U.S. automobile production as compiled by the Department of Commerce is released. The index currently stands at 33.0, a rise of six points from the previous week, and a decline of 66 percent from the corresponding week one year ago.		The German musical comedy Ronny premiers in the German capital of Berlin. The film is directed by Reinhold Schunzel and stars Willy Fritsch, both of whom are German Film Award winners.	Dec. 22
Census officials report that the number of foreign aliens living in the United States has increased by 2 percent since 1921.		Freight car loadings for the past week amounted to 613,534 cars, according to figures published by the American Railway Association. The total is 22,832 cars less than the previous week, and a decline of 33 percent from the corresponding week last year. The drop from last week was attributable to losses in grain products, forest products, and livestock.		Ben-Hur: A Tale of the Christ, starring Hollywood Walk of Fame recipients Ramon Novarro, Francis X. Bushman, and May McAvoy, is re-released in Finland. A cultural artifact of its time, the film will be archived in 1997 by the National Film Preservation Board for the enjoyment of future generations.	Dec. 23
		The Annalist releases its weekly list of U.S. wholesale commodity prices. At 96.5, the index is a reduction of 0.7 points from the previous week and a decline of 17 percent from the corresponding week a year ago. Economists say the drop from the previous week was caused by losses in food products, textile products, fuels, and building materials. . . . Dun's Review releases its weekly index of U.S. business failures. At 163.9, the figure is a rise of 22 points from the previous week, and a decline of 15 points from the corresponding week one year ago.			Dec. 24
		Dun's Review releases its weekly index of the U.S. federal reserve ratio. At 83.9, the figure is a drop of 1.4 points from the previous week, and a decline of 14 points from the corresponding week one year ago. Dun's Review releases its weekly index of U.S. bank debits. At 87.2, the figure is a rise of 13 points from the previous week, but a decline of 32 points from the corresponding week one year ago. . . . The U.S. Department of Commerce reports that bank clearings for the past week amounted to $5,447,761,000, a rise of $500 million from the past week, but a decline of $2 billion from the corresponding week one year ago.		The women's prison movie Ladies of the Big House is released throughout the United States. The film stars Hollywood Walk of Fame recipients Sylvia Sydney and Gene Raymond.	Dec. 25
		Prof. Irving Fisher of Yale University releases his weekly index of international stock prices. The figure is 49.2, a drop of 5.2 points from the preceding week, and a decline of approximately 47 percent from the corresponding week a year ago.	The National Electric Light Association reports U.S. electric power output for the past week amounted to 1,675,653,000 kilowatt hours, 4 million kilowatt hours greater than the preceding week, but a decline of 5 percent from the corresponding period one year ago.	Paramount Pictures' Morocco, starring Hollywood Walk of Fame recipients Gary Cooper, Marlene Dietrich, and Adolphe Menjou, and directed by Academy Award-nominee Josef von Sternberg, is released in Portugal. The film would garner four Academy Award nominations, including Best Actress, Best Art Direction, Best Cinematography, and Best Director.	Dec. 26
New York City Health Commissioner Shirley Wynne appoints a special commission to study the causes of the spread of tuberculosis.		The Annalist releases its weekly index of U.S. business activity. At 63.1, the figure is a drop of 0.2 points from the previous week, and a decline of 20 percent from the corresponding period last year. Economists say the drop from last week was caused by losses in freight car loadings, steel mill activity, and electric power production.		The comedy short film The Pottsville Palooka is released throughout the United States. The film is written by Lewis Foster, who later won the 1940 Academy Award for Best Original Screenplay for the Jimmy Stewart classic Mr. Smith Goes to Washington.	Dec. 27
		Prof. Irving Fisher of Yale University releases his weekly index of international commodity prices. The figure is 66.7, a decline of 0.3 points from the preceding week, and a reduction of approximately 15 percent from the corresponding week a year ago.		Academy Award-nominated director Michael Powell's short film Two Crowded Hours is released throughout the United States.	Dec. 28

F	G	H	I	J
Includes elections, federal-state relations, civil rights and liberties, crime, the judiciary, education, healthcare, poverty, urban affairs, and population.	Includes formation and debate of U.S. foreign and defense policies, veterans affairs, and defense spending. (Relations with specific foreign countries are usually found under the region concerned.)	Includes business, labor, agriculture, taxation, transportation, consumer affairs, monetary and fiscal policy, natural resources, pollution, and accidents.	Includes worldwide scientific, medical, and technological developments, natural phenomena, U.S. weather, and natural disasters.	Includes the arts, religion, scholarship, communications media, sports, entertainment, fashions, fads, and social life.

	World Affairs	Europe	Africa & The Middle East	The Americas	Asia & The Pacific
Dec. 29		France and Germany enter into an economic agreement whereby the latter will annually sell significant quantities of nitrate to the former.		Argentina delays the settlement of a proposed tripartite economic pact between itself, Uruguay, and Brazil, requesting further negotiation of terms.	
Dec. 30	The moderate German newspaper *Socialist Vorwaerts* (*Socialists Forward*) prints an editorial stating that Europe has grown bitter and cynical over the issue of World War I reparation payments. "Every child in Europe knows that the United States benefits most from German payments."		World Zionist Organization president Nahun Sokolow attends the annual convention of the Junior Hadassah, a Zionist young women's organization.		Fearing an onslaught by advancing Japanese forces, Chinese Gen. Chang Hsueh-liang orders all troops serving in the Chinchow region to retreat.
Dec. 31		Ireland drastically raises tariffs on imported bacon, effectively placing an embargo on it.		Brazil, Argentina, and Uruguay enter into a tripartite economic pact, avoiding a potential deadlock by Argentina. Among the provisions of the pact is a shared meat inspection program.	

A	B	C	D	E
Includes developments that affect more than one world region, international organizations, and important meetings of world leaders.	Includes all domestic and regional developments in Europe, including the Soviet Union.	Includes all domestic and regional developments in Africa and the Middle East.	Includes all domestic and regional developments in Latin America, the Caribbean, and Canada.	Includes all domestic and regional developments in Asian and Pacific nations (and colonies).

U.S. Politics & Social Issues	U.S. Foreign Policy & Defense	Economics & Great Depression	Science, Technology & Nature	Culture, Leisure & Lifestyle	
Vice President Charles Curtis declares that the U.S. federal budget can be reduced by $500 million annually by eliminating excessive bureaucracy.		The weekly index of U.S. automobile production as compiled by the Department of Commerce is released. The index currently stands at 39.8, a rise of 6.8 points from the previous week, but a decline of 59 percent from the corresponding week one year ago.		German Film Award winner Reinhold Schunzel's *Der Kleine Seitensprung* (*The Little Escapade*) is released in the United States. The film stars German Film Award recipients Hermann Thimig and Hilde Hildebrand.	Dec. 29
		Freight car loadings for the past week amounted to 581,733 cars, according to figures published by the American Railway Association. The total is 31,801 cars less than the previous week, and a decline of 29 percent from the corresponding week last year. The drop from last week was attributable to losses in coal, coke, grain, and livestock.		Paramount Pictures' *Dr. Jekyll and Mr. Hyde*, based on the novel by Robert Louis Stevenson, is released throughout the United States. The film is directed by Rouben Mamoulian, and stars Fredric March and Miriam Hopkins. A critical favorite, *Dr. Jekyll and Mr. Hyde* will be nominated for three Academy Awards, including Best Actor, Best Cinematography, and Best Screenplay.	Dec. 30
Senator James Couzens of Michigan suggests to his colleagues to pass legislation reducing the salaries of Congressmen by an average of 25 percent.		*The Iron Age* releases its weekly index of U.S. steel mill activity. The index currently stands at 32.4, a rise of 1.7 points from the previous week, but a decline of approximately 38 percent from the corresponding week one year ago.		*A Nous La Liberte*, a French musical comedy written and directed by legendary filmmaker Rene Claire, is released throughout the United States. The film will be nominated for a 1932 Academy Award for Best Art Direction, becoming the first foreign-language film to receive an Oscar nomination.	Dec. 31

F	G	H	I	J
Includes elections, federal-state relations, civil rights and liberties, crime, the judiciary, education, healthcare, poverty, urban affairs, and population.	*Includes formation and debate of U.S. foreign and defense policies, veterans affairs, and defense spending. (Relations with specific foreign countries are usually found under the region concerned.)*	*Includes business, labor, agriculture, taxation, transportation, consumer affairs, monetary and fiscal policy, natural resources, pollution, and accidents.*	*Includes worldwide scientific, medical, and technological developments, natural phenomena, U.S. weather, and natural disasters.*	*Includes the arts, religion, scholarship, communications media, sports, entertainment, fashions, fads, and social life.*

1932

Amelia Earhart speaks to a crowd in England after being the first woman to fly solo across the Atlantic Ocean.

	World Affairs	Europe	Africa & The Middle East	The Americas	Asia & The Pacific
Jan.	The Turkish and Persian governments agree to establish the boundary between the two nations in the vicinity of Mount Ararat.	The Spanish Republican government abolishes the Jesuit Order and seizes the order's property as part of the government's new social program. . . . Negotiations between the Romanian and Soviet governments in Warsaw, under Polish mediation, fail to settle the Bessarabian question.	French forces occupy the oasis of Tafilet, effectively bringing to an end the conflicts with Moroccan tribes.	Four thousand protesting farmers are killed by the Salvadorian army.	The Japanese army completes the occupation of Manchuria. The Republic of Manchukuo is established as a puppet state. . . . British authorities in India arrest Gandhi and outlaw the Indian Nationalist Party. . . . The Japanese government orders an attack against Shanghai to force the Chinese to stop their economic boycott.
Feb.	The Permanent Court of International Justice holds its 24th session in The Hague. . . . Sixty nations take part in the Geneva Conference on the Reduction and Limitation of Arms. In spite of hopes, the conference fails to find a common agreement.	The Soviet and Latvian governments sign a nonaggression pact. . . . The Oslo Conventions establish economic cooperation between Denmark, Norway, Sweden, Belgium, Luxemburg, and the Netherlands.			
Mar.	The League of Nations Assembly holds a special session in Geneva to discuss the Manchurian crisis. . . . With reference to the Japanese occupation of Shanghai, the League of Nations unanimously adopts the Stimson Doctrine of nonrecognition of violations of the Pact of Paris.	Former French foreign minister and co-author of the Paris Pact Aristide Briand dies. . . . Eamon De Valera is elected Irish prime minister on a manifesto which asks for abolishment of all loyalty to the British Crown. . . . In Finland, the fascist Lapua Movement causes widespread riots.			Japanese forces occupy Shanghai, driving out the Chinese Nationalist Army from one of the country's most important harbors. . . . Former Chinese Emperor Henry Pu-Yi becomes Regent of Manchukuo, but all the important governmental functions are taken by Japanese officials.
Apr.	The International Labor Organization holds its 16th session in Geneva. . . . The Permanent Court of International Justice holds its 25th session in The Hague.	Representatives from Britain, France, Germany, and Italy meet in London to discuss problems in the Danube region. . . . Paul von Hindenburg is re-elected president of Germany, with Adolf Hitler coming second. However, Hitler's party makes important gains in state elections, becoming first in four states.	The citizens of Southwest Africa form the Farmers' and Labor Party, whose goal is to establish the region as an independent territory with responsible government. . . . Kurds rebel against the Iraqi government, which subdues the revolt. . . . King Faisal of Iraq conducts a state visit to Persia.		
May	The League of Nations Council holds its 67th session in Geneva.	Turkey and Italy renew their non-aggression pact for another five years. . . . French president Paul Doumer is killed. Albert Lebrun becomes the new president.	Socal is the first American firm to discover oil in the Middle East (Bahrain). . . . Rebel forces from Trans-Jordania invade Nejd, fighting against the centralizing policies of Ibn Saud.		The Chinese and Japanese governments reach an agreement establishing a neutral zone around the International Settlement in Shanghai and a termination of the Chinese boycott against Japanese goods. The Japanese subsequently agree to withdraw from Shanghai. . . . Japanese Prime Minister Tsuyoshi Inukai is assassinated.
Jun.	Representatives from Belgium, Britain, France, Germany, Italy, and Japan meet in Lausanne, Switzerland, with the mediation of the League of Nations, to negotiate Germany's reparation program.	German President Paul von Hindenburg makes Franz von Papen the prime minister, dismissing Chancellor Heinrich Brüening. Von Papen lifts the ban on German stormtroopers.		A military coup takes place in Chile.	Hailstones kill more than 200 people in the Chinese province of Hunan. . . . A coup ends absolute monarchy in Thailand.
Jul.	The League of Nations Assembly holds its second special session of the year to continue negotiations with the Japanese over the Manchurian crisis. . . . The League of Nations agrees to give Austria a loan of 300 million schillings provided it does not join Germany before 1952. . . . The League of Nations admits Turkey into the organization.	Norway announces the annexation of southern Greenland. . . . France and Britain sign a treaty of friendship. . . . Antonio de Oliveira Salazar becomes premier and dictator of Portugal. . . . Hitler's National Socialist Party becomes the first party in the German parliament.		Years of tensions between Bolivia and Paraguay over the Chaco region escalate into a full war. . . . The Ottawa Imperial Conference starts.	
Aug.		The Austrian Assembly approves the League of Nations loan to help the country's economy in spite of the clause barring union with Germany. . . . Hitler refuses to serve as Franz von Papen's deputy. . . . In England, 200,000 textile workers go on strike. . . . Nazi leader Hermann Goering is elected president of the Reichstag.			
Sept.	The German government withdraws from the League of Nations Disarmament Conference because Germany is not granted equal rights with other participants.	Delegates meet in Stresa, Italy, to discuss problems relating to central and eastern Europe. . . . The Belgian parliament gives the government extraordinary powers to deal with the economic depression. . . . The Spanish government grants a new charter for Catalonia. . . . The German government led by Franz von Papen falls.	The Kingdom of the Hejaz and Nejd officially changes its name to Saudi Arabia.	Relations between the Peruvian and Colombian governments become tense over the Leticia region, an area claimed by both countries.	The Japanese and Manchukuo governments sign an agreement that officially makes Manchukuo a Japanese protectorate. . . . Gandhi starts a hunger strike against the treatment of Untouchables.

A	B	C	D	E
Includes developments that affect more than one world region, international organizations, and important meetings of world leaders.	*Includes all domestic and regional developments in Europe, including the Soviet Union.*	*Includes all domestic and regional developments in Africa and the Middle East.*	*Includes all domestic and regional developments in Latin America, the Caribbean, and Canada.*	*Includes all domestic and regional developments in Asian and Pacific nations (and colonies).*

U.S. Politics & Social Issues	U.S. Foreign Policy & Defense	Economics & Great Depression	Science, Technology & Nature	Culture, Leisure & Lifestyle	
Hattie W. Caraway, a Democrat from Arkansas, becomes the first woman elected to the Senate. . . . Oliver Wendell Holmes quits the Supreme Court at 90 years of age. . . . New York Governor Franklin Delano Roosevelt announces his candidacy for the Democratic presidential nomination.	Secretary of State Henry Stimson officially protests against the Japanese occupation of Manchuria.				Jan.
Al Capone loses his appeal and is sent to prison in Atlanta for tax evasion.	The U.S. delegation at the Geneva Disarmament Conference calls for the abolition of all offensive weapons as a basis for negotiation but encounters strong opposition. . . . Secretary of State Henry Stimson invites other countries not to recognize acts that violate the Pact of Paris.	The Glass-Steagall Act is passed, giving the Federal Reserve the right to expand credit in order to increase money circulation.	An explosion in a coal mine in Boissevain, Va., causes 38 deaths.	New York Governor Franklin D. Roosevelt opens the Winter Olympic Games at Lake Placid, N.Y. . . . The musical *Face the Music* by Irving Berlin premieres in New York.	Feb.
Charles Lindbergh, Jr., the infant son of Charles and Anne Lindbergh, is kidnapped from the family home in New Jersey. A $50,000 ransom is demanded. . . . Riots at the Ford factory in Dearborn, Mich., cause the death of four people. . . . George Eastman, founder of Eastman Kodak, commits suicide.	Secretary of State Henry Stimson suggests to the British Foreign Secretary John Simon that the two governments jointly protest against the Japanese attack against Shanghai, but Simon refuses.			The first of the *Tarzan* films opens with Olympic gold medal swimmer Johnny Weissmuller in the title role.	Mar.
Charles Lindbergh pays the $50,000 ransom asked for his son, but the infant is not returned.			C.C. King of the University of Pittsburgh isolates vitamin C. . . . A vaccine for yellow fever is announced.	*Too True to be Good* by George Bernard Shaw premieres in New York. . . . American poet Hart Crane drowns after jumping from a steamer.	Apr.
Al Capone begins his conviction in an Atlanta prison. . . . The corpse of Charles Lindbergh's son is found. . . . Luigi Malvese, bootleg gangster, is ambushed and shot to death in San Francisco.	Congress changes the name of Porto Rico to Puerto Rico. . . . An estimated 17,000 veterans, calling themselves the Bonus Expeditionary Force, march on Washington demanding cash for their bonus certificates.			Pearl S. Buck is awarded the Pulitzer Prize for *The Good Earth*. . . . Walter Duranty of the *New York Times* wins a Pulitzer Prize for his series on the Soviet Union that praises Josef Stalin. . . . Amelia Earhart is the first woman to fly solo across the Atlantic. She takes off from Newfoundland for Ireland.	May
President Herbert Hoover and Vice President Charles Curtis are renominated at the Republican national convention in Chicago.	Veterans repeatedly march on Washington to demand cash payment of their bonuses for service in World War I. The Senate rejects the Veterans' Bonus Bill.	The Revenue Act is passed creating the first gas tax in the United States.		Heavyweight Max Schmeling loses a title fight against Jack Sharkey.	Jun.
New York Governor Franklin Roosevelt is nominated as presidential candidate by the Democratic Party Convention in Chicago.	The United States signs a treaty with Canada to develop the St. Lawrence Seaway. . . . President Hoover orders the Army to evacuate the thousands of war veterans demonstrating in Washington for their war bonuses.			The Summer Olympic Games open in Los Angeles. . . . The George Washington quarter goes into circulation.	Jul.
Presidential candidate Franklin Roosevelt announces a nationwide tour to support his campaign.		The stock market drops 8.4 percent, halting a month's steady rise.	Carl D. Anderson discovers the first positron. . . . A 5.1-kg. chondrite-type meteorite breaks into different fragments and strikes earth near the town of Archie in Cass County, Missouri.	Auguste Piccard reaches a record altitude of 16,500 meters with an air balloon.	Aug.
New York Mayor Jimmy Walker resigns due to charges of graft and corruption in his administration. . . . A traditional Republican stronghold, the state of Maine elects a Democratic governor.		A five-day working week is established for General Motors workers.	The steamboat *Observation* explodes in New York's East River. Seventy-one people die.	The New York Yankees win the World Series.	Sept.

F	G	H	I	J
Includes elections, federal-state relations, civil rights and liberties, crime, the judiciary, education, healthcare, poverty, urban affairs, and population.	*Includes formation and debate of U.S. foreign and defense policies, veterans affairs, and defense spending. (Relations with specific foreign countries are usually found under the region concerned.)*	*Includes business, labor, agriculture, taxation, transportation, consumer affairs, monetary and fiscal policy, natural resources, pollution, and accidents.*	*Includes worldwide scientific, medical, and technological developments, natural phenomena, U.S. weather, and natural disasters.*	*Includes the arts, religion, scholarship, communications media, sports, entertainment, fashions, fads, and social life.*

	World Affairs	Europe	Africa & The Middle East	The Americas	Asia & The Pacific
Oct.	The League of Nations admits Iraq to the organization. . . . The Lytton Report on Manchuria, ordered by the League of Nations, condemns the Japanese invasion and invokes the constitution of an autonomous state under Chinese sovereignty.	Julius Goemboes becomes Hungarian prime minister. He will seek closer ties with Mussolini's fascist Italy. . . . Vladko Machek, the leader of the Croat Peasant Party, is arrested. . . . Oswald Mosley forms the British Union of Fascists.		The Rubio administration renews tensions between the Mexican state and the Catholic Church.	
Nov.	British medical authorities meet with central African, South African, and Indian officials to address regional healthcare issues.	The Croat Peasant Party denounces the arrest of its leader and demands regional autonomy. . . . A Finnish court finds Gen. Kurt Wallenius and 50 other leaders of the Lapua movement guilty in their failed uprising. The movement is dissolved. . . . Russia signs nonaggression treaties with Poland and France.	The Persian government cancels the Anglo-Persian oil concessions of 1901 and 1909.	Saavedra Lamas, foreign minister of Argentina, publishes the South American Anti-War Pact. . . . A strong tornado kills about 1,000 people in Cuba.	Delegates of the British government and Indian leaders meet in London to discuss the future of India.
Dec.	The League of Nations Assembly holds its third special session of the year in Geneva to continue discussion on the Japanese occupation of Manchuria. . . . The German government agrees to return to the Disarmament Conference after delegates sign the Geneva Protocol, which establishes the equality of rights among the participants.	The French parliament rejects the government's proposal to pay the scheduled installment of war debt to the United States. . . . The Catalonian government meets for the first time.	In spite of its rich gold deposits, the Union of South Africa government withdraws from the gold standard.	The Mexican government withdraws from the League of Nations.	Japanese forces from Manchukuo invade the Chinese province of Jehol in an attempt to extend their influence over China. . . . A massive earthquake in Kansu, China, kills about 70,000 people.

A	B	C	D	E
Includes developments that affect more than one world region, international organizations, and important meetings of world leaders.	Includes all domestic and regional developments in Europe, including the Soviet Union.	Includes all domestic and regional developments in Africa and the Middle East.	Includes all domestic and regional developments in Latin America, the Caribbean, and Canada.	Includes all domestic and regional developments in Asian and Pacific nations (and colonies).

U.S. Politics & Social Issues	U.S. Foreign Policy & Defense	Economics & Great Depression	Science, Technology & Nature	Culture, Leisure & Lifestyle	
		The stock market drops 7.2 percent.	The world's biggest dam is put into operation in the Soviet Union.	George Kaufman and Edna Ferber's *Dinner at Eight* premieres in New York.	**Oct.**
Franklin Roosevelt becomes the 32nd president of the United States, defeating Herbert Hoover in a landslide victory.				Groucho Marx first performs on the radio. . . . The musical *Gay Divorcee* by Cole Porter premieres in New York.	**Nov.**
Marlin R.M. Kemmerer draws a revolver in the House of Representatives. Melvin Maas, a Republican from Minnesota, convinces him to drop the gun.	Congress decrees that no debt owed to the United States should be cancelled. Finland will be the only country to pay its debt in full. . . . The United States government negotiates a No Force Declaration with Britain, France, Germany, and Italy. Present or future differences between them will never be settled by force.			Fred Astaire and Ginger Rogers make their first movie together, *Flying Down to Rio*. . . . Radio City Music Hall opens in New York.	**Dec.**

F	**G**	**H**	**I**	**J**
Includes elections, federal-state relations, civil rights and liberties, crime, the judiciary, education, healthcare, poverty, urban affairs, and population.	*Includes formation and debate of U.S. foreign and defense policies, veterans affairs, and defense spending. (Relations with specific foreign countries are usually found under the region concerned.)*	*Includes business, labor, agriculture, taxation, transportation, consumer affairs, monetary and fiscal policy, natural resources, pollution, and accidents.*	*Includes worldwide scientific, medical, and technological developments, natural phenomena, U.S. weather, and natural disasters.*	*Includes the arts, religion, scholarship, communications media, sports, entertainment, fashions, fads, and social life.*

	World Affairs	Europe	Africa & The Middle East	The Americas	Asia & The Pacific
Jan. 1	Former secretary of war Newton Baker urges the United States to enter the League of Nations, the organization that he was instrumental in creating during the administration of President Woodrow Wilson.	The British Earl of Willingdon, Viceroy of India, sends a telegram to Mohandas Gandhi threatening force if civil disobedience campaigns continue.			Japan asks for additional time in the evacuation of the region of Manchuria.
Jan. 2		France appropriates 4 billion francs ($160 million) to provide public works projects for the unemployed.		Canadian Prime Minister Richard Bennett tells his countrymen in a New Year's radio address that "the worst is over. Canada has survived the economic crisis."	Ceding to international pressure, Japan establishes the Republic of Manchukuo in the disputed war-torn region of Manchuria. Although officially controlled by Chinese Emperor Pu-yi, later evidence would prove that Manchukuo's affairs were managed by Japan. Fifty-seven of the members of the League of Nations refused to formally recognize the nation as an independent entity.
Jan. 3	A group of professors of Harvard University calls on the League of Nations to condemn the Italian practice of requiring all educators to recite a Fascist oath before receiving their teaching license.			Uruguay calls for a South American economic conference for itself, Brazil, and Argentina.	The British Viceroy in India arrests Indian revolutionary leader Mohandas Gandhi following a breakdown in negotiations with the All-India National Congress.
Jan. 4		Newspapers in London, England, praise the British Viceroy in India's decision to imprison Indian revolutionary leader Mohandas Gandhi. . . . Belgium purchases 60 war planes from the British Fairey Aviation Company at a cost of $1.5 million. It is the largest single purchase from the British aircraft industry by a foreign government.	Muslim leader M.A. Jinnah lays blame on the British government for ongoing unrest in India.	Remnants of the deposed regime of President Hipolito Irigoyen of Argentina begin an invasion of the South American country from Uruguay. Argentine newspapers describe the rebels' invasion attempt as futile.	
Jan. 5		Chancellor Heinrich Bruening of Germany declares that his country is absolutely unable to pay its foreign debts. The announcement causes a furor in international circles.		A group of rebels who invaded Argentina on January 4 engage in a full-scale retreat.	Great Britain declares the All-India National Congress to be an illegal organization. Henceforth, the declaration states, all peaceful demonstrators will be subject to arrest and possible deportation.
Jan. 6		Romania signs a nonaggression pact with the Soviet Union.			Joseph Lyons is sworn in as the new prime minister of Australia. Lyons succeeds James Scullin, who was voted out of office for failure to protect his country from the economic avalanche of the Great Depression. . . . British imperial authorities arrest former Indian Legislative Assembly president Vithalbhai Patel.
Jan. 7		French War Minister Andre Maginot dies at the age of 54 in the French capital of Paris following a two-week battle with typhoid fever. Maginot had an apt understanding of the aggressively militaristic nature of Germany following World War I, as he advocated the strengthening of defense fortifications along the French-German border. This doctrine would come to be known as the Maginot Line.		Tensions between Argentina and Uruguay worsen as Argentina issues a note of protest against Uruguay's decision to grant exile to members of the deposed regime of President Hipolito Irigoyen.	Great Britain releases a statement warning the Indian populace that "civil disobedience cannot be carried on without violence."
Jan. 8	Sir Philip Cunliffe-Lister, British Secretary of State for Colonies, sends a cablegram to the Zionists of America organization in which he pledges Great Britain's full support in adhering to the 1917 Balfour Declaration.	Police in the German capital of Berlin round up 176 suspected Communists.		The Bolivian Treasury Ministry files suit against the newspaper *La Republica*, contending that it illegally contributed campaign funds to opponents of President Carlos Galindo.	

A	B	C	D	E
Includes developments that affect more than one world region, international organizations, and important meetings of world leaders.	Includes all domestic and regional developments in Europe, including the Soviet Union.	Includes all domestic and regional developments in Africa and the Middle East.	Includes all domestic and regional developments in Latin America, the Caribbean, and Canada.	Includes all domestic and regional developments in Asian and Pacific nations (and colonies).

U.S. Politics & Social Issues	U.S. Foreign Policy & Defense	Economics & Great Depression	Science, Technology & Nature	Culture, Leisure & Lifestyle	
A strike of the Chicago Broadcasters' Association is averted as employers capitulate, agreeing to a shorter workweek.		The number of British idle workers falls to 2,506,719, a decline of 65,883 from the previous week.			Jan. 1
Police in a dozen U.S. cities uncover an anti-fascist bomb plot directed against prominent Italian-Americans.		*Dun's Review* releases its weekly index of U.S. business failures. At 138.3, the figure is a drop of 25.6 points from the previous week, and a decline of 8.1 points from the corresponding week one year ago.	The American Association for the Advancement of Science awards $1,000 to Dr. Carl Speidel for his contributions to the study of neurology.	The comedic short film *Detectuvs* is released throughout the United States.	Jan. 2
The U.S. national debt rises to $17,838,214,704.	The submarine *S-4* is transferred by naval authorities from New London, Conn., to Pearl Harbor. It was constructed in 1917 by the Portsmouth Navy Yard.	*The Annalist* releases its weekly index of U.S. business activity. At 62.1, the figure is a drop of 2.2 points from the previous week, and a decline of 22 percent from the corresponding period last year. Economists say the drop from last week was caused by losses in freight car loadings and cotton cloth production.		Cowboy legend Gary Cooper's western film, *The Texan*, starring Hollywood Walk of Fame recipient Fay Wray, is released in Finland. . . . The drama film *Transatlantic*, winner of the 1932 Academy Award for Best Art Direction, is released in Finland. The film is directed by William Howard and stars Edmund Lowe, both of whom are Hollywood Walk of Fame recipients. . . . The German-language film *Secrets of the Orient* is released throughout the United States.	Jan. 3
The New York City Welfare Council releases a statement saying that immediate action is needed to prevent the creation of a "pauper class."		Prof. Irving Fisher of Yale University releases his weekly index of international commodity prices. The figure is 66.3, a drop of 0.4 points from the preceding week, but a decline of approximately 16 percent from the corresponding week a year ago.		Hollywood Walk of Fame recipient Buck Jones's western, *Ridin' for Justice*, is released throughout the United States.	Jan. 4
Rep. John Cochran of Missouri introduces a bill on the House floor that would create a federal public works department in the executive branch.	Naval Secretary Charles Francis Adams announces he will support the proposed $616 million naval budget bill that is awaiting Congressional approval.	The U.S. Department of Commerce releases its weekly index of electric power production. At 74.7, the figure is a reduction of 0.7 points from the previous week, and a decline of 14 percent from the corresponding week one year ago.		Metro-Goldwyn-Mayer's adventure film *Hell Divers* is released throughout the United States. The film features performances by Academy Award-winning actors Wallace Beery and Clark Gable.	Jan. 5
Famed American explorer Roy Chapman Andrews tells students of the all-women Barnard College that women are not physically able to explore uncharted territories. . . . The First National Bank of Gary, Ind., closes its doors following an excessive amount of withdrawals, known commonly as a "bank run." . . . Members of the American Anti-Saloon League tell reporters that the organization is nearing insolvency.	Army officials report the United States currently has a standing army of approximately 118,000 men.	Prof. Irving Fisher of Yale University releases his weekly index of international stock prices. The figure is 48.8, a drop of 1.1 points from the preceding week, and a decline of approximately 47 percent from the corresponding week a year ago.			Jan. 6
		The Iron Age releases its weekly index of U.S. steel mill activity. The index currently stands at 26.8, a reduction of 5.6 points from the previous week, and a decline of approximately 48 percent from the corresponding week one year ago.			Jan. 7
Rumors circulate in Washington that Democratic National Committee chairman Jacob Raskob will establish a "third liquor party."		The weekly index of U.S. automobile production as compiled by the Department of Commerce is released. The index currently stands at 43.1, a rise of 3.3 points from the previous week, but a decline of 24 percent from the corresponding week one year ago.		Citing a much-debated official policy of excluding foreign artists, the British Ministry of Labor deports the African-American musical group The Four Harmony Kings.	Jan. 8

F	G	H	I	J
Includes elections, federal-state relations, civil rights and liberties, crime, the judiciary, education, healthcare, poverty, urban affairs, and population.	*Includes formation and debate of U.S. foreign and defense policies, veterans affairs, and defense spending. (Relations with specific foreign countries are usually found under the region concerned.)*	*Includes business, labor, agriculture, taxation, transportation, consumer affairs, monetary and fiscal policy, natural resources, pollution, and accidents.*	*Includes worldwide scientific, medical, and technological developments, natural phenomena, U.S. weather, and natural disasters.*	*Includes the arts, religion, scholarship, communications media, sports, entertainment, fashions, fads, and social life.*

	World Affairs	Europe	Africa & The Middle East	The Americas	Asia & The Pacific
Jan. 9		Aristide Briand resigns as French Foreign Minister, effective in one week's time. Briand attributes his decision to an undisclosed illness.		Cuban President Gerardo Machado proposes a general amnesty for all political prisoners, contingent upon Congressional approval.	Great Britain pledges not to ally itself with the United States in the ongoing conflict between China and Japan.
Jan. 10	Belgium and Romania officially become two of the 17 nations that would participate in the third Winter Olympics Games, held in Lake Placid, N.Y.	A statue of Antarctic explorer Ernest Shackleton is unveiled in London, England.		Dwight Davis announces his resignation as Governor-General of the Philippines. President Herbert Hoover submits to the Senate his nomination of Theodore Roosevelt, Jr., Governor of Puerto Rico, as Davis's successor.	
Jan. 11	The Women's International League calls on U.S. President Herbert Hoover to assist the world's nations in achieving universal disarmament.		At the request of the Iraqi government, a consortium of American educational experts travels to Iraq to investigate the Middle Eastern country's school system.	As news of decreased customs receipts surface, Colombian lawmakers reduce their country's federal budget for 1932 by 7 million pesos.	
Jan. 12	British economists release a statement declaring that the All-India National Congress's boycott of British goods has resulted in a 25 percent loss of commerce to India.... Charles Dawes announces his intention to resign as U.S. Ambassador to Great Britain.	Dutch officials express agreement toward a proposed cancellation of all of Germany's World War I debts.			A force of Chinese bandits numbering 5,000 attack a Japanese army company in Sinmin, Manchuria, resulting in the company's near annihilation.
Jan. 13	Prime Minister Ramsay MacDonald of Great Britain guarantees full autonomy for Burma if it completely severs its ties with India.			Argentine economists report that the amount of exports has increased by 4.1 percent since the beginning of 1931.	
Jan. 14	American citizen Eddie Cullens is executed by hanging in London, England, for the murder of vacationing Turk Achmet Musa.	Austria bans the practice of dentists filling patients' cavities with gold, fearing that dentists will begin hoarding it.... American citizen Laurence Benet is awarded the title of Grand Officer in the Legion of Honor by the French government.	A $100,000 copy of the Koran, the holy book of Islam, is reported stolen from the El-Aska mosque in Jerusalem.		
Jan. 15		Legendary comedian Buster Keaton's German-language film Casanova wider Willen (Casanova Against His Will), is released in Germany.... The number of unemployed German workers rises to approximately 6 million.		A petition is signed by more than 6,000 Mexicans protesting a recent government decision to limit the number of Catholic priests able to serve in Mexico City.	Australian Attorney General John Latham recommends to Prime Minister Richard Bennett the banning of all imported Communist literature.
Jan. 16	The annual convention of the League of Nations Association is held in Philadelphia, Pa., where 1931 Nobel Peace Prize winner Nicholas Murray Butler urges the United States to officially become a member of the League of Nations. . . . Brazil and Belgium enter into a most-favored-nation economic agreement.	Germany announces it will send a team to the third Winter Olympic Games in Lake Placid, N.Y., reversing an earlier policy.		Approximately 15,000 employees of major Cuban tobacco manufacturers go on strike, protesting low wages.	

A	B	C	D	E
Includes developments that affect more than one world region, international organizations, and important meetings of world leaders.	*Includes all domestic and regional developments in Europe, including the Soviet Union.*	*Includes all domestic and regional developments in Africa and the Middle East.*	*Includes all domestic and regional developments in Latin America, the Caribbean, and Canada.*	*Includes all domestic and regional developments in Asian and Pacific nations (and colonies).*

U.S. Politics & Social Issues	U.S. Foreign Policy & Defense	Economics & Great Depression	Science, Technology & Nature	Culture, Leisure & Lifestyle	
	The destroyer *Dallas* is transferred by naval authorities from Charleston, S.C., to the Pacific Coast. Constructed in 1919 by the Newport News Shipbuilding Company, *Dallas* would eventually be awarded a Presidential Unit Citation for service in World War II.	*Dun's Review* releases its weekly index of U.S. business failures. At 150.4, the figure is a rise of 12.1 points from the previous week, and a gain of 17.2 points from the corresponding week one year ago.		*The Woman from Monte Carlo* is released throughout the United States. The film is directed by Michael Curtiz, and stars Walter Huston and Warren William, all of whom are Hollywood Walk of Fame recipients. . . . World featherweight boxing champion Bat Battalino forfeits his title after failing to meet the maximum weight requirements. Battalino measured in at 135 pounds, the requirement being 126 pounds.	Jan. 9
Representatives of major U.S. auto manufacturers protest a proposed 5 percent automobile sales tax, contending that manufacturers already pay "$1 billion" in taxes annually.		*The Annalist* releases its weekly index of U.S. business activity. At 63.7, the figure is a rise of 1.4 points from the previous week, but a decline of 17 percent from the corresponding period last year. Economists say the rise from last week was caused by gains in freight car loadings, automobile production, and cotton cloth production.		*Afoot In Italy*, a book detailing an American's experiences in fascist Italy, is published. . . . The German-language film *Der Kleine Seitensprung (The Little Escapade)* is released in Finland. The film features the performances of German Film Award winners Hermann Thimig and Hilde Hildebrand.	Jan. 10
Supreme Court Justice Oliver Wendell Holmes announces his retirement.	The U.S. Navy transfers the gunboat *Sacramento* from the Panama Canal Zone to the Pacific Coast. Constructed by the William Cramp & Sons Shipbuilding Company in 1914, *Sacramento* would service American sailors in both World War I and World War II.	Prof. Irving Fisher of Yale University releases his weekly index of international commodity prices. The figure is 65.3, a decline of 1.0 points from the preceding week, and a reduction of approximately 17 percent from the corresponding week a year ago. . . . The Gadsen National Bank of Alabama closes its doors following a bank run. Bank officials say the run was caused by wild speculation.		The comedic film *Three Wise Girls* is released throughout the United States. The film stars Jean Harlow and Andy Devine and is directed by William Beaudine, all of whom are Hollywood Walk of Fame recipients. . . . The science-fiction film *Just Imagine*, starring Hollywood Walk of Fame recipients Maureen O'Sullivan, Frank Albertson, and Herbert Bosworth, is released in Denmark. The film offers a prophecy for life in New York in 1980: a heavily bureaucratized society featuring personalized commuter airplanes, pill meals, and state-sanctioned marriage and procreation.	Jan. 11
Following a special election to fill the vacant Senate seat left by the death of her late husband, Hattie Caraway is confirmed as the United States' first elected female Senator. Rebecca Felton had earlier served as a Georgia Senator in 1922, albeit for only a single day. . . . Prohibition Bureau Director W. Woodcock releases a report showing that a total of 38,018 arrests were made by his bureau during the last six months of 1931, an increase of 7,000 from the same period in 1930.		The U.S. Department of Commerce releases its weekly index of electric power production. At 75.1, the figure is a rise of 0.4 points from the previous week, but a decline of 13 percent from the corresponding week one year ago.			Jan. 12
New York City reduces its budget by $110 million in an effort to decrease wasteful and unnecessary spending.		Prof. Irving Fisher of Yale University releases his weekly index of international stock prices. The figure is 48.7, a drop of 0.1 points from the preceding week, and a decline of approximately 51 percent from the corresponding week a year ago.		Cass Canfield is elected president of the National Association of Book Publishers.	Jan. 13
Treasury Secretary Andrew Mellon estimates in testimony before the House Ways and Means Committee that the U.S. federal budget deficit will rise to $2.8 billion by the end of 1932. It is an increase of $600 million from an earlier estimate.		*The Iron Age* releases its weekly index of U.S. steel mill activity. The index currently stands at 28.6, a rise of 1.8 points from the previous week, but a decline of approximately 44 percent from the corresponding week one year ago.		First National Pictures' *Union Depot* premiers in New York City. The film is directed by Alfred Green and stars Douglas Fairbanks and Joan Blondell, all of whom are Hollywood Walk of Fame recipients.	Jan. 14
	Assistant Secretary of Commerce for Aviation Col. Clarence Young reports that the number of U.S. airfields has increased by 311 since 1931.	The weekly index of U.S. automobile production as compiled by the Department of Commerce is released. The index currently stands at 51.4, a rise of 9 points from the previous week, but a decline of 27 percent from the corresponding week one year ago.		*Forbidden*, directed by legendary filmmaker Frank Capra, is released throughout the United States. The film stars Hollywood Walk of Fame recipients Barbara Stanwyck, Ralph Bellamy, and Adolphe Menjou.	Jan. 15
During remarks on the Senate floor, Senator Robert Wagner of New York advocates the issuance of a $2 billion bond for public works projects.		*Dun's Review* releases its weekly index of U.S. business failures. At 181.6, the figure is a rise of 31.2 points from the previous week, and a gain of 43.3 points from the corresponding week one year ago.	Researchers at Cornell University announce the creation of a new compound, sodium rhodanate, which doctors say can assist in combating morphine addiction.	The musical comedy film *Manhattan Parade* is released throughout the United States. The film's director, Lloyd Bacon, its writer, Robert Lord, and its star, Charles Butterworth, are all Hollywood Walk of Fame recipients.	Jan. 16

F	G	H	I	J
Includes elections, federal-state relations, civil rights and liberties, crime, the judiciary, education, healthcare, poverty, urban affairs, and population.	Includes formation and debate of U.S. foreign and defense policies, veterans affairs, and defense spending. (Relations with specific foreign countries are usually found under the region concerned.)	Includes business, labor, agriculture, taxation, transportation, consumer affairs, monetary and fiscal policy, natural resources, pollution, and accidents.	Includes worldwide scientific, medical, and technological developments, natural phenomena, U.S. weather, and natural disasters.	Includes the arts, religion, scholarship, communications media, sports, entertainment, fashions, fads, and social life.

	World Affairs	Europe	Africa & The Middle East	The Americas	Asia & The Pacific
Jan. 17				Officials of the Panama Canal report that total toll revenue through the canal during the last six months of 1931 amounted to $11,671,143, 16 percent less than the total from the same period in 1930. . . . Costa Rican economists report that 1932's coffee crop, the chief export of the Latin American nation, will be approximately 50,000 less than 1931's total.	China alleges in a letter to the League of Nations that Japan is deliberately targeting civilians during bombing raids.
Jan. 18	Chinese Vice Minister of Foreign Affairs Fu Ping-chang invokes Article XVI of the League of Nations covenant in calling for sanctions against Japan.	Austrian economists report that their country's total exports have fallen by over 20 percent since the beginning of 1931. . . . Nazi leader Adolf Hitler expresses opposition to a proposed measure to prolong the presidency of Paul von Hindenburg without the consent of the people's vote. Hitler claims that this would be in violation of Germany's constitution. He advocates a "legal" overthrowing of President Paul von Hindenburg's regime.			A group of Chinese Communist bandits seize the Chinese city of Nanchang, capital of the Kiangsi province.
Jan. 19	Japan issues a statement describing the invasion of Manchuria as a "police action" similar to when the United States invaded the Mexican territory of Veracruz in 1914.	Citing a lack of funds, the British Air Ministry announces it is halting plans to create a "transatlantic flying boat service." . . . In the Hungarian capital of Budapest, 114 jobless demonstrators shouting "We want work and bread" are arrested by police authorities.		In an effort to improve trade relations, Paraguay and Argentina create commissions whose purpose it will be to study ways to increase commerce between the two nations.	
Jan. 20			A team of excavators in Jerusalem discover the remnants of a "massive" iron tower that officials say dates back to the Early Iron Age.	Argentina drastically raises taxes in an effort to balance the federal budget. Those earning more than $6,500 annually will be subject to a "graduated" tax. Sales taxes on gasoline, matches, tobacco, and perfume are also increased. . . . Bolivia rejects a proposed nonaggression treaty offered by Paraguay.	
Jan. 21	A petition advocating worldwide disarmament containing the signatures of 2,123,629 Britons is sent to the League of Nations headquarters in Geneva, Switzerland.	Three Italians and one Frenchman accused of spying are expelled from Austria.		President Herbert Hoover nominates James Beverly as the new Governor of Puerto Rico. The nomination requires Congressional approval. If confirmed, Beverly will replace Theodore Roosevelt, Jr., who was nominated to succeed the retiring Dwight Davis as Governor-General of the Philippines.	
Jan. 22		Several hundred university students in the Yugoslavian capital of Belgrade engage in peaceful demonstrations against the regime of Pera Zivkovich.			In a sign of desperation to uphold its status as the world's foremost colonial power, Great Britain offers any Indian woman 20 cents a day to join the imperial police force.
Jan. 23		Berlin University is closed down following a preliminary student election that dissolved into utter chaos involving the competing parties of the National Socialists, Socialists, and Communists.	Abyssinia formally apologizes to U.S. diplomat Addison Southard, who was unlawfully assaulted by a traffic policeman a week earlier.	President Renato Pacheco of Brazil announces that his country will participate in the upcoming Winter Olympic Games, to be held in Lake Placid, N.Y.	Great Britain expresses apathy toward China's threat of military action if Japan fails to fully evacuate from Manchuria.
Jan. 24		Two thousand Hollanders march on the capital of Amsterdam, demanding worldwide universal military disarmament. . . . Chancellor Heinrich Bruening of Germany describes Adolf Hitler's refusal to support the prolonging of President Paul von Hindenburg's term as "purely partisan."			Chinese diplomats express agreement toward U.S. State Secretary Henry Stimson's statement that the United States would not recognize any peace settlement achieved through the violation of international treaties.
Jan. 25	The 60th session of the League of Nations commences in Geneva, Switzerland.	Soviet and Polish diplomats sign a nonaggression pact.	Turkey and Persia sign a treaty establishing Mount Ararat as the dividing line between the two countries' respective territories.		

A	B	C	D	E
Includes developments that affect more than one world region, international organizations, and important meetings of world leaders.	Includes all domestic and regional developments in Europe, including the Soviet Union.	Includes all domestic and regional developments in Africa and the Middle East.	Includes all domestic and regional developments in Latin America, the Caribbean, and Canada.	Includes all domestic and regional developments in Asian and Pacific nations (and colonies).

U.S. Politics & Social Issues	U.S. Foreign Policy & Defense	Economics & Great Depression	Science, Technology & Nature	Culture, Leisure & Lifestyle	
Former secretary of state Bainbridge Colby urges the United States to ask itself, "What would Ben Franklin do?" in solving political and economic crises around the globe.		The Annalist releases its weekly index of U.S. business activity. At 64.4, the figure is a rise of 0.7 points from the previous week, but a decline of 18 percent from the corresponding period last year. Economists say the rise from last week was caused by increases in steel mill activity, electric power production, automobile production, and cotton cloth production.		Legendary performer Bing Crosby's musical comedy short, Dream House, is released throughout the United States.	Jan. 17
		Prof. Irving Fisher of Yale University releases his weekly index of international commodity prices. The figure is 65.2, a drop of 0.1 points from the preceding week, and a decline of approximately 17 percent from the corresponding week a year ago.		France enacts a quota on imported radio receivers that officials say will most negatively affect the United States.	Jan. 18
		The U.S. Department of Commerce releases its weekly index of electric power production. At 73.8, the figure is a drop of 1.3 points from the previous week, and a decline of 13 percent from the corresponding week one year ago.		Tony Conzeri loses his title of world junor welterweight champion, succumbing to challenger Johnny Jadick in 10 rounds. . . . A couple in the New York City borough of the Bronx name their newborn baby girl Norma Depression Jacobs.	Jan. 19
Senator William Borah introduces a bill cutting government salaries that would reduce the burden placed upon American taxpayers by $200 million annually.		Prof. Irving Fisher of Yale University releases his weekly index of international stock prices. The figure is 53.0, a rise of 4.2 points from the preceding week, but a decline of approximately 45 percent from the corresponding week a year ago.		The Associated Press releases the results of a survey showing that baseball is America's most popular sport, with football being a close second. Golf came in third, and boxing was a distant fourth.	Jan. 20
The New York State Educational Department releases the results of a study showing that disabled workers are both less tardy and less accident-prone than fully able-bodied workers.		The Iron Age releases its weekly index of U.S. steel mill activity. The index currently stands at 29.8, a rise of 1.2 points from the previous week, but a reduction of approximately 45 percent from the corresponding week one year ago.		The film Der Ungetreue Eckehart (The Ungrateful Eckehart) is released throughout the United States. The film stars Hollywood Walk of Fame recipients Paul Horbiger and Paul Henckels.	Jan. 21
Atlantic City drastically reduces sales taxes in an effort to increase tourism.	Rep. Joseph Byrns of Tennessee urges the merger of the Army and Navy Departments to create a Department of National Defense, which he says would save American taxpayers $100 million annually.	The weekly index of U.S. automobile production as compiled by the Department of Commerce is released. The index currently stands at 46.1, a decline of 5.3 points from the previous week, and a reduction of 28 percent from the corresponding week one year ago.		Academy Award-winning screenwriter Sidney Buchman's dramatic film No One Man is released throughout the United States. The film features the performances of Hollywood Walk of Fame recipients Carole Lombard, Ricardo Cortez, and Paul Lukas.	Jan. 22
		Dun's Review releases its weekly index of U.S. business failures. At 191.9, the figure is a gain of 10.3 points from the previous week, but a decline of 3.7 points from the corresponding week one year ago.		Taxi!, starring Academy Award-winning actor James Cagney, is released throughout the United States. The film also features a performance by Academy Award-winning actress Loretta Young.	Jan. 23
Senate Foreign Relations Committee chairman William Borah criticizes President Herbert Hoover's proposed moratorium on World War I debts, saying that it is "like postponing the operation until the patient is so weak he cannot survive it."		The Annalist releases its weekly index of U.S. business activity. At 63.0, the figure is a drop of 1.1 points from the previous week, and a decline of 19 percent from the corresponding period last year. Economists say the drop from last week was caused by losses in freight car loadings, electric power production, automobile production, and cotton cloth production.		Stan Laurel and Oliver Hardy's comedy short Helpmates is released throughout the United States.	Jan. 24
Sixty-five people in Plainfield, N.J., are arrested on the grounds of violating the city's "blue law," which forbids the showing of motion pictures on any given Sunday. . . . An official report is released showing total tax revenue for New York City during the whole of 1931 amounted to $1,413,867,997. Expenditures amounted to $1,446,399,616, netting a deficit of $33 million.		Prof. Irving Fisher of Yale University releases his weekly index of international commodity prices. The figure is 65.1, a drop of 0.1 points from the preceding week, and a decline of approximately 17 percent from the corresponding week a year ago.	Clarence D. Chamberlain sets a world altitude record for diesel engine vessels at 22,000 feet.		Jan. 25

F	G	H	I	J
Includes elections, federal-state relations, civil rights and liberties, crime, the judiciary, education, healthcare, poverty, urban affairs, and population.	Includes formation and debate of U.S. foreign and defense policies, veterans affairs, and defense spending. (Relations with specific foreign countries are usually found under the region concerned.)	Includes business, labor, agriculture, taxation, transportation, consumer affairs, monetary and fiscal policy, natural resources, pollution, and accidents.	Includes worldwide scientific, medical, and technological developments, natural phenomena, U.S. weather, and natural disasters.	Includes the arts, religion, scholarship, communications media, sports, entertainment, fashions, fads, and social life.

	World Affairs	Europe	Africa & The Middle East	The Americas	Asia & The Pacific
Jan. 26	During remarks before the League of Nations, Chinese diplomat Dr. W.W. Yen describes Japanese military policy as "cynical" and "ruthless."	The British submarine *M-2* is accidentally sunk off the Isle of Portland during a routine exercise. Officials express the belief that the sinking was caused by water entering one of the submarine's entrances. All of the submarine's crew, approximately 60 people, drowns.		An unsuccessful revolt in El Salvador results in the deaths of over 600 people at the hands of El Salvadoran National Guardsmen.	Eugene Chen announces his resignation as Chinese Foreign Minister. Chen disagrees with his colleagues over the response to the Japanese invasion of Manchuria.
Jan. 27		A hundred of Berlin's blind population march on City Hall, demanding increased poverty relief funds. . . . A bill is introduced on the floor of the House of Commons that would make insanity and habitual drunkenness grounds for divorce. . . . The Hamburg National Socalists hold their first formal reception in Athens, Greece.			Indian education official K.C. Chatterjee is arrested by British imperial authorities. Officials claim that the schools Chatterjee oversees are "breeding places of sedition."
Jan. 28		The entire Austrian Cabinet resigns in a move to force the ousting of Foreign Minister Johann Schober. . . . Student riots break out in the Yugoslavian capital of Belgrade. Thousands demand the overthrow of Premier Zhivkovitch's regime, and shouts of "Down with Zhivkovich!" are heard echoing throughout the streets.	Prominent Arabs in Jerusalem announce plans for the creation of a Pan-Arab Federation, the goal of which would be to seek independence for all Arab nations.	El Salvador rejects the United States' offer of a squadron of Marines to assist the Latin American country in preventing ongoing small-scale riots from escalating into civil war.	British diplomats express sympathy with Japan over the invasion of Manchuria, contending that Japan's actions are in no way different from when British troops were dispatched into China in 1927 in an effort to end a boycott against imported British goods. . . . Two dozen prominent Indian commercial organizations suspend operations in a protest against the imprisonment of Mohandas Gandhi by British imperial forces. . . . One thousand Japanese troops are dispatched to the Chinese city of Harbin to engage in combat with Chinese soldiers.
Jan. 29	During a visit to the United States, future British prime minister Winston Churchill advocates the strengthening of ties between the United States and Great Britain: "We must be the strong central nucleus at the council board of the nations."	The dramatic German-language film *Kameradschaft* (*Comradeship*), directed by German Film Award winner Georg Pabst, is released in France. It is the story of a group of trapped French miners who are heroically saved by a group of conscientious Germans.			The film *Haru wa gofujin kara* (*Spring Comes the Ladies*) is released in Japan.
Jan. 30		Austria's new Cabinet is sworn in. Among the new members is Foreign Minister Karl Buresch, War Minister Carl Vaugoin, and Education Minister Emmerich Czermak.		Canadian Minister of Trade and Commerce Harry Stevens lays blame for his country's adverse trade balance on the 1930 Smoot-Hawley Tariff Act.	
Jan. 31				Colombia discontinues the practice of using the word "coolie," referring to laborers, in its official documents.	The American-owned Chinese newspaper *The Shanghai Evening Post and Mercury* condemns the Japanese bombing of the Chinese city of Shanghai.
Feb. 1	The 24th session of the Permanent Court of International Justice commences in The Hague, the Netherlands. . . . U.S. Undersecretary of State William Castle expresses the hope that the hostile military actions by Japan against China will inspire the world to engage in universal disarmament.		The Smithsonian Institution announces plans to establish a solar observatory in the Sinai Peninsula, the area where Biblical scholars claim that God gave the Ten Commandments to Moses.	The Mexican newspaper *El Nacional* condemns Japan for "disregarding international pacts," and compares Japan's actions in China to Germany's immediately prior to World War I.	Japanese snipers in the war-torn Chinese city of Shanghai begin targeting American diplomats near the U.S. Consulate. . . . A battle between Chinese and Japanese forces near the Chinese city of Harbin results in the deaths of over 500 Chinese soldiers.

A	B	C	D	E
Includes developments that affect more than one world region, international organizations, and important meetings of world leaders.	Includes all domestic and regional developments in Europe, including the Soviet Union.	Includes all domestic and regional developments in Africa and the Middle East.	Includes all domestic and regional developments in Latin America, the Caribbean, and Canada.	Includes all domestic and regional developments in Asian and Pacific nations (and colonies).

U.S. Politics & Social Issues	U.S. Foreign Policy & Defense	Economics & Great Depression	Science, Technology & Nature	Culture, Leisure & Lifestyle	
The state of Massachusetts reduces its annual budget by approximately $8 million. . . . Albert Einstein declares in a speech that Western civilization has been "critically shaken" by the effects of the Great Depression.		The U.S. Department of Commerce releases its weekly index of electric power production. At 73.9, the figure is a rise of 0.1 points from the previous week, but a decline of 13 percent from the corresponding week one year ago.			Jan. 26
A group of criminologists reports that more thefts occurred in the United States in 1931 than in any other year in the nation's history.		Prof. Irving Fisher of Yale University releases his weekly index of international stock prices. The figure is 52.4, a drop of 0.6 points from the preceding week, and a decline of approximately 45 percent from the corresponding week a year ago.			Jan. 27
American Federation of Labor president William Green estimates the number of unemployed Americans has risen to 8.3 million. He urges Congress to enact high taxes against the wealthy as a solution to the matter. . . . The Vermont Democratic State Committee unanimously votes to endorse the candidacy of New York Governor Franklin Roosevelt for the 1932 presidential election.		The Iron Age releases its weekly index of U.S. steel mill activity. The index currently stands at 32.0, an increase of 3.2 points from the previous week, but a decline of approximately 43 percent from the corresponding week one year ago.	In Miami Beach, Fla., American Gar Wood sets the world speedboat record at 110.785 miles per hour. Wood eclipses the previous record by 0.562 miles per hour.		Jan. 28
The Federal Reserve Board reports a total of 2,290 bank failures in the United States during the whole of 1931, the highest yearly total record. Deposits in the failed banks amounted to $1,759,484,000.	As Japan begins its occupation of Shanghai, four U.S. destroyer ships are dispatched to the waters near Shanghai to protect American interests in the region. The dispatch creates rumors that the United States has declared war on Japan.	The weekly index of U.S. automobile production as compiled by the Department of Commerce is released. The index currently stands at 42.1, a decrease of 4.8 points from the previous week, and a decline of 35 percent from the corresponding week one year ago.		The Menace, starring Hollywood Walk of Fame recipients H.B. Warner and Bette Davis, is released throughout the United States. . . . Boxer Bat Battalino is fined $5,000 by the Cincinnati Boxing Commission for failure to meet the maximum weight requirement for the featherweight division.	Jan. 29
	A bill is introduced on the floor of the House of Representatives that would reduce the number of enlisted men in the Army by 10,000. Opponents of the bill say that its authors will face "the fight of their lives" in attempting to pass it.	Dun's Review releases its weekly index of U.S. business failures. At 210.1, the figure is a rise of 18.2 points from the previous week, and an increase of 35.2 points from the corresponding week one year ago.		The comedic film High Pressure is released throughout the United States. The film is directed by Mervyn LeRoy and stars William Powell and Evelyn Brent, all of whom are Hollywood Walk of Fame recipients. . . . The dramatic film Hell House, starring Hollywood Walk of Fame recipients Bette Davis and Pat O'Brien, is released throughout the United States.	Jan. 30
Senate Foreign Relations Committee chairman William Borah expresses fierce opposition to a proposed economic boycott against Japan, describing it as "the first step toward war."	Naval Secretary Charles Francis Adams describes Rep. Joseph Byrns's proposal to merge the Navy and Army Departments to create a unified National Department of Defense as "a step in the wrong direction."	The Annalist releases its weekly index of U.S. business activity. At 62.9, the figure is a drop of 0.2 points from the previous week, but a decline of 19 percent from the corresponding period last year. Economists say the drop from last week was caused by losses in freight car loadings and automobile production.		Metro-Goldwyn-Mayer's Inspiration, featuring performances by Academy Award-winning actors Greta Garbo, Robert Montgomery, and Lewis Stone, is released throughout the United States. The film's director is five-time Academy Award-nominee Clarence Brown.	Jan. 31
	The destroyer Barry is transferred by naval authorities to the Pacific Coast. Barry was constructed in 1920 by the New York Shipbuilding Company. . . . Retired Gen. Smedley Butler declares in a speech that "the Japanese have been getting ready for the China invasion for the past 10 years." He asserts that Japan waited until the effects of the Great Depression hit before undertaking military action. . . . Secretary of State Henry Stimson declares that the United States will refrain from declaring war on Japan, but will implement a policy of "unqualified resistance" in response to the Japanese militaristic actions on China.	The Department of Commerce reports that total automobile production in 1931 is the lowest yearly total in nearly a decade. . . . Prof. Irving Fisher of Yale University releases his weekly index of international commodity prices. The figure is 64.5, a drop of 0.7 points from the preceding week, and a decline of approximately 16 percent from the corresponding week a year ago.		The third Winter Olympic Games commence in Lake Placid, N.Y. Future president Franklin Roosevelt hosts the opening ceremony. . . . Hollywood Walk of Fame director Oscar Micheaux's film Veiled Aristocrats is released throughout the United States.	Feb. 1

F	G	H	I	J
Includes elections, federal-state relations, civil rights and liberties, crime, the judiciary, education, healthcare, poverty, urban affairs, and population.	Includes formation and debate of U.S. foreign and defense policies, veterans affairs, and defense spending. (Relations with specific foreign countries are usually found under the region concerned.)	Includes business, labor, agriculture, taxation, transportation, consumer affairs, monetary and fiscal policy, natural resources, pollution, and accidents.	Includes worldwide scientific, medical, and technological developments, natural phenomena, U.S. weather, and natural disasters.	Includes the arts, religion, scholarship, communications media, sports, entertainment, fashions, fads, and social life.

	World Affairs	Europe	Africa & The Middle East	The Americas	Asia & The Pacific
Feb. 2		Berlin Mayor Heinrich Sahm officially endorses German President Paul von Hindenburg for reelection, calling him the candidate of the common man.		Canadian economists report that total Canadian automobile production has fallen by nearly 50 percent since the beginning of 1930.	
Feb. 3	The long-awaited conference on worldwide military disarmament opens in Geneva, Switzerland, with 232 delegates representing nearly 60 nations present. Chairman Arthur Henderson urges all signatories of the Kellogg-Briand Pact to uphold their pledge to eliminate war throughout the world, especially in the Far East. . . . Governor Franklin Roosevelt of New York expresses opposition to the potential entry of the United States into the League of Nations, as well as the cancellation of World War I debts.			Ecuadorian soldiers recapture the Tulcan Armory in the city of Guayaquil, seized by rebel forces a few days prior.	Thirty-six American citizens situated in the Chinese city of Nanking evacuate, fearing a possible Japanese attack.
Feb. 4	International creditors renew a $100 million loan to Germany for an additional month.			Canadian Prime Minister Richard Bennett reorganizes his Cabinet. Among the changes is the appointment of former premier Arthur Meighen as a general minister.	Several banks in the Chinese city of Shanghai that had been closed for a week due to ongoing violence officially reopen.
Feb. 5	Former U.S. secretary of the treasury Andrew Mellon is appointed to the post of U.S. Ambassador to Great Britain.	Latvia and the Soviet Union sign a nonaggression pact. . . . British Chancellor of the Exchequer Neville Chamberlain introduces a bill in the House of Commons that would drastically raise tariffs on imported goods, effectively ending a century-long British tradition of free trade. . . . Members of the French Military Affairs Committee allege that Germany is violating the terms of the Treaty of Versailles by engaging in military rearmament.	Prominent Arab leaders in Palestine tell British imperial authorities that they desire that Palestine be divided into two separate "provinces," one for Arabs and one for Jews.		Japanese military officials dispatch an additional army division to the Chinese city of Shanghai.
Feb. 6	At the international disarmament conference in Geneva, Switzerland, French War Minister Andre Tardieu recommends the creation of an "international police force."	Spokesmen for Adolf Hitler officially deny that the 42-year-old author of *Mein Kampf* is seeking the German presidency, declaring that he will seek "a Cabinet post to begin with." . . . German Defense Minister General Groener lifts a ban prohibiting any member of the National Socialist Party to serve in the nation's army.			The U.S. destroyer *Whipple* suffers severe damage in a collision with the British steamer *Rosalie Moller* near the Chinese city of Shanghai.
Feb. 7	Viscount Robert Cecil of Chelwood urges a global reduction of 25 percent in armament expenditures.	Denmark, Norway, Sweden, Belgium, Luxemburg, and the Netherlands enter into a free-trade agreement known as the Oslo Convention.			China reduces government employee salaries to a fixed rate of 115 yuans ($25) per month.
Feb. 8				An international study reveals that Canada's total life insurance policies amount to $7,392,706,000, the third highest total of any of the world's nations.	Japanese Admiral Kiochi Shiozawa declares that only intervention by Western military powers "can stop China's interminable civil wars and political intrigue."
Feb. 9	At the international disarmament conference in Geneva, Switzerland, British Foreign Secretary John Simon proposes the abolition of submarines and chemical weapons in warfare.	The number of unemployed Britons rises to 2,131,298, an increase of 218,490 from the beginning of January 1932.	South African diplomat Jan Smuts expresses opposition to France's proposal for the creation of an international police force governed by the League of Nations. "The object of the League is and must remain pacific," he says.	In the Cuban capital of Havana, a bomb explodes near the home of Assistant Secretary of the Interior Giordano Hernandez, causing considerable damage. Officials blame the incident on a group of university students.	British imperial authorities officially forbid Indian newspapers from publishing the names of those arrested for participating in the civil disobedience campaign.

A	B	C	D	E
Includes developments that affect more than one world region, international organizations, and important meetings of world leaders.	Includes all domestic and regional developments in Europe, including the Soviet Union.	Includes all domestic and regional developments in Africa and the Middle East.	Includes all domestic and regional developments in Latin America, the Caribbean, and Canada.	Includes all domestic and regional developments in Asian and Pacific nations (and colonies).

U.S. Politics & Social Issues	U.S. Foreign Policy & Defense	Economics & Great Depression	Science, Technology & Nature	Culture, Leisure & Lifestyle	
Laurence Olivier, who would go on to become considered one of the greatest actors of all time, is forced to leave the United States as his work visa expires. . . . Aviator/movie producer Howard Hughes offers to purchase the airship *Los Angeles* from the U.S. Navy for use in future motion picture projects.	Army Chief of Staff Douglas MacArthur appears before the House Military Affairs Committee to express opposition to a proposed cut in Army personnel. . . . In response to the Japanese attack on the Chinese city of Shanghai, the U.S. Navy transfers the destroyer *Smith Thompson* to the region to protect American lives and interests.	Prof. Irving Fisher of Yale University releases his weekly index of international stock prices. The figure is 49.8, a drop of 2.6 points from the preceding week, and a decline of approximately 49 percent from the corresponding week a year ago.	The 45th annual Groundhog Day celebration is held in Punxsutawney, Pa. Punxsutawney Phil, the city's most reliable "weatherhog," emerges from seclusion at 9:11 a.m., and his furry body casts a long, dark shadow, indicating another six weeks of cold, bitter winter.	Paramount Pictures' multimillion dollar adventure film *Shanghai Express* premiers in New York City. The film features the performances of Hollywood Walk of Fame recipients Marlene Dietrich and Clive Brook. *Shanghai Express* would win the 1932 Academy Award for Best Cinematography.	Feb. 2
	The destroyers *Hopkins* and *Tracy* are transferred to Cuba to provide medical aid to those affected by a massive earthquake. . . . The U.S. Navy transfers the destroyer *Waters* to Hawaii. *Waters* was constructed in 1917 by William Cramp & Sons.			Oscar-winning screenwriter Sidney Howard's *The Greeks Had a Word for Them* is released throughout the United States. The film stars Hollywood Walk of Fame recipients Joan Blondell, Madge Evans, and Ina Claire.	Feb. 3
Senator Warren Barbour of New Jersey officially endorses President Herbert Hoover for reelection.	The submarine *Narwhal* is transferred from Mare Island Navy Yard to Hawaii by U.S. naval authorities. . . . The U.S. Army and Navy Departments simulate an attack on the Pearl Harbor naval base in Hawaii.	*Dun's Review* releases its weekly index of U.S. business failures. At 199.5, the figure is a drop of 10.6 points from the previous week, but an increase of 37.2 points from the corresponding week one year ago.		First National Pictures' crime drama film *The Hatchet Man*, starring Academy Award winners Edward G. Robinson and Loretta Young and directed by Academy Award winner William Wellman, premiers in New York City.	Feb. 4
		The weekly index of U.S. automobile production as compiled by the Department of Commerce is released. The index currently stands at 39.0, a decrease of 3.1 points from the previous week, and a decline of 37 percent from the corresponding week one year ago.		The comedic film *Man Braucht Kein Gold*, starring German Film Award winners Heinz Ruhmann and Hans Moser, premiers in the German capital of Berlin.	Feb. 5
	The 31st U.S. Infantry, numbering 1,168 men, arrives in the Chinese city of Shanghai to protect American interests.	*The Iron Age* releases its weekly index of U.S. steel mill activity. The index currently stands at 30.1, a drop of 1.9 points from the previous week, and a decline of approximately 47 percent from the corresponding week one year ago.		The comedic film *The Passionate Plumber* is released throughout the United States. The film is directed by Edward Sedgwick and stars Buster Keaton, Jimmy Durante, and Polly Moran, all of whom are Hollywood Walk of Fame recipients.	Feb. 6
The Bureau of Efficiency reports that a proposed 10 percent reduction in all federal government employees' salaries would result in a savings of only $55,383,465.		*The Annalist* releases its weekly index of U.S. business activity. At 62.2, the figure is a drop of 0.6 points from the previous week, and a decline of 19 percent from the corresponding period last year. Economists say the drop from last week was caused by losses in freight car loadings, steel mill activity, and automobile production.		The horror film *The Monster Walks*, starring Oscar-nominated actress Mischa Auer, is released throughout the United States. . . . Aldous Huxley publishes *Brave New World*, considered by literature experts to be one of the greatest utopian novels ever written.	Feb. 7
New York City Health Commissioner Shirley Wynne reports that the city's death rate is currently at its lowest in more than 30 years.	U.S. Senator William Borah heaps heavy criticism upon French War Minister Andre Tardieu's proposal for an "international police force."	Prof. Irving Fisher of Yale University releases his weekly index of international commodity prices. The figure is 64.2, a drop of 0.3 points from the preceding week, and a decline of approximately 16 percent from the corresponding week a year ago.		*Huckleberry Finn*, the film adaptation of the Mark Twain novel, is released in Finland.	Feb. 8
		Prof. Irving Fisher of Yale University releases his weekly index of international stock prices. The figure is 49.3, a drop of 0.5 points from the preceding week, and a decline of approximately 51 percent from the corresponding week a year ago.		Future Hall of Fame baseball player Waite Hoyt is released by the Philadelphia Athletics.	Feb. 9

F	G	H	I	J
Includes elections, federal-state relations, civil rights and liberties, crime, the judiciary, education, healthcare, poverty, urban affairs, and population.	Includes formation and debate of U.S. foreign and defense policies, veterans affairs, and defense spending. (Relations with specific foreign countries are usually found under the region concerned.)	Includes business, labor, agriculture, taxation, transportation, consumer affairs, monetary and fiscal policy, natural resources, pollution, and accidents.	Includes worldwide scientific, medical, and technological developments, natural phenomena, U.S. weather, and natural disasters.	Includes the arts, religion, scholarship, communications media, sports, entertainment, fashions, fads, and social life.

	World Affairs	Europe	Africa & The Middle East	The Americas	Asia & The Pacific
Feb. 10		Two prominent members of the German National Socialist Party are fined 100 marks each by a court in Berlin for inciting anti-Semitic incidents on New Year's Day of this year. . . . Bulgaria announces it will no longer pay any reparations pertaining to World War I. . . . Spain exiles 109 Communist demonstrators who participated in a recent revolt in the region of Catalonia. . . . In the German city of Hamburg, 2,100 taverns refuse to sell beer to their patrons, protesting a recent government decree that forced the taverns to slash the price of beer.		Ecuador officially goes off the gold standard, effective until November 1932.	
Feb. 11	Newly appointed U.S. Ambassador to Denmark Frederick Coleman presents his credentials to Danish King Christian X. . . . Italian Foreign Minister Dino Grandi urges the abolition of "capital ships, submarines, aircraft carriers, heavy artillery, tanks, bombing aircraft, and chemical weapons."	Pope Pius XI confers with Italian Premier Benito Mussolini in Vatican City.	At the Hebrew University in Jerusalem, a small riot instigated by Zionist demonstrators occurs during a lecture given by former Palestinian attorney general Norman Bentwich. Bentwich's lecture, entitled, "Jerusalem, City of Peace," was criticized by some as being naively pacifistic.		T.M. Ainscough, the British trade commissioner in India, reports that Mohandas Gandhi's civil disobedience campaign has resulted in a trade loss of $86,250,000 to India over the past year.
Feb. 12		The British Board of Trade reports that Great Britain's total exports have fallen by £1,263,000 since December 1931. . . . Polish Commissioner of Danzig H. Strasserburger announces his resignation, citing pressure from the German National Socialist Party to do so.		President Ortiz Rubio of Mexico announces his intention to create a central banking system similar to the United States' Federal Reserve Board.	
Feb. 13	British Foreign Secretary John Simon states in a report that despite slavery being abolished in most major nations since the mid-19th century, there still exist approximately 5 million slaves throughout the world.	French lawmakers introduce a bill granting suffrage to women. The bill would be defeated; French women's suffrage will not occur until the end of World War II.		Argentine economists report that Argentina's exports in January 1932 amounted to $29,656,000, a decline of 7.8 percent from January 1931.	
Feb. 14			The American Palestine Campaign releases the results of a study showing that the Jewish population in Palestine is on "a much sounder basis" than the Jewish population in other industrialized nations.		
Feb. 15	Referring to France, German Chancellor Heinrich Bruening demands in a radio interview that "the limitation of armaments imposed on us must also be applied to them."	In an effort to lessen the importation of meat, Greek lawmakers pass a measure prohibiting citizens from consuming meat during three days each week.			All-India National Congress President Sirdar Singhi is arrested by British imperial authorities. . . . Muslim leader Maulana Shaukat Ali accuses Indian revolutionary leader Mohandas Gandhi of "betraying" the Muslim community.
Feb. 16		The British Actors' Equity Association requests British lawmakers to eliminate the quota system on foreign-born thespians.		Cuba commemorates the 34th anniversary of the sinking of the USS Maine, the event that ignited the Spanish-American War, leading to eventual independence for Cuba.	
Feb. 17		Prices on the German stock exchange rise in anticipation of the ousting of French President Pierre Laval.	Nobel Prize-winning author George Bernard Shaw sustains serious injuries in an automobile accident in South Africa.	A violent Costa Rican rebellion led by Manuel Castro Quesada forces President Cleto Viquez to take refuge in a fortified artillery garrison.	

A	B	C	D	E
Includes developments that affect more than one world region, international organizations, and important meetings of world leaders.	Includes all domestic and regional developments in Europe, including the Soviet Union.	Includes all domestic and regional developments in Africa and the Middle East.	Includes all domestic and regional developments in Latin America, the Caribbean, and Canada.	Includes all domestic and regional developments in Asian and Pacific nations (and colonies).

U.S. Politics & Social Issues	U.S. Foreign Policy & Defense	Economics & Great Depression	Science, Technology & Nature	Culture, Leisure & Lifestyle	
Lawyers of convicted gangster Al Capone request an appeal.				The dramatic film *The Man Who Played God* is released throughout the United States. The film is written by Julien Josephson and stars George Arliss and Bette Davis, all of whom are Academy Award nominees.	**Feb. 10**
1931 Nobel Peace Prize winner Nicholas Murray Butler urges U.S. lawmakers to end Prohibition. . . . The National Urban League releases a report stating that African Americans have been disproportionately affected by the Great Depression.		*Dun's Review* releases its weekly index of U.S. business failures. At 191.6, the figure is a decrease of 7.9 points from the previous week, but a rise of 35.5 points from the corresponding week one year ago.			**Feb. 11**
President Herbert Hoover meets with legendary entertainer Will Rogers. The pair discuss such issues as the Japanese invasion of Manchuria.		The weekly index of U.S. automobile production as compiled by the Department of Commerce is released. The index currently stands at 37.9, a drop of 1.1 points from the previous week, and a decline of 40 percent from the corresponding week one year ago.	The British Royal Aero Club awards its annual Britannia Trophy to Australian aviator Bert Hinkler for his flight from New York to London.	The crime drama film *Final Edition*, starring Hollywood Walk of Fame recipient Pat O'Brien, is released throughout the United States.	**Feb. 12**
People's Lobby executive secretary Benjamin Marsh declares in a speech that "a public works program of at least $3 billion annually is essential to reduce unemployment." . . . In testimony before the Senate, Constitutional Rights Association of America national secretary Stanley Shirk estimates that upholding Prohibition has cost American taxpayers $6 billion since 1919.	The destroyer *Jacob Jones* is transferred to the Pacific Coast. *Jacob Jones* was constructed in 1918 by the Bethlehem Shipbuilding Corporation.	*The Iron Age* releases its weekly index of U.S. steel mill activity. The index currently stands at 30.5, a rise of 0.4 points from the previous week, but a reduction of approximately 47 percent from the corresponding week one year ago.	U.S. aviation officials report that the number of U.S. air passengers has increased by 83,000 since February 1931.	The film *Ein Steinreicher Mann (A Tremendously Wealthy Man)* is released in Germany. The film stars German Film Award winners Curt Bois and Dolly Haas.	**Feb. 13**
Congress members officially reject a bill proposed by Senator William Borah that would have reduced government salaries by a significant amount. . . . Officials of the Catholic Church report that there are currently 21,887,606 Catholics within the United States, an increase of 2,552,397 over the past decade.	House Military Affairs Committee chairman John McSwain recommends the merging of the Army and Navy Departments. . . . Senate Foreign Relations Committee Chairman William Borah expresses opposition to a proposed trade boycott against Japan.	*The Annalist* releases its weekly index of U.S. business activity. At 62.8, the figure is a rise of 0.6 points from the previous week, but a decline of 19 percent from the corresponding period last year. Economists say the rise from last week was caused by increases in freight car loadings and electric power production.		The film noir motion picture *The Beast of the City*, starring Hollywood Walk of Fame recipient Wallace Ford, is released throughout the United States.	**Feb. 14**
		Prof. Irving Fisher of Yale University releases his weekly index of international commodity prices. The figure is 63.6, a drop of 0.6 points from the preceding week, and a reduction of approximately 16 percent from the corresponding week a year ago.		The U.S. bobsled team is awarded the gold medal at the third Winter Olympic Games in Lake Placid, N.Y. Team member Eddie Eagen becomes the world's first athlete to win a gold medal in both the Summer and Winter Olympic Games. . . . *Clara, Lu & Em*, the first daytime soap opera, debuts on the NBC radio network.	**Feb. 15**
President Herbert Hoover nominates New York State Court of Appeals Chief Judge Nathan Cordoza to fill the Supreme Court seat vacated by retiring Justice Oliver Wendell Holmes. The nomination is lauded by both Congressmen and political analysts alike. . . . American Federation of Labor president William Green leads a strike of 30,000 dressmakers in New York City.		Prof. Irving Fisher of Yale University releases his weekly index of international stock prices. The figure is 47.5, a drop of 1.8 points from the preceding week, and a reduction of approximately 54 percent from the corresponding week a year ago.		Paramount Pictures' $1 million film, *Dr. Jekyll and Mr. Hyde*, based on the 1886 novel by Robert Louis Stevenson, is released in Denmark. The film will receive three Academy Award nominations, including Best Actor, Best Cinematography, and Best Screenplay.	**Feb. 16**
By a vote of 48–35, the Senate rejects a bill that would have provided $375 million in charitable aid to idle workers.		The salaries of the directors of the Canadian National Railways are lowered by an average of 10 percent in an effort to reduce federal budget deficits. . . . American economic officials report that total foreign trade in January 1932 amounted to $286 million, the lowest monthly total since 1914.			**Feb. 17**

F	G	H	I	J
Includes elections, federal-state relations, civil rights and liberties, crime, the judiciary, education, healthcare, poverty, urban affairs, and population.	Includes formation and debate of U.S. foreign and defense policies, veterans affairs, and defense spending. (Relations with specific foreign countries are usually found under the region concerned.)	Includes business, labor, agriculture, taxation, transportation, consumer affairs, monetary and fiscal policy, natural resources, pollution, and accidents.	Includes worldwide scientific, medical, and technological developments, natural phenomena, U.S. weather, and natural disasters.	Includes the arts, religion, scholarship, communications media, sports, entertainment, fashions, fads, and social life.

	World Affairs	Europe	Africa & The Middle East	The Americas	Asia & The Pacific
Feb. 18		British economic officials report that Great Britain experienced an adverse trade balance of £110 million during the whole of 1931, compared with a trade surplus of £28 million during the whole of 1930.	Spokesmen for the De Beers diamond company announce the company is closing its mines in the South African city of Cape Town, a decision owing to a "dismal" diamond market.	The entire Cabinet of President Daniel Salmanaca Urey of Bolivia resigns amid heavy internal tension.	Chinese military officials estimate that there are currently 120,000 troops stationed in and around the city of Shanghai to defend against a possible Japanese attack.
Feb. 19	At the international disarmament conference in Geneva, Switzerland, the chief German delegate recommends the universal abolition of frontier defense fortresses, warfare aviation, and military conscription.				Great Britain expresses the fear that ongoing tensions between China and Japan will "have disastrous repercussions in India."
Feb. 20	Former U.S. secretary of war Newton Baker urges the League of Nations to impose economic sanctions on Japan.			Gen. Agustin Pedro Justo is inaugurated as Argentina's newest president. Justo succeeds Jose Felix Uriburu, who following a military coup in September 1930, pledged to reinstitute a democratic government. . . . Bolivia designates February 22 as a national holiday to commemorate the 200th anniversary of the birth of George Washington.	
Feb. 21	Denmark dispatches a destroyer ship to the Chinese city of Shanghai to protect Dutch interests in the region.	German President Paul von Hindenburg officially announces his candidacy for reelection.			Chinese officials report that massive floods that devastated areas near the Yangtze River late in 1931 caused damages exceeding $2 billion.
Feb. 22	The League of Nations annual *Armaments Yearbook* is published. The book shows that China has the world's largest army; Great Britain, the world's largest navy; and France, the world's largest air force.	The German federal budget deficit rises to 1,187,000,000 marks, an increase of 95 million marks from the beginning of 1931. . . . The German National Socialist Party nominates future dictator Adolf Hitler as its candidate for president.		A strike of 1,700 garment workers in the Canadian city of Montreal ends as employees capitulate to employers' demands of a 10 percent wage reduction.	Japan cables a message to the League of Nations claiming that Japan is acting in "self defense" in its attack on the Chinese city of Shanghai.
Feb. 23		The number of unemployed Germans rises to 6,127,000, an increase of 85,000 since the beginning of February 1932.	The Jewish National Fund of America announces plans to create a 500,000-tree forest in Palestine. . . . Arab leaders select the holy city of Mecca as the location for an upcoming Pan-Arabian Congress, during which the creation of an Arab League of Nations will be considered.	A bomb explodes in the Ville Clara Theater in the Cuban capital of Havana, injuring several theatergoers. Officials place blame for the incident on a local student revolutionary movement.	
Feb. 24	British Foreign Secretary John Simon announces that his government will oppose any effort by the League of Nations to impose economic sanctions upon Japan.	Austrian Chancellor Karl Buresch is stricken with a severe case of influenza.		Canadian census officials report their country's population has increased by 15 percent since 1921, from 8,788,483 to 10,374,196.	
Feb. 25		Future Nazi Propaganda Minister Joseph Goebbels describes the German Socialist Party, the party with the most representation in the German Reichstag, as "the party of traitors and deserters." German Defense Minister Wilhelm Groener assails Goebbels's remarks, calling them an insult to the German people.		Argentine economists report that total trade to the United States has declined by nearly 50 percent since January 1930.	In an effort to restrict the flow of undesirable immigrants, the Philippines closes all immigration ports, with the exception of those in the capital of Manila.
Feb. 26		In a speech made before the Reichstag, German Chancellor Heinrich Bruening refers to Adolf Hitler by saying, "The accusations of betrayal of the fatherland by the Weimar Republic in 1919 are made by men who then had not yet discovered to what country they belonged."			Australia reduces tariffs on imported iron, steel, porcelain, cotton yarns, glassware, and confectionary sugar. . . . Chinese forces prevent the Japanese army from advancing into the city of Miaoshin. . . . Japan sends five army divisions to the Chinese city of Shanghai, increasing the number of Japanese troops in the city to 100,000.
	A	B	C	D	E
	Includes developments that affect more than one world region, international organizations, and important meetings of world leaders.	Includes all domestic and regional developments in Europe, including the Soviet Union.	Includes all domestic and regional developments in Africa and the Middle East.	Includes all domestic and regional developments in Latin America, the Caribbean, and Canada.	Includes all domestic and regional developments in Asian and Pacific nations (and colonies).

U.S. Politics & Social Issues	U.S. Foreign Policy & Defense	Economics & Great Depression	Science, Technology & Nature	Culture, Leisure & Lifestyle	
		Dun's Review releases its weekly index of U.S. business failures. At 170.3, the figure is a reduction of 21.3 points from the previous week, but a rise of 39.2 points from the corresponding week one year ago.		Norwegian Sonja Henie is awarded the women's gold medal for figure skating for the second consecutive time at the third Winter Olympic Games in Lake Placid, N.Y. Henie would go on to claim more Olympic medals than any woman figure skater in history. . . . The Marx Brothers' film *Monkey Business* is released in Japan.	Feb. 18
As economic conditions worsen, the city of Chicago is forced to dismiss 2,479 city employees. . . . *The Literary Digest* publishes the results of a nationwide survey showing that 84 percent of the American public favors repeal of Prohibition.	The U.S. Navy transfers the submarine *S-20*, constructed in 1918 by the Bethlehem Shipbuilding Corporation, to the Mare Island Navy Yard in Vallejo, Calif.	The weekly index of U.S. automobile production as compiled by the Department of Commerce is released. The index currently stands at 38.4, a rise of 0.5 points from the previous week, but a decline of 36 percent from the corresponding week one year ago.		The animated short *A Romeo Monk*, directed by John Foster, who created more than 100 animated shorts over the span of a 13-year career, is released throughout the United States. . . . By shooting a 69, golfer Bobby Jones establishes a one-round record for the Augusta Country Club, the home of the annual Masters' tournament.	Feb. 19
Rep. Frederick Britton introduces a bill that would make Saturday a legal holiday throughout the United States.	The USS *Wright* arrives at the Naval Air Station North Island, located off the waters of San Diego, Calif. *Wright* was constructed as a miscellaneous auxiliary vessel in 1920 by the Tietjen and Lang Dry Dock Co.	*The Iron Age* releases its weekly index of U.S. steel mill activity. The index currently stands at 28.9, a drop of 1.6 points from the previous week, and a decline of approximately 49 percent from the corresponding week one year ago.		The horror film *Freaks* is released throughout the United States. The film is directed by Hollywood Walk of Fame recipient Tod Browning. *Freaks* will be archived in 1994 by the U.S. National Film Preservation Board for the enjoyment of future generations.	Feb. 20
Senate Foreign Relations Committee chairman William Borah expresses fear that a proposed boycott of Japanese trade could be interpreted by other nations as "an act of war."		*The Annalist* releases its weekly index of U.S. business activity. At 62.5, the figure is a drop of 0.3 points from the previous week, and a decline of 19 percent from the corresponding period last year. Economists say the drop from last week was caused by losses in steel mill activity and electric power production.		Metro-Goldwyn-Mayer releases the dramatic film *Dance, Fools, Dance*. The film is directed by Harry Beaumont and stars Joan Crawford and Clark Gable, all of whom are Academy Award nominees. . . . Norway is awarded the gold medal for speed skating at the third Winter Olympic Games in Lake Placid, N.Y.	Feb. 21
	The airship USS *Akron* suffers severe damages to its tail while being lifted from its hangar in Lakehurst, N.J.	Prof. Irving Fisher of Yale University releases his weekly index of international commodity prices. The figure is 63.7, a rise of 0.1 points from the preceding week, but a decline of approximately 16 percent from the corresponding week a year ago.		Universal Pictures releases *Murders in the Rue Morgue*, based on the story by legendary author Edgar Allen Poe. The film stars Hollywood Walk of Fame recipient Bela Lugosi.	Feb. 22
Former New York governor Al Smith, who lost in a landslide to Herbert Hoover in the 1928 presidential election, announces his intention to run for the presidency in 1932 under the Democratic ticket.	The U.S. Navy transfers the heavy cruiser *Indianapolis* to the Panama Canal Zone. She became legendary after delivering across the Pacific the atomic bomb that was eventually dropped on the Japanese city of Nagasaki.	Prof. Irving Fisher of Yale University releases his weekly index of international stock prices. The figure is 53.3, a rise of 5.8 points from the preceding week, but a decline of approximately 50 percent from the corresponding week a year ago.		The French film *Tu seras Duchese* (*You Will Be a Duchess*) premiers in Paris.	Feb. 23
The Senate Judiciary Committee unanimously approves the appointment of Ben Cardoza to fill the Supreme Court seat vacated by retiring Justice Oliver Wendell Holmes. . . . Governor William Murray of Oklahoma announces his candidacy for the 1932 presidential election. If elected, Murray claims, he will uphold a policy of neutrality toward the conflict between China and Japan.		Canadian economists report a favorable trade balance of $4,948,962 for the month of January 1932.			Feb. 24
By a vote of 40–9, the New York State Senate passes a bill creating a centralized state banking board comprised of nine prominent economists. . . . In Boston, 3,500 members of the International Ladies Garment Workers Union go on strike. Spokeswomen for the strike claim that workers are receiving "starvation wages."	The destroyer *Mayer* is sold for scrap by U.S. naval authorities. *Mayer* was constructed in 1919 by the Bethlehem Shipbuilding Corporation. . . . The destroyer *McDermott* is sold for scrap by U.S. naval authorities. *McDermott* was constructed in 1918 by the Bethlehem Shipbuilding Corporation, and spent most of its years as a member of the Atlantic Fleet.	*Dun's Review* releases its weekly index of U.S. business failures. At 184.5, the figure is a rise of 14.2 points from the previous week, and an increase of 7.1 points from the corresponding week one year ago.	Briton Malcolm Campbell establishes the world automobile speed record of 253.968 in Daytona Beach, Fla. Campbell eclipses his own record by 8.235 miles per hour, set in the same location in 1931.	First National Pictures' *Alias the Doctor* is released throughout the United States. The film is directed by Lloyd Bacon and stars Richard Barthelmess, both of whom are Hollywood Walk of Fame recipients.	Feb. 25
An explosion in a coal mine in Boissevain, Va., results in the deaths of 38 miners.	The U.S. Navy sells the destroyer *Yarborough* for scrap. *Yarborough* was constructed in 1919 by the Bethlehem Shipbuilding Corporation. . . . In accordance with the London Naval Treaty, the U.S. Navy sells the destroyer *Rizal* for scrap. A member of the Pacific Fleet, *Rizal* was named after Filipino revolutionary Jose Rizal.	The weekly index of U.S. automobile production as compiled by the Department of Commerce is released. The index currently stands at 37.1, a drop of 1.3 points from the previous week, and a decline of 34 percent from the corresponding week one year ago.			Feb. 26

F	G	H	I	J
Includes elections, federal-state relations, civil rights and liberties, crime, the judiciary, education, healthcare, poverty, urban affairs, and population.	Includes formation and debate of U.S. foreign and defense policies, veterans affairs, and defense spending. (Relations with specific foreign countries are usually found under the region concerned.)	Includes business, labor, agriculture, taxation, transportation, consumer affairs, monetary and fiscal policy, natural resources, pollution, and accidents.	Includes worldwide scientific, medical, and technological developments, natural phenomena, U.S. weather, and natural disasters.	Includes the arts, religion, scholarship, communications media, sports, entertainment, fashions, fads, and social life.

	World Affairs	Europe	Africa & The Middle East	The Americas	Asia & The Pacific
Feb. 27	U.S. Senate Foreign Relations Committee chairman William Borah declares in an interview with *The Presbyterian* that the worldwide military disarmament is impossible "as long as we have the Versailles Treaty. It must be rewritten either peaceably or forcibly."	Austrian-born revolutionary Adolf Hitler is granted German citizenship. . . . The Finnish anti-Communist Lapua Movement undertakes a failed coup attempt in the city of Mantsala. . . . German Chancellor Heinrich Bruening survives a confidence vote in the Reichstag. After the vote's defeat, members of the National Socialist Party describe the Reichstag as a "monkey show."		Cuban census officials report that Cuba's population increased by 37 percent over the past decade, from 2,889,004 to 3,962,344.	
Feb. 28		The Berlin Municipal Bureau of Statistics reports that the city's population declined by 42,721 during 1931. Officials attribute the loss to increased emigration owing to depressive economic conditions.		President Enrique Herrera of Colombia issues a proclamation officially banning all demonstrations by the Liberal Party. . . . Costa Rica eliminates all of its diplomatic representation in Europe in an effort to reduce federal budget deficits.	
Feb. 29	Theodore Roosevelt, Jr., is officially installed by the United States as Governor-General of the Philippines. He pledges to commit himself to the administrative aspects of the Philippines and to refrain from either encouraging or preventing plans for Filipino independence.	Four thousand members of the Finnish fascist movement amass in the city of Mantsala, threatening a violent march on the capital of Helsinki if Interior Minister Baron von Born refuses to capitulate to the fascists' demand for his resignation.		In Cuba, alcohol sales are temporarily suspended for 24 hours to provide for peaceful municipal elections in which 710,593 Cubans cast ballots.	Japanese diplomat Nobuo Fujimura declares in a radio address that Japan's economic prosperity is being threatened by rising tariffs and trade barriers.
Mar. 1		Campaign propaganda for the 1932 German elections begins to appear in Berlin. Chancellor Heinrich Bruening makes use of Germany's state-owned radio by delivering a speech broadcast nationwide. The National Socialists announce plans to counter Bruening's oratorical prowess by distributing 6 million campaign posters.		Cuban newspapers predict that President Gerardo Machado will be easily elected in the Caribbean island nation's upcoming presidential elections.	
Mar. 2	Belgian Premier Jules Penkin expresses support for U.S. Secretary of State Henry Stimson's uncompromisingly belligerent stance over the Japanese attacks on China.			Bermudan women send to lawmakers a petition containing the signatures of over 1,000 Bermudans who desire the granting of women's suffrage. . . . The Central Bank of Chile reduces its bank rate by 0.5 percent, from 6 percent to 5.5 percent.	Japan announces the capture of the Chinese city of Miaoshin.
Mar. 3	The British newspaper *The Daily Telegraph* describes the kidnapping of Charles Lindbergh's infant son as a "monstrous crime," and says that it indicates that a pervasive lawlessness exists throughout the United States.		Nathan Straus is elected New York chairman of the Jewish Agency for Palestine.		
Mar. 4				The Colombian state of Antioquia defaults on all of its loans to international creditors. . . . Higinio Arbo is appointed as the new Foreign Minister of Uruguay.	Chinese newspapers criticize Gen. Chiang Kai-shek for his failure to uphold his pledge to provide 100,000 troop reinforcements to the 19th Army.
Mar. 5	German newspapers express apathy toward the kidnapping of famed aviator Charles Lindbergh's infant son. They claim that the concept of kidnapping for ransom is entirely unfamiliar to the German people. . . . J.P. Morgan & Co. grants a loan of $150 million to the British government.	Belgian newspapers demand the end of partial Prohibition.		By a vote of 83–28, the Canadian parliament passes a bill reducing government employee salaries by an average of 10 percent.	

A	B	C	D	E
Includes developments that affect more than one world region, international organizations, and important meetings of world leaders.	Includes all domestic and regional developments in Europe, including the Soviet Union.	Includes all domestic and regional developments in Africa and the Middle East.	Includes all domestic and regional developments in Latin America, the Caribbean, and Canada.	Includes all domestic and regional developments in Asian and Pacific nations (and colonies).

U.S. Politics & Social Issues	U.S. Foreign Policy & Defense	Economics & Great Depression	Science, Technology & Nature	Culture, Leisure & Lifestyle	
The Glass-Steagall Act is passed, officially removing the United States from the gold standard, as well as enabling the Federal Reserve Board to greatly expand its credit resources. . . . Governor Franklin Roosevelt of New York signs into law a tax bill that officials estimate will increase the state's treasury reserves by $76 million in 18 months.	The destroyer *Hart*, constructed in 1918 by the Union Iron Works Company, is sold for scrap in accordance with the London Naval Treaty. *Hart* spent most of its years cruising the waters of the Pacific. . . . The armored cruiser *Rochester* is officially made a member of the Pacific Fleet. A relic of sorts, she was constructed in 1890 by William Cramp & Sons.	*The Iron Age* releases its weekly index of U.S. steel mill activity. The index currently stands at 27.7, a drop of 1.2 points from the previous week, and a decline of approximately 52 percent from the corresponding week one year ago.		Metro-Goldwyn-Mayer's drama film *Polly of the Circus* is released throughout the United States. The film stars Hollywood Walk of Fame recipients Marion Davies, Clark Gable, C. Aubrey Smith, and Raymond Hatton.	Feb. 27
	The U.S. Navy sells the destroyer *William Jones* for scrap. A member of the Pacific Fleet, *William Jones* was constructed in 1918 by the Bethlehem Steel Corporation. . . . The destroyer *Meyer*, constructed in 1919 by the Bethlehem Shipbuilding Corporation, is sold for scrap in accordance with the London Naval Treaty. . . . The U.S. Army announces plans for construction of the world's largest nonrigid airship at a cost of $125,000. The ship, to be known as the *TC-13*, will have a length of 233 feet.	*The Annalist* releases its weekly index of U.S. business activity. At 61.2, the figure is a drop of 1.2 points from the previous week, and a decline of 21 percent from the corresponding period last year. Economists say the drop from last week was caused by losses in freight car loadings, steel mill activity, and automobile production.		The western film *Law and Order* is released throughout the United States. The film stars Hollywood Walk of Fame recipients Walter Huston, Harry Carey, and Raymond Hatton.	Feb. 28
A tax bill is introduced on the House floor that would increase federal tax revenue by approximately $1 billion annually. . . . The American Federation of Labor releases a report estimating the number of unemployed Americans to be 8.3 million. AFL president William Green declares that "the only solution is to shorten working hours."	U.S. Commerce Department officials warn members of Congress that a proposed economic boycott against Japanese imported goods would have disastrous consequences.	France and Italy sign an economic agreement eliminating most trade barriers and tariff restrictions between the two countries.		Swimmer Eleanor Holm ties the U.S. 100-meter backstroke record with a time of one minute and 22.4 seconds.	Feb. 29
Charles Lindbergh, Jr., 20 months old, son of the world famous aviator, is reported kidnapped from his home in Hopewell, N.J. The incident sparks a media firestorm. Journalist H.L. Mencken would call the story "the biggest since the Resurrection of Jesus Christ."	The U.S. Navy transfers the destroyer *Ellis* to the waters off San Francisco, Calif.	In Philadelphia, Pa., four officials of the Upper Darby Bank, which declared its insolvency on May 9, 1931, are arrested on charges of defrauding the state of $350,000. . . . Solicitor General Thomas D. Thacher releases a report showing that the number of annual U.S. bankruptcies has quadrupled over the past decade, from 15,000 in 1921 to 60,000 in 1931.		Universal Pictures' dramatic romance film *Stowaway*, starring Hollywood Walk of Fame recipient Fay Wray, is released throughout the United States.	Mar. 1
The Metropolitan Life Insurance Company reports that the death rate in New York City has declined by approximately 7.6 percent over the past year.	The destroyer *Williamson*, constructed in 1919 by the New York Shipbuilding Corporation, is transferred by U.S. naval authorities from the Atlantic Coast to the Pacific Coast.			The dramatic film *Impatient Maiden* is released throughout the United States. The film stars Hollywood Walk of Fame recipients Lew Ayres, Mae Clarke, and Andy Devine.	Mar. 2
Presidential candidate Governor Bill Murray of Oklahoma adopts "Bread, Butter, Bacon, and Beans" as his official campaign song. Murray campaigners express the hope that the song, along with "Hoover Made a Soup Houn' Out o' Me," will enchant potential voters. . . . Postal officials in Hopewell, N.J., intercept a postcard addressed to Charles Lindbergh that reads, "Baby safe. Instructions later. Act accordingly." Oddly, the letter's author misspelled the famed aviator's name as "Linberg."	The minesweeper *Bobolink* is transferred by naval authorities from the Atlantic Coast to the waters off San Diego, Calif. *Bobolink* was constructed in 1918 by the Baltimore Dry Dock and Shipbuilding Company.			The comedic short film *Runt Page*, directed by Academy Award nominee Ray Nazarro, is released throughout the United States.	Mar. 3
In response to the Lindbergh kidnapping, members of the Kentucky House of Representatives pass a resolution urging Congress to enact federal legislation to make kidnapping a crime punishable by life imprisonment.	The destroyer *Goff*, constructed in 1920 by the New York Shipbuilding Corporation, is recommissioned by the U.S. Navy after more than a month of inactivity. She will receive two battle stars for her service in World War II.	Prof. Irving Fisher of Yale University releases his weekly index of international commodity prices. The figure is 62.9, a drop of 0.8 points from the preceding week, and a decline of approximately 17 percent from the corresponding week a year ago.			Mar. 4
The Census Bureau reports that total budget expenditures for New York City have increased by 187 percent since the end of World War I.		*Dun's Review* releases its weekly index of U.S. business failures. At 156.5, the figure is a drop of 28 points from the previous week, and a reduction of 5.4 points from the corresponding week one year ago.		Metro-Goldwyn-Mayer's short *Olympic Events*, detailing the training exercises by athletes preparing for the 1932 Summer Olympic Games, is released throughout the United States.	Mar. 5

F	G	H	I	J
Includes elections, federal-state relations, civil rights and liberties, crime, the judiciary, education, healthcare, poverty, urban affairs, and population.	Includes formation and debate of U.S. foreign and defense policies, veterans affairs, and defense spending. (Relations with specific foreign countries are usually found under the region concerned.)	Includes business, labor, agriculture, taxation, transportation, consumer affairs, monetary and fiscal policy, natural resources, pollution, and accidents.	Includes worldwide scientific, medical, and technological developments, natural phenomena, U.S. weather, and natural disasters.	Includes the arts, religion, scholarship, communications media, sports, entertainment, fashions, fads, and social life.

	World Affairs	Europe	Africa & The Middle East	The Americas	Asia & The Pacific
Mar. 6	American author Dorothy Thompson publishes *I Saw Hitler*, a detailed account of the rise to power of the man who is considered by many to be history's most destructive individual. The book describes Hitler's manifesto, *Mein Kampf*, as "an 800-page speech of pathetic gestures and unlimited self-satisfaction."			President Jose Uriburu of Argentina reorganizes his Cabinet to include the appointments of Alberto Hueyo and Leopoldo Melo as Minister of Finance and Minister of the Interior, respectively.	
Mar. 7		During "Red Fighting Day," 90 Austrians are arrested for participating in Communist demonstrations in Vienna. . . . Dutch economists report that total Dutch real estate value has fallen by 50 percent since the beginning of 1930.		President Luis Cerro of Peru sustains injuries in an attempted assassination in the capital of Lima but narrowly survives. Police prevent the assassin, a Peruvian youth with ties to a radical U.S. political group, from being lynched by indignant city residents.	U.S. Consul General in Shanghai Edwin Cunningham formally protests the attack by Japanese citizens on American missionary Rose Marlowe.
Mar. 8	Condolences are expressed worldwide over the death of French Foreign Minister Aristide Briand. An ardent pacifist, Briand was co-author of the 1928 Pact of Paris, which outlawed war "as an instrument of national policy." Nobel Peace Prize winner Austen Chamberlain characterizes him as "the greatest European of us all."	Polish lawmakers introduce a bill that would lower the daily minimum wage from 84 cents to 56 cents.			Chinese Gen. Chiang Kai-shek is put in command of all of China's military forces.
Mar. 9		Rising federal budget deficits force Austria to reduce budget expenditures by $15 million.		American A.L. Randall is deported from Chile on the grounds of writing an article describing the Chilean workmen as lazy. . . . The Argentine Finance Minister announces plans for the creation of a central banking system similar to U.S. Federal Reserve Board.	
Mar. 10		Belgium increases tariffs on most dutiable goods by an average of 15 percent. . . . British economists report a favorable trade balance of £34,640,000 for the month of February 1932. . . . Former Austrian chancellor Ignaz Seipel expresses support for French Premier Andre Tardieu's proposal for a Central European "economic bloc."		Chile arrests former ambassador Carlos Davila for engaging in seditious activities.	
Mar. 11		Five bombs explode simultaneously in the Spanish city of Huelva in what police describe as an elaborate terrorist action perpetrated by syndicalist organizations.		Canadian economists report that total Canadian wheat exports in the past seven months amount to $68,382,448.	The Japanese navy announces plans for the construction of a $2 million airbase in the city of Yokosuka. . . . The Canadian federal budget deficit rises to £3,560,000.
Mar. 12	Members of the League of Nations sign a resolution stating that the League will not formally recognize any treaty derived "by means contrary to the League of Nations Covenant or to the Pact of Paris." Japan abstains from signing the resolution.	Funeral services are held for the late French foreign minister Aristide Briand.		Argentina announces plans for the construction of an oil refinery at a cost $1,250,000 to be located in the city of La Plata.	
Mar. 13		Presidential elections are held in Germany. Incumbent Paul von Hindenburg receives 49.6 percent of the vote, while runner-up Adolf Hitler of the National Socialist Party receives 30 percent of the vote.		In an effort to boost domestic agriculture, President Gerardo Machado of Cuba issues a decree requiring all Cuban bakers to manufacture bread containing at least 40 percent yucca flour.	Anti-Kuomintang demonstrators instigate a violent riot in the Chinese city of Peiping.
Mar. 14		The German Reichsbank reduces its discount rate by 1 percent, from 7 percent to 6 percent.		The Chilean newspaper *Comercio* warns of an impending Communist coup that will likely result in the deaths of all members of President Luis Cerro's Cabinet. . . . The Canadian steamship *Prince David* accidentally sinks off the coast of Bermuda. Luckily, all of the ship's crew and its passengers survive.	Filipino revolutionaries threaten a boycott of all U.S. goods if their demands for full independence are not met.

A	B	C	D	E
Includes developments that affect more than one world region, international organizations, and important meetings of world leaders.	Includes all domestic and regional developments in Europe, including the Soviet Union.	Includes all domestic and regional developments in Africa and the Middle East.	Includes all domestic and regional developments in Latin America, the Caribbean, and Canada.	Includes all domestic and regional developments in Asian and Pacific nations (and colonies).

U.S. Politics & Social Issues	U.S. Foreign Policy & Defense	Economics & Great Depression	Science, Technology & Nature	Culture, Leisure & Lifestyle	
	The Portsmouth Navy Yard completes construction on the submarine *Dolphin*. *Dolphin* will be stationed at the Pearl Harbor naval base during the Japanese sneak attack on December 7, 1941, and will later receive a battle star for services in World War II. . . . Navy Capt. William D. Puleston is appointed as the new commander of the battleship *Mississippi*.	*The Annalist* releases its weekly index of U.S. business activity. At 60.8, the figure is a drop of 0.7 points from the previous week, and a reduction of 21 percent from the corresponding period last year. Economists say the drop from last week was caused by losses in freight car loadings, electric power production, automobile production, and cotton cloth production.		The comedic film *The Expert* is released throughout the United States. The film is directed by Archie Mayo, and stars Lois Wilson, both of whom are Hollywood Walk of Fame recipients.	Mar. 6
		Prof. Irving Fisher of Yale University releases his weekly index of international stock prices. The figure is 52.4, a rise of 0.8 points from the preceding week, but a decline of approximately 51 percent from the corresponding week a year ago.			Mar. 7
Charles Lindbergh receives a letter from his son's kidnappers demanding a ransom sum of $50,000 for the safe return of the 20-month-old infant.	The destroyer *Sturtevant* is recommissioned by the U.S. Navy after more than three months of inactivity. Constructed in 1918 by the New York Shipbuilding Company, *Sturtevant* would become the victim of a mine detonation off the coast of Florida on May 8, 1942.	The weekly index of U.S. automobile production as compiled by the Department of Commerce is released. The index currently stands at 36.5, a decrease of 0.5 points from the previous week, and a decline of 38 percent from the corresponding week one year ago.		In an exhibition rematch of the 1931 World Series, the Philadelphia Athletics defeat the St. Louis Cardinals by a score of 4–2.	Mar. 8
The Senate passes a bill appropriating $188 million for the Agriculture Department.	The U.S. Navy recommissions the destroyer *Reuben James* after more than a year of being out of service. Constructed in 1919 by the New York Shipbuilding Corporation, *Reuben James* will be sunk by the German submarine *U-552* near Iceland on October 31, 1941, an incident that will increase tensions in the run-up to the U.S. entry into World War II.	*The Iron Age* releases its weekly index of U.S. steel mill activity. The index currently stands at 28.9, a rise of 1.2 points from the previous week, but a decline of approximately 52 percent from the corresponding week one year ago.			Mar. 9
The Associated General Contractors of America urges Congress to issue a $3 billion bond for public works projects. . . . An editorial in the *New York Times* declares that the Lindbergh kidnapping indicates that the United States has descended into "moral bankruptcy."	The destroyer *Bainbridge* is transferred by U.S. naval authorities to the Rotating Reserve Division 19, effectively placing it in reduced commission. *Bainbridge* was constructed in 1920 by the New York Shipbuilding Corporation.	*Dun's Review* releases its weekly index of U.S. freight car loadings. The index currently stands at 60.8, a drop of 0.7 points from the previous week, and a decline of approximately 22 percent from the corresponding week one year ago.		RKO Pictures' drama film *The Lost Squadron*, starring Hollywood Walk of Fame recipients Mary Astor and Richard Dix, is released throughout the United States.	Mar. 10
Convicted gangster Al Capone offers to use his seedy underworld connections to locate the missing infant son of Charles Lindbergh if released from prison.		Prof. Irving Fisher of Yale University releases his weekly index of international commodity prices. The figure is 63.3, a rise of 0.4 points from the preceding week, but a decline of approximately 17 percent from the corresponding week a year ago.		The Academy Award-winning film *Shanghai Express* is released in Denmark. . . . The dramatic film *The Big Timer* is released throughout the United States. The film stars Hollywood Walk of Fame recipients Ben Lyon, Constance Cummings, and Thelma Todd.	Mar. 11
The First National Bank of Chicago reduces its annual dividend rate from 18 percent to 12 percent.	The U.S. Navy transfers the destroyer *Fairfax* from the Atlantic Coast to the Pacific Coast. *Fairfax* was constructed in 1917 by the Mare Island Navy Yard, and would become one of many ships given to Great Britain as part of the U.S.-U.K. Destroyer for Bases Agreement.	*Dun's Review* releases its weekly index of U.S. business failures. At 161.9, the figure is a rise of 5.4 points from the previous week, and a gain of 11 points from the corresponding week one year ago.		The comedic short film *The Nickel Nurser* is released throughout the United States. The film stars Charley Chase, Thelma Todd, and Billy Gilbert, all of whom are Hollywood Walk of Fame recipients.	Mar. 12
Gold prospectors discover a large quantity of gold in the Platte River near Denver, Colo. . . . *The American Banker* reports that a total of 11 banking institutions with deposits amounting to $990,000 have closed their doors since March 1, 1932.		*The Annalist* releases its weekly index of U.S. business activity. At 60.7, the figure is a drop of 0.3 points from the previous week, and a decline of 21 percent from the corresponding period last year. Economists say the drop from last week was caused by losses in freight car loadings and cotton cloth production.		The dramatic romance film *Bought* is released throughout the United States. The film is directed by Archie Mayo and stars Constance Bennett and Ben Lyon, all of whom are Hollywood Walk of Fame recipients.	Mar. 13
		Prof. Irving Fisher of Yale University releases his weekly index of international stock prices. The figure is 54.0, a rise of 1.6 points from the preceding week, but a decline of approximately 50 percent from the corresponding week a year ago.		The Portuguese-language dramatic film *Anchieta Entre o Amor e Religiao* is released in Brazil. . . . The dramatic romance film *I Take This Woman*, starring Hollywood Walk of Fame recipients Gary Cooper and Carole Lombard, is released throughout the United States.	Mar. 14

F	G	H	I	J
Includes elections, federal-state relations, civil rights and liberties, crime, the judiciary, education, healthcare, poverty, urban affairs, and population.	Includes formation and debate of U.S. foreign and defense policies, veterans affairs, and defense spending. (Relations with specific foreign countries are usually found under the region concerned.)	Includes business, labor, agriculture, taxation, transportation, consumer affairs, monetary and fiscal policy, natural resources, pollution, and accidents.	Includes worldwide scientific, medical, and technological developments, natural phenomena, U.S. weather, and natural disasters.	Includes the arts, religion, scholarship, communications media, sports, entertainment, fashions, fads, and social life.

	World Affairs	Europe	Africa & The Middle East	The Americas	Asia & The Pacific
Mar. 15			Capitulating to pressure exerted by prominent Arab leaders, Great Britain bans the showing of the film *Tell England*, which depicts the military prowess of the British army, in the city of Jerusalem.		
Mar. 16	U.S. Secretary of State Henry Stimson tells reporters that the domestic situation in China is "as peaceful as a young mother on a May evening."	A bill is introduced in the Icelandic parliament that would permit the sale of beer with an alcoholic content of less than 4 percent.			Four munitions factories in the Chinese city of Canton are destroyed by massive explosions. Officials blame the incident on Communist bandits.
Mar. 17		The French Committee for European Cooperation proposes an international five-year public works program. . . . American bodybuilder Bernarr MacFadden is given the ceremonial title of Commander of the Order of the Crown of Italy by King Victor Emanuel. . . . Great Britain purchases 2.1 million cubic meters of timber from the Soviet Union. . . . St. Patrick's Day is celebrated throughout Ireland.		Police in Havana, Cuba, receive an anonymous tip that the missing infant of aviator Charles Lindbergh was spotted in the Mariano district. A subsequent exhaustive search lasting hours proves futile.	Ten Japanese miners working underground in Nagasaki are killed by a sudden gas explosion. . . . Fifty thousand Chinese soldiers are dispatched to the city of Kiangsi to protect against a possible Communist subversion plot.
Mar. 18		Fernando de Rosa, who attempted to assassinate Prince Humber of Italy in October 1929, is released from prison.			Two divisions of Communist troops are slaughtered by an overwhelming force of Chinese soldiers in the city of Kiangsi.
Mar. 19	British statesman Winston Churchill characterizes Indian revolutionary Mohandas Gandhi as a "half-naked holy man."	French Ambassador to the United States Paul Claudel predicts the imminent creation of a United States of Europe.			A Chinese Communist horde mounts an unsuccessful campaign to capture the Chinese city of Hankow, and is driven off by the Chinese National Army. Casualties on both sides number in the thousands.
Mar. 20	U.S. Ambassador to Japan W. Cameron Forbes announces his retirement. His post is succeeded by U.S. ambassador to Turkey Joseph Grew. Emperor Hirohito of Japan praises Cameron as a skilled statesman.			Eighteen Nicaraguan National Guardsmen quell a putsch attempted by a force of bandits numbering 250 men.	China and Japan agree to a preliminary armistice agreement. Negotiations are conducted between Chinese Vice Foreign Minister Quo Tai-chi and Japanese Ambassador to China Mamoru Shiegemitsu.
Mar. 21			Egyptian Premier Ismail Pasha narrowly escapes an assassination attempt in the capital of Cairo. A bomb explodes on a street only minutes before Pasha's arrival.	Brazilian newspapers report that the Brazilian state of Rio Grande do Sul has descended into revolt, refusing to continue "political relations" with President Getulio Vargas's national government.	
Mar. 22	Brazilian Ambassador to the United States R. de Lima e Silva plays down repeated reports of a revolt in the state of Rio Grande do Sul.	Police in Spain uncover a Communist plot financed by the Soviet Union, the intent of which was to overthrow the existing political order in April 1932. Ramon Casanellas, who assassinated Premier Eduardo Dato in 1921, is arrested in connection with the plot.		The Canadian Dominion Bureau of Statistics reports that the Province of Quebec's population has increased by 17 percent since 1921, from 2,361,655 to 2,874,255.	

A	B	C	D	E
Includes developments that affect more than one world region, international organizations, and important meetings of world leaders.	Includes all domestic and regional developments in Europe, including the Soviet Union.	Includes all domestic and regional developments in Africa and the Middle East.	Includes all domestic and regional developments in Latin America, the Caribbean, and Canada.	Includes all domestic and regional developments in Asian and Pacific nations (and colonies).

U.S. Politics & Social Issues	U.S. Foreign Policy & Defense	Economics & Great Depression	Science, Technology & Nature	Culture, Leisure & Lifestyle	
A bill is introduced on the House floor that would grant independence to the Philippines eight years after its passage. . . . U.S. economic officials report that the total 1931 federal income tax revenue was the lowest yearly total since the end of World War I.		The weekly index of U.S. automobile production as compiled by the Department of Commerce is released. The index currently stands at 36.9, a rise of 0.3 points from the previous week, but a decline of 39 percent from the corresponding week one year ago.	The Ontario Cancer Commission predicts that if a cure for cancer is not found, "at least one in ten of the adults now alive" will contract the disease within their lifetime.	The dramatic film *Vanity Fair* is released throughout the United States. The film is written by F. Hugh Hubert and stars Myrna Loy, both of whom are Academy Award nominees.	Mar. 15
		The Iron Age releases its weekly index of U.S. steel mill activity. The index currently stands at 29.3, a rise of 0.4 points from the previous week, but a decline of approximately 50 percent from the corresponding week one year ago.		The comedic film *The Wiser Sex*, starring Academy Award winners Claudette Colbert and Melvyn Douglas, is released throughout the United States. . . . The animated short *Crosby, Columbo, and Vallee*, directed by Academy Award nominee Rudolf Ising, is released throughout the United States.	Mar. 16
		Dun's Review releases its weekly index of U.S. freight car loadings. The index currently stands at 60.6, a drop of 0.7 points from the previous week, but a decline of approximately 22 percent from the corresponding week one year ago.		Metro-Goldwyn-Mayer's pro-Prohibition drama film *The Wet Parade* is released throughout the United States. The film is directed by Victor Fleming and stars Robert Young, Lewis Stone, Walter Huston, Jimmy Durante, Myrna Loy, and Neil Hamilton, all of whom are Hollywood Walk of Fame recipients.	Mar. 17
Senator Warren Barbour attributes the Lindbergh kidnapping to Prohibition, claiming that the Eighteenth Amendment has created a culture of crime within the United States. . . . Rep. John Moore of Kentucky introduces a bill that would reduce U.S. annual immigration by quotas by more than 90 percent.		Prof. Irving Fisher of Yale University releases his weekly index of international commodity prices. The figure is 63.1, a drop of 0.2 points from the preceding week, and a decline of approximately 17 percent from the corresponding week a year ago.		The dramatic romance film *Love Affair*, starring Hollywood Walk of Fame recipient Humphrey Bogart, is released throughout the United States.	Mar. 18
The American Tobacco Company reports a record yearly profit of $46,189,741 for 1930. The increased tobacco sales are likely attributable to consumers' stress caused by depressive economic conditions. . . . Senator Thomas Connally of Texas introduces a bill that would suspend payment of all federal government employees' salaries until June 30, 1933.		*Dun's Review* releases its weekly index of U.S. business failures. At 168.3, the figure is a rise of 6.4 points from the previous week, and a gain of 29.3 points from the corresponding week one year ago.		The adventure film *Carnival Boat* is released throughout the United States. The film stars Hollywood Walk of Fame recipients William Boyd, Ginger Rogers, Hobart Bosworth, Marie Prevost, and Edward Kennedy. . . . The German language film *Funf von der Jazzband* (Five of the Jazzband), starring German Film Award winner Jenny Jugo, is released in Austria.	Mar. 19
Predicting his defeat in the 1932 presidential election, Illinois Republicans request President Herbert Hoover to withdraw his name for his party's nomination.		*The Annalist* releases its weekly index of U.S. business activity. At 60.1, the figure is a drop of 0.3 points from the previous week and a reduction of 23 percent from the corresponding period last year. Economists say the drop from last week was caused by losses in freight car loadings, steel mill activity, and automobile production.		The musical comedy short *Billboard Girl* is released throughout the United States. The film is written by Lewis Foster and stars Bing Crosby, both of whom are Academy Award winners.	Mar. 20
	The Veterans' Administration estimates that total expenditures relating to providing relief to veterans of all past American wars, including the Civil War and the Spanish American War, will rise to $16 million by 1933.	Prof. Irving Fisher of Yale University releases his weekly index of international stock prices. The figure is 50.9, a drop of 3.1 points from the preceding week, and a decline of approximately 53 percent from the corresponding week a year ago.		The German-language comedy film *Der Sieger* (The Victor) is released in Germany. The film is co-written by legendary filmmaker Billy Wilder, winner of five Academy Awards. . . . The western film *Whistlin' Dan*, starring Hollywood Walk of Fame recipient Ken Maynard, is released throughout the United States.	Mar. 21
	The U.S. Navy transfers the destroyer *Sicard* from Hawaii to the waters off San Diego, Calif. *Sicard* was constructed in 1919 by the Bath Iron Works Co.	The weekly index of U.S. automobile production as compiled by the Department of Commerce is released. The index currently stands at 34.8, a drop of 2.1 points from the previous week, and a decline of 43 percent from the corresponding week one year ago.		The musical-comedy film *One Hour with You* is released throughout the United States. The film is directed by George Cukor and stars Maurice Chevalier, Jeanette MacDonald, Genevieve Tobin, Charles Ruggles, and Roland Young, all of whom are Hollywood Walk of Fame recipients. *One Hour with You* would be nominated for the 1932 Academy Award for Best Picture.	Mar. 22

F	G	H	I	J
Includes elections, federal-state relations, civil rights and liberties, crime, the judiciary, education, healthcare, poverty, urban affairs, and population.	Includes formation and debate of U.S. foreign and defense policies, veterans affairs, and defense spending. (Relations with specific foreign countries are usually found under the region concerned.)	Includes business, labor, agriculture, taxation, transportation, consumer affairs, monetary and fiscal policy, natural resources, pollution, and accidents.	Includes worldwide scientific, medical, and technological developments, natural phenomena, U.S. weather, and natural disasters.	Includes the arts, religion, scholarship, communications media, sports, entertainment, fashions, fads, and social life.

	World Affairs	Europe	Africa & The Middle East	The Americas	Asia & The Pacific
Mar. 23		British economists predict that Great Britain's federal budget surplus will rise to $50 million by the end of the current fiscal year.		Cuban revolutionaries, or "terrorists" as they are referred to by police authorities, detonate a bomb near the home of Senator Horacio Diaz Pardos.	American economists report that Indian revolutionary Mohandas Gandhi's civil disobedience campaign has had the unintended consequence of lessening U.S. trade to India by more than 40 percent.... Chinese military officials report that total losses resulting from the Japanese invasion of Manchuria amount to over $500 million.
Mar. 24		President Eamon de Valera of Ireland declares that his citizens will no longer pay tribute to Great Britain by reciting the oath of allegiance of the Free State Dail to the British Crown. . . . The German Reichstag sets its federal budget for the upcoming fiscal year at $2 billion.		The German airship *Graf Zeppelin* flies over the skies of Brazil, delighting the skyward-gazing Brazilian crowd.	Japan begins to formulate plans to colonize the war-torn region of Manchuria with Japanese settlers.
Mar. 25	The League of Nations calls on its members to grant liberal financial loans to Austria, which is struggling under mounting burdens of debt.				
Mar. 26		The French Chamber of Deputies issues a $139 million bond for public works projects to provide employment to idle workers.		President Getulio Vargas of Brazil appoints Rio Grande do Sul Governor Flores de Cunha to the post of Justice Minister.	Japanese War Minister Gen. Sadao Araki threatens that his country will withdraw from the League of Nations if international hostility toward Japan's military actions in the Far East continues.
Mar. 27	A German organization, The Committee for Saving the Scottsboro Victims, pleads with U.S. President Herbert Hoover to federally pardon the Scottsboro Boys, eight African Americans sentenced to death for the rape of a white woman in Scottsboro, Ala.	The doctor of the late French foreign minister Aristide Briand reveals to reporters that Briand's intense worry over whether his 1928 Pact of Paris would achieve its objective contributed to his ailing health.		Bolivia raises tariffs on imported liquor. Funds gained from the increased tariffs will be used to finance education, officials say.	
Mar. 28	Diplomats at the League of Nations express the belief that Japan will not take the initiative to withdraw from the League of Nations.			A bill is introduced in the Peruvian Congress that would nationalize Peru's oil industry.	
Mar. 29		A group of Moldavian rebels allege that during the past three months, a total of 1,000 Moldavians have been shot at and killed by Soviet police authorities while trying to cross the border and emigrate into Romania.		In a special session of Congress, Argentina reduces its federal budget by 24,864,952 pesos.	
Mar. 30		The French Chamber of Deputies passes a bill raising tariffs on most dutiable items by an average of 2 percent. . . . The German airship *Graf Zeppelin* returns from its tour of Brazil.		The U.S. Ambassador to Nicaragua, Matthew Hanna, sails to the capital of Managua to oversee upcoming presidential elections.	Two Chinese army regiments start a mutiny, breaking free from their superior officers and seizing the city of Piangshek.

A	B	C	D	E
Includes developments that affect more than one world region, international organizations, and important meetings of world leaders.	Includes all domestic and regional developments in Europe, including the Soviet Union.	Includes all domestic and regional developments in Africa and the Middle East.	Includes all domestic and regional developments in Latin America, the Caribbean, and Canada.	Includes all domestic and regional developments in Asian and Pacific nations (and colonies).

U.S. Politics & Social Issues	U.S. Foreign Policy & Defense	Economics & Great Depression	Science, Technology & Nature	Culture, Leisure & Lifestyle	
Senator Alben Barkley of Kentucky officially endorses New York Governor Franklin Roosevelt for the 1932 presidential election.		*The Iron Age* releases its weekly index of U.S. steel mill activity. The index currently stands at 28.0, a drop of 1.3 points from the previous week, and a decline of approximately 52 percent from the corresponding week one year ago.		The comedic film *Disorderly Conduct* is released throughout the United States. The film is directed by John Considine and stars Spencer Tracy, Ralph Bellamy, and Ralph Morgan, all of whom are Hollywood Walk of Fame recipients.	Mar. 23
House Appropriations Committee chairman Rep. Joseph Byrns introduces a bill that would reduce all government employee salaries by 11 percent, saving the American taxpayer approximately $67 million annually.		*Dun's Review* releases its weekly index of U.S. freight car loadings. The index currently stands at 59.0, a drop of 0.9 points from the previous week, and a decline of approximately 24 percent from the corresponding week one year ago.		The German-language mystery film *Das Blaue Licht (The Blue Light)* is released throughout Germany. The film features the performance of future Nazi propagandist Leni Riefenstahl, creator of *The Triumph of the Will*. Eerily, one of the film's characters is an infant played by a one-month-old boy named Beni Fuhrer.	Mar. 24
Rep. Patrick J. Boland calls for an embargo on Soviet coal, contending that most of it is produced through forced labor. Treasury Secretary Ogden Mills responds by saying that a complete embargo is impossible under present tariff agreements. . . . By a vote of 6–1, the Alabama Supreme Court upholds a lower court ruling of guilt for eight African Americans who were accused in early 1931 of raping a white girl in the city of Scottsboro. The date for their execution is scheduled for May 13, 1932.		Prof. Irving Fisher of Yale University releases his weekly index of international commodity prices. The figure is 63.0, a drop of 0.1 points from the preceding week, and a decline of approximately 17 percent from the corresponding week a year ago.		The action adventure film *Tarzan the Ape Man* is released throughout the United States. The film is directed by W.S. Van Dyke and stars Johnny Weissmuller, Neil Hamilton, Maureen O'Sullivan, and C. Aubrey Smith, all of whom are Hollywood Walk of Fame recipients.	Mar. 25
Senator William Borah publicly advocates the cutting of government expenditures in order to balance the federal budget.	The destroyer *Evans* is transferred by the U.S. Navy from the Atlantic Coast to the Pacific Coast. *Evans* was constructed in 1918 by the Bath Iron Works Co., and will become one of many ships transferred to Great Britain as part of the U.S.-U.K. Destroyers for Bases Agreement.	*Dun's Review* releases its weekly index of U.S. business failures. At 174.0, the figure is a rise of 1.7 points from the previous week, and a gain of 39.1 points from the corresponding week one year ago.		The German-language film *Das Geheimnis des Femdenlegionars (Sergeant X)* is released throughout Germany. The film stars German Film Award winner Trude von Molo.	Mar. 26
Senator Warren Barbour of New Jersey delivers a statewide radio address in which he asks the people of New Jersey to fully support him in his efforts to eliminate "overlapping and unnecessary government activity."		*The Annalist* releases its weekly index of U.S. business activity. At 61.3, the figure is a rise of 0.3 points from the previous week, but a decline of 22 percent from the corresponding period last year. Economists say the rise from last week was caused by gains in freight car loadings.		The dramatic film *Are You Listening?* is released throughout the United States. The film is directed by Harry Beaumont and stars William Haines, Madge Evans, Anita Page, and Neil Hamilton, all of whom are Hollywood Walk of Fame recipients. . . . The comedic short film *The Flirty Sleepwalker*, starring Hollywood Walk of Fame recipient Betty Grable, is released throughout the United States.	Mar. 27
The National Committee of Republican Women for the World Court criticizes Senate Foreign Relations Committee chairman William Borah for his efforts to delay the vote on a proposal for the United States to join the Permanent Court of International Justice. . . . *The Pathfinder* releases the results of a mock presidential election. Of the 235,000 polled nationwide, 115,042 voted for Herbert Hoover, while 49,626 voted for New York Governor Franklin Roosevelt.		Prof. Irving Fisher of Yale University releases his weekly index of international stock prices. The figure is 49.0, a drop of 1.9 points from the preceding week, and a decline of approximately 50 percent from the corresponding week a year ago.		The comedy film *The Cohens and Kellys in Hollywood* is released throughout the United States. The film stars Hollywood Walk of Fame recipient Charles Murray.	Mar. 28
By a vote of 203–132, the House votes down a bill that would have provided $100 million in relief for needy farmers. . . . The annual Easter egg roll ceremony is held at the White House with 11,000 participants.		*The Iron Age* releases its weekly index of U.S. steel mill activity. The index currently stands at 27.2, a drop of 0.8 points from the previous week, and a decline of approximately 53 percent from the corresponding week one year ago.	An unseasonable blizzard on the East Coast of the United States claims 12 lives.	The Swedish-language film *Landskamp* is released throughout Sweden. The film features the first appearance of Ingrid Bergman, considered by many film critics to be one of the greatest actresses of all time.	Mar. 29
	The destroyer *Wainwright*, constructed in 1914 by the New York Shipbuilding Company, is transferred by U.S. naval authorities to the waters near St. Petersburg, Fla.	*Dun's Review* releases its weekly index of U.S. freight car loadings. The index currently stands at 62.1, a rise of 0.7 points from the previous week, but a decline of approximately 22 percent from the corresponding week one year ago		The Danish-language comedic film *I kantonnement* is released in Denmark. The film stars Bodil Award winner Poul Reichhardt. . . . The German-language film *Der Raub der Mona Lisa*, starring German Film Award winners Trude von Molo and Willi Frost, is released throughout the United States.	Mar. 30

F	G	H	I	J
Includes elections, federal-state relations, civil rights and liberties, crime, the judiciary, education, healthcare, poverty, urban affairs, and population.	Includes formation and debate of U.S. foreign and defense policies, veterans affairs, and defense spending. (Relations with specific foreign countries are usually found under the region concerned.)	Includes business, labor, agriculture, taxation, transportation, consumer affairs, monetary and fiscal policy, natural resources, pollution, and accidents.	Includes worldwide scientific, medical, and technological developments, natural phenomena, U.S. weather, and natural disasters.	Includes the arts, religion, scholarship, communications media, sports, entertainment, fashions, fads, and social life.

	World Affairs	Europe	Africa & The Middle East	The Americas	Asia & The Pacific
Mar. 31	Turkey and Yugoslavia announce the signing of an economic pact designed to stimulate cooperation between each country's opium trade.	As a measure to decrease traffic congestion, Germany limits the number of taxi cabs able to cruise the streets of the capital of Berlin each day.			Chinese Gen. Chiang Kai-shek hosts a group of diplomats sent by the League of Nations to investigate ongoing tensions between China and Japan.
Apr. 1	The League of Nations Financial Committee reports in Geneva that tariffs and debts are blocking the way to world recovery from the Depression. It is especially worried about Austria, Greece, Bulgaria, and Hungary.	Thousands flee the Italian village of Villa Santo Stefano, as their homes sink into a series of caves beneath the town. Premier Benito Mussolini orders nearby towns to provide accommodations for the refugees.	Sixty Akamba youths in Kenya who were convicted of killing a woman thought to be a witch have their death sentences commuted by the governor.		Japan sends 5,000 soldiers to Manchuria to help the 30,000 already there to quell disturbances. Foreign observers think it will take twice that many.
Apr. 2	League of Nations leaders are pleased that U.S. Secretary of State Henry Stimson is coming to Geneva. He will be the first U.S. Secretary of State to sit in on a League session.		British archaeologist John Gerstang writes that the walls of Jericho fell as the result of an earthquake, not because Joshua blew his trumpet as the Biblical account claims.	Sixteen bandits who wrecked a train going from Laredo to Mexico City and killed four trainmen are shot by a firing squad. The government is looking for about 35 more bandits who were involved in the attack.	Chinese Gen. Chiang Kai-shek insists that Manchuria is still part of China and Manchukuo does not exist. He says the Chinese will resist a Japanese takeover of the area.
Apr. 3	Sir James Arthur Salter, finance director of the League of Nations, believes the hope of the world depends on America's ability to pull out of the Depression.	In spite of plans to abolish the oath of allegiance to the Crown, the Irish Free State still wants to maintain ties with Great Britain. President Eamon de Valera accepts a bid to the Ottawa conference.			Fighting continues in Manchuria, as combined Japanese and Manchukuo forces defeat a large insurgent army at Ningtuo. The Japanese rush in more troops from Korea, 80 miles away.
Apr. 4	Naotake Sato, Japanese delegate to the League of Nations, denies that Japanese authorities have seized Manchurian revenue.	After 15 hours of discussion, British Prime Minister Ramsay MacDonald and French Premier Andre Tardieu agree on three points. The Danubian states, including Austria, Romania, Czechoslovakia, Yugoslavia, and Hungary, should have their own conference and the four powers should not be part of it. They also agree on the need for aid to the Danubian states.	Abyssinian emperor Haile Selassie promises to end slavery in the country within 15 years. Slave trading has already been banned and carries a death penalty.	Rafael Sanchez Aballi, former ambassador to the United States from Cuba, dies in Havana. Before becoming ill, Aballi had been Secretary of Communications in the current administration.	In a revolt against the dictatorship of the governing Koumintang party of China, north China leaders secede from the party. The development comes as a shock, since the party members had been hand-picked to assure their loyalty.
Apr. 5	The League of Nations Committee on Traffic in Women and Children rejects a proposal by Germany that it look into the effect that times of economic depression have on vice.	At the flying field in Danzig, Germany, 35,000 people assemble to enthusiastically cheer Adolf Hitler.	Margery Durant is delayed at Kampala, East Africa, with propeller trouble on her plane. Durant, daughter of the pioneer automobile manufacturer, is in Africa on a hunting trip with her pilot and mechanic.	In Newfoundland, an angry mob of approximately 10,000 people wrecks the legislative building in St. John. The mob also beats Prime Minister Richard Squires until he promises to resign.	India announces that the All-India Congress will hold a special session in New Delhi at the end of April. India will attend the Imperial Economic Conference to be held at Ottawa.
Apr. 6	The financial committee of the League of Nations is reported to want U.S. Ambassador Norman H. Davis to serve as an envoy from the League to the Danubian states in the upcoming conference. Davis says he has heard of the plan, but declines to discuss it since no official action has been taken.	Britain refuses to recognize that the new state of Manchukuo exists. They do not answer a communication asking them to open diplomatic relations with the new country.	Brig. Gen. Henry Rowan-Robinson, Inspector General of the Iraq Army, is wounded by a bullet from Kurdish snipers.	Chile reports that Bolivia has amassed nearly 100 planes in the disputed Chaco area, supposedly in preparation for an attack on Paraguay. La Paz denies the reports. . . . In an attempt to balance the budget, Canada will raise taxes for a total increase of $55 million.	Chinese Vice Minister of Foreign Affairs Quo Tai-Chi announces that armistice talks with Japan will probably be cut off and the matter put into the hands of the League of Nations.
Apr. 7	The Danubian parley fails as Italy and Germany refuse to give favored-nation status to the Danubian states.	After Adolf Hitler sends stormtroopers to distribute pamphlets during the election, Bavaria bans the Nazis from assembling between Saturday and Monday.	Astronomers at the Cape of Good Hope Royal Observatory in South Africa discover a new comet, located near the south pole of the skies.	Chile's Cabinet resigns after a run on the Central Bank alarms the government. The president requests martial law.	
Apr. 8	Japan threatens to withdraw from the League of Nations if Article XV, which would involve the League in the Manchurian dispute, is applied.	Followers of German President Paul von Hindenburg jam the square in Berlin, demonstrating for him and against the Nazis.		Bolivia accuses Paraguay of being bellicose because of its refusal to consider a nonaggression pact. Bolivia says it has no plans to attack Paraguay.	
Apr. 9	Four League of Nations meetings will be in progress in Geneva next week. They include the arms conference, the Danubian parley, the annual conference of the international labor organization, and discussion of the Far East conflict.	France reports it has cut the number of men in its army but has added officers, so more officers are commanding fewer units.	The Union of South Africa and the Protectorate of Southwest Africa reach agreement on naturalization, parliamentary powers, and adoption of three languages.	Brazilians living in the northeastern states of that country are driven into the cities in search of food due to a severe drought.	
Apr. 10		Paul von Hindenburg beats Adolf Hitler by 6 million votes in the German elections. Communists are also badly defeated.	British Arabic scholar H. St. John Philby discovers the capitals of two ancient kingdoms buried beneath the Arabian Desert.	The Ecuadorian navy is in the hands of rebels who continue to menace the port of Guayaquil, even though the government says the port is reopened.	Chinese Gen. Ting Chao is believed to have been assassinated by his own men in Manchuria. His aides were dissatisfied with his attitude toward Japan.

A	B	C	D	E
Includes developments that affect more than one world region, international organizations, and important meetings of world leaders.	*Includes all domestic and regional developments in Europe, including the Soviet Union.*	*Includes all domestic and regional developments in Africa and the Middle East.*	*Includes all domestic and regional developments in Latin America, the Caribbean, and Canada.*	*Includes all domestic and regional developments in Asian and Pacific nations (and colonies).*

U.S. Politics & Social Issues	U.S. Foreign Policy & Defense	Economics & Great Depression	Science, Technology & Nature	Culture, Leisure & Lifestyle	
		The weekly index of U.S. automobile production as compiled by the Department of Commerce is released. The index currently stands at 33.5, a drop of 1.3 points from the previous week, and a decline of 43 percent from the corresponding week one year ago.		Howard Hughes's crime drama film *Scarface* is released throughout the United States by The Caddo Co. The film is directed by Howard Hawks and stars Paul Muni and Ann Dvorak, all of whom are Hollywood Walk of Fame recipients. An artifact of its time, *Scarface* will be archived in 1994 by the U.S. National Film Preservation Board for the enjoyment of future generations.	Mar. 31
Thirty days after the Lindbergh baby's kidnapping, Maj. Charles H. Schoeffel of the New Jersey Police is on his way to England to check a new development in the case.		Speakers at the Eastern Regional Conference of the Child Welfare of League of America stress the importance of job security for parents in assuring the future welfare of children.	The League of Nations signs a convention regulating whaling. Right whales, calves, immature whales, and female whales accompanied by calves may not be killed.		Apr. 1
	The U.S. Army Air Corps tests equipment that makes it possible for a pilot to land in fog by use of instruments alone. The tests are done at Patterson Field in Dayton, Ohio.	Five leaders of the strike against the anthracite coal companies are fired, including Thomas Maloney, president of the Stanton Local Union in Pennsylvania.	Dr. William Hale Charch, an Ohioan living in Buffalo, receives the Jacob P. Schoelkopf gold medal for 1932 for his development of moisture-proof cellophane.		Apr. 2
The White House Conference on Child Health and Protection reports that 5,630,000 children in the United States are handicapped in their learning and need special help.	A Navy submarine chaser receives serious damage off the coast of California. *Eagle Boat P-34* collides with the freighter *Javanese Prince* six miles south of Point Vicente. No one is injured in the collision.		Marie Curie, co-discoverer of radium, has surgery on a cut on her elbow sustained in a fall last week. The cut has become infected.	Both NBC and CBS broadcast a message from Pope Pius XI, blessing all who aid peace and praising those striving to end the Depression.	Apr. 3
Senator Alben W. Barkley of Kentucky is chosen temporary chairman of the Democratic National Convention, which will begin on June 28. . . . The Philippine Independence Bill passes in the House.	Maj. Gen. William R. Smith announces his retirement from his position as Superintendent of the U.S. Military Academy at West Point, effective April 30.	The National Industrial Conference Board reports the cost of living in the United States has dropped 17 percent during the two-year period ending December 1931.	Several low-cost "parasol" monoplanes are shown at the National Air Show in Detroit. Prices range from $399 for an unassembled model to $1,990.	Stanley Cup play begins tonight as the New York Rangers meet the Toronto Maple Leaves at Madison Square Garden.	Apr. 4
President Hoover says that Secretary of State Henry Stimson is going to Geneva only to participate in the disarmament conference and will not participate in any discussions on war debts.	Ten people in New York City are indicted for trying to bribe U.S. Coast Guard members working on the south shore of Long Island to let them smuggle in liquor.	The Department of Agriculture gives crop loans to 125,448 farmers. The loans total $15,480.000. About 83,000 others applied.	A Mexican archaeologist discovers that the ancient Toltec pyramid is built over and around other ancient buildings. Exploratory tunnels are being dug and stone stairways and walls have already been discovered.		Apr. 5
John Curtis, who claims to have been in contact with an agent of the Lindbergh baby's kidnappers, says he met with that agent last weekend and was assured the baby was alive and well.		It is reported that over the past 15 fiscal years, U.S. government spending has exceeded its revenue by about $23.5 billion. The deficit was greatest during World War I.	On landing in Germany, Dr. Albert Einstein says he is very pleased with his interaction with American astronomers and physicists in Pasadena. He praises the United States for its interest in disarmament and its sympathy for Germany's economic problems.	The Boston Braves announce they will admit women for half-price on Monday, Tuesday, Wednesday, and Thursday. Admission for them will be free on Fridays.	Apr. 6
	At their seventh annual convention, the Chaplains' Association of the Army opposes any reduction in officer personnel and favors bringing the Navy up to treaty strength.		Trees along the Potomac in Washington are showing pink and white buds, heralding the famous cherry blossom season in the nation's capital.	The Boston Braves are the first team in the National League to put numbers on the uniforms of its players.	Apr. 7
A move in the House to abolish the Farm Board fails, as Congressmen vote 152–23 to retain it.	Twenty packing cases of petitions, containing 2,240,030 names, are delivered to the capital by over 1,200 veterans calling for early payment of their veterans' bonus.	The Department of Agriculture reports the winter wheat crop is down 42 percent from last year. About 12 percent was due to the abandonment of acreage and the rest to drought.	Johns Hopkins psychiatrist Dr. Adolf Meyer urges recognition of psychobiology, a new science that treats the mind and body together.	The North American semi-finals of the Davis Cup will be played in New Orleans and will pit Mexico against the winner of the United States vs. Canada match.	Apr. 8
A White House conference between President Herbert Hoover and the House Economy Committee recommends cutting salaries of the President, Cabinet, and Congress. . . . The government tries to trace serial numbers of bills used by Lindbergh to pay a $50,000 ransom to the kidnappers of his baby.	Hugh Gibson, acting chairman of the U.S. delegation to the arms conference, pushes to end the use of submarines and poison gas.	The proposed program of the House Economy Committee would reduce appropriations, cut salaries, and authorize charges for certain services.	The U.S. Coast and Geodetic Survey announces it has discovered a large submerged volcano about 30 miles off the coast of the Philippines.	Movie comedian Harpo Marx, one of the famous Marx Brothers, is seriously injured in an automobile accident in Hollywood.	Apr. 9
Although the Constitution forbids cutting a President's pay while he is in office, President Herbert Hoover says he will be willing to take a pay cut.		Hearings resume in the Senate Finance Committee, as Congress hopes to rush a tax bill through.	In a radio address from London, British astrophysicist James Jeans identifies the six top achievements in science. He names the discovery of electricity, discovery of the expanding universe, and the contributions of Newton, Einstein, Copernicus, and Darwin.	The Toronto Maple Leafs triumph over the New York Rangers to take the Stanley Cup, sweeping the series in a record-setting three games. They are the youngest team in professional hockey.	Apr. 10

F	G	H	I	J
Includes elections, federal-state relations, civil rights and liberties, crime, the judiciary, education, healthcare, poverty, urban affairs, and population.	Includes formation and debate of U.S. foreign and defense policies, veterans affairs, and defense spending. (Relations with specific foreign countries are usually found under the region concerned.)	Includes business, labor, agriculture, taxation, transportation, consumer affairs, monetary and fiscal policy, natural resources, pollution, and accidents.	Includes worldwide scientific, medical, and technological developments, natural phenomena, U.S. weather, and natural disasters.	Includes the arts, religion, scholarship, communications media, sports, entertainment, fashions, fads, and social life.

	World Affairs	Europe	Africa & The Middle East	The Americas	Asia & The Pacific
Apr. 11	The Chinese delegation asks the League of Nations committee to meet as soon as possible to review the situation in the Far East.	Even though Paul von Hindenburg won the German election, the French press worries about Adolf Hitler's gain in support, saying it bodes ill for the Geneva and Lausanne parleys.		The Argentine government offers to act as mediator in the dispute between Bolivia and Paraguay. Relations were broken off last July.	Japan pledges to ensure the safety of Chinese statesman Dr. Wellington Koo as he accompanies the League of Nations investigators on their tour of Manchuria.
Apr. 12	The Germans acclaim the arms proposal brought forth in Geneva by U.S. diplomat Hugh Gibson, but the French are opposed to it.	In a special session, the Prussian Diet amends its bylaws to require the premier to be elected by a majority in an attempt to keep the Nazis from coming to power.	Zionist leader Chaim Weizmann suffers from ptomaine poisoning after a dinner in his honor in Durban, South Africa. Thirty other guests also become ill.	The Paraguayan Cabinet meets to discuss Bolivian troop movements in the Chaco area, but dismisses the reports as "Bolivian sword rattling."	A troop train carrying 154 Japanese soldiers to Harbin is blown up by explosives. Eleven are dead and 93 injured.
Apr. 13	Sentiments at the arms parley in Geneva are divided, with Italy, Brazil, and Turkey backing the U.S. position and Poland, Uruguay, and Yugoslavia on the side of France.	It is reported that Irish Free State head Eamon de Valera will ask for an early election, giving him a mandate for an independent Irish republic.			Gen. Ma Chen-shan, who was believed to be a Japanese puppet in the Manchukuo government, announces he will oppose the new regime there.
Apr. 14	Japan refuses to participate in League of Nations discussions in Geneva about the situation in Shanghai.	German police implement President Paul von Hindenburg's decree to dissolve the Nazi stormtroopers with raids on 150 Nazi gathering places. Adolf Hitler says the decree will not put an end to the stormtroopers.	Starving Bedouins from northern Arabia are crossing into Trans-Jordan and begging for food. Some are well-known sheikhs.		Hundreds of jobless riot in the streets of Aukland, New Zealand. Most shop windows are broken and three policemen are seriously injured.
Apr. 15	League of Nations leaders look forward with interest to the arrival tomorrow of U.S. Secretary of State Henry Stimson. They are speculating on whether he will discuss Far Eastern matters, disarmament, or other issues.	Adolf Hitler says he will get the best lawyers to contest the legality of German President Paul von Hindenburg's edict to dissolve the Nazi stormtroopers.		Ash from the Chilean volcano that erupted last week has traveled 1,800 miles to Rio de Janeiro.	An all-day battle in the city of Changchow kills 2,000 Chinese Communists. A number of British missionaries are able to escape.
Apr. 16	The Earl of Lytton, chairman of the League of Nations inquiry commission, receives a long letter from Chinese Gen. Ma, who denounces Japanese imperialism. Ma is in Russia.		An American, W.H. Heinrichs, is appointed head of the Jerusalem YMCA.	Canada's parliament accepts the new budget, which increases federal taxes by 16 percent.	Schools close in Hankow, China. Teachers go on strike protesting more than four months without pay.
Apr. 17	The armament conference meeting in Geneva, Switzerland, must decide whether the arms reduction should be based on draft conventions, whether all criteria in Article VIII of the League covenant should be met, and whether the principle of qualitative reduction will be admitted.	German Communists, Nazis, and nationalists are defeated in their attempt to dissolve the Saxon Diet, as the referendum fails by 510,000 votes.		The Nicaraguan National Guard receives reports that Gen. Augusto Sandino plans an attack on the country next month.	Tens of thousands are killed by an earthquake in the northeastern Hupeh area of China. Reports say 70 percent of the houses in the town of Macheng crumbled with their inhabitants inside.
Apr. 18		Rumors throughout Scandinavia hold that Swedish industrialist Ivar Krueger fled from Paris to Sumatra rather than committing suicide. Paris police deny a cover-up.	An expedition led by Dr. William Bade determines that Tell en Nabesh is the ancient Biblical Mizpah, where Saul was chosen King.	The Chilean Chamber of Deputies passes a bill that will take the country off the gold standard. The president is expected to sign it.	All Americans are evacuated from areas of the interior of China that are believed to be unsafe due to a threat to the city of Changchow.
Apr. 19	The League of Nations asks Japan to completely evacuate Shanghai at once. The resolution is stronger than had been expected.	British Chancellor of the Exchequer Neville Chamberlain omits war debts from the budget, both those owed to the United States and those that Germany owes Britain.	Rev. Rowland H. Evans, head of the West Africa Mission of the Presbyterian Church, dies in Cameroon, West Africa.	A presidential decree in Havana requires all foreigners living in Cuba to obtain certificates, which they must carry with them at all times, from the Department of the Interior.	A 20-year-old Chinese girl leads irregulars in battle against Manchukuo troops in Manchuria. Locals call her the Chinese Joan of Arc.
Apr. 20		The bill that proposes to drop the oath of allegiance from the Irish Free State Constitution passes on its first reading, with only one no vote.		With 7,000 Bolivian troops amassed near the border, an attack on Paraguay appears imminent, according to Argentine papers.	The Japanese Minister of War says more troops will be sent to Manchuria if rebels continue to threaten the new government.
Apr. 21	The British Prime Minister, the French Premier, the German Chancellor, the U.S. Secretary of State, and the British and Italian Foreign Ministers meet in Geneva to discuss world problems. . . . Talks in Geneva on the Shanghai armistice are at a standstill, as both Japanese delegate Nagoaka and Paul Hymans, president of the 19-power commission, remain firm in their positions.	Britain's new tariff, averaging 20 percent on manufactured goods, is expected to cause great hardship for the United States. Over one-third of U.S. exports to Great Britain are manufactured goods.	The Iraqi government signs an oil contract with the British Oil Development Company, with the understanding that the British will be in control of development.	Thirty-five men are executed in Mexico for their parts in the attack last week on Paso del Macho. Twelve are released after proving they were forced to participate.	The Chinese government evacuates the port of Amoy as rebels are expected to capture the city at any time.
Apr. 22	The disarmament conference makes progress, adopting two resolutions. One approves the principle of qualitative disarmament and the other decides to do a study of air, land, and sea armaments.	The Hungarian parliament extends for one year the extraordinary economic powers it gave the government a few months ago.	British Col. Josiah Wedgwood, speaking to the House of Commons, accuses British officials in Palestine of being hostile to Jews.	The Peruvian government is authorized to petition the World Court, asking permission to collect taxes on oil-rich land leased by a British company.	Japan expresses irritation with the intention of the League of Nations to fix a date for Japanese troops to be withdrawn from Shanghai.

A	B	C	D	E
Includes developments that affect more than one world region, international organizations, and important meetings of world leaders.	Includes all domestic and regional developments in Europe, including the Soviet Union.	Includes all domestic and regional developments in Africa and the Middle East.	Includes all domestic and regional developments in Latin America, the Caribbean, and Canada.	Includes all domestic and regional developments in Asian and Pacific nations (and colonies).

U.S. Politics & Social Issues	U.S. Foreign Policy & Defense	Economics & Great Depression	Science, Technology & Nature	Culture, Leisure & Lifestyle	
	The U.S. Navy practices "force-firing" off the coast of California, with 104 ships and nearly 300 aircraft simulating a modern naval battle.		The new Patent Office in Washington, D.C., opens with many distinguished inventors and scientists attending the ceremony.	President Hoover throws out the first ball for the Washington Senators' opening game of the baseball season. The Senators defeat the Boston Red Sox.	Apr. 11
The Democratic Convention in Louisville, Ky., instructs its delegates to vote for Franklin Roosevelt as the presidential candidate. They favor Alben W. Barkley for vice president.		The United States exports 1,902,000 bushels of grain in the past week, which is four times the amount shipped out in the same period last year.	Prof. Ralph McKee of the Department of Chemical Engineering at Columbia University announces a scientific process to manufacture diamonds larger than any artificial diamonds ever made.	The University of Missouri football team goes on strike to protest the resignation of head coach Gwinn Henry. It is rumored that Henry was asked to resign.	Apr. 12
The "wets" in the House of Representatives have a petition bearing 96 names to sell 2.75 beer. They need 84 more to force a vote on the beer bill.	R. L. Sprague, U.S. Consul to Gibraltar, celebrates the 100th anniversary of his family's service there. His grandfather was appointed on April 30, 1832, his father succeeded him, and he was appointed following his father's death.		A new flashing electrical device expected to save money is introduced to the New York Electrical Society. The device could be used in railroad signals, moving street signs, and traffic signals.		Apr. 13
Col. Charles Lindbergh and his wife issue a statement emphasizing the importance of secrecy in dealing with the kidnappers of their infant son.		Andrew Mellon, new Ambassador to the Court of St. James in London, expresses optimism that the United States and Britain will be instrumental in helping world recovery from the Depression.	Vincent Astor's yacht returns from a cruise in the South Seas, bearing specimens for the New York Aquarium. These include penguins, tortoises, and brightly-colored tropical fish.		Apr. 14
	On its maiden voyage from Buffalo to Anacosta Naval Base near Washington, the U.S. Navy's newest seaplane becomes stuck in the ice. Divers clear away the ice and the boat is pulled to shore.	Bond prices on the Stock Exchange soar, helping to ease recent losses. Many commodities are up 1 to 6 points.	Dr. J.D. Long of the U.S. Public Health Service goes to inspect work being done on bubonic plague in Peru. He has directed the project for several years.	Well-known potter Susan Frackelton, creator of award-winning Frackelton blue and gray ware, dies at the age of 85.	Apr. 15
President Herbert Hoover explains his plan for government economy, which would save over $225 million through staggered furloughs for federal employees rather than pay cuts.	Rear Admiral Jehu V. Chase replaces Rear Admiral Mark L. Bristol as head of the Navy General Board. Bristol will retire May 1.		Engineers Allen Carpe, E.P. Beckwith, and Theodore Coven head for Alaska, where they will measure the cosmic rays on Mt. McKinley.	Coleman Clark of Chicago wins the Parker Cup, denoting him national U.S. amateur ping pong champion.	Apr. 16
Raids by Prohibition agents on speakeasies and illicit stills increase in Chicago, as they attempt to "clean up" the city before the political conventions.	The new Navy seaplane XP2Y1, its largest, flies from Buffalo to the Anacosta Naval Air Station near Washington in just three hours and 10 minutes.	Vessels sailing from the East Coast are delayed as longshoremen strike in protest against lowering of wages.	Smoke from a New Jersey industrial plant is determined to be hazardous to the health of those who live nearby. Fumes also kill vegetation in the area.	Twelve teams compete in Montreal's six-day bicycle race. The U.S. team of Reggie McNamara and Horace Horan is one of the favorites.	Apr. 17
	A veteran who chauffeured Gen. John Pershing and President Herbert Hoover appeals to the House Ways and Means Committee to pass the Bonus Bill.	The House Economy Committee agrees to incorporate all economy proposals into one bill as President Herbert Hoover requested.	Dr. Louis Leakey's expedition discovers an ancient jawbone near Lake Victoria in Africa. It is believed to be that of the earliest modern man.	The Mason-Dixon tennis tournament opens, with members of the Davis Cup team participating. These include Ellsworth Vines, John Van Ryn, Frank X. Shields, and Wilmer Allison. . . . U.S. cyclists Reggie McNamara and Horace Horan lead in the Montreal bicycle race.	Apr. 18
Senator William Borah, in a speech to the Senate, opposes cancellation of European war debts at this time.	Even though Admiral Pratt has warned that further reductions in the U.S. Navy's budget could threaten security, the House Appropriations Committee recommends sharp reduction.	A House banking subcommittee approves Herbert Hoover's home loan bank bill with little change. It now goes to the full committee.		Attendance drops at American League games, while holding steady in the National League during the first week of the major league baseball season.	Apr. 19
The 50th day since the kidnapping of Charles Lindbergh, Jr., passes with no word of the missing baby.	Navy fliers protest slashes in flying pay, saying civilians in hazardous jobs receive higher pay. Army fliers worry their pay will also be cut.	President Herbert Hoover worries that the Senate's stringent economies will cost the country 6,000 jobs.	Dr. E. Starr Judd, president of the American Medical Association, says human life expectancy has reached 58 years, up from 33 years in 1800.	Teachers at the annual convention of the American Physical Education Association urge changes in women's basketball rules to make it more like the men's game.	Apr. 20
The House Economy Committee agrees on a plan to reduce costs. It includes 11 percent pay cuts in federal salaries and combining the War and Navy Departments.			Dr. George W. Crile tells the American Philosophical Society that animal energy is derived from explosions in the cells.	Olympic officials prepare for an average of 350,000 people per day attending the upcoming Olympic Games in Los Angeles, Calif.	Apr. 21
Newton D. Baker, former secretary of war and possible Democratic candidate for president, still backs the repeal of Prohibition, saying control belongs with the states.	Fear of a war between Japan and Russia fuels the sudden interest in the Senate to recognize Russia. Proponents of recognition want to be able to back Russia if tensions escalate.	Railroads drastically reduce passenger miles in an attempt to meet economy measures recommended by the Interstate Commerce Commission.	Physics professor Dr. Jesse W. Beane explains his invention of a top that spins 500,000 times a minute and produces centrifugal force 1 million times that of gravity.	Stockholm reports Greta Garbo will marry and retire from films. She is to marry Swede Wilhelm Sorensen.	Apr. 22

F	G	H	I	J
Includes elections, federal-state relations, civil rights and liberties, crime, the judiciary, education, healthcare, poverty, urban affairs, and population.	*Includes formation and debate of U.S. foreign and defense policies, veterans affairs, and defense spending. (Relations with specific foreign countries are usually found under the region concerned.)*	*Includes business, labor, agriculture, taxation, transportation, consumer affairs, monetary and fiscal policy, natural resources, pollution, and accidents.*	*Includes worldwide scientific, medical, and technological developments, natural phenomena, U.S. weather, and natural disasters.*	*Includes the arts, religion, scholarship, communications media, sports, entertainment, fashions, fads, and social life.*

	World Affairs	Europe	Africa & The Middle East	The Americas	Asia & The Pacific
Apr. 23	Japan indicates it may accept the resolution on Shanghai made by the League of Nations, but wants some modifications.	Germany says it cannot pay reparations and looks to the Lausanne conference in June to come up with a solution to economic problems.	King Albert of Belgium returns from a month-long inspection trip of the Belgian Congo. He notes it is no longer "Darkest Africa."		A band of 3,000 irregulars occupies the Chinese Eastern Railway Station, interrupting service between Harbin and Changchun.
Apr. 24	Plans for the Lausanne conference on interallied debts move very slowly. French Premier Andre Tardieu and U.S. Secretary of State Henry Stimson deny having discussed debt and reparations issues.	Growing support for Adolf Hitler is demonstrated by the Austrian elections. After not being previously represented in the Vienna Diet, the Hitlerites elect 15.	The Iraq army, with help from the British Royal Air Force, inflicts 120 casualties on rebels led by the Sheikh of Barzan.	Puerto Rican women rush to register to vote. About 150,000 are expected to vote for the first time in the November election.	The Philippines mobilize forces to fight locusts, leaf-eaters, and rats that threaten the crops.
Apr. 25	The disarmament parley takes a two-week recess, due in part to the upcoming French elections.	The Greek chamber considers a bill for the abandonment of the gold standard.	Thousands are out of work in Algeria because of mine shutdowns due to the cost of shipping minerals out of the country.	Puerto Rico is shown to be the United States' best customer to the south. Last year it bought more than all of Central America combined.	Philippine Governor Gen. Theodore Roosevelt will travel to the north end of Luzon Island, where it is reported that Japanese are fishing illegally and stealing timber from the forests.
Apr. 26	Reports in Nanking say Dr. Wellington Koo will become the Chinese Ambassador to France when he completes his duties as assessor for the League of Nations inquiry commission.	Unemployed residents of Zyradow, Poland, storm City Hall when money is not available to pay the unemployment dole. Several are injured.		Nine more rebels are shot in Mexico for their part in the recent raids on the village of Paso del Macho.	Chinese officials say they believe Amoy is safe from the Chinese Communist army. Regular troops advance against Communist troops at Changchow.
Apr. 27	The French are upset by recent events in Geneva involving disarmament and feel their plan is being scrapped by other leaders.	Eamon de Valera says he is ready to lead the drive for an independent Irish republic. . . . Cattle graze in Amsterdam on the reclaimed Wieringermeer Poulder, which was under the waters of the Zuider Zee two years ago.	The Depression has spread to Algeria, forcing the closing of three branches of the Franco-Algerian Bank.	Fighting is expected in Costa Rica between supporters of two recent contenders in the elections. Schools are closing and many families are leaving the area before Congress begins May 1.	Chinese authorities report that 30,000 could starve to death unless the National Flood Relief Commission can obtain more American wheat.
Apr. 28	Secretary of State Henry Stimson postpones his departure from Geneva so he can attend the League of Nations Assembly session on the conflict between China and Japan.	A near riot occurs in the Irish Dail as Eamon de Valera's bill to abolish the oath of allegiance to England is discussed.		W.A. Gordon, Canadian Minister of Labor and Immigration, introduces a new plan in the parliament whereby jobless who are drawing relief would be placed on farms owned by the Crown.	Eight high-ranking Japanese officials are injured as a bomb explodes in Shanghai.
Apr. 29	At a consultation in Geneva with the delegates of the U.S., British, German, Italian, and French governments, it was agreed that disarmament is a matter of urgency and that the talks will resume in about two weeks.	An attorney for Adolf Hitler institutes action against the election board, alleging that President Paul von Hindenburg was the only candidate allowed radio time. Radio in Germany is controlled by the state.		The National University in Mexico City is allotted 1 billion pesos for the construction and equipment of primary schools. The money should build about 30 schools, but some will be in communities outside the city.	A group of 6,000 Chinese irregulars manage to hold several detachments of Japanese at bay in the eastern Kirin province of Manchuria. The Chinese lose 200 men in the two-day battle near Hailin.
Apr. 30	The League of Nations approves a formula for the early evacuation of Shanghai by the Japanese. Japan abstains from voting, but says it will do everything in its power to bring the Shanghai negotiations to a successful conclusion.	At the request of Ambassador Andrew Mellon, 21 American women will be presented to King George and Queen Mary at this year's four courts. They will be presented by the wife of the French ambassador.	In Arabia, starving Bedouins straggle into the Jordan Valley, hoping for a handout. Streams in the desert have dried up, and fruits are no longer growing in the oases.	The Trinidad legislature votes to allot $27,000 to the fight against witchbroom disease. The blight is affecting trees on the cocoa plantations. An export tax of about three cents per 100 pounds of cocoa will be levied to recover the money.	Eleven Koreans are arrested in Shanghai, accused of involvement in the Hongkew bombing. The men were said to have been previously involved in anti-Japanese activities.
May 1		One million Soviets march in a three-hour-long military parade in Moscow to commemorate May Day. Included in the parade are bombers, tanks, and anti-aircraft batteries.	The Hebrew University in Jerusalem celebrates its seventh anniversary, and Jewish leaders from the United States, France, and Germany participate in a broadcast to help celebrate.	In a peaceful turnover, the Costa Rican Congress selects Ricardo Jimenez Oreamuno as its next president, to succeed Cleto Gonzalez Viquez, whose term is expiring.	The rival Chinese governments of Nanking in the north and Canton in the south fail to come to an agreement on retaining their southwestern political council. Nanking wants to abolish it.
May 2	Leaders in Geneva are pleased with the results of the French election, believing that newly elected Edouard Herriot will be more accommodating than Premier Andre Tardieu has been.	The German government announces that it will resist with all its forces a predicted Polish coup at Danzig.		Argentine President Agustin Justo urges the Congress to make the sacrifices necessary for Argentina to pay the payments that are due.	The Japanese claim they killed hundreds of Chinese and lost only six men in fighting at Paiyantala, about 100 miles west of the Manchukuo capital of Changchun.
May 3	The parliaments of Canada and New Zealand ratify a trade treaty between the two countries.		Archaeologists identify three skulls found in Palestine as those of Neanderthal man. They were discovered in a small cave at the foot of Mt. Carmel.	A U.S. National Guard unit clashes with insurgents in Lucaya, Nicaragua. One Nicaraguan is killed and two injured, while two Guardsmen are wounded slightly.	The Hougomout, a bark carrying wheat from Australia to Europe, is lost and believed adrift in the rough waters of the Indian Ocean.
May 4	Experts at the Geneva parley clash over whether or not submarines and aircraft carriers are offensive weapons.	London and Moscow are linked as public telephone services between the two cities open.		President Luis M. Sanchez Cerro of Peru returned to his duties a few days ago after recuperating from a gunshot wound from a would-be assassin, but now is ill again.	Chinese and Japanese representatives sign a truce, ending the hostilities between them in Shanghai.

A	B	C	D	E
Includes developments that affect more than one world region, international organizations, and important meetings of world leaders.	Includes all domestic and regional developments in Europe, including the Soviet Union.	Includes all domestic and regional developments in Africa and the Middle East.	Includes all domestic and regional developments in Latin America, the Caribbean, and Canada.	Includes all domestic and regional developments in Asian and Pacific nations (and colonies).

U.S. Politics & Social Issues	U.S. Foreign Policy & Defense	Economics & Great Depression	Science, Technology & Nature	Culture, Leisure & Lifestyle	
	Members of the Army Air Corps are kept warm by a new flying suit made from horsehide and wool. It is lighter and warmer than the old suits.			About 35 million residents of 15 states are affected as those areas adopt daylight savings time, which will continue until September 25.	Apr. 23
Eliot Ness, who obtained the evidence that led to Al Capone's indictment on liquor law violations, is promoted to chief investigator of Chicago's federal forces.		A huge economy bill addressing 22 points will be introduced in the House today. Three of President Herbert Hoover's recommendations are not included.	Thomas A. Edison and George Eastman are honored with a memorial service by the National Inventors Congress in San Francisco.		Apr. 24
	Three guard patrols of U.S. Marines clash with Nicaraguans who had killed three U.S. Marine officers. Three outlaws are killed and four wounded.	General Motors shows a sharp decline in sales for the first quarter. They sold 143,514 cars, compared to 231,881 last year.	Clinical and experimental research shows that the common cold is due to a virus, reports Dr. Alphonse Dochez at a symposium of the New York Academy of Medicine.		Apr. 25
The House Economy Committee completes its report on the Economy Bill, while the Ways and Means Committee holds hearings on the Bonus Bill.	Secretary of State Henry Stimson arranges a meeting between German Chancellor Heinrich Bruening and French Premier Andre Tardieu in an attempt to mediate their differences on the arms plan.	William Green, president of the AFL, estimates the number of unemployed at 7,950,000, saying this is the first time in five years that unemployment has risen in April.	German archaeologists find an ancient temple in Smyrna while searching for the ancient Greek theater located there.	Helen Wills Moody, tennis star, leaves for England where she will captain the U.S. team playing abroad.	Apr. 26
The House of Representatives tears the Economy Bill apart, throwing out all amendment curbs and raising salary exemptions.			The observatory in Heidelberg, Germany, confirms the discovery of a new comet by astronomer Rafael Carrasco at the Madrid Observatory.	Laura Adams Armer wins the John Newbery Medal for the best children's book of the year for her first novel, *Waterless Mountain*.	Apr. 27
	Marine Sgt. Orville B. Simmons receives the Navy Cross for his actions in Nicaragua. He fought off outlaws and aided a pilot whose plane crashed.	Austria plans import embargoes on many products it buys from the United States, which will cause great losses in U.S. trade.		In Davis Cup play, Ellsworth Vines, America's 20-year-old tennis champion, beats Canadian ace Dr. Jack Wright. Another American player, Wilmer Allison from Texas, downs Canadian Marcel Rainville.	Apr. 28
	Rear Admiral Frank E. Clark is named to succeed Vice Admiral Arthur L. Willard as commander of the scouting force.	E.H. Westlake, vice president of the Tennessee Corporation, stresses the need for a tariff on copper. He states that most of the copper companies in the United States will be unable to stay in business unless an import duty is enacted.	The American Geophysical Union is told that the depths of the Pacific Ocean contain a billion tons of radium, and the sediments on the bottom of the ocean are 12 times as rich in radium as rocks on dry land.	Movie star James Cagney offers to work in three movies for Warner Bros. without pay if they would then cancel the remainder of his five-year contract. The company refuses. Cagney has been suspended because of his refusal to work in any more films until his $1,400-a-week salary is raised. Another studio offers to take over his contract for $150,000, but Warner Bros. refuses that offer as well.	Apr. 29
Arnold Peterson calls the convention of the Socialist Labor Party to order in New York. He mentions the Democratic and Republican conventions in Chicago, but insists this convention is the only important one.	The House rejects a bill to merge the Army and Navy in order to save $50 million. Under the bill, the War Department and the Navy Department would have been merged into one department, called the Department of Defense.	The American Bankers Association suggests five amendments to the Glass Banking Bill, although they are generally in favor of the bill overall.	Dr. E.E. Free makes it possible for radio listeners to hear the sound of deadly radium particles reverberating in the bones of a poison victim. The use of hydrogen causes the particles to give off an audible noise.	Dr. Alexander Alekhine of Paris, chess champion of the world, agrees to participate in the Post-Olympic Chess Congress beginning in Pasadena, Calif., on August 15.	Apr. 30
	Army and Navy officers are concerned with a clause in the Economy Bill that gives the President the power to restrict the transfer of military personnel from one post to another.	Delegates from 50 nations meet in Berlin to discuss ways to restore prosperity and stimulate world trade.		Eleanor Holm sets a national record for the backstroke. . . . The U.S. Olympic Committee faces an unprecedented shortage of funds as only $34,000 of a projected $350,000 needed has been raised.	May 1
At the American Conference on Institutions for the Establishment of International Justice, President Herbert Hoover stresses that the entire social structure is erected on justice and that it is a safeguard of peace.	Dr. E.A. Goldenweiser, research economist for the Federal Reserve Board, tells the House Ways and Means Committee that prepayment of the veterans' bonus would prolong the Depression and cripple the system.	The Senate Finance Committee adds several more taxes to the billion-dollar tax bill due to go to the floor of the Senate.	George E. Merritt tells the Seismological Society of America about the tiltmeter he has invented. He says that with the help of this instrument, scientists should be able to predict the time and place where quakes will appear.	The radio show of comedian Jack Benny airs for the first time.	May 2
Al Capone enters the federal penitentiary in Atlanta after his conviction for income-tax evasion.	Two naval reserve pilots manage to maintain control of their planes and land safely after colliding in midair over Floyd Bennett Field while practicing a bombing dive maneuver.	After the first 10 months of the fiscal year, the government deficit stands at $2,334,105,142.	Acoustics experts report that hearing begins to deteriorate after the age of 20 and each decade causes more problems in hearing high tones.	*New York Times* writer Walter Duranty wins a Pulitzer Prize for a series on the Soviet Union, while Pearl S. Buck wins one for her novel, *The Good Earth*. Gen. John Pershing also receives a Pulitzer Prize for his memoirs.	May 3
The House discovers duplications in the omnibus Economy Bill, which shrink estimated savings from $38,124,500 to about $30 million.		Coca-Cola sues two candy-store chains for selling other drinks similar to theirs. Pepsi-Cola, in return, sues Coca-Cola for interfering with their contract with one of the chains.		In a spectacular performance, Boiling Water wins the feature horserace at Churchill Downs by a length.	May 4

F	G	H	I	J
Includes elections, federal-state relations, civil rights and liberties, crime, the judiciary, education, healthcare, poverty, urban affairs, and population.	*Includes formation and debate of U.S. foreign and defense policies, veterans affairs, and defense spending. (Relations with specific foreign countries are usually found under the region concerned.)*	*Includes business, labor, agriculture, taxation, transportation, consumer affairs, monetary and fiscal policy, natural resources, pollution, and accidents.*	*Includes worldwide scientific, medical, and technological developments, natural phenomena, U.S. weather, and natural disasters.*	*Includes the arts, religion, scholarship, communications media, sports, entertainment, fashions, fads, and social life.*

	World Affairs	Europe	Africa & The Middle East	The Americas	Asia & The Pacific
May 5	The Japanese and Chinese agree to a neutral zone around the International Settlement in Shanghai. China agrees to end its boycott against Japanese products.	It is reported that revenues of the Reich fell far below the budgetary estimate in the past fiscal year. The deficit would have been larger had several taxes not been increased.	Egypt asks the French, Italian, and British governments to negotiate on payment of debt bonds, but all three countries refuse.	The Toronto Industrial Commission states that after two years of the Great Depression, Canada is better off than the United States. It points to the fact that U.S. exports have dropped more than Canadian exports.	Japanese troops clash with Chinese insurgents near Nantienmen, Manchuria, killing 24. One Japanese soldier is killed.
May 6	The World Bank shows a profit of $2,895,000 in its second year, which is an increase over last year's profit.	French President Paul Doumer is assassinated in Paris by Paul Gorguloff.	A 10-minute delay in his train schedule saves the life of Egyptian Premier Sidky Pasha. A bomb explodes on the tracks at the place where the train should have been.	As crowds protest, Peruvian radical leader Victor Raul Haya de la Torre is arrested as an accomplice to the assassin who shot President Luis Cerro.	A typhoon in the Philippines leaves 99 dead on the island of Sulu, while destroying all buildings, leaving 140,000 homeless.
May 7	Representatives of France, Britain, and the United States, along with the Secretary-General of the League of Nations, have agreed upon a policy regarding Manchuria. They will not recognize Manchukuo, but believe Japanese strategies will fail, so will not intervene now.	The War Minister of Austria dissolves an army unit of Hitler followers, saying they engaged in propaganda during the elections instead of tending to their military duties.	Southwest Africa Airlines will operate an internal mail service within the area of southwest Africa, covering nearly all the populated area.	Both parties in Panama charge fraud in issuing voting certificates for the upcoming election of the president and National Assembly members.	Eugene Chen, former foreign minister of China, believes Japan is planning war on the United States. . . . The Tienmen district in China is experiencing famine brought on by Communist armies using all the food.
May 8	The League of Nations mourns the sudden death of Albert Thomas, Director-General of the League's International Labor Office.			Mexicans are highly insulted by a new U.S. movie called *Girl of the Rio*. The picture, which stars Mexicans Dolores Del Rio and Leo Carillo, will probably be barred in Mexico.	Japanese forces begin evacuation of Shanghai, according to the League of Nations agreement.
May 9	U.S. Consul General at Shanghai Edwin S. Cunningham is named to chair a committee to oversee the withdrawal of Japanese troops from Shanghai.	Detectives have found evidence that Dr. Paul Gorguloff, who assassinated French Premier Paul Doumer, planned to head an anti-Soviet dictatorship in Russia.		A mutiny planned on two of Peru's navy cruisers is foiled by a loyal sailor who swims to shore and warns the government. Communists are blamed for the plot.	
May 10	The disarmament conference disbands and will not meet again until June. Technical committees will continue working.	Albert Lebrun succeeds to the presidency of France.	Crown Prince Asfoaw Wessen of Abyssinia marries the daughter of the governor of Northern Abyssinia.	Ricardo Jiminez Oreamuno, new president of Costa Rica, appoints a Cabinet headed by Defense Minister Leonidad Pacheco.	The 24,000 men of the Japanese 14th Division move from Shanghai to Dairen. Rumors say the Japanese plan an invasion inside the Great Wall.
May 11	A committee in Geneva debates how wide the mouth of a mobile cannon must be in order to consider it an offensive weapon.	Britain wants the Danubian states to abandon the gold standard, while France urges they retain it.	Jesuit archaeologists from Rome unearth what they believe to be the cities of Sodom and Gomorrah, finding paintings and pottery with writing on it.	Cuban President Gerardo Machado names the ambassador to the United States, Dr. Orestes Ferrarra, Secretary of State.	Cabinet member Stanley Bruce intimates that Australia may soon quit the gold standard for sterling.
May 12		The British Cabinet is waiting for the Lausanne Conference in June before it decides whether it can pay its war debt to the United States in full on December 15.	American archaeologists in Mesopotamia believe they have found the Tower of Babel mentioned in the Bible in the city of Akshak.		
May 13	Sir John Simon of Great Britain maintains an attitude of qualified optimism toward disarmament. He tells the House of Commons he has no idea where the United States stands on an international monetary conference.	Yugoslavia requests a free hand in its negotiations with Germany over reparations as the Little Entente opens in Belgrade to discuss the Danubian question.	Ugandan climbers Capt. G.N. Humphreys and George Oliver complete their ascent of Weissman Peak in the Ruwenzori Mountains in Kenya. Some areas they covered had not been explored before.	Planes drop flame-smothering liquid on burning oil tanks in Tampico, Mexico. The fire apparently started with someone burning his fields and has been raging for two days.	Jack Lang, premier of New South Wales, Australia, is dismissed by Sir Phillip Game, the state governor.
May 14	Japan and China give conflicting reports to the League of Nations on Manchuria. Japan accuses the former rulers of a campaign to stir up disorder in northern Manchuria, while China accuses the Japanese of burning, pillaging, and bayoneting women.	The British government is already economizing, but Neville Chamberlain, chancellor of the Exchequer, hints at drastic measures in order to pay Britain's debt to the United States. Economies may affect old-age pensions and schools.		Mexico severs diplomatic relations with Peru when the Peruvian government declares the minister from Mexico as a persona non grata. Peru accuses Juan Cabral of having close ties with Communists who are a threat to the government of Peru.	
May 15	League of Nations leaders express doubt that there will be any serious repercussions from the assassination of Japanese Premier Tsuyoshi Inukai. They are shocked, but say the slaying will not affect the world situation.	The Little Entente charges that nationalism is causing economic havoc. The group does not offer any solution, but does pledge its cooperation with any proposed solution.		The Brazilian government sends two airplanes and two warships to the state of Sao Paolo, which is torn apart by strikes.	Japanese Prime Minister Tsuyoshi Inukai is assassinated. . . . Hindus and Muslims riot in Bombay, killing 30 and injuring hundreds.
May 16		A French liner, the *Georges Phillipar*, burns at the mouth of the Gulf of Aden. Other ships take on 663 of the passengers and crew, but the other 237 are unaccounted for. Before the ship sailed, the French secret service warned the owners of the vessel of threats to destroy the ship.	American scientists Theodore E. McCown of the University of California and H.J. Movius of Harvard discover the remains of five Neanderthal men in a cave in Palestine, about 10 miles south of Haifa.	Peru says it meant no disrespect to Mexico when it asked the Mexican minister to Peru to leave. The government says he abused the post by consorting with Communist leaders. Washington believes Lima was within its rights.	Japanese forces pour into Harbin and are sent east on the Chinese Eastern Railway. The 10th Division and 14th Division have been brought in from Shanghai. At the request of the United States, Nanking sends troops to Anwhei to combat the Communists there.

A	B	C	D	E
Includes developments that affect more than one world region, international organizations, and important meetings of world leaders.	*Includes all domestic and regional developments in Europe, including the Soviet Union.*	*Includes all domestic and regional developments in Africa and the Middle East.*	*Includes all domestic and regional developments in Latin America, the Caribbean, and Canada.*	*Includes all domestic and regional developments in Asian and Pacific nations (and colonies).*

U.S. Politics & Social Issues	U.S. Foreign Policy & Defense	Economics & Great Depression	Science, Technology & Nature	Culture, Leisure & Lifestyle	
	The War Appropriation Bill comes before the House after the committee slashes it to $24,380,000 under the budget. Numbers of enlisted men remain the same, but 2,000 officers will be retired.	Government bonds close near the record high after making large gains.			May 5
A mob of 1,000 Communists attacks Chicago police when told to disperse. Eight are wounded by machine-gun fire.		A 10 percent cut in salaries does not stop the drop in railroad earnings, with gross revenues down 22 percent for the first three months of the year.		A field of 20 horses is named for tomorrow's Kentucky Derby at Churchill Downs.	May 6
	The Military Order of Foreign Wars asks for postponement of the veterans' bonus issue, but condemns cuts in appropriations for national defense.	Businessmen and industrial executives are asked to support the revised bankruptcy act.		Burgoo King wins the Kentucky Derby by five lengths. This is the third time a horse owned by E.R. Bradley has won the Derby, setting a record.	May 7
George W. Wickersham, chairman of President Herbert Hoover's committee to study Prohibition, believes a national referendum on the topic is necessary.		Winston Churchill, member of the British parliament, states that problems with the monetary system have caused the Great Depression, and urges the United States and England to work together to correct the problems.	A new treatment for arthritis is demonstrated to the American Medical Association. Treatment involves submerging the patient in water to take stress off the affected limbs.	The Catholic Church gives its approval to only four of the 50 plays produced on the New York stage between December 5 and April 15.	May 8
The Los Angeles Times backs President Herbert Hoover's plan for a five-day workweek and also endorses his idea of a staggered workweek instead of a pay cut for federal workers.		Opponents of a proposed tariff hike on sugar charge American sugar refiners want the tariff to put Cuba out of business.	British flier Amy Johnson will wed James Mollison, Australian distance flier. Johnson was the first woman to fly alone from England to Australia.	American dancer Adele Astaire weds British Lord Charles Cavendish in London.	May 9
		Senator Carter Glass charges that some Chicago banks have bribed Congressmen to vote against the branch banking section in the McFadden Bill.	The 1932 Daniel Guggenheim gold medal for aeronautics goes to Spaniard Juan de la Cierva, who invented the autogiro.		May 10
		The new Senate Economy Committee meets with President Herbert Hoover and agrees on several suggestions for reducing government spending.	A group of physicians in New York City seeks to ban use of radium water, saying prolonged use of it can be fatal.		May 11
The baby son of Col. Charles Lindbergh and his wife is found dead in Hopewell, N.J. He was missing for 10 weeks.			William Bebee will sail soon for Bermuda, where he and assistant Vincent Palmer will again study sea creatures from the bathysphere.	Walt Disney's Mickey's Revue introduces a new character, known as Goofy or Dippy Dawg.	May 12
Col. Charles Lindbergh identifies the body of the baby found in the woods and confirms that it is his son. The baby's body is then cremated.	The House votes to drop 2,000 Army officers, although the War Department opposes the cuts. Democrats believe the dropping of ROTC and citizen training camps will also be passed.	The House Committee on Coinage reports favorably on a resolution asking President Herbert Hoover to call an international monetary conference to consider the reevaluation of silver and discuss the gold standard and international exchanges.	Several hundred inventors at the International Patent Convention in New York pause a moment to pay tribute to the memories of Thomas A. Edison and George Eastman.		May 13
	The State Department reports that the 31st U.S. Infantry, which was sent to Shanghai, will return to its permanent station in Manila since Japan and China have agreed to an armistice.	Bankers believe a successful conference in Lausanne is necessary if the world is to recover from the worldwide depression. They say quick action is needed.	Fruit farmers in upstate New York are hiring swarms of bees to transfer pollen between trees. There are no longer enough bees in the wild to pollinate the trees, so farmers rent bees from the south to do the job, then they are returned.	Proponents of abolishing Prohibition hold a "We Want Beer" parade in New York City, led by Mayor James Walker. . . . Bradley's Derby winner, Burgoo King, wins the Preakness horserace by a head.	May 14
New Jersey police believe they know the identities of a gang of five men and one woman who they think may have kidnapped and killed the Lindbergh baby.	J.T. Taylor, vice chairman of the American Legion's legislative committee, urges the House to pass the bill that provides pensions for World War II veterans' widows and orphans.	Prices in the livestock market are the lowest they have been since 1911. Hog prices are at a record low of $3.30.	Explorer Lincoln Ellsworth selects a new monoplane that he will use in his upcoming exploration of Antarctica. The plane has a speed of 230 miles per hour.	Dr. I.M. Rubinow, international secretary of B'nai B'rith, says the American Jew is being driven out of commerce. He says "the door is nearly closed" in some lines of work, and urges a study of the problem.	May 15
The Senate votes down a proposal for wartime income taxes, 49–31.	Admiral Frank H. Schofield, commander in chief of the nation's fleet, says the naval dirigible Akron will start its flight east from California about May 30.	The Salvation Army asks for support from the public in its drive, saying that requests for help are up 700 percent since the beginning of the Depression. The Army needs $1,090,000 in order to continue its work.	Theodore Koven and Allen Carpe, scientists who headed an expedition to Mt. McKinley to study cosmic rays, have died there. Koven's body is found, but Carpe is believed to have fallen into a crevasse and the body is not seen.	It is announced that Henry Ford's son, Edsel, will drive the pace car for the 500-mile automobile race in Indianapolis on May 30. Ford will practice on the track for several days, as he needs to lead the cars at 90 miles per hour.	May 16

F	G	H	I	J
Includes elections, federal-state relations, civil rights and liberties, crime, the judiciary, education, healthcare, poverty, urban affairs, and population.	Includes formation and debate of U.S. foreign and defense policies, veterans affairs, and defense spending. (Relations with specific foreign countries are usually found under the region concerned.)	Includes business, labor, agriculture, taxation, transportation, consumer affairs, monetary and fiscal policy, natural resources, pollution, and accidents.	Includes worldwide scientific, medical, and technological developments, natural phenomena, U.S. weather, and natural disasters.	Includes the arts, religion, scholarship, communications media, sports, entertainment, fashions, fads, and social life.

	World Affairs	Europe	Africa & The Middle East	The Americas	Asia & The Pacific
May 17		French Minister of the National Defense, Francois Pietri, is rescued when the seaplane in which he is traveling is forced down in the Mediterranean Sea. He is taken aboard the training ship *Gueydon* and is unhurt.	A scientific expedition from Belgium will leave soon to explore the western slopes of the Ruwenzori Range in Africa, which lie partly in Uganda and partly in the Belgian Congo. Snow or rain occurs here 320 days of the year, constituting the greatest hazard.	Due to the oversupply of coffee in Brazil, the National Coffee Council announces it has destroyed 6,244,897 bags of coffee. Between 300,000 and 400,000 coffee trees are also destroyed.	The Seiyukai Party in Japan expresses its willingness to compromise and form a coalition government. They hope this is acceptable to the army, whose attitude remains ambiguous.
May 18		The Belgian government, under Jules Renkin, informs King Albert of its resignation. Party leaders are working on forming a new Cabinet.	The League of Nations will be asked to send a representative to Liberia to try to restore security. Forty-four villages have been burned, killing 81 men, 49 women, and 29 children. Another 12,000 tribesmen have fled into the bush, where they have no food or shelter.	A bomb is found in the Argentine oil fields at Rivadavia where a strike is underway. Twenty workers are arrested and transported to Buenos Aires. Communists are believed to be behind the plot.	A battle that began last night still rages along the north bank of the Sungari River near Harbin. Both the Japanese forces and the Chinese insurgents are suffering heavy losses.
May 19	The League of Nations Council approves the terms under which Iraq may join the League. It includes a bill of rights for Iraqis and assures most-favored-nation status for League members for 10 years.	Germany, already discouraged by the rejection of its disarmament proposals, is even more upset that the Geneva conference has rejected its proposal to ban all military aircraft.	Thirty-four survivors of the *Georges Phillipar* disaster are joyously reunited with friends and relatives at Aden. They were brought to Aden by the steamer *Andre LeBon*.	Liberals and conservatives clash in Colombia for the third straight day. At least 100 liberals flee across the border to Venezuela and eight are known dead, plus more than 20 have been wounded.	Japan says it will not increase its forces in Manchuria. It puts little credence in reports that Russia is mobilizing its army reserves of four years.
May 20	Bacteriological war weapons are unanimously banned by the disarmament conference's commission on gas and germ warfare. There is more controversy over banning gas, as it can take several forms.	Dr. Engelbert Dollfuss forms a coalition cabinet for Austria, which includes members of the Farmers' Party, the Christian Social Party, and the Heimwehr. The Pan Germans are not included.	A plan for the rehabilitation of Liberia is approved by the Council of the League of Nations. The League will send a representative to the Kru region where many natives were recently killed by the Liberian militia.	In a decree made public by the Ministry of Labor, Brazilian women have won the guarantee of equal pay if they perform the same job that a man holds.	Japanese sports enthusiasts want to buy the houses in which their victorious Olympic athletes are housed and move them to Japan to serve as monuments to them.
May 21	Samuel Reber, Jr., the U.S. representative on the Liberian committee in Geneva, wants to send a single representative to Liberia to advise the country on reforms. He cites economic reasons.	Relatives of the late statesman Georges Clemenceau refuse to attend the unveiling of a statue to honor him, saying it is derisive. They also criticize the ceremony and the site.		The Bolivian government says it will grant about five acres of gold-washing land to any unemployed man who wants it. If he makes money from gold mining, each man must pay the government a 12.5 percent royalty.	Chinese irregulars kill 80 Korean farmers in the southern Kirin province of Manchuria.
May 22	Japan invites the United States to participate in a conference of the ambassadors of the five principal powers in an attempt to ensure safety of foreign lives and property in China, particularly in Shanghai.	Former Hungarian premier Count Bethlen criticizes the idea of a Danubian union, saying it is a ploy to make people of the defeated nations forget the mutilations suffered at the hands of the victors.		Harvard Museum explorer Donald S. Wees confirms the existence of blond white Indians living in Paraguay. They are naked and live in the desert with no shelters of any kind.	A bomb explosion during the marketing hour in the Japanese Concession in Tientsin causes panic. Two women are taken to the hospital with slight injuries.
May 23	The League of Nations begins the Conference of Institutions for the Scientific Study of International Relations. It is hoped this will improve the ability of countries to relate to one another.	The Austrian Heimatschutz or "Home Guard" has been placed under the supreme command of Nazi Adolf Hitler.	Prof. H.P. Lamont of Pretoria is tarred and feathered there as a protest against anti-Afrikaners sentiment they say was contained in his book, *War, Wine and Women*. Lamont had already offered to remove the offending passages from future editions.		Chinese delegate W.W. Yen warns the League of Nations that unless the League warns Japan to stop hostile acts against China, there is every possibility of another world war.
May 24	U.S. Ambassador Norman H. Davis has been named by the Financial Committee of the League of Nations as a member of the commission to study the Danubian situation.	The Reich tells Poland that any attempt on its part to interfere with the Free City of Danzig would be considered an affront to Germany.			Gen. Honjo opens a new offensive drive pushing back 4,000 Chinese irregulars to a point four miles from Harbin. They take 500 prisoners, three armored cars, and several field guns, while suffering only seven injuries.
May 25		Turkey and Rome renew their Non-Aggression Pact as Turkish Foreign Minister Twefik Rushdi visits Rome.	A riot between Arabs and Jews in Aden leaves 69 injured. The fighting broke out when the Arabs attacked a group of Jews whom they accused of defiling a mosque.	Bolivia says it will offer its services to try to mediate the problems between Mexico and Peru, which arose from Peru's expulsion of the Mexican minister.	In an attempt to quell political disturbances, Burma sentences 70 rebels to death and will deport 22 more.
May 26	The International Touring Alliance protests touring restrictions, appealing to both the League of Nations and their respective governments. The group includes representatives from Europe, Asia, Africa, and America.	Queen Mary of England celebrates her 65th birthday with a luncheon for members of the royal family. She is honored by a 20-gun salute in Hyde Park.	The German airline Deustche Lufthansa will begin regular flights across the South Atlantic between British Gambia, Africa, and Natal, Brazil. They will station a six-ton steamship in the mid-Atlantic to serve as a refueling station.	E.H. Magoon of the Rockefeller Foundation arrives in Managua, Nicaragua, where he will assist the government in its campaign against malaria. A severe epidemic occurred last year.	
May 27	A world oil agreement is held up by disagreement between the Soviet representatives and the rest of the representatives on fundamental points.	Italian King Victor Emannuel views American art at the American Academy of Fine Arts in Rome. The King showed a lively interest in pieces on display.	German war veteran Oskar Daubmann, believed dead for 16 years, writes to his parents from Italy, where he is alive and well. Daubmann says he was a French prisoner of war and was deported to Africa, where he has been ever since.	Bolivia refuses to let 370 Mennonites settle on land in the Chaco territory given to them by Paraguay. Bolivia says Paraguay has no authority to grant land in the Chaco.	Forty Chinese are missing after the steamer *Iling* struck a rock in the Yangtze River and sank. About 100 of the passengers and crew are picked up by Chinese junks below the wreck.

A	B	C	D	E
Includes developments that affect more than one world region, international organizations, and important meetings of world leaders.	*Includes all domestic and regional developments in Europe, including the Soviet Union.*	*Includes all domestic and regional developments in Africa and the Middle East.*	*Includes all domestic and regional developments in Latin America, the Caribbean, and Canada.*	*Includes all domestic and regional developments in Asian and Pacific nations (and colonies).*

U.S. Politics & Social Issues	U.S. Foreign Policy & Defense	Economics & Great Depression	Science, Technology & Nature	Culture, Leisure & Lifestyle	
The name Porto Rico is officially changed to Puerto Rico by Congress. . . . After several days of questioning by police, John Curtis admits his story of negotiating with the kidnappers of the Lindbergh baby was all a hoax.		Senator William Borah proposes a 20 percent cut in the salaries of Senators and Representatives, and would also eliminate the mileage allowance of the members of Congress.	After exploring the area where scientist Theodore Koven's body was found, Minneapolis mountaineer A.D. Lindley and Mt. McKinley Park Superintendent Harry J. Leik believe Allen Carpe fell into a crevasse in a glacier and Koven fell in himself while trying to rescue him. He managed to climb out, but died from his injuries and exposure.		May 17
The House Judiciary Committee approves capital punishment for kidnappers and makes it a capital offense to transport a kidnapped person across a state line. The measure had already been in committee, but representatives waited to act until the Lindbergh baby was found, for fear the news would cause the kidnappers to harm the baby.	Civil War veteran and Indian fighter George Crow, 102, dies in his Lancaster, Ohio, home.	The circulation of counterfeit money is at an all-time high, according to William H. Moran, chief of the Secret Service. It is believed that many bootleggers have turned to counterfeiting since the Depression started.		In the first day of the British Open, Helen Hicks and Maureen Orcutt are defeated.	May 18
	The Army Bill passes in the House after it restores the training camp activities that had been cut. However, the House refuses to consider reinstating the 2,000 officers cut by the bill.			The slump in cigarette production shows how the Depression has affected the number of smokers in the country. The output of cigarettes in April is down almost 2 million from the same month last year.	May 19
President Herbert Hoover notifies Senate administration leaders that he expects them to take action on essential legislation before recessing.	Admiral Richard H. Leigh is named to take over as commander in chief of the U.S. naval fleet, succeeding Admiral Frank H. Schofield.	The Banking Committee reports favorably to the House on President Herbert Hoover's home loan bank bill. The bill will create a federal home loan board and a system of 8–12 home loan banks.	U.S. aviatrix Amelia Earhart Putnam flies from the United States to Northern Ireland in just 14 hours and 54 minutes.	American Broadway musical star Libby Holman marries Smith Reynolds, son of the tobacco financier. It is Holman's first marriage and Reynolds's second.	May 20
At a follow-up of the White House conference on child health and protection, some speakers express concern that the Depression is having an adverse effect on children in several ways. Many are malnourished and both truancy and delinquency are up.		The Senate debates for three hours but still does not bring the lumber and copper tariffs to a vote. Duties on oil and coal passed fairly easily yesterday.		Chairman George Graves of the Olympic finance committee announces the donation of $8,000 worth of clothing for American Olympic athletes. The donations come from 18 different firms.	May 21
John Curtis, the boatbuilder who pretended to negotiate with the Lindbergh baby's kidnappers, is charged with giving false information and hindering the investigation.	Over 300 Bonus veterans from Oregon take over a freight train in St. Louis, but the B&O Railroad refuses to move the train. The veterans are on their way to Washington, D.C., to demand early payment of their bonus.	Some Midwest farmers are turning to horses to cultivate their fields, due to the high cost of fuel for their tractors.		Eleven Americans are included in the field of golfers who will compete in the British Open tomorrow. Dave Martin, the California champion, heads the U.S. contingent.	May 22
The Beer Bill is voted down in the House, 228–169. The measure would have legalized 2.75 percent beer with a tax of three cents per pint.			Senator Walcott of Connecticut says he will introduce a resolution in Congress to award Amelia Earhart Putnam a Congressional Medal for her transatlantic flight.	Atlantic City officials announce the types of bathing apparel they will allow on the beach this summer. Banned are costumes made of lace or net and costumes consisting of trunks only, with a strap across the shoulder.	May 23
Police once again search the site of the Lindbergh kidnapping, interviewing people who live near the home.	A group of 78 American Gold Star Mothers arrives in Paris on their pilgrimage to visit the battlefields where their sons died in combat. More than 700 Gold Star Mothers will visit France before August 25.		The Heidelberg Observatory in Germany announces the discovery of a new planetoid that could come within 7 million miles of the earth. Dr. Karl Reinmuth names it 1932 H.A.		May 24
The House of Representatives holds services honoring the three Senators and 16 Representatives who have died since the 1930 election.	The Indiana National Guard arranges to provide trucks to transport Bonus veterans across the state to the Ohio line.	Senator Robert Wagner introduces a relief bill amounting to $2.3 billion for federal works and loans for self-liquidating enterprises, as well as state loans for unemployment. The bill includes detailed instructions as to the use for public works.	At the annual conference for the National Advisory Committee for Aeronautics, improvements in airplanes are showcased. Important advances in safety have been made and engines and propellers are more efficient. Orville Wright is present.	All three remaining Americans are eliminated from the British golf championships today, as Dave Martin and Robert and Charles Sweeney all lose their matches.	May 25
	Speaker of the House John Garner makes public his own economic proposal for a $2.1 billion unemployment relief bill. He will introduce it in the House tomorrow.	A research group in Toronto tests a diabetes antitoxin. Doctors have developed the toxoid from nasal sinus germ cultures. Those trying it for two months have shown some improvement.	The Ziegfeld Broadway show Hot-Cha, which was scheduled to close, will now continue with a cut in ticket prices from $5.50 to $4.40. This was made possible by voluntary pay cuts taken by the cast, except for Buddy Rogers, who will be replaced by Art Jarrett.		May 26
	Marine Corp. Hilmer N. Torner receives the Distinguished Flying Cross for an act of "self-sacrificing heroism." Torner, who had never flown a plane, took over the controls when the pilot he was flying with fainted. Torner managed to land the plane safely.		A 10-inch snowfall in some parts of North Dakota helps to kill off the serious invasion of grasshoppers. Scientists say the young insects could not withstand the cold.	Helen Wills Moody moves into the finals of the French tennis championships in Paris.	May 27

F	G	H	I	J
Includes elections, federal-state relations, civil rights and liberties, crime, the judiciary, education, healthcare, poverty, urban affairs, and population.	Includes formation and debate of U.S. foreign and defense policies, veterans affairs, and defense spending. (Relations with specific foreign countries are usually found under the region concerned.)	Includes business, labor, agriculture, taxation, transportation, consumer affairs, monetary and fiscal policy, natural resources, pollution, and accidents.	Includes worldwide scientific, medical, and technological developments, natural phenomena, U.S. weather, and natural disasters.	Includes the arts, religion, scholarship, communications media, sports, entertainment, fashions, fads, and social life.

	World Affairs	Europe	Africa & The Middle East	The Americas	Asia & The Pacific
May 28	Norman Davis, member of the U.S. delegation to the disarmament conference, leaves Geneva for Paris, where he will participate in a meeting of the League's commission on relief for Austria, Bulgaria, Greece, and Hungary.		Governor of the Abyssinian province of Gojam Ras Hailou and his son are seized in connection with a reported plot to poison Emperor Haile Selassie.	Many young men in north Brazil are enlisting in the army due to the famine there. Unable to find work, the army will provide them with food and shelter.	
May 29	British Prime Minister Ramsay MacDonald urges broadening the scope of the Lausanne conference to address international trade, as well as war debts and reparations.	Poles are alarmed over anti-Polish feeling in Germany and the Reich's recent statement about Danzig. The Foreign Office refuses to comment on reports of Polish drilling near Danzig.	Persia cedes the mountain of Little Ararat to Turkey, in exchange for land farther south. Mt. Ararat, which is associated with Noah's Ark, is made up of Little Ararat and Great Ararat.	In an attempt to increase its trade, Argentina sends commercial delegates to Paraguay, Bolivia, and Chile. They will also try to settle outstanding economic questions.	The Rajah of Jubal, which lies in Punjab at the foot of the Himalayas, arrives in San Francisco on his world tour.
May 30	A delegation of committees from the League of Nations meets with auto manufacturers from around the world. U.S. manufacturers refused the invitation.	German President Paul von Hindenburg asks Franz von Papen to form a new government upon the resignation of Chancellor Heinrich Bruening.		The National Guard in Nicaragua reports two clashes with rebels. It suffered no casualties while defeating the rebels.	Japanese bombs set fire to the city of Hailun, 150 miles north of Harbin in Manchuria. A fierce battle is also underway between the two cities, as a column of Japanese marching north is attacked by the Chinese cavalry.
May 31	British Earl Stanhope reports at the disarmament conference in Geneva that his country is ready to scrap all tanks over 25 tons.	The Romanian government under Nicholas Iorga fails as it is unable to secure a badly needed loan from France.		Bolivia is not likely to sign a treaty on the Chaco, proposed by a committee of neutrals in Washington, D. C., in its present form. It opposes holding future negotiations in Buenos Aires.	The Nanking government's 48th Division wins an important victory, slaying more than 2,000 Communists in a battle northwest of Hankow. It also captures 2,000 transport junks.
Jun. 1	British Foreign Minister Sir John Simon tells the House of Commons he wants the United States to participate in the Lausanne conference.	After being ousted as German Chancellor, Heinrich Bruening suffers what his doctors call a nervous heart attack and is unable to confer with his successor, Franz von Papen.	The bark *Cariolanus*, which in 1877 set a sailing record between London and Calcutta, will sail out of Boston to engage in trade with Africa.	Former Cuban ambassador to the United States Dr. Orestes Ferrara is named Secretary of State of Cuba.	After being held in China for four and a half months, American Capt. Charles Baker is released.
Jun. 2		The fascist newspaper *La Tribuna* in Rome says that because of the United States' stand on debts, any economic parley will be futile.	A congress is held in the Union of South Africa by delegates who favor the secession of Natal from the Union. The people of Natal do not like Premier J.B. Hertzog's attitude toward Great Britain.	Gen. Juan Cabral, ousted Mexican minister to Peru, arrives home and denies the charges that he had close ties with Communists in Peru. He says he never mixed in local politics.	Japanese Premier Makoto Saito says there is absolutely no danger of war between Japan and Russia, but asks Russia not to send more troops to Siberia.
Jun. 3	Speaking at the disarmament conference as an experienced journalist, Senator Louis de Brouckere of Belgium denounces censorship of all kinds. He says the suppression of official news agencies is dangerous to peace.	King Carol of Romania calls former premier Nicholas Titulesco to try to form a coalition cabinet. The liberals say they will refuse to join such a Cabinet, but are willing to form one of their own.		A violent earthquake rocks Mexico, killing 23 and injuring more. Property damage is estimated at $300,000 in Colima, which was hardest hit.	A petition signed by 32,000 Japanese farmers is presented to the Diet, asking for a grant of 50 million yen to help them emigrate to Manchuria.
Jun. 4		Statistics show that about one-eighth of Germany's population was helped under comprehensive social insurance during the past year. . . . Edouard Herriot is installed as the new premier of France.	British archaeologist John Garstang, who is working on excavating the city of Jericho, believes the evidence points to the walls having fallen due to an earthquake.	A military coup occurs in Chile. Carlos Davila, leader of the revolution, has long been a leader in the government of Chile and once served as ambassador to the United States.	Japan says there is no friction between Korea and Japan that would lead to any serious consequences. Gen. Sadao Araki, Minister of War, says Korea is not opposed to Japan's policies in Manchuria.
Jun. 5	Irish President Eamon de Valera still says his country will be represented at the Ottawa parley, but the delegates need to sail before the outcome of the oath bill is known.	A government spokesman in Berlin flatly denies the rumor that President Paul von Hindenburg will retire to make way for the return of former Crown Prince Friedrich Wilhelm.		According to a Bolivian newspaper, Paraguay has violated the confidence of Bolivia by revealing the terms of the nonaggression pact they are negotiating.	New U.S. Ambassador to Japan Joseph Grew arrives in Yokohama with his wife and daughter. He is installed in the Embassy at Tokyo and meets with American correspondents.
Jun. 6		The Reichstag election, the fourth in four months, is set for July 31. The rumor that the monarchy might be restored may have hastened the election.	Dr. Cuthbert Christy, expert in tropical diseases, naturalist, and explorer, dies in the Belgian Congo. Christy had also served with the League of Nations.	The Canadian Department of Agriculture lifts its ban on garden produce, so farmers in California, Oregon, Arizona, and Nevada will again be able to sell vegetables to the Canadians.	The Nanking government approves resumption of diplomatic relations with Soviet Russia in a secret meeting. Relations were cut off when Russians and Chinese were fighting in Manchuria in 1929.
Jun. 7	In a 40-year-old boundary dispute between France and Switzerland, the World Court rules in favor of Switzerland by a 6–5 vote.	Due in part to the inability of Prussia to balance its budget, the Reich is expected to appoint a federal commissioner to replace the Prussian ministry.		Bolivia jails two Paraguayan officers accused of spying in central Bolivia near the Chaco.	Japanese farmers are in such dire straits that some have resorted to eating animal feed and selling their young daughters. Premier Makoto Saito takes steps to draft emergency measures to help them.

A	B	C	D	E
Includes developments that affect more than one world region, international organizations, and important meetings of world leaders.	Includes all domestic and regional developments in Europe, including the Soviet Union.	Includes all domestic and regional developments in Africa and the Middle East.	Includes all domestic and regional developments in Latin America, the Caribbean, and Canada.	Includes all domestic and regional developments in Asian and Pacific nations (and colonies).

U.S. Politics & Social Issues	U.S. Foreign Policy & Defense	Economics & Great Depression	Science, Technology & Nature	Culture, Leisure & Lifestyle	
Three indictments are handed down by the Hunterton County, N.J., grand jury regarding the kidnapping of the Lindbergh baby, but they remain secret. It is believed that one of them is against John Curtis, whose negotiator hoax led police astray in their investigation.	America's newest symbol, the Tomb of the Unknown Soldier, is expected to receive a large number of visitors on Memorial Day. It is estimated that the total number of visitors for 1932 will surpass one million people.	Congress debates three forms of relief. They include financing of self-liquidating improvements by the federal government, financial aid to states for unemployment relief, and bond issue for public works construction.	Holland reclaims 500,000 acres of farm land by building a dike and turning the Zuider Zee into a huge lake, called Ijsselmeer, or Ijssel Lake.		May 28
President Herbert Hoover cuts short his stay at his Rapidan camp in order to meet at the White House with a group of Republican Senators about the tax bill.	Memorial Day ceremonies held at Arlington Cemetery are attended by 25,000 people.	All livestock prices remain low, but hog prices, at $3.20, are the lowest they have been since 1898.	The department of biological chemistry of Harvard plans a three-month field study in Boulder City, Nev., of heat prostration among workers on Hoover Dam.	Forty auto racers enter the 500-mile race at Indianapolis.	May 29
	Washington, D.C., is concerned by the influx of Bonus veterans who arrived yesterday. The 500 men say they will stay until the bonus is paid.	In a speech at Gettysburg, former ambassador Henry P. Fletcher calls the Economy Bill sent to the Senate a joke. He charges the government is incompetent and extravagant.		Three U.S. women golfers remain in the running for the British Open championship. Two favorites, Helen Hicks and Maureen Orcutt, are beaten, but Virginia Van Wie, Glenna Collett Vare, and Leona Cheney remain.	May 30
The Supreme Court settles a 100-year controversy when it rules bills may be signed by the President within 10 days after Congress adjourns.	Naval Ensign D.S. Stillman of Milwaukee, Wisc., disappears from his ship, the USS *Peary* en route from Manila to Shanghai.	Socal becomes the first American firm to discover oil in the Middle East when it strikes oil in Bahrain.	Marie Peary Stafford, who was known as "Snow Baby" when she was born to her parents at the Arctic Circle, will place a flag on the monument being built to her father at the Arctic Circle.		May 31
	The Washington police superintendent appears before a Senate committee, asking for $75,000 to feed the veterans who are encamped in the capital to pressure Congress to prepay their bonus.	As the fiscal year nears an end, the U.S. deficit stands at $2.7 billion, which is an increase of over $2 billion in the last 11 months.	The newly finished Hall of Science for the 1933 World's Fair is dedicated in Chicago with an elaborate celebration, including music and balloons. Many schoolchildren attend.	Although she does not play her best game, Helen Wills Moody advances to the semi-finals in the women's singles event of the French tennis tournament.	Jun. 1
Jeanette Rankin, the first woman elected to the House of Representatives, leaves Washington, D.C., on an automobile speaking tour to promote peace. She will arrive in Chicago on the eve of the national conventions.	The Coast Guard takes seven rum-running vessels trying to escape detection at night. They confiscate $100,000 worth of liquor and take several prisoners.	Passage of the Economy Bill is delayed because of lack of agreement on the proposal to cut federal salaries 10 percent.	A Harvard expert presents evidence that a cold can only be caught from another person. Dr. Wilson Smillie cites a year-long study on two islands, one in the Virgin Islands and one above the Arctic Circle. Colds are caused by germs, not exposure to cold temperatures.		Jun. 2
	About 2,000 Bonus marchers swarm over the Pennsylvania Railroad yards in Cleveland, vowing to stop business until a freight train is provided to take them to Washington, D.C.	President Herbert Hoover will hold an economic conference at his Rapidan getaway tomorrow with Arthur A. Ballentyne, Undersecretary of the Treasury; Paul Bestor of the Federal Farm Loan Board; and members of the Reconstruction Finance Corporation.	Broderick Haskell, Jr., of the Guaranty Company tells a meeting of scientists that industrial research is leading the United States out of the Depression and back to prosperity.	Lou Gehrig hits four straight home runs, tying the record and leading the New York Yankees to a victory. . . . John J. McGraw, for 30 years the manager of the New York Giants baseball team, resigns because of ill health. He will stay with the club as vice president and adviser. First baseman Bill Terry is named as his successor.	Jun. 3
After a seven-hour debate and nine roll calls, the Senate finally votes to cut federal salaries by 10 percent starting July 1. Savings are estimated at $117,150,000. Salaries under $1,000 will not be affected. . . . John Curtis pleads not guilty to charges of providing false information regarding the kidnapping of the Lindbergh baby, and his trial is set for June 27.	Police Superintendent Pelham Glassford tells the Bonus Army that he will furnish trucks to transport them 50 miles from Washington, D.C.	Railroad stocks lead the advance as bonds soar on the stock exchange to create the strongest bond market in recent years.	The International Soaring Society will meet at Elmira, N.Y., on July 11 to test their silent gliders on the hills of Chemung County. . . . There is no news of aviator Stanislaus Hausner, who left Newfoundland on a flight to Poland.	Actor John Barrymore is "too excited to comment" as a son is born in Los Angeles to him and his wife, Dolores Costello.	Jun. 4
	With 8,000 Bonus veterans already in the capital and 5,000 more on the way, Washington police term the situation as desperate. The Bonus Army pledges no violence, but refuses to leave.	Farmers in southeastern Idaho appeal to the state for help as millions of grasshoppers and crickets spread across the area and other parts of the west.	The 6,000 delegates to the National Electric Light Association convention in Atlantic City see a demonstration of a surgeproof transformer that defies lightning.	Norman Armitage, 1929 and 1930 champion, regains the national outdoor saber title in a competition in New York City.	Jun. 5
The Revenue Act of 1932 creates the first federal gasoline tax in the United States at 1 cent per gallon.	The last surviving officer of the 21st Illinois Volunteer Infantry dies in Cincinnati, Ohio. John A. Jones was a friend of General Ulysses S. Grant.		There is still no word on the fate of flier Stanislaus Hausner, who left for Poland on Friday. His fuel should be exhausted, and some think he may have landed in the moors of Newfoundland.	According to the 1930 census, Americans are marrying later. The percentage of divorced people rises for both sexes.	Jun. 6
John H. Curtis will call Col. Charles Lindbergh as a defense witness in his trial for obstructing the search for Lindbergh's kidnapped baby. Lindbergh will be called to show that Curtis received no pay for his activities.	A Bonus Army parade of 7,000 veterans in Washington remains orderly, despite reports that Communists would cause a disturbance.	President Herbert Hoover's economic plan contains four recommendations that aim to help industry, the states, farmers, and labor.	Dr. William Harvey King of New York asserts that laughter is important to health and recovery from illness, and a good joke may be worth more than a pill.	Kanzi Nakamura, a Japanese artist who has lived in the United States since 1908, dies in Cambridge, Mass. Nakamura's work may be seen at the Fogg Museum at Harvard and the Boston Art Museum.	Jun. 7

F	G	H	I	J
Includes elections, federal-state relations, civil rights and liberties, crime, the judiciary, education, healthcare, poverty, urban affairs, and population.	*Includes formation and debate of U.S. foreign and defense policies, veterans affairs, and defense spending. (Relations with specific foreign countries are usually found under the region concerned.)*	*Includes business, labor, agriculture, taxation, transportation, consumer affairs, monetary and fiscal policy, natural resources, pollution, and accidents.*	*Includes worldwide scientific, medical, and technological developments, natural phenomena, U.S. weather, and natural disasters.*	*Includes the arts, religion, scholarship, communications media, sports, entertainment, fashions, fads, and social life.*

	World Affairs	Europe	Africa & The Middle East	The Americas	Asia & The Pacific
Jun. 8	The air commission of the disarmament conference agrees that bombing is a grave threat to civilians, but is unable to define a bomber. The United States, Japan, France, Britain, and 14 other countries think the weight of an empty plane indicates its offensive capacity, but 21 others, including Italy, Russia, and Germany disagree.	The Nazis in Austria are trying to absorb the Heimwehr into their party in order to take over that party's large supply of arms and munitions.	Archaeologist Theodore McCown notifies Yale that his group has found four more skeletons in the ruins they are excavating near Haifa, Palestine.		A huge battle rages in Honan between 20,000 insurgents and the Chinese provincial forces. Provincial troops vow to crush the rebels and have brought in reinforcements, including a squadron of planes.
Jun. 9	The League of Nations gold delegation urges the world to return to the gold standard, saying it is the world's "best available monetary mechanism."	In court for his suit against journalist Werner Abel, Adolf Hitler refuses to answer questions. He is fined for contempt of court and disorderly conduct for insulting the defense lawyers.	Abyssinia's former emperor Yeassu, who has been in captivity for 15 years, escapes dressed as a woman and gathers a large army to challenge present Emperor Haile Selassie.	The condition of crops in eastern Canada is generally below those of last year, with the exception of winter wheat in Ontario.	Gen. Ma, a leader of the forces fighting the Japanese in Manchuria, has fled, taking all the money in the treasury with him. It is believed a Russian emissary helped him escape.
Jun. 10	The U.S. Congress and administration are pleased with the League of Nations call to return to the gold standard, but still oppose cancellation of the war debt.	Protests pour in as new French Premier Edouard Herriot and his Finance Minister Louis Germain-Martin propose a 10 percent cut in both civil service pay and armaments appropriations.		Premier John Bracken of Manitoba receives a letter threatening his life if he wins the election in July.	A spokesman for the Chinese government states that China is ready to negotiate with Soviet Russia for a nonaggression treaty, since the Chinese desire to promote world peace.
Jun. 11	The League of Nations reports that 15 European nations have agreed to barter, rather than buying and selling goods. Eleven countries have abandoned the gold standard.	Talks on reparations begin in Paris between Britain's Prime Minister Ramsay MacDonald and French Premier Edouard Herriot.	An excavation led by Prof. A. Speiser of the University of Pennsylvania uncovers the remains of an ancient city in Iraq. The most interesting relic found is a stamp seal on clay depicting the story of Adam and Eve.	Brazil celebrates its Navy Day by a presidential decree to modernize its navy. President Getulio Vargas signs the decree providing $33.5 million to be used to build 24 or 25 ships in the next 12 years.	None of the Chinese newspapers has published a word of thanks or appreciation for the efforts of the U.S., British, French, and Italian ministers who framed the Shanghai agreement.
Jun. 12		The Soviets announce the discovery of vast oil fields in the Ural Mountains. The deposits are estimated to contain hundreds of millions of tons of oil.	Premier H.U. Moffat of Southern Rhodesia arrives in London en route to the Ottawa parley. He says Rhodesia hopes for help in marketing its tobacco.	Carlos Davila resigns only a week after his coup in Chile brings him to power. It is believed his partner in the coup, Juan Esteban Montero, forced Davila out because he believes his views are too moderate.	Japanese Premier Makoto Saito asks Count Yasuya Uchida to be foreign minister. Uchida will not take the office unless he can reach an understanding with the army about their policies.
Jun. 13	At a short board meeting in Switzerland, the World Bank plans to study the role of the bank in economic reconstruction. The board indicates it will renew Austria's loan next month.	King Carol dissolves the Romanian Cabinet and decrees that new elections be held starting July 17.	The former Abyssinian emperor Lij Yeassu, who escaped last week, is recaptured. He planned to launch an attack on Emperor Haile Selassie at the end of the rainy season.	In a surprise move, leftist parties pledge their support to new Argentine President Agustin Justo.	The Mexican government seizes the Japanese fishing boat *Kumano* in the Bay of California, off the coast of Guaymas. Officials refuse to discuss the incident.
Jun. 14	The arms parley is recessed until next week, as many leaders leave for Lausanne, Switzerland, for the reparations parley there.		A clash in Morocco between soldiers and tribesmen trying to stop a shipment of rations kills five Moroccan soldiers and one French soldier.	President Gerardo Machado's government arrests hundreds of Cubans in a drive against alleged terrorism. The jails in Havana are overflowing.	Count Yasuya Uchida accepts the post of Japanese foreign minister. He is said to favor recognition of Manchukuo.
Jun. 15		Twelve people are on trial before a military court in Belgrade, charged with conspiracy against the state.	Former Abyssinian emperor Lij Yeassu remains at large, despite false reports of his capture. Three thousand troops are combing the Gojam Hills for him.		The United States asks the Chinese government to provide armed escort for 18 American missionaries trying to reach Tsinan from Kaichow.
Jun. 16	The reparations conference begins in Lausanne, Switzerland, under the auspices of the League of Nations.	The Franz von Papen government lifts the ban on Nazi stormtroopers in Germany, but forbids street brawls.	The League of Nations names Dr. Melville Mackenzie as commissioner to ensure humane treatment of the Krus in Liberia. He has gained the confidence of the native group, who call him "Boss."	In a counter-revolutionary movement, Col. Marmaduke Grove, who led the coup in Chile 12 days ago, is captured. Airplanes and troops with machine guns take over the palace.	
Jun. 17	At the Lausanne Conference, Britain expresses its willingness to wipe out all debts due to it if other European governments will do the same. Germany frankly states it cannot pay its debt.	Eamon de Valera insists on an Irish republic with loose ties to Great Britain, but Britain refuses to discuss the matter.		The army that overthrew the government of Chile's Col. Marmaduke Grove withdraws and Carlos Davila, former ambassador to the United States, again heads the government.	A fierce battle rages at the entrance to the harbor of Macao, 75 miles south of Canton, as a 5,000-man army routs a fleet of Nanking gunboats.
Jun. 18	Canadians have high hopes for the empire conference to be held at Ottawa in July. It will address trade, tariff, currency, and exchange issues.		Excavations in Palestine uncover the ancient city of Sichem. Its huge towers, walls, and temples are evidence of the powerful culture of the Canaanites.		Chinese bandits pose a big problem in eastern Manchuria, and the government of Manchukuo seems to have no authority to stop them. Japanese troops have only made matters worse for the Chinese peasants.
Jun. 19	U.S. Senator Claude A. Swanson makes it clear to the leaders of France and Britain that the United States will not give up its plan for limiting arms effectives.	British Prime Minister Ramsay MacDonald and French Premier Edouard Herriot meet to try to resolve their differences on the war debt situation.		Puerto Ricans are pleased with references to Puerto Rico in the Republican platform and hope recognition of the island as part of the country will eventually lead to statehood.	
	A Includes developments that affect more than one world region, international organizations, and important meetings of world leaders.	**B** Includes all domestic and regional developments in Europe, including the Soviet Union.	**C** Includes all domestic and regional developments in Africa and the Middle East.	**D** Includes all domestic and regional developments in Latin America, the Caribbean, and Canada.	**E** Includes all domestic and regional developments in Asian and Pacific nations (and colonies).

U.S. Politics & Social Issues	U.S. Foreign Policy & Defense	Economics & Great Depression	Science, Technology & Nature	Culture, Leisure & Lifestyle	
	Unconfirmed reports say Army posts near Washington are taking precautionary moves due to the numbers of Bonus veterans demonstrating in the city.	The Economy Bill finally passes, with President Herbert Hoover's furlough plan replacing the 10 percent pay cut for federal workers. Savings are cut from $238 million to less than $156 million.	Dr. W.S. Adams and Dr. Theodore Dunham of the Carnegie Institute discover that carbon dioxide is probably present in the atmosphere of Venus.	Finnish distance runner Paavo Nurmi will come to Los Angeles even though he is under suspension from the International Amateur Athletic Federation. He hopes the suspension will be lifted in time for him to compete in the Olympics.	Jun. 8
Former president Calvin Coolidge defends the agreement made by his administration as he opposes revision of war debts.	Washington officials ask the states to try to stem the influx of veterans into the capital. Doctors who inspect the site say conditions are "frightful" and they fear an epidemic.	The Senate passes the War Department appropriations bill after restoring the 2,000 officers cut by the House.	Paul Siple, who went with Admiral Byrd on his expedition to the South Pole, receives a Bachelor of Science degree from Allegheny College. Siple interrupted his college career to make the trip. His thesis, "The Biological Report of the Byrd Expedition" won him the Heckel Prize in science.		Jun. 9
	William Howard Gardiner, president of the Navy League of the United States, stresses that the U.S. Navy needs to be strong enough to protect the country abroad. . . . The Bonus Army wants to increase their number to 50,000.		Divers of the salvage ship *Artiglio* recover large amounts of paper money from the sunken liner *Egypt*, but they are worthless since the issue has been cancelled.	Gene Sarazen's victory in the British Open means that American golfers have won the British Open in 11 of the last 12 years. A British golfer won in 1923.	Jun. 10
Ambassador Walter Edge says that rumors he will become chairman of the Republican Party are only gossip.		President Herbert Hoover calls an unexpected meeting of Republican members of the Economy Committee at the White House and tells them the budget is not balanced yet. He wants Congress to remain in session until it is balanced.	After being missing for eight days, flier Stanislaus Hausner is picked up from his plane, which is floating off the coast of Europe. . . . Asteroid #1222 Tina is discovered by Delporte.	The Wightman Cup in Wimbledon, England, goes to the American women's tennis team, 4–3. . . . Burgoo King, winner of the Kentucky Derby and the Preakness, comes up lame and will miss the American Derby and the Arlington Classic.	Jun. 11
As the Republican convention is about to begin, President Herbert Hoover is mainly interested in two issues—Prohibition and the vice presidential candidate. He says he will not accept a repeal plank in the platform.	Members of the Bonus Army wait eagerly for the House to vote on the Bonus Bill.	The Carnegie Steel Company resumes operations in Youngstown, Ohio, putting 2,500 people back to work.	Amelia Earhart Putnam is cheered as she arrives at the airport in Brussels, tours the city, and attends a dinner in her honor. Tomorrow she will meet King Albert, who pilots a plane himself.	Babe Ruth hits his 19th and 20th home runs of the year, to lead the New York Yankees to a victory over the Cleveland Indians.	Jun. 12
Rep. Henry Rainey is sworn in to serve as a temporary replacement for Speaker John Garner, who is suffering from a bad attack of the grip.	Bonus Army veterans are pleased when the House votes to consider the bill to pay an immediate bonus. However, enough were opposed to practically ensure that the House would not be able to override a presidential veto.		Missing German seaplane Capt. Hans Bertram and his crew are believed to be alive after natives in northwestern Australia find a silver cigarette case with the initials HB and a message scratched on it in German.	American actress Adele Astaire, who recently married British Lord Charles Cavendish, is reported to be getting ready to be presented to the King and Queen at the next session of Court.	Jun. 13
The Republican National Convention opens in Chicago with a keynote speech by Senator L.J. Dickinson, for which the listeners show little enthusiasm. . . . While pleading on the floor of the House for passage of the Bonus Bill, Rep. Edward Esliek dies.	Rear Admiral Harry G. Hamlet is sworn in as Commandant of the Coast Guard, succeeding the late Rear Admiral F.C. Billard, who recently died of pneumonia.	Senate leaders conclude that due to confusion surrounding relief and economic legislation, Congress will need to stay in session at least another week.	Capt. Hans Bertram's plane is found near Wyndham, Australia, and an intensive search is being made for him and his crew.	J.H. Loucheim's horse, Economic, the favorite for the American Derby, develops a lame leg and is doubtful for the race. Burgoo King already had to be scratched, as did Evening, Tick On, and Top Flight.	Jun. 14
Gaston Means, former Department of Justice agent, receives a 15-year sentence for fraud in the Lindbergh kidnapping.	The House of Representatives passes the Bonus Bill, 209–126, but it is not expected to pass in the Senate.	Foreign trade falls once more during May, with the $132 million in exports the lowest since 1914. However, imports are also down, so a favorable balance of trade is maintained.	Mexican archaeologist Enrique Juan Palacios discovers that the Totonac Indians of southeast Mexico used the Mayan system of hieroglyphics.		Jun. 15
The Republican National Convention in Chicago renominates President Herbert Hoover and Vice President Charles Curtis.	The Senate passes the Navy appropriations bill, but says none of the $318 million may be used to send Marines to Nicaragua to supervise elections there.		With a brilliant flash of light, a huge meteorite crashes to the ground in Igusassu Falls, Brazil. People miles away hear the explosion.	In a disagreement with the St. Louis Cardinals, pitcher Dizzy Dean leaves the team in Philadelphia and goes home. He says his contract is not binding because he was not 21 when he signed it. Vice President Branch Rickey of the Cardinals says Dean was 22 and that he will be severely punished if he does not return.	Jun. 16
	The cash-now Bonus Bill is defeated in the Senate, while 10,000 veterans surround the Capitol. They remain orderly.	The United States remains detached from the Lausanne parley and says decisions made there will not affect the country.	Edward Miles, 54, completes his four-year around-the-world journey. Miles sailed alone in a 37-foot schooner.	Dizzy Dean agrees to rejoin the Cardinals and says if he is given a chance to pitch tomorrow, he will show the manager "how games should be pitched."	Jun. 17
The Democratic Convention needs to make four major decisions: a presidential nominee, a vice presidential nominee, a permanent chairman, and a platform plank on Prohibition.		Copper producers say the industry will be forced to reorganize when the new four-cent tariff on copper takes effect.	A precedent is set in broadcasting as a tiny lapel microphone is introduced at the Republican Convention. The one-inch microphone clips to the lapel or pocket, freeing the speaker's hands.	Gusto, grandson of Man O' War, surprises everyone by winning the American Derby, beating Osculator by two and a half lengths.	Jun. 18
New York Governor Franklin Roosevelt confers for many hours with lawyers about the evidence in the corruption case against Mayor Walker. Some expect a decision soon.	Rep. Loring A. Black, who introduced a bill for $125,000 to maintain the Bonus Army in Washington, D.C., now proposes the money be used to send the veterans home on trains.	Unemployment in the United States is estimated at between 9 million and 11 million. AFL figures put it at 10,634,000.	Capt. O. Scharf of the German liner *Stuttgart*, sights two 25-foot blue sharks near the Grand Banks. The man-eating sharks are usually found in tropical waters.	Two of Paavo Nurmi's world records are shattered by another young Finn, Lauri Lehtinen. During Olympic trials, he beats the records for the 5,000 meters and the three-mile run.	Jun. 19

F	G	H	I	J
Includes elections, federal-state relations, civil rights and liberties, crime, the judiciary, education, healthcare, poverty, urban affairs, and population.	*Includes formation and debate of U.S. foreign and defense policies, veterans affairs, and defense spending. (Relations with specific foreign countries are usually found under the region concerned.)*	*Includes business, labor, agriculture, taxation, transportation, consumer affairs, monetary and fiscal policy, natural resources, pollution, and accidents.*	*Includes worldwide scientific, medical, and technological developments, natural phenomena, U.S. weather, and natural disasters.*	*Includes the arts, religion, scholarship, communications media, sports, entertainment, fashions, fads, and social life.*

	World Affairs	Europe	Africa & The Middle East	The Americas	Asia & The Pacific
Jun. 20	A three-power conference takes place in Geneva with representatives of France, Britain, and the United States. With all compromising slightly, it seems an arms settlement may be getting closer.	The Benelux customs union is negotiated by Belgium, the Netherlands, and Luxemburg. They invite other nations to join them.		Former U.S. Navy pilot Donald Terry is found in Peru after being missing for several days. Terry, a pilot for Fawcett Airways in Peru, says he was forced to land due to a shortage of gasoline.	The American missionaries in the Tamingfu area of China are all safe, as the rebels have fled from the area.
Jun. 21	At 2:00 a.m., the League of Nations rushes out notices of a general meeting to be held this afternoon. It is believed the U.S. delegation asked for the meeting in order to present their effectives plan.	Premier Edouard Herriot says, "France will never yield on the question of the complete immediate cancellation of reparations."	On his return from Palestine, Emanuel Neumann declares the Depression is not being felt there. Neumann, an executive of the Jewish Agency for Palestine, says trade is thriving in the country.		Japanese Viscount Kikujiro Ishii says the Manchurian campaign was undertaken as a self-defense measure against Chinese aggression.
Jun. 22	The U.S. arms reduction proposal is presented to the League of Nations. It proposes cutting armies, navies, and planes by nearly a third of their present strengths. Germany sees President Herbert Hoover's arms proposal as a genuine move for settlement of the arms question.		Abbe De Moor, who recently returned from a 20,000-mile tour of Africa, says certain native chiefs still practice a system of slavery.	Bolivia sends a slightly modified copy of the proposed pact between it and Paraguay to the neutral arbitrators in Washington, and hopes Paraguay will accept it.	A German Catholic missionary, Father Conrad Rapp, is reported to have been killed by a Japanese soldier in Manchuria. British nationals are told to evacuate the area.
Jun. 23	Two nations, Italy and Russia, fully approve the Hoover plan for disarmament. The Germans seem favorable and even Great Britain is discussing it. France is against it and Japan is lukewarm.	Sir John Simon, British foreign secretary, flies from Geneva to London to meet with the British Cabinet on the Hoover armament proposal.	The jewels of Egyptian Princess Sat-Hathor-Iunut, daughter of King Senusert II, are on display at the Metropolitan Museum in New York.	In Havana, President Gerardo Machado signs a bill keeping himself in office until 1935.	A hailstorm in the Hunan province of China kills 200 people. . . . A relatively bloodless coup by the military ends the absolute monarchy in Siam and it becomes a constitutional monarchy.
Jun. 24	The League of Nations Commission of 19 asks for more time to study the problems between Japan and China in Manchuria. Both China and Japan must approve the delay.	The Munich government tells the Reich to keep its hands off Bavaria, which does not want Nazi stormtroopers in its streets. Hitler wants martial law and demands that Communists be suppressed.	The Sheikh of Barzan surrenders to Kurdish forces near the Iraqi border. The capture marks the end of a two-year struggle to establish law and order in that area.		All Americans evacuate Kwangchow in the province of Honan, China, to avoid threatened Communist attacks against the city.
Jun. 25	The world spends $4 billion a year on armaments, but with U.S. President Herbert Hoover's plan, it would save $10–15 billion over the next 10 years.	England unveils a fast new bomber plane, which brings recriminations from some since the world is now involved in trying to cut armaments.	Skulls found recently in Palestine are believed to be a new species. They were first thought to be those of Neanderthal men, but the head is rounder and the limb bones are bigger.	The drought in north Brazil causes a famine that affects at least 500,000 people. The exodus of people to surrounding areas is causing problems there.	A Chinese government report states 500,000 people have been killed or are missing due to drives of Chinese communists and bandits in the past three months.
Jun. 26		In Bucharest, former premier Dr. Julius Maniu is expected to resume leadership of the National Peasant Party after he speaks to 50,000 at a mass meeting.	An archaeology expedition from the University of Pennsylvania excavates a palace at Tepe Hissar in northwestern Persia. It is believed to be 4,000 years old.		Chinese rebel commander Admiral Chan Chak captures a Chinese liner delivering 5,000 rifles to Cantonese regular forces in the south. Three planes bomb his gunboat in a vain attempt to get back the loot.
Jun. 27	Sir John Simon is expected to return to Geneva from London with a compromise proposal, combining U.S President Herbert Hoover's proposal with the British one.	Adolf Hitler's chief lieutenant Joseph Goebbels tells the press that the Nazis will not compromise with the Franz von Papen government.	The Kerr Steamship Line announces a new freight service from California and the Gulf Ports to South Africa.		The Chinese bomb the British gunboat Moorhen, mistaking it for the rebel gunboat that stole 5,000 rifles from a Chinese liner.
Jun. 28	Great Britain's delegation tries all day to bring together the Germans and French, but neither will budge on their positions on reparations.	A British submarine collides with an excursion ship, endangering the lives of 150 passengers. Luckily, there are no casualties.		Dr. Donald Wees is cleared of a hoax in the story of the white Indians in Paraguay. Wees says he was misquoted and he did not see white Indians with blond hair.	It seems that China is trying to mollify relations with Japan, as it offers to suppress the boycott and admit some Japanese rights and interests in Manchuria.
Jun. 29		The British Labor Party approves U.S. President Herbert Hoover's disarmament proposal, calling it "a substantial first step toward total disarmament."		F.C. Alderdice, new premier of Newfoundland, names the country's new Cabinet. He also has promised to appoint a committee to study the feasibility of governing the country by commission.	The city of Nanchang, China, is threatened by floods that have already killed hundreds of farmers in the valley. Thousands are homeless and a cholera epidemic is beginning.
Jun. 30	A committee of the five powers at Lausanne works all day and hopes to finish their plan for reparations by evening. Agreement is not likely, however. Germany still insists it can pay no reparations at any time. . . . Both Japan and China accept the request of the League of Nations for more time to study the conflict between them. The Assembly will ratify the extension tomorrow.	The Prince of Wales, who was to address the delegates to the Ottawa conference at a dinner tonight, becomes ill and is unable to attend. Prince George reads his address, which asks for the cooperation of all the delegates at the Ottawa parley.	Borrah Minnevitch, reported missing on a yacht between North Africa and France, is believed to have been found.	Marine Sgt. Edward H. Schmierer is murdered in his sleep at his post in Nicaragua. Authorities believe Lt. Roberto Gonzalez of the Nicaraguan National Guard is responsible. Gonzalez and four friends have deserted.	

A	B	C	D	E
Includes developments that affect more than one world region, international organizations, and important meetings of world leaders.	Includes all domestic and regional developments in Europe, including the Soviet Union.	Includes all domestic and regional developments in Africa and the Middle East.	Includes all domestic and regional developments in Latin America, the Caribbean, and Canada.	Includes all domestic and regional developments in Asian and Pacific nations (and colonies).

U.S. Politics & Social Issues	U.S. Foreign Policy & Defense	Economics & Great Depression	Science, Technology & Nature	Culture, Leisure & Lifestyle	
	A House bill providing for extension of insurance for veterans passes the Senate.	The Senate Banking and Currency Committee turns in a favorable report on a bill to buy up silver each month.	New York City welcomes Amelia Earhart Putnam on her return to the United States, a month and a day after she embarked on her trans-atlantic flight.	Platinum blonde movie star Jean Harlow files her intention to wed in Los Angeles. She will marry Paul Bern, a 42-year-old Metro-Goldwyn-Mayer executive.	Jun. 20
Congressional conferees fail to agree on whether or not to cut 2,000 officers from the Army appropriations bill.	Superintendent of Police Pelham Glassford is negotiating with railroads about returning Bonus Army members to their homes under an old provision that calls for transportation of groups of indigents at low fares.	Senate conferees decide to recommend to the Senate that they accept the modified furlough plan that the House adopted.	Dr. Charles H. Herty, president of the American Chemical Society, reveals a new process by which white paper can be made from the pulp of Georgia pines.	Jack Sharkey beats Max Schmeling for the heavyweight title. Joe Jacobs, Schmeling's manager, exclaimed, "We was robbed!"	Jun. 21
President Herbert Hoover signs the Federal Kidnapping Act, making transporting a kidnapped person across state lines a federal offense.	The Pennsylvania and B&O Railroads offer a rate of one cent per mile to transport Bonus veterans to their homes. This is less than a third of the normal rate.	The Senate approves $500 million in bonds for relief works.	Mexican archaeologists discover a rare plaque made of turquoise and jade in a Mayan tomb beneath the Castillo Pyramid in Chichen Itza.	In his last practice round before the U.S. Open, Gene Sarazen, winner of the British Open, shoots a par 70.	Jun. 22
Franklin Roosevelt says he will go to Chicago to the Democratic Convention if there is a deadlock in naming the presidential nominee or if he is nominated and his presence is deemed necessary by his advisers.		Canada's imports of U.S. products drop in every category, while their imports from Great Britain are up. . . . Louis Cates of the Phelps Dodge Corporation believes the new tariff on copper will help the copper-producing industry to get back on a sound basis.	A California farm, an experiment in farming without soil, grows vegetables in water using pills containing nutrients usually obtained from the soil.	American tennis players Frank Shields, Ellsworth Vines, Wilmer Allison, Gregory Mangin, Helen Jacobs, and Sarah Pelfrey advance in the Wimbledon tennis tournament. John Van Ryn and Dorothy Andrus Burke are eliminated.	Jun. 23
New York Governor Franklin Roosevelt's aides send him word from the Democratic Convention in Chicago that no real efforts have been made to stop his nomination.	A remnant of the Confederate Army parades past statues of Confederate generals Robert E. Lee, J.E.B. Stuart, Stonewall Jackson, and Confederacy president Jefferson Davis.	The Senate returns the Economy Bill to conference without a vote.	An expedition headed by Sherman Pratt returns from Ecuador with over 50 animals, snakes, and birds, which will be given to the Philadelphia Museum. Pratt will give the 15,000 feet of film he shot to the Museum of Natural History.	People are swarming to theaters to see Frank Buck's new movie, Bring 'Em Back Alive. Filming the movie took eight months, and none of the fierce fights between animals was staged.	Jun. 24
	Walter Waters, head of the Bonus Army, quits after most of the men ignore his order to march on the Capitol. Vice Commander Thomas Kelly is named to take his place but cannot be found.	The House will address minor matters over the next three days until members return from the Democratic Convention. The Economy Bill and Relief Bill must be dealt with before adjournment.	The Daniel Guggenheim Airship Institute opens at Akron, Ohio. The building includes the largest wind tunnel in the world, which will be used for aeronautic experimentation.	Albert Einstein cables the American Jewish Congress as it opens in Washington, D.C., supporting the international organization to defend the rights of Jews.	Jun. 25
	Father Duffy, Chaplain of the "Fighting 69th," dies in New York, where he has been ill for three months. The United States awarded him the American Distinguished Service Cross and France gave him the Croix de Guerre for heroism under fire.			A new shrine at St. Cecelia's Roman Catholic Church in Englewood, N.J., is dedicated to St. Therese, the "Little Flower of Jesus."	Jun. 26
The trial of John Curtis opens in New Jersey, and he is expected to say police forced him to make a confession on charges that he obstructed the investigation of the Lindbergh baby kidnapping. Col. Charles Lindbergh will testify.	The Bonus Army still refuses to leave Washington, saying they will get along somehow even though food is exhausted.	Realizing the necessity of passage, the Senate asks the House to return the Economy Bill it rejected as a conference report.		The Eastern Intercollegiate Association decides to ban radio broadcasting of its games, due to a drop in gate receipts. . . . Helen Wills Moody and Helen Jacobs make it to the semifinals at Wimbledon.	Jun. 27
Col. Charles Lindbergh's testimony at the trial of John Curtis, accused of a hoax in the Lindbergh kidnapping investigation, is cross-examined.	The Senate passes a bill offering to pay the Bonus veterans' way home. It now goes to the House.	The Senate passes the Economy Bill, which will now go to the President for his signature.	Recent developments in sound reproduction make it possible to provide the blind with "talking books," which will be produced in the near future.	Annie Swan Coburn dies in Chicago and leaves most of her fine art collection to the Chicago Art Institute. Ten other paintings go to the Fogg Museum at Harvard in memory of her husband, Lewis Coburn, who is a Harvard graduate.	Jun. 28
Democrats vote for a platform plank asking for the repeal of the Eighteenth Amendment. Only seven states favor a milder plank.	After a week of dissension, the Bonus veterans elect Walter Waters as their head for the third time, this time with unlimited powers.	The annual convention of the Montana State Federation of Labor passes a resolution asking Congress to coin 25 million silver dollars and the same number of half-dollars in an attempt to stimulate the silver market.		Delegates at the Democratic Convention are entertained during the afternoon recess by Amos & Andy, Will Rogers, and other radio personalities.	Jun. 29
Nominating speeches at the Democratic Convention are met with cheers, boos, and noisy floor parades.	As stated in his acceptance of the leadership of the Bonus Army, Walter Waters supervises a drill in the Bonus camp. Police watch to be sure he does not take his powers too far. He clashed with police last night over who has authority in the camp.	On the last day of the fiscal year, the U.S. federal deficit stands at $2,852,035,008. Last year at this time it was $875,752,335.	The National Society for the Prevention of Blindness recommends a ban on toys that can injure the eyes. The list includes air rifles, cap pistols, slingshots, darts, toy guns, and bows and arrows. It also asks the prohibition of the sale of fireworks.	U.S. tennis champion Ellsworth Vines will meet the British first-ranking player, H.W. (Bunny) Austin, in the men's finals at Wimbledon. It will be the first British-American match in the finals in the 55-year history of the tournament.	Jun. 30

F	G	H	I	J
Includes elections, federal-state relations, civil rights and liberties, crime, the judiciary, education, healthcare, poverty, urban affairs, and population.	Includes formation and debate of U.S. foreign and defense policies, veterans affairs, and defense spending. (Relations with specific foreign countries are usually found under the region concerned.)	Includes business, labor, agriculture, taxation, transportation, consumer affairs, monetary and fiscal policy, natural resources, pollution, and accidents.	Includes worldwide scientific, medical, and technological developments, natural phenomena, U.S. weather, and natural disasters.	Includes the arts, religion, scholarship, communications media, sports, entertainment, fashions, fads, and social life.

	World Affairs	Europe	Africa & The Middle East	The Americas	Asia & The Pacific
Jul. 1	Action was delayed on the Chinese-Japanese conflict at a special session of the League of Nations Assembly, in order to wait for the report of the Lytton commission.	Unemployment in the top six industrial nations of Europe doubled in the past year. The International Labor Office in Geneva, Switzerland, reported that almost 12 million people are without jobs in these countries.		Bolivia accuses four of its soldiers of plotting for Paraguay. Two of the soldiers are executed and the other two imprisoned for life.	Shops are closed in Bombay, India, because of rioting. Policemen fire on the mobs, killing 10 and injuring 200. . . . The Australia Broadcasting Commission is established.
Jul. 2	Great Britain's war loan conversion is predicted to aid in worldwide recovery. . . . The British market shows large gains, as loan bonds are purchased by banks and dealers.	The owner of the largest copper mine in the world, located in Africa, pulls out of Copper Exporters, Inc. A Belgian Company, the Union Minière du Haut Katanga, follows other companies in leaving the selling cooperative.		A volcanic eruption in the Andes blankets several cities in Chile with ashes. Cities affected include Santiago, Talca, and Curico. Earthquakes are felt in Argentina.	
Jul. 3	Manchukuo, a new nation created from part of Manchuria, accuses Russia of trying to start another world war by fomenting the Shanghai conflict between Japan and China.	The Austrian parliament approves construction of the Alpine Highway. The road will be the third-highest in Europe and will be named the Glockner Road.			
Jul. 4			Cairo reports an arbitrator has decided in favor of Egypt in the famous Salem case. The case had been pending for more than ten years before George T. Salem, a naturalized American citizen and former resident of Egypt, agreed to arbitration.	Argentine President Agustín P. Justo sends greetings to the American people on Independence Day, saying that his people have been inspired by the Declaration of Independence.	After a six-week search, German aviators Hans Bertram and Adolf Klausman are found alive in a remote area of Australia where their plane had crashed. Aboriginals had found them and are credited with saving their lives.
Jul. 5	The disarmament conference in Geneva adjourns until fall.	Dr. Antonio de Oliveira Salazar becomes prime minister of Portugal.	Italy marks the 50th anniversary of becoming a colonial power. The nation owns 800,000 square miles in Africa.	Venezuela and Italy announce a joint expedition to search for the source of the Orinoco River.	The ousted governor of Manchuria, Chang Hsiao-liang, claims that Japan plans to send Manchukuo armies through the Jehol mountains to attack Peiping and Tientsin.
Jul. 6	Many American scientists attend the fifth International Electrical Conference in Paris. Other scientists send papers to be read.				
Jul. 7	Turkey is invited to join the League of Nations.	Sixty-six are killed when the French submarine Prométhée sinks off the coast of Cherbourg.		Uruguayan Minister of Foreign Affairs Dr. Juan Carlos Blanco denies that Uruguay is a haven for Communists.	Four hundred Japanese fishermen who work at a Russian crab-canning plant on Ptchichi Island are imprisoned by the Russians. The Japanese make a formal protest to Moscow.
Jul. 8	James Mattern and Bennett Griffin's attempt to break the round-the-world record of Post and Gatty comes to an abrupt end today when their plane crashes in Borisov, Russia.	The British press expresses relief at the cancellation of reparations and declares the meetings at Lausanne a big success. . . . Antonio Oliveira Salazar attempts to organize a less military regime in Portugal, as the people there have expressed a desire for a freer government.		Mobs seize the town of Trujillo in northern Peru. Many are killed in the clash between the mobs and police and military troops.	
Jul. 9	The reparation conference in Lausanne agrees on five resolutions, including an agreement on Germany's reparations to the former Allies. The agreement also extends a moratorium on intergovernmental debts.	Divers have still received no response from the French submarine Prométhée 56 hours after the boat goes down.	Col. E.H. Rothery, who helped fix one of Liberia's boundaries, dies. The newspaperman and diplomat represented the African Republic in Philadelphia.	E.J. Carlyle, general secretary of the Canada Institute of Mining and Metallurgy, predicts that great opportunities lie ahead for the mining industry in Canada.	
Jul. 10	Neville Chamberlain, chancellor of the exchequer for Great Britain, envisions a new era for Europe. On his return from Lausanne, Chamberlain expresses his belief that old suspicions between nations will disappear.		Eric H. Luow, minister at Washington from the Union of South Africa, advocates international consultation and action in order to meet the demands of this modern era.		
Jul. 11	German Nazi leader Adolf Hitler predicts at a campaign meeting that after the Nazis win the elections, the Lausanne Pact will be worth about 75 cents.	Holland's Olympic athletes arrive in the United States. Despite being one of the smallest nations to compete, they have 20 athletes entered in seven sports.		It is reported that four states in Brazil have joined São Paulo in a revolt against the government. The port of Santos is closed, and reports indicate the uprising is more serious than the government will admit.	
Jul. 12	International oil companies meeting in Paris find it necessary to change their plan to try to stabilize oil markets outside the United States. The change is due to the reluctance of Soviet oil interests to participate in an international conference.	The French are uneasy over what they term an "inaccurate version" of the Lausanne agreement that was published in the United States. . . . Norway appropriates another strip of land in Greenland. Denmark last year referred the dispute to the Permanent Court of International Justice at The Hague.		The 118 faculty members of the University of Havana vote not to reopen the university until political conditions in Cuba stabilize.	The civil war between two Cantonese factions ends with military commander Gen. Chen Chia-tang holding Canton.
	A Includes developments that affect more than one world region, international organizations, and important meetings of world leaders.	**B** Includes all domestic and regional developments in Europe, including the Soviet Union.	**C** Includes all domestic and regional developments in Africa and the Middle East.	**D** Includes all domestic and regional developments in Latin America, the Caribbean, and Canada.	**E** Includes all domestic and regional developments in Asian and Pacific nations (and colonies).

U.S. Politics & Social Issues	U.S. Foreign Policy & Defense	Economics & Great Depression	Science, Technology & Nature	Culture, Leisure & Lifestyle	
Franklin Roosevelt, governor of New York, is nominated as the Democratic presidential candidate on the fourth ballot. A deadlock is broken when California and Texas, which had been committed to John Nance Garner, cast their votes for Roosevelt.		Democratic leaders believe the Depression will overshadow Prohibition as an issue in the presidential campaign. The party pledges to reduce government expenditures by $1 billion.		Helen Wills Moody of the United States defeats fellow American Helen Jacobs to win the women's singles title for the fifth straight year at Wimbledon. Moody has not lost a single set during those five years.	Jul. 1
Around 10,000 people welcome Franklin Roosevelt, presidential candidate, who arrives in Chicago for the Democratic Convention.	Around 5,000 members of the Bonus Army gather on the steps of the Capitol to protest the adjournment of Congress without passing a bill to make payments to them.	At its annual convention, The National Education Association calls upon the federal government to provide aid for schools. They declare education to be "the chief bulwark of the nation against the destructive forces of extreme radicalism."		Former opera star Marian Talley secretly marries a German pianist. The young singer, who retired after four years with the Metropolitan Opera, weds Michael Raucheisen in White Plains, N.Y.	Jul. 2
John H. Curtis, convicted the day before of perjury in the Lindbergh case, appeals to the Supreme Court. Curtis's testimony prevented the arrest of the kidnapper of the Lindbergh baby.	The world is startled by a disarmament proposal by President Herbert Hoover. He suggests cutting battleships and submarines by one-third and abolishing aggressive weapons such as bombers, poison gas, and tanks.	The Commerce Department reports that bank debits outside New York City were higher in the past week than at any other time during June.	Dr. George Burgess, well-known scientist and director of the Bureau of Standards, dies at his desk. . . . Millions of white moths swarm over New York City and into northern New Jersey.	Lawrence Val Coleman, director of the American Association of Museums, states that every two weeks a new museum is established and a new museum building or wing is built every 15 days.	Jul. 3
New York Governor Franklin Roosevelt returns to Albany from the Democratic Convention in Chicago. Despite the rain, he is greeted by thousands.		Minority Leader Bertrand Snell predicts that President Herbert Hoover will call an extra session of Congress if the legislature does not pass an unemployment relief bill.		The Pittsburgh Pirates tighten their hold on first place by defeating the Chicago Cubs in a doubleheader.	Jul. 4
New York City Mayor Jimmy Walker, a Democrat, says that he will support his party's ticket, even if Governor Franklin Roosevelt removes him from office.	The Bonus Army again parades down Pennsylvania Avenue to the Capitol.				Jul. 5
Bill Jurges, shortstop for the Chicago Cubs, is shot twice by his enraged girlfriend. Jurges's injuries are not critical. . . . The price for a first-class postage stamp is raised from two cents to three cents.			Secretary of Agriculture Arthur Hyde announces the appointment of Sam G. Anderson of Eutchinson, Minn., as an additional member-at-large of the Advisory Board, Migratory Bird Treaty Act.	A growing fad of white duck caps in New York City gives employment to several thousand people. Fifty factories spring up to manufacture them.	Jul. 6
The Prohibition Party nominates William D. Upshaw for the presidency. Upshaw, a former Representative, agrees to withdraw if it is possible to get an outstanding leader like Senator William Borah of Idaho to head the party.	The United States refuses to discuss details of naval cuts with Great Britain until land forces in Europe are reduced.	The Department of Commerce reports that American exports to Great Britain in May exceeded those in April by $2 million.	Marie Curie presents a paper on the electron to the International Electrical Conference in Paris. There have been reports that Curie has discovered a new radioactive material and scientists had hoped she would confirm.		Jul. 7
	President Herbert Hoover signs a bill to provide $100,000 to pay fares to send the members of the Bonus Army back home. The veterans have been camped near the Capitol for two months, demanding to be paid a bonus voted them in 1924. The bonus is supposed to be paid in 1945, but the veterans want it now.	In an address at Chautauqua, N.Y., Eleanor Roosevelt, wife of the Democratic presidential nominee, claims the over-centralization of big business was a factor in the Depression and the nation should realize the interdependence of agriculture, industry, and trade.	Col. Clarence M. Young, head of the Aeronautics Branch of the Department of Commerce, announces that certificates for airplanes will only be valid for four years, to ensure that they are airworthy.	A 48-hour search of the Atlantic turns up no trace of the yacht Curlew, which had been missing since it left Montauk Point on June 25.	Jul. 8
James Farley, chairman of the Democratic National Committee, announces that the Democrats will run their campaign as economically as possible, as they did the campaign for Franklin Roosevelt's nomination.	Politicians on Capitol Hill protest the idea that the United States would be willing to consider further war debt cuts.	Thomas O'Connor, chairman of the Shipping Board, proposes to President Hoover that a moratorium of one year be placed on repayment of construction loans. These loans, amounting to $111 million, are due from American steamship lines.	American scientist Nicolai Tesla declares on his 76th birthday that his talents are at their peak. . . . The remains of a 16-foot armadillo are discovered in volcanic ash on the Argentine pampas.	The missing yacht Curlew is found by the Coast Guard off the coast of Nantucket, far from where it should have been.	Jul. 9
		The Department of Commerce reports that business conditions in foreign markets remain generally unfavorable. However, there are some improvements in the Canadian, Chinese, and Philippine markets.		A statue of Leif Ericsson, a gift from the United States to Iceland, will be dedicated this month. Ericsson visited North America over 900 years ago.	Jul. 10
Governor Franklin Roosevelt suggests that he and President Herbert Hoover meet to discuss the development of the St. Lawrence Waterway. Hoover refuses, saying the treaty is not yet completed.	Out of the 7,500 members of the Bonus Army, only 802 apply to the Veteran's Administration today for train fare home. The rest will stay and hope to change the mind of the Congress about paying their bonus.	Livestock prices are the highest of the season for both cattle and hogs. Cattle are $3.50 a hundredweight higher than they were in May, and hogs are up five cents	Mrs. Joyce Borden Babalocovik ends her around-the-world cruise in New York. She manned a two-masted schooner on the 35,000-mile trip while her violinist husband practiced five hours a day.		Jul. 11
		The New York City Health Department denies that a rise in suicides is due to the Depression. The rise in suicide rates began during the boom of 1928–29. The rate of male suicides in the city has risen sharply during the past two years, while the rate for females has risen only slightly.	Amelia Earhart attempts to break Hawks's record for a flight from the West Coast to the East Coast of the United States. She takes off at 5:11 a.m. for her attempted nonstop flight to Newark.	The U.S. Army team comes from behind to beat Shelburne in polo in the Meadow Brook Club Tournament on Long Island.	Jul. 12

F	G	H	I	J
Includes elections, federal-state relations, civil rights and liberties, crime, the judiciary, education, healthcare, poverty, urban affairs, and population.	Includes formation and debate of U.S. foreign and defense policies, veterans affairs, and defense spending. (Relations with specific foreign countries are usually found under the region concerned.)	Includes business, labor, agriculture, taxation, transportation, consumer affairs, monetary and fiscal policy, natural resources, pollution, and accidents.	Includes worldwide scientific, medical, and technological developments, natural phenomena, U.S. weather, and natural disasters.	Includes the arts, religion, scholarship, communications media, sports, entertainment, fashions, fads, and social life.

	World Affairs	Europe	Africa & The Middle East	The Americas	Asia & The Pacific
Jul. 13	Envoys from Great Britain, India, Rhodesia, and South Africa set sail from Britain for Canada. There they will participate in the Imperial Economic Conference in Ottawa. London newspapers are skeptical about the conference's success.		The Shipping Board approves an agreement between the Pacific Coast-South and East Africa Lumber Conference. They will maintain freight rates as agreed upon by the conference on shipping of lumber and logs.	United Fruit announces they will cut acreage of bananas in Costa Rica by 1,800 acres.	
Jul. 14	Prime Minister Edouard Herriot of France says, after reading the Franco-British "treaty of conference," that the United States must treat with France and Great Britain together.	Prime Minister Edouard Herriot says the recent pact between Britain and France relates to Europe and does not cover the debts the two countries owe to the United States. He says he was misquoted in earlier press releases.		Argentina and Uruguay break diplomatic relations. Brazilian Ambassador Assis Brasil offers to mediate between the two countries.	Foreign Minister Yasuya Uchida of Japan assures the Inquiry Commission of the League of Nations that Manchuria is free.
Jul. 15	Austria is granted a loan of 300 million schillings by the League of Nations, but Austrians are protesting a condition that they must agree not to enter into an economic or political union with Germany before 1952.	Adolf Hitler opens his Reichstag election campaign by demanding "honor, liberty, and bread."		Heavy rains in Saltillo, Mexico, cause flooding in the city. Nine people are killed.	In his first message to the legislature there, Theodore Roosevelt, Governor-General of the Philippines, asks for more cuts to balance the budget. In an effort to aid the "small man," Roosevelt is pushing homesteading, crop diversification, and expansion of credit.
Jul. 16	The League of Nations calls a world economic and monetary conference, as was recommended at Lausanne. A committee is formed to draft an agenda and to set a date and meeting place.	The Irish cheer President Eamon de Valera on his return from England, where he tried unsuccessfully to negotiate with Prime Minister Ramsay MacDonald.		Chile rejects the quotas proposed for them at the nitrate conference in London. The Minister of Finance says he would prefer ruthless competition to accepting the proposed quotas.	
Jul. 17		Fifteen people die on "Bloody Sunday" following Nazi street violence in Altona, Germany. . . . General elections are held in Romania. The fascist Iron Guard wins 70,000 votes and elects five deputies.			
Jul. 18	Norway appeals to the World Court at The Hague, asking them to declare their occupation of southeastern Greenland to be valid. . . . Turkey enters the League of Nations as its 56th member.	French Ambassador to the United States Jean Jules Jusserand dies. President Herbert Hoover sends condolences to his widow as many in Washington mourn his loss.		Rebel forces in São Paulo, Brazil, offer little resistance as they lose three towns to federal forces sent by President Getulio Vargas.	At a conference on rural distress in Tokyo, governors report acute poverty and virtual bankruptcy across a large area of rural Japan.
Jul. 19	The United States wins a victory as an arbitrator rules that it did not detain Swedish ships during the war as had been charged. . . . Arms conferees in Geneva agree upon air bombing, tanks, and budgetary limitations, but are still at odds on land artillery.	The Ouchy Agreement, which includes reduction of trade and economic barriers, is concluded by Belgium, the Netherlands, and Luxemburg.		Bolivian and Paraguayan troops battle in the remote Chaco region, which is disputed by the two countries.	Chinese government officials fear the clash between China and Japan in Jehol will be used as an excuse by the Japanese to oust Marshal Chang Hsiao-liang from Peiping. . . . More than 700 Chinese in seven cities die from cholera.
Jul. 20	As one of Great Britain's major trading partners, the Dutch feel that Holland has a stake in the Ottawa parley.	The Reich government takes control of Prussia, ousting Otto Braun, who had been premier for the last 12 years, except for a few weeks in 1925.		Argentina rejects United States aid in its dispute with Uruguay.	
Jul. 21	Silas Strawn, chairman of the American Committee of the International Chamber of Commerce, lauds the spirit of the Lausanne pact. He stresses the importance of war debt revision.	New Irish tariffs on British products go into effect. Products being taxed include shoes, cement, coal, and electrical goods.	Tension develops between Bedouins and Jewish farmers in the Valley of Jezreel.	Mexico orders striking workmen of the Southern Pacific Railroad back to work. The strike is declared legal and Southern Pacific will have to pay the workers back pay.	
Jul. 22					
Jul. 23	Agents from 11 nitrate-producing countries meeting in London come to a tentative agreement to revive the nitrate cartel. China and 10 European nations will agree on the division of markets.	British, American and Romanian oil producers come to an agreement that should help stop the price war. Prices will be increased and production in Romania limited.		Fighting in Brazil intensifies and many wounded are removed to Rio de Janeiro. The government claims gains, but Washington receives contradictory reports saying the rebels are holding their own.	The Chinese mobilize forces to defend Jehol. The Japanese warn Marshal Chang that he will be guilty of a hostile act if he sends troops to the area.
Jul. 24					In Thailand, a palace coup at dawn brings the Thai absolute monarchy to an end.
	A Includes developments that affect more than one world region, international organizations, and important meetings of world leaders.	**B** Includes all domestic and regional developments in Europe, including the Soviet Union.	**C** Includes all domestic and regional developments in Africa and the Middle East.	**D** Includes all domestic and regional developments in Latin America, the Caribbean, and Canada.	**E** Includes all domestic and regional developments in Asian and Pacific nations (and colonies).

U.S. Politics & Social Issues	U.S. Foreign Policy & Defense	Economics & Great Depression	Science, Technology & Nature	Culture, Leisure & Lifestyle	
Delegates from the Women's International League for Peace and Freedom put their program before President Hoover. They want revisions of war debts and tariffs, universal disarmament, and recognition of the Soviets.		At their annual meeting, the American Federation of Labor asks Congress for aid on jobs for the unemployed. They report that an average of 23 percent of their members are unemployed.	A German-built glider piloted by Martin Schempp of Pittsburgh stays in the air for seven hours in Elmira, N.Y. The pilot has to land so he can attend a dinner held for the pilots and officials of the Soaring Society of America. . . . Amelia Earhart fails to beat Hawks's record for a coast-to-coast flight, but her time is the best held by a woman.	A new dance called the "Earhart Hop" is demonstrated at the Dancing Teacher's Congress. The dance, dedicated to Amelia Earhart, simulates her flights through a series of sways, dips, and whirls.	Jul. 13
The Relief Bill ends in a deadlock between the House and Senate, as the House insists that loans to banks be made public and the Senate disagrees. It is also reported that the President threatens to veto the bill.		A $390 million War Department bill is signed in Washington.			Jul. 14
The National Prohibition Board of Strategy refuses to support President Hoover for the presidency. The Board urges dry voters to vote for candidates who support the Eighteenth Amendment.		Former president Calvin Coolidge endorses a proposal for a general sales tax, rather than high taxes levied on the wealthy. He sees excessive taxation of a few as a "grave threat to the whole structure of American democracy."	Inventor Linn Boyd Benton dies. He was known as the "Edison of the Typographic Industry."	It is reported that Finnish long-distance runner Paavo Nurmi will not be reinstated by the Amateur Athletic Federation Council and will not be allowed to compete in the Olympic Games in Los Angeles. Nurmi reportedly received an excessive sum of money for expenses on a trip to Germany in 1929.	Jul. 15
A bank robber disguised as an armored truck driver walks away from a New York City bank with $56,325.	The Bonus Army says that it is prepared to camp in Washington until 1945 unless their bonuses are paid before that time.	The legislative council of the American Federation of Labor endorses a plan for a five-day week for government workers. They believe the shorter workweek would spread to private industry and would be a "great economic and social achievement."		Ticket sales for the Olympics break sales records with 854,000 tickets sold.	Jul. 16
Franklin Roosevelt marks the start of his presidential campaign with his first public appearance since the Democratic Convention, addressing a crowd at Hampton Beach.		President Herbert Hoover announces his intention to sign the amended Relief Bill.	In a message read at the dedication of the Owyhee Dam, now the highest dam in the world, President Herbert Hoover sends his greetings and congratulations. The dam is located on the Snake River in Oregon.		Jul. 17
National Democratic leaders decide to run Franklin Roosevelt's presidential campaign out of New York, rather than having branch headquarters in Chicago and either Los Angeles or San Francisco.	The United States and Canada sign a treaty to govern the development of the St. Lawrence River into an ocean lane. The project, which will take ten years, will open the Great Lakes to the world.	President Herbert Hoover praises Congress for its cooperation as he prepares to sign an unemployment relief bill. He had vetoed an earlier version.		Babe Ruth is helped from the field after he falls chasing a fly ball. The Yankees have to play without Ruth for three weeks.	Jul. 18
Robert Reynolds, Democratic nominee for the Senate from North Carolina, says his state will go for Franklin Roosevelt in the presidential election. Hoover carried the state in the last election.		It was hoped that the adjournment of Congress would produce a rally in the stock market. However, stocks decline. Fifty assorted stocks show a net decline of $1.34.		Playdale, a horse from French Lick Springs Stable, breaks the track record at Arlington Park. In doing so, Playdale wins the coveted Ravinia purse.	Jul. 19
President Herbert Hoover issues an executive order abolishing the Radio Division of the Department of Commerce. The Federal Radio Commission will take over these duties.	Harmodio Arias, president-elect of Panama, visits the White House. . . . U.S. Ambassador to England Andrew Mellon sets sail for the United States for a one-month visit.	A Georgia mill begins making newsprint from the pulp of pine trees. The new industry will use local resources. . . . The five-day workweek goes into effect for all Detroit city employees when Mayor Frank Murphy signs an ordinance, which also cuts all salaries 14.5 percent.	At least 21 deaths are attributed to the heat wave that still lingers throughout the country, with many areas recording temperatures above 100°F.	Yankee player Herman "Babe" Ruth reports that his injured leg is improving and he says he hopes to be back in uniform next week.	Jul. 20
President Herbert Hoover signs into law the federal relief bill passed by Congress. The bill makes available $3.8 billion. . . . During an excursion to Washington, D. C., 350 people contract ptomaine poisoning at a river resort.		The executive council of the American Federation of Labor calls on President Herbert Hoover to summon leaders of labor and industry for talks. They criticize industry for not introducing a five-day workweek and hope Hoover can work out such a plan with industrial leaders.		Athletes continue to arrive at the Olympic Village in Los Angeles. Today's arrivals include the U.S. track and field team, the entire German Olympic team, and the Czechoslovakians.	Jul. 21
Billy Jurges, who was shot on July 6 by his enraged girlfriend, returns to the starting lineup of the Chicago Cubs.		President Herbert Hoover signs the Home Loan Bank Bill, which establishes discount banks for home mortgages.		Mickey Cochrane of the Philadelphia Athletics "hits for the cycle," meaning he hits a single, double, triple, and home run in the same game.	Jul. 22
		The National Association of Real Estate Boards reports that the country is ready for a building boom.	An ancient seal showing a man and woman slinking away from a serpent is found in Tepe Cawra. Dr. E. A. Speiser, of the University of Pennsylvania, dates the seal at 4000 B.C.E.		Jul. 23
The baseball team of the Southern Pacific Railroad plays the San Quentin "All-Stars" at California's notorious San Quentin State Prison.				The six-minute black-and-white cartoon Spring is Here is released by Educational Pictures and the Fox Film Corporation.	Jul. 24

F	G	H	I	J
Includes elections, federal-state relations, civil rights and liberties, crime, the judiciary, education, healthcare, poverty, urban affairs, and population.	Includes formation and debate of U.S. foreign and defense policies, veterans affairs, and defense spending. (Relations with specific foreign countries are usually found under the region concerned.)	Includes business, labor, agriculture, taxation, transportation, consumer affairs, monetary and fiscal policy, natural resources, pollution, and accidents.	Includes worldwide scientific, medical, and technological developments, natural phenomena, U.S. weather, and natural disasters.	Includes the arts, religion, scholarship, communications media, sports, entertainment, fashions, fads, and social life.

	World Affairs	Europe	Africa & The Middle East	The Americas	Asia & The Pacific
Jul. 25	The Germans agree to accept the Anglo-British invitation to join their "European confidence pact." The British receive formal notification from German Chargé d'Affaires Count von Bernstorff.	A series of nonaggression pacts are signed between Russia and the countries of Poland, Estonia, and Finland.		The United States may lose about a fourth of the nation's anthracite coal market in Canada. Under an agreement between Canada and Great Britain, Canada will buy more British anthracite.	
Jul. 26		Germany's Minister of Defense, Lt. Gen. Kurt von Schleicher, says that if other nations don't disarm, Germany will reorganize its army.	A prehistoric human skull, said to be either Neanderthal or Rhodesian, is found among bones of extinct animals in South Africa.	Latin American countries unite in an effort to prevent a war between Bolivia and Paraguay. Argentina, Chile, Brazil, and Peru have begun diplomatic negotiations.	Japan recalls Lt. Gen. Shegiru Honjo from his post as head of the army in Manchuria.
Jul. 27	The French are concerned that the Versailles Treaty is being threatened by both Schleicher's talk in Germany and Senator William Borah's insistence on tying arms reduction to debt reduction.	The German naval training ship *Niobe* sinks in the Baltic Sea with 69 people aboard, including two-thirds of the year's naval class.		The settlers in the Irish and Welsh colony in Argentina are forced to flee because of flooding.	India says it will not join any agreement at the economic parley in Ottawa aimed at restricting its trade with other members of the British Empire. Sir Atul Chatterjee says trade with the United States will not be cut.
Jul. 28		Spain's Finance Minister says that his country will start an income tax in 1933. The measure is expected to be a serious blow to the landed classes.		A new rebel plot comes to light in Cuba. The signal for the uprising was to be the assassination of Machado on August 13 or 15.	
Jul. 29	The League of Nations invites the United States to participate in an economic parley.	German Chancellor Franz von Papen tells Americans in a radio address that he has no intention of becoming a dictator. He also demands equality and calls the peace treaty a "source of German despair."		Bolivians attack Paraguayans in the Chaco region and claim victory at two forts, Corrales and Colonel Bolgado.	The atmosphere is grave in Peiping as the Political Council opens a session to discuss threatening situations in north China and Jehol.
Jul. 30	The Summer Olympics open in Los Angeles. More than 2,000 athletes from 38 countries will compete in 14 sports. Approximately 1.5 million tickets have been sold for the event.	Austria defaults on its $126 million loan from the League of Nations. European nations that guaranteed the bonds may have to make good on the loan.		Bolivia rejects any overtures to settle its differences with Paraguay peacefully. A declaration of war is expected.	A new crisis between Japan and China ensues when Chinese Finance Minister T.V. Soong announces his country will withhold the $150,000 Japanese portion of the Boxer indemnity.
Jul. 31				Although war has not been formally declared, it is apparent that a state of war exists in Chaco between Bolivia and Paraguay. Planes and tanks are amassed on the border and La Paz has sent 50,000 men to the area.	The Japanese headquarters in Manchuria announces that Chinese Gen. Ma Chen-Shan has been killed.
Aug. 1	Italy's delegate to the world disarmament conference charges that every decision was made only by France, England, and the United States.	British government bonds show an increase and the average of fixed-interest securities is the highest in nine years.	The two-month-long revolt against the King of Hejaz in Arabia ends with the death of the rebel leader, chieftain Hamad Ibn Rafada.	Seven hundred jobless Canadians criticize President Herbert Hoover and demand emergency relief.	Flooding causes 500 deaths in China and leaves 50,000 homeless. Many are also dying from cholera and bubonic plague in China.
Aug. 2	Edward P. Warner, former assistant secretary of the Navy for aeronautics, suggests a disarmament plan that would cut the air forces of the world by 80 percent.	Austria's former chancellor Ignax Seipel dies in Vienna.		Gen. Abelardo Rodriguez succeeds Gen. Plutarco Elias Calles as Mexican Secretary of War.	The Chinese prepare to intervene in north China where Japanese forces threaten to attack the province of Jehol as well as in Tientsin and Peiping.
Aug. 3	U.S. Ambassador to France Walter Edge is in Paris attempting to negotiate a trade treaty with the French.	Riots erupts in Germany, leaving three dead. . . . Norway loses its case as the World Court refuses to stop the Danes from occupying Greenland.			Manchuria is flooded after 21 days of uninterrupted rain, and thousands of acres of grain and soybeans are lost.
Aug. 4	President Herbert Hoover signs two treaties to help victims of war. The treaties address the treatment of prisoners of war and injured and sick soldiers in the field.	The riots in Germany cause tension between Adolf Hitler and Chancellor Franz von Papen. Hitler's Nazis are involved in most of the rioting.		The efforts of 19 American nations to avert war between Bolivia and Paraguay fail. Bolivian Col. Alfonso Peña begins bombarding an area of the disputed Chaco region.	Jolaro Yamamoto is expected to be named Japan's new ambassador to the United States, succeeding Katsuji Debuchi.
Aug. 5	At the Ottawa parley, the British government rejects Canadian proposals for reciprocity in trade.	Residents of the French Riviera, clad in bathing suits, attack a night club in protest of the mayor's decree that businesses must close at 10:00 p.m.	Scientists hail the discovery of human fossils of men in Palestine, but disagree on which theory on the beginnings of man the remains support.	Bolivia's proposal to settle its dispute with Paraguay over the Chaco territory is turned down by the committee of neutral countries trying to help settle the problem. They recommend arbitration.	According to Japanese accusations, the Chinese are encouraging the boycotts at Shanghai. Meanwhile the Manchurians claim they have captured Tungliao.

A	B	C	D	E
Includes developments that affect more than one world region, international organizations, and important meetings of world leaders.	Includes all domestic and regional developments in Europe, including the Soviet Union.	Includes all domestic and regional developments in Africa and the Middle East.	Includes all domestic and regional developments in Latin America, the Caribbean, and Canada.	Includes all domestic and regional developments in Asian and Pacific nations (and colonies).

U.S. Politics & Social Issues	U.S. Foreign Policy & Defense	Economics & Great Depression	Science, Technology & Nature	Culture, Leisure & Lifestyle	
	U.S. Ambassador to Great Britain Andrew Mellon says he will not resign. He arrives home for a three-week holiday and refuses to discuss the Lausanne conference or the Pact of Paris.	Heavy trading on Wall Street shows a sharp advance in securities. The fifth day of successive gains causes optimism to spread through Wall Street.		Nine U.S. gymnasts are barred from the Olympic Games by the international body.	Jul. 25
Arthur Sellers, a Republican nominee for Congress from Pennsylvania, commits suicide. He was accused of embezzlement.		A general advance in stocks and bonds is noted in the past two days. Many stocks, including all the railways, show advances of two to three points.	Frank J. Sprague, who invented the trolley line, rapid transit, electric elevators, and remote control, is honored on his 75th birthday by a gathering of scientists, engineers, educators, inventors, and others, including President Hoover.	U.S. Olympic athletes are not being allowed to eat soup or pastries or drink coffee.	Jul. 26
		A National Economy League is formed to fight governmental extravagance. The League is endorsed by both President Herbert Hoover and New York Governor Franklin Roosevelt. The League calls for the elimination of annual grants to veterans who suffered no disability while serving in the Spanish-American or the World War.	Georgetown scientists will study the July 31 eclipse in order to test Einstein's theory.	Polish pianist Arthur Rubenstein marries in London. He weds Amelia Munz whose father, Emil Mlynarski, is conductor of the Warsaw Opera.	Jul. 27
The Institute for Politics opens in Williamstown, Mass. with a speech on "International Coopera-tion" by Dr. Inazo Nitobe. This is the 12th annual session for the Institute, which is a forum to discuss international problems.	Troops set fire to the Bonus Army camp in Washington, D.C.	The worth of the American dollar improves on the foreign market, coinciding with the strengthening of the gold position in the United States.		It is announced that the 1936 Winter Olympics will take place in Germany, although a specific town has not yet been chosen.	Jul. 28
	President Herbert Hoover orders a grand jury to investigate charges concerning the Bonus Army. It is alleged that the leaders in the Bonus Army riots are Communists and other radicals, rather than ex-servicemen.	Hog prices fall, with the price per hundred pounds in Chicago down 15 cents. The supply of hogs increases.	Professor T.F. Zucker of Columbia extracts vitamin D from cod liver oil, after 10 years of research. He says the tasteless product can be used in foods to cure rickets.	Comedian Aubrey Lyles dies. Lyles appeared with Floarney Miller in *Shuffle Along* and was in many other Broadway musical shows.	Jul. 29
		Senator Pat Harrison, Democrat from Mississippi, charges President Herbert Hoover with waiting "two long years after the economic collapse" before taking measures to act on the Depression.		The Americans win the Davis Cup Doubles, with Wilmer Allison and John Van Ryn defeating their French challengers.	Jul. 30
Col. Theodore Roosevelt returns from the Philippines, where he is Governor-General, to participate in the campaign to reelect President Hoover.		Presidential candidate Franklin Roosevelt states that tariff revision would lead to the lowering of trade barriers. He believes this would make it unnecessary to cancel war debts owed to the United States.	American engineers begin their second year of work on the Hoover Dam.		Jul. 31
Maj. Gen. Smedley D. Butler advises the members of the Bonus Army to go home.	Seven soldiers, including four officers, are lost in the Waianae Mountains of Hawaii. A search is organized to find the men.	President Herbert Hoover sends Secretaries Doak and Lamont to meet with a delegation of New Englanders to discuss a five-day workweek.	Excavators from the University of Chicago Oriental Institute discover relics in the Tigris Valley that link the cultures of India and Babylonia.	Five Olympic records are broken on the first day of the games, including two by Americans. Leo Sexton betters the Olympic shot-put record, while Mildred Didrikson breaks the world record for the javelin throw.	Aug. 1
Atlee Pomarene, chairman of the board of directors of the Reconstruction Corps, says politics will be forgotten in attempts to relieve the effects of the Depression.	The United States says it will participate in the League of Nations International Monetary and Economic Conference. Negotiations on tariffs, reparations, and money owed the United States are barred.	A treaty signed between France and Belgium threatens the loss of millions of dollars to U.S. business interests.		William Veeck, president of the Chicago Cubs, announces that Rogers Hornsby has been released as manager.	Aug. 2
Secretary of Commerce Robert Lamont resigns from the Cabinet. President Herbert Hoover announces the appointment of Roy Dikeman Chapin to take his place.	American delegates Claude Swanson and Norman Davis believe real cuts are likely at the arms parley.	All grains advance at the Chicago Board of Trade. Wheat leads, but rye, corn, and oats are also up.	Albert Einstein joins the Institute for Advanced Study at Princeton University.	America wins four Olympic medals in track and field. William Miller takes the pole vault, Eddie Tolan wins the 200-meter, John Anderson breaks the discus record, and George Saling triumphs in the 100-meter hurdles.	Aug. 3
Libby Holman Reynolds, former Broadway singer, is indicted in the murder of her husband, Z. Smith Reynolds, heir to the R.J. Reynolds tobacco fortune. Also indicted are Reynolds' secretary and boyhood friend, Ab Walker.		Prices of preferred stock rise sharply on the New York Stock Exchange in the most active market since December.		Pearl Buck returns to the United States from China. She says she was surprised to win the Pulitzer Prize for her novel *The Good Earth*.	Aug. 4
Democratic campaign chairmen are being sought for every state by James A. Farley, chairman of the Democratic National Committee. Leaders will gather in New York next week in order to coordinate campaign efforts.		At the American Institute of Cooperation in Durham, N.H., Carl Williams reports that the Farm Board has broken even on its loans.		The United States wins two races as the eight days of Olympic yacht racing begin. Gilbert Gray and Owen Churchill are the winning skippers.	Aug. 5

F	G	H	I	J
Includes elections, federal-state relations, civil rights and liberties, crime, the judiciary, education, healthcare, poverty, urban affairs, and population.	Includes formation and debate of U.S. foreign and defense policies, veterans affairs, and defense spending. (Relations with specific foreign countries are usually found under the region concerned.)	Includes business, labor, agriculture, taxation, transportation, consumer affairs, monetary and fiscal policy, natural resources, pollution, and accidents.	Includes worldwide scientific, medical, and technological developments, natural phenomena, U.S. weather, and natural disasters.	Includes the arts, religion, scholarship, communications media, sports, entertainment, fashions, fads, and social life.

	World Affairs	Europe	Africa & The Middle East	The Americas	Asia & The Pacific
Aug. 6	American fliers Bennett Griffin and James Mattern say they were amazed at the enthusiastic reception they got in Europe after "cracking up a perfectly good ship." The pair, who crashed in Russia, wants to try again for an around-the-world flight.	Swedish Prime Minister Carl Ekman resigns among accusations that he accepted donations from the late Ivar Krueger. . . . The first Venice Film Festival is held.	The revolt continues in Arabia, fueled by drought, depression, and discontent with Ibn Saud's rule.	Bolivian President Daniel Salamanca Urey says in a speech to Congress on Bolivia's Independence Day that the arbitration efforts of the Pan-American Union in the Chaco situation are making things worse.	
Aug. 7		A huge bas-relief Breton monument is destroyed in France. The monument commemorated the union of Brittany with France.		Paraguayan troops capture two Bolivian fliers from a plane shot down over Chaco. Argentina, Chile, Brazil, and Peru pledge neutrality in an effort to help settle the conflict.	It is believed the United States will experience a huge loss of trade if the Filipinos gain their independence. They pay $12 million yearly for steel and more than that for farm products from the United States.
Aug. 8	Upon their return from international meetings in Geneva, Senator Claude Swanson and Rep. Andrew Montague say they expect no change in the situation of war debts owed to the United States by European nations.	An earthquake in the Azores leaves 2,000 people homeless.		A committee of neutrals asks Bolivia for a truce tomorrow at daybreak in the Chaco area. . . . Two are killed in an Argentine tornado.	Manchurian leader Marshal Chang Hsiao-liang resigns, turning over power in north China to two councils. It is feared there will be new civil wars. . . . Japan names Gen. Nobuyoshi Muto as both its military and its diplomatic representative in Manchuria.
Aug. 9	Britain and Canada try to compromise at the imperial economic conference being held in Ottawa. Trade and tariff programs are at stake.	All the German political leaders are to meet soon in Berlin to determine Adolf Hitler's role in the government to be presented to the Reichstag.		Harold Foard, a chemist who returned from Ecuador where he sought medical herbs and new ore deposits, tells of the death by starvation of his student companion.	All 11 members of the Cabinet at Shanghai resign in a protest against Chang's policies. . . . Chinese bandits shoot and wound an American woman after her servants pursue them as they try to abduct her.
Aug. 10	A worldwide trade group, the International Apple Association, holds a world rally at the Waldorf Astoria in New York.	Many in Madrid are awakened by the sound of machine guns at 4:00 a.m. as Communists attack the Ministry of War. . . . A Nazi coup is rumored in Germany, as the president approves a resolution providing the death penalty for all political killings.	A number of ancient relics, some of which bear inscriptions, are found in a cave in Jerusalem. Included are 23 ossuaries, some from the Greek period.	Commander in Chief of the Brazilian forces Gen. Góes Monteiro reports that his troops are encountering no opposition from rebel forces as they march westward.	
Aug. 11	Secretary of State Henry Stimson states that war anywhere should be the concern of those who signed the Paris peace pact, leading the League of Nations to assume the Monroe Doctrine is no longer in effect.	Plans to make Adolf Hitler Chancellor of Germany hit a snag when President Paul von Hindenburg balks at the move because the Nazis do not have a majority in the Reichstag.		Mexico refuses to allow the Bonus Army to establish a colony there. President Ortiz Rubio says any available jobs there must go to unemployed Mexican citizens.	
Aug. 12	The deadlock between Great Britain and Canada is broken at the parley in Ottawa. The two countries reach an agreement on free entry and tariff preferences.	Paris, France, has its hottest day in 21 years. . . . Prussia bans beauty contests and nudist groups.	Qavam-ul-Mukl, one of the wealthiest tribal chieftains in Persia, is forced to exchange his ancestral lands in the Shiraz area for government lands in central and northern Persia.	Mexico City reports that the country is in the midst of a sugar crisis. They expect they will have a surplus of 100,000 tons at the end of the year.	Japan decides to attack Jehol immediately. They are upset because the man who led an official mission there, Gonshiro Ishimoto, is still in captivity after 26 days of negotiations.
Aug. 13	India reports it will participate in the 1933 World's Fair in Chicago, even though the government has decided not to take part officially.	Adolf Hitler refuses the secondary post in the German government and demands the office of dictator. Paul von Hindenburg is trying to bar the action.		Paraguay retakes a fort in the Chaco from Bolivia. This is the fourth time the fort has changed hands. . . . Four hundred students seize the University of Chile, but the riot quickly subsides when the police move in. All of Chile is now under martial law.	
Aug. 14	The first Jewish world conference opens today at Geneva. Twenty-five countries are represented by 100 delegates. Twelve million Jews live in those countries. The delegates are discussing the "grave conditions" facing Jews in many nations.	A World Library will soon be available to students from all countries who study in Geneva, Switzerland, as Count Johann von Bernstorff, Germany's Ambassador to the United States from 1908–17, donates his private library.		Argentine women receive the right to vote, but in return they must assume all the civic duties of men, with the exception of military service.	A fire sweeps through Manila, in the Philippines, causing $2.5 million in damage. Three city blocks are destroyed, as well as two colleges and many government records. U.S. troops help to fight the flames.
Aug. 15	Relations ease between the Japanese and the Soviets as a result of a Pacific fishing treaty.	The Soviet Union forms a bloc in the eastern Mediterranean. They have no intention of asking for United States recognition. . . . Czechoslovakia is in shock over the death of young Dr. Vaclav Vojtek, who was killed in a boating accident on the Elbe River. Vojtek was a member of Admiral Byrd's expedition to the South Pole.	According to reports to the first World Jewish Conference in Geneva, Switzerland, Palestine is the only place where Jews are doing well both materially and spiritually.	The Brazilian government reports that it turned back 700 rebel troops on the southern front. A total of 26 are reported dead.	In Anwhei, China, crops are ruined by locusts.
Aug. 16	Great Britain sets an electoral plan for India, under which both women and members of the Untouchable caste will be allowed to vote. The system is expected to be in place for at least 10 years.	A legislative proposal allowing the government to seize the estates of nobles involved in the "recent revolutionary movements" is signed by Spanish President Niceto Alcalá Zamora.		At President Gerardo Machado's request, doctors employed by mutual aid societies in Cuba delay for three days a threatened strike to protest use of their services by patients who are unable to pay.	

A	B	C	D	E
Includes developments that affect more than one world region, international organizations, and important meetings of world leaders.	Includes all domestic and regional developments in Europe, including the Soviet Union.	Includes all domestic and regional developments in Africa and the Middle East.	Includes all domestic and regional developments in Latin America, the Caribbean, and Canada.	Includes all domestic and regional developments in Asian and Pacific nations (and colonies).

U.S. Politics & Social Issues	U.S. Foreign Policy & Defense	Economics & Great Depression	Science, Technology & Nature	Culture, Leisure & Lifestyle	
	Lovell Hall Jerome, hero of the Indian Wars in the early 1870s, turns 83.	The ocean liner *Columbia* is launched at Newport News, Va. . . . Wheat prices soar to their highest point in the last 60 days.	Prof. Auguste Piccard of Switzerland prepares for a second flight into the upper stratosphere on Monday.	Jim Bausch of the United States sets a world record as he wins the decathlon at the 10th Olympic Games in Los Angeles.	Aug. 6
	Brown University president Rev. Dr. Clarence Barbour backs Senator William Borah on arms cuts. He agrees cuts must occur before debt cancellation can be considered.	Prices of beef steers in Chicago drop 10 cents from the past week.		It is reported from Paris that Lanvin's newest fashions feature full skirts, hats worn straight instead of tilted, and coats with a Cossack influence.	Aug. 7
Both Prohibitionists and non-Prohibitionists in the Republican Party believe that President Herbert Hoover will interpret the Prohibition plank in the Republican platform to suit them. . . . Former president Calvin Coolidge says he will campaign for Herbert Hoover.	Three new White House aides are naval officers. They include Lt. Donald Tallman, Lt. Junior Grade Harold Pound, and Lt. Junior Grade Charles Weeks.	The Federal Home Loan is established, offering relief to home owners. . . . The Interstate Commerce Commission insists that the Missouri Southern Railroad agree not to pay any of its executives or officials over $10,000 for the life of the loan it approves today.		Greta Garbo is greeted in Stockholm by a large crowd of admirers. She denies that she has bought the former Krueger villa.	Aug. 8
President Herbert Hoover promotes Federal District Attorney George Johnson, who planned the case against Al Capone, to a federal judgeship.	Walter Waters, leader of the Bonus Army, says the veterans have won their war and are sure to get their bonuses next December.	The price of cotton soars as crop estimates are found to be low. At one point at the New York Cotton Exchange, the price reaches $5 a bale.	A newly invented skinning machine is being used to process salmon in Alaska. The Beegle Packing Company is trying out the device in hope that it will improve the packing of salmon.	Helen Wills Moody, holder of the national women's tennis title, confirms that she will not defend that title this year, but will remain in Europe.	Aug. 9
It is predicted that President Herbert Hoover's home state of Iowa, which usually goes Republican, is likely to vote Democratic this year in the presidential election. . . . Senator Hattie Carroway of Arkansas is renominated by a landslide in the Arkansas primary.		The price of wheat rises, because of increased demand.	A meteorite strikes near Archie, Mo., breaking into at least seven pieces. . . . A Belgian expedition reaches the summit of the highest peak in Belgian territory. Ruwenzori Peak, located in Belgian Congo, soars to a height of 16,732 feet.	The Catholic Church changes its position on when a child should receive first Communion. Now they must be age six and a half or seven. . . . American Clarence Crabbe captures the 400-meter freestyle swimming event, while American Georgia Coleman is victorious in three-meter springboard diving.	Aug. 10
New York City Mayor Jimmy Walker faces Governor Franklin Roosevelt concerning a formal demand for his removal from the mayor's office. . . . In his acceptance speech for the Republican presidential nomination, President Herbert Hoover admits that Prohibition has failed.		Stocks fall slightly, but bonds soar, with the heaviest trading since last December. Net gain is 1 to 12 points, as 4,402,000 shares are traded.	Storms in New England cause fires and flooding.	Groucho Marx and his three brothers star in *Horse Feathers*. Filmgoers are amused at Chico's language problems, Harpo's pantomime, and Groucho's characteristic off-beat humor.	Aug. 11
John Thomas Scopes, who was convicted of teaching evolution in the "Scopes Monkey Trial," decides to run for Congress. . . . Democratic candidate Franklin Roosevelt meets with his running mate, John Nance Garner.		Stocks show the greatest decline since last October, but bonds hold steady.	A meteor shower is seen across the nation, with several small meteorites landing on a farm in Missouri.		Aug. 12
Democratic candidate Franklin Roosevelt begins to tour the nation for a period of three weeks.		The Amalgamated Clothing Workers of America ask department-store owners to support the principles for which they are striking. Their president, Sidney Hillman, sends out a letter asking stores not to handle merchandise made in sweat shops.	German scientist Prof. Erich Regener of Stuttgart University measures cosmic rays by sending an unmanned balloon to the altitude of 92,000 feet. His findings upset the theory of constant intensity gain.	A rare Egyptian robe is donated to the Metropolitan Museum of Art by its owner, Edward Harkins. Repairs are made to the ancient linen robe so it can be put on display.	Aug. 13
The Children's Bureau is concerned about the large numbers of transient boys in the United States. These boys who have taken to the road are a product of the Depression and are causing a strain on social agencies.	The White House receives a complaint because troops were used to evict the members of the Bonus Army. Roy Howard, of Scripps-Howard newspapers, and Dr. John Dewey, the famous educator, are among the 41 people who sign the protest.		The total eclipse of the sun, which will occur on August 31, is predicted to be the best one until 2017.		Aug. 14
The national convention for the Jobless-Liberty Party is scheduled to be held in St. Louis.		A farmers' strike in Iowa grows in intensity. The farmers, who are demanding higher prices for wheat, blockade roads around Sioux City and the leaders, who are meeting in Des Moines, consider extending their movement to other states.	A hurricane in South Texas kills 17 and injures at least 50. Property damage is estimated at many thousands of dollars.	The 10th Olympic Games close in Los Angeles, with 95,000 people attending the closing ceremonies. The United States finishes with the most medals, far ahead of the closest competitor.	Aug. 15
The Republican National Committee establishes their campaign headquarters at the Waldorf Astoria Hotel.	A naval survey of Kodiak Island is completed. This expedition to Alaska results in meteorological information and clues to the origins of the Native American.	A report by the National Industrial Conference Board states that the average factory worker has about 27 percent less buying power than he had three years ago. Average pay is now $16.24 a week.	The German Electric Company announces that it has been able to harness atomic power in experiments.	Eddie Cantor signs a five-year movie contract with Samuel Goldwyn. . . . A record-breaking crowd of 17,000 people gather in Lewisohn Stadium in New York to hear a George Gershwin program.	Aug. 16

F	G	H	I	J
Includes elections, federal-state relations, civil rights and liberties, crime, the judiciary, education, healthcare, poverty, urban affairs, and population.	Includes formation and debate of U.S. foreign and defense policies, veterans affairs, and defense spending. (Relations with specific foreign countries are usually found under the region concerned.)	Includes business, labor, agriculture, taxation, transportation, consumer affairs, monetary and fiscal policy, natural resources, pollution, and accidents.	Includes worldwide scientific, medical, and technological developments, natural phenomena, U.S. weather, and natural disasters.	Includes the arts, religion, scholarship, communications media, sports, entertainment, fashions, fads, and social life.

	World Affairs	Europe	Africa & The Middle East	The Americas	Asia & The Pacific
Aug. 17		Italy says it will retire nearly one-third of its navy, including the only two battleships. The ships will also include 12 submarines and 25 destroyers.	The Jewish conference at Geneva adjourns after demanding an end to anti-Semitism, denouncing the Nazi regime, and asking for aid from the League of Nations. Another conference is planned for the summer of 1934.	Levrinhas, Brazil, is expected to fall as the federal infantry advances on the rebel lines.	Workers are working day and night in munitions plants in Japan. Japanese imports of potential war materials also increase.
Aug. 18		Temperatures in London reach 92°F.		American oil companies operating in Argentina may be forced out of business if legislation now before the Argentine Senate passes. The plan will regulate production of petroleum in the country.	The government of Manchukuo demands withdrawal of all Russian troops stationed within sight of Manchouli. . . . Fifty-seven generals send a warning to the head of the Nanking government, Chiang Kai-shek. The generals say they will resign if Marshal Chang Hsiao-liang is forced to give up his command of the Peiping area.
Aug. 19	Rabbi Stephen Wise declares the Jewish Congress in Geneva a success. He believes that Jews from all over the world will band together to improve their status.	While a record heat wave causes all of Europe to swelter, Michigan has light snow. Temperatures of 99°F in London and 96°F in Paris are recorded.		The Brazilian regime reports they are close to defeating the rebels as they continue to bombard the insurgents in the mountains. . . . Labor leader Luis Morones is arrested in Mexico City. The government accuses Morones of spreading subversive propaganda.	Yasuya Uchida is expected to introduce the idea of a "Monroe Doctrine" for Asia when he speaks to the Diet on foreign policy.
Aug. 20	Delegation leaders at the Ottawa parley agree that it is urgent to take international action to raise wholesale prices throughout the British Commonwealth.		The discovery of synthetic clove oil threatens the prosperity of Zanzibar, which has been important in the spice trade for centuries.	Bolivians turn back Paraguayan attackers at Fort Arce in Chaco.	The truce between Japan and China is broken, as the Chinese intensify their boycott of Japan. Groups in both Shanghai and Nanking are trying desperately to halt any trade with Japan.
Aug. 21	According to the agreement signed at the Ottawa parley, members of the dominion are granted free trade of natural products with Great Britain.	The number of unemployed Germans has risen 16,000 since June, and now totals 5.5 million.	A Belgian expedition scales the high peaks of the Ruwenzori Range in Belgian Congo.		The Japanese bomb four villages in Jehol and capture Nanking. The Chinese appeal to Peiping for aid.
Aug. 22		A Yugoslavian government newspaper accuses Italy and Hungary of conspiring in recent bombings in Yugoslavia. Public buildings and railway coaches have been the targets of the bombs.	Opinion on the pact signed at the Ottawa parley is divided in South Africa, with one newspaper lauding the pact and another saying that little was accomplished.	Both sides claim gains in the fighting in Brazil. Rebels claim explosions during the night were part of their revolutionary tactics, but federals deny the claim. . . . Brazil welcomes another 1,000 Japanese settlers, bringing the total of Japanese living in Brazil to 130,000.	Prime Minister Joseph Lyons says Australia is pleased with the pact signed at the Ottawa parley. It is believed that no Australian industry will suffer ill effects from the plan.
Aug. 23	President Herbert Hoover says the silver question will be discussed at the World Economic Conference, and that he will appoint someone from the west with silver mining interests as a delegate.	Despite restrictions on cooperation with Germany, the Austrian Parliament ratifies the loan from the League of Nations.	Former prime minister Jan Smuts of South Africa does not believe that the agreement reached at the Ottawa parley will help his country.		Kojiro Matsukata of Japan visits Baku, Russia, in an attempt to find another source of oil in case the United States decides to boycott the Japanese market.
Aug. 24	British, Canadian, and American economists at the Institute of World Politics being held in Williamstown, Mass., agree that America's Hawley-Smoot tariff was mainly responsible for the parley held in Ottawa.	Denmark seeks to protect Danish farmers by negotiating a trade agreement with Great Britain.	Southern Rhodesia is satisfied with the results of the Ottawa parley. They are interested mostly in the effect on the tobacco and copper trades.	The Canadian National Railways will cut 55 officials, according to S.J. Hungerford, acting president. Salaries of the remaining officials will also be cut.	Reports say Canton is preparing to punish Marshal Chang Hsaio-liang for "failure to resist the Japanese invasion" in Manchuria.
Aug. 25		British author Kenneth Grahame's body is exhumed from a temporary grave in Berkshire. Through the efforts of his widow, Grahame will be reburied next to his only son, Alistair, in Oxford.		Anti-Argentine demonstrations take place in several parts of Bolivia. Police turn back an attempt to mob the Argentine legation at La Paz last week.	Four bombs are thrown into a store in Hankow, China. Anti-Japanese boycotters are protesting the fact that the store carries Japanese goods. Two are injured and the store is destroyed.
Aug. 26	Secretary Kaku Mori says Japan may be forced to quit the League of Nations. He anticipates worse relations with the United States and does not believe the League is necessary for Japan. He advocates isolationism for his country.	Several British newspapers criticize Japan's intention of recognizing Manchukuo's government.		Ecuador's Congress in Quito approves keeping Provisional President Baquerizo Moreno in office until presidential elections can be arranged. It has been determined that since he is not a citizen, President-elect Neptali Bonifaz is ineligible for the office.	Chinese evacuate the Chapei district of Shanghai in a panic after seeing large numbers of sightseeing Japanese marines in the area. It is rumored that reinforcements are arriving in Shanghai daily, disguised as reservists.
Aug. 27	Now that the Ottawa parley is over, the British seek to conclude trade pacts with other nations not in the Dominion. In the next few months, they will have trade talks with Denmark, Sweden, Argentina, and Germany.	Italian Premier Benito Mussolini orders Umberto Giordano, a well-known Italian composer, to compose a new national anthem.		The four South American countries bordering Bolivia and Paraguay plan a blockade to prevent the two countries from receiving war supplies to be used in the war in Chaco. Argentina, Peru, Chile, and Brazil will declare a state of war if the fighting does not cease.	In the Chihli province, which borders Manchuria on the south, 2,500 Chinese soldiers are killed according to Japanese military authorities.

A	B	C	D	E
Includes developments that affect more than one world region, international organizations, and important meetings of world leaders.	Includes all domestic and regional developments in Europe, including the Soviet Union.	Includes all domestic and regional developments in Africa and the Middle East.	Includes all domestic and regional developments in Latin America, the Caribbean, and Canada.	Includes all domestic and regional developments in Asian and Pacific nations (and colonies).

U.S. Politics & Social Issues	U.S. Foreign Policy & Defense	Economics & Great Depression	Science, Technology & Nature	Culture, Leisure & Lifestyle	
Secretary of Labor William Doak reports that for the first time in history, the number of aliens leaving the country exceeded the number of immigrants admitted for residence.		Pennsylvania is attempting to enact a sales tax in an effort to raise money for unemployment relief. The measure is passed by the House and advances to the Senate.	Swiss Prof. Auguste Piccard begins the balloon ascent he hopes will take him 12 miles up into the stratosphere. Piccard and his aide, Max Cosyns, take off at 5:06 a.m. Swiss time and in 10 minutes the balloon disappears from view. Piccard will study cosmic rays.	The New York Yankees extend their winning streak to 10 as Babe Ruth hits his 34th home run of the year.	Aug. 17
In St. Louis, the Jobless-Liberty Party splits, with each party naming its own candidate for president. The Jobless Party names Father James Cox of Pittsburgh, and the Liberty Party names W.H. Harvey of Arkansas.	At the annual convention of the National Aeronautic Association, Senator Hiram Bingham, president of the group, calls for a reserve of 100,000 competent aviators who can be ready to respond in any emergency.	All bonds listed on the Stock Exchange show gains. The advance is led by domestic railroads and industrial securities, followed by foreign loans and public utility issues. Government bonds also increase.	Auguste Piccard reaches 16,500 meters in his balloon.		Aug. 18
	Chief of Naval Aeronautics Rear Admiral William Moffett contends that spending a billion dollars a year for relief of World War veterans makes it impossible to get needed funds for national defense.	According to a monthly survey conducted by the Bureau of Labor Statistics, employment fell 3 percent in July and payrolls decreased 6.1 percent.	Maryse Hilz sets a new aviation record as she soars 33,456 feet above France. . . . German scientists believe cancer can be treated with a new type of beta ray.		Aug. 19
Republican Senator Smith Brookhart of Iowa blames the Hoover administration for the Depression.		An upswing in business across the nation is fueled by an increase in wholesale buying and industrial activity.	Two American physicians report on their use of ultraviolet light as an antiseptic in a speech to the International Congress of Light in Copenhagen. The doctors used the light rays successfully in 200 surgical cases.	Dr. Alexander Alekhine of Paris takes the lead in the International Master's tournament in chess with a perfect 4–0 score.	Aug. 20
Roosevelt aides are alarmed by a movement in some midwestern states to write in Alfred Smith's name for president on election ballots in November.		The American Federation of Labor fights to get back pay and privileges lost when the Economy Bill passed.	The body of Theodore Koven is recovered on the slopes of Mt. McKinley where he died, along with Allen Carpe, as they attempted to scale the peak to study cosmic rays. Carpe's body has not been recovered.		Aug. 21
American businessmen in the Philippines are concerned about Governor-General Theodore Roosevelt's absence. Roosevelt will take part in President Hoover's campaign for reelection.	The battleship Maryland wins the annual naval Engineering Trophy.	Iowa farmers picket at the state border in an attempt to stop shipments of hogs to Omaha. Two hundred farmers block the roads at Missouri City, Iowa, twenty miles north of Omaha.	The American Chemical Society opens two days of meetings in Denver. Discussions will include ways to improve agriculture and mining, news of motor fuel research, new methods of food preservation, innovations in science teaching, and ways to treat cancer.	Many world trapshooting records are broken at the 33rd annual Grand American Handicap Tournament in Vandalia, Ohio. Five shooters break 200 straight targets.	Aug. 22
The Children's Bureau of the federal government celebrates its 20th birthday. Created in 1912, the bureau works to help children in the areas of schooling, healthcare, and family and social relationships.	Norman Davis, one of the delegates to the disarmament conference in Geneva, expresses optimism as he tells President Herbert Hoover that arms cuts are likely.	Cotton prices are the highest in a year, closing up 15–20 points. Buying is stimulated by reports of boll weevil damage to this year's crop.	The Bureau of Standards in Washington, D.C., determines that radio waves can be transmitted farther in damp cool weather than when the weather is hot and dry.	Joe Wolcott is taken to the hospital with a heart attack. Wolcott was the welterweight champion of the world 30 years ago, but now lives in poverty.	Aug. 23
	President Herbert Hoover presents Commander Claude Jones with the Congressional Medal of Honor for heroism shown when his ship Memphis was destroyed in 1916 by a hurricane off Santo Domingo.	Farmers blockading roads into Omaha clash with sheriff's deputies.		Charlie Chaplin sues to keep his former wife, Lita Grey Chaplin, from putting their two young sons, Charles and Sidney Earl, in motion pictures. He says he wants the children to lead normal lives.	Aug. 24
President Herbert Hoover sends a congratulatory message to President Gabriel Terra of Uruguay on the anniversary of his country's independence.		Pennsylvania shows a 16 percent decrease in employment of miners of anthracite coal in July.			Aug. 25
Speaker John Garner, in his acceptance speech for his nomination as Democratic candidate for vice president, declares the Republican Party is to blame for the government's $3 billion deficit.	Robert E. Lee Week ends with a ball designed to raise money to pay for a statue of Lee on his horse, Traveler, to be erected in Richmond, Va.	Cotton prices soar to the highest of the year.	A great national air pageant begins at Cleveland, Ohio. About 70 aircraft are being readied for the races. Prizes include $10,000 and two automobiles.	Famous vaudeville comedienne Eva Tanguay faces eviction from the small Hollywood cottage where she lives. She is critically ill and is partially blind.	Aug. 26
Cleveland has a plan to eliminate slums in the city. The plan will build sets of model homes and tenements for slum areas.	Assistant Secretary of War F. Trubee Davison charges that Communists have been counterfeiting World War discharge papers. This enables them to infiltrate the ranks of the American Legion.	Recent gains in wholesale and retail trade seem to be stimulating industry as a whole. The demand for automobiles is up and the textile industry is also improving.	Scientists report that life on earth is only possible because of the ozone layer in the upper atmosphere. This ozone layer keeps damaging rays of ultraviolet light from reaching the earth.	The recently ended Chicago Art Fair is proclaimed as the "art sensation of the decade." The 13-day-long fair was held outdoors in Grant Park and admission was free.	Aug. 27

F	G	H	I	J
Includes elections, federal-state relations, civil rights and liberties, crime, the judiciary, education, healthcare, poverty, urban affairs, and population.	*Includes formation and debate of U.S. foreign and defense policies, veterans affairs, and defense spending. (Relations with specific foreign countries are usually found under the region concerned.)*	*Includes business, labor, agriculture, taxation, transportation, consumer affairs, monetary and fiscal policy, natural resources, pollution, and accidents.*	*Includes worldwide scientific, medical, and technological developments, natural phenomena, U.S. weather, and natural disasters.*	*Includes the arts, religion, scholarship, communications media, sports, entertainment, fashions, fads, and social life.*

	World Affairs	Europe	Africa & The Middle East	The Americas	Asia & The Pacific
Aug. 28	The Warsaw Conference of eight nations asks for an end to trade barriers. The eastern and central European agricultural bloc asks special concessions from Britain, France, and the United States.	The Fall Fair begins in Leipzig, Germany. The 700-year-old fair has 7,000 exhibits. Many Christmas items, especially German-made toys, are on display.		The rebellion in Ecuador seems to be ending, as loyal troops advance on Quito with no bloodshed.	Mohandas Gandhi is in the Yeravda Jail in Poona, but in what is seen as a peace move, a member of the viceroy's council is on the way to interview him.
Aug. 29	Australia asks for changes in the British Empire's naval defenses. Sir George Pearce, Commonwealth Minister of Defense, says the present defenses are unsatisfactory for a widespread empire like the British Empire.	*Voelkischer Beobachter*, the newspaper controlled by Hitler, reports his rejection of Franz von Papen's economic program.		Heriberto Wilford, an American, is arrested in Havana, Cuba, after a bomb explodes in the residence of the chief of police. Wilford is the son of John Wilford, the American editor of the *Havana American News*.	Manchuria announces that Chinese irregulars kill and wound scores of people. Fire destroys the airplane of Chang Hsiao-liang, which had been seized by the Japanese earlier.
Aug. 30	The International Physiological Conference in Rome hears Dr. William S. Collens of Brooklyn speak. He tells of a method of administering insulin through the nose which is just as effective as injections.	Dutch sailors walk out after a second wage cut is proposed. While they are negotiating, one of the shipping companies transfers its fleet to a British company, hiring British sailors and flying the British flag.	The press in Baghdad, Iraq, announces that a Pan-Arab parley is planned. The Arab situation, including the proposed union of Iraq and Syria, will be discussed by delegates from Iraq, Syria, Palestine, Egypt, Trans-Jordan, and Hejaz.	Mexico ships 51 known Communists to the federal penitentiary on the island of Maria Madre.	India is now buying Soviet gasoline. Western India Oil denies rumors that it is trying to start a price war among Russia, Britain, and the United States.
Aug. 31	The Japanese are boycotting British gasoline, saying it is too expensive. All suppliers have increased their prices from 35 cents to 42 cents a gallon.	A special emergency session of the Belgian parliament is called to act upon fiscal measures to help rehabilitate the economy.		Rebels renew the battle in Ecuador. They refuse to surrender unless they are given amnesty, and the government refuses it.	About 5,000 Chinese irregulars are reported to have attacked Japanese headquarters at Mukden in Manchuria. Tokyo denies these reports.
Sept. 1	The *Ottawa Journal* criticizes President Herbert Hoover's radio speech, saying he read it in a cold, colorless monotone, mispronouncing a number of words.	Britain retaliates against Germany's higher tariffs by raising the tariff on gloves, most of which Britain buys from Germany.		The Cuban government confiscates all copies of the American magazine *Plain Talk* because it contains an article they believe defames the present administration. . . . Peruvians and Colombians accept an offer by the League of Nations to mediate their dispute in the Leticia region.	Thirty thousand people have died of cholera in the Shasi province of China. Flooding has intensified the epidemic. . . . Tokyo announces that a treaty will be signed between Japan and Manchukuo. Japan will defend the Manchurian state and may station troops there.
Sept. 2	London announces that the Royal Geographical Society will send an expedition in 1933 to try again to reach the top of Mt. Everest. The last British expedition, in 1924, came within 900 feet of the summit but would have required oxygen masks to go on. The Dalai Lama gives consent for the British to visit Tibet.	The Albanian Minister to Belgrade admits that there is danger of a revolt in his country. It is reported that a number of prominent Albanians have been arrested and threatened with execution.	Cairo celebrates the symbolic ceremony of the "Cutting of the Khalig" with fireworks and elaborate decorations. It signifies that the annual rise of the Nile River has reached its full height.	Mexican President Pascual Ortiz Rubio resigns to go to the United States for treatment of illness. His entire Cabinet also resigns.	The cholera epidemic in the province of Shasi subsides, but bubonic plague breaks out in the city of Paoteh and spreads through the countryside.
Sept. 3	The International Astronomical Union meets at Harvard. The first meeting to be held in the United States was scheduled to coincide with the eclipse on August 31.	In the foothills of the French Pyrenees, archaeologist J. Townsend Russell unearths what may have been a tool factory for cavemen 50,000 years ago. The Smithsonian Institution regards the discovery as significant.		Federal headquarters in Rio de Janeiro reports that federals have captured a rebel airport in São Paulo, but many of the planes escape.	Chinese War Lord Chang Tsung-Chang is slain by two youths in a railroad station in Tsinanfu. Chang's misrule impoverished millions of Chinese and caused thousands to flee to Manchuria.
Sept. 4	The Congress of Stresa begins, to discuss problems in eastern and central Europe.	Several supporters of Irish Free State President Eamon de Valera are beaten at Trim, County Meath, by members of the Army Comrades Association.		Chile's Minister of War Gen. Pedro Lagos publishes an open letter to military organizations citing the improvements since his group took over the government.	A special session of the Japanese Diet fails to ease farm debts but does pass most of its relief issues.
Sept. 5	Britain's Prime Minister Ramsay MacDonald asks the League of Nations to agree to preliminary talks before the World Economic Conference in Geneva.	A federation of 450 French syndicates speaks out against a possible Franco-American treaty, charging that the United States will not lower its high tariffs.	The International Astronomical Union urges France to send scientists to study a meteorite in the Sahara Desert at Adrar in North Africa.	Two men are arrested for throwing a bomb into a school in Havana, Cuba. No one was injured, but the building was badly damaged and windows in buildings within a two-block radius were shattered by the blast.	The Japanese say the League of Nations Lytton Report on Manchuria is less severe than they had anticipated.
Sept. 6	The Trades Union Congress in England adopts a resolution asking for the abolition of all war debts.	French Premier Edouard Herriot is said to be drafting a veto of Germany's arms proposal. Meanwhile, Kurt von Schleicher of Germany says his country will go ahead with defense plans.	Three American consular officials who were kidnapped by Lur tribesmen are rescued by Persian troops and taken to Teheran.	The United States and Haiti sign a treaty which provides for less U.S. intervention in Haiti. Under the plan, some of the U.S. Marines stationed on the island will be withdrawn.	
Sept. 7	Pope Pius XI expresses a hopeful view of world affairs to Bishop John Gannon of Erie, Pa.	As the September 25 elections approach, Greeks fear a *coup d'etat*. . . . Italy considers a five-day work-week in order to provide jobs for a million unemployed.		Chile's recovery plan goes into effect. It is hoped the scheme will eradicate unemployment and stimulate production in agriculture, mining, and industry.	Mongolian princes and leaders meet in Peiping to try to offset alleged activities of Japanese agents in Mongolia. It is charged that the Japanese agents are trying to convince Mongol leaders to raise an army and join Manchukuo.

A	B	C	D	E
Includes developments that affect more than one world region, international organizations, and important meetings of world leaders.	*Includes all domestic and regional developments in Europe, including the Soviet Union.*	*Includes all domestic and regional developments in Africa and the Middle East.*	*Includes all domestic and regional developments in Latin America, the Caribbean, and Canada.*	*Includes all domestic and regional developments in Asian and Pacific nations (and colonies).*

U.S. Politics & Social Issues	U.S. Foreign Policy & Defense	Economics & Great Depression	Science, Technology & Nature	Culture, Leisure & Lifestyle	
Franklin Roosevelt is endorsed by the semi-annual meeting of the State Federation of Labor in Rhode Island.	Massachusetts Governor Joseph Ely believes only a Democratic victory in the presidential election can bring about a change in foreign policy regarding tariffs. He believes that will pull the country out of the Depression.	Chicago reports trade in all areas is steadily increasing.		The Philadelphia Orchestra has barred modern music from its programs and will only present classics.	Aug. 28
The Children's Bureau announces that its costs for June have risen 91 percent above the costs they incurred in the same period last year.	Seventy-two wartime vessels are retired. The retirement is expected to be permanent, but the ships are all termed "desirable" and would be available in case of emergency.		Dr. C.C. Little tells the Genetics Conference that in mice there is a correlation between the color of the mouse and the incidence of cancer. He does not yet know if there is any human application of the research.	*The Folies Bergere* closes suddenly in Newark before it was scheduled to open in New York. It is said there were differences between the director, Max Rudnick, and the star, James Barton.	Aug. 29
Governor-General Theodore Roosevelt decides to stay in the Philippines rather than coming to the United States to help in Hoover's campaign.	It is announced in Fort Dodge, Iowa, that William Hughes, believed to be the oldest living Civil War veteran, has died. Hughes was 107.	Sheriff Keeling and 30 deputies disperse farmers picketing in Des Moines. The head of the Iowa Farmer's Union, Milo Reno, says the strikers will not give up.	Diver Headon Locke sets a record in Sydney, Australia, by staying 165 feet under water for an hour, then being brought to the surface in three and a half minutes. Locke suffers no problems from rising so quickly. He wears a new diving suit invented by E.R. Clifford and J. Cantor.		Aug. 30
		American banking interests agree to back the Swedish Match Company.	In most of the northeast, clouds mar the view of the total eclipse of the sun. Americans in Bermuda have good views of the eclipse. Scientists say the eclipse proves that the course of ultraviolet rays is straight.		Aug. 31
New York Mayor Jimmie Walker resigns and President of the Board of Aldermen Joseph McKee succeeds him. Samuel Seabury, sponsor of the main charges that brought on the hearings before the governor, sees the resignation as an admission of guilt.	American businessmen protest new tariffs levied by the Reich on American products. The protest is not likely to be successful. . . . Four Navy fliers are killed in a plane crash in the Panama Canal Zone.	Cotton prices decrease for the fourth straight day, with losses of 8–13 points.	Dr. G. S. Carter reports to the British Association for the Advancement of Science that sleep is connected with the amount of iodine in the blood.	Americans are favored to win the series today as they take a 4–0 lead in the Walker Cup golf tournament.	Sept. 1
The week of October 9 is named Fire Prevention Week by President Herbert Hoover. He cites "deplorable loss of life and property" and urges people to take notice.	Secretary Charles Adams approves the recommendation of the Navy Board of Awards to make Marines and Navy men who served after the Armistice on November 11, 1919, eligible to be awarded the Victory Medal.	Farm leaders protest to President Herbert Hoover that the Reconstruction Finance Corporation has superseded both the Farm Board and the Department of Agriculture. They fear that their cooperatives will not be able to obtain sufficient funds through loans.	A group of scientists who photographed the total eclipse of the sun from Acton Vale, Quebec, on October 31 say they have twelve clear photos from which much scientific data can be obtained.	Charlie Chaplin wins his suit against his ex-wife. The ruling prevents her from having their sons work in movies without his consent.	Sept. 2
	A report by the Foreign Policy Association charges that the United States Army is unsound. It says that a well-trained reserve is necessary, but Congress rejected the idea when the War Department asked for a reserve corps. . . . The annual convention of the Jewish War Veterans of the United States opens at Atlantic City.	Hugh Frayne, American Federation of Labor organizer in the east, denies any discrimination against African Americans. Several African Americans disagree, admitting that membership is open to them but contending that they are discriminated against after they join, and preference in jobs is given to white workers.	Canadian J. A. Marsh reports that a photograph taken through a blue filter shows the corona of the sun, which he believes has never before been seen in a photograph.	Dorothy Irene Hann of Camden, N. J., is named Miss America. She receives $1,000 in gold and a trophy.	Sept. 3
Franklin Roosevelt makes a plea for party unity in a speech in Connecticut. He is aware that many in New England are disappointed that Al Smith is not the candidate for president.	The Navy concludes a project it has worked on for 25 years with the publication of a new chart of Cuba. Twenty-three thousand miles of coastline are charted.		Fourteen inches of rain strands 400 in a train in Mexia, Texas, when flooding washes out several stretches of track.	Fred Waring and the Pennsylvanians perform at the Palace in New York City.	Sept. 4
Financier Bernard Baruch hails Franklin Roosevelt as "a defender of the nation's institutions."	J.G. Friedman, an attorney from Jersey City, is unanimously elected to head the Jewish War Veterans as their conference draws to a close.	The American Federation of Labor favors an unemployment compensation law to protect workers.	Dr. Raymond Ditmars gives up his search for the bushmaster in Panama, but he says he obtained valuable data on its habitat. The snake is one of the fiercest and most poisonous of tropical snakes.	Al Fraser dies in a fiery crash at a stock car race on the Readville track in Boston.	Sept. 5
A federal judge rules that Postmaster John Kelly of New York was within his rights when he refused to mail two issues of the *American Freeman* containing articles advocating that the American working class should take the law into its own hands.	Three veterans who were with the Bonus Army in Washington, D.C., swear in affidavits that there were guns and dynamite in the camps.	The leaders of the striking Iowa farmers meet to discuss demands. The group plans to ask the Midwest governors' parley for a Midwest food embargo.	Dr. William Bebee prepares to descend half a mile under the ocean in his bathysphere. Bebee's quarter-mile descent in 1930 is the deepest man has yet gone into the ocean.		Sept. 6
		The Teamsters' Union urges the Hoover administration to prevent wage cuts for railroad workers.	The University of Texas and the University of Chicago join forces to build an observatory on a peak in the Davis Mountains in western Texas. The observatory will house an 80-inch reflecting telescope.	Protestant church leaders ask for a week of prayer, beginning on October 1. They urge everyone to pray for peace and power.	Sept. 7

F	G	H	I	J
Includes elections, federal-state relations, civil rights and liberties, crime, the judiciary, education, healthcare, poverty, urban affairs, and population.	*Includes formation and debate of U.S. foreign and defense policies, veterans affairs, and defense spending. (Relations with specific foreign countries are usually found under the region concerned.)*	*Includes business, labor, agriculture, taxation, transportation, consumer affairs, monetary and fiscal policy, natural resources, pollution, and accidents.*	*Includes worldwide scientific, medical, and technological developments, natural phenomena, U.S. weather, and natural disasters.*	*Includes the arts, religion, scholarship, communications media, sports, entertainment, fashions, fads, and social life.*

	World Affairs	Europe	Africa & The Middle East	The Americas	Asia & The Pacific
Sept. 8	The French and German plans for central European rehabilitation presented to the Stresa convention are very similar, and it is believed that an agreement will soon be reached. . . . Irish Free State President Eamon de Valera is named to lead the Irish delegation to the League of Nations.	Britain has decided not to postpone the next payment on the loan to the United States, even though Britain has the right to do so. The $95 million payment is due on December 15.		The Argentine Senate considers a new petroleum bill which will keep foreign interests from controlling the oil industry.	Dr. Inazo Nitobe states that Japan would find it necessary to withdraw from the League of Nations if the Lytton Report on the Far East were found to be unfavorable to Japan.
Sept. 9	The Vienna World Peace Conference adopts resolutions they hope will lead to world peace. As the conference adjourns, it warns of increasing militarism in the world.	Spain passes an agrarian bill which dispossesses all the nobility of their land holdings and gives the land to those who work it.		Nicaraguan rebels threaten to create chaos during the coming elections.	China's imports from Japan are down $4.9 million for the first six months of the year. The boycott and fighting in Shanghai have a large effect.
Sept. 10	Two hundred thousand Croatian immigrants to Argentina petition the League of Nations to be released from Serbian rule.	British extend credit limits from 12 to 18 months in order to garner more trade from Russia.		Argentine Foreign Minister Saavedra Lamas foresees an early solution to the problems between Argentina and Uruguay.	Chinese from all parts of the world contribute $11 million in gifts to help finance military opposition to the Japanese in Shanghai.
Sept. 11		The British ascribe the recent recovery in sterling to the revival of the London stock market. The British are investing there rather than on Wall Street, as they perceive the American stock market to be risky.	American expeditions working in North Persia discover the remains of a large building which was destroyed by fire. The body of a girl, posed in dancing position, is found. She wears all kinds of silver and copper jewelry with lapis and turquoise stones.	Bolivians turn back 5,000 Paraguayans in their third attack on Fort Boqueron in Chaco. People in the streets in La Paz celebrate the victory.	Tibetan forces hope, with British backing, to declare Greater Tibet independent.
Sept. 12	Foreign Minister Saavedra Lamas says Argentina will rejoin the League of Nations. The nation will propose a universal League policy to not recognize territorial changes resulting from force.	Germany, France, and Italy agree at the Stresa Conference on a plan which gives preferential treatment in European markets to the Danubian countries. Britain is unlikely to participate. . . . The Franz von Papen government in Germany insists the Reichstag be dissolved.		Cuba frees 84 political prisoners by order of President Gerardo Machado. Most of the group, which includes 10 women, are university students. About 60 students remain in jail.	Australian workers throughout the country plan to strike against the reduction of wages, which they believe will lower the standard of living in Australia.
Sept. 13	China plans to ask the League of Nations to boycott Japan. They believe Japan's actions in Manchuria are in violation of the Nine-Power Treaty.	Britain refuses at the Stresa Conference to aid the countries of the Danube. Britain believes that tariff cuts would end the crisis in the area.		The battle in the Chaco intensifies as the Bolivians manage to hang on to Fort Boqueron during the fifth straight day of attacks.	India is upset by Mohandas Gandhi's threat to starve himself to death in his prison cell. Dr. B.M. Ambedkar, leader of the Untouchables, calls it a publicity stunt.
Sept. 14		Germany withdraws from the disarmament conference, arguing that it did not have equal rights with the other countries. . . . The Belgian legislature grants the government great powers to try to turn the Depression around.	*Homo Helmei* is the name chosen for the species of man whose skull was found in South Africa by Dr. Drayer of Grey University. Drayer believes this skull furthers the thesis that each continent developed its own species of man.	The committee of neutrals urges Bolivia and Paraguay to create a demilitarized zone 20 kilometers wide between the two armies. They believe this plan would stop the bloodshed long enough for negotiations to take place.	Prime Minister George Forbes of New Zealand believes the worst of the Depression is over, even though 56,456 are still unemployed.
Sept. 15	Japan asks the League of Nations to delay its study of the Lytton Report for six weeks so the Japanese can study the report and send a representative to Geneva.	Italians search in vain for a lost plane carrying American nurse Edna Newcomer. It is believed the plane was lost over the ocean.		Paraguay is vigorously opposed to the demilitarized zone proposed by the neutrals.	Manchukuo becomes a Japanese Protectorate as the two governments sign a protocol.
Sept. 16	The League of Nations asks Washington permission to mediate in the Chaco dispute. The United States asks for more time, as the neutrals still hope they can mediate the clash between Bolivia and Paraguay.	Chancellor Franz von Papen nearly overcomes resistance of Bavaria and other southern states to absorbing Prussia and other small states. There would only be five states in the Reich under this plan.	Gold is discovered in the Italian colony of Eritrea, Africa.	Bolivia replies with an encouraging note to the suggestion by the neutrals that a demilitarized zone be set up between the Bolivian and Paraguayan armies in the Chaco.	Dr. M. Ambedkar, leader of the Untouchables, says he's willing to listen to any proposal that Mohandas Gandhi has, but he refuses to attend a conference called on Monday, because he believes any conference is useless unless Gandhi's ideas are known.
Sept. 17		Italian Premier Benito Mussolini calls democracy a worn-out doctrine and hails fascism as the creed of the century.	The Right Honorable Jacob de Villiers, Chief Justice of South Africa, dies in London. De Villiers fought in the Boer War and at one time served as High Commissioner of the Union of South Africa.	Argentina says that the nation will only join the League of Nations with an announcement that the country does not recognize the Monroe Doctrine as a regional agreement. September 27 is the date set for the vote on Argentina's entry into the League.	Prof. Nobutake Takagi explains Japan's reasons for wanting to withdraw from the League of Nations. He cites the League's attempts to settle the problems in Manchuria without complete information.
Sept. 18	The League of Nations wants to know where the United States stands on the Japan-China issue, and whether the United States will back their belief that Japan is the aggressor.	The French are pleased with Britain's stance opposing revision for the Reich. France is against any move that will allow an increase in arms for Germany.		The Bolivians want to end the hostilities with Paraguay, but say that the Paraguayans must first agree.	Japan and Russia reach an agreement whereby large quantities of Russian oil will be exported to Japan.
Sept. 19	Doctors from 40 nations are meeting at a medical conference in Vichy, France, to discuss diseases of the gall bladder, liver, and intestines.	The Danubian Plan is adopted at Stresa, Italy. A group based in Basel, Switzerland, will direct the project. A fund of $14.5 million is provided.		Officers from the Chaco say the fighting at Boqueron is one of the largest engagements to ever take place between South American nations.	China's new civil war stretches across the Shantung Peninsula. General Ho and General Chang both try to end it, but the fighting continues.

A	B	C	D	E
Includes developments that affect more than one world region, international organizations, and important meetings of world leaders.	Includes all domestic and regional developments in Europe, including the Soviet Union.	Includes all domestic and regional developments in Africa and the Middle East.	Includes all domestic and regional developments in Latin America, the Caribbean, and Canada.	Includes all domestic and regional developments in Asian and Pacific nations (and colonies).

U.S. Politics & Social Issues	U.S. Foreign Policy & Defense	Economics & Great Depression	Science, Technology & Nature	Culture, Leisure & Lifestyle	
Col. Raymond Robins, a personal friend of the President, disappears. Kidnapping is suspected.		Anthracite miners protest a proposed wage cut, but producers are adamant that slashing salaries is the only way to stabilize the coal mining industry.	Astronomers report that the next two total eclipses of the sun will only be seen well from remote sites. The one in 1934 will only be visible from a few tiny islands in the Pacific, while the eclipse expected in 1936 will best be viewed from the middle of Siberia.	Pittsburgh Pirates catcher Robert Earl Grace ends his string of errorless chances at 444, as he makes a wild throw to second base, allowing the runner to score from third.	Sept. 8
President Herbert Hoover plans to make a few speeches, but decides that he will not make a campaign tour of the country.	In Washington, D. C., oil producers ask for a tariff on naphtha from Russia and Romania. They want the 0.5-cent tax raised to 2.5 cents per gallon.	Sales in department stores for the first eight months of the year are down 24 percent from sales for the same eight months last year. . . . The boilers on the steamer *Observation* explode, killing at least 37 and injuring 64 more.	Louis Gellerman of Yale reports that young chimpanzees that are brought up like children will learn more than human children by the age of two.	Eleanor Holm sets a world record in the 220-yard backstroke.	Sept. 9
	The United States announces its position on Manchuria. Secretary of State Henry Stimson says that the United States will not recognize any agreement or situation brought about by means which are contrary to the Pact of Paris.	Workers undergo great difficulties in order to build a scenic road in Glacier National Park in Montana. Parts of the road are carved from the solid rock cliffs on the sides of Mt. Pollack.	Prof. Henry Fairfield Osbourne reports the finding of a 1.5-ton dinosaur fossil.. He estimates the bones to be about 70 million years old.	Noel Coward receives a huge ovation in London as his play *Cavalcade* ends after 400 performances.	Sept. 10
African Americans ask President Herbert Hoover's help in assuring that they get a fair share of public works jobs.	Norman Armour, who has been with the U.S. Embassy in Paris, sails for home. After a month, he will take up new duties in Port-au-Prince as U.S. Minister to Haiti. J. Theodore Mariner replaces him in Paris.	Representatives of nine midwestern states come up with an economic plan to aid farmers in their area. They favor revision of tariffs, an orderly marketing program, and a moratorium on farmers' debts.			Sept. 11
Democratic nominee Franklin Roosevelt embarks on a 9,800-mile train journey to campaign throughout the midwest and the west.	The United States and several countries from South America meet at the International Cocoa Conference to try to increase consumption of cocoa and come up with improved production methods.	For the fifth straight week, business failures in the United States decrease. Comparison with a year ago is also favorable.	At Presidio, Texas, the flooding Rio Grande washes away a bridge and three federal buildings. The Concho River, which flows into the Rio Grande just above Presidio, rises 38 feet.	Columbia, Harvard, Army, and Navy say they will broadcast their college games in accordance with the Eastern Intercollegiate Association's new policy of letting the individual schools make their own decisions about airing their games.	Sept. 12
Democrats triumph in Maine, electing the governor, two Congressmen and many county and state officials. The state is traditionally Republican. Vice presidential candidate John N. Garner predicts a Democratic sweep across the nation.	An Army flier sets a bombing record when he hits seven circles on the ground from 5,000 feet. The Army Air Corps believes Lt. Charles O'Conner's feat is a world record for consecutive hits.	The average cost of living is lower than it has been since 1917. Food prices are the same as they were in 1913 and clothing costs what it did in 1916. Rents are about the same as they were in 1919.	Skeletons of 49 Mound Builders are found near Pittsburgh. The natives lived there 10,000 years ago. The bodies were arranged in a circle, with their faces upward.	The New York Yankees beat the Cleveland Indians to clinch the American League pennant.	Sept. 13
Franklin Roosevelt is cheered by 10,000 people as he speaks from the steps of the Kansas State Capitol in Topeka. He outlines a Six-Point Plan to combat the effects of the Depression.	President Herbert Hoover names Hugh Wilson, U.S. Minister to Switzerland, to represent the United States at the Bureau meeting of the arms parley to be held in Geneva on Wednesday.	Representatives of striking coal miners in Ohio agree to terms to end the strike. The membership still needs to vote on the proposal.			Sept. 14
President Herbert Hoover opens the Welfare and Relief Mobilization Conference at the White House with a vow that no one should go hungry this winter.	Secretary of State Henry Stimson refuses to comment on Japanese recognition of Manchukuo. Apparently the United States will wait for the Lytton Report to the League of Nations before commenting.	Railway workers do not believe cutting wages would do anything to help the Depression and they are adamantly against it.	Engineers for the Westinghouse Electrical and Manufacturing Company announce an invention which can cook food over a distance by radio waves. They say that eventually every radio will have a cooking apparatus attached to it.	John Tammaro dies after falling with his horse at Belmont on Tuesday. He is the third steeplechase rider to be killed by falling in the past six weeks.	Sept. 15
In a statement from the executive office in Albany, Governor Franklin Roosevelt wishes a happy new year to the Jews of New York State on the occasion of Rosh Hashanah.	Only Estonia, Latvia, and Poland ask to delay payments on the principals of their loans.	Foreign trade rises $13.7 million in August. This was the first upturn in trade since March.	Hieroglyphics found recently in India by Sir John Marshall match those found on tablets on Easter Island in the Pacific. The find was disclosed in a paper read to the French Society of Sciences by Paul Pelliot.		Sept. 16
Changing his mind after seeing the reception Franklin Roosevelt has received in the west, Herbert Hoover considers a four-week campaign tour.	In a note to the United States, China charges that Japan constitutes a menace to the world and asks for help in combating the Japanese aggression. The note states that Machukuo is nothing but a Japanese puppet.	J.C. Barry, vice president of the General Electric Company, believes that for electrical companies, the Depression is a thing of the past. He says all business signs are favorable.	New radios with clearer reception are being introduced. A small gadget which hooks onto the antenna is said to eliminate man-made static.	Kerry Patch wins the Futurity at Belmont. Jockey Jimmy Burke was scheduled to ride the winning horse, but was delayed by a flat tire and jockey Pete Wills was assigned to take his place.	Sept. 17
Prohibition leader Rev. Daniel Poling will make a campaign tour of the country by plane on behalf of President Herbert Hoover.	The Newport Conference passes a resolution calling for a conference of international economic representatives to meet in the United States.	Farmers of the midwest and the south are set to strike tomorrow, withholding grain and livestock products from the market. The highest cattle prices of the year are seen in Chicago.	Thousands of fossils of fish with legs are found on the Newfoundland shore. Scientists are calling the creature a missing link, halfway between toads and fish.	Actress Peg Entwhistle commits suicide by jumping from the letter H of the Hollywood sign.	Sept. 18
	Ambassador Edge and Senator Reed inform French Prime Minister Edouard Herriot that the United States opposes rearmament by the Reich.	Farmers picket roads in Minnesota in an attempt to keep shipments from reaching Sioux City, N.Dak. They are hoping to bring about higher prices for their goods.	A new process to extract vitamin A has lowered the price. The price had been about $11,000 a pound for the vitamin.		Sept. 19

F	G	H	I	J
Includes elections, federal-state relations, civil rights and liberties, crime, the judiciary, education, healthcare, poverty, urban affairs, and population.	*Includes formation and debate of U.S. foreign and defense policies, veterans affairs, and defense spending. (Relations with specific foreign countries are usually found under the region concerned.)*	*Includes business, labor, agriculture, taxation, transportation, consumer affairs, monetary and fiscal policy, natural resources, pollution, and accidents.*	*Includes worldwide scientific, medical, and technological developments, natural phenomena, U.S. weather, and natural disasters.*	*Includes the arts, religion, scholarship, communications media, sports, entertainment, fashions, fads, and social life.*

	World Affairs	Europe	Africa & The Middle East	The Americas	Asia & The Pacific
Sept. 20	The Japanese are apprehensive about Irish President Eamon de Valera being named President of the League of Nations Council. The Japanese feel their request for a six-month delay in discussing the Lytton Report will be granted.	David Lloyd George criticizes the British arms policy, charging it has antagonized Italy, Germany, and Russia. He says if the Lausanne conference turns out to be a success, he will then support the British government again.		Diplomats in Buenos Aires doubt if Argentina, Brazil, Chile, and Peru will continue to participate in the Chaco negotiations. Peru's occupation of Leticia in Colombia causes the negotiations to be dropped.	India's Mohandas Gandhi begins his hunger strike in his prison cell in Poona. He turns down a release from prison.
Sept. 21	The disarmament conference resumes work in Geneva. Germany's demand for equality is read and they adjourn discussion of the topic until an answer to their reply is received from German Foreign Minister Baron von Neurath.	The Hungarian Cabinet resigns. Regent Admiral Horthy asks Premier Count Karolyi to continue to conduct affairs until a new government is formed.	The State Department warns Americans not to emigrate to Ethiopia, as there are no jobs open there for Americans and no relief agencies to care for the destitute.	Chile extends the state of martial law until October 21. Provisional President Gen. Bartolomé Blanche says he will not turn the government over to anyone but the person elected president in the October election.	The civil war in China is halted by torrential rains. Gen. Chiang Kai-shek is using armored motor boats to navigate the canals and rout out the Communists. It is working so well that Chiang declares he will have the area free of Communists in three months.
Sept. 22	France agrees with the United States and has no intention of recognizing the new nation of Manchukuo. It is believed London feels the same.	Unemployment in Europe is at a record level as of the first of June. This count stands at 11.3 million people in 19 countries.	The Kingdom of Jehaz and Nejd changes its name officially to Saudi Arabia.	Paraguay announces the takeover of 100 meters of Bolivian trenches in the Chaco, killing 72 Bolivians. Paraguay also rejects proposed truce terms.	The Chinese threaten to kill the two British subjects they have been holding hostage. A message arrives from Mrs. Kenneth Pawley, begging her father to pay the ransom they ask for her and Charles Corkran. The Chinese say they will cut off their ears, then shoot them in one week.
Sept. 23	The 86th session of the League of Nations Council opens in Geneva.	Sir Winston Churchill believes giving Germany arms equality with France would constitute a grave danger to peace in Europe. He offers the opinion that even though partially disarmed, Germany is still the strongest power in Europe.	King Victor Emmanuel of Italy sails for Africa to visit Eritrea, where gold was recently discovered. The King hopes his trip will arouse interest among Italians in the colonies in Africa.	The commission of neutrals sends identical notes to Bolivia and Paraguay, asking for a truce. The neutrals say they will withdraw recognition of either country if it accepts the truce, then breaks it.	A draft agreement is being prepared for Mohandas Gandhi, as he weakens from lack of food. He says he will not quit his fast until the British government approves the agreement.
Sept. 24		A new socialist government comes into power in Sweden with Per A. Hansson as prime minister.	The rivalry between two towns across the Nile River from each other in Egypt flares. Residents of Akhmin invade Sohag, which dispatches 150 police to the waterfront. Thirteen drown.	The committee of neutrals declines the offer of Bolivia to declare a truce only in the Bequeron sector. Paraguay has not replied to the proposal from the neutrals.	The Untouchables abandon their demand for a separate vote and their leaders and those of the Hindus sign an accord to which Gandhi gives his assent.
Sept. 25		Spain grants Catalonia a new charter of autonomy, giving the region its own flag, president, parliament and government. Catalan is also recognized as the official language.		Fort Boqueron in the Chaco still stands on the 18th day of attacks. Reinforcements depart from La Paz.	Prime Minister Ramsay MacDonald approves the agreement reached in India and ends Gandhi's hunger strike.
Sept. 26		Because of the Cabinet crisis, King George returns to London from Scotland, where he was vacationing. It is anticipated that several members may resign because of Prime Minister Ramsay MacDonald's liberal attitude toward the Ottawa agreements.	Egypt has agreed to trade its cotton for Germany's potassium nitrate. It is believed that this may lead to the two countries trading other goods.	Bolivia says that the nation's last note was misunderstood, and that Bolivia is ready to declare a truce in the entire Chaco area. The previous note mentioned the Fort Bequeron area because that is the only place hostilities are currently taking place.	Mohandas Gandhi ends his six-day hunger strike in his prison cell in Poona, as a Britain approves terms of a settlement between the Hindus and the Untouchables. His doctors allowed him a few sips of orange juice and in the morning he will be given barley water and goat's milk.
Sept. 27	Foreign Minister Peter Munch of Denmark is sponsoring a plan at Geneva which attempts to compromise with Hoover's plan of reducing armaments by one third, while guaranteeing security by an international agreement.	An earthquake in Greece kills 150 and injures 1,000 more. . . . The Prince of Wales shocks the Danish at a luncheon they hold in his honor. He wears a cutaway suit with a soft striped shirt with soft collar.	A joint expedition of the University of Chicago and the Royal Geographical Society leaves for the Libyan Desert to study the "Rock People." The expedition will take two months and cover about 1,000 miles.	The government of Brazil reports that forces have recaptured four cities. There were many lives lost on both sides during the combat.	Cholera kills 150,000 people in China during the past five months. This is the worst epidemic since 1919.
Sept. 28	The Argentine Chamber of Deputies votes to join the League of Nations, but say they will not recognize the Monroe Doctrine as a regional agreement.	Prussian statistics show that 115 people have died in political riots so far this year.		Chile cuts off war supplies for Bolivia, which protests to Santiago. The United States confers with the League of Nations about the conflict in the Chaco.	Several cities in three areas of Manchuria are captured by Chinese rebels. After fierce fighting, rebels also take over 100 miles of the Chinese Eastern Railway.
Sept. 29	At the meeting of the League of Nations Assembly, French Premier Edouard Herriot praises Secretary of State Henry Stimson's August 8 speech. He also calls Hoover's plan "essential for any discussion of disarmament."	Ambassador Edge tries to push the trade treaty with France. He says he is confident that President Herbert Hoover will win reelection.		A storm hits Puerto Rico killing 212, injuring over 2,000, and leaving 245,000 homeless. Rumors that another storm is coming are denied by the Weather Bureau.	
Sept. 30	German Foreign Minister Baron von Neurath insists that Germany will not return to arms talks at Geneva unless they have a guarantee of equality with other nations.	A new Hungarian Cabinet is formed in Budapest under Premier and Minister of War Julius Goemboes.		The Remington Arms Company in Bridgeport, N.Y., receives a very large order for arms from Bogota, Colombia, as part of its preparation for war with Peru.	A series of hearings on Philippines independence ends in Manila. The Hawes-Cutting bill in the U.S. Congress would grant the territory its freedom in the next 15 years.

A	B	C	D	E
Includes developments that affect more than one world region, international organizations, and important meetings of world leaders.	Includes all domestic and regional developments in Europe, including the Soviet Union.	Includes all domestic and regional developments in Africa and the Middle East.	Includes all domestic and regional developments in Latin America, the Caribbean, and Canada.	Includes all domestic and regional developments in Asian and Pacific nations (and colonies).

U.S. Politics & Social Issues	U.S. Foreign Policy & Defense	Economics & Great Depression	Science, Technology & Nature	Culture, Leisure & Lifestyle	
Franklin Roosevelt is cheered in Seattle as he advocates revision of tariffs in order to restore trade.	President Herbert Hoover wants the Reich to remain a part of the arms parley, but does not comment on Germany's plea for equality.	Increasing employment continues through August, according to the Employment Service of the Department of Labor. Harvesting of cotton and other crops has provided employment for many workers.		The Chicago Cubs of the National League win the pennant with a 5–2 win over the Pittsburgh Pirates in the first game of a doubleheader.	Sept. 20
According to *Literary Digest*'s presidential poll, President Herbert Hoover is leading in the east, while Franklin Roosevelt is running ahead in the western states.	Ambassador Edge leaves France for the United States, bringing France's counter-proposals on the most-favored-nation pact. It is believed the United States will have to make tariff concessions before a treaty is agreed upon.		The *Graf Zeppelin* sets a record, flying from Pernambuco, Brazil, to Friedrichshafen, Germany, in 17.5 hours. The journey usually takes 84 hours.	Kansans raise money to buy land for a public park as a memorial to the famed Knute Rockne, former Notre Dame football coach, and the other seven passengers killed with him in an airplane accident in Kansas.	Sept. 21
A delegation from the National Woman's Party visits President Herbert Hoover, asking for his support for extending women's rights. Amelia Earhart points out that equality now exists in the area of flying and it should be extended to all fields of endeavor.		Economists back Hoover on his stand against paying the Bonus Army their bonuses before they are due in 1945. They say doing so would imbalance the budget.	William Bebee takes his bathysphere 2,200 feet below the surface of the ocean, a distance of almost half a mile. While 1,500 feet below the surface, Bebee begins a radio broadcast which ends when he reaches 2,200 feet.		Sept. 22
Franklin Roosevelt speaks to a crowd in San Francisco. He accuses Republicans of not addressing the issues and he comes out for the repeal of Prohibition.	Secretary of State Henry Stimson waives the policy of sending delegations only on U.S. ships. Norman Davis, U.S. delegate to the disarmament conference, will sail on a fast German liner in order to arrive in time for the conference.	The National Chamber of Commerce asks industrial, commercial, and other employers to go to a 40-hour week in order to alleviate unemployment.	Noted physicist Dr. Akitsune Imamura claims the earth's center is solid and made of a material 2.5 times as hard as steel. Most scientists agree that the core of the earth is fluid. Imamura reached his conclusion by studying waves from an earthquake.	Lillian Gish returns from Europe, and plans to appear in a revival of *Camilla*.	Sept. 23
In a speech in Washington, D.C., vice presidential nominee John Garner praises Franklin Roosevelt's ideas for fighting the Depression.	The Reconstruction Finance Corporation approves $9 million in loans to be used for emergency relief work. The money goes to five states—Illinois, Ohio, Michigan, Kentucky, and Missouri.			Rogers Hornsby protests being left out of the World Series money. He says he picked the members of the Cubs team and whipped them into shape before being relieved of his duties as manager, so he deserves a share of the money.	Sept. 24
Eleanor Roosevelt flies to Arizona to join her husband, Democratic presidential nominee Franklin Roosevelt.	The Coast Guard Academy moves to six modern buildings in New London, Conn. Now those training in the Coast Guard will have facilities comparable to those of the Army at West Point and the Navy at Annapolis.	According to the nonpartisan Fact-Finding Committee, business recovery is really on the way in the United States. Economist Roger Babson thinks the worst is definitely over.	Sixteen hot-air balloons from eight countries take off from Basel, Switzerland, in a race. The United States has two balloons in the race.		Sept. 25
The Republicans and President Herbert Hoover plan to campaign aggressively for the next six weeks. Hoover's first campaign speech will be in Des Moines, Iowa, on October 4.		President Herbert Hoover asks heads of railroads and unions to put their talks about wage cuts on hold until January. He believes the economic situation may be better by then, and wages may not need to be slashed.	It is believed that one of the U.S. balloons in the race in Basel is the winner. All other balloons except the two U.S. entries are known to be grounded. The Navy balloon was last seen near Warsaw, while the Goodyear balloon hasn't been seen since takeoff.	Phillies' outfielder Chuck Klein is named most valuable player in the National League, while Jimmy Foxx of the Athletics is the American League most valuable player.	Sept. 26
Democratic vice presidential nominee John Garner refuses to discuss the bonus payments for veterans, and says he will not discuss them at any time during the campaign.	President Herbert Hoover appoints Georgian Charles Crisp to the Tariff Commission. Crisp has been a member of Congress for 20 years.	New car production dropped 20,814 below the July output in 144 factories.	Dr. Robert Greenbough from Massachusetts General Hospital reports that cancer treatments are on the increase.	Both CBS and NBS will carry play-by-play broadcasts of the World Series games between the New York Yankees and the Chicago Cubs.	Sept. 27
Charles Lindbergh receives an anonymous letter which leads to the arrest of a suspect in the baby kidnapping case. Dennis Lawrence is being held in the Saline County, Ill., jail. He admits he was in Passaic, N.J., at the time of the kidnapping, but denies any knowledge of the crime.	The National Council of American Shipbuilders announces that private shipyards have offered to finance the building of three Navy ships until June 30 if the Navy will let them start building the ships now. They already are ordered, but the money is not yet available from the Navy Department.			James Cagney settles his wage dispute with his studio, Warner Bros. First National Studio. He will make $1,750 a week.	Sept. 28
In a speech at a women's conference, President Herbert Hoover urges an end to child labor. He emphasizes the importance of child welfare and education.	President Herbert Hoover is urged by the Chicago Board of Trade to back a plan whereby the Reconstruction Finance Corporation will finance loans to European countries to buy American corn.	The American Federation of Labor reports slight gains in employment by union members in August and early September, the first since 1929.		The Yankees lead the Cubs, two games to none in the World Series.	Sept. 29
A crowd of 200,000 greets Democratic presidential nominee Franklin Roosevelt in Chicago. Mayor Anton Cermak predicts Roosevelt will have a clean sweep in the Midwest.		Textile mills are busy, clothing sales are increasing, and St. Louis reports the best shoe sales in 18 months.		George Cohan makes his debut in talking movies in *The Phantom President*, a musical farce based on a book by George Worts.	Sept. 30

F	G	H	I	J
Includes elections, federal-state relations, civil rights and liberties, crime, the judiciary, education, healthcare, poverty, urban affairs, and population.	Includes formation and debate of U.S. foreign and defense policies, veterans affairs, and defense spending. (Relations with specific foreign countries are usually found under the region concerned.)	Includes business, labor, agriculture, taxation, transportation, consumer affairs, monetary and fiscal policy, natural resources, pollution, and accidents.	Includes worldwide scientific, medical, and technological developments, natural phenomena, U.S. weather, and natural disasters.	Includes the arts, religion, scholarship, communications media, sports, entertainment, fashions, fads, and social life.

	World Affairs	Europe	Africa & The Middle East	The Americas	Asia & The Pacific
Oct. 1	The Disarmament Committee in Geneva adopts a program based on President Herbert Hoover's plan. The plan would cut existing armed forces by about 1.25 million men.	Adolf Hitler addresses 30,000 young people from all over Germany in a huge youth rally in Potsdam.	An African tribal war in Liberia is settled by an envoy from the League of Nations. Dr. Melville MacKenzie gets tribal chiefs to meet with him and agree to a peace pact.	Admiral C.H. Woodward urges Nicaraguans to vote in the coming election. The chairman of the U.S. electoral mission to Nicaragua promises an election that is free, fair, and honest.	Japan's new slogan, "Back to Asia!" shows a loss of faith in the Western world. Kaku Mori of Japan wants to return to the culture and ideals of the Orient. . . . Gen. Liang Kuan-ying orders his troops to help farmers harvest their crops in the Anhui province.
Oct. 2	The British press characterizes the Lytton Report as wise and fair, but French newspapers are skeptical.	President Paul von Hindenburg is hailed throughout Germany on his 85th birthday. Adolf Hitler ignores the occasion.		Peace negotiations break down in Brazil and fighting resumes. The federals easily seize several cities from the rebels.	The Japanese Foreign Office says the Lytton Report will not deter Japan in Manchukuo. Japanese leaders accuse the commission of prejudice and say they may find it necessary to quit the League of Nations.
Oct. 3	Iraq is formally admitted to the League of Nations, after agreeing to several stipulations. This ends the British mandate over Iraq.	Three ships are wrecked off Finland, but the American steamer *Bird City* avoids a similar fate. Signals from a Finnish Coast Guard boat save the American ship.	It is believed that Syria and Palestine may soon become members of the League of Nations, following in the footsteps of fellow Middle Eastern country Iraq.	Tension builds in Mexico between the Roman Catholic Church and the Rubio administration over church and state issues.	Manchukuo expresses regret that the Lytton Report fails to recognize the independence of the state.
Oct. 4	The Lytton Report on the situation in Manchuria is introduced in the League of Nations. Findings are that the Japanese have violated Chinese sovereignty in Manchuria. They recommend that Manchuria become an autonomous Chinese state, while recognizing Japanese economic interests.	Julius Goemboes formally takes over as the new premier of Hungary. He wants to change Hungary's boundaries with the cooperation of Italy.	A report of the Palestine Economic Corporation shows growth in industry.	Bolivians are stirred to action by the loss of Fort Boqueron after 600 Bolivians held off 8,000 Paraguayans for three weeks. Bolivians are rushing to enroll in the army to try to win back the fort.	The Chinese press and political leaders are bitterly disappointed in the outcome of the League of Nations discussion of the Lytton Report. They had expected Japan would be told to evacuate Manchuria immediately.
Oct. 5	A meeting in Brussels of the sugar-producing countries agrees on concessions for Cuban sugar growers. As a result, Cuba's export quota will be increased.	Portugal celebrates its 22nd anniversary as a republic.		Chile's new civic administration formally takes office, with Javier Angel Figueroa as Minister of the Interior. Their first priority is to push the sale of nitrates.	Australian Postmaster Gen. J.E. Fenton resigns. Fenton says he will support the government on all other issues, but he refuses to back the tariff proposals and the trade agreements of the Ottawa Imperial Conference.
Oct. 6	The Earl of Lytton, chairman of the committee for the Lytton Report on the Japan/China situation, praises the U.S. stance on the issue.	Adolf Hitler predicts a complete Nazi victory in the Reichstag elections coming up in a month. He says if the government denies power to the Nazis, "we will swamp you."	A band of Syrian brigands invades Turkey. A battle ensues, and one bandit is killed, 20 wounded, and others captured.	Puerto Rico has less damage than feared in the recent hurricane. The coffee crop shows little damage and the sugar crop will probably be average. However, the citrus fruit crop is devastated and many people are without homes.	The civil war in the Szechuan province of China now involves about 300,000 soldiers in an area 135 miles long. Seven or eight provincial warlords are involved, and thousands of refugees stream out of the area into Chefoo.
Oct. 7	The League of Nations attempts to name a successor to Secretary-General Sir Eric Drummond, but Germany blocks the vote.	Monaco announces that it may stop producing postage stamps and use French stamps. Philatelists are anxiously awaiting the decision.		The new Panamanian government discharges hundreds of employees in order to cut its payroll. When the new regime took over, workers salaries were two months in arrears and the treasury was empty.	Business improves in the Far East. China has excellent crops and Japan's exports increase. Trade is also active in New Zealand.
Oct. 8	France is relieved by the delay in the arms parley in Geneva. The delay gives France some time to decide whether to advocate equality for Germany or continue to refuse it.	The Bavarians are concerned about the militarist tendencies of Franz von Papen's Cabinet. A return to the parliamentary system in the German government would please Bavaria.	The Egyptian envoy in Washington hosts a huge reception in honor of the 15th anniversary of King Fuad's succession to the throne.	Acting Governor E.J. Waddington sees a gloomy outlook for the economy of Bermuda, although the winter vegetable trade with Canada was good and the tourist trade is improving.	China extends its boycott to include all Japanese goods. Japan contends that a boycott is a form of economic warfare. America will feel the effects of the boycott, because China buys raw materials from the United States to manufacture goods usually sold to China.
Oct. 9	A new effort is made to rescue British captives Mrs. Kenneth Pawley and Charles Corkran who are being held in Manchuria. A Japanese army captain and 30 men are sent to negotiate with the kidnappers.	Premier Edouard Herriot reports that a new plan for peace and progressive disarmament will soon be on the table at Geneva.	South African pioneer Henry Hull dies in Cape Town. He was active in South African politics and finance.	The head of a coffee-exporting firm in Brazil urges exporters to set the price at 12 cents a pound. He does not believe that is high enough to weaken the demand for coffee in other countries.	Australian Prime Minister Joseph Lyons rebukes the Laborites for saying if they came to power, they would terminate the Ottawa agreements. Lyons holds that the pacts must be honored, even though they lower Australian tariffs.
Oct. 10	Former Shanghai judge Liang Yuen-Li accuses Japan of thwarting the League of Nations.	Sir Winston Churchill leaves the hospital on a stretcher, but he is smiling and smoking a cigar. A bulletin says he is doing well, but will be confined to his bed for rest and quiet for some time.	A group of 17th-century frescoes from Persia will be shown at the Museum of Modern Art in New York.	Brazil releases 6,000 prisoners of war, retaining only the officers. According to a government announcement, only the instigators will be punished.	The Japanese army begins an intensive drive in southern Manchuria. The object of the attack is to drive the rebels back into the mountains, then starve them out. Bombers will be used, and the United States asks Japan to take special care to avoid hitting U.S. missions in the area.
Oct. 11	Prospects for an agreement on disarmament seem brighter in Geneva and Franco-American relations seem less strained.	British cotton mills are busy filling a flood of orders that came in when the weavers' strike ended. Workers' wages will be cut 8.5 percent next Monday. Spinners will agree to the wage cut if they can be guaranteed a 48-hour week.	Tourists wanting to visit Palestine will have to prove that they have either a business or property at home, as well as a return ticket. The purpose is to keep people from remaining in the country after being admitted as tourists.	Brazilian bankers meet at Rio de Janeiro to discuss costs of the civil war, the coffee market, and the paper money issued by São Paulo.	Naotake Sato, Japan's representative to the League of Nations, surprises other delegates by opposing the League's move to abolish its branch offices.

A	B	C	D	E
Includes developments that affect more than one world region, international organizations, and important meetings of world leaders.	*Includes all domestic and regional developments in Europe, including the Soviet Union.*	*Includes all domestic and regional developments in Africa and the Middle East.*	*Includes all domestic and regional developments in Latin America, the Caribbean, and Canada.*	*Includes all domestic and regional developments in Asian and Pacific nations (and colonies).*

U.S. Politics & Social Issues	U.S. Foreign Policy & Defense	Economics & Great Depression	Science, Technology & Nature	Culture, Leisure & Lifestyle	
Prohibitionists oppose the stands of both presidential candidates, so they concentrate on trying to elect members of Congress who will block repeal of the Eighteenth Amendment.	Congress discusses the Bonus Bill and the unfairness of the Bonus Army's stand is pointed out. The veterans are reminded that when the legislation passed in 1924 to pay the bonus in 1945, they were satisfied with the terms.	It is believed Henry Ford will replace his four-cylinder car with a six-cylinder model, while continuing to produce the V-8. . . . The recent $120 million loan to the states for road building is seen as a step toward a national highway system.	Forty are believed dead in the flash-flooding of a California canyon. A forty-foot wall of water rushed through the Tehachapi, washing out fifteen bridges and large sections of the Southern Pacific and Santa Fe railroads.	The Chicago Cubs go down to a third straight defeat in the World Series at the hands of the New York Yankees. Babe Ruth and Lou Gehrig lead the Yankee offense, and their manager, Joe McCarthy, thinks they will take the Series in four games.	Oct. 1
Ambassador Walter Edge begins to campaign for President Herbert Hoover. He is optimistic about the chances of a Republican victory.	Funeral services are held at the Naval Academy Chapel in Annapolis for Vice Admiral Joel Roberts Poinsett Pringle.	Corn crops are considered average. The crop nationwide is estimated at around 4 billion bushels.		The New York Yankees win the World Series in four straight games over the Chicago Cubs. . . . John Barrymore, Billie Burke, and Katharine Hepburn star in the film *A Bill of Divorcement*.	Oct. 2
President Herbert Hoover speaks in Des Moines, personally addressing arguments put forth by Democratic nominee Franklin Roosevelt.	Washington will await League of Nations action before it comments on the Lytton Report, in order to avoid a quarrel with Tokyo.	A number of factories reopen in the Pittsburgh area, sending 3,600 employees back to work. It is expected that 1,830 more jobs will be restored within the next week.	A German expedition in the Andes finds the ruins of an ancient Incan City. A glacial canal built by the Indians still holds water there.	Yale University dedicates its new divinity building, made possible by the generosity of John Sterling.	Oct. 3
	A new organization, the National Committee Against Prepayment of the Bonus, has been formed. Members plan to carry their fight into all Congressional districts in all states.	In the first half of 1932, 40 percent of U.S. exports go to Great Britain, while 30 percent of imports come from there. Canada, Poland, Germany, and France are also major partners.	Scientists at McGill University in Montreal, Canada, discover a method of taking X-ray photographs of the liver and spleen. They believe the same methods could be applied to taking photographs of other organs.	Charlie Chaplin improves after being ill for three days. The actor's ailment is believed to be food poisoning.	Oct. 4
At Ft. Wayne, Ind., President Hoover accuses Roosevelt of "deliberate, intolerable falsehoods." He does not name the Democratic nominee, but his meaning is clear.	At a conference in Uniontown, Pa., the Bonus Army votes not to stage another march. They agree to have a committee carry their demands to President Hoover and Congress.		Amelia Earhart, who proved a woman could fly the Atlantic alone, is given the Gimbel Award in Philadelphia for Outstanding Woman of the Year.	The newspaper *Tigningenn* in Stockholm, Sweden, mentions British poet laureate John Masefield as a possible contender for the Nobel Prize in literature for 1932.	Oct. 5
Secretary of the Treasury Ogden Mills speaks on the tariff and why it is important to back President Herbert Hoover for reelection because of his stand on the tariff.		Farmers again blockade roads going into Sioux City to keep grain and livestock from getting to South Dakota's largest city.	Recent rains provide some relief to the middle eastern states which had been suffering from drought. It is the first significant rainfall since June.	Mae West signs a long-term contract with Paramount which will keep her in Hollywood. This means she will not be seen on Broadway in the near future.	Oct. 6
Former president Calvin Coolidge is amused by all the rumors linking him with open posts in Washington. "If there is a position anywhere in creation that is open," he says, "my name always seems to be mentioned."	Norman Davis confers in London with Foreign Secretary Sir John Simon and others about Hoover's arms plan. He says they will discuss the disarmament conference at Geneva and the World Economic Conference. The possibility of cutting the British navy may also be discussed.			The new substitution rule in football is more liberal, but a player who is withdrawn may not return to play in the same quarter. Players are not permitted to leave the field during the one-minute intermissions between quarters.	Oct. 7
	U.S. diplomat Norman Davis meets with Ambassador Andrew Mellon to go over topics he thinks will come up in his talks with members of the British government.	General Motors sales drop in September, but it is a much smaller drop than in the same time period last year.	In a speech in New York, Dr. George Bigelowe cites 300 cases of cured cancer as proof that if diagnosed early, cancer can be cured with a combination of surgery, radiation, and X-ray. He also said that bootleg liquor does not cause stomach cancer, as some had thought.		Oct. 8
Al Smith is on the road, campaigning for the Democratic ticket. His efforts will be concentrated in New England and New Jersey.	The Veteran's Aid Fund, which helps needy veterans and their families, is harmed by the demands of the Bonus Army. Donations are down appreciably this year.	Ohio dairy farmers consider a strike in an attempt to raise milk prices. The possible strike would involve 300 eastern Ohio dealers and dairymen.	William Bebee reports observing strange white-skinned fish from his bathysphere off the coast of Bermuda.	Sideshow performer Alpine Blitch, known as the world's fattest woman, dies in Richmond, Va. The 732-pound woman was still performing and performed the night before her death.	Oct. 9
Vice presidential nominee John Garner meets with Franklin Roosevelt to plan their proposed speaking tour. . . . Vice President Curtis defends the tariff to farmers in Montana, saying that it protects them. He charges a Democratic tariff would let in a flood of cheap goods that would compete with theirs.		The Mummers Parade in Philadelphia will be canceled due to the Depression. The city does not have the finances to provide the prizes. The parade has been seen on New Year's for 31 years.	South Dakota sets new records for early cold temperatures and snow, with six inches of snow and a temperature of 14°F. Wisconsin, Nebraska, Colorado, and Minnesota also have their first snows of the year.	Humorist Will Rogers arrives in Panama on the first leg of the South American tour he has planned since he went to Central America last year.	Oct. 10
The Democrats are the first to use television in a campaign when a half-hour program is aired. . . . A candidate for the Woodbury, N.J., City Council withdraws after it is learned he is not a U.S. citizen. Christopher J. Sanderson came to the United States from England when he was four and did not realize that he was not a citizen.	Newton Baker, former secretary of war, believes isolationism causes other countries to view the United States with suspicion. He asserts in a speech in Cincinnati that U.S. policy since 1921 has prevented harmony in Europe.	A.A. Busch, Jr., asserts legalizing beer would aid in the recovery of the nation from the Depression. He states the manufacture of beer would provide jobs for hundreds of thousands of workers. Millions of dollars would also be spent for the manufacturing equipment.	To commemorate the 100th anniversary of the telegraph, Clarence Mackay of the Postal Telegraph Company, sends a message around the world in the record time of four minutes and 45 seconds.	Thirteen Lutheran seminaries in the United States merge into five new schools across the country. . . . Joe McCarthy, manager of the world champion New York Yankees, receives a three-year contract.	Oct. 11

F	G	H	I	J
Includes elections, federal-state relations, civil rights and liberties, crime, the judiciary, education, healthcare, poverty, urban affairs, and population.	Includes formation and debate of U.S. foreign and defense policies, veterans affairs, and defense spending. (Relations with specific foreign countries are usually found under the region concerned.)	Includes business, labor, agriculture, taxation, transportation, consumer affairs, monetary and fiscal policy, natural resources, pollution, and accidents.	Includes worldwide scientific, medical, and technological developments, natural phenomena, U.S. weather, and natural disasters.	Includes the arts, religion, scholarship, communications media, sports, entertainment, fashions, fads, and social life.

	World Affairs	Europe	Africa & The Middle East	The Americas	Asia & The Pacific
Oct. 12	Further delay in discussions at the arms parley in Geneva seems imminent, as the German Foreign Minister cannot attend and the new French security plan will not be ready for at least two weeks.	In a speech beginning his election campaign, Adolf Hitler said he will play second fiddle to no man, and that it is ridiculous to expect him to cooperate with the present Cabinet.	The League of Nations reveals a plan for governing Liberia. Under the plan, a foreign adviser would have full authority to administer the government. The adviser will be appointed by the League of Nations.	Cuba says it will cut sugar exports in 1933 to comply with quotas established at the conference at Brussels.	Manchurian bandits kill Mrs. E.T. Woodruff as she tries to prevent them from kidnapping her three children. Two of the bandits are killed by Chinese policemen.
Oct. 13	Disarmament president Arthur Henderson says both the issue of German equality and that of French security must be addressed by the conference. . . . The League of Nations Assembly announces it will elect two deputy secretaries-general instead of one. One will be from a smaller power.	France's arms exports increase over the past eight months, as Japan continues to increase imports from there. It is not known if France is sending arms to Japan, but other items useful in times of war are being supplied.		Bolivian military leaders meet in La Paz. Gen. Montes reports excellent morale. He names transportation in the Chaco area as the biggest problem. Gen. Lanza says the importance of the loss of Fort Boqueron has been exaggerated.	The Chinese bandit who killed Mrs. E.T. Woodruff yesterday is lynched by an angry mob.
Oct. 14	The World Court opens its 26th session at The Hague.	Progress is made in the Anglo-Irish talks over land annuities.		The neutrals report satisfactory progress in their efforts to mediate the crisis in Chaco between Bolivia and Paraguay. Both countries accept the sending of a commission of neutrals to the area.	Member of the Manchukuo Privy Council Li Yi-Hsun dies after being hacked with an axe by Gen. Chen Shieh-yuan, former governor of Heilungkiang province.
Oct. 15	In a secret session, the League of Nations unanimously elects Joseph Avenol of France as Secretary-General. He succeeds Sir Eric Drummond.	Anglo-Irish talks break off abruptly, and the Irish accuse the British of "waving a big stick" and not showing a conciliatory attitude.	Telephone service is now available between Belgium and Leopoldsville in the Belgian Congo. A three-minute conversation costs about $11.14 American.	Bolivian envoy E. Diez De Medina says Bolivia's policy has always been to settle disputes peacefully. He asserts that Paraguayan stubbornness is blocking the way to a settlement.	Tata Airline makes its first flight. It is the forerunner of Air India. . . . Several hundred Japanese colonists settle in Brazil each month. Colonists are required to be farmworkers.
Oct. 16	Chancellor Franz von Papen tells Germany's foreign creditors that keeping tariffs high keeps them from being able to repay their loans.	London newspapers report Prime Minister Edouard Herriot of France will travel to Italy on October 21 for the purpose of negotiating a new treaty with the Italians.	The Johannesburg Chamber of Mines reports that output of gold in the Transvaal in the first nine months of the year breaks the record. A total of 8,619,265 ounces has been mined so far this year.	Finance Minister Hueyo of Argentina announces that he will submit a balanced budget to an extra session of Congress this week.	Muslims in India agree on a plan to bring about a Muslim-Hindu accord. A committee is appointed to negotiate with the Hindus.
Oct. 17	British diplomats fail again in attempts to get Germany to come back to Geneva for a four-power arms conference. Foreign Minister Konstantin von Neurath tells Prime Minister Ramsay MacDonald that under no circumstances will Germany attend.	The Yugoslav government arrested the leader of the Croat Peasant Party, Dr. Vlado Machek. . . . Albert Einstein attempts to resign his professorship in Berlin, but the government will not allow it.	The Smithsonian Institution plans an observatory atop Mt. St. Katherine in the Sinai Desert. Some say this is the mountain where Moses received the Ten Commandments from God.	Members of the Liberal and Conservative parties clash in Havana, resulting in the wounding of nine people. Military reinforcements are sent to the towns where the shootings occurred.	Reports from friends of Mohandas Gandhi say that he suffered a stroke in his Poona prison cell soon after concluding his hunger strike. The news is being withheld from the Indian people.
Oct. 18		Great Britain terminates its trade treaty with Russia, saying it would be in violation of the Ottawa agreements. J.H. Thomas, dominions minister, said negotiations will begin immediately for a new pact with Russia that will not violate the new system.	Istanbul reports that the Turks and the French are near an agreement on the border between Turkey and Syria.	During the past eight years, over 300,000 Canadians who had come to the United States to make a better life returned to their native country.	Dr. B.D. Ambedkar, leader of the Untouchables, visits Mohandas Gandhi in prison and says he is completely healthy. This squelches yesterday's rumor about his health.
Oct. 19	Albert Halsted, in his last talk before retiring as American Consul General in London, stresses the importance of tariff reform to save the world from disaster.	Prince Gustav Adolf of Sweden marries Princess Sibylla of Sachse-Coburg.	Remains of the first kangaroo ever found in Africa are unearthed in the Union of South Africa. The small marsupial was about the size of a rat and carried its young in a pouch, like its Australian relative.	Havana announces the Cuban Congress will enact a drastic law providing the death penalty for anyone convicted of terrorist activities or illegal possession of firearms or explosives.	The state of Bohr in India abolishes Untouchability in schools, courts, offices, and other public places.
Oct. 20	Two British subjects kidnapped 44 days ago are freed by Manchurian bandits. Mrs. Kenneth Pawley and Charles Corkran gain their freedom in exchange for $30,500, some winter clothing, and 250 pounds of opium. Mrs. Pawley is hospitalized with a severe cold and fever.	Romania's new premier, Dr. Julius Maniu, forms a new Cabinet. King Carol and Maniu agree to cooperate and work closely together for the good of the country.		Bolivian Fort Arce in the Chaco is holding out against great odds. Paraguayans outnumber Bolivians 5 to 1 in the area. The Bolivians report heavy Paraguayan casualties.	Clashes in the Szechwan province of China claim over 7,000 lives in the past few days. Efforts for mediation fail and commands to cease fire are ignored.
Oct. 21	A radio-telegraph parley held in Madrid brings pressure to bear on China, but that country will not take a stand against censorship. Mexico, Canada, and the United States unite against Europe on the question of allocation of wavelengths.	The illness of Premier Frantisek Udrzal prompts the resignation of his Cabinet in Prague. Jan Malypetr, president of the Chamber of Deputies, forms a new Cabinet, making only four changes in the regime from the past three years.			About 3,000 people lose their homes in a fire raging through Komatsu, Japan. The fire starts in a movie theater and spreads to consume 600 homes. No casualties are reported.
Oct. 22		Six European countries attend the third Balkan conference held in Bucharest, Romania. The aim is to promote cooperation and possibly an eventual union among the Balkan nations.	Gold is discovered in a 40-mile extension of a reef in South Africa, following an elaborate two-year survey. The reef is believed to contain a possible 278 million tons of gold.	American flyer Orton Hoover is still being held as a political prisoner in São Paulo, Brazil. Hoover, a former aviation instructor for the state of São Paulo, is held in connection with a recent revolutionary movement.	Gen. Ho Hsien-tsu is accused of killing hundreds because they could not pay the exorbitant taxes he levied against them.

A	B	C	D	E
Includes developments that affect more than one world region, international organizations, and important meetings of world leaders.	Includes all domestic and regional developments in Europe, including the Soviet Union.	Includes all domestic and regional developments in Africa and the Middle East.	Includes all domestic and regional developments in Latin America, the Caribbean, and Canada.	Includes all domestic and regional developments in Asian and Pacific nations (and colonies).

U.S. Politics & Social Issues	U.S. Foreign Policy & Defense	Economics & Great Depression	Science, Technology & Nature	Culture, Leisure & Lifestyle	
The prediction of Democratic nominee John Garner that beer will be on sale by March arouses Prohibition leaders to fight the plan. They declare November 6 a day of prayer, and pledge to unite immediately after the election to prevent passage of any legislation legalizing the sale of beer.		Wanamaker's opens the largest men's store in the world in Philadelphia.	The Meyers Research Laboratory demonstrates a new radio tube containing "cold light." The tube is ideal for use in television, as it responds instantly to the fluctuations of radio waves carrying images. The new tube is twenty times as efficient as the best incandescent.	Dr. Alexander Alekhine of Paris wins his fifth straight chess game in the tournament in Mexico City. He beats his last opponent, the Mexican champion, in only 50 moves.	Oct. 12
Franklin Roosevelt labels Herbert Hoover's relief policies belated and uncoordinated. In a radio address, he lays out his own plan for recovery from the Depression.	President Herbert Hoover is cordial to a delegation from the Bonus Army, but says the needs of the country must come first. They give him a petition censuring him for evicting them last summer and a list of new demands.	Senator William Borah says three issues must be settled before the nation can recover from the Depression. He addresses farm debts, reparations, and arms cuts.		Conductor Arturo Toscanini's performance with the Philharmonic at Carnegie Hall is brilliant and squelches rumors that he is in poor health.	Oct. 13
At a conference on child welfare, Dr. Thomas Darlington, former health commissioner in New York, says that cuts in budgets may lead to higher infant mortality.	Annapolis ensigns are barred from marrying until they put in two years' service, putting an end to the famous graduation day weddings in the chapel there.		Sir Lenthal Cheatle, foremost British cancer authority, reports that a dye can be used to distinguish between normal cells and cancer cells. Cancerous cells will not take the stain.	Baseball Commissioner K. M. Landis rules Rogers Hornsby is not eligible for a share of World Series money. A World Series rule says only those eligible to participate in the Series may receive a share. Hornsby is ineligible, since he was released in August.	Oct. 14
The Corn Belt pays little attention to Prohibition as an issue. People in the area are primarily concerned about economic issues, including farm prices.		Production of both anthracite and bituminous coal is on the rise. Anthracite shows a gain of 548,631 tons in the last month. Also bituminous mines have reopened in the Pittsburgh area.	Prof. Yandell Henderson of Yale University believes whooping cough may be effectively treated with carbon dioxide. The gas is already used to treat children with pneumonia.	Harvard beats Penn State 46–13 before a crowd of 15,000. Left halfback Jack Crickard thrills the spectators with two touchdowns for Harvard.	Oct. 15
Father Hammer of St. Patrick's Cathedral charges in a sermon that there is a move to keep Catholics from being elected to high offices. He states that one cannot be a good Catholic and a bad citizen.		An open petition signed by 180 economists arrives at the White House. It asks President Herbert Hoover to consider lowering tariffs in order to aid in world recovery.	Albert Einstein states in a speech in Berlin that he believes the earth is at least 10 billion years old, which is at least double other scientists' estimates.	Michigan improves its chances in the Big Ten race with a victory over Ohio State. They are now tied with Purdue and Indiana for the league lead.	Oct. 16
The Ford Motor Company sends bulletins to all Ford offices in the country, urging employees to vote for President Herbert Hoover.		Trading in stocks is the lightest it has been in nearly three months. Stock prices close slightly lower. . . . Delegates to the International Institute of Agriculture in Italy express regret that the United States is not participating.	An Italian doctor shows a meeting of medical doctors in London an "elixir of life," which he says will add 10 years to a person's life. The inventor spent 20 years working on the preparation and says it will arrest senile decay.	Jockey Eddie Arcaro rides Hot Shot to victory at Sportsmen's Park in Chicago, establishing a new track record. Arcaro also wins races today with horses Raffles Chance and Princess Black.	Oct. 17
Child labor in the United States decreases. According to the 1930 census, the number of workers between the ages of 10 and 17 decreased slightly. However, over two million children are still employed.	Stanley Hornbeck, chief of the Far Eastern division of the State Department, says U.S. foreign policy in the Orient is based on keeping peace. He stresses that the United States is impartial in events occurring between countries in the area.	Average food prices in 51 cities show a decrease of about half a percent in the past month, with a 16 percent decrease for the year.	Twelve associates and several family members of Thomas Edison laid a wreath on his grave at 3:24 a.m., exactly a year after his death.	The Church of Latter Day Saints buys a tract of land near Kennett, Mo. on which they plan to build the ideal farming community.	Oct. 18
President Herbert Hoover schedules 13 stops on his trip to Detroit. He will speak from the back of the train at 10 towns in Ohio and three in West Virginia.			Dr. C. William Hoeflich, president of the Associated Anesthetists of the United States and Canada, urges colleagues to treat patients with inoperable cancer with the acidosis method developed by Dr. Willy Myer.	Sentiment in the American League grows against broadcasting ballgames on the radio. Baseball leaders contend that broadcasts keep people from attending games.	Oct. 19
Both Filipinos and Japanese object to proposed raises in tariffs alluded to by Governor-General Theodore Roosevelt in a recent speech. Some believe the intent of the tariff is to aid American exports, rather than to help the Philippines.		Gains in gold reserves this week amount to $24 million. Also this week, monetary gold stocks rise $19 million.	More than half of the world's more than 30 million radio sets are located in the United States. The Department of Commerce also reports that the country boasts about half the broadcasting companies in the world.	The National Symphony Orchestra opens its second season in Washington, D.C. Hans Kindler conducts the orchestra at Constitution Hall.	Oct. 20
President Herbert Hoover leaves on a tour of the Midwest.		Continuous gains are shown by business, especially in textiles and steel production.	Aeronautical experts study the feasibility of a plane which could fly 1,000 miles per hour and fly around the world in 24 hours. Gasoline burning in long tubes would propel the plane.	Well-known painter of landscapes and still lifes John Ten Eyck dies at his home in Connecticut.	Oct. 21
Arthur Barry, a gem thief who has been a fugitive for three years, is arrested in New Jersey. Barry, who preyed on the society set, has stolen more than $2 million in gems.	For the first time, the Army gives the members of its Air Corps permission to make cross-country flights. The men will fly to the semi-annual convention of the Air Reserve Association in Kansas City.	Bankers attending the Investment Bankers Association of America convention believe recovery has begun and the worst of the Depression is now past.	A new serum to cure typhoid fever is used successfully in Cuba.		Oct. 22

F	G	H	I	J
Includes elections, federal-state relations, civil rights and liberties, crime, the judiciary, education, healthcare, poverty, urban affairs, and population.	Includes formation and debate of U.S. foreign and defense policies, veterans affairs, and defense spending. (Relations with specific foreign countries are usually found under the region concerned.)	Includes business, labor, agriculture, taxation, transportation, consumer affairs, monetary and fiscal policy, natural resources, pollution, and accidents.	Includes worldwide scientific, medical, and technological developments, natural phenomena, U.S. weather, and natural disasters.	Includes the arts, religion, scholarship, communications media, sports, entertainment, fashions, fads, and social life.

	World Affairs	Europe	Africa & The Middle East	The Americas	Asia & The Pacific
Oct. 23	Premier Benito Mussolini announces that Italy will not resign from the League of Nations. He backs Germany in that nation's demand for equality and appeals to the United States to cut debts.	Adolf Hitler again insists on full power over the German government and says he will accept no less. He says Franz von Papen's "doom is sealed."		The Argentine government asks to see the books of several meat-packing houses, including Armour and Swift. The packers believe the law requiring them to do so is unconstitutional.	Some Chinese royalists predict Henry Pu-Yi will become Emperor of China, saying most provinces are tired of civil war and would voluntarily give their allegiance to him. Japan thinks such a move is unlikely.
Oct. 24	Norman Davis, U.S. delegate to the disarmament conference, confers with British Prime Minister Ramsay MacDonald, Foreign Secretary Sir John Simon, and Stanley Baldwin, Lord President of the Council on disarmament topics. Britain is believed to be ready to cooperate with Hoover's plan for a one-third arms reduction.	The jobless of Scotland, Wales, and England march on London to ask for help. The march is orderly and in many cities labor organizations provide sleeping quarters and food.		Cuba protests the deportation of 27 Cuban musicians employed in France. The French charge that the musicians violated immigration laws.	Chinese farmers revolt at Yangchow, less than 50 miles from Nanking. The entire farming population invades the city after 50 peasants are arrested for not paying taxes.
Oct. 25	George Norlin, president of the University of Colorado, in a speech in Berlin makes an appeal for unity in the world and urges the United States to join the League of Nations.	The British House of Commons defends its recognition of El Salvador, which is said to displease Secretary of State Henry Stimson. British Undersecretary for Foreign Affairs Capt. Anthony Eden explains that the present government of El Salvador has shown itself to be a stable regime.		The Canadian House of Commons had considered paying prairie wheat farmers a bonus of five cents per bushel, but Premier Bennett reports that the Dominion is not able to pay it this year.	Japan says it will present its own plan for cutting naval resources to the conference at Geneva. Japan calls Hoover's plan a "crude and unfair method."
Oct. 26	The League of Nations gives the U.S. government permission to publish and sell cheap copies of the Lytton Report for 50 cents each. The League sells copies for $2.50, but they include maps, which the U.S. copies do not.	The French arms plan cuts military training from one year to nine months. If approved by the Council of National Defense, the plan will be presented to the arms convention in Geneva.		Both Bolivia and Argentina tell the Commission of Neutrals that they are ready to negotiate peace in the Chaco. Bolivia has lost a dozen forts in the last month and its government has changed twice.	A tornado cuts a 300-mile-wide swath of destruction across a part of New Zealand. Trees are uprooted, roofs blown off, and homes razed, but no injuries or deaths are reported.
Oct. 27	French Prime Minister Edouard Herriot believes the Chamber of Deputies should debate the disarmament question, but he is dead set against any discussion of debts.	Due to U.S. complaints about treatment of American students during anti-Semitic riots at Vienna University, Chancellor Dollfuss cordons off the school, only allowing students taking examinations to enter.		A Canadian government bill designed to effect far-reaching changes in the country's transportation system is introduced in the Senate.	Rev. Bert Nelson, an American who has been a captive for two years, is reported killed in China by Honan Communists. Nelson was a medical missionary.
Oct. 28		Police have an all-night guard set up at the home of Montague Norman, governor of the Bank of England, after he receives threats. An anonymous caller says unemployed people will attack the home.		Argentina agrees to send Vice President Julio Roca to try to negotiate new treaties with the British. The British Foreign Office says their government is highly pleased with the choice of Roca.	A privately owned news agency in Shanghai reports that China has rejected the Lytton proposals, saying an autonomous Manchukuo is not consistent with China's sovereignty.
Oct. 29	U.S diplomat Norman Davis hears the French plan for disarmament from French Prime Minister Edouard Herriot and War Minister Boncour. Colonial needs are ignored in the plan. Davis believes the Germans will rejoin the talks.	Turkey celebrates the ninth anniversary of the republic's founding with a parade and a display of military airplanes. Large crowds struggle to catch a glimpse of President Mustapha Kemal.	The French Foreign Legion digs in for the winter after building roads and fighting belligerent natives in Morocco. They are trying to connect Morocco and Algeria by road.	Auto owners in Brazil object to the mixture of gasoline and alcohol being sold in all service stations in Rio de Janeiro. A gas company official says pure gasoline will be available when the supply of alcohol runs out in the end of November.	American aid saves thousands of lives in China by making it possible for farmers to relocate to areas with canals for irrigation.
Oct. 30		Operatives in the spinning department of the British cotton mills strike. If the strike of the 170,000 spinners lasts any length of time, the weaving department will grind to a halt, idling 200,000 weavers.		Today's presidential election in Ecuador is accompanied by much disorder. Authorities decide to search voters, as some fire revolvers into the air. Incomplete returns show Martinez Mera, the Liberal candidate, with a large lead.	Rebels in Manchouli free 120 Japanese women and children who had been held for 32 days. Soviet intervention brings about the release.
Oct. 31	The World Monetary and Economic Conference opens in Geneva with a meeting of the preparatory committee. Joseph Avenol, Secretary-General-elect of the League of Nations, warns that the situation is "so grave as to make success absolutely indispensable."	The British Ambassador to Argentina sharply criticizes the Argentines' unfriendly attitude toward British interests in the country.	An earth tremor shakes the South African city of Johannesburg, but causes no serious damage. The quake is attributed to the collapse of a mine.	The National Revolutionary Party in Mexico writes a provision into its platform whereby anyone who has served as president of Mexico or governor of one of the states may not serve in that office again.	The Laono district of Manila is threatened with a new outbreak of Moro bandits. Major J.A. Green will send a constabulary force of 100 to try to capture the notorious outlaw Dimacaling, who says he cannot be taken.
Nov. 1	The Jewish Agency for Palestine gives its annual report to the League of Nations. It takes a generally optimistic view of developments in Palestine.	Britain tells Canada that Canadian wheat will not receive preferences if it is stored in the United States.		Canada begins enforcing its 12-mile limit law which was passed in 1931. The purpose is to stop the rum runners who work along the coast.	The Chinese report that Communists have killed Rev. Burt Nelson, an American missionary. . . . News from Shanghai says Japanese soldiers are massacring hundreds of Koreans in southern Manchuria. Many are reported to be women and children.
Nov. 2	The new arms plan France will present at Geneva Friday includes an anti-war pact with the United States. It also suggests a European Military Staff be created to keep peace.	Adolf Hitler says his plan of government for Germany would not in any way resemble the old regime. He charges that Franz von Papen brought nothing of use with him, but what he, Hitler, brings will be priceless to the Nazis.	Both Herbert Hoover and Franklin Roosevelt send greetings to Palestine as that state marks the 15th anniversary of the Balfour Declaration.	Panama Canal traffic increased in October, with 21 transits more than in September, and the highest in a year. Traffic is up because of grains and fruits from the Pacific Coast.	Australia is pleased to learn that October was the best month since the Depression set in. This is due in part to the Ottawa Pact. The government expects a large surplus at the end of the year, most of which will be applied to the floating debt.

A	B	C	D	E
Includes developments that affect more than one world region, international organizations, and important meetings of world leaders.	Includes all domestic and regional developments in Europe, including the Soviet Union.	Includes all domestic and regional developments in Africa and the Middle East.	Includes all domestic and regional developments in Latin America, the Caribbean, and Canada.	Includes all domestic and regional developments in Asian and Pacific nations (and colonies).

U.S. Politics & Social Issues	U.S. Foreign Policy & Defense	Economics & Great Depression	Science, Technology & Nature	Culture, Leisure & Lifestyle	
The Lame Duck Amendment proposed to the Constitution is almost certain to pass. It will eliminate the session of Congress in December, when many of the legislators have already been defeated for the next term. Also the inauguration date for the President will be moved forward from March 4 to January 20.		The week's trading in oats and rye is very light. The dealing in oats was the lowest in history.	Professor J.A. Curtin of D'Youville College predicts a cold winter with heavy snow. His prediction is based on four months spent studying sunspots.	Utah is the only unbeaten and untied team remaining in the Rocky Mountain Conference and has a good chance at a fifth straight title.	Oct. 23
President Herbert Hoover attacks Franklin Roosevelt for not taking a stand on the issue of recognizing Russia.		Five railroads show their income is up from that of a year ago. This was the seventh consecutive increase for the Reading Railroad. . . . President Herbert Hoover requests more data on 16 commodities in order to determine whether higher tariffs are needed or would benefit workers.	Dr. David Kaliski tells the New York Academy of Medicine that sentimental people who stand in the way of experimentation with animals are enemies of civilization. He says animals are absolutely necessary in cancer research.		Oct. 24
Dr. Carl Buck fears that a decline in public health will be a delayed outcome of the Depression. He is especially concerned about children and their nutrition.		The American Bankers Association states that the elimination of 10,000 banks has strengthened the banking structure of the United States. These banks were called uneconomical. . . . New Jersey Governor Moore attacks tariffs and says he thinks the decline in exports is linked to the Smoot-Hawley tariff.		Columbia University is charged with professionalism in intercollegiate athletics. Charges state that players are shown favoritism in obtaining jobs and in maintaining their scholarship standing. . . . Rogers Hornsby signs as a player with the St. Louis Cardinals. He is not being considered as a future manager.	Oct. 25
President Herbert Hoover now plans to visit 22 cities in his last-minute campaign trip through the Midwest. He will make 18 short speeches from the back platform of the train.	In a Navy Day Eve address, President Hoover states that if the disarmament convention in Geneva fails, the U.S. must enlarge its Navy.	Alexander Noyes, financial editor of The New York Times, speaks to the Canadian Club in Ottawa, citing eight signs he says point to the lessening of the Depression.	William Bebee escapes injury when his bathysphere nearly hits a jagged outcropping of rock beneath the sea.		Oct. 26
Franklin Roosevelt promises better days ahead in his radio address and predicts a smashing victory. He also asks people to put party differences aside and work together for the good of the country.	Norman Davis wins the British over to support Hoover's one-third plan at the disarmament parley in Geneva.	The output of dressed meat in the United States is up 8 percent in September.	Professor E.D. Adrian and Sir Charles Sherrington, British scientists, receive the 1932 Nobel Prize for Medicine. They are awarded the prize because of their joint discoveries about how neurons function.	Charles Laughton, Raymond Massey, and Boris Karloff star in the film The Old Dark House, based on the novel by J.B. Priestly.	Oct. 27
Vice presidential nominee John Garner's secretary denies rumors that Garner is affiliated with the Ku Klux Klan. He credits recent statements about it to the Republicans.	Admiral Henry E. Wiley warns against cutting the U.S. Navy, saying a strong navy is insurance in time of war and a guarantee of peace.	A big decrease in bank failures is seen compared to October a year ago.	John Hammond demonstrates a new musical instrument that combines radio and the piano to produce the tonal effects of a massive organ.		Oct. 28
A report from the Republican National Committee shows a total of $1.4 million has been donated since June for the Republican campaign.	Recent revisions in the regulations for soldiers' rations provide for each soldier to receive six ounces of sugar-cured bacon rather than the usual salt pork. The change will benefit both the soldier and the farmer.				Oct. 29
Franklin Roosevelt is winding up his campaigning with a trip through the New England states.	The Tariff Board investigates the effect of depreciated foreign money on production costs abroad.	New York Central president F.E. Williamson contends that taxes are stifling the purchasing power of the railroads.	Engineers of the General Electric Company develop a new vacuum tube which can measure one quintillionth of an ampere. In cooperation with an "electric eye," the tube will measure light from faraway stars.	Rev. Rollin Dodd, rector of the All Souls Protestant Episcopal Church in New York, defies his Bishop by conducting services for a mixed congregation of whites and African Americans.	Oct. 30
President Herbert Hoover concludes his campaign for reelection with a speech at Madison Square Garden in New York City.	The Norfolk Navy Yard announces the historic ship Constitution is to be overhauled prior to making a voyage to the Pacific Coast.	A group of 10,000 unemployed Chicagoans hold a hunger march, chanting "We want bread." The march is orderly and the demonstrators are peacefully dispersed.	Scientists and historians in Uniontown, Pa., use an electromagnetic device in an attempt to find a cannon said to be buried there.	Henry Hadley, composer and former associate director of the New York Philharmonic, attacks conductors for playing mediocre foreign music and ignoring the best American works.	Oct. 31
Crowds in New England wait for hours in the rain to cheer Democratic presidential nominee Franklin Roosevelt. . . . President Herbert Hoover adds a speech in St. Paul to his western trip.	In a campaign speech, Newton Baker warns that the greatest danger to America is Herbert Hoover's stand on the tariff. He says the tariff has destroyed foreign trade.	R.J. Hamilton, president of the National Radiator Company, is optimistic about the future as he addresses the Architectural League.	The first electric train makes a test run in England. The train goes from London to Brighton successfully, with a top speed of 55 miles per hour.	The San Francisco Opera House opens its doors.	Nov. 1
President Hoover decides to go by train to California, where he will vote. He will make 28 stops in the Midwest on his way.	Payments to World War veterans are increasing and now total about $2.7 million annually. So far, 400,000 have applied for benefits, but it is predicted that another 500,000 will apply.	General Motors declares a regular quarterly dividend of 25 cents per common share.	F.M. Starr, engineer with the General Electric Company, wins the Nobel Prize for his paper entitled "Equivalent Circuits."	Pearl Buck, author of The Good Earth, speaks to 2,000 women at a luncheon in her honor. She emphasizes that America needs better missionaries.	Nov. 2

F	G	H	I	J
Includes elections, federal-state relations, civil rights and liberties, crime, the judiciary, education, healthcare, poverty, urban affairs, and population.	*Includes formation and debate of U.S. foreign and defense policies, veterans affairs, and defense spending. (Relations with specific foreign countries are usually found under the region concerned.)*	*Includes business, labor, agriculture, taxation, transportation, consumer affairs, monetary and fiscal policy, natural resources, pollution, and accidents.*	*Includes worldwide scientific, medical, and technological developments, natural phenomena, U.S. weather, and natural disasters.*	*Includes the arts, religion, scholarship, communications media, sports, entertainment, fashions, fads, and social life.*

	World Affairs	Europe	Africa & The Middle East	The Americas	Asia & The Pacific
Nov. 3	Argentine Foreign Minister Saavedra Lamas believes the Chaco dispute is a matter for the League of Nations, not for the neutrals.	An unauthorized strike of employees of the Municipal Transit Company left everyone in Berlin walking in the rain. The strike was led by Communists and Nazis.	The U.S. State Department notifies Britain that the United States feels it has a right to be consulted about the administration of Iraq when the British mandate ends.	Apparently the committee of Neutrals meeting in Washington, D.C., to try to mediate the Chaco dispute has failed. Bolivia says Paraguay thinks it has won and is making unreasonable and unacceptable demands.	
Nov. 4	British Prime Minister Ramsay MacDonald is named to head the British delegation at the Round Table Conference on Indian Affairs.	Royalist leader Panayoti Tsaldaris forms a Cabinet in Greece, a coalition of all the anti-Venizelist parties. This gives the Cabinet an overwhelming majority in the Chamber of Deputies.	Britain replies that the United States has no say on what happens in Iraq, since that country has joined the League of Nations.	Cuba's sugar crop in 1933 will be the smallest in 20 years, due to a decree by President Gerardo Machado limiting the crop to 2 million tons, which is 23 percent less than this year's yield.	Tokyo reports that China is seeking to resume diplomatic relations with Russia. Chinese delegate to Geneva W.W. Yen was seen approaching Soviet Commissar Maxim Litvinoff about the subject.
Nov. 5	Leaders at Geneva credit American Norman Davis with defusing the explosive situation with the French last month. They believe if Roosevelt is elected, he will name Davis Secretary of State.	As a result of a vote by British card-room workers and spinners, the mill strike in Manchester, England, will end tomorrow.	Lady Broughton returns to her home in London after spending four months photographing animals in their native environment in Uganda and the Belgian Congo. She also brings specimens of vegetation for the British Museum to use in their gorilla exhibit.	Wheat farmers in Alberta vote overwhelmingly to support a nationwide strike of Canadian farmers to take place next spring. The province of Alberta hopes Manitoba and Saskatchewan will join in the farm strike. . . . Plantations of the United Fruit Company in Costa Rica are found abandoned.	Another civil war breaks out in the Szechuan province of China. Gen. Liu Wen-hui has not paid his soldiers for several months, but levies high taxes. Gen. Tien Sung-yao is attempting to oust him.
Nov. 6	The League of Nations requests input from the Soviet Union and the United States while trying to solve the problems in the Far East. Leaders there also attach great importance to Norman Davis's talks with Benito Mussolini and other Italian officials.	After German elections, the Reichstag is so divided that Franz von Papen's rule is expected to continue. Hitler loses votes as Nazis lose 35 seats, Communists gain 11, the Nationalists 13, and the People's Party 4.		Fort Platanillos falls to the Paraguayans in a key battle in the Chaco. Most of the Bolivian army is concentrated around Munoz, and the Paraguayans are headed that way with a force of 8,000, which they expect to be joined by reinforcements numbering 6,000.	The Filipino legislature demands independence for the country. In a resolution they ask for more autonomy, the swiftest possible transition, and a trade agreement with the United States.
Nov. 7	A tentative agreement is reached by the Bureau of the disarmament conference. U.S. diplomat Norman Davis is pleased with his talks with Italian Premier Benito Mussolini, as he finds their views are similar.	Czechoslovakian Foreign Minister Eduard Benes believes that 1933 is an important year in determining whether Europe moves toward war or peace. He thinks the only way to avoid war is to negotiate a Continental European pact.	Howard Unwin Moffat, premier of Southern Rhodesia, announces he will retire after the next legislative session. He has served as premier since 1927.	The wreckage of a Swedish freighter is in flames off the coast of Newfoundland. The ship was wrecked in September and officials believe boys set fire to the ruin.	Baroness Keichi Ishimoto from Japan is in the United States to study methods of birth control, since the high birth rate in Japan is a vital issue.
Nov. 8	U.S. diplomat Norman Davis continues his talks on disarmament with the Italian leaders, as Premier Benito Mussolini honors him at a dinner.	Two Americans are sentenced to 16 months in prison in Hungary for passing counterfeit British notes. George Cuomo and W.F. Dante admit they took 5,000 of the notes to Europe to get them into circulation.		A German party braves heavy snow and bitter cold to scale Mt. Aconcagua in the Andes, the highest peak in the Western Hemisphere at 23,100 feet.	During their lunch hour, Japanese crowds eagerly grab extra editions of newspapers to read American election results. Most seem pleased with Franklin Roosevelt's election, but officials say it would be discourteous to comment.
Nov. 9	Leaders in the League of Nations foresee cooperation from the Democrats on world problems. They believe Norman Davis has a better grasp of League affairs than any other American.	Russian leader Josef Stalin's second wife dies at 30. No reason for death is given. . . . Riots in Geneva kill 12 and injure 60 as police armed with machine guns open fire on a group of Socialists trying to break up an anti-Socialist meeting.	The Egyptian University has discovered tombs painted like stage scenery at the famous site of Hermopolis, 150 miles south of Cairo.	A hurricane cuts a 100-mile-wide swath across Cuba, killing at least 1,000. Jamaica is also affected by the storm.	Fifty-nine Japanese soldiers have been missing in Manchuria for eleven days and Tokyo fears they have been slain by guerilla fighters.
Nov. 10	Speaking to the International Good Will Congress, Prof. Andre Philip of the University of Lyon in France says he believes if the disarmament conference fails, there will be war within five years.	Many mourners file past the body of Mrs. Josef Stalin as it lies in state at the Hall of the Executive Committee in Red Square. . . . The jobless riot in Reykjavik, Iceland. Twenty policemen and many of the demonstrators are injured.	Palestine is happy with the election of Franklin Roosevelt, as they believe the Democrats will repeal the Eighteenth Amendment, and they will again have a good market in the U.S. for their wine.	A Venezuelan prospector discovers a rich gold field which yields $500,000 worth of gold in less than three weeks, giving credence to the idea of many Venezuelans that their country will profit more from gold than from oil.	A group of Japanese leaders leave for Siberia, where they hope to negotiate with Gen. Hsu Pingwen about Manchuria. However, Hsu has not answered messages asking for negotiations.
Nov. 11	Countries around the world mark the 14th anniversary of the armistice ending the World War.	The French disarmament plan is completed and agreed upon at a three-hour conference between Premier Edouard Herriot and other French leaders.	Chemist Colin G. Fink discovers that the Egyptians knew the process of electroplating 5,000 years ago. He made the discovery while restoring ancient Egyptian metal art objects.	Soldiers search through debris for bodies in Santa Cruz, Cuba, after the town was leveled by a hurricane. Bodies are being burned because of their condition and the climate.	Nobumi Ito, delegate to Geneva, denies rumors that Japan is fortifying the former German Pacific Islands which are under Japanese mandate. Ito insists there are no naval bases on the islands.
Nov. 12	British Foreign Secretary Sir John Simon intends to present a disarmament plan calling for, among other things, the abolition of long-range guns, the reduction of submarines, and banning of aerial bombing.	The French reveal some of the contents of a secret dossier on Germany. They claim that German warships have three times the amount of ammunition they are allowed and the fleet is much more powerful than is sanctioned.		Bolivian planes bomb a Paraguayan troop center, resulting in many casualties.	Marshal Feng Yu-hsiang, known as the "Christian Marshal," comes out of retirement and heads for Shansi by train. Leaders of the Nanking government are dismayed, but nobody dares to stop him.
Nov. 13	The League of Nations wants input from both the Soviet Union and the United States on the crisis in the Far East. They consider setting up a General Consultative Committee, of which both nations would be members.	Anti-Semitic rioting breaks out in Warsaw, as 1,000 Nationalist students smash hundreds of windows in Jewish-owned stores. Forty students are arrested and eight are injured.	Gold production in the Transvaal by the Johannesburg Chamber of Mines is up 10 percent over production in 1929.	Ecuador calls all men between the ages of 20 and 25 to register for military service as a precautionary measure as the Ecuadorian government believes Peru and Colombia will soon be at war.	The Australian gold rush in the desert is being aided by planes. Prospectors face constant thirst, heat, no fresh food, and the threat of attacks by the Aborigines.
	A *Includes developments that affect more than one world region, international organizations, and important meetings of world leaders.*	**B** *Includes all domestic and regional developments in Europe, including the Soviet Union.*	**C** *Includes all domestic and regional developments in Africa and the Middle East.*	**D** *Includes all domestic and regional developments in Latin America, the Caribbean, and Canada.*	**E** *Includes all domestic and regional developments in Asian and Pacific nations (and colonies).*

U.S. Politics & Social Issues	U.S. Foreign Policy & Defense	Economics & Great Depression	Science, Technology & Nature	Culture, Leisure & Lifestyle	
President Herbert Hoover proclaims Thursday, November 24, Thanksgiving Day, then reads George Washington's original Thanksgiving Day Proclamation.		The largest increase of money circulation in weeks is reported by the Federal Reserve Bank, with a rise of $32 million.		Greta Garbo will remain in Sweden until after Christmas and has "half-promised" to appear in a stage version of *Grand Hotel* during Christmas week.	Nov. 3
A crowd of 14,000 cheers Franklin Roosevelt and Al Smith in Brooklyn.		Ford Motor Company dealers throughout the country receive a letter denying that Henry Ford was trying to coerce employees to vote for Herbert Hoover.	The Leonid meteors are due to appear between November 12 and 17 and astronomers hope they will actually be seen well. If the planet Jupiter is too close to the meteors, its gravity will draw them beyond the Earth's atmosphere.	World chess champion Dr. Alexander Alekhine wins 38 of 39 matches in Baltimore, tying the other with S. Bowie Smith.	Nov. 4
Both major parties heavily cut the costs of their presidential campaigns. They spend $3.3 million this year, as opposed to the $11.6 million spent on the 1928 campaign.	Domestic manufacturers will seek an anti-dumping law at the December Lame Duck Congress. The law would keep foreign competitors from dumping products here at lower prices than similar American-made products sell for.	James Rand, Jr., chairman of the board of Remington Rand, Inc., predicts in a radio address that 50 percent of the country's unemployed will be back at work by the first of the year.			Nov. 5
On Tuesday night, presidential election results will be signaled from the Times Tower in New York. A circle of white lights around the flagpole will show Hoover leading, while a circle of red lights will show Roosevelt ahead. When results are final, a searchlight will shine to the south if Roosevelt is elected or to the north if Hoover is the choice.		Wheat hits a new low this week, which is partly ascribed to the fact that due to Britain's interpretation of the Ottawa pacts, most Canadian wheat will not be shipped to England through the United States' ice-free ports this winter.	About 250 people enjoy the opening of the nation's first night club on wheels. Located on a train which runs from St. Paul to New Richmond, Wisc., the club has two cars with special floors for dancing, parlor cars with bridge tables, and refreshment bars.	Five Japanese art critics visiting cities of the world to view their art museums arrive in New York, where they will visit the Metropolitan Museum and others before moving on to San Francisco. They have already visited London, Paris, Berlin, and Rome.	Nov. 6
Both Herbert Hoover and Franklin Roosevelt claim they are assured of a victory at the polls tomorrow. . . . The two major networks, NBC and CBS, will air all-night broadcasts on Tuesday so listeners can keep up with election results.	U.S. naval vessels rush to the aid of a freighter endangered by a hurricane off the coast of Nicaragua. The minesweeper *Swan* and the destroyer *Overton* offer help to the *San Simeon*, which has a broken steering gear and jammed rudder.	Ford Motor Company denies the rumor that all its assembly plants will be concentrated in six locations on the eastern seaboard.	Dr. Shirley Wynne and Dr. H.C. Sherman address 1,000 nutrition experts at the 50th annual convention of the American Dietetic Association. Both stress the importance of calcium in the diet, while Sherman also informs attendees of the importance of vitamin A.	The first radio broadcast of *Buck Rogers in the 25th Century* airs.	Nov. 7
Franklin Delano Roosevelt is elected in a landslide, getting 472 electoral votes. The House will be heavily Democratic and they will have a smaller majority in the Senate.	The U.S. Navy ship *Phemius*, which was feared lost in the Panama Canal Zone, is located by a salvage tug.	Mayor L.L. Stokey of Patokee, Fla., reports nearly all the residents of that area of the Everglades are in desperate need of aid. Most have lost their homes and over 4,000 will be without food in a few days if they do not get help. Much of the bean crop, in which they had invested all their money, is ruined.		World chess champion Alexander Alekhine plays simultaneous games against 200 challengers in the 7th Regiment Armory in New York as a crowd of 1,000 watches.	Nov. 8
President-elect Roosevelt in a short speech to the American people pledges to lift the country out of the Depression. He believes his victory transcends party lines.		Money circulation falls $26 million in contrast to last October, with $293 million for the month.	More than 300 representatives of the media viewed the new models at the Dodge Brothers factory in Detroit. The new six-cylinder car is streamlined, with a low-hung chassis and has 81 horsepower.	The Vienna Boys' Choir delights the audience in their New York debut. The choir has been in existence since 1498, with only a six-year hiatus after the war.	Nov. 9
No clues have been found in the kidnapping of 10-year-old Paul Marciante who was snatched from his aunt on his way to school. Ten Italian-speaking detectives are on the case.	Both Britain and France ask for postponement of their war debt due the United States on December 15. . . . Veterans' leaders believe there is little hope of the next Congress voting to prepay the Bonus.	Police in Washington, D.C., say they will not interfere with a farmers' march as long as their protest is peaceful.	The Nobel Prize in Chemistry goes to Dr. Irving Langmuir of Schenectady, N.Y., who invented the gas-filled tungsten lamp and was also a pioneer in radio.		Nov. 10
Josephus Daniels, who was Secretary of the Navy during the Wilson administration, wants to change the emblem of the Democrats from a donkey to a rooster.	A cenotaph is dedicated at the World War Memorial Plaza in Indianapolis. It bears the name of James Bethel Gresham of Evansville, Ind., the first member of the American Expeditionary Force to be killed in the World War.	Prof. Sumner Schlicter, who teaches business economics at the Harvard Graduate School, advocates setting up the best dole system for America. He believes a federal board should deal with unemployment for the next two years.	Dr. J.G. Davidson claims the United States leads the world in the use of ethylene. He said uses range from making anti-freeze to using it for the artificial ripening of oranges in warehouses.	Author Mary Roberts Rinehart gets none of her husband's estate, as he states in his will that she wanted it to all go to their three sons. She is the beneficiary of his insurance policies, however.	Nov. 11
President-elect Franklin Roosevelt says his philosophy is the same as Thomas Jefferson's—to do the greatest good for the greatest number of people.	President Herbert Hoover is remaining silent on the subject of the war debts and it is believed he will leave it to President-elect Franklin Roosevelt to deal with the problem.	Christmas Club savings at banks throughout the country total about $500 million this year, down about $100 million from last Christmas.	Engineer Gordon Long finds a novel way to lower a new bridge into place. He has six 400-pound blocks of ice placed under the span. As the ice melts, the bridge settles nicely into place.	Notre Dame plays a brilliant game to defeat Northwestern in front of a crowd of 42,000.	Nov. 12
President Herbert Hoover invites President-elect Franklin Roosevelt to confer with him on war debts, disarmament, and the economic parley.	A new Bonus Army march is being planned in New York City and is supposed to reach Washington, D.C., on December 5. Only veterans with accredited bonus certificates may participate.		A year's work pays off as the mighty Colorado River is diverted into a man-made hole in the canyon wall to leave room for excavation. The project will take another three years to complete.		Nov. 13

F	G	H	I	J
Includes elections, federal-state relations, civil rights and liberties, crime, the judiciary, education, healthcare, poverty, urban affairs, and population.	*Includes formation and debate of U.S. foreign and defense policies, veterans affairs, and defense spending. (Relations with specific foreign countries are usually found under the region concerned.)*	*Includes business, labor, agriculture, taxation, transportation, consumer affairs, monetary and fiscal policy, natural resources, pollution, and accidents.*	*Includes worldwide scientific, medical, and technological developments, natural phenomena, U.S. weather, and natural disasters.*	*Includes the arts, religion, scholarship, communications media, sports, entertainment, fashions, fads, and social life.*

	World Affairs	Europe	Africa & The Middle East	The Americas	Asia & The Pacific
Nov. 14	Britain is not entered in the Chicago Exposition next year because of the high costs involved.	The Prince of Wales orders a twin-engine plane which is capable of flying 130 miles per hour and is large enough to carry him and several friends.	After January 15, the Union of South Africa will not recognize British silver coins as legal currency.	The American colony at La Gloria, Cuba, appeals to American Ambassador Harry Guggenheim for immediate aid in obtaining clothing and medical supplies.	The Shantung Civil War, which began two months ago, ends and Gen. Liu Chen-nien's defeated forces are being sent to Hupeh province.
Nov. 15	The World Court rules that the 1919 convention against women working at night still stands and applies to women executives not engaged in manual work.		The British government sternly warns Haile Selassie, Emperor of Abyssinia, that if he cannot control his subjects, they will have to take appropriate action.		Japan will present a naval limitations program at Geneva that differs in several ways from the plans of Great Britain and the United States.
Nov. 16		A new decree permits Soviet workers to be dismissed for an absence of one day. They may also lose their rations and even their housing, if it is provided by the factory.	Lewis French, director of the Palestine Development scheme, resigns. He is said to have a difference of opinion with British High Commissioner Lt. Gen. Sir Arthur Wauchope.	Mexican Minister of Foreign Affairs Manuel Tellez admits that his country has closed its offices at the League of Nations, but says that does not necessarily mean Mexico will quit the League.	Australia ratifies the Ottawa pact with no amendments, even though the Laborites do not approve.
Nov. 17	In a speech before the Bureau of the General Disarmament Conference, American delegate Norman Davis makes a plea for action on disarmament.	German Chancellor Franz von Papen and his Cabinet resign after they fail to get the backing of the Reichstag. President Paul von Hindenburg is likely to discuss the situation with Adolf Hitler of the Nazi party.		Argentina reveals a pact for enforcing peace which has already been approved by several South American nations. Neither the United States nor the Central American countries are asked to join.	England and India resume their final Round Table Conference. The framework of the constitution is already in place, but details need to be filled in. The biggest problem is finance, since England feels it should control them and India does not agree.
Nov. 18	At Geneva the United States drops its opposition to supervision of private manufacturers of arms, but insists on public arsenals. However, Japan is adamantly against them.	The Reich tightens its control on Prussia, as President Paul von Hindenburg issues a decree giving the Chancellor full control over the area. He says the move was necessary to restore public safety and order.	Amy Johnson lands safely at Cape Town, shaving 10.5 hours off her husband's time. She flew from Lympne, England, to Cape Town in four days, six hours and 56 minutes. She had a total of about five hours sleep on the trip.	Cuba's new Ambassador to the United States, Oscar Cintas, meets with President Herbert Hoover and expresses his country's desire for closer economic ties.	Japan's army cuts its budget by one-third, as it scales back its plan for mechanization.
Nov. 19		Danish Minister of Defense Laurkz Rasmussen calls Denmark's defense worse than nothing. He says the navy is useless and the army cannot defend the borders. Rasmussen plans to resign next week.		Bolivia says it is ready to go to arbitration on the Chaco territory, but it has some conditions. Bolivia wants a harbor on the Paraguay River and also wants to limit the decision to the frontier zone.	Japan sends 480 young ex-servicemen to work farms in Manchuria. The group is given a 35,000-acre area of fertile land in the Sungari Valley. The move is an experiment to see whether it is practical to colonize the area.
Nov. 20	Dr. W.W. Yen, Chinese delegate to Geneva, says his country accepts the Lytton Report, which he says "bears out all charges." He believes Japan is using the Geneva proceedings as a respite during which that nation is planning new warfare.	The Swedes predict that on Saturday an engagement will be announced between Princess Ingrid of Sweden and Prince George of England. There has been no official denial of the engagement.	A conference on Palestine held in Omaha and attended by leaders of seven national Jewish organizations agrees on a unified program for building up the Jewish homeland in Palestine.	Paraguay announces that it has killed over 6,000 Bolivians and captured 1,500 more since the dispute about the Gran Chaco began last summer.	Muslims reject the communal representation proposal agreed upon by the Hindus and the Sikhs.
Nov. 21	The arms parley attempts to get the Reich to return to the talks. Norman Davis will talk with Foreign Minister Konstantin von Neurath, who is pleased with the speech by British Foreign Secretary Sir John Simon.	Leon Trotsky, exiled Soviet leader, arrives by ship in Marseilles. A police boat is sent several miles out of the harbor to pick up Trotsky and his party and they enter Marseilles without being detected.	A Belgian expedition to the Ruwenzori Mountains in the Belgian Congo brings back enough gold to pay for the expedition. The three leaders are decorated by King Albert.	Bolivia cables Geneva to charge that Paraguayans are forcing Bolivian prisoners to work, which is a violation of international law.	Delegates at the Round Table on Indian Affairs in London show approval of the Marquess de Lothian's report on the franchise. The plan increases the franchise fivefold, including giving the vote to 6.6 million women.
Nov. 22	England upholds the Lytton Report and strongly urges all other countries to refrain from recognizing Manchukuo.	Adolf Hitler makes no decision about putting together a Cabinet, as he receives conflicting advice from aides.	Nineteen-year-old aviator Victor Smith is safe after crossing the Sahara in a 21-hour and 34-minute flight. He will leave Oran, Algeria, in the morning and attempt the return flight to London.	Canada approves new trade treaties with South Africa, Southern Rhodesia, the Irish Free State, and the United Kingdom.	There are heavy losses on both sides as two government divisions fight against Chinese Communists who are being aided by farmers in the Hupeh province.
Nov. 23	Japanese spokesman Yosuke Matsuoka loses his effort to silence the Lytton Commission now that they have given their report. He insists they should have no more input, but Eamon de Valera says the committee has not been dissolved, so is still active.	Adolf Hitler says it is impossible to form a cabinet under the conditions set by Paul von Hindenburg.	The League of Nations is disappointed to hear that negotiations between the Finance Corporation of America and Liberia have not yet begun and will not begin until next year.		In an effort to stop the fall of the yen, Japan orders banks to make daily reports on all transactions.
Nov. 24	The League of Nations hears the Lytton Report and Sir John Simon of England takes the strongest stand yet against the Japanese.	Two-thirds of the Russian people are not expected to have sufficient food this winter. Crop yields are much lower than in 1931 and livestock has fallen 50 percent from five years ago.	In an address in Buffalo, Rabbi Wolf Gold asks all Orthodox Jews to unite in building up Palestine as the Jewish homeland.	Representatives of business and commerce in Argentina meet to plan a nationwide tax strike to protest government proposals for increasing taxes.	The Chinese Foreign Office declares that Japanese with machine guns recently massacred 2,700 Chinese peasants in northern Manchuria.

A	B	C	D	E
Includes developments that affect more than one world region, international organizations, and important meetings of world leaders.	Includes all domestic and regional developments in Europe, including the Soviet Union.	Includes all domestic and regional developments in Africa and the Middle East.	Includes all domestic and regional developments in Latin America, the Caribbean, and Canada.	Includes all domestic and regional developments in Asian and Pacific nations (and colonies).

U.S. Politics & Social Issues	U.S. Foreign Policy & Defense	Economics & Great Depression	Science, Technology & Nature	Culture, Leisure & Lifestyle	
A rum runner in a Boston jail alleges that Col. Raymond Robins, missing since September, was thrown overboard from a boat and drowned after being abducted on the order of a New Jersey beer baron.	The United States makes an official statement that it will not attend a general meeting on war debts, but will negotiate individually with debtor nations.	After informal discussions, the World Bank is optimistic about the world monetary situation.	Calvin Goddard, of the Scientific Criminal Detection Laboratory at Northwestern University, reveals a method by which the age of a person can be determined by examination of a single hair.	Cuban boxer Kid Chocolate, featherweight champion of the world, defeats challenger Pete Nebo in a 10-round battle.	Nov. 14
Noted architect Frank Lloyd Wright receives notes threatening he will be kidnapped and held for ransom.	The Committee Against Prepayment of the Bonus believes that a bill for prepayment would not pass in the Lame Duck Congress.	It is announced that the Ford Motor Company will close its factory in Cork in the Irish Free State.	Amy Johnson, who is flying a perilous route across the Sahara Desert in an effort to beat her husband's record, is long overdue to land at Niamey, French West Africa.	Yankee's baseball club owner Col. Jacob Ruppert believes the Yankees have a good chance to win the pennant in 1933 and is not concerned about signing Babe Ruth to a contract.	Nov. 15
Sir Percival Perry, chairman of the Ford Motor Company of Britain, denies that the plant in Cork in the Irish Free State is closing.	Dr. Nicholas Murray Butler, president of Columbia University's National Economic League, states in a speech that the $450 million spent yearly on veterans is the biggest waste in the nation's budget. He believes only soldiers injured in the war should draw pensions.		Amy Johnson lands safely after a difficult flight across the Sahara, then continues on her flight, still ahead of her husband's time.	At a meeting in Washington, D.C., the Catholic hierarchy unanimously votes to condemn indecent books. They believe the increasing flood of immoral literature is a threat to the national well-being.	Nov. 16
	Dr. John Grier Hibben asserts that Europe cannot recover from the Depression without U.S. help. He believes the United States needs to cancel war debts and join the League of Nations.	Wholesale prices fall one and one-third percent in October, continuing the downward trend. They are eight and one-third percent lower than wholesale prices last October.	Belgian scientist Abbé Georges LeMaître announces he will travel to Southern California next month to study at the Mount Wilson Observatory.	A crowd of 60,000 to 75,000 is expected to attend the annual Notre Dame-Navy game in Cleveland on Saturday. 55,000 tickets have already been sold. Notre Dame is heavily favored to win.	Nov. 17
Ten-year-old Paul Marciante is released by his kidnappers near his uncle's store. . . . Col. Raymond Robins, who disappeared on his way to confer with his close friend President Herbert Hoover, has been found living in the mountains of North Carolina as a prospector. He appears to be suffering from amnesia.		A survey by the New York State Commission on Old Age Security finds that 59 percent of jobs are closed to older men, although another survey shows a very low drop in efficiency with age.	A memorial to the Wright Brothers is unveiled at Kill Devil Hills in Kitty Hawk, N.C., where they made their first flight.	At the annual Academy Awards, Helen Hayes wins Best Actress for her role in *The Sin of Madelon Claudet*, while Fredric March is named Best Actor for his role in *Dr. Jekyll and Mr. Hyde*. *Grand Hotel* is named Best Motion Picture of 1932.	Nov. 18
Col. Raymond Robins does not know his identity and fails to recognize his wife, saying, "I don't know this woman." His wife does not believe he is faking.	Maj. Gen. Benjamin Foulois, Chief of the Air Corps, reports that the corps is 396 fliers under strength. He believes the only way to remedy the situation is to call in fliers from the Reserves.	Exports for October are up $21 million over those in September, marking the second consecutive month that they have risen over $20 million.	Dr. Charles Abbott of the Smithsonian Institution has developed a device to measure sun rays. He believes it will help him in his quest to find the cause of weather cycles on earth.	In an interview after a wild taxi chase in Copenhagen, Greta Garbo refuses to divulge any future plans, including whether or not she will return to Hollywood.	Nov. 19
Vice President-elect John Garner rushes back to Washington from his home in Texas to participate in a meeting with President-elect Franklin Roosevelt and Democratic leaders.		The Lame Duck Congress will take a look at the job relief plan set up by the last session of the legislature, and will probably make some changes.	Wax models are being used to simulate human flesh in a British hospital in an attempt to determine the proper strength of radium used in treating cancer.	Libby Holman's manager says she will not return to the stage after being cleared of the death of her late husband, Z. Smith Reynolds. Holman will remain in seclusion until after the birth of her child.	Nov. 20
		It is the slowest day on the New York Stock Exchange since August 13, 1928, as bonds are weak and trading sluggish.	Strong winds from the sea blow a flock of auks, small birds which breed in Iceland and Greenland, into New York City. The exhausted little birds are taken to the Bronx Zoo.		Nov. 21
The Democrats are expected to pigeonhole over 100 appointments that will be recommended by President Hoover in the Lame Duck assembly.	According to Maj. Gen. J. F. Preston, the number of Army desertions in 1932 is only half the 1931 total. He believes it is due to the Depression.	Aid to the poor has risen sharply in the last year. Aid to families is 144 percent higher than last year. Money paid out in relief in September totaled $22.6 million.	The American Cotton Cooperative Association is concerned that the boll weevil is spreading throughout the south and new areas may be affected next year.	A symposium on the arts concludes that emphasis on sex in the arts is waning. They say the trend is evident in literature, drama, and music.	Nov. 22
	President-elect Franklin Roosevelt is considering five men for the three posts of Assistant Secretary of War, Assistant Secretary of Commerce, and Assistant Secretary of the Navy. Being considered are C.V. Whitney, Maj. J. Carrol Cone, Maj. Gen. James E. Fechet, Maj. Reed Landis, and John Dwight Sullivan.	Cotton prices fall to nearly $1 a bale in heavy trading. The drop is attributed to the news about war debts.	Dr. William Beebe's bathysphere will be exhibited at the Chicago Exposition in 1933. The huge metal globe has three glass windows and can hold three persons.	Stanford's football coach "Pop" Warner believes the dead ball rule is contrary to the spirit of the game. He says there's no sense in it at all.	Nov. 23
	Upon his return to the United States from Europe, Gen. John Pershing says war is unlikely.		The FBI Scientific Crime Detection Laboratory officially opens in Washington, D.C.	Approximtely 500,000 children and adults enjoy Macy's Thanksgiving Day Parade, with its bands, clowns, and thousands of balloons. . . . Halbert Blue of Aberdeen, N. C., wins the 17th annual Carolina golf tourney at Pinehurst.	Nov. 24

F
Includes elections, federal-state relations, civil rights and liberties, crime, the judiciary, education, healthcare, poverty, urban affairs, and population.

G
Includes formation and debate of U.S. foreign and defense policies, veterans affairs, and defense spending. (Relations with specific foreign countries are usually found under the region concerned.)

H
Includes business, labor, agriculture, taxation, transportation, consumer affairs, monetary and fiscal policy, natural resources, pollution, and accidents.

I
Includes worldwide scientific, medical, and technological developments, natural phenomena, U.S. weather, and natural disasters.

J
Includes the arts, religion, scholarship, communications media, sports, entertainment, fashions, fads, and social life.

	World Affairs	Europe	Africa & The Middle East	The Americas	Asia & The Pacific
Nov. 25	The League of Nations asks the Washington Neutrals to act at once in the Chaco dispute between Bolivia and Paraguay. It says the two countries, as member of the League, need to put an immediate stop to the fighting.	Conservative women in the Finnish Parliament ask for a ban on the American play *The Green Pastures* because they say it is wounding religious feelings.	Dr. J.E. Halloway, Director of Census and Statistics in the Union of South Africa, visits the United States and is amazed by the gains made in the status of the African Americans.	The Alberta Wheat Pool, with support from Saskatchewan and Manitoba, asks the Canadian government to sponsor a world wheat parley to take steps toward stabilizing the marketing of wheat.	The Japanese Foreign Office says if the League of Nations proposes to transfer the problems in Manchuria to a conference of signatories of the Nine-Power Treaty, Japan will reject the proposal. Japan claims that the treaty does not apply to Manchukuo.
Nov. 26	The State Department announces that Norman Davis has not been instructed to confer with anyone at Geneva about the Lytton Report, and if he does so, it is not official. Reports say he met with Japanese delegate Yosuke Matsuoka.	It is pointed out that there are only seven eligible princesses in all of Europe and there are quite a few more bachelor princes.	Reports from the eighth national convention in Palestine say great progress is being made in agriculture in the country.	As expected, the House of the Assembly in Bermuda votes not to ratify the Ottawa trade agreement until the Finance Committee has more time to study it.	From Shanghai comes news of the bombing of several Japanese businesses in Tientsin by Chinese. Tokyo absolutely denies the recent story of a Japanese massacre of 2,700 Chinese peasants.
Nov. 27		It is evident the Liberals are losing in the Belgian election, while the Socialists and Catholics are gaining seats in the new parliament.		Members of the Brooklyn Museum Brazil Expedition fail to locate the fabled white Indians and Pygmy Indians said to be living in the northern part of the country.	Two groups of Japanese salvagers claim to have found the hull of the *Admiral Nachimov*, a Russian cruiser that was sunk in 1905 with 11 million pounds in British sovereigns on board. They will try to salvage the gold in the spring.
Nov. 28	A special League of Nations session is called for December 6 to discuss the Manchurian clash. Japan says it may be forced to quit the League.	Lt. Gen. Kurt von Schleicher attempts to put together a new Cabinet for Germany that would at least tide the country over until after the holidays. If a Christmas truce is blocked, President Paul von Hindenburg is expected to reappoint the von Papen government.	A London report says Aircraftman Shaw, also known as Lawrence of Arabia, may visit Arabia, the scene of his World War exploits, when his term in the Royal Air Force is up in three years. Others think he will reenlist.	The Panama Canal is closed today when the Chagres River pours 200,000 cubic feet of water per second into the spillway. The river was 25 feet above its normal level. Engineers believe the canal will reopen tomorrow, barring heavy rains during the night.	Six generals who were either neutral or on the side of Gen. Liu Hsiang have gone over to the side of Gen. Liu Wen-hui in the civil war taking place in Szechuan province.
Nov. 29	French Premier Edouard Herriot tells Norman Davis he is willing to go to Geneva Friday for the Five-Power disarmament talk that is planned.	Albanians celebrate the 20th anniversary of their independence by paying homage to King Zog in Tirana.	While Britain worries about Persia canceling the Anglo-Persian Oil Company contract, the United States expects Persia to give automobile and tire concessions to General Motors and Firestone.	A battle rages in the Chaco over Fort Saavedra. Bolivia is better supplied with guns and ammunition, but the Paraguayans have access to water in the River Verde, near Fort Arce.	
Nov. 30	The meeting of the Five Powers scheduled for Friday will have to be postponed, as French Premier Edouard Herriot cannot attend.	Moscow is pleased with the signing of the Russo-Franco nonaggression treaty. Newspapers call it a great triumph.	To celebrate the cancellation of the Anglo-Persian Oil Company contract, Teheran theaters admit all moviegoers free.	The 38-member crew of the tanker *Margit* is rescued as the ship, loaded with gasoline, burns and sinks in the harbor at Concepción, Chile.	The Japanese mount a surprise offensive in Manchuria and advance 100 miles in sub-zero weather.
Dec. 1	Officials at the disarmament conference in Geneva are concerned about rumors that the United States wants to get the conference over with soon or even withdraw from the conference. A U.S. spokesman denies that the United States is considering withdrawing.	Adolf Hitler sends a letter to President Paul von Hindenburg demanding he be made Chancellor. . . . Sir Frederick Whyte, a former adviser to China, believes that if England, France, and the United States were to unite and confront Japan about Japanese actions in Manchuria, Japan might withdraw all forces from the area.	The Persian government issues a statement denying that the end of the concession granted to the Anglo-Persian Oil Company signaled unfriendly feelings on the part of the Persian government toward the British-based company.	President Gerardo Machado ends two years of martial law in most of Cuba. Only the Havana province will remain under military control.	Shanghai terrorist organizations threaten three British insurance companies. They say if the companies do not immediately settle fire losses from the fighting in Chapei last February, their insurance offices in Shanghai will be bombed.
Dec. 2	French Gen. Emil Adolfe Taufflieb declares that the League of Nations is impotent. He charges that when Germany asks for equality, that nation really means building its army to the strength it was in 1919.	Kurt Von Schleicher is named Chancellor of Germany, in a move that pleases Adolf Hitler's opponents, who believe this is a sign that his strength is beginning to wane.	South African Premier Hertzog believes that cancellation of German reparations is helping to restore confidence that the world can recover from the Depression.	Bolivia accepts all the terms laid out in the Commission of Neutrals proposal for ending the fighting in Chaco. Bolivia would prefer a smaller neutral zone, arguing that establishing a large zone would encourage Paraguay to lay claim to the Chaco. Fighting continues.	Japan says it will consider negotiating with China about Manchuria if Manchukuo also joins the discussion.
Dec. 3	U.S. diplomat Norman Davis has convinced British Prime Minister Ramsay MacDonald of his views on disarmament, and he already got the support of French Premier Edouard Herriot when he was in Paris. The Italians also seem to be in agreement. . . . Mexico informs the League of Nations of its intent to withdraw from the organization.	The Bulgarians are upset by increasing Communist activities in the country. Meanwhile, the plight of the peasants worsens, and in order to buy a box of matches, they must sell a kilogram of wheat. . . . A circus manager in Budapest pays his back taxes with 7 lions and 13 apes. The city accepts them.			Despite the Japanese attacks, conditions in some parts of China show improvement. Railways have given better service, air travel has increased, and road building has been extended.
Dec. 4	The Americans and British have made lists of what they think needs to be included in the disarmament agreement. They have exchanged lists, as well as sharing them with the French and Italians.	Leon Trotsky, exiled Russian revolutionary, arrived at the port of Antwerp on the liner *Bernsdorff*, but Belgium would not allow him to go ashore.	Canon John Roscoe, an authority on the tribes of Uganda, dies. Roscoe spent 25 years as a missionary in East Central Africa.	Bolivia claims that a flier trained in the U.S. Army has damaged planes carrying bombs which were to be dropped on Fort Saavedra. The plane crashed, causing the bombs to detonate. The explosion killed the pilot and his passenger. Bolivian troops buried the bodies of the Paraguayans.	The Japanese cross the Khingan in Manchuria in minus 40°F weather and move into Mientuho. Forces are advancing westward.

A	B	C	D	E
Includes developments that affect more than one world region, international organizations, and important meetings of world leaders.	*Includes all domestic and regional developments in Europe, including the Soviet Union.*	*Includes all domestic and regional developments in Africa and the Middle East.*	*Includes all domestic and regional developments in Latin America, the Caribbean, and Canada.*	*Includes all domestic and regional developments in Asian and Pacific nations (and colonies).*

U.S. Politics & Social Issues	U.S. Foreign Policy & Defense	Economics & Great Depression	Science, Technology & Nature	Culture, Leisure & Lifestyle	
Julian Marcelino, a Filipino who killed six and wounded thirteen in Seattle, says his "mind turned over" after his savings were stolen. He went on a rampage through the south end of the city, stabbing anyone who got in his way.	The Treasury Department has determined that both Britain and Germany are exempt from the new tax on coal, due to provisions of past treaties.	A group of 350 hunger marchers leaves Chicago to march to Washington, D.C. Washington civic organizations warn them that they cannot and will not give them free food and lodging in the city when they arrive.	Dr. George Hale, director emeritus of the Mt. Wilson Observatory at Pasadena, Calif. is one of eight who will be awarded medals by the Royal Society in England. Dr. Hale will receive his award for work he has done on the magnetic field of the sun.	Marie Dressler and Polly Moran star in a new musical comedy about family friction and banking troubles. The film *Prosperity* showcases Dressler, who won an Academy Award in 1931.	Nov. 25
Congress will attempt to reduce the cost of the federal government, as Democrats call for cutting billions of dollars in expenses.	The State Department notifies Poland and Czechoslovakia that their war debt payments will be expected on December 15. However, Hoover says he will recommend that Congress create an agency to review the matter of war debts.	Business begins its annual Christmas upswing as people shop for gifts. Some also find seasonal employment as stores take on extra help for the season.	Guglielmo Marconi says the world's first wireless telephone, which he invented, is being tested between Vatican City and the Pope's summer home at Castel Gandolfo. He foresees the phone being in everyday use.	Christian churches throughout the United States plan to observe Bible Sunday, which is sponsored each year by the American Bible Society.	Nov. 26
The National Child Labor Committee begins a campaign to send 2 million children working in industry back to school, thereby leaving their jobs open for unemployed adults.	A group of 250 Marines leaves Nicaragua and sails for California. The evacuation will be complete on January 2.	Henry Ford rests quietly at Ford Hospital, where he underwent major surgery yesterday. The doctor says there is some danger of infection.	Visitation to U.S. national parks is up about 6 percent over last year, despite the Depression, reports Harold Allbright, director of the National Park Services.	Texas Christian University, with an unbeaten and untied record, wins the Southwest Conference championship.	Nov. 27
Speaker John Garner, who submitted a resolution to repeal Prohibition to the Judiciary Committee for study, will try to force a vote by rules suspension if necessary.	President Herbert Hoover wants to wait for further developments on Manchuria before commenting on the suggestion of the League of Nations for a committee of conciliation that would include Russia.	At the American Federation of Labor convention, president William Green says labor is losing patience with management and will fight for the five-day week and the six-hour day.	Vessels coming into Porto Alegre, Brazil, notice a huge raft of floating dead locusts several miles wide about 50 miles offshore. The dead insects apparently had been carried out to sea by a high wind.	Last summer's Olympic winner of the 100-yard and 200-yard dash, Eddie Tolan from Michigan, is working in vaudeville to help his family and save money for medical school. He supports his mother and several brothers and sisters.	Nov. 28
President-elect Franklin Roosevelt works on refining his plan for a "New Deal." His priorities are unemployment relief and measures to prevent another Depression.	Gen. Douglas MacArthur, Chief of Staff of the Armed Forces, recommends increasing the regular Army to 14,000 officers and 165,000 enlisted men.	A committee of three hunger marchers was sent ahead to meet with the District of Columbia commissioners. They demand food, shelter, and a meeting place.	A steamship is en route from Ketchikan, Alaska, to Seattle with several tons of specimens from Alaska for the Smithsonian Institution.	Maurice Cleary's suit to collect $45,000 from Gloria Swanson for acting as her agent opens in Los Angeles. Cleary testifies that one film alone netted the actress $1.2 million.	Nov. 29
Senator McKellar charges that President Herbert Hoover placed 2,619 people in civil service jobs without having them take the examinations. Most are Republicans.	Naval maneuvers in the Pacific have been ordered for the United States fleet during the first three months of 1933. The fleet will drill in Hawaiian waters.	At its convention in Cincinnati, the American Federation of Labor reverses its former stand and comes out strongly for jobless insurance.	American and Canadian universities will finance Auguste Piccard's fourth trip into the stratosphere, somewhere in the Hudson Bay region. He has made two trips from Switzerland and will make one from Belgium next summer, before he comes to America.	Spanish pianist Jose Iturbi appears before a near-capacity audience at Carnegie Hall.	Nov. 30
Congressional leaders refuse to reconsider Britain's debt payment after receiving another note from the British, asking again to postpone the December 15 deadline.	Assistant Secretary of War F. Trubee Davison reports that the United States ranks fourth in the world in air strength. The Army, National Guard, and Reserves have a total of 1814 planes, but 210 are said to be unserviceable.	The chairman of the Post Office Committee of the House of Representatives announces hearings will start on Monday on a bill to drop the price of a stamp from three cents to two cents. Rep. Collier says revenue has fallen off since stamps increased to three cents. However, the Post Office Department says cutting the cost of stamps would lose them $100 million.	A new monoplane with an air-controlled robot pilot is revealed in Los Angeles. Lt. Cdr. Frank Hawkes will use the *Sky Chief* as a flying laboratory for research. The robot pilot feature will relieve the pilot on long flights.	Marilyn Miller, musical comedy star, and her reported fiancé, movie star Don Alvarado, are reported to be stowaways on an ocean liner bound for France. Apparently the two, along with five friends, went aboard to bid farewell to friends, and did not leave when the "all ashore" call went out.	Dec. 1
The House Judiciary Committee votes 13–6 against sponsoring John Garner's proposal for a repeal of Prohibition. Garner says on Monday he will move for the suspension of rules and the adoption of his proposal.		A movement for compulsory unemployment insurance is afoot in New York, Pennsylvania, Massachusetts, New Jersey, and Connecticut.	Dr. Robert Millikan offers evidence that cosmic rays are photons, not electrons, as his rival, Dr. Arthur Compton, claims. In a speech in Pasadena, Calif., Millikan cites evidence that the sun has no direct effect on the intensity of cosmic rays.	The convention of the American Association of Pools and Beaches calls upon bathing suit manufacturers to make their new models for 1933 more conservative.	Dec. 2
Eleanor Roosevelt believes politics gives one a chance to serve humanity and cautions young people not to go into politics to make money.	Democratic Senator Hull believes the first step to economic recovery should be a 10 percent cut in world tariffs. He says since the United States led the way to high tariffs, the United States should now lead tariffs in the other direction.		The new post office in High Point, N.C., will have the first electric eye of any federal building in the country. If the sun throws too much light on a window, the electric eye is supposed to let in only the required amount of light.		Dec. 3
The current short session of Congress contains 144 "Lame Ducks," the name given to those who sought reelection and were defeated. Thirty others did not run for reelection and four have died, so 178 of the members in this session will not be at the next session.	In a radio symposium, two internationally known economists advocate reducing the war debts further. The two, R.A. Seligman and Irving Fisher, point out that most of the money borrowed from the United States by the Allies is spent in this country.	The Farm Bonus Plan, which would provide the farmer with a bonus paid by the consumer, seems to be gaining favor. It would work somewhat like the tariff, but would be levied on farm products used at home.	The Children's Science Fair opens at the Museum of Natural History in New York, showcasing projects and experiments of 7,000 schoolchildren. Exhibits include mechanical devices, live animals, and models.		Dec. 4

F	G	H	I	J
Includes elections, federal-state relations, civil rights and liberties, crime, the judiciary, education, healthcare, poverty, urban affairs, and population.	Includes formation and debate of U.S. foreign and defense policies, veterans affairs, and defense spending. (Relations with specific foreign countries are usually found under the region concerned.)	Includes business, labor, agriculture, taxation, transportation, consumer affairs, monetary and fiscal policy, natural resources, pollution, and accidents.	Includes worldwide scientific, medical, and technological developments, natural phenomena, U.S. weather, and natural disasters.	Includes the arts, religion, scholarship, communications media, sports, entertainment, fashions, fads, and social life.

	World Affairs	Europe	Africa & The Middle East	The Americas	Asia & The Pacific
Dec. 5	The Big Five—Britain, France, Germany, Italy, and the United States—meet for the first time since the disarmament conference began.	Prof. Friedrich Siegmund-Schulze says unemployed Germans are sleeping till noon in an economy move. The practice keeps them warm and wards off hunger.	Undersecretary for Foreign Affairs Anthony Eden tells the House of Commons that England will not tolerate interference by Persia in the matter of oil leases in that country. He points out the concession was granted in 1901 for 60 year, and there is no provision for its cancellation.	Archaeologists believe an empty tomb uncovered in Monte Albán in Mexico was raided by Spaniards during the Conquest. The stone ceiling of the tomb was broken.	Tokyo believes the League of Nations is overestimating the chance that Japan will make concessions on the Manchurian issue. Japan points out that an acceptable solution can only be reached if Manchukuo is recognized.
Dec. 6	Big Five disarmament talks in Geneva result in a formula on security and equality. German Foreign Minister Konstantin von Neurath is expected to have an answer from Berlin when talks resume tomorrow morning.	President Herbert Hoover's message to Congress ends London's hope of delaying the debt payment due on December 15. The installment will probably be paid in gold.		The Jamaican Governor opens a session of the legislature to try to provide relief for banana growers in the area. The Attorney General will authorize a short-term loan to provide assistance to the hurricane victims.	Governor-General Theodore Roosevelt reports the capture of a Japanese vessel and 34 men fishing illegally in Philippine waters. . . . China arranges to transport Chinese troops who fled into Russia back to Shanghai.
Dec. 7	The League of Nations Assembly convenes without Germany, since the delegate is waiting for instructions from Berlin. The American plan is discussed. It would be a three-year pact with a ban on bombing and gas warfare. It also calls for bringing France and Italy into the London Naval Accord.	The British government demands an apology from Russia for an article which appeared in a Moscow newspaper, charging British agents were told to falsify documents linking Communism with the Soviet government if they could not find genuine documents.	Egyptian officials demand an apology from Turkish President Kemal for suggesting the Egyptian Minister remove his fez after a banquet. Fezzes are banned in Turkey.	Guayaquil announces the formation of a new Ecuadorian Cabinet by President Juan de Dios Martínez Mera.	The Chinese Foreign Office announces it has protested to the Japanese government, protesting a massacre. China claims 2,700 Chinese villagers in Manchuria were slaughtered.
Dec. 8		Russia refuses to apologize to Great Britain for an article in a Moscow paper, laying the blame on the newspaper. The Soviet ambassador to Britain claims his government is not responsible for anything printed in the papers.	Great Britain sends an ultimatum to Persia concerning oil concessions there. Britain says if concessions are not returned by Thursday, the British government will turn the matter over to the World Court as a matter of urgency.	The Cuban schoolteachers' strike fails to materialize today. The teachers have not been paid for the past six to eight months. Secretary of the Interior Octavio Zubizaretta said teachers on the committee planning the strike would be arrested and jailed, and any teacher not showing up for work today would be dismissed.	The Japanese attack the border of Jehol. The attack is seen as the start of a campaign to annex the province to Manchukuo.
Dec. 9	A clash is averted in the League of Nations today when the Manchuria question is referred to a committee. The "small four," consisting of Ireland, Sweden, Spain, and Czechoslovakia, had framed a statement censuring Japan. . . . Experts at Geneva hope to be able to reach a formula today for equality. The Big Five powers will meet in the morning to try to work out the details and make the plan agreeable to all five nations.	The Reichstag adjourns indefinitely, giving Chancellor von Schleicher a reprieve before they consider his programs. A revolt occurs in Adolf Hitler's ranks, with several of his top aides resigning.		A newspaper in Santiago, Chile, charges that the great powers of the world, especially the United States, are responsible for the economic crisis in the world today.	Japanese forces invade Jehol, a Chinese province, in their quest to expand their holdings in northern China.
Dec. 10	Japan's Naval Plan, made public today by the League of Nations, would cut the American big cruiser tonnage by half, while only cutting their own by less than 30 percent.		A bomb explodes in the residence of the British High Commissioner in Cairo, raising dinner guests out of their seats, but injuring no one and doing little damage. British believe it was merely a warning to Sir Percy Loraine not to interfere in Egyptian politics.	The provisional government of Brazil issues a decree denying political rights to hundreds for three years. Included are those involved in the São Paulo revolts and those connected with the federal government under the Ruiz regime.	Japanese leader Kaku Mori dies of pneumonia at the age of 49.
Dec. 11	Delegates to the disarmament conference sign the Geneva Protocol, giving participants equal rights in the deliberations. Germany agrees to return to the talks.	The British are not pleased with the new Japanese naval proposal. Tokyo's plan would give Japan supremacy in the Far East. Japan wants to keep submarines, while Britain wants them abolished.	A newspaper in Jerusalem reports problems on the property in Abadan where the offices of the Anglo-Persian Oil Company are located. Troops have to be called in to protect officials from an angry mob, and oil wells are damaged.	The Bolivians fight all day, forcing the Paraguayans back to their second line. La Paz says Bolivia lost only five defenders, while slaying 460 of the enemy. Bolivians again complain of Paraguayans killing stretcher bearers.	
Dec. 12	Russia and China reinstate diplomatic relations.	Poland feels uneasy about the Geneva agreement, since part of Polish territory is claimed by Germany. Countries like Poland and Czechoslovakia will feel the need to increase arms if Germany is rearmed.	It is reported to the House of Commons in England that the British made only slightly less money on the oil fields in Persia than the Persians themselves earned.	It is learned that Bolivia is now using tanks in the war against Paraguay in the Chaco. La Paz says the light tanks were used successfully at Saavedra.	A spokesman for the Japanese government says Japan is not happy about the resumption of diplomatic relations between China and Russia. He says China has made a big mistake in allying herself with Russia.
Dec. 13	At the League of Nations Committee of Nineteen's drafting committee meeting, Sir John Simon of England opposes setting up a commission on Manchuria without the help of the United States and Russia.	The Belgian Cabinet, headed by Count Charles de Broqueville, resigns after sending the United States a note saying it is necessary for Belgium to default on their December 15 payment. The nation lost a large amount of revenue when the Lausanne agreement deprived Britain of payments from Germany.	Reports from Teheran say Persia will report threats and pressure from Great Britain in the Anglo-Persian Oil Company dispute to the League of Nations.	Buenos Aires reveals that Argentina borrowed $20 million in 1923 from the United States to buy arms, and the same amount again in 1926.	Japan instructs the Japanese delegate to Geneva to reject any proposal that the United States and Russia should be part of the conciliatory commission studying the Manchurian question. . . . China is delighted with the accord with the Soviet Union, hoping it might help curb Japanese activity in Manchuria.

A	B	C	D	E
Includes developments that affect more than one world region, international organizations, and important meetings of world leaders.	Includes all domestic and regional developments in Europe, including the Soviet Union.	Includes all domestic and regional developments in Africa and the Middle East.	Includes all domestic and regional developments in Latin America, the Caribbean, and Canada.	Includes all domestic and regional developments in Asian and Pacific nations (and colonies).

U.S. Politics & Social Issues	U.S. Foreign Policy & Defense	Economics & Great Depression	Science, Technology & Nature	Culture, Leisure & Lifestyle	
The petition of D.C. Stephenson, former dragon of the Ku Klux Klan, to be released from his life imprisonment is denied. He is serving the term for the murder of Madge Oberholtzer in 1925.		Crude oil production falls in October, with the daily average 64,000 barrels lower than in September. Stocks decline 893,000 barrels, even though the production of motor oil increases.	Albert Einstein is angered by 45 minutes of questioning by the U.S. Consulate General about his fitness to enter the United States. He left and in a phone call said if he does not have a visa by noon tomorrow, he will cancel his visit.	Babe Didrikson, Olympic star, is barred from the Amateur Athletic Union because her picture appeared in an advertisement for an automobile. She denies authorizing the ad and says she will fight for reinstatement.	**Dec. 5**
About 1,500 Hunger Marchers start home after they present their demands for unemployment insurance to Congressional leaders. The parade of 3,000 marchers covered a six-mile route.	In its annual report, the Veterans' Administration asks for a Congressional study and a new plan for veterans' relief. They back President Herbert Hoover's statement to eliminate abuses stemming from ill-considered legislation. . . .The War Department motorizes its first and most famous cavalry unit.	Democrats plan to fight for a greatly broadened plan of relief. The program aims to remove from the RFC the power to grant federal loans to the states.	The National Exposition of Power and Mechanical Engineering introduces new technological developments from the past year. Two new forms of copper have been developed. One is as thin as a sheet of paper and the other is in an alloy and is as hard as iron, stronger than steel, and looks like gold. It is hoped these developments will put some surplus copper to good use.	Minister of the Irish Free State Michael MacWhite and his wife are guests of honor at an art exhibit at the Sears and Roebuck Gallery in Washington, D.C. On display are photographs, etchings, paintings, and modern architectural models, all by modern artists. . . . Since they lack passports, England and France have barred Marilyn Miller and her party from entering the countries.	**Dec. 6**
The present short session of Congress is faced with the possibility of being a "do-nothing session." The repeal move and a review of war debts are both blocked. Members were also hostile to President Herbert Hoover's recommendation of a sales tax.	Italian economist Mario Alberti calls U.S. policy on debts fair and asks, "Why should America sacrifice herself on the altar of European folly?"	The exterior of the 70-story RCA Building in Rockefeller Center in New York is finished. It took 102 days to build the 850-foot façade, which used 530 carloads of Indiana limestone. The new studio and office building is scheduled to open on May 1, 1933.	The first electric train begins service between New Brunswick and Jersey City in New Jersey. A small stretch from New Brunswick to Trenton has not yet been electrified, but should be by the end of the month.	The Pope dedicates a new gate into the Vatican Museum. Although he was only in the street outside Vatican territory for five minutes and was only a few yards away, it was considered significant, since it was only the fourth time a pope has left Vatican City since the accord ending the "voluntary imprisonment" of popes.	**Dec. 7**
The Philippines Independence Bill is hung up on the floor of the Senate, as Senator Royal S. Copeland speaks for two hours on his belief that Congress has no legal right to free the country, but that they must vote for independence.	Plans for a 20,000-ton aircraft carrier are submitted to the Secretary of the Navy.	The total inventory of new cars at General Motors dealerships is the lowest it has ever been, as is the total of used cars.		Brooklyn Dodgers manager Max Carey is released from the hospital, where he has been recuperating from influenza since last Monday.	**Dec. 8**
	Gen. Frank Hines asks Congress for a sound national policy on veterans' relief. He would rank veterans with those injured in combat at the top.	An explosion traps 23 men in the Zero mine in Harlan, Ky. Ten bodies have been found, and little hope is held that others are alive.	Scientists are equipping a yacht to serve as their base on a trip to the Caribbean, where they will study the ocean bottom and collect specimens. They have a six-mile cable with which they hope to sound the depths of the Puerto Rico Deep.	Cuban boxer Kid Chocolate retains his featherweight boxing championship when he beats Fidel La Barba, but it takes him fifteen rounds to do it. It was a very close decision and many of the spectators did not agree with the judges.	**Dec. 9**
Representatives of 30 organizations attend a child labor parley in Washington, D.C. They will discuss school attendance and child labor legislation.	A group of veterans in the southern and eastern parts of the country have set up an organization against the immediate payment of the bonus to veterans.	Teachers in Chicago have not been paid for weeks, and are now facing pay cuts. Since the teachers have jobs, they do not qualify for any kind of relief, even though they are not getting paid.			**Dec. 10**
Both Democrats and Republicans send letters to U.S. Senators, asking them to vote to ratify the three treaties pending which would assure United States adherence to the World Court.	The American Veterans' Association makes recommendations to Congress that could save $450 million if adopted. They advocate repeal of benefits to veterans not disabled in the war and stand against prepayment of the bonus.				**Dec. 11**
The Senate Judiciary Committee begins work on drafting a resolution for repeal of Prohibition.	Senator MacKellar of Tennessee submits a resolution to the Senate asking them to create a five-man committee to investigate the eviction of the Bonus Army.	Fifteen thousand auto workers go back to work in the factories in Detroit, and with new models coming out, it is expected many more will soon be recalled.		Mexican authorities bar American author Edna Ferber from entering the country. They charge that after her last visit, she wrote a magazine article calling the country a land of dogs and fleas.	**Dec. 12**
Leaders of the dry organizations of the country charge Congress cannot legalize beer without amending the Constitution by repealing the Prohibition Amendment.	John Taylor, vice chairman of the legislative committee of the American Legion, denounces those who want to cut veterans' benefits. He charges the United States Chamber of Commerce and the National Economy League with running a campaign of misinformation about veterans' affairs.	Chairman Jones submits a tentative farm bill to the House Agricultural Committee. The bill entails farmers curtailing production of some products in exchange for government subsidies.		Babe Didrikson is suspended from further amateur participation in sports after an investigation into the charges that she endorsed an automobile for advertising purposes.	**Dec. 13**

F	G	H	I	J
Includes elections, federal-state relations, civil rights and liberties, crime, the judiciary, education, healthcare, poverty, urban affairs, and population.	Includes formation and debate of U.S. foreign and defense policies, veterans affairs, and defense spending. (Relations with specific foreign countries are usually found under the region concerned.)	Includes business, labor, agriculture, taxation, transportation, consumer affairs, monetary and fiscal policy, natural resources, pollution, and accidents.	Includes worldwide scientific, medical, and technological developments, natural phenomena, U.S. weather, and natural disasters.	Includes the arts, religion, scholarship, communications media, sports, entertainment, fashions, fads, and social life.

	World Affairs	Europe	Africa & The Middle East	The Americas	Asia & The Pacific
Dec. 14	Britain had planned to bring the Anglo-Persian Oil Company dispute before the World Court, but Persia's request for the League of Nations to settle the dispute makes that impossible. Therefore, Britain also requests that the League of Nations put the dispute on its agenda for discussion.	England has arranged to send the United States 200 tons of gold bars to make their December 15 payment, instead of the usual way of paying with treasury bonds. The $95.5 million worth of gold should arrive in about six weeks.		A young American is convicted of bombing the home of a police officer in Havana. Herbert Wilford, 19, is the son of the American editor of a Havana newspaper. He has not been sentenced yet, but the judge advocate asks for life in prison.	
Dec. 15	In response to U.S. rejection of the Lausanne agreement, most Allied governments default on their war debts to the United States.	Instead of sailing for home as planned, Ambassador Mellon is staying over in London and will confer with Neville Chamberlain, chancellor of the exchequer for England, tomorrow. Presumably the discussions will center around revision of Great Britain's debt-funding agreement.	The Persian government asks the League of Nations to delay action on the problem between Persia and the Anglo-Persian Oil Company, in hope they can settle the problem amicably on their own. However, the Council is expected to discuss the question tomorrow.	After a clash between police and civilians in Buenos Aires results in the injury of a precinct captain, the city orders machine guns, bullet-proof vests, tear gas, and gas masks for the Buenos Aires Police.	The Legislative Assembly in Delhi, India, approves the Ottawa tariff bill, while turning down proposed amendments.
Dec. 16	The League of Nations is charged with lacking interest in Latin America and being mainly concerned with European affairs. Carlos Garcia Palacios, as a spokesman for the League's Information Bureau, denies the charges, saying the League is showing great interest in the situations in the Chaco and Leticia.	Great Britain hires seven ocean liners to transport the gold being used to pay the nation's debt installment to the United States. The last shipment will leave London on December 31.	Three employees who refused to join a transit strike in Cape Town, South Africa, were separately kidnapped, beaten, and left lying unconscious along the road.... According to a 30-page statement Great Britain gives the League of Nations, no American oil experts are involved in the controversy between Persia and the Anglo-Persian Oil Company.	At a dinner in his honor in London, Canadian Prime Minister R.B. Bennett vows that Canada would never default on any debts to Great Britain.	Japan's representative to the League of Nations, Yosuke Matsuoka, says Japan is not happy about the proposal that the United States and Russia should sit in with the Committee of 19 when they act on the Manchurian situation. Japan wants so many changes in the resolution that some League officials think the whole resolution may need to be scrapped.
Dec. 17	A deadlock occurs in Geneva in the attempt of the League of Nations to settle the problems between Japan and China in Manchuria. It is unlikely a settlement will be reached before the Christmas holidays.	Now that their debt payment has been made, the British people seem to harbor no ill will toward the United States, but seem to feel a pride in paying their debt. London asks that revision talks include discussion of political and economic problems.		After a fiery five-hour-long debate, the Chamber in Buenos Aires approves a law enabling the president to declare a state of siege for Argentina for the next 30 days. Now the bill goes to the Senate. Under the new law, freedoms of speech and the press will be suspended, and the government will be authorized to deport anyone it deems dangerous to the country.	The Philippines threaten a boycott of U.S. products to retaliate against the United States because of the Senate passage of the Hawes-Cutting independence bill. Provisions restricting imports to America from the Philippines and barring Filipino immigration from America are the main objections to the bill.
Dec. 18	China maintains the position that any attempts at conciliation by the League of Nations Assembly must be preceded by a refusal to recognize Manchukuo.	The Little Entente parley opens in Belgrade, in connection with revision of peace treaties. Yugoslavia's and Romania's relations with Italy will also be discussed.		Paraguay considers withdrawing from the peace parley in Washington, D.C., after refusing to accept the Neutrals' most recent peace plan.	A spokesman for the New Zealand government says it will resume payments on its debt to Great Britain, even though the British had offered to postpone the payments.
Dec. 19	The Committee of Nineteen discusses the Lytton Report and the deadlock between Japan and China which is blocking a settlement. The committee will probably adjourn until mid-January and most negotiation until then will be through diplomatic channels.		The date for opening arguments on the Anglo-Persian Oil Company dispute is set for January 23. It is the first time a strong country like Great Britain has turned to the League for help in settling a dispute with a smaller country such as Persia.	President Herbert Hoover asks Congress for the right to put an embargo on shipment of arms to warring countries. It does not mention Bolivia or Paraguay, but would apply to the Chaco dispute.	
Dec. 20	China prepares a final statement to Japan on the dispute on Manchuria, but it will probably not be released until Thursday.	Fire does considerable damage to one wing of the Royal Palace in Brussels, Belgium, but the royal family was not there. The King is in Antwerp and the Queen is traveling abroad.	T.A. Brocklebank, noted rower for Cambridge, will join the British expedition attempting to climb Mt. Everest in 1933.	Cattle are starving in Chile, where pastures are being covered by fine volcanic ash from two volcanoes, Descabezado and Quizapu. The ash is keeping 300,000 head of cattle on the eastern slopes of the Andes from getting to the grass, putting them in danger of starvation.	A large crowd of Sikhs visits Kartarpur in India to see the Granth Sahib, a 250-year-old religious manuscript in the handwriting of Arjan, the fifth guru.
Dec. 21			The Persian Shah approaches jewelry dealers in Britain and France with a tentative offer to sell the Peacock Throne, worth almost $20 million, and a gem-studded globe two feet in diameter. He says financial difficulties in his treasury cause him to make the move.	The neutrals in Washington receive a communication from Paraguay, affirming the country's refusal to accept their December 15 proposal. Paraguay leaves open the possibility of renewing negotiations if offered suitable security.	Members of the America-Japan Society in Tokyo present a gold clock to Prince Iyesato Tokugawa on the occasion of his golden wedding anniversary.
Dec. 22	U.S. diplomat Norman Davis returns from Geneva and asserts that while no concrete plans have come out of the arms parley, there has been much progress made in laying the groundwork for an agreement.	Ambassador Walter Edge goes back to Paris with instructions from the State Department concerning negotiation of a treaty with the French.		Pope Pius XI convinces Bolivia and Paraguay to agree to a Christmas Day truce in the Chaco. It will run from midnight on December 24 to midnight on December 25.	Kenzo Adachi, former Japanese home minister, forms a new Fascist party. He states the party will try to establish a controlled economy in order to cut down on unemployment and raise purchasing power.

A	B	C	D	E
Includes developments that affect more than one world region, international organizations, and important meetings of world leaders.	Includes all domestic and regional developments in Europe, including the Soviet Union.	Includes all domestic and regional developments in Africa and the Middle East.	Includes all domestic and regional developments in Latin America, the Caribbean, and Canada.	Includes all domestic and regional developments in Asian and Pacific nations (and colonies).

U.S. Politics & Social Issues	U.S. Foreign Policy & Defense	Economics & Great Depression	Science, Technology & Nature	Culture, Leisure & Lifestyle	
In a close vote, the Senate approves the time frame in the House bill to grant the Philippines their independence in eight years.	A group of men representing the Rank & File Veterans present a petition to Vice President Charles Curtis and House Speaker John Garner. Curtis objects to a sentence censuring Hoover for the eviction of the Bonus Army, and crosses it out. Police do not allow the men to march in formation back to their headquarters.		Hawaiians spot a giant octopus along the shore of the island of Maui. The octopus is said to have tentacles 20 feet long and a head three times as big as that of a man. They believe it was driven close to shore by high winds.	Major league baseball owners are expected to change the method of selling World Series tickets. Heretofore tickets have only been sold in blocks of three, but probably will be available for single games next fall.	Dec. 14
The Ways and Means Committee votes 17–7 to give a favorable report on the Collier Bill, which would legalize the sale of beer and decide to bring it up in the House next Tuesday.	Poland, France, Estonia, Belgium, and Hungary default on their debt payments to the United States. Latvia, Lithuania, Czechoslovakia, England, Italy, and Finland make their payments on time.	According to the Department of Agriculture's final crop report, cash crops, including tobacco, wheat, rice, and cotton, show a big decline for 1932. They attribute this to the back-to-the-farm movement, in which much of the land that formerly grew cash crops was planted with garden crops.	Thirty-three Rhodes scholars will enter Oxford University in October 1933. They are chosen from among 615 applicants throughout the country. Four Princeton students are named, and two each from the University of Wisconsin, the University of Virginia, and the University of Oklahoma.		Dec. 15
The House of Representatives passes the first of the new appropriations bills, providing funds for the Treasury and Post Office departments. They rejected a proposal by President Herbert Hoover for an 11 percent wage cut for federal employees making more than $1,000.	A House committee considering reduction in the Marine Corps heard from Secretary Adams today. He believes the move would interfere with the efficiency of the Marines. Several high-ranking naval officers also testified against the proposed cut.	Wage negotiations for railway workers hit a snag when the two sides have basic differences in their interpretation of the Willard agreement. The pact was signed January 31 and provided for a 10 percent wage cut for a year. The problem is whether or not the former wage rate will automatically be restored on January 31, 1933.	Dr. Donald Menzel of the Harvard College Observatory lists two exciting discoveries in the world of physics this year. He cites the discovery of the neutron, as well as the discovery of the hydrogen isotope.	Two Indiana golfers, Johnny Watson and J. Russell Stonehouse, tie at 67 to win the annual best ball tourney in Miami. This is one of three events leading up to the annual Miami Open which will run from December 30 to January 1.	Dec. 16
A nationwide study of children and the Depression finds problems to include loss of homes, delinquency, and undernourishment. Grace Abbott, chief of the Children's Bureau of the Department of Labor, stresses the importance of greater relief efforts in these areas.		Alfred Bernheim, director of a research organization for labor, advocates a 30-hour workweek, while maintaining wages. He asserts this would put two million unemployed industrial workers back to work.	The six new Chevrolet models introduced for 1933 have more power and speed and greater economy. They also have larger, lower bodies, easier starting, and shatterproof glass in the windshields.		Dec. 17
After 576 are arrested in vice raids in Chicago, Mayor Anton Cermak asserts that Al Capone's power over the gambling and liquor syndicate has been broken.	In a radio address, Dr. Julius Klein, assistant secretary of commerce, says both tariff issues and international debts must be discussed at the coming world economic parley.	Kansas Senator Capper discusses the latest farm relief proposal, the domestic allotment plan. He explains that the plan would increase the farmers' income, which would help the economy, help create jobs, and stimulate industry.	A large crowd in London cheers aviatrix Amy Johnson when she lands at Croyden after setting another flying record. Her time on the London to Cape Town to London flights was the best in both directions. In spite of being grounded in the Sahara for two days by blinding storms, she made the return trip in seven days, seven hours, and five minutes.	The Chicago Bears win the Professional Football League Championship on a touchdown by Red Grange. . . . Red Sox first baseman Dale Alexander leads the American League in batting for 1932 with a .367 batting average, three points ahead of the Athletics' Jimmy Foxx, who leads in home runs, runs scored, and total bases.	Dec. 18
			Australian astronomers believe they have observed Tempel's Comet, which has not been seen since 1866. A number of observers have confirmed the sighting.	Olympic golfer Babe Didrikson is named Outstanding Woman Performer of the year. . . . About 150 delegates attend the Foreign Mission Conference of North America in Briarcliff Manor, N.Y. Many different foreign mission boards are represented at the four-day conference.	Dec. 19
President-elect Franklin Roosevelt does not like the idea of linking war debts to the arms or economic parleys. He believes the ability of debtors to pay their debts can be assessed through existing diplomatic channels.	Brig. Gen. J. Fred Pierson dies of a heart attack at the age of 83. He was the oldest surviving Union general from the Civil War.	The International Typographical Union announces it will go to a five-day workweek for employees on January 1. Printing plants will still work six days a week, but each employee will miss one day of work a week, and a substitute will be employed.	An earthquake jars a large section of the West, from Rawlins, Wyo., to Long Beach, Calif., but there was little damage. The most severe shock was felt in Nevada.	Lefty Groves's 2.84 ERA leads American League pitchers for the fourth straight year.	Dec. 20
The House of Representatives passes the bill to legalize beer, and it now goes to the Senate, where its fate is in doubt.	President-elect Franklin Roosevelt resists setting up a commission to deal with war debts now. He prefers to wait until he becomes President on March 4.	Last-minute shoppers fill the stores, needy children attend parties and receive gifts, and many get ready to travel for the Christmas holidays. The extra business has given temporary jobs to at least 25,000 people who are working in the city stores.		Golfer Babe Didrikson announces that she will turn pro, since she has been banned by the Amateur Athletics Union. She says she will write, do some film work, and attempt to swim the English Channel.	Dec. 21
The Senate passes a bill granting the Philippines independence after a period of 10 years. Only 50 Filipinos a year will be allowed to immigrate to the United States, although the Secretary of the Interior can up that number if workers are needed in Hawaii. The House is expected to pass the bill, then after the President signs it, the Filipino Legislature will vote on it.				Babe Didrikson is reinstated to amateur status by the Amateur Athletic Union, but her announcement that she is turning pro would bar her from amateur participation for one year, even if she did not do any professional work.	Dec. 22

F	G	H	I	J
Includes elections, federal-state relations, civil rights and liberties, crime, the judiciary, education, healthcare, poverty, urban affairs, and population.	Includes formation and debate of U.S. foreign and defense policies, veterans affairs, and defense spending. (Relations with specific foreign countries are usually found under the region concerned.)	Includes business, labor, agriculture, taxation, transportation, consumer affairs, monetary and fiscal policy, natural resources, pollution, and accidents.	Includes worldwide scientific, medical, and technological developments, natural phenomena, U.S. weather, and natural disasters.	Includes the arts, religion, scholarship, communications media, sports, entertainment, fashions, fads, and social life.

	World Affairs	Europe	Africa & The Middle East	The Americas	Asia & The Pacific
Dec. 23		The British refuse to allow Americans to broadcast the Christmas Eve service at the Church of the Nativity in Bethlehem. It would have required the installation of a microphone, which would have been intrusive to the people of the church.	Liberia finds it necessary to suspend payments to Firestone because of the Depression. They took 55 percent of the government's revenue in 1931.	The premier of Peru resigns. Carlos Zavala Loayza has been in poor health, so his resignation was expected.	In Tokyo, the Emperor has the Aksaka Palace opened so Mrs. Theodore Roosevelt, widow of the former president, can tour the gardens. Mrs. Roosevelt is on her way to Manila to visit her son, Theodore, Jr., who is Governor-General of the Philippines.
Dec. 24	Czechoslovakian Foreign Minister Eduard Benes warns that any arms agreement must put an end to big powers dictating to smaller countries. He says the Little Entente will not be dictated to.		Long lines of autos and carriages travel through Bethlehem, while chimes sound from the belfries commemorating the Nativity. A large star lights up at midnight and a nativity scene is illuminated. Many American travelers are among those who visit Bethlehem on Christmas Eve and Christmas Day.	Costa Rican President Jimenez Oreamuno signs a decree in which Costa Rica denounces the Central American Peace Pact which bans recognition of revolutionary regimes.	Sir Samuel Hoare, India's secretary of state, announces that the government is seriously considering releasing Mohandas Gandhi and other political prisoners in India.
Dec. 25		British subjects all over the world hear King George's Christmas message broadcast on the radio. He delivers a friendly greeting, ending with "God bless you."	Ancient tombs in Tepe Gawra in Mesopotamia are found to be 500 years older than the tombs of Ur.	The people of Conceica de Araguaya in Brazil say their town was sacked by the fierce Caipos Indians, who murdered seven white people and kidnapped nine children. They also stole large stores of food and ammunition.	An earthquake in the Kansu province of China leaves 70,000 people dead. The tremors are picked up by seismographs in London.
Dec. 26	Pierre Comert, head of the information section of the League of Nations for 13 years, resigns. He prefers to resign, rather than fight against the extremist German opposition.	Newspapers report that Russian meteorologists have discovered a hut at the northernmost tip of Asia that is said to have been used by Norwegian explorer Roald Amundsen in 1918–19 when ice forced him to camp there. Amundsen has been missing since 1928.	The South African Cabinet meets in emergency session brought on by the reentry into politics of Judge Tielman Roos. He is backed by farmers, who hope the gold standard will be abandoned.	The Christmas Day truce in the Chaco, arranged by the Pope, is followed by air raids, as Bolivian bombers twice bombard Paraguayan troops.	
Dec. 27		Canada and Germany agree on an interim trade agreement to begin January 1 and last for three months, when it is hoped a permanent pact will be put in place.	The Union of South Africa, after prolonged debate, decides to quit using the gold standard, even though it has rich gold deposits.	Brazil has ordered several units of the First Naval Division to guard the frontier in the Upper Amazon area. A squadron of bombers will also help to maintain neutrality in Brazilian waters, as Peru and Colombia clash over Leticia.	Tokyo police reveal that they arrested four reactionaries who were plotting the assassination of Premier Makoto Saito.
Dec. 28	Eleven nations will begin enforcing sea safety regulations on Sunday, as their new pact goes into effect. The agreement came out of the international conference in London in 1929. The United States is not included.	French and German diplomats amend their trade treaty to allow either side to change important tariffs with a two-week notice.	After a Jewish colonist dies of injuries sustained from a bomb last week, other colonists in Nahalai demand better protection for Jews. The Palestine government offers a reward for apprehending the bombers.	Bolivian troops advance three miles, driving Paraguayan troops out of the Fort Jordan area of the Chaco, where they had been firmly entrenched.	Japan's project for modernizing the army aims to bring it up to the standards of the Russian army. Most of Japan's peacetime force of 230,000 soldiers will be based in Manchuria.
Dec. 29		The Irish attempt to end the economic war with Britain by combined efforts of the opposition parties against President Eamon de Valera's government.		Expecting more conflict with Peru over Leticia, Colombia arms a 375-mile strip along the Putamayo River. Troops and warships are gathering in the area.	After a long and bitter debate, Filipino legislators adopt a compromise plan for independence. Americans living in Manila believe the independence measure would be fatal to the Philippines, and would cause the islands to decline into political and economic disorder.
Dec. 30		The French Senate approves a $14 million loan to Austria after a hard-fought battle. Keeping the Danube area strong was emphasized, but many senators disapproved, since France had defaulted on its debt to the United States.	The value of the pound falls in South Africa without the gold standard, but the move to drop it is believed expected to increase profits to both the mines and the government.	Argentina experiences a heat wave, with the official temperature in Buenos Aires at 102, the hottest in two years.	China temporarily gives in to protests from London, Paris, and Washington, D.C., and decides not to censor foreign-owned publications in China.
Dec. 31	The League of Nations is concerned about the failure of President Herbert Hoover and President-elect Franklin Roosevelt to cooperate. Geneva believes U.S. diplomat Norman Davis is the only American who really understands the workings of the League.	France's chief worry going into the new year is the government's debt and the refusal of the Chamber of Deputies to make the scheduled December 15 payment to the United States.		Since the British Treasury ruled that Canadian grain shipped through American ports such as Buffalo is not eligible for preferential treatment, Canada announces that it will ship wheat this winter through Canadian ports.	The Japanese War Office says it's keeping an eye on the situation in Jehol, where Chinese troops are said to be congregating. As of now, they feel the situation is not serious enough to warrant a statement.

A	B	C	D	E
Includes developments that affect more than one world region, international organizations, and important meetings of world leaders.	Includes all domestic and regional developments in Europe, including the Soviet Union.	Includes all domestic and regional developments in Africa and the Middle East.	Includes all domestic and regional developments in Latin America, the Caribbean, and Canada.	Includes all domestic and regional developments in Asian and Pacific nations (and colonies).

U.S. Politics & Social Issues	U.S. Foreign Policy & Defense	Economics & Great Depression	Science, Technology & Nature	Culture, Leisure & Lifestyle	
The Senate votes 48–23 against the beer bill which passed in the House recently. The bill called for immediate legalization of beer. The Senate wants time to consider the matter.			The Japanese beetle quarantine area in the northeastern states has been extended to cover more area. The Department of Agriculture announces the ban becomes effective on January 1.	George A. Jacobus, new president of the PGA, assures the country that there will be a team of American golf professionals in England in 1933 for the Ryder Cup. He says money is available and the team will be selected in late February.	Dec. 23
		The Corn Belt is facing a hard winter. Employment has steadily declined because farmers do not have money to spend. The bright spot is that the farmers should have plenty to eat.			Dec. 24
	A service at Valley Forge, Pa., pays tribute to George Washington and his underfed and underclothed troops who spent the winter of 1777 there.	A group of 1,200 jobless people receive a charter for land in Bucks County, Pa., where they plan to start a cooperative farming community where they can support themselves.			Dec. 25
Speaker John Garner believes that if President Herbert Hoover does not sign measures for farm relief and legalization of beer, an extra session of Congress will be necessary early in the Roosevelt administration.	An amphibious plane belonging to the U.S. Marines is lost from its squadron today and a low gas supply forces it to land at Oaxaca City, Mexico. The 16-plane squadron was en route to Panama.	Bodies of 39 miners, mangled by an underground explosion, have been returned to the surface by rescue workers. Hope remains for only five miners, while the other 10 are believed to have burned to death in the shaft.		At their annual meeting which opens today, the American Football Coaches' Association evaluates the new rules in football. The decrease in injuries during the past season shows the rules have made the game safer. Many believe the extra point should be eliminated.	Dec. 26
Chairman Byrns of the House Appropriations Committee begins a movement to fix governmental expenses. He says President Hoover's proposals along these lines are inadequate in scope.	Rep. Black of New York demands that the House investigate the eviction of the Bonus Army from Washington, D.C., last summer. A similar bill has been introduced in the Senate by Senator McKellar.	A nationwide clearing house is set up for the exchange of goods and services by the barter method by unemployed workers. A similar statewide system has been in use in California.	The annual winter meeting of the American Association for the Advancement of Science hears that between 100,000 and a million years ago, the earth probably collided with a giant comet larger than Halley's comet.	Finnish sportsman Karl A. Hilli says he plans to ask the AAU to consider reinstating Paavo Nurmi, running star from Finland.	Dec. 27
Japan's Institute of Research in National Economy considers inviting President Herbert Hoover to act as the institute's adviser after he leaves office on March 4.		Subcommittees in the Senate will begin hearings on the five-day workweek on January 5.	The Franklin Institute Museum in Philadelphia will preserve the plane in which Amelia Earhart made her solo flight across the Atlantic.	Jockey M. Bonaventure rides the winners in all four races at the steeplechase in Nice.	Dec. 28
Democrats agree to give Franklin Roosevelt the power to consolidate and eliminate bureaus of the government in order to economize. Roosevelt asks that Congress give him until the first regular session of Congress next December to finalize his economic program.	A U.S. Coast Guard cutter is on its way to aid the five-masted schooner, Edna Hoyt, which is taking on water at a rate of six inches an hour. The schooner is off the coast of Cape Hatteras, N.C., on its way from Venezuela to Baltimore with a load of fertilizer.		The joint convention of the American Geological, Paleontological, and Mineralogical Societies hears about the great Sargasso Sea which millions of years ago covered over half of today's United States. Fossilized evidence has helped scientists to trace where the sea once was.	The District Court of Appeals in San Francisco backs actress Lillian Gish in her breaking of a movie contract with Inspiration Pictures.	Dec. 29
Congress avoids economic and tax problems, showing a tendency to leave the door wide open for Roosevelt to act in these areas.			According to Dr. Arthur Compton, cosmic rays at the equator differ in intensity from those in polar or temperate regions.	Cleveland Indians' outfielder Charley Jamieson, a 17-year veteran of the major leagues, is given his unconditional release, due to age and declining health.	Dec. 30
Lewis McHenry Howe, a leading aide in the Roosevelt campaign, says he has never seen a campaign so dominated by the candidate. He says Roosevelt himself made all major decisions, even setting the schedule and stops for his train trips.	Maj. Gen. B.D. Foulois, Chief of the Army Air Corps, points to a shortage of 396 pilots last June, and says prospects are not bright for alleviating that shortage in 1933.	A.C. Tozzer, president-elect of the Associated General Contractors of America, believes the launch of a great public construction program would get people back to work and help bring an end to the Depression.	Dr. Hans Jensen of Johns Hopkins Medical School is studying insulin in hope that diabetics will be able in the future to take the hormone orally rather than having to take daily injections.		Dec. 31

F	G	H	I	J
Includes elections, federal-state relations, civil rights and liberties, crime, the judiciary, education, healthcare, poverty, urban affairs, and population.	Includes formation and debate of U.S. foreign and defense policies, veterans affairs, and defense spending. (Relations with specific foreign countries are usually found under the region concerned.)	Includes business, labor, agriculture, taxation, transportation, consumer affairs, monetary and fiscal policy, natural resources, pollution, and accidents.	Includes worldwide scientific, medical, and technological developments, natural phenomena, U.S. weather, and natural disasters.	Includes the arts, religion, scholarship, communications media, sports, entertainment, fashions, fads, and social life.

1933

Franklin (left) and Eleanor Roosevelt greet the crowd as they ride in the motorcade up Pennsylvania Avenue after Roosevelt's 1933 inauguration.

	World Affairs	Europe	Africa & The Middle East	The Americas	Asia & The Pacific
Jan.	Economic problems in Romania lead the League of Nations to launch a four-year program to supervise the country's finances.	Adolf Hitler becomes German chancellor. The rise of the fascist government implies a closer cooperation between Germany and Italy. . . . An uprising in Barcelona against the slow social reforms of the government is repressed by the army.	Jan Smuts asks for the resignation of the South African government and an end to racial discrimination.		Japanese forces continue their occupation of the Chinese region of Jehol.
Feb.	The Permanent Court of International Justice holds its 27th session in The Hague. . . . The Disarmament Conference begins in Geneva with delegates from 60 countries. . . . The League of Nations Assembly holds its fourth special session to discuss the deteriorating situation in Manchuria and Japanese aggression.	In the face of rising fascism and Nazism in Europe, the nations adhering to the Little Entente make their pact indefinite in duration. . . . Hitler dissolves parliament and calls for new elections. The campaign is marked by the burning of parliament by National Socialists, an event that Nazis successfully manage to blame on Communists.	The Anglo-Persian Oil Company resumes operations in exchange for tax and revenue concessions to the Persian government. . . . Arabs begin a boycott of British goods in Palestine when the British government refuses to restrict Jewish immigration.		Sailors on the Dutch training ship Zeven Provincien mutiny in East Indian waters in response to a reduction in pay. The Dutch recapture the ship.
Mar.	The British government proposes a new disarmament plan to reduce international tensions and military expenditures.	The Austrian Premier, Engelbert Dollfuss, suspends parliamentary government and prohibits political parades in Austria to contain the rise of National Socialism. . . . The National Socialists together with their Nationalist allies obtain the absolute majority at the Reichstag. . . . Poland occupies the free city of Danzig.		The British government appoints a Royal Commission to investigate the economic crisis in Newfoundland.	In response to the nonrecognition of Manchukuo, Japan withdraws from the League of Nations.
Apr.	The Permanent Court of International Justice rules against the Norwegian annexation of the east coast of Greenland. Norway accepts without protest.	A national boycott of Jewish goods and businesses is launched by the new German government. . . . German leaders Hermann Goering and Franz von Papen conduct an official visit to Rome. . . . Goering becomes premier of Prussia.	The Persian government awards Danish and Norwegian firms the construction of the Trans-Persian Railway.	The Canadian government withdraws from the gold standard.	Western Australians vote two to one to secede from the Commonwealth of Australia.
May	The Permanent Court of International Justice holds its 28th session in The Hague. . . . The Canadian and French governments sign a trade agreement that goes into effect on June 10, 1933. The agreement provides for reciprocal tariff preference on 1,148 items to stimulate trade between the two countries.	The Austrian government decrees the expulsion of National Socialist agitators. Relations with Germany become tense. . . . The Finnish government prohibits the establishment of military units linked to political parties. . . . The Spanish government nationalizes all church properties and forbids members of religious orders to engage in industry or trade.	The Persian government grants the Anglo-Persian Oil Company a new oil production concession.	The Paraguayan government officially declares war against Bolivia.	The Australian government assumes authority over one-third of Antarctica. . . . The Chinese Nationalist government and Japan sign the Tangku Truce.
Jun.	Because of the economic depression, the governments of Britain, Czechoslovakia, Italy, Latvia, Lithuania, and Romania offer symbolic token payments to the United States for their war debts. . . . The International Labor Organization holds its 17th session in Geneva. . . . The International Economic Conference opens in London.	Tensions between Italy and Albania lead to the closing of all Italian schools in Albania. . . . The Austrian government expels Theodor Habicht, Hitler's "Inspector of Austria." The outbreak of terrorist activity in Austria leads to the dissolution of the National Socialist Party. . . . National Socialists seize power in the free city of Danzig.	Anti-missionary and anti-Christian rioting breaks out in Egypt.	The new U.S. Ambassador to Cuba serves as a mediator between President Gerardo Machado and opposition groups.	The Japanese Crown Prince Akihito is born.
Jul.	The League of Nations holds its 74th session in Geneva. . . . The Economic Conference in London fails. . . . Representatives of Britain, France, Germany, and Italy sign a revised version of Premier Benito Mussolini's Four-Power Pact proposal. . . . The Vatican and Germany sign a new Concordat.	The Russian and Romanian governments sign a Non-Aggression Pact. . . . All political parties except the National Socialist Party are dissolved in Germany.	The Saudi and Trans-Jordanian governments sign a Treaty of Friendship.		The All-India Congress meets in Poona and, under Gandhi's leadership, launches a new civil disobedience campaign.
Aug.	The League of Nations hosts a conference on wheat production in London. Argentina, Australia, Canada, the Soviet Union, and the United States sign the International Wheat Agreement limiting exports and planted acreage.	The death penalty is declared in Germany for anti-fascists. . . . Portuguese dictator António Salazar forms the Portuguese secret police.	Due to the rise of National Socialism, tensions break out between British and German colonists in Southwest Africa. . . . Iraqi troops massacre Christian Assyrians.	The Cuban army forces Gerardo Machado out of power and Carlos Manuel de Cespedes becomes the new president of Cuba.	Due to the resumption of the civil disobedience campaign, British authorities arrest Gandhi who, however, is released after only a few days.
Sept.	The League of Nations Assembly holds its 14th session in Geneva.	Alejandro Lerroux forms a new government in Spain. . . . The Greek and Turkish governments sign a 10-year nonaggression pact. . . . The trial of Marinus der Lubbe opens. He is accused of burning the Reichstag.		The Cuban army, led by Fulgencio Batista, replaces Carlos Manuel de Cespedes with Grau San Martin.	The Nationalist Chinese government launches a campaign against Communists in Nanjing.
Oct.	The League of Nations holds an international conference against prostitution. . . . The League of Nations holds an international conference on the plight of refugees around the world.	King Alexander of Yugoslavia conducts state visits to Sofia and Istanbul as part of a series of visits by Balkan rulers. . . . An assassination attempt on Austrian Premier Engelbert Dollfuss fails. . . . Germany withdraws from the League of Nations Disarmament Conference.		At Rio de Janeiro, representatives of Brazil, Argentina, Chile, Mexico, Paraguay, and Uruguay sign a non-aggression treaty.	The Filipino parliament rejects the Hawes-Cutting Plan for Philippine independence.

A	B	C	D	E
Includes developments that affect more than one world region, international organizations, and important meetings of world leaders.	Includes all domestic and regional developments in Europe, including the Soviet Union.	Includes all domestic and regional developments in Africa and the Middle East.	Includes all domestic and regional developments in Latin America, the Caribbean, and Canada.	Includes all domestic and regional developments in Asian and Pacific nations (and colonies).

U.S. Politics & Social Issues	U.S. Foreign Policy & Defense	Economics & Great Depression	Science, Technology & Nature	Culture, Leisure & Lifestyle	
The construction of the Golden Gate Bridge in San Francisco begins. . . . Calvin Coolidge, the 30th president of the United States, dies in Northampton, Mass.	U.S. troops finally evacuate from Nicaragua, ending the occupation that began in 1912. . . . Congress passes the Hawes-Cutting Bill, which calls for a 12-year transitional period for the Philippine Commonwealth under a Filipino executive.			The first episode of the radio series *The Lone Ranger* is broadcast. The program will continue for 21 years on ABC radio.	Jan.
The Twentieth Amendment to the Constitution comes into effect, reducing the time that defeated members in Congressional elections, or "lame ducks," remain in office. . . . President-elect Franklin Roosevelt escapes an assassination attempt in Miami. . . . Congress passes the Twenty-first Amendment, ending Prohibition.	The Stimson formula of nonrecognition of Manchukuo is adopted by the League of Nations.	Frances Perkins is appointed Secretary of Labor. She is the first woman in the U.S. Cabinet.		The first issue of *Newsweek* is published.	Feb.
Franklin Roosevelt is inaugurated president of the United States.	In his inaugural address, President Roosevelt outlines his Good Neighbor Policy, a clear break with the interventionist stance of previous administrations in Latin American affairs. . . . The National Association for the Advancement of Colored People begins a campaign to stop segregation and discrimination.	President Roosevelt closes all banks for four days and forbids the exportation of gold to protect the U.S. reserve. . . . Congress passes the Emergency Banking Relief Act, which authorizes the President to regulate transactions in credit, currency, gold, silver, and foreign exchange.	An earthquake in Long Beach kills more than 100 people.	*King Kong* premieres in New York. The film saves RKO from bankruptcy.	Mar.
President Roosevelt signs an amendment to the Volstead Act that makes wine and beer containing up to 3.2 percent alcohol legal.		The U.S. government withdraws from the gold standard to have greater control on monetary policy.	The dirigible *Akron* crashes into the Atlantic off the coast of New Jersey, killing 73 of its passengers.		Apr.
Nellie T. Ross becomes the first female director of the U.S. Mint. . . . The Tennessee Valley Authority Act is signed by President Roosevelt to build dams in the Tennessee Valley.		The Federal Emergency Relief Administration and the Agricultural Adjustment Administration are established to provide help for the needy and farmers. . . . President Roosevelt passes the Federal Securities Act.	Karl Jansky reports the detection of radio waves from the center of the Milky Way galaxy.	Archibald Macleish is awarded the Pulitzer Prize. . . . The Century of Progress World Fair opens in Chicago.	May
In Kansas City, the mob kills an FBI agent, a gangster, and four policemen.	Congress plans to punish those countries who refuse to pay their war debts to the United States.	Congress cancels the gold clause from all obligations. . . . The U.S. Employment Service is established. . . . Congress passes the National Recovery Act.		Richard M. Hollingshead, Jr., auto products salesman, opens the first drive-in movie theater in Camden, N. J. . . . Actor Roscoe "Fatty" Arbuckle dies.	Jun.
	President Roosevelt condemns the negotiators at the International Economic Conference in London for focusing solely on currency stabilization and excluding tariff reduction.			The first All-Star baseball game takes place. . . . American aviator Wiley Post completes the first solo flight around the world.	Jul.
	U.S. warships are sent to Cuba due to the continuous disorders and political instability.		A fire breaks out in Tillamook, Ore., that is not extinguished until September. An estimated 311,000 acres burn.		Aug.
	The United States refuses to recognize the new Cuban regime led by Grau San Martin.				Sept.
John Dillinger escapes from a jail in Allen County, Ohio. . . . Albert Einstein immigrates to the United States due to the rise of National Socialism and anti-Semitism.	President Roosevelt meets President Harmodio Arias of Panama. They agree that Panama will control all of the commercial rights within the Canal Zone.		The first synthetic detergent, Dreft, by Procter and Gamble goes on sale.	Eugene O'Neill's comedy *Ah, Wilderness!* premieres in New York. . . . The first issue of *Esquire* is published.	Oct.

F	G	H	I	J
Includes elections, federal-state relations, civil rights and liberties, crime, the judiciary, education, healthcare, poverty, urban affairs, and population.	*Includes formation and debate of U.S. foreign and defense policies, veterans affairs, and defense spending. (Relations with specific foreign countries are usually found under the region concerned.)*	*Includes business, labor, agriculture, taxation, transportation, consumer affairs, monetary and fiscal policy, natural resources, pollution, and accidents.*	*Includes worldwide scientific, medical, and technological developments, natural phenomena, U.S. weather, and natural disasters.*	*Includes the arts, religion, scholarship, communications media, sports, entertainment, fashions, fads, and social life.*

	World Affairs	Europe	Africa & The Middle East	The Americas	Asia & The Pacific
Nov.	The French and Syrian governments sign a treaty that pledges France to support Syria's admission into the League of Nations within four years.	Germans overwhelmingly support the government's decision to withdraw from the League of Nations. . . . Spanish Basques vote for independence.	The French open the Moroccan-Tunisian Railway, which unites the French North African colonies.	The Royal Commission appointed to investigate the huge debt of Newfoundland blames the incompetence and corruption of government.	
Dec.		Hungarian Premier Julius Goemboes rejects the Franco-Czech plan for a Danubian Federation. . . . Czar Boris of Bulgaria conducts a state visit to Belgrade. This visit marks the beginning of the Bulgarian-Yugoslavian reconciliation. . . . . Romanian Prime Mminister Ion Duca is assassinated by members of the Iron Guard, a fascist organization.	Jews protest against British restrictions imposed on immigration in Palestine. The protests escalate into riots.	The seventh Pan-American Conference takes place in Montevideo, Uruguay. . . . Newfoundland loses its status of Dominion and reverts to Crown Colony status. . . . Paraguay makes important progress in the Chaco conflict, capturing thousands of Bolivian prisoners.	

A	B	C	D	E
Includes developments that affect more than one world region, international organizations, and important meetings of world leaders.	Includes all domestic and regional developments in Europe, including the Soviet Union.	Includes all domestic and regional developments in Africa and the Middle East.	Includes all domestic and regional developments in Latin America, the Caribbean, and Canada.	Includes all domestic and regional developments in Asian and Pacific nations (and colonies).

U.S. Politics & Social Issues	U.S. Foreign Policy & Defense	Economics & Great Depression	Science, Technology & Nature	Culture, Leisure & Lifestyle	
Pennsylvanians vote for permitting Sunday sports. . . . Brooke Hart is kidnapped from the parking lot of the family-owned department store in San Jose, Calif. He is later killed.	U.S. and Soviet representatives begin negotiations that end in the mutual recognition of the two countries.	President Roosevelt creates the Civil Works Administration, designed to create jobs for more than 4 million unemployed.	A huge dust storm hits North Dakota.		Nov.
Utah is the 36th state to ratify the Twenty-first Amendment to the U.S. Constitution, thus repealing Prohibition.	At the seventh Pan-American Conference, U.S. Secretary of State Cordell Hull supports a treaty that declares that no state has the right to interfere in the internal or external affairs of another state. This policy is the application of President Franklin Roosevelt's Good Neighbor Policy.			Jack Kirkland's *Tobacco Road* premieres in New York. . . . The ban on James Joyce's *Ulysses* is lifted.	Dec.

F
Includes elections, federal-state relations, civil rights and liberties, crime, the judiciary, education, healthcare, poverty, urban affairs, and population.

G
Includes formation and debate of U.S. foreign and defense policies, veterans affairs, and defense spending. (Relations with specific foreign countries are usually found under the region concerned.)

H
Includes business, labor, agriculture, taxation, transportation, consumer affairs, monetary and fiscal policy, natural resources, pollution, and accidents.

I
Includes worldwide scientific, medical, and technological developments, natural phenomena, U.S. weather, and natural disasters.

J
Includes the arts, religion, scholarship, communications media, sports, entertainment, fashions, fads, and social life.

	World Affairs	Europe	Africa & The Middle East	The Americas	Asia & The Pacific
Jan. 1		Government officials of Turkey and Greece exchange New Year's greetings, demonstrating the growing friendliness between the two nations.	In order to aid the transition of Abyssinia from a feudal system to a more modern one, Emperor Haile Selassie cuts magistrate fees in half and cancels many fines.	Argentine farmers hold their wheat crops, many not even harvesting them, since the price of grain has dropped so low.	Filipino Senator Benigno Aquino states in a speech in Chicago that he is in favor of the Philippine Independence Bill passed by Congress. He says Filipinos have waited 400 years for their freedom, so another 10 years is nothing to them.
Jan. 2	London is optimistic that the signing of the Ottawa Pacts with the other countries in the British Empire will help trade in the coming year.	In his newspaper, Adolf Hitler demands the ouster of Germany's Chancellor Kurt von Schleicher and the lowering of interest payments on the country's debts.	Sir John Simon has the British Foreign Office inform the Anglo-Persian Oil Company that no negotiations can take place until the League of Nations acts on the points the British government raised about the situation.	Four Colombian warships steam up the Amazon River, heading for the Putumayo River. Peru's air force gathers and bombers are expected to attack the ships when they reach the Leticia area.	Japanese troops have taken Shanhaikwan, the gateway between Manchuria and North China, and are pushing on toward Peiping and Tientsin.
Jan. 3		Three Communist officials in the south Ukraine are sentenced to death for sabotage of grain collections for the state and stealing grain. They also incited peasants to fulfill only 40 percent of their grain collection.		The Bolivians bomb the Paraguayan gun boat *Humaita* at Bahia Negra in Paraguay.	The head of the Chinese delegation says China may be forced to quit the League of Nations if reasonable progress is not made to apply the League's principles in the Far East.
Jan. 4		British officials deny a story in a London newspaper that says Britain is sending a delegation to the United States to negotiate about war debts.		Salvadorean President Maximiliano Hernandez Martinez's new government is recognized by Austria.	
Jan. 5		France happily interprets Senator William Borah's speech to mean that if France does not pay its war debt to the United States, then the United States would enter negotiations to readjust the debt.			Chinese flee from the area around Shanhaikwan. An estimated 100,000 people pile into unheated boxcars on trains headed for Peiping and Tientsin. Hundreds of wounded Chinese are also transported by train.
Jan. 6	Economic circles in Geneva are disappointed to learn that the United States will not attend the conference on universal adoption of the 40-hour week. U.S. presence was expected to be influential, since many companies there have gone to shorter workweeks. . . . Heads of state from around the world send condolences to the United States on the loss of former president Calvin Coolidge. Those sending messages include King George of England, President von Hindenburg of Germany, Premier Benito Mussolini of Italy, and Foreign Minister Yasuya Uchida of Japan.		Little business is being done in South Africa since the country abandoned the gold standard on December 30. Many U.S. orders are cancelled.	Many in southern Chile flee as erupting volcanoes spew ash, smoke, and lava into the air. Scientists had predicted the eruptions, based on underground rumblings and earth tremors in the area.	China asks Great Britain and the United States to send neutral military observers to the area of Shanhaikwan so they can report what is happening there.
Jan. 7		Users of electricity in Moscow are told they must cut their consumption in half in the next four months. If they fail to obey the order, they will be charged triple.	The Shah has recalled the Persian Minister, Mirza Ali Gohli Kahn Ansari, to London. It is believed he is unhappy with the way the Minister has conducted himself during the oil dispute between England and Persia.	Colombia and Peru agree to allow Brazil to mediate their conflict on Leticia. It is in Brazil's best interests to settle the matter because of the proximity of Leticia to Brazil. Spokesmen in Rio de Janeiro say they will allow no fighting on Brazilian territory.	General Muto enlarges Japan's holdings in Manchuria, and Japan talks of plans to take Jehol. No action is taken by the League of Nations on the conflict between Japan and China.
Jan. 8	Information published today shows a deadlock between Japan and the League of Nations. Japan demands invitations to the United States and Russia to sit in be withdrawn. They also demand that only League members with important interests in China be on the conciliation committee.	Communists rise up in Spain and battle troops for two hours in Barcelona. The city is virtually under martial law after five are killed.		Rebellions break out in two Argentine towns, and President Justo cuts short his holiday at the beach. The government downplays the incident.	The Japanese carry their aerial warfare into the Jehol province, bombing the Chinese Sixteenth and Nineteenth Brigades east of Jehol City.
Jan. 9	The League of Nations sends out a memorandum answering Colombia's complaint sent to them last week. It says the question is an internal one, since Leticia was seized by a group of Peruvians acting on their own, not by the Lima government.	Socialist newspapers in Vienna report that freight cars loaded with machine guns and rifles arrive in Vienna from Italy, then are shipped on to Hungary. Other newspapers deny the report.	Persian Foreign Minister Aly Khan Farrughi stresses that the recall of the Minister to London is in no way connected with the problems with the Anglo-Persian Oil Company.	In a surprise attack, the Bolivians take both the old and new Forts Lopez from the Paraguayans. The attack follows a lull dictated by heavy rains in the area.	Five Chinese brigades construct fortifications on the Jehol frontier in anticipation of Japanese attacks. Japan has already bombed a Chinese column 35 miles within the borders of Jehol.

A	B	C	D	E
Includes developments that affect more than one world region, international organizations, and important meetings of world leaders.	Includes all domestic and regional developments in Europe, including the Soviet Union.	Includes all domestic and regional developments in Africa and the Middle East.	Includes all domestic and regional developments in Latin America, the Caribbean, and Canada.	Includes all domestic and regional developments in Asian and Pacific nations (and colonies).

U.S. Politics & Social Issues	U.S. Foreign Policy & Defense	Economics & Great Depression	Science, Technology & Nature	Culture, Leisure & Lifestyle	
	The Coast Guard sends four cutters and a plane to look for another Coast Guard plane that made a forced landing along the coast of Florida. The endangered plane had gone in search of a boy lost in a boat, and when the rescuers saw that he had found his way ashore, they started back and ran into rough weather.	The farm parity bill is expected to pass this week as Democrats in Congress invoke a special rule to rush it through. They believe if President Herbert Hoover vetoes the bill, President-elect Franklin Roosevelt will call a special session of Congress to pass it as soon as he takes office on March 4.	Flood conditions in the south improve after days of rain. Only Nashville and the area around Tallahatchie, Miss., are expected to still have rising water tomorrow.	The annual Tournament of Roses Parade takes place in Pasadena, Calif. Some of the 155 floats decorated with blossoms contain over 100,000 flowers. Actress Mary Pickford serves as grand marshal.	Jan. 1
	The last of the U.S. Marines leave Nicaragua, as 815 men and 80 officers sail on two transports. The United States had occupied the country since 1912.	A group of economists recommends to President-elect Franklin Roosevelt a three-part program to lift the country out of the Depression. The program maintains the gold system, lowers tariffs, and settles war debts.	A loud explosion causes a huge section of the side of Carbon Mountain in Colorado to break off and thunder down the mountainside. A 75-foot heap of boulders and soil lies at the foot of the mountain. Scientists believe a coal bed deep within the earth ignited, causing the explosion.	England's poet laureate John Masefield arrives in the United States for a tour of the country. No other poet laureate has come to America.	Jan. 2
The parity farm bill, which incorporates President-elect Franklin Roosevelt's ideas on farm relief, is introduced in the House.	President Herbert Hoover asks Congress to approve $300,000 so that President-elect Franklin Roosevelt will have funds to pay for delegations to the World Disarmament Conference and the World Economic Parley.		Prof. Auguste Piccard sails for the United States, where he plans a lecture tour. He announces that he has invented a rocket that he believes will eventually be made practical to transport mail and passengers across the Atlantic.	Actress Nita Naldi, who played opposite Rudolph Valentino in several movies, files for bankruptcy. She became known for playing vampire parts.	Jan. 3
Senator Pat Harrison asks the Senate Finance Committee to do a study of the economic problems facing the nation today. He emphasizes that it should include anything that might help pull the country out of the Depression.	Capt. John W. Thomason, Jr., a novelist and a member of the U.S. Marines, praises China for the fight it has put up against a stronger and better-armed Japan.	Congress considers giving more power to the Reconstruction Finance Corporation so that it might accept collateral. It would then be able to make loans to the railroads for their immediate needs.			Jan. 4
Former president Calvin Coolidge dies suddenly in his Northampton home, where his wife finds him when she returns from shopping. Doctors say the cause of death is a heart attack. Coolidge's death leaves the nation with no living former presidents.		The new economy bill, which could save the nation over $30 million, is passed by the Senate Appropriations Committee. The bill would give President-elect Franklin Roosevelt the most power Congress has ever conferred on a President in peace time.	American aviator Amelia Earhart receives two awards in one day. In the afternoon the Jeanne d'Arc Medal is given to her by Le Lyceum, an organization of French women in New York. In the evening she receives the first gold medal to be awarded by the Society of Woman Geographers.	Tallulah Bankhead, who has not appeared on Broadway for 10 years, will star in the play Forsaking All Others. Arch Selwyn will be the producer.	Jan. 5
Three employees of the cemetery in Plymouth, Vt., dig a grave on the hillside to serve as a final resting place for former president Calvin Coolidge. He will lie between his mother and his son, Calvin, Jr. He refused to improve the lot, saying, "I don't want my lot to look any better than my neighbors'."		President-elect Franklin Roosevelt confers with Democratic leaders, asking them to give him as much power as possible to help him effect economies in order to balance the budget.	A plane of Air Express, Inc. establishes a new record for a flight from Los Angeles to New York as it makes the trip in 14 hours and 20 minutes elapsed time.		Jan. 6
Rain and hail pour down as former president Calvin Coolidge is laid to rest in the cemetery in Plymouth, Vt. The graveside service lasts less than five minutes, then the casket is lowered and covered with four truckloads of flowers sent in the president's memory.		Several auto manufacturers announce price reductions for the 1933 models. Cuts range from $50 to $1,000.		The Big Ten begin their conference basketball schedule. Indiana is at Ohio State, Purdue at Minnesota, Michigan at Iowa, Northwestern at Illinois, and Chicago at Wisconsin for the openers.	Jan. 7
Grace Coolidge, wife of the recently deceased former U.S. president Calvin Coolidge, attends church as usual in Northampton.	Bonus Marcher Royal W. Robertson sues the Veteran's Bureau for $10,000 because he fell out of a Navy hammock and sustained injuries. He charges that after he drew a pension for several years, the government arbitrarily canceled his pension.		Dr. Irving Langmuir, winner of the Nobel Prize in Chemistry in 1932, devises a method to measure the speed and charge of atoms.	American author Edna Ferber is very ill, suffering from influenza in a London hotel. She is in London to attend the premiere of Dinner at Eight, a play which she co-authored.	Jan. 8
Senators Johnson and Borah exchange sharp words as the Senate debates the problem of war debts owed to the United States.	The U.S. Military Academy at West Point cancels several athletic contests with other schools due to a serious outbreak of influenza among its cadets.	General Motors reports that sales in December ran far ahead of their sales for November, but are less than for the same period last year. The increase is attributed to the release of the new 1933 models in December.	A federal court in Baltimore sets aside an 8,240-acre tract as a bird sanctuary. The sanctuary is the result of a treaty reached with Great Britain that provides care for birds migrating from Canada.	Forty trotters register for the Hambletonian, which is the richest harness horse race in the world. This is the biggest field in the history of the trotting classic.	Jan. 9
F Includes elections, federal-state relations, civil rights and liberties, crime, the judiciary, education, healthcare, poverty, urban affairs, and population.	**G** Includes formation and debate of U.S. foreign and defense policies, veterans affairs, and defense spending. (Relations with specific foreign countries are usually found under the region concerned.)	**H** Includes business, labor, agriculture, taxation, transportation, consumer affairs, monetary and fiscal policy, natural resources, pollution, and accidents.	**I** Includes worldwide scientific, medical, and technological developments, natural phenomena, U.S. weather, and natural disasters.	**J** Includes the arts, religion, scholarship, communications media, sports, entertainment, fashions, fads, and social life.	

	World Affairs	Europe	Africa & The Middle East	The Americas	Asia & The Pacific
Jan. 10	The parley in Geneva on the shorter workweek begins, with representatives from 34 nations in attendance. Belgian representative Ernest Mahaim is elected president. Both Russia and the United States decline the invitation to attend.	The rebellion in Spain spreads, with the situation the worst in Seville. The Cabinet authorizes Premier Manuel Azano to declare martial law.	The Zionist Organization of America is informed that Dr. Louis Cantor, chief sanitary engineer for the Palestine government, has died. He has been there since World War I.	In response to Colombian ships heading up the Amazon, Peru warns Colombia that "progress of a Colombian expedition toward Leticia means the initiation of hostilities." Colombia Commander Alfredo Vasquez Cobo replies that his mission is peaceful.	The Japanese and Chinese battle for possession of the Chumen Pass in the Great Wall of China, leading into the province of Jehol. Four Japanese planes bomb the Chinese lines. This afternoon Peiping announces the Chinese still hold the southern end of the pass.
Jan. 11		The U.S. Embassy in Paris receives a letter from an American, Fletcher N. Candell, charging that he has been held at Villejulf Asylum for five months and the confinement is unjustified. The letter sounds quite coherent, so the Consulate will investigate the situation tomorrow.	Gen. Jan Smuts is cheered when he arrives in Capetown, South Africa, this morning. He speaks of the possibility of a coalition with Tielman J. de V. Roos, who will return to South Africa on Saturday.	A newspaper in Mexico City begs President-elect Franklin Roosevelt not to replace Reuben Clark, U.S. Ambassador to Mexico. The article is in response to rumors that Clark will retire on February 15.	The Philippine Legislative Mission calls at the White House to urge President Herbert Hoover to sign the Independence Bill. It is believed that Hoover is considering vetoing it.
Jan. 12	It seems that the Committee of Nineteen of the League of Nations will abandon their efforts to settle the Far East question and turn it back to the Assembly. The small powers are adamant about wanting the League to condemn Japan and some even want the country expelled from the League.	Belgium sees many socialist demonstrations protesting food taxes, decreases in unemployment relief, and taking the dole away from married women. Demonstrations are also held in Louviers where 4,000 workers go out on strike.		South American diplomats renew their efforts to end hostilities in Bolivia and Peru when threats of more air raids cause an immediate reaction.	
Jan. 13	Japan seems less likely to quit the League of Nations after receiving a resolution from the Committee of Nineteen, which Japan says is a great improvement over earlier attempts. However, it still contains an invitation to the United States and Russia to sit in, and Japan insists that be eliminated.	The Turkish Cabinet approves granting a concession to Britain for the first time since World War I. The British will run a train ferry service from Sirkeji at the European edge of Turkey and across the Bosporus, at the Asiatic edge.	Wallace Murray, chief of the Division of Near Eastern Affairs of the U.S. State Department, praises England for the good administration of its Iraq mandate, which ends with Iraq becoming an independent nation and a member of the League of Nations.	La Paz vehemently denies that her planes bombed Concepcion, saying the flights were merely for reconnaissance. It is believed they did drop handbills addressed to the Paraguayans.	China begins a drive, sending 30,000 troops to attack the Japanese army at the southeast corner of Jehol. England warns Japan that their fighting menaces British interests.
Jan. 14		Jewelers remodel the British crown for King George. It was made for Queen Victoria in 1838 and some of the jewels were insecure. The entire gold framework is taken apart and the jewels reset. Many of the precious stones in the crown are much older than the gold framework.	Persian Minister of Justice Ali Akbar Khan Davar challenges the right of the British government to intervene in the Anglo-Persian oil dispute. He asserts it is an internal matter and only Persians have a right to take part in it.	Sir John Aird, president of the Canadian Bank of Commerce, suggests that trade would be greatly encouraged if all nations would immediately reduce their tariffs by 10 percent.	
Jan. 15	The agenda for the economic parley in Geneva is nearly set, but most agree that not much can be accomplished until the matter of war debts is resolved. No one is sure what President-elect Franklin Roosevelt's position will be on the subject.	King Boris of Bulgaria is criticized for having his infant daughter, Maria Luisa, baptized into the Orthodox faith. It was assumed that he had promised the Pope when he married that all of his children would be brought up in the Roman Catholic faith.	Tielman Roos calms a South African riot as he speaks from his hotel balcony. In his calm talk, he wins support for a coalition government.		Over 3,000 Chinese troops flee across the border into Russia as Japan takes Hulin.
Jan. 16	The League of Nations gives Japan 48 hours to agree to conciliation. . . . A committee of the World Bank believes war debts must be settled before any other economic business can be transacted. It says countries that have gone off the gold standard need to stabilize their currencies at new parities.	Poland executes three Germans convicted as spies. Jan Kropidlowski is shot, while Paul Gliebe and Ernest Koch are hanged.	A rescue plane leaves Nairobi to try to rescue two fliers whose plane crashed between Nairobi and Tanganyika. Joan Page and Audrey Salebarker were en route from Capetown to England. Search planes spot their plane and one of the women waves to them, but the other is not seen.	The Bolivians mount another offensive in the Chaco. It is said that a new plan for peace will be presented soon by the ABC group—Argentina, Brazil, and Chile.	Japan negotiates with Great Britain to buy the old White Star liner *Megantic*, which served as a troop ship for the Canadian army during the World War.
Jan. 17	France believes it will be difficult for the League of Nations to conciliate the Far East dispute and maintain League prestige. M. Paul-Bancour calls it a severe test for the League.			Foreign Minister Mello Franco of Brazil says his country is happy to sign the anti-war pact proposed by Argentina, but would like to open the pact up to all countries of the world.	The Chinese believe Japan will try to take Jehol, and worry that the Yangtse Valley might also be in Japan's sights. Planes leaving Peiping are filled with Chinese fleeing to Shanghai and Nanking, while trains going the other way carry troops.
Jan. 18		Irish President Eamon de Valera is cheered in Cork as he is well received by his opponent's constituency.	The Archbishop of Canterbury is concerned with the British policy of mining gold on land in Kenya that is set aside for use by the native Kenyans. The government says the gold belongs to the Crown, rather than to the Kenyans or the British.	Paraguay charges the Bolivian army is using dum-dums, soft-nosed bullets that spread. These are prohibited by international law.	The Chinese military sends a trainload of camels to Jehol, presumably to be used as transportation. . . . The Chinese press reports 360 Chinese soldiers in thin summer uniforms have frozen to death at their posts in Manchuria.

A	B	C	D	E
Includes developments that affect more than one world region, international organizations, and important meetings of world leaders.	*Includes all domestic and regional developments in Europe, including the Soviet Union.*	*Includes all domestic and regional developments in Africa and the Middle East.*	*Includes all domestic and regional developments in Latin America, the Caribbean, and Canada.*	*Includes all domestic and regional developments in Asian and Pacific nations (and colonies).*

U.S. Politics & Social Issues	U.S. Foreign Policy & Defense	Economics & Great Depression	Science, Technology & Nature	Culture, Leisure & Lifestyle	
Senator Long's three-hour filibuster halts action on the Glass Bank Bill. He says there is no way it will ever pass after March 4. . . . President Herbert Hoover deeds his Rapidan Camp to the state of Virginia. It will eventually become part of the Shenandoah National Park. . . . A. R. Erskine, president of the Studebaker Corporation, warns there are many unsafe automobiles on the roads. He says eventually there comes a time when operating an old car is both expensive and hazardous, and then it needs to be replaced.	Col. E.M. House and James W. Gerard call on President-elect Franklin Roosevelt to discuss foreign affairs. Both Democrats have had extensive experience in diplomacy.			E.R. Bradley's three-year-old colt, Thrush, drops dead at the finish line on the track at Hialeah. Jockey Smith was pinned beneath the horse, but was not injured. . . . Actress Libby Holman has a baby boy in a Philadelphia hospital.	Jan. 10
A resolution to allow the President to ban arms sales to other countries if he determines that such sales encourage the use of force in a dispute is rushed before the Senate. President Herbert Hoover requested the granting of such authority.	The House Naval Committee protests to the House Appropriations Committee against their recommendation to cut the Marine Corps. The group argues that the country needs more marines, not fewer.	The Anthracite Institute states that production of hard coal in 1932 is 10,296,000 tons below production in 1931.	A violent windstorm in California kills at least two and does over $1 million in property damage. The wind reaches 80 miles per hour in places, blowing down 200 oil derricks in southern California.	Amos Parrish, whose spring fashion clinic is attended by buyers from around the country, says women's fashions for spring show a mannish tendency. Some have broad shoulders and narrow skirts, and many tailored women's suits are double-breasted and made of menswear fabrics.	Jan. 11
The House passes the farm relief bill. . . . The filibuster in the Senate continues with Senator Long talking for five hours. Senator Thomas takes over the filibuster, and Congress finally adjourns without making a decision on the Glass Bill.	The House Appropriations Committee agrees to maintain the regular Army at its present strength and says it will increase funding for the National Guard.	Over 1,500 members of the Needle Trades Unemployment Council riot in New York City streets, led by their Communist leaders. They are finally dispersed by 150 policemen.	Prof. Auguste Piccard arrives in the United States and meets his twin brother, Jean, and the two of them joke with reporters. He plans to visit laboratories and confer with other scientists on such topics as cosmic rays, rocket planes, and the stratosphere.		Jan. 12
The House of Representatives overrides President Herbert Hoover's veto of the Hawes-Cutting bill on Philippine independence. The bill goes to the Senate on Monday.	The War Department begins preparing for the annual pilgrimage of mothers and widows of soldiers who died in World War I. The group will travel to cemeteries in Europe where their sons and husbands are buried.		Charles A. Devila, Romanian Minister to the United States, awards the Romanian order of Virtutea Aeronautic to Col. Charles A. Lindbergh and Amelia Earhart. This highest aeronautic honor of the Romanian government is given in the name of King Carol.	The National Collegiate Athletic Association is investigating allegations that Japanese swimmers in the Olympics were given oxygen or some other stimulant. Doctors doubt the theory, saying any effect would last for a very short time.	Jan. 13
Nicholas Schreiber, who came to the United States from Germany as a boy, dies. He served as a drummer boy in the Civil War. Only one member of his G.A.R. post survives.		President-elect Franklin Roosevelt says that when he revamps the Reconstruction Finance Corporation, he will strictly enforce his New Deal principles, saying he wants to humanize the board. Some believe he will name Al Smith to head the agency.		The Southern Conference asks for an investigation into allegations of recruiting and subsidizing athletes by colleges.	Jan. 14
	The last Marines who were stationed in Nicaragua arrive in the United States. The Second Brigade is welcomed at Quantico, Va., after being gone for four years.		University of Arizona's Archaeology Department Head, Dr. Byron Cummings, announces that he and a group of advanced students have uncovered seven large pueblos once occupied by the Sobapuri Indians.		Jan. 15
The parity bill for farm relief is being debated in the Senate. Many Senators believe that since the bill is of an experimental nature, it should only cover wheat and cotton.	Secretary of State Henry Stimson reaffirms his opposition to recognition of Manchukuo. He also denies a Japanese rumor that the United States has an agreement to supply China with arms in the event of a war between Japan and China.	In a nationwide radio address, Secretary Mills renews his call for a sales tax, saying that is the only way to balance the budget.		The bestseller list for 1932 lists two books each for Pearl Buck and Ely Culbertson. *Culbertson's Summary* tops the list, with *The Fountain* by Charles Morgan in second place.	Jan. 16
The Cutting-Hawes Philippine Independence Bill becomes law, as the Senate votes to override President Herbert Hoover's veto, as the House did a week ago.		In an address to Congress, President Herbert Hoover stresses the need for budget cuts and advocates a sales tax. He points out that a balanced budget is one of the most useful things he and the Congress can contribute to the Roosevelt administration.	Two scientists in Calcutta, India, produce vitamin B by the action of ultraviolet rays on adenine sulphate. The vitamin was first isolated in its pure form a year ago.	Lily Pons returns to the Metropolitan Opera after several weeks of illness. She is scheduled to play the role of Gilda in *Rigoletto* on Monday.	Jan. 17
A House committee works on a plan to give Samoans U.S. citizenship without taking away their unique culture.	The Twenty-Third Bombardment Squad hangar at Luke Field in Hawaii is swept by fire. Loss is estimated at $150,000. There is a bomber in the hangar. This is the second fire in 18 months.	Foreign trade for the United States in 1932 is the lowest since 1905.	Dr. Vesto M. Slipher, director of the Lowell Observatory in Flagstaff, Ariz., is awarded the Gold Medal of the Royal Astronomic Society in England. He wins for his spectroscopic research on planets, stars, and nebulae.	Cuban featherweight world champion Kid Chocolate sails from Havana on his way to New York for a championship bout with Seaman Tom Watson, the English titleholder. The match will be fought on January 27.	Jan. 18

F	G	H	I	J
Includes elections, federal-state relations, civil rights and liberties, crime, the judiciary, education, healthcare, poverty, urban affairs, and population.	*Includes formation and debate of U.S. foreign and defense policies, veterans affairs, and defense spending. (Relations with specific foreign countries are usually found under the region concerned.)*	*Includes business, labor, agriculture, taxation, transportation, consumer affairs, monetary and fiscal policy, natural resources, pollution, and accidents.*	*Includes worldwide scientific, medical, and technological developments, natural phenomena, U.S. weather, and natural disasters.*	*Includes the arts, religion, scholarship, communications media, sports, entertainment, fashions, fads, and social life.*

	World Affairs	Europe	Africa & The Middle East	The Americas	Asia & The Pacific
Jan. 19	In Geneva the Preparatory Economic Commission approves a report containing the six-point agenda for the economic conference to be held in London. They strongly advise settling the war debts matter and returning to the gold standard.	London banker F.C. Goodenough says Britain should not pay the United States another payment on its debt until the whole matter has been discussed and settled satisfactorily.		The Nicaraguan Senate approves a state of siege for nine departments of the country. There have been no problems yet, but they anticipate problems with Gen. Sandino.	Tokyo police think they have halted most of the labor rioting at the Singer Sewing Machine Company factory that erupted yesterday. Damage is estimated at several thousand yen.
Jan. 20	Part 2 of the report of the Preparatory Economic Commission is released and calls for cutting wages and a return to the gold standard. It also emphasizes the role of the World Bank in world recovery from the Depression.	Germany is pleased with the decision of the United States to discuss war debts with the British. Hans Dieckhoff from the Foreign Office says they realize the United States will play a tremendous role in the settlement of the war debt problem.		Chile's proposal for ending hostilities in the Chaco includes each side withdrawing 10 miles and submitting the problem for arbitration within a month of signing the agreement. Reports say if Bolivia and Paraguay turn down the proposal, Chile will not allow arms to be shipped through its territory.	The business outlook in Japan looks gloomy for 1933. Profits will be smaller as production costs increase. Imported raw materials cost more because of the decrease in the yen.
Jan. 21	Bolivia notifies the League of Nations that it believes Paraguay is making asphyxiating war gas at Asuncion, where 500 women are also manufacturing gas masks. Bolivia hopes the League will take action against Paraguay.	A small-scale exodus from Moscow begins among those who do not qualify for passports being given out to those engaged in "socially useful" work. They hope the passport system will not spread throughout the country.	The third son of King George, who is the Duke of Gloucester, kills an elephant with 60-pound tusks on his big game hunt in Sudan.	Labor unions of Cuba attempt to form a new Socialist Labor Party. They back the six-hour day and the five-day week for workers.	The name of Changchun, capital of Manchukuo, has been changed to Hsinking, which means "new capital." A building boom takes place in the city. New government buildings are erected, as well as a State Bank and a palace for the Chief Executive.
Jan. 22		Nazi troops demonstrate in the center of the Communist district of Berlin. The demonstration is at a cemetery where a young Nazi killed by Communists in 1930 is buried. Adolf Hitler attends and delivers a brief address.		Jean Mermoz, French mail pilot, breaks the record for flying from France to Argentina. He is cheered by Argentineans when he lands after making the 7,500-mile flight in 54 hours, 33 minutes flying time.	
Jan. 23	The disarmament conference resumes in Geneva, and the first eight articles of the treaty are approved.	Czechoslovakian authorities are worried about a fascist bombing of the army barracks at Brno. General Gajda, who is head of the Fascist Party in Czechoslovakia, is arrested. Authorities fear a coup.	Arabs threaten to overthrow Emir Abdullah of Trans-Jordan if he leases part of his personal property to a Jewish company.	Bolivia goes on the offensive along the 95-mile Chaco front. Other Bolivian objectives are Fort Boqueron and Fort Arce.	A spokesman in the Japanese Diet says that unless relations with the United States improve, they will lead to renewed armaments or another world war.
Jan. 24		Neville Chamberlain, Chancellor of the Exchequer, reveals Britain's plan for the war debt it owes the United States. The two-point program stresses that the settlement must be final and that the amount owed must not necessitate Britain resuming a claim on Germany for reparations.		Argentine farmers in the Santa Fe province vote to strike on February 1, stopping all farming activities unless the government acts on relief measures.	Reports from Peiping say Marshal Chang Hsiao-liang is ready to quit as military leader of north China. The reports are not confirmed.
Jan. 25	The League of Nations Finance Committee reports that the financial situation in Hungary has grown much worse. It gives the country some suggestions to alleviate the problems.		John D. Rockefeller, Jr. donates a collection of Assyrian sculpture to the Metropolitan Museum of Art. Most of the sculptures are from the palace of King Ashur-nasir-apal II at Nimrud.	The ABC nations of South America (Argentina, Brazil, and Chile) seek a new peace policy. They would like to help settle the problems in the Chaco and Leticia.	
Jan. 26	The League of Nations Council hears arguments about the Anglo-Persian Oil Company. Sir John Simon speaks for England, while Minister of Justice Davar presents Persia's case.	Irish Free State President Eamon de Valera's party is likely to have a majority in the Irish legislature, Dail Eirann, capturing 52 seats. William Cosgrove's party wins 31, with 50 yet in doubt.		The Bolivian army advances steadily in the Ayala area, wiping out "nests" of Paraguayan machine gunners in islands of trees in the prairie.	China denies rumors it might withdraw from the League of Nations. The country awaits the outcome of the League's new efforts.
Jan. 27	The League of Nations report on the Far East conflict clears China of any wrongdoing. It also says it is justifiable to invoke a boycott against a nation which has attacked. The British criticize the findings as too general. . . . Colombia appeals to the League in the matter of Peru's action at Leticia.	Two fascist leaders in the Czechoslovakian uprising on Sunday are arrested, and Gen. Gajda and Lt. Gejdi surrender in Yugoslavia, asking for political immunity.	Egyptian Premier Sidky is ill with congestion of the brain, but Egypt reports his condition is improving. . . . American friends give Albert Einstein $100,000 to be used in projects he supports in Jerusalem.	Bolivian Commander Gen. Hans Kundt meets with President Salamanca and his Cabinet in La Paz. Kundt is optimistic about developments in the Chaco.	The Chinese retake Chaoyang, a key city in Jehol, which has been occupied by Japan for several months.
Jan. 28	Leaders of the League of Nations consider recent U.S. moves concerning war debts, Manchuria, and economic considerations to be a bit tardy.	British Chancellor of the Exchequer Neville Chamberlain insists Britain will not go back to the gold standard unless they are sure it will work. He stated there would have to be international accord first.		The Argentine government extends relief to farmers in areas where crops were damaged by locusts and drought.	The Japanese use 12 armored cars and 10 planes in a frontal attack on the Chinese, forcing them to retreat. The Chinese fight back and regain their original position.
Jan. 29	Japan welcomes friendly intervention by the British and is hopeful that the League of Nations will be able to help in the situation in Manchuria.	French President Albert Le Brun asks War Minister Edouard Daladier to form a new Cabinet. He needs the support of the Socialists, but can't afford to alienate the right and center-right, either.	Rumors from Capetown are that Prime Minister Hertzog's South African government will resign if a coalition can be formed between Gen. Jan Christian Smuts and Tielman Roos.	The Canadian National and Canadian Pacific Railroads serve notice that they will reduce the wages of employees by 20 percent on the basic rate on March 3. This will bring wages to 17 percent below those for U.S. railroad workers.	Japanese planes once again bomb Kailu in northeast Jehol. One hundred houses are destroyed and many people killed.

A	B	C	D	E
Includes developments that affect more than one world region, international organizations, and important meetings of world leaders.	*Includes all domestic and regional developments in Europe, including the Soviet Union.*	*Includes all domestic and regional developments in Africa and the Middle East.*	*Includes all domestic and regional developments in Latin America, the Caribbean, and Canada.*	*Includes all domestic and regional developments in Asian and Pacific nations (and colonies).*

U.S. Politics & Social Issues	U.S. Foreign Policy & Defense	Economics & Great Depression	Science, Technology & Nature	Culture, Leisure & Lifestyle	
The "Kingfish," Senator Huey Long, tells the Senate that he is going to talk turkey with President-elect Franklin Roosevelt. He goes to Roosevelt's suite, telling reporters, "I ain't afraid of anything except the people." He later emerges from Roosevelt's suite with a big smile, but refrains from telling reporters anything.	A British publication, *Brassey's Naval Shipping Annual*, criticizes the U.S. battleships *Colorado*, *West Virginia*, and *Maryland*, saying they are slow and are equipped with fewer guns than British ships.	The Cotton Textile Institute, Inc. would face great losses if the farm parity bill became law, says its president, George A. Sloan. He gives examples of how retail prices of cotton staples would be affected.	Albert Einstein says in Los Angeles that he will organize a group of the 25 greatest minds in the world to work for the best interests of mankind. He believes the committee, which would include six Americans, would "become the most potent moral and idealistic force of the world."	World featherweight champion Kid Chocolate from Cuba is deported because he does not have a permit from the Secretary of Labor to enter the United States.	Jan. 19
	Capt. A.A. DeWar succeeds Capt. Patrick McNamara as Naval Attaché to the British Embassy in Washington.	Henry Ford is served a subpoena while at a dance. The local sheriff's office has had it for several weeks but are unable to find Ford, so when they read in the paper that he is to attend a dance, they take it there. It is in regard to a suit Ford filed against the Sweeten Automobile Company of Philadelphia.		Claudette Colbert and Fredric March star in a mythical romance called *Tonight Is Ours*. The film is an adaptation of Noel Coward's play *The Queen Was in the Parlor*.	Jan. 20
The American Automobile Association expects record numbers of people to travel to Washington, D.C., for the March 4 inauguration. They will try to provide maximum travel facilities.		The garment industry appeals to women not to buy clothing made in sweatshops. A spokesman said such concerns are driving legitimate garment makers out of business and he urged nationwide action against them.	In an attempt to keep oysters from extinction, local citizens on Edisto Island, S.C., advocate replanting the oyster beds, which are one of the main sources of food on the island.	The Girl Scouts in the United States report a gain of 20,642 members in 1932. More girls earned the health-winner badge than any other. Second and third were the first-aid badge and the scholarship badge.	Jan. 21
President-elect Franklin Roosevelt works on shaping his Cabinet, trying to get a good balance of liberals and conservatives.	Two young Boston fishermen disappear in a thick fog on heavy seas. Seven Coast Guard patrol boats, three planes, and three fishing boats carry on the search and finally locate the men after three days.	Senator William Borah contends it is impossible to balance the budget without first stabilizing prices and adjusting currency. He calls a sales tax cruel. . . . Ford Motor Company recalls 1,000 workers to its Windsor, Ontario, plant, where work is beginning on the new model.		The New York Giants sign Mel Ott to a contract for the 1933 season. Ott, who is not quite 24, will be playing his ninth season with the Giants. Outfielder Carl Hubbel is also under contract.	Jan. 22
	Secretary of the Treasury Ogden Mills says there is no foundation for a statement in a San Francisco newspaper saying he wants to abolish the Coast Guard. Mills issues a formal denial.	Income tax collections for July–December are down $137,660,448 from the same period last year.	F.M. Starr wins the Nobel Prize in Engineering with a paper on equivalent circuits. Starr is an electrical engineer with General Electric Company in New York City.		Jan. 23
The farm bill has passed both houses and is sent to the President for his signature. It provides $90 million for crop loans.	The Congress finally passes the Army Bill, with the Reserve Corps and Citizen Camp funds intact. The bill now goes to the Senate.	President-elect Franklin Roosevelt spends the day conferring with financier Bernard Baruch on reorganizing the government for economy, war debts, rehabilitation of the railroads, and refunding of Treasury obligations.	During an operation in Stockholm, Dr. Clarence Crawford stops a woman's heart from beating for four minutes, then restarts it. It was necessary in order to remove a blood clot in the heart. The woman is recovering.	A new novel by Sinclair Lewis, the only American author who has won a Nobel Prize for Literature, is published. The book, entitled *Ann Vickers*, is his first since 1929.	Jan. 24
President Herbert Hoover helps his first teacher, Molly Brown Carran, by appointing her son as a rural mail carrier in West Branch, Iowa.		The Senate passes the Glass bank reform bill, 54–9. Senator Huey Long, who filibustered for hours against the bill, is not there for the vote.		A trapeze performer is paralyzed when he falls 20 feet to the stage in a theater in Lowell, Mass. Harry Borcherding sustains a cervical fracture and compression of the spine.	Jan. 25
The Glass banking reform bill goes to the House, where Republicans predict it will die in the Banking and Currency Committee.	The War Department awards a contract to build 38 new planes, high-speed bombers said to be the most powerful weapon ever devised.	U.S. delegates Edmund Day and John Williams return from the world economic parley's preparatory commission saying the "Buy American" movement negates the idea of dependence among nations.	Prof. Colin G. Fink of Columbia University says the age of aluminum is coming. We have a vast supply and he thinks it will be used for ships, trains, and buildings.		Jan. 26
President Herbert Hoover says he will deliver his farewell speech to the nation at Lincoln's birthday celebration on February 13.				A survey by Iowa educator Irving Harlow Hart shows *Quo Vadis* is the most popular novel issued since 1895, and Pearl S. Buck's *The Good Earth* is second in popularity.	Jan. 27
President-elect Franklin Roosevelt invites British Ambassador Sir Ronald Lindsay to his Warm Springs, Ga., home, where they confer informally about war debts.	The House of Representatives assures there will be a vote on February 13 on the bill to increase tariffs against nations with depreciated currency.	Robert D. Kohn, chairman of the National Committee for Trade Recovery, says the only way to put millions of unemployed back to work is through a federal program of public works.		At a special match for baseball players at a gun club in Philadelphia, Athletics first-baseman Jimmy Foxx wins with 62 out of 75.	Jan. 28
The Silk Association of America appeals to President Herbert Hoover to veto the farm parity bill, which it calls "a most unjust form of legislation."		Employees of the Briggs Manufacturing Company, which makes car bodies for Ford, picket in the bitter cold. Strikers number 6,000. The strike also idles 4,500 Ford employees.		Poet Sara Teasdale is found dead in her bathtub. She has been despondent over illness and authorities suspect suicide. . . . Melvin Johnson of Detroit and Kit Klein of Buffalo win the national speed skating championships in Wisconsin.	Jan. 29

F	G	H	I	J
Includes elections, federal-state relations, civil rights and liberties, crime, the judiciary, education, healthcare, poverty, urban affairs, and population.	Includes formation and debate of U.S. foreign and defense policies, veterans affairs, and defense spending. (Relations with specific foreign countries are usually found under the region concerned.)	Includes business, labor, agriculture, taxation, transportation, consumer affairs, monetary and fiscal policy, natural resources, pollution, and accidents.	Includes worldwide scientific, medical, and technological developments, natural phenomena, U.S. weather, and natural disasters.	Includes the arts, religion, scholarship, communications media, sports, entertainment, fashions, fads, and social life.

	World Affairs	Europe	Africa & The Middle East	The Americas	Asia & The Pacific
Jan. 30	The League of Nations discusses use of gas in future wars, but is unable to reach a conclusion. Germany and France strongly oppose reprisals against violators, while Italy and Britain back reprisals.	Adolf Hitler is appointed Chancellor of Germany. Communists in Berlin urge a strike at 7 a.m. tomorrow in protest of Hitler's Cabinet. They pass out handbills to that effect in working-class districts until police break up the crowds.			China believes independent conversations between Tokyo and Nanking could work if a neutral country such as Great Britain or the United States serves as a go-between.
Jan. 31	The League of Nations upholds China's boycott of Japan and rejects Tokyo's plea of self-defense in the conflict in Manchuria.	Centrist leaders in Germany ask Adolf Hitler to clarify his policies as Chancellor. Many believe von Papen is still in control and has the power to veto any rash moves Hitler might make.	Sesostris Sidarouss Pasha, Egyptian Envoy to the United States, retires.	Almost 100,000 farmers in four grain-raising provinces of Argentina strike, refusing to either plant or harvest grain.	In today's Chinese Times, China warns Britain that those who side with China's enemies may see reprisals in the form of trade restrictions.
Feb. 1	Tokyo sends what it says is its final offer to the League of Nations. It says it will accept conciliation if recognition of Manchukuo is not ruled out. It also makes it clear that the committee is to assist, not conduct the negotiations between Japan and China.	Britain denies a rumor that it is siding with Japan in the Far East dispute so that Japan will give her a free hand in Tibet. . . . It is believed that King Alexander of Yugoslavia and King Carol of Romania have signed a secret pact.	Persia and Great Britain agree to resume negotiations on the Anglo-Persian Oil Company dispute. . . . A fire in an Armenian refugee camp in Syria leaves 10,000 Armenians homeless. Those who lived there fled from Turkey in 1922–23.	A parley begins between Argentina and Chile to discuss the Chaco situation, inter-American tariff agreements, and commercial relations.	The poorly equipped army of the Chinese is not dressed warmly enough to withstand the bitter cold in north China. Their War Ministry says the Japanese are equipped with plenty of the latest weapons.
Feb. 2	Japan's senior delegate to the League of Nations, Yosuke Matsuoka, reveals the concessions Japan is willing to make in order to settle its dispute with China. It still insists on recognition of Manchukuo.	Chancellor Adolf Hitler forbids Communists to hold any outdoor meeting in Germany, and indoor meetings will be closely monitored. The Reich is also searching, without search warrants, the homes of all Communists. . . . Portugal expects to readopt the gold standard soon.	Great Britain and Persia reach a provisional agreement in the matter of the cancellation of the Anglo-Persian Oil Company's concession in Persia. The agreement is reached through the League of Nations.		A Japanese sentry on duty threatens American Lt. Robert Skidmore, assigned to Intelligence in Peiping. He blocks Skidmore's way and thrusts his bayonet against his abdomen. Skidmore pushes the weapon away, but does not attempt to disarm the soldier. When the soldier puts a cartridge into his rifle's chamber, Skidmore quietly returns to his barracks and reports the incident.
Feb. 3	Leaders in the League of Nations doubt that Japan would try to annex the Pacific Islands under her mandate if she quit the League. If Japan did that, it would have no legal right to the islands. This also opens the question of whether the League could relieve Japan of its mandate if it quit the League.	The Chamber of Deputies gives a vote of confidence to Edouard Daladier's government with a vote of 370–200. Former French prime minister Herriot gives the Daladier government the official support of his Radical Party. His position is far from secure, though.	The agreement between Great Britain and Persia is revealed. Britain concedes that a new contract needs to be negotiated rather than restoring the old one. Persia will allow the company to operate, pending negotiations. Both countries thank Edward Benes of Czechoslovakia for serving as peacemaker.	The ABC-Peru group, which came out of the meetings between the Foreign Ministers of Argentina and Chile, says it will arbitrate all future disputes on the South American continent. They will settle the Chaco dispute with no intervention from the United States.	Nineteen Japanese troop trains head south toward Jehol. An official dispatch from Mukden says a statement will be made soon concerning the coming Jehol campaign.
Feb. 4	The League of Nations says Japan's proposals are not a suitable basis for conciliation of the conflict in Manchuria between Japan and China.		Actor Otis Skinner, who has played an Arab role in Kismet, is off to North Africa to determine whether his portrayals are faithful.	The American Chamber of Commerce and a group of U.S. businessmen in Rio de Janeiro plan a campaign to remove obstacles to trade with Brazil. They want free importation of Brazilian products that do not compete with U.S. products as long as Brazil reciprocates.	Australia is making a swift recovery from the financial reverses of 1930–31. The federal government shows a surplus and is able to reduce taxes. Unemployment drops and business is reviving.
Feb. 5	In May, the presidency of the League of Nations Council will pass, in alphabetical order, from Italy to Japan. A Japanese citizen is also president of the World Court. With the League finding Japan at fault in the Far East dispute, people anticipate some discomfort with the situation. In fact, some are hoping Japan will drop out of the League.	Romanian Premier Vaida-Voevad is relieved that the first Sunday under martial law passes without incident. He believes there would have been trouble had the government not invoked martial law.	South African gold shares are rising in the London market and the boom resembles the famous one of 1895.		Japan believes its rights to the Caroline Islands and Marshall Islands, which it administers, stem from the Versailles treaty and not from the League of Nations.
Feb. 6	The Committee of Thirteen of the United Nations recommends not only nonrecognition of Manchukuo, but also noncooperation with the country. All recommendations are based on the Lytton Report.	It is believed in London that Sir Ronald Lindsay and Franklin Roosevelt agreed that a lump sum payment would be the best way of settling Britain's war debt to the United States. If so, negotiations will focus on the amount of the payment, which would probably be made by floating British government bonds in the United States.	Prof. Selim Hassan discovers an unknown sphinx near the second pyramid. He also finds 12 mastabas, which were ancient Egyptian tombs. Hassan is connected with the archaeology department of the University of Cairo.	An armed clash is expected this week in Leticia. Word comes that Colombia is afraid Peru will block the Pacific ports of Tumaco and Buenaventura with a cruiser and submarines.	Three thousand cases of treasures from the old palace museum in Peiping are loaded onto two trains and carried south to Shanghai. The city is illuminated with floodlights and troops stand guard in case of an anticipated attempt to stop the removal.
Feb. 7	League of Nations Secretary-General Sir Eric Drummond and other League leaders confer with Japanese delegate Yosuke Matsuoka about Japan's attitude toward the League's condemnation of its policy in Manchuria.	The crew of a Dutch battleship mutinies to protest a cut in pay. The ship, De Zeven Provincien, is in East Indian waters. Dutch ships are in pursuit.		A Canadian syndicate in Winnipeg negotiates with a group in Russia to barter cattle for coal and oil. Reports say 100,000 cattle would be sent to Russia.	The Chinese report the Japanese capture the south Manchurian port of Hulutao. China had hoped to make it into a terminus for its railroad.

A	B	C	D	E
Includes developments that affect more than one world region, international organizations, and important meetings of world leaders.	*Includes all domestic and regional developments in Europe, including the Soviet Union.*	*Includes all domestic and regional developments in Africa and the Middle East.*	*Includes all domestic and regional developments in Latin America, the Caribbean, and Canada.*	*Includes all domestic and regional developments in Asian and Pacific nations (and colonies).*

U.S. Politics & Social Issues	U.S. Foreign Policy & Defense	Economics & Great Depression	Science, Technology & Nature	Culture, Leisure & Lifestyle	
President-elect Franklin Roosevelt stresses that the only agreement between him and Sir Ronald Lindsay is on the physical arrangements for the coming debt negotiations in Washington. There is no agreement on revision of the debt.	A resolution to give the President authority to declare an arms embargo is introduced by House Foreign Affairs Committee Chairman Sam McReynolds.	The Bankruptcy Bill passes the House of Representatives by a vote of 201–43.		An autopsy shows that poet Sara Teasdale's death was not a suicide. Dr. Charles Norris says death was due to "general viscera condition and unresolved pneumonia" paired with "accidental immersion."	Jan. 30
Senator Robinson, Democratic leader of the Senate, proposes acting on the farm mortgage problem, and leaving more substantial farm relief to the new Congress, as they will have more time to study it.	Rep. Woodruff of Virginia asks for a 10 percent cut in veterans' benefits, which he says would amount to a savings of $58 million.		According to Dr. A. F. Erdmann, music calms patients undergoing anesthesia.	Thirty-three nations enter the Davis Cup tennis tournament. Ellsworth Vines, ranked the world's leading player, is expected to help the United States bring home the Cup.	Jan. 31
It is rumored that Rep. Ewin F. Davis, brother of Norman Davis, may be appointed to the Senate seat of Senator Hull in the likely event that Hull is chosen to be part of Roosevelt's Cabinet.		The Ford Motor Company resumes production as the Briggs Manufacturing Company delivers car bodies. Briggs says 3,000 are back at work after a strike, but most are new employees.	Dr. Reid Blair of the Bronx Zoo says no one has called this year wanting to use the zoo's groundhog, Secundus, to predict the length of winter. He said the animal has failed them five years in a row.	College football coaches attending the rules meeting in New York have ideas for rule changes. Northwestern coach Dick Hanley would like to be able to pass from anywhere behind the line of scrimmage, while Coach McLaughry is against the second-half kickoff.	Feb. 1
The House of Representatives passes the $966,838,634 appropriation for veterans' benefits without debate.	Eleven members of the Coast Guard are being held on charges they kept liquor seized from a rum runner for their own use. Capt. B.M. Chiswel believes this can be handled as an internal matter by the Coast Guard.	The government deficit at the end of January stands at $1,271,721,030. Experts predict that when Franklin Roosevelt takes office next month it will be $1,350,000.		The National Ski Tournament, planned for this weekend in Salisbury, Conn., has to be postponed because snow brought in from another mountain melts in above-average temperatures.	Feb. 2
Rep. James Buchanan of Texas introduces a farm mortgage bill in the House of Representatives. Passage of the Hull bill, which provides a two-year moratorium on farm foreclosures, is urged.		Eggs sell wholesale in Chicago at less than a penny apiece, which is said to be the lowest wholesale price on eggs in 30 years. . . . Reports indicate that during the last quarter of 1932, the Reconstruction Finance Corporation lent out $330,145,572.		Actress Lola Lane is granted a divorce from actor husband Lew Ayres. She claims he stays away for several days and tells her it is none of her business. She is awarded $35,000 and told she may keep her clothes and jewelry.	Feb. 3
President-elect Franklin Roosevelt waits to see whether Senator Carter Glass will accept his offer of the Secretary of the Treasury job. If he does not, that may mean a shuffling of other tentative Cabinet members.	A survey conducted by the sons of Confederate veterans shows that the number of living Confederate veterans has shrunk to 10,406. Most still live in former Confederate states.	A South Dakota milk farmer is near death after he and his two sons are shot trying to run a blockade of 100 pickets near Sioux City. The men were trying to deliver 1,000 gallons of milk to Sioux City.	George Engelberger of Lawrence, Kans., says his lettuce and cabbage grows better in electrified ground. Engelberger buried wires just below his germinating beds, arranged so as to heat the whole beds.	One hundred entries are expected for the Kentucky Derby. . . . Actor Douglas Fairbanks sails for Europe for an extended tour. He is accompanied by Thomas Garaghty. Fairbanks will be joined by his wife, Mary Pickford, as soon as she finishes filming her new movie, Secrets.	Feb. 4
With just 23 days remaining in the short session of Congress, neither Republican nor Democratic leaders believe much more significant legislation will be passed. President-elect Franklin Roosevelt is expected to lay out his whole reconstruction plan in his inaugural address.	Speaker of the House Garner receives a telegram from the Ketchikan, Alaska, Chamber of Commerce asking for immediate action on the depreciated currency tariff legislation. Most residents are salmon fishermen, and with their seasonal work, they need to make enough to see them through the winter.		Dr. Arthur Duel of New York reports that he and Sir Charles Balance of London have collaborated on a method of restoring impaired muscle control in those with facial paralysis. The injured nerve is repaired by taking an autoplastic graft from a healthy nerve.	Bob Carey wins the 100-mile race on the dirt track at Oakland, Calif. Carey, of Indianapolis, was the national automobile racing champion last year. His time is 59 minutes, 33.9 seconds, and he is believed to have broken all track records. AAA officials clock his average speed at 100.7023 miles per hour.	Feb. 5
Secretary Henry Stimson announces that the Lame Duck Amendment passes, as it has been ratified by 39 states. It provides that Congress will meet on January 3 and the President and Vice President will be inaugurated on January 20.	The Senate drafts a broad relief bill and adds $300 million to the Reconstruction Finance Corporation's fund. The bill also reduces the interest rate on the loans.			Former heavyweight champion James "Gentleman Jim" Corbett is confined to his bed with heart problems, but tells his old friend, John T. McGraw, that he will get better. His condition is considered serious.	Feb. 6
The Senate's Sergeant-at-Arms David S. Barry is ousted by a vote of 53–17. In an article, Barry wrote that "not many" Senators take money for their votes.	Democratic Rep. Rainey calls for a Democratic caucus after Republicans charge Democrats are afraid to call a caucus to unite members to fight against the depreciated currency bill. Both he and Garner believe one-third of Democrats will pledge to vote the bill down.	The average daily output of crude oil in the United States is up to 19,550 barrels a day. Refineries are operating at 56.8 percent of capacity.	The worst blizzard in years sweeps across the Midwest, bringing temperatures as low as 55 degrees below zero. Four deaths in Chicago are attributed to the storm, which extends from the Texas Panhandle to Chicago and continues to move east.	Baseball's National League shifts its schedule around, sending the western teams east earlier in the year. They believe that will help to balance the pennant race. They wait to set the entire schedule until they learn whether Pennsylvania will pass a bill allowing Sunday baseball in Philadelphia and Pittsburgh.	Feb. 7

F	G	H	I	J
Includes elections, federal-state relations, civil rights and liberties, crime, the judiciary, education, healthcare, poverty, urban affairs, and population.	*Includes formation and debate of U.S. foreign and defense policies, veterans affairs, and defense spending. (Relations with specific foreign countries are usually found under the region concerned.)*	*Includes business, labor, agriculture, taxation, transportation, consumer affairs, monetary and fiscal policy, natural resources, pollution, and accidents.*	*Includes worldwide scientific, medical, and technological developments, natural phenomena, U.S. weather, and natural disasters.*	*Includes the arts, religion, scholarship, communications media, sports, entertainment, fashions, fads, and social life.*

	World Affairs	Europe	Africa & The Middle East	The Americas	Asia & The Pacific
Feb. 8	Dr. Syngman Rhee of Korea asks the League of Nations to act in Korea's behalf, since Japan annexed Korea in 1910. Since then, the country has been governed by a Japanese governor. Rhee says he represents 23 million Koreans.	The Dutch battleship *De Zeven Provincien* is in communication with pursuing ships and the mutineers say they will surrender if their pay is restored. . . . The Catholic Bavarian People's Party, who have a majority in the state, scoff at Adolf Hitler's Third Reich and do not believe he will do anything to aid business in Germany.	Although some in the House of Lords and the House of Commons deplore removing Kenyan natives from their land so the British can mine gold there, the measure to do so is approved.	The Argentine corn crop has been hit by both locusts and drought, destroying more than 25 percent of the maturing crop.	In an effort to reduce the national deficit, the New Zealand House of Representatives approves an increase in tariffs on sugar, pipe tobacco, and gold.
Feb. 9	The League of Nations tells Japan to stay out of Jehol and Japan responds that it is not the League's business. . . . At the disarmament conference in Geneva, France and Germany disagree on the meaning of the December 11 Big Five agreement. France believes the whole conference needs to act on the issues of equality and security, while Germany believes those issues were settled by the Big Five.	The Dutch battleship *De Zeven Provincien* is bombed by seaplanes when mutineers refuse to surrender.		Brazil's frontier guard commander General Almerido de Mouro, makes a secret visit to Fort Tabatinga, just outside Leticia. It is believed Brazil may be getting ready to take over Leticia preparatory to restoring it to Colombia.	Japan reports 1,000 Chinese troops cross the border from Jehol into Fengtien province, where they attack two villages. Japanese troops are sent to the area.
Feb. 10	After three hours of debate, the disarmament conference's bureau approves a proposal to refer the security question to the political commission and the question of effectives to the general commission.	Reports say 18 men die on the Dutch ship *De Zeven Provincien* when it is bombed. The ringleaders of the mutiny are imprisoned on an island in the East Indies.		Brazil again offers to hold Leticia for two months while the Colombians and Peruvians negotiate. If negotiations are not successful, it would revert to Colombia.	Tokyo reports Eugene Chen, former war minister of China, has negotiated a treaty with Russia, but Chen denies it, remarking that "The Japanese Foreign Office has been seeing ghosts again."
Feb. 11	Tokyo says it will defend Manchukuo at any cost and refuses to heed the actions of the League of Nations.	France announces it will renew negotiations with the Soviet Union on pre-war debts. It is possible the French may give the Russians credits in return for payments.	The Catholic University of America confers an honorary Doctor of Law degree on Egypt's retiring Envoy to the United States, Sesostris Sidarouss Pasha.	Canadian negotiator Joseph de Champlain, with permission of Newfoundland Premier Alderice, works on a proposal for Canada to buy Labrador from Newfoundland.	Chinese General Ho Chu-kuo has 40,000–50,000 troops entrenched in the Shanhaikwan area, waiting for the Japanese to mount an offensive.
Feb. 12	Japan replies to the League of Nations that it cannot renounce Manchukuo.	Fritz Schaeffer, leader of the Bavarian People's Party, the largest party in Germany, says his party is strongly opposed to a dictatorship for the Reich.	A committee from Princeton University discovers a mosaic sidewalk at Daphne, near Antioch, Syria. The age cannot be determined until archaeologists finish excavating the building in which it is found.		It is reported that the Kaotal earthquake in China kills 70,000. The earthquake registers on seismographs as far away as London, but it is in a remote area and word is slow to reach Peiping.
Feb. 13	Japan reaffirms her intention to remain in Jehol and Manchukuo, and the League of Nations prepares to ask the United States and the Soviet Union to consult with League members on the subject. Japan is expected to withdraw from the League.	Prime Minister Ramsay MacDonald states that the Depression in England is halted and the economy shows definite signs of recovery.		Thousands of women fill the galleries of Congress in Santiago, Chile, demanding the right to vote in municipal elections. President of the Chamber Gabriel Gonzalez agrees they should have the same rights of suffrage as men.	Sir Samuel Hoare, Secretary for India, says freeing Mohandas Gandhi from prison will not be considered unless he convinces the government he will not resume his civil disobedience campaign.
Feb. 14	The League of Nations Committee of Nineteen unanimously adopts the report condemning Japan for her actions....The disarmament conference's political commission opens its meeting by deciding to discuss Britain's proposal to outlaw force rather than war, along with France's proposal for a European mutual assistance pact.	Denmark and Sweden protest German tariff increases and threaten to retaliate with new tariffs of their own.	Archaeologist L.C. Goodrich of Columbia University asserts that Egyptian culture predates Chinese culture. He says this has been determined by recent archaeological finds in China.	Ambassador J. Reuben Clark, Jr., is touched as Mexicans turn out to say farewell as he leaves Mexico City. A Mexican orchestra plays and Clark's wife and daughter are showered with flowers. . . . The Colombian government orders their Minister to Peru, Fabio Lozano, Jr., to come home. Colombia learned yesterday that Peru had bombed their gunboat, *Cordoba*, on the Putumayo River.	Japan gives China an ultimatum to get out of Jehol. The League of Nations assembly will act on it.
Feb. 15	In invoking the Nine-Party Treaty, the League of Nations asks for U.S. help. . . . Britain wants the disarmament conference to set up a committee composed of representatives of the principal air powers. It wants to ban bombing and other military use of planes and otherwise regulate aviation.	The Little Entente, consisting of Czechoslovakia, Romania, and Yugoslavia, is made permanent, resulting in greater solidarity among the members. . . . The Dutch Cabinet resigns, in accordance with a royal decree ordering the dissolution of the Second Chamber. Elections will be held on April 26.	Lord Bradbourne, chairman of the Consolidated Gold Fields of South Africa, dies suddenly aboard the liner *Carnarvon Castle*.		Yosuke Matsuoka, Japan's Special Consul in Geneva, cables the Japanese Foreign Office seeking permission to stop in the United States on his way home to talk to Franklin Roosevelt soon after the inauguration. The Foreign Office gives permission, but says this is not an official mission.
Feb. 16	The League of Nations adopts Britain's proposal and appoints a committee of 18 countries, including all the great countries and Canada, to study abolishing war aviation and establishing international control of civil aviation.	The committee of international bankers that has been considering Germany's finances gives the country a one-year extension of foreign credits.	A British-American archaeological expedition in the Judean Hills in Palestine discovers a tomb containing pottery from the era of King Solomon. It finds another tomb with burials from the Byzantine era.	Peru reports that Brazil has closed portions of the upper Amazon to Colombia and Peru because of the fighting over Leticia.	About 50,000 men, including Japanese troops and Manchukuo's army, steadily make their way toward the Jehol border, on their way to attack. About half the force fought in the Manchuria campaign last year.

A	B	C	D	E
Includes developments that affect more than one world region, international organizations, and important meetings of world leaders.	*Includes all domestic and regional developments in Europe, including the Soviet Union.*	*Includes all domestic and regional developments in Africa and the Middle East.*	*Includes all domestic and regional developments in Latin America, the Caribbean, and Canada.*	*Includes all domestic and regional developments in Asian and Pacific nations (and colonies).*

U.S. Politics & Social Issues	U.S. Foreign Policy & Defense	Economics & Great Depression	Science, Technology & Nature	Culture, Leisure & Lifestyle	
President Herbert Hoover urges passage of the tariff bill, feeling that imports are a threat to U.S. laborers. Democrats hold a caucus and vote 161–4 against voting for the Crowther bill, which provides automatic tariff adjustments.	Senator Hiram Bingham refuses to withdraw his motion to reconsider the arms embargo resolution that was passed by the Senate. He believes if the resolution passes, war might result. Bingham does oppose sale of arms to revolutionists.	General Motors Corporation reports the sharpest increase in sales since July 1931 in their January report. The company sells 72,274 cars to dealers, who in turn sell 50,653 of those to consumers.		Singer, actor, and African-American impersonator Al Jolson returns to films, starring in *Hallelujah, I'm a Bum*. Jolson plays a romantic hobo who reigns over the other tramps in Central Park.	Feb. 8
After only three hours discussion, the Senate passes the Department of Agriculture appropriations bill for $100,275,000. A couple of amendments are suggested but do not pass.	Secretary of State Henry Stimson pleads with the House Foreign Affairs committee to immediately adopt President Herbert Hoover's proposed arms embargo resolution.	Wall Street is given hope by a $538,591,137 rise in bonds in January. Brokers are reassured by the sustained improvement in bond prices since January 1.	It is reported that 12 comets were observed in 1932, with one of them being a new discovery, the Peltier-Whipple-Sase comet. The Schvassmann-Wachmann comet was unusual in that it flared up to 100 times its usual brilliance.	Famous evangelist Billy Sunday becomes ill in Des Moines, Iowa, where he is leading a revival. Doctors say he suffers a heart attack, brought on by indigestion.	Feb. 9
The Senate restores Army officer cuts in the War Department appropriation bill and adds $500,000 to the bill.	Secretary Adams opposes the 5 percent Navy cut in the Bratton amendment, saying it would reduce ships to only 66 percent of the vessels Great Britain has and 56 percent of Japanese vessels. It would also idle 14,650 people. The aircraft industry opposes the amendment.	Senator Hastings presents a new bankruptcy bill to his Judiciary subcommittee. It includes a section on railroads and also carries a provision for farmers.		L.D. Cheney wins the Southern California woman's golf title, defeating national champion Virginia Van Wie. . . . The American Football Coaches Association meets and discusses rules, with the aim of speeding up the game and making it safer. Five new rules are proposed to those ends.	Feb. 10
President and Mrs. Hoover host the members of the diplomatic corps at the White House. The dinner is attended by 85, and 100 more come later for a musicale in the East Room.	The Atlantic fleet of the U.S. Navy will remain in the Pacific. Indications are that both Hoover and Roosevelt had input into the decision. Japan is not happy and seems not to believe it is for economy measures.		Pope Pius is pleased with a short-wave telephone system which Guglielmo Marconi sets up for him between the Vatican and his summer residence, Castel Gandolfo, about 15 miles south of Rome.	Canada retains the North American curling championship, beating the United States 259–164. It is the fourth year in a row that Canada has won the Gordon International Curling Medal.	Feb. 11
A poll in the House of Representatives shows that the Crowther bill on increasing tariffs will be defeated tomorrow.		Attorney Clarence Darrow meets in Chicago with a delegation of striking employees from the Briggs Automotive Company in Detroit. He advises them to request federal, state, and city inquiries into working conditions and wages.	President Herbert Hoover sets aside a portion of California's torrid Death Valley as a National Monument. The area contains over 500 species of plants, may of which are found nowhere else.	Britain rules that any U.S. tennis player who participates in the U.S. Open against both pros and amateurs will lose his amateur standing and will not be allowed to compete at Wimbledon.	Feb. 12
President Herbert Hoover arrives in New York City, where he gives his farewell speech to the nation at the National Republican Club's annual Lincoln Celebration. The speech is broadcast across the nation.	The Senate adds $2 million to the Army bill in order to provide for 88,000 homeless boys. Senator Couzens introduces the amendment, which provides that unemployed boys aged 15–21 will be eligible to spend a year in a Citizen's Military Training Camp.	The bankruptcy bill is trimmed down to include only farmers and individual debtors, leaving out railroads and corporations. Senators think this is the most that can pass in this session and note the urgency of farm aid.		With spring training just two weeks away, half the New York Yankees baseball team remains unsigned. Only three of those who have signed could be called regulars. Babe Ruth angrily returns a contract that calls for a drop in salary from $75,000 to $50,000 and Lou Gehrig is also unsigned.	Feb. 13
President Herbert Hoover and his wife entertain six justices and their wives in the State Dining Room at the White House, after receiving their guests in the Blue Room.		The Hull-Wolcott Bill to use $600 million of federal credit to postpone foreclosures for two years for farmers and homeowners gets bipartisan support on the floor of the Senate. It would also reduce interest rates.			Feb. 14
In an unsuccessful attempt to assassinate President-elect Franklin Roosevelt in Miami, Giuseppe Zangara of Hackensack, N.J., shoots five other people, including Chicago Mayor Anton Cermak who is in critical condition with a bullet lodged in the back of his abdomen. "I'm glad it was I, not you," he tells Roosevelt.	The House passes the arms embargo act after it is amended to include only the Western Hemisphere. It was turned down earlier because Congressmen feared it would entangle the United States in the Far East situation.	After Franklin Roosevelt takes office, the railway unions, supported by the AFL, will make a concerted drive for a six-hour workday law.	Professor Carl N. Correns of Berlin University, who last year was awarded the Darwin Medal by the Royal Society of Great Britain, dies. Correns is one of three scientists who rediscovered Gregor Mendel's lost laws.	Cartoonist Patrick Sullivan, who created the comic strip *Felix the Cat*, dies of pneumonia in New York, where he lives. He was born in Sydney, Australia.	Feb. 15
A new constitutional amendment addresses the assassination attempt on Franklin Roosevelt that occurred the previous day. Now if the President-elect dies before taking office, the Vice-President-elect will be inaugurated. . . . Mayor Anton Cermak is still in critical condition, but is resting easily.	The Treasury objects to a House committee's proposal for free-trade zones, saying there is too much likelihood of smuggling goods through such zones.	Henry Ford says he still believes in high wages and as soon as business picks up, he will raise the wages of his employees.	P.M.S. Blackett, a young physicist in Cambridge, England, has a new theory on cosmic rays. He says they contain a new kind of particle, which he calls a positive electron. Dr. Blackett says his findings confirm the findings of Dr. Carl. D. Anderson.		Feb. 16

F	G	H	I	J
Includes elections, federal-state relations, civil rights and liberties, crime, the judiciary, education, healthcare, poverty, urban affairs, and population.	*Includes formation and debate of U.S. foreign and defense policies, veterans affairs, and defense spending. (Relations with specific foreign countries are usually found under the region concerned.)*	*Includes business, labor, agriculture, taxation, transportation, consumer affairs, monetary and fiscal policy, natural resources, pollution, and accidents.*	*Includes worldwide scientific, medical, and technological developments, natural phenomena, U.S. weather, and natural disasters.*	*Includes the arts, religion, scholarship, communications media, sports, entertainment, fashions, fads, and social life.*

	World Affairs	Europe	Africa & The Middle East	The Americas	Asia & The Pacific
Feb. 17	The League of Nations reports its censure of Japan to the world in a 10-hour broadcast and invites Russia and the United States to join in the discussion.	A Hitler aide says democracy is dead in Germany. He says there is not just a new government, but a new regime whose first priority is to stamp out Communists.	Captain H.S. Lawson, an experienced pilot with 13,000 hours flying time, crashes his plane in Africa while doing a stunt called the "falling leaf." He and his radio operator, E. Ross, are both killed instantly. They were members of Sir Alan Cobham's flying circus, and Lawson had just married during the previous week.	Four Cuban rebel chiefs who sought refuge in the Mexican Embassy plan to leave Cuba tomorrow bound for Key West, Fla.	China refuses to renew the trade treaty with Japan, hoping to strike a blow against that country's trade.
Feb. 18	Peru requests an urgent meeting about the Leticia situation. The Council of the League of Nations will meet and discuss it with both Peru and Colombia.	In spite of the Depression, the number of automobiles in France keeps steadily rising. According to recently released statistics, taxes were paid on 1,251,538 passenger vehicles in the 1931–32 year.		The Cuban government is in arrears paying veterans' pensions, and at least 20 veterans have starved to death during the past two months.	Unconfirmed reports say Japan is quitting the League, but the Cabinet meeting scheduled for today is postponed. Some think Premier Makoto Saito is trying to postpone the decision.
Feb. 19	Both President Herbert Hoover and President-elect Franklin Roosevelt receive copies of a League of Nations communication urging an immediate embargo on shipment of arms to South America and the Far East. They are asked to cooperate with that embargo.	German people are worried about the health and well-being of President von Hindenburg. He is rarely seen in public and sees few people in private.	Dr. G. Wiet, director of the Egyptian government's Arab Art Museum, discovers examples of medieval Muslim art in Egypt. The frescoes are believed to be from the Fatamid period, in the 10th and 11th centuries.	A decree, dated February 17, is published today. It forbids Peruvians 21–25 years of age from leaving the country. President Luis M. Sanchez Cerro tells Peruvians in a broadcast to defend their honor against Colombia and to meet force with force.	Japan decides to secede from the League of Nations as soon as the League formally adopts its proposed condemnation of Japan in Manchuria. . . . Formal warfare between Japan and China seems imminent. Experts wonder if Japan would dare blockade Shanghai, which as an international port is guarded by ships from France, Italy, Britain, and the United States.
Feb. 20	The committee of the disarmament conference which was set up to study aviation recommends civil air control.	French Foreign Minister Joseph Paul-Bancour says he wants to talk with the United States about their war debts after Roosevelt takes office.	King Victor Emmanuel of Italy arrives in Cairo for a two-week visit. He and Queen Elena and Princess Maria are met at the station by King Fuad and his Cabinet members. The Egyptians attach great political importance to the visit.	Bolivia reports all is quiet in the Chaco, except for an exchange of artillery at Fort Nanawa, also known as Ayala.	Japan decides to withdraw from the Disarmament Conference in Geneva, as well as the League of Nations. It says there is a "hostile atmosphere" at the arms conference.
Feb. 21	In spite of its friendship with Tokyo, France supports the League of Nations in its action in the case of Manchuria. France hopes some sort of compromise can be reached so Japan will remain a member.	The trade unions of the Austrian railroad decide to have a two-hour strike on March 1 to protest wage cuts and the paying of wages in installments.		Bolivian planes are controlling the air around Nanawa so the Paraguayans cannot receive any help. Yesterday a Bolivian plane machine-gunned a Paraguayan truck taking water to the troops.	Great Britain sells war materials to both Japan and China. During 1932, Britain sold China 7,735,000 small-arms cartridges and sold Japan 5,361,450. China purchased 312,256 pounds of high explosives, while Japan bought twice as many. Japan also bought 740 machine guns.
Feb. 22	President-elect Franklin Roosevelt announces that Norman Davis will be retained as a delegate to the disarmament conference in Geneva. Roosevelt said he would not change the U.S. attitude toward disarmament.	The British Cabinet meets for a second time tonight to discuss the League of Nations embargo. They make no decision, saying they want to see what the League does this week on the Manchurian question. It is believed they are also waiting to see what the United States does about an embargo.		Nicaraguan President Juan B. Sacasa is informed that all Sandinistas have turned in their weapons, which will be sent to Managua. The only exceptions are 100 Sandinistas who are now government auxiliaries.	The London Daily Herald reports that a group of British financiers have been meeting with high Japanese officials and that they have made a secret deal to sell the Japanese a large quantity of arms.
Feb. 23	Leaders of the League of Nations decide in a secret meeting to name a consultative committee to consider the Japanese affair. It would be composed of the Committee of Nineteen, Holland, Canada, Russia, and the United States.	The Earl of Lytton, chairman of the Far East Commission of the League of Nations, says he backs the arms embargo, although he would see nothing wrong with selling arms to China, since it is the victim. He admits that under the circumstances, it would be difficult to be sure the arms would not end up in Japan's possession.	Gen. Jan Christian Smuts and Prime Minister J.B.M. Hertzog tentatively agree to call an election in July, after dissolving the House of Assembly next week. Mr. Hertzog would keep his position as Prime Minister, and he would give Gen. Smuts a Cabinet position.		The Japanese onslaught on Jehol includes 30,000 troops, plus tanks, artillery, and planes with bombs.
Feb. 24	The League of Nations Assembly votes unanimously to accept the report censuring Japan for its activities in Manchuria. Japan votes no, but a disputing party's negative vote does not count. Siam abstains.	Chancellor Adolf Hitler arms Nazi storm troopers and uses them as police, as the atmosphere in Germany becomes more oppressive. The press is curbed and people in the south are told it is useless to resist.		Panama believes Colombia will send troops down the Cotuhe River to attack Leticia from land, although an air raid is possible.	Chinese troops are retreating northwest, as Japanese keep pushing on in spite of frigid weather and blinding snow.
Feb. 25	The new Committee of Twenty-one of the League of Nations begins discussion on whether to put an arms embargo on Japan. They decide to wait for input from the United States and Russia.	Bulgarian newspaper editor Christo Christoff is sentenced to six months imprisonment for libel because he published an article saying President von Hindenburg is mad. The sentence is suspended on the condition that he not libel anyone else.	A delegation of eight Arab leaders asks Lt. Gen. Sir Arthur Wauchope, British High Commissioner for Palestine, to ban sale of land to Jews. They also want him to restrict immigration of Jews into the country. Wauchope refuses.	Police in Chile uncover an extensive Communist plot for a naval revolt. They arrest many members of the Chilean Workers' Federation.	In a Cabinet meeting in Tokyo, Japan decides that even though it has withdrawn from the League of Nations, it still might participate in the world economic, disarmament and labor conferences. A decision may not be made for some time.

A	B	C	D	E
Includes developments that affect more than one world region, international organizations, and important meetings of world leaders.	Includes all domestic and regional developments in Europe, including the Soviet Union.	Includes all domestic and regional developments in Africa and the Middle East.	Includes all domestic and regional developments in Latin America, the Caribbean, and Canada.	Includes all domestic and regional developments in Asian and Pacific nations (and colonies).

U.S. Politics & Social Issues	U.S. Foreign Policy & Defense	Economics & Great Depression	Science, Technology & Nature	Culture, Leisure & Lifestyle	
Dr. E.C. Thomas, county physician, declares Joseph Zangara, the man who tried to kill Franklin Roosevelt, to be sane. Mayor Cermak is improving and is expected to recover.	The Marines and the Army will help the Washington, D.C., police with security on Inauguration Day.	Secretary of Agriculture Arthur Hyde announces that in order to be eligible for crop-production loans, farmers must reduce by 30 percent the acreage planted in cash crops. Congress has made $90 million of RFC money available for farm loans.	The House Rules Committee agrees to make way for a bill creating the Morristown National Historic Park in New Jersey. The area is said to be "so primitive and so beautiful as to excite the admiration of any lover of nature."	The Vatican announces that Pope Pius will revive an old tradition. On Easter Sunday, he will celebrate Mass in St. Peter's, then go out on his balcony and bless the crowd in St. Peter's Square.	Feb. 17
Although some people think President Herbert Hoover's farewell to the nation sounded as if he might run in 1936, his close friends say he is ready to retire for good.			Coyotes have become so bold in Kansas that farmers have strung up hundreds of square yards of chicken wire around their feed lots to protect their lambs, a favorite food of the coyote. Some gray wolves have also been seen recently.	James "Gentleman Jim" Corbett, ex-heavyweight champion of the world, dies of cancer at the age of 66. He thought he was suffering from heart trouble.	Feb. 18
	The U.S. Navy urges that the country replace obsolete ships with new ones. Worn-out and outmoded destroyers are a critical problem, and the U.S. submarines are also old.	Gains are shown in January in employment in the shoe, hosiery, and silk manufacturing businesses, while factory employment stays about the same.	Robert G. Aitken and his staff at Lick Observatory on Mount Hamilton have been watching a new comet. It appears soon after sunset and seems to be going north and east. L.T. Peltier discovered it the previous week while in Delphos, Ohio.	National outdoor speed-skating champion Kit Klein suffers a leg injury in a race in Chicago and will be out for the rest of the season.	Feb. 19
Senator Carter Glass turns down Franklin Roosevelt's bid to be Secretary of the Treasury in favor of remaining in the Senate.	Admiral Richard H. Leigh, commander in chief of the U.S. fleet, urges that the United States should build the U.S. Navy up to parity. He says the Japanese equal in battleships and exceed in other kinds of craft the capabilities of the United States.			King George and Queen Mary of Great Britain plan to see the movie Good Companions on February 28. It will be the first talking picture they have seen.	Feb. 20
Mayor Anton Cermak takes a turn for the worse, and doctors call it a crisis. His temperature is 101 and his body racked with pain from acute enteritis caused by blood seeping into his intestines from the area around the gunshot wound he suffered during an assassination attempt on Franklin Roosevelt.	Cordell Hull believes in tariffs for revenue only. He is chosen by President-elect Franklin Roosevelt to head his Cabinet.	The American Federation of Labor is vehemently opposed to the United States recognizing the Soviet Union.	Ohio Dr. Theodore T. Zuck says treatments with hormones can help children grow. Each child needs a different combination of hormones and each case must be studied individually.		Feb. 21
Senator William Borah objects to giving President-elect Franklin Roosevelt what he refers to as "dictatorial powers." He argues that the Constitution covers any situation the new President might face.	Congress believes that President-elect Franklin Roosevelt will build up the Navy gradually to meet treaty strength.		The deepest known sea depth is measured from a yacht in the Atlantic off the coast of Puerto Rico by Dr. Paul Bartsch. He measures a depth of 44,000 feet, or almost nine miles.	Sir Malcolm Campbell breaks his own speed record of 253 miles per hour, replacing it with a record of 272 miles per hour, but he is not satisfied. He says his car has a potential of at least 300 miles per hour and he should have been able to go at least 285. However, he was favoring an injured arm.	Feb. 22
Frances Perkins becomes the first woman Cabinet member, as President-elect Franklin Roosevelt names her Secretary of Labor. . . . President Herbert Hoover's "Little Cabinet" entertains him at the Mayflower Hotel and gives him the gift of the chair he used in his office at the White House. The group is made up of the assistant secretaries of the 10 Cabinet departments.	The House of Representatives passes the Navy bill, appropriating $15,419,000.	One hundred police officials, sheriff's deputies, and volunteers disperse a crowd of farmers protesting mortgage foreclosures at Kankakee, Ill. They plan to send a delegation of farmers to Springfield to talk with Governor Horner.		The Indoor Polo Association of America announces a reorganization of its annual championships. The finals will be played in Chicago in April.	Feb. 23
The new Chinese Minister to the United States calls on President Herbert Hoover to present his credentials. Dr. Sao-ke Alfred Sze does not refer to the confrontation in Manchuria.		Ford Motor Company advertising manager Fred Black quits after 15 years with the company. He was also an adviser to Henry Ford during the building of Greenfield Village.		Buster Crabbe, the Olympic swimming champion, stars in a new motion picture entitled King of the Jungle. He plays a young man who has lived on his own in the jungle since he was three years old.	Feb. 24
Absence of leadership in the Lame Duck Congress causes it to shelve many bills. Congress has enacted 700 laws, but a total of 16,000 measures were introduced during the whole session.	Secretary of State Henry Stimson confers with Cordell Hull, who will replace him on March 4, about foreign affairs, especially regarding the League of Nations. It is believed the United States will cooperate with the new advisory committee.	Congress enacts the Couzens amendment to the national banking bill and it is signed into law by President Herbert Hoover. It gives the President power over the banks in a crisis, with the approval of the Secretary of the Treasury.	London reports that a number of experimental vehicles are running on compressed coal gas instead of gasoline, and it is proving efficient. The British see this as a help for their depressed coal industry.	George Jacobus, president of the Professional Golfers Association of America, announces the U.S. team to compete with the British in the Ryder Cup. Veteran golfer Walter Hagen will be the team captain.	Feb. 25

F	G	H	I	J
Includes elections, federal-state relations, civil rights and liberties, crime, the judiciary, education, healthcare, poverty, urban affairs, and population.	Includes formation and debate of U.S. foreign and defense policies, veterans affairs, and defense spending. (Relations with specific foreign countries are usually found under the region concerned.)	Includes business, labor, agriculture, taxation, transportation, consumer affairs, monetary and fiscal policy, natural resources, pollution, and accidents.	Includes worldwide scientific, medical, and technological developments, natural phenomena, U.S. weather, and natural disasters.	Includes the arts, religion, scholarship, communications media, sports, entertainment, fashions, fads, and social life.

	World Affairs	Europe	Africa & The Middle East	The Americas	Asia & The Pacific
Feb. 26	League of Nations leaders are pleased to have the moral support of the United States when they receive a note from Secretary of State Henry Stimson approving the Manchuria report. Japanese spokesman Yosuke Matsuoka is disturbed by the note and warns the United States to "think twice."	In Moscow, Josef Stalin and Premier Molotoff sign a decree providing for the loan for 613,000 tons of seed to socialized farms in the Ukraine and the Kuban region.		Three new submarines leave Taranto, Italy, where they were built, on their way to Buenos Aires. The Argentine submarines, the Salta, Santa Fe, and Santiago Delestero are given an enthusiastic farewell as they leave on their 7,000-mile journey.	Jehol City swarms with Chinese troops, as they prepare to defend the area from the attacking Japanese. Hundreds of camels carrying munitions as well as long lines of oxcarts and donkey carts carrying supplies line the roads and cross the mountain passes.
Feb. 27	Both Peru and Colombia notify the League of Nations that they have ordered fighting to cease in the Leticia area, as the League had asked them to do. The Committee of Three confers with delegates from the two countries.	Budapest is alarmed by the announcement of the Little Entente pact and wonders if the League of Nations will protect Hungary if it is attacked by members of the Little Entente.	The Arabs in Jerusalem announce they will boycott British goods and will refuse to pay taxes. This is a reaction to British High Commissioner Arthur Wauchope's refusal to bar Jews from buying land or immigrating to Palestine.	Chile believes Communists in Montevideo, Uruguay, were plotting a Communist takeover of Chile, beginning with an infiltration of the lower ranks of the army and the crews of warships.	General Chiang Kai-shek lets it be known that he will not go to Jehol to help with the fighting there. He believes the northern generals would resent his intrusion and would not obey him.
Feb. 28	Colombia accepts the League of Nations plan for conciliation in the Leticia conflict, but Peru has not yet replied to the proposal. . . . The Disarmament Conference accepts Britain's proposal to outlaw the use of force, but limits it to Europe.	Ramon Casanelles, alleged to have assassinated Spanish Prime Minister Eduardo Dato in 1921, is arrested in Barcelona. Police say he has spent several months in the city, engaged in Communist activities.		A truck filled with dynamite is parked in front of the secret service building in Havana, in an attempt to blow up the headquarters. However, police become suspicious and munitions experts turn off the motor, which would have triggered the explosion.	The Chinese stand firm at the Paishihtsumen Pass, about 50 miles north of the Great Wall on the border of Jehol and Manchuria. The Japanese continue their advance in the Kailu area, where the temperature is now 30 degrees below zero.
Mar. 1	Arthur Henderson, chairman of the disarmament conference, is notified by Japanese delegate Shichtaro Yada that Japan has decided to continue its participation in the conference. . . . The only world armament agreement ever made expires without fanfare. Last November it was extended for four months, due to the disarmament conference. Leaders say it is too full of loopholes to be practical.	Two Czechoslovakian fascists are extradited from Yugoslavia where they had fled. Lieutenants Kobsinek and Gaidl are jailed for organizing the fascist uprising at Bruenn on January 26 when 50 men seized the barracks.		Bolivia accepts the proposal of the ABC-Peru group for renewing peace negotiations with Paraguay "in principle and with reservations."	
Mar. 2	The political commission of the disarmament conference adopts a resolution outlawing war among European nations. . . . Chinese delegate Dr. Wellington Koo explains the rumor that the Chinese delegation is quitting the League. He said he and the others had asked to be relieved because of fatigue, but were told to stay on.	France and England plan to discuss war debt negotiations with the United States. It is believed that Premier Edouard Daladier will go to London to meet Prime Minister Ramsay MacDonald.		Chile announces it is ready to sign a commercial treaty with Argentina, covering tariffs, barter, and international railroads.	
Mar. 3	When Japanese Admiral Osami Nagano and Gen. Taketomi return to Geneva, they will report to the disarmament conference that Japan plans to increase its army.	Ernst Thalmann, who was a German presidential candidate, is arrested at his apartment. Thalmann is head of the Communist Party in Germany. Other Communists are arrested during the day and Communist publications suppressed.		In an executive session, Paraguay's Senate approves a bill to declare war on Bolivia over the Chaco conflict.	The U.S. Army and Navy aid Japanese affected by the massive earthquake. . . . Japan demands that China remove all troops from Tiensin. The Nanking government refuses and may move the capital to Changsha in the Hunan province.
Mar. 4	The disarmament conference is the scene of an alliance between France, the Continent's strongest capitalist nation, and the Soviet Union, the strongest Communist power. Many consider it significant, since it comes on the eve of German elections.	Austrian Chancellor Engelbert Dollfuss dissolves the parliament of Austria and prohibits political parades and assemblies in an effort to stave off Nazism.	A Cairo museum official discovers quarries in the desert west of the Nile that have been lost for 3,500 years. Diorite, a gray rock containing amethystine quartz, is found there.	Reports of rebel gatherings of civilians and military in southern Brazil are met by the government with a vow to stamp out any rebel movement.	China is losing its territories, one by one. Russia has made Outer Mongolia a Soviet republic, while the Japanese control Inner Mongolia and Manchuria under the guise of the republic of Manchukuo. China is losing its hold on Jehol, and Tibet has also made war on China.
Mar. 5	Many League members believe that by withdrawing from the League of Nations, Japan will sacrifice its permanent seat in the Council. Some believe that seat may be given to China.	The Nazi party wins 44 percent of the vote in the German elections. It joins with the Nationalists to obtain a slight majority in the Reichstag.	The Mt. Everest explorers who left Baghdad yesterday become separated during a sandstorm and are finally reunited at Bushire on the Persian Gulf today.	A flood in Puerto Rico destroys 500 homes and kills at least 20. Scores of people are missing and property loss exceeds $1,000,000.	China closes the Great Wall, but is unable to keep the Japanese from taking some of the passes. The final phase of the Jehol campaign produces the fiercest fighting yet.
Mar. 6	From remarks made by Sir John Simon it seems likely that Great Britain will drop the arms embargo it instituted last week, since no other countries have followed suit and it is losing out on trade. . . . The free city of Danzig complains to the League of Nations because Poland brings in 100 additional policemen. The League has limited Poland to a military guard of 88 men in Danzig.			Bolivians practically annihilate 400 Paraguayans who try to break through their lines surrounding Fort Nanawa.	Nanking military leader General Chiang Kai-shek flies to Peiping to confer with Marshal Chang Hsiao-liang and other leaders. The Chinese face a grave situation after the fall of Jehol.
Mar. 7	The League of Nations committee of three on Latin American conflicts asks the Council to meet in regard to the undeclared war in the Chaco between Paraguay and Bolivia. . . . The League tells the Polish government to withdraw the 100 police it just sent to Danzig.	Worried about Hitlerism in Germany, Austrian Chancellor Engelbert Dollfuss bans meetings and parades and suspends freedom of the press.		It is believed that Bolivia has 12,000 men clustered in the Fort Toledo area of the Chaco.	The Japanese detain a ship carrying 110 trucks from the Ford factory in Japan. A U.S. firm had bought them, and then sold them to the Chinese for use in Marshal Chang's army. . . . Chang is replaced as the Chinese military leader.
	A Includes developments that affect more than one world region, international organizations, and important meetings of world leaders.	**B** Includes all domestic and regional developments in Europe, including the Soviet Union.	**C** Includes all domestic and regional developments in Africa and the Middle East.	**D** Includes all domestic and regional developments in Latin America, the Caribbean, and Canada.	**E** Includes all domestic and regional developments in Asian and Pacific nations (and colonies).

U.S. Politics & Social Issues	U.S. Foreign Policy & Defense	Economics & Great Depression	Science, Technology & Nature	Culture, Leisure & Lifestyle	
Mayor Anton Cermak still fights for his life in a Miami hospital, but he has developed pneumonia in the lung that was grazed by the bullet, lessening his chances. He asks his son-in-law in Bohemian, "Am I going to get well?"	The National Economy League urges President Herbert Hoover to veto the bill on veterans' benefits, since it disregards his recommendations on nonwar disabilities.	Economic bills take top priority in this final week of the Lame Duck Congress. They will attempt to pass bills on mortgages, bankruptcy, and banking.		Ethel Barrymore will resume her leading role in the play *Encore*, which was forced to close when she was taken ill. Barrymore will also manage the production and will take it on tour, starting in Providence.	Feb. 26
The Senate passes the bankruptcy bill, which will help railroads, individuals, and farmers to readjust their debts without resorting to formal bankruptcy.	General John A. Lejeune, formerly Commandant of the Marine Corps, is gradually recovering from a fractured skull suffered in a fall. Lejeune is now the Superintendent of the Virginia Military Institute.		Forestry officials say hundreds of deer are starving to death in Columbia National Park in the state of Washington. Many are so weak they can be caught easily by hand. The problem was discovered a week ago, and hay and feed were brought in, but it was too late for most of them.	The six-day bike race at Madison Square Garden is in its second day and 13 of the 15 teams remain.	Feb. 27
The House is said to be sure to pass the bankruptcy bill, under the influence of President-elect Franklin Roosevelt.	Rear Admiral Edwin Stewart, who was the oldest naval officer, dies at his home in New Jersey at the age of 96. Stewart was a veteran of both the Civil War and the Spanish-American War.	In the past five months, the General Motors Corporation has added 29,292 workers to its factories.	Dr. John Belling, a leading geneticist at the Carnegie Institute, dies in Berkeley, Calif. He was noted for his microscopy and work with chromosomes.		Feb. 28
The House agrees to the Senate's amendment, passing the Bankruptcy Bill, 207–26. The bill now goes to President Herbert Hoover. The bill was backed by both the President and President-elect Franklin Roosevelt.	The Army air expansion program begun in 1926 is completed with the approval of five new air squadrons.	Six states declare bank holidays to prevent runs on the banks.		American composer Werner Janssen makes his debut in Berlin, Germany. He conducts the Berlin Philharmonic Orchestra and is well received by the German audience.	Mar. 1
Washington is shocked and saddened by the sudden death of Senator Thomas Walsh, who was slated to be President Franklin Roosevelt's Attorney General.	Newton D. Baker, former Secretary of War, advocates a government policy prohibiting the sale of arms to aggressive nations.	January car exports increase 22 percent over December, while truck exports are up 38 percent.	A device that replaces the carburetor in a car engine makes it possible to burn fuel oil instead of gasoline. Fuel oil gets 18 percent better mileage. . . . Japan is hit by the most powerful earthquake in 180 years.	Fay Wray stars in the premiere of *King Kong*. The movie uses an 18-inch model to portray King Kong.	Mar. 2
	Retiring Secretary of the Navy Charles Francis Adams sends a farewell note to every ship, praising the Navy personnel.		Dr. James Ewing, director of cancer research at New York's Memorial Hospital, says cancer research among patients at clinics is making substantial progress.	The California bank holiday finds many movie stars unprepared, as Noah Beery has forty-five cents in his pocket, Irene Dunne and Cary Grant sign restaurant checks, and Maurice Chevalier borrows $2 from a gas station operator.	Mar. 3
In Washington, D.C., Franklin D. Roosevelt is inaugurated for his first term. In pledging the lead the country out of the Depression, he says, "We have nothing to fear but fear itself."		Wholesalers and producers agree to "business as usual" in spite of the bank holiday. Many are encouraged by Roosevelt's speech and his quick action.	Broadcasters assert that television is clearer than it was in 1930, but that they can go no further with the present transmitting apparatus. They hope experimenters will be able to use bigger pictures and better illumination so the viewer can tell a cat from a Scottie dog.		Mar. 4
	Beginning at dawn, 134 U.S. Navy ships will begin maneuvers off the coast of California. About 34,000 officers and men will be involved.	President Franklin Roosevelt orders a four-day bank holiday in order to prevent people from withdrawing large sums of money from the banks.		German scientist Albert Einstein sits patiently while sculptor Frederick Schweigardt works on a bust of him in Los Angeles.	Mar. 5
Chicago Mayor Anton Cermak dies of wounds from the February 15 shooting when Giuseppe Zangara tried to shoot Franklin Roosevelt. . . . Senator Thomas Walsh's funeral is held in the Senate chamber.	When George H. Dern takes office as Secretary of War, he is greeted by the heads of all the War branch departments in uniform.	President Franklin Roosevelt forbids exportation of gold in order to protect the gold reserve in the country. . . . Executives of six motion picture companies meet to decide what to do since they cannot meet their payrolls. Due to the bank holiday, they cannot get money from New York and may have to shut down.	Doctors report that oxygen aids in the digestion of protein. They say the discovery may have a bearing on cancer research.		Mar. 6
The minority party Republicans name Senator Charles McNary as president pro tempore of the Senate.	Secretary of the Navy Claude Swanson urges building the U.S. Navy up to the strength prescribed in the London Naval Treaty.			The Brooklyn Dodgers will add 4,000 new bleacher seats to Ebbets Field. Cost for a bleacher seat is 55 cents. . . . Movie star Janet Gaynor sues her husband, screenwriter Lydell Peck, for divorce, charging jealousy.	Mar. 7

F	G	H	I	J
Includes elections, federal-state relations, civil rights and liberties, crime, the judiciary, education, healthcare, poverty, urban affairs, and population.	*Includes formation and debate of U.S. foreign and defense policies, veterans affairs, and defense spending. (Relations with specific foreign countries are usually found under the region concerned.)*	*Includes business, labor, agriculture, taxation, transportation, consumer affairs, monetary and fiscal policy, natural resources, pollution, and accidents.*	*Includes worldwide scientific, medical, and technological developments, natural phenomena, U.S. weather, and natural disasters.*	*Includes the arts, religion, scholarship, communications media, sports, entertainment, fashions, fads, and social life.*

	World Affairs	Europe	Africa & The Middle East	The Americas	Asia & The Pacific
Mar. 8		Prime Minister Ramsay MacDonald and Sir John Simon of Great Britain go to Paris to confer with Premier Eduoard Daladier before returning to Geneva the next day for a last effort at an arms agreement.		Reliable sources in Paraguay believe Bolivia's reply to the ABC-Peru Armistice proposal amounts to a virtual rejection, as Bolivia places so many conditions on the agreement.	Word is received about the heroism of Harriet Minns, a missionary and the only American in Jehol. During the capture of Lingyuan, she took a group of Chinese children to a dugout she had prepared. Two American flags she had made caused Japanese aviators to spare the shelter.
Mar. 9		Nazi storm troopers in Annaberg, Germany, arrest all Jewish merchants, including the manager of the electric company.	The British field in Cairo where the Coldstream Guards are stationed is rocked by a bomb thrown over the wall by a man in an automobile. There are no casualties.		In an attempt to kill Cantonese General Chen Chi-tang, an assassin kills four others in a bomb explosion.
Mar. 10	A five-hour discussion in Paris between French and British leaders centers on how to keep Germany from rearming in defiance of the Treaty of Versailles.	The new Greek Cabinet is sworn in under the leadership of Premier Panayoti Tsaldaris.	South Africa will not host the British Empire games as planned, committee chairman Sir James Leigh Wood announces. They will be held in London instead.	The British would like to take over the coal market in Canada from the United States. They say they can ship it cheaper than the United States.	According to reports from China, Japan now holds all the gateways through the Great Wall. The Kupei Pass is the last to fall.
Mar. 11	British Prime Minister Ramsay MacDonald and Sir John Simon talk with many League of Nations leaders about disarmament upon their arrival in Geneva.	Moderate Austrians fear that parliamentary government may not be able to endure in Austria with the strong Nazi movement in Germany.	War relics believed to be from 701 B.C.E. are dug up in the ancient city of Lachish in Palestine. A British-American group, the Wellcome-Colt Archaeological Expedition, is exploring the ruins.	A pillar now marks the border of Brazil, British Guiana, and Venezuela. The 200-year-old dispute will end as soon as the countries ratify the agreement.	
Mar. 12		President Paul von Hindenburg takes down the German Republic's flag and replaces it with the swastika and the empire banner, flown side by side.		Fighting continues along the whole front in the Chaco. Bolivia takes Fort Alihuata but suffers 2,000 casualties in a clash with Paraguayans near Fort Toledo.	China's formerly powerful warlord, Marshal Chang Hsiao-liang, returns to private life. He refuses to grant reporters an interview.
Mar. 13	The United States accepts the League of Nations invitation to cooperate with the Manchurian advisory committee, which is working to end the Far East conflict.	Joseph Goebbels, Chancellor Adolf Hitler's right-hand man, becomes Nazi Minister of Information and Propaganda.	Fourteen ancient churches are found in Nubia, Egypt. However, excavations must cease because the area will be under water due to the building of the Aswan Dam.	Toronto hockey players are involved in a brawl with Boston players after they play an exhibition game in Berlin. Spectators join in the melee.	
Mar. 14	The League of Nations settles the problem in Danzig and Poles agree to withdraw their troops.	Winston Churchill of Great Britain wants to boost England's air defense. . . . German refugees in Vienna report Nazi torture of Communists, Jews, newspapermen, and others in Germany.	The Hebrew University in Jerusalem is in danger of having to suspend some of its scientific activities due to lack of funds. The school is researching malaria under the auspices of the League of Nations.	The Foreign Ministers of Bolivia and Colombia sign a trade treaty to facilitate the exchange of goods and aid financial relations.	China refuses Japanese conditions for peace. They reject the idea of a neutral zone and refuse to cease resistance against the Japanese.
Mar. 15	One League of Nations subcommittee works on the question of an arms embargo in the Far East, while another considers the nonrecognition of Manchukuo.	Former German minister Richard von Kuhlmann asserts that the Reich has no desire for conflict and scoffs at rumors of war.	The Shah of Persia celebrates his birthday and receives a congratulatory message from President Franklin Roosevelt.	Colombia concentrates 10,000 troops along the Putumayo River, since Brazil has prevented them from attacking Leticia by water.	The Chinese are convinced the Japanese will move to capture north China, although all is quiet. Chinese attacks block Japanese troops at Sifeng.
Mar. 16	The British present a new disarmament plan to help reduce military spending and tensions between countries.	The Belgian government increases military expenditures in order to reinforce fortifications along the Meuse River.		Both Bolivia and Paraguay report gains in the Chaco. Most fighting is behind the lines.	Thousands of Filipinos bid Governor General Theodore Roosevelt goodbye as he sails for home after retiring.
Mar. 17	Baron Ki-ichiro Hiranuma, vice president of the Privy Council in Japan, rebukes the Cabinet for letting the news out about Japan quitting the League of Nations. . . . The Brazilian government offers to barter with Japan—coffee for warships. Japan is considering the idea.	A Berlin newspaper says Albert Einstein's declaration that he will not set foot on German soil as long as the present conditions continue is good news.			Japanese Minister of War Sadao Araki says his army will take "proper steps" if the Chinese do not stop resistance at the Great Wall. . . . The British offer India limited self-government.
Mar. 18	A report adopted by the League of Nations Council tells Peru to withdraw its troops from Colombia and give up the disputed Leticia area. . . . U.S. diplomats are surprised to hear of the resolution in the French Chamber of Deputies to pay the United States the war debt installment owed since December.	Leaders of the Heimwehr party in Austria want to join the Nazis, and Chancellor Engelbert Dollfuss confiscates an official Nazi newspaper.	King Ibn Saud, the most powerful ruler on the Arabian Peninsula, puts down an uprising and drives rebelling tribes back into the mountains.	Alaskans propose a highway to connect Alaska with the continental United States. It would run from Seattle to Fairbanks and construction is estimated at $40 million.	The Chinese continue their hold on Sifeng Pass in the Great Wall of China, despite heavy Japanese bombing.

A	B	C	D	E
Includes developments that affect more than one world region, international organizations, and important meetings of world leaders.	*Includes all domestic and regional developments in Europe, including the Soviet Union.*	*Includes all domestic and regional developments in Africa and the Middle East.*	*Includes all domestic and regional developments in Latin America, the Caribbean, and Canada.*	*Includes all domestic and regional developments in Asian and Pacific nations (and colonies).*

U.S. Politics & Social Issues	U.S. Foreign Policy & Defense	Economics & Great Depression	Science, Technology & Nature	Culture, Leisure & Lifestyle	
In an article in *Pictorial Review*, Eleanor Roosevelt gives her interpretation of the New Deal. She writes that people must learn to look ahead, live simply, and quit being so concerned over material things.	The Army honors Major John Wesley Bean, the first retired army officer to turn 100. Bean, who lives in Massachusetts, is a Civil War hero.	Many governors throughout the United States issue proclamations asking the people to support President Franklin Roosevelt in his endeavors to restore the economy of the nation.	The Clavilux, or color organ, accompanies Julie Peters, lyric soprano, at a recital at Carnegie Hall. Forms of color move and change in rhythm on a large screen.	The racehorse Ebony Lady wins the Cermak Memorial purse at Hialeah Park.	Mar. 8
President Franklin Roosevelt calls Congress into a special session to work on enacting his New Deal.	The new Navy cruiser *San Francisco*, built under the Washington Treaty of 1922, is launched at the Mare Island Navy Yard in California. The ship is a 10,000-ton "pocket battleship."	Congress passes the Emergency Banking Relief Act, giving the President power to regulate banking transactions. They hope to divert a national banking crisis.	Scientists in California finish their experiments in measuring the speed of light, but they say it will take six months to sift through the figures and come to a conclusion.		Mar. 9
Eleanor Roosevelt attends a tea given by the Congressional Club for the wives and daughters of new Congress members. . . . Nevada becomes the first state in the United States to regulate narcotics.		Irving J. Reuter, president and general manager of the Buick Motor Company, closes the plants because of the present monetary crisis. Chevrolet will follow suit. However, both plants believe the economic measures undertaken by President Franklin Roosevelt will allow the plants to reopen soon.	An earthquake registering 6.3–6.4 on the Richter scale hits Long Beach, Calif., killing 115 people. Fires rage and people run through the streets seeking shelter as buildings crumble. . . . Dr. Albert Einstein is so engrossed in his conversation with Dr. Beno Gutenburg as they walk across a California campus that they do not even notice the earthquake until they see people running from the buildings.		Mar. 10
	The sister airship of the *Akron* is christened in Akron, Ohio. The wife of William A. Moffett, chief of the Navy's Bureau of Aeronautics, christens the *Macon*, pulling a red, white, and blue cord to release 48 pigeons.		French physician G.J. Stefanopoulo reports his discovery that mosquitoes carry yellow fever in Africa.	Two New Yorkers, John Blomshield and Loring Farnsworth, leave Shanghai to sail around the world in a Chinese junk. The *New Horizons*, as its name means in English, is equipped with an auxiliary motor and measures 68-feet-long by almost 14-feet-wide.	Mar. 11
The "fireside chat" is born, as President Franklin Roosevelt delivers his first radio address as President. He tells the country what he is doing to deal with the Depression.	Many veterans throughout the nation pledge their support to President Franklin Roosevelt for cuts in veterans' compensation.	Many banks throughout the nation reopen for business, but Connecticut, South Carolina, Kentucky, and Virginia extend their bank holidays.	Mexican scientists discover the 12-century-old ruins of the capital city, which include 15 pyramids. . . . Nineteen-year-old flier Victor Smith lands at Walfish Bay, South Africa, in his attempt to better the flying time of Amy Johnson Mollison from London to Cape Town. So far he is 10 hours ahead of her time.	The movie industry faces a crisis as all studios plan to close tomorrow. Producers and members of the Motion Picture Academy of Arts and Sciences meet but money talks are deadlocked.	Mar. 12
A subcommittee of Democrats from the House Ways & Means Committee drafts a bill to allow the manufacture of 3.2 beer. President Franklin Roosevelt urges passage because of the much-needed tax revenue.		The Administration Relief Bill nears completion, as Senator Robert F. Wagner and Secretary of Labor Frances Perkins put the finishing touches on it. The bill will put 200,000 to 300,000 unemployed back to work on development projects.		Negotiations between Babe Ruth and Yankee management end in a deadlock. . . . The Chicago Art Institute reports it is assembling world-famous paintings to be shown during the World's Fair there.	Mar. 13
President Franklin Roosevelt's $500 million economy bill is held up in the Senate while amendments are discussed.			An exhibit of the work of Albert Einstein and other scientists opens at Columbia University on Einstein's birthday today.		Mar. 14
	The Navy is pleased by the performance of the airship *Akron* under tropical conditions on a trip from Miami to the Canal Zone.	The American Bankers Association favors a proposal for more clearing houses.	A device is introduced to the New York Electrical Society which would reduce the danger of marine disasters that sometimes occur because other ships fail to receive an SOS. The device rings a bell on ships in the area when another ship sends an SOS.		Mar. 15
The Senate passes the Beer Bill, 43–30, after cutting alcohol content from 3.2 to 3.05. It also legalizes wine with the same alcoholic strength.		In speaking with the British, German, and French Ambassadors, President Franklin Roosevelt urges the earliest possible date for the World Economic Conference.	Amazon explorer Carl Griem returns with 2,000 rare fish, including 12 vicious piranhas.	Chancellor Adolf Hitler promises that he will fully support the 1936 Olympic Games, which are to be held in Berlin.	Mar. 16
Harry L. Engelbright of California is named Republican whip, according to Minority Leader Representative Bertrand H. Snell.	Norman Davis, delegate to the disarmament conference, helps President Franklin Roosevelt shape his foreign policy toward disarmament.	The State Bank Bill hits a snag in the House of Representatives, as members want more time to study the Steagall Amendment.	Dr. George Curme, winner of the Chandler medal, says many products may soon be produced synthetically. He cited vitamins, drugs, explosives, and textiles as examples.	Joan Crawford announces her separation from her husband, Douglas Fairbanks, Jr. She says they do not plan to divorce. . . . In New York City, 400,000 spectators view the St. Patrick's Day parade.	Mar. 17
Senators Bulkley and Smith, both strong Roosevelt supporters, put forth a simpler version of the President's Farm Aid Bill.					Mar. 18

F	G	H	I	J
Includes elections, federal-state relations, civil rights and liberties, crime, the judiciary, education, healthcare, poverty, urban affairs, and population.	Includes formation and debate of U.S. foreign and defense policies, veterans affairs, and defense spending. (Relations with specific foreign countries are usually found under the region concerned.)	Includes business, labor, agriculture, taxation, transportation, consumer affairs, monetary and fiscal policy, natural resources, pollution, and accidents.	Includes worldwide scientific, medical, and technological developments, natural phenomena, U.S. weather, and natural disasters.	Includes the arts, religion, scholarship, communications media, sports, entertainment, fashions, fads, and social life.

	World Affairs	Europe	Africa & The Middle East	The Americas	Asia & The Pacific
Mar. 19	Colombia is thrilled with the League decision on the Leticia conflict and hopes it might also impose penalties on Peru.	Italian dictator Benito Mussolini confers with British Prime Minister Ramsay MacDonald, but an official communiqué says they did not discuss arms plans.		Bolivia reports 2,000 Paraguayans are fleeing from its cavalry and planes. They say the Paraguayan siege of Fort Saavedra is ended.	Most Indian leaders are expected to back the British proposal for partial Indian self-government, although the Nationalists are against it.
Mar. 20	The Japanese Navy Office telegraphs its delegates at the disarmament conference that it objects to limiting war planes and to the limitations on naval strength in the London and Washington treaties.	Britain halts trade treaty negotiations with the Soviets because of the arrest of British engineers in Russia.	Palestinian Jews are upset by the display of the Nazi flag bearing a swastika at German Consulates in Jerusalem and Tel Aviv.	Bolivians expect the war in the Chaco to end very soon, as their troops keep advancing on the Paraguayans.	The Japanese steamer, *Canadian Seigneur*, which had been in danger near Alaska from the seas and wind, jettisons 250 logs and is able to continue on its own.
Mar. 21	The disarmament conference decides that on Thursday, instead of discussing Britain's disarmament plan, they will adjourn for four or five weeks.	The U.S. State Department responds to the plea of the American Jewish Congress by asking the U.S. Embassy in Berlin to make a complete report.	Persia promises to provide a refuge for 20,000 Iraq Assyrians whose positions are untenable since Iraq is no longer a British protectorate.	Canada will avoid a deficit by increasing both income taxes and excise taxes.	The Japanese are reported to have captured a village seven miles south of the Sifeng Pass, but Japan is not expected to launch an attack on north China from the Jehol province.
Mar. 22	The Leticia advisory committee of the League of Nations asks other countries to join in an embargo against Peru if it does not pull out of Leticia. Delegate Hugh Wilson urges the United States to join in.	France will soon issue its first silver coins since the World War. The new 10-franc coins are about the size of a U.S. quarter dollar.	New Iraq Prime Minister Ali Beg El Gailani tells newspapermen that one of his main goals is Anglo-Iraq cooperation.	Brazilian President Getulio Vargas is reported to have agreed to permit thousands of political exiles to return to the country.	
Mar. 23	In a dramatic change of plans, the arms parley decides not to adjourn. Tomorrow they will begin consideration of Prime Minister Ramsay MacDonald's disarmament plan.	The Enabling Act, granting Chancellor Adolf Hitler dictatorial powers, is adopted by the Reichstag in Germany.			North China's War Minister General Ho Ying-ching says he will not give up until the Chinese flag again flies over Jehol and Manchuria.
Mar. 24	The League of Nations disagrees with Japan's view that it holds Pacific Islands because of a secret agreement with the Allies. The League says its mandate at the end of the war supersedes any prior agreement. . . . Yosuke Matsuoka, Japanese delegate to the League of Nations, states in New York that Japan will be a vassal to no country, including the United States. He believes Japan will quit the League and denies that China is a nation.	Dutch police have trouble dispersing angry crowds that gather when the German Embassy flies the Nazi flag with the swastika.		An accident near Mexico City kills 12 road workers as their truck plunges into a 900-foot ravine.	
Mar. 25	The Little Entente opposes Italian Premier Benito Mussolini's arms plan, saying it violates the rights of the smaller countries.	Chancellor Adolf Hitler's Nazi regime is hearing criticism from countries around the world on its policy of anti-Semitism.	Farmers who have settled in East Africa are having elephant problems. The huge wild beasts, in mobs of 100 or more, eat crops down to the ground, walk through fences, and knock down barns.	Doctors at the Pan-American Medical Congress ask all in the Americas to help fight yellow fever. Doctors are keeping it in check in Brazil, but it has now appeared in Bolivia and Colombia.	The Silk Association of America urges Japan to promote the use of silk in the United States and to educate the purchasing public about the qualities of silk.
Mar. 26	Germany is skeptical of the proposed world economic parley. It thinks the conference will aid mostly those on the gold standard.	Poland seeks a peace pact with the Little Entente, as well as one with Czechoslovakia.	Abyssinian Princess Senaba-Ouorq dies in Makalla, North Abyssinia, after nine months of marriage. She is the second daughter of the Emperor.	The historic St. Jacques Church in Montreal is a target of arsonists during Mass today. The church, which holds 2,000, is nearly full. Several people are injured, but none seriously. Loss is set at between $300,000 and $500,000.	
Mar. 27	The international arms conference recesses for a month. . . . Japan leaves the League of Nations in response to the adoption of the Lytton Report by the League. Japan plans to keep its mandates in the Pacific, however.	In Spain, the Minister of Agriculture exempts the lands of a Columbus descendent, the Duke of Veragua, from expropriation without compensation.	The Union of South Africa seeks to buy mine rights from the British South African Company for a sum of £2 million. The company accepts with reservations.	The Argentine delegation takes the proposed trade treaty with Chile home for consideration by the government. It includes railroad construction and tariff reform.	Japan talks about seizing Peiping and insists the Chinese must stop attacking Japanese forces along the Great Wall.
Mar. 28	Chinese Foreign Minister Dr. Lo Wen-kan asserts that Japan cannot be released from its obligations to the League until two years after its withdrawal takes effect.	The Nazis ban all Jews from businesses, schools, and professions in Germany. Jewish businesses, physicians, and lawyers are to be boycotted.	Jews in Cairo boycott German goods, but the government forbids a demonstration they had set for tomorrow meeting to protest German policies.	Colombian and Peruvian planes clash above Guepi on the Putumayo River. Four Colombians are killed and seven wounded, while Peruvian casualties include 10 dead and many wounded.	An official assures the U.S. Embassy that Japan will investigate the bombing of an American missionary residence there.

A	B	C	D	E
Includes developments that affect more than one world region, international organizations, and important meetings of world leaders.	Includes all domestic and regional developments in Europe, including the Soviet Union.	Includes all domestic and regional developments in Africa and the Middle East.	Includes all domestic and regional developments in Latin America, the Caribbean, and Canada.	Includes all domestic and regional developments in Asian and Pacific nations (and colonies).

U.S. Politics & Social Issues	U.S. Foreign Policy & Defense	Economics & Great Depression	Science, Technology & Nature	Culture, Leisure & Lifestyle	
The Jewish Sheltering and Immigrant Aid Society asks President Franklin Roosevelt to ease restrictions on immigration in order to admit Jews from Germany trying to escape persecution.		A conference for economic reconstruction is called for May 6 and 7. About 5,000 delegates from all over the country are expected to come to Washington. . . . Shipment of Canadian grain out of the Port of New York is at a standstill due to new British regulations that want products shipped directly and not through a third nation.		Babe Ruth still refuses to sign a contract for $50,000, and Col. Jacob Ruppert says that is the most the Yankees will offer.	Mar. 19
Giuseppe (Joe) Zangara dies in the electric chair for his assassination attempt on President Franklin Roosevelt. Chicago Mayor Anton Cermak died as a result of that attack.		Secretary of the Navy Claude Swanson says that his plan for bringing the Navy fleet to treaty strength would benefit the unemployed, as 85 percent of construction costs go to pay laborers.		The British reject all proposals to alter playing conditions for the British Open, which will start on July 3.	Mar. 20
Members of both parties in the House criticize President Franklin Roosevelt's Farm Aid Bill, but say they will vote for it. The bill is expected to pass tomorrow.		President Franklin Roosevelt introduces his unemployment relief plan to Congress and hopes it will pass soon enough that he can begin recruiting public works employees in two weeks.	Surgeon General Hugh S. Cumming tells the Pan-American Medical Council that governments must not economize on public health.		Mar. 21
President Franklin Roosevelt signs a bill to legalize wine and beer containing up to 3.2 percent alcohol.	It is reported that President Franklin Roosevelt will ask Congress to enable him to negotiate treaties based on mutual tariff concessions within certain limits.	Members of the Senate and House Labor and Education committees meet with President Franklin Roosevelt at the White House, and he lays out his unemployment relief measures.	Harvard astronomer Dr. P.M. Millman determines the chemical elements in nine meteors by studying their spectra in photographs he took.	Babe Ruth agrees to a one-year contract for which he will be paid $52,000 to play for the New York Yankees.	Mar. 22
Forty-four newspapers raise money to build a 20 by 40-foot pool in the White House where President Franklin Roosevelt can do his needed exercises.	Authorities on tariffs report that reciprocity and most-favored-nation statuses can be reconciled. They think plurilateral treaties might work for the United States.	A farm mortgage refinancing bill is approved in the White House and expected to become part of the Farm Aid Bill.	The Chicago Daily News will sponsor air races of balloons and an air meet in conjunction with the World's Fair in September.	John D. Rockefeller, Sr., attends a village street fair in Ormond Beach, Fla., and awards the prizes.	Mar. 23
Fifteen hundred people gather to pay tribute to Frances Perkins, who was recently named as Secretary of Labor in the Roosevelt Cabinet. Perkins has a long history of service in New York State.		AFL president William Green criticizes President Franklin Roosevelt's Conservation Corps for Reforestation as "smacking of fascism," saying it proposes regimentation of labor.	An Arizona doctor shares his theory at the Pan-American Medical Congress: Dr. Fred Valles believes germs can be carried from other planets to earth. . . . Mt. Everest fliers encounter problems in Egypt and Persia as they overcome sandstorms, tropical dews, and high winds on a difficult flight from London to India.	Film stars Maurice Chevalier and Ramon Novarro sail for Europe. Chevalier is on vacation, while Novarro will sing on the concert stage in several European capitals.	Mar. 24
Former majority leader of the House John Q. Tilson praises President Franklin Roosevelt's record so far and asks Republicans to back him and his programs.		AFL president William Green urges states to ratify a child labor amendment to the Constitution, which would protect young people and open up jobs for adults. . . . President Franklin Roosevelt says he expects U.S. debtors to pay promptly on June 15, but most other government officials are ready to write off the debts. The State and Treasury departments do not include those receipts in their estimated revenue calculations.		A collection of Americana from the estate of Bostonian Charles Tyler will be auctioned. Items include an etching by Whistler and a series of Currier & Ives prints. . . . Detroit is torn by controversy over a series of murals done by Mexican artist Diego Rivera. Catholic groups charge a panel in the garden court of the Detroit Institute of Art is a caricature of the Holy family and wants it removed.	Mar. 25
The first order by President Franklin Roosevelt under his new powers calls for all federal agricultural credit agencies to consolidate. It also abolishes the Federal Farm Board.	Republican Rep. George Tinkham construes the proposed arms embargo as a hostile move toward Japan and a possible step toward war in Asia.	General Motors president Alfred P. Sloan is optimistic about the future of the automobile industry. He believes the obsolescence of cars will accelerate the rate of recovery from the Great Depression.	The Guggenheim Foundation awards 11 research grants to scientists in the United States and Latin America.	Gains are seen in the public's interest in the fine arts, as attendance at 19 fine arts museums across the country increases, with the exception of museums in Boston and Philadelphia.	Mar. 26
In New York City, 55,000 people demonstrate against Adolf Hitler's rise to power.	Troop maneuvers at Ft. Benning, Ga., are canceled, as passage of unemployment compensation pending in Congress might require the participation of the Army.	The 15 percent pay cut for federal employees is to take effect on April 1. Reports show the cost of living in the United States has dropped 23 percent since 1928.		Noted architect H.B. Herts dies. His invention of the arch design for theaters allowed the elimination of balcony pillars. He also designed the Polo Grounds in the Bronx and the Brooklyn Academy of Music.	Mar. 27
Virginians ask President Franklin Roosevelt to use former president Herbert Hoover's fishing camp in Rapidan as a getaway. The President says he may go there occasionally.	The House Committee on Foreign Affairs approves arms embargo power for President Franklin Roosevelt when the possibility of war exists.		Dr. Harry Dietz tells the American Chemical Society that only 40 percent of the world's insects are controlled by chemical means and says the loss by farmers due to insects costs more than the education of their children.	During the World's Fair in Chicago, attendees will be able to view more art in three days than they would be able to see in three weeks in Europe. The Chicago Art Institute amasses a huge collection of paintings, sculpture, and prints lent to them by 25 museums and 225 private collectors.	Mar. 28

F	G	H	I	J
Includes elections, federal-state relations, civil rights and liberties, crime, the judiciary, education, healthcare, poverty, urban affairs, and population.	Includes formation and debate of U.S. foreign and defense policies, veterans affairs, and defense spending. (Relations with specific foreign countries are usually found under the region concerned.)	Includes business, labor, agriculture, taxation, transportation, consumer affairs, monetary and fiscal policy, natural resources, pollution, and accidents.	Includes worldwide scientific, medical, and technological developments, natural phenomena, U.S. weather, and natural disasters.	Includes the arts, religion, scholarship, communications media, sports, entertainment, fashions, fads, and social life.

	World Affairs	Europe	Africa & The Middle East	The Americas	Asia & The Pacific
Mar. 29	The French see Japanese withdrawal as a detriment to the League of Nations, depriving it of a strong Asian influence. However, France supports the League in the Lytton Report.	Austrian Nazis stage a demonstration in spite of the government's attempts to suppress German nationalism in Austria.	South Africa cites economy as the reason for closing its New York office and says the action in no way indicates any change in the country's attitude toward trade with the United States. Business will now be conducted from the Washington office.	Panama protests to the United States of alleged competition between private business and canal commissaries.	Chinese pirates kidnap four British officers from the British ship *Nanchang* while the ship waits for high tide in the Newchwang Bar. They also loot the ship's cabins and injure two of the Chinese crew.
Mar. 30	After consultation between U.S. diplomat Norman Davis and British Prime Minister Ramsay MacDonald, it is believed the World Economic Conference will get under way in May. The committee of arrangements will be put into action and the three-month waiting period between the setting of the date and the conference will be waived.	Hungarian Foreign Minister Kanya denies that Hungary has a secret pact with Germany and Italy.		Peru reports it has retaken Guepi and that Colombian ships have withdrawn. A squadron of Peruvian planes convinces the enemy to retire.	The Japanese, with the help of Manchukuoan forces, attack the town of Dolan Nor in Inner Mongolia. It is located in the province of Chahar, which adjoins Jehol on the west.
Mar. 31	The League of Nations believes the German Jews have grounds for appeal. First, the League covenant says the League may achieve peace by maintaining justice. It also may deal with "any matter that affects the peace of the world." Third, League members are to try to maintain fair and humane conditions for all.	The Swiss rule that Jews fleeing Germany may be admitted as temporary refugees only and may not accept work or buy land in Switzerland.		The plane carrying Canada's basketball champions, the Winnipeg Toilers, crashes in Kansas, killing two team members and four others. Six members of the team are injured, some critically. The pilot and copilot also die, along with the team's business manager.	The kidnappers of four Britons from the ship *Nanchang* are traced to Ehrcheih, where they continued inland with their captives.
Apr. 1	The League of Nations ratifies the narcotics pact. . . . Leaders in Geneva hail the return of Norman Davis and are glad that President Franklin Roosevelt has asked him to continue in his role as diplomatic representative of the United States.	The boycott of Jewish-owned businesses in Nazi Germany begins. . . . Heinrich Himmler is made Police Commander of Germany. . . . The Nazis seize the funds in Prof. Albert Einstein's bank account, supposedly to "prevent their use for treasonable purposes." The Prussian Academy accepts his resignation without regret and accuses him of spreading propaganda in the United States.	Teheran newspaper *Shafagh Sorch* charges that Russian ships are seizing Persian fishing boats and their crews at the mouth of the River Gurgan, which is at the east end of the Caspian Sea. The area is about 20 miles from the Soviet frontier.	President Getulio Vargas leads a Cabinet meeting in Rio de Janeiro to discuss the calling of a Constituent Assembly to revise the Constitution.	The Chinese town of Shihmenchai falls to the Japanese after a seven-hour battle. The city is located seven miles below the Great Wall in north China.
Apr. 2		It is believed the boycott of Jews in Germany will be called off. Wide protest is heard from Germans, as well as the rest of the world, and even a majority of the Cabinet is against it.	Baghdad reports that Persia plans to bar all imports from Russia, with the possible exception of oil.	Canadians hold meetings throughout the country to protest treatment of the German Jews by Adolf Hitler's Nazi regime.	The Chinese in Tientsin fear the Japanese occupation of Shihmenchai is a prelude to Japanese occupation of a large part of China proper.
Apr. 3	President Franklin Roosevelt's diplomatic representative, Norman Davis, hints the world economic conference may be delayed up to two months in deference to Tokyo and the Reich.	The British Parliament will act on a measure to put an embargo on products from Russia to protest the arrest of six British engineers in Russia.	An appeal is made in the British House of Commons to relax immigration restrictions in Palestine in order to allow Jews fleeing from Germany to emigrate there.	Governor Cevera of Colon province of Panama asks for two naval planes to check reports that the San Blas Indians are torturing 20 Panamanian turtle fishermen and threatening to kill them in reprisal for the death of an Indian girl killed by a Panamanian.	
Apr. 4	President Franklin Roosevelt defers the matter of World Court protocols as Senator Robinson moves to hold the matter in the Committee of Foreign Relations for this session. The purpose is to make time for emergency legislation to help fight the effects of the Depression.	France shows its eagerness for reciprocal trade agreements with the United States by dropping quota restrictions on U.S. products, including radios, asparagus, apples, and pears. Otherwise the French fear they will lose the chance of selling wine to Americans.		The Canadian Department of National Revenue announces the ban on exporting 3.2 beer and wine to the United States will be lifted after April 6, since the United States has legalized these beverages.	Some Chinese leaders conspire to oust General Chiang Kai-shek, charging him with not resisting the Japanese.
Apr. 5	The World Court rules against Norway's claim to the east coast of Greenland, which the Norwegian government had annexed in the past two years. . . . British newspapers disagree with Tokyo's claim, insisting the League of Nations is in charge of mandates.	Norman Davis denies he negotiated on debt settlements on his recent visit to London. He labels reports in London papers erroneous.	Israel B. Brodie, president of the American Economic Committee for Palestine, urges Palestine to loosen immigration restrictions so Jews fleeing from Hitlerism can settle there.	Bolivia makes a bid for peace in the Chaco, asking the neutrals to induce Paraguay to define the area being claimed.	

A	B	C	D	E
Includes developments that affect more than one world region, international organizations, and important meetings of world leaders.	*Includes all domestic and regional developments in Europe, including the Soviet Union.*	*Includes all domestic and regional developments in Africa and the Middle East.*	*Includes all domestic and regional developments in Latin America, the Caribbean, and Canada.*	*Includes all domestic and regional developments in Asian and Pacific nations (and colonies).*

U.S. Politics & Social Issues	U.S. Foreign Policy & Defense	Economics & Great Depression	Science, Technology & Nature	Culture, Leisure & Lifestyle	
	The Foreign Relations Committee delays action on a report to the Senate on the World Court protocol. . . . President Franklin Roosevelt commends the spirit of the people and endorses the plans for an Army Day celebration. . . . U.S. diplomat Norman Davis arrives in London and confers with U.S. Ambassador to Belgium Hugh Wilson before his appointment with Prime Minister Ramsay MacDonald tomorrow.	France assures President Franklin Roosevelt that it will make the delayed payment of debt due last December before the World Economic Conference begins.	Prof. Albert Einstein, a Jew, renounces his Prussian citizenship. Einstein says he was a citizen of Switzerland before he became a Prussian citizen.	American composer Werner Janssen, who is to conduct the Berlin Philharmonic Orchestra on April 8, is told he cannot play Rubin Goldmark's *Gettysburg*, because "we are having trouble with America right now."	Mar. 29
The Forestry Camp Act goes to the president and he will sign it. . . . A bill sent to Illinois Governor Henry Horner authorizes the city council to fill the unexpired term of Mayor Anton Cermak, who died from a gunshot wound during an assassination attempt on Franklin Roosevelt. The person named will exercise all rights and powers until a successor is elected.	In an argument for the merger of the Army and Navy, Brig. Gen. Mitchell tells the House Military Affairs Committee that the United States really does not have an air force. He believes merging the services would save from $150–300 million per year.	The $500 million unemployment relief bill, which is the first to allow direct federal grants to the states, passes in the Senate and will go to the House on Monday. It will end the lending of money by the Reconstruction Finance Corporation to the states.	A New York expedition of botanists reaches Trinidad after cruising the West Indies for five months, gathering flower and fruit specimens for the New York Botanical Society.	Actress Mary Pickford returns from her European trip and wants to appear in an animated film by Walt Disney in which she would be the only live character. She likes both *Alice in Wonderland* and *Peter Pan*. She says people have had enough of sex and gangsters in movies. . . . J. Rogers Mathieu, who recently completed an 8,000-mile trip across the Sahara Desert by car, dies suddenly at a reception in his honor in Marseilles, France. Mathieu was also known for other exploits in the desert and for his bravery during the Moroccan War.	Mar. 30
Congress creates the Civilian Conservation Corps (CCC) to help relieve unemployment. It provides jobs for young men in conservation, national forests, and road construction.	Maj. Gen. Benjamin Foulois, Chief of the Army Air Corps, asserts that the United States needs 880 more planes and recommends a thorough study of the nation's entire national defense setup.		Members of the Mt. Everest flying expedition spend four hours taking infrared photographs near Mt. Kanchenjunga.	The club officials of the Pittsburgh Pirates say they will not sell beer in the ballpark. The New York clubs—the Giants, Dodgers, and Yankees—will make beer available to their fans, as will the Chicago Cubs and White Sox.	Mar. 31
The Departments of War, Interior, Agriculture, and Labor receive thousands of queries about the 250,000 Civilian Conservation Corps jobs to be filled soon.		Proposed pay cuts are being based on the drop in the cost of living, but while the total cost is down, some items cost double what they did in 1913 or 1923, years which are often used as a base. . . . Veterans' benefits are reduced by $400 million per year. Spanish-American and World War veterans who were injured or contracted diseases while in the service may collect, as may widows, children, and dependent parents of those who died in the service during the war.		Mexican artist Diego Rivera is again the center of controversy as he works on a mural in the new RCA Building in Rockefeller Center in New York. Rivera says he takes a good deal of pleasure in being attacked.	Apr. 1
Senator Samuel Colcord of the Committee on Educational Publicity announces that more than 20 senators already support Senator King's bill to outlaw war by enactment of an international law. . . . The Intercollegiate Conference, a student group in the San Francisco area, labels war absurd and pledges to fight any attempt at conscription.		Most trade union pension systems in the United States are in grave danger and cannot continue much longer under existing financial conditions.	Dr. Hermann Von Schrenk, a lumber expert from St. Louis, Mo., believes a famous cypress tree near Oxaco City, Mexico, is 4,000 years old, making it the oldest living thing in the world.	Norman Church's four-year-old colt, Gallant Sir, sets a new course record in winning the Agua Caliente Handicap. He breaks the record set last year by Australian wonder horse, Phar Lap.	Apr. 2
	The Navy's famous dirigible, the *Akron*, crashes off New Jersey. Most aboard are killed as the ship goes down in the Atlantic Ocean during a lightning storm. . . . President Franklin Roosevelt names prominent Democrat Claude Bowers, an editorial writer and author of political books, as U.S. Ambassador to Spain.	President Franklin Roosevelt names Massachusetts labor leader Robert Fechner as Director of Unemployment under the Unemployment Reforestation Act. They hope to have 25,000 men working in the forest camps in two weeks.	The British expedition finishes its first flight and aerial photography survey over Mt. Everest, battling high winds and extreme cold in their open-cockpit planes.	The longest hockey game in the history of the sport is played as the Toronto Maple Leafs down the Boston Bruins by a score of 1–0.	Apr. 3
Congressmen predict the end of dirigible use as the House Committee on Naval Affairs gets ready to meet tomorrow to start an investigation into the tragic accident of the *Akron*.	Naval planes and ships search in vain for more *Akron* survivors. Four were picked up, but one later died from exposure. Among the 73 dead is Rear Admiral William A. Moffett, chief of the Navy's Bureau of Aeronautics.	William Green, president of the AFL, reports that according to union reports, unemployment increased in February. Government estimates agree. Over 13 million are believed to be unemployed.	Col. Blacker, chief observer on the Mt. Everest flight, reports the planes battled downdrafts and cold as the photographers fumbled with frigid photographic gear. Blacker says all were awed by the majestic beauty and grandeur of the mountain. . . . The first direct telephone line between Germany and Palestine is opened. A trial call is successful.		Apr. 4
The Senate Agricultural Committee merges the two pending bills on agriculture. The Senate will probably act on it tomorrow.	President Franklin Roosevelt uses his new authority to cut tariffs on several types of agricultural hand tools. He will soon need to make a decision on cutting tariffs on sugar.			American author Earl Biggers, creator of the Charlie Chan series, dies of a heart attack. He was one of the foremost mystery writers in the country.	Apr. 5

F	G	H	I	J
Includes elections, federal-state relations, civil rights and liberties, crime, the judiciary, education, healthcare, poverty, urban affairs, and population.	*Includes formation and debate of U.S. foreign and defense policies, veterans affairs, and defense spending. (Relations with specific foreign countries are usually found under the region concerned.)*	*Includes business, labor, agriculture, taxation, transportation, consumer affairs, monetary and fiscal policy, natural resources, pollution, and accidents.*	*Includes worldwide scientific, medical, and technological developments, natural phenomena, U.S. weather, and natural disasters.*	*Includes the arts, religion, scholarship, communications media, sports, entertainment, fashions, fads, and social life.*

	World Affairs	Europe	Africa & The Middle East	The Americas	Asia & The Pacific
Apr. 6	British Prime Minister Ramsay MacDonald accepts U.S. President Franklin Roosevelt's invitation to come to the United States to talk about economics and disarmament.	The entire board of directors of the Federation of German Industries resigns under Nazi pressure. The Nazis now control business. U.S. businesses in Germany are concerned.	Churches of all denominations in Jerusalem are filled as Easter pilgrims flood into the city. Many are U.S. citizens.	President Franklin Roosevelt and Ambassador Tomas Le Breton of Argentina issue a joint statement on the need for "economic disarmament." A trade treaty in July is likely.	The Japanese ship *Kyodo Maru 36* is damaged when it collides with a Chinese steamer off Shantung.
Apr. 7	Based on the Geneva covenant of 1879, Bolivia asks Uruguay to mediate the transfer of Bolivian Medical Corps prisoners held by Paraguay.	The German Cabinet approves a complete constitutional reorganization of Germany, making states into provinces of one state ruled over by Adolf Hitler.	A newspaper in Teheran announces Persia has arranged a number of 15-year trade agreements with the Persian-American Trading Corporation of New York.	Peru states its squadron of warships that passed through the Panama Canal is headed for the Upper Amazon, beyond Leticia.	China drops its native coin, the tael, and adopts the silver dollar.
Apr. 8	Foreign traders believe U.S. President Franklin Roosevelt's talks with world leaders on trade will help smooth out the agenda for the World Economic Conference to be held in London.		King Fuad of Egypt arranges with European railroads for travelers to be able to go from Paris to Cairo without changing trains.	Radio news broadcasts in Canada are limited to material approved by the *Canadian Press*, with the exception of local news.	Western Australia votes to secede from the Commonwealth of Australia in protest of the federation system, which they believe discriminates against the agricultural states.
Apr. 9	U.S. diplomat Norman Davis says Germany will not send a leader to Washington for President Franklin Roosevelt's economic talks, but Adolf Hitler assures him that Germany will not pull out of the disarmament talks.	A bloodless revolution in the tiny republic of Andorra gives all men in the country the right to vote. According to custom, only landowning family heads could vote, and a man could not vote as long as his father was alive.	Jews in Palestine and around the world begin celebrating Passover at sundown tonight.	Seven areas in the Chaco are attacked from land and air by Bolivia. Bolivian planes bomb the Paraguayans at four points.	Hachiro Saionji, adopted son of Japanese Prince Saionji, is accused of keeping money from the sale of government land and from running the Emperor's horses.
Apr. 10		Since President Franklin Roosevelt has been inviting representatives of European countries to come to Washington to talk over economics, the Little Entente—Poland, Belgium, and Spain—wonder why they have not been invited.		After 11 months of fighting and 50,000 casualties, Paraguay formally declares war on Bolivia over the Chaco.	The Japanese push below the Great Wall in four places as they launch a new offensive on China.
Apr. 11	British Prime Minister Ramsay MacDonald hopes the talks at the White House bring about an Anglo-American accord before the World Economic Conference.	German government leaders Franz von Papen and Hermann Goering visit Rome. As a result of this official visit, Germany agrees to join the Four-Power Pact.	The new Teheran-Caspian Road, which crosses a 10,000-foot pass, is ready to open. It is the shortest route from Teheran to the sea.	Chileans finally reach a cordial agreement on nitrate with the rest of the nitrate industry.	American missionary Dr. Niels Nielsen is kidnapped by bandits in Manchuria and held for $500,000 ransom.
Apr. 12	The League of Nations is delighted the pact on narcotics is assured of enough votes to ratify it and put it into effect.	The Chamber of Deputies in Paris is in the process of creating a professional chair at the College de France for Prof. Albert Einstein.	Egypt, Persia, and the Union of South Africa are among the 42 nations invited to send representatives to talk to U.S. President Franklin Roosevelt about the economy.	Colombia notifies Geneva it accepts the settlement of the Leticia dispute, including Peruvian evacuation of the area and League jurisdiction of Leticia.	
Apr. 13	Japan hints that as well as quitting the League of Nations, it might also withdraw from the Permanent International Court of Justice at The Hague.	Sir John Simon denies the British engineers on trial in Russia are spies. He states that none of the men has ever been connected with the British Intelligence Service.		Brazil restores the Imperial Order of the Southern Cross, to be bestowed upon foreigners who perform noteworthy scientific and humanitarian deeds on behalf of Brazil.	Japan sends six additional warships to Hankow, China, making a total of 11.
Apr. 14	Pierre Lanux, official of the League of Nations, says the French are pleased with the way President Franklin Roosevelt has taken on the role of mediating chairman.		Arabs accuse the British of establishing a branch of the YMCA in Palestine expressly to try to convert Muslims.	Many Mexicans in the state of Veracruz are forced to flee their homes as the long-dormant San Martin volcano erupts.	The Maharajah of Nepal honors members of the Mt. Everest flight expedition, having them ride on elephants in a procession.
Apr. 15	The Celtic League of Nations will meet in Brest in July for its organizational meeting. Delegates will come from Ireland, Wales, Scotland, the Isle of Man, and Brittany.		The Belgian colonial government, attempting to curb polygamy in the Belgian Congo, levies a tax on each extra wife.	Colombian diplomat Alphonso Lopez is welcomed to Lima, where he will meet with Peru's President Oscar Benavides.	Emperor Hirohito sends a message to the Japanese troops, thanking them for the energy and courage they displayed in the Jehol campaign.
Apr. 16	The Zionist Organization of America takes the first step toward negotiating with Great Britain and the League of Nations regarding German Jewish settlers in Palestine.	The Irish army criticizes Eamon de Valera's government as being too friendly to England and advocates using force against the "internal enemies of Irish freedom."	A search is on in Algeria for Captain William Lancaster, whose plane left Morocco on Wednesday as he attempted a record flight from London to Cape Town.	Special Brazilian envoy J.F. de Assisi-Brasil arrives in Washington, where he and President Franklin Roosevelt will confer about South American commerce and tariffs.	Japanese troops sweep into cities on the Chinese coast. The territory captured includes U.S. Army and Marine bases.
Apr. 17	Former French premier Edouard Herriot sails for the United States to talk with President Franklin Roosevelt, but is not unduly optimistic. He hints he may make an offer on war debt payment.	Austrian Chancellor Engelbert Dollfuss says on his return from Italy that he is confident of that nation's backing for Austria against the Nazis.		U.S. Ambassador William Culbertson delivers a note concerning President Franklin Roosevelt's suggestions for a nonaggression pact to President Jorge Alessandri of Chile.	Chinese Finance Minister T.V. Soong sails for the United States, where he will confer with President Franklin Roosevelt on economics. Manchuria may be included in the talks.

A	B	C	D	E
Includes developments that affect more than one world region, international organizations, and important meetings of world leaders.	*Includes all domestic and regional developments in Europe, including the Soviet Union.*	*Includes all domestic and regional developments in Africa and the Middle East.*	*Includes all domestic and regional developments in Latin America, the Caribbean, and Canada.*	*Includes all domestic and regional developments in Asian and Pacific nations (and colonies).*

U.S. Politics & Social Issues	U.S. Foreign Policy & Defense	Economics & Great Depression	Science, Technology & Nature	Culture, Leisure & Lifestyle	
	Rear Admiral Hutch Cone, chairman of the U.S. Shipping Board, says the United States must never again rely on foreign vessels. He asserts it would be a grave mistake to revert to pre-war naval status.	The heaviest buying in several years sends grain prices soaring to a season's high.	President Franklin Roosevelt plans to have 36,000 new trees planted on his Hyde Park estate before fall. The 15 species of trees will be planted through an agreement between the President and Syracuse University.	President Franklin Roosevelt accepts an invitation to attend the American League opening day baseball game in Washington. He praises baseball for helping to keep morale up in the country during the Depression.	Apr. 6
President Franklin Roosevelt signs the amendment to the Volstead Act, making 3.2 beer legal.	Army, Navy, and Marine Corps officers and others crowd St. Patrick's Cathedral in New York at a special Mass for those who died on board the Akron.	Senator Carter Glass and Rep. Henry Steagall, chairman of the House Banking and Currency Committee, jointly sponsor the President's banking reform bill.	Prominent chemist A.M. Comey dies. He was a retired official of the Du Pont Company and his dictionary of chemical solubilities is a well-known reference book.	The National Association of Basketball Coaches will vote on a dozen proposed rule changes, but few are expected to pass.	Apr. 7
Senator Royal S. Copeland makes an appeal for donations to the International Save the Children Fund, saying children in sections of the southern states are in need of food and medicinal supplies.	Democratic leaders in Congress believe President Franklin Roosevelt will call for the War and Navy departments to spend $200 million less in the next fiscal year. This amount will be slashed from the $658 million appropriated for those departments by the last Congress.	The first 25,000 unemployed men selected for President Franklin Roosevelt's reforestation program begin two weeks of conditioning in army camps. They will then go to the forest camps to work on reforestation projects.		John Ringling says that although the circus has grown bigger and better in the past 50 years, its appeal remains the same.	Apr. 8
	A committee of seven veterans plans a new Bonus March on the capital. The American Legion; last year's leader Walter Waters; and his aide, Doak Carter, are all opposed to the move.	President Franklin Roosevelt is expected to recommend another unemployment plan to Congress. This one will develop Mussel Shoals and the Tennessee Valley. . . . Room is cleared in the Allegheny Forest of Pennsylvania for the first forest work camp. The 220 men who arrive April 20 will begin planting seedlings.	Specialists have a new technique to treat curved spines. It was developed after the infantile paralysis epidemic of 1931 left many children with that problem. Doctors apply a plaster jacket, which bends the spine in the opposite direction of the curvature.	Ellsworth Vines, Wilmer Alison, John Van Ryn, and George M. Lott, Jr., are named to the U.S. Davis Cup team.	Apr. 9
	Secretary of Commerce Daniel C. Roper, in a radio address, urges the United States to make it clear to the world that the country is now committed to a policy of fair play in international economic relations.	Governors of five states—Iowa, Minnesota, Wisconsin, Indiana, and Illinois—appeal to President Franklin Roosevelt to make farm mortgage interest rates consistent with what farmers can pay.	Bell Telephone Laboratories comes up with a new sound reproduction system called Wide Range, which is being installed in movie theaters. They say it offers "a faithful and undistorted quality of sound."	Appleton publishes a new biography of Alfred Mond, whose mission in life was to raise $70 million to bring the Jews back to Palestine.	Apr. 10
The President wants the power to negotiate reciprocal agreements at the World Economic Conference.	Testimony of the three survivors of the Akron disaster establishes that the airship did not break up in the air but upon impact with the water.		British aviator William Lancaster sets out to try to break the speed record from London to Cape Town.		Apr. 11
	At a special session of the Pan American Union, President Franklin Roosevelt pleads for peace in the Americas and adoption of a good neighbor policy.	The steel industry rallies sharply and even scrap steel and pig iron prices are up fifty cents a ton.	Biologists find that light exercising helps digestion, but violent movements are not good because they stop the action of stomach acids.	The baseball writers will have the task of naming the Most Valuable Player in each league.	Apr. 12
Edward J. Kelly, friend and adviser of the late Chicago mayor Anton Cermak, is the unanimous choice of the city council to replace him.	Argentina is the only one of the first 11 countries invited by President Franklin Roosevelt to send a representative to discuss economics that has not replied.	President Franklin Roosevelt urges Congress to pass a measure to help homeowners. His plan saves homes valued at $10,000 or less from foreclosure and cuts the interest rate on mortgage loans.			Apr. 13
Republicans in the House of Representatives oppose giving President Franklin Roosevelt arms embargo power.	Fifty administrative officers and bureau chiefs of the Navy meet to draft an economy plan.	Secretary of Labor Frances Perkins announces the members of a committee to study the statistical system of the Labor Department.	Prof. Albert Einstein accepts the invitation of the Sorbonne. His duties will consist mainly of conferences and discussions and will not interfere with previous engagements at Princeton University and other places.	Washington Park officials set the date for the American Derby. The race for three-year-olds will be run on June 3.	Apr. 14
The National Consumers League congratulates President Franklin Roosevelt on his support of legislation setting minimum wages.		George MacDonald, former president of the Chicopee National Bank, asks for a law to guarantee deposits in national banks and trust companies.	An experiment by Dr. Raphael Zon, director of the Lake States Forest Experiment Station, shows the importance of erosion control for forestry, flood control, and agriculture.		Apr. 15
	More debris from the Akron is found at sea, including part of the outer cover. Admiral William V. Pratt, Chief of Naval Operations, says the search will end Wednesday unless more evidence is found. . . . Rep. Hamilton Fish, Jr., urges the United States to put diplomatic pressure on Cuba to oust Machada and hold elections, since the Machada regime is so oppressive.		The famous barometer that Charles Darwin carried on his voyage on the Beagle is on display at his home in Kent, which is now a science museum.	Col. E.R. Bradley, whose horses have won three Kentucky Derbies, chooses Boilermaker and Broker's Tip to enter in this year's race at Churchill Downs.	Apr. 16
The arms embargo resolution is adopted by the House by a 253–109 vote, but is expected to face some opposition in the Senate.		A fight begins in the Senate on the proposed St. Lawrence Waterway. Senator Royal S. Copeland believes it may hurt U.S. commerce by diverting shipments from railroads and ocean liners.		Actor Fred Terry dies in London at the age of 69. Terry was the brother of actress Ellen Terry.	Apr. 17

F	**G**	**H**	**I**	**J**
Includes elections, federal-state relations, civil rights and liberties, crime, the judiciary, education, healthcare, poverty, urban affairs, and population.	Includes formation and debate of U.S. foreign and defense policies, veterans affairs, and defense spending. (Relations with specific foreign countries are usually found under the region concerned.)	Includes business, labor, agriculture, taxation, transportation, consumer affairs, monetary and fiscal policy, natural resources, pollution, and accidents.	Includes worldwide scientific, medical, and technological developments, natural phenomena, U.S. weather, and natural disasters.	Includes the arts, religion, scholarship, communications media, sports, entertainment, fashions, fads, and social life.

	World Affairs	Europe	Africa & The Middle East	The Americas	Asia & The Pacific
Apr. 18	Japan minimizes its clash with Russia over the Chinese East Railroad and says the state departments will not be involved unless the Russians try to use force.	A Czechoslovakian worker in France tells police he thinks he knows the man who was responsible for the kidnapping of the child of famed aviator Charles Lindbergh.	Persian experts study the trade situation between Persia and Russia after annulling the 1931 Persian-Soviet Treaty.	As talks between U.S. President Franklin Roosevelt and Alberto Pani of Mexico end, it seems likely trade will resume between the two countries.	Japanese bombing nearby endangers the lives of 200 American children attending a private school in Peiping.
Apr. 19			Algerian planes conduct an aerial search in the Sahara Desert for British flier William Lancaster, who has been missing for a week.	Fascists riot in Buenos Aires. It takes 1,000 police, armed with tear gas, machine guns, and a high-power fire truck to quell the demonstration.	Japanese arrest two U.S. sailors at Chinwangtao for taking photographs. They keep the camera and let the men go.
Apr. 20	The United States is expected to make representations to Japan for losses of American-owned property bombed by the Japanese in China. Japan says it will pay only if it is proven the institutions were not sheltering enemy troops.	New German flags are ordered flown in the country today in celebration of Adolf Hitler's 44th birthday. The old flag can be flown alongside the Nazi flag. . . . Dutch Minister J.H. Von Royen visits Secretary of State Cordell Hull and asks how long the embargo on gold will last. He said his country will work with the United States in an effort to reduce tariffs.		Mexican Postmaster General Arturo Elias bars *Time* magazine from the Mexican mail because it has "printed defamatory material about Mexico and Mexicans."	Chinese leader Gen. Ma, long believed dead, arrives in Berlin, where he insists that the Chinese people will never submit to Japan.
Apr. 21	The arms conference reopens on Tuesday, but delegates will probably stall for time, waiting for the results of the talks in Washington between British Prime Minister Ramsay MacDonald and U.S. President Franklin Roosevelt.	The Nazi regime in Germany bans the kosher ritual shechita.	Danish and Swedish concerns sign a contract to build a 600-mile-long railroad from the Persian Gulf to the Caspian Sea.	The Canadian Department of Finance reports the country remains on the gold standard, as it makes two shipments of gold to London.	The Japanese worry that Britain will penalize Japan for its attitude toward the League by curbing the textile trade between Japan and India.
Apr. 22	In trying to form a New Deal for foreign affairs, U.S. President Franklin Roosevelt follows the same formula he did to come up with his domestic New Deal. He collects pertinent information, gets opinions of people involved, then sifts through his research to come up with a plan of action.		Dr. C.H. Barlow works to rid Egypt of an ancient disease caused by carrier snails. The flatworm disease infects 65–70 percent of the Egyptian population. . . . Turkey's government negotiates a new debt repayment plan, which reduces its debt from 107 million Turkish pounds to 8 million Turkish pounds.	Brazil believes the U.S. withdrawal from the gold standard will benefit Brazilian trade, as the lowering of the value of the dollar will help in its loan payments to the United States.	Manchukuo threatens the Soviet Union with drastic consequences unless Chinese Eastern Treaties are revised.
Apr. 23	U.S. diplomat Norman Davis goes back to Geneva, leaving Allen Dulles in Paris to keep in contact with French leaders.	Large areas of France are hit by drought. This is the 34th day without rain, and frost has also damaged the fruit crops.	Anatolia in Asia Minor is the epicenter of a violent 30-second earthquake that kills several in the Near East.		
Apr. 24	Foreign Secretary Sir John Simon calls the organizing committee of the economic conference to London for a meeting Saturday. U.S. diplomat Norman Davis will attend.	Karl Vaugoin, Austrian Minister of War, says he will use the Austrian army against the Nazis if he has to, calling them a great danger to the peace of the country.		The Colombian government contradicts releases from Lima that say Peruvian forces bombed a Colombian gunboat on the Putumayo River. It says Peru bombed a Brazilian launch.	Marshal Chang Hsiao-liang, ousted governor of Manchuria, arrives in India, where he expresses disgust with Chinese politics.
Apr. 25	As the arms parley resumes in Geneva, France restates its demands, and delegates discuss the British plan to bring the United States and Russia into an agreement to consult whenever the five powers think peace is threatened.	Poland denies it is joining the Little Entente, although it admits that Poland plans closer ties with France and the Little Entente in order to fight Italian Premier Benito Mussolini's plan for treaty revision.		Canada joins the United States and other countries no longer on the gold standard, due to the worsening of international financial conditions.	C.C. Julian, wanted in Oklahoma for mail fraud, is found in Shanghai. He claims he is a Canadian citizen, so extradition to the United States is impossible.
Apr. 26	U.S. diplomat Norman Davis speaks up at the arms parley, saying some security measures are necessary for disarmament. He states that international supervision of disarmament and abolition of aggressive weapons are the two most important considerations.	The Gestapo is established in Nazi Germany. . . . All Jewish children are barred from attending school in Germany.	Y. Azodi, Chargé d'Affaires, reports that negotiations have already begun in Teheran between the Anglo-Persian Oil Company and the Imperial Persian government.	President Getulio Vargas of Brazil suffers a broken leg when a rock from an avalanche crashes through the roof of his automobile.	Bandits with machine guns wreck a train in Mukden and capture the Russian stationmaster and his two Russian assistants.

A	B	C	D	E
Includes developments that affect more than one world region, international organizations, and important meetings of world leaders.	Includes all domestic and regional developments in Europe, including the Soviet Union.	Includes all domestic and regional developments in Africa and the Middle East.	Includes all domestic and regional developments in Latin America, the Caribbean, and Canada.	Includes all domestic and regional developments in Asian and Pacific nations (and colonies).

U.S. Politics & Social Issues	U.S. Foreign Policy & Defense	Economics & Great Depression	Science, Technology & Nature	Culture, Leisure & Lifestyle	
	Naval ships find the hulk of the *Akron* and divers bring up pieces of the frame and equipment. No bodies have been found yet, but it is expected many of the 67 still missing will be found in the wreckage. . . . The Senate approves an inquiry into the accident that wrecked the *Akron*.	Bethlehem Steel chairman Charles M. Schwab says the Depression is over and business will now continue to improve.	Malaria is wiped out in the Italian province of Istria by over a million little American fish, which eat all the larvae of the mosquitoes that carry the disease.		Apr. 18
First Lady Eleanor Roosevelt criticizes the relief system, saying it tends to neglect single men and women.		President Franklin Roosevelt issues a proclamation taking the United States off the gold standard.	The British airmen on the Mt. Everest expedition make an unauthorized flight over the peak and obtain the photographic results they want. They disregard orders from London to come home and one photographer thinks he got "the finest shot of mountain scenery ever obtained."	Maurice Chevalier stars with a one-year-old child in a new film, *Bedtime Story*. Chevalier plays the part of a philanderer who suddenly finds himself a foster father.	Apr. 19
The Justice Department presents a bill to the House Interstate Commerce Committee that addresses unlawful interstate shipping of oil.	William C. Bullitt is appointed as special assistant to Secretary of State Cordell Hull. His duties will mainly be concerned with the economic discussions with foreign diplomats.	Organized labor is unhappy with Secretary Frances Perkins's suggested amendments to the Black 30-hour bill, saying they grant her "most unusual power."		German violinist Adolf Busch refuses to participate in the Brahms centennial celebration in Hamburg because Jewish pianist Rudolf Serkin is barred from the festival. . . . Dr. I.H. Holmes, noted anthropologist who retired last summer from his position as director of the National Museum of Art, dies at the home of his son in Royal Oak, Mich.	Apr. 20
Ishbel MacDonald, daughter of Britain's Prime Minister, is greeted at the White House by President and Mrs. Roosevelt and their daughter.	President Franklin Roosevelt impresses foreign diplomats who come to discuss economy with him. Prime Minister Ramsay MacDonald is amazed when a smiling President meets him on the front porch of the White House. MacDonald says Roosevelt's great spiritual power will go far to help the nations of the world.	The United States was due to lose about $600 million in gold reserves when the President issued the gold embargo order.	An endangered species vanishes. Since 1928, scientists have agreed that only one heath hen remained on Martha's Vineyard. Scientists searched in vain for a mate for her, and now she cannot be located. The last time she was seen was March 11, 1932.	Eddie Cantor eulogizes the late showman Flo Ziegfeld as many stars pay a final tribute to him at Loew's Ziegfeld Theater.	Apr. 21
The British are impressed with President Franklin Roosevelt's leadership and believe it will be a decisive factor in world affairs. They would like to see a Triple Entente, including the United States, Great Britain, and France. . . . House leaders expect to finish action on President Roosevelt's administrative bills this week. Majority Leader Joseph Byrns says debate on all bills will be limited and no amendments may be made except those by the committees.	Governor A. Harry Moore of New Jersey sends President Franklin Roosevelt a telegram, saying the National Guard cuts would be detrimental to the country's national defense.		Dr. Vesto Slipher of Lowell Observatory reports that cosmic radiation, as well as starlight, illuminates the night sky.	As guest conductor of the Pasdeloup Orchestra in Paris, American Fabien Sevitsky of the Boston Symphony introduces the French to the work of two American composers. He chooses *Sinfonietta* by Edward Burlingame Hill and Arkady Dubensky's *Fugue for Strings*.	Apr. 22
Premier Edouard Herriot of France arrives in Washington for economic talks with President Franklin Roosevelt. . . . Canadian Premier R.B. Bennett is en route to Washington to confer with President Roosevelt on economic matters.			Aviator William Lancaster is feared dead. He took off from North Africa in difficult flying conditions with a strong northwest wind on a moonless night. Lancaster was trying to break the speed record from London to Cape Town. . . . Bishop William Moreland insists there is enough scientific evidence of the resurrection of Christ to convince the Supreme Court.	Outstanding tennis player Daniel Prenn is barred from Germany's Davis Cup team because he is Jewish.	Apr. 23
Investigators believe two small boys who died after eating food given to the family by the Emergency Unemployment Relief Committee did not die from food poisoning, as earlier believed. Their sister remains hospitalized.	When Admiral William V. Pratt retires as Chief of Naval Operations, Vice Admiral William Standley will succeed him. Pratt will remain at his post during the disarmament conference.	The Bank of America notes three factors that contributed to an upswing in business in the Far West recently. Building permits are up 28.1 percent, prices of hops and barley have risen sharply, and $182 million in engineering contracts has been awarded this year.	The father of missing flyer William Lancaster and his invalid mother are disconsolate after their son has been missing for 12 days. The father hangs around the newspaper offices in London, but authorities have all but given up hope of finding Lancaster alive, believing his plane crashed in a sandstorm.		Apr. 24
The Immigration Committee of the House votes against the Equalization Bill, which would have given full citizenship to the alien children of American women or women who are naturalized citizens.	As part of the *Akron* inquiry, the joint Congressional committee members will study its sister ship, the newer *Macon*.	At a meeting of the National Economy League, Admiral Richard E. Byrd quits as chairman of the group, citing personal affairs. He will remain a member of the group.	Deaf children hear their first sounds through a new invention. The device works on the principle of bone conduction. It clamps over the child's head on a metal band and carries vibrations through the skull to the brain.	Abyssinian wrestler Reginald Siki wrestles to a 30-minute draw with Leo Pinetzki of Poland. At 255 pounds, Pinetzki outweighs Siki by 45 pounds.	Apr. 25
Frances Perkins, Secretary of Labor, closes the Job Bureau, saying that the service started by the last administration was "too unsatisfactory to warrant continuance."	Gen. Douglas MacArthur, Chief of Staff of the Army, tells the House Military Affairs Committee that cutting 4,000 of the 12,000 officers will leave the Army short of officers. He cites the fact that about 4,000 officers will be overseeing the reforestation camps.	Frances Perkins, Secretary of Labor, asks mineworkers to hold up negotiations on pay cuts for 30 days, due to a possible rise in prices.		Edward Laurillard, theatrical agent for Francis Lederer, sues Lederer for $50,000 he says is due him. Lederer starred in *Autumn Crocus*.	Apr. 26

F	G	H	I	J
Includes elections, federal-state relations, civil rights and liberties, crime, the judiciary, education, healthcare, poverty, urban affairs, and population.	Includes formation and debate of U.S. foreign and defense policies, veterans affairs, and defense spending. (Relations with specific foreign countries are usually found under the region concerned.)	Includes business, labor, agriculture, taxation, transportation, consumer affairs, monetary and fiscal policy, natural resources, pollution, and accidents.	Includes worldwide scientific, medical, and technological developments, natural phenomena, U.S. weather, and natural disasters.	Includes the arts, religion, scholarship, communications media, sports, entertainment, fashions, fads, and social life.

	World Affairs	Europe	Africa & The Middle East	The Americas	Asia & The Pacific
Apr. 27	Ecuador, which has been a member of the League but has never had representation, sends Dr. Cesareo Carrara to Geneva as its representative.	Germany and Great Britain negotiate a trade agreement that they believe will stimulate their economic relations.	The Persian-Caspian Fisheries Company signs an agreement with a Soviet business to sell all fish caught for one year to the Soviet government.	Seven army aviators leave Rio de Janeiro to pick up planes ordered from the United States by Brazil.	Chinese military leaders claim their forces reoccupy Chinwangtao.
Apr. 28	The League of Nations committee studying the problems of Danzig meets in London to discuss the free city's nationality, customs, and postal issues. . . . Former French premier Edouard Herriot says U.S. President Franklin Roosevelt's talks with individual leaders have saved the upcoming trade parley.	Viscount Grey, who was Britain's Foreign Secretary when the World War began, denounces the Hitler regime, saying it threatens world peace and security.	The Anglo-Persian Oil Company assures Persia of a minimum of $4,850,000 a year.	President Agustin Justo honors retiring U.S. Ambassador Robert Bliss on the eve of his departure from Argentina.	The Chinese say they pushed back the Japanese flanks and held their ground in the bloodiest fighting since Japan penetrated the Great Wall.
Apr. 29		Dr. Vladko Machek, leader of the Croat national movement, is found guilty of treason by a Yugoslav court and imprisoned for three years.	A Belgian newspaper reports the discovery of important new deposits of tin, casserite, and gold in the Belgian Congo.	Argentina bars display of the Nazi flag, saying only the national flag of Argentina and flags of nations on friendly diplomatic terms with the country may be flown.	The Chinese are building a Big Sword Corps. However, all their successes with swords have been surprise attacks at night on the Japanese, who now have police dogs to warn them of anyone approaching.
Apr. 30	Delegates from Italy, Germany, and Argentina will meet with U.S. President Franklin Roosevelt this week to discuss economic problems.	Russia plans its greatest May Day celebration, featuring decorated buildings, store windows, and streets, and 50-foot photos of Marx, Lenin, and Stalin.	Louis Lipsky, Zionist leader, urges settling of German Jews in Palestine.	Peruvian President Sanchez Cerro is assassinated, despite attempts of a civil guard to shield him. The assassin is shot and killed.	Mohandas Gandhi says he will begin a three-week fast on May 8 in his Poona jail cell to help end untouchability.
May 1	Negotiations in London on the World Trade Parley halt as Sir John Simon is taken ill.	A million people hail Chancellor Adolf Hitler as he speaks at a May Day celebration. He introduces a plan for compulsory manual labor for every young German.	An ancient city believed to be 4,000 years old is discovered in Persia, 17 miles northeast of the ancient Babylonian capital of Kish. Scientists believe it may be part of a whole chain of Sassanian cities.	Argentina signs a new trade agreement with the British at their Foreign Office in London.	Australia increases its defense budget. Most of the extra money will go for upkeep on the cruisers and submarines it is borrowing from Great Britain.
May 2	Bolivia notifies the League of Nations that President Elgio Ayala of Paraguay has threatened to carry out reprisals against Bolivian prisoners.	Chancellor Adolf Hitler bans trade unions when Gleichschaltung goes into affect.	Egypt announces it will allow 200 exiled Jewish doctors and lawyers to live and practice in Egypt. . . . The new lease the Persian government gives to the Anglo-American Oil Company cuts the company's oil area in half.	Argentine President Augustin P. Justo announces he is ending martial law, which has been in effect since December 19. He is aware of some rebels still plotting against his government.	Viscount Ishii declares Japan wants a bigger navy. He asserts that the Japanese people do not feel safe with the present ratio.
May 3	The British and the Germans agree at the arms conference on militarized police.	A big crowd hails British Prime Minister Ramsay MacDonald on his return from the United States. He says he is pleased with his trip and thinks it will aid the economic conference.			Japan is buying thousands of tons of scrap steel from the United States in the form of old freight cars that have been junked. Southeastern Railroads have sold them 2,000 cars.
May 4	The Arms Committee of the disarmament parley adopts the Belgian plan for identifying the aggressor in an armed conflict.	Austria outlaws the wearing of uniforms by political parties, as it tries to force the Nazis out of the country.		Bolivia requests that Uruguay appoint a commission to evaluate treatment of the Chaco prisoners by both Bolivia and Paraguay.	Marshal Chang Hsiao-liang, recently commander-in-chief of Chinese troops in Jehol, arrives in Italy for a long stay. Chang is also a former Manchurian warlord.
May 5	U.S. Secretary of State Cordell Hull says that haggling over tariffs would prevent progress at the upcoming World Economic Conference.	The German and Soviet governments renew the Treaty of 1926 and the Treaty of 1929.		Havana's Navy Chief of Staff says a Peruvian cruiser nearing Havana may not stay in Cuban waters more than 24 hours so no one will question Cuba's neutrality in the undeclared Chaco war.	
May 6	U.S. Special Ambassador Norman Davis cancels plans to go to Geneva as he receives instructions to stay in London and press the British for an immediate tariff truce. . . . The German Minister of Defense categorically denies the rumor that Gen. Hans von Seeckt is in China, organizing and training a national army.	It is rumored that Russia is secretly sending munitions parts to the Far East. Recently several shiploads supposedly containing salt, but weighing 90,000 tons, set out for Vladivostock, Siberia. A shipload of salt weighs only 20,000 tons.		Chile's Premier Horacio Hevia resigns after he is unable to dissuade a fascist group from demonstrating in the streets of Santiago.	

A	B	C	D	E
Includes developments that affect more than one world region, international organizations, and important meetings of world leaders.	Includes all domestic and regional developments in Europe, including the Soviet Union.	Includes all domestic and regional developments in Africa and the Middle East.	Includes all domestic and regional developments in Latin America, the Caribbean, and Canada.	Includes all domestic and regional developments in Asian and Pacific nations (and colonies).

U.S. Politics & Social Issues	U.S. Foreign Policy & Defense	Economics & Great Depression	Science, Technology & Nature	Culture, Leisure & Lifestyle	
News releases from Paris intimate that the United States will not press for France's June 15 war debt payment if it pays the defaulted December 15 payment. The White House denies making any such arrangement.		After a conversation with President Franklin Roosevelt today, French representative Edouard Herriot is finally convinced that the World Economic Conference will be held. He asks that a tariff truce begin at once.	Expert Dr. T.H. Von Karman believes that the Akron was crushed between two opposing polar fronts, which were moving at great speed. He says no airship could have withstood such a collision of fronts.	The portrait Louisa, Countess of Mansfield, painted by John Hoppner, brings $35,000 at an auction at the American Art Association—Anderson Galleries, Inc. Also sold were paintings by Goya and John Singer Sargent.	Apr. 27
	The National Foreign Trade Council recommends giving President Franklin Roosevelt broad powers to negotiate tariff duties.	A Senate report says that Americans have lost over $25 billion by investing in worthless stocks. Therefore, the Banking and Currency Committee urges Congress to pass the administration's security control bill.	Dr. Ross Gunn of the Naval Research Laboratory says his tests show the stars in the Milky Way are moving away from the center of the galaxy. His experiments support the theory of an exploding universe.	Actor Ronald Colman says he may quit the movie business. Colman speaks from Spain, where he says personal happiness is more important than acting.	Apr. 28
Major, the White House dog, bites Senator Hattie Caraway at a party First Lady Eleanor Roosevelt gives for Secretary of Labor Frances Perkins. The bite is not serious.		The National Association of Cost Accountants will hold its Annual Meeting in New York City on May 12–15. They will discuss present economic conditions. . . . Special Ambassador Norman Davis informs the rest of the planning committee for the economic conference that at the opening of the conference, the United States will propose a tariff truce.	Cars showing a century of progress in the automotive industry will be exhibited at the Chicago World's Fair. The autos will be displayed in the Travel and Transport Building.	The RCA Building opens to the public in New York City. The 70-story building contains a mural by Diego Rivera. It also boasts the "top of the Rock" observatory.	Apr. 29
	The London Telegraph reports a hostile response to U.S. diplomat Norman Davis's call for a tariff truce, saying it would block pending agreements.	Senator Homer Bone urges the National Economy League to refinance War Bonds. Exchanging them for low-interest securities would save the government money.	Dr. Francis W. Pannell, curator of botany at the Academy of Natural Sciences, predicts 1933 will be a record year for wildflowers. Abundant rainfall has created ideal conditions.	Film star Greta Garbo lands in San Diego. When reporters try to interview her, she is as reticent as ever about her plans for her career.	Apr. 30
Senator Carter Glass announces that the Senate Banking Committee has finished revising his banking reform bill and it is ready for a final conference with President Franklin Roosevelt.	President Franklin Roosevelt faces a fight as he asks Congress for authority to cut tariffs when he makes trade agreements with other countries.	Four states receive loans from the Reconstruction Finance Corporation for use during May. The loans go to Wisconsin, Maryland, Missouri, and California.	Judge Advocate Ralph G. Pennoyer tells a naval court of inquiry that the question of what caused the Akron to crash into the Atlantic Ocean will never be answered.	U.S. Immigration workers hold film star Greta Garbo's luggage while they check on conflicting declarations she made about her citizenship. . . . AP reporter Francis Jamison receives the $1,000 Pulitzer Prize for "best example of a reporter's work" for his coverage of the Lindbergh kidnapping.	May 1
Guillermo Estevez, member of the insular council, assails President Franklin Roosevelt for appointing Robert Gore as governor of Puerto Rico. He believes a native should have been appointed.	The U.S. Army transport Republic, along with 10 other ships, is marooned in New York Bay for 24 hours by a thick fog.	Secretary of State Cordell Hull declares in a speech that the old policy of isolationism and high tariffs has failed. He says that to meet the challenge of world conditions today, people must realize they cannot ignore these conditions.	The first modern sighting of the Loch Ness monster occurs.	The 30th May Festival in Cincinnati, Ohio, opens with a presentation of Handel's oratorio Samson. The Cincinnati Symphony participates, as well as 400 trained singers.	May 2
President Franklin Roosevelt chooses Senator Sam G. Bratton as federal judge in the 10th Circuit. He asks Bratton to finish this session of Congress before taking the new position.		Nellie T. Ross, named by President Franklin Roosevelt as the first female director of the U.S. Mint, takes office.	A white buffalo calf is born in western Montana.	Screen star Ann Harding nearly drowns when the 20-foot sailboat she is riding in capsizes off the Havana coast. Harding, her secretary Maria Lombard, and actor Alexander Kirkland cling to the overturned boat for three hours before being rescued. Sharks kill a sailor who tries to swim for help.	May 3
Former Cabinet Member Robert Lamont fights the 30-hour workweek bill, saying it would hurt both the steel industry and workers.	The national executive committee of the American Legion drafts a policy on veterans' legislation that stresses federal care of disabled veterans.	The April output of autos is reported to be 62 percent higher than the output in March, and is the highest in the last 21 months, since July 1931.	Dr. John C. Merriam, president of the Carnegie Institute, says new data puts the age of the earth at 2,000 million years old. The evidence is furnished by dating the rocks in the Grand Canyon of Arizona. . . . The Royal Aeronautics Society of Great Britain presents medals to two fliers who set a distance record on a nonstop flight from England to South Africa in February.	Archibald Macleish wins the Pulitzer Prize for poetry.	May 4
The only item holding up the administration's farm relief bill is disagreement on the cost-of-production guaranty plan.	A five-year-old girl pins a "buddy poppy" on the President's lapel to kick off the Decoration Day Week sale of 6 million poppies to benefit disabled veterans. Little Imogene Laura Stone is the daughter of a deceased veteran.	The U.S. dollar is at a new low in foreign exchange, with the British pound rising to $4 and the French franc also rising. Trading on the New York Stock Exchange is the fifth heaviest of the year.	A rare and bright type of solar halo is visible over eastern New York State. The sun is surrounded by a rainbow of colors. The phenomenon is caused by the sun shining through ice crystals in the clouds.	U.S. tennis champion Helen Jacobs defeats England's number-one ranked player, Mary Heeley. The win, her second of the day, puts her into the finals of the British hard court tennis tournament. She will also play in the French championships and at Wimbledon.	May 5
Grace Abbott, head of the Children's Bureau, makes a special appeal to the communities of the United States to provide recreational facilities for young people who graduate from high school and cannot find employment.			Dr. Leslie. N. Gay of Johns Hopkins University reports those suffering from hay fever or asthma can find relief by installing an air-conditioning apparatus in their homes.	Horse owner E.R. Bradley scores his fourth Kentucky Derby win and the second in a row. Broker's Tip wins by a nose over Head Play at Churchill Downs.	May 6

F	G	H	I	J
Includes elections, federal-state relations, civil rights and liberties, crime, the judiciary, education, healthcare, poverty, urban affairs, and population.	Includes formation and debate of U.S. foreign and defense policies, veterans affairs, and defense spending. (Relations with specific foreign countries are usually found under the region concerned.)	Includes business, labor, agriculture, taxation, transportation, consumer affairs, monetary and fiscal policy, natural resources, pollution, and accidents.	Includes worldwide scientific, medical, and technological developments, natural phenomena, U.S. weather, and natural disasters.	Includes the arts, religion, scholarship, communications media, sports, entertainment, fashions, fads, and social life.

	World Affairs	Europe	Africa & The Middle East	The Americas	Asia & The Pacific
May 7	The Reich sends a note to the disarmament conference insisting on the same rights as Italy and France, who are building 26,000-ton warships.			Cockfighting is legalized in Puerto Rico, after being outlawed for 30 years. The sport is very popular and still follows the old Spanish rules from 1825.	The American-owned Sungari Flour Mills in Harbin complains that a Manchukuoan tax inspector from Japan is installed inside the mill to check output of flour and collect a new Manchukuoan stamp tax.
May 8	The committee studying the conflict between Peru and Colombia for the League of Nations asks neutral nations not to aid Peru's ships in any way if they come into their ports.		The Persian government grants the America-Persia Corporation a trading monopoly in furs, automobiles, and tires.		India's Mohandas Gandhi is released from Poona Prison and goes to the home of Lady Vittal Das Thackersey, where he begins a three-week hunger strike designed to help overcome untouchability.
May 9	U.S. diplomat Norman Davis tells Adolf Hitler's chief foreign affairs adviser, Dr. Alfred Rosenberg, that Germany's new plan for increasing military strength imperils the disarmament conference.	Students in Berlin collect 25,000 "un-German" books for a huge bonfire.	The transdesert motor mail service between Baghdad and Damascus is discontinued, except to those willing to pay an extra charge beyond the postage.		Mohandas Gandhi's physician is called when he becomes ill with nausea on the second day of his fast.
May 10	The 28th session of the Permanent Court of International Justice begins in The Hague.	The Nazis stage massive public book burnings in front of 40,000 people to underline censorship.		Paraguay declares war on Bolivia as a result of the fierce fighting in the Chaco.	British and French ministers propose an armistice, but the Japanese Commander in north China rejects the proposal.
May 11	Disarmament talks in Geneva break down as the conference reaches a deadlock on effectives. The problems are between Germany and the other nations.	Viscount Hailsham, British Secretary for War, warns Germany that if it breaks from the disarmament conference, it will be liable to have sanctions applied, as outlined in the Treaty of Versailles.		Chile's nitrate company, Cosach, reaches an agreement with the nitrate industry in general, which marks the end of a long period of misunderstanding.	A spokesman in Tientsin says the Japanese plan an advance on Peiping. They are already marching along the Mandarin highway toward the city.
May 12		Switzerland also bans the wearing of political uniforms in response to the Nazi activities in Europe.	U.S. Zionist Appeal chairman Nathan Straus believes Palestine will prove to be "a haven of refuge for persecuted Jews in Germany." He believes the persecution is not random but is here to stay.	The Canadian government signs a trade agreement with the French government.	Bombs are found in the residence of Myrl Myers, the U.S. Consul General in Mukden, Manchuria, and in the British Consulate. They are safely removed.
May 13	The debate in Geneva is held up while the conference waits to hear what Chancellor Adolf Hitler has to say to the Reichstag on disarmament.	France fears that Chancellor Adolf Hitler will announce that Germany plans to rearm. It has just been determined that sanctions covered by the Versailles Treaty do not apply in this case.	Haverford College announces that students on a geological trip to Beth Shemesh in Palestine unearthed a scarab carved from Egyptian limestone, believed to be from the wedding celebration of King Tut's grandfather.	All Argentine Cabinet members sign a decree issued by President Agustin Justo. It declares Argentina's neutrality in the Chaco war between Paraguay and Bolivia.	China is in an uproar over the disappearance of 15 valuable paintings. Chang Tsaio-liang took them from the Summer Palace to Peiping, and after he resigned, they disappeared.
May 14	Great Britain agrees to the tariff truce suggested by U.S. diplomat Norman Davis, and London newspapers applaud the decision.	Factions put Vienna in a turmoil as 30,000 members of the Heimwehr Party march, and hostile Nazi crowds pelt them with eggs.		The 122nd anniversary of Paraguayan independence is celebrated in the city of Asuncion.	The Chinese make a stand north of Peiping as Japanese troops advance on the city and occupy Lwanchow, on the Shanhaikwan-Tientsin Railway.
May 15	The League of Nations asks a committee to draft a plan for restoring peace to the Chaco. It cannot decide who is the aggressor, so a commission of inquiry will be sent to the Chaco.	Prince Louis of Monaco announces that he will return constitutional government to the tiny principality. Elections will be held in June and July.	A French trimotor plane, piloted by Jean Murmoz, arrives safely in Dakar, French Africa, after the crew makes mechanical repairs in midair.	General Lázaro Cárdenas resigns as War Minister of Mexico in order to run for the presidency.	The International Express arrives in Shanghai full of bullet holes after bandits attack the train and kill a Manchukuo guard. Two Chinese passengers are injured, as well.
May 16	A London committee urges a conference on League of Nations loans. Of nine loans given out, only Danzig and Estonia have met their obligations to pay back the money.	Former French premier Andre Tardieu accuses the United States of trying to use the London parley to benefit and says he opposes any French concessions.	An assassination attempt on the life of Egyptian Premier Ismail Sidky Pasha fails. Police capture the assailant.	Alfonso Lopez, peace envoy from Colombia, visits President Oscar Benevides in Lima, raising Peruvian hopes for peace.	Fighting suddenly ceases in north China and Japanese Gen. Muto and War Minister Araki announce the Japanese army will return to the Great Wall if the Chinese will "abandon their provocations."
May 17	German Chancellor Adolf Hitler's conciliatory talk makes little impression on the British government. It wants deeds, not words, to convince it of the Nazis' desire for peace.	The German government outlaws strikes. . . . Nasjonal Samling, the nationalist-socialist party of Norway, is formed by Johan Bernhard Hjort and Cidkun Quisling.	The coalition between J.B.M. Hertzog and Jan Smuts in South Africa wins 94 of the 100 seats reported in the election today.	Peruvian ports remain open to Bolivian vessels, in accordance with commercial treaties between the two countries. Lima holds this does not violate Peru's neutrality in the Chaco war.	Swedish missionaries who had been captured at Chinese Turkestan are released and told to leave India in eight days.
May 18	The League of Nations Council adopts a peace plan for the Chaco, which it will present to Paraguay and Bolivia tomorrow.	French officials urge Premier Edouard Daladier to have face-to-face talks with German Chancellor Adolf Hitler to try to settle the disarmament problem.		After a four-hour talk with Gerald Wright, who sponsored the Trinidad plan for a world conference of cocoa producers, Augusto Amaral says Brazil will support the plan.	The British Consul protests to Manchukuo on plans to deport Lenox Simpson, editor of a newspaper in Harbin.

A	B	C	D	E
Includes developments that affect more than one world region, international organizations, and important meetings of world leaders.	*Includes all domestic and regional developments in Europe, including the Soviet Union.*	*Includes all domestic and regional developments in Africa and the Middle East.*	*Includes all domestic and regional developments in Latin America, the Caribbean, and Canada.*	*Includes all domestic and regional developments in Asian and Pacific nations (and colonies).*

U.S. Politics & Social Issues	U.S. Foreign Policy & Defense	Economics & Great Depression	Science, Technology & Nature	Culture, Leisure & Lifestyle	
Governors of the northwestern states ask for early action on the Columbia River development, which is one of the great waterway projects President Franklin Roosevelt has undertaken.	More than 200 veterans leave Johnson City, Tenn., on a freight train to deliver a plea to President Franklin Roosevelt to restore recent cuts in disability compensation. All have been patients at the Veterans' Hospital there.	Labor leader D.B. Robinson warns that reaching an agreement on the debt problem is vital to business in this country and a failure to do so would cause U.S. credit to collapse and destroy the country's world trade.	A swirling sandstorm forces Col. Charles Lindbergh to land his plane in the Texas panhandle. He and his wife eat and sleep in the plane, which is stocked with a 30-day supply of food and a mattress.		May 7
Rep. Henry Watson of Pennsylvania says that giving President Franklin Roosevelt "dictatorial powers" has not helped the country's economic recovery.	Col. Charles Stanton, known for saying, "Lafayette, we are here!" dies in San Francisco. The saying is often attributed to Gen. John J. Pershing, but it was actually Stanton who said it at the Picpus Cemetery in Paris.		Famed Italian flyer Gen. Francesco de Pinedo, who has been incognito in the United States for some time, plans a solo flight nonstop from New York to Persia, a distance of 6,200 miles.	Two jockeys draw penalties for rough riding in the Kentucky Derby. Donald Meade, who rode the winner, Broker's Tip, is suspended for 30 days, while Herb Fisher, rider of second-place finisher Head Play, gets a 35-day suspension. Films show each guilty of "grasping the equipment of the other."	May 8
In Scottsboro, Ala., 3,000 whites and blacks march in an effort to bring the plight of nine black youths to the attention of President Franklin Roosevelt. The men were convicted of assault and maintain their innocence.	The Navy League of the United States criticizes President Franklin Roosevelt's proposal for a "rotation reserve," whereby a third of the Navy's ships would be laid up at any one time.	The House of Representatives votes 283–108 to reject the cost-of-production amendment the Senate had put into the farm relief inflation bill. The Senate is expected to agree to the change.	Eighteen sites are chosen in New York State forests for conservation work projects under President Franklin Roosevelt's recovery program. Four are on private land, while the rest are on state-owned land.		May 9
	President Franklin Roosevelt promises to review the program on cuts for veterans' benefits, with an eye toward making the cuts less severe.	The Senate passes the farm relief and inflation act, after sharp debate on the "cost-of-production" issue.	Legislation protecting game animals, birds, or fish was debated or enacted in 30 states in the past year.	Helen Wills Moody, American tennis player, cables her entry to Wimbledon. She is the defending champion in women's singles.	May 10
President Franklin Roosevelt blocks the cash Bonus Army move, but shows concern for unemployed veterans by letting 25,000 enlist in the Citizens' Conservation Corps to work in the forests.	The National Institute of Social Sciences awards a gold medal to Newton D. Baker, former Secretary of War, for his care of soldiers during the World War.	Cotton makes gains of 30–34 points on the Cotton Exchange, as the broadest demand in years drives the price up.	The German liner *Westfalen*, rebuilt to provide a floating airport for flights between Africa and South America, proves effective in a test by Spanish and German naval officials.	Mexican artist Diego Rivera loses his contract for a mural General Motors had asked him to paint for the World's Fair. It was believed to be a reaction to his dismissal from the Radio City mural by J.D. Rockefeller.	May 11
A group of "mortgage marchers" is assured at the White House that "Mr. Roosevelt is moving heaven and earth to do something for you folks." . . . The Bonus Marchers have dwindled from 200 to 100, but those still in Washington continue to oppose the alleged Communist leadership at the Fort Hunt camp.		Farmers and the needy get help when the Federal Emergency Relief Administration and the Agricultural Adjustment Administration are established.		Actress Joan Crawford is granted a divorce from her husband, Douglas Fairbanks, Jr., son of the actor who is married to Mary Pickford. She says Fairbanks was insanely jealous.	May 12
	Rear Admiral H.G. Hamlet, Commandant of the Coast Guard, announces cuts in watercraft and personnel to meet the necessary budget cuts. A number of boats will be cut, as well as 1,650 men.	Gains in April retail sales are the most encouraging sign in two years that the economy is recovering, as department stores make their best comparative showing since July 1931.	The exhibits at the Chicago World's Fair will emphasize that developments in industry and engineering during the past century were made possible by physics, chemistry, biology, and geology.		May 13
Louisiana Senator Huey Long accuses the United States of meddling in European affairs.	The VFW gives Secretary of the Navy Claude Swanson a six-foot anchor covered with poppies to honor members of the Navy and Marines who died in action.		In Cincinnati, Ohio, a record 5.3 inches of rain in 24 hours pushes the Ohio River to flood stage. It is expected to crest at 56 feet. Flooding leaves four dead and damages crops.	Recurrence of an old injury is blamed for Broker's Tip's poor showing in the Preakness horse race. He is out of commission until fall.	May 14
A voice amplification system is used for the first time in the Senate. . . . Druggists report no big wave of business as restrictions on prescriptions for medical liquor are lifted. They say bootleg liquor is still cheaper.	Army planes carry out extensive maneuvers over Ohio as they stage a mock air battle over Cincinnati, which is supposed to represent a mass of smoldering ruins.	Raymond L. Collier, director of the Steel Founders Society, says manufacturers, labor, and the public hail the proposed national industrial recovery act.		Ellsworth Vines, Frank Shields, and Keith Gledhill will represent the United States at Wimbledon. For the first time since 1927, the whole U.S. Davis Cup team is not entered.	May 15
The First Lady, Eleanor Roosevelt, visits the veterans' bonus camp at Fort Hunt. After wading through ankle-deep mud, she leads the men in singing *There's a Long, Long Trail*. They applaud her as she tells about her experiences during the war.	The first graduating class at the new Coast Guard Academy in New London, Conn., has 32 cadets.	The number of store failures declines from the total a month ago and is substantially lower than the number that failed a year ago.	The New York City area is infested with huge swarms of termites. They eat wood from the inside, munching until only a thin outer shell is left. Termites also cause damage in New Jersey, California, and the southern states.	The New York Yankees' first home game of the year, against the Detroit Tigers, is rained out.	May 16
After visiting the President in the White House, Senator Royal S. Copeland, who is a physician, declares President Franklin Roosevelt to be in splendid health and says he ranks higher than the Cabinet members in physical fitness.	President Franklin Roosevelt receives nearly unanimous praise from both parties in both houses of Congress for his disarmament message.	The Bureau of Labor Statistics reports that employment increased 1.6 percent in April, and payrolls advanced 4.5 percent in that same period.	The Franklin Institute in Philadelphia awards a medal to Orville Wright for contributions to aviation by him and his brother Wilbur.		May 17
President Franklin Roosevelt creates the Tennessee Valley Authority so that the government can go ahead with building dams on the Tennessee River.	Members of the Bonus Army reject President Franklin Roosevelt's offer of jobs with the CCC. They also adopt a resolution demanding immediate payment of the bonus.	It is announced at the National Conference on Old Age Security that the long battle for old age pensions is half won, with 25 states providing some sort of relief for the aged.	In his new book, *The Background of Science*, Sir James Jeans says that the science of the idealist explains the universe better than does that of the realist.	*The Chicago Tribune* will sponsor a baseball game between the All-Star players of the American and National Leagues on July 6.	May 18

F	G	H	I	J
Includes elections, federal-state relations, civil rights and liberties, crime, the judiciary, education, healthcare, poverty, urban affairs, and population.	*Includes formation and debate of U.S. foreign and defense policies, veterans affairs, and defense spending. (Relations with specific foreign countries are usually found under the region concerned.)*	*Includes business, labor, agriculture, taxation, transportation, consumer affairs, monetary and fiscal policy, natural resources, pollution, and accidents.*	*Includes worldwide scientific, medical, and technological developments, natural phenomena, U.S. weather, and natural disasters.*	*Includes the arts, religion, scholarship, communications media, sports, entertainment, fashions, fads, and social life.*

	World Affairs	Europe	Africa & The Middle East	The Americas	Asia & The Pacific
May 19		The Albanian administration replaces all Italian officials with Albanians, due to a disagreement about Albania's debt to Italy.		Bolivia reports it has begun a drive on Fort Arce in the Chaco, after utterly defeating the Paraguayans at Alihuata. . . . Colombian envoy Alfonso Lopez leaves Peru after attempts to settle the Leticia conflict fail.	The Chinese are angry about a rail deal in which Russia proposes to sell its shares in the Chinese Eastern Railway to Japan.
May 20		Chancellor Adolf Hitler delivers a speech on Nazi goodwill toward the world and eases the pressure on Austria.	A Harvard University expedition to Palestine finds a stele, or slab of stone, dating to the time of the Assyrian occupation of Samaria.	Canada clamps down on immigration fraud, deporting 1,100 people. It also charges five Japanese, including one official, with trafficking in false papers.	The Japanese army is closing in on Peiping and it is reported that Tokyo plans to occupy territory at least as far south as the Yellow River.
May 21	Washington is pleased with the news that Germany, Italy, France, and Great Britain have signed a Four-Power Pact. It is believed it will help U.S. President Franklin Roosevelt in his plans for disarmament and solving economic problems internationally.	Ten thousand Nazi storm troopers celebrate the 12th anniversary of their defeat of the Poles at Annaberg, Upper Silesia.		Argentina holds up 5,000 cases of gasoline and 3,000 bags of flour meant for Bolivian troops in its first action since declaring its neutrality.	
May 22	U.S. diplomat Norman Davis presents the United States' stand on disarmament. It is willing to reduce armaments as much as other countries, abolish aggressive weapons, and consult other countries if there is a threat to peace. It also wholeheartedly accepts the British plan.	The British government kicks off a huge housing program, which is designed to end slums in five years by providing houses with cheap rent for workingmen.	Seven elders of an African tribe are jailed for instructing a 14-year-old boy to commit suicide because he had accidentally struck and killed a friend while practicing spear throwing.	Guerilla fighters in Cuba gain strength, destroying a section of railroad and sniping at government military posts in their mission to overthrow President Gerardo Machado.	Tokyo says Japanese troops do not plan to occupy the city of Peiping, but Gen. Ho Ying-ching, Nanking War Minister, formally orders all Chinese troops to evacuate the city.
May 23	Germany hails U.S. diplomat Norman Davis's address on armaments, while the French give it a cool reception.	Great Britain signs a trade treaty with Iceland, the sixth such treaty in the past few weeks. The others are with Argentina, Sweden, Norway, Denmark, and Germany.		Because of a clash yesterday, Costa Rica will deport seven Communist agitators. Several of the men are Venezuelans.	Tokyo's Foreign Office announces that the Chinese will sign a truce in Miyun tomorrow, creating a neutral zone which both sides agree not to cross.
May 24	Peru accepts the plan already approved by Colombia for the peaceful transfer of Leticia. The seized land will be evacuated and the League of Nations will have jurisdiction over the disputed land.		Oswin B. Bull, director of technical education in Basutoland, South Africa, announces plans for vocational training for future tribal chiefs.	Two young Cuban revolutionists die attempting to dynamite a bridge. As they are planting the bomb, a bullet from a guard causes it to explode.	Col. Takayoshi Matsumuro, chief of the Japanese special mission in Jehol, dies in a plane crash there. Chinese bandits are believed to have shot down the plane.
May 25	Former French premier Edouard Herriot condemns the Four-Power Pact, believing it to contradict the policy of the League of Nations.	Greece asks Jewish newspapers there to stop their anti-Nazi campaign, following a complaint by the German Minister. Germany is the second biggest purchaser of Greek tobacco.		Colombia's Foreign Minister telegraphs Sean Lester, member of the Secretariat of the League of Nations, that hostilities between Colombia and Peru have ceased.	Tokyo reports that accredited representatives of Chinese and Japanese commanders have pledged orally that their troops will not pass the Miyun-Tungchow-Ningho line.
May 26	Japanese delegate Naotake Sato warns the Geneva arms parley that Tokyo will not sign any agreement that is based on ratios. . . . The League of Nations asks the United States to provide an Army officer who speaks Spanish to serve as one of three members on the League's Leticia Commission.	Former French Premier Edouard Herriot tells the Chamber of Deputies that U.S. President Franklin Roosevelt told him the French must pay their missed December payment before he will negotiate on debt settlement.	South Africa leads all countries in the production of gold for April, with a valuation of $238,931,000.		
May 27			Belgium plans to turn parts of the Belgian Congo into vast tracts of oil-bearing palm trees. Existing palms will be burned to prevent them from crossing with the new variety.	Brazil has a colorful election, as candidates set up "offices" in automobiles and along the streets. They provide typewriters so voters can add write-in votes.	Chinese rebels under the "Christian General" Feng Yu-siang will defy the China-Japanese truce and continue trying to drive the Japanese from their country.
May 28	Chancellor Engelbert Dollfuss asserts that Austria will fight Germany to the end to avoid being absorbed by the Nazi regime.	In the Danzig elections, the Nazis win a majority of the Senate seats.		Argentina changes its stance, closing its ports to Bolivia, effectively cutting off supplies of gasoline, beef, and wheat from troops of the landlocked nation.	Two hundred Chinese prisoners overpower guards and smash their way out of the Manchukuoan prison at Changchun.
May 29	The Reich rejects the League of Nations Council report on Silesia. The report charges that Germany's anti-Semitic laws violate its Silesian convention with Poland.	The Dutch struggle to stay on the gold standard, as they face deficits at home and in their colonies. They do have large stocks of gold in their banks.		Again, there are conflicting reports from the Chaco. Paraguay reports it captured Fort Betty, but Bolivia claims Paraguayan attacks in the area were repulsed.	Japanese Viscount Ishii praises President Franklin Roosevelt's candor and says in a radio address that they have reached an agreement on many issues.

A	B	C	D	E
Includes developments that affect more than one world region, international organizations, and important meetings of world leaders.	Includes all domestic and regional developments in Europe, including the Soviet Union.	Includes all domestic and regional developments in Africa and the Middle East.	Includes all domestic and regional developments in Latin America, the Caribbean, and Canada.	Includes all domestic and regional developments in Asian and Pacific nations (and colonies).

U.S. Politics & Social Issues	U.S. Foreign Policy & Defense	Economics & Great Depression	Science, Technology & Nature	Culture, Leisure & Lifestyle	
President Franklin Roosevelt appoints Harry Hopkins, New York State administrator of relief, as Federal Relief Administrator.	In his daily column, comedian Will Rogers lauds President Franklin Roosevelt's handling of the Bonus Army.	Debate on the Glass Bank Bill opens in the Senate. An amendment is added, which insures all deposits up to $2,500 for a year.	It is unofficially reported through news agencies that the British expedition has failed in its attempt to scale Mt. Everest. However, their sponsor, the Royal Geographical Society, has had no word confirming this.	The Catholic Theater Movement approves only two Broadway plays. They are *Music in the Air* and *One Sunday Afternoon*. . . . The Union of South Africa wins the first two of its Davis Cup tennis matches against Switzerland.	May 19
The Supreme Court puts teeth in the Radio Act with its decision in the Chicago radio case. It gives the Radio Commission the power to change station assignments and to make sure all stations are serving the public.	Naval men are upset about inequality of pay, as pay cuts hit junior officers much harder than other government employees.		Philip G. Johnson, president of United Airlines, says the company's new planes are equipped with the latest in "airobots" or automatic pilots. The devices can relieve the pilot from manipulating the controls.		May 20
President Franklin Roosevelt confers with Secretary of State Cordell Hull on whether to ask Congress for authority to deal with tariffs and debts.	The Women's International League for Peace and Freedom asks President Franklin Roosevelt to call for a Senate investigation of the private manufacture of arms.	Banks are reopening at the rate of 125 a week, and fewer banks are applying to the RFC for loans. Jesse H. Jones, head of the RFC, sees both as signs of economic recovery.	The American Museum of Natural History in New York plans to build a planetarium, inspired by the success of the Chicago Planetarium.	The parents of Barbara Hutton announce the New York heiress will marry Prince Alexis Mdivani in Paris. Hutton is heir to the Woolworth fortune. . . . South Africa advances in Davis Cup play by eliminating Switzerland from the competition.	May 21
President Franklin Roosevelt asks for power from Congress to choose a Hawaiian governor who lives outside the islands, if he feels he is the best man for the job.	The Bonus Army march ends, with 350 veterans accepting the offer of free train travel back to their homes.		The Italian liner *Count di Savoia* crosses the Atlantic from Italy to New York in 5 days and 22 hours, but does not break the records of the German liners the *Bremen* and the *Europa*.	A crash at the Indianapolis Speedway injures Al Aspen and his mechanic, Mitz Davis, when their car hits the wall at 109.5 miles per hour.	May 22
Secretary of Agriculture Henry Wallace authorizes the calling of a wheat congress so that wheat growers can come up with recommendations for making the Farm Relief Act apply to wheat.	A cadet missing from West Point leaves a note, but police refuse to divulge whether it mentions suicide.	The House approves the Steagall Bank Deposit Guarantee Bill by a vote of 262–19. The Senate approves the conference report on the securities bill.		Billie Burke, widow of Flo Ziegfeld, will present a new "Ziegfeld Follies of 1933" in Hollywood, beginning in August. . . . Forty-one Arab merchants and artisans from Tunis and Morocco arrive to take part in the Chicago World's Fair. Their dress is a cross between European and Arabian clothing.	May 23
House Republicans decide to force a vote on the manufacturers' sales tax issue on Friday.	The Navy decides to abandon its lay-up plan, as Secretary of the Navy Claude Swanson overrules it. A special board, headed by Assistant Secretary Henry Roosevelt, is working on other economic cuts.	Business continues to pick up in May, with industrial production rising seven points in the Federal Reserve Board's index.	A group from the New York Academy of Medicine plans a nationwide drive to try to reduce the 50,000 deaths that occur each year from asphyxiation.	Fans are voting on players for the All-Star Game in Chicago in July. Al Simmons of the White Sox leads Babe Ruth. Lou Gehrig is the top vote-getter among the first basemen.	May 24
	President Franklin Roosevelt orders the Secretaries of all departments to submit an economy draft. The Army and War departments are said to oppose proposed personnel cuts.	The Senate passes the Glass Banking Bill, which provides for insuring of deposits in banks up to $2,500 a year.	Passengers on the Delaware, Lackawanna, and Western Railroad will have a more comfortable journey this summer. Sleeping and dining cars at Hoboken and Scranton will be cooled to 70°F.	Yale wins the Eastern Intercollegiate Association golf championship for the fourth time in six years. . . . Rev. Dr. Melvin G. Kyle, leader of several archaeological expeditions to the Holy Land, dies at his home in Pittsburgh. Dr. Kyle made many important archaeological discoveries.	May 25
Senator Arthur Capper offers a revised version of the oil control measure to the Senate Finance Committee. It would create an Administrator of Petroleum Conservation to oversee the oil industry, rather than leave this responsibility with the Secretary of the Interior.	Assistant Secretary of the Navy Henry Roosevelt tells those graduating from the Naval War College that his department hopes to bring the Navy up to treaty strength.	Many stocks show huge advances following the announcement of the New York Reserve Bank's reduction in its rediscount rate.	Plastic surgeons warn that it is dangerous for plastic surgery to be practiced in beauty shops by unqualified persons.	Mary Astor and Edward G. Robinson star in a new picture called *The Little Giant*, based on a story by Robert Lord.	May 26
	The New York Society Standing Committee of the Military and Naval Officers of the World War urges the President and Congress to reconsider cuts in the nation's military budget.	President Franklin Roosevelt signs the Federal Securities Act into law. It requires all securities to be registered with the Federal Trade Commission.	Dr. Frank Mallory believes cirrhosis of the liver is not produced directly by alcohol, but is caused by phosphorus in steel and iron alcohol containers.	The 1933 World's Fair, the Century of Progress, opens in Chicago.	May 27
President Franklin Roosevelt weathers a dangerous storm on the Potomac River in the presidential yacht. Secretary of the Treasury William Woodin called it "the greatest scare of my life." . . . The 116 passengers and crew of the steamer *George M. Cox* arrive in Houghton, Mich., aboard the Coast Guard cutter *Crawford*. They took refuge in a lighthouse when the steamer wrecked yesterday.		It is predicted that if the upturn in the economy continues through the summer, many new products will be seen in the fall. Production of new machinery and items requiring capital investment has been slow.	Dr. George G. Simpson will spend his summer assembling the fossilized bones of a 45 million-year-old Patagonian snake, which will be displayed in the American Museum of Natural History.	Tragedy strikes at the Indianapolis Speedway again, as William Denver and his mechanic, Robert Hurst, are killed as they crash in the same car Al Aspen was driving in last week's crash.	May 28
	Since more than 6,000 Army officers will supervise the Civilian Conservation Corps camps, plans for cutting officers have practically been abandoned.	The House passes the gold repeal resolution by almost a 5–1 vote. Federal and private obligations may be paid in legal tender, as this resolution cancels the gold clause in the contracts.	Prentiss Gray donates a mounted specimen of a giant sable antelope from Angola, West Africa, to the Harvard Museum. The antelope's horns measure 59 inches. The species is nearly extinct.	Thousands throng the grounds of the Chicago World's Fair, causing it to be termed a success. . . . F. Trubee Davison, director of the American Museum of Natural History, is given a farewell dinner before he leaves for four months in Africa to hunt big game by airplane.	May 29

F	G	H	I	J
Includes elections, federal-state relations, civil rights and liberties, crime, the judiciary, education, healthcare, poverty, urban affairs, and population.	*Includes formation and debate of U.S. foreign and defense policies, veterans affairs, and defense spending. (Relations with specific foreign countries are usually found under the region concerned.)*	*Includes business, labor, agriculture, taxation, transportation, consumer affairs, monetary and fiscal policy, natural resources, pollution, and accidents.*	*Includes worldwide scientific, medical, and technological developments, natural phenomena, U.S. weather, and natural disasters.*	*Includes the arts, religion, scholarship, communications media, sports, entertainment, fashions, fads, and social life.*

	World Affairs	Europe	Africa & The Middle East	The Americas	Asia & The Pacific
May 30	Delegates of four big wheat-producing countries meet in London to attack the problem of the low price of wheat. Canada, Argentina, Australia, and the United States are represented.	French Premier Edouard Daladier sways the Chamber of Deputies to his viewpoint on the Four-Power Pact.	Nineteen African tribesmen armed with spears attack a Scottish farmer in Nairobi, East Africa. They seize him and throw him in a gully.	Argentina prohibits immigration of Jewish settlers under the provision of the immigration law that bars large groups. Several Jewish organizations had hoped exiled German Jews could settle in Argentina.	Kie Tsai-shou, well-known Chinese educator, dies. Kie was one of the first Chinese students to be educated in the United States, graduating from Hartford High School and attending Yale.
May 31	Legalistic thinkers in Berlin say Franz Bernheim, who petitioned the League of Nations on behalf of Jews in Upper Silesia, has no standing since he is not a member of the civil service or any of the professions affected by the Reich's "Aryan Enactment."	The French hear rumors of a Nazi-Polish plot to seize land in the Ukraine from the Soviets. Poland would cede land in the Polish Corridor to Germany and in return would receive land in the Ukraine.	French gold mining shares fall because of new taxes levied on gold in South Africa.	Canada reports a new export balance for 1932 of $23 million. The country had a $72 million excess of exports over imports.	
Jun. 1	Intolerant treatment of German university professors is charged in a protest filed at the League of Nations by the American Association of University Professors.	Germany imposes a 1,000-mark fee on Germans who visit Austria, ruining the Austrian tourist trade.	Deputy Prime Minister Jan Christian Smuts sails for London, where he will represent South Africa at the World Economic Conference.	Diplomatic relations are strained between Argentina and Bolivia as Argentina protests aerial bombardment of Paraguay.	Peiping and Tientsin return to normal as Chinese and Japanese troops evacuate the neutral zone specified by the truce signed yesterday.
Jun. 2	The League of Nations Secretariat appoints U.S. Col. Arthur Brown as one of the three members of the Leticia Commission, which will investigate the conflict between Colombia and Peru in the Upper Amazon.	Britain's policy for the World Economic Conference, as submitted to the House of Commons by Neville Chamberlain, Chancellor of the Exchequer, is much like President Franklin Roosevelt's plan.		Finance Minister Alberto Hueyo says Argentina must be very careful to guard its credit rating, as it needs foreign capital. It urgently needs to decrease its public debt, as it absorbs nearly 45 percent of its public revenues.	The U.S. cruiser *Houston* pays a courtesy visit to Japan. The Japanese people regard the visit as an easing of a two-year tension between the two countries and outdo themselves to show Admiral Taylor and his men a good time.
Jun. 3	Delegates from 66 countries are making their way toward London for the World Economic Conference. The main topics of discussion will be raising the world price level, lowering international tariffs, and remedying problems in many countries' money systems.	Eamon de Valera's government pushes a plan for small farms with an upcoming Land Bill. His aim is a land of small farmers who can meet most of the needs of the Irish state.	The Belgian Congo will soon dispatch its first shipment of bananas to Antwerp, the Belgian government reports. Bananas will be transported in refrigerated cars on the Congo Railroad, then in a cooled room in the hold of a Congo mailboat.	Chile and Argentina sign a trade treaty, ending their six-month trade war. The pact may be revised in one year if the trade balance proves to be unfavorable to either country.	Chinese War Minister Ho Ying-ching reports that renegade troops of Japanese and Chinese fire on Chinese outposts near Lutai.
Jun. 4		Europe is upset by the new gold payment ban passed by the U.S. Congress and many believe it will severely damage U.S. credit, which has always been impeccable.		A bomb blast damages a railroad bridge near Coliseo in the Matanzas province of Cuba. It is the first incident in Cuba since President Gerardo Machado declared he will serve his complete term.	President Franklin Roosevelt approves extending a $50 million credit to the Republic of China. The credit will be used to purchase U.S. wheat and cotton.
Jun. 5		President Jaan Tonisson of Estonia is hit by a rocket as students demonstrate after he speaks, shouting and shooting off fireworks. He is not injured, but martial law is declared in the town of Dorpat where the rioting occurred.	A Roman Catholic home for native girls in the Belgian Congo becomes a refuge for African brides who have been sold by their parents, against their will, to polygamists. The mission usually buys the bride from her husband, and when she later marries someone of her choice, he pays the mission back.	Bolivia replies to a protest from Argentina because Bolivian bombers damaged property in the Gran Chaco that belongs to an Argentine citizen. The reply is believed to be conciliatory in nature.	Chinese Generals Ma Chen-shan and Su Ping-wen are hailed as heroes when they return to Shanghai by way of Germany, Italy, and Russia. General Ma, a hero of the Manchurian fighting, double-crossed the Japanese and was reported killed many times. General Su was also an antagonist of the Japanese.
Jun. 6	U.S. Special Ambassador Norman Davis takes a strong stand at the disarmament conference, saying that if an agreement can be reached on arms reduction, effective control and supervision, and a system for manufacturing and exporting arms, he thinks the problem of private manufacture of arms will solve itself.	On his return from Rome, Chancellor Engelbert Dollfuss says Italy backs a free Austria. He sends Heimwehr Party supporters armed with machine guns to guard the border with Germany.		Paraguay outlines a peace proposal for the Chaco conflict that includes an immediate cease-fire, withdrawal of both armies, and sending a League of Nations commission to establish responsibility. It also suggests the League try to provide access to the sea for both countries.	Twenty people are killed in India when a mail train hits a bus at a grade crossing. Three others on the bus are injured.
Jun. 7	U.S. Special Ambassador Norman Davis, backed by the British, will seek concessions from French Premier Edouard Daladier during talks in Paris.		Gen. Theodore Roosevelt suffers a painful injury in Teheran, Persia, when a waiter spills a kettle of boiling water on his legs. He will spend two days in the hospital.	A cold wave in Brazil causes heavy damage to crops. In some areas, the coffee crop is completely destroyed by frost; last night frost damaged coffee trees in Sao Paolo by destroying the buds.	Three ammunition magazines explode at Hamamatsu, Japan, damaging most of the country's heavy bombing aircraft and injuring 59 people.
Jun. 8	The 17th session of the International Labor Conference opens in Geneva. Giuseppe de Michelis of Italy is chairman.	President Niceto Zamora of Spain dismisses Premier Manuel Azana, showing a lack of confidence in Azana and his Cabinet, which promptly resigns.		Cuban President Gerardo Machado's declaration that there would be constitutional reform and a vice president would be appointed is interpreted by the people as an admission that he is stepping down. Their enthusiasm causes him to invoke military censorship over the newspapers.	Dr. Nils Ambolt, who had been missing in Tibet since November, is in Hotien, south Turkestan. Ambolt was a member of a Chinese-Swedish expedition doing research in central Asia.

A	B	C	D	E
Includes developments that affect more than one world region, international organizations, and important meetings of world leaders.	Includes all domestic and regional developments in Europe, including the Soviet Union.	Includes all domestic and regional developments in Africa and the Middle East.	Includes all domestic and regional developments in Latin America, the Caribbean, and Canada.	Includes all domestic and regional developments in Asian and Pacific nations (and colonies).

U.S. Politics & Social Issues	U.S. Foreign Policy & Defense	Economics & Great Depression	Science, Technology & Nature	Culture, Leisure & Lifestyle	
Senator Robert La Follette charges that J.P. Morgan dominates the N.Y. Chamber of Commerce, and through that is leading opposition to plans for the St. Lawrence Seaway.	Five thousand attend the beachfront memorial service for those who died aboard the *Akron* in April.	Most domestic markets are closed for Memorial Day, but the New Orleans Cotton Market remains open. The market closes with cotton $1.10–$1.15 higher than yesterday afternoon.	Astronomer William L. Elkin, former director of the Yale Observatory and the first scientist to successfully photograph meteors, dies in New Haven, Conn., at the age of 78.	Louis Meyer becomes only the second man to win the Indianapolis 500 twice, but two other drivers and a mechanic are killed in the race.	May 30
In an address in London, Ambassador Robert W. Bingham emphasizes the recovery the United States has made in the two months since Franklin Roosevelt became President.		The House passes the Farm Credit Bill after voting down all amendments. Now it will be sent to the Senate in its original form. . . . Secretary of State Cordell Hull hopes for lower tariffs as he sets out for the Economic Conference in London.	An expedition from the Field Museum in Chicago views a group of 500 rare sea elephants near Guadalupe Island, Mexico.		May 31
The Senate Commerce Committee approves an investigation into racketeering, but a $25,000 appropriation needs to be approved by the Contingent Expenses Committee.	Three die as an Army transport plane crashes into a mountain in the fog. The pilot, Lt. C.M. McHenry, thought he could clear a foothill below the summit of Cajon Pass near San Bernardino, Calif.	Because of heavy demand by fabricators, the price of copper advances one-eighth of a cent to 8 cents a pound, the highest price this year.	Rear Admiral Richard E. Byrd accepts the vice presidency of the National Aeronautic Association. He will work with them until he leaves for his Antarctic expedition in September.		Jun. 1
Rep. George Tinkham demands President Franklin Roosevelt recall Special Ambassador Norman Davis from Europe, as he charges Davis was guilty of fraud in a Cuban land deal.	Although a new Navy Department regulation forbids graduates of Annapolis to marry until two years after graduation, two new graduates are wed at the academy chapel. Both young men have quit the service.	The federal deficit decreases $1 million in the last fiscal year due to reduced expenditures.	Frank Smythe and E.E. Shipton of the Mt. Everest expedition wait in their 27,400-foot-high camp for the strong northwest winds to die down so they can attempt to reach the summit.	Fay Wray and Ralph Bellamy star in a new melodrama, *Below the Sea*, which deals with a search for sunken gold.	Jun. 2
Congress endeavors to finish passing major legislation so it can adjourn next week, but there is much work to be done.		The U.S. Customs Court rules against a tariff collected from Great Britain and Germany on coal imports. Thousands of dollars collected since June 1932 must be returned. . . . The first business upturn since 1929 continues in the southeastern part of the country, as jobs increase and the retail trade shows gains.		Pope Pius XI releases his encyclical, "On Oppression of the Church in Spain."	Jun. 3
	State quotas are set for the number of veterans who will be enlisted for the emergency conservation camps in national and state forests. Preference is given to veterans of the World War.	President Franklin Roosevelt asserts that if necessary he will stay on the job all summer in order to balance the budget.	Bud Sutherland of Detroit sets a new world record when he makes 39 loops in his glider. About 25,000 attending the glider exposition in Detroit witness the feat. . . . Texan flyer James Mattern is missing on his attempted flight around the world. He should have arrived in Paris by noon yesterday.	Pope Pius XI canonizes Andre-Hubert Fournet as 50,000 people watch in Rome. Fournet was a Frenchman who martyred himself in the Church's defense during the French Revolution.	Jun. 4
The House passes the McKeown Bill, which will enable corporations to avoid bankruptcy proceedings. The corporation will be able to reorganize the business with the consent of the majority of its stockholders and two-thirds of its creditors.	The House accepts the Vinson bill, with the Senate's amendment that suspends one year's sea pay to midshipmen who do not receive commissions when they graduate from Annapolis.	Police in Dearborn, Mich., stop several hundred marchers who are taking a list of demands to the Ford factory there. Their demands include relief for unemployed Ford workers and better wages and working conditions.	James Mattern is fine after a rough landing on a stony Norwegian beach, which he thought was the coast of Scotland. He sleeps two hours, and then repairs a wing damaged by ice. He takes off before dawn and lands in Moscow ahead of Post and Gatty's record.	Alma Gluck, noted opera singer, is recovering from bruises received in an automobile accident near her summer home in Hartford, Conn.	Jun. 5
Conferees come to no decision on the Glass-Steagall Banking Bill. President Franklin Roosevelt, who opposes the Vandenberg amendment, calls Glass to the White House for discussion, but Glass does not disclose what took place.	The American Veterans' Association backs the Independent Offices Bill without the amendment that limits pension reductions for veterans with service-related disabilities.	The U.S. Employment Service is created.	In filling a vacancy, the French Academy of Sciences recommends Dr. Pieter Zeeman over Dr. Albert Einstein.	In Camden, N.J., auto products salesman Richard Hollingshead, Jr., opens the first drive-in theater. . . . Jockey Eddie Arcaro breaks two ribs in a fall from his mount at Washington Park.	Jun. 6
Senator William E. Borah and Senator Robert Wagner debate the Industry Bill, which Borah believes would be a big step toward concentrating the country's wealth. Wagner says the program will provide opportunities for owners of small businesses.		Chain stores show a marked recovery in their business and their sales are only slightly below those of a year ago, after a downward trend previously.	The Women's Medical College of Pennsylvania awards medical degrees to 27 women from 14 states and 4 foreign countries.		Jun. 7
	The United States will continue talks with Britain and France during the disarmament conference break.	General Motors sells more cars in May than it has in any month since July 1931. Consumers buy 85,969 automobiles.	New information on Mars rules out human life there. It only has 1 percent of the amount of oxygen on earth, and the temperature in the summer ranges from 79°F to far below zero.	In a boxing upset, American Max Baer knocks out German Max Schmeling in the 10th round. Schmeling lost the heavyweight title to Jack Sharkey last year.	Jun. 8

F	G	H	I	J
Includes elections, federal-state relations, civil rights and liberties, crime, the judiciary, education, healthcare, poverty, urban affairs, and population.	Includes formation and debate of U.S. foreign and defense policies, veterans affairs, and defense spending. (Relations with specific foreign countries are usually found under the region concerned.)	Includes business, labor, agriculture, taxation, transportation, consumer affairs, monetary and fiscal policy, natural resources, pollution, and accidents.	Includes worldwide scientific, medical, and technological developments, natural phenomena, U.S. weather, and natural disasters.	Includes the arts, religion, scholarship, communications media, sports, entertainment, fashions, fads, and social life.

	World Affairs	Europe	Africa & The Middle East	The Americas	Asia & The Pacific
Jun. 9	Edwin S. Smith becomes the first American to address the League of Nations International Labor Conference when he supports a unanimous resolution urging improved labor conditions and stabilization of currency.	The royal family of Great Britain attends a ceremony, the Trooping of the Colors, honoring King George on his 68th birthday.	Explorer F. Trubee Davison has a lot to look for on his trip to Kenya. The American Museum of Natural History would like four elephants, one elephant skeleton, a dongo, a gerenuk, pygmy and sable antelopes, a hartebeest, and a red duiker.	President Agustin Justo of Argentina issues a decree forbidding Standard Oil of Argentina from merging with its subsidiaries or increasing its capital.	Japan signs a trade treaty with Holland, and the Foreign Office denies rumors that it plans retaliatory tariffs against the British.
Jun. 10		The Austrian government bars Nazi newspaper *Voelkische Beobachter* by withdrawing postal privileges for one year.	The Shah of Persia receives Col. Theodore Roosevelt and invites him to a big-game hunt in north central Persia.	John Bracken, Prime Minister of Manitoba, says wheat farmers there believe it is important to restrict wheat acreage in wheat-exporting countries.	Japanese banker Tetsujiro Shidachi urges his country to show leadership and statesmanship and help turn the ebbing tide of its economic life at the World Economic Conference in London.
Jun. 11		A raging blizzard in northern Siberia endangers the lives of 600 members of a fishing fleet. High winds tear the ships from their anchors and send them scuttling down the river.		President Getulio Vargas reviews 21 Brazilian ships as part of the country's Navy Day celebration.	Generals Tsai Ting-kai and Pai Chung-hsai call a meeting in Canton, supposedly to discuss anti-Communist strategies.
Jun. 12	The International Economic Conference opens in London to try to stabilize currency and come to an agreement on trade barriers.	Ousted Spanish Premier Manuel Azana manages to put together a Cabinet, after three other politicians try and fail.	Egyptian Princes Youssouf Kamal and Mohamed Abdel Monelm arrive in New York to begin their four-month tour of the United States and Canada.	In Havana, a huge crowd of Cubans greets the *Cuatro Vientos*, plane of Spanish round-the-world fliers Mariano Barbaran and Joaquin Collar.	Australian wheat farmers balk at the idea of restricting wheat crops. They say they need to sell more wheat in order to come back from economic disaster.
Jun. 13	The question of war debts comes up again at the London parley. Italian delegate Guido Jung believes that question must be addressed before other economic problems can be settled. . . . Jan Christian Smuts of South Africa, speaking at the economic parley, accuses the United States of shirking the responsibility accorded it by the Lausanne Conference.	The Gestapo (German Secret State Police) is organized.		Bolivia suggests to the League of Nations that it urge Paraguay to accept direct arbitration in the Chaco conflict.	The Cotton Spinners Federation in Tokyo resolves to boycott cotton from India, as India has raised tariffs on cotton six times since 1930.
Jun. 14	The League of Nations sends out a report on Manchukuo, recommending a policy of nonrecognition of the new nation. . . . U.S. Secretary of State Cordell Hull pleads with the Economic Conference delegates to cooperate in lowering tariffs, which he holds to be the biggest bar to trade.	Cheers are heard in the House of Commons as Neville Chamberlain announces that the United States will accept $10 million in silver in lieu of the $75,950,000 debt payment due on June 15. . . . Austria expels German Chancellor Adolf Hitler's "Inspector of Austria," Theodor Habicht.	The foreign service office in Accra, Africa, is one of the 53 foreign offices the U.S. Commerce Department says it will close for economy reasons.	The Sugar Producers Association in San Juan announces that Puerto Rico's sugar crop is down 21 percent from last year, due to a hurricane.	Filipinos welcome their new governor, Gen. Frank Murphy, who says in his inauguration speech that he will maintain a hands-off policy on the topic of Philippine independence.
Jun. 15	The World Economic Conference concludes its opening round of speeches and appoints two committees—one economic and the other monetary.	Chancellor Engelbert Dollfuss of Austria is pleased that Britain, France, and Italy agree to the $40 million loan promised at Lausanne. The nations want to help Austria defend itself against German Chancellor Adolf Hitler's advances.		In a note to the League of Nations, Bolivia says Paraguay's claims in the Gran Chaco area are "monstrous" and it wants Paraguay to reduce those claims so negotiations will be possible.	Manchukuo responds to the League of Nations report, saying it will discriminate against those who refuse to recognize the country.
Jun. 16	The Economic Board of the London parley, headed by Dutch Premier Hendrick Colijn, begins its work by asking each nation to submit a proposal.	Nazi editor Edgar Starn-Rubarth asserts that Jews are a secondary people, not equal to gentiles in Germany.	At the London parley, the Reich says it wants to recover its former colonies in Africa.	Brazilian Finance Minister Oswaldo Aranha denies rumors of an agreement to barter coffee for other goods.	Shanghai reports that thousands have starved to death in the Shensi province, and some have resorted to cannibalism. There has been no rain since 1928.
Jun. 17	The German delegation to the World Economic Conference disavows Minister Alfred Hugenberg's demand for African colonies for Germany.		German Jews are shocked to hear that Dr. Chaim Arlosoroff has been slain in Tel Aviv. He was working on a plan to help them resettle in Palestine.	Chile and Belgium sign a commercial treaty calling for bartering of nitrate for textiles, with no money exchanging hands.	The Philippines try out two six-cylinder International Harvester trucks that run on alcohol, which is plentiful there.
Jun. 18	The Argentine delegation to the Economic Conference hopes to work out a wheat acreage plan that Australia can accept.	If parents resist the Nazi movement, German Chancellor Adolf Hitler threatens to take away their children. . . . The former Prince of Spain, who gave up his rights to the throne, will marry a commoner, Edelmira San Pedro of Cuba, in Switzerland.	About 75,000 march in the funeral procession in Tel Aviv, Palestine, for Dr. Chaim Arlosoroff, slain Jewish leader. The assassins are still at large.	The League of Nations Commission for Leticia is on its way to the embattled area. U.S. Col. A.W. Brown and his companions land at Pedrero and will spend four days on a cruiser going up the Amazon.	An earthquake rocks a 2,000-mile-long area of Japan, but no damage is reported.
Jun. 19	The German delegation pulls out of the World Economic Conference, charging they were insulted by delegates from other countries.	France grants political asylum to Russian Leon Trotsky. . . . The Austrian government dissolves the Nationalist Social Party in the country.	Four Nubian tombs, each the burial place of a king and his slaves, are discovered in Upper Egypt. Each tomb consists of several rooms. . . . A suspect is arrested in Jerusalem on suspicion of murdering Dr. Chaim Arlosoroff.	The Nicaraguan President is granted power to negotiate a loan of 1,500,000 cordobas from the Bank of Nicaragua to cover a budget deficiency and to loan to coffee growers in an attempt to stimulate trade.	A wave of terrorism by bandits sweeps the Mukden area of Manchuria. Manchukuoan officials seem unable to check the outbreak.
Jun. 20	Countries in the European gold bloc may demand adjournment of the economic parley until the United States stabilizes its dollar.	The Nazis take control of the Danzig government and conform its policies to those of Germany.	King Faisal, ruler of Iraq, arrives in London, where he will be the guest of King George.	Argentine President Agustin Justo refuses to explain to Congress why the country is participating in the wheat parley in London.	Australian Minister of Defense Sir George Pearce asks London for advice on strengthening its air force. It is prepared to spend £1 million additional on its defense program.

A	B	C	D	E
Includes developments that affect more than one world region, international organizations, and important meetings of world leaders.	Includes all domestic and regional developments in Europe, including the Soviet Union.	Includes all domestic and regional developments in Africa and the Middle East.	Includes all domestic and regional developments in Latin America, the Caribbean, and Canada.	Includes all domestic and regional developments in Asian and Pacific nations (and colonies).

U.S. Politics & Social Issues	U.S. Foreign Policy & Defense	Economics & Great Depression	Science, Technology & Nature	Culture, Leisure & Lifestyle	
	The Coast Guard destroyer *Wainwright* comes to the aid of the steamer *Arizpa*, which has a fire blazing in one of its holds. They hope the fire can be contained while the destroyer escorts the ship to Boston.	The New York Stock Exchange reports that bonds in May gained $1,643,649,795. . . . The House reaches an agreement on revenue items, which include reducing local postage from 3 to 2 cents, retaining the 1-cent tax on gasoline, and transferring a 3 percent power tax to the producer from the consumer.	Inventor Minor Gouverneur, a former associate of Thomas Edison, dies in Baltimore. Several of his electrical devices are still in use.	Max Schmeling's defeat at the hands of Max Baer is almost forgotten by Germans as they learn that he will wed German film star Anny Ondra.	Jun. 9
Rep. Hamilton Fish complains of the lack of "real Republicans" at the Economic Conference, saying Republican James Couzens takes a bipartisan stance in Congress.		In the first four months of 1933, shipments by air are up 250 percent over last year. Photos for newspapers and film for movie companies top the list, followed by food and flowers.	Two German scientists find they can generate helium, which is rarer than gold in the universe, in a laboratory.	The art exhibit assembled at the World's Fair is an impressive collection of American art through the years. Included is the work of Gilbert Stuart, Benjamin West, Grant Wood, and Harold Weston.	Jun. 10
Ten peace organizations back President Franklin Roosevelt's attempts at disarmament, world cooperation, and peace.	President Franklin Roosevelt says he will not modify his stand on veterans' benefits and hopes Congress will adopt his program and adjourn soon.	Newton D. Baker, former Secretary of War, leads the nationwide mobilization of welfare services planned for this fall. Nearly all social services in America will join in.	An exhausted James Mattern sleeps in a Siberian hotel while his plane is tuned up and refueled for the next leg of his round-the-world trip.		Jun. 11
At the National Conference of Social Work in Detroit, Mich., David C. Coyle advocates expanding social services.	Secretary of State Cordell Hull tells the delegates to the Economic Conference that economic peace is just as important as the ban on war.	The American dollar falls to a new low level, while the British pound rises to $4.19 and many other currencies hit record highs.	The Soaring Society of America offers the first soaring camp in Elmira, N.Y., for owners of gliders. Between 50 and 100 students are expected.	Con Amore, the favorite in the Broomstick Handicap in Belmont, is sponged. Someone stuffed a sponge up her nose to hamper her breathing during the horse race.	Jun. 12
	In a speech to West Point graduates, Gen. Douglas MacArthur warns against economizing at the expense of the national defense.	The Bank Reform Bill passes and goes to President Franklin Roosevelt, who says it is the best banking law since the creation of the Federal Reserve System.	The heat wave in the east is ended by a thunderstorm, which lowers the temperature to a refreshing 68°F. Several people had died from the prolonged heat.	Tennis players Elizabeth Ryan and Helen Wills Moody play in doubles at the Kent tennis championship to get ready for Wimbledon, where they were eliminated in the final round last year.	Jun. 13
The House approves the conference report on the $3.6 billion deficiency bill, most of which will go for a public works program.		One positive development for the United States is likely to come out of the London parley: shipments of Canadian grain through U.S. ports to England will probably be revived.	Doctors learn at the annual American Medical Association (AMA) conference in Milwaukee, Wisc., that bone disorders may be caused by problems with any of five glands.	The Chicago Opera Company performs Verdi's *La Forza del Destino* for an audience of 4,500.	Jun. 14
Congress finally adjourns after the Senate approves President Franklin Roosevelt's veterans' plan, 45–36.	Special Ambassador Norman Davis says he will return home to discuss the disarmament conference with President Franklin Roosevelt. The State Department denies Davis will resign.	France defaults again on its war debt to the United States. French newspapers make no comment on the action.	Texas flyer James Mattern is missing again, this time on his flight from Siberia to Alaska. There has been no word from him and it is estimated that he should be out of fuel.	The Red Sox beat the Yankees. It is the first time they have lost four games in a row since 1931.	Jun. 15
Washington reports that only 1 percent of the bills introduced in the last session of Congress passed.	U.S. diplomat Norman Davis arrives in London and has a long talk with U.S. Secretary of State Cordell Hull about disarmament. He sails tomorrow for the United States to report personally to President Roosevelt.	The Federal Deposit Insurance Corporation (FDIC) takes effect.	A new theory on the common cold is advanced at the AMA conference. Some studies show that colds are caused by a combination of a virus and bacteria.	Irreplaceable books, paintings, and manuscripts are burned or destroyed by water as author F. Scott Fitzgerald's home burns.	Jun. 16
The Union Station Massacre occurs in Kansas City, Mo., when gangster Pretty Boy Floyd kills four unarmed FBI agents in an attempt to free fugitive Frank Nash.		Lack of mortgage money is held to be the chief factor holding back construction across the country.	Dr. R. Plato Schwartz of Strong Memorial Hospital in Rochester, N.Y., invents a device called the electrobasograph, which measures a person's gait and gives him information to help the person correct the way he walks.		Jun. 17
On the first day of President Franklin Roosevelt's cruise along the New England coast, he is forced by a squall to port in Edgartown, Mass.	Before sailing from London, Norman Davis emphatically denies that he will resign as Special Ambassador. Rep. George Tinkham renews his attacks on Davis.		The new Boulder Dam contains a huge refrigeration system that is being embedded in the dam to cool the cement as it hardens to prevent it from cracking.		Jun. 18
Bernard Baruch, close friend and adviser to President Franklin Roosevelt, will serve as an aid to the President while Assistant Secretary of State Raymond Moley is in London for the World Economic Conference.	Henry L. Roosevelt, acting Secretary of the Navy, announces that bids will be taken from private shipyards for the building of 16 of the 32 new vessels. The rest will be built in government Navy yards.	Government coordinator Joseph B. Eastman announces he will meet tomorrow with railroad executives and representatives of labor in an attempt to settle the rail wage dispute.	The American Physical Society hears of a new atom-gun which can be hurled by a powerful magnet, then shot into the heart of a lithium atom, liberating 1,000 percent of the energy it puts in.	National League owners gather for their annual meeting. They will finalize selection of the team to play against American League All-Stars in Chicago next month.	Jun. 19
President Franklin Roosevelt consults for two hours with Assistant Secretary of State Raymond Moley on economic issues. Moley sails for London tomorrow to attend the World Economic Conference.	After extensive testing, the airship *Macon* will be accepted for commission by the Navy. After commissioning in Washington, the *Macon* will proceed to Lakehurst, where it will be based this summer.	Washington does not consider that stabilizing the U.S. dollar is necessary before the economic parley can discuss other issues.	President Franklin Roosevelt authorizes the buying of six to eight million acres of land in the south and east for National Parks. It will be used in the reforestation program.	Heiress Barbara Hutton and Prince Alexis Mdivani of the Russian Republic of Georgia marry in Paris. . . . Film director George Hill saves actress Fay Wray from drowning near Los Angeles.	Jun. 20

F	G	H	I	J
Includes elections, federal-state relations, civil rights and liberties, crime, the judiciary, education, healthcare, poverty, urban affairs, and population.	*Includes formation and debate of U.S. foreign and defense policies, veterans affairs, and defense spending. (Relations with specific foreign countries are usually found under the region concerned.)*	*Includes business, labor, agriculture, taxation, transportation, consumer affairs, monetary and fiscal policy, natural resources, pollution, and accidents.*	*Includes worldwide scientific, medical, and technological developments, natural phenomena, U.S. weather, and natural disasters.*	*Includes the arts, religion, scholarship, communications media, sports, entertainment, fashions, fads, and social life.*

		World Affairs	Europe	Africa & The Middle East	The Americas	Asia & The Pacific
Jun. 21		The World Economic Conference seeks an end to trade barriers. Most countries do not favor a horizontal tariff cut such as the United States government suggests.	Germany forbids all non-Nazi parties. . . . The Nazi Senate in Danzig submits an enabling act giving them dictatorial powers until 1937.	Dr. Edward Chiera, professor of Assyriology at the University of Chicago, dies. Dr. Chiera's expedition to Iraq in 1928 uncovered the palace at Khorsabad.	The ABC-Peru group that has tried to mediate peace in the Chaco gives up and leaves the task to the League of Nations.	Seven workers drown in China as the Yangtse River breaks through an embankment, and floods cover a large area of the country.
Jun. 22		The U.S. delegates persuade others at the World Economic Conference to drop the idea that the dollar needs to stabilize before other issues can be discussed.	German Chancellor Adolf Hitler compares Nazi Germany to the United States, saying the United States also has immigration curbs to keep out unwanted immigrants. He says Germany does not want eastern European Jews, and that it is the same principle.		A number of Mexican planes, including 30 military planes, search for Spanish flyers Mariano Barberan and Joaquin Collar, whose plane has been missing since takeoff from Havana on Tuesday.	According to a rumor in a Tokyo newspaper, Japan expects Russia to cede Vladivostok to Japan when it completes the purchase of the Chinese Eastern Railroad.
Jun. 23		The subject of debts is brought up again at the World Economic Conference, as Hungary and Bulgaria suggest solutions for the problem.	British and Soviet statesmen plan to meet to try to iron out their differences. Britain hopes to obtain the release of two Britons imprisoned there and Russia wants the British boycott of its products dropped.	The Anglo-Persian Oil Company announces profits are up over last year and dividends rise to 7.5 percent.	High offshore winds in Buenos Aires necessitate closing the port, as the average depth of the harbor drops from 23 feet to 19 feet.	As China's two great rivers, the Hwang (Yellow) and the Yangtse, continue to rise, the government takes emergency action. Some cities and thousands of acres of farmland are already underwater.
Jun. 24		Nationalism holds back the Economic Conference, as the different countries have conflicting domestic considerations.	Over 1,000 Communists and Macedonians are arrested by the Bulgarian government to prevent political disorder.	South Africa's boycott of German goods angers the Exporters' Association of Hamburg, which petitions the Reich to forbid importation of South African products.	Argentina learns that former Gen. Severo Teranzo asked for support from Bolivian authorities for a revolt against President Agustin Justo of Argentina.	Philippine Gen. Emilio Aguinaldo, leader of the 1901 insurrection, says he would never submit the independence act to a vote of the people. He would decide himself.
Jun. 25			For 19 hours, no one in Bulgaria is allowed to leave home, while every house is searched for revolutionaries who have been terrorizing the country.	Giraffes rubbing their necks against telephone wires cause serious static in Nairobi, Africa. The poles will be raised to solve the problem.	The Chilean government's goal is to expand trade beyond its frontiers, according to statements made in Santiago.	
Jun. 26		The labor parley in Geneva ends with H.B. Butler, director of the International Labor Office, praising the United States for its cooperation in the social and economic field, here and in London.	The Soviet-British commercial war seems about to end, as the two nations discuss renewing trade.	An Egyptian native, Demetrio Solamon, now a citizen of Spain, is arrested for a bomb explosion in St. Peter's in Vatican City.	Bolivia prepares for a possible Paraguayan attack at Fort Nanawa, but hopes a League of Nations task force can help bring peace to the Chaco.	About 3 million people have starved to death during the famine that has lasted since 1928 in the Shensi province of China. Cannibalism continues to increase.
Jun. 27		The arms parley in Geneva recesses. President Arthur Henderson is authorized to negotiate solutions to the remaining deadlocks during the three-month hiatus.	The German Press Association ousts five Jewish members, saying if they were allowed to remain, "the reputation of the association would be grossly damaged."	Dr. Chaim Weizmann, president of the Hebrew University in Palestine, is honored by the American Jewish Physicians Committee at a dinner in New York	The Washington Neutrals, appointed by the Pan American Union to negotiate peace in the Chaco, give way to the League of Nations.	A squadron of five Chinese navy vessels deserts and is believed to be heading for the demilitarized zone, which some Chinese generals last week declared to be independent of China.
Jun. 28		Australia instructs its delegates to the Economic Conference to consider the wheat plan, but say restrictions must be applicable to all wheat-producing countries.	Eight are injured in Spain when monarchists and socialists clash.	Dr. Chaim Weizmann, president of the Hebrew University in Palestine, proposes sheltering 250,000 Jewish victims of Nazi anti-Semitism in Palestine. Weizmann estimates the cost at $25 million.	The League of Nations negotiators for the Leticia conflict are quartered on the ship *Morona*. Peruvian forces have evacuated the area.	Japan denies a charge by Russia that the Japanese destroyer *Tachikaze* illegally entered Russian waters to investigate the killing of three Japanese fishermen, allegedly by the Russian coast guard.
Jun. 29		The world economic parley is at a crisis, with the gold bloc and Britain telegraphing President Franklin Roosevelt to ask him to join a declaration to stop speculation in dollar exchange.	Chancellor Adolf Hitler confers with President von Hindenburg at his East Prussia estate. Radical Nazi farm leader Richard Darre replaces Alfred Hugenberg as National Minister of Economics and Agriculture, while Nazis Kurt Schmidt and Gottfried Feder are named Minister of Economics and Undersecretary of the Ministry.	Dr. Chaim Weizmann criticizes Jewish scientist Albert Einstein for turning down a professional post at the Hebrew University in Palestine. He hopes they will still succeed in bringing Einstein to Jerusalem.	Ministers in Peru's new Cabinet are sworn in at Lima soon after their appointment.	Japan says its government is willing to stabilize its currency if Great Britain, France, and the United States do so first.
Jun. 30		The world economic conference subcommittee considering gold clauses rejects Romania's proposal that central banks in agricultural countries should adapt their banking programs to the needs of agriculture.	Official reports say progress is being made in talks between Russia and England. Another meeting will be held between Sir John Simon of England and Foreign Commissar Litvinoff of the Soviet Union.	The Presbyterian Theological Seminary of Chicago reports that its excavations in Palestine have produced the remains of a wine shop for old warriors at Beth-zur, which is on the road to Jerusalem.	Peace talks begin in Havana between President Gerardo Machado's regime and its opposition. The two factions will talk separately tomorrow with U.S. Ambassador Sumner Welles, who is mediating.	The Imperial Household Ministry in Japan announces the Empress is expecting another child in January. The court and the nation hope the child will be a boy, since there is not yet a son to inherit the throne.
Jul. 1		The Australians agree to limit wheat production, so now all the main wheat-growing countries are in agreement. . . . T.V. Soong, China's finance minister, asks the League of Nations for its continued help, and asks that a technical officer be named to ensure further collaboration. He says liaisons in the areas of health and transit are especially helpful.	The Nazi regime bans married women from working.	Muslims in Egypt open a campaign to get rid of missions, saying they try to convert children to Christianity.	Canadians report signs that their economy is reviving. They cite higher wheat prices, less unemployment, and improved car loadings and canal traffic.	

A	B	C	D	E
Includes developments that affect more than one world region, international organizations, and important meetings of world leaders.	*Includes all domestic and regional developments in Europe, including the Soviet Union.*	*Includes all domestic and regional developments in Africa and the Middle East.*	*Includes all domestic and regional developments in Latin America, the Caribbean, and Canada.*	*Includes all domestic and regional developments in Asian and Pacific nations (and colonies).*

U.S. Politics & Social Issues	U.S. Foreign Policy & Defense	Economics & Great Depression	Science, Technology & Nature	Culture, Leisure & Lifestyle	
So far 237,984 have been enrolled in the Civilian Conservation Corps, with another 70,000 expected soon. By the end of June, there will be 1,433 camps.	Four of the new naval ships to be built have been allotted to Navy yards, two in Portsmouth, one in New York, and the other in Charleston.	Czechoslovakia, Latvia, and Romania receive promises from the United States to negotiate with them on debt revisions. All three countries made token payments on their debts on June 15.		The United States retains its lead in the international chess tournament after beating Lithuania and splitting with Hungary.	Jun. 21
	Four nations—Canada, Russia, Argentina, and the United States—agree on a plan to restrict wheat acreage and limit exports. Australia has not decided yet.	William Green, head of the AFL, notes a rise in employment over the past two months of about 1.2 million people.		A preview of the Gelattly Art Collection is held in the National Museum of Art. The collection, valued at $4 million, will be open to the public tomorrow. . . . Former president Herbert Hoover will assume duties as librarian when his war library at Stanford University is completed.	Jun. 22
Col. and Mrs. Charles Lindbergh turn over their estate in New Jersey, the site of their baby's kidnapping, to be used as a refuge for children.	U.S. diplomat Norman Davis returns home and says there is a growing realization in Europe that security lies in disarmament. He will confer with the President and attend his son's wedding.	The Federal Home Loan Bank Board will appoint a manager in each state by July 1, then soon after hopes to begin making loans to those whose homes are threatened by mortgage foreclosure.	The New York State Conservation Department attributes the deaths of thousands of perch, whitefish, and carp in the Mohawk River to molasses seeping from a sunken barge, which kept them from breathing by sticking their gills together.	Max Schmeling sails for the United States, saying negotiations are in progress for a return bout with Max Baer, who defeated him in their last heavyweight fight.	Jun. 23
	The Boston Navy Yard is assigned the contract to build two of the 1,500-ton destroyers in the new Navy program.	Passage of the Glass-Steagall Banking Bill ushers in a new epoch in banking. It strengthens the Federal Reserve, as well as guarantees deposits.	Prof. C. Judson Herrick of the University of Chicago reveals that the number of connections between brain cells is a number so huge that it would take 30 full-sized books to print out that number.		Jun. 24
A destroyer takes U.S. diplomat Norman Davis to the *Amberjack II*, on which President Franklin Roosevelt is vacationing. The two will confer on economic matters.	Four Army fliers are killed when their bomber crashes into the James River in Virginia.	The small grain crop is endangered in the northwestern states. A drought and unusually high temperatures damage crops of oats, rye, and corn.	Sixty vessels containing germs of malaria, anthrax, and cholera are found buried in a Berlin garden and are destroyed. However, some were broken.	MGM announces that in the coming cinema season, it will produce 56 two-reel subjects, 46 feature films and 104 newsreels. . . . Japanese swimmer Shozo Makino breaks the world's 800-meter freestyle record with a time of 10 minutes, 8.6 seconds.	Jun. 25
President Franklin Roosevelt's schooner may be held up for days as fog maroons him at Roque Island, Maine. . . . Senator William E. Borah undergoes major surgery at Johns Hopkins.	In an interview, Secretary of State Cordell Hull says the economic conference must agree to end high embargoes and that the whole aim of the conference is to stimulate international trade.	Automobile output rises to the highest level of 1933. Chevrolet shows the sharpest increase.	Engineers devise the iconoscope, a human-like eye that may make the use of television in the home practical.	The first electronic pari-mutuel betting machine is unveiled at Arlington Park racetrack near Chicago.	Jun. 26
	Chrysler Motor Company is accused of evading the tariff on their cars manufactured in Canada, then shipped to England. Accusers say they do not meet the 50 percent empire content requirement.	Wheat makes huge gains at the Chicago Board of Trade; corn, oats, rye, and barley are also up.	Three flyers begin a search in Alaska for James Mattern, missing for 12 days...*The Jeller*, a Danish ship that will serve as a base for Col. Charles Lindbergh's exploration and mapping of an air route to Europe, sails for Greenland.	Singer Bing Crosby and his wife have a son, whom they name Gary. . . . Americans advance at the British tennis tournament at Wimbledon.	Jun. 27
Cotton textile manufacturers ban child labor in their mills, setting the minimum age of workers at 16.	As part of the Roosevelt administration's economy program, 5,000 technicians at arsenals across the country face layoffs.	Employment in the silk industry is up 15.2 percent in May over April, and it was 48 percent higher than last May.	Two hundred delegates at the congress of the International New Thought Alliance try out music therapy, which is said to cure pain and disease, as well as soothe mental and emotional disturbances. Several say it cured their headaches.	U.S. track stars gather in Chicago to compete in the U.S. title meet at Soldier Field.	Jun. 28
Canadians at Campobello Island greet President Franklin Roosevelt enthusiastically. It is the first time Roosevelt has visited his home there since he was carried out on a stretcher, a victim of infantile paralysis, which many thought would ruin his life.	Secretary of the Navy Claude Swanson outlines his naval policy, including building and operation of ship, aircraft, and personnel.	About 5,000 workers, members of the International Pocketbook Workers Union, go on strike, demanding better working conditions, a 40-hour week and no pay cuts.	The committee in London recalls the Mt. Everest climbing expedition, saying it is too dangerous due to heavy snowstorms and the danger of avalanches.	Actor Roscoe "Fatty" Arbuckle, who had starred in the Keystone comedies, dies. . . . Italian challenger Primo Carnera knocks out Jack Sharkey to become the heavyweight champion of the world.	Jun. 29
The widow of racketeer Jack "Legs" Diamond is murdered in her Brooklyn apartment. Police say Alice Diamond had been dead two days when they found her lying on the floor in her living room. She had said she was tired of protecting underworld figures.	Admiral William V. Pratt, Chief of Naval Operations, ends 47 years with the Navy as he retires. In tomorrow's ceremony, he will turn over his command to his successor, Admiral William Harrison Standley.	*Dun & Bradstreet, Inc.* says the recovery of business in the last three months is "doubtless without parallel in the history of the country."	The American Institute of Electrical Engineers hears from research engineer L.W. Schad about a system of heating homes that would use the heat of the human body as the principal source of indoor heat.	Augusto Rosso, Italian Ambassador to the United States, presents the Right Rev. James Edward Freeman, Bishop of Washington, with an ornately carved stone from a tomb on the Appian Way. It will be incorporated into the walls of the Cathedral of Sts. Peter and Paul.	Jun. 30
	Secretary of State Cordell Hull shocks London when he tells of President Franklin Roosevelt's rejection of the request by Britain and the gold bloc that the world should return to the gold standard as soon as practical and should check speculation in exchange.	The Miller-Bennett report confirms the crop damage in the west from the record heat and dry weather in June. The yield of wheat is predicted to be the lowest since 1896, corn the lowest since 1913, and oats since 1932. The aggregate crop of all grains is the smallest since 1903.	The ancient skeleton of a prehistoric rhinoceros is found in deposits of clay at Bellevue, near the French Riviera. Geologist Paul Goby believes it dates back about a million years.	Seven of America's best track and field stars sail for Europe on Wednesday for a competitive tour through six countries. . . . The opera *Arabella*, by Strauss-Hofmannsthal, premiers in Dresden.	Jul. 1

F	G	H	I	J
Includes elections, federal-state relations, civil rights and liberties, crime, the judiciary, education, healthcare, poverty, urban affairs, and population.	Includes formation and debate of U.S. foreign and defense policies, veterans affairs, and defense spending. (Relations with specific foreign countries are usually found under the region concerned.)	Includes business, labor, agriculture, taxation, transportation, consumer affairs, monetary and fiscal policy, natural resources, pollution, and accidents.	Includes worldwide scientific, medical, and technological developments, natural phenomena, U.S. weather, and natural disasters.	Includes the arts, religion, scholarship, communications media, sports, entertainment, fashions, fads, and social life.

	World Affairs	Europe	Africa & The Middle East	The Americas	Asia & The Pacific
Jul. 2	London financiers blame the United States for a split in the economic conference and think the failure of the conference to act is due to the U.S. reluctance to stabilize the dollar.	Russia frees the two Britons convicted there of being spies. The two engineers, William MacDonald and Leslie Thornton, leave for London and the embargoes end.		Puerto Rican Governor Robert Gore's speech, advocating the compulsory sharing of land for food crops, is held by some to be radical.	German Walter Miller and Swiss Arthur Gautschi are arrested in Manchuria, charged with being part of a group of five pirates who killed 10 people on the steamer *Chengan*. The others are already in captivity.
Jul. 3	The London Convention defines an aggressor nation under international law. Delegates from Turkey, Russia, Romania, Poland, Persia, Latvia, Estonia, and Afghanistan sign it.	The Dutch are unhappy with President Franklin Roosevelt's attitude toward gold-standard countries and fears it will wreck the World Economic Conference.	In discussing the tariff truce proposed by the Americans at the World Economic Conference, Abdul Wahab Pasha of Egypt says the truce would work to the advantage of the already protected United States.	New figures show Canadian immigration is down 39.3 percent in April and May, compared to those months last year.	The Soviet Union and Manchukuo are far from agreeing on a price for the Chinese Eastern Railway. The amount Russia is asking would be about $132.6 million, but Manchukuo is only willing to pay one-tenth of that.
Jul. 4	The British Empire wants to continue the World Economic Conference, and hopes that U.S. President Franklin Roosevelt will cooperate in revival attempts.	Chancellor Engelbert Dollfuss asks writers for the foreign press to make it clear that Austria is safe for travelers. He said small incidents have been treated sensationally by the press.		U.S. Marines in Brazil celebrate Fourth of July in Rio de Janeiro. The Marine Bugle Corps sounds reveille on the steps of the U.S. Embassy.	Mohandas Gandhi is sentenced to prison again.
Jul. 5	A committee of the Big Four wheat-growing nations still meets, but the United States doubts if European wheat-growing countries will join the pact, as Australia requires for its participation.	The Reich dissolves religious political parties in Germany, including the Catholic parties.	Artifacts found in a house unearthed in Palestine predate the house by centuries, branding the owners as antique collectors. The house is 2,700 years old, and the artifacts 1,000 years older than that.	The Bolivians blow up Paraguayan trenches for 1,200 feet around Fort Ayala, killing 1,000.	Manchukuo sees hope of being recognized by the Soviet Union if it completes the deal with Russia to buy the Chinese Eastern Railway.
Jul. 6	U.S. delegates at the World Economic Conference say they are willing to discuss any economic topic except the temporary stabilization of the dollar.	Nazis arrest two former Bavarian Cabinet members in Munich, charging them with talking against the Reich and Chancellor Adolf Hitler.		Cuban Secretary of War Gen. Alberto Herrera announces all political prisoners will be released. U.S. Ambassador Sumner Welles served as mediator.	
Jul. 7	Japan wants big tanks and guns. A document filed at the disarmament conference calls for 20-ton tanks rather than 16-ton, saying the topography of the Far East requires bigger tanks. It also wants 155mm guns instead of 115mm.		The French ship *Nicolas Paquet* is a total loss after going aground east of Tangier. The 26 passengers and 117 crewmembers survive. . . . France is concerned that unrest in Tunis, caused by economic problems, may cause a loss of allegiance to France.	The Cucuracha slide is sliding again in the Canal Zone, but canal traffic is not interrupted as a dipper dredge is removing the displaced soil.	Chinese Marshal Chiang Kai-shek claims a victory in the Kiangsi province, saying his troops have killed 3,000 Communists.
Jul. 8	Six nations agree to adhere to the gold standard against speculation. France, Italy, Holland, Switzerland, Belgium, and Luxemburg make the decision.	Austrian Minister of Justice Kurt von Schuschnigg confirms the rumor that Austria is considering revival of the death penalty. He says if martial law is ever necessary, that is the only penalty military courts could impose.		The Bolivians turn back a Paraguayan offensive with hand-to-hand fighting near Gondra in the Chaco.	A 1,700-year-old coin found at Mohanad, a village in south Bengal, proves India had gold coins in the second century.
Jul. 9	The League of Nations narcotics treaty goes into effect, limiting manufacture of these drugs to the legitimate medical and scientific needs of the world.	Berlin condemns the U.S. dollar policy, calling it inadvisable and impractical, but says artificially stabilized U.S. prices would not be internationally valid.	Archaeologist Richard Stillwell announces the finding of a beautiful mosaic floor in an ancient Corinthian temple.	Canada's annual Calgary Stampede opens in Alberta, featuring a huge parade, calf roping, bronco busting, chuckwagons and more.	Chinese bandits attack a convoy of 4,000 Koreans on their way to Manchuria. They kill or wound 32 Koreans and 3 Japanese guards.
Jul. 10	The 29th session of the Permanent Court of International Justice opens in The Hague.	Floods in Czechoslovakia render 3,000 homeless. The village of Upla at the foot of the Carpathian Mountains is almost completely under water.		Representatives from the United States, Canada, Mexico, Costa Rica, Cuba, El Salvador, Guatemala, Honduras, and Nicaragua meet in Mexico for the first North and Central American Regional Radio Conference.	Japan plans to bring its navy up to full strength under the London Treaty. The cost will be about $156 million.

A	B	C	D	E
Includes developments that affect more than one world region, international organizations, and important meetings of world leaders.	Includes all domestic and regional developments in Europe, including the Soviet Union.	Includes all domestic and regional developments in Africa and the Middle East.	Includes all domestic and regional developments in Latin America, the Caribbean, and Canada.	Includes all domestic and regional developments in Asian and Pacific nations (and colonies).

U.S. Politics & Social Issues	U.S. Foreign Policy & Defense	Economics & Great Depression	Science, Technology & Nature	Culture, Leisure & Lifestyle	
First Lady Eleanor Roosevelt flies home from her trip to Campobello Island. She will be at the White House for two days, then go to New York to see son Franklin, Jr., off on a school trip to Europe.	Allen Dulles, U.S. delegate to the disarmament conference, returns and says he believes the conference will be successful.	Damage to grain crops is said to be worldwide. Experts believe that the surplus of grain will be depleted if there are two or three years like this.	Frank Lutz, director of the department of insect life at the American Museum of Natural History, discovers that bees are able to distinguish small intricate patterns in ultraviolet colors, as well as most of the colors we see.	United Artist Studio's Samuel Goldwyn starts a movement to employ actors and actresses who have been excluded from the German film industry.	Jul. 2
	The military forces of the Army, Navy, and Marines join in the activities at the 1933 National Air Races at Los Angeles. Their flying maneuvers thrill the crowd.	President Franklin Roosevelt condemns negotiators at the World Economic Conference for focusing on stabilizing U.S. currency.... Auto retail sales bounce back sharply, as the output of automobiles is the highest of any month in the last two years.	Cold weather hits the East Coast, with snow flurries reported in Kane, Pa., and a record-breaking low of 55°F for this date in New York City.	The crowd at the Chicago World's Fair breaks the previous one-day record, as over 200,000 attend. A cool day and the fact that it was Jewish Day bring out more people.	Jul. 3
	President Franklin Roosevelt asks U.S. representatives at the World Economic Conference to try to keep the conference alive until the most important problems have been solved.	As a result of the administration's economy program, 8,000 federal employees have lost their jobs. Hundreds of them are taken on by new agencies set up to fight the Depression.... Salmon fishermen in Alaska end their strike just in time for the salmon season, which starts tomorrow. Local buyers agree to a price nearly three times as high as the lowest price paid last season.	Work begins on building the Oakland Bay Bridge in California.	Dark Secret beats Kerry Patch by a neck at the historic Brooklyn Handicap horse race at Aqueduct. Dark Secret is a son of Kentucky Derby winner Flying Ebony.	Jul. 4
School board elections in Kentucky leave eight dead in three different districts, due to arguments over whether or not the polls are already closed.	U.S. Special Ambassador Norman Davis cancels his plans to sail for Europe. He will meet with President Franklin Roosevelt in Washington before returning to Europe.	Chinch bugs ravage the corn crop in the Midwest, causing prices of corn to soar. In Iowa alone, 20 million to 25 million bushels are lost.	Arno B. Cammerer is appointed to head the National Parks System. Cammerer will begin his duties on August 9.		Jul. 5
	Canadian Prime Minister Richard Bennett gives Secretary of State Cordell Hull strong backing as he speaks to the importance of continuing the economic conference.	According to Dun & Bradstreet, the number of business failures for June is the smallest number since 1929.	Ahto Walter sails a 26-foot sloop from Gambia, on the coast of West Africa, to New York in 50 days, beating the British cutter Enterprise, which left on the 4,000-mile journey at the same time.... Lincoln Ellsworth embarks on his journey to New Zealand, where he will prepare for his flight of exploration to the South Polar region.	In the first All-Star Baseball Game in Chicago, the American League beats the National League, 4–2, with the help of a home run by Babe Ruth.	Jul. 6
	President Franklin Roosevelt drafts a message for the World Economic Conference, setting forth the U.S. position. Roosevelt has a long conference with advisers, including U.S Special Ambassador Norman Davis, before preparing the statement. Some experts fear that President Roosevelt's stand at the conference will cause the United States to lose European trade and may serve to unite 15 nations against the United States.	The British pound rises, while the U.S. dollar continues its downward plunge, ending at 70 percent of its former gold value.	The U.S. Coast Guard cutter Northland receives word that round-the-world flyer James Mattern is safe in a small Siberian trading post 2,600 miles north of Vladivostok.	American tennis star Ellsworth Vines loses the finals of the men's singles at Wimbledon to Australian star Jack Crawford in a hard-fought match.	Jul. 7
Henry Morgenthau, Jr., of the Farm Credit Administration says the farm mortgage plan has been tested in Wisconsin to his satisfaction and will soon be extended to other states.	Secretary of State Cordell Hull has quiet talks with representatives of several countries as he tries to put together a program that does not only represent U.S. policy. The main goal is to raise the world price level.... Russia has no objections to the U.S. Coast Guard sending a boat to pick up James Mattern from the isolated village where his plane crashed.	William Taylor, vice president of the Valley Camp Coal Company, proposes a code in the bituminous coal industry designed to put 150,000 men back to work at $4 per day for five six-hour days per week.		American Helen Wills Moody retains her title as Wimbledon Women's Singles Champion by defeating Dorothy Round of Great Britain.	Jul. 8
	The Navy Department estimates that the naval construction approved under the Industrial Recovery Act will provide more than 2,430,000 "man-weeks" of employment.	The U.S. delegation to the World Economic Conference wants a year's extension on the tariff truce, giving the countries involved more time to come up with other options.... President Franklin Roosevelt signs the textile code, establishing a 40-hour workweek, abolishing child labor, and setting a minimum wage of $13 per week in the north and $12 per week in the south.	American archaeologist Arthur Kingsley Porter drowns off the coast of Ireland near Donegal, when his boat overturns in a storm.	Rev. Dr. W. Russell Bowie recommends printing the Bible attractively and binding it into 56-volume editions. He believes that would make it more attractive and readable to the modern public.	Jul. 9
President Franklin Roosevelt promises Senator Royal S. Copeland he will do everything he can to help in the war on racketeering. He puts all government facilities at Copeland's disposal.	The U.S. delegation to the World Economic Conference decides to propose an international policy of higher wages and a shorter workweek.	The committee drafting a code for coal workers is deadlocked, but the miners and operators will continue to meet. Agreement on wages seems near.	Flyer James Mattern's backers work to find a plane in which he can finish his round-the-world trip.... Eastchester Township, N.Y., pioneers the first police radio system.	Actress Tallulah Bankhead announces she will star in the Broadway play, Jezebel.... Fourteen large packing cases from Nairobi, East Africa, arrive at the American Museum of Natural History, sent by Alfred J. Klein. Included are birds, animal skins, and trees.	Jul. 10

F	G	H	I	J
Includes elections, federal-state relations, civil rights and liberties, crime, the judiciary, education, healthcare, poverty, urban affairs, and population.	Includes formation and debate of U.S. foreign and defense policies, veterans affairs, and defense spending. (Relations with specific foreign countries are usually found under the region concerned.)	Includes business, labor, agriculture, taxation, transportation, consumer affairs, monetary and fiscal policy, natural resources, pollution, and accidents.	Includes worldwide scientific, medical, and technological developments, natural phenomena, U.S. weather, and natural disasters.	Includes the arts, religion, scholarship, communications media, sports, entertainment, fashions, fads, and social life.

	World Affairs	Europe	Africa & The Middle East	The Americas	Asia & The Pacific
Jul. 11	The economic parley compromises and decides on limited discussion of monetary matters and indebtedness.	The Nazis confiscate a motorboat and a yacht belonging to Prof. Albert Einstein. They say there was a plot to smuggle the boats out of the country.	Abyssinian Emperor Haile Selassie sends his son-in-law, Prince Ras Deste Demtu, to return the U.S. Special Mission's visit to Abyssinia in 1930.	Paraguay reports Bolivians rush reinforcements to their troops near Fort Ayala in the Chaco. They believe Bolivia is reorganizing its troops for another attempt to capture the fort. . . . A crowd in Halifax, Nova Scotia, enthusiastically greets Col. Charles Lindbergh and his wife upon their arrival there. They will spend the night, but he refuses to say where they will go next.	Japanese arrest 49 in raids on superpatriotic societies. The government believes they were plotting a fascist coup and the assassination of some government leaders.
Jul. 12		French manufacturers are concerned about their government abandoning quota restrictions on imports, even though raising tariffs makes them unnecessary.			Four Japanese planes bomb Dolon Nor, on the Jehol-Chahar border. Reports say Gen. Feng declares himself "the people's anti-Japanese forces," declaring he will recapture Jehol from the Japanese.
Jul. 13	Even though the World Economic Conference is faltering, the committees continue their discussions.	A new Nazi decree forces employees throughout the Reich to sign a declaration that they are not of Jewish lineage.	Palestine is borrowing about $9.5 million from England to develop works such as deepening the Haifa Harbor and improving Jerusalem's water supply.	After four days of fighting in the Chaco last week, there are 3,000 dead and 12,000 other casualties. Bolivia says it will file a complaint with the League of Nations against Paraguay.	
Jul. 14	The League of Nations calls for a truce between Paraguay and Bolivia in the Chaco. Both armies are told to adopt a purely defensive attitude. A commission will go to the scene in August.	France celebrates Bastille Day with an air show featuring troops parading, 100 planes, and people dancing in the streets. . . . The Nazi party becomes the only legal political party in Germany.	Desert life in Arabia may be transformed, as King Ibn Saud grants an oil concession to the Standard Oil Company of California.	U.S. Chargé d'Affaires Walter Thurston presents the final proposal for a trade agreement between the United States and Brazil at the Brazilian Foreign Office.	A Japanese group that calls itself the Sacred Warriors planned to steal guns and massacre the Japanese Cabinet, then exterminate bankers, capitalists, and financiers.
Jul. 15	The Four-Power Pact is signed by Italy, Germany, France, and Great Britain.	A movement is afoot in Paris to suppress France's Devil's Island penal colony in French Guiana.	An Egyptian mob of Muslims attacks two Roman Catholic nuns at Kafr el Zayat as they return home after taking two Muslim children to the railway station.		Mohandas Gandhi opens the All-India Congress in Poona.
Jul. 16	Great Britain suggests that when and if the economic parley resumes, it should do so in Washington. U.S. delegates are against the idea.	Italy believes the countries on the gold standard will be able to remain on it and thinks that although the U.S. is having a momentary reawakening of confidence, it will have problems down the road.		The Paraguayans say they completely wiped out Fort Gondra and began an attack on Fort Alihuata, killing 450 and injuring another 550. The Bolivians deny the report.	Manila police estimate 60,000 Filipinos join in a parade urging independence on the eve of the opening of the annual 100-day legislative session.
Jul. 17	Arthur Henderson, president of the disarmament conference, discusses disarmament in various European capitals. He has been to Paris and Rome and is now in Berlin.	Germany is building a giant air ship, twice as big as the *Graf Zeppelin*. The huge ship will have 26 cabins, a dining room, smoking room, social room, and reading and writing room.		The Bolivians report they have turned back seven Paraguayan attacks since July 11.	A spokesman for the Japanese army says Gen. Feng's presence in Dolon Nor is contrary to the spirit of the Tangku truce and threatens action if Feng does not withdraw his forces.
Jul. 18	Secretary of State Cordell Hull is scheduled to speak to the World Economic Conference before it adjourns on July 27. He will stress that it is not ending, but just starting a continuing job of solving international difficulties.	U.S. Ambassador Claude Bowers is scheduled to talk to Spanish Premier Manuel Azana about five Americans held prisoner in Majorca.	Palestine provides a refuge for the 4,000 German Jews who have immigrated there in the past three months. About half of them are already self-supporting.	The Gran Chaco area of Argentina has what is believed to be the first snowfall ever. The temperature is down to 21°F.	Mohandas Gandhi announces the temporary cessation of mass civil disobedience in India. Individual civil disobedience will be pursued now.
Jul. 19		Reports say Irish President Eamon de Valera may be willing to compromise with Great Britain, so an end to the tariff war may be in sight.		Canada's exports to the British Empire last month are up 46 percent over its exports in June 1932.	
Jul. 20	German Chancellor Adolf Hitler meets in Munich with Arthur Henderson, president of the World Disarmament Conference, for informal discussions. Henderson hopes to pave the way for a meeting between Hitler and Premier Edouard Daladier of France.	The Nazi government signs a Concordat with the Vatican, defining the Catholic Church's position in Germany. Spain's Prime Minister Manuel Azana releases five Americans on bail after talking to U.S. Ambassador Claude Bowers.	Both Egypt and South Africa sharply curtail trade with Germany in protest of the Reich's treatment of Jews.	Nicaragua names its baseball teams after teams in the U.S. major leagues, and Nicaraguan newspapers devote a good deal of space to their idol, Babe Ruth.	Manuel Roxas loses the Speakership of the House of Representatives in the Philippines because he backs the Hawes Act for independence.

A	B	C	D	E
Includes developments that affect more than one world region, international organizations, and important meetings of world leaders.	Includes all domestic and regional developments in Europe, including the Soviet Union.	Includes all domestic and regional developments in Africa and the Middle East.	Includes all domestic and regional developments in Latin America, the Caribbean, and Canada.	Includes all domestic and regional developments in Asian and Pacific nations (and colonies).

U.S. Politics & Social Issues	U.S. Foreign Policy & Defense	Economics & Great Depression	Science, Technology & Nature	Culture, Leisure & Lifestyle	
Workers at Civilian Conservation Corps forest camps across the country will hear President Franklin Roosevelt via a nationwide radio hookup.	Secretary of State Cordell Hull works on a five-year recovery program to present to the World Economic Conference in London.	Farm Loan Commissioner Albert Goss orders interest rates on loans through the Federal Land Bank.	James Mattern backer H.B. Jameson says Pan American Airlines offers to send a seaplane from Fairbanks, Alaska, to Anadyr, Siberia, so Mattern can finish his round-the-world solo flight.		Jul. 11
	The fourth group of Gold Star Mothers sails on the *President Harding* for their pilgrimage to France, where their sons were killed. . . . President Franklin Roosevelt announces that the United States is ready to begin trade talks with several South American countries. Argentina, Brazil, and Colombia have already been contacted.	The electrical manufacturing industry and the shipbuilding industry have filed codes for their respective industries.		Musical-comedy actor Fred Astaire marries New York socialite Phyllis Livingston Potter. They delayed marrying until she got full custody of her four-year-old son.	Jul. 12
Due to the number of recent kidnappings, the Secret Service has extended its services to guard the four Roosevelt grandchildren. No threats have been received, however.	Rep. David J. Lewis urges the United States to join both the League of Nations and the World Court.	Chrysler sales increase so much that it sells as many cars in the first six months of 1933 as it did in the whole year of 1932.	A new elevator in the RCA Building can move 1,400 feet in one minute. It can go from the first to the 61st floor in 37.1 seconds and is supposed to be the fastest passenger elevator.		Jul. 13
Elliot Roosevelt, second son of the President, files for divorce in Nevada, charging his wife, the former Elizabeth Donner, of "extreme cruelty." The couple has an infant son, William Donner Roosevelt.		The International Ladies' Garment Workers' Union criticizes the proposed code for the clothing industry. They say a 40-hour week is too long and wages are much lower than the union feels is fair.	After 23 years of research on the role heredity plays in cancer, Maud Slye determines that susceptibility to cancer is carried in a single gene.	Fifteen-year-old Ralph Flanagan breaks Buster Crabbe's one-mile record at the National AAU outdoor swimming championships in Chicago.	Jul. 14
Arguments are still being advanced both for and against recognition of Russia, but the U.S. relations with that country have improved in the past month.		The price of bread increases as a tax of $1.38 is levied on each barrel of flour. . . . William Green, president of the AFL, believes the steel industry's code provides for too long a workweek and too low wages.	American aviator Wiley Post begins his solo flight around the world. . . . A crowd of 100,000 people greets Balbo's Italian Air Armada as the first of their huge seaplanes lands on Lake Michigan. Covering 6,100 miles in 47 hours and 52 minutes, they finish the greatest mass flight in aviation history.		Jul. 15
Alabama, Arkansas, and Tennessee are believed to be leaning toward voting for the repeal of Prohibition.	President Franklin Roosevelt's secretary, Louis Henry Howe, says if the President's disarmament suggestions are adopted, they will save the world more than $1 billion a year.	Henry Stehli, head of the silk and rayon weavers' planning board of the Silk Association of America, is pleased that President Franklin Roosevelt has brought silk workers under the textile code, saying it will put at least 20,000 back to work.	American aviator Wiley Post is the first to fly nonstop from New York to Berlin.	Dorothy Duggan of Greenwich, Conn., sets three world records in archery in a tournament in Westchester County, N.Y.	Jul. 16
The New Deal is in effect, as 1 million people either get higher wages or a shorter workweek.		Crude rubber and cocoa make large advances in the stock market, with all staples up and many cash prices the highest they have been all year.	Earle S. Draper, presidential aide, says the main purpose of the Tennessee Valley Authority is to conserve natural resources in the area, and says the government will avoid competition with existing power companies.	Billy Rose announces his new revue, starring Fannie Brice and Phil Baker, will open in Detroit October 1, then go to Chicago and New York.	Jul. 17
Attorney General Homer Cummings presides over the Executive Council as it meets to coordinate the activities of the recovery agencies and eliminate any that overlap.	There is a positive outlook for a Pan-American alliance. Chile and Uruguay formally apply to join in the negotiations.	In an address to the Governors' Conference in San Francisco, President Franklin Roosevelt plans to outline his plans for the Recovery Act. . . . Secretary of the Interior Harold Ickes already sees the effects of funds being put into the Public Works Administration as part of the National Recovery Act. He says thousands are already at work building needed roads.			Jul. 18
The National Child Labor Committee asks that all codes include a child labor clause, barring workers under 16 years of age. . . . Acting Secretary of State William Phillips hosts Prince Ras Deste Demtu of Ethiopia at a dinner. President Franklin Roosevelt cancels a planned luncheon with him because of illness.	Reports that a treaty with Japan is being held up by a Far East Monroe Doctrine are emphatically denied by Secretary of State Cordell Hull, who says he has heard of no treaty negotiations.	Financier J.P. Morgan arrives in London, where he will visit his friend, Monthagu Norman, governor of the Bank of England. He says they may discuss currency stabilization.	Fog prevents Col. Charles Lindbergh from making any survey flights over Labrador in connection with his aerial mapping project.	Marlene Dietrich stars in a new version of *The Song of Songs*. It is said to be a beautiful film, although drastically revised from the original.	Jul. 19
The telegram President Franklin Roosevelt sends to the U.S. Davis Cup team provides great inspiration.	News from Paris holds that Secretary of State Cordell Hull tries to negotiate continuance of the tariff truce, while Senator Key Pittman advocates a return to the gold standard.	President Franklin Roosevelt urges all employers in business and industry to voluntarily meet the minimum wage and workweek guidelines set up in the National Industrial Recovery Act.	When Rear Admiral Richard E. Byrd heads for the South Pole, he will take a duplicate of the cosmic ray "trap" used in Prof. Arthur Compton's worldwide cosmic ray study. A trained physicist will go along to operate the equipment.	Tennis player Helen Wills Moody returns to the United States after retaining her title at Wimbledon. She expects the United States to win both the Davis Cup and the Wightman Cup.	Jul. 20

F	G	H	I	J
Includes elections, federal-state relations, civil rights and liberties, crime, the judiciary, education, healthcare, poverty, urban affairs, and population.	*Includes formation and debate of U.S. foreign and defense policies, veterans affairs, and defense spending. (Relations with specific foreign countries are usually found under the region concerned.)*	*Includes business, labor, agriculture, taxation, transportation, consumer affairs, monetary and fiscal policy, natural resources, pollution, and accidents.*	*Includes worldwide scientific, medical, and technological developments, natural phenomena, U.S. weather, and natural disasters.*	*Includes the arts, religion, scholarship, communications media, sports, entertainment, fashions, fads, and social life.*

	World Affairs	Europe	Africa & The Middle East	The Americas	Asia & The Pacific
Jul. 21	The League of Nations insures the lives of the three men on the Chaco commission for $54,000 each. . . . U.S. Secretary of State Cordell Hull is slated to present a plea to the World Economic Conference at its final session. He will ask international cooperation in raising prices.	A crowd of hundreds of Jews threatens Isaac Angel, a toy importer in London, for importing toys from Nazi Germany. Angel sends back the goods, which he had ordered before the ban on Nazi imports.	Haifa Harbor opens in Palestine.	Argentine President Agustin Justo urges farmers to hold back corn under the financing plan of the Bank of the Nation. Government agents will teach the farmers to prepare corn for long storage.	The Nanking government urges military leaders in Peiping to let up the pressure on Gen. Feng and to try to come to an amicable agreement with him. Feng sends a new peace plan to Peiping.
Jul. 22	The World Economic Conference proves that 61 nations are not ready to make the concessions necessary to come up with an international economic plan.	Romania prohibits the Makkabi, the Jewish Olympic Games, scheduled to open there on August 30. Instead they will begin in Prague, Czechoslovakia, on August 25.	The president of the Suez Canal Company denies British allegations that they are losing business due to high tolls on the canal.	The Canadian government issues new regulations to protect the walrus, its largest mammal. No one may kill a walrus except for food for himself, his family, and his dog team. Even natives are limited to seven walrus a year.	Gen. Feng evacuates Dolon Nor, and asks the government to make it a demilitarized zone.
Jul. 23	Delegates hope the negotiators from the wheat-growing nations can come to a definite agreement before the World Economic Conference ends on Thursday.	Many fascists are arrested in Spain for passing out handbills designed to incite people to riot.	A large dam will be built in Ethiopia to control the headwaters of the Blue Nile. Egypt and Sudan will also profit from the dam, as water will be made available to irrigate thousands of acres there.	Five hundred conservatives and Communists demonstrate in Ecuador, calling for the resignation of President Martinez Mera. The police disperse them easily.	Tokyo police arrest 16 rural "patriots" who planned a demonstration and possible terrorism in the city.
Jul. 24	The League of Nations is unable to settle the Chaco dispute, and turns it back to the ABC-Peru group for arbitration. Bolivia refuses to cease hostilities until Paraguay agrees to negotiate.	The Austrian government charges the Nazis helped Baron Werner von Alversleben after he shot Tyrol Security Director Dr. Richard Steidle. Munich police refused to arrest him, and they gave him a false passport.		The Brazilian state Rio Grande do Sul will finish paying off its foreign debt by the end of the year if unforeseen circumstances do not occur. . . . President Franklin Roosevelt telegraphs the head of the Pan-American Society, hailing Simon Bolivar as a man who loved peace. A celebration of the 150th anniversary of Bolivar's birth is held in Central Park in New York.	Japanese police question African-American author James Langston Hughes for six hours, and "suggest" he leave Japan immediately. He books passage on the next ship. They suspect him of being a Communist.
Jul. 25	The British Parliament hears a government proposal for a trade parley in India among India, Japan, and Great Britain.	Recent clashes in The Hague between Dutch fascists and Communists or between fascists and socialists leave several injured.		The Silver Java Pacific Line in Canada is awarded the subsidy for a shipping line that runs from Canada to South Africa.	
Jul. 26	Both Bolivia and Paraguay ask the League of Nations to transfer negotiations on the Chaco dispute back to the ABC-Peru group.			A serious political crisis is reported in the state of Sao Paulo in Brazil. Reports say President Getulio Vargas removes Gen. Waldomiro Lima as Federal Interventor, but Lima refuses to leave office.	The Japanese government studies nine small islands between French Indo-China and the Philippines, with the idea of disputing French ownership.
Jul. 27	Secretary of State Cordell Hull and the rest of the U.S. delegation to the World Economic Conference leave London with no farewell from British officials.	Former French premier Edouard Herriot praises U.S. President Franklin Roosevelt's radio address on recovery and says France should cooperate with the United States.	The Trans-Jordanian and Saudi governments end years of conflict by signing a Treaty of Friendship. . . . Abyssinian Prince Ras Deste Demtu says he would like to build a "fun park" in Ethiopia.	Mexico, rated second in the world in silver production, awaits further details on the silver agreement reached at the World Economic Conference before deciding whether to join. Much depends on the world price that is set.	China and Japan are two of France's biggest customers for arms this year. Japan spends 19.7 million francs on mounted arms and 7 million francs on cartridges. China is the largest customer, purchasing 40 percent of France's exported mounted arms and cartridges.
Jul. 28	Police executives from important cities in Europe, Canada, and the United States meet and establish an international police force. They tentatively plan offices in Vienna and Washington.	While Austrian Security Minister Maj. Emil Fey is speaking in Graz, a large tear-gas bomb explodes, injuring five people.			Field Marshal Nobuyoshi Muto, Japan's chieftain in Manchuria, dies suddenly of jaundice. Muto directed the recent campaign in Jehol and north China.
Jul. 29	The total expense to all nations for the World Economic Conference in London is about $5 million, including entertainment.	The British House of Commons rushes a measure whereby Prof. Albert Einstein will become a naturalized British citizen. Although a five-year residence is usually required, Einstein will be allowed citizenship in three months.		Mexico is adding 15 gunboats, launches, and transports to its navy. The ships will be built in Spain.	According to a Tokyo newspaper, Japan is reorganizing and reinforcing its troops in Manchuria. Three separate forces will guard different areas of the railroad.
Jul. 30	Dr. Hjalmar Schact, president of the Reichsbank, considers the economic parley a failure and says from now on, Germany will negotiate with only those nations that are directly involved.	Austrian Minister of Commerce Friedrich Stockinger arrives in Budapest for a three-day trade conference with Premier Julius Goemboes and his aides.		For the first time in 20 years, Canada gets a loan from England. Since the beginning of the World War, it has borrowed from the United States.	Missionaries from the Catholic Foreign Missionary Society of America send a group of missionaries to the Philippines, Japan, Korea, Manchuria, and south China.
Jul. 31		Many Austrian officials are on the list of 4,800 Nazi party members that was obtained by the Vienna police.		Argentina has 333,997 unemployed, a jump of 115,000 since January 1932.	Chinese fishermen are ordered to leave seven small islands that France has just annexed between the Philippines and French Indo-China.

A	B	C	D	E
Includes developments that affect more than one world region, international organizations, and important meetings of world leaders.	Includes all domestic and regional developments in Europe, including the Soviet Union.	Includes all domestic and regional developments in Africa and the Middle East.	Includes all domestic and regional developments in Latin America, the Caribbean, and Canada.	Includes all domestic and regional developments in Asian and Pacific nations (and colonies).

U.S. Politics & Social Issues	U.S. Foreign Policy & Defense	Economics & Great Depression	Science, Technology & Nature	Culture, Leisure & Lifestyle	
President Franklin Roosevelt approves a new list of projects for his Public Works program. Aides say enough funds have been allotted to employ every jobless man in the country for one week.		Chrysler raises wages 10 percent, effective July 31. About 40,000 workers are affected.	Buckminster Fuller's "Dymaxion," a new three-wheeled automobile shaped like a bullet, can go 70 miles per hour.		Jul. 21
Albert Bates and "Machine-Gun" Kelly kidnap Oklahoma oilman Charles Urschel and demand $200,000 ransom.	West Point appoints Rev. Roscoe Thornton Foust as chaplain of the United States Military Academy.	Both imports and exports increase in June, but imports total more. Most are raw materials used in manufacturing.	Wiley Post becomes the first aviator to complete a solo round-the-world flight. It took seven days, 18 hours, and 45 minutes.	The U.S. bridge team, led by Ely Culbertson, wins the Schwab Trophy in London, beating the British team.	Jul. 22
	Secretary of State Cordell Hull favors setting a definite date to reconvene the World Economic Conference, preferably no later than early November.	Employers and workers in the garment industry cannot agree on a code. They are deadlocked on the subject of wages, and negotiations end after a four-day session in Washington fails to produce an agreement. . . . Wheat farmers will receive bonuses totaling $90 million this fall for curtailing their wheat production.		The U.S. track team that is traveling in Europe wins every event in a meet against the Sundsvall Athletic Club in Sundsvall, Sweden.	Jul. 23
Judge Edward F. Hanify turns down Kenneth Buck's request for a new trial in the kidnapping of 10-year-old Peggy McMath. Buck is serving a 25-year sentence, but says his confession should not have been admitted at the trial.		In a radio speech, President Franklin Roosevelt makes a direct appeal to the country's 5 million employers to agree to his "blanket code" proposal so that 6 million people can be put back to work. The code reduces working hours and raises wages.	Sir Arthur Smith Woodward, British anthropologist, believes the Garden of Eden, where human life began, was located somewhere in East Africa.		Jul. 24
President Franklin Roosevelt receives more than 10,000 messages, pledging support to his blanket code for higher wages and shorter hours.	The National Recovery Administration has not yet approved the shipbuilders' code on the eve of bids opening for the largest naval building program in history.	The Chicago & Northwestern Railroad asks approval from the Interstate Commerce Commission for a $3,863,000 loan it wants from the Reconstruction Finance Corporation.	New York City reports 31 cases of typhoid fever in the past week, and 6 are fatal. Doctors say the people were infected by bathing in polluted water or eating clams or mussels dug from unapproved sources.	Movie production runs at about 50–60 percent of normal, as movie industry sound technicians strike. Only 2 of the 794 cameramen in the union are working.	Jul. 25
	Coast Guard boats capture a rum boat, the Oblay, after a chase and a fire. A tracer bullet from a Coast Guard boat sets the craft ablaze. After the fire is doused, the boat is confiscated and the liquor unloaded.	The National Automobile Chamber of Commerce, representing 42 companies, has its code nearly ready and will raise wages for 200,000 workers on August 1. The Ford Motor Company is not included.	Crowds honor flier Wiley Post with a ticker tape parade down Broadway in New York. He then flies to Washington, where President Franklin Roosevelt praises his accomplishment.	Rogers Hornsby, formerly a player for the Cardinals, is signed to manage the St. Louis Browns. He plans to be a playing manager and to build a competitive ball club.	Jul. 26
A granite headstone is placed on the grave of former president Calvin Coolidge. It is simply inscribed with the words, "Calvin Coolidge—1872–1933" and bears the U.S. coat of arms.		Federal Administrator Henry Hopkins urges relief administrators in all states to address the problem of the transient unemployed. He will provide federal unemployment relief funds to aid transients.	Austrian geologist Prof. Bruno Sander believes one can reconstruct the movements of the forces that built the mountains by studying the crystalline structure of the rocks in the mountain.	The New York Giants defeat the Brooklyn Dodgers to pull five games ahead of the second-place Chicago Cubs in the National League pennant race.	Jul. 27
In a message to Young Democrats, President Franklin Roosevelt challenges youths to help in the drive for national recovery.	President Franklin Roosevelt approves the promotion of two members of the Naval Medical Corps to Rear Admiral. Capt. Middleton Elliott and Capt. James Pryor receive promotions.	The National Automobile Chamber of Commerce announces approval of its wage-work code. It provides a 35-hour week and a wage of 40–43 cents per day.	Dutch astronomer Willem de Sitter changes his ideas on the expansion of the universe. He now believes the galaxies were compressed into a smaller space, then separated a few billion years ago.	Singer Rudy Vallee receives the first singing telegram for his birthday. . . . The NFL divides into two divisions, each with five teams.	Jul. 28
Attorney General Home Cummings appoints J. Edgar Hoover head of the new Division of Investigation, which President Franklin Roosevelt created. It will combine the present bureaus of investigation, Prohibition, and identification. . . . Senator William Borah leaves Johns Hopkins Hospital.		Secretary of the Interior Harold Ickes announces that the Cabinet Advisory Board has found a way to advance money for road-building projects to states that are "financially embarrassed."	Dr. Karl G. Zwick of Cincinnati warns of the dangers of sunburn, saying it can lead to skin cancer. He says people often think the spots are warts and do not get treatment.	At least 200 thoroughbreds competing in races on U.S. tracks in the last eight months were doped, according to the Federal Narcotics Commission. Seven horse handlers are arrested at Chicago's Arlington Park. . . . A new book, Congo Solo, relates the adventures of author Emily Hahn on her trip to the Belgian Congo.	Jul. 29
It is learned that Charles "Pretty Boy" Floyd plotted to kidnap a Hollywood actress from her home in Malibu Friday night and fly her to a remote island in Mexico. He expected her producer to pay $500,000 ransom.		Checks totaling about $6 million go out to about 300,000 people named to receive allotments from members of the Civilian Conservation Corps.	A tropical storm in Florida does serious damage to the citrus crops. Damages are estimated at $1 million.	Washington, D.C., sees a revival of bicycle riding. The bicycle craze is believed to have come from Hollywood, where it is quite a fad.	Jul. 30
Farm Act Administrator George Peek and Secretary of Agriculture Henry Wallace issue a joint statement asking farmers to support the NRA.	Martial law is declared in New Orleans to protect the grand jury in a case of election fraud.	The nationwide chain grocery store, the A&P, puts its code into effect. It employs 90,000 workers and expects to hire thousands more in the next few months.	Dr. William Beebe returns from the Gulf of Panama with nearly 40 varieties of fish hitherto unknown to scientists.		Jul. 31

F	G	H	I	J
Includes elections, federal-state relations, civil rights and liberties, crime, the judiciary, education, healthcare, poverty, urban affairs, and population.	Includes formation and debate of U.S. foreign and defense policies, veterans affairs, and defense spending. (Relations with specific foreign countries are usually found under the region concerned.)	Includes business, labor, agriculture, taxation, transportation, consumer affairs, monetary and fiscal policy, natural resources, pollution, and accidents.	Includes worldwide scientific, medical, and technological developments, natural phenomena, U.S. weather, and natural disasters.	Includes the arts, religion, scholarship, communications media, sports, entertainment, fashions, fads, and social life.

	World Affairs	Europe	Africa & The Middle East	The Americas	Asia & The Pacific
Aug. 1		The death penalty is declared for anti-fascists in Germany.	The Spanish government works to rescue 300 Spanish soldiers they believe have been held prisoner by the Moors in the Sahara since 1921.	An explosion rocks Managua, Nicaragua, as the government arsenal blows up. Several buildings are destroyed, but no deaths are reported.	The British government arrests Mohandas Gandhi when the All-India Congress votes to resume the civil disobedience campaign. They sentence him to 12 months in prison.
Aug. 2	Sir Robert Baden-Powell, founder of the Boy Scouts, speaks at the fourth annual Boy Scout Jamboree in Budapest to 30,000 Boy Scouts from 53 countries.	Poland and Danzig sign a pact guaranteeing fair treatment for Poles in Danzig.	Sir Graham John Bower dies in London. Bower served as imperial secretary to the High Commissioner for South Africa, then was Colonial Secretary of Mauritius.	The entire country of Nicaragua is under martial law after the explosion that destroys most of the government's ammunition.	For the second night, British Royal Air Force planes bomb a Kotkai village in India. The Indian government believes tribesmen there are sheltering the pretender to the Afghan throne.
Aug. 3	Argentina and Chile reject the League of Nations proposal for Chaco peace negotiations, but say if the League hands the matter back to the ABC-Peru group they are willing to mediate.	The Third Reich's execution choice is now the hangman's axe. Hanging or shooting will be permitted only by court order.	The Spanish newspaper *La Voz* reports the 350 Spanish soldiers missing since 1921 have been found in Morocco.	A general transportation strike in Cuba appears imminent, as railway workers prepare to join bus and taxi drivers and streetcar conductors and motormen.	A Chinese force revolts, looting the villages of Yaohsien and Sansui, and raising a Communist flag above them. The troops kill 156 and capture 64, whom they hold for ransom.
Aug. 4	Henry Morgenthau, U.S. delegate to the wheat parley, tells President Franklin Roosevelt he believes war is imminent, as Europe is "bristling with arms" and seems to have no interest in peace.	Austria arrests five German newspapermen for allegedly writing articles attacking the Austrian government.		Cuban President Gerardo Machado warns he will return the country to martial law if the transportation strike and other strikes in Cuba do not end.	Gandhi is released from jail, but is sent back in an hour because he refuses to leave Yerovda.... As part of a new defense plan, Australia places 9.2-inch guns in strategic places along the coast.
Aug. 5	U.S. Secretary of State Cordell Hull denies that the World Economic Conference has failed and believes if such a conference had been held 20 years ago, it could have averted the World War.	The French and British Ambassadors in Berlin object to German planes dropping leaflets criticizing Chancellor Engelbert Dollfuss in Austria, saying that is contrary to the Four-Powers Pact.		Canada's Royal Canadian Mounted Police celebrate their 60th anniversary. The force, which began with 300 men in 1973, now consists of 2,500 officers and men.	Manchukuo's navy begins, as a 220-ton coast guard cutter is launched at the Kawasaki dockyards in Japan. It is one of four armored patrol boats ordered by the country.
Aug. 6		Austria forces 27 Nazis to climb a 6,000-foot cliff and erase a huge swastika painted at the top. A new law makes all Nazis responsible for crimes committed by unidentified persons believed to be Nazis.	Three hundred Assyrians cross the Tigris River and attack the Iraqi army. Some Assyrians are killed and the rest are driven into the mountains around Zakho.	A U.S. sailor, Daniel Kennedy, is charged with homicide in Panama City. He allegedly struck a woman and then threw her from a 30-foot balcony, killing her.	Marshal Feng Yu-Hsiang's revolt falls apart and he hands over control of the Chahar province to Gen. Sung Che-yuan. Feng says he is retiring.
Aug. 7	James M. Cox, U.S. delegate to the World Economic Conference, says the world was simply not ready for the parley. He does not believe that war is brewing in Europe.	Thieves steal 16 masterpieces from the art collection of Eugene Greggory of Cannes, France. The haul included paintings by artists including Manet, Corot, and Renoir.	The government in Cape Town, South Africa, is concerned by the rate at which the Nazi movement is increasing in Southwest Africa.	The uprising in Havana against President Gerardo Machado seems to be spontaneous and is believed by many to foreshadow the end of Machado's leadership in Cuba.	American missionaries in the Lung-yen area of the Fukien province of south China are evacuated to Amoy due to the hostilities in their region.
Aug. 8	Austria is expected to appeal to the League of Nations concerning violation of its independence by German Chancellor Adolf Hitler's government. Britain and France are prepared to back up Austria's appeal.		French flyers Paul Codos and Maurice Rossi beat the world's long-distance record for a direct flight, landing in Syria after a 56-hour flight from New York. They cover about 5,713 miles.	The League of Nations has never adopted a flag, but the Leticia commission adopts one and it flies over Leticia. The white rectangle is inscribed in dark blue: "League of Nations Commission of Leticia."	Chinese Communists take over the city of Liencheng in western Fukien.
Aug. 9	The Iraqi government protests to the League of Nations, blaming French Syria for the recent Assyrian attack on its troops.	Premier Hermann Goering of Prussia requires all city workers to submit evidence of their wives' Aryan background, including birth certificates of the wives' parents.	In a surprise attack, dissident tribesmen at Djebel Babou, Morocco, kill 42 French soldiers in fierce, hand-to-hand fighting.	Former president Mario Menocal of Cuba predicts that within 48–72 hours, revolt will break out all over Cuba or the United States will publicly renounce President Gerardo Machado.	A Belgian priest reports that the Japanese drop more than 20 bombs on a mission about 120 miles north of Peiping, killing more than a score of civilians.
Aug. 10		The French station troops on the German border near Mulhouse, France, as a precaution against Nazi attacks.	W.M. Jardine, U.S. Ambassador to Egypt, cables Washington with his resignation.	Victor Raul Haya de la Torre, head of the Alianza Popular Revolucianara Americana, or Apra, who has been imprisoned in Peru since May 1932, is freed and promises to help the government.	Japanese newspapers allege the United States is negotiating with Mexico to build a naval base in lower California on the Pacific Coast. It believes the base would violate the Washington treaty.
Aug. 11	Since the ABC-Peru group appointed by the League of Nations is not succeeding at mediating the Chaco conflict, it is believed that Brazil may act alone to facilitate negotiations between Bolivia and Paraguay.	Estonia bans uniformed groups and declares a state of emergency. The government also regulates public meetings and tightens control of the press.	The Wahabi King threatens hostilities because Zaidi Imam of Yemen invades his territory in Nagram. The area has been disputed for a long time.		Most of the $40 million China borrowed from the RFC will be spent for cotton in Houston. The area expects to ship more than 500,000 bales to China.
Aug. 12	Austria is alarmed by the refusal of Italy to commit itself with the other nations in the Four-Powers Pact to protest Germany's treatment of Austria to the League of Nations.	Ten thousand farmers in southern England revolt to protest payment of the traditional tithe, which has upset them for some time.	In the Rand district of South Africa, gold miners have to go as far as 1.5 miles below the surface to mine gold. More than 3.5 tons of rock must be blasted to produce one ounce of gold.	President Gerardo Machado of Cuba is overthrown by the Cuban army and Carlos Manuel de Cespedes becomes president.	The U.S. Consul in China attempts to rescue eight American missionaries believed to be safe in the city of Yuanchow. It asks a truce allowing the missionaries to leave.

A	B	C	D	E
Includes developments that affect more than one world region, international organizations, and important meetings of world leaders.	*Includes all domestic and regional developments in Europe, including the Soviet Union.*	*Includes all domestic and regional developments in Africa and the Middle East.*	*Includes all domestic and regional developments in Latin America, the Caribbean, and Canada.*	*Includes all domestic and regional developments in Asian and Pacific nations (and colonies).*

U.S. Politics & Social Issues	U.S. Foreign Policy & Defense	Economics & Great Depression	Science, Technology & Nature	Culture, Leisure & Lifestyle	
President Franklin Roosevelt maps out his war on kidnapping. J. Edgar Hoover and the Justice Department start preliminary action.		Tens of thousands of stores and businesses display the Blue Eagle, the insignia showing that the establishment has accepted the President's re-employment program.	The heat wave in the eastern United States kills 23 in New York and the surrounding area in four days. The temperature is 95°F.	Giants' pitcher Carl Hubbel breaks the National League record for consecutive scoreless innings pitched, totaling 45.	Aug. 1
In an interview, Dr. John Condon, who was the "Jafsie" of the Lindbergh kidnapping case, says he still is convinced he was dealing with the real kidnappers. He has since received a letter saying the man he paid the ransom to met a "sudden death."	President Franklin Roosevelt approves $46 million worth of Navy Department contracts for naval construction. The contracts will help provide work for the unemployed.	The petroleum industry wants to establish a "cost-recovery formula," while the government believes the only necessary price-fixing is the establishment of a maximum price.			Aug. 2
Secretary of State Cordell Hull and his wife and niece accept an invitation to spend the weekend at Hyde Park with the Roosevelts. Hull reports to the President on the World Economic Conference. They also discuss debts and bilateral trade treaties.	Assistant Secretary of the Navy Henry Roosevelt arrives in the Canal Zone to inspect the Coco Solo Marine base and the fleet air base.	Iowa coal miners strike over failure of their employers to sign the National Recovery Act code.	Texas oil refiners sue the federal government for curtailing the output of oil, due to conservation orders.	Chicago dedicates a bronze statue of Columbus in Grant Park and celebrates Italian Day at the World's Fair.	Aug. 3
	National Council of American Shipbuilders president H. Gerrish Smith estimates that $105 million will go for labor to build the 21 new Navy ships. The total cost is $130 million.	President Franklin Roosevelt approves a compromise code for the garment industry. Garments sold without the NRA insignia will be considered "sweatshop" production.	Dr. Dorothy V. Whipple of the University of Pennsylvania touts oysters as a "brain food," since they contain a good deal of vitamin B.	Helen Hayes and Robert Montgomery star in *Another Language*, said to be an excellent pictorial adaptation of the stage play by Rose Franken.	Aug. 4
President Franklin Roosevelt appoints a seven-person board to settle all disputes in industry.	Senator Robert Wagner of New York visits with League of Nations officials in Geneva and explains U.S. foreign policy. He is very impressed with the League and their leaders are impressed with him.	The railroads pledge their help to President Franklin Roosevelt in his recovery program, saying they will continue to provide as much employment as they can.	Vermont debates the idea of a skyline highway that could be built with federal funds. The Green Mountain Club charges it would spoil the natural beauty of the area.	Trainloads of Catholics rush to Beauraing, Belgium, where it is reported the Virgin Mary has made several miraculous appearances. . . . The U.S. women win the Wightman Cup in tennis for the third year in a row.	Aug. 5
President Franklin Roosevelt assures Secretary of State Cordell Hull that he has confidence in him and says he wants to work with him on setting up a Pan-American alliance.		Government contracts will be adjusted under the National Recovery Act to meet cost increases.	H.E. Burton, the principal astronomer at the Naval Observatory, observes a white spot on Saturn's equator. He believes the spot is about 20,000 miles long by 12,000 miles wide.	James Mattern tells the story of his plane crash, including setting his clothes on fire when he tried to dry them, in a theater newsreel.	Aug. 6
Assistant Secretary of State Raymond Moley, who was appointed by President Franklin Roosevelt to investigate the crime situation, confers with the Attorney General and others at the Justice Department.	Secretary of State Cordell Hull thinks his policy of vigorous international trade expansion is feasible, with 46 countries still adhering to the tariff truce.	President Franklin Roosevelt asks financial institutions to give relief to homeowners by exchanging mortgages for home loan bonds.	A huge run of crawfish covers five miles of the highway between New Orleans and Baton Rouge.	Two horseshoe pitchers, Theodore Allen and James Lecky, break the ringer record. Allen, the world champion, has a percentage of 79.7 to better his own record of 73.5, while Lecky has a 78.1 percentage.	Aug. 7
Kidnappers are warned that when they are caught, they will pay a severe penalty— either a long term in prison or the death penalty.	General Frank T. Hines, veterans' administrator, names three new boards to review cases of disability among veterans. They are to give reasonable doubt to those whose disabilities are from war service.	Striking coal miners heed a plea by President Franklin Roosevelt and go back to work, pending the adoption of the coal code after hearings.			Aug. 8
	The Army is asking for 60 recruits, "of good moral, physical, and mental qualifications" who will be assigned to service in Panama and Hawaii.	Nearly a million people in Illinois, Wisconsin, and Iowa are placed in jobs under the new codes of the National Recovery Act.	Robert Fechner, director of emergency conservation work, stresses that the 300,000 men working in conservation camps are doing much to reduce loss of forests by fire, insects, and disease.	Lou Brouillard, the new middleweight boxing champion, held the welterweight title in 1931.	Aug. 9
Messages from around the world pour in as former president Herbert Hoover celebrates his 59th birthday with a quiet dinner at home with his wife and a few friends.	The Navy blimp *K-1* arrives in Lakehurst, N.J., where it will be put into commission after being reconditioned at the Goodyear factory in Akron, Ohio.	First Lady Eleanor Roosevelt urges equal pay for women, noting that several of the codes have different wages for men and women. She will discuss the matter with Secretary of Labor Frances Perkins and Gen. Hugh Johnson of the NRA.	Col. Charles Lindbergh laughs at reports that he had been killed in a crash when flying from Greenland to Copenhagen. The Danes are not amused.	Seventeen-year-old Ralph Miller of Seattle, Wash., wrests the national archery title from Russell Hoogerhyde of Bristol, Conn.	Aug. 10
	Senator James H. Lewis of Illinois believes the new foreign policy of the United States will stress negotiations with individual nations rather than participation in world parleys.		American explorer Lincoln Ellsworth arrives in Auckland, New Zealand, where he waits for a ship to bring the plane and equipment for his Antarctic expedition.	Actor Douglas Fairbanks's manager says rumors that Fairbanks seeks British citizenship are ridiculous. He and his son are making a movie in London. . . . Pope Pius XI tells Bishop John Gannon of Erie, Pa., that he admires President Franklin Roosevelt and is hopeful about the situation of the United States.	Aug. 11
President Franklin Roosevelt travels 180 miles, inspecting five forest camps and eating steak with the workers. He is pleased with what he sees in the CCC camps.		Harry L. Hopkins, relief administrator, approves $431,005 in national grants to New Mexico, Colorado, and South Carolina to match relief expenditures there during the second quarter.	A number of sharks have been seen off the New Jersey coast this summer, but fishermen deny they are coming in to eat garbage they dump offshore.	The ban on smoking at professional boxing matches in Madison Square Garden in New York, which has caused controversy, is expected to be lifted before the season starts.	Aug. 12

F	G	H	I	J
Includes elections, federal-state relations, civil rights and liberties, crime, the judiciary, education, healthcare, poverty, urban affairs, and population.	Includes formation and debate of U.S. foreign and defense policies, veterans affairs, and defense spending. (Relations with specific foreign countries are usually found under the region concerned.)	Includes business, labor, agriculture, taxation, transportation, consumer affairs, monetary and fiscal policy, natural resources, pollution, and accidents.	Includes worldwide scientific, medical, and technological developments, natural phenomena, U.S. weather, and natural disasters.	Includes the arts, religion, scholarship, communications media, sports, entertainment, fashions, fads, and social life.

	World Affairs	Europe	Africa & The Middle East	The Americas	Asia & The Pacific
Aug. 13	Carrie Chapman Catt, women's suffrage leader and peace advocate, gathers signatures from 9,000 women around the world protesting German Chancellor Adolf Hitler's treatment of Jews. She will send it to the League of Nations.	Reports say Austria and Germany begin unofficial talks in Switzerland in an attempt to end their differences.		A party of Catholic dignitaries is rescued by small fishing boats when the ship they are on goes aground on a reef near Caribou Island, Quebec.	Reports from Amoy claim that the Chinese 19th Route Army has recaptured Lienchien from the Communists.
Aug. 14	Senator Key Pittman tells President Franklin Roosevelt that the adoption of a resolution stabilizing silver was a definite accomplishment of the World Economic Conference.	Albanian fruit merchant Ephraim Tselo shoots former Albanian premier Hassan Bey Pristina in Saloniki, Greece, where Pristina was in exile. Tselo says Pristina urged him to assassinate King Zog of Albania.	Cairo announces that the Wahabi delegates who were held by Zaidi Imam in Yemen when they went to negotiate a treaty have been released.	Americans living in Havana celebrate the resignation of President Gerardo Machado. They believe both commerce and relations with the United States will improve.	Bombay editor K. Natarajan predicts that the caste system in India will be completely changed in five years. He says great progress has been made toward eliminating the Untouchables as a caste.
Aug. 15		In an open letter to President Paul von Hindenburg of Germany, the American Jewish League asks him to save 600,000 Jews from "certain extermination" by removing Chancellor Adolf Hitler from office.	The London Times claims 500 Assyrians, including 200 not involved in the recent raids, have been killed by Iraqi soldiers.	The Canadian Cabinet is expected to act soon on a U.S. request to send gold to Canada for smelting and refining.	Belgian Bishop Leon Desmedt says the bombing of the mission in China was not provoked and that no soldiers were nearby. Ten bombs were dropped on the mission, so he believes the mission had to be the target.
Aug. 16	The Institute of Pacific Relations discusses a number of economic issues at their parley in Banff, Alberta, Canada.	After the United States protests having a number of its products placed on the maximum tariff list, France backs down and places them in the categories where they were before.		Cuba's new president, Manuel Carlos de Cespedes, asks the United States to agree to a trade treaty giving Cuba better terms on selling sugar to the United States in order for Cuba to prosper again.	The government of India allows Mohandas Gandhi to carry on propaganda for the Untouchables from his prison cell. Therefore, he calls off his scheduled "fast to the death."
Aug. 17	Austria is pleased that Herr Theodor Habicht, a member of the Reichstag, said in a radio address that Germany would like the dispute between the two countries to be put before the League of Nations "in its true light."	A bomb intended for former Bulgarian premier Alexander Tzankoff misses him and injures one of his bodyguards.	King Faisal postpones his trip to Switzerland, so he will be in Iraq to talk to British Ambassador Sir Francis Humphreys. Faisal says the reports of attacks on Assyrians are exaggerated.	Paraguay renews the air war in the Chaco, with seven planes flying over Bolivian territory. Bolivia says three of its planes chase the Paraguayan planes away, killing one pilot and destroying some planes.	
Aug. 18	The Parisian newspaper Le Temps criticizes the United States for building up its navy, saying that action does not fit well with statements by U.S. Special Ambassador Norman Davis and others, urging disarmament.	Amsterdam denies persistent rumors that Holland will resume formal trade relations with Russia.	Iraq deports Mar Shimun, leader of the Assyrians there, for refusing to declare his loyalty to King Fisal.		Since he is so weak after a 48-hour fast, the Indian government offers to release Mohandas Gandhi immediately if he will cease civil disobedience activities.
Aug. 19			Asmara is to be the site of new cosmic ray testing by Italy. It is located in the Italian colony of Eritrea in east Africa.	Cubans who were in exile in the United States because of their anti-Machado stand sail for Cuba. Included are leaders Col. Carlos Mendieta and Col. Mendea Penate.	Japanese War Minister Araki says he wants a peace treaty with the United States and says he will do all in his power to promote friendship between the two countries.
Aug. 20	The wheat parley resumes in London with delegates from 16 countries. The United States is optimistic.	President Eamon de Valera's speech in Thurles, Ireland, is cheered as he vows he will not allow force to take over the country.		Argentine grain crops face disaster if it does not rain immediately. The crops, classed as being in poor condition, need an abundance of rain if they are to produce.	A new area of China is threatened by flooding as dikes on the Yellow River in Upper Honan are shaky and may collapse.
Aug. 21	The League of Nations hosts a World Wheat Conference in London, attended by Argentina, Australia, Canada, the Soviet Union, and the United States.	Austria sends 8,000 troops to guard its border against Nazi attacks. Austria will probably seek approval from France, Britain, and Italy to increase her army in order to protect the German frontier.	The British colony of Kenya, in east Africa, takes up the sport of baseball. A league of teams in east Africa may be formed.	Argentine President Agustin Justo makes two Cabinet changes, appointing Federico Pinedo Minister of Finance and Luis Duhau Minister of Agriculture.	Mohandas Gandhi's weight drops to 93 pounds as he gets progressively weaker. His wife is released from prison to spend time at his bedside in the hospital.
Aug. 22	Reports say President Franklin Roosevelt tells U.S. Special Ambassador Norman Davis that U.S. action depends on the rest of the world disarming.	Exiled Austrian Nazis use loudspeakers to broadcast propaganda against Austrian Chancellor Engelbert Dollfuss across the Inn River from Germany. Austrians retaliate with loud patriotic music and finally a live band.	The Iraqi government plans a big reception for the troops that quelled the Assyrian attack on August 6 and denies charges that troops massacred 200 Assyrians not involved in the attacks.	About 20 Cuban refugees who were involved with the Machado government arrive in New York aboard the Oriente, but none will admit to being refugees.	
Aug. 23	Europeans study a plan for world recovery whereby payments on debts would be used to finance public works, which would provide employment for the jobless.		A team of South African polo players leaves for Buenos Aires, where they will play a South American team.	La Paz, Bolivia, holds a contest for the best essay on George Washington written in English. Winner is Henry Merubia, son of a Bolivian teacher, who was educated in the United States.	Mohandas Gandhi, who weighs only 90 pounds after a week-long fast, is given an unconditional release from prison by the Indian government.
Aug. 24	Canada will invoke the Ottawa accords in an attempt to make Britain reduce her imports of timber from Russia.	The famine Russia is experiencing is said to be as severe as the one in 1921. Many die from starvation and cannibalism is reported.	Fourteen Assyrian leaders send King Faisal of Iraq a telegram praising his accomplishments on the anniversary of his coronation.	The Ecuadorian Congress guarantees full freedom, including the right to disseminate their doctrines, to socialists and Communists.	
Aug. 25	In London, 21 nations reach a wheat agreement that will raise prices, restrict production, and reduce tariffs.	The French approve of Italian Premier Benito Mussolini's plan to aid Austria financially and politically, since it may prevent German Chancellor Adolf Hitler from taking over the country.		Cubans celebrate President Manuel Carlos de Cespedes's act to return the country to the Constitution of 1901.	Emperor Hirohito reviews Japan's naval fleet, and a Tokyo newspaper makes it clear that Japan's aim is to dominate the seas in the western Pacific with its navy.

A	B	C	D	E
Includes developments that affect more than one world region, international organizations, and important meetings of world leaders.	Includes all domestic and regional developments in Europe, including the Soviet Union.	Includes all domestic and regional developments in Africa and the Middle East.	Includes all domestic and regional developments in Latin America, the Caribbean, and Canada.	Includes all domestic and regional developments in Asian and Pacific nations (and colonies).

U.S. Politics & Social Issues	U.S. Foreign Policy & Defense	Economics & Great Depression	Science, Technology & Nature	Culture, Leisure & Lifestyle	
The Colorado board to review veterans' claims draws criticism because a majority of the members named to the board are veterans.	President Franklin Roosevelt says he is sending warships to Cuba, not to intervene, but to protect Americans who are there.		A tiny octopus found on a dock on Staten Island was probably caught in a crab pot by fishermen, authorities say, since octopus stay in clean waters and the waters in the area are polluted.	American golfer Gene Sarazen captures the PGA title in Milwaukee, Wisc., defeating Willie Goggin in a close duel.	Aug. 13
Elmore Clark, one of three black youths seized yesterday by a mob, is found alive. National Guardsmen take him to Birmingham, Ala., for protection. His two companions had been killed and he was wounded.	Edward A. Filene, long an advocate of low tariffs, changes his stand. He also believes the United States needs to follow the European trend toward nationalism and economic isolation.	About 60,000 dress workers threaten to strike as a result of a clash over the code for the garment industry.	Loggers in Tillamook, Ore., start a forest fire that destroys 240,000 acres.	A series of studies shows that watching some movies affects children's ability to sleep, while other movies have a calming effect.	Aug. 14
Chicago's request is granted to have Al Capone brought there to stand trial with 23 others on racketeering charges. If convicted, he will finish serving his present term before starting to serve another.	Statistics for the first six months of 1933 show improvement in foreign trade, although it is still not up to pre-Depression standards.	Secretary of the Treasury William Woodin may recommend cutting the amount put aside for the sinking fund each year in order to relieve the strain on federal finances.		American tennis player Helen Jacobs sets a trend as she wears shorts when she beats her opponent, Eunice Dean, in her first match of the Women's National Championships in tennis.	Aug. 15
It is understood that when U.S. Special Ambassador Norman Davis returns to Geneva, he will not take the lead in the disarmament talks, but will wait to see what moves Europe makes.	Attorney General Homer Cummings studies the shipping code, as it is thought to conflict with laws already in effect. Also, foreign ship owners do not want to submit to National Recovery Act standards.	Army engineers reject a plan to build a canal between the Delaware River and Chesapeake Bay, saying the amount of traffic it would get would not justify the expense.	The Italian ocean liner *Rex* sails 3,181 miles from Gibraltar to New York in 4 days, 13 hours, and 58 minutes to set a record.	Yankee player Lou Gehrig ties the record for most consecutive games played with his 1,307th game in a row.	Aug. 16
Postmaster General James Farley announces that with President Franklin Roosevelt's approval, all non-emergency communications will be sent by air mail rather than telegram.	Pope Pius XI blesses the U.S. Navy after having an audience with 80 cadets from the schoolship *Annapolis*.	President Franklin Roosevelt gives the bituminous coal operators an ultimatum, saying they must come up with a code by Saturday.	Dr. Albert Claude discovers a group of chemicals that duplicate the action of bacteria that breaks down the body's resistance. It is hoped the discovery can be applied to medical research.	The U.S. traveling track team finishes its tour of Europe with a win in Paris. The team beat every team it faced.	Aug. 17
President Franklin Roosevelt praises the United Flag Association for its "crusade against crime."		President Franklin Roosevelt announces he has decided to continue the Civil Conservation Corps at full strength through the winter, but asks that those with offers of jobs accept them, so others can take their places.		A judge grants film star Carole Lombard a divorce from her husband, actor William Powell, on charges that he was temperamental and cruel.	Aug. 18
President Franklin Roosevelt impresses coal, oil, and steel men with his knowledge of their industries, as he gives them an ultimatum on their codes.	Controversy rages in California over whether to locate the navy base in Los Angeles or San Francisco. Ships have generally sailed from the Los Angeles area, but both cities want the base.	Beet sugar growers accept a quota of 1,750,000 tons in an effort to work out an agreement that will raise prices.	As part of his New Deal, President Franklin Roosevelt encourages use of public domain land. Forests are being used as conservation camps and fences have been removed in public domain land so free range cattle can graze there.	Betty Nuthall of England wins six games in a row to beat U.S. player Alice Marble and move on to the semifinals of the U.S. title tennis tournament. Now she faces Helen Wills Moody.	Aug. 19
A number of national organizations ask President Franklin Roosevelt to issue a proclamation proclaiming the fifth anniversary of the Kellogg-Briand pact.	Governor Paul McNutt of Indiana, speaking in Michigan, calls on the American Legion to join in the war against the Depression, saying it is as "real and grim as any other war."	Striking anthracite coal workers in Pennsylvania return to the mines pending a hearing on their code.	Buds swell on a century plant due to bloom for the first time in a Bronx park. . . . The famous Weather Kiosk on Boston Commons goes on the sale block for economic reasons.	The 34th Grand American Handicap, the annual national trapshooting tournament, opens today in Vandalia, Ohio.	Aug. 20
In a dinner speech, Postmaster General James Farley says he is confident that President Franklin Roosevelt's accomplishments will assure his reelection in 1936.	A customs patrol boat follows the 60-foot yacht *Pueblos* and arrests the crew, confiscating $60,000 worth of liquor.	In Chicago, 7,500 dress shop workers strike to protest the failure of owners to adopt a suitable NRA code.		Ned Lilly, 17, breaks 199 out of 200 clay targets to win the North American Clay Target Crown at the Grand American Handicap in Vandalia, Ohio.	Aug. 21
Postmaster General James Farley appeals in a radio address to the people of Texas to vote for repeal of Prohibition.	Secretary of State Cordell Hull still believes it will be possible to remove some of the barriers to world trade. He proposes that the existing tariff truce be maintained and strengthened.	The NRA may allow the soft coal industry to put their code to a 90-day trial period. Wages and workweek have not been agreed upon as yet.	Charles B. Gray sues Eastman Kodak for allegedly using a push-button shutter control, which he invented, on their cameras.		Aug. 22
The Senate is expected to vote for a measure giving wider powers to the Attorney General in his fight against racketeering.	Over 200 employees of the Navy yard in Brooklyn protest cuts in hours and pay ordered by the Secretary of the Navy.	Secretary of the Interior Harold Ickes urges public works that open up new jobs for the unemployed, warning that the money appropriated must not lie idle.	A hurricane batters the East Coast, from the Carolinas northward. At least 10 are dead and property loss is estimated in the millions.	The National Labor Board ends the strike of movie technicians in Hollywood.	Aug. 23
	President Franklin Roosevelt warns the French that their unpaid debt is hurting their relations with the United States.	President Franklin Roosevelt intervenes again to settle the soft coal stalemate, while automobile men make progress toward a code. However, they are still debating the open shop issue.	Public Health Service figures show a direct correlation between being overweight and early death.	Newsreels at theaters this week showcase evangelist Aimee Semple McPherson, Col. and Mrs. Charles Lindbergh, Gen. John Pershing, and Mr. and Mrs. Herbert Hoover.	Aug. 24
Former president William Howard Taft's cousin, William F. Wood, escapes his kidnapper by shouting at a policeman as he is forced to shop for supplies with his captor. The kidnapper is killed after shooting the policeman.	Mrs. Ruth Bryan Owen, U.S. Minister to Denmark, says in a radio speech that the world is watching as President Franklin Roosevelt leads.	General Hugh Johnson, administrator of the NRA, asks strikers of the International Ladies Garment Workers Union to go back to work immediately.		The United States wins the Pro Tennis Series as William "Big Bill" Tilden beats Henri Cochet of France.	Aug. 25

F	G	H	I	J
Includes elections, federal-state relations, civil rights and liberties, crime, the judiciary, education, healthcare, poverty, urban affairs, and population.	Includes formation and debate of U.S. foreign and defense policies, veterans affairs, and defense spending. (Relations with specific foreign countries are usually found under the region concerned.)	Includes business, labor, agriculture, taxation, transportation, consumer affairs, monetary and fiscal policy, natural resources, pollution, and accidents.	Includes worldwide scientific, medical, and technological developments, natural phenomena, U.S. weather, and natural disasters.	Includes the arts, religion, scholarship, communications media, sports, entertainment, fashions, fads, and social life.

	World Affairs	Europe	Africa & The Middle East	The Americas	Asia & The Pacific
Aug. 26	The United States, Soviet Union, Canada, Australia, and Argentina sign the International Wheat Agreement, limiting exports and planted acreage of wheat.	Spanish Premier Manuel Azano allows increasing freedom to the Spanish people and gives full freedom to opposition newspapers.	Iraqi Muslim troops march through Baghdad upon their return from subduing the Assyrian Christians. A band plays *Marching Through Georgia* as thousands cheer.	The new Cuban government pays passage home for 42 young Cuban exiles who took refuge in the United States during the Machado regime.	The United States asks Governor Ho of Honan province to release seven American Catholic missionaries who were captured June 25 when the city of Yuanchow fell.
Aug. 27		Chancellor Adolf Hitler asserts that Germany will never relinquish the Saar Basin, long disputed between France and Germany. The Treaty of Versailles awarded it to France.		American soldier Capt. Ralph Osman faces court-martial in the Canal Zone. Osman is accused of espionage.	
Aug. 28	Australian Prime Minister Joseph Lyons praises the wheat pact, but says he wishes it did not necessitate the slowing up of normal agricultural development.	The Nazis report they have made a deal with Palestine. They say they will barter German goods for Jaffa oranges from Palestine and Syria. Palestine denies having made such a deal.	The French army ends a 30-year drive to subdue the wild Berber tribes in Morocco. Only two small pockets of rebels remain.	Employment is up in Canada according to the Dominion Bureau of Statistics, which reports that 24,000 people went back to work in July.	Liu Shih, governor of the Honan province in China, is accused of cutting Yellow River dikes there, causing the flooding in western Shantung which left 3 million homeless.
Aug. 29	Japanese cotton spinners are on their way to England to seek a pact with the British. They will also protest the 75 percent duty imposed on the goods they export to India.	Sean O'Kelly, vice president of the Irish Free State, says the aims of former president William Cosgrove's party and those of the Blue Shirts, led by Gen. Owen O'Duffey, are identical.	Turkish frontier guards deny reports that they killed 50 Assyrians who tried to cross the border as they fled from Iraq.	Secretary of State Cordell Hull and others confer with Brazilian Ambassador R. de Lima e Silva about revising an existing trade treaty with South America.	Japanese silk producers plan a three-year campaign to popularize silk in the United States.
Aug. 30	The League of Nations agenda for its next session does not mention the persecution of Jews in Germany.	Air France begins operation....Theodor Lessing is assassinated in Marienbad, Czechoslovakia.	The League of Nations plans to discuss the Anglo-Persian oil agreement when it meets on September 22.	When the Mexican Congress opens tomorrow, President Abelardo Rodriguez will review the past year's accomplishments, and then outline his six-year plan for economic recovery.	Chinese banditry revives in the Chinwangtao area of China, where 5,000 Chinese have clustered around the Japanese barracks for protection.
Aug. 31	Luis Duhau, Argentine Minister of Agriculture, tells his people that the country will not have to reduce the acreage now planted in wheat under the new pact.	Czechs are aroused by the murder of Prof. Theodor Lessing, German Jewish exile. Police suspect Max Epker, who had been heard discussing Lessing with a German. Epker is believed to have escaped to Germany.		Cuban President Manuel Carlos de Cespedes creates a consultative commission, which will propose emergency legislation to him until a new Congress is elected.	Japan orders warships to speed to the port of Amoy to stop an advancing Communist invasion.
Sept. 1	U.S. Special Ambassador Norman Davis denies he will discuss war debts on his present trip to Europe. He will confer with leaders in London and Paris before the disarmament conference in Geneva reopens.	Eight people are under arrest in Czechoslovakia, in connection with the murder of Theodor Lessing, a German Jewish exile in the country. Two are women, suspected of being Nazi couriers.	The Jewish Agency for Palestine reports that 6,000 Jews have immigrated to Palestine in the past six months and they expect the number to double by the end of the year.	A bill in the Colombian Congress establishes the fact that all unclaimed lands in the country are in the public domain. The bill allows the government to regulate exploitation of forests and to prohibit deforestation.	The Szechwan Civil War ends in China, but the fiercest fighting yet between the Cantonese troops and the Communists goes on in south China.
Sept. 2	The U.S. disarmament delegation sees new hope as it believes current negotiations between France and Germany may help bring about arms reduction.	The Belgian government borrows $60 million to be used to strengthen fortifications along the German frontier. . . . The U.S. government protests to Germany because of another attack on an American there. Samuel Bossard was watching a parade of youth in Nazi uniforms when several attacked him, knocking him to the ground.		Argentina will use airplanes to fight locusts by spraying their wintering breeding grounds in the jungle districts of the north.	B.E.J. Burge becomes the third successive British Magistrate in three years to be assassinated in the Midnapur district of India. One attacker is killed and another seriously injured.
Sept. 3	The French think President Franklin Roosevelt's economic recovery program will run into trouble when it becomes necessary to maintain high enough prices to cover higher wages called for by NRA.	Austrian Chancellor Engelbert Dollfuss asks 8,000 more men to enlist in the Austrian army....A new government is formed in Spain by Alejandro Lerroux.	H. Malcolm Ross, a land agent in Tanganyika, says when he worked in Germany he saw a skull he believes is the long-lost skull of Sultan Mkwawa. The Versailles treaty ordered Germany to return the skull to Africa, but it did not.	At a special Cabinet meeting, Cuba appropriates $50,000 for hurricane relief in the Santa Clara and Matanzas provinces where 100 died and 650 were injured.	Martial law is declared in the Chinese city of Peitaiho, where thousands of refugees crowd in to escape bandits seven miles away.
Sept. 4	Japanese Foreign Minister Yasuya Uchida says Japan will stick to its demand for equality in the naval conference scheduled for 1935.	France's former premier Edouard Herriot praises Russia's Josef Stalin, saying his Six Points show a high degree of intelligence and courage.		Privates and noncommissioned officers take over the Cuban army, demanding removal of commissioned officers who had supported President Gerardo Machado.	
Sept. 5		Tension grows in Austria as the government sends seven private planes to patrol the Bavarian-Tyrolean border. The Treaty of St. Germain forbids Austria to have any military planes.	M. Peyrouton, French Resident General in Tunis, arrives in Paris for talks and says the economic situation in Tunis is bad and France must help or risk losing its whole establishment in North Africa.	A committee of enlisted army and navy men ousts President Carlos Manuel de Cespedes and his Cabinet from office in Cuba. They say they are not Communists, and their move is aimed at getting rid of the rest of Gerardo Machado's followers.	Nanking announces that the earthquake in the Szechwan province August 25 was the worst in China in the last hundred years.
Sept. 6	U.S. Special Ambassador Norman Davis confers with Britain's Sir John Simon, trying to convince him of the importance of strict supervision of disarmament, as the United States and France want.		Premier Sidky of Egypt decides not to resign, which is taken to mean that the palace has surrendered to his demands and will not interfere.		China denies the persistent rumor that most of the cotton it bought with the money loaned by the United States is being sold to the Japanese at 30 percent below what China pays the United States for it.

A	B	C	D	E
Includes developments that affect more than one world region, international organizations, and important meetings of world leaders.	*Includes all domestic and regional developments in Europe, including the Soviet Union.*	*Includes all domestic and regional developments in Africa and the Middle East.*	*Includes all domestic and regional developments in Latin America, the Caribbean, and Canada.*	*Includes all domestic and regional developments in Asian and Pacific nations (and colonies).*

U.S. Politics & Social Issues	U.S. Foreign Policy & Defense	Economics & Great Depression	Science, Technology & Nature	Culture, Leisure & Lifestyle	
President Franklin Roosevelt's 2,000-acre farm near Warm Springs, Ga., is a model for other farms. He personally supervises selection of crops. He says his aim is to "make this a farm that can be imitated by any farmer that chooses."	The War Department rules that no nonmilitary passengers shall be transported in U.S. Army planes except in "cases of emergency involving life or catastrophe."	The garment workers agree on a code for the National Recovery Act and both sides say they are pleased with it.	Scientists study the effect of weather on crops, with the aim of reducing damages by making sure crops are planted in the proper climates.	Back pain forces Helen Wills Moody to default in the third set of the final round of the U.S. tennis championships, making Helen Jacobs the winner.	Aug. 26
Washington is surprised by the resignation of Raymond Moley, Assistant Secretary of State. Secretary of State Cordell Hull denies he asked him to resign. Moley will edit a new weekly magazine, Newsweek.	The Women's International League for Peace and Freedom urges President Franklin Roosevelt to curtail military spending.	Mine owners revise their labor clause, proposing one that is similar to that of the auto workers' code.	American scientist Frank R. Perret opens a volcanological museum in St. Pierre, on the island of Martinique.	The eight winners of Paramount's film contest in the British Empire sail for Hollywood, where they hope to start careers as film actors and actresses.	Aug. 27
Attorneys at the annual American Bar Association convention pledge their assistance in fighting the war against racketeers and kidnappers.		President Franklin Roosevelt and Secretary of the Interior Harold Ickes confer on the Public Works program. Ickes says he suggested setting a timeframe within which a project must be started.	The two sides clash at the Agricultural Department's hearing on baiting wild water fowl. A proposed regulation would make it illegal to spread corn or feed within 100 feet of a hunting blind.	Baseball Commissioner K.M. Landis refuses to back down after appointing official scorers for the series between the Cubs and the White Sox without consulting the baseball writers.	Aug. 28
In a speech in Milwaukee, Louisiana Senator Huey Long lambastes newspapers, denounces his foes, and says the administration can go to hell.		The Cotton Exchange submits its code, which follows the recommendations for hours and wages and bans child labor.	The incidence of encephalitis, also known as sleeping sickness, is on the decline in New York City, with only 44 cases reported this year and 27 resulting deaths.	Alice Brady and Maureen O'Sullivan star as mother and daughter in the new film, Stage Mother.	Aug. 29
President Franklin Roosevelt and his family attend the Dutchess County Fair, near their Hyde Park home. His son, John, wins a blue ribbon with the President's horse, New Deal.	U.S. Special Ambassador Norman Davis sails for Europe with messages from President Franklin Roosevelt for heads of various European governments.	After conferring with Governor Eugene Black of the Federal Reserve Board and representatives of the office of the Controller of the Currency, RFC head Jesse Jones says ways and means of extending credit may be announced tomorrow.		In writer Gertrude Stein's new book, strangely titled The Autobiography of Alice B. Toklas, she says that she, Pablo Picasso, and Alfred Whitehead are the only geniuses she has ever met.	Aug. 30
	Parents of Ralph Osman, convicted of espionage in the Canal Zone, plan to appeal the case. He is sentenced to two years in prison and a $10,000 fine or 20 years in prison if he does not pay the fine.		An Indian chief's attempt to entice a deer across a rustic bridge in Watkins Glen State Park fails. The deer has been trapped on the ledge for six days.	The new weekly magazine Today, to be edited by Raymond Moley, former Assistant Secretary of State, will first appear on the newsstand on October 1.	Aug. 31
President Franklin Roosevelt enjoys his first day of total rest since March 4 aboard a yacht off Montauk.	Secretary of the Navy Claude Swanson signs contracts for 17 new war vessels, which should make the U.S. Navy second to none. Included are a 10,000-ton cruiser, eight 1,800-ton destroyers, six 1,500-ton destroyers, and two submarines.	Many believe that Henry Ford will choose to go it alone rather than sign the NRA auto code. He may raise wages back to $5 per day to show he pays better than the code prescribes.	J.C. Hunsaker, vice president of the Goodyear Zeppelin Corporation, believes the crash of the Akron was due to the Navy policy of shifting commanding officers around from craft to craft.	Attendance at the World's Fair in Chicago passes that of the St. Louis fair in 1904. Its total was 12,804,000, a mark eclipsed by the Century of Progress about noon today in its 97th day. The St. Louis fair ran for 187 days.	Sept. 1
	Senator Key Pittman says the Monroe Doctrine is out of date and thinks abolishing it would stimulate friendships between the United States and Central and South American countries.	The federal debt at the end of August stands at $229,685,457 as opposed to $663,949,644 on the same date a year ago.		Virginia Van Wie holds onto her title as Women's National Golf Champion by beating Helen Hicks in the finals.	Sept. 2
James Roosevelt, eldest son of the President, speaks in Iowa, appealing for public support of his father's recovery programs.		In a Labor Day message to the workers of the nation, Secretary of Labor Frances Perkins asks them to support the NRA.	The Smithsonian Institution discovers the skeletons of two ancient cats that lived before the Ice Age in Idaho. One is similar to a small saber-toothed cat and the other resembles a puma.		Sept. 3
	The Army changes its command in the Canal Zone, sending Maj. Gen. Harold B. Fiske to replace Maj. Gen. Preston Brown, who will be headquartered in Chicago.	The deadline for Henry Ford to accept the NRA code passes, and there is no word from Ford, who remains in the North Woods. The company says it already lives up to the NRA code.	The recent storm on the eastern seacoast nearly wiped out a 300-year-old herd of wild ponies on Chincoteague Island. It is believed only three out of hundreds of ponies survived.		Sept. 4
	U.S. action in Cuba is seen as inevitable. Many Cubans would welcome a group from the United States, headed by someone familiar with Cuba, to help reconcile factions, restore morale, bring about reforms, and prepare for elections.	Cotton leaders from five southeastern states oppose the government's acreage control plan and ask for a plan that controls the number of bales instead.		John D. Rockefeller, Sr., returns a portrait painted by an art student in Chicago. He asks Michael Matsakas if he would change the color of the tie in the portrait to match his own tie. Matsakas does, and returns the portrait.	Sept. 5
	Over 1,000 Marines assemble at Quantico, Va., awaiting orders to go to Cuba, if necessary.	Oscar B. Ryder, whose tariff views are similar to those of the President, is appointed to the NRA, as NRA Administrator Hugh Johnson gets ready to consider the need for higher duties to offset higher production costs.		In the fourth round of the men's national tennis championships, George Lott and John Van Ryn are defeated, but Frank Shields, Ellsworth Vines, and Jack Crawford are still in the running.	Sept. 6

F	G	H	I	J
Includes elections, federal-state relations, civil rights and liberties, crime, the judiciary, education, healthcare, poverty, urban affairs, and population.	Includes formation and debate of U.S. foreign and defense policies, veterans affairs, and defense spending. (Relations with specific foreign countries are usually found under the region concerned.)	Includes business, labor, agriculture, taxation, transportation, consumer affairs, monetary and fiscal policy, natural resources, pollution, and accidents.	Includes worldwide scientific, medical, and technological developments, natural phenomena, U.S. weather, and natural disasters.	Includes the arts, religion, scholarship, communications media, sports, entertainment, fashions, fads, and social life.

	World Affairs	Europe	Africa & The Middle East	The Americas	Asia & The Pacific
Sept. 7	South American leaders hope the United States will not find it necessary to intervene in Cuba, believing it might hurt the Pan-American Conference to be held soon.	A secret conference is reported among representatives of Russia, Romania, and Poland. It is believed they are discussing starting an anti-German front.	It is feared that war may break out in Arabia, since the British destroyers *Delight*, *Duncan*, and *Diamond* sail for the Red Sea. Saudi Arabian King Ibn Saud is preparing for possible hostilities with Yemen.	Bolivia protests to the Argentine government, alleging it sent 3.5 million cartridges to Paraguay.	The Chinese government reveals a gigantic program of railroad, highway, and irrigation, which it hopes will bring China closer to economic security.
Sept. 8	The Jewish World Conference in Geneva closes after asking the League of Nations to intervene on behalf of the German Jews, especially in facilitating their emigration to Palestine.	Henry Berenger, French senator, says that if Germany were to annex Austria, a new European conflict would be sure to ensue.	King Faisal of Iraq suddenly dies of a heart attack in Berne, Switzerland. His son, Ghazi, who was educated in England, succeeds to the throne.	Argentine Foreign Minister Carlos Saavedra Lamas asks the United States to refrain from intervening in Cuban affairs, no matter what happens.	The Japanese send an expedition to rescue three British ship officers who were held in Manchuria for 23 weeks. Chief Officer Johnson, Second Officer Hargraves, and Second Engineer Blue of the *Nanchang* are free.
Sept. 9	Bolivia says it will allow no more White Russians from Manchuria to settle in the Chaco until Bolivian demands are settled by the League of Nations.		Cairo deeply regrets the departure of William Jardine, who has been the U.S. Ambassador to Egypt for three years. He is equally popular with the American colony in Cairo.	The monthly commercial letter of the Bank of Canada reports that mining is now the second largest business in Canada, after agriculture. It noses out forestry, which was second for many years.	Rafael Alunan, head of the Philippine Sugar Association, predicts serious problems for his country, due to the sugar stabilization agreement signed in Washington. The Philippines quota calls for a 32 percent reduction.
Sept. 10	A parley on British Commonwealth relations begins in Toronto. Delegates will discuss consultation, action, and improved communications among the members of the Commonwealth.	As President Paul von Hindenburg nears the age of 86, most people think Adolf Hitler will take his place as president, or *Führer* (leader), of the Reich.	Iraq expects no serious problems after the death of King Faisal, as King Ghazi is extremely popular with his subjects.	Fulgencio Batista pulls off another coup in Cuba, deposing President Carlos Manuel de Cespedes and taking over as dictator.	
Sept. 11		The management of the Dutch Industries Fair, being held in Utrecht, sues the General Committee against Terror and Persecution in Germany for handing out propaganda that causes loss of profits to them.	Premier Rashid Ali Beg of Iraq pledges to continue its alliance with Great Britain. King Ghazi reappoints his father's entire Cabinet.		The Japanese public is surprised by the procurator's demand for the death penalty for three involved in the killing of Premier Ki Inukai.
Sept. 12	Joseph Avenol, the new Secretary General of the League of Nations, says the world is looking for profitable lessons from the economic recovery program of the United States.	British flier Amy Johnson Mollison says commercial flying in the United States is at least two years ahead of the system in Great Britain.	A British admiral is sent to Africa to investigate reports that a native chief has sentenced a European to flogging. The laws of the Bechuanaland protectorate ban a native court from dealing with Europeans.	Mexico notifies the ABC countries that it will not join with them in an appeal to Cuba to form a strong government.	Japanese War Minister Sadao Araki wants to cover defense appropriations by a $267 million domestic loan.
Sept. 13	Japanese Minister of War Sadao Araki says U.S. sympathy to China and the continued presence of the U.S. fleet in the Pacific is dangerous and makes it necessary for Japan to immediately strengthen its navy.	The Dutch lower chamber approves two new tariffs—a 5 percent duty on manufactured goods and a 12 percent duty on luxury items.	A British Court of Inquiry banishes Briton Phineas Mackintosh, who was sentenced to flogging by a tribal chief, from all native areas of South Africa after evidence shows his immorality.	Argentine President Agustin Justo says he will go to Rio de Janeiro to sign seven new treaties with Brazil.	Japanese Foreign Minister Yasuya Uchida resigns and is replaced by Koki Hirota, who is said to be even more nationalistic.
Sept. 14	Jurists from seven nations hold a hearing in London to determine who was responsible for setting the Reichstag building on fire on February 27.		In Haifa, 100,000 Arabs from four nations gather to pay homage to Iraqi King Faisal, whose body arrives there aboard the British cruiser *Dispatch*.	Three Spaniards are arrested at Cristobal, Canal Zone, when they try to smuggle six pounds of opium and a quarter of a pound of cocaine on the ship *Juan Sebastion el Cano*.	Mohandas Gandhi agrees to commit no acts of civil disobedience until August 2, 1934. . . . The British combine air and infantry attacks to subdue hostile tribesmen in India who are interfering with the building of a military road there.
Sept. 15	The French adopt a disarmament plan and will begin talks next week with U.S. Special Ambassador Norman Davis and Sir Anthony Eden of Great Britain.	The governments of Turkey and Greece sign a 10-year Non-Aggression Pact.	Persia apologizes to Great Britain because Persian naval officers landed on Basidu Island in the Persian Gulf and pulled down the British flag.	Employees of the Panama Canal Zone will not be allowed to buy spare parts for their Ford cars until Henry Ford signs the NRA code.	Japanese planes drop leaflets on the town of Kalgan, warning the Chinese to evacuate the town or they will bomb it. They say the Chinese are violating the truce.
Sept. 16		The United States enters into a complete aviation agreement with Sweden that will go into effect on October 9.	A witchcraft trial in Tanganyika, east Africa, leads to the conviction of 71 Africans who killed a mother and daughter they believed were witches. . . . Most of the 6,000 German Jews who have settled in Palestine have found jobs, and many professionals are working as farmers.	Argentina has a new plan to deal with locusts. It is spending about $5 million for sheet iron barriers it believes will keep locusts out of sprouting wheat fields.	Japan says it desires amity with China, but Foreign Minister Koki Hirota says better relations between the countries depend on China's recognition of Manchukuo.
Sept. 17	The Jewish Board of Deputies in London takes steps to bring the issue of Germany's anti-Semitic campaign before the League of Nations Council meeting on Friday.	Albania cuts its arms budget in half, saying that national defense has been taking up too large a proportion of the budget in recent years.	The output of gold drops in the Transvaal in Africa, partly due to treatment of a lower grade of ore.	U.S. officials in Havana fear an economic collapse in Cuba and stress to the Cuban government the need for strong rule to prevent chaos.	The Filipino Veterans' Association rejects the Hawes-Cutting Independence Law, saying it does not fulfill the Filipinos' desire for genuine independence.

A	B	C	D	E
Includes developments that affect more than one world region, international organizations, and important meetings of world leaders.	*Includes all domestic and regional developments in Europe, including the Soviet Union.*	*Includes all domestic and regional developments in Africa and the Middle East.*	*Includes all domestic and regional developments in Latin America, the Caribbean, and Canada.*	*Includes all domestic and regional developments in Asian and Pacific nations (and colonies).*

U.S. Politics & Social Issues	U.S. Foreign Policy & Defense	Economics & Great Depression	Science, Technology & Nature	Culture, Leisure & Lifestyle	
President and Mrs. Roosevelt meet their son, Franklin, Jr., as his ship, *The Manhattan*, docks in New York. Also aboard the liner is Col. Theodore Roosevelt, son of the late president.	The Army sets up a laboratory in St. Louis to study encephalitis and try to find a cure for it.	Controller of the Currency James F.T. O'Conner names Democrat Walter Joseph Cummings and Republican E.G. Bennett as directors of the Deposit Insurance Corporation.	The Department of Agriculture sets up a program for scouting out trees infected with Dutch elm disease. The only possible cure is early removal of infected limbs.	Dr. C.A. Wills, father of tennis star Helen Wills Moody, says she cannot touch a racquet for six months. Her injury is due to pressure on the sciatic nerve and could recur.	Sept. 7
President and Mrs. Roosevelt appeal to the people of the United States to help the needy on an individual basis, as relief programs cannot do it all.	Seven Army planes get lost in thick fog over New York City on their way to Mitchel Field. Two finally land there and two make forced landings at an airport in Queens, but three crash. Their two-man crews parachute to safety.	The Treasury sets the price of gold mined on and after August 29 at $29.62 an ounce. The permanent fixed purchase price was $20.67.	Explorer Bob Bartlett observes red walrus, the first he has ever seen in the Atlantic. He watches the red-throated loon teaching her young to fly and visits with Eskimo families.		Sept. 8
To his duties as Secretary of the Interior, Harold Ickes has added a new duty—he is the administrator in charge of enforcing the oil industry code.	Leaders in the U.S. Army Air Corps want pursuit planes that can go 300 miles per hour with a load. They would also like interceptor planes of the type used by the British forces.		Dr. Robert H. Gault of Northwestern University introduces scientists to the "telefactor," a device that allows a person to distinguish slight variations in sound through the fingertips.	A one-armed tennis star from Washington wins the veterans' national tennis championship for the third time. By beating Jarvis Adams of Long Island, Clarence Charest gains permanent possession of the trophy.	Sept. 9
The National Conference on Financing Education asks the government to provide federal aid for education, not only during this emergency, but all the time.	Latin Americans praise President Franklin Roosevelt for consulting representatives of Latin American countries on the Cuban situation. All leaders are opposed to U.S. intervention.	Governor I.C. Blackwood of South Carolina invites cotton-growing states to a meeting to try to immediately raise the price of cotton.		Frederick Perry of Great Britain defeats Jack Crawford of Australia to win the U.S. men's tennis title, the first Briton to do so since 1903.	Sept. 10
	President Franklin Roosevelt says U.S. intervention in Cuba looks less likely now, and Secretary of State Cordell Hull says the United States will welcome a regime that keeps order and has the support of the people. . . . Secretary of the Navy Claude Swanson arrives in Colon, where he inspects the fleet, air, and submarine bases at the Atlantic side of the Panama Canal.	Henry Ford returns home to Dearborn, Mich., and eludes reporters. He remains silent on the NRA.	Chemists in Chicago hear of a new "weighing machine" which can weigh electrons, protons, and deutons. Professor Frank H. Spedding of the University of California devised the "scales" from light beams.	Two balloonists missing for a week are found in the Canadian wilds, 40 miles north of Sunbury, Ontario. W.T. Van Orman and Frank Trotter landed in a tree, which tore the balloon apart. They cut down a telephone pole to disrupt service and get attention.	Sept. 11
Three more states vote for the repeal of Prohibition. Minnesota, Maine, and Maryland vote wet.	A former member of the Coast Guard is accused of selling information on the movements of Coast Guard ships to rum runners, giving them a free run for seven years.		Prof. Albert Einstein works hard in England to prepare a treatise setting forth a new angle he has discovered concerning his theory of relativity.	In the qualifying round for the national amateur golf championship, Johnny Fischer shoots a 69, the lowest qualifying score in the history of the tournament.	Sept. 12
	Gen. John Pershing celebrates his 73rd birthday quietly in Paris, where he is inspecting war memorials.	NRA Administrator Hugh Johnson believes that Henry Ford is observing the auto code even though he has not signed it, and will probably take no action unless he violates some provision of that code.	Prof. Richard Willstaetter of Munich, winner of the Nobel Prize for Chemistry, tells a reporter in Chicago that both the secret of life and of cancer can be traced to newly discovered enzymes.	The Giants lead the Cubs and Pirates by 6.5 games in the National League, while the Senators are 8.5 games ahead of the Yankees in the American League.	Sept. 13
The widow of the late president Theodore Roosevelt appeals to the Needlework Guild of America to help provide more than 1 million garments for the needy for the coming winter.	A new destroyer being built at the Navy Ship Yard in New York is named *Dale*, after Capt. Richard Dale, who served with John Paul Jones.	President Franklin Roosevelt calls mine owners and leaders of the United Mine Workers to the White House and demands a code, which they agree to provide by 9 p.m.	A new theory by Prof. Paul Kunze of Rostock holds that the human body ages from being bombarded by cosmic rays.	British artist Frank Brangwyn is having trouble finishing his huge mural of the Sermon on the Mount for the RCA Building, since he is told not to paint Jesus in the picture.	Sept. 14
Aides to Secretary of the Interior Harold Ickes hint at dissention within the department, saying Theodore Walters, First Assistant, may file a protest on the way the department is being run.		Automakers say the situation with them is improving and seasonal decline is less than expected. Production for September is up 100 percent from last September.	Dr. James H. Hutton of Chicago finds that treating the insane with hormones results in 27 percent being able to return home, as opposed to 17 percent who receive only psychiatric treatment.	The U.S. women's field hockey team, which is traveling in Europe, wins its fourth straight victory, defeating the Leipzig Sports Club.	Sept. 15
	None of the United States' European debtors asks for a legal postponement of their war debt payments, but the United States expects many will default on the December 15 payment, as they did on June 15.		An Amsterdam newspaper says it has it on good authority that Prof. Albert Einstein is next on the Nazis' "Murder Bureau" list. It says an assassin will be paid 10,000 to 20,000 marks.		Sept. 16
	Senator William Borah of Idaho can foresee no condition under which he would agree with U.S. intervention in Cuba.	The U.S. dollar reaches the lowest point of depreciation yet.	Admiral Richard E. Byrd plans to attempt broadcasts from Antarctica during his expedition next winter. Technicians expect to learn much about remote control radio from the broadcasts.	George Dunlap, new amateur golf champion of the United States, sets his sights on the British Amateur. Dunlap's 68 round in the finals is called "as fine a round as I ever saw played anywhere" by golfer Bob Jones.	Sept. 17

F	G	H	I	J
Includes elections, federal-state relations, civil rights and liberties, crime, the judiciary, education, healthcare, poverty, urban affairs, and population.	*Includes formation and debate of U.S. foreign and defense policies, veterans affairs, and defense spending. (Relations with specific foreign countries are usually found under the region concerned.)*	*Includes business, labor, agriculture, taxation, transportation, consumer affairs, monetary and fiscal policy, natural resources, pollution, and accidents.*	*Includes worldwide scientific, medical, and technological developments, natural phenomena, U.S. weather, and natural disasters.*	*Includes the arts, religion, scholarship, communications media, sports, entertainment, fashions, fads, and social life.*

	World Affairs	Europe	Africa & The Middle East	The Americas	Asia & The Pacific
Sept. 18	Tariff talks open in India between Indian mill owners and the Lancashire textile delegation from England on problems in the textile industry. Several Japanese representatives are also involved in the discussion.	The national executive council of Britain's Labor Party praises President Franklin Roosevelt's industrial recovery program.	The Dowager Queen of Bamangwato in South Africa begs Great Britain to free her son, the chief convicted of ordering a white man to be flogged.	A shortage of drinking water forces Bolivian forces to abandon positions gained at heavy cost. A Bolivian patrol, wandering in the desert for three days, succumbs to sunstroke, and then is captured.	
Sept. 19	The League of Nations cuts its budget for 1934 by 10 percent. Money appropriated for the disarmament conference is cut from $330,000 to $210,000.	Queen Wilhelmina urges the Dutch parliament not to undertake any risky monetary or economic experiments.		Argentina may decide to reenter the League of Nations. The League has always considered Argentina a member, but its senate failed to ratify the covenant.	China will sell cotton recently acquired under a $50 million U.S. loan to Japan.
Sept. 20	An article by Newton D. Baker, former U.S. Secretary of War, defends the idea of enforcing peace by international action and hails the League of Nations as the "embodiment of the principles of pacific settlement."	Chancellor Engelbert Dollfuss and Major Emil Hey, leader of the Heimwehr, form a fascist Cabinet for Austria, with Dollfuss holding five of the Cabinet posts.		Buenos Aires reports that Bolivia has tightened its censorship, which makes Argentina believe there is some sort of political crisis in the country. . . . American citizens in Cuba are ordered to take refuge on the nearest U.S. war vessel, as Communists increase activities in the country.	Tokyo denies that Japan is fortifying the Bonin Islands in the Pacific and building an air base there, which would violate the Washington Naval Treaty.
Sept. 21	Acting as president, Norwegian Premier John Mowinckl opens the session of the League of Nations Council in Geneva.	Marinus van der Lubbe, a Dutchman, goes on trial for allegedly starting the Reichstag fire on February 27.	Negotiations are going on for the release of a group held captive in the Sahara Desert by Moors for 12 years.	A prospector in Brazil finds the second-largest diamond ever recorded. It weighs 2,000 carats and is appraised at $800,000.	The Japanese military seeks approval to reestablish four army divisions eliminated in 1925. They say they are necessary to meet commitments under the treaty with Manchukuo.
Sept. 22	An agreement appears close in a three nation parley involving the United States, France, and Great Britain. They outline an eight-year disarmament plan for the world.	David Lloyd George entreats the British government not to bully the Reich to the point where a Communist takeover would occur.		Peru fights the spread of malaria in the southern part of the country. The government purchases large quantities of quinine sulfate to aid in the fight.	Russia charges that Manchukuo plans several infractions of Russian rights on the Chinese Eastern Railway. It says Japan must take responsibility, since Manchukuo is powerless.
Sept. 23	A decree in Panama makes hundreds of children born there to American parents natural-born citizens of Panama, in addition to being U.S. citizens.	Major Emil Fey, acting Chancellor of Austria while Engelbert Dollfuss is in Geneva, will establish concentration camps for Austrian Nazis, who will be detained at their own expense.	Police in Alexandria take precautions as King Fuad plans to form a Cabinet in which the Premier is the least important member. A few members of the Sidky Pasha Cabinet will remain.	The stage is set for the end of hostilities in the Chaco, as Bolivia accepts the ABC-Peru plan, which Paraguay had already accepted.	The "Buy Philippine" movement is revived as a Trading Center and Exchange is set up in Manila.
Sept. 24	An article by a London writer states that the Germans plan to invade France by going through Switzerland. France and other countries are skeptical of any German talk of peace in Geneva.		Yehia Pasha, who is vacationing in Europe, is called back to Cairo to form a nonpartisan Cabinet for Egypt.	Police shoot and kill three rebels who are in a secret meeting, planning an armed uprising and a series of kidnappings in Jalisco State in Mexico.	Russia issues a strong warning to Japan as to consequences if it seizes the Chinese Eastern Railway.
Sept. 25	The Argentine Senate votes unanimously to join the League of Nations. The League has considered it a member for 13 years.	London denies rumors that Princess Juliana of the Netherlands will marry the Duke of Gloucester. Amsterdam also denies it.	Workers leveling land for a football field just outside Alexandria, Egypt, find beautifully painted walls. They are believed to be part of an ancient tomb.		Some roads in Manchuria are closed to traffic, due to an epidemic of pneumonia and bubonic plague, which is proving fatal to 90 percent of those who get it.
Sept. 26		The British delegation, headed by Frederick Leith-Ross, chief economic adviser, sails for the United States to take part in debt revision talks.	The Abyssinian Empress visits Palestine as the first stop on her tour of Christian shrines. She will also dedicate a new Abyssinian church in Jerusalem.	A tornado destroys the town of Tampico in Mexico. At least 20 are killed and over 850 injured.	Eighteen unmarried Chinese women become the first Chinese policewomen in Peiping. They have had three months of intensive training, and carry revolvers and batons while on patrol.
Sept. 27	U.S. Special Ambassador Norman Davis and Briton Sir John Simon fight a proposal by Germany and Italy to delay arms talks and transfer them to Italy.	Denmark plans to supply its citizens with gas masks to guard against chemical warfare. They will sell for about $5.08. Gas-proof rooms are also being built, since children cannot wear the masks.	Abdel Fatta Yehia Pasha heads the new bipartisan Egyptian Cabinet. Sidky Pasha virtually ran the last Cabinet, but this Cabinet has several strong members.		New regulations give the Chief of Staff of the Japanese navy enough power to make it almost independent of the Cabinet.
Sept. 28	Former U.S. president Herbert Hoover is being recommended for a League of Nations post the Dutch want created. He would be High Commissioner for German Refugees.	The British believe the tariff truce negotiated by U.S. Special Ambassador Norman Davis last spring is on its way out, since both Sweden and Holland have abandoned it.	The British decide to reinstate African chieftain Tshekedi, who was banished from his territory in South Africa because he ordered the flogging of a white man.	Disorder grows rapidly in Cuba, with soldiers removing large guns from the police departments after a rumor that police might join an uprising.	Tokyo's war office insists it needs to increase its armed forces because Russia has 10 divisions stationed in the Far East.
Sept. 29	Austrian Chancellor Engelbert Dollfuss returns home, satisfied after the League of Nations assembly applauds his determination to keep Austria free.		Exiled Mar Shimun, Patriarch of the Assyrians, leaves for Geneva to plead his peoples' case before the League of Nations.	All those invited to the Pan-American talks accept Uruguay's invitation to Montevideo. Since Bolivia and Paraguay both accept, Uruguay thinks the Chaco War may end before the talks.	China's Wellington Koo warns the League of Nations that war will come soon in the Far East and asks the League to stand with China against Japanese aggression.

A	B	C	D	E
Includes developments that affect more than one world region, international organizations, and important meetings of world leaders.	*Includes all domestic and regional developments in Europe, including the Soviet Union.*	*Includes all domestic and regional developments in Africa and the Middle East.*	*Includes all domestic and regional developments in Latin America, the Caribbean, and Canada.*	*Includes all domestic and regional developments in Asian and Pacific nations (and colonies).*

U.S. Politics & Social Issues	U.S. Foreign Policy & Defense	Economics & Great Depression	Science, Technology & Nature	Culture, Leisure & Lifestyle	
	Secretary of State Cordell Hull denies that Great Britain has asked the United States to abandon its planned naval reconstruction program.	The new sugar stabilization agreement to go to President Franklin Roosevelt calls for larger quotas for Cuba and the Philippines and asks RFC funds to hold surplus in reserve. . . . Christian A. Herter, a friend of former president Herbert Hoover, charges that President Franklin Roosevelt's policies are leading the nation toward an economic morass.		Movie actress Jean Harlow elopes from Hollywood with cameraman H.G. Rosson.	Sept. 18
Eugene L. Vidal is named Director of Aeronautics for the Department of Commerce.	Rep. Walton Moore of Virginia succeeds Raymond Moley as Assistant Secretary of State. Moore may be put in charge of debt revision talks beginning soon.		The National Association of Audubon Societies urges the extermination of stray cats because they prey on birds.	The Giants clinch the National League pennant for the 30th time, tying the Chicago Cubs for the most pennants won.	Sept. 19
		Senator James Couzens says he will press bank reform, saying Judge Harry Keidan did not allow him to finish testifying to a grand jury investigating two large banks in Michigan.	The Radio-Electrical Show at Madison Square Garden emphasizes small radio sets as being in vogue.	Rosh Hashanah, the Jewish New Year, began last night and continues through tomorrow. Yom Kippur, the Day of Atonement, will be on September 30.	Sept. 20
A gang of four bandits toting machine guns holds up the Farmers State Bank in Hays, Kans., taking 12 hostages. They take them on a wild ride in stolen cars, then release them at the Oklahoma border.	In order to combat smuggling, which is predicted to increase after the repeal of Prohibition, $14.8 million is allotted to the Coast Guard. The money will cover construction of seaplanes, cutters, and patrol boats.		The American Dahlia Show at the Hotel Pennsylvania in New York features a new bloom named the Eleanor Roosevelt. The pure white flower is the formal decorative type of dahlia.	Author Mary Roberts Rinehart says that after 25 years of writing, she will take a year off from her regular writing to write a book to please herself.	Sept. 21
	The Navy refuses to surrender Lt. John Henry Cross for civil trial in the Canal Zone. He is charged with involuntary manslaughter when a passenger in his car dies in an accident.	Henry Ford puts his 50,000 workers on a 32-hour workweek, which complies with the NRA code he has not signed.	Canadian astronomer Dr. J.B. Marsh, who led the study of the total eclipse last year, dies at his home in Hamilton, Ontario.	Maureen Orcutt wins the New Jersey Women's Golf Championship for the third time. . . . President Franklin Roosevelt congratulates the Washington Senators on their American League pennant win and says he will attend at least one game of the World Series.	Sept. 22
Secretary of War George H. Dern announces the administration will press for ratification of the St. Lawrence Treaty with Canada.	The Veterans' Administration and the Department of Labor are selecting 75,000 more men for the Civil Conservation Corps. Present members will be allowed to re-enlist, but are encouraged to take other jobs if they can find them.	President William Green predicts the AFL will join the boycott of German goods being organized by trade unions in Europe.	Canada moves about 1,000 buffalo from Wainwright, Alberta, to a larger preserve in the Northwest Territories. The park has 17,300 square miles where the animals can roam and graze.		Sept. 23
	U.S. warships in Cuban ports are given authority to land forces if it is necessary to protect lives.	Secretary of Agriculture George Peek speaks out against inflation, saying only restoration of world trade or cutting of excess acreage planted during the war will help farmers.	A bloodsucking aquatic leech kills thousands of ducks in the United States and Canada by getting into their throats and nostrils and either choking or smothering them.	Babe Ruth's name is mentioned as a possible successor to Bucky Harris as manager of the Detroit Tigers. Ruth says he has not heard about the proposal.	Sept. 24
The National Women's Party urges President Franklin Roosevelt to halt dismissals of married women from federal jobs. They ask that he provide these women with furloughs with retention of their civil service status.		Officials in Washington expect President Franklin Roosevelt to appoint a Corporation of Foreign Security Holders. It will act in the interests of Americans holding foreign bonds.	Radiologists meeting in Chicago hear that light rays hold the secret of the universe. The American Society for the Control of Cancer praises radiation for curing many cancers.	The New York Giants vote on division of shares of World Series money, voting equal shares to the 21 players, 3 coaches, the club secretary, and the club trainer.	Sept. 25
A witness in court testifies that Chicago mayor Anton Cermak had full knowledge of the plot to assassinate him, and had said that Louis "Little New York" Campagna was being imported to do the job.	Washington denies reports from Havana that the U.S. government will take temporary custodianship of Cuba.	Three thousand workers strike at the Chester plant of the Ford Motor Company. . . . Charles Coiner, who designed the Blue Eagle insignia of the NRA, applies for a patent, but signs it over to the U.S. government.	Scientist C.P. Haskins tells the American Congress of Radiology that x-rays can artificially alter hereditary traits in living things.	Chicago baseball writers defy Commissioner K.M. Landis and appoint their own two scorers for the World Series—sports writers Herb Simons and Eddie Munzel.	Sept. 26
Postmasters from across the nation gather in Rochester, N.Y., where Postmaster General James Farley will address the convention.		Former Undersecretary of the Treasury Arthur Ballantine charges the United States is headed toward a bigger deficit than in any year since 1919.	Admiral Richard E. Byrd says his expedition will be unable to go to Antarctica unless a few thousand dollars can be raised to purchase things "vital to the safety of the men."		Sept. 27
	A gang of 20 rumrunners abandons 500 cases of liquor on the New Jersey coast after a 20-minute gun battle with the Coast Guard, which had received a tip.		Robert Fechner, conservation director, announces that the Forest Conservation Corps will buy 250 million feet of lumber to build forest camps, which will stimulate the lumber business.	Actress Greta Garbo buys land in Dyvik, Sweden, where an old friend, Max Gumpfel, is designing a castle for her.	Sept. 28
Secretary of War George H. Dern returns to Washington after a 1,200-mile trip inspecting the Great Lakes/St. Lawrence waterway. He says that President Franklin Roosevelt is solidly behind the project.		Col. William Chevalier is appointed an industrial advisor for the construction machinery distributing trade.	A Belgian officer, Major R. von Rolleghem, demonstrates a new material that will make a plane immune to fire. He puts two mice in the cockpit of a model plane covered with the material, then sets a fire in the nose of the plane. The mice are unharmed.		Sept. 29

F	G	H	I	J
Includes elections, federal-state relations, civil rights and liberties, crime, the judiciary, education, healthcare, poverty, urban affairs, and population.	*Includes formation and debate of U.S. foreign and defense policies, veterans affairs, and defense spending. (Relations with specific foreign countries are usually found under the region concerned.)*	*Includes business, labor, agriculture, taxation, transportation, consumer affairs, monetary and fiscal policy, natural resources, pollution, and accidents.*	*Includes worldwide scientific, medical, and technological developments, natural phenomena, U.S. weather, and natural disasters.*	*Includes the arts, religion, scholarship, communications media, sports, entertainment, fashions, fads, and social life.*

	World Affairs	Europe	Africa & The Middle East	The Americas	Asia & The Pacific
Sept. 30	The ABC-Peru group declines the mandate by the League of Nations and gives up on trying to make peace in the Chaco between Bolivia and Paraguay.	Spain endeavors to solve the problem of the large numbers of beggars by placing them in concentration camps.	The University of Pennsylvania Museum and the Boston Museum of Fine Arts team up to excavate the ancient city of Ray, located six miles south of Teheran, Persia.	Canada is building a 2-million bushel grain elevator at Fort Erie, which Americans are afraid will compete with the ones across the river in Buffalo.	
Oct. 1	U.S. Special Ambassador Norman Davis supports continuation of the disarmament conference, fearing failure of the conference will mean that all will depend on the signers of the Four-Powers Pact.	The Belgian middle class shows its unhappiness with excessive taxation by a huge demonstration in Brussels. Delegations come from nine provinces.		Discovery of a Communist revolt plot has Argentine troops on guard at government buildings in Buenos Aires and may necessitate martial law.	An overloaded excursion vessel carrying 130 people capsizes in Japan. Seventy are rescued and the rest are believed to have drowned, although only 33 bodies have been found so far.
Oct. 2	The League of Nations creates a 15th seat on its council. Argentina, Denmark, and Australia are elected for three-year terms, replacing the Irish Free State, Guatemala, and Norway.	French Foreign Minister Joseph Paul-Bancour assures the Austrian delegate to the League of Nations that "France is with you."		President Ramon Grau San Martin is said to be a virtual prisoner in Cuba and a coup is believed imminent. Col. Fulgencio Batista, head of the army, says he will establish a free government with fair elections.	Japan says it will withdraw a third of its troops that have remained in the neutral zone in north China.
Oct. 3		Austrian Chancellor Engelbert Dollfuss is seriously injured in an assassination attempt. . . . Yugoslavian King Alexander arrives in Sofia, Bulgaria, to help establish a Balkan Pact against the Nazis.	Noted traveler and writer William Joseph Harding King, who explored the Libyan Desert as well as the Sahara, dies in Devon, England, at the age of 64.	Rumors that the U.S. Embassy in Havana would be bombed necessitate a special guard around the building. The public also learns that 30 shots were fired at an armored car carrying President Ramon Grau San Martin.	Japan's government will reduce acreage planted with rice in 1934, since a bumper crop, plus surplus left from last year, is causing a problem for farmers.
Oct. 4	William Ormsby-Gore of Great Britain attacks the Nazis' view on race at the League of Nations Assembly Commission, saying the mixture of races "holds the British Empire together."	Konrad Henlein, leader of the Student National Socialist Party in Czechoslovakia, dissolves the party because he thinks the government will ban it.		There is talk of rebuilding the town of Tampico, Mexico, which was devastated by hurricanes. The city is still three-quarters covered with water, and residents want to rebuild on higher ground.	Official dispatches from Nanking state that the Executive Yuan has approved the issuing of $100 million in treasury notes.
Oct. 5	The League of Nations Economic and Financial Commission reports that stabilized currency is necessary to a lasting recovery for the world.	Britain speeds up its naval construction, awarding the first contract six months early. The London Times says the contract time was possibly advanced because of shipbuilding activity in other countries.	In a joyful ceremony, Tshekedi is reinstated as Chief of the Bamangwato tribe in South Africa. He was banished for sentencing a white man to be flogged.	British explorer Col. H.P. Fawcett and his son are again reported to be alive in the jungles of Brazil, after disappearing there eight years ago. They are reported prisoners of the Cuicuru tribe.	
Oct. 6	The League of Nations recommends appointment of a High Commissioner for Refugees. Italy objects to a clause that assumes nations that have not received many German refugees will provide employment for refugees.	Strong-arm tactics by Catalonia's Governor General averts what could have been one of the most serious strikes in Spain in recent years. Utility employees had threatened to walk out.		Brazil has destroyed $200 million worth of coffee since July 1931. That figure equals a full year's consumption for the entire world.	The Filipino Senate votes 15–4 to reject the Hawes-Cutting plan for independence. However, leaders agree that this is not a final vote.
Oct. 7	Argentina thanks the League of Nations for its election to the Council and pledges its cooperation in seeking world peace.	The British government defends its criticism of the U.S. Navy, saying the size of new U.S. cruisers may stimulate a new rivalry for bigger navies.		Bolivia asks the League of Nations for a formula for arbitration between itself and Paraguay in the Chaco conflict.	Japanese Gen. Kosio plays down the tension between Russia and Japan, saying there will be no war unless Russia challenges Japan.
Oct. 8	Dr. Rudolf Nadolny, German delegate to the disarmament conference, asks U.S. Special Ambassador Norman Davis to arrange a meeting between French and Germans on their disarmament differences.	Diego Martinez Barrios forms a coalition Cabinet in Spain, incorporating all republican parties except the Socialists, who do promise their support.	Timurtash Khan, former aide to the Shah, dies in a Persian prison where he was sent after being convicted of bribery and embezzlement.	Brazil's President Getulio Vargas urges unity among South American countries; Argentina's President Agustin Justo agrees.	Japan and India extend their trade pact for one month to give them time to work on revising it.
Oct. 9	The League of Nations hosts the Conference for the Repression of the Traffic in Women in an effort to stop prostitution around the world.		South African Defense Minister Oswald Pirow proposes a fighting air squadron as part of the country's plan to strengthen its defense.	Guatemala names its delegates to the Pan-American conference. They are Carlos Sanchez, Ramiro Fernandez, Foreign Minister Alfredo Skinner Klee, and Finance Minister Jose Gonzalez Campos.	Russia is emphatic in warning Japan that it will not tolerate action against the Chinese Eastern Railway. A Russian newspaper accuses Japan of a plot to seize the railroad, which Japan angrily denies.
Oct. 10	The governing board of the new refugee aid organization of the League of Nations will include non-member countries and private organizations. The United States is expected to be invited to sit on the board.	The trial on the Reichstag fire continues, with witnesses disagreeing on whether they saw one man or two enter the building. When asked if anyone else helped him, defendant Marinus van der Lubbe says, "I can't say."		Six Latin American nations sign an anti-war treaty, plus treaties on commerce, navigation, and extradition. Signing are Argentina, Brazil, Chile, Mexico, Paraguay, and Uruguay.	Peace negotiations between rebel Gen. Fang Chen-wu and the Chinese government break down, threatening further hostilities.

A	B	C	D	E
Includes developments that affect more than one world region, international organizations, and important meetings of world leaders.	*Includes all domestic and regional developments in Europe, including the Soviet Union.*	*Includes all domestic and regional developments in Africa and the Middle East.*	*Includes all domestic and regional developments in Latin America, the Caribbean, and Canada.*	*Includes all domestic and regional developments in Asian and Pacific nations (and colonies).*

U.S. Politics & Social Issues	U.S. Foreign Policy & Defense	Economics & Great Depression	Science, Technology & Nature	Culture, Leisure & Lifestyle	
Former president Herbert Hoover urges Republican leaders to support President Franklin Roosevelt's NRA program.	Eighty-four West Point graduates will begin training in Randolph Field, Texas, for their air corps commissions.	AFL leader William Green tells laborers they should be slow to strike and should give the NRA time to mature and work out any problems.	A study of their skulls links Peking man with Neanderthal man, with both showing a distinctly human type of brain.	Iowa scores a major upset in Big Ten football, beating Northwestern, 7–0, to score its first Big Ten victory in four years.	Sept. 30
President Franklin Roosevelt decides at the last minute to go to Chicago and address the American Legion Convention about economies that affect veterans. He and Eleanor Roosevelt will also visit the Century of Progress World Fair.	Secretary of State Cordell Hull holds a mass meeting in Washington to start a nationwide campaign on behalf of an international disarmament treaty. Dr. Mary Wooley, delegate to the conference in Geneva, also speaks.	AFL president William Green reports that since the NRA was enacted, AFL membership has increased by 1.3 million, giving them a total of 4 million members.	Scientists at Princeton University create "heavy water," a compound in which each hydrogen atom has a mass of two instead of one.	A Hans Holbein painting of England's King Henry VIII is discovered in the home of Geoffrey Howard near York. The painting, which was covered with four layers of paint, bears Holbein's signature and the year 1542.	Oct. 1
When President Franklin Roosevelt returns from Chicago, he will confer with Assistant Secretary Dean Acheson about debt negotiations with the British, which will take place next week.	The United States will only land troops in Havana if it is necessary for the safety of U.S. citizens. The State Department praises Ambassador Sumner Welles, who managed to extricate 24 Americans while avoiding U.S. intervention.	Questionnaires are being sent to 3 million employers asking for data on changes in the past four months, as President Franklin Roosevelt attempts to evaluate the progress being made by the NRA.	Guglielmo Marconi, inventor of the telegraph, spends time with President Franklin Roosevelt at the World's Fair in Chicago.	The Giants beat the Senators in the first game of the World Series at the Polo Grounds. . . . Eugene O'Neill's *Ah, Wilderness*, a comedy, premieres in New York City.	Oct. 2
President Franklin Roosevelt signs 17 codes and confers with Hugh S. Johnson, NRA Administrator.		About 80,000 dressmakers, members of the International Ladies Garment Workers Union, hold a victory celebration because of improvements in hours, wages, and working conditions due to the NRA.	James and Amy Mollison encounter difficulties as they attempt to take off for Baghdad from Ontario. The plane gets off the ground, but winds force it down on the beach, necessitating taking it to Toronto for repairs. . . . The Eighth General Conference on Weights and Measures, being held in Paris, is expected to propose worldwide adoption of the metric system.	Abbott and Dunning announce Helen Mencken will star in *The Drums Begin*. However, the Theatre Guild says she will be seen in *Mary of Scotland*. The Actors Equity Association will decide which play she is to do.	Oct. 3
Assistant Attorney General Pat Malloy quits his job, charging that Attorney General Homer Cummings failed to prosecute a financier on tax evasion and failed to back Malloy's speech to the American Bar Association in August.	The Bonus movement is dead, but the American Legion asks Congress for a $50 million per year payment to World War veterans instead.	The NRA says there must be no exceptions to the ban on child labor and says if the child's earnings are vital to the family, it will receive relief.		The first issue of *Esquire* magazine is published.	Oct. 4
	The American Legion speaks out against inflation, saying veterans are getting little enough money as it is. It is against arms reduction and says the government is responsible for care of disabled veterans.	A survey shows that as many as a million people may be employed by winter, working on projects under the government's Public Works program.	Soviet Arctic expert N.G. Datsky discovers that the ice cap is receding in the north of Russia, causing the barren tundra to show new growth of plants.	Bill Veeck, president of the Chicago Cubs, dies in Chicago of leucocythaemia. He had asked that the city series between the Cubs and White Sox not be called off if he died. . . . President Franklin Roosevelt, along with many other government officials, sees the Washington Senators win over the New York Giants in the third game of the World Series.	Oct. 5
President Franklin Roosevelt greets the delegation from Great Britain and they talk a few minutes, but do not go into any detail on debts. Meetings will begin on Monday.		President Franklin Roosevelt signs an order dropping the provision for a 40-hour week during six weeks of this year. Now all employees will work a 35-hour week.	French physician Dr. Jacques Le Mee believes leprosy is not contagious and says that his research indicates the disease is transmitted by soil.	Mel Ott's home run in the 10th inning carries the Giants past the Senators to win the World Series, four games to one.	Oct. 6
	Reciprocity treaties with countries in South America will be a first step away from isolation for the United States, in conjunction with President Franklin Roosevelt's recovery program.	Both the nation's forests and the men participating in the Civil Conservation Corps are found to have benefited during the first six months of the program.	A scarab unearthed by the Haverford expedition in Palestine tells the story of the marriage of Amenhotep III and Queen Tiy of Egypt.		Oct. 7
Ten heavily armed guards take Harvey Bailey and Albert Bates to Leavenworth to begin their life sentences for the kidnapping of Charles E. Urschel. . . . The Federal Council of Churches of Christ in America, representing 25 Protestant denominations, asks Secretary of State Cordell Hull to demand cuts in arms at the Geneva disarmament parley.		The Roosevelt administration scraps the proposed sugar stabilization agreement, but still plans limitations on sugar beets and sugar cane crops.	Cornell University astronomers on an Arizona mountaintop photograph the ultraviolet rays of stars, with the help of a new aluminum mirror.		Oct. 8
Chicago gang leader Gus Winkler is slain in a shotgun execution for being an informer.	Naval authorities in the Canal Zone refuse to surrender Lt. J.H. Cross to the civil courts on a charge of involuntary manslaughter. The Navy will conduct a trial by court-martial.	Farm leaders charge they are not benefiting from the New Deal and that the Farm Relief Bill is not functioning. They are asking aid from the rail unions and will meet with them on October 17.	Dr. Joseph Bloodgood of Johns Hopkins University says three types of cancer can be easily eradicated. They include cancer of the mouth, cancer of the skin, and cancer of the cervix.	Former national amateur tennis champion Ellsworth Vines turns pro. He signs with William Tilden and will make his pro debut on January 10 at Madison Square Garden.	Oct. 9
President and Mrs. Roosevelt give a state dinner at the White House in honor of President Harmodio Arias, who is visiting from Panama.			Guglielmo Marconi, inventor of the telegraph, is amazed by the advanced state television has reached in the United States. Marconi visits the television lab of the RCA Victor Company in Camden, N.J.	Actress Renee Adoree, who died Thursday, leaves no will. Her only heir is her mother, Mrs. Victoria Adoree, in England.	Oct. 10

F	G	H	I	J
Includes elections, federal-state relations, civil rights and liberties, crime, the judiciary, education, healthcare, poverty, urban affairs, and population.	*Includes formation and debate of U.S. foreign and defense policies, veterans affairs, and defense spending. (Relations with specific foreign countries are usually found under the region concerned.)*	*Includes business, labor, agriculture, taxation, transportation, consumer affairs, monetary and fiscal policy, natural resources, pollution, and accidents.*	*Includes worldwide scientific, medical, and technological developments, natural phenomena, U.S. weather, and natural disasters.*	*Includes the arts, religion, scholarship, communications media, sports, entertainment, fashions, fads, and social life.*

	World Affairs	Europe	Africa & The Middle East	The Americas	Asia & The Pacific
Oct. 11	In a meeting with Sir John Simon of Britain and Joseph Paul-Bancour of France, U.S. Special Ambassador Norman Davis suggests that they ask Germany to submit a list of its demands.	The Dutch city of Zaandam, near Amsterdam, adopts a resolution to boycott German goods due to the Hitler regime in Germany.		The Navy sends the battleship *Wyoming* to Guantanamo Bay, Cuba, but stresses the move is only part of regular training of marines. It may replace the *New Mexico*, which has been stationed there.	Russians bitterly resent Japanese actions in the Harbin area, where Soviet officials of the Chinese Eastern Railway are being seized and their offices searched. Additionally, 300 Soviet Russians working on a new railway are replaced by White Russians.
Oct. 12	The League of Nations invites the United States to be one of 15 nations sitting on the board of the new body being set up for the relief of German refugees.	French diplomat Joseph Paul-Bancour appears optimistic as he tells the French Cabinet of the British and U.S. stand against the rearmament of Germany.	Jerusalem police, worried about the number of Arabs coming into the city to march against Jews immigrating to Palestine, enlist the help of the military in planning extra security.	Canadian and U.S. Chambers of Commerce meet and recommend elimination of regulations hindering free trade between the two countries at points on the border.	Siam reports that two regiments of soldiers have mutinied and have taken over the Donmuang airdrome. Martial law is proclaimed.
Oct. 13	France decides to withdraw from the tariff truce drawn up by Secretary of State Cordell Hull at the economic conference in London. Withdrawal will be effective in 30 days.	Plans are under way for a meeting of three Balkan kings. King Boris of Bulgaria, King Carol of Romania, and King Alexander of Yugoslavia will be included in the meeting.	Eleven people are hurt in a clash between Arabs and police in Jerusalem. The Arabs are protesting immigration of German Jews into Palestine.	Cuban former president Gerardo Machado and his aides disappear from Montreal and are believed to be headed to the United States.	Japanese War Minister, Lt. Gen. Sadao Araki, says he wants to clear up mis-understandings, stating that Japan has no desire for a war with Russia.
Oct. 14	Air forces become one of the main topics of debate at the disarmament conference in Geneva. They will also discuss civil aviation, as it could be converted to military.		E.G. Boulenger, director of the British Zoological Society, says if it were not for wildlife preserves, African mammals would soon be extinct. Africa has 20 of them, including the Kruger National Park.	Gen. Hans Kundt, German commander of the Bolivian army, says the country has resources enough to continue the fight in the Chaco for another year, if necessary.	Australia takes steps to protect the country against aggressors, as it worries about the Japanese policy in the East.
Oct. 15	A Santiago newspaper says Germany's withdrawal has killed the League of Nations. Chileans are concerned that the Reich will start a new war.	The Scandinavians are upset by Germany's withdrawal from the League and even those newspapers that are usually pro-German condemn the move. . . . Austria also expresses concern that Germany may be even more dangerous outside the League.		The Chilean Foreign Minister asks members of earlier Pan-American conferences to be prepared to discuss a list of topics at the Montevideo conference.	Inner Mongolia wants autonomy, and if the Nanking government does not grant its demands, it will ask Manchukuo for help in cutting itself off from China.
Oct. 16	The arms parley recesses until October 26, after telling Germany its reasons for quitting were not valid. . . . The Russians foresee an end to Germany's "fake pacifism" and say they have heard that Germany and Japan have a definite agreement about joint military action.	Austria arrests 20 Nazis after uncovering a plot to seize the Linz garrison. All are charged with high treason.		Alberto Salamanca, son of Bolivia's president, dies in a battle in the Chaco War.	
Oct. 17	Delegates from many countries attend the opening of the Institute of International Affairs at William & Mary College in Virginia.	Three men confess to being involved in the bomb blast in the Vatican in June, which injured two and threw the crowd into a panic.		President Franklin Roosevelt and President Harmodio Arias of Panama meet in Washington and release the Panama Canal Declaration, whereby Panama controls the commercial rights within the Canal Zone.	A revolt in Siam is blamed on the return of exiled radical leader Luang Pradit. The rebels say they could capture the capital any time they wished.
Oct. 18	German Chancellor Adolf Hitler refuses to send delegates back to the disarmament parley until equality is assured.	Premier Thorvald Stauning announces that the southern border of Denmark will be defended to the limit. He has reinforced military units along the German border.		The Ecuadorian Senate votes unanimously to impeach President Juan Martinez. Three other presidents have also been ousted in a short time.	Flier Bert Hall is arrested in Tangku, China, and accused of being paid for German ammunition and never delivering it.
Oct. 19	The president of the disarmament conference, Arthur Henderson, is against resorting to use of the Four-Powers Pact because he thinks it could arouse suspicion and damage both the treaty and the conference.	British holders of German bonds ask their government to protest against the favored treatment Germany gives Dutch and Swiss bondholders.	Dr. William J. Schieffelin, president of the American Mission of Lepers, reports completion of a new leper colony in Addis Ababa, Abbyssinia.	Brazil opens bids in an attempt to barter manganese, cocoa, cotton, rubber, nuts, and oil for the construction of the 28 new warships it has authorized.	
Oct. 20	The 30th session of the Permanent Court of International Justice opens in The Hague.	The Dutch test their air defenses at a small town three miles from the German border, as army planes are sent up and pretend to drop bombs. Sirens wail, telling people to take shelter. This is the first such test the Dutch have ever performed.		The Leticia parley is delayed, since some of the members, including Colombian Foreign Minister Roberto Urdaneta, have not yet arrived. Ecuador is also trying to get a place at the conference.	Prince Sithiporn, one of the leading agriculturists in Siam, is arrested in connection with the revolt there. His brother, Prince Bovoradej, was the leader of the revolt.
Oct. 21	People in official circles in Brazil say the country is seriously considering rejoining the League of Nations, and if it does, Foreign Minister Afranio Mello Franco would resign to become Brazil's delegate.	Austria arrests German Prince Bernhard von Sachsen-Meiningen and his wife, Princess Margot, charging them with a Nazi conspiracy against Austria.	A conference will be held in London on October 31. The purpose is to formulate an international plan to protect Africa's wild animals and plants, some of which are threatened with extinction.	Canada has marked nearly 200 historic sites and monuments since a plan to do so was put into operation in 1919. One of the latest is a monument to Capt. George Vancouver in British Columbia.	Chinese leaders believe the main purpose of the talks between the United States and Russia is to prepare a united defense against Japanese menacing in the Far East.

A	B	C	D	E
Includes developments that affect more than one world region, international organizations, and important meetings of world leaders.	Includes all domestic and regional developments in Europe, including the Soviet Union.	Includes all domestic and regional developments in Africa and the Middle East.	Includes all domestic and regional developments in Latin America, the Caribbean, and Canada.	Includes all domestic and regional developments in Asian and Pacific nations (and colonies).

U.S. Politics & Social Issues	U.S. Foreign Policy & Defense	Economics & Great Depression	Science, Technology & Nature	Culture, Leisure & Lifestyle	
Eleanor Roosevelt celebrates her 49th birthday by entertaining Guglielmo Marconi and his wife, Marchesa, at lunch, hosting a tea for women delegates to the AFL, and enjoying a family dinner.		John Cornwell, general counsel for the B&O Railroad, says the merger of that road with the Pennsylvania Railroad could cause the loss of 300,000 jobs.	Dr. Charles Mayo of the Mayo Clinic tells a Chicago medical meeting that the average man can add 10 years to his life by personal care and may keep the brain functioning well with exercise and new interests.	An Associated Press survey of 34 colleges shows football attendance is up 41 percent this year over last year.	Oct. 11
	Hugh Wilson, U.S. Ambassador to Switzerland, sits in on the League of Nations Council meeting concerning the Central Opium Board. . . . Secretary of State Cordell Hull meets with German Ambassador Dr. Hans Luther concerning attacks on U.S. citizens in Germany.	NRA Administrator Hugh Johnson, Agricultural Adjustment Administrator George Peek, and Secretary of Agriculture Henry Wallace meet to try to coordinate recovery efforts.	A Soviet army flier sets a record by falling 23,124 feet before pulling the rip cord on his parachute, when he is only 150 meters above the ground. He lands safely.	The newly organized Screen Actors Guild, with Eddie Cantor as its head, threatens to strike if the motion picture code provides for fixed salaries.	Oct. 12
John Dillinger's gang helps him escape from a jail in Allen County, Ohio.	The U.S. Department of Justice acquires the U.S. Army disciplinary barracks on Alcatraz Island to use as a federal penitentiary.	The AFL Convention ends after approving compulsory unemployment insurance and averting a debate on unionism.	Prof. Harry Holmes of Oberlin University tells the American Chemical Society that he has produced a nearly pure vitamin A oil, 9,200 times as potent as cod liver oil.	The Hialeah Race Track plans to adopt a "dope box" system as used in France and England. Each horse is examined to make sure it has not received any stimulants.	Oct. 13
	The Army rushes construction of 63 Civil Conservation Corps camps in New York and New Jersey. They are to be used as winter headquarters for the workers.		J.B. Thompson, RCA engineer, invents a tiny radio tube called the acorn, which can pick up small radio waves and make it possible for more stations to broadcast in an area without interference. . . . More human bones and primitive instruments are unearthed in the Choukoutien, 40 miles south of Peiping.		Oct. 14
Kicking off the four-week 1933 Mobilization for Human Needs drive, President Franklin Roosevelt appeals to the nation to provide local aid for the needy, as the government cannot do it all.	Senator William E. Borah calls German Chancellor Adolf Hitler's regime the "fruits of Versailles" and believes the world is facing the possibility of another war.	The code for banks takes effect today and will eliminate waste and provide desired reforms. Clearing houses will make banking more economical.		The National Symphony opens its third season under Dr. Hans Kindler with a "popular" concert in Constitution Hall.	Oct. 15
Senator Huey Long is booed and hissed as he attacks President Franklin Roosevelt in a speech at the Louisiana State Fair in his home state.	Officials in Washington say the United States will remain aloof from the inter-capital conferences taking place in Europe, as they mainly address European concerns.	Harry Hopkins, Federal Emergency Relief Administrator, announces the purchase of huge amounts of beef and butter to be distributed to the needy this winter. Much pork has already been bought.	A new unit illustrating bird life in northern Europe is presented to the American Museum of Natural History and dedicated to British ornithologist Lord Grey and Theodore Roosevelt.		Oct. 16
President Franklin Roosevelt is victim of a practical joke by Harvard undergraduates, who write to ask permission to name a carillon after him. When he learns it was a hoax, he says he would rather have a baby or a puppy named for him.		In a move to convince doubters, the Cabinet plans a radio address summarizing the improvement in the nation's economic situation. The President may make a final summation.	Prof. Albert Einstein arrives in the United States, where he will live as a refugee from Nazi Germany.	Anastasia Scott, 19, swims the mile and a half from Alcatraz Island to the mainland in 43 minutes, a feat many escaping prisoners could not manage.	Oct. 17
At a luncheon, Eleanor Roosevelt tells 300 YMCA and YWCA leaders they must provide spiritual leadership to the youth with whom they work.		The dollar moves up in exchange value as the franc drops the lowest it has been in years. Experts believe it is due to alarm in France about the European political situation.	Dr. James W. McKean, former head of a hospital in Siam, says he has a remedy for leprosy that will cure it if it is caught in the early stages. He uses chaulmoogra oil.		Oct. 18
Most senators and representatives favor President Franklin Roosevelt's recent move to open diplomatic discussions with Russia.	The United States is likely to play an active role in the World Bank since George L. Harrison, governor of the Federal Reserve Bank of New York, is elected to the board of the World Bank.	In spite of Governor William Langer's embargo, designed to raise the price of wheat, North Dakota farmers ship carloads of wheat by railroad.	Dr. Thomas H. Morgan of Pasadena, Calif., wins the Nobel Prize for Medicine for his studies of chromosomes.	Babe Ruth receives a warm welcome from 10,000 fans as he arrives in Honolulu. He will play in exhibition games there.	Oct. 19
Senator William Borah praises President Franklin Roosevelt's initiation of talks with Russia and says recognition of Russia would be "a stroke of genius."		Fewer than half the veterans receiving disability pay will continue to do so. Brig. Gen. Frank Hines, Veterans Administrator, asks President Franklin Roosevelt to extend the October 31 deadline so more cases can be reviewed.		Jean Harlow and Lee Tracy star in a hilarious comedy entitled Bombshell, which is about a motion picture actress and a studio publicity man.	Oct. 20
Making an unexpected speech at Washington College, President Franklin Roosevelt urges his 10,000 listeners to cooperate as people did in pioneer days. He asks people to be patient and to seek the right perspective.	Coast Guard officers expect no let-up in the smuggling of liquor after Prohibition is repealed. Since liquor needs to be aged four years, most sold in the United States in the immediate future will be imported and the Coast Guard wants to make sure the duty is paid.	The Public Works Administration allots $25 million to the Army and Navy for national defense. The funds will be used for motorization and mechanization of the Army and new planes.		Screen comedian Buster Keaton re-weds his wife, May Scrivens Hawley, after their marriage in Mexico is not recognized in California because his divorce from Natalie Talmadge was not final at the time of the wedding.	Oct. 21

F	G	H	I	J
Includes elections, federal-state relations, civil rights and liberties, crime, the judiciary, education, healthcare, poverty, urban affairs, and population.	Includes formation and debate of U.S. foreign and defense policies, veterans affairs, and defense spending. (Relations with specific foreign countries are usually found under the region concerned.)	Includes business, labor, agriculture, taxation, transportation, consumer affairs, monetary and fiscal policy, natural resources, pollution, and accidents.	Includes worldwide scientific, medical, and technological developments, natural phenomena, U.S. weather, and natural disasters.	Includes the arts, religion, scholarship, communications media, sports, entertainment, fashions, fads, and social life.

	World Affairs	Europe	Africa & The Middle East	The Americas	Asia & The Pacific
Oct. 22	Businessmen in Germany fear the withdrawal from the League of Nations and the disarmament parley mark the beginning of an era of bad relations between Germany and the rest of the world.		Former Egyptian premier Adly Yeghen Pasha dies in Paris after surgery. He is a cousin to King Fuad of Egypt.	Eight people in Peru are arrested in a plot to kill President Oscar Benavides with a bomb.	
Oct. 23		Turkey and Hungary renew the Turko-Hungarian treaty of neutrality and conciliation for five years.		Wheat farmers in Argentina threaten to not harvest their crops unless the government sets a minimum price that at least covers the cost of production.	Japanese Ambassador to the United States Debuchi is called home, supposedly to confer with the Foreign Minister on improving relations between Japan and the United States.
Oct. 24	In another step toward severing its relations with other countries, Germany withdraws from the International Labor Office.	An express train bound from Cherbourg to Paris derails and plunges into a river, killing 30 and injuring 32. A cause has not been determined.		Chile had expected a shortage of wheat, but finds out production exceeds national consumption by 800,000 tons, causing prices to slump.	Russia believes one reason Japan has not replied to its publication of "secret" Japanese documents is that United States recognition of Russia seems near.
Oct. 25	The Geneva arms parley votes to recess until December 4, but the bureau will continue discussions on various topics related to the conference.	The British Embassy protests the arrest of Neil Panter, a British newspaper correspondent in Munich. He is charged with exaggerating the military aspect of storm troopers appearing before Chancellor Adolf Hitler.		Negotiations begin on settling the Leticia dispute, with both Colombia and Peru eager for a settlement. An agreement is expected soon.	Manchuria releases American Dr. Niels Nielsen after he spends six months as a prisoner. Nielsen is in fair health and it is believed the ransom paid was small.
Oct. 26	The League of Nations Intergovernmental Conference on Refugees begins in Geneva.	An Italian court is lenient with Enrico Caruso, son of the late tenor, who is found guilty of assaulting and seriously injuring a farmer. He receives a suspended sentence of two and a half years.	Arabs in Jaffa, Palestine, are determined to defy police, who say they may not march through the streets tomorrow in a demonstration against immigration of Jews into Palestine.	Striking Mexican students who demand the resignation of rector Diaz de Leon surrender peacefully to police.	Nanking reports an important victory, claiming the slaying of 7,000 Communists in a 48-hour battle. Conflicting reports say the Reds destroy strategic bridges and make vigorous raids.
Oct. 27	After talking with U.S. Special Ambassador Norman Davis, Arthur Henderson, president of the World Disarmament Conference, says he may convene the bureau on November 3 instead of November 9.	The Reich withdraws from the World Court and cancels cases that Germany has pending.	Arab riots in Palestine kill 20 and injure about 130 as Arabs clash with police while attempting to demonstrate against Jewish immigration into Palestine.		It is believed that China's Finance Minister Soong has resigned, leaving militarists to control the government. The rumors cause bonds to drop.
Oct. 28	Hope grows in Geneva that negotiations may bring Germany back to the disarmament parley.	Czechoslovakia celebrates the anniversary of the nation with a military parade in Prague.		The Paraguayan War Minister announces his country's troops have advanced six miles, as fighting begins again in the Chaco.	China has a new policy that requires civil servants to buy Chinese goods. A $5 fine will be levied on anyone buying or wearing foreign apparel.
Oct. 29	Japanese War Minister Sadao Araki proposes a peace conference on the Far East to be held in Tokyo. He invites the United States, Great Britain, China, India, Russia, France, Holland, and Manchukuo.	Denmark is encouraged by Prime Minister of Sweden Per Albin Hansson's talk of closer cooperation among the Scandinavian nations.	More rioting in Jerusalem leaves three dead and 70 injured.	Plans are being made for a bridge across the Parana River connecting Uruguayana, Brazil, to Paso de los Libres, Argentina. The mile-and-a-half-long structure will cost $2.5 million.	A railway station in the Hilli section of the Eastern Bengal Railway is raided by 15 armed men resembling policemen. They grab the registered mail and escape.
Oct. 30		Former Reich labor leader Martin Pletti says that workers in Germany feel increasingly bitter toward Chancellor Adolf Hitler.	Because of recent Arab rioting, Palestine's High Commissioner, Sir Arthur Grenfell Wauchope, proclaims the Palestine Defense Order, which gives him military and dictatorial powers.		
Oct. 31	An international conference on saving African animals from extinction opens in London with representatives from countries with colonies in Africa. The United States is observing.	A French spokesman says London will accept a quota system in exchange for France lifting the tariff on British goods.	Arabs in Baghdad, Iraq, plan a demonstration against Jewish immigration into the Holy Land.	Bolivia asks the International Red Cross to investigate the mistreatment and exploitation of Bolivian prisoners in Paraguay.	American wartime pilot Bert Hall pleads guilty to illegally importing arms into China to sell to the military, then keeping the money.
Nov. 1	U.S. Special Ambassador Norman Davis leaves Geneva. He will stop in Paris to talk to War Minister Joseph Paul-Bancour on his way home. He refuses an invitation from Sir John Simon to stop in London as well.	Germany announces it will free British correspondent Neil Panter, who was arrested on charges of espionage and treason. Panter will be expelled from Germany.	In an attempt to pacify Arabs there, Palestine publishes an Arabic edition of the news, posting it on public bulletin boards and sending it to elders of Arab villages.		India wants Japan to agree to take a specified amount of Indian raw cotton in exchange for India purchasing a fixed amount of textiles from Japan, but Japan has objections.
Nov. 2	U.S Special Ambassador Norman Davis tells French War Minister Joseph Paul-Bancour that the United States will not return to the World Disarmament Conference until some progress has been made concerning the impasse with Germany.	The *Graf Zeppelin* returns to Germany after its trip to the Chicago World's Fair. Lt. Gen. Hermann Goering greets the captain and crew and presents them with letters of congratulations.	The road just built across the Ziff country of Morocco officially opens, making it possible to reduce the Moroccan army by 8,000 men.	Brazil decides to reduce its workweek for bankers to 36 hours. Reductions of hours in other lines of work will follow in an effort to fight the Depression.	The United States complains to the League of Nations about the opium menace Manchukuo creates for the world, saying it violates the laws of China. Poland calls for a world embargo on narcotics trade with Manchukuo.

A	B	C	D	E
Includes developments that affect more than one world region, international organizations, and important meetings of world leaders.	Includes all domestic and regional developments in Europe, including the Soviet Union.	Includes all domestic and regional developments in Africa and the Middle East.	Includes all domestic and regional developments in Latin America, the Caribbean, and Canada.	Includes all domestic and regional developments in Asian and Pacific nations (and colonies).

U.S. Politics & Social Issues	U.S. Foreign Policy & Defense	Economics & Great Depression	Science, Technology & Nature	Culture, Leisure & Lifestyle	
Thousands cheer former presidential candidate Alfred E. Smith and his wife as he attends the Chicago World's Fair as "just an ordinary citizen from New York."		U.S. bankers and economists are confused by President Franklin Roosevelt's newly announced plan to control the price level by the control of exchange and the buying and selling of gold.	The discovery of a 2,200-year-old axe in Virginia convinces scientists that man lived in that area during the time of Christ.	Heavyweight champion of the world, Primo Carnera, holds onto his title as he defeats Paulino Uzcudun in front of 70,000 spectators.	Oct. 22
A Senate subcommittee meets in Chicago to investigate the increase in kidnapping and racketeering in the Midwest and the rest of the nation.	Secretary of State Cordell Hull plans to visit government authorities in Chile, Argentina, and Peru on his way to Montevideo, Uruguay, for the Pan-American Conference, which opens December 3.	The immediate reaction to President Franklin Roosevelt's new gold program is an advance in sugar, coffee, and cocoa futures as well as gains in raw silk, crude rubber, silver, copper, and tin.	Weather prophets in British Columbia predict a long Indian summer, based on showers of beetles and roads covered with thousands of frogs.	Thirty-two college football teams in the United States are unbeaten and untied, but West Virginia school Davis-Elkins leads the list, with 284 points in six consecutive wins.	Oct. 23
	The keel is laid for the first Navy ship to be built under the NRA program. The U.S. submarine *Shark* is being built at the Groton, Conn., shipyard of the Electric Boat Company.	President Franklin Roosevelt issues an executive order fixing a procedure to administer provisions of the NRA that will control imports that are a menace to U.S. products.	Astronomers J.H. Menzel and J.C. Boyce of Harvard discover that the sun's corona is composed at least partially of oxygen, which explains why the corona is seen in eclipses of the sun.		Oct. 24
The Justice Department considers a requirement to register machine guns in an effort to get them out of the hands of criminals.	NRA Administrator Hugh Johnson orders a data study that will provide statistics on which President Franklin Roosevelt can base tariff action.	Henry Ford's failure to sign the auto code keeps him from participating in the $10 million U.S. Army motorization program. Only companies under the code will get contracts for the equipment.	An Arctic gale brings the season's first severe snowstorm to Canada and the northern part of the United States.	Comedian Ed Wynn resigns as president of the Amalgamated Broadcasting System, saying he is a better showman than radio official. . . . Film actress Edwina Booth sues MGM, saying that her health was ruined by working in Africa for the filming of the movie *Trader Horn*.	Oct. 25
	Secretary of State Cordell Hull postpones his sailing for South America so he can be in Washington when Maxim Litvinoff, envoy from Russia, arrives for recognition talks with President Franklin Roosevelt.	As opposition grows in western Iowa to the Farmers National Holiday Association strike, the National Guard assigns 30 Guardsmen to protect the farmers involved.		George Brent walks off the set of *Mandelay* in a dispute over salary. Lyle Talbot will take his place, starring with Kay Francis.	Oct. 26
	Navy Day is celebrated in New York City by an air show in which five planes from Floyd Bennett Field demonstrate parachute jumping and bombing.	President Franklin Roosevelt agrees with NRA Administrator Hugh Johnson that the Ford Motor Company is not eligible for contracts under the NRA, since it did not submit to the code.	Mrs. Horst Van der Goltz, an aquarist, says her many years of observing fish have taught her that fish think and that certain species have a well-regulated family life, like birds.		Oct. 27
The debt conference with England is expected to end soon. Reports say the British want to pay only 25 percent of their debt, while the United States wants them to pay 75 percent.		The NRA Board begins distributing the final third of its $3.3 billion fund for public works. It hopes to use all of the money to fund projects before the end of December.	The Darwin Memorial Expedition, made up of 20 men and 2 women, sails for the Galapagos Islands on December 12. The scientific expedition will last two and a half years.	The Ballet Jooss, a dance company organized in Essen, Germany, two years ago, arrives in the United States for a tour of the country.	Oct. 28
	The entire cadet corps at West Point turns out to greet the Army football team as it returns from its victory over Yale.	After meeting with experts at the White House, President Franklin Roosevelt announces that the government will buy gold from world markets through machinery set up by the RFC.	The Smithsonian Institution reports that a mere one-eighth of an inch of ozone keeps people from being killed by the "death rays" of the sun.	Former Detroit Tigers manager Bucky Harris signs a one-year contract to manage the Boston Red Sox, replacing Marty McManus.	Oct. 29
	Washington is pleased that only four nations—Holland, Sweden, Ireland, and Venezuela—have denounced the tariff truce. . . . U.S. officials are skeptical about a conference on the Far East to be held in Japan and they do not think most countries will accept the bid.	The VFW charges that the National Economy Act, which stipulates cuts in benefits to veterans, shifts the burden of caring for them from the government to the taxpayer.	Prof. Albert Einstein and his wife move from an inn where they have been staying into a two-family house in Princeton, N.J., where he accepted an appointment at Princeton's Institute for Advanced Study.	Opera singer Lily Pons signs a contract to sing at the Colon Theater in Buenos Aires next season. . . . Canadian Herman Lindner wins the All-Around-Cowboy title at the eighth annual rodeo held at Madison Square Garden.	Oct. 30
Former president Calvin Coolidge's widow visits her new granddaughter, Cynthia Coolidge, daughter of son John and his wife, Florence. Cynthia is her only grandchild.	Germany and Italy see U.S. Special Ambassador Norman Davis's return to the United States as the end of the disarmament parley in Geneva, but others are still hopeful.	Henry Ford announces his intention to report wage scales and hours of labor in his plants, in compliance with the NRA code.	Dr. T. Gilbert Pearson, president of the National Association of Audubon Societies, says wild waterfowl are in need of a New Deal. He says unemployment increases incidents of poaching.	The O. Henry Memorial Prize awards go to Marjorie Kinnan Rawlings, Pearl S. Buck, and Nancy Hale.	Oct. 31
President Franklin Roosevelt talks to British envoys, then announces that the debt parley with them will continue. Efforts are being made to avoid the appearance of British default on their upcoming December 15 debt payment.	Germany defaults on interest payments on 14 loans from the United States, while Uruguay defaults on its two loans.	Henry Ford concedes to his employees the right to bargain, but refuses to agree to a 35-hour week with a $5 per day minimum wage.	Canadian Dr. F. B. Banting, discoverer of insulin, develops a means of preventing silicosis, which is a condition caused by tiny particles of silica which irritate the lungs.	Champion horse Equipose will be retired to its owner's farm in Kentucky, where he will be used for stud service. . . . The Century of Progress Exhibition of Art at the World's Fair in Chicago closes after breaking all records for attendance at art shows in the United States.	Nov. 1
	The Conference of Younger Churchmen sees the U.S. naval program as a threat to world peace, and thinks Japan interprets it as a direct challenge to its position. . . . Secretary of State Cordell Hull says he pledges himself to the "good neighbor" program President Franklin Roosevelt mentioned in his inaugural speech.	Five midwestern governors and President Franklin Roosevelt work out a program to raise farm prices on wheat, corn, rye, and other products.	Carnegie Institute's Wilson Observatory reports the beginning of a new cycle of sunspots, which are disturbances within the sun that resemble tornadoes.	Ignace Jan Paderewski, the great Polish pianist, is forced to cancel his American tour for this year because he is suffering from acute and persistent neuritis. He hopes to reschedule it for next year.	Nov. 2

F	G	H	I	J
Includes elections, federal-state relations, civil rights and liberties, crime, the judiciary, education, healthcare, poverty, urban affairs, and population.	*Includes formation and debate of U.S. foreign and defense policies, veterans affairs, and defense spending. (Relations with specific foreign countries are usually found under the region concerned.)*	*Includes business, labor, agriculture, taxation, transportation, consumer affairs, monetary and fiscal policy, natural resources, pollution, and accidents.*	*Includes worldwide scientific, medical, and technological developments, natural phenomena, U.S. weather, and natural disasters.*	*Includes the arts, religion, scholarship, communications media, sports, entertainment, fashions, fads, and social life.*

	World Affairs	Europe	Africa & The Middle East	The Americas	Asia & The Pacific
Nov. 3		The Spanish navy guards Barcelona, where the electric light strike threatens to plunge the coast into darkness. Warships with searchlights stand by to illuminate the coastline.	A mob of Africans damages a German newspaper office in Pretoria, South Africa, in a protest against Nazism.	Canadian farmers in Manitoba propose cutting high tariffs so goods could be exchanged freely with other nations willing to trade on an equal basis.	Japan will build an airfield on Saipan Island, one of its protectorates in the Pacific. The airfield will assist fisheries, try to improve communications, and study atmospheric conditions.
Nov. 4	A delegation of workmen from the Free State of Danzig complains to the League of Nations that the Nazis have dissolved their Free Trades Unions' Federation.	Georgi Dimitrov acts as his own defense in his trial on burning the Reichstag, and is acquitted.		Brazil plans to build a 14-story skyscraper in Rio de Janeiro that will house the Brazilian Ministry of Labor and Commerce. Several semi-official agencies will also be housed in the million-dollar building.	China orders the arrest of Gen. Liu Chen-hou for needlessly surrendering the city of Suiting to the Communists. He will be severely punished, as will other generals who surrender when it is not absolutely necessary.
Nov. 5	On his return from the meeting of the International Chamber of Commerce in Paris, Thomas J. Watson reports that he sees a definite improvement in trade and finance in the principal countries of Europe.	Spanish Basques vote for autonomy. The Basque state will be made up of the three provinces of Guipuzcoa, Alava, and Viscaya.	High Commissioner of Palestine Arthur Wauchope releases 15 Arabs who had been held prisoner in Acre because of their involvement in the riots in Jaffa on October 27.	The Cuban government under Ramon Grau San Martin attempts to restore public order by a series of stern measures. A law of national defense gives the government extraordinary powers to meet such emergencies.	Russia reports that nine Japanese planes flew 20 miles into Russian territory over the Amur River last Friday.
Nov. 6	Two hundred people attend the ceremony as the last stone is laid for the new League of Nations Palace. Flags of all 57 members are flown, along with the U.S. flag, in recognition of American gifts to the League.	Germany's Foreign Minister Konstantin von Neurath charges that the League of Nations is just a tool to perpetuate the Treaty of Versailles and to allow the victors of the World War to get their way.	King Victor Emmanuel of Italy names Air Marshal Italo Balbo as governor of the Italian colony in Libya in northern Africa.	A strict new passport rule in Chile bars socialists. The new passports, which require proof of job and good health, will be required of foreigners entering the country.	The Philippine Senate approves a women's suffrage bill. The bill was approved by the House in 1932 and can still be revived.
Nov. 7	The League of Nations Conference of Government Press Bureaus opens in Madrid to promote dissemination of international news.	Rioting Nazis drive the Jewish students off the campus of the university in Budapest, Hungary.		In a new revolt in Cuba, three planes circle Havana, then drop bombs on Camp Columbia, headquarters of Col. Fulgencio Batista. The rebels want to return Carlos Manuel de Cespedes to office.	London announces the new loan to India for £10 million at 3.5 percent interest replaces an old 6 percent loan that matures on December 15.
Nov. 8	Premier Joseph Paul-Bancour of France refuses to join in a disarmament agreement, the League of Nations will be able to curb Germany by applying economic sanctions.	The University of Edinburgh in Scotland celebrates its 350th anniversary. The Chancellor, Sir James Barrie, presides.	Abdullah ibn Hussein, Emir of Trans-Jordan, calls for an Arab parley to discuss the situation in Palestine.	U.S. destroyers stationed in Havana Bay move out of range of danger as rebels bomb the Patria and the Cuba, gunboats loyal to the new Cuban regime.	Japan abandons its plan to cut its army in Manchuria to peacetime strength, alarming the Soviets.
Nov. 9	In spite of the recess in the World Disarmament Conference, the steering committee resumes work, attempting to draft the convention.	Czechoslovakian Foreign Minister Edvard Benes warns that Czechoslovakia is armed and that it will defend its borders against attacks from Germany or Hungary.	Nine European countries with possessions in Africa sign a pact to protect African wildlife. National parks are recommended in all African countries.	The U.S. battleship Wyoming leaves Tampa to sail for Cuba. It is said to be a routine move.	Russia warns Japan not to repeat the incident that occurred recently, when nine Japanese planes flew over Russian territory. Tension between the two countries continues to increase.
Nov. 10		Discontent with Nazi rule grows among Bavarians and many are arrested for expressing private opinions.	King Ghazi asks new Iraqi Premier Jamil Beg Midfai to form a new Cabinet to succeed the Raspig Ali Beg Cabinet.	President Agustin Justo decrees import licensing for Argentina. Under the plan, the country will limit imports from any nation to the value of the goods it exports to that country.	The bubonic plague spreads to two more areas in Manchuria, leaving 1,100 dead. A quarantine station opens on the north bank of the Sungari River opposite Harbin.
Nov. 11	The French stand firm in their desire to keep the World Disarmament Conference in Geneva rather than moving it to Rome or somewhere else.		British archaeologist Sir Charles Marston explains the significance of 1,400-year-old tablets found in Syria. The cuneiform writing contains some passages from Isaiah 27 in the Bible.	The main goal of the Pan-American Conference in Montevideo is to set up an effective mechanism for peacefully settling disputes. . . . Canada has to kill 2,000 of its buffalo herd because of the high rate of natural increase.	The Canton government in China prepares strenuously for war, importing armored cars, tanks, and a large supply of automatic weapons.
Nov. 12		Over 92 percent of German votes go to the Nazis in the first Reichstag election. Also, 93 percent of German voters approve of Germany leaving the League of Nations.	A squadron of 30 French airplanes, called the Black Squadron, flies from Colomb-Bechar, Morocco, to Adrar in the Sahara. They are making a 15,525-mile tour of Africa.	Gen. Ismael Montes, former president of Bolivia, is gravely ill with thrombosis and gangrene in his right leg. He is too weak to undergo surgery.	The Soviets charge Japan is creating an armed base in Manchukuo in order to start a war, and threaten retaliation by aerial bombardment if attacked.
Nov. 13	The commission investigating the conflict in the Chaco for the League of Nations arrives in Buenos Aires, where the members talk with Argentine diplomat Carlos Saavedra Lamas about details of the ABC-Peru efforts.	Romanian Liberal Dr. Ion Duca tells King Carol that he is unable to form a Cabinet with his bitter enemy, George Bratiano, who is the leader of the Liberal Party.		Manuel Musquiz Blanco, a Mexican poet, is killed in a car crash. His chauffeur is so distraught that he pulls out a gun and shoots himself in the head.	Mohandas Gandhi denies a report in The Evening News of India saying people threw eggs at him as he sat on a platform at a public meeting in Nagpur.
Nov. 14	Britain, "with regret," joins in the race for big cruisers, spurred by concern about Japan beefing up its army.	In Stockholm, thieves steal Rembrandt's Jeremiah Mourning for the Destruction of Jerusalem from the home of art collector M. Herman Rasch, along with other works worth $25,000.	Afghans and Indians in Teheran are disturbed by the presence of former king Inayatullah of Afghanistan in Persia.		Senator Manuel Quezon of the Philippines denies that Filipinos want protection from U.S. armed forces. He says if they are fully independent, they need to be able to protect themselves.
Nov. 15	Arthur Henderson, president of the disarmament conference, pressures all the powers, including the Reich, to get back to work on establishing a plan for world disarmament.		The Jewish Agency Executive issues a statement saying that Palestine could economically absorb many more Jewish immigrants than the government says it can.	Brazilian Finance Minister Oswaldo Aranha believes his country will soon be engaged in talks with Russia aimed at giving it formal recognition. . . . The Northern Railway, which runs from San Jose to Limon in Costa Rica, receives so much damage from recent heavy rains that mail and freight have to be rerouted.	

A	B	C	D	E
Includes developments that affect more than one world region, international organizations, and important meetings of world leaders.	*Includes all domestic and regional developments in Europe, including the Soviet Union.*	*Includes all domestic and regional developments in Africa and the Middle East.*	*Includes all domestic and regional developments in Latin America, the Caribbean, and Canada.*	*Includes all domestic and regional developments in Asian and Pacific nations (and colonies).*

U.S. Politics & Social Issues	U.S. Foreign Policy & Defense	Economics & Great Depression	Science, Technology & Nature	Culture, Leisure & Lifestyle	
	President Franklin Roosevelt orders the U.S. naval fleet back to the Atlantic Coast next spring, after three years on the Pacific. The move is seen as friendly toward Japan.	The National Association of Manufacturers objects to the Swopes plan, saying it does not want to lose its identity by merging with other groups to create a National Chamber of Commerce and Industry.	Dr. K.W. Ney, professor of neurosurgery, claims that 89 percent of the epileptics he has treated by removing the top of the skull have made either complete or nearly complete recoveries.	The Russian government sells two famous paintings by artist Hubert van Eyck to the Metropolitan Museum of Art. They are *The Crucifixion* and *The Last Judgment*. When combined, the two form a diptych.	Nov. 3
Reports say negotiations with Britain on debt revision are over. British Ambassador Sir Ronald Lindsay refuses an interview.	President Franklin Roosevelt orders the establishment of an import division of the NRA where manufacturers can lodge complaints about harmful foreign competition.		Nash offers a new line of autos, comprising five body types. They all have twin-ignition valve-in head engines and bodies are streamlined.	A new four-page newspaper, designed to help immigrants learn English and keep up on the news, appears in New York. *News of the Week for New Americans* will use only a 900-word vocabulary.	Nov. 4
Yesterday's meeting between President Franklin Roosevelt and the British envoy seems to have been strictly to arrange another token payment for December 15. Negotiations will be resumed later.		NRA Administrator Hugh Johnson sets out for the Midwest, where he will try to counter opposition to and discontent with the NRA.			Nov. 5
Six states—Kentucky, North Carolina, Ohio, Pennsylvania, South Carolina, and Utah—vote on repeal of the Eighteenth Amendment. If any three of them vote to pass the issue, Prohibition will end.		At a press conference, Eleanor Roosevelt emphasizes her desire to include women and girls in employment relief programs.	H.B. Meller, head of the Air Pollution Investigation of the Carnegie Mellon Institute of Industrial Research, says noxious gases and smoke from chimneys, which hangs over cities, can cause cancer.	Spanish pianist Jose Iturbi says the future of music lies in the United States, praising the quality and discrimination of the American concertgoer.	Nov. 6
The Eighteenth Amendment is repealed after 14 years of Prohibition. . . . Fiorello LaGuardia is elected mayor of New York City.	Briton David Lloyd George chides the United States for preaching peace, while at the same time increasing armaments.	A joint communiqué issued by London and Washington puts an official end to the debt revision negotiations between the United States and Great Britain.	A Memphis inventor, N.J. Verret, sues the Navy for patent infringement for a device enabling small planes to be attached to and launched from the dirigible *Macon*. He says he patented the device in 1929.	Pennsylvania voters, to permit sports on Sundays, overturn blue laws. This will be a big boon to baseball.	Nov. 7
	The United States backs the League of Nations on nonrecognition of Manchukuo and suggests barring Manchukuo from multilateral treaties, as well as barring the narcotics trade with Manchuria.	President Franklin Roosevelt announces the creation of the Civil Works Administration, designed to create jobs for 4 million of the nation's unemployed.	Restrictions on waterfowl hunting are likely, since the Biological Survey shows a continual decrease in the number of ducks while the number of hunters continues to increase.	Leaders in major league baseball are pleased with Pennsylvania's vote to allow Sunday sports in the state. John Heydler, president of the National League, says it will make scheduling easier.	Nov. 8
Washington, D.C., will remain dry until Congress has a chance to enact control legislation for the District of Columbia.	VO-Squadron 7M of the Quantico Marines is awarded the Herbert Schiff Trophy for compiling the largest number of flying hours without a serious accident.	NRA Administrator Hugh Johnson returns from his trip to the Midwest and says not more than 1 percent of the American people oppose the NRA.		Master chefs are ecstatic about the repeal of Prohibition and are building wine cellars so they can add fine wines to their many meat and dessert recipes, which were not of the highest quality under the alcohol restrictions.	Nov. 9
President Franklin Roosevelt approves $16,678,675 to build 237 new post offices around the country.	New York lawyer Louis Waldman represents Ralph Osman as he appeals his conviction on charges of selling secrets to Communists in the Canal Zone.	The anthracite union calls off a strike planned by 60,000 workers after Senator Robert Wagner guarantees all their jobs if they will go back to work.	The Black Blizzard, a combined snowstorm and dust storm, ranges from South Dakota to the Atlantic Coast.	Well-known Canadian author William A. Fraser is dead. His best-known works are *Brave Heart* and *Thoroughbred*.	Nov. 10
The nation observes the 16th anniversary of the Armistice, as President and Mrs. Roosevelt put flowers on the tomb of the Unknown Soldier. The United States also observes the traditional two minutes of silence.		NRA Administrator Hugh Johnson is surprised to receive a warm welcome when he speaks in Ft. Worth, Tex. He expected to have to "sell" the NRA, but says he finds it is already "sold."	The first of the great dust storms that will create the Dust Bowl strips topsoil from farmland in South Dakota.		Nov. 11
President Franklin Roosevelt endorses the work of the Citizens Family Welfare Committee, saying the public's generosity is needed, along with government programs, to ensure full recovery.	Rear Admiral Ridley McLean, who saw action in the Spanish-American War, the Boxer Rebellion, and the Philippine insurrection, dies on board his flagship, the *Nevada*. Ridley was Commander of Battleship Division Eight of the U.S. fleet.	President Franklin Roosevelt and his financial advisers meet and decide to continue purchasing small amounts of foreign gold.	Three British scientists discover a new chemical preparation that can be used to replace thyroid extract in treating certain thyroid disorders.		Nov. 12
	The United States receives a cable from Geneva, asking the early return of U.S. Special Ambassador Norman Davis and U.S. delegate Mary Wooley to the disarmament conference.	The first modern sit-down strike begins in Austin, Minn., at the Hormel meat packing plant. . . . Comedian Eddie Cantor will meet with President Franklin Roosevelt at Warm Springs to present the film actors' views on the code for the movie industry.			Nov. 13
	The U.S. delegation to the Pan-American Conference meets on board the *American Legion* to organize for the conference.	The NRA reverses an earlier decision in deciding that tips are not wages, averting a strike of 150,000 waiters in New York City.	Tuberculosis authorities are skeptical of Dr. Stephen Maher's claim to be close to finding a cure for the disease. They say his discoveries were already known and they do not constitute a cure.	Leopold Stokowski and the Philadelphia Orchestra present an evening of Russian music at Carnegie Hall in Pittsburgh.	Nov. 14
President Franklin Roosevelt favors a new food and drug bill that increases safeguards.	The airship *Macon* is tested at sea to see if it could work with the U.S. fleet. Its planes would serve as scouting and observation units, as well as bombing planes.	It appears the NRA will concede to newspaper publishers, who insist "freedom of the press" must be included in their code.	Dr. James Bond tells the American Ornithology Union that so-called collectors and scientists are causing the extinction of some species of birds and stresses the need for more bird protection.	Eight of Britain's foremost artists agree that a newly found portrait of Henry XIII was not painted by Hans Holbein. They believe it may have been done by a student of Holbein.	Nov. 15

F	G	H	I	J
Includes elections, federal-state relations, civil rights and liberties, crime, the judiciary, education, healthcare, poverty, urban affairs, and population.	*Includes formation and debate of U.S. foreign and defense policies, veterans affairs, and defense spending. (Relations with specific foreign countries are usually found under the region concerned.)*	*Includes business, labor, agriculture, taxation, transportation, consumer affairs, monetary and fiscal policy, natural resources, pollution, and accidents.*	*Includes worldwide scientific, medical, and technological developments, natural phenomena, U.S. weather, and natural disasters.*	*Includes the arts, religion, scholarship, communications media, sports, entertainment, fashions, fads, and social life.*

	World Affairs	Europe	Africa & The Middle East	The Americas	Asia & The Pacific
Nov. 16	Britain sends Sir John Simon and Sir Anthony Eden to Geneva to confer on disarmament with the French and possibly the Italians.	A Paris newspaper publishes what it say are secret instructions from Joseph Goebbels, Nazi Propaganda Minister, to agents abroad to step up propaganda efforts, especially in the Americas.	The French Black Squadron of planes flies in formation over French West Africa, arriving in Senegal.	Brazil's President Getulio Vargas gets an overwhelming vote of confidence when special discretionary powers are granted to him until a constitution can be adopted.	Arms expenses in Japan are the second highest they have been since 1921, when an arms race was in progress. The Japanese military budget exceeds $445 million.
Nov. 17	Japan says it will still administer its mandated islands in the Pacific, and that it will continue to report to the League of Nations.	The leading Estonian Laborite paper, *Rahva Sana*, accuses the German Nazis of a campaign to take over the government of Estonia.		Several agrarians are arrested and a quantity of arms seized at a secret meeting near Chontia in the state of Veracruz, Mexico. The men were plotting against the government.	Tokyo says it welcomes the news of U.S. recognition of Russia, but that it will not affect the situation in the Far East either economically or politically.
Nov. 18	No real progress is made as representatives from Great Britain, France, and Italy meet in Geneva for preliminary disarmament talks.	Austrian officials hope a 7 p.m. curfew and a ban on bicycle traffic between 6 p.m. and 5 a.m. will help to suppress Nazi activities.	A colony of rare hammer-headed storks has been found near Nairobi, Kenya. The storks build nests like haystacks.	Interest in British Columbia in the building of the projected Midnight Sun Highway, connecting Alaska with the rest of the United States, revives as the United States votes an $18 million allotment for the project.	The long parley between China and Japan ends without the formal treaty Japan had wanted. Japan says an agreement cannot be reached until China recognizes Manchukuo.
Nov. 19	Three Italian newspapers publish strong hints that Italy may quit the League of Nations. It is believed the Fascist Grand Council will discuss the matter.	The Nazis are delighted that the marriage rate in Germany is up 53 percent this year in big cities, which should help them to further their goal of multiplying the Aryan race.	A meeting of the Palestine Arab Executive decides that on January 17, every town should hold a demonstration against Jewish immigration into Palestine. Demonstrations will be led by members of the Arab Executive.		Canton is alarmed by a growing revolt in the Fukien province. It is rumored that leaders have removed a reserve of bullion worth $2 million, which causes runs on Chinese banks.
Nov. 20	Secret meetings with the Big Four continue in Geneva on the subject of disarmament. Italy denies it will quit the League.	The Reich seizes all property belonging to Jewish Albert Einstein and his wife, deeming them "enemies of the state."	The 28 planes of the French Black Squadron arrive in Dakar from Kayes, Upper Senegal.	Six die and eight are wounded in Uruguay in a clash between police and bandits trying to rob the Montevideo mansion of gambling king Marcos Caneriza.	Japan's former premier Reijiro Wakatsuki escapes two would-be assassins with daggers as police intercept them. One, Susumu Noguchi, is a well-known boxer in Japan.
Nov. 21	Secretary General of the League of Nations Joseph Avenol is in Italy, where he will confer with Premier Benito Mussolini, probably about Italy's possible withdrawal from the League.	German Chancellor Adolf Hitler tells Paris that after the Saar question is settled, there will be nothing to separate Germany and France and they will draw closer.	A delegation of Palestinians calls upon High Commissioner Arthur Wauchope, informing him of their concerns on Jewish immigration into Palestine.	Because of its financial crisis, Newfoundland will revert to its status as a crown colony and be ruled by Great Britain.	Japan tells its delegates to terminate meetings with India on the barter of Japanese cloth for Indian cotton if its last demands are not accepted.
Nov. 22	The steering committee of the disarmament conference approves the proposal by the conference president, Arthur Henderson, to postpone the December 4 meeting until mid-January.	Turkey, Greece, Yugoslavia, and Romania are ready to sign a Balkan Pact. They will invite Bulgaria and Albania to join. . . . Austria criticizes U.S. Ambassador to Austria George H. Earle III because he accepts an invitation to visit President Tomas Masaryk in Czechoslovakia.		Chile and Peru are hard at work preparing a commercial treaty for the two countries.	Nanking's air force is held in readiness near the border of the Chekiang and Fukien provinces. It believes it can quickly crush the Fukien rebellion.
Nov. 23	Italy is pleased with the recess of the disarmament conference and believes the Big Four need to meet and come up with a preliminary plan before the parley reconvenes.	Britain says its three new cruisers will be privately built, because the government yards have all the work they can do. This seems to indicate it is increasing its navy to the limits of the London Naval Treaty.	For their flight back to the United States, Col. and Mrs. Charles Lindbergh will take off from Senegal in west Africa.	El Salvador urges setting up an American League of Nations and a Court of International Justice for the Americas.	Tokyo tells Japanese in China not to interfere with the Fukien movement unless Japanese nationals are endangered.
Nov. 24	Geneva newspapers believe economic problems will arise from the gold bloc formed by Italy, Poland, Belgium, Switzerland, France, and Holland.	The Reich charges an unarmed German soldier practicing skiing near the border was shot and killed by an Austrian patrol. Austria is investigating, but doubts the soldier was unarmed.		Jefferson Cafferty will go to Cuba as President Franklin Roosevelt's special representative and serve as an observer rather than an ambassador, to avoid recognizing the Grau regime.	Japanese imports from the United States increase, but due to the falling dollar and economic uncertainty in Japan, the future is obscure.
Nov. 25	The League of Nations would like to work with the Pan-American Union, believing the tie would strengthen both bodies.		Construction is finished on the Iraqi pipeline linking Kirkuk, Haifa, and Tripoli. . . . South Africa will abolish its navy and Britain will guard its coastline, as it did before 1922.	The Weston-Carr expedition studying the Goajira Indians in Colombia reports that the tribe members have no religion, but they do believe in an afterlife during which they will wander the earth in an invisible form.	
Nov. 26		Camille Chautemps announces the formation of a new French "public safety" Cabinet. He will serve as Premier and Minister of the Interior, and the Cabinet includes four former premiers.	The Union of South Africa is one of three countries that economists find are on solid economic footing, identified with Finland and Lithuania as being unaffected by the Depression.	Washington is ready to sign a reciprocal trade treaty with Colombia. It will be the first treaty under President Franklin Roosevelt's commercial policy.	The French steamer *Commandant Henri Riviere* falls victim to pirates in Hong Kong, as 20 men who had boarded as passengers seize the ship, loot it, and rob the passengers.
Nov. 27	The wheat parley resumes in London. Despite huge surpluses this year, members have high hopes that limiting crops will improve things for next year.	Hungary's Premier, Julius Goemboes, visits Chancellor Engelbert Dollfuss in Vienna. The two men will go on a hunting trip while discussing mutual concerns.		Sixty-five exiled former Cuban leaders from three parties urge a coalition. They hope the manifesto they sign will cause public opinion in Cuba to put an end to the Grau regime.	
Nov. 28	Japanese Foreign Minister Koki Hirota wants to initiate preliminary negotiations among the chief naval powers in order to prepare for the 1935 naval conference.	Austria apologizes for the death of a German soldier, but refuses to take responsibility, since it claims he had crossed the border. Germany says he did not.	The Moroccan-Tunisian Railway is opened by the French to unite the French North Africa colonies.		The Empress of Japan, in an ancient ceremony, dons the ceremonial girdle made of raw silk. This signifies the ninth month of her pregnancy.

A	B	C	D	E
Includes developments that affect more than one world region, international organizations, and important meetings of world leaders.	Includes all domestic and regional developments in Europe, including the Soviet Union.	Includes all domestic and regional developments in Africa and the Middle East.	Includes all domestic and regional developments in Latin America, the Caribbean, and Canada.	Includes all domestic and regional developments in Asian and Pacific nations (and colonies).

U.S. Politics & Social Issues	U.S. Foreign Policy & Defense	Economics & Great Depression	Science, Technology & Nature	Culture, Leisure & Lifestyle	
	President Franklin Roosevelt sends a telegram to Soviet leader Maxim Litvinoff, in which he expresses hope that U.S.-Soviet relations will "forever remain normal and friendly."	Foreign deposits in U.S. banks are down $3 million in the last week.	A new airplane safety device, invented by Harry Trusty, is demonstrated at Roosevelt Field on Long Island. The pilot pulls a lever and four passengers, still in their seats, parachute to safety.	The National Bureau of Casualty and Surety Underwriters offers a safety code for roller skaters, since the fad is sweeping the country and accidents have increased.	Nov. 16
	The United States officially recognizes the Soviet government in Russia. . . . Secretary of State Cordell Hull receives the news of Russian recognition while aboard the *American Legion*. He is pleased, saying he believes the world situation is improving.	After the 90-day trial proves satisfactory, the steel industry petitions for and receives a six-month extension of its code.	Dr. V. Pardo-Castello tells the Southern Medical Association that because pressure from shoes is causing atrophy, children in a few generations may be born with no nails on their little toes.	Baseball's Southern Association eliminates the intentional base on balls, or "walk," by a new rule stating that if the pitcher throws four consecutive balls, the hitter goes to first and all other base runners advance two bases.	Nov. 17
President Franklin Roosevelt recalls U.S. Ambassador Sumner Welles from Havana and urges Cuba to stabilize its government.		In a speech to 30,000 people in Savannah, Ga., President Franklin Roosevelt defends his experiments and says the country is on the road to recovery.	The United States decides to try a Seadrome, as outlined 20 years ago by Edward R. Armstrong. The Seadrome is like a floating airport in the ocean.	The Amateur Athletic Union will meet with the American Olympic Association to decide how to handle Germany's nonrecognition of Jews during the Olympics.	Nov. 18
	Col. Frederick Palmer, a veteran of three wars and former head of Gordon Institute, dies in Georgia at the age of 70. Palmer participated in the last Indian War, the Spanish-American War, and the World War.	The National Export Trade Company announces that the NRA exempts more than 60 industries that are involved mainly in exporting from the NRA codes.	The New York Academy of Medicine says that 65 percent of the mothers who die in childbirth could be saved with proper procedures. It blames doctors for 61 percent of the deaths.		Nov. 19
Due to overcrowding in Moscow, the U.S. diplomatic staff may be temporarily quartered in a hotel.	The Canal Zone dismisses charges of involuntary manslaughter against Navy Lt. John H. Cross. Cross had already been acquitted of the charges in a court-martial.	The U.S. budget for 1934 is expected to be about $2.6 billion, including $800 million for interest on the national debt.	A hot air balloon is missing after rising 11 miles into the stratosphere. Navy Lt. Commander T.G.W. Settle and Marine Major Chester Fordley are missing somewhere over New Jersey.	The Amateur Athletic Association decides to boycott the 1936 Olympic Games in Berlin unless the Nazi government changes its stand toward Jews.	Nov. 20
In his Thanksgiving Proclamation, President Franklin Roosevelt rebukes greed and selfishness. He forgoes the formal language usually found in such proclamations and says to be thankful for the "passing of dark days."	President Franklin Roosevelt names Joseph P. Chamberlain as the U.S. member of the League of Nations Committee to Aid Jewish Refugees.		Rockefeller Center research finds that the virus causing infantile paralysis enters the body through the nose and then goes to the brain by way of the olfactory nerve.	Film star Lee Tracy, accused of "offending public morals" and "insulting the Mexican government," flees from Mexico by plane.	Nov. 21
	The Navy Department awards contracts for $4,188,050 for naval projects, with $2,789,600 to go to developing the greatest navy base in the Pacific, in Pearl Harbor, Hawaii.	Acting Secretary of the Treasury Henry Morgenthau asks St. Louis banker Tom K. Smith to confer with him about a new position as an adviser to the Treasury on banking.	The National Academy of Sciences hears about a new superspeed motion picture camera that can take up to 6,000 pictures per second.		Nov. 22
In an unexpected move, President Franklin Roosevelt announces that U.S. Ambassador to Cuba Sumner Welles will be replaced by Jefferson Cafferty, currently an Assistant Secretary of State. Welles will resume his post in the State Department.	President Franklin Roosevelt must make a decision as to whether or not the Coast Guard should be made part of the Navy to reduce expenses. The Coast Guard is against it, fearing it will be swallowed up in the larger Navy.	President Franklin Roosevelt asks the banks to quickly cash checks from the 1 million employees of the Civil Works Administration who will be paid tomorrow.		The final day of the auction of Arthur Hind's stamp collection is today. He had the finest collection of Confederate stamps to ever be sold at auction.	Nov. 23
	Russian Commissar for Foreign Affairs Maxim Litvinoff and President Franklin Roosevelt end their meeting, both pledging cooperation and enduring friendship.	The NRA names Boaz W. Long as Deputy Administrator for Puerto Rico. He has been with NRA since its inception.	Rear Admiral Richard E. Byrd plans to set up a hut covered with snow to use as a base for his observations in the Antarctic. Meanwhile he will be isolated from the rest of the party.	Amelia Earhart has designed a line of sports clothes for women, including flying outfits. It goes on sale in December.	Nov. 24
	America's new Seadrome project is seen in Geneva as proof that the United States is not isolationist.	Forty business leaders in Cincinnati, Ohio, send a telegram urging President Franklin Roosevelt to go back to the gold standard.	California doctors James Rinehart and Stacy Mettier believe vitamin C may be the clue in curing rheumatic ills. Mice fed on orange juice resisted infection in experiments.	In their traditional rivalry, Army beats Navy in the annual football match. One player says it is the "hardest, toughest game we ever played."	Nov. 25
President Franklin Roosevelt backs the Christmas Seal Sale to raise money for tuberculosis, saying that "protection of public health has long been one of the fundamental responsibilities of government."	Gen. Douglas MacArthur says the U.S. Army is "below the danger line" as far as personnel and materials. Retirements and economic cutbacks have caused the shortage of personnel.		American doctor John Long helps Chile fight typhus fever, which has been prevalent there for several weeks. The death rate has been over 22 percent of those afflicted.	James Dunn, Lillian Roth, and June Knight star in the film version of the musical comedy *Take a Chance*.	Nov. 26
Bills for the remonetization of silver are sure to be introduced in Congress in January. One plan calls for fixing the price of silver certificates at 75 cents and backing them up with 25 cents worth of gold.		Secretary of Labor Frances Perkins says in a speech at Yale that the NRA has succeeded beyond expectations.	A mysterious malady kills 100 San Blas Indian children in Panama. Most of those killed are under the age of five.	Philadelphia announces that the traditional mummers' parade on New Year's Day has been canceled due to the economy.	Nov. 27
British Attorney General Sir Thomas Inskip criticizes President Franklin Roosevelt's recovery program, calling it a "rash and hazardous experiment."	The Army quits buying all food grown or processed in foreign countries.		Dr. Robert J. Van de Graeff produces a 7,000,000-volt lightning bolt, using the giant electrostatic generator he designed. A few scientists witness the test of the device.	Screen actor Gary Cooper will marry Veronica Balfe, whose screen name is Sandra Shaw.	Nov. 28

F	G	H	I	J
Includes elections, federal-state relations, civil rights and liberties, crime, the judiciary, education, healthcare, poverty, urban affairs, and population.	*Includes formation and debate of U.S. foreign and defense policies, veterans affairs, and defense spending. (Relations with specific foreign countries are usually found under the region concerned.)*	*Includes business, labor, agriculture, taxation, transportation, consumer affairs, monetary and fiscal policy, natural resources, pollution, and accidents.*	*Includes worldwide scientific, medical, and technological developments, natural phenomena, U.S. weather, and natural disasters.*	*Includes the arts, religion, scholarship, communications media, sports, entertainment, fashions, fads, and social life.*

	World Affairs	Europe	Africa & The Middle East	The Americas	Asia & The Pacific
Nov. 29	The British accuse Japan of being dishonest in trade by underselling them in manufactured cotton goods. They say some are labeled to look like British goods.	The Chautemps Cabinet and ministry are not expected to last a week as there is great unrest in France.	France will encourage the settlement of Assyrian Christians in French Guiana. The Assyrians are anxious to avoid clashes with the Iraqis in their homeland.	The government of Newfoundland is reorganized after the Royal Commission finds its huge debt is due to corruption and incompetence.	Japan's government begins persecuting Communists.
Nov. 30		The Nazis behead six Communists in Cologne Jail for shooting two Nazi storm troopers.		Chile and Peru say they will erect a large statue of Christ atop Morro de Arica as a symbol of a new era of peace between the two nations.	The latest official figures in India show that civil disobedience has declined and fewer people are being jailed for that offense.
Dec. 1	Joseph Chamberlain, U.S. representative to the governing body of the High Commission for Refugees from Germany, arrives in Geneva. The Commission will meet in Lausanne, Switzerland, to organize its work.	Nazi storm troopers become an official organ of the Reich, and Ernst Roehm and Rudolf Hess are named ministers in the German government.	The bride of Iraqi King Ghazi, whom he married by proxy, arrives from Istanbul. Princess Aliyah and the King meet for the first time.	The administration of the Panama Canal takes the blame for a November 22 accident to the Standard Shipping Company's *Standard*. Damages are estimated at $23,000.	
Dec. 2	Sir Cecil Hurst of Great Britain succeeds Mineichiro Adachi of Japan as president of the Permanent Court of International Justice in The Hague.	The Poles feel safer than they have for a long time after they sign a non-aggression treaty with Russia and Chancellor Adolf Hitler assures them that Germany has renounced the use of force in its relations with Poland.	Bert Fish, the U.S. Ambassador to Egypt, arrives in Cairo and presents his credentials to King Fuad at the royal palace. Fish is received with elaborate court ceremonies.	The Haitian delegation wants the Pan-American Conference to adopt a resolution asking the United States to promise to terminate "all extra-territorial occupation, both financial and military."	Berlin's former police chief Albert Grzesinski and his deputy, Bernhard Weiss, arrive in Shanghai. They have been hired to reorganize the Chinese police system.
Dec. 3	League of Nations members in Geneva doubt that German Chancellor Adolf Hitler will denounce the Versailles treaty as he has threatened, saying the Reich would lose more than it gained by such a step.		Col. Charles Lindbergh tries twice to take off for Brazil from Gambia, British West Africa, but lack of wind makes takeoff impossible. He unloads some of his fuel and decides to wait until early morning.	At the Pan-American parley in Montevideo, Uruguay, President Gabriel Terra says solutions are needed to the economic problems of the 21 participating nations.	Australia says its aim in sending diplomats to China and Japan is to promote goodwill, rather than to negotiate trade issues.
Dec. 4	Observers from Portugal and Spain will sit in on the Pan-American Conference in Montevideo.	Dominions Secretary J.H. Thomas is expected to make a statement to the Irish House of Commons that will force President Eamon de Valera to call for a vote on whether or not to secede from the British Commonwealth.	Col. Charles Lindbergh and his wife work on the plane, as the weather in Gambia is still too calm to take off. He has not asked to refuel at the German refueling ship.	At the Pan-American Conference, Mexico suggests inter-American systems of currency and banking.	
Dec. 5	Arthur Henderson, president of the World Disarmament Conference, confers with France's Foreign Minister Joseph Paul-Bancour about the future of the negotiations on disarmament.	French wine growers are disappointed by the amount of wine they can sell to the United States. They believe California wine is competing, plus they do not like the red tape posed by quotas and tariffs.	Leaders of the Arab riots in Palestine in October are sentenced. Jamal Husseini and Edmond Rock receive one month each and Sheekh Muzzafar is released on the condition of one year's good behavior.	The Pan-American Conference will not attempt to solve the Chaco problem, but will leave that to the League of Nations.	The Nanking Foreign Office charges that Japan is supplying money and ammunition to the rebels in the Fukien province.
Dec. 6	Italian officials say its call for reform of the League of Nations was meant to bring back Japan and Germany and to cause the United States and Russia to join.	According to British Financial Secretary of the Treasury Leslie Hore-Bellisha, Britain has the highest per capita tax burden of any country, amounting to about $74.51.	The Lindberghs fly from Gambia, British West Africa, to Natal, Brazil, in 16 hours.	The National Revolutionary Party nominates former minister of war Gen. Lázaro Cárdenas for president of Mexico. He is expected to be elected.	Civil War in Outer Mongolia pits the Nationalists against the Soviets, according to Japanese reports. They say revolts are a result of recent Russian efforts to tighten control in the area.
Dec. 7	When the League of Nations Commission seeking a solution to the Chaco conflict arrives in La Paz, Bolivians cheer them, throw flowers, and ask for "an honorable peace."	Irish Free State President Eamon de Valera says Ireland would be free in 24 hours if the British would lift their threat of force.	Former Egyptian premier Ismail Sidky Pasha retires from Egyptian politics. He was serving as a member of the chamber and as president of his party.	Premier Benito Mussolini of Italy informs Argentine Foreign Minister Carlos Saavedra Lamas that Italy wants to sign the Argentine anti-war pact. That would obligate Italy not to declare war on South American countries.	A Filipino delegation arrives in Washington with the slogan, "Independence at any price." They will confer with Secretary of War George H. Dern, and want to talk directly to President Franklin Roosevelt.
Dec. 8		The Prince of Wales urges faster planes for his country, charging the British lag behind in commercial aviation.		Fifteen are killed by the explosion of a steam boiler at a sugar cane mill near Monterrey, Mexico. Many houses are destroyed and scores of people injured.	Japanese Count Yamamoto, who twice served as premier, dies at the age of 81. Yamamoto was also a naval hero in the war with Russia and served as minister of the navy for eight years.
Dec. 9	Italian dictator Benito Mussolini proposes rewriting the covenant of the League of Nations since he believes the League is ineffective. France is against the idea.	The Iberian Anarchist Confederation tries for the fourth time to overthrow the government of Spain. Several hundred are injured and 42 killed as police put down the rebellion.	After seven years at the head of the Persian government, the Shah can point to many accomplishments. The tribes are peaceful, communications have improved, many roads have been built, and national pride is growing.	The Ecuadorian ambassador to the United States Colon Eloy Alfaro refuses to run for president of Ecuador and returns to his post in the United States. He believes the Liberals are too disorganized.	Japan sends ships to the west coast of Formosa to watch the events of the Chinese rebellion in the Fukien Province.
Dec. 10		Bulgaria's King Boris visits Belgrade and receives an enthusiastic reception. This marks a reconciliation between Bulgaria and Yugoslavia.	A Harvard expedition uncovers the tower of Jezebel in Samaria. The 25 to 35-foot-high tower has been buried for 2,000 years, according to Dr. Kirsopp Lake, leader of the expedition.	Martial law is declared in the Santiago province of Cuba after six people are critically injured in a bomb blast.	

A	B	C	D	E
Includes developments that affect more than one world region, international organizations, and important meetings of world leaders.	*Includes all domestic and regional developments in Europe, including the Soviet Union.*	*Includes all domestic and regional developments in Africa and the Middle East.*	*Includes all domestic and regional developments in Latin America, the Caribbean, and Canada.*	*Includes all domestic and regional developments in Asian and Pacific nations (and colonies).*

U.S. Politics & Social Issues	U.S. Foreign Policy & Defense	Economics & Great Depression	Science, Technology & Nature	Culture, Leisure & Lifestyle	
President Franklin Roosevelt appoints Joseph H. Choate, Jr., as "liquor czar." He will serve as director and chairman of the Federal Alcohol Control Committee.	The United States will use control of imports of liquor and wine to promote reciprocal trade treaties with big alcohol exporters and to level tariffs on American goods.		A severe earthquake lasting 10 seconds occurs in Acapulco, Mexico. The damage from the quake has not yet been assessed.	Comedian Ed Wynn, his agent, and his secretary are accused of attacking a process server who came to his apartment to serve legal papers.	Nov. 29
The *Daily Express*, a London paper that often criticizes U.S. affairs, says the country is lucky to have Franklin Roosevelt as President.	Two army fliers, Staff Sergeants Preston Miller and James Dodge, die as their personal plane loses a wing in high winds and crashes on the West Virginia side of the Potomac.	Dr. Murray Nicholas Butler, president of Columbia University, asks for donations for the United Hospital Fund of New York, saying hospitals have never been in such need.		The Cardinal Hayes Literature Committee makes public the Catholic "white list" of books for this quarter. It includes many biographies, travel books, novels, essays, and historical and scientific books.	Nov. 30
For the second time, a federal judge refuses the plea of Al Capone to be released from the Atlanta penitentiary. His attorneys say they will appeal to the Supreme Court.		Chicago will assign 49,000 jobs through the Civil Works Administration by a lottery in which 300,000 jobless will participate. Winners will have 90 days of employment at wages ranging from $15 to $36 per week.		Comedian Ed Wynn is acquitted on charges of beating a process server at his apartment, but his secretary is found guilty and fined $10.	Dec. 1
The Federal Emergency Relief Act helps to keep kindergartens and nursery schools open. Classes for young children are deemed especially important to children of the needy and unemployed because of their health and educational benefits.	President Franklin Roosevelt is told that the United States ranks no higher than fourth in the strength of its air force. The aircraft industry asks for $79 million of Public Works funds to build military planes for the Army and Navy.		A small group of scientists will erect a monument to British scientist Charles Darwin on Chatham Island in the Galapagos Islands. The island, just off the coast of Ecuador, is where Darwin did much of his research.		Dec. 2
	The President's Cup remains with the West Coast Navy as it defeats the San Francisco Marines in the battle for the national service football championship. President Calvin Coolidge established the cup in 1924.	Eleanor Roosevelt predicts that with the plans under consideration, unemployed women will receive more adequate provisions in relief programs soon.	J.G. Vail, Philadelphia scientist, is awarded the Chemistry Industry Medal for his work on sodium silicates.		Dec. 3
When the Senate committee investigating air and ocean mail contracts resumes its meeting tomorrow, it will study the contracts awarded to the Lykes Brothers, who operate 52 ships.	Secretary of the Navy Claude Swanson says that Japan has a perfect right to carry out the naval program it proposes, as it is within the guidelines of the London Treaty. . . . Italian Ambassador Augusto Rossi and Acting Secretary of State William Phillips discuss Italy's debt in Washington. Italy offers a token payment of $1 million on December 15. It is believed the United States accepts the offer.	Harry Hopkins, Civil Works Administrator, announces Civil Works funds will be used to build airports. He will name 500 aides to serve as advisers on aeronautics.	Dr. Nathan Rosenthal, hematologist, finds that minute amounts of venom from moccasin snakes will successfully stop bleeding.	Chuck Klein wins the batting championship in the National League with a .368 mark.	Dec. 4
Cyril Clemens, cousin of Mark Twain, visits the White House to award the gold medal of the International Mark Twain Society to President Franklin Roosevelt, who recalls that Twain was the first to use the phrase "new deal."		Cotton gains 16 to 18 points on the stock market, with the current crop estimated at 13,175,000 bales.		The donors who made it possible get a sneak peek at the Franklin Institute Museum in Philadelphia. Officials hope it will be open to the public the first of the year, but some exhibits are not yet in place.	Dec. 5
	A Coast Guard official says a slight haze hangs over "Rum Row," but Coast Guard boats manage to keep a tail on six of 12 rum-running boats trying to come into New York.		Automatic doors, operated by a laser beam, are in use now at the main waiting room of the Pennsylvania Station. As a person approaches the door, it breaks the beam, triggering the mechanism to open the door.		Dec. 6
Discussion in Washington shows little interest in Italy's ploy to try to get the United States to join the League of Nations.		Striking workers at the Ford plant in Edgewater, N.J., telegraph President Franklin Roosevelt that they want government action in their struggle for collective bargaining rights.	Dr. T.P Hyatt holds that clean teeth are immune to decay. He says diet has no effect on tooth decay. Hyatt states that food debris in the mouth starts decay if it is not removed by brushing the teeth.	Actor John Barrymore appears in a film version of Elmer Rice's play, *Counsellor-at-Law*. He plays the part of George Simon, a highly successful lawyer who has managed to rise from the ghetto.	Dec. 7
President Franklin Roosevelt asks George M. Peek to head a new division in the State Department. Peek will try to find new markets for U.S. products abroad on the basis of American demand for imported wines and liquors.	During the Pan-American Conference at Montevideo, President Franklin Roosevelt announces a policy of non-intervention in Latin America and adopts the "good neighbor" policy.	Henry Bruere, who was "on loan" from the Bowery Savings Bank to serve as a special aide to President Franklin Roosevelt, leaves the administration after staying three weeks longer than agreed upon. He is very enthusiastic about the recovery program.	Jack Miner, of Kingsville, Ontario, reports that Canada geese are migrating quickly this year. His refuge has received many tagged geese from Illinois, Indiana, and Ohio.	Pope Pius XI canonizes the 14-year-old French peasant girl whose visions of the Virgin Mary in 1858 resulted in the building of the grotto at Lourdes. The girl will be known as St. Bernadette Soubirous.	Dec. 8
Dr. Carlos Alden, dean of the University of Buffalo Law School, believes high tariffs and taxes on liquor will provide more business for the bootleggers.		This week's advance in domestic corporation bonds is the largest it has been since the week of April 29.	Pilots practice blind landings in low-hanging clouds and drizzle. A new instrument perfected by engineers at Transcontinental and Western Air works well.	The original Charlie Chan, Chinese detective Chang Apana, dies in Honolulu. Apana was the inspiration for the detective in Earl Biggers's famous series.	Dec. 9
Representatives of the Foreign Service greet William Bullit, new U.S. Ambassador to Russia, at the border of Russia.		Membership in the Home Loan system has grown from just 116 agencies on January 1 to 2,026.	Soviet scientists at the Metchnikoff Institute announce they have cultivated the typhus germ, which they believe will eliminate the disease. The serum is being prepared for injection.		Dec. 10

F	**G**	**H**	**I**	**J**
Includes elections, federal-state relations, civil rights and liberties, crime, the judiciary, education, healthcare, poverty, urban affairs, and population.	*Includes formation and debate of U.S. foreign and defense policies, veterans affairs, and defense spending. (Relations with specific foreign countries are usually found under the region concerned.)*	*Includes business, labor, agriculture, taxation, transportation, consumer affairs, monetary and fiscal policy, natural resources, pollution, and accidents.*	*Includes worldwide scientific, medical, and technological developments, natural phenomena, U.S. weather, and natural disasters.*	*Includes the arts, religion, scholarship, communications media, sports, entertainment, fashions, fads, and social life.*

	World Affairs	Europe	Africa & The Middle East	The Americas	Asia & The Pacific
Dec. 11	Joseph Avenol, Secretary General of the League of Nations, says he favors a flexible League but states that it must be flexible within the bounds of the covenant.	France asks German Chancellor Adolf Hitler what role the storm troopers play in his government, believing that adding storm troopers may be a way of adding members to the military.		President Ramon Grau San Martin abruptly breaks off conciliation negotiations in Cuba, saying he has no intention of resigning.	The Japanese charge 2,000 Korean revolutionists are trying to start a war along the Manchurian-Siberian border.
Dec. 12		Tension subsides and things are back to normal in Spain, but the socialists charge "grave excesses" in government suppression of the anarchist rebellion.	The French planes of the Black Squadron become the first group of planes to cross the Sahara Desert in one day as they start home to France.	Gen. Jose Lanza is appointed chief of staff of the Bolivian army. Paraguay's claims of great victory are said to be greatly exaggerated.	The Mongol Conference at Pangtiang rejects a Mongol autonomy agreement between Mongol princes and Nanking.
Dec. 13		Spain estimates 80 dead and 250 injured during the recent rebellion. The Cabinet is expected to resign now that order has been restored.	An Italian expedition to Asmara in the Italian colony of Eritrea in Africa discovers that the earth's magnetic field bends cosmic rays.	The Pan-American Conference decides to save economic problems to discuss at a third Pan-American financial conference, which will tentatively be held in Santiago, Chile.	Wu The-chen, mayor of Shanghai, warns that anyone "starting rumors prejudicial to public peace" will be severely punished.
Dec. 14	A radiophone link between Japan and the United States will be operational by April.	Chancellor Adolf Hitler puts out a call for the best athletes in the country to get ready for the 1936 Olympics. He does not mention race or creed, so many assume his ban on Jews in the Olympics has been lifted.	A mail plane crashes between Durban and Johannesburg in South Africa. The pilot and three passengers are killed, while the other passenger and the wireless operator escape injury.	The Pan-American Conference praises Secretary of State Cordell Hull's introduction of a new U.S. tariff policy that would result in lower tariffs.	Bandits attack and derail a Chinese Eastern Railway train near Tsitsihar. Seven passengers are killed and eight are wounded.
Dec. 15		The family of Marinus van der Lubbe, condemned to death for the burning of the Reichstag, says it will present a petition for mercy.... Czechoslovakia's Foreign Minister, Edvard Benes, continues his conversation with the French, saying that for him and his country, the future of the League of Nations is a great concern.		The parley at Montevideo comes to a halt as members go to a football game between Argentina and Uruguay.	Russia strongly protests the continued arrests of Russian citizens in Manchukuo. Vladivostok frontier guards say they will defend the Soviet frontier in the Far East.
Dec. 16			Belgium is seeking agriculturists, artisans, and small tradesmen with some capital to settle in the Belgian Congo.	Statistics show that the average Canadian has a longer life expectancy than the average American in the United States.	China plans to add six customs stations along the Great Wall. They expect the move to reduce smuggling of Japanese and Manchurian goods into the country.
Dec. 17	U.S. Secretary of State Cordell Hull will explain why the United States will not support League sanctions in the Chaco, but will back any solution formulated by the Pan-American countries.			Cubans burn the plant of the newspaper El Pais. Four are killed and 10 injured in the rioting, as a mob armed with army rifles attacks the building.	The Nacionalista Party of the Philippines splits, with advocates of the Hawes Act for Independence forming the new Nacionalista Party for Independence.
Dec. 18	The League of Nations Peace Commission and the Bolivian government agree on "concrete points" for resolution of the conflict in the Chaco. The group goes to Paraguay tomorrow.	Well-informed circles say Germany is willing to attend a four-power meeting to settle the disarmament impasse. However, it will still push for arms equality.	Egypt's Ismail Sidky Pasha changes his mind and decides he will not quit since he does not want to cause the dissolution of the Egyptian parliament.	Chile asks for action from the Pan-American Conference on the Chaco conflict, saying the parley will be a failure if it does not settle the dispute.	The Fukien rebel regime tries to revive anti-foreign slogans like the ones that were popular in China in 1926–27.
Dec. 19	Germany says reforms in the League of Nations would not win it back and it will definitely remain out of the League.	The French army bill wins a big majority in the Chamber of Deputies. The military service age will shift to ensure an army strength of about 100,000 men.	An accident in a Johannesburg, South Africa, mine kills 10 natives and two Europeans when a platform they are standing on crashes to the bottom of the mine shaft.	Latin American leaders give Secretary of State Cordell Hull the credit for ending the Chaco War. He had a plan ready when he arrived at the Pan-American Conference.	The Nanking government commandeers all motor buses to transport troops to fight the Fukien rebels and Communists in the south.
Dec. 20		The German Olympic Committee formally invites all nations to the Olympics in Berlin in 1936.... Hitler's government announces the sterilization of 400,000 people because of hereditary defects.	Prince Lucien Murat, great-grandson of the King of Naples who ruled in Napoleon's time, dies in Morocco where he fled from Russia during the revolution. His mother was Russian.	Bolivia charges bad faith in the truce as Paraguay takes four forts in the Chaco. The Pan-American Conference in Uruguay nearly breaks up over the announcement.	The British expect the death of the Dalai Lama in Tibet will result in anti-British Lamas taking control.
Dec. 21	France opposes German armament proposals, while Sir John Simon of Great Britain is cautiously optimistic about Germany's proposed nonaggression pact with all its neighbors.			Bolivia charges Paraguay is violating the truce by taking more forts and not continuing truce talks.	Communists hold part of the Fukien front as clashes increase in south China. Both Fukienese and Nanking planes are in the area, so aerial encounters are expected soon.
Dec. 22	Bolivia and Paraguay agree to let the League of Nations Commission on the Chaco determine whether or not the Paraguayan seizure of four forts violates the truce.	Archduchess Adelheid is the first of the Austrian royal family to visit Vienna since her father, Emperor Karl, lost his throne in 1918.		The Pan-American Conference takes the first steps toward making Secretary of State Cordell Hull's tariff proposal a reality.	Nationalist government aviators bomb Changchow in the Fukien province.

A	B	C	D	E
Includes developments that affect more than one world region, international organizations, and important meetings of world leaders.	Includes all domestic and regional developments in Europe, including the Soviet Union.	Includes all domestic and regional developments in Africa and the Middle East.	Includes all domestic and regional developments in Latin America, the Caribbean, and Canada.	Includes all domestic and regional developments in Asian and Pacific nations (and colonies).

U.S. Politics & Social Issues	U.S. Foreign Policy & Defense	Economics & Great Depression	Science, Technology & Nature	Culture, Leisure & Lifestyle	
The president of Metropolitan Life Insurance reports that a study shows heart disease is the leading cause of death in the United States, with cancer second and tuberculosis third.	Secretary of State Cordell Hull makes it clear that he wants the Pan-American Conference to be kept separate from the League of Nations.	Jesse Jones, chairman of the Reconstruction Finance Corporation, says 1,512 banks have joined the RFC plan, selling preferred stocks or capital notes worth about $440 million.	Dr. Lincoln Ellsworth's ship, The Wyatt Earp, battles its way through subpolar storms on its way to the Antarctic.	Eleanor Roosevelt conceives a plan to hire 2,500 artists to decorate federal and other public buildings across the country. Harry Hopkins of the Civil Works Administration approves the plan.	Dec. 11
In Paris, Postmaster General James Farley encourages people to support President Franklin Roosevelt, saying that criticism will not deflect him from carrying out his plans.	The Women's International League for Peace and Freedom wants Congress to investigate the munitions industry and to prevent further spending on arms.	Both France and Belgium decide to default again on their war debt payments due to the United States on December 15.		Actress Mary Pickford is greeted by dozens of fans when she arrives very early in the morning at Pennsylvania Station. She refuses to discuss her divorce proceedings from Douglas Fairbanks.	Dec. 12
	President Franklin Roosevelt backs bilateral trade pacts. He believes general tariff reductions should be an objective, but feels that will be hard to accomplish.	The Farm Bureau's annual convention in Chicago approves President Franklin Roosevelt's recovery program for agriculture.	Dr. Arthur Kennelly, who was Thomas Edison's chief electrical assistant, receives the Edison medal for 1933.	Irvin "Ace" Bailey, Toronto Maple Leafs' hockey player, fights for his life after he sustains a fractured skull in a game against the Bruins at Boston Garden.	Dec. 13
U.S. Ambassador to Britain Robert Bingham denies that President Franklin Roosevelt has recalled him as he sets sail for the United States for the Christmas holidays.	The Navy Department announces that the Marine Corps has been placed under the commander in chief of the fleet. Brig. Gen. Charles H. Lyman will command the new force.	President Franklin Roosevelt holds to his policy of buying gold, saying the RFC gold purchases will continue indefinitely.	Admiral William E. Byrd's ship in the Antarctic finds itself among icebergs, which present a hazard in foggy weather.	Dance masters invent a new "champagne step" that they hope will revive the waltz.	Dec. 14
The Chicago Daily News calls upon all patriotic Americans to support President Franklin Roosevelt and his programs, saying it is their duty.	Congress cables Secretary of State Cordell Hull in Montevideo, telling him to sign the Nationality Treaty, as a step toward abolishing gender discrimination in laws and practices.	Harry Hopkins, Administrator of the Civil Works Administration, tells the U.S. Conference of Mayors that 4 million people have been put to work on CWA projects.	Tests by Dr. Francis Pease and Fred Pearson show that the speed of light changes daily. They say they cannot explain the irregularities.	Thirty baseball players in the American League and 15 in the National League have been traded or sold since the season ended.	Dec. 15
	For the first time since Prohibition began, a Navy cruiser is christened with champagne. The 10,000-ton U.S. Navy cruiser Astoria is launched in Puget Sound.	Business is booming in the California wine areas since the repeal of Prohibition. About 20,000 men are now at work in the wine industry there.	Interviewed on the anniversary of his famous Kitty Hawk flight, Orville Wright explodes the myth that a toy helicopter got him and his brother interested in flying. They were actually inspired by reading about German scientist Otto Lilienthal.	The newly organized Chicago Grand Opera Company will kick off the season with opera singer Jeritza singing the leading soprano role in La Tosca.	Dec. 16
The National Economy League asks Congress to reduce future expenditures under the recovery program.	Secretary of State Cordell Hull is pleased with the Montevideo Conference as he obtains a pledge to cut tariffs and improves relations for the United States.	Secretary of Labor Frances Perkins summarizes the progress of President Franklin Roosevelt's recovery program in a newsreel now showing in the theaters.	Dr. Karl Compton of MIT announces the development of a new atom gun that fires nine times as many protons per given time. Dr. Edward Lamar and Dr. Overton Luhr developed it.	The Chicago Bears beat the New York Giants 23–21 in the first world championship football game.	Dec. 17
Maine becomes the 19th state to ratify the Child Labor Amendment, meaning more than half the number of states needed for adoption have now passed it.	Acting Secretary of the Treasury Henry Morgenthau rejects all construction bids for nine Coast Guard cutters because they total more than the $13.5 million allotted by the public works fund.		A four-year-old chimpanzee named Meshie is guest of honor at the annual dinner of the New York Academy of Science. She sits in her high chair and eats with a spoon. Harry Raven brought her from the Cameroon in Africa in 1931.	In the midst of a ceremony to award him a medal, cartoonist Walt Disney rushes to the hospital where his wife, Lillian, has just had a baby. The little girl is named Dianne Marie.	Dec. 18
	Secretary of State Cordell Hull pledges the United States will not intervene in other nations. He also backs recognition of Cuba.		Winters seem to be getting milder, according to a trend spotted by Joseph B. Uincer, chief climatologist of the Weather Bureau. Records show 18 of the last 21 winters were warmer than average.	Jimmy Foxx of the Philadelphia Athletics wins the American League batting title with a .356 average.	Dec. 19
The National Women's Party rejoices as word comes that the United States will sign the nationality treaty. It is the first treaty drafted by a woman to receive official recognition.		Acreage sown in winter wheat is down 4 percent from last year, with even those wheat farmers who did not sign bonus agreements cutting production.			Dec. 20
Attorney General Homer Cummings says the Department of Justice is considering a plan by which federal investigators in all branches of government would have the authority to enforce all laws.	After conferring with maritime leaders in Europe, Robert Lee of the American Export Line says they favor international agreements to reduce the excess tonnage that is costing ship lines millions of dollars.	Will Hays, president of Motion Picture Producers and Distributors, Inc., says the industry is doing well and employment in the movies is up to the 1929 level.	Rear Admiral Richard Byrd's ship enters new territory south of the Arctic Circle.	Famous jockey Tod Sloan dies at the age of 59. Sloan had a remarkable career, pioneering a new style of riding and winning and losing several fortunes.	Dec. 21
A special staff is needed at the White House to sort gifts and cards. Each of the last two days sees 25,000 letters and cards arriving, and seasoned staff says this year's volume is about 10 times more than usual for a President at Christmas.		A report on the strike at the Edgewater, N.J., Ford plant charges Henry Ford with violating the NRA mandate for collective bargaining.	A new cold treatment that has been tried on students in Minnesota seems effective. The drug is a combination of codeine and paverine.	Hockey player "Ace" Bailey is on the road to recovery after sustaining a life-threatening head injury.	Dec. 22

F	G	H	I	J
Includes elections, federal-state relations, civil rights and liberties, crime, the judiciary, education, healthcare, poverty, urban affairs, and population.	Includes formation and debate of U.S. foreign and defense policies, veterans affairs, and defense spending. (Relations with specific foreign countries are usually found under the region concerned.)	Includes business, labor, agriculture, taxation, transportation, consumer affairs, monetary and fiscal policy, natural resources, pollution, and accidents.	Includes worldwide scientific, medical, and technological developments, natural phenomena, U.S. weather, and natural disasters.	Includes the arts, religion, scholarship, communications media, sports, entertainment, fashions, fads, and social life.

	World Affairs	Europe	Africa & The Middle East	The Americas	Asia & The Pacific
Dec. 23	The League of Nations cites big gains in 1933, including an increase in U.S. cooperation, improvement in relations with Russia, progress with the arms conference, and the League's assistance in ending both South American wars.	Marinus van der Lubbe receives the death sentence for starting the Reichstag fire.	An Egyptian woman, Loutfieh El Nadi, beats out 29 men to win a big international air race in Cairo. She flies from Cairo to Alexandria and back in two hours and five minutes.	Three main factors cause a rise in wheat prices in Winnipeg: the U.S. government's silver-buying policy, anxiety about European crops, and freer purchasing by exporters.	Swedish scientist Erik Norin, lost for five months in the wilderness of Western China, returns to Peiping.
Dec. 24		A train crash in Lagny, France, kills over 150 people.		Dr. Victor Grossi, a Chilean health officer, says that drug traffic flourishes in South and Central America because of collusion of police officials.	
Dec. 25		The number of dead from Saturday's train wreck in France climbs to 191. The cause is attributed to use of wooden cars. Joseph Paganon, Minister of Public Works, will immediately introduce a bill to supply funds for steel cars.	Syrian nationalists campaign against a new treaty that agrees to a 25-year alliance with France. Nationalist deputies ask parliament to reject the treaty without consideration.	Paraguay insists Bolivia evacuate the war zone in the Chaco before it will begin peace negotiations.	A volcanic eruption, followed by a typhoon and tidal wave, kills 13 Filipinos and causes much property damage in the Philippines.
Dec. 26	Former French premier Edouard Herriot calls French policy shortsighted and believes France is distancing itself from both the British and the Americans.		The American Economic Committee for Palestine says inquiries have been received from 1,379 potential settlers, about 70 percent of whom are German.	U.S. Col. Arthur Brown, president of the League of Nations Commission, is off to Leticia.	Gen. Liu Kwei-tang and his army turn against the government and loot the town of Chihcheng in southeastern Chahar. Liu Kwei-tang, a former bandit, has shifted allegiance between Japan and China several times.
Dec. 27		German Foreign Minister Konstantin von Neurath insists that the Nazi storm troopers are not soldiers trained for war, but serve only as a defense against the Communists.	Sir Arthur Henry Hardings dies. He served as Acting Consul General at Cairo, Consul General for the British East Africa Protectorate, and Minister to Teheran.	Mexicans greet Ramon Franco, who was the first Spaniard to fly across the Atlantic. He comes to look for fellow officers Capt. Barberian and Lt. Collart, who disappeared in Mexico after flying the Atlantic.	The signing of a cotton pact between India and Japan is jeopardized by proposed Indian tariffs.
Dec. 28	President Franklin Roosevelt says the United States will adopt a policy of nonintervention. He says it will not join the League of Nations, but praises its work and says the United States will continue to work with the League.	Spain will introduce a system of import quotas to help regulate its trade with foreign countries.		Negotiators on the Chaco conflict are discouraged, as Paraguay refuses to extend the truce.	Brazil reports a record number of Japanese immigrants. The total for the year is 22,310.
Dec. 29		Members of the Iron Guard assassinate Romanian Prime Minister Ion Duca.		Brazil's ministers of finance and foreign affairs quit the Cabinet because of dissension over federal commissionership for the state of Minas Geraes.	The United States sends the destroyer *Fulton* to the Foochow area, where it is ready to protect American lives and property if necessary.
Dec. 30	Secretary General Joseph Avenol says both the League of Nations and the disarmament and economic conferences struggle against selfish nationalism.	More than 3,000 attend a fiesta in Granada, Spain, in honor of American author Washington Irving, who did much of his writing while living there.		President Harmodio Arias of Panama sees a better understanding among the Americas, due to the Pan-American Conference. . . . Mexico is delighted with the new U.S. policy and says, "We now, with love and trust, join our northern sister."	Japan hails a whole new era as it greets a baby prince. It believes the birth of a boy as the heir is a sign of approval of the gods.
Dec. 31	The League of Nations honors American Arthur Sweetser by appointing him to the rank of director.	Mario Merighi, convicted of sending 38 packages of explosives through the mail, is sentenced to 25 years in prison. Over a 10-year period, 38 were injured by his bombs.		Another clash with Argentine rebels kills between 70 and 80 people in Concordia in the Entre Rios province.	Former Chinese minister of finance, Dr. T.V. Soong, says the Chinese people have watched with interest President Franklin Roosevelt's experiment and says he hopes the Chinese can get a new deal next year.

A	B	C	D	E
Includes developments that affect more than one world region, international organizations, and important meetings of world leaders.	*Includes all domestic and regional developments in Europe, including the Soviet Union.*	*Includes all domestic and regional developments in Africa and the Middle East.*	*Includes all domestic and regional developments in Latin America, the Caribbean, and Canada.*	*Includes all domestic and regional developments in Asian and Pacific nations (and colonies).*

U.S. Politics & Social Issues	U.S. Foreign Policy & Defense	Economics & Great Depression	Science, Technology & Nature	Culture, Leisure & Lifestyle	
Ambassador to Great Britain Robert Bingham discusses with President Franklin Roosevelt the great improvement in Britain's economic situation. He attributes the 600,000 re-employed to the decision to give up the gold standard.		In Kansas, 43,000 farmers will share in a $15 million payment for cutting farm acreage.	The government helps forests on two fronts. Reforestation by the CCC improves and extends the government's forests, while the NRA code for the lumber industry emphasizes conservation of private forests.	Pope Pius XI condemns the Nazi's new sterilization program.	Dec. 23
	The Interstate Commerce Commission urges strict regulations of vessels carrying explosives in U.S. harbors and rivers.	The millinery code goes into effect today, with one of the shortest workweeks in industry at 37.5 hours. Minimum wages increase, affecting about 35,000.	Doctors in Great Britain say if tapeworm larvae reach the brain, they can cause epileptic seizures.	A robber who holds up a party at movie executive Matthew Levine's house strikes him with a pistol when he will not give up a ring his wife bought him.	Dec. 24
White House police allow Christmas carolers to go to the front steps of the White House, where the Roosevelt family hears them.	Only four vacancies exist in the U.S. foreign service, and two should be filled in the next few days. President Franklin Roosevelt is expected to appoint Ambassadors to the Netherlands and Czechoslovakia.	The Civil Works Administration has put 100,000 women back to work in an effort spurred by the President's wife, Eleanor Roosevelt.	Travel to National Parks in October and November is up 22 percent over the same period a year ago.	Ginger Rogers, Joel McCrea, and Marian Nixon star in a comical movie entitled Chance at Heaven.	Dec. 25
	Some members of Congress believe the United States cannot act on tariff agreements made at the Pan-American Conference until the U.S. economic program is completed.	Retailers plan a series of conferences in the new year at which time they will seek to modify their code.	German Willy Merkl, who commanded an unsuccessful expedition last year, will try again to climb the 26,629-foot peak of Nanga Parbat in Kashmir.		Dec. 26
	Secretary of State Cordell Hull is encouraged by the trade outlook, believing that European nationalism has caused the Latin American countries to turn to the United States as a trade partner.		Dr. R.L. Kahn tells scientists that the skin is the body's first line of defense against germs, with its immunity being over 10 times as great as that of the bloodstream.	In the first film she has made in more than 18 months, Greta Garbo plays the part of Queen Christina of Sweden in a film called simply Queen Christina.	Dec. 27
Congress pledges support for Secretary of State Cordell Hull, saying he has achieved much in relations with Latin America.		Gen. Hugh Johnson, NRA Administrator, approves fair practice rules for banks that will ensure they do not operate at a loss and will prevent unfair competition between large and small banks.	Scientists say that a pint of fairly strong coffee will offset the effect of a stiff shot of gin. In order to be effective, the person must drink the coffee at the same time or immediately after drinking the gin.	National amateur champion golfer George T. Dunlap, Jr., defeats F.C. Robertson in his first match at the midwinter golf tourney at Pinehurst, N.C.	Dec. 28
A Jewish group in New Jersey, under a federal project, begins a 1,000-acre farm community. Applicants accepted will receive a home and an acre of land.	President Franklin Roosevelt says that U.S. Special Ambassador Norman Davis will return to Geneva after the League of Nations Council meeting and that he will focus only on disarmament.		Canadian scientist Dr. Francois Henroteau develops an electronic telescope that can magnify the stars as much as a telescope with a 2,000-inch reflecting mirror.	The father of grand opera star Hope Hampton dies in Los Angeles. Harry Kennedy was 58 years old.	Dec. 29
		The CCC will recruit another 30,000 workers in the next 10 days.	Tombs found at Soings-en-Sologne, France, contain ancient Roman coins, jewelry, urns, and utensils. The burial ground there contains several thousand tombs.	Uncle Donald, the 10–1 favorite, puts on a burst of speed and beats Little Lad by three lengths at the Jefferson Park horse track.	Dec. 30
The Roosevelts will celebrate the New Year quietly, without a formal White House reception.	A Navigation Bureau report urges returning the U.S. Navy to full strength, saying both Japan and Britain have more naval personnel than the United States.	The NRA finds jobs for 4 million workers and helps five times that many by reducing their work hours and getting them higher pay.		In an interview, Johnny Goodman says his chief objective for 1934 is to win another U.S. Open golf championship.	Dec. 31

F	G	H	I	J
Includes elections, federal-state relations, civil rights and liberties, crime, the judiciary, education, healthcare, poverty, urban affairs, and population.	Includes formation and debate of U.S. foreign and defense policies, veterans affairs, and defense spending. (Relations with specific foreign countries are usually found under the region concerned.)	Includes business, labor, agriculture, taxation, transportation, consumer affairs, monetary and fiscal policy, natural resources, pollution, and accidents.	Includes worldwide scientific, medical, and technological developments, natural phenomena, U.S. weather, and natural disasters.	Includes the arts, religion, scholarship, communications media, sports, entertainment, fashions, fads, and social life.

The Hoover Dam, along the border between Arizona and Nevada, under construction in 1934. It would be completed in 1935.

1934

	World Affairs	Europe	Africa & The Middle East	The Americas	Asia & The Pacific
Jan.	The International Labor Office in Geneva reports that 20 countries successfully managed to reduce unemployment in 1933. The United States has the most marked reduction. . . . The League of Nations starts its 78th Council session in Geneva.	The Bayonne pawnshop scandal extends and involves members of the French Cabinet, particularly Albert Dalimier, Minister for the Colonies. . . . Reichbishop Ludwig Mueller suppresses the self-government of the German Protestant Church in an attempt to stop the protests against Hitler's anti-Semitic policies.	The Italian colony of Libya is reorganized into four provinces. . . . Arab Muslims march throughout Palestine to protest against the selling of land to Jews.	Cuban President Ramon Grau resigns and is replaced by Carlos Mendieta. . . . Paraguay and Bolivia resume fighting in the Chaco region as their armistice expires.	An infant found in the outskirts of Lhasa, Tibet, is officially declared to be the 14th Dalai Lama. . . . A violent earthquake in India and Nepal kills 10,700 people and damages the unique Mahabuddha Temple in Patan, Nepal.
Feb.	The British, Indian, and Yemeni governments sign a treaty of friendship. . . . The League of Nations Chaco Commission submits to Bolivia and Paraguay a formal proposal to end the Chaco conflict.	The German government outlaws all monarchist parties to restrain political opposition from the right. . . . The Austrian Socialist Party is officially outlawed. Its leaders are arrested. . . . King Albert I of Belgium dies in a mountaineering accident. Prince Leopold, age 32, succeeds to the throne.	The British and Saudi governments conclude the Treaty of Sanaa, which establishes 40 years of friendly relations between the two governments. . . . Berbers start an uprising against the French in Morocco.	Paraguayan troops make important advances in the Chaco conflict. . . . The Liberal leader Alfonso Lopez is elected president of Colombia. He favors a peaceful solution of the Leticia controversy with Peru. . . . The leader of the Sandino insurrection in Nicaragua, Gen. Augusto Sandino, is murdered.	Australian States demand to the Commonwealth government to have a larger share of the central government's revenues.
Mar.	The League of Nations Chaco Peace Committee announces it is unable to settle the war between Bolivia and Paraguay. The committee will soon return to Europe.	The Italian, Austrian, and Hungarian governments sign the Rome Protocols. They include agreements for closer trade relations, consultation, and common policy. . . . The new Austrian constitution makes the country a dictatorship.	After several border incidents, the Saudi King Ibn Saud ends the truce with Yemen and launches a military offensive.	President Mendieta suspends all constitutional guarantees in an effort to halt the spreading of strikes throughout Cuba. . . . The Paraguayan army threatens the main Bolivian military base at Fort Ballivian. . . . The Constituent Assembly reelects Gabriel Terra as president of Paraguay for the 1935–39 term.	Henry Pu-Yi is crowned as Emperor of Manchukuo. Japanese officials continue to hold key places in the empire.
Apr.	The Italian educator Giovanni Bosco is the first saint to be canonized on Easter Sunday. . . . The Holy Year ends.	The Soviet government signs a 10-year nonaggression pact with the Baltic States. . . . Exiled Russian Communist Leon Trotsky is discovered living in Fontainebleau, France, under false identity.	The Actions Committee of the World Zionist Organization ends its 12-day meeting in Jerusalem without reaching internal unity.	Cuban Minister of Justice, Col. Roberto Mendez Penate, commits suicide over disagreements with his lifelong friend, President Mendieta. . . . Paraguayans are halted in their advance toward Fort Ballivian.	Gandhi suspends the Indian civil disobedience campaign against British authorities. . . . Foreign Office spokesman Eiji Amau says Japan will intervene if it judges that China is endangering the peace in East Asia. This declaration is interpreted as a warning to countries that are selling arms and planes for China's army.
May	A committee is named in Geneva to preside over the plebiscite that will decide the fate of the Saar Valley. . . . The League of Nations announces that its jurists have devised a legal formula to prohibit the sale of arms to Bolivia and Paraguay, the belligerent nations in the Chaco conflict. . . . The League of Nations disarmament conference opens in Geneva.	The president of the British Board of Trade, Walter Runciman, tells Japan's Ambassador Matsudaira that Britain will impose quotas to check the inflow of Japanese goods in British colonies. . . . The Irish Dail (lower chamber) passes a Bill to abolish the Senate, where the Eamon De Valera government does not have a clear majority.	An armistice is announced in the war between Saudi Arabia and Yemen.	The Paraguayan advance in the Chaco region is halted by the Bolivians who are deeply entrenched in their positions in Fort Ballivian. . . . Rafael Trujillo is reelected president of the Dominican Republic. He is the sole candidate in the election.	The National Congress Party adopts a resolution to favor the repudiation of India's debt to the British. . . . Chinese peasants revolt against Japanese authorities in northern Manchukuo. Three hundred Chinese are killed and several Japanese are wounded.
Jun.	The 18th session of the International Labor Conference opens in Geneva. . . . The World Disarmament Conference adjourns until the fall without having reached an agreement.	French Foreign Minister Louis Barthou arrives in Bucharest on an official visit for a conference with the Little Entente. . . . To prevent a plot against the regime, Chancellor Adolf Hitler summarily executes 77 people, many of whom had been leaders of the party. The event become known as the Night of the Long Knives.	The Shah of Persia makes official visits to Tunisia and Turkey.	Cuba begins a three-day celebration for the abrogation of the Platt Amendment and its establishment as an independent nation. . . . A parade of 80,000 militants of the ABC revolutionary organization is attacked in Havana by gunmen. Fourteen people are killed and more than 60 are injured.	The peasant uprising in the Ilan province in northeastern Manchuria is subdued only after the killing of 2,000 Chinese. . . . Gen. Chiang Kai-shek, head of the Chinese national government, announces that his campaign against the Communist rebels in the Kiangsi province is successfully concluded.
Jul.	The British and Italian governments sign an agreement finalizing the border between Libya and Anglo-Egyptian Sudan.	In an attempt to halt the spreading of fascism, the Belgian government prohibits the formation of military units and the wearing of political uniforms. . . . The National Socialists fail in their coup to seize power in Austria. Chancellor Engelbert Dollfuss is assassinated. Dr. Kurt Schuschnigg forms a new government.	The French open a new railway line that connects Brazzaville, in the French Congo, to the Atlantic coast at Pointe Noire. . . . The Mosul-Tripoli oil pipeline opens, allowing the shipment of oil from Iraq to the Mediterranean coast.		The Australian government adopts a three-year defense program designed to expand the country's air force, naval power, and army mechanization. . . . A constitutional convention gathers in the Philippines to discuss the future institutional structure of the country.
Aug.		A national plebiscite combines the offices of president and chancellor for Adolf Hitler after German president Paul von Hindenburg dies.	Arab nationalists launch a series of violent attacks on Jews in Constantine and other Algerian cities.		
Sept.	The League of Nations Assembly holds its 15th session. . . . The League of Nations admits the Soviet Union as a member state and the Soviets accept the sixth permanent seat on the Council. . . . The League of Nations accepts Afghanistan as a member state.	Ivan Mihailov, the leader of the Macedonian independence movement, flees to Turkey to escape imprisonment by the Bulgarian government. . . . The Estonian, Latvian, and Lithuanian governments sign a number of agreements that provide for common action in defense and foreign affairs.	Tunisia begins its movement for independence.	Ecuador joins the League of Nations to support its claims in the Amazon Basin during the Leticia dispute between Peru and Colombia.	A typhoon strikes Honshu Island, Japan, and kills 4,000 people.

A	B	C	D	E
Includes developments that affect more than one world region, international organizations, and important meetings of world leaders.	*Includes all domestic and regional developments in Europe, including the Soviet Union.*	*Includes all domestic and regional developments in Africa and the Middle East.*	*Includes all domestic and regional developments in Latin America, the Caribbean, and Canada.*	*Includes all domestic and regional developments in Asian and Pacific nations (and colonies).*

U.S. Politics & Social Issues	U.S. Foreign Policy & Defense	Economics & Great Depression	Science, Technology & Nature	Culture, Leisure & Lifestyle	
William Woodin resigns as Secretary of the Treasury because of ill health and is replaced by Henry Morgenthau, Jr.	The Hawes-Cutting Act regarding Philippine independence expires and a new plan for the independence of the island is submitted to President Roosevelt. . . . Alexander Troyanovsky arrives in the United States, the first Soviet ambassador since the two countries ceased diplomatic relations in 1918. . . . President Roosevelt announces the U.S. recognition of Cuba.	President Roosevelt's budget message presents a huge financing program, estimated at $10 billion. Wall Street reacts negatively. . . . Congress completes approval of President Roosevelt's Money Bill. The act authorizes President Roosevelt to devalue the dollar at 50 to 60 cents by reduction of its gold content.	Heavy floods in Los Angeles cause the death of 38 people and $5 million in damages. . . . Dr. George E. Vincent announces the discovery of a serum that immunizes human beings to yellow fever.	The Metropolitan Opera Company revives Richard Strauss's *Salomé*, a scandalous opera based on Oscar Wilde's work. . . . Baseball player Babe Ruth signs a record contract for $35,000. . . . Six thousand dinner parties celebrate President Roosevelt's 52nd birthday.	Jan.
President Roosevelt orders the cancellation of all existing airmail contracts and orders the army to fly the mail during the emergency created by his decision.	In the Senate, a coalition of Democrats and Republicans approves amendments to the Independent Offices Bill, which restores all benefits for veterans canceled by the Economy Act.	The Fletcher-Rayburn Stock Exchange Regulation Bill is introduced in Congress. It provides strict federal control of the stock market.	French physicists Joliot and Curie produce artificial radioactivity. It is hoped that this radioactivity will be used for medical treatment.	The Stein-Thomson opera *Four Saints in Three Acts* opens in Broadway to enthusiastic audience reactions. The opera will become the longest-running in Broadway history. . . . Frank Capra's romantic comedy *It Happened One Night* opens at Radio City Music Hall.	Feb.
Bank robber and murderer John Dillinger escapes from Lake County jail using a wooden pistol. . . . President Roosevelt faces his first major defeat when the Senate rejects the St. Lawrence Seaway treaty, 46–42. A two-thirds majority is necessary for the approval.	The House of Representatives approves the Patman Bonus Bill, which gives cash payments to war veterans. Breaking with the administration are 231 Democrats, who join with Republicans in approving it. . . . President Roosevelt signs the McDuffie Bill, which grants the Philippines independence in 1945 or soon after.	President Roosevelt issues an executive order that makes the National Labor Board independent from the NRA. This will enable the Labor Board to obtain prompt enforcement of its decisions.	The California Institute of Technology announces the production of artificial radioactivity from nonradioactive material.	Primo Carnera beats Tommy Loughran in Miami and keeps the world heavyweight championship. . . . The Detroit Red Wings win the National Hockey League championship by defeating the Toronto Maple Leafs.	Mar.
The U.S. government begins a nationwide campaign aimed to eliminate bootleggers and illicit distillers. . . . John F. Curry is the first leader of Tammany Hall to be deposed by its executive committee.	President Roosevelt confers with Haiti's President Vincent about the definite withdrawal of U.S. Marines from the island. . . . The United States says it has no intention of changing its "open door" policy toward China. All nine powers that signed the 1922 treaty are to have equal opportunities in commerce with China.	Former Republican Secretary of State Henry Stimson urges Congress to give President Roosevelt the authority of negotiating new tariffs with foreign countries. It is the first time a Republican leader publicly endorses an important Roosevelt policy.	Dr. Hubble of Mount Wilson Observatory calculates that the diameter of the physical universe is 6 billion light-years.	The Chicago Black Hawks beat the Detroit Red Wings, capturing the Stanley Cup and the world hockey championship. . . . The 1934 championship baseball season begins.	Apr.
Former Secretary of the Treasury William H. Woodin dies at 65. . . . The Senate votes 42–24 to abolish the Electoral College, but the constitutional amendment does not reach the required two-thirds. . . . Gangsters Clyde Barrow and Bonnie Parker are killed in Louisiana in a police ambush.	President Roosevelt prohibits the sale of arms to Bolivia and Paraguay in an attempt to stop the Chaco War. . . . Congress approves the abrogation of the Platt Amendment, making Cuba an independent country.	The Darrow report on the National Recovery Administration is made public. The report criticizes the NRA, finding that its codes lead toward monopoly and damage small businesses.	A large fire, described as the worst since 1871, breaks out in Chicago's stockyards, causing damages of $10 million.	The U.S. Davis Cup team wins the American zone series. . . . A renovated and improved Century of Progress exposition opens in Chicago.	May
Henry P. Fletcher is elected chairman of the Republican National Committee. . . . W.E.B. Du Bois resigns as editor of *Crisis*, the monthly magazine of the National Association for the Advancement of Colored People. . . . The 73rd Congress adjourns.	The United States receives payment for war debts by Finland only. All other countries notify they will not pay. . . . President Roosevelt orders an embargo on arms and other military equipment for Cuba except under licenses from the State Department.	Congress approves the Fletcher Rayburn Bill for Stock Exchange Control in its final form. . . . The Reciprocal Tariffs Bill is finally approved by the House and goes to the President for signing.	Italian scientist Enrico Fermi artificially produces a new chemical element. . . . President Roosevelt says that drought in the western states has reached the proportion of national disaster. Yet, because of the ample food surplus, there is no danger of famine.	The animated short *The Wise Little Hen* is released, marking the debut of Donald Duck. . . . Italy beats Czechoslovakia 2–1 and wins the 1934 football championship. . . . Max Baer beats Primo Carnera and becomes the world heavyweight champion.	Jun.
San Francisco mayor Angelo Rossi orders the police to repress the maritime strike. The police kill several people and wound hundreds. . . . John Dillinger is shot to death by FBI agents in Chicago. . . . The Supreme Court of North Dakota suspends Governor William Langer, announcing that Ole Olsen is the legitimate governor.			The first x-ray photograph of an entire body is made in Rochester, N.Y. . . . "Madame" Marie Curie-Sklodovska, Polish-born French chemist and Nobel Prize winner, dies in Paris of leukemia due to her long exposure to radiation.	The Hollywood Motion Picture Production Code, formalized in 1930, goes into effect.	Jul.
The U.S. Court of Appeals upholds a lower court ruling striking down the government's attempt to ban the controversial James Joyce novel, *Ulysses*. . . . The U.S. government opens a maximum security prison on Alcatraz Island in San Francisco Bay.	The U.S. government makes arrangements for the complete termination of American control of Haiti. . . . The Roosevelt administration accepts membership in the International Labor Organization.	The U.S. and Cuban governments negotiate a reciprocal trade agreement designed to expand trade between the two countries.		The satirical comic strip *Li'l Abner*, created by Al Capp, makes its debut. . . . William Beebe and Otis Barton establish a new world diving record at 3,028 feet.	Aug.
Bruno Hauptmann is arrested in New York for the kidnapping and murder of the Lindbergh baby. . . . Bank robber Baby Face Nelson is shot dead by FBI agent Sam Cowley, who also dies in the shooting.			The luxury liner *Morro Castle*, en route from Havana to New York, catches fire which results in 134 deaths.	Babe Ruth makes his farewell appearance as a regular player with the New York Yankees in a game against the Boston Red Sox.	Sept.

F	G	H	I	J
Includes elections, federal-state relations, civil rights and liberties, crime, the judiciary, education, healthcare, poverty, urban affairs, and population.	*Includes formation and debate of U.S. foreign and defense policies, veterans affairs, and defense spending. (Relations with specific foreign countries are usually found under the region concerned.)*	*Includes business, labor, agriculture, taxation, transportation, consumer affairs, monetary and fiscal policy, natural resources, pollution, and accidents.*	*Includes worldwide scientific, medical, and technological developments, natural phenomena, U.S. weather, and natural disasters.*	*Includes the arts, religion, scholarship, communications media, sports, entertainment, fashions, fads, and social life.*

	World Affairs	Europe	Africa & The Middle East	The Americas	Asia & The Pacific
Oct.	The Permanent Court of International Justice holds its 33rd session in The Hague. . . . The Naval Disarmament Conference opens in London.	The leftist political parties in Spain call for a general strike in support of the Socialist government. . . . A Macedonian revolutionary assassinates King Alexander of Yugoslavia and Louis Barthou, the French foreign minister. . . . The Greek-Turkish Mixed Commission, established to settle unresolved disputes between the two countries, ends its meetings.		Newfoundland announces it will lower most import duties for the colony.	The British establish the Royal Indian Navy as an independent naval force. . . . Mao Tse-Dong is forced to leave his headquarters in Nanking due to attacks by Chiang Kai-shek and the Nationalists and begins his Long March. . . . Gandhi withdraws from the Indian National Congress.
Nov.	The League of Nations helps to settle the Leticia dispute between Colombia and Peru.	German theologian Karl Barth surrenders to Nazis.	The Moroccan Nationalist Movement starts with the publication of "A Plan of Moroccan Reforms," an agenda designed by intellectuals educated in Europe. . . . The new Egyptian Prime Minister, Mohammad Tewfik Nessim, suspends the Constitution of 1930.	Lázaro Cárdenas begins his term as president of Mexico.	The Chinese Nationalist government announces its withdrawal from the silver standard.
Dec.	The major naval powers fail to find an agreement at the London Naval Disarmament Conference. . . . The League of Nations Council holds its 83rd session in Geneva. . . . . Weekly airmail service between England and Australia begins.	Sergei Kirov, a close collaborator of Stalin, is assassinated in Leningrad. The murder is followed by a large purge. . . . Hungary and Yugoslavia accept League of Nations mediation to settle their dispute after the assassination of King Alexander. . . . The Spanish government suspends the Catalonian Statute.	Italian and Ethiopian troops clash at Ualual on the border with the Italian colony of Somalia.	Due to the repeated defeats in the Chaco War, the Bolivian army overthrows President Daniel Salamanca. Vice President Luis Tejada Sorzano assumes the presidency.	The Japanese government formally withdraws from the Naval Treaties of 1922 and 1930. The country can now start to build a massive fleet.

A	B	C	D	E
Includes developments that affect more than one world region, international organizations, and important meetings of world leaders.	Includes all domestic and regional developments in Europe, including the Soviet Union.	Includes all domestic and regional developments in Africa and the Middle East.	Includes all domestic and regional developments in Latin America, the Caribbean, and Canada.	Includes all domestic and regional developments in Asian and Pacific nations (and colonies).

U.S. Politics & Social Issues	U.S. Foreign Policy & Defense	Economics & Great Depression	Science, Technology & Nature	Culture, Leisure & Lifestyle	
Bruno Hauptmann, a carpenter and illegal alien, is indicted for murder in the death of the infant son of Charles A. Lindbergh. . . . Described as a 20th-century Jesse James, or as the most dangerous man alive, Charles Floyd is killed by federal agents in Ohio.				Jean Piccard and Jeanette Ridlen attain a record balloon height of 17,341 meters.	Oct.
Gloria Vanderbilt's mother is considered unfit for her custody by a court. . . . The gangster Baby Face Nelson is shot by the FBI.	The United States agrees with Britain to build 5 million tons of naval ships.		American chemist Harold C. Urey is awarded the Nobel Prize for Chemistry for his work on deuterium.	Lillian Hellman's *The Children's Hour* premieres in New York. . . . The musical *Anything Goes* by Cole Porter premieres at the Alvin Theatre, New York.	Nov.
				Parker Brothers purchase the game of Monopoly from George Darrow.	Dec.

F
Includes elections, federal-state relations, civil rights and liberties, crime, the judiciary, education, healthcare, poverty, urban affairs, and population.

G
Includes formation and debate of U.S. foreign and defense policies, veterans affairs, and defense spending. (Relations with specific foreign countries are usually found under the region concerned.)

H
Includes business, labor, agriculture, taxation, transportation, consumer affairs, monetary and fiscal policy, natural resources, pollution, and accidents.

I
Includes worldwide scientific, medical, and technological developments, natural phenomena, U.S. weather, and natural disasters.

J
Includes the arts, religion, scholarship, communications media, sports, entertainment, fashions, fads, and social life.

	World Affairs	Europe	Africa & The Middle East	The Americas	Asia & The Pacific
Jan. 1	British Prime Minister Ramsay MacDonald and Foreign Secretary Sir John Simon give a cold reception to U.S. President Franklin Roosevelt's proposal for world disarmament.	German President Paul von Hindenburg praises Chancellor Adolf Hitler for his "spiritual regeneration" of Germany. . . . Two hundred thousand Romanians render homage to the corpse of former premier Ion Duca, assassinated by the fascist movement of the Iron Guard.	The Italian colony of Libya is reorganized into four provinces.	Fighting continues in Argentina between supporters of President Agustin Justo and rebels asking for increased democracy. . . . Mexico introduces the minimum wage.	
Jan. 2		The ashes of Anatol Lunacharsky, former Soviet commissar for education, are solemnly deposited in the Kremlin in Moscow. . . . British Foreign Secretary Sir John Simon meets fascist Italian leader Benito Mussolini in an attempt to further the disarmament process in Europe and overcome the Franco-German deadlock.		Cuban President Ramon Grau announces free elections for April and his intention to step down as president afterward. . . . A revolutionary plot is discovered in Chile, leading to a tightening of censorship.	Intense fighting in the northern Fukien region of China is reported between government forces and Communist rebels.
Jan. 3		Lt. Gen. Werner Von Fritsch is appointed commander in chief of the German army. . . . Constantine Angelescu resigns as prime minister of Romania after only five days in office.			India and Japan reach an agreement that settles long disputes over the exchange of Indian raw cotton and Japanese cotton textiles.
Jan. 4	The official Vatican directory shows an increase in almost all activities of the Holy See in spite of fiscal difficulties.	Violin prodigy Yehudi Menuhin refuses a Nazi plea to help Germany improve its image in the world of arts and music. . . . Near Osseg, Czechoslovakia, 120 miners die while trapped in a coal mine. . . . The Bayonne pawnshop scandal extends and involves members of the French Cabinet, particularly Albert Dalimier, Minister for the Colonies.		Talks among leading Cuban political factions identify Col. Carlos Mendieta as a possible successor to Ramon Grau to the presidency.	Intense fighting between rebels and government forces continues in southern China.
Jan. 5	The International Labor Office in Geneva reports that 20 countries successfully managed to reduce unemployment in 1933. The United States has the most marked reduction.	In a joint communiqué, Italian premier Benito Mussolini and British Foreign Secretary John Simon consider complete disarmament an impractical solution. . . . Austrian Chancellor Engelbert Dollfuss faces new pressures from Heimwehr fascists to have more ministerial seats in his government. . . . The meeting of the German Lutheran Bishops fails to oust Reichbishop Ludwig Mueller, who enjoys Chancellor Adolf Hitler's favor.	The Egyptian Bar Association protests the regime's decision to prohibit the election to the lawyers' syndicate of any person condemned by the Judicial Disciplinary Council. This is seen as a move to oust the popular Bar Association head, Makram Ebeid.	In Cuba, students demonstrate against President Ramon Grau and his Head of Staff, Col. Fulgencio Batista.	King Prajadhipok of Siam announces a five-month journey to the United States and Europe.
Jan. 6		Reichbishop Ludwig Mueller suppresses the self-government of the German Protestant Church in an attempt to stop the protests against Chancellor Adolf Hitler's anti-Semitic policies. . . . Sir Stafford Cripps, former Solicitor General, shocks the British with his criticism against the King, the City of London, and the House of Lords.		The Chaco armistice between Bolivia and Paraguay expires, and fighting resumes.	
Jan. 7		Six thousand pastors in Berlin defy the Nazis, insisting that they will not be muzzled. . . . The Turkish government launches a five-year plan to industrialize the country. . . . Gen. Owen O'Duffy, leader of the United Ireland Party, attacks the Eamon De Valera government at a large rally in Wexford.	Six people are killed in a train crash in South Africa.		Gen. Chiang Kai-shek announces that his forces are making important gains in the Fukien region against rebels. . . . Manuel Roxas launches the "Young Philippines," a youth fascist movement.
Jan. 8	France and Great Britain increase quotas for U.S. products.	The Austrian government increases the number of fascist patrols. . . . Seven meetings of protest against Reichbishop Ludwig Mueller take place in Berlin. . . . The only leftist minister of the Spanish government, Rico Avello, resigns as Minister of the Interior. . . . Alexandre Stavinsky, the leading figure in the Bayonne pawnshop scandal, commits suicide and Minister Albert Dalimier resigns.		Fourteen Peruvian army officers admit to have taken part in an abortive revolutionary plot. . . . Cuban military authorities strengthen their forces to face uprisings against President Ramon Grau.	

A	B	C	D	E
Includes developments that affect more than one world region, international organizations, and important meetings of world leaders.	Includes all domestic and regional developments in Europe, including the Soviet Union.	Includes all domestic and regional developments in Africa and the Middle East.	Includes all domestic and regional developments in Latin America, the Caribbean, and Canada.	Includes all domestic and regional developments in Asian and Pacific nations (and colonies).

U.S. Politics & Social Issues	U.S. Foreign Policy & Defense	Economics & Great Depression	Science, Technology & Nature	Culture, Leisure & Lifestyle	
William Woodin resigns as Secretary of the Treasury because of ill-health and is replaced by Henry Morgenthau, Jr. . . . Fiorello LaGuardia is inaugurated mayor of New York and promises to clean the city from corruption and rackets. . . . William N. McNair is inaugurated mayor of Pittsburgh. He is the first Democratic mayor since 1906. . . . Walter White, the secretary of the National Association for the Advancement of Colored People, denounces the steady increase of lynching.	The Foreign Policy Association and the World Peace Foundation urge President Franklin Roosevelt to grant independence to the Philippines.	The new year opens with hope of economic recovery. It is announced that, for 1933, financial and industrial activities in the United States exceeded those of the previous year, the first time since 1929. . . . Chester C. Davis, the new director of the Agricultural Adjustment Administration, announces a complete restructuring of the agency.	Thirty-eight people die in Los Angeles due to heavy floods.	The Columbia Lions beat Stanford 7–0 in the Rose Bowl.	Jan. 1
	The U.S. government follows Great Britain in protesting to the German government against the arbitrary reduction of the interest payments on German foreign indebtedness.	An NRA report foresees substantial industrial recovery for 1934. . . . Secretary of State Edward J. Flynn orders the dissolution of 8,500 stock corporations for their failure to file annual franchise tax returns for five years.	The damages of the heavy floods in the Los Angeles area are estimated at $5 million.	Doris Warner, daughter of film producer Harry M. Warner, marries director Melvyn LeRoi.	Jan. 2
		President Franklin Roosevelt addresses Congress in a joint session and illustrates the economic progress achieved since the launch of his New Deal.		A diamond necklace and breastplate owned by the late Edith Rockefeller McCormick are auctioned for a record sum of $15,000. . . . The painter and mural artist Edwin Howland Blashfield is awarded the golden medal from the National Academy of Design.	Jan. 3
Senators Edward Costigan and Robert Wagner introduce an anti-lynching bill that includes harsher penalties for officers who fail to act against mob assaults.		President Franklin Roosevelt's budget message presents a huge financing program, estimated at $10 billion. Wall Street reacts negatively.			Jan. 4
In his annual report, Attorney General Homer Cummings proposes to reduce the sale of weapons as a measure of crime prevention. . . . The House of Representatives passes the Liquor Tax Bill.		President Franklin Roosevelt urges Congress for a quick approval of his budget without major modifications.		The annual meeting of the American Horse Show Association names, for the first time in its history, three women to its board. . . . The earliest manuscript of Francis Scott Key's "Star-Spangled Banner" is auctioned for $24,000.	Jan. 5
Thousands of farmers picket, preventing milk deliveries in Chicago. Farmers protest against the proposed reduction of price for their milk.	The National Council of Jewish Federations and Welfare Funds begins its first assembly in Chicago to coordinate relief of German-Jewish refugees.		Four 25,000-gallon crude oil stills explode at the Atlantic Refining Company's plant in South Philadelphia.	The National Automobile Show opens in New York, displaying innovative car models that combine comfort with economy of operation.	Jan. 6
A report of the American Federation of Labor cites the reduction of unemployment and of working hours as important gains for workers obtained in 1933. . . . A group of 75 New York Democrats asks for the resignation of John F. Curry as New York Democratic Party leader, blaming him for the defeat of the Democratic ticket in the municipal election.	Alexander Troyanovsky arrives in the United States, the first Soviet Ambassador since the two countries ceased diplomatic relations in 1918.			The International Baseball League votes to retain for the second consecutive year the play-off system. . . . The first *Flash Gordon* comic strip, drawn by Alex Raymond, is published.	Jan. 7
The Republican opposition introduces a Veterans' Bill in the Senate. . . . Henry Morgenthau, Jr., is confirmed Secretary of the Treasury by the unanimous vote of the Senate.	Senator William E. Borah of Idaho advocates a foreign policy of isolationism and speaks against international political commitments.	Travis H. Whitney, Civil Works Administrator and founder of the "people's lobby," dies of pneumonia. . . . Walter White, the secretary of the National Association for the Advancement of Colored People, declares that African-American workers are systematically excluded from New Deal benefits.		More than 200 motor representatives from 38 foreign countries take part in the International Day at the National Automobile Show.	Jan. 8

F	G	H	I	J
Includes elections, federal-state relations, civil rights and liberties, crime, the judiciary, education, healthcare, poverty, urban affairs, and population.	*Includes formation and debate of U.S. foreign and defense policies, veterans affairs, and defense spending. (Relations with specific foreign countries are usually found under the region concerned.)*	*Includes business, labor, agriculture, taxation, transportation, consumer affairs, monetary and fiscal policy, natural resources, pollution, and accidents.*	*Includes worldwide scientific, medical, and technological developments, natural phenomena, U.S. weather, and natural disasters.*	*Includes the arts, religion, scholarship, communications media, sports, entertainment, fashions, fads, and social life.*

	World Affairs	Europe	Africa & The Middle East	The Americas	Asia & The Pacific
Jan. 9		France and Russia agree on a new commercial agreement that is seen also as a political pact against Germany and Japan. . . . Finland places an embargo on important German products.	The Algiers observatory announces the discovery of two small planets in a group of asteroids circulating between Mars and Jupiter.	Paraguayan forces capture important Bolivian positions in the Chaco region.	An infant found on the outskirts of Lhasa, Tibet, is officially declared to be the 14th Dalai Lama.
Jan. 10	The League of Nations reports that talks on disarmament scheduled to take place in Geneva at the end of January may be delayed for two or three weeks.	Dutch Communist Marinus van der Lubbe is guillotined in Berlin for having set fire to the Reichstag. . . . Nazi violence spreads throughout Austria with a dozen bombings in Vienna alone. . . . President Eamon De Valera summons Irish government and Fianna Fail deputies to defend his economic policies.		Liberal and Conservative supporters clash in Santander, Colombia. . . . Oswaldo Aranha and Afranio De Mello Franco rejoin the Brazilian government as Ministers of Finance and Foreign Affairs, ending the Cabinet crisis.	The Japanese government announces the planned visit of Ambassador Hiroshi Saito to the United States in February to restore cordial relations between the two countries.
Jan. 11	The French government backs U.S. and British protests against German decisions to reduce the interest payments on foreign indebtedness.	German police raid the homes of dissident clergy in Berlin. . . . The Paris police clash with royalist youth during a demonstration against the corruption exposed by the Bayonne scandal. . . . France and Russia sign the Franco-Soviet Trade Treaty.		A flood in the Andes causes severe damage and kills more than 20 people in the Argentinean province of Mendoza. . . . The Cuban army breaks up a demonstration of teachers on strike.	The rebels experience heavy defeats in the Chinese Fukien province.
Jan. 12		The French parliament rejects the proposal of the opposition for a parliamentary commission on the Bayonne scandal.		Robert H. Gore resigns as governor of Puerto Rico and is replaced by Maj. Gen. Blanton Winship.	King Prajadhipok leaves Siam for a journey to the United States and Europe. He will never return to his country and will abdicate in March 1935.
Jan. 13	The 14 nations bound by the Chadbourne sugar agreement ask the United States to take part in talks for an international sugar convention.	The Italian Senate approves Benito Mussolini's economic reforms to make Italy a "corporative state." . . . French Premier Camille Chautemps announces a bill modifying the civil code to fight public corruption more effectively.		Argentina starts mediation for peace in the Chaco War. . . . Brazil resumes talks with the United States for a reciprocity treaty.	Foochow, the capital of the rebels in the Chinese province of Fukien, is captured by the government army. . . . Manchukuoan officials announce that former Chinese emperor Henry Pu Yi is considering accepting the throne of Manchukuo.
Jan. 14		The Russian Communist Party announces its reorganization at its forthcoming 17th congress. . . . Viscount Rothermere praises the Black Shirt movement, stating that fascism can save Britain.	Valuable Roman temples and statues are uncovered by Italian excavations in Leptis Magna, near Tripoli, Libya.		
Jan. 15	The League of Nations starts its 78th council session in Geneva.	Nazi terrorism increases in the French region of Saar, which is disputed by the Reich. . . . The Esquerra, Catalonia's left-wing party, overwhelmingly wins the municipal elections.		Cuban President Ramon Grau resigns. Carlos Hevia is designated as the new Cuban president, but fears of an armed conflict between opposed political factions remain.	A violent earthquake in India and Nepal kills 10,700 people and damages the unique Mahabuddha Temple in Patan, Nepal.
Jan. 16	The World Bank praises President Franklin Roosevelt's decision to revalue the dollar, but criticizes his decision to take ownership of all the gold of the Federal Reserve System.	In Germany, the "law for the organization of labor" cancels collective bargaining, the right to strike, and unions. . . . Winston Churchill praises U.S. President Franklin Roosevelt. . . . Ivan Michailoff, leader of Macedonian revolutionaries, welcomes the prospective Balkan Pact with Greece and Yugoslavia.			Rebels flee from the southern part of the Fukien region, which is taken over by the nationalist forces.
Jan. 17	Two economic and workers' organizations of the Saar region denounce the intimidation and violence of Nazi groups to the League of Nations.	The leader of the Norwegian Labor Party, Johann Nygaardsvold, is elected president of the Storting (parliament). It is the first time that a radical leader is elected to that office. . . . The Dutch government declares it is against reform of the League of Nations.	Arab Muslims march throughout Palestine to protest the selling of land to Jews.	Carlos Hevia resigns as Cuban president after only two days in office. Carlos Mendieta, leader of the Nationalist Party, is designated president. . . . NRA codes will be extended to the industries of Puerto Rico.	The Hawes-Cutting Act regarding Philippine independence expires and a new plan for the independence of the island is submitted to President Franklin Roosevelt.

A	B	C	D	E
Includes developments that affect more than one world region, international organizations, and important meetings of world leaders.	Includes all domestic and regional developments in Europe, including the Soviet Union.	Includes all domestic and regional developments in Africa and the Middle East.	Includes all domestic and regional developments in Latin America, the Caribbean, and Canada.	Includes all domestic and regional developments in Asian and Pacific nations (and colonies).

U.S. Politics & Social Issues	U.S. Foreign Policy & Defense	Economics & Great Depression	Science, Technology & Nature	Culture, Leisure & Lifestyle	
Former postmaster general Walter F. Brown is charged with burning official documents and setting up more than 5,000 airmail line extensions without competitive biddings. . . . Emma Goldman, militant anarchist deported by the United States in 1919, receives a permit to enter the country to visit her relatives.				George Blumenthal, retired banker and philanthropist, is elected president of the Metropolitan Museum of Art.	Jan. 9
The Senate unanimously passes the Liquor Tax Bill. . . . The Rockefeller Group is sued for $10 million for unfair competition and coercion in obtaining tenants for Rockefeller Center. . . . President Franklin Roosevelt urges the Senate to ratify the St. Lawrence Canal treaty to increase navigating facilities for farmers and to produce cheaper electrical power.		Henry Ford speaks in favor of President Franklin Roosevelt's measures for economic recovery.	Six naval seaplanes leave from San Francisco to Honolulu for the longest overseas flight ever attempted.	A record crowd of 16,000 people watch the tennis match between William Tilden and Ellsworth Vines. Tilden wins.	Jan. 10
The House of Representatives adopts by a narrow margin a special "gag rule" to prevent hostile amendments to all economic sections of appropriation measures. . . . Senator Royal S. Copeland introduces 14 bills to prevent the illegal possession of firearms by gangsters.	William C. Bullitt is confirmed by the Senate as U.S. Ambassador to the Soviet Union. . . . Secretary of State Cordell Hull visits Peru to talk about the difficulties of Latin American countries in paying their debts in the middle of the economic depression.		Six naval seaplanes reach Honolulu in a record flight covering 24,000 miles in less than 25 hours. . . . Lincoln Ellsworth flies over Antarctica with his Polar Star plane.		Jan. 11
		The Supreme Court invalidates the emergency measures of the State Bank Act.		European lightweight champion Cleto Locatelli beats Jackie Berg in Madison Square Garden. . . . American baritone Lawrence Tibbet, Spanish pianist José Iturbi, and violinist Jascha Heifetz raise $10,000 in a concert for destitute German professionals. . . . Soviet dancers make their debut at Carnegie Hall with the official permission of their government, resuming cultural relations between the two countries.	Jan. 12
	Government representatives of the Irish Free State and the United States gather to discuss the development of trade relations.	Speculator David Lamar, also known as the "Wolf of Wall Street," dies in poverty in New York. . . . The League of Nations Labor Office praises the New Deal and says the U.S. economy is recovering.		The Metropolitan Opera Company revives Richard Strauss's *Salomé*, a scandalous opera based on Oscar Wilde's adaptation.	Jan. 13
A plot to extort $25,000 from Gerhardus H. Van Senden, a vice president of the Shell Union Oil Corporation, is revealed.			After a serious accident, Lincoln Ellsworth abandons his plan to fly over Antarctica with his Polar Star plane.		Jan. 14
President Franklin Roosevelt admits that opposition to the ratification of the St. Lawrence Canal treaty mainly comes from his own party. . . . New York Democratic leaders cannot agree on a common candidate to replace John F. Curry as party leader. They thus propose a triumvirate or a committee of seven to lead Tammany Hall.	U.S. naval forces land in Foochow where fighting between nationalists and rebels resumes.	President Franklin Roosevelt announces his monetary plan to revalue the dollar and seize the profit on gold held by the Federal Reserve System. . . . William Green, leader of the American Federation of Labor, argues for an extension of the Railway Emergency Transportation Act to Pullman porters.		Baseball player Babe Ruth signs a record contract for $35,000. . . . More than 8,000 people attend the opening of the memorial exhibit on Bishop Dunn's missionary activities in New York.	Jan. 15
Democratic opposition endangers the bill designed by Mayor Fiorello LaGuardia and Governor Herbert Lehman to empower the New York City Board of Estimate to make drastic cuts in the city's administration.		Most Congressmen back President Roosevelt's monetary plan.	The University of California develops a neutron beam, more powerful than X-rays or radiation from radium.	Jacoby Four win the first annual U.S. bridge tournament against Malowan team.	Jan. 16
The Conference on Birth Control and National Recovery urges President Franklin Roosevelt to change the criminal code to allow the dissemination of birth control material.		Attorney General Homer Cummings states in front of the Senate Banking and Currency Committee that President Franklin Roosevelt's monetary plan is entirely constitutional. . . . The Garment Manufacturers Association challenges the National Recovery Act as unconstitutional. . . . Ralph Pulitzer accepts an NRA position as deputy administrator in charge of the newspaper and graphic art codes.		David Sarnoff, president of the Radio Corporation of America, is elected to be a director of the Metropolitan Opera Association. . . . Prof. Albert Einstein plays the violin in a charity concert to raise funds for "some of his scientific friends in Berlin."	Jan. 17

F	G	H	I	J
Includes elections, federal-state relations, civil rights and liberties, crime, the judiciary, education, healthcare, poverty, urban affairs, and population.	*Includes formation and debate of U.S. foreign and defense policies, veterans affairs, and defense spending. (Relations with specific foreign countries are usually found under the region concerned.)*	*Includes business, labor, agriculture, taxation, transportation, consumer affairs, monetary and fiscal policy, natural resources, pollution, and accidents.*	*Includes worldwide scientific, medical, and technological developments, natural phenomena, U.S. weather, and natural disasters.*	*Includes the arts, religion, scholarship, communications media, sports, entertainment, fashions, fads, and social life.*

	World Affairs	Europe	Africa & The Middle East	The Americas	Asia & The Pacific
Jan. 18	The League of Nations tries to agree on a date when disarmament talks should resume.	The Portuguese government suppresses a revolutionary movement led by the Communists and the General Confederation of Labor. . . . French Premier Camille Chautemps hopes the United States will end its neutrality.		Carlos Mendieta is sworn in as Cuban president in the midst of public celebrations.	
Jan. 19		Leo Gallagher, the American attorney of Georgi Dimitroff, a Bulgarian Communist charged with the burning of the Reichstag, is ordered to leave Prussia immediately. . . . The Reich rejects the French proposal of step-by-step disarmament, opting instead for an immediate process. . . . In Vienna, the police clash with Nazi demonstrators, arresting 500.	Prince George begins an official visit to South Africa.	President Franklin Roosevelt announces he hopes to officially recognize the Cuban government led by Carlos Mendieta.	
Jan. 20	The League of Nations forms a committee to safeguard the Saar plebiscite from Nazi violence. . . . The League decides to postpone any decisions on when the disarmament commission should gather.	The Italian Undersecretary for Foreign Affairs declares that Austria's independence must be guaranteed. . . . Nazi Protestants claim they are the majority of the German church. More anti-Nazi priests are arrested. . . . Parisian police suppress demonstrations by royalists over the Bayonne scandal.	Edouard Renard is appointed governor of Algeria.		Japan officially complains about the U.S. policy of nonrecognition. . . . The 19th Route Army announces that the new rebels' capital in Fukien is Cahngchow.
Jan. 21		Nazi acts of violence spread in the Saar, Austria, and Danzig. . . . The Swedish Ministry of Health announces a bill for the sterilization of the unfit. . . . Having reformed the university system, the Turkish government announces a reform of secondary education. . . . Workers' demonstrations throughout France protest against the government's budget.	The South African government launches a policy to prevent land erosion by hiring unemployed whites to build dams.	Admiral Sir David Anderson is appointed governor of Newfoundland.	Lt. Gen. Sadao Araki resigns as Japanese Minister for War. . . . Japan protests against Soviet propaganda that claims the Japanese invasion of Russia is imminent. . . . Britain starts heavily arming its military base in Singapore.
Jan. 22		Austria officially demands that Germany stop its aggressive policy against Austrian independence. . . . Riots between the royalists and the police on the one hand and between Communists and the police on the other continue in Paris. An estimated 750 people are arrested. . . . In London, 700 unemployed Scots start their march. . . . A bomb on a Yugoslav train kills three people as the Little Entente conference opens.		The new Cuban government led by Carlos Mendieta hopes to establish fruitful trade relations with the United States.	Japanese Foreign Minister Koki Hirota tells the Japanese Diet he wants to establish friendly diplomatic relations with the United States.
Jan. 23		Vienna is shaken by Nazi acts of violence and by reports that set January 30 as the date of annexation to the Reich. . . . Estonian Prime Minister Constantin Paets assumes the presidency, and Estonia becomes a fascist state. . . . The Reich asks the British government to take part in the bilateral Franco-German talks on disarmament. . . . In Romania, an uprising of the fascist Iron Guard is feared. . . . The Little Entente conference ends in Zagreb.	Sir Malcom Campbell, holder of the world's automobile speed record, and Sir Alan Cobham announce an aerial expedition to the South African desert to find a gold reef.	President Franklin Roosevelt officially recognizes the new Cuban government led by Carlos Mendieta. . . . The Canadian liner *Duchess of York* is hit by three tidal waves that cause 28 to be injured.	The Eastern Sinkiang province, on the western border of China, declares its independence.
Jan. 24	The big European powers—France, Britain, and Italy—discuss the possibility of becoming guarantors of Austria's independence.	The Czech crown loses 7 percent of its value because of international concerns over the financial policies of Minister Englis. . . . Twelve Protestant pastors in key positions in the German church announce their resignations against Reichbishop Ludwig Mueller. . . . King Alexander accepts the resignation of the Yugoslav Cabinet.	Egyptian brokers go on strike as the Finance Minister accuses them of exploiting poor cotton producers. . . . The Mixed Tribunal of Egypt rejects a Jewish suit against the publication of an allegedly anti-Semitic pamphlet.	Cuban troops set an ammunition deposit on fire in Santiago. Medical strikes resume. . . . Violent clashes between Conservatives and Liberals push Colombia to the edge of a civil war.	The session of the Japanese Diet is critical of the positions of former Minister of War Koki Hirota. The Foreign Minister confirms he wants to establish friendlier relations with the United States and the Soviet Union. . . . Chinese rebels advance in the Ningsia region, getting close to its capital. . . . A violent flood of the Yellow River kills 10 people and makes more then 4,000 homeless.

A	B	C	D	E
Includes developments that affect more than one world region, international organizations, and important meetings of world leaders.	*Includes all domestic and regional developments in Europe, including the Soviet Union.*	*Includes all domestic and regional developments in Africa and the Middle East.*	*Includes all domestic and regional developments in Latin America, the Caribbean, and Canada.*	*Includes all domestic and regional developments in Asian and Pacific nations (and colonies).*

U.S. Politics & Social Issues	U.S. Foreign Policy & Defense	Economics & Great Depression	Science, Technology & Nature	Culture, Leisure & Lifestyle	
Edward G. Bremer, head of the Commercial State Bank, is kidnapped. A $200,000 ransom is asked.		Gen. Hugh Johnson, National Recovery Administrator, defends the NRA from its critics, saying recovery in business is on its way.	The anthropology division of Harvard University traces a new racial type in America.		Jan. 18
Postmaster General James A. Farley announces his resignation as Chairman of the Democratic National Committee. . . . President Franklin Roosevelt amends the Economy Act to raise the pensions of war veterans.	Ambassador William Bullitt warns the United States against selling goods on credit to the Soviet Union. He favors an exchange with Russian goods.			The Annual Beaux-Arts Ball takes place at the Waldorf Astoria, drawing the attendance of more than 3,000 people. . . . The 29th Motor Boat Show opens at Grand Central Palace. The models on display stress comfort and safety.	Jan. 19
Edward J. Brundage, former Attorney General of Illinois and powerful Republican leader, is found dead of a bullet wound in his home.		The House of Representatives passes the Gold Bill, thus backing President Franklin Roosevelt's new monetary policy. . . . The Interstate Commerce Commission report on the Emergency Railroad Transportation Act suggests a tentative plan for the public ownership of the railroads.		Frank Shields defeats George Lott in the Canadian tennis final.	Jan. 20
John Henry McCooey, powerful Democratic leader from New York, dies.	Upon his return from the seventh International Conference of American States, Secretary of State Cordell Hull declares that the conference has established friendlier relationships between the United States and Latin American countries.	A report by the Department of Commerce shows a 40 percent decline in individual income between 1929 and 1932. Production income fell by 54 percent.			Jan. 21
President Franklin Roosevelt backs the bill for a full treaty Navy. This is considered vital for U.S. defense. . . . Mayor of New York Fiorello LaGuardia discloses his intention to compel the retirement of all municipal employees over age 70.		President Franklin Roosevelt considers asking Congress for an emergency appropriation of $1.2 billion to continue the Civil Works Administration, the Civilian Conservation Corps, and direct federal relief.			Jan. 22
The cooks and waiters of the Waldorf Astoria suddenly go on strike to protest against the discharge of a fellow worker member of the Amalgamated Food Workers' Union. . . . The only African-American Rep., Oscar De Priest, demands that the House decide whether African Americans can eat at the House restaurant.		The Department of Justice begins an investigation of alleged graft in the Civil Works Administration. President Franklin Roosevelt maintains the CWA will stop its activities in May as scheduled. . . . The Treasury Department offers $1 billion in treasury notes and certificates of indebtedness to finance the administration's recovery program.		Several American Jewish organizations present Italian conductor Arturo Toscanini the certificate of inscription in the Golden Book of the Jewish National Fund.	Jan. 23
The Amalgamated Food Workers' Union calls for a general strike of its 15,000 members to stop intimidations against the union. . . . New York Mayor Fiorello LaGuardia announces "payless paydays" for public employees unless his Emergency Economy Bill is passed. . . . John Klorer is defeated in the New Orleans Democratic mayoralty primary. His defeat represents a setback for the powerful Louisiana Senator Huey Long, one of his backers. . . . An investigation in the Welfare Island penitentiary describes it as a gangsters' paradise, where convicts are the actual rulers of the institution.	A resolution introduced by Senator Millard Tydings asks the Senate to express its condemnation of Hitler's anti-Semitic policies. . . . For the first time, U.S. representatives join standing committees of the League of Nations International Labor Office. . . . Finance Secretary Henry Morgenthau lifts three bans on U.S.-Soviet trade.	Fifteen hundred white-collar employees of the Civil Works Administration protest against pay cuts.		Thirteen foreign countries announce their participation in the Motor Boat Race in Florida scheduled for March.	Jan. 24

F	G	H	I	J
Includes elections, federal-state relations, civil rights and liberties, crime, the judiciary, education, healthcare, poverty, urban affairs, and population.	*Includes formation and debate of U.S. foreign and defense policies, veterans affairs, and defense spending. (Relations with specific foreign countries are usually found under the region concerned.)*	*Includes business, labor, agriculture, taxation, transportation, consumer affairs, monetary and fiscal policy, natural resources, pollution, and accidents.*	*Includes worldwide scientific, medical, and technological developments, natural phenomena, U.S. weather, and natural disasters.*	*Includes the arts, religion, scholarship, communications media, sports, entertainment, fashions, fads, and social life.*

	World Affairs	Europe	Africa & The Middle East	The Americas	Asia & The Pacific
Jan. 25		Chancellor Adolf Hitler and President Paul von Hindenburg examine the crisis in the national Protestant Church in Germany. . . . The King and Queen of Bulgaria go on an official visit to Romania. . . . The Soviet Union grants Turkey an $8 million loan for the purchase of machineries for the industrialization of the country. . . . The Fascist Grand Council announces a new electoral system for the next Italian election in March. Voters will simply approve or reject a single list drawn up by the Council.	King Ghazi of Iraq marries Princess Aliyah. . . . The Chicago Field Museum sends an expedition to West Africa to collect specimens of African birds and record native music.	A vast building program to help the Canadian unemployed is announced in a Throne Speech. . . . Peru and Colombia resume talks over the Leticia region, which almost caused a war between the two nations. . . . Bolivians recapture important positions in the Chaco War.	
Jan. 26		Germany and Poland sign a Non-Aggression Pact that guarantees the preservation of the countries' borders for 10 years. . . . Poland adopts a new constitution granting the president the power to appoint the premier, the head of the Supreme Court, the commander in chief of the army, and 40 senators. . . . Riots between conservative groups and the police continue in Paris.	Jews and moderate Arabs blame the Palestinian government for having allowed Arabs to march in protest against Jewish immigration.	President Franklin Roosevelt officially recognizes the Martinez government in El Salvador.	
Jan. 27	Pope Pius XI firmly condemns materialism, atheism, and Communist and Protestant proselytism.	The French government led by Camille Chautemps resigns as a result of the Bayonne scandal, in which many of its ministers were involved. . . . A decree of the Reich orders that all active members of the World War I veterans' league (faithful to the monarchy) be absorbed and controlled by the Reich stormtroopers. . . . Soviet leader Josef Stalin warns capitalist countries that war cannot be a way to solve economic depression. On the contrary, war may result in a new wave of revolutions. . . . The president of the Irish Free State, Eamon de Valera, stresses the economic successes of his government that will soon make the Free State self-sufficient.		Several fishing villages in Nova Scotia suffer from starvation and infectious illness as they are cut off from the rest of the world by adverse weather conditions. . . . A plot to kill President Harmodio Arias is discovered in Panama.	As a result of the tension between Russia and Japan in Manchuria, White Russians riot in front of the Soviet Consulate.
Jan. 28		The British government sends a new plan for disarmament to France, Germany, and Italy to resume talks after Germany's withdrawal from the League of Nations. . . . Lenin's widow, Nadezhda Krupskaya, praises Stalin's policies. . . . Rev. Martin Niemoeller, leader of the Pastors' Emergency League, which is protesting the subordination of the German church to the policies of the Reich, is arrested. He is released after a few hours of detention, but is ordered to report daily to the police. One hundred members of the Pastors' Emergency League are suspended from their church positions.	Two Christian villages are raided and burn in a religious war between tribesmen in Kenya.	The Canadian government successfully reaches the area in Nova Scotia affected by famine and severe food shortage. Supplies for about 3,000 people and for cattle are provided. . . . The Nationalist Party holds a large demonstration in Havana in support of the new Cuban government led by Carlos Mendieta. . . . South Central Mexico is hit by a strong earthquake, causing many casualties and seriously damaging several buildings.	The rebellion in the Chinese Fukien province ends with the surrender of the 19th Route Army.
Jan. 29		The Soviet Press reacts coldly to the German-Polish pact, fearing that it will lead to Poland's isolation in Europe. . . . The Austrian Peasant Association adopts an anti-Nazi resolution, calling for a big demonstration in support of the Engelbert Dollfuss government. . . . French President Albert Lebrun appoints Radical Socialist Edouard Daladier prime minister after the resignation of the Chautemps's Cabinet.	An assassin fails in his attempt to kill Hashin Khan, premier of Afghanistan.	The American Jewish Congress reports Nazi activity and propaganda in South America. . . . Bolivian patrols break up a heavy attack by two Paraguayan divisions in the Chaco War. . . . Traffic in the Peruvian capital of Lima halts because of an unexpected transportation strike. . . . The new Cuban government announces that elections for a constituent assembly will take place before the end of the year.	Important gold quartz discoveries are made in the Chinese province of Sikang. Because the boundaries of the province are not well-defined, it is feared that the King of Muli, the neighboring region, may start a civil war for the possession of the gold fields.

A	**B**	**C**	**D**	**E**
Includes developments that affect more than one world region, international organizations, and important meetings of world leaders.	*Includes all domestic and regional developments in Europe, including the Soviet Union.*	*Includes all domestic and regional developments in Africa and the Middle East.*	*Includes all domestic and regional developments in Latin America, the Caribbean, and Canada.*	*Includes all domestic and regional developments in Asian and Pacific nations (and colonies).*

U.S. Politics & Social Issues	U.S. Foreign Policy & Defense	Economics & Great Depression	Science, Technology & Nature	Culture, Leisure & Lifestyle	
Correction Commissioner, Austin MacCormick, vows to make Welfare Island a model penitentiary. . . . John Dillinger and three members of his criminal band are seized by policemen in Arizona.	U.S. Minister to Austria George Earle praises Austrian efforts to retain the country's independence.	The Senate announces a federal investigation into the operation of large banks before and during the Depression. . . . The Ways and Means Committee of the House of Representatives passes radical modifications to the income tax law, which will increase its yield by $200 million. . . . The General Motors Corporation announces a substantial rise in its profits during 1933.	Dr. George E. Vincent announces the discovery of a serum that immunizes human beings to yellow fever.	The director of the American Civil Liberties Union, Roger Baldwin, criticizes film censorship as causing great damage to cinema.	Jan. 25
The general strike of the Amalgamated Food Workers' Union has only a limited impact on hotel operation. . . . At the biannual convention of the United Mine Workers of America in Philadelphia, coal operators and miners agree to put aside disagreements to cooperate for the preservation of the Coal Code.	The U.S. government announces it will ship food products to Cuba for the sum of $2 million. Jefferson Caffery is appointed Ambassador.	The Ways and Means Committee of the House of Representatives continues to modify the income tax laws to safeguard U.S. interests abroad and impose more taxes on foreign business branches in the United States.		The State Athletic Commission approves a new set of stricter regulations for wrestling. . . . Baseball champions Lou Gehrig and Russell Van Atta sign their contracts with the New York Yankees. For two consecutive years, Gehrig gets $23,000.	Jan. 26
		President Franklin Roosevelt asks Congress for an additional sum of $950 million to continue the activities of the Emergency Relief Administration and the Civil Works Administration. . . . The Senate passes Roosevelt's money bill.			Jan. 27
Three thousand Armenians gather into Mecca Temple in New York in a mass demonstration against the murder of Archbishop Leon Tourian on December 24, 1933.	The American Committee on Religious Rights and Minorities protests against the Nazi persecution of Jews and the attempt to make Christian churches subordinate to the central government.	A national survey of the road projects of the Public Works Administration shows that they employ more than 133,000 men.		U.S. skaters win in all four divisions of the North American speed-skating championships on Fowler Lake. . . . Neil Sullivan wins the Atlantic Coast squash championship. . . . The first U.S. rope ski tow begins operation in Woodstock, Vt.	Jan. 28
Mayor of New York Fiorello LaGuardia faces strong opposition by Democrats for his Emergency Economy Bill in spite of Governor Herbert Lehman's support. The bill gives the Board of Estimate the power to cut salaries and reorganize the city's administrative structure. . . . The Amalgamated Hotel and Restaurant Workers Union continues its protests against the Waldorf Astoria for the hotel's failure to recognize the union. The union addresses a telegram of protest to President Franklin Roosevelt for his choice of celebrating his birthday at that hotel.		Congress completes approval of President Franklin Roosevelt's Money Bill. The act authorizes Roosevelt to devalue the dollar at 50 to 60 cents by reduction of its gold content. The measure also sets up a $2 billion stabilization fund. . . . Former secretary of the treasury Ogden L. Mills attacks Roosevelt's economic policy, criticizing it for hindering recovery. Mills urges a modification of U.S. tariffs and an end to the nation's intense nationalism.	The temperature in the center and the east of the United States suddenly drops by an average of 50 degrees.	James Bryant Conant, president of Harvard University, emphasizes in his first annual report the emergence of Harvard as a truly national university. He also calls for the establishment of new scholarships to attract more students and staff to the university.	Jan. 29

F	G	H	I	J
Includes elections, federal-state relations, civil rights and liberties, crime, the judiciary, education, healthcare, poverty, urban affairs, and population.	Includes formation and debate of U.S. foreign and defense policies, veterans affairs, and defense spending. (Relations with specific foreign countries are usually found under the region concerned.)	Includes business, labor, agriculture, taxation, transportation, consumer affairs, monetary and fiscal policy, natural resources, pollution, and accidents.	Includes worldwide scientific, medical, and technological developments, natural phenomena, U.S. weather, and natural disasters.	Includes the arts, religion, scholarship, communications media, sports, entertainment, fashions, fads, and social life.

	World Affairs	Europe	Africa & The Middle East	The Americas	Asia & The Pacific
Jan. 30		Adolf Hitler celebrates the first anniversary of the establishment of a National Socialist regime in Germany. The Reichsrat, which represents German states, is abolished, making Germany a national state. . . . Juan Figueras Soler, leader of Catalan anarchist terrorists, is arrested in Spain. . . . Irish Premier Eamon De Valera is concerned that the spread of violent acts in southern Ireland may bring the country to the edge of a civil war. . . . Edouard Daladier forms a new government in France. However, it is predicted that the new government will not survive the confidence vote.		Argentine trade has dropped by 5 percent during 1933, marking the reversal of a positive trend in previous years.	In the Philippines there is vast discontent against the U.S. proposal to tax coconut oil. To the Filipinos, the tax represents an unfair and discriminatory act against an American possession. According to their estimate, it would also result in high unemployment. . . . Former Japanese ambassador to the United States Katsuji Debuchi invites American businessmen to extend their trade in Eastern Asia with the help of Japan. . . . Sir Robert Henry Clive replaces Sir Francis Lindley as British Ambassador to Japan.
Jan. 31	The conference between Germany and its creditors ends with a compromise agreement that raises German interest payments over its obligations to 77 percent of the contractual amount.	Great Britain and Italy issue two new disarmament proposals. They both agree that Germany should return to the League of Nations and the disarmament conference in ex-change for its right to rearm.		Strikes spread in Havana and in the interior of Cuba, pushing the island to the edge of a general strike. The political turmoil may result in the loss of the sugar crop. . . . Paraguayan troops bring strong attacks against Bolivian military points in the Fort Platanillos sector of the Chaco region. However, Bolivians manage to hold on to their positions.	
Feb. 1	The League of Nations deplores the British and Italian proposals for German rearmament as a victory for munitions makers. . . . The Permanent Court of International Justice starts its 31st session in The Hague.	The Reich responds to the official complaint filed by Austria of Nazi interference in its domestic policy. The reply considers Austria to be part of the Reich. . . . Bulgaria says it is not prepared to join in the Balkan Pact. However, the country is willing to sign a nonaggression treaty with Romania. . . . Parisian taxi drivers go on strike against a new tax on gasoline.		The Chaco peace talks are deadlocked on the question of how much of the Chaco territory should be included in the arbitration. Paraguay refuses to include in the arbitration the part of its territory received by U.S. President Rutherford B. Hayes.	The session of the Japanese parliament is dominated by criticism against the army for its efforts to influence Japanese politics. . . . The trade turnover of Manchuria since the founding of Manchukuo has decreased considerably.
Feb. 2		The Soviet All Union Party Congress is informed that more than 17 percent of the members of the Communist Party have been expelled in the last year. . . . Alfred Rosenberg is appointed philosophical chief of the Nazi Party. . . . In Lower Austria, 100,000 peasants take part in a rally in support of Chancellor Engelbert Dollfuss. . . . Parisian taxi drivers continue their strike and violently clash with the police. . . . The German government outlaws all monarchist parties to restrain political opposition from the right.	Fifteen hundred delegates of New York Jewish organizations meet to discuss means of encouraging German-Jewish refugees to settle in Palestine.		The trials against the terrorists who tried to overthrow the Japanese government in 1932 end in Tokyo.
Feb. 3		After French Prime Minister Edouard Daladier dismisses the prefect of the Paris police, two of his Cabinet ministers resign, starting a new government crisis. . . . Andrew Jameson, director of the Bank of Ireland, criticises the policies of the Eamon De Valera government.		The employees of the Cuban Electric Company go on strike against the appointment of a new manager.	Hiroshi Saito, the new Japanese Ambassador to the United States, leaves for America. . . . Violent clashes between Hindus and Muslims break out in Kashmir.
Feb. 4		Austria is increasingly threatened by Germany as the three other main European powers (Britain, France, and Italy) avoid confrontation. . . . In Paris, taxi drivers continue their strike. . . . Ion Mastia, the deputy leader of the anti-Semitic Iron Guard, is arrested in Bucharest.		During a demonstration against the occupation of a hospital by military forces, the Cuban army opens fire and kills two people. . . . Argentina decides to exclude European nations from the benefits of trade agreements between South American countries.	
Feb. 5		The Austrian Cabinet entrusts Prime Minister Engelbert Dollfuss to appeal to the League of Nations against Nazi threats to the country's independence. . . . The Polish Foreign Minister Joseph Beck declares Poland's wish to establish friendly relations with the Soviet Union.		Maj. Gen. Blanton Winship becomes governor of Puerto Rico and announces his plans to extend NRA codes to the island. . . . The Paraguayan War Minister announces the capture of the Bolivian stronghold Fort Lachina, a key position in the Chaco War. . . . A 24-hour general strike is called in Havana in solidarity with the workers of the Cuban Electric Company.	Tribesmen opposing the Kashgar independence movement in Sinkiang, Chinese Turkestan, make important military progress.

A	B	C	D	E
Includes developments that affect more than one world region, international organizations, and important meetings of world leaders.	*Includes all domestic and regional developments in Europe, including the Soviet Union.*	*Includes all domestic and regional developments in Africa and the Middle East.*	*Includes all domestic and regional developments in Latin America, the Caribbean, and Canada.*	*Includes all domestic and regional developments in Asian and Pacific nations (and colonies).*

U.S. Politics & Social Issues	U.S. Foreign Policy & Defense	Economics & Great Depression	Science, Technology & Nature	Culture, Leisure & Lifestyle	
Mayor Fiorello LaGuardia's Emergency Economy Bill is rejected by the New York Assembly. . . . The House of Representatives passes the Vinson Navy Replacement Bill, which establishes the largest peacetime fleet in U.S. history. . . . More than 4,000 people participate in the mass picketing demonstration organized by the Amalgamated Hotel and Restaurant Workers Union through the main hotel district in New York City.	Secretary of State Cordell Hull says the United States is insisting in its mediation between Paraguay and Bolivia for a peaceful solution to the Chaco conflict.	President Franklin Roosevelt signs the Money Bill and immediately calls for a conference of his financial advisers to devalue the dollar.	Most of the Atlantic coast of the United States continues to be in the grip of cold weather. Two people die in New Jersey. Special measures for the poor and the homeless are adopted in New York. . . . A sharp earthquake is felt in different western regions of the United States. . . . The Soviet civil stratosphere balloon Osoaviakhim 1 exceeds the world's altitude record by reaching the height of 67,585 feet.	President Franklin Roosevelt celebrates his 52nd birthday. . . . The noted publisher Frank Nelson Doubleday dies at the age of 72 in Miami.	Jan. 30
Verne Sankey, a suspect in the kidnapping of Col. Charles Lindbergh's child and other violent crimes, is arrested in Chicago by federal agents. . . . Carl R. Gray, president of the Union Pacific Railroad Company, announces that railroad business is increasing steadily. . . . The United Mine Workers of America ends its conference, putting on top of its agenda a 30-hour working week and an increase in wages.	The U.S. State Department considers the possibility of calling a conference with Japan to discuss naval ratios. It is anticipated that the Japanese Navy will surpass the American one in auxiliary vessels by 1936.	As a result of the Money Bill, the dollar is revalued at 59.06 cents, the gold price is fixed at $35 an ounce, and a $2 billion stabilization fund established. . . . West Coast stock exchanges are positively affected by the announcement of the gold price. They reach their highest peak in turnover since July 1933.	French airplane designer René Cousinet starts the construction of an airplane, which he hopes will cross the Atlantic to America next July or August traveling in the stratosphere.	Raymond Pond is appointed coach of Yale's football team, ending a long debate over the team's coaching staff. . . . A record crowd of 20,200 people watch the wrestling match between Jim Landos and former football star Joe Savoldi at Chicago Stadium. Landos is the winner.	Jan. 31
The government starts investigating several distillery groups charged with having formed monopolies to keep liquor prices at high levels. . . . The government starts a suit against William Dwyer, "king of bootleggers," to recover more than $4,256,002 of unpaid taxes. . . . Ralph Pulitzer resigns as NRA administrator of the newspaper code because of opposition to his appointment by the American Newspaper Guild.		Secretary of the Treasury Henry Morgenthau expresses his hope that other governments will cooperate with the United States to keep the dollar at its new level. The bank rate is reduced from 2 percent to 1.5 percent. . . . President Franklin Roosevelt issues an executive order stating that the representatives chosen by the majority of workers for collective bargaining with employers will deal for all employees.	French physicists Frédéric Joliot and Irène Curie produce artificial radioactivity. It is hoped that this radioactivity will be used for medical treatment.		Feb. 1
New York taxi drivers start a sudden strike against a five-cent tax imposed by the former city administration. . . . William P. MacCracken, assistant secretary of commerce under President Herbert Hoover, is arrested by the order of the Senate. The arrest comes as part of the Senate investigation of ocean and airmail contracts.		President Franklin Roosevelt urges the state directors of the National Emergency Council to keep politics out of relief programs.		American baritone John Charles Thomas debuts at the Metropolitan Opera in La Traviata. . . . Former lightweight champion Tony Canzoneri defeats Cleto Locatelli in Madison Square Garden.	Feb. 2
The strike of New York taxi drivers continues, causing major disruptions. More than 4,000 drivers gather at Madison Square Garden.			A scientific expedition heads for the crater of the Quizapu volcano in the Andes mountains. The volcano was the center of violent explosions in 1932, scattering its ashes over a vast area. It is the first time that the crater of the Quizapu has been explored. . . . A huge avalanche of stones and snow kills 39 people in Corsica.		Feb. 3
New York taxi drivers end their strike, thanks to the mediation of Mayor Fiorello LaGuardia. LaGuardia proposes that the five-cent tax imposed by the previous mayor be shared among the drivers, their customers, and the operating companies.	Senator William King asks for an official condemnation of Germany's anti-Semitic policies and the severing of diplomatic relations.	Even the staunchly conservative National Association of Manufacturers endorses President Franklin Roosevelt's plan to stabilize the dollar. The organization shows optimism for future industrial commitments.		The American Olympic Committee avoids the discussion of whether to accept or reject Germany's invitation for 1936.	Feb. 4
The Supreme Court rules that all prosecutions linked to Prohibition crimes that started after the repeal of the Eighteenth Amendment are illegal. . . . New York taxi drivers reject Mayor Fiorello LaGuardia's proposal and resume demonstrations. . . . A riot breaks out between policemen and striking hotel and restaurant workers in front of the Waldorf Astoria. . . . William Sutton, a fugitive involved in many armed robberies, is arrested in Philadelphia.		New Deal policies benefit Alaska's economy, which makes good progress on the road to recovery. . . . Jesse H. Jones, chairman of the Reconstruction Finance Corporation, urges banks to provide proper credit for private enterprise.		Maxie Rosenbloom keeps the light-heavyweight title in his fight against Joe Knight.	Feb. 5

F	G	H	I	J
Includes elections, federal-state relations, civil rights and liberties, crime, the judiciary, education, healthcare, poverty, urban affairs, and population.	*Includes formation and debate of U.S. foreign and defense policies, veterans affairs, and defense spending. (Relations with specific foreign countries are usually found under the region concerned.)*	*Includes business, labor, agriculture, taxation, transportation, consumer affairs, monetary and fiscal policy, natural resources, pollution, and accidents.*	*Includes worldwide scientific, medical, and technological developments, natural phenomena, U.S. weather, and natural disasters.*	*Includes the arts, religion, scholarship, communications media, sports, entertainment, fashions, fads, and social life.*

	World Affairs	Europe	Africa & The Middle East	The Americas	Asia & The Pacific
Feb. 6		The French premier Edouard Daladier wins two confidence votes in parliament. Yet, major riots erupt in Paris and other French cities in response to the Stavisky scandal. . . . During a parliamentary debate, British Foreign Secretary Sir John Simon says that Germany's right to have equal weapons with other countries cannot be resisted. . . . Heimwehr groups occupy Linz, demanding the establishment of a fascist state in Austria. . . . Hungary recognizes the Soviet regime and resumes diplomatic relations.		Members of the Democratic Revolutionary Alliance stage demonstrations in Lima protesting against the arrest of their deputy leader. . . . Peru and Ecuador agree to send delegations to Washington to settle a boundary dispute. In case the two delegations do not agree on a settlement, President Franklin Roosevelt will act as arbiter. . . . The police open fire against a demonstration of more than 3,000 students in Havana, killing one person and injuring 10.	Responding to interpellations in the Japanese parliament, the government declares that military expenditures cover 40 percent of the national budget.
Feb. 7		After the riots caused by royalist and fascist militants, French Premier Edouard Daladier resigns. Former president Gaston Doumergue is called to form a new Cabinet. . . . In Russia, the Communist Party Congress ratifies the Second Five-Year Plan, setting the annual growth of industry at 16.5 percent. . . . Heimwehr groups tighten their control of Austrian provinces, which are virtually under fascist rule. . . . The Spanish government, led by Alejandro Lerroux, wins a confidence vote over its ability to cope with a Socialist revolution.		Paraguayan troops continue their advance in the Chaco War.	
Feb. 8		In Austria the police raid Socialist centers and newspapers, finding weapons for an alleged coup. The raids take place when Premier Engelbert Dollfuss is on an official visit to Budapest. . . . Gaston Doumergue appeals to all French political parties to form a wide coalition. The army guards the city of Paris and its public buildings. . . . Italy starts modernizing its heavy battle fleet. . . . General O'Duffy is reelected leader of the fascist United Ireland Party. . . . General Manuel Gonzalez and six of his aides are found guilty by the Spanish Supreme Court of having taken part in the Seville Rebellion in 1932. They are sentenced to 12 years' imprisonment.		Many political prisoners in Venezuela are said to have escaped from prison as their leader Gen. Urbina visits Panama.	Baron Nakajima resigns as the Japanese Minister of Commerce. He is replaced by Joji Matsumoto.
Feb. 9		The Turkish, Greek, Romanian, and Yugoslav governments sign the Balkan Pact. The four governments agree to mutually guarantee the security of the Balkan frontiers and pledge not to take any action with regard to any Balkan nonsignatory state without previous consultation. . . . Deputies of Austria's Christian Social Party join forces with the Socialists to oppose the Heimwehr demands to turn Austria into a fascist dictatorship. . . . Former French president Gaston Doumergue forms a new government of national union and safety.		Cuban President Carlos Mendieta praises President Franklin Roosevelt's setting of quotas on sugar.	Hiroshi Saito, the new Japanese Ambassador to the United States, arrives in Washington, stating his country's peaceful intentions. He claims the rumors that Japan wants to extend its territory to the Philippines, Siberia, and Alaska are ridiculous.
Feb. 10		The new French Cabinet led by Gaston Doumergue views Austrian independence as a vital issue. . . . The Czech government announces the devaluation of its currency to protect export trade. . . . Soviet Foreign Trade Commissar Rosengoltz announces Russia will reduce its imports. . . . The Spanish Cabinet takes drastic measures to suppress strikes and revolutionary movements.		U.S. Secretary of State Cordell Hull praises the spirit of cooperation between the United States and Latin American countries, which he witnessed at the recent Pan-American Conference in Montevideo. . . . The presidential elections take place in Colombia. The only opponent to Alfonso Lopez is a Communist candidate.	Official celebrations for the birth of the Crown Prince Akihito begin in Japan. The Emperor announces a general amnesty for prisoners. . . . The King and Queen of Siam arrive in France en route to the United States. . . . The Chinese government approves the building of a 2,000-mile highway and a railway from the coast to the inland province of Sinkiang.

A	B	C	D	E
Includes developments that affect more than one world region, international organizations, and important meetings of world leaders.	Includes all domestic and regional developments in Europe, including the Soviet Union.	Includes all domestic and regional developments in Africa and the Middle East.	Includes all domestic and regional developments in Latin America, the Caribbean, and Canada.	Includes all domestic and regional developments in Asian and Pacific nations (and colonies).

U.S. Politics & Social Issues	U.S. Foreign Policy & Defense	Economics & Great Depression	Science, Technology & Nature	Culture, Leisure & Lifestyle	
A new plan is devised to end the taxi strike in New York. Operators announce their intention of resuming service under police protection. . . . Governor Lehman urges Democrats to vote in favor of Mayor Fiorello LaGuardia's Emergency Economy Bill.	L.S. Rowe, director general of the Pan-American Union, says that the Pan-American Conference has marked a new era in the relations between the United States and Latin American countries.	Organized labor submits to the National Labor Board a complaint charging that delays in settling disputes under the labor provision of the Recovery Act lead to the defeat of unions. . . . Twenty thousand Ford workers receive a 10 percent wage increase. . . . The National Emergency Council approves a plan to increase the funds for the Civil Works Administration to $2.5 billion to continue the operation of the program until January 1935.		Club owners of the National League ratify the 1934 baseball schedule, equally distributing Sunday home matches among its members for the first time.	Feb. 6
A crowd of about 500 striking New York taxi drivers causes a violent riot, damaging cars and clashing with the police. . . . The chairman of the Senate committee investigating ocean and airmail contracts says the former Postmaster General Walter Brown may be called to testify in the inquiry. . . . The Treasury orders the stamping of whiskey bottles to help customers identify illegal bottles. . . . Senator James Hamilton Lewis is appointed Chairman of the Democratic Senatorial Campaign Committee.		President Franklin Roosevelt favors a cut in interest rates. He views the rate of many outstanding obligations of industry, municipalities, and foreign governments held by Americans as too high to allow repayments.			Feb. 7
Bank president Edward G. Bremer is released after 22 days of captivity. A ransom of $200,000 dollars is paid to his kidnappers. . . . Kidnapper Verne Sankey hangs himself in his cell in a South Dakota prison. . . . Postmaster General James Farley confers with President Franklin Roosevelt and Attorney General Homer Cummings to cancel airmail contracts as result of a Senate investigation. . . . All representatives of unionized New York taxi drivers sign a settlement for the cab strike.	President Franklin Roosevelt's message on sugar quotas is read as an important step in the economic rehabilitation of Cuba.	President Franklin Roosevelt urges Congress to include sugar beets and sugar cane as basic commodities under the Agricultural Adjustment Act and to set quotas for all sugar producers. This would stabilize the price of sugar in the United States and increase the purchase power of Cuba for U.S. products. . . . The National Republican Committee publishes a pamphlet that sharply criticizes the Civil Works Administration. The publication charges the CWA as being a covert political set-up that diverts public funds to carry the 1934 elections. . . . The American Federation of Labor's monthly business report expresses fears that the NRA administrative machine may favor the interests of owners and industrialists, thus endangering the aims of the Recovery Act.	A new cold wave sweeps the entire region east of the Rocky Mountains.	A cast made up entirely of African-American singers performs Gertrude Stein's opera Four Saints at the new Avery Memorial Theatre in Hartford.	Feb. 8
President Franklin Roosevelt orders the cancellation of all existing airmail contracts and orders the Army to fly the mail during the emergency created by his decision. The Assistant Secretary of Commerce under President Herbert Hoover, William P. MacCracken, refuses to appear in front of the Senate committee investigating the airmail contracts.		The Fletcher-Rayburn Stock Exchange Regulation Bill is introduced in Congress. It provides strict federal control of the stock market.	A cold wave continues to sweep the east, causing six deaths.	Lillian Evanti, an African-American soprano, sings at the White House in honor of Mary Bewson, head of the women's division of the National Democratic Committee. . . . Chicago heavyweight King Levinski beats Charley Massera on points. . . . Werner Janssen is the first American to conduct an orchestra in Finland.	Feb. 9
During an unauthorized parade of hotel and restaurant workers in the New York theatrical district, four hotels are damaged.	The American Section of the Universal Christian Council expresses grave concerns regarding the situation of the German church. . . . President Franklin Roosevelt appoints Joshua Wright as Minister to Czechoslovakia. George Messersmith succeeds Wright as Minister to Uruguay.	President Franklin Roosevelt announces his intention to ask Congress for more funds to continue the Civilian Conservation Camps until mid-October.		Postmaster General James Farley opens the National Stamp Exhibition at the Rockefeller Center in New York. The first unperforated ungummed U.S. stamp is issued for the occasion. . . . Harry Hanson's new opera, Merry Mount, opens at the Metropolitan to an enthusiastic reception.	Feb. 10

F	G	H	I	J
Includes elections, federal-state relations, civil rights and liberties, crime, the judiciary, education, healthcare, poverty, urban affairs, and population.	Includes formation and debate of U.S. foreign and defense policies, veterans affairs, and defense spending. (Relations with specific foreign countries are usually found under the region concerned.)	Includes business, labor, agriculture, taxation, transportation, consumer affairs, monetary and fiscal policy, natural resources, pollution, and accidents.	Includes worldwide scientific, medical, and technological developments, natural phenomena, U.S. weather, and natural disasters.	Includes the arts, religion, scholarship, communications media, sports, entertainment, fashions, fads, and social life.

	World Affairs	Europe	Africa & The Middle East	The Americas	Asia & The Pacific
Feb. 11	The British, Indian, and Yemeni governments sign a treaty of friendship. . . . The Italian government and the Vatican celebrate the anniversary of the Lateran Treaty.	Four days of violence against Socialists start in Vienna. Premier Engelbert Dollfuss reaches agreement with Heimwehr leaders to dissolve provincial governments and all political parties except his own. . . . Bulgaria criticizes the Balkan Pact, particularly the section that forbids any agreements with nonsignatory Balkan nations without previous consultations with the other members.	The British and Saudi governments conclude the Treaty of Sanaa, which establishes 40 years of friendly relations between the two governments.	The Liberal leader Alfonso Lopez is elected president of Colombia. He favors a peaceful solution of the Leticia controversy with Peru. . . . Paraguay makes important gains in the Chaco War.	Generalissimo Chiang Kai-shek prepares his army to subdue the semi-independent Chinese province of Canton.
Feb. 12	Pope Pius XI celebrates the 12th anniversary of his coronation and appoints four American Bishops.	Clashes between Socialists and Heimwehr forces lead Austria to the brink of a civil war. The Socialist Party calls for a general strike to protest raids on its headquarters. Premier Engelbert Dollfuss responds by outlawing it, and 129 people are killed in the riots. . . . French left-wing parties and labor organizations organize a strike against the fascist and royalist elements that caused the riots of February 6. . . . The Finnish High Court at Abo starts the trial of 28 people suspected of being spies for the Soviets.		The first conference of South American Chambers of Commerce takes place in Chile to foster more commercial cooperation between Latin American countries. . . . Due to a government decree outlawing strikes, the employees of the Cuban Electric Company return to their workplace but refuse to perform any work. . . . The Paraguayan army continues to advance westward in the Chaco conflict, pushing back the Bolivian army.	The Chinese government prepares its army for a possible Tibetan invasion of the Szechwan province. . . . Tensions between the Canton province and the central Chinese government may lead to an armed conflict.
Feb. 13	The Sacred Congregation of Rites places two Nazi books on religion by prominent Nazi leaders on the index of forbidden books. . . . Pope Pius XI warns against the spread of violent ideologies that aim to drag the world back into paganism.	The Spanish government imposes strict restrictions on carnival celebrations in fear of a Socialist coup. . . . Socialist resistance in Vienna is defeated by government troops. . . . The French government issues a note to the Reich saying it will not disarm to prevent Germany's rearmament.			Hostilities between the central government and the Canton province wane as Canton agrees to help in the repression of Communists. . . . The Japanese House of Representatives approves the budget. Military expenditures rise considerably.
Feb. 14		In Austria, Socialist and government forces continue to fight. Chancellor Engelbert Dollfuss offers amnesty for those Socialists who surrender. . . . The Czech government resigns as the Czech National Democrats leave the coalition. They disagree with the government decision to devalue the crown. . . . Reich Chancellor Adolf Hitler signs a decree abolishing the Reichsrat (Federal Council). Hitler thus abolishes the last federal institution still surviving in the Reich.		The Paraguayan army conquers Fort Cabezon from the Bolivians. The Paraguayans now control a vast area of the Chaco region and are protected against a flank or rear attack.	
Feb. 15		Socialist resistance in Vienna collapses completely. Party leaders leave the country. . . . French Premier Gaston Doumergue obtains the confidence of the parliament.	Wrestling is barred by Johannesburg city councilors as brutal.	Puerto Rico's Democratic Party asks Governor Winship for an extension of the New Deal to the region.	The Japanese Cabinet is endangered by a financial scandal that involves several ministers.
Feb. 16		The British and Russian governments sign a trade treaty, also in an effort to improve relations between the two countries. . . . The conference between Germany and its foreign creditors ends with the decision of leaving the interest rate unchanged for another year. . . . After days of violent clashes between Socialists and government troops, Vienna and the Austrian provinces are again under control. It is estimated that some 600 Socialists and more than 100 soldiers have died during the fighting.	Afghani King Zahir Shah issues a proclamation ordering a general election for a new National Assembly.	Newfoundland gives up its status as dominion of the British Empire, formally surrendering self-government. The area is governed by a commission appointed by the Crown.	Australian States demand of the Commonwealth government to have a larger share of the central government's revenues. The demand is seen as a further act of discontent by the Australian States after Western States voted for secession from the Commonwealth.
Feb. 17	The International Congress for Peace closes in Brussels. Many delegates regret that the final resolutions do not include any comments by the United States on a reformed League of Nations. . . . The League of Nations Saar committee gathers in Geneva to discuss the plebiscite by which Saar inhabitants will decide whether to stay with France, pass under Reich control, or remain under the administration of the League of Nations.	King Albert I of Belgium dies in a mountaineering accident. Prince Leopold, age 32, succeeds to the throne. . . . Britain, Italy, and France issue a joint declaration stressing the importance of Austria's independence. . . . France suspends any further talks with Germany on disarmament while the Reich rearms. . . . Nazi terrorist attacks resume in Vienna.			The bribe inquiry that is shaking the Japanese government moves ahead. The Minister of Education admits taking 50,000 yen, claiming, however, that the sum was a gift, not a bribe.

A	B	C	D	E
Includes developments that affect more than one world region, international organizations, and important meetings of world leaders.	Includes all domestic and regional developments in Europe, including the Soviet Union.	Includes all domestic and regional developments in Africa and the Middle East.	Includes all domestic and regional developments in Latin America, the Caribbean, and Canada.	Includes all domestic and regional developments in Asian and Pacific nations (and colonies).

U.S. Politics & Social Issues	U.S. Foreign Policy & Defense	Economics & Great Depression	Science, Technology & Nature	Culture, Leisure & Lifestyle	
Basil Banghart, who was involved in kidnappings and holdups, is arrested in Baltimore. . . . Col. Charles Lindbergh criticizes President Franklin Roosevelt's decision to cancel all existing airmail contracts.				The Fine Arts Foundation is established in New York to promote American painting and sculpture.	Feb. 11
The National Association for the Advancement of Colored People celebrates its 25th anniversary with mass meetings and dinners. . . . Fifteen long-term convicts unsuccessfully try to escape from the Walla Walla penitentiary in Washington. Seven convicts and a guard are killed. . . . Postmaster General James Farley announces that the government will initially operate only 14 airmail routes instead of the 26 now flown by mail contractors.		At their annual Lincoln Day dinner, Republicans attack President Franklin Roosevelt's New Deal as unconstitutional and as endangering individual rights.		The Rockefeller Center cancels the $21,000 mural painted by Diego Rivera. The work is considered offensive because it portrays Soviet leader Lenin.	Feb. 12
Transcontinental and Western Air sues the government for its cancellation of all airmail contracts. . . . The workers of the Amalgamated Hotel and Restaurant Union continue their strike. The Hotel Men's Association submits a proposal for a settlement that the Union rejects.				A group of artists withdraw their works from the Municipal Art Show to be held at the Rockefeller Center at the end of February in protest against the destruction of the Rivera mural.	Feb. 13
For the second time, Mayor Fiorello LaGuardia's City Economy Bill is defeated in the Assembly. In spite of Governor Lehman's plea only seven Democrats vote for the bill. . . . William MacCracken, who refused to testify before the Senate in the airmail contracts scandal, is sentenced to 10 days in prison for Senate contempt. . . . Postmaster General James Farley defends the cancellation of all existing airmail contracts, claiming that the law calling for competitive bidding was ignored.	President Franklin Roosevelt urges U.S. Minister to Austria George H. Earle to go back to his post in Austria to observe in person the political situation.	The Senate grants Roosevelt $950 million to continue relief operations, including the Civil Works Administration, until May 1.			Feb. 14
Walter F. Brown, former Postmaster General, denies that airmail contracts were given out without following legal procedures. . . . The strike of hotel workers in New York ends. The Amalgamated Hotel and Restaurant Union accepts a settlement that reinstates dismissed workers. . . . President Franklin Roosevelt speaks against a further reduction in the salaries of railroad workers.	Ambassador William C. Bullitt sails for Russia.	New York Mayor Fiorello LaGuardia attacks the relief methods of the Civil Works Administration as ineffectual in aiding the poor. . . . Five thousand workers employed by the Civil Works Administration march through New York in protest against planned cuts to the CWA. . . . Representatives of governors of 44 states gather in Washington to devise a model Labor Code common to all.			Feb. 15
Federal Judge John C. Knox rejects a motion to restrain Postmaster General James Farley from canceling all existing airmail contracts. The motion was presented by Transcontinental and Western Air. . . . The largest shipment in gold in history worth $100 million arrives in New York from Europe. . . . Thousands of Socialists and Communists clash at a rally in Madison Square Garden in New York.		President Franklin Roosevelt destines $500 million of the $950 million obtained for relief to the Civil Works Administration. . . . President Roosevelt signs the codes for restaurant and laundry jobs.		After two years of research, Mary Cunard publishes the 855-page anthology The Negro, one of the first that is entirely devoted to the condition and culture of blacks in America, Europe, Africa, and the West Indies.	Feb. 16
President Franklin Roosevelt supports the prohibition of ginning of cotton in excess of 9.5 million bales from the 1934 crop. . . . In spite of the settlement agreement signed on Friday, members of the Amalgamated Hotel and Restaurant Union continue their strike and picketing of the main hotels and eating places in New York. . . . Hilton Crouch, a member of the infamous Dillinger gang, is sentenced to 20 years for bank robbery.		President Franklin Roosevelt signs the code for the graphic arts industries, one of the most bitterly contested of those approved so far.			Feb. 17

F	G	H	I	J
Includes elections, federal-state relations, civil rights and liberties, crime, the judiciary, education, healthcare, poverty, urban affairs, and population.	Includes formation and debate of U.S. foreign and defense policies, veterans affairs, and defense spending. (Relations with specific foreign countries are usually found under the region concerned.)	Includes business, labor, agriculture, taxation, transportation, consumer affairs, monetary and fiscal policy, natural resources, pollution, and accidents.	Includes worldwide scientific, medical, and technological developments, natural phenomena, U.S. weather, and natural disasters.	Includes the arts, religion, scholarship, communications media, sports, entertainment, fashions, fads, and social life.

	World Affairs	Europe	Africa & The Middle East	The Americas	Asia & The Pacific
Feb. 18	Presidents and prime ministers of many nations send their condolences for the death of King Albert I of Belgium. . . . The criticism of the papal nuncio against the Spanish government makes diplomatic relations between the Vatican and Spain extremely tense. The Holy See demands that the Spanish government revise its choice of Foreign Minister Leandro Pita Romero as Ambassador to the Vatican.	Paris taxi drivers continue their 18-day strike, rejecting a government settlement. . . . The new film code is passed in Germany, tightening censorship on both German and foreign films. . . . The number of people who died in Austria in the clashes between Socialists and government troops rises to more than 1,000.	The Jewish National Fund of America votes for a resolution to gather $500,000 to purchase Palestinian soil and establish more Jewish settlements.	A two-ton dose of quinine is shipped to Puerto Rico as a first measure to fight malaria.	
Feb. 19	The Soviet Union amasses a large number of troops along the Soviet-Manchurian border as relations with Japan become increasingly tense. In case of war, the troops will have to defend the Trans-Siberian Railway, a strategic link between east and west. . . . The Spanish Cabinet refuses to change its appointment of Leandro Pita Romero as Ambassador to the Vatican.	Large crowds witness the transportation of the coffin of King Albert I to the Royal Palace in Brussels from the royal castle in Laeken. . . . In Austria, more Socialist leaders are arrested and put on trial. . . . German President Paul von Hindenburg signs a decree introducing the swastika, the Nazi Party symbol, into the army and navy. . . . Christian Rakovsky, former Russian ambassador, is the last of Leon Trotsky's followers to ask the Soviet Communist Party for forgiveness.		The late Peruvian dictator Augusto B. Leguia is honored by a large crowd at a memorial service in the capital, Lima.	The chief whip of the majority party in the Japanese Diet resigns as he demands a full inquiry into the bribe allegations against the Minister of Education.
Feb. 20	Japanese are alarmed by Soviet maneuvers along the Manchurian border. They fear Russia may start a war against Japan and Manchukuo.	More than 100,000 people put flowers on the bier of King Albert I in Brussels. . . . The Department of Defense of the Irish Free State announces the recruiting of 15,000 men for a new territorial force. The force will be modeled after British territorial units and will work for the unity of the Irish State. . . . The Reich announces that in three and a half years of economic depression they have been able to cut their foreign debt by 46 percent. . . . Martial law is suspended in Vienna as Premier Engelbert Dollfuss honors those who fought for the government against the Socialists.			
Feb. 21		Albert Prince, the prosecutor in the Stavisky case that has shaken French politics, is found dead beside railroad tracks in Dijon. . . . An Italian delegation goes on an official visit to Hungary to discuss closer economic cooperation between the two countries. . . . Anthony Eden, British Privy Seal, and Chancellor Adolf Hitler discuss possible disarmament plans. Germany may consider returning to Geneva to the League of Nations commission on disarmament.	Berbers start an uprising against the French in Morocco.	The provincial government of San Juan, Argentina, is overthrown by rebels. It was the last provincial government still led by a Radical Party leader. . . . Uruguayan President Gabriel Terra calls for national elections on April 8 to approve the new constitution and to choose a new national administration. The opposition says they will boycott the election.	Japanese forces have lost seven planes and 14 men in the past two weeks due to several plane crashes. . . . Another financial scandal is revealed in Japan as several bankers are accused of fraud.
Feb. 22		The funeral of King Albert I of Belgium takes place in Brussels. Almost every country in the world is represented. . . . Austrian Premier Engelbert Dollfuss announces the drafting of a new constitution that should be ready in two to three weeks. The constitution will avoid fascist and socialist extremes. . . . Anthony Eden ends his diplomatic visit to Berlin for disarmament talks. The Reich seems to have changed its position on arms, demanding only defensive weapons.	Snow falls in North Africa, an exceptional event for the region.	The leader of the Sandino insurrection in Nicaragua, Gen. Augusto Sandino, is murdered. A state of siege is declared in the country. . . . Federal troops restore order in the province of San Juan, where rebels had overthrown the provincial government. However, the governor is not reinstated to his position.	Chinese bankers warn President Franklin Roosevelt that a rise in the value of silver would seriously damage the Chinese economy.
Feb. 23	Charles Wingfield is named British Minister to the Vatican.	Prince Leopold is crowned King of Belgium. . . . France announces a vast three-year expansion of its aviation program. . . . The Irish Dail (lower chamber of parliament) passes a bill that makes it a criminal offense to wear the blue shirt of the Irish Fascist movement. . . . Official celebrations and military parades take place in Moscow to celebrate the 16th anniversary of the Red Army. . . . The Free Evangelical Synod of the Rhineland urges pastors to refuse obedience to the ordinances of Reichsbishop Ludwig Mueller.	A tablet dug from excavations in Iraq reveals the succession of Assyrian kings.	The Cuban army intervenes in a riot between two factions of students in Santiago. Five students and two soldiers are injured.	Speaking before the Japanese parliament, Foreign Minister Hirota says he expects relations with the United States to improve. He also claims a naval agreement for new ratios can be reached by the two nations.

A	B	C	D	E
Includes developments that affect more than one world region, international organizations, and important meetings of world leaders.	*Includes all domestic and regional developments in Europe, including the Soviet Union.*	*Includes all domestic and regional developments in Africa and the Middle East.*	*Includes all domestic and regional developments in Latin America, the Caribbean, and Canada.*	*Includes all domestic and regional developments in Asian and Pacific nations (and colonies).*

U.S. Politics & Social Issues	U.S. Foreign Policy & Defense	Economics & Great Depression	Science, Technology & Nature	Culture, Leisure & Lifestyle	
The national Democratic chairman and Postmaster General James Farley try to persuade New York Democrats to vote in favor of Mayor Fiorello LaGuardia's Economy Bill, which has already been rejected twice. New York Democratic leaders refuse. . . . Following allegations of corruption in the airmail contract investigation, Col. Charles A. Lindbergh issues a statement of his financial transactions since joining the staff of Pan American Airways and Transcontinental and Western Air.		Secretary of Agriculture Henry A. Wallace supports a radical cut in tariffs to allow an increase of imports. . . . About 20,000 owners of cleaning and dyeing businesses close their shops in New York. Their action is supported by workers' unions demanding fairer application of the category's industrial code.	Secretary of Agriculture Henry A. Wallace supports a radical cut in tariffs to allow an increase of imports.	The International Beer and Wine Show begins in the Grand Central Palace in New York. It is described as the largest collection of alcoholic drinks ever assembled under one roof.	Feb. 18
The government takes over from private companies the operation of the airmail system.		The $200 million in gold that has arrived in the United States from abroad in the past four days swamps the United States Assay Office, which has to ask the federal government for additional help. . . . President Roosevelt signs the code for daily newspapers.			Feb. 19
The continuation of the hotel workers' strike in New York leads Mayor Fiorello LaGuardia to criticize the hotel association. The mayor threatens the closure of those hotels that fail to meet sanitary provisions.	President Franklin Roosevelt appoints Maj. Gen. John H. Russell head of the Marine Corps.	The federal government intervenes in the lockout of cleaning and dyeing businesses, asking for an injunction that compels chain stores to respect the price-fixing provisions of the industry's code. . . . President Franklin Roosevelt directly intervenes to assure beet-sugar producers that their request for protection will be taken into serious consideration. This averts a likely crisis over the question of sugar-production quotas.	The New England coast is swept by a heavy snowstorm, one of the heaviest since 1888. Transports are heavily delayed, up to 10 hours. At least 13 people die in the New York region.	The Stein-Thomson opera Four Saints in Three Acts opens on Broadway to enthusiastic audience reactions. The opera will become the longest-running in Broadway history.	Feb. 20
Acting on Mayor Fiorello LaGuardia's orders, inspectors of the Health Department raid several New York hotels to identify possible sanitary violations. The raids represent LaGuardia's reaction against hotel managers whose attitude toward the hotel workers' strike the mayor finds unjustifiable. . . . President Franklin Roosevelt expresses grave concern over the high prices of liquor and launches a new fight against high prices and bootleggers.	President Franklin Roosevelt refuses to discuss a possible U.S. recognition of Manchukuo. However, Far East experts claim that the U.S. government will take an increasingly conciliatory stance toward Manchukuo.	Senator Fletcher, one of the authors of the bill to regulate the stock exchange, charges the stock market with sponsoring nationwide propaganda to avoid federal regulation. . . . The House of Representatives overwhelmingly approves the Tax Bill designed to provide $258 million of new revenues.	Parts of New York, Long Island, and New England are still covered by snow. Transports are still difficult.		Feb. 21
Roger Touhy and two members of his gang are sentenced to 99 years for the kidnapping of wealthy speculator John Factor. . . . After hotel raids by the Health Department inspectors, the representatives of the Hotel Men's Association tell Mayor Fiorello LaGuardia they will cooperate in a quick settlement of the hotel strike in New York.	The Senate rejects an amendment to the Independent Offices Bill. The amendment would have restored to veterans all the benefits that were precluded to them by the Economy Act.	Secretary of Agriculture Henry Wallace charges unjustifiable practices by processors and distributors of meat and dairy products. This is part of the Agricultural Adjustment Administration's policy to obtain higher prices for farmers. . . . Richard Whitney, president of the New York Stock Exchange, attacks the Fletcher-Rayburn bill that is intended to regulate financial markets. Whitney presents an alternative proposal, entailing the establishment of a Federal Stock Exchange Coordinating Authority.		Frank Capra's romantic comedy It Happened One Night opens at Radio City Music Hall. . . . The New York Rangers inflict the first defeat in 14 matches on the Detroit Red Wings.	Feb. 22
The crash of a plane delivering airmail brings the total deaths since the beginning of airmail operations by the Army to five. Army officials say flying airmail at such short notice is almost an impossible task for the Army, whose members have been trained for entirely different tasks. . . . Three persons are killed and 11 injured due to an explosion in Yonkers, N.Y., caused by a short-circuit. . . . Republicans replace Senator Capper on the Republican Senatorial Campaign Committee for his endorsement of the New Deal.		The Federal Alcohol Control Administration announces a decrease in the price of whiskey due to an agreement with Canadian distillers for a reduction of the price of liqueurs shipped to the United States.	All of the volcanoes in the Aleutian Islands are erupting ashes. . . . Dr. P.I. Wold challenges the theory of the expanding universe. He claims that the shift of the lines of the spectra from distant nebulae toward the red end of the spectrum can be due to the reduction of the velocity of light through space.	Johnny Layton wins the world's three-cushion billiard championship, defeating titleholder Welker Cochran. . . . English composer Sir Edward Elgar dies in London. He is hailed as the greatest British composer since Purcell.	Feb. 23

F	G	H	I	J
Includes elections, federal-state relations, civil rights and liberties, crime, the judiciary, education, healthcare, poverty, urban affairs, and population.	Includes formation and debate of U.S. foreign and defense policies, veterans affairs, and defense spending. (Relations with specific foreign countries are usually found under the region concerned.)	Includes business, labor, agriculture, taxation, transportation, consumer affairs, monetary and fiscal policy, natural resources, pollution, and accidents.	Includes worldwide scientific, medical, and technological developments, natural phenomena, U.S. weather, and natural disasters.	Includes the arts, religion, scholarship, communications media, sports, entertainment, fashions, fads, and social life.

	World Affairs	Europe	Africa & The Middle East	The Americas	Asia & The Pacific
Feb. 24	The League of Nations Chaco Commission submits to Bolivia and Paraguay a formal proposal to end the Chaco conflict. . . . Pope Pius XI denounces contemporary tendencies toward paganism in a speech that is interpreted as a covert criticism of the Reich's policies.	Rumors from Vienna's political circles anticipate a march on the Austrian capital by Heimwehr troops to force Premier Engelbert Dollfuss to accept the establishment of a dictatorship. . . . Russians continue to amass army troops along the Soviet-Manchurian border. . . . Anthony Eden, British Privy Seal, continues his diplomatic mission in Europe to encourage disarmament talks. He arrives in Rome hoping Italian Premier Benito Mussolini will help him to bridge the French and the German positions.	A crowd of 10,000 tribesmen welcomes Prince George on his official visit to South Africa. . . . The French Foreign Legion and two desert armies begin a military campaign to conquer the remaining Moroccan territory that is still under tribesmen's control.	Argentine President Agustin Justo warns the army to take the necessary precautions to prevent revolutionary uprisings in the Tucuman province. . . . Cuban President Carlos Mendieta appeals to the nation in a radio broadcast to cooperate for the restoration of peace and economic stability.	Prince Tokugawa, former president of the Japanese House of Peers, dismisses in a nationwide broadcast the possibility of a Japanese-American conflict. . . . Disbanded soldiers violate the tombs of Pu Yi's parents as he is preparing to be crowned emperor of Manchukuo.
Feb. 25	More details about the League of Nations proposal for the Chaco War are revealed. The area is to be policed by an international force and submitted for arbitration to an international tribunal.	Twelve thousand policemen guard London during a vast demonstration against the government's Unemployment Bill. . . . Lord Tyrrell resigns as British Ambassador to Paris and is replaced by Sir George Clerk. . . . One million of Adolf Hitler's followers swear their loyalty to the Chancellor through a spectacular radio broadcast.	During heavy clashes with tribesmen in the Bani mountain regions in Morocco, the French Foreign Legion loses five men.	The Cuban police discover a plot led by former army officers against the Mendieta regime.	A plot to overthrow the Dutch administration is exposed in the East Indies. Members of the radical National Indonesian Party are arrested.
Feb. 26		A monarchist demonstration of about 4,000 is held in Vienna. Premier Engelbert Dollfuss sends his greeting to the meeting, which is presided by Duke Max Von Hohenberg, the son of Franz-Ferdinand. . . . During a meeting with British Privy Seal Anthony Eden, Italian Premier Benito Mussolini accepts the British memorandum on disarmament as a basis for discussion. . . . The High Court of Dublin declares the Irish Blue Shirts a legal movement. The sentence is seen as a major setback for the Eamon De Valera government, which had asked for the action to be dismissed.		Peruvian President Oscar Benavides asks for closer commercial relations between Peru and the United States.	The insistence of the Japanese army to have a central role in the enthronement ceremony of Pu Yi as Manchukuo emperor causes tensions between Japanese and Manchurian officials. . . . The Chinese government announces it will soon launch another offensive against Communist rebels in the Kiangsi and Fukien provinces.
Feb. 27	Pope Pius XI appoints Cardinal Von Faulhaber as Papal Legate, a title that grants him immunity from Nazi arrest.	Following a Soviet request, German authorities release the Bulgarian Communist Georgi Dimitroff and two fellow comrades whom they had unsuccessfully tried for the burning of the German parliament building. . . . Prince Starhemberg, leader of the Heimwehr, declares Austria is a now a fascist and totalitarian state and that Premier Engelbert Dollfuss agrees with the Heimwehr political agenda.		Former Cuban senator Wilfredo Fernandez, a close political ally of former president Gerardo Machado, commits suicide in his prison cell. . . . Fernando Gonzalez Roa is appointed Mexican Ambassador to the United States.	A final dress rehearsal for Pu Yi's enthronement takes place in Manchukuo.
Feb. 28		Soviet planes rescue more than 200 fishermen stranded on ice in the Caspian Sea. . . . Reichsbishop Ludwig Mueller claims that all pastors within the German church should adhere to the principles of National Socialism.		Former Bolivian president Carlos Saavedra is exiled to Chile. . . . Four workers are killed by Cuban policemen at two different demonstrations.	The Japanese government protests against alleged Soviet plane violations of the Korean border. . . . In spite of the corruption allegations against some of his ministers, Japanese Premier Saito remains in power.
Mar. 1	The League of Nations commission for the Saar region announces its ban on political marches and display of political uniforms and symbols.	Former Greek premier Eleftherios Venizelos criticizes the Balkan Pact. . . . The Spanish coalition government headed by Alejandro Lerroux resigns because of disagreements between monarchists and republicans. . . . British Privy Seal Anthony Eden meets French Premier Gaston Doumergue, but he does not receive a definite answer on the British memorandum for disarmament. . . . The Nazi secret state police reports that 8,000 Germans are held in prison for political crimes.		Sugar mill workers in the Cuban provinces of Oriente, Camaguey, and Santa Clara go on strike. Because of increasing workers' agitation, managers fear the crop may not reach the amount decreed by the authorities.	Henry Pu Yi is crowned as Emperor of Manchukuo. Yet, Japanese officials continue to hold key places in the empire. Chinese newspapers describe the Emperor as a mere puppet in the hands of the Japanese.

A	B	C	D	E
Includes developments that affect more than one world region, international organizations, and important meetings of world leaders.	Includes all domestic and regional developments in Europe, including the Soviet Union.	Includes all domestic and regional developments in Africa and the Middle East.	Includes all domestic and regional developments in Latin America, the Caribbean, and Canada.	Includes all domestic and regional developments in Asian and Pacific nations (and colonies).

U.S. Politics & Social Issues	U.S. Foreign Policy & Defense	Economics & Great Depression	Science, Technology & Nature	Culture, Leisure & Lifestyle	
Mayor Fiorello LaGuardia warns that vast dismissal of New York municipal employees will be the only way to balance the city budget if his Economy Bill is rejected. . . . After six hours of intense debate, the House of Representatives passes the Brunner Bill, allowing the use of the Army Air Corps to carry the mail. Republican representatives sharply criticize the cancellation of airmail contracts. . . . A crowd of 2,000 people attends a Mass in honor of King Albert of Belgium at St. Patrick's Cathedral in New York. . . . The motions for a new trial for Heywood Patterson and Clarence Norris in the Scottsboro case are rejected as they were not filed within the statutory time limits.	Secretary of State Cordell Hull urges a more liberal commercial policy in foreign trade.	Col. Robert H. Montgomery resigns from his position of chief of the National Recovery Administration's Research and Planning Division.	Dr. Vladimir Zworykin announces the invention of a powerful microscope that will be combined with television to make visible for the first time ultra-microscopic viruses.	Glenn Cunningham sets the new world record in the indoor 1,500 meters.	Feb. 24
Nine Dartmouth students are found dead in their fraternity house due to carbon monoxide poisoning. . . . A report to the executive committee of the National Education Association stresses the need for a fundamental reform of the American school system.			Heavy snowstorms sweep the northern part of the United States. Three tornadoes leave 23 victims in Alabama, Mississippi, and Georgia.	John J. MacGraw, who was manager of the Giants for 30 years, dies in the New Rochelle Hospital. He is celebrated as one of the greatest figures in the world of baseball.	Feb. 25
President Franklin Roosevelt encourages the creation of a Federal Communication Commission to control transmission by phone, telegraph, wireless, and cable. . . . Five people die and many others are injured in Pittsburgh when a train derails from a viaduct into a city street. . . . After the death of John McCooey, the powerful Brooklyn Democratic organization will be ruled by a triumvirate representing the different factions of the party.	President Franklin Roosevelt announces his intention to veto the Patman Bonus Bill, which would give World War veterans immediate cash payment of their promised endowment.	Independent cleaning and dyeing businesses in New York end their lockout as NRA officials assure them that everything possible will be done to enforce the category's code.	Snow still falls on the northern part of the United States, causing damages and shortages in coal as well as food supplies. Windstorms continue to affect southern states. A total of 60 dead due to these adverse weather conditions is reported throughout the country.		Feb. 26
	In the Senate, a coalition of Democrats and Republicans approves amendments to the Independent Offices Bill, which restores all benefits for veterans canceled by the Economy Act.	John W. Davis, Democratic presidential candidate in 1924, criticizes the New Deal for its limitations on personal liberties. Gen. Hugh Johnson, NRA Administrator, listens to more criticism of the National Recovery Administration from businessmen, labor spokesmen, and consumers. . . . Senator Robert Wagner, Chairman of the National Labor Board, announces a bill to strengthen the powers of the board.		The Metropolitan Opera announces it will carry on the next season without public funds. The necessary resources for its operation will be raised among the friends and patrons of opera.	Feb. 27
New York Mayor Fiorello LaGuardia denounces the persecution of Jews in central Europe and urges religious toleration in the United States. . . . The strike of hotel and restaurant workers, which lasted for more than a month, is suspended. Dismissed workers will be reemployed and union members will not be discriminated against at their workplaces.	The Senate approves a resolution allowing the President to prevent the shipment of arms or ammunitions abroad.	President Franklin Roosevelt announces a new relief program designed to pay full attention to the different needs of the unemployed in rural and urban areas.			Feb. 28
For the first time, President Franklin Roosevelt sends Congress a veto message against the honorable discharge of a deserter. . . . A check by former airmail operators indicates that, in some cases, the airmail cargoes have been reduced by half since the Army took over.	The Speaker of the House of Representatives refers the Independent Offices Bill, which would give veterans considerable cash benefits, to the subcommittee that originally drafted it. The measure is taken to delay the bill approval, which would be vetoed by the President.	Senator Robert Wagner introduces a bill to create a permanent National Labor Board that can settle disputes through arbitration. The bill also abolishes company unions and recognizes the majority representatives of labor unions in collective bargaining. . . . President Franklin Roosevelt and Secretary of the Treasury Henry Morgenthau ask Congress to delay the establishment of a monetary authority to be in a better position to evaluate the effects of the government's gold plan.	The California Institute of Technology announces the production of artificial radioactivity from nonradioactive material.	Primo Carnera beats Tommy Loughran in Miami and keeps the world heavyweight championship title.	Mar. 1

F	G	H	I	J
Includes elections, federal-state relations, civil rights and liberties, crime, the judiciary, education, healthcare, poverty, urban affairs, and population.	Includes formation and debate of U.S. foreign and defense policies, veterans affairs, and defense spending. (Relations with specific foreign countries are usually found under the region concerned.)	Includes business, labor, agriculture, taxation, transportation, consumer affairs, monetary and fiscal policy, natural resources, pollution, and accidents.	Includes worldwide scientific, medical, and technological developments, natural phenomena, U.S. weather, and natural disasters.	Includes the arts, religion, scholarship, communications media, sports, entertainment, fashions, fads, and social life.

	World Affairs	Europe	Africa & The Middle East	The Americas	Asia & The Pacific
Mar. 2	U.S. President Franklin Roosevelt announces his intention to propose a universal pact of nonaggression as a supplement to any general disarmament convention.	The stubs of checks paid out by Alexandre Stavisky, the main figure in the financial scandal that unsettled French politics, are recovered. It is believed these stubs bear the names of the recipients of Stavisky's favors. Stavisky's widow is arrested. . . . President Eamon De Valera proposes that all arms in the Irish Free State should be put under neutral control until after the general election. . . . Spanish President Niceto Zamora asks Alejandro Lerroux to remain prime minister. He will attempt to form a center-right Cabinet.			The Chinese government orders the Military Affairs Commission to dispatch troops for a punitive campaign against the rebel state of Manchukuo.
Mar. 3		Reichsbishop Ludwig Mueller abolishes the General Synod and deprives all provincial synods of deliberative powers. He thus strengthens his control over the German church. . . . Italian dictator Benito Mussolini announces a meeting to take place in mid-March with Austrian and Hungarian premiers to talk about the future of Danubian countries. This is seen as a reaction against Germany's attempt to expand its rule on German-speaking populations in central Europe. . . . Germany and Holland sign a commercial agreement that puts an end to a critical year for German-Dutch trade relations.		Thousands of Brazilian workers gather outside the Constituent Assembly to protest against the draft constitution. . . . Several changes take place in the Cuban Cabinet. The Minister of Interior resigns and a new Minister of Labor is appointed. . . . The Central Bank of Chile reports that the country is successfully fighting the economic depression, although more time will be needed for the normal purchasing power of the people to be restored.	
Mar. 4	The League of Nations still waits for an answer from Bolivia and Paraguay to its proposal on the Chaco region. However, it is believed that neither country will accept the League's proposal.	More than 20,000 supporters of the government in the fascist stronghold of Carinthia cheer at Chancellor Engelbert Dollfuss's propositions for a new constitution for Austria. . . . The Soviets react positively to the U.S. proposal for disarmament and a universal nonaggression pact.		The Paraguayans continue to advance in the Chaco region.	The Japanese army returns the Kupei, the most important pass in the Great Wall, to China.
Mar. 5		The Austrian government is planning to cancel the ban on the Hapsburgs so that they will be able to enter the country. . . . The Hungarian government starts a campaign to check the spread of Nazi ideology among the German minorities in western Hungary. . . . Forty-four people, including a Nationalist Party deputy, are arrested at a monarchist meeting in Spain.	Two young travelers, a German and an American, are killed by Bedouins in Iraq.	Four officials linked to the Machado regime are sentenced to death in Havana. The government of Carlos Mendieta tightens the military control over Cuba as more workers join the strike movement. . . . In the Chaco War, Paraguayans push back Bolivian forces behind the 62nd meridian, which was proposed as the western boundary of a neutral zone in previous proposals for the settlement of the conflict.	The leader of the League of Native Samoans, O.F. Nelson, is convicted of sedition and is expected to be exiled. . . . The steamer Szehui sinks on the Pearl River midway between Hong Kong and Canton. Forty people die.
Mar. 6		The Austrian government issues a decree that unifies all trade unions under a single union, which will be placed under the control of the Ministry of Social Welfare, led by a Heimwehr leader. . . . The third Lerroux government appears before the Spanish parliament. Socialists attack it, but are unable to force a confidence vote.		President Carlos Mendieta suspends all constitutional guarantees in an effort to halt the spreading of strikes throughout Cuba. . . . Both Bolivia and Paraguay reject the terms of the League of Nations proposal to settle the Chaco conflict.	
Mar. 7		The former prefect of the Paris police says former interior minister Eugene Frot was plotting a coup to establish a left-wing dictatorship. . . . Due to the spreading of strikes throughout the country, the Spanish government declares "a state of alarm," the second of Spain's three degrees of martial law.		In addition to the suspension of all constitutional guarantees for 90 days, President Carlos Mendieta signs two other decrees. They provide heavy penalties for native labor agitators and speedy deportation of foreigners convicted for labor disturbances. An attempt to assassinate the Cuban Secretary of State fails.	
Mar. 8		For the first time, the Labor Party gains control of the London County Council with a landslide victory. . . . The lawyer of a central figure in the Stavisky trial tries to commit suicide in Paris.		In spite of the repressive measures taken by the Mendieta regime, strikes continue to spread throughout Cuba.	The Japanese government plans to expand its naval fleet. This is seen as a measure against the approval of the Vinson Bill by the U.S. Congress, which devotes more financial resources to the enlargement of the Navy. . . . Sanji Muto, publisher of the Japanese newspaper Jiji, is shot and wounded by an unemployed salesman. The shooting is related to the newspaper campaign against financial scandals.

A	B	C	D	E
Includes developments that affect more than one world region, international organizations, and important meetings of world leaders.	Includes all domestic and regional developments in Europe, including the Soviet Union.	Includes all domestic and regional developments in Africa and the Middle East.	Includes all domestic and regional developments in Latin America, the Caribbean, and Canada.	Includes all domestic and regional developments in Asian and Pacific nations (and colonies).

U.S. Politics & Social Issues	U.S. Foreign Policy & Defense	Economics & Great Depression	Science, Technology & Nature	Culture, Leisure & Lifestyle	
The House of Representatives votes an inquiry into all phases of Army procurement for the War Department and the leasing of government buildings.	President Franklin Roosevelt urges Congress to revive the Hawes-Cutting Philippine Independence Act bill by removing the provision for U.S. military and naval bases on the islands. The original bill established a Philippine commonwealth over a 12-year transition period. . . . President Roosevelt asks Congress to enable him to establish a new tariff policy to stimulate foreign trade by reciprocal agreements with other nations.	NRA Director Hugh Johnson thanks critics of the National Recovery Administration for pointing out possible improvements to the program.			Mar. 2
On the anniversary of his first year in the presidency, President Franklin Roosevelt praises the people's renewed interest in politics and public administration. He also pledges to continue his campaign to eradicate corruption from public life. Republicans criticize the administration for excessive spending and bureaucracy. . . . Chicago utilities operator Samuel Insull is expelled from Greece, where he is hiding from U.S. authorities wanting to prosecute him on charges of embezzlement and grand larceny. . . . Bank robber and murderer John Dillinger escapes from Lake County jail.	President Franklin Roosevelt's demands to Congress for a new tariff policy on foreign trade meet with opposition from Democrats and Republicans alike.	President Franklin Roosevelt issues an executive order that makes the National Labor Board independent from the NRA. This will enable the Labor Board to obtain prompt enforcement of its decisions.		Mrs. August Belmont becomes president of the Motion Picture Research Council. She commits herself to reforms to eliminate block-booking and to promote the educational and cultural value of motion pictures.	Mar. 3
The police launch a hunt across four states to capture the fugitive robber John Dillinger. . . . The district leaders of the New York Democratic Party oppose the confirmation of John F. Curry as leader of Tammany Hall.		The NRA Consumers Advisory Board submits to NRA Director Hugh Johnson a report stressing the need to reform the National Recovery Administration policies.	The eastern states of the United States are threatened by floods due to heavy rains and rising temperatures.	One thousand subscribers to the Theatre Guild take part in a symposium on the Guild's latest play, They Shall Not Die, on the Scottsboro case.	Mar. 4
The car used by fugitive robber John Dillinger to escape from prison is found in Chicago. . . . The Supreme Court upholds in a 5–4 vote New York State's right to fix milk prices.	Richard Washburn Child, former U.S. Ambassador to Rome, is appointed special adviser to Secretary of State Cordell Hull for Europe. He will be sent to Europe to investigate the economic situation.	President Franklin Roosevelt tells a large audience of business and industrial leaders that the recovery program as represented by the NRA and other government agencies will be permanent features of U.S. social and economic policy. . . . NRA Director Hugh Johnson asks for a 10 percent cut in working hours and an equal rise in salaries. . . . Harry L. Hopkins, Civil Works Administrator, announces that the CWA will end on March 30, a month in advance of the scheduled closing announced by President Roosevelt.	Floods still menace the eastern states. Thousands of families seek refuge, fleeing their homes.	Mother-in-law's Day is first celebrated in Amarillo, Texas.	Mar. 5
The Senate passes the Vinson Bill, which devotes increased funds to the strengthening of the U.S. Navy. . . . Invalid physician Dr. Alice Wynekoop is found guilty of the murder of her daughter. She is sentenced to 25 years in prison. . . . President Franklin Roosevelt appoints Florence E. Allen as judge of the Sixth Circuit Court. She is the first woman to be appointed to this rank.		Industry representatives on code authorities oppose the proposal for a cut in working hours and an increase in salaries. Yet, the Labor Committee of the House of Representatives approves the Connery Bill, which provides a maximum workweek of 30 hours for all professions under NRA codes.	Adverse weather causes the crash of a 10-passenger American Airways plane. Four people die.		Mar. 6
President Franklin Roosevelt urges the return of airmail deliveries to private companies with new rules. Contracts should be awarded for a period of three years and on the basis of free and fair competition.	Twenty thousand people take part in a mass meeting at Madison Square Garden in New York to denounce the crimes of Nazism. The meeting takes the form of a mock-trial against German Chancellor Adolf Hitler.	President Franklin Roosevelt says he expects Congress to pass legislation in the present session to regulate the stock exchange. . . . NRA Administrator Gen. Hugh Johnson says it is the full responsibility of business leaders to find ways to stimulate national recovery.		Densmore Shute and Al Espinosa win the annual international four-ball championship in Miami.	Mar. 7
	Three Cabinet members, Secretaries Cordell Hull, Henry Wallace, and Daniel Roper urge Congress to give President Franklin Roosevelt the authority to negotiate reciprocal tariff agreements with foreign partners.	In their caucus, the majority of House Democrats vote against President Franklin Roosevelt's indication that the Independent Offices Supply Bill should not include increases for war veterans. . . . Secretary of the Treasury Henry Morgenthau recommends a constitutional amendment to tax future issues of federal, state, and municipal securities.	Infrared photographs of distant galaxies taken by Harvard University show for the first time that they are void and empty, in contrast with nearer interstellar spaces.	Prince Sigvard of Sweden surrenders his royal rights and marries actress Erika Patzek in London.	Mar. 8

F	G	H	I	J
Includes elections, federal-state relations, civil rights and liberties, crime, the judiciary, education, healthcare, poverty, urban affairs, and population.	Includes formation and debate of U.S. foreign and defense policies, veterans affairs, and defense spending. (Relations with specific foreign countries are usually found under the region concerned.)	Includes business, labor, agriculture, taxation, transportation, consumer affairs, monetary and fiscal policy, natural resources, pollution, and accidents.	Includes worldwide scientific, medical, and technological developments, natural phenomena, U.S. weather, and natural disasters.	Includes the arts, religion, scholarship, communications media, sports, entertainment, fashions, fads, and social life.

	World Affairs	Europe	Africa & The Middle East	The Americas	Asia & The Pacific
Mar. 9		Princess Ileana of Romania joins the fascist Heimwehr Party. Her husband, the Archduke Anton of Hapsburg, says the members of the Hapsburg family living in Austria have long been members of the movement. . . . The British film *Catherine The Great* is banned in Germany as it stars Jewish actress Elisabeth Bergner. . . . The Spanish government orders raids on the headquarters of left and right-wing extremist groups and bans all their newspapers.	Two French fliers find what they believe are the ruins of the capital of Sheba, southeast of Jerusalem.	President Carlos Mendieta signs a decree that dissolves all labor unions refusing to comply with his strike regulations. Several unions retaliate, announcing a 24-hour protest strike.	Bao Dai, emperor of Annam, announces his wedding to common-er Nguyen Hu Hao. . . . The armies of Canton and Nanking pledge cooper-ation to contain Communist forces. This virtually ends the independent status of Canton and extends the power of the central Chinese govern-ment.
Mar. 10	Pope Pius XI urges the Order of Dominicans throughout the world to follow the example of their founder and fight religious heresies.	The Greek government reaches an agreement with the opposition for the ratification of the Balkan Pact. . . . The day after joining the Heimwehr, Princess Ileana of Hapsburg speaks in support of Heimwehr leaders and government ministers at a rally of 3,000 people,		The Cuban government employs 500 strikebreakers, putting them to work on the docks that have been para-lyzed for several days. Labor unions threaten a general strike. . . . President Getulio Vargas signs the Brazilian Economic Readjustment Act, which authorizes the government to help farmers with their mortgages.	Sanji Muto, president of the newspa-per *Jiji*, dies in the hospital from wounds he received when shot by an unemployed salesman.
Mar. 11	Pope Pius XI canonizes Luisa de Marillac, cofounder of the Daughters of Charity. Thousands of people take part in the ceremony in the Vatican.	The French veterans' association Croix de Feu announces its support for the establishment of a corporative state modeled on fascist Italy. . . . It is announced that Dr Benno Walter, leader of the powerful German Jewish fraternity B'nai B'rith, was arrested by the German secret police at the end of February.	The new Einstein Institute of Physics opens at Hebrew University in Jerusalem.	Paraguay accepts Bolivia's offer of direct negotiations to settle the Chaco conflict under the mediation of the League of Nations. . . . Cuban dock workers and newspaper employees vote to suspend their strikes and go back to work.	A Japanese officer is killed and 10 others are wounded in a peasants' revolt in Manchuria.
Mar. 12	The League of Nations Chaco Peace Committee announces it is unable to settle the war between Bolivia and Paraguay. The committee will soon return to Europe.	German anti-Jewish laws are applied to the army and the navy, and mem-bers who cannot prove their Aryan descent will be expelled by the end of May. . . . The British House of Commons approves a bill that author-izes building up the navy to the limits set by the 1930 London Treaty. . . . The Yugoslav government protests the alleged restoration of the Hapsburgs in Austria and Hungary. . . . Estonian President Konstantin Paets abolishes all political parties and suspends civil liberties, establishing a dictatorship.		Most Cuban unions call off their strikes. Tensions arise when dock workers go back to work and find that strikebreakers have been retained. The strike of the telephone company continues. . . . The children of the late Nicaraguan rebel Augusto Sandino are reported to have been killed by the National Guard.	The Japanese torpedo boat *Tomotsuru* capsizes with 113 people aboard. Three people are successfully rescued.
Mar. 13		Hungarian and Austrian Premiers Julius Gomboes and Engelbert Dollfuss begin a series of meetings with Italian dictator Benito Mussolini to agree on an economic strategy to revive the central European economy. . . . The German Minister for Economics announces a complete restructuring of German business and the creation of a new business code. . . . Dr. Benno Walter, leader of the Jewish fraternity B'nai B'rith, is released.		Due to the dissolution of many unions, Cuban industries are hiring new employees as well as taking back those who agree to stop striking. The telephone company also resumes operations. In some cases, operations resume under military protection.	Ten more sailors are rescued from the Japanese torpedo boat *Tomotsuru*.
Mar. 14	Italy joins several Latin American countries to sign the Argentine anti-war pact, which calls for peaceful set-tlement of international disputes.	Several people are hurt in Madrid as a result of riots between Communists and socialists. Negotiations to end widespread strikes continue. . . . Sweden is the first country to grant the Soviet Union a long-term loan with reduced interest.		More than 250 people are killed and 1,000 wounded when seven tons of dynamite blow up on a train in front of an explosive warehouse, 22 miles south of San Salvador. The dynamite was being moved when the train came to a sudden stop, setting off the blast. . . . The Bolivian Cabinet resigns over its inability to solve the Chaco conflict with Paraguay.	A U.S. gunboat is destroyed by fire while patrolling the Chinese coast. All crew members are saved by British ships.
Mar. 15	The League of Nations Chaco Commission urges American coun-tries to impose sanctions on Bolivia and Paraguay to force them to end the Chaco conflict.	Samuel Insull, the Chicago utilities operator wanted in the United States for fraud, escapes from his heavily guarded apartment in Greece while extradition procedures are being finalized by the Greek Cabinet.	The "Blue Sultan," leader of the Moor rebels in French Morocco, gives him-self up to a garrison in Spanish Morocco as a political exile.	Many arrests of railway workers are made in the Cuban city of Camaguey following the bombing of a train operated by soldiers.	The Chinese central government launches a heavy offensive against Gen. Sun's 50,000 rebels in eastern Ningsia.

A	B	C	D	E
Includes developments that affect more than one world region, international organizations, and important meetings of world leaders.	*Includes all domestic and regional developments in Europe, including the Soviet Union.*	*Includes all domestic and regional developments in Africa and the Middle East.*	*Includes all domestic and regional developments in Latin America, the Caribbean, and Canada.*	*Includes all domestic and regional developments in Asian and Pacific nations (and colonies).*

U.S. Politics & Social Issues	U.S. Foreign Policy & Defense	Economics & Great Depression	Science, Technology & Nature	Culture, Leisure & Lifestyle	
President Franklin Roosevelt announces that his administration will fight excessive liquor prices by temporarily removing all restrictions on imports and domestic manufacture.... Fugitive robber and murderer John Dillinger escapes capture in Chicago.... The administration introduces its bill to restore airmail service to private carriers. The Republican opposition accuses President Roosevelt of being responsible for the deaths of Army fliers who crashed while carrying the mail.		The Commerce Department reports an increase in private employment and moderate improvement in business activity in the new year.... The representatives of the refractory industry are the first to agree with President Franklin Roosevelt's proposal to cut working hours by 10 percent and raise salaries by the same percentage.			Mar. 9
Attorney General Homer Cummings announces that he will soon begin tax evasion suits against former secretary of the treasury Andrew W. Mellon and James J. Walker, former mayor of New York.... President Franklin Roosevelt orders the Army to fly airmail only on safe routes.		Publisher William Randolph Hearst criticizes the NRA, doubting its effective capacity for the country's economic recovery.... The Schenley Products Company is the first company in the United States to adopt Roosevelt's proposal for a 10 percent cut in working hours and a matching rise in salaries.		Columbia's Lions win the polo championship of the Intercollegiate Swimming Association. It is the first time since 1920.	Mar. 10
The Chief of the Air Corps orders the grounding of all planes flying airmail until further notice. A further cut of 20 percent in airmail routes is foreseen.	Former assistant attorney general Charles Warren urges Congress to pass legislation to ensure U.S. neutrality in case of a European or Far Eastern war. This would include a ban on the sale of arms to all belligerent states.	In his annual report for stockholders, Myron Taylor, chairman of the United States Steel Corporation, says the steel industry is recovering.	The South African Institute of Electrical Engineers calculates the speed of lightning, which they found varying from 14,900 to 68,400 miles per second.	The annual Operatic Surprise Party takes place at the Metropolitan Opera House with a huge cast of stars and an excellent reception by the audience.	Mar. 11
New York Mayor Fiorello LaGuardia criticizes the President's decision to end the Civil Works Administration by April 1. He says the city is not ready to take the burden of 160,000 CWA employees who should be absorbed by the city administration.... The Senate resumes the debate on the St. Lawrence seaway treaty. Opposition to the bill increases.	The House of Representatives approves the Patman Bonus Bill, which gives cash payments to war veterans. The administration is against the bill, but 231 Democrats join with Republicans in approving it.		Severe earthquakes are reported in northern Utah and southern Idaho.	The Museum of Modern Art receives the Bliss collection of modern paintings.... Film attendance in 1933 averaged 60 million weekly. The survey shows there was a marked increase toward the end of the year.... Bob Pastor wins the Golden Gloves, the largest New York boxing tournament.	Mar. 12
Manny Strawl is convicted for the kidnapping of Lt. John J. O'Connell. Basil Banghart, member of the Touhy gang, is sentenced to 99 years for his part in the abduction of John Factor. Another gang member is found murdered.... Secretary George Dern appoints Orville Wright, Charles A. Lindbergh, and Clarence Chamberlain to a special committee to study the Army's operation of the airmail.		Henry Ford and the National Automobile Chamber of Commerce announce their plans to comply with President Franklin Roosevelt's proposal to shorten working hours and raise salaries. Ford restores the $5 daily minimum wage.	America's largest and longest-range plane is made available for inspection at the Sikorsky Aviation Corporation. This is the first of six transoceanic planes to be completed for Pan American Airways, based on a project by Charles A. Lindbergh.	Harry Wolf retains the title of U.S. squash champion by beating Milton Baron.	Mar. 13
Orville Wright and Charles Lindbergh decline to serve on the government's committee to study the Army airmail operations. Lindbergh refuses to participate because he thinks the cancellation of private airmail contracts was unfair.... President Franklin Roosevelt faces his first major defeat when the Senate rejects the St. Lawrence seaway treaty, 46–42. A two-thirds majority would have been necessary for the approval.	A petition signed by 250,000 Americans of different religious faiths urges President Franklin Roosevelt to condemn the Reich's persecution of Jews.			The Navajo Council expels previously adopted Hollywood stars such as Douglas Fairbanks and Mary Pickford from their tribe. Navajos also ask that American Indians on screen be played by Native Americans, not by other races.... Sixteen thousand people attend a charity figure-skating carnival at Madison Square Garden. Norwegian champion figure skater Sonja Henie takes part in the gala.	Mar. 14
Aviator Charles Lindbergh agrees to appear before Congress to talk about the airmail operations, but still refuses to serve on the government committee.	The Board on Reorganization of the American Navy discourages the implementation of radical changes. President Franklin Roosevelt approves the Board's reports. His approval is interpreted as a rejection by the administration of the Vinson Bill, which calls for a radical restructuring of the Navy.	The NRA claims it will be forced to impose a code on the wire communication industry unless a satisfactory code of standards is submitted.... NRA Administrator Gen. Hugh Johnson and the National Labor Board join forces to prevent a strike in the Detroit automobile industry. The strike may seriously endanger the economic recovery program.	More quakes are reported in Utah.	Lt. William B. Kunzig wins the national junior saber championship.	Mar. 15

F	G	H	I	J
Includes elections, federal-state relations, civil rights and liberties, crime, the judiciary, education, healthcare, poverty, urban affairs, and population.	Includes formation and debate of U.S. foreign and defense policies, veterans affairs, and defense spending. (Relations with specific foreign countries are usually found under the region concerned.)	Includes business, labor, agriculture, taxation, transportation, consumer affairs, monetary and fiscal policy, natural resources, pollution, and accidents.	Includes worldwide scientific, medical, and technological developments, natural phenomena, U.S. weather, and natural disasters.	Includes the arts, religion, scholarship, communications media, sports, entertainment, fashions, fads, and social life.

	World Affairs	Europe	Africa & The Middle East	The Americas	Asia & The Pacific
Mar. 16		The Polish Senate is unable to approve the country's new constitution before the end of its session. . . . The French parliament approves Premier Gaston Doumergue's proposal for a two-month break of parliamentary activities, leaving him the power to balance the budget and the tariffs by decree.			Several members of the British Consulate are killed along with 2,000 local civilians in Kashgar, Chinese Turkestan. The massacre is caused by fighting between the native population and the forces of the newly proclaimed independent government.
Mar. 17	An international committee arrives in Vienna to investigate the status of Socialist prisoners held in Austrian jails. . . . Pope Pius XI announces his intention to extend the Holy Year beyond its end on April 2.	Samuel Insull leaves Greece and is said to be heading toward the British protectorate of Aden in the Red Sea. . . . The Italian, Austrian, and Hungarian governments sign the Rome Protocols. They include agreements for closer trade relations, consultation, and common policy. . . . The Soviet Central Executive Committee approves a decree to reform Russian industry and agriculture and reduce bureaucracy.		The police raid a secret meeting of Communists in Lima and arrest 18 people, including the well-known leader Nicolas Terreos.	Japan repeals the Geneva Convention and resolution of 1927 that commits its signatories not to increase tariffs.
Mar. 18		Fascist Italian dictator Benito Mussolini says Germany should be allowed to rearm if other countries fail to disarm. . . . Heimwehr leaders reject Austrian Chancellor Engelbert Dollfuss's demand to place the party under his control. . . . Poland's largest industrial unit, the Upper Silesian Coal and Steel Company, asks for a voluntary receivership to prevent bankruptcy.		Bolivia and Paraguay amass their armies in preparation for the decisive battles of Fort Avanti and Fort Ballivian.	The Japanese government prepares a bill to limit the influence of the army over Japanese politics. . . . Mohandas Gandhi urges cooperation with the British administration to relieve the distress caused by an earthquake at Bihar.
Mar. 19	Pope Pius XI presides at the ceremonies for the joint canonization of three saints: Teresa Redi, Father Pompilio Pirrotti, and Father Giuseppe Cottolengo.	Two Americans arrested in Paris for spying admit their guilt and name other members of their group. It is believed they work for the Soviets. . . . Tensions between Poland and Czechoslovakia grow as Czechs are accused of persecuting the Polish minority in their country. . . . Sir Esmond Ovey is appointed British ambassador to Belgium and Luxemburg.	Fifteen Arab leaders on trial for the illegal demonstrations in Jaffa in October 1933 are found guilty by a Palestinian court.	Venezuelan dictator Juan Gomez is reported to be severely ill.	Chinese government forces make important advances against Gen. Sun's rebel army. The rebels are forced to leave the city of Tengkow.
Mar. 20		France announces the fortification of Corsica with the construction of a military airfield, only 60 miles from the coast of Italy. . . . The German regime starts a new campaign to boycott Jewish shops. . . . A Soviet government decree requires that all workers falling short of the quota set for their jobs will have a corresponding pay deduction.			The passing of the McDuffie Bill, which provides for complete independence of the Philippines, is greeted with no sign of enthusiasm in the islands.
Mar. 21	The Saar Economic Association forwards a petition to the League of Nations. The petition complains about the repeated Nazi interference and propaganda campaign against those who favor control of the region by the League. . . . International powers consider Geneva as a serious candidate to host the international navy parley in 1935.	Russian authorities announce that nine days ago the crash of two trains caused the death of 33 people. . . . Chancellor Adolf Hitler claims in a speech in Munich that the Reich government has a plan to put 2 million Germans to work. More than 3 million Germans are unemployed. . . . The Senate of the Irish Free State rejects the bill putting a ban on wearing blue shirts or other political uniforms.		The Constituent Assembly reelects Gabriel Terra as president of Paraguay for the 1935–39 term.	Hakodate, the largest city north of Tokyo, is completely destroyed by fire. More than 1,500 are killed and 200,000 are left homeless.
Mar. 22		The word "republic" is excised from the new constitution. Austria is now a "federal state." . . . The Spanish government drafts a bill designed to prevent unexpected strikes. Public utilities employees must first give 30 days' notice. . . . Irish President Eamon De Valera introduces a bill to the Lower House of Parliament to abolish the Senate.		Forty rebels are killed in Nicaragua by the National Guard, and weapons are seized.	The Japanese government says its has no intention of interfering with U.S. policies in the Philippines. . . . The cooperation between Canton and the Chinese government will extend to centralized control of Canton's army, air forces, and naval units.
Mar. 23		France rejects all British proposals for disarmament that were sent for consideration at the end of January. . . . Italy celebrates the 15th anniversary of the founding of the Fascist Party. . . . The German government passes a law forcing companies with dividends of 6 percent or more to invest their surplus in state loans.	After several border incidents, the Saudi King Ibn Saud ends the truce with Yemen and launches a military offensive.		The rebel movement led by Gen. Sun surrenders to the central Chinese government.

A	B	C	D	E
Includes developments that affect more than one world region, international organizations, and important meetings of world leaders.	*Includes all domestic and regional developments in Europe, including the Soviet Union.*	*Includes all domestic and regional developments in Africa and the Middle East.*	*Includes all domestic and regional developments in Latin America, the Caribbean, and Canada.*	*Includes all domestic and regional developments in Asian and Pacific nations (and colonies).*

U.S. Politics & Social Issues	U.S. Foreign Policy & Defense	Economics & Great Depression	Science, Technology & Nature	Culture, Leisure & Lifestyle	
Charles Lindbergh attacks the new airmail bill before the Senate. He condemns the cancellations of all contracts held by private carriers as unjust.		The administration proposes establishing intermediate credit banks in all Federal Reserve districts to make direct loans to industry or contribute to such loans with private banks. A bill in this direction is introduced in Congress.		Katharine Hepburn and Charles Laughton win the Motion Picture Academy Awards for outstanding actress and actor of the year. *Cavalcade* wins as best film, and its director Frank Lloyd is awarded as best director.	Mar. 16
Thousands battle the police in the streets of Harlem, protesting the Scottsboro trial. . . . Twenty thousand Irish-Americans march in New York's St. Patrick's Day parade. . . . Spokesmen for the railway unions reject the proposal for the continuation of the 10 percent salary reduction. . . . New York taxi drivers go on strike. They are unable to disrupt service to the extent they did in February.	The War Department orders the Army to resume carrying the airmail.			President Franklin Roosevelt and his wife celebrate their 29th wedding anniversary with a dinner at the White House. . . . Glenn Cunningham establishes the world record for the indoor mile at Madison Square Garden.	Mar. 17
The Regional Labor Board intervenes to end the taxi drivers' strike in New York.	The Army Air Corps resumes its mail service on eight routes. . . . Rep. Lewis announces he will introduce a bill for U.S. membership in the World Court.		A meteor explodes in Central Alberta with such force that it destroys several homes.	Italian Antonio Becchi wins the world speed championship for 12-liter motorboats in Florida. Chicagoan Horace Tennes wins the International Class X title race.	Mar. 18
Going against Secretary Henry Morgenthau's opinion, the House of Representatives passes the Dies Silver Purchase Bill. It provides for the exchange of surplus agricultural products for foreign silver.	Air Corps Chief Gen. Foulois orders that all flights carrying airmail be canceled unless good weather conditions exist, as defined in the Army flight regulations. . . . . The House passes the McDuffie Bill, which provides for complete independence of the Philippines in 12–14 years. The bill now goes to the Senate.	A bill to establish intermediate credit banks in all Federal Reserve districts to make direct loans to industry is transmitted to Congress by President Franklin Roosevelt.		Twenty-five thousand New Yorkers take part in the opening of the annual flower show at Grand Central Palace.	Mar. 19
The Speaker of the House of Representatives condemns the Reich persecution of Jews and other groups. The House approves an investigation of Nazi activities in the United States. . . . President Franklin Roosevelt intervenes in the dispute over railway wages. He urges both sides to continue the existing rates for another six months.	William Wallace MacDowell, U.S. Minister to the Irish Free State, arrives in Dublin.	NRA Administrator Hugh Johnson fails to settle the possible strike of Detroit automobile workers. He conveys to the unions and manufacturers President Franklin Roosevelt's invitation for a meeting at the White House. The unions accept to delay their strike.	In London, Sir Henry Greer, chairman of Baird Television, addresses shareholders by a ultra-short-wave television. This is a further step in the development of television technology.	The parents of actress Mary Astor file suit against her for maintenance.	Mar. 20
New York Democratic district leaders tell John F. Curry, leader of Tammany Hall, that he should resign or face removal from office. The loss of confidence is due to his opposition to the nomination of Franklin Roosevelt as the presidential candidate and Herbert Lehman as governor of New York. . . . Violence erupts throughout New York as taxi drivers continue their strike.	Secretary of State Cordell Hull and the Foreign Minister of Japan exchange direct communications about general relations between the two countries. Both politicians commit to amity.			Brewster & Co., a subsidiary of Rolls Royce, starts the production of a new line of luxury cars which, for the first time, will have a Ford engine.	Mar. 21
After a long meeting with President Franklin Roosevelt, automobile union leaders agree to delay the strike call for 48 hours. . . . Police break up a parade of 2,500 taxi drivers on strike in Times Square to avoid the violence of the day before.	Army mail fliers are running into debt to pay hotel bills and transportation as Congress has not yet approved a $5 per day allowance. . . . The Senate approves the McDuffie Bill for Philippine independence.	The Stock Exchanges of the main American cities are united in their opposition to the Fletcher-Rayburn Stock Exchange Bill. Richard Whitney, president of the New York Stock Exchange, suggests changes and amendments before the House Committee on Interstate Commerce.			Mar. 22
New York Mayor Fiorello LaGuardia blames both sides for the taxi drivers' strike. He demands a permanent settlement and calls a meeting in which he will act as a mediator.		Thomas Jefferson Coolidge, vice president of the First National Bank of Boston, is appointed special fiscal adviser to Secretary Henry Morgenthau. . . . Eugene R. Black, governor of the Federal Reserve Bank, gives his support to the Fletcher-Rayburn Stock Exchange Bill.		Dorothy Paget wins the Grand National Steeplechase, attended by a huge crowd of 25,000 people, setting the fastest time of the event.	Mar. 23

F	G	H	I	J
Includes elections, federal-state relations, civil rights and liberties, crime, the judiciary, education, healthcare, poverty, urban affairs, and population.	Includes formation and debate of U.S. foreign and defense policies, veterans affairs, and defense spending. (Relations with specific foreign countries are usually found under the region concerned.)	Includes business, labor, agriculture, taxation, transportation, consumer affairs, monetary and fiscal policy, natural resources, pollution, and accidents.	Includes worldwide scientific, medical, and technological developments, natural phenomena, U.S. weather, and natural disasters.	Includes the arts, religion, scholarship, communications media, sports, entertainment, fashions, fads, and social life.

	World Affairs	Europe	Africa & The Middle East	The Americas	Asia & The Pacific
Mar. 24	The monetary committee of the International Chamber of Commerce urges governments to stabilize their currencies and stop depreciation.	In a radio address to the nation, French Premier Gaston Doumergue says tensions and riots in the country should stop as they may lead to foreign invasion. . . . The Westphalian Synod announces its secession from the German Evangelical Church in protest against Reichsbishop Ludwig Mueller.			C.C. Julien, an oil promoter under fraud charges in the United States, commits suicide in Shanghai.
Mar. 25		Italians overwhelmingly approve the list of 400 members of parliament prepared by the Fascist Grand Council. . . . Right- and left-wing militants battle in the streets of Toulon and Tours. France fears more riots. . . . The new Austrian Constitution eliminates all democratic principles, making Austria a fascist state. . . . Eighteen Czech citizens resident in Poland are expelled as a retaliation for alleged Czech persecution of Polish minorities.		Puerto Rico asks for full autonomy from the United States.	The Japanese parliament ends its session, passing the budget and reforming the electoral system.
Mar. 26	Pope Pius XI praises U.S. President Franklin Roosevelt for his policies in favor of the unemployed.	The Austrian government imposes a "security tax" to cover the costs of the struggle against the Socialists. . . . Switzerland bans all offensive references to state institutions in the press, threatening the suppression of those publications which do not comply with the ban.			Gen. Han Fu-chu, governor of the Shantung province, launches a military offensive against bandits in his province.
Mar. 27		The French government announces that salaries and pensions of veterans and civil servants will be slashed. . . . Production in Soviet heavy industry shows a marked increase in the first quarter of 1934.		Governor Blanton Winship sets up a commission to regulate the high price of gasoline in Puerto Rico.	
Mar. 28		In spite of Premier Gaston Doumergue's appeal to bear with the sacrifices needed to balance the budget, French civil servants' unions call mass meetings to protest against cuts in their salaries. . . . Chancellor Adolf Hitler urges Reichsbishop Ludwig Mueller to pacify the German Protestant church by May 1. . . . France and Britain are preparing a new international conference on disarmament.		Paraguayans continue to advance in the Chaco region, capturing 950 Bolivian prisoners and wiping out an entire Bolivian regiment.	
Mar. 29		General Roehm, Reich Minister and chief of the storm troopers, arrives in Dubrovnik, where German and Yugoslav delegations are discussing a new trade pact. . . . French President Albert Lebrun signs a decree stating that arms sellers must keep a registry of all purchasers. The Council of Ministers approves Premier Gaston Doumergue's measures to balance the budget. . . . The Austrian government bans 100 foreign publications and orders the removal of all nude statues from city streets.	Two French explorers find prehistoric carvings in an area 800 miles south of Algiers. The carvings depict a rich flora and fauna. This leads scientists to believe that there once was jungle life in the middle of the Sahara Desert.	The Mexican National Labor Chamber criticizes the United States for the displacement of Mexican workers in favor of unemployed Americans. The Chamber appeals to the Mexican president to apply the same policy to American workers in Mexico.	The construction of several railroads in Manchuria is seen with suspicion by the Soviets as they fear increased Japanese domination of the areas closer to the Soviet border.
Mar. 30		For the first time since the republican revolution of 1931, the traditional Holy Week processions take place throughout Spain. . . . An interpellation to the French Minister of Interior asks for the dissolution of the Freemasons association that was involved in the Stavisky scandal.		The Congress of the Pan American Medical Association ends. The final statement says the Congress has been a definite step in advancing cooperation between American people.	
Mar. 31		Samuel Insull, who faces legal prosecution in the United States for fraud, arrives in Turkey from Greece. . . . The British government completes its financial year with a surplus of more than £30 million, probably the largest since the start of the Depression. . . . The repeated riots in February enlarge the French deficit. . . . The Berlin daily *Vossische Zeitung* ends publication after 230 years. In its last editorial, it criticizes Nazi control of the press.		Several Mexican politicians are killed in the political campaign in the State of Puebla. . . . A Jewish synagogue is bombed in Buenos Aires while 700 people are present. No one is hurt. . . . Brazilian exporters put pressure on the government for the conclusion of a trade pact with the United States.	Seven young reactionaries are indicted in Japan for plotting to murder two leading Japanese politicians.

A	B	C	D	E
Includes developments that affect more than one world region, international organizations, and important meetings of world leaders.	Includes all domestic and regional developments in Europe, including the Soviet Union.	Includes all domestic and regional developments in Africa and the Middle East.	Includes all domestic and regional developments in Latin America, the Caribbean, and Canada.	Includes all domestic and regional developments in Asian and Pacific nations (and colonies).

U.S. Politics & Social Issues	U.S. Foreign Policy & Defense	Economics & Great Depression	Science, Technology & Nature	Culture, Leisure & Lifestyle	
Despite a long meeting between drivers' unions, taxi companies, and the mayor, violence erupts again in New York in connection with the taxi strike. . . . Rail workers' unions reject proposals to settle the wage controversy. . . . Detroit automobile manufacturers and unions cannot reach an agreement. President Franklin Roosevelt is to act as mediator.	President Franklin Roosevelt signs the McDuffie Bill, which grants Philippine independence after 1945. . . . The Perkins committee recommends the retention of immigration restrictions as imposed by the present law. Asylum for refugees from racial and political persecution should be granted within the immigration quotas.	The Chamber of Commerce of the United States attacks the Wagner Labor Bill, designed to establish collective bargaining, as stirring labor unrest. . . . Seven hundred representatives of CWA workers parade in Washington to protest the end of the relief program.			Mar. 24
President Franklin Roosevelt averts the Detroit automobile strike scheduled for tomorrow. The terms of the agreement guarantee collective bargaining, the right of workers to organize in groups, and an independent board to settle discrimination disputes. . . . Five of seven Scottsboro convicts are put in solitary confinement after disturbances in the Jefferson County jail.		More than 8,000 CWA workers and sympathizers gather in Madison Square Garden to protest the planned end of the Civil Works Administration.	The glass for what is planned to be the world's largest telescope is molded at a factory in Corning, N.Y. The 200-inch reflecting telescope will be operated by the Department of Astrophysics at the California Institute of Technology.	A sword belonging to Grand Duke Vladimir, uncle of the last Czar of Russia, is stolen from the Hammer Galleries in New York. . . . Albert Einstein and his wife are officially welcomed as residents of New Jersey at a formal reception. . . . Arturo Toscanini celebrates his 67th birthday conducting the symphony orchestra at Carnegie Hall. . . . The Montreal Maroons eliminate titleholders New York Rangers for the hockey Stanley Cup.	Mar. 25
Two investigations are begun in the behavior of the police and city administrators in connection with the New York taxi strike.	President Franklin Roosevelt intends to veto the Independent Offices Bill, which contains sharp increases in veterans' pensions.	President Franklin Roosevelt urges Congress to pass a bill that contains effective regulation of the Stock Exchange.		In his annual report, Will Hays, president of the Motion Pictures Producers and Distributors of America, praises the efforts to raise the standards of the film industry.	Mar. 26
Postmaster General James Farley announces that the administration will return mail delivery to private operators as soon as possible.	President Franklin Roosevelt signs the Vinson Bill (authorizing a naval and air force build-up), although he states that he favors continual limitation of naval armaments. . . . The House of Representatives overrides President Roosevelt's veto on the increases in veterans' pensions.		Capt. Flavel Williams wins the gold medal of the American Museum of Safety for his invention of the fog camera, which allows safer navigation. . . . Research chemists F.C. Schmelkes and H.C. Marks discover azochloramid, a powerful agent to destroy bacteria.		Mar. 27
The City Economy Bill designed by New York Mayor Fiorello LaGuardia is defeated for the fourth time. . . . Postmaster General James Farley says aviation lines whose airmail contracts were cancelled will be allowed to bid on temporary contracts if they reorganize and replace officers unacceptable to the administration. . . . Negotiations to solve the rail wage dispute are still deadlocked.	Following the House, the Senate also overrides the presidential veto on the Independent Offices Bill, which considerably increases veterans' pensions. This is the first setback by Congress to Roosevelt's Depression policies.		Dr. Earl W. Flosdorf announces to the American Chemical Society that he is developing a process to preserve life-saving serums against bacteria and viral diseases for indefinite periods without losing their anti-bacterial powers.		Mar. 28
The Senate approves the application of a 75 percent tax on the value of all cotton in excess of 10 million bales that may be ginned during 1934. It is the first time such a crop control measure has been introduced. . . . New York taxi drivers get rid of Communist elements in their leadership and seek a settlement to their strike.	The House authorizes President Franklin Roosevelt to enter into trade negotiations with foreign nations and to raise or reduce tariff rates as much as 50 percent.	Soft-coal miners in the Appalachian area obtain a reduced workweek of 35 hours over a five-day week and a pay raise. . . . President Franklin Roosevelt may ask Congress to approve new taxes to cover the extra expenditures caused by the increase of veterans' pensions.		Banker Otto Khan, philanthropist and patron of the arts, dies in New York. . . . Celebrations for Passover, the ancient feast in which Jews commemorate their escape from Egypt, start today and continue for eight days.	Mar. 29
Joseph Eastman, appointed mediator by the President in the railroad wage dispute, is unable to lead parties to an agreement. The issue returns to the President. . . . The Post Office Department invites bids for temporary airmail contracts over 21 routes.	Secretary of State Cordell Hull commemorates the 80th anniversary of the first treaty negotiated between the United States and Japan. Hull commits the United States to continue friendly cooperation with Japan.	Gen. Hugh Johnson, NRA Administrator, urges setting up sections of the NRA to quickly settle labor disputes that may lead to strikes.		An exhibition of Salvador Dali's surrealist drawings and etchings opens at the Julien Levy Gallery in New York. . . . The Detroit Red Wings win the National Hockey League championship by defeating the Toronto Maple Leafs.	Mar. 30
The fugitive robber John Dillinger escapes once more from the police after a shooting. . . . The New York taxi strike ends after three weeks. The recognition of the union is rejected. . . . Joseph Eastman, railroad coordinator, proposes the creation of a national board that would address disputes between the railroads and their workers.		The Civil Works Administration ends. . . . Representatives of the flour milling industry decide to operate without a code of fair competition. . . . Federal Judge John C. Knox upholds the NRA right to price-fix.	The Skeidarar volcano in Iceland erupts, breaking the ice cap on its top and melting glaciers.		Mar. 31

F	G	H	I	J
Includes elections, federal-state relations, civil rights and liberties, crime, the judiciary, education, healthcare, poverty, urban affairs, and population.	*Includes formation and debate of U.S. foreign and defense policies, veterans affairs, and defense spending. (Relations with specific foreign countries are usually found under the region concerned.)*	*Includes business, labor, agriculture, taxation, transportation, consumer affairs, monetary and fiscal policy, natural resources, pollution, and accidents.*	*Includes worldwide scientific, medical, and technological developments, natural phenomena, U.S. weather, and natural disasters.*	*Includes the arts, religion, scholarship, communications media, sports, entertainment, fashions, fads, and social life.*

	World Affairs	Europe	Africa & The Middle East	The Americas	Asia & The Pacific
Apr. 1	The Italian educator Giovanni Bosco is canonized by Pope Pius XI on Easter Sunday. It is the first time in history that a saint is canonized at Easter.	The Turkish Cabinet decides to turn fugitive Chicago speculator Samuel Insull over to U.S. authorities. . . . The Reich stops the educational activities of the Carnegie Endowment for International Peace in Berlin. . . . Both the Catholic and the Protestant churches complain about the Reich's intervention in religious matters.	Thousands of pilgrims of different faiths gather in Jerusalem to celebrate Easter.	President Eligio Ayala says before parliament that Paraguay is ready to offer Bolivia a peaceful settlement of the Chaco conflict.	Gen. Sun, leader of the defeated rebel army in the northwest of China, retires to private life.
Apr. 2	Pope Pius XI addresses a message to Catholic Youth organizations in Germany encouraging them to resist the forces of paganism. The message is interpreted as a criticism of the Reich's intervention in religious matters. . . . The Holy Year for the celebration of the 19th centenary of Christ's passion, death, and resurrection closes at noon. Forty thousand people gather at St. Peter's Basilica in Rome.	Chicago fugitive speculator Samuel Insull is arrested in Turkey, but extradition to the United States is expected to take a long time. . . . Several Heimwehr militants and former Socialists who betrayed the party during the February riots are found murdered throughout Austria. This hints to a secret Socialist organization that is taking its revenge on the people who led to their February defeat. . . . After the general election, Italian Premier Benito Mussolini is thinking of making large changes to his government.	The Spanish government orders the occupation of the Ismi region in Spanish Morocco. The measure is taken to help the French fight the Moors. . . . Abyssinian Prince Lij Araya calls off his marriage to Masako Kuroda, daughter of a Japanese Viscount. The end of the engagement is seen as the result of Italian influence, as Italian Premier Benito Mussolini is eager to stop Japanese influence in Africa.	Gilberto Valenzuela, former Mexican minister of the interior and presidential nominee, will not be allowed to return from his exile in the United States unless he is prepared to face prosecution for his participation in the 1929 Escobar revolt.	The Japanese government led by Saito receives the support of the elder and respected statesman Saionji, thus strengthening its leadership.
Apr. 3	The Holy Year is extended for another year to be devoted to worldwide prayers.	A German court rules that the Catholic press is a superfluous element and that parish bulletins are enough. . . . Carl Severing, former Prussian minister of the interior and head of police, publicly denies his conversion to National Socialism.	French and Spanish military posts in North Africa are warned of possible Nazi shipments of arms to Moor rebels.		Japanese and Manchukuo reinforcements are amassed at the Jehol frontier with China. Japanese authorities put pressure on China for definitive settlement of the outstanding issues with north China.
Apr. 4		The Soviet government signs a 10-year nonaggression pact with the Baltic States. . . . The measures adopted by French Premier Gaston Doumergue to balance the budget cause unrest in the public sector. . . . The Soviet Union starts a campaign to persuade the remaining individualist farmers to enter collective units. No coercive measures will be taken.		Cuban Minister of Justice, Col. Roberto Mendez Penate, commits suicide over disagreements with his lifelong friend President Carlos Mendieta. . . . Pedro José Zepeda, leader of the Sandino movement, announces he will lead a peaceful campaign to restore legal power in Nicaragua.	The Emperor of Manchukuo is planning a journey in North China to visit the tombs of his ancestors, although the two countries do not recognize each other.
Apr. 5	Pope Pius XI addresses 300 young Germans in the Vatican, urging them to be prepared for further sacrifices to defend the rights of the Church.	Hungary opposes the return of Archduke Otto von Hapsburg to Austria, saying that if he returns to live in Austria as a private citizen, he will spoil the chances for the restoration of the monarchy in Hungary. . . . The trial for the murder of Romanian Premier Joh Duca ends with life sentences for the three murderers, but acquittal of the leaders of the fascist Iron Guard. . . . French Premier Gaston Doumergue issues an appeal to civil servants to bear the sacrifices necessary to balance the country's budget.	The Actions Committee of the World Zionist Organization ends its 12-day meeting in Jerusalem without reaching internal unity. Negotiations between the more moderate representatives and those of the *Mizrachi* (religious orthodox) fail.	Argentina abolishes the Exchange Control Commission. The decision follows the discovery that members of the commission were speculating together with bank employees and brokers. . . . Protests throughout Cuba follow the suicide of Minister of Justice Col. Roberto Mendez Penate and the appointment of a conservative to the State Council. . . . A revolt against President Daniel Salamanca breaks out in La Paz, Bolivia. It is led by military cadets, but is short-lived.	The Japanese government will soon ask the Chinese administration to pay for the unsecured debts owed to Japanese citizens.
Apr. 6		Luis Calderon is appointed Ambassador of Spain to the United States. . . . The head of police in Cologne announces the military simulation of an air raid defense for April 18. It will be the first to be staged in the demilitarized left bank of the Rhine, thus breaching the Treaty of Versailles. . . . Hundreds of Protestant ministers are arrested throughout Germany.			The British and Belgian legations of the north China demilitarized zone issue a request to the Chinese government to protect foreign residents and the area's mine plant from armed gangs.
Apr. 7	The International Wheat Advisory Commission debates at its meeting in Rome how to solve the problem of low wheat prices.	France and Britain agree that the next meeting of the Disarmament Conference Bureau should call a general session of the conference for May 23. . . . The Spanish government suspends the martial law introduced to counter the widespread labor agitations.		Three ministers resign from the Cuban Cabinet. . . . Another military revolt breaks out in Bolivia, this time in the city of Cochabamba. The exact extent of the unrest is unknown due to heavy censorship. . . . Brazilian rail workers go on strike, halting milk deliveries into Rio de Janeiro.	Gandhi suspends the Indian civil disobedience campaign against British authorities in response to widespread violence and riots.

A	B	C	D	E
Includes developments that affect more than one world region, international organizations, and important meetings of world leaders.	Includes all domestic and regional developments in Europe, including the Soviet Union.	Includes all domestic and regional developments in Africa and the Middle East.	Includes all domestic and regional developments in Latin America, the Caribbean, and Canada.	Includes all domestic and regional developments in Asian and Pacific nations (and colonies).

U.S. Politics & Social Issues	U.S. Foreign Policy & Defense	Economics & Great Depression	Science, Technology & Nature	Culture, Leisure & Lifestyle	
The gang of Bonnie and Clyde kills two policemen and kidnaps a housewife in Texas.		In his pamphlet report for 1933, Alfred P. Sloan, president of the General Motors Corporation, says industrial recovery is now on the way "with irresistible force."	Archaeologist Frank Beckwith discovers a vast deposit of dinosaur bones in Utah.	Lester Stoefen is appointed to the team from which the U.S. Davis Cup squad will be formed.	Apr. 1
Several taxi drivers involved in the New York riots connected to their strike have their licenses revoked or suspended.		Myron Taylor, chairman of the United States Steel Corporation, defends the NRA as beneficial to industrial recovery and stabilization. . . . The NRA opens hearings to establish a code of fair practice for the telegraph industry.		A huge crowd of more than 50,000 attend the annual egg-rolling festivities at the White House. . . . The eastern racing season opens at Bowie. John Roosevelt, son of the President, is among the 10,000 people in the audience.	Apr. 2
The deadlock over the City Economy Bill, proposed by New York Mayor Fiorello LaGuardia and rejected several times by the Assembly, ends as Democratic members and the mayor agree on amendments. . . . Eugene Green, a member of John Dillinger's band, is shot and critically wounded by policemen in Minnesota.	The government officially thanks Turkey for the arrest of Samuel Insull and for its decision to turn him over to the United States.	The Treasury offers holders of called 4.5 percent bonds to convert them. The move is part of the Treasury's new policy to get rid of short-term bonds and contain the immediate debt. . . . NRA Administrator Gen. Hugh Johnson says he agrees to allow the licensing provision of the NRA to expire in June as originally planned. . . . Opposition to the Fletcher-Rayburn bill for the regulation of stock markets gains unexpected strength in both the House and Senate committees.	Spring floods in Wisconsin and Minnesota send rivers out of their bounds, flooding cities in Chippewa Valley and causing eight deaths.	The Chicago Black Hawks beat the Detroit Red Wings in the first hockey game of their series for the Stanley Cup.	Apr. 3
		General Motors Corporation announces increases in car prices. . . . A special House commission will be appointed for the revision of the Fletcher-Rayburn bill for stock exchange regulation.	The flood of the Washita River in western Oklahoma kills 16 people.		Apr. 4
A personal dispute between two Democratic Senators delays the approval of the Tax Bill. The La Follette amendment to raise income tax from 4 to 6 percent is rejected. . . . Fifteen hundred employees of the Detroit Motor Products Corporation go on strike to protest against the company's failure to raise their wages.		Virgil Jordan, president of the National Industrial Conference Board, attacks the economic measures of the New Deal, which he critically refers to as "state socialism."		The Chicago Black Hawks beat the Detroit Red Wings for the second time in the hockey contest for the Stanley Cup.	Apr. 5
A rioting crowd of about 4,000 people forces the Minneapolis city council to approve several measures on relief and employment. . . . The inquiry into the airmail contracts causes a shakeup in the Post Office Department. One official is suspended and many others are transferred.	Norman Davis, U.S. Ambassador in Europe, meets British Foreign Secretary John Simon. The U.S. government says it will not back vague disarmament proposals.	The Allied Dye and Print Works, Inc., is the first firm to be prosecuted for violations of an NRA code. The firm is fined a sum of $1,000.		Leonard Spence sets the world record in the 220-yard breaststroke, taking the Amateur Athletic Union's title.	Apr. 6
Samuel Leibowitz, the defendants' lawyer in the Scottsboro case, charges his clients have been tortured in Jefferson County jail.		NRA Administrator Gen. Hugh Johnson urges all Code Directors to bring violators of NRA codes to trial in federal courts.	A huge cliff falls into the Norwegian Sea causing a wave that inundates two nearby villages. Fifty-seven people drown.	Twenty thousand Brooklyn residents parade on the streets to celebrate the 100th anniversary of the granting of a Charter for the Old City of Brooklyn.	Apr. 7

F	G	H	I	J
Includes elections, federal-state relations, civil rights and liberties, crime, the judiciary, education, healthcare, poverty, urban affairs, and population.	Includes formation and debate of U.S. foreign and defense policies, veterans affairs, and defense spending. (Relations with specific foreign countries are usually found under the region concerned.)	Includes business, labor, agriculture, taxation, transportation, consumer affairs, monetary and fiscal policy, natural resources, pollution, and accidents.	Includes worldwide scientific, medical, and technological developments, natural phenomena, U.S. weather, and natural disasters.	Includes the arts, religion, scholarship, communications media, sports, entertainment, fashions, fads, and social life.

	World Affairs	Europe	Africa & The Middle East	The Americas	Asia & The Pacific
Apr. 8		Pastor Martin Niemoeller challenges the authority of Reichsbishop Ludwig Mueller, and although he is suspended, addresses a large audience from his pulpit. . . . Twenty-five thousand Belgian war veterans pay homage to the late King Albert, marching past Laeken Castle and then onto the King's tomb.	Fossilized remains of Dicynodon reptiles are discovered in South Africa.	Colonel Grove, a Socialist candidate, wins a seat in the Chilean Senate. He has run his campaign from a prison cell where he was confined for alleged conspiracy against the government. . . . The Paraguayan army continues its advance in the Chaco conflict, arriving only 25 miles from the main Bolivian military camp. . . . Rodolfo Baquerizo Moreno is appointed new prime minister of Ecuador.	Gen. Von Seekt arrives in China from Germany to become chief military adviser to the Chinese Nationalist government.
Apr. 9	For the first time, Pope Pius XI receives all foreign correspondents in the Vatican to thank them for contributing to the success of the Holy Year.	One hundred Romanian civilians are detained in connection with a plot to kill King Carol at Easter service. . . . British Foreign Minister John Simon says at a parliamentary debate that he awaits explanations from Germans about the increased expenditures in the Reich budget. . . . The Belgian Nationalist movement of the Blue Shirts causes widespread riots in Brussels.	The Spanish government orders the military occupation of Ifni, a coastal area of Morocco allotted to Spain in 1860.	Brazilian rail workers end their strike following an appeal by President Getulio Vargas. . . . The Chamber of Commerce of Puerto Rico criticizes the U.S. economic policies toward the dominion, saying U.S. recovery is funded by the impoverishing of Puerto Rico.	Japan asks China to fully observe the Tangku truce, resuming railway traffic along the Peiping-Mukden Railways and the postal service to Manchukuo.
Apr. 10	The Disarmament Conference Bureau in Geneva calls for a general meeting on May 23.	Joseph Goebbels, the Reich propaganda minister, announces a huge celebration for May Day to celebrate the progress in Adolf Hitler's reformation of labor. . . . Two bombs are thrown at the son of the late dictator and leader of the Spanish Fascist Party, José Antonio Primo de Rivera. The bombs fail to explode. . . . French civil-servant unions start to organize protests against the proposed cuts to salaries necessary to balance the budget.	In spite of denials in Berlin, Palestinian and Egyptian officials confirm that German Interior Minister Frick visited Palestine as an Easter Pilgrim.	The victory of Col. Grove, an extreme left-wing politician, in the Chilean Senate race threatens the stability of the Cabinet led by Jorge Alessandri.	Japanese Ambassador Saito asks the United States to let in Japanese immigrants on the same proportionate quota basis as Europeans.
Apr. 11	Vatican authorities deny a definite rupture with Nazi Germany saying that negotiations for the full application of the Concordat still continue.	Romanian censors tighten their grip on the press to prevent details of the plot to kill King Carol from becoming known abroad. . . . Poland demands an international conference on minorities in Europe to be held in 1935. . . . President Thomas Masaryk, age 85, is the only candidate for the Czech presidency for the May election.	Liberia rejects the League of Nations plan for the country's reconstruction.	Canadian Premier Richard Bennett asks for a revision of the British North America Act, the Canadian Constitution, to bring it more in line with the modern era. . . . Hector Castro, former foreign minister, is named El Salvador's envoy to the United States. . . . In spite of requests from several coalition parties, Governor Winship refuses to appoint a new Treasurer for Puerto Rico. . . . Paraguayans open the battle for Fort Ballivian, the main Bolivian army base in the Chaco area.	Japanese Minister of War Hayashi resigns as his brother is involved in a financial scandal. The Premier asks him to withdraw his resignation.
Apr. 12	The advisory committee of the League of Nations on the Leticia region warns that Colombia and Peru are purchasing arms to get ready for a possible war.	Samuel Insull, Chicago fugitive speculator, starts his journey back to the United States where he will face trial for fraud. . . . The German government responds to the British Foreign Secretary on the increased military expenditures of the Reich. Germany says there is nothing in the Versailles treaty to prevent increasing the military budget. . . . French war veterans partially accept the economic sacrifices asked by Premier Gaston Doumergue to balance the budget. They ask the government to eliminate corruption.	Reich Minister of Interior Frick, whose department has the biggest role in persecuting German Jews, is in Palestine for his honeymoon.		Governor Murphy criticizes the three-cent coconut-oil tax in the new tax bill as an injustice to the Philippines. . . . Japanese Minister Hayashi leaves his resignation in the hands of the Chief of General Staff. He will decide whether Hayashi should resign following the conviction of his brother.
Apr. 13	The International Labor Office of the League of Nations reports that the favorable trend in employment begun in 1933 has continued in the first three months of 1934.	Italian Premier Benito Mussolini says Italy is willing to resume disarmament talks. To this end, he agrees with the French proposal to establish guarantees of performance. . . . The Spanish parliament fails to pass the Amnesty Bill. The law was promised by Premier Lerroux to right-wing militants imprisoned for their participation in riots against the republic.		Paraguayan troops arrive within 15 miles of Fort Ballivian, the main Bolivian military base, thus marking another important victory in the Chaco War.	

A	B	C	D	E
Includes developments that affect more than one world region, international organizations, and important meetings of world leaders.	Includes all domestic and regional developments in Europe, including the Soviet Union.	Includes all domestic and regional developments in Africa and the Middle East.	Includes all domestic and regional developments in Latin America, the Caribbean, and Canada.	Includes all domestic and regional developments in Asian and Pacific nations (and colonies).

U.S. Politics & Social Issues	U.S. Foreign Policy & Defense	Economics & Great Depression	Science, Technology & Nature	Culture, Leisure & Lifestyle	
Workers of the Detroit Motor Products Corporation reject a tentative settlement of the strike reached by representatives of employees and employers before the Labor Board. . . . Republican leaders criticize the government's airmail bill and present an alternative bill to Congress. . . . Vincenzo Tisbo, hunted all over the world for the bankruptcy of his bank in 1923, is arrested in New York, where he manages a wine cellar. . . . Riots between Nazis and Communist sympathizers break out during a Nazi rally in New York attended by more than 9,000 people.			A slide from Storm King Mountain, near West Point, N.Y., falls across the Storm King Highway, killing a family of three and wrecking several cars.	The Detroit Red Wings beat the Chicago Black Hawks, keeping alive their chances of winning the Stanley Cup.	Apr. 8
Mayor Fiorello LaGuardia's City Economy Bill for New York is finally passed after four rejections. . . . President Franklin Roosevelt pays tribute to the Red Cross as a factor in national recovery at the American convention of the organization.	The U.S. Ambassador to the Irish Free State dies suddenly at a dinner given in his honor.	The NRA manages to settle the automobile workers' strike in Detroit. . . . The Senate Banking and Currency Committee approves several amendments to the Fletcher-Rayburn bill for the control of stock exchanges. Rayburn opposes them as they weaken the regulations of the markets.			Apr. 9
The Illinois primaries for the November polls show a bigger participation of Democrats than Republicans. Almost all Democratic members of Congress are reconfirmed.		School Superintendent William Wirt is heard by a special House committee that questions him on his allegations that President Franklin Roosevelt's "brain trust" was plotting the destruction of the existing social order. . . . The Senate rejects the Couzens amendment to increase taxes a further 10 percent.		Soviet Ambassador Troyanovsky and his wife give their first official reception in Washington. . . . The Chicago Black Hawks beat the Detroit Red Wings, capturing the Stanley Cup and the world's hockey championship. . . . The United States Football Association selects the players who will represent the United States at the world football championship that will begin on May 24 in Italy.	Apr. 10
The Annual Convention of the American Red Cross approves several resolutions pledging continued cooperation with President Roosevelt's recovery program.	U.S. and Japanese delegations in New York renew mutual friendship between the two countries.	After having rejected it the day before, the Senate reconsiders the Couzens amendment for a general 10 percent increase of taxes and approves it. . . . The grand jury investigating the reaction of the city administration to the long and violent New York taxi drivers' strike criticizes Mayor Fiorello LaGuardia and the police for failing to prevent the disorders.	Italian Commander Renato Donati achieves a new airplane altitude record.		Apr. 11
Detroit auto toolmakers announce a strike due to the failure of the Automotive Tool and Die Manufacturers Association to grant workers a 20 percent wage increase, a 7-hour working day, and a 5-day week.		President Franklin Roosevelt and NRA Administrator Hugh Johnson study basic changes to the National Recovery Administration. They also plan to drive through the remainder of the administration's legislative program.	Explorer Lincoln Ellsworth announces a new Antarctic expedition to map a new part of the world.		Apr. 12
American students stage demonstrations throughout the nation against war. . . . Three officials of the Union Trust Bank, including Joseph Nutt, former treasurer of the Republican National Committee, are indicted for fraud.		The Senate passes the tax bill increasing the government's revenue by $220 million above the amount passed by the House.	In western Massachusetts and southern New Hampshire, rivers continue to swell. Three people die.		Apr. 13

F	G	H	I	J
Includes elections, federal-state relations, civil rights and liberties, crime, the judiciary, education, healthcare, poverty, urban affairs, and population.	Includes formation and debate of U.S. foreign and defense policies, veterans affairs, and defense spending. (Relations with specific foreign countries are usually found under the region concerned.)	Includes business, labor, agriculture, taxation, transportation, consumer affairs, monetary and fiscal policy, natural resources, pollution, and accidents.	Includes worldwide scientific, medical, and technological developments, natural phenomena, U.S. weather, and natural disasters.	Includes the arts, religion, scholarship, communications media, sports, entertainment, fashions, fads, and social life.

	World Affairs	Europe	Africa & The Middle East	The Americas	Asia & The Pacific
Apr. 14		The Soviet government announces large economic cuts to limit administrative expenses. . . . The Fascist government reduces the salaries of Italian state employees in an attempt to contain the general deficit. . . . The French parliamentary subcommission to reform the constitution approves two important changes that give the government and the president of the Republic more powers. . . . Reichbishop Ludwig Mueller declares a general amnesty for the rebel members of the German clergy.		Chilean President Jorge Alessandri refuses to give up his emergency powers as demanded by the Socialist party.	Chinese officials fear renewed tensions with Japan unless China agrees to resume railway and postal service to Manchukuo.
Apr. 15		Exiled Russian Communist Leon Trotsky is discovered living in Fontainebleau, France, under false identity. . . . Rudolph Diels, head of the Prussian secret police, resigns over disagreements on reform plans. . . . All Austrian fascist military formations will be unified in the Patriotic Front, which will be placed under the control of Premier Dollfuss and his Heimwehr Deputy Prince von Starhemberg.		Paraguayans are halted in their advance toward Fort Ballivian by heavily entrenched Bolivian forces. The Paraguayans suffer severe losses in their repeated attacks against the fort, a key position in the Chaco conflict. . . . Widespread protests throughout Cuba lead to the resignation of the president of the Council of State.	Japanese military leaders and the Chief of General Staff persuade War Minister Hayashi to withdraw his resignation from the post.
Apr. 16	The president of the League of Nations, Joseph Avenol, leaves for Rome where he will talk to Italian Premier Benito Mussolini about possible Soviet entry into the League. . . . James G. MacDonald, League of Nations High Commissioner for German Refugees, pays an official visit to Czechoslovakia to discuss the refugee problem.	Riots in Rhodes between the Greek population and Italian authorities cause several deaths and hundreds of arrests. . . . The strike called to protest against pay cuts in civil servants' salaries fails to stop French public services.		Bolivian authorities announce the overwhelming defeat of Paraguayan troops in the battle for Fort Ballivian. After a series of retreats, Bolivian forces retain their main military base and halt the Paraguayan army. . . . The Puerto Rican Senate ratifies three Cabinet appointments made by Governor Winship.	
Apr. 17		The British budget cuts income taxes. No mention is made of payment of war debts to the United States. . . . . In a note to the British government, France bars any possibility of accepting the rearmament of Germany. . . . Leon Trotsky's residence permit is revoked by the French government.	Walter C. Teagle, president of the Standard Oil Company of New Jersey, says the new Iraq Petroleum Company's oil output should be divided between U.S., French, and British interests in proportion to their company holdings.	The Cuban government approves a wide program of social reforms and unemployment relief. Prisoners arrested for violations of the government's strike decree are freed under a general amnesty. . . . Twenty-one people are killed in Mexico during the electoral campaign for the State of Puebla.	Foreign Office spokesman Eiji Amau says Japan will intervene if it judges that China is endangering the peace in east Asia. This declaration is interpreted as a warning to the United States and other Western countries that are selling arms and planes to China's army.
Apr. 18		As more details of the French note on disarmament become known, it is apparent that bilateral negotiations are over and that the whole matter should go back to the League of Nations in Geneva. The French justify their firm standing by the increased German army budget. . . . The fears of anti-fascist outbreaks at the May Day demonstrations lead the Austrian government to arrest hundreds of Socialists throughout the country.	A report of the Jewish National Home shows that more than 11,000 Jewish refugees entered Palestine in the last eight months of 1933.	The Central Post Office in Havana is bombed. The striking workers of the telephone sector receive an ultimatum that unless they return to work within 72 hours they will be definitely discharged. . . . Three Cabinet members of the Chilean Radical Party resign, so President Jorge Alessandri will form a new government.	
Apr. 19	Pope Pius XI receives Prince von Starhemberg, the leader of the Heimwehr, the Austrian fascist party.	Eighty-one political opponents of the Austrian government are placed in a detention camp without trial for an indefinite period.		Cuba will ask the United States to extradite for prosecution former president Gerardo Machado and his chief of staff, Gen. Alberto Herrera. . . . President Jorge Alessandri forms a new coalition government in Chile, which represents many political forces but excludes the leftwing.	The Japanese note threatening intervention if China upsets the peace in the Far East stirs indignant reactions in Chinese circles. Chinese officials say Japan wants to establish its own protectorate in China. . . . India and Japan reach a preliminary agreement for a commercial treaty after seven months of negotiations.
Apr. 20		Riots between the police and 6,000 demonstrators break out in front of the Paris city hall. Socialists and Communists are protesting government economic measures. One thousand are arrested. . . . Chancellor Adolf Hitler celebrates his 45th birthday away from the capital. There are no official celebrations, but the Chancellery becomes the object of pilgrimage for thousands of Germans. . . . Violent riots break out in Madrid in front of the Parliament while it approves an amnesty bill mainly for right-wing political prisoners.		The Cuban government starts to train a special squad of 250 people to face labor demonstrations with modern equipment rather than firearms. This should prevent further bloodshed.	Japanese leaders criticize Foreign Office spokesman Amau for his declaration, which virtually set up a protectorate over Chinese relations with Western powers. Amau is seen as having nullified Premier Hirota's efforts to improve Japanese relations with the rest of the world.

A	B	C	D	E
Includes developments that affect more than one world region, international organizations, and important meetings of world leaders.	Includes all domestic and regional developments in Europe, including the Soviet Union.	Includes all domestic and regional developments in Africa and the Middle East.	Includes all domestic and regional developments in Latin America, the Caribbean, and Canada.	Includes all domestic and regional developments in Asian and Pacific nations (and colonies).

U.S. Politics & Social Issues	U.S. Foreign Policy & Defense	Economics & Great Depression	Science, Technology & Nature	Culture, Leisure & Lifestyle	
President Franklin Roosevelt confers with leaders of the Senate and Secretary of the Treasury Henry Morgenthau to plan a legislative program for the rest of the congressional session.	President Franklin Roosevelt urges the elimination of the three-cent coconut-oil tax in the new tax bill. The tax may endanger the relationship with the Philippines. . . . Richard Washburn Child, special economic adviser to Secretary of State Cordell Hull, meets French Cabinet members and businessmen to develop new trade relations.	President Franklin Roosevelt signs an executive order that all budgets and assessments of Code Authorities for financing the administration of codes be approved by NRA Administrator, Gen. Hugh Johnson. . . . The House is hostile to many amendments to the new tax bill approved by the Senate. . . . The Conference of Methodist Episcopalian Ministers condemns President Franklin Roosevelt because NRA policies have not been carried far enough to produce lasting economic reform.	The Bishop Museum of Science Expedition announces the departure of a six-month mission for an ethnological and natural history survey of the islands of Polynesia.	Francis Shields wins the 16th annual North and South tennis championship.	Apr. 14
President Franklin Roosevelt plans to adjourn Congress in early May, after the approval of the Stock Exchange Regulation Bill and amendments to the most controversial sections of the Security Act of 1933. The President will also ask Congress for a supplementary sum of $1.5 billion to finance relief measures.	Former U.S. envoy to Austria, George H. Earle, bitterly criticizes the German Reich in a speech before the Union of American Hebrew Congregations.	Postmaster General James Farley announces the resumption of full postal service because of the marked increase in postal revenues. . . . Senator Robert Wagner, head of the National Labor Board, says that the sudden increase in strikes during February and March shows that a minority of large employers still adopts behaviors contrary to industrial peace.		Conductor Arturo Toscanini starts a series of three Sunday concerts devoted to Richard Wagner at Carnegie Hall.	Apr. 15
William Langer, governor of North Dakota, is indicted for forcing political contributions from federal employees in his state.		President Franklin Roosevelt asks Congress to authorize a commission to study a broad policy for American aviation.	The convention of the American College of Physicians opens with reviews of new treatments for pneumonia and results on new studies of tuberculosis.		Apr. 16
Two companies of Louisiana National Guardsmen are employed to defend the Caddo parish courthouse when a mob of 3,000 tries to seize Fred Lockhart, who confessed the murder of a 16-year-old girl. . . . Four airmail companies file a personal suit against Postmaster General James Farley for his decision to cancel all existing airmail contracts.	President Roosevelt confers with Haitian President Vincent about the definite withdrawal of U.S. Marines from the island.		Physicists at Columbia University determine the diameter of a neutron to be 1/10,000,000,000,000 (one ten-trillionth) of an inch.	The 1934 baseball season begins. The world champion Giants beat the Phillies.	Apr. 17
President Franklin Roosevelt voices his firm opposition to the McLeod Bill, which would provide government payment of in full to depositors in closed banks now in receivership.	The United States says it has no intention of changing its "open door" policy toward China. All nine powers that signed the 1922 treaty are to have equal opportunities in commerce with China. Japanese objections against the United States selling military planes to China contravene this principle.	The Senate subcommittee in charge of redrafting the Rayburn-Fletcher Exchange Bill completes its work. . . . At a meeting in Birmingham, Ala., 300 southern industrialists oppose the emanation of wage differentials between north and south as they fear the NRA may propose.		Paul Cadmus's picture *The Fleet's In* is removed from the Navy Department at Secretary Claude Swanson's request. According to Navy authorities, the picture is an insult to the Navy as it represents sailors as a debauched and drunken crowd.	Apr. 18
The government begins a nationwide campaign aimed at eliminating bootleggers and illicit distillers. . . . The Post Office Department receives 45 bids to operate, under temporary contracts, 17 airmail routes.		The Senate passes the Costigan Bill. The Bill makes sugar cane and sugar beets basic agricultural commodities under the Agricultural Adjustment Act. It also establishes fixed domestic production and gives Secretary of Agriculture Henry Wallace the authority to decide quotas for importation of sugar from outside the United States.		Dave Komonen wins the 38th Boston marathon.	Apr. 19
John F. Curry is the first leader of Tammany Hall to be deposed by its executive committee. He will be replaced by a committee.		President Franklin Roosevelt says he is against currency inflation and the remonetization of silver. He urges an international agreement to make silver a monetary commodity.	A giant sun-spot 16,000 miles in width appears on the sun surface. Astronomers predict storms and climactic upheavals.		Apr. 20

F	G	H	I	J
Includes elections, federal-state relations, civil rights and liberties, crime, the judiciary, education, healthcare, poverty, urban affairs, and population.	Includes formation and debate of U.S. foreign and defense policies, veterans affairs, and defense spending. (Relations with specific foreign countries are usually found under the region concerned.)	Includes business, labor, agriculture, taxation, transportation, consumer affairs, monetary and fiscal policy, natural resources, pollution, and accidents.	Includes worldwide scientific, medical, and technological developments, natural phenomena, U.S. weather, and natural disasters.	Includes the arts, religion, scholarship, communications media, sports, entertainment, fashions, fads, and social life.

	World Affairs	Europe	Africa & The Middle East	The Americas	Asia & The Pacific
Apr. 21		There is a violent explosion in the Kakanj coal mine, the largest in Bosnia, and 250 miners are trapped. . . . International military observers are convinced that the Reich is giving military training to German youths to prepare a full-sized army. . . . French Foreign Minister Barthou leaves for Poland and Czechoslovakia to strengthen bonds between the countries.		Bolivians inflict more casualties to the Paraguayan army as both countries get ready for a new battle for Fort Ballivian, a key military position in the Chaco War.	Chinese Foreign Minister Wang says its government will not enter any negotiation with Japan that could lead to the recognition of Manchukuo.
Apr. 22	League of Nations reports on the Chaco war show the plight of Indians, who have been massacred by both sides.	Sir Oswald Mosely launches his Black Shirts movement with a mass meeting at the Royal Albert Hall in London, attended by 10,000 people. . . . Ten thousand German Protestants demonstrate in south Germany to ask for fewer government interventions in the internal affairs of the Church. . . . Catholic and Socialist forces violently clash in Madrid.	Four Arabs are put on trial in Iraq for the murder of the American tourist Ray Fisher.		Akira Ariyoshi, Japanese Minister to China, says Japan will not tolerate China building up a large air force.
Apr. 23		French Foreign Minister Barthou is reassured by Polish Premier Pilsudski of the Franco-Polish alliance. . . . Twenty-four Finns are convicted of espionage for the Soviet Union. . . . Joachim von Ribbentrop is appointed by German President Paul von Hindenburg as Commissioner for the Disarmament Question.	The trial against three Jewish revisionists accused of killing Labor Party leader Arlosoroff begins in Jerusalem. . . . Prince George leaves South Africa, where he has been on an official trip for two months, to return to Britain.	Students' demonstrations spread throughout Cuba when soldiers fire on several students in Santa Clara in the Camaguey province. . . . The Bolivian army resists repeated Paraguayan attacks in the Las Conchitas area in northern Chaco.	The British government sends an official note to Japan saying that it stands by the Nine-Power Treaty signed in 1922.
Apr. 24		French Foreign Minister Barthou leaves Poland, having obtained Polish backing on France's firm stand against Germany on the disarmament question. . . . The Spanish government reaches an agreement with the President of the republic on the application of the recently approved amnesty, thus averting a Cabinet crisis.		Mexico and the United States sign a convention that provides a lump-sum settlement for American claims against Mexico during the revolutionary period from 1910 to 1920. . . . Bolivians hold their positions in the Conchitas sector, pushing back all attacks from the Paraguayan army.	China asks Britain and the United States to take leading roles among the nine signatories of the 1922 treaty to contain Japanese influence in Asia. . . . The ban against Filipino immigration to the United States, the coconut tax, and retroactive sugar limitation spread concerns in the Philippines over the impending independence.
Apr. 25	The Chinese delegate to the League of Nations says China intends to continue the country's reconstruction through the League.	German officials say that foreign debts should not prevent the Reich from carrying out its National Socialist program. . . . Although President Zamora signs the amnesty designed by Spain's Lerroux government, he sends the Prime Minister a list of moral faults he finds in the act. The government feels this is an act denoting lack of confidence in its operations and resigns. Martial law is proclaimed throughout the country.		Former Cuban president Gerardo Machado is sought throughout the United States to face charges of massacre in his native country. . . . Cuban President Carlos Mendieta signs a decree increasing the salaries of public employees. . . . Bolivians repulse Paraguayans in the Chaco conflict. A series of consecutive defeats have had a demoralizing effect on Paraguayan troops.	
Apr. 26		French Foreign Minister Barthou arrives in Prague to strengthen the Franco-Czech Alliance. . . . All Spanish left-wing leaders urge President Zamora to dissolve the parliament and call for new elections.	Public sentiment in Palestine is overwhelmingly with the defendants indicted in the murder of Labor Party leader Arlosoroff. Many leading Jews make appeals for funds to support the defense of the accused.	An agricultural commission headed by Governor Winship leaves Puerto Rico to confer with Secretary of Agriculture Henry Wallace on the fixing of the sugar quota.	Mohandas Gandhi is attacked by a crowd of Hindus who disapprove of his campaign to help the Untouchables.
Apr. 27		The Austrian parliament is summoned to approve the new constitution, which will set up a Christian and corporative state. . . . Ricardo Samper, former minister of industry and commerce, is appointed Prime Minister by Spanish President Zamora.		A Paraguayan reconnaissance party is captured by the Bolivians in the Chaco area. The prisoners admit that the recent defeats in the conflict have caused rifts in the Paraguayan army. . . . Thirteen American nations sign the Argentine anti-war pact. Signatory nations include the United States and the two nations involved in the Chaco War, Bolivia and Paraguay. . . . Many labor leaders are arrested in Cuba as more strikes are called for the May Day celebrations.	The Japanese Foreign Office sends an official note to the British and U.S. Embassies reassuring both countries about its policy on China. . . . Chinese officials fear a Japanese invasion of Inner Mongolia.

A	B	C	D	E
Includes developments that affect more than one world region, international organizations, and important meetings of world leaders.	Includes all domestic and regional developments in Europe, including the Soviet Union.	Includes all domestic and regional developments in Africa and the Middle East.	Includes all domestic and regional developments in Latin America, the Caribbean, and Canada.	Includes all domestic and regional developments in Asian and Pacific nations (and colonies).

U.S. Politics & Social Issues	U.S. Foreign Policy & Defense	Economics & Great Depression	Science, Technology & Nature	Culture, Leisure & Lifestyle	
The union leaders of railway workers reject Roosevelt's proposal for an extension of the pay cut for another six months. . . . President Roosevelt signs the Bankhead Bill for compulsory control over cotton production.		Rexford G. Tugwell, Assistant Secretary of Agriculture, defends Roosevelt's New Deal as preserving American democracy.	A study by the Rockefeller Institute shows that genes may determine a person's length of life as well as susceptibility to diseases.	The return to an open betting system attracts a record crowd of 18,000 horserace followers to the Jamaica track.	Apr. 21
A new wage structure is approved for soft-coal workers. President Roosevelt asks 50,000 striking workers to return to their jobs. . . . John Dillinger, fugitive robber and murderer, is surrounded in a wooded area in Wisconsin.			The King of Italy dedicates the world's longest double-track railway tunnel, which cuts through the Etruscan Apennines.	Frank Shields wins the Mason-Dixon tennis championship for the second year in a row.	Apr. 22
John Dillinger escapes for the second time in 24 hours from police and federal agents. In the shooting two men are killed, five wounded. . . . Secretary of Agriculture Henry Wallace says he approves of control of tobacco production as designed in the Kerr limitation plan. The plan, however, does not contain compulsory features as does the Bankhead Act on cotton limitation.		Secretary of State Cordell Hull says the New Deal embodies the American traditions of democracy and liberalism.	Dr. Hubble of Mount Wilson Observatory calculates that the diameter of the physical universe is 6 billion light-years.	A Bay Ridge court rules that the sentence "You can go to hell" is not a slur. . . . Actress Gloria Swanson announces she will file for divorce from her husband, F. Michael Farmer.	Apr. 23
Secretary of the Treasury Henry Morgenthau sends the Senate a list of holders of silver. The list reveals that two of the Senators who support the remonetization of silver have large quantities of the metal. . . . Rexford Tugwell, a member of the "brain trust," is appointed by the President as Undersecretary for Agriculture. . . . Five thousand men are on the hunt for fugitive John Dillinger.	William Phillips, Undersecretary of State, meets Japanese Ambassador Saito to discuss the recent declaration concerning Japanese policy in China.	Given the doubts of many Democratic Senators on the Reciprocity Tariff Bill, administration leaders decide to actively support this measure, which gives the President authority to agree to new tariffs with foreign nations.	Prof. Arthur Compton shows the first photographs of the atom at the National Academy of Sciences meeting.	The new devalued dollar encourages tourists from Europe to visit the United States. . . . President Roosevelt tosses the first ball to inaugurate the baseball season in Washington.	Apr. 24
More agents and policemen are employed in the hunt for bank robber John Dillinger, but with no success.	President Roosevelt informally announces at a press conference that he will ask Congress to authorize him to use an indeterminate amount of public works funds for naval construction in the fiscal year beginning in July. This new policy may be due to recent Japanese declarations of its intention to act as a stabilizing force in Asia.	Senators manage to persuade Representatives of the necessity of higher taxes. The tax bill for 1934 will eventually add at least $417 million to the income of the federal government.	The city of San Francisco awards Italian inventor Guglielmo Marconi its honorary citizenship.	President Roosevelt and his building advisers are considering employing Public Works Administration artists to decorate public buildings with murals rather than gold leaves and scrolls.	Apr. 25
Senator Fletcher urges the approval of the Stock Exchange Control Bill, describing it as the only way to subordinate security trading to the general welfare. . . . Union leaders and railway operators reach an agreement that will gradually restore the 10 percent pay cut in workers' salaries. . . . More than 1,000 Arizona citizens take part in the manhunt for the kidnapping of 6-year-old June Robles.		Secretaries Cordell Hull and Henry Wallace speak before the Senate of the necessity to approve the Reciprocity Tariff Bill.	A.G. McNish and G.R. Wait report at the annual meeting of the American Geophysical Union that they have found radium in thunderstorms.		Apr. 26
Bishop James Cannon is declared innocent of concealing campaign contributions in 1928. The Bishop had allegedly used money to campaign in Virginia and other southern states against Alfred E. Smith. . . . The American Federation of Labor announces that unemployment in March decreased from 11,467,000 to 10,905,000.	The NRA and the American Iron and Steel Institute will make a survey of the Steel Code, which expires on May 31, to devise possible changes.	Norman Davis, chief U.S. delegate to the Geneva Disarmament Conference, tells President Franklin Roosevelt and Secretary of State Cordell Hull that prospects for disarmament in Europe are very poor.		At New York's second Opera Ball, the Metropolitan Opera Association announces that a new season is assured.	Apr. 27

F	G	H	I	J
Includes elections, federal-state relations, civil rights and liberties, crime, the judiciary, education, healthcare, poverty, urban affairs, and population.	Includes formation and debate of U.S. foreign and defense policies, veterans affairs, and defense spending. (Relations with specific foreign countries are usually found under the region concerned.)	Includes business, labor, agriculture, taxation, transportation, consumer affairs, monetary and fiscal policy, natural resources, pollution, and accidents.	Includes worldwide scientific, medical, and technological developments, natural phenomena, U.S. weather, and natural disasters.	Includes the arts, religion, scholarship, communications media, sports, entertainment, fashions, fads, and social life.

	World Affairs	Europe	Africa & The Middle East	The Americas	Asia & The Pacific
Apr. 28		Italian King Victor Emanuel opens the 29th session of the Italian Parliament saying Italy hopes for a long period of peace and stability in Europe, adding that the best guarantee of peace comes from the efficiency of armed forces. . . . Former Austrian chancellor Otto Ender says the new constitution will not abolish democracy. . . . The German government suspends the publication of the leading Catholic daily *Koelnische Volkszeitung* for 10 days.		Bolivian President Salamanca visits his troops entrenched in the Las Conchitas sector of the Chaco region. He says Bolivia will fight until it wins the conflict.	
Apr. 29	Most of the countries involved in the production of rubber sign a five-year plan in London for the regulation and control of all rubber exports.	Two million Germans are expected to take part to the May Day demonstration, the biggest parade organized by the Nazis. . . . Riots break out in Mantes, near Paris, when the results of the local parliamentary by-election are announced. . . . Meetings of the fascist Blue Shirt movement cause widespread riots throughout the Irish Free State. . . . Socialist leaders announce large demonstrations in Spain for May Day against the new government.	The British government is planning to set up a Jewish colony in the Portuguese west African colony of Angola.		At the National Buddhist Convention in Hangchow, China, it is announced that the Panchen Lama, exiled former spiritual leader of Tibet, will return to his country. . . . Manuel Quezon, president of the Philippine Senate, returns to the Philippines from the United States, where he has been negotiating his country's independence. He receives an enthusiastic welcome.
Apr. 30		Prussian Premier Hermann Goering resigns as Minister of the Interior. Wilhelm Frick is appointed to the post. . . . The Austrian parliament approves the new constitution, which makes Premier Dollfuss a dictator and gives the government the functions of the parliament.		Cuba receives a loan from the Second Import-Export Bank of Washington. The loan is designed to stimulate foreign trade. . . . Thousands of Peruvians take part in the memorial service for former president Sanchez Cerro, who was killed a year ago.	The Philippines approve the Tydings-McDuffie Act, taking the first step toward the country's independence.
May 1		Violent riots break out in Paris between the police and Communist militants who are celebrating May Day. . . . In Berlin, a huge crowd of 2 million Germans gathers to hear Chancellor Adolf Hitler speak of how National Socialism is ennobling labor. . . . A huge demonstration of workers and an impressive military parade take place in Moscow under the eyes of Josef Stalin. . . . Prince von Starhemberg, leader of the Heimwehr, becomes Austrian vice chancellor.		The Colombian government issues a decree setting an eight-hour standard working day. . . . Soldiers fire against a May Day demonstration in Havana, wounding 10 people.	New Zealand announces a plan to increase its air forces as part of a general scheme to strengthen its defenses.
May 2		A former Polish army officer is arrested in France on espionage charges for the Reich. . . . The new Spanish Cabinet formed by Ricardo Samper gains the vote of confidence of the parliament. . . . France is forced to keep Russian exile Leon Trotsky as no other government will accept him.	The military forces of the Saudi Arabian Kingdom make important advances in the war against Yemen. The ruler of Yemen is reported dead as a revolt against him spreads in the capital of Sana.	The Supreme Court orders the indictment of Cuban army head, Col. Fulgencio Batista, on contempt of court charges for failing to hand over soldiers and army leaders to the court for prosecution.	Nationalist commander in chief Chiang Kai-shek orders the amassing of 1 million soldiers in the Kiangsi province as tensions rise in the Canton areas.
May 3		The president of the British Board of Trade, Walter Runciman, tells Japanese Ambassador Matsudaira that Britain will impose quotas to check the inflow of Japanese goods in British colonies. . . . Germany and Yugoslavia sign a trade treaty that is hailed as a decisive step in the economic cooperation between Germany and Danube countries. . . . The National Socialist government establishes the People's Court to try cases of treason.	It becomes increasingly apparent that Ibn Saud, ruler of the Saudi Arabian Kingdom, is fast completing his conquest of the Kingdom of Yemen. . . . Tel Aviv, the first entirely Jewish city in Palestine, celebrates the 25th anniversary of its founding.	Soldiers fire against students demonstrating against the death of a student who died after his arrest at a May Day demonstration. One person is killed and 15 wounded.	Baron Ikki, linked to the liberal spectrum of Japanese politics, is appointed to the presidency of the Privy Council, replacing the conservative Baron Kuratomi.
May 4	A committee of three people is named in Geneva to preside over the plebiscite that will decide the fate of the Saar Valley. The Saar, now a League of Nations protectorate, is disputed between Germany, to whom it belonged before the World War, and France.		The Palestinian government issues a £2 million loan that Britain will guarantee.	General Daltro, commanding the Second Military District at Sao Paolo, is exonerated by President Getulio Vargas on disloyalty charges.	Japanese Foreign Minster Hirota says his country will not enter any international parley on Far Eastern affairs, but that it is willing to meet with any nation individually. . . . Two hundred Soviet soldiers and 700 Mongol rebels are killed in an anti-Soviet uprising in Outer Mongolia, 70 miles from Urga.

A	B	C	D	E
Includes developments that affect more than one world region, international organizations, and important meetings of world leaders.	*Includes all domestic and regional developments in Europe, including the Soviet Union.*	*Includes all domestic and regional developments in Africa and the Middle East.*	*Includes all domestic and regional developments in Latin America, the Caribbean, and Canada.*	*Includes all domestic and regional developments in Asian and Pacific nations (and colonies).*

U.S. Politics & Social Issues	U.S. Foreign Policy & Defense	Economics & Great Depression	Science, Technology & Nature	Culture, Leisure & Lifestyle	
Joseph Choate, director of the Federal Alcohol Control Administration, denounces that bootlegging and illicit distilling are still widespread in the United States in spite of the end of Prohibition. . . . Police investigations link the kidnapping of Edward Bremer to the gang of John Dillinger. Chicago politician John McLaughlin is arrested in connection with the kidnapping.		The Senate Banking and Currency Committee approves Senator Glass's loan plan to extend the facilities of the Federal Reserve System to private industries.		The brown gelding Captain Kettle wins one of the most prestigious hunt racing prizes, the Maryland Cup.	Apr. 28
Brotherhood Day, sponsored by the National Conference of Jews and Christians, is celebrated throughout the United States. President Roosevelt, as well as other important politicians and personalities, asks Americans to overcome suspicion and prejudice against other faiths and religions.		The Durable Goods Industries Committee warns the National Recovery Administration against indiscriminate wage increases and reductions of working hours. . . . Former Republican Secretary of State Henry Stimson urges Congress to give President Roosevelt the authority to negotiate new tariffs with foreign countries. It is the first time a Republican leader publicly endorses an important Roosevelt policy.		Babe Ruth and Lou Gehrig lead the Yankees to victory against the Red Sox. . . . Veteran tennis player Walter Kinsella wins the first open court tournament held in the United States.	Apr. 29
William Green, president of the American Federation of Labor, asks President Roosevelt to set the standard workweek for all industries at 30 hours.	With an official note by the U.S. Ambassador in Japan, Joseph C. Grew, the United States takes a firm stand on China. The declaration calls for the observance of international rights and obligations in China.	The Treasury sets up a $2 billion stabilization fund to protect the value of the dollar abroad. . . . A study by the member organizations of the Chamber of Commerce of the United States reports widely differing views on the successes and failures of the NRA.			Apr. 30
President Franklin Roosevelt vetoes the Postal Wage Bill, which would have set minimum incomes for post-office substitute employees. . . . Five thousand Roman Catholics witness the consecration of Stephen Donahue to Auxiliary Bishop of New York. . . . Peaceful demonstrations for May Day take place throughout the United States.		New York Stock Exchange member firms and members operating as individuals show considerable profits from 1928–33 in spite of the economic depression. . . . The House rejects the 10 percent additional levy on individual tax returns that had been proposed by the Senate. . . . The Senate passes the Municipal Bankruptcy Bill. It allows insolvent cities to scale down their debts and refinance themselves in the next two years.			May 1
President Roosevelt says he will soon launch a housing program of unprecedented size that will be the next step in his recovery policy.		Gen. Hugh Johnson, NRA Administrator, announces a large public campaign to revive interest in code enforcement. He warns that public enthusiasm in the National Recovery Administration is waning.		The gold medal of the American Institute of Architects is awarded to Swedish architect Ragnar Ostberg. . . . Former Broadway and vaudeville star Stella Mayhew dies in New York. The stock exchange crash had left her penniless. . . . Col. John S. Hammond and a group of associates gain control of the famous sports arena Madison Square Garden.	May 2
Former Secretary of the Treasury William H. Woodin dies at 65. . . . Attorney General Cummings says the Department of Justice intends to use fast armored cars, special rifles, airplanes, and machine guns against crime. . . . Postmaster General James Farley announces the award of 15 temporary airmail contracts for three months.		The Senate gives up its amendment for a 10 percent additional levy on individual tax returns that the House had rejected. The tax bill goes to President Franklin Roosevelt for signing. . . . Before the Chamber of Commerce of the United States, President Roosevelt tells business interests that it is time to cooperate to advance national recovery.	A fierce fire breaks out at an old Brooklyn pier. Cargoes with a total value of $3 million are destroyed, and one man is killed. . . . William E. Boeing is awarded the Daniel Guggenheim Medal for his pioneering in aircraft manufacture and air transportation.	Vince Dundee successfully defends the world middleweight title against Al Diamond. . . . The U.S. fencing team retains the Robert M. Thompson International Trophy, beating Britain.	May 3
It is announced that some private operators such as United Airlines will resume carrying airmail within a week.	President Roosevelt announces that within two weeks he will send a message to Congress regarding the war debts owed by European countries to the United States.	The House passes the Stock Exchange Control Bill, which now goes to the Senate. . . . The closing session of the U.S. Chamber of Commerce criticizes some points of the government's economic recovery program, but avoids a complete condemnation. . . . In spite of Senator Long's obstructionism, the Senate passes the Corporate Bankruptcy Bill.		The American Artists Professional League complains to the Postmaster General about the inaccurate reproduction of Whistler's portrait of his mother on the new three-cent stamp.	May 4

F	G	H	I	J
Includes elections, federal-state relations, civil rights and liberties, crime, the judiciary, education, healthcare, poverty, urban affairs, and population.	Includes formation and debate of U.S. foreign and defense policies, veterans affairs, and defense spending. (Relations with specific foreign countries are usually found under the region concerned.)	Includes business, labor, agriculture, taxation, transportation, consumer affairs, monetary and fiscal policy, natural resources, pollution, and accidents.	Includes worldwide scientific, medical, and technological developments, natural phenomena, U.S. weather, and natural disasters.	Includes the arts, religion, scholarship, communications media, sports, entertainment, fashions, fads, and social life.

	World Affairs	Europe	Africa & The Middle East	The Americas	Asia & The Pacific
May 5	Western powers such as Italy and Great Britain consider with great anxiety Ibn Saud's advances in Yemen.	Two thousand Russian editors and newspaper writers gather for their national meeting. They firmly put the press to the service of the Revolution and the Soviet government. . . . Russia and Poland sign an extension of their nonaggression pact. . . . The first stone of the new Reichsbank building is laid in Berlin during an elaborate ceremony before a crowd of 10,000 Germans. . . . In Spain, a five-week general strike in Saragossa leads the city's industry to the verge of bankruptcy.		Argentine President Agustin Justo issues a decree that confirms the country's participation in the postal union of Spain and the Americas, thus reversing a previous decision. . . . In an attempt to sedate the disorder that is spreading throughout Cuba, prosecuting attorneys at Havana Courts say they will prosecute newspapers and journalists that publish news of an alarming nature.	The Filipino parliament votes for constitutional elections to take place on June 26. Women will not vote this time, but they will be enfranchised for future elections.
May 6		The Italian government announces it has increased the funds devoted to the improvement of the country's navy. . . . Several bombs explode in Vienna's most important railway stations. . . . Joseph Goebbels, Reich Minister for Propaganda, starts his campaign to win the plebiscite to return the Saar region to Germany. . . . The British King and Queen celebrate the 24th anniversary of the King's accession to the throne.	Saudi troops are pushing their way to the capital of Yemen, Sana, to complete their conquest of the country.	The Cuban government creates a bureau to control the press and censor newspapers.	The National Congress Party adopts a resolution to favor the repudiation of India's debt to the British. This is interpreted as a victory for the faction that favors complete independence of India from Britain.
May 7	Poland threatens to withdraw from the League of Nations to obtain the status of "Great Power" before Russia is admitted to the body.	The British government cuts Japanese cotton and rayon textile imports to its colonies by 57 percent. . . . Hungarian Premier Julius Goemboes says that his signing of the Rome Protocols should not be interpreted as a stance against Austro-German *anschluss*.	The army of the Imam of Yemen converges on the capital, Sana, to defend it from the steady advance of the Saudi Arabian army.	Argentine socialists attack the government for its foreign exchange and grain policies. . . . The Brazilian parliament starts to vote on the new constitution. . . . Paraguayans' efforts to advance in the Chaco area are rejected by Bolivians. The Paraguayan army is forced to withdraw, leaving behind more than 100 dead.	Admiral Matsushita, a high official of the Japanese army, says Japan is close in spirit to Germany.
May 8	Geoffrey Knonx, Saar Commissioner, warns the League of Nations Council that several reports describe a Nazi coup in the Saar region as likely. . . . Persia and China restore diplomatic relations after a break of 1,300 years.	Ehm Welk, an editor whose newspaper was suppressed by the Nazis for criticizing the Reich, is freed. . . . The British government says it will not formulate another disarmament proposal.		The Bolivian government announces it will not need to impose new taxes to finance the Chaco conflict thanks to the increase in the production of tin and other metals.	Governor General Frank Murphy informs the War Department that the government of the Philippines closes the fiscal year with a surplus of 500,000 pesos. The decline of the country's economy seems, thus, to have stopped. . . . Sir John Anderson, governor of Bengal, escapes assassination at the Lebong races.
May 9		The official Soviet newspaper, *Pravda*, accuses the widow of Lenin of depicting him as soft and sentimental in her memoirs. . . . The Soviet Union plans to settle 12,000 dispossessed Jews in the Far East in the province of Biro-Bidjan. . . . Italy reforms its economic organization, dividing its productive forces into 22 corporative groups gathered into three main classes. . . . The general strike of Saragossa, which started on April 4, ends, allowing 30,000 Spanish workers to return to work. . . . The budget of the Irish Free State shows a deficit of about £6 million.	A violent battle takes place between the Arabian and Yemeni armies in the region surrounding the Yemeni capital, Sana.		In an official note, Japan says it resents the British decision to cut Japanese cotton and rayon textile imports to its colonies by 57 percent.
May 10		Von Ribbentrop, Hitler's personal negotiator on rearmament, meets British Foreign Secretary John Simon, but fails to obtain his support for German rearmament. . . . The Soviet Commissar for War launches a campaign to intensify physical training in the Red Army.		Brazilian farmers attack a Japanese settlement, killing five and wounding 16. . . . The Chilean Fascist Party urges rejection of the extremist political and economic demands of the left. . . . Paraguay begins reprisals against Bolivian prisoners in retaliation for Bolivian air raids.	Chinese peasants revolt against Japanese authorities in northern Manchukuo. Three hundred Chinese are killed and several Japanese are wounded.
May 11	The League of Nations Chaco Commission makes public its report on the conflict between Bolivia and Paraguay. The war is described as futile and the two belligerents share responsibility for the conflict together with all the countries that sold them weapons and ammunitions. . . . Uruguay and Japan sign a trade treaty granting each other the most favorable conditions.	Alarmed by Germany's plans to enlarge its air corps, Britain prepares to strengthen its own aviation. . . . Reich Minister for Propaganda Goebbels threatens Jews, warning Germans will soon vent their rage against them. . . . About 100,000 people render homage to the body of Vyacheslaf Menjinsky, chief of the Soviet secret police, Ogpu.	The Palestinian government receives a £2 million loan from the British government to enable important public works.	An extradition warrant for murder is issued in the United States for Gen. Alberto Herrera, provisional Cuban president for a few hours after President Gerardo Machado's resignation. . . . Argentina refuses to join the international agreement to fix minimum wheat prices.	China feels oppressed by Japanese influence and may invoke the principles of the Nine-Power Treaty against the Japanese.

A	B	C	D	E
Includes developments that affect more than one world region, international organizations, and important meetings of world leaders.	*Includes all domestic and regional developments in Europe, including the Soviet Union.*	*Includes all domestic and regional developments in Africa and the Middle East.*	*Includes all domestic and regional developments in Latin America, the Caribbean, and Canada.*	*Includes all domestic and regional developments in Asian and Pacific nations (and colonies).*

U.S. Politics & Social Issues	U.S. Foreign Policy & Defense	Economics & Great Depression	Science, Technology & Nature	Culture, Leisure & Lifestyle	
President and Mrs. Roosevelt attend the funeral of former Secretary of the Treasury Woodin in New York. . . . New York City Controller W. Arthur Cunningham dies of a heart attack at 39. Democrats will try to fight for the vacant post, which would enable them to control the policy of Mayor Fiorello LaGuardia. . . . Friends of former president Herbert Hoover say he will not run for president in 1936. However, he intends to play an active part in the reorganization of the Republican Party.	Attorney General Homer Cummings rules that Finland, Great Britain, Czechoslovakia, Italy, Latvia, and Lithuania are not in default to the United States for their war debts obligations. On the contrary, the Soviet government is held in default.			Cavalcade wins the 60th running of the Kentucky Derby at Louisville before a record crowd of 60,000 spectators. . . . The Association of Motion Pictures Producers announces that it will ban movie stars from advertising wines, beers, and liqueurs.	May 5
Louis J. Moss, president of the United Synagogue of America, urges the members of the Jewish organization to support President Roosevelt and his New Deal.	The State Department instructs the U.S. Ambassador in Berlin to protest any discrimination toward American holders of German bonds that may result from the international conference on German debt in Berlin. . . . Soviet Ambassador Troyanovsky takes issue with the ruling of Attorney General Homer Cummings, who had faulted Russia for its war debts with the United States.	Twenty-eight prominent American industrialists join in a strong appeal for the modification of the Fletcher-Rayburn Bill on stock exchange control.		British Douglas Dexter wins the U.S. outdoor fencing title.	May 6
After two years of exile abroad, Samuel Insull, a Chicago speculator charged with fraud, returns to the United States and faces trial. . . . New York Governor Herbert Lehman urges city planning that decentralizes factories and industries to encourage decentralization of urban populations.		The National Recovery Administration decides to impose a complete code on the telegraph industry. . . . The Senate and House Banking Committees approve plans to loan more than $500 million to industry.	A forest fire burns over an area of 10 miles from early afternoon until midnight in the state of New York.	Pulitzer Prize winners for 1933 are announced at Columbia University. Caroline Miller wins for her novel, Lamb in His Bosom, and Sidney Kingsley for his play, Men in White. . . . Actress Jean Harlow separates from her husband, cameraman Hal G. Rosson.	May 7
A gang armed with machine guns raids a Brooklyn branch of the Prudential Savings Bank, escaping with $22,939. . . . Samuel Insull is put in jail when he is unable to pay the $200,000 bail set by the court. Insull's bail is the highest set by a Chicago federal court. . . . Former Secretary of the Treasury Andrew Mellon is cleared by a federal grand jury of tax-evasion charges.		Amendments designed to lessen the penalties provided in the Stock Exchange Control Bill are rejected by the Senate.		Dr. Theodor Lewald, German representative on the Olympic Executive Committee, confirms that Germany will not discriminate against Jewish athletes at the 1936 Olympic Games. . . . Walt Disney receives the gold medal of the American Art Dealers' Association for his service to American art. . . . Actress Katharine Hepburn obtains a divorce from her husband, Ludlow Smith, in a Mexican court.	May 8
New York Mayor LaGuardia appoints Joseph McGoldrick as Controller of the city. McGoldrick is hostile to Tammany Hall.	President Roosevelt does not rule out a possible agreement with war-debtor nations for the upcoming June payments. At the same time, he does not object to Congress's policy of not accepting token payments any longer.	President Roosevelt signs the Costigan-Jones Bill, which puts the production of sugar under federal control. The duty on imported sugar is reduced by 25 percent.	Large forest fires spring up again across New Jersey and in eastern parts of Long Island.	In the baseball championship, the St. Louis Browns break the string of successes of the Yankees, beating them 9–8.	May 9
Retired oil millionaire William F. Gettle is kidnapped during a party in California. . . . The Senate passes a bill, already approved by the House, removing all discriminatory measures against women in the nationality laws.	The State Department informs war-debtor countries that token payments will be accepted for the June repayment installment. Yet, they will not be enough to prevent the countries from being considered in default according to terms of the Johnson Act approved by the Senate.			The New York Yankees inflict an overwhelming defeat on the Chicago White Sox.	May 10
President Roosevelt denies attempts to curtail the freedom of the press and praises the work of journalists in helping national recovery. . . . Two different ransom demands are received by the family of oil millionaire William Gettle. . . . Samuel Insull, detained in a Chicago jail for fraud, pays his bail and is released.	American manufacturers of plane engines and aircraft say there has been a considerable increase in their exports to Germany in the last few months. However, they stress, aviation products were exported mainly for commercial reasons, not military ones. . . . President Roosevelt opposes a general conference with war-debtor nations. He urges treating each case individually.		An estimated 330 million tons of dust, the topsoil in the valleys of the Missouri and Mississippi rivers, are swept over half of the United States by a strong northeastern wind. New York is covered by a vast dust cloud for five hours.	The United States Walker Cup golf team gains an unexpected lead over the British team.	May 11

F	G	H	I	J
Includes elections, federal-state relations, civil rights and liberties, crime, the judiciary, education, healthcare, poverty, urban affairs, and population.	Includes formation and debate of U.S. foreign and defense policies, veterans affairs, and defense spending. (Relations with specific foreign countries are usually found under the region concerned.)	Includes business, labor, agriculture, taxation, transportation, consumer affairs, monetary and fiscal policy, natural resources, pollution, and accidents.	Includes worldwide scientific, medical, and technological developments, natural phenomena, U.S. weather, and natural disasters.	Includes the arts, religion, scholarship, communications media, sports, entertainment, fashions, fads, and social life.

	World Affairs	Europe	Africa & The Middle East	The Americas	Asia & The Pacific
May 12	The League of Nations Chaco Commission pleads to the nations of the world to help end the Chaco conflict by stopping arms sales to Paraguay and Bolivia. . . . The League of Nations announces that Hungary has issued a request asking for a board to investigate Yugoslav frontier killings.	The British government says it will reconsider its policy of war-debt repayments. . . . The French Radical Socialist Party assures its collaboration with the Doumergue government in its conference. . . . The Lapua Movement, the Finnish Fascist Party, is dissolved by court decision.		Paraguayans attack Bolivian positions in the Chaco region with their bombardment planes.	Japan says it will continue to observe the League of Nations Covenant in its administration of the Caroline and Marshall Islands.
May 13	The Reich Debt Conference in Berlin is deadlocked over disagreements between the British and American delegations.	Before a huge crowd of supporters, the president of the Irish Free State Eamon De Valera says he is ready to enter an economic agreement with Great Britain. . . . A large demonstration takes place in Paris to honor the day of Joan of Arc. . . . Leon Koslowski is appointed Polish prime minister.	Spain reports that North African rebels in the Ifni area have been completely disarmed without difficulties. . . . An armistice is announced in the war between Saudi Arabia and Yemen. Yemen will either be annexed or retain virtual independence under Saudi rule.	The opposition condemns as farcical the Dominican elections in which current President Trujillo is the sole candidate. . . . Peruvian Premier Aguero resigns after the National Assembly passes the divorce law.	The Communist army led by Gen. Ho Lung makes important advances in the Szechwan province and kidnaps two missionaries.
May 14	The League of Nations Council starts its 79th session in Geneva.	Eight trade agreements are signed in Rome between Hungary, Italy, and Austria to put into effect the Rome protocols signed in March. . . . French Premier Doumergue says France will not make any steps toward war against other countries. He stresses that France is disarming while other countries are rearming. . . . The Bulgarian government resigns due to the withdrawal of the Agrarian Party from the Cabinet when its demand for more ministers is rejected.	Twenty people are killed in the area of Tiberias due to violent rain and hail storms. . . . After the armistice, Yemen accepts the peace proposals of Saudi Arabian King Ibn Saud.	The Foreign Offices of the ABC-Peru entente (Argentina, Brazil, Chile, and Peru) are drafting a new peace proposal for the resolution of the Chaco War. The League of Nations is criticized for its inaction.	
May 15	The League of Nations establishes a plebiscite commission and a plebiscite tribunal to control the Saar. The region will decide whether to return to Germany. . . . The Permanent Court of International Justice opens its 32nd (extraordinary) session in The Hague.	The German government restricts the freedom of movement of peasants who intend to seek jobs in urban areas. . . . Negotiations between the German government and delegates of Catholic bishops are delayed until the next month.	More floods hit the area of Tiberias, though no additional casualties are reported.	Bolivia bombs three Paraguayan towns.	The Japanese government instructs its Ambassador in London to protest officially against the decision to impose quotas on Japanese goods sold to British colonies.
May 16	Delegates at the forthcoming League of Nations disarmament conference in Geneva show little hope of reaching an agreement.	Josef Stalin signs a decree establishing the teaching of history and geography in Soviet primary and secondary schools for the first time. . . . The Latvian government declares martial law to prevent disorder from radicals. Prime Minister Ulmanis becomes a virtual dictator. . . . The British parliament blocks the introduction of a bill against the use of military uniforms for political purposes. The bill was designed against the fascist movement of the Black Shirts. . . . The Archbishop of Canterbury protests German anti-Semitism.		Colombia objects to the agreement for the Leticia dispute worked out by Brazil. Peru, on the contrary, fully accepts the proposal.	Hiroshi Saito, Japanese Ambassador to the United States, denies that Japan wants to trespass upon the rights of other powers in China.
May 17	Great Britain urges the League of Nations to resume negotiations for an arms embargo against Bolivia and Paraguay to end the Chaco War.	Statistics of the Central German Bank show a continuous decrease of German foreign trade.		Rafael Trujillo is reelected president of the Dominican Republic.	Japan will ask for a revision of the navy-ratio principle at the international conference in 1935. It will ask for the reduction of U.S strength in certain types of ships, particularly aircraft carriers.
May 18	The League of Nations announces that its jurists have devised a legal formula to prohibit the sale of arms to Bolivia and Paraguay, the belligerent nations in the Chaco conflict. . . . Foreign Soviet Commissar Litvinoff has a series of meetings in Geneva regarding the Soviet Union's entry into the League of Nations.	Der Angriff, the official organ of German propaganda, says only Nazis have the right to free speech in the Reich. All critics, it is threatened, should remain silent. . . . Great Britain expresses pessimism over the disarmament conference to take place in Geneva and says it is getting ready for a new war. . . . The French parliament rejects a Socialist motion against the Doumergue government by a large majority.	A peace conference between the delegates of Saudi Arabia and Yemen opens at Taif in Arabia.	The Argentine Senate votes in favor of keeping emergency rule until July 15 to stop demonstrations and disorder by radical militants. . . . Former Cuban president Ramon Grau comes back to Cuba and is cheered by a crowd of 20,000.	
May 19	Britain suggests the League of Nations should consider the expulsion of Liberia for its treatment of native populations such as the Kroos.	A military coup establishes a fascist regime in Bulgaria. Kimon Gueorguieff is the new premier. . . . Italian Premier Benito Mussolini and German Chancellor Adolf Hitler's personal representative for the disarmament question try to agree on a common disarmament proposal. . . . The Reich refuses radio broadcast of the Pentecost sermon of the Berlin Catholic Bishop.		The fiercest battle in the Chaco War, involving more than 60,000 people, takes place. A great number of casualties are reported on both sides. . . . Peru and Colombia reach a peaceful settlement for the Leticia controversy. Both nations will observe all existing treaties. . . . Former Cuban president Ramon Grau blames his fall on former American ambassador Sumner Welles. Grau says he is ready to serve again as president if the people of Cuba ask him to.	The Japanese Vice Minister of Finances, Hideo Kuroda, is arrested for a financial scandal involving the selling of stocks under market value with official connivance.

A	B	C	D	E
Includes developments that affect more than one world region, international organizations, and important meetings of world leaders.	*Includes all domestic and regional developments in Europe, including the Soviet Union.*	*Includes all domestic and regional developments in Africa and the Middle East.*	*Includes all domestic and regional developments in Latin America, the Caribbean, and Canada.*	*Includes all domestic and regional developments in Asian and Pacific nations (and colonies).*

U.S. Politics & Social Issues	U.S. Foreign Policy & Defense	Economics & Great Depression	Science, Technology & Nature	Culture, Leisure & Lifestyle	
The lawyer of oil millionaire William Gettle reports a first contact with the kidnappers. . . . The International Longshoremen's Association calls a strike that involves 10,000–15,000 workers.		The Senate approves the Fletcher-Rayburn Stock Exchange Bill, which goes to conference for decisions on the differences between the House and Senate bills. . . . James M. Cox, Democratic presidential candidate in 1920, defends Roosevelt's New Deal, stating it aims to recreate a stable social order.	The Federal Relief Administration and the Farm Administration survey the damages of prolonged drought in midwestern areas. The drought has damaged crops.	Mother's Day is celebrated throughout the United States. . . . Winnie the Pooh, the famous bear for whom A. A. Milne named his children's book, dies in the London Zoo at 20 years of age. . . . The United States golf team wins the Walker Cup for the eighth time in a row.	May 12
Four district leaders announce they will run for the leadership of Tammany Hall. . . . Labor strikes in different industries spread throughout the United States, pointing to the rise of a mass movement for labor organization. . . . New York Governor Herbert Lehman legalizes the sale of hard liquors in bars from July 1.			The National Forest Reservation Commission plans to acquire more than 3 million acres for the federal domain. . . . A violent rain and hail storm on the Serra da Estrella, Portugal's highest mountain ridge, leaves more than 2,000 peasants homeless.	Charles Johnson, an amateur, wins the seventh annual outboard marathon on the Hudson from Albany to New York.	May 13
Millionaire William Gettle and six-year-old June Robles are found alive and rescued from their kidnappers.		President Roosevelt sends Congress a message illustrating his program for house construction and renovation, his latest incentive to economic recovery. . . . The Senate approves the Glass-Barley bill, which provides loans for business enterprises.	George Pond and Cesare Sabelli start a transatlantic flight from New York to Rome in their monoplane.	The U.S. Davis Cup team, which will play against Canada at the end of May, is named.	May 14
The kidnappers of millionaire William Gettle are sentenced to life imprisonment only 24 hours after their arrest. . . . William P. Kenneally is named provisional leader of Tammany Hall. . . . The Senate approves six anti-crime bills.	After a meeting with President Roosevelt, Norman H. Davis announces he will represent the United States at the next disarmament conference in Geneva at the end of May.	President Roosevelt sends a message to Congress asking that relief funds be limited to the amount of $3.1 billion as fixed in January so that a balanced budget can be reached in 1936. . . . An address by Eleanor Roosevelt at the Waldorf-Astoria, the cotton garment industry adopts an NRA code.	George Pond and Cesare Sabelli are forced to land near Dublin during their transatlantic flight to Rome.		May 15
A nationwide poll shows a 2 to 1 approval of President Roosevelt's policies.	The Senate Foreign Relations Committee hears the opinion of politicians and diplomats against the joining of the United States to the International Court of Permanent Justice.	The leaders of the Senate group that favors the nationalization of silver accept President Roosevelt's offer that leaves to the President's discretion the time and manner in which this should be done. . . . The annual conference of the National Association of Mutual Savings Banks approves a statement that praises the New Deal but asks for a return to greater private initiative.			May 16
Twenty thousand Nazi sympathizers gather in Madison Square Garden to defend Hitler's policies and denounce the Jewish boycott of Germany.		Republican Senator William E. Borah denounces President Roosevelt's reciprocal tariffs program as yet another step away from constitutional democracy.	The midtown Hudson Tunnel, which will cost $37 million and will link Manhattan to New Jersey, is inaugurated.	North Carolina is the fourth state to obtain federal funds for its symphony orchestra. . . . The Long Island golf team wins for the second consecutive year the Golf Illustrated Trophy.	May 17
Signing six anti-crime bills, President Franklin Roosevelt denounces the romanticizing of crime and the toleration of known criminals. . . . President Roosevelt supports the changes to the Agriculture Adjustment Act proposed by Secretary of Agriculture Henry Wallace. According to these changes, Wallace would have the power to control through licenses the producers and handlers of food products.	With specific reference to the Chaco War, President Roosevelt urges international action to limit the traffic of arms. A resolution is introduced in the Senate empowering the President to prohibit the sale of arms to Paraguay and Bolivia to stop the Chaco conflict.	Gen. Hugh Johnson confirms the continuation of his campaign to obtain a 10 percent cut in working hours and a corresponding 10 percent rise in salaries to revive the National Recovery Administration.	The Pullman Car and Manufacturing Corporation presents new types of high-speed subway cars.		May 18
Senator LaFollette and his followers found the Progressive Party in Wisconsin. . . . Former Republican Secretary of the Treasury Ogden L. Mills attacks Roosevelt's New Deal, charging it wants to achieve "the regimentation of the American people."	Secretary of State Cordell Hull hopes an international arms embargo against Bolivia and Paraguay will soon be established.		A large fire, described as the worst since 1871, breaks out in Chicago's stockyards, causing damages of $10 million.	Yale varsity rowing crew wins the Carnegie Cup.	May 19

F	G	H	I	J
Includes elections, federal-state relations, civil rights and liberties, crime, the judiciary, education, healthcare, poverty, urban affairs, and population.	Includes formation and debate of U.S. foreign and defense policies, veterans affairs, and defense spending. (Relations with specific foreign countries are usually found under the region concerned.)	Includes business, labor, agriculture, taxation, transportation, consumer affairs, monetary and fiscal policy, natural resources, pollution, and accidents.	Includes worldwide scientific, medical, and technological developments, natural phenomena, U.S. weather, and natural disasters.	Includes the arts, religion, scholarship, communications media, sports, entertainment, fashions, fads, and social life.

	World Affairs	Europe	Africa & The Middle East	The Americas	Asia & The Pacific
May 20	Pope Pius canonizes the German Capuchin monk Conrad of Parzham. He admonishes against a revival of paganism in Germany. . . . Japan and Germany are seen in diplomatic circles as increasingly close to each other.	The new Bulgarian government announces it will divide Macedonia so as to restore good relationships with Yugoslavia. Bulgarian Premier Gueorguieff announces he is ready to sign nonaggression pacts with all Balkan states.		Paraguayan soldiers reject a Bolivian counter-attack near Fort Ballivian. . . . Military displays and parades take place throughout Cuba to celebrate the 32nd anniversary of Cuban independence.	The Japanese government orders all governors to exercise vigilance over members of patriotic society. It is feared that the new financial scandal involving the government may lead to renewed right-wing disorders.
May 21		Great Britain voices its concerns over the Japanese decision to abandon the ratio principle at the next naval conference in 1935. . . . The new Bulgarian government is accepted by the people without public disturbances. . . . The Austrian government orders the release of all but two prominent Socialist leaders under arrest since the February riots.		Violent clashes between the Paraguayan and the Bolivian armies continue in the Chaco conflict. . . . El Salvador is the second state after Japan to recognize the state of Manchukuo. . . . Governor Calles of the State of Sonora, Mexico, closes all Catholic churches in his state.	
May 22	League of Nations officials condemn the recognition of Manchukuo by El Salvador.	Belgrade students are forced by the police to leave the university, which they had occupied two days before. . . . Diplomatic relationships between France and Russia are increasingly marked by military cooperation.		The Cuban Cabinet prohibits the exportation of gold and orders the treasury department to call in all Cuban gold coinage to reduce its gold content. . . . Mexico is the first country to bar the shipment of arms to Paraguay and Bolivia, the two countries engaged in the Chaco War.	Japanese political circles believe that the government led by Viscount Saito will be brought down by the latest financial scandal. The rising star of Japanese politics is the liberal Gen. Issei Ugaki.
May 23		All of the important leaders of the Macedonian revolutionary movement are arrested except Vantcho Mikhailoff.	A general strike of Jews in Palestine leads to violent clashes between strikers and the police. The strike is called to protest the limitation on Jewish immigration.	The Bolivian High Command reports a crushing defeat of the Paraguayan army in a violent battle of the Chaco conflict.	An 11th-century city is discovered in the Cambodian jungle. The city dates back to the Khmer civilization.
May 24	The League of Nations holds a conference of academics in Paris to promote peaceful international relationships.	Leading personalities of the Stahlhelm (German League of Front Soldiers) are arrested throughout the country for discouraging members of their organization to join the storm troop. . . . Archduke Eugene of Hapsburg goes back to Austria after 15 years in exile. . . . Thomas Masaryk is reelected president of Czechoslovakia for the third time.		Bolivian authorities report a complete rout of the Paraguayan army in a counter-offense in the Chaco War. Six thousand Paraguayans are said to have been killed.	
May 25	In addition to the United States, the British government invites Japan, Italy, and France to bilateral talks on naval problems preliminary to the 1935 conference. . . . A report to the League of Nations opium advisory committee describes Bulgaria as the center of the illicit traffic of narcotics.	The Irish Dail (lower chamber) passes a bill to abolish the Senate. . . . French Foreign Minister Barthou promises that his country will always be committed to peace.		Paraguay launches another offensive in the Las Conchitas section of the Chaco region.	
May 26		Italian Premier Benito Mussolini says the country will strengthen its naval and air fleets. . . . France and Russia agree on technical cooperation between their military forces. . . . The leading organ of German propaganda, Der Angriff, bitterly attacks German intellectuals for their criticism of the Reich. . . . The French Cinema Owners Association requests that more American films be shown in France.		Reports from Cuba expose plots to kill U.S. envoy Jefferson Caffrey. . . . Heavy rains and floods extend from northern to southern Chile, affecting Santiago and other large urban areas. Thousands of people are made homeless. . . . Peruvian President Oscar Benavides orders the release of all political prisoners to celebrate the signing of the Leticia peace agreement with Colombia.	Japan demands that the naval conference of 1935 be limited to naval issues and exclude talk of Far Eastern politics.
May 27	France and Great Britain plan a joint session with U.S. representatives on their war-debt payments.	Turkey plans to ask for the remilitarization of the Dardanelles for the country's more effective defense. . . . Italy announces the construction of three battleships by 1940 for a total cost of $85 million. . . . Germany is concerned over the military cooperation between France and Russia.		Gunmen fire several shots against the home of the U.S. envoy in Cuba, Jefferson Caffrey. . . . The Bolivian army reports more military gains in the Chaco area.	The central Chinese government prepares an ambitious military expedition to bring the Sinkiang province completely under its control.
May 28		The Reich imposes a further reduction on imports as a result of its shrinking export trade. . . . Official Soviet press approves Russia's likely entrance to the League of Nations. . . . In the first demonstration after the establishment of the dictatorship, 20 Macedonians are arrested in Sofia, Bulgaria.		Four Cuban terrorists attack the car of H. Freeman Matthews, First Secretary of the U.S. Embassy. . . . Brazilian President Getulio Vargas concedes a general amnesty for all political prisoners and refugees.	

A	B	C	D	E
Includes developments that affect more than one world region, international organizations, and important meetings of world leaders.	Includes all domestic and regional developments in Europe, including the Soviet Union.	Includes all domestic and regional developments in Africa and the Middle East.	Includes all domestic and regional developments in Latin America, the Caribbean, and Canada.	Includes all domestic and regional developments in Asian and Pacific nations (and colonies).

U.S. Politics & Social Issues	U.S. Foreign Policy & Defense	Economics & Great Depression	Science, Technology & Nature	Culture, Leisure & Lifestyle	
President Roosevelt, his Cabinet, the Supreme Court, and the diplomatic corps all celebrate the centenary of the Marquis De Lafayette's death.		The Darrow report on the National Recovery Administration is made public. The report criticizes the NRA, finding that its codes lead toward monopoly and damage small businesses.			May 20
Sixteen policemen and 19 strikers are injured in a violent riot in Minneapolis in connection with a truck drivers' strike. . . . Socialist leader Norman Thomas is arrested in Taylorville, Ill., as he tries to speak without the permission of city officials. . . . The Senate votes 42–24 to abolish the electoral college, but the constitutional amendment does not reach the required two-thirds.	President Franklin Roosevelt expects both the House and the Senate to approve the arms embargo against Bolivia and Paraguay within the week.	Gen. Hugh Johnson, NRA Administrator, finds the criticism of the NRA in the Darrow report unjustified. . . . Republican Senators propose a large series of amendments to President Roosevelt's reciprocal trade agreements bill, which make it inoperative.		Vassar College lifts its ban on married students.	May 21
The Regional Labor Board orders the end of the truck drivers' strike after the violent riots in Minneapolis. . . . For the second consecutive time, the constitutional amendment to abolish the electoral college does not obtain the necessary two-thirds of the Senate to be approved.	The House Committee on Foreign Affairs reports favorably on the administration's resolution to empower the President to prohibit the sale of arms to Paraguay and Bolivia, the belligerent states in the Chaco conflict.	The NRA approves the limitation of the cotton textile industry machineries to 75 percent of the maximum hours for 12 weeks. . . . President Roosevelt proposes legislation to Congress to increase the use of silver in monetary stocks.	Maritime Day is observed throughout the United States. It marks the 115th anniversary of the sailing of the *Savannah*, the first American steamship to cross the Atlantic.		May 22
Gangsters Clyde Barrow and Bonnie Parker are killed in Louisiana in a police ambush. . . . Seven hundred National Guardsmen are employed in Toledo to control the riots between strikers and workers at the Electric Auto-Lite Company plant.	The House approves the arms embargo against Paraguay and Bolivia.	The House passes the Direct Loans to Industry Bill which provides for $440 million in loans to small businesses. . . . The NRA Advisory Board condemns the Darrow report and asks for its termination through an Executive Order of the President.			May 23
National Guardsmen open fire against strikers in Toledo, Ohio: Two are killed, 25 injured. . . . The United States is the first country in the world to ratify an international agreement that guarantees equal nationality rights to men and women.	The United States and Britain start formal talks for a preliminary agreement on naval issues before the 1935 international conference. . . . The Senate approves the arms embargo against Paraguay and Bolivia.			The United States beats Canada in the first two Davis Cup tennis matches.	May 24
Prompted by the eruption of major strikes and violent riots, the Senate Committee on Education and Labor approves a revised version of the Wagner Bill. . . . Violent riots continue in Toledo as strikers reject compromise.	Soviet Ambassador Troyanovsky voices his hope that the Soviet Union and the United States may find common ground to secure complete or partial disarmament.	Gen. Hugh Johnson, NRA Administrator, invites all members of his organization who are dissatisfied to resign without waiting for the adjournment of Congress.	At the conference of the American Urological Association, Dr. George Smith reports that a diseased bladder can be removed and the patient can continue to live.	The Metropolitan Opera Association announces that its new season will open on December 24.	May 25
More than 600 radicals protest against New York's system of home and work relief. . . . Riots continue in Toledo, although some progress is made at the negotiations for a settlement.		Complete agreement between the Senate and the House on the Stock Exchange Regulation Bill is reached. A new agency called the Securities and Exchange Commission will regulate the stock market.	Burlington's streamlined train, the *Zephyr*, opens a new era in railroad transportation. Its first journey from Denver to Chicago is the longest and the fastest in the history of the railroad. . . . French pilots Maurice Rossi and Paul Codos attempt a nonstop flight from Paris to San Diego, in an effort to beat their own previous record from New York to Syria.	The U.S. Davis Cup tennis team defeats Canada and qualifies to meet Mexico in the final round of the American zone. . . . A renovated and improved Century of Progress exposition opens in Chicago.	May 26
Rioting ceases in Toledo as federal mediators work on a settlement for the automotive strike.		An executive order by President Franklin Roosevelt exempts the service industries from some of the fair trade practices of NRA codes. The exemption does not apply to minimum wages, maximum working hours, child labor, and collective bargaining.	French pilots Maurice Rossi and Paul Codos are confident they will succeed in the Paris-San Diego non-stop flight in spite of adverse weather conditions.	The U.S. soccer team is eliminated by Italy from the world football championship.	May 27
In San Francisco, striking longshoremen violently clash with the police.	President Roosevelt prohibits the sale of arms to Bolivia and Paraguay in an attempt to stop the Chaco War.	President Roosevelt urges Congress to reconsider the tax on coconut oil, as this violates the Philippines Independence Act. . . . Following the President's executive order, Gen. Hugh Johnson exempts seven industries from the fair trade practices of their codes.	French pilots Maurice Rossi and Paul Codos are forced to land at Floyd Bennett Field because of structural problems with their plane.	Barney Ross captures the welterweight boxing title, defeating Jimmy McLarnin at the Madison Square Garden Bowl. . . . Ellsworth Vines wins the first eastern professional tennis championship.	May 28

F	G	H	I	J
Includes elections, federal-state relations, civil rights and liberties, crime, the judiciary, education, healthcare, poverty, urban affairs, and population.	Includes formation and debate of U.S. foreign and defense policies, veterans affairs, and defense spending. (Relations with specific foreign countries are usually found under the region concerned.)	Includes business, labor, agriculture, taxation, transportation, consumer affairs, monetary and fiscal policy, natural resources, pollution, and accidents.	Includes worldwide scientific, medical, and technological developments, natural phenomena, U.S. weather, and natural disasters.	Includes the arts, religion, scholarship, communications media, sports, entertainment, fashions, fads, and social life.

	World Affairs	Europe	Africa & The Middle East	The Americas	Asia & The Pacific
May 29	The League of Nations disarmament conference opens in Geneva. . . . The German debt conference ends in Berlin with a compromise that does not completely satisfy either Germany or its creditors.	The issue of the payment of war debts to the United States causes the first serious rift within the French government.		A new violent tornado hits the Chilean coast, causing more damages. . . . Cubans celebrate the abrogation of the Platt Amendment and their country's complete independence.	Japanese Admiral Heihachiro Togo, the hero of the Russo-Japanese conflict, dies at 86 of throat cancer.
May 30	Britain and France clash at the Geneva disarmament conference over the Reich rearming.	The Irish Senate strongly protests the Abolition Bill, which should eliminate the upper chamber of the Irish Free State. . . . Opponents of the policies of Reich Bishop Ludwig Mueller gather in a free synod in Westphalia.		President Herrera changes the Colombian government, naming five liberals and four conservatives.	Nanking and Canton military forces join in an action against Communist rebels along the Fukien-Kiangsi border. . . . Kusho Lungshar, former commander in chief of Tibet and a favorite of the Dalai Lama, is killed for plotting against the prime minister.
May 31		The Polish government is disturbed by the gains of the Nationalists in the municipal elections. Several big urban centers, such as Lodz, are taken by the Nationalist opposition, whose campaign was built on anti-Semitism. . . . The founding family of the *Frankfurter Zeitung*, the last of Germany's liberal newspapers, relinquishes control on the daily. . . . The French Chamber of Deputies rejects a motion for the dissolution of parliament and the calling of new elections.		Bolivia invokes the intervention of the League of Nations Council in the Chaco War in an attempt to delay the proposed arms embargo.	
Jun. 1	The League of Nations Council will examine again the Chaco conflict between Bolivia and Paraguay. . . . France, Germany, and the League of Nations agree on voting procedures for the Saar plebiscite scheduled for January 13.	The Reich Free Synod that gathered in Westphalia decrees its independence from the rule of Reichbishop Ludwig Mueller. His positions, including anti-Semitism, are condemned by the free synod. . . . An additional sum of 3 billion francs is voted by the French parliament for military expenses.		After the abrogation of the Platt Amendment in Cuba, Panama expects the United States will give up its right of intervention in Panama too.	The peasant uprising in the Ilan province in northeastern Manchuria is subdued only after the killing of 2,000 Chinese.
Jun. 2	Delegates from 39 nations sign an international agreement in London to protect trademarks, patents, and copyrights.	France and Britain are disappointed by President Franklin Roosevelt's message on war debts, as he did not specify whether another token payment would absolve both nations from a default.		The Mexican National Labor Chamber plans a general strike in support of the strikers at the Eagle Oil Company. . . . Bolivians report a huge arms seizure in the Chaco conflict. They also say Paraguay has lost two-thirds of its soldiers in battle.	
Jun. 3		The British King, George V, celebrates his 69th birthday with a quiet family gathering at Buckingham Palace.		Negotiations are carried out within the Cuban Cabinet to dissuade those ministers who intend to resign because of conflicts between military and civil authorities.	
Jun. 4	The 18th session of the International Labor Conference opens in Geneva. . . . The Council of the League of Nations adopts the report of its Saar committee, which lays down the rules for the plebiscite.	Britain announces it will stop paying its war debts to the United States pending a revision of its debt situation.		The Argentine government expresses its satisfaction with the U.S. decision to cancel the Platt Amendment, thus granting Cuba full independence.	A violent election campaign ends in the Philippines. The two major groups are led by Senator Manuel Quezon and Sergio Osmena-Manuel Roxas.
Jun. 5	Arthur Henderson, president of the World Disarmament Conference in Geneva, threatens to resign following a bitter attack by French Foreign Minister Barthou.	The House of Commons supports the decision of the British government not to pay anything on the war debt to the United States. . . . Communist leader Josef Stalin issues a decree reorganizing the Russian railways, which he says are still the greatest handicap to Russian industry.		The Cuban government approves a further 90-day extension of military rule. All constitutional rights are suspended.	The first electoral results in the Philippines assign the Senate to the faction led by Quezon, but the House to Roxas.

A	B	C	D	E
Includes developments that affect more than one world region, international organizations, and important meetings of world leaders.	Includes all domestic and regional developments in Europe, including the Soviet Union.	Includes all domestic and regional developments in Africa and the Middle East.	Includes all domestic and regional developments in Latin America, the Caribbean, and Canada.	Includes all domestic and regional developments in Asian and Pacific nations (and colonies).

U.S. Politics & Social Issues	U.S. Foreign Policy & Defense	Economics & Great Depression	Science, Technology & Nature	Culture, Leisure & Lifestyle	
Negotiations with strikers fail in Toledo. The units of the American Federation of Labor get ready for a general strike.	The United States and Cuba sign a treaty abrogating the Platt Amendment. The treaty assures Cuba complete independence from the United States, which only retains the naval base at Guantanamo.	A Delaware federal district court refuses to issue a preliminary injunction to restrain the Weirton Steel Company from interfering with the independent election of a spokesman for collective bargaining. This is a setback for the government, the NRA, and organized labor.			May 29
New labor disputes arise across the nation. Cotton textile workers threaten a general strike, and unionists in the steel industry criticize the changes made to their code.... In his speech at the Gettysburg battlefield, President Franklin Roosevelt hails the new unity among American citizens.... The majority of Republican members of Congress is in favor of the election of a party chairman from the liberal wing of the party.	Veterans of different wars parade in New York to commemorate their fallen comrades.			Fox Film Corporation announces its productions for the 1934–35 season. Its most ambitious projects include the filming of Dante's *Inferno* and Sinclair Lewis's *Work of Art*.... Bill Cummings wins the 500-mile Indianapolis automobile race.... The U.S. Davis Cup team wins the first two matches against Mexico in the American zone final.	May 30
Toledo's labor unions ask President Franklin Roosevelt to intervene directly to avert their general strike.	President Franklin Roosevelt reviews the U.S. fleet as it makes its entrance into New York Harbor.... The Senate approves the treaty between the United States and Cuba, which cancels the Platt Amendment.	Gen. Hugh Johnson starts talks to avoid the threatened strikes in the steel and textile industries.... In light of the severe drought that has badly affected many states, the Agricultural Adjustment Administration considers revising its policy on production curtailment.	Dr. Looney and Dr. Hoskins report at the annual meeting of the American Psychiatric Association that they are testing a new drug for the treatment of schizophrenia that stimulates the oxidative processes.	Actor Lew Cody, the star of many silent films, dies in his sleep in Los Angeles.... The U.S. Davis Cup team wins the American zone series.	May 31
A number of distillers and manufacturers of bottles ask the Federal Alcohol Control Commission for direct governmental control of liquor production in an attempt to diminish the sale of illicit liquor.... The National Convention of the Socialist Party in Detroit votes down by a narrow margin a resolution calling for revolution and the dictatorship of the proletariat.... In Toledo, the possibility of a general strike seems to lose ground as electric workers get a salary increase and union status.	In a message to Congress, President Franklin Roosevelt confirms that he is against a general parley on war debts and that the case of each nation should be treated separately.	Harry L. Hopkins, Relief Administrator, allocates a preliminary sum of $5,476,000 for farmers damaged by the worst drought in American history.... Congress approves the Fletcher-Rayburn Bill for Stock Exchange Control in its final form.		Important personalities in the U.S. diplomatic, political, and social network take part in the U.S. Fleet Ball at the Waldorf Astoria ballroom.	Jun. 1
The general strike in Toledo is definitely called off as the two major labor disputes are settled.... The Socialist Convention in Detroit faults the NRA for its lax application, which gives no advantages to workers.		Gen. Hugh Johnson, NRA Administrator, averts the strike by the cotton textile industry.... The House Appropriation Committee passes the Deficiency Appropriation Bill, which puts in the President's hands a relief fund between $2.5 billion and $6 billion.	High temperatures continue to affect the western United States, damaging the crops.		Jun. 2
The left wing of the Socialist Party, led by Norman Thomas, gains control of the organization.... The National Committee of the Republican Party gathers in Chicago to discuss reorganization of the party.			The exceptional dry spell is broken in the Rocky Mountain region. Scattered rains are reported throughout the territory struck by drought.	Hundreds of thousands of Americans inspect the fleet in New York.... United Artists announces its releases for the 1934–35 season, anticipating a new comedy by Charlie Chaplin.... The U.S. Olympic Committee defers acceptance of the German invitation to the Olympic Games. Its president, Avery Brundage, is to study the condition of Jews before accepting.	Jun. 3
President Franklin Roosevelt approves a $525 million relief program for the regions of the United States heavily damaged by the drought.... The Republican Party National Committee announces the adoption of a strong platform declaring opposition to some New Deal measures.		The Senate passes the Reciprocal Tariff Bill, which gives President Roosevelt power to negotiate tariffs with foreign nations.	Rain gives the Midwest relief from heavy drought.... Italian scientist Enrico Fermi artificially produces a new chemical element. He subjects uranium to a bombardment of neutrons produced by decomposition of berlyium through radium.	Albert Einstein's collection of writings, *How I See the World*, criticizes American attitudes toward debts and disarmament.... Warner Brothers Pictures will produce 60 films during the 1934–35 season, including film adaptations of *The Magnificent Ambersons* and Sinclair Lewis's *Babbit*.	Jun. 4
The Republican National Committee is unable to agree on whom to elect as party chairman.	The German Ambassador and the German Consul General in New York are accused before a House special committee of having helped to finance Nazi and anti-Semitic propaganda in the United States.	President Franklin Roosevelt presents his plan for drought relief to the members of Congress of the 14 states most severely damaged.		Eight thousand people take part in the first open-air dance in Central Park, N.Y.	Jun. 5

F	G	H	I	J
Includes elections, federal-state relations, civil rights and liberties, crime, the judiciary, education, healthcare, poverty, urban affairs, and population.	Includes formation and debate of U.S. foreign and defense policies, veterans affairs, and defense spending. (Relations with specific foreign countries are usually found under the region concerned.)	Includes business, labor, agriculture, taxation, transportation, consumer affairs, monetary and fiscal policy, natural resources, pollution, and accidents.	Includes worldwide scientific, medical, and technological developments, natural phenomena, U.S. weather, and natural disasters.	Includes the arts, religion, scholarship, communications media, sports, entertainment, fashions, fads, and social life.

	World Affairs	Europe	Africa & The Middle East	The Americas	Asia & The Pacific
Jun. 6		Ten people are killed in the farm workers' strike in Andalusia, Spain.... The brother of former Spanish dictator Damaso Berenguer is killed. The former dictator is unharmed.... Jacques Z. Suritz, a Jew, is named Soviet Ambassador to Berlin.		The mother of Gen. Augusto Sandino, slain revolutionary leader of Nicaragua, surprisingly endorses her son's enemy, General Somoza, for the presidency.	The final electoral results in the Philippines avert divided control of parliament. Senator Manuel Quezon's group will have a majority in both chambers, although his majority in the lower house will be only slight. ... Prince Chichibu, the Japanese Emperor's brother, arrives to Manchukuo on an official visit.
Jun. 7	Pope Pius XI celebrates the fifth anniversary of the Lateran Pacts with Italy, which made the Vatican an independent state.	The British Secretary of Air, the Marquess of Londonderry, is hurt as his plane crashes while landing.... Rudolph Poetch, Austrian Socialist leader, is found hanged at Woellersdorf concentration camp, where he was detained.... Former Lithuanian premier Waldemaras attempts a coup, which fails.			The Japanese Vice Consul in Nanking disappears.
Jun. 8	The British and French governments will try to persuade Germany to join the World Disarmament Conference.	The Little Entente officially recognizes Soviet Russia. In addition, Poland, Romania, and Russia agree to safeguard their present frontiers. For the first time, the Soviet government officially recognizes the loss of Bessarabia to Romania.... German Chancellor Adolf Hitler and Italian Premier Benito Mussolini will soon meet to discuss their worsening diplomatic relationships.... Carol II, King of Romania, celebrates the fourth anniversary of his enthronement.	Abraham Stavsky is sentenced to death for the murder of Chaim Arlosoroff, labor leader. The trial has stirred the interest of Palestinian public opinion, which has sided with the defendant.... Negotiations open for the establishment of air service between Paris and Cape Town.	A violent hurricane in El Salvador damages the capital, leaving 500 homeless and eight casualties.... Paraguay opposes the mediation of Argentina, Chile, Brazil, and Peru in the Chaco conflict. This is due to the training of the Bolivian army by Chilean retired officers.	
Jun. 9	The League of Nations abandons its plans for an arms embargo against Bolivia and Paraguay to stop the Chaco War.	The Reich suspends payments owed to other countries for commercial transactions for two weeks.... French Foreign Minister Barthou is invited to meet Italian Premier Mussolini.... A government decree transfers the functions of trying and punishing traitors from the Ogpu, Russia's secret police, to the normal courts.		Cuba begins a three-day celebration of the abrogation of the Platt Amendment and its establishment as a sovereign and independent nation.	
Jun. 10	The general feeling at the World Disarmament Conference is one of pessimism.	Socialist and Communist militants clash with the police throughout France as they try to prevent meetings of right-wing organizations.... Former kaiser Wilhelm is willing to return to the throne if Germans want him to.... The Nazi Publicity Bureau announces the veterans' organization *Stahlhelm* will be dissolved into the Nazi Storm Troops.		News reaching the capital of El Salvador from the interior reports that the violent hurricanes and storm of last week have left hundreds dead.	Tensions between Japan and China increase as a result of the disappearance of Japanese Vice Consul Kuramoto. The Japanese believe Kuramoto has been killed.
Jun. 11	The World Disarmament Conference adjourns until the fall without having reached an agreement.	The Italian government makes clear that the meeting between Italian Premier Benito Mussolini and German Chancellor Adolf Hitler was requested by Germany. ... In an attempt to stop Nazi terrorism, the Austrian government extends martial law to cover all kinds of bombing activities. ... Belgian Premier de Broqueville forms a new government.		The town of Sampacho in the Argentine province of Cordoba is destroyed by a strong series of quakes. Six thousand are left homeless.	
Jun. 12	The League of Nations holds its second conference on the standardization of vitamins.	French Foreign Minister Barthou announces that France will not pay the installment of its war debt to the United States. ... German soldiers are reported to have trespassed into the demilitarized Rhine Zone, breaching the Treaty of Versailles.	The Union of South Africa pays its war-debt installment to Britain.	Argentina continues to be shaken by violent earthquakes and storms extending over an area of 47,000 square miles.	The Japanese government says it will hold Chinese authorities responsible for the fate of the Japanese Vice Consul, who has been missing since Friday.
Jun. 13		British politicians and economists reject Secretary of State Cordell Hull's offer to pay the British war debt to the United States through commodities. ... Bulgarian Premier Gueorguieff decrees that Macedonian societies can no longer collect taxes. In addition, all arms and ammunition must be turned in to authorities. These moves are intended to suppress the Macedonian revolutionary movement.		Cuban President Carlos Mendieta denies that his government's failure to restore constitutional rights is turning the country into a military dictatorship.	The Japanese Vice Consul at Nanking, Eimei Kuramoto, is found on the outskirts of Nanking. Because of reprimands, the diplomat decided to desert his job. His disappearance almost caused a diplomatic incident between China and Japan, which believed its Vice Consul had been kidnapped.... Japanese Foreign Minister Hirota says he is ready to meet President Franklin Roosevelt to discuss Japanese-American questions.

A	B	C	D	E
Includes developments that affect more than one world region, international organizations, and important meetings of world leaders.	Includes all domestic and regional developments in Europe, including the Soviet Union.	Includes all domestic and regional developments in Africa and the Middle East.	Includes all domestic and regional developments in Latin America, the Caribbean, and Canada.	Includes all domestic and regional developments in Asian and Pacific nations (and colonies).

U.S. Politics & Social Issues	U.S. Foreign Policy & Defense	Economics & Great Depression	Science, Technology & Nature	Culture, Leisure & Lifestyle	
Henry P. Fletcher is elected chairman of the Republican National Committee.		Gen. Hugh Johnson fails to persuade steel union leaders to call off their strike planned for June 16. . . . The Reciprocal Tariff Bill is finally approved by the House and goes to President Franklin Roosevelt for signing. . . . President Roosevelt signs the Stock Exchange Control Bill.	President Franklin Roosevelt says that drought in western states has reached the proportion of national disaster. Yet, because of the ample food surplus, there is no danger of famine.	The Giants win against the Boston Braves and take first place in the baseball league.	Jun. 6
Former president Herbert Hoover congratulates Henry Fletcher upon his election to chairman of the Republican National Committee. . . . Tommy Carroll, a member of John Dillinger's gang, is killed by police in Iowa.		Big corporations start to reorganize under the new bankruptcy law. . . . The NRA officially gives up price-fixing to allow freer competition. . . . The American Iron and Steel Institute says it could agree to establishing a board as a medium for labor relations in the industry.	Coleman S. Williams, a member of the second Scarritt Expedition to Patagonia sponsored by the American Museum of Natural History, comes back to the United States with 49 boxes of specimens. Many are believed to be new to scientists.	Atlantic City prohibits women from drinking in bars. . . . Mae West asks the former king Alfonso of Spain to be the male lead in her next film.	Jun. 7
President Franklin Roosevelt urges Congress to pass legislation in its next session that would ensure the security of American people. This would include: the building or modernization of homes, better use of land and water resources, and social insurance against unemployment and old age.		Members of the steel workers' union attack Gen. Hugh Johnson's plan, agreed to with the American Iron and Steel Institute, to avert the threatened steel strike of June 16. . . . The new policy of the National Recovery Administration of abandoning price-fixing will not apply to approved codes.	The Federal Crops Reporting Board predicts that the wheat crop for 1934 will be one of the smallest since 1893.	Cardinal Dougherty of Philadelphia orders a film boycott throughout his diocese. Films are condemned as attacking the core values of Christian civilization. . . . Bobby Cruickshank takes the lead in the national open golf championship.	Jun. 8
In spite of mediation by Postmaster General and Democratic Party Chairman James Farley, members of Tammany Hall are still unable to agree on whom to elect as their leader.		President Franklin Roosevelt sends a message to Congress illustrating his plan for drought relief and asking for an appropriation of $525 million. . . . Leaders of the steel workers' union ask President Roosevelt to intervene directly in their labor dispute as Gen. Hugh Johnson is "discredited" as mediator.	Rains are forecast in the area of the United States heavily hit by drought. In North Dakota, the spring wheat yield is 27 percent of the normal amount.	Olin Dutra wins the 38th U.S. Open golf championship. . . . The animated short The Wise Little Hen is released, marking the debut of Donald Duck.	Jun. 9
The American College of Surgeons launches a campaign to provide better medical service through the system of voluntary and prepaid health insurance.		Senator Robert Wagner, head of the National Labor Board, says the board has helped more than 1.5 million workers in less than a year.		Hollywood is alarmed that criticism leveled at the film industry in the past weeks may result in federal censorship. . . . Italy beats Czechoslovakia 2–1 and wins the 1934 football championship.	Jun. 10
W.E.B. Du Bois resigns as editor of Crisis, the monthly magazine of the National Association for the Advancement of Colored People.	The State Department is informed by Belgium and Czechoslovakia that they will not pay their war debt installments on June 15.	For four hours, the Senate Agriculture Committee examines Rexford Tugwell, central member of Roosevelt's "brain trust," for his confirmation as Undersecretary of Agriculture. . . . The Senate approves the Silver Purchase Bill, which then goes to the House. . . . The second Darrow report on NRA operations describes Gen. Hugh Johnson, NRA Administrator, as "a military dictator."	A nine-ton airliner that went missing on Sunday is found wrecked on a Catskills peak. All its seven passengers are dead. . . . A Pan American–Grace Airways airplane flying from Buenos Aires to Santiago crashes, killing five people and injuring five.	Actress and singer Maggie Cline dies in New Jersey. She was nicknamed "Irish Queen of the 1890s."	Jun. 11
President Franklin Roosevelt confers with Democratic Party leaders to avert the steel strike and devise legislation to settle labor disputes. . . . President Roosevelt signs the Airmail Bill, which makes new rules for contracting airmail to private operators.	Secretary of State Cordell Hull offers Britain the option to pay its war debt in goods.	The Senate Agriculture Committee favorably reports on the appointment of Rexford Tugwell as Undersecretary of Agriculture.	At the 85th American Medical Association meeting, a team of seven doctors reports the discovery of anti-hormones in the human body. The discovery is expected to shed light on diseases such as diabetes and goiter, as well as on cancer.		Jun. 12
The House passes the Housing Bill. . . . President Franklin Roosevelt's policies continue to enjoy vast approval in the Literary Digest nationwide poll.	Secretary of State Cordell Hull tells the Bolivian government that the United States will keep the arms embargo in spite of Bolivian protests.	President Franklin Roosevelt sends a message to Congress proposing a four-point program to resolve labor disputes and replace the pending Wagner Bill. Under the proposed legislation, the President would have the authority to establish boards for all industries to settle labor disputes. . . . George Peek, special adviser to the President on foreign trade, argues that in the past 38 years the United States has had a loss of $22 billion in foreign accounts.			Jun. 13

F	G	H	I	J
Includes elections, federal-state relations, civil rights and liberties, crime, the judiciary, education, healthcare, poverty, urban affairs, and population.	Includes formation and debate of U.S. foreign and defense policies, veterans affairs, and defense spending. (Relations with specific foreign countries are usually found under the region concerned.)	Includes business, labor, agriculture, taxation, transportation, consumer affairs, monetary and fiscal policy, natural resources, pollution, and accidents.	Includes worldwide scientific, medical, and technological developments, natural phenomena, U.S. weather, and natural disasters.	Includes the arts, religion, scholarship, communications media, sports, entertainment, fashions, fads, and social life.

	World Affairs	Europe	Africa & The Middle East	The Americas	Asia & The Pacific
Jun. 14		The Reich suspends all payments on foreign debts.... Italian Premier Benito Mussolini and German Chancellor Adolf Hitler meet in Rome. The content of their long conversation is kept secret. . . . In France, five bombs are delivered through the mail by a mysterious group called the Three Judges of Hell. The president and various politicians are threatened. . . . French Premier Doumergue announces a larger budget for national defense.		Cuban military authorities, looking for arms, inspect many buildings in Havana. This follows the threat by radicals to attack a huge ABC revolutionary party rally on Sunday.	
Jun. 15		Polish Interior Minister Pieracki is shot and killed in Warsaw. . . . Italian Premier Benito Mussolini and German Chancellor Adolf Hitler agree that Austria's independence should be preserved. Mussolini also backs Germany's request for arms parity rights.		Cuban President Carlos Mendieta is slightly injured when a bomb explodes at a luncheon given in his honor.... Paraguay reports wide gains in the Chaco conflict.	
Jun. 16	Germany is believed to be considering its return to the League of Nations.	British Conservative Party leaders fear the old parties are losing strength to the fascist Black Shirt movement led by Sir Oswald Mosley. . . . The Bulgarian army hunts the few remaining Macedonian rebels in the Piren mountain range.	The Shah of Persia arrives in Turkey for an official visit to President Mustapha Kemal Pasha.	The Chaco War enters its third year. Peace between Paraguay and Bolivia is still far off. . . . ABC revolutionary party militants clash with radicals in Havana.	
Jun. 17		German Vice Chancellor von Papen defends the right to criticize the regime and asks for a freer press.... The pilgrimage to the grave of 18th-century Irish patriot Theobald Tone leads to violent clashes between the opposing factions of the Irish Republican Army and the Irish Congress.	The Kenyan government blames the rise of crimes on witch doctors of the Lumbwa tribe.	A parade of 80,000 militants of the ABC revolutionary organization is attacked in Havana by gunmen. Fourteen people are killed and more than 60 are injured. . . . The southern and central parts of Argentina suffer from an intense cold wave.	Gen. Chiang Kai-shek, head of the Chinese national government, announces that his campaign against the Communist rebels in the Kiangsi province is successfully concluded.
Jun. 18	Preliminary talks between Britain and the United States start in London in preparation for the 1935 naval conference.	Joseph Goebbels, the Reich's minister for propaganda, suppresses in all newspapers and radio broadcasts Vice Chancellor von Papen's speech in which he defended the right to criticize the regime. . . . A strong heat wave hits France and causes forest fires throughout the country.	The French open a new airline linking the French Congo and Algeria.	The Bolivian army suffers a serious defeat by the Paraguayans northeast of Fort Ballivian in the Chaco region.	
Jun. 19	The League of Nations commission turns Leticia back to Colombian civil authorities.	The German President, Paul von Hindenburg, praises the Vice Chancellor's speech on the right of people to criticize the Reich. . . . Communists and other radical groups clash with police forces in Lyon and Toulouse, France.		A Cuban commission investigating U.S. loans for about $60 million to the previous regime describes them as illegal. The commission recommends to the government not to pay.... After 25 years, the Liberal Party comes back to power in Ontario.	
Jun. 20	British Prime Minister Ramsay MacDonald explains to Anglo-American representatives at preliminary talks on naval issues that Britain needs a larger fleet.	An earthquake in Turkey causes widespread damage. . . . French Foreign Minister Barthou arrives in Bucharest on an official visit for a conference with the Little Entente (Romania, Czechoslovakia, and Yugoslavia). . . . Members of the National Radical Party (an outlawed fascist party) are arrested throughout Poland.		The Paraguayan army continues its advance toward Fort Ballivian, trying to overwhelm the entrenched Bolivian army.	The official newspaper, *Asahi*, argues the case of Japan's increase of its naval ratio.
Jun. 21	At the preliminary talks for the 1935 naval conference, Britain gives U.S. delegates full details of its plans to enlarge its fleet. There is complete Anglo-American agreement on rejecting Japanese claims for equality with the two powers.	Germany threatens to suspend all relationships with countries that retaliate against its decision to suspend payments of its foreign debts. . . . French Foreign Minister Barthou says France will oppose any revision to Romanian borders.... The Greek government begins a full-scale repression of the Communist Party. Two Communist mayors are removed from office and a bill is introduced to establish harsher sentences for agitators.		A violent battle rages along the Fort Ballivian front in the Chaco War. Eighty thousand men are involved in the conflict, but neither Paraguay nor Bolivia manages to make definite gains.	
Jun. 22	The International Labor Organization unanimously invites the United States to join.	Germany establishes a rationing system that limits its daily foreign payments to its daily foreign income. . . . Finland announces that its 15-year war against liquor smuggling has been won and that no liquor illegally enters the country any longer.		The new Salvadorian envoy to the United States, David Castro, sails for Washington. . . . Cuban President Carlos Mendieta negotiates with the ABC revolutionary party to prevent its withdrawal from his government.	

A	B	C	D	E
Includes developments that affect more than one world region, international organizations, and important meetings of world leaders.	Includes all domestic and regional developments in Europe, including the Soviet Union.	Includes all domestic and regional developments in Africa and the Middle East.	Includes all domestic and regional developments in Latin America, the Caribbean, and Canada.	Includes all domestic and regional developments in Asian and Pacific nations (and colonies).

U.S. Politics & Social Issues	U.S. Foreign Policy & Defense	Economics & Great Depression	Science, Technology & Nature	Culture, Leisure & Lifestyle	
The House passes the Liquor Bottle Bill, which authorizes the Treasury to control the size, branding, marking, and sale of liquor containers. The legislation was invoked by Secretary of the Treasury Henry Morgenthau to limit bootlegging. . . . The returns of the *Literary Digest* nationwide poll on President Roosevelt suggest that 47 states support the President.		William Green, president of the American Federation of Labor, is disappointed by the replacement of the Wagner Bill. . . . The Senate confirms Rexford Tugwell as Undersecretary of Agriculture.	The Philadelphia Academy of Natural Sciences sponsors an expedition of ornithologists to Greenland to obtain specimens of rare birds.	Max Baer beats Primo Carnera and becomes the world heavyweight champion.	Jun. 14
Republicans and Democrats agree on a bipartisan truce to adjourn Congress by Sunday.	The United States receives payment for war debts from Finland only. All other countries give notification that they will not pay.	The impending strike of steel workers is averted as they accept the mediation of a board appointed by President Roosevelt. . . . The National Recovery Administration celebrates its first anniversary. . . . The Senate passes the Deficiency Appropriation Bill, setting, however, a lower limit for the President's relief actions than the version originally approved by the House.	Reports from the meeting of the American Medical Association point to a definite link between unbalanced equilibrium of the internal secretion glands and cancer.	The President's daughter, Anna Roosevelt, admits she wants to divorce her husband, Curtis Dall. . . . Writer Dorothy Parker discloses that she married actor Alan Campbell last October.	Jun. 15
A minor banking bill keeps the Senate from adjourning. . . . The Senate passes the Housing Bill, which is now sent to conference.	U.S. Special Ambassador Norman H. Davis arrives in London to start preliminary talks with Britain on naval issues in view of the 1935 naval conference.	President Franklin Roosevelt praises the National Recovery Administration for its first year of operation and praises its head, Gen. Hugh Johnson. . . . Congress accepts President Roosevelt's new labor plan, which replaces the Wagner Bill. Roosevelt is given the power to appoint independent boards to settle labor disputes. . . . American public debt surpasses the 1919 peak.		Glenn Cunningham sets a new world record for the mile at Palmer Stadium in Princeton, N.J. . . . California's eight-oared varsity crew retains the Poughkeepsie championship, first won in 1932. . . . The U.S. team beats Great Britain at Wimbledon, keeping the Wightman Cup.	Jun. 16
The Democratic leaders of Tammany Hall are still unable to elect a leader who will succeed John F. Curry.	An investigating committee of the House unanimously asks the Secretary of War to remove Gen. Benjamin Foulois as chief of the Army Air Corps.	Union leaders meet in Washington and express their disappointment in the Roosevelt administration's failure to support the Wagner Labor Bill.	Russia's new eight-motored plane, Gorki, takes 40 people over Moscow in its first trial flight. . . . Hurricanes in Louisiana and Mississippi cause six deaths.	Eighty thousand people pay a farewell visit to the U.S. fleet on its last day in New York Harbor. . . . At a rally of the League of Decency, 50,000 Catholics pledge to boycott indecent movies.	Jun. 17
The 73rd Congress adjourns after approving all the important measures President Roosevelt had requested. Both chambers pass the Housing Bill, as suggested in the conference report.	Secretary of State Cordell Hull instructs the U.S. Ambassador in Berlin to protest the German moratorium on its international debts. . . . The U.S. fleet leaves New York after 18 days.	Secretary of Agriculture Henry Wallace says President Roosevelt will be careful in using his new tariff powers.		The Metropolitan Opera Association selects a new American opera, *The Eunuch*, by John Laurence Seymour, for its next season.	Jun. 18
President Franklin Roosevelt chooses Secretary of Labor Frances Perkins to represent him in all labor disputes. . . . Joseph Harriman, former president of the Harriman National Bank and Trust Company, is convicted of 16 illegal bank acts.		President Roosevelt assures he will allot $500 million to the Public Works Administration.		RKO announces 50 new films for the 1934–35 season, including two with Katharine Hepburn.	Jun. 19
William Kenneally, chairman of the Tammany executive committee, says the committee will meet soon to elect the new leader. . . . Rexford Tugwell takes the oath as first Undersecretary of Agriculture.	G. P. Baldwin, General Electric vice president, gives a strong defense of the NRA at a League of Nations labor conference in Geneva. He counters European critics of Roosevelt's policies.	The cleaning and dyeing industry suspends the fair-trade practice provisions, accusing the NRA of bad faith. . . . Speaking before a Yale gathering, President Franklin Roosevelt says his "brain trust" will continue to play a central role in the policies of the administration.		Paramount Pictures and MGM announce their films for the new season, which include an adaptation of Capek's celebrated play *R.U.R.*	Jun. 20
At Harvard University, anti-Nazi demonstrations are held against Ernst Hanfstaengl, Hitler's personal liaison officer for the Anglo-American press in Germany, who is at the university for the annual reunion of his class.		Secretary of Labor Frances Perkins indicates that the new Labor Board to be chosen by President Roosevelt will be composed of members outside the ranks of labor and industry. . . . The Consumers Advisory Board of the NRA claims a revision of all codes is necessary.	The development of the first American synthetic rubber tires is announced by the Du Pont Company and Dayton Rubber Manufacturing.		Jun. 21
	Secretary of State Cordell Hull receives Britain's proposals for a larger navy. Hull says these are mere suggestions at this stage.	The Public Works Administration sets aside $25 million for slum clearance in New York.	A report to the meeting of the American Association for the Advancement of Science illustrates for the first time the constitution of the atmospheres of Jupiter, Saturn, Uranus, and Neptune. They consist of hydrogen, nitrogen, and carbon.	The Federal Council of the Churches of Christ in America recommends to its members to join forces with Catholics to boycott immoral movies. . . . The Yale crew beats Harvard in varsity regatta before an audience of 80,000 people, including President Roosevelt.	Jun. 22

F	G	H	I	J
Includes elections, federal-state relations, civil rights and liberties, crime, the judiciary, education, healthcare, poverty, urban affairs, and population.	*Includes formation and debate of U.S. foreign and defense policies, veterans affairs, and defense spending. (Relations with specific foreign countries are usually found under the region concerned.)*	*Includes business, labor, agriculture, taxation, transportation, consumer affairs, monetary and fiscal policy, natural resources, pollution, and accidents.*	*Includes worldwide scientific, medical, and technological developments, natural phenomena, U.S. weather, and natural disasters.*	*Includes the arts, religion, scholarship, communications media, sports, entertainment, fashions, fads, and social life.*

	World Affairs	Europe	Africa & The Middle East	The Americas	Asia & The Pacific
Jun. 23		Soviet Foreign Commissar Litvinoff and French Foreign Minister Barthou state that future European treaties should be open to all nations. . . . In a rally for the Saar plebiscite, German Vice Chancellor von Papen praises Hitler as the country's savior from political collapse.	With the mediation of Great Britain, Saudi Arabia and Yemen sign a peace treaty that preserves Yemen's independence but modifies the boundaries between the countries in favor of Saudi Arabia.	Paraguayans suffer heavy losses in their attempt to conquer the Bolivian positions at Fort Ballivian. . . . A naval rebellion is suppressed in Cuba. Members of the ABC organization resign from the Mendieta cabinet.	
Jun. 24	After meetings held in Geneva, a Mediterranean security pact is considered by Italy, France, Yugoslavia, Greece, and Turkey.	Kiev is reestablished as the capital of Ukraine. The city had lost its capital status during the civil war. . . . Chancellor Adolf Hitler says Germany will retaliate against international boycotts of its goods. . . . France will oppose any revision of the naval clauses of the Versailles Treaty that would allow Germany to expand its naval fleet.		President Carlos Mendieta tries to persuade the ABC revolutionary party not to withdraw its members from the Cuban Cabinet.	Leaders of southern Chinese provinces gather to discuss military action against the central government.
Jun. 25		Britain claims that the Low Countries should be helped in maintaining their independence from aggression. . . . The Italian government sends its fleet to Albania as a result of tensions between the two countries. . . . The House of Commons unanimously gives the British government the power to wage a trade war against Germany.		The Cuban Cabinet resigns after the ABC's withdrawal of its support. . . . The new liberal Prime Minister of Ontario announces he will abolish the office of Lieutenant Governor, which represents the British King in Canadian provinces.	A bomb is thrown at a car in which Mohandas Gandhi should have been riding. The terrorist attack is blamed on orthodox Hindus critical of Gandhi's anti-Untouchability campaign.
Jun. 26		French Foreign Minister Barthou is received as guest of honor by the Yugoslav parliament, where he speaks against revision of present European borders. . . . Acts of Nazi terrorism continue throughout Austria in spite of the Hitler-Mussolini agreement on the independent future of Austria.	The Shah of Persia arrives in Istanbul on an official visit.	Paraguayan Foreign Minister Pastor Benitez is replaced by Rogelio Ibarra for his favoring of a peaceful settlement of the Chaco dispute.	
Jun. 27		German Chancellor Adolf Hitler rejects the demand of the most radical Nazi elements to dissolve the *Stahlhelm* (war veterans' organization). . . . The Marquess of Londonderry, Secretary of State for Air, says before the House of Commons that Britain has lost all hope for disarmament. The Cabinet has therefore decided to build an air force to protect the country.		The Dominican government denies that former Cuban president Gerardo Machado is hiding in Santo Domingo.	Violent rioting breaks out in Shanghai between 400 Japanese and the Chinese police.
Jun. 28		The Reich Propaganda Ministry announces that today, the anniversary of the Versailles Treaty, flags will be at half-staff on public buildings. . . . Several Nazi terrorist attacks in Vienna mark the 15th anniversary of the Versailles Treaty. . . . Partial results of the Irish local elections show that the two biggest parties, Eamon De Valera's Fianna Fail and the United Ireland Party, have about equal support.		Bolivian forces continue to resist Paraguayan attacks against their entrenched positions at Fort Ballivian.	
Jun. 29		Angered by repeated demands by the Storm Troops to dissolve the conservative veterans' organization, *Stahlhelm*, German Chancellor Adolf Hitler orders silence on the issue.		Governor Winship says President Roosevelt has approved his plan for relief for farmers and the unemployed in Puerto Rico. . . . The Paraguayan army slowly advances toward Fort Ballivian, where Bolivians are entrenched.	
Jun. 30	Unemployment statistics for the second quarter of 1934 by the International Labor Office in Geneva show a general improvement, consistent with the trend for the last three quarters of 1933 and the first of 1934. The only countries that show a decrease of employment are France, Portugal, Spain, Bulgaria, Poland, and Ireland.	To prevent a plot against the regime, German Chancellor Adolf Hitler summarily executes 77 people, many of whom have been significant leaders of the party. This drastic move is directed against the more radical, social revolutionary wing of the National Socialist party. Leading victims include Gen. Kurt von Schleicher, Ernst Roehm, Gregor Strasser, and Erich Klausener. The event becomes known as the Night of the Long Knives.			

A	B	C	D	E
Includes developments that affect more than one world region, international organizations, and important meetings of world leaders.	Includes all domestic and regional developments in Europe, including the Soviet Union.	Includes all domestic and regional developments in Africa and the Middle East.	Includes all domestic and regional developments in Latin America, the Caribbean, and Canada.	Includes all domestic and regional developments in Asian and Pacific nations (and colonies).

U.S. Politics & Social Issues	U.S. Foreign Policy & Defense	Economics & Great Depression	Science, Technology & Nature	Culture, Leisure & Lifestyle	
Attorney General Homer Cummings announces a $10,000 reward for the capture of John Dillinger. . . . Six members of the North Dakota cabinet refuse to recognize Governor Langer's authority because of his recent conviction for felony.			Nobel Prize winner Robert A. Millikan finds further evidence for his theory that cosmic rays are the result of the building up of matter in space.	President and Mrs. Roosevelt meet their daughter-in-law for the first time.	Jun. 23
Supporters of James Dooling as leader of Tammany Hall seek the support of the faction led by Edward Ahearn.	Secretary of State Cordell Hull welcomes Colombian President Alfonso Lopez to Washington on his official visit.	President Franklin Roosevelt allocates $150 million of the $525 million set aside for drought relief.		Joseph Breen, administrator of the production code of the motion picture industry, declares that Hollywood will be more careful of the movies it makes as a result of recent criticism over the moral values of the industry.	Jun. 24
The Recovery Party intends to organize primaries in every district if the Tammany executive committee fails to elect James Dooling or a leader favored by the Roosevelt administration.		Harry Hopkins, Relief Administrator, says that relief should be provided on a permanent basis through industry stimulation and the establishment of unemployment insurance.	Richard du Pont establishes a new world distance record for motorless airplane flight. He flies 155 miles nonstop, while the previous record was 136 miles.	Jim Londos wins the world heavyweight wrestling title in the Madison Square Garden Bowl.	Jun. 25
President Franklin Roosevelt appoints a labor board to deal with the longshoremen's strike, applying his new labor legislation for the first time. . . . After two years of public accusations, general counsel for the Interborough Rapid Transit receivership admits before a Senate committee that the receivership was arranged.		Federal Judge John P. Barnes grants an injunction restraining the government from enforcing the provisions of the Agricultural Adjustment Administration milk-licensing agreement against six independent milk dealers in the Chicago milkshed area. The decision is a serious blow to the New Deal.	A short circuit throws into uncontrollable panic 600 passengers of a subway train in Brooklyn. Ten people are slightly injured.	The mother of President Franklin Roosevelt is received by the British King and Queen in Buckingham Palace for tea. . . . The directors of the Metropolitan Opera and Real Estate Company approve plans for the immediate modernization of the old Metropolitan Opera House.	Jun. 26
President Franklin Roosevelt urges his political aides to follow his example and refrain from engaging in active politics while he is away from Washington. He also says he will not take part in the campaign for the Congressional election in the fall as his administration is dedicated to public good, not party service.		Gen. Hugh Johnson denounces the second Darrow report on the NRA as even more inaccurate than the first.			Jun. 27
President Franklin Roosevelt creates the National Steel Labor Board, thus averting the possibility of a steel strike. . . . The Alabama Supreme Court unanimously upholds the death sentences of Scottsboro boys Heywood Patterson and Clarence Norris.	Secretary of State Cordell Hull blames Nazi policies for Germany's inability to pay its foreign debts.	Secretary of the Treasury Henry Morgenthau orders an embargo on exports of silver to avoid speculation. . . . President Franklin Roosevelt addresses the nation in a radio message. He asks American citizens to compare their lives now to that of a year ago to judge the progress of his recovery program.		Zaro Agha, who claims he is 160 years old, dies in Turkey. . . . Tony Canzoneri beats Frankie Klick, confirming he is the outstanding challenger for the world lightweight championship.	Jun. 28
North Dakota Governor William Langer is sentenced to 18 months and a fine of $10,000 for defrauding the United States.	President Roosevelt orders an embargo on arms and other military equipment to Cuba, except under licenses from the State Department. Such licenses will have to be requested directly from the Cuban government through its U.S. Embassy. . . . Secretary of State Cordell Hull will be in charge of negotiating the reciprocity pacts with foreign nations under the tariff-bargaining act.	President Franklin Roosevelt signs an executive order allowing bidders on government contracts to submit prices up to 15 percent below those established by their code authorities. . . . Senator McAdoo advocates the constitution of a reserve fund through which industries will share their surplus profits with workers. . . . President Roosevelt appoints the Committee on Economic Security that, with the assistance of economic advisers, will have the task of formulating economic and social provisions for the recovery of the nation.	A heat wave hits the United States and causes several deaths throughout the nation.	Two new poems by Rudyard Kipling are read at the opening performance of the great Pageant of Parliament at Albert Hall in London.	Jun. 29
Before embarking on a month-long cruise, President Franklin Roosevelt appoints two commissions: one for the control of the stock exchanges and one to control operations of telegraph, telephone, and radio companies. . . . John Dillinger robs the Merchants National Bank in South Bend, Ind., and escapes with $28,000. One policeman is killed in the shooting and four are wounded.		Gen. Hugh Johnson, NRA Administrator, announces that his 10-month dispute with the Ford Motor Company is near settlement. Ford will accept the NRA automobile code.	A torrid heat wave continues for the second consecutive day throughout the country.	The theater adaptation of Sherwood Anderson's novel, Winesburg, Ohio, opens in Philadelphia. . . . Bill Bonthron sets a new world record for the 1,500 running race in Milwaukee, Wisc.	Jun. 30

F	G	H	I	J
Includes elections, federal-state relations, civil rights and liberties, crime, the judiciary, education, healthcare, poverty, urban affairs, and population.	*Includes formation and debate of U.S. foreign and defense policies, veterans affairs, and defense spending. (Relations with specific foreign countries are usually found under the region concerned.)*	*Includes business, labor, agriculture, taxation, transportation, consumer affairs, monetary and fiscal policy, natural resources, pollution, and accidents.*	*Includes worldwide scientific, medical, and technological developments, natural phenomena, U.S. weather, and natural disasters.*	*Includes the arts, religion, scholarship, communications media, sports, entertainment, fashions, fads, and social life.*

	World Affairs	Europe	Africa & The Middle East	The Americas	Asia & The Pacific
Jul. 1		German Chancellor Adolf Hitler executes an estimated 200 "rebels," orders stormtroopers to remain in their houses, and bans the carrying of knives. Austria and Germany guard their borders to prevent Germans from entering Austria. Germans want to restrain fugitives; Austria wants to keep radicals out after Hitler's executions. . . . Four bombings in Austria result in one Nazi death at Rattenberg, Tyrol. Austrian Chancellor Engelbert Dollfuss condemns the violence. . . . The European wheat crop is estimated at 25–30 percent under the previous year's. . . . British stock and employment indices are up.		A Sikorsky bimotor airplane arrives in La Paz, Bolivia. The plane will shorten the trip from the gold mines in northwest Bolivia from 20 days to one hour. A boom in the gold industry is expected. . . . Pro-American Lázaro Cárdenas is elected president of Mexico.	The Cabinet of Premier Makato Saito is expected to resign on July 2 over a financial scandal. The Emperor of Japan is expected to refuse to allow the resignations. . . . Japanese mobs attack a Pole and an American in Shanghai. . . . Young Japanese naval officers call for abrogation of the naval treaties, increasing concern that the military is getting involved in politics.
Jul. 2	At the Geneva disarmament conference, despite Great Britain's reservations and without the participation of Germany, Italy, and Japan, a proposal for control of the arms trade is agreed. The measure next goes to the participating governments. . . . In Hendon, the British display their new aircraft—including a fighter capable of 250 miles per hour and a bomber with a top speed of 200 miles per hour—to over 2,000 representatives of virtually every country in the world.	Britain gives Germany a delay in debt repayment.		Pan American Airways and Railway Express team up to provide fast service to 30 countries of Central and South America. Maximum door-to-door delivery is seven days.	Chinese and Japanese troops guard the first train on the Peiping-Mukden Railway in Manchukuo after an explosion that killed four the previous day, presumably done by objectors to the resumption of Chinese service to Manchukuo. . . . Financial scandal brings down the Japanese Cabinet.
Jul. 3	Britain begins subsidizing shipping for the first time in 80 years. France and the United States also subsidize merchant shipping.	Austria, suffering internal turmoil and sabotage, refuses to allow the return of those who went to Germany. . . . German Vice Chancellor von Papen resigns. Adolf Hitler ends the summary executions and meets with President Paul von Hindenburg.	Zionists ask for a seat in the League of Nations.	Chilean rebels destroy crops and livestock and murder people in the countryside. Federal troops are sent to control the area.	Under pressure from military demands for a strong leader, the Emperor of Japan selects Admiral Okada to head the new government.
Jul. 4	After Germany defaults, the United States asks for French aid in getting Germany to pay debt service on Dawes and Young loans. France is reluctant.	The Austrian bombings continue. . . . Belgium prepares to undertake a "New Deal" to tighten controls over taxes, loans, government salaries and pensions, industry, utility rates, and provincial budgets. . . . Germany represses Catholics and shuts down newspapers that reported the recent uprising. President von Hindenburg refuses to remove Vice Chancellor von Papen from office. . . . Romania bans Nazi organizations and uniforms. . . . Macedonian Protogeroffist leftist rebels in Bulgaria disband after severe government repression. Mikhailloffist rebels are on the run but are expected to revive.		Canadian wheat exports and revenues rise. . . . Mexico holds the losing presidential candidate in custody to prevent a revolt. . . . Police teargas rioting students in Havana, Cuba. The students and labor unions are supporting the 100 political prisoners in the sixth day of their hunger strike.	
Jul. 5	Germany and France are in a diplomatic dispute because Germany used illegal entanglement with France as justification for one of its political murders.	Dutch Nazi membership drops to 18,500 from 30,000. . . . South Albanians rise against King Zog.	Turkey denies attacks on Jews in the Dardanelles and Thrace. Despite Turkish promises to protect them, Jews are departing.	A seamen's strike in Rio de Janeiro, Brazil, has halted operations of the Brazilian government line. . . . Marta Vergara, Chilean Communist leader and delegate to the Pan-American Convention, is arrested along with 200 others. Rebels are reported to be scattered by federal troops. . . . President Franklin Roosevelt promises to withdraw the U.S. Marines from Haiti. . . . In El Salvador, water service resumes after a recent hurricane.	
Jul. 6	Germany suspends attacks on France.	A potato shortage is occurring in Germany, and the harvest estimate is far below normal. The hoarding of imported goods is increasing as Germany attempts substitution of local products. Germany asks single workers to give their jobs to married men. . . . Riots in Amsterdam after a reduction in the dole leave nine dead.		Turmoil in Cuba continues with the arrests of army officers on conspiracy charges. Bombings and arson continue, but the student strike is broken. . . . The Mexican economy is improving, and the demand for steel pushes bank loans up 200 percent.	Chinese citizens complain that Chinese government tariff policy is advantaging the Japanese at Chinese expense. Chinese foreign trade is below 1933 levels.

A	B	C	D	E
Includes developments that affect more than one world region, international organizations, and important meetings of world leaders.	*Includes all domestic and regional developments in Europe, including the Soviet Union.*	*Includes all domestic and regional developments in Africa and the Middle East.*	*Includes all domestic and regional developments in Latin America, the Caribbean, and Canada.*	*Includes all domestic and regional developments in Asian and Pacific nations (and colonies).*

U.S. Politics & Social Issues	U.S. Foreign Policy & Defense	Economics & Great Depression	Science, Technology & Nature	Culture, Leisure & Lifestyle	
Airmail rates are reduced to 6 cents from 8 cents for the first ounce, 13 cents for each additional ounce. The expectation is that increased volume will offset the rate reduction. . . . African Americans in Oklahoma City decry the National Recovery Administration's discrimination.		The U.S. government authorizes bidders for NRA contracts to secretly bid up to 15 percent below the fixed price. This is an effort to eliminate price fixing and restore competition. . . . The Journal of the American Bankers Association reports that bankers agree the economy rebounded in June. The Bank of America reports its six-month earnings are up 17 percent from the previous year. . . . Civilian Conservation Corps enrollment for the year is set at 160,000; the budget for drought relief is $50 million.	Vassar College's Summer Institute of Eugenics opens. . . . Popular Science reports that meteors emit sound at the speed of light. . . . The U.S. weather service begins attaching meteorographs to the wings of airplanes, allowing them to gather weather information in the upper atmosphere instead of solely on the ground. . . . In Rochester, N.Y., the first x-ray of the entire human body is taken.	Best sellers include: Caroline Miller's *Lamb in His Bosom*, Robert Graves's *I, Claudius*, Hervey Allen's *Anthony Adverse*, and Thomas Mann's *Joseph and his Brothers*. Alexander Woollcott, Agatha Christie, and Isak Dinesen also make the list. . . . In Marietta, Ga., the Unknown Soldier of the Civil War, a casualty of the battle of Kenesaw Mountain, is laid to rest with both the Stars and Stripes and the Stars and Bars. . . . Bill Terry, the New York Giants' player-manager, leads the All-Star voting, followed by Charley Gehringer of the Detroit Tigers and Frankie Frisch of the St. Louis Cardinals. . . . Joe Louis wins his first professional bout. He will win 12 fights this year, 10 by knockout.	Jul. 1
The NAACP reports that the NRA codes are discriminatory, allowing 20–40 percent pay differentials; that whites refuse to pay even the lower rates; and that blacks are coerced into accepting lower wages.		Business failures in the United States and Canada are down from the previous week and from the same week the previous year. . . . Samuel Insull, Jr., pleads not guilty to mail fraud. Other charges are still pending against his Public Service Company of Northern Indiana.			Jul. 2
The Louisiana legislature passes a two-cent tax on newspaper advertising. Critics charge that Huey Long is trying to stifle the opposition press.	The U.S. War Department announces plans to spend $10 million to buy 1,551 trucks to motorize the National Guard.			A Chicago gasoline price war ends with agreement to raise the prices. Regular is up two cents, to 17.3 cents per gallon. Bargain grade is 15.3 cents. . . . Justin Dupee, inventor of the Cyclone, Wildcat, and other amusement park rides, dies of heat stroke at age 43. . . . Motion picture code implementation is delayed until August 15.	Jul. 3
There were six lynchings in the first half of the year, compared to eight in the first half of 1933 and five for the first half of 1932. All occurred in the south.		President Franklin Roosevelt reinstitutes the Davis-Bacon Act requiring that government contractors pay the wage prevailing in the community. The act had been suspended temporarily. . . . Troops armed with vomiting gas prepare to take on striking dock workers in San Francisco.	Madame Curie is mourned. . . . A coal-burning British steam truck is being tested in North Carolina. . . . The National Bureau of Standards' effort to standardize doses of x-rays in treating cancer is regarded as a breakthrough. . . . The Tennessee Valley Authority finds potash and other components for artificial fertilizer in Tennessee.	A report shows the suicide rate dropped from 21.3 to 19.1 per 100,000 people in 1933. . . . Three American scullers and two crews are victorious in opening rounds of the Henley Regattas.	Jul. 4
A *Literary Digest* poll reveals that respondents in 9 of 10 cities support President Franklin Roosevelt and the New Deal.		The auto industry cancels its auto shows, citing the cost and the need to keep car prices down. . . . Drought in Texas is the worst in 40 years, but the cotton crop is still expected to match the 1933 yield of 10 million bales. . . . The West Coast dock strike continues, with two dead and 115 injured in San Francisco. Federal arbitrators armed with new legal authority are waiting for the various parties to come to the table.	Dr. Maurice Brodie and two other New York physicians test their newly developed infantile paralysis (polio) vaccine on themselves and report no deleterious effects.	Mischa Elman performs to packed houses in Argentina after successes in Brazil. . . . The National Conference of Jews and Christians reports that the fight for decency in films and fairness in industry practices (such as the elimination of block booking) is bringing about a historic unity of Protestants, Catholics, and Jews.	Jul. 5
		Silver, cotton, lead, and copper prices are down. Coffee remains strong. . . . The cost of living is still 20.2 percent below 1928, so 5 percent reductions in government salaries continue. . . . Loans by the Home Owners Loan Corporation exceed $1 billion in the HOLC's first year. Of 1.5 million applicants, over 341,000 receive help.		The Hays group appoints Joseph Breen as voluntary censor of films and enforcer of the production code in order to head off government intervention. . . . Englishman Fred Perry routs Australian Jack Crawford at Wimbledon to take the first title for England since the first Wimbledon meet in 1909.	Jul. 6

F	G	H	I	J
Includes elections, federal-state relations, civil rights and liberties, crime, the judiciary, education, healthcare, poverty, urban affairs, and population.	*Includes formation and debate of U.S. foreign and defense policies, veterans affairs, and defense spending. (Relations with specific foreign countries are usually found under the region concerned.)*	*Includes business, labor, agriculture, taxation, transportation, consumer affairs, monetary and fiscal policy, natural resources, pollution, and accidents.*	*Includes worldwide scientific, medical, and technological developments, natural phenomena, U.S. weather, and natural disasters.*	*Includes the arts, religion, scholarship, communications media, sports, entertainment, fashions, fads, and social life.*

	World Affairs	Europe	Africa & The Middle East	The Americas	Asia & The Pacific
Jul. 7	In Paris, the International Conference of Women resolves in favor of arms limitations—including chemical and bacteriological weapons, international control of airspace, and the arms trade in general. . . . Finland makes its war debt payment. Secretary of State Cordell Hull reminds other countries that their debts are outstanding and repayment is necessary to maintain the credit system. Poland plans to repay in local currency rather than the dollar as required.	Rioting in Amsterdam is crushed with six dead. Tanks are used to prevent uprisings in other Dutch cities. . . . Fianna Fail gains six seats in Irish elections, with eight more seats likely. . . . Storm troopers are defeated by authorities in Beuthen, Germany. . . . Poland opens its third "isolation camp" for political prisoners.	Bulgarians join Jews and Greeks fleeing Thrace.	Chile quells its agrarian rebellion. . . . Cuba defeats the uprising of former military officers. . . . Saskatchewan farmers plan a hunger march to protest evictions. The Mounties arrest 11 strike leaders in Manitoba.	John Latham, Australian Minister of External Affairs, returns from a goodwill trip to Asia and encourages increased trade as the path to preserving peace.
Jul. 8	Japan agrees to attend the 1935 naval conference.	In Amsterdam, rioting resumes. . . . German industry in May was reportedly 60 percent under capacity. . . . Spain plans to implement a public works program. Spain also prepares to fortify the Balearic Islands.		The Brazilian bank clerk strike ends. . . . Mexican troops prevent rebellion in Nuevo Leon after rebels attack the tax collector. . . . Paraguay claims it kills 200 Bolivians at Fort Ballivian in the Chaco War.	
Jul. 9	The Commander of the Russian Air Force tests a Fokker S-36 passenger plane in Amsterdam. . . . At a meeting in London, the French government seeks two mutual assistance agreements, but not military alliances. Italy opposes the plan. . . . The World Bank protests the preferential treatment of Britain in German repayments and urges Germany to pay all of its debts.	The Dutch riots end. . . . German Chancellor Adolf Hitler's stormtroopers are to be disarmed and reduced from 2.5 million to 800,000. . . . Germany increases imports of potatoes from Holland, Belgium, and Italy.		Puerto Rican sugar growers object to the lowering of their quota from 1.1 million tons to 803,000. The U.S. representative advises that if they do not set a quota voluntarily, then he will set it for them. . . . Bolivia claims to shoot down a Paraguayan plane as its forces hold steady at Fort Ballivian. . . . Brazilian banks are open again. Clerks win a pension plan. . . . Cubans call a general strike to protest Fulgencio Batista's imprisonment of former officers.	Japan protests that China is failing to safeguard the newly reopened Japanese Consulate in Yunnanfu. . . . The dowager Maharani of Mysore dies in India. With her husband she helped modernize the principality in a pre-feminist era.
Jul. 10	The Soviet Union is hesitant to participate in the naval conference because it wants to build rather than limit its navy.	Famine is reported in Russia. . . . The Soviet Union abolishes its secret police, the Ogpu.	Turkey begins protecting Jews in Thrace, jails attackers, and orders the return of items taken from Thracian Jews.		A fatal drought and heat strike in Shanghai, with 63-year-record temperatures, cause the rivers to dry; bubonic plague breaks out in Amoy. Floods in Manchuria isolate towns and allow banditry.
Jul. 11	Britain and Norway are in a dispute over Norwegian naval interference with British trawlers in Norwegian waters. Britain threatens to send a warship. . . . The funeral cortege of Prince William, the royal Dutch consort, is viewed by 1 million before he is laid to rest in Delft, Netherlands.	Austria's Chancellor Engelbert Dollfuss takes on the security, war, and foreign portfolios and vacates the Berlin legation in an effort to strengthen his hand against the Nazis.		After the Chilean rebellion is crushed, some Longuimay rebels head to Argentina. . . . Paraguayan forces nearly have Fort Ballivian surrounded and are driving against entrenched Bolivian troops at Canada el Carmen. . . . The Canadian wheat crop of 185 million bushels is about 82 percent of normal.	The bubonic plague spreads in Manchukuo.
Jul. 12	France and Britain agree to urge a 25,000-ton limit for warships.	The Austrian Nazis' attempt to discourage tourism by bombing Salzburg injures four Nazis and two tourists. The death penalty for bombers is proposed. . . . Germany prepares to implement compulsory labor service and opens a campaign against food bootlegging.		Bolivians claim to have repulsed Paraguayans with heavy losses to Paraguayan forces and machines. Paraguay claims 70,000 troops are engaged on the 100-mile front. . . . Argentina bans the Nazi flag.	Shanghai's temperature reaches a record 104°F. Floods occur in northern Manchuria.
Jul. 13	British trade and industry and Spanish and Hungarian agriculture are reported up. Italy struggles with its deficit and balance of payments.	Germany establishes a people's treason court to try Communists and Roehm conspirators under "Germanic principles" rather than law.		The Bolivian counter-attack at Canada el Carmen is reportedly repulsed. Bolivians are withdrawing in Chaco.	
Jul. 14	Anti-Nazi paraders are arrested in Philadelphia and London.	French tornado damage is estimated at 10 million francs. . . . Drought and heat in Europe cut Hungarian rye production in half.	Northern Rhodesians, discontented with British rule and taxation, contemplate merger with Southern Rhodesia, not rebellion.	Chile reportedly is intervening on Bolivia's behalf. Bolivia claims success at Canada el Carmen. . . . Mexican authorities investigate a rumored uprising of former military officers in Chihuahua. The government alleges that Antonio Villareal, defeated presidential candidate, is planning a rebellion.	Floods in western Assam and Japan kill hundreds. . . . New Zealand increases spending on military defense. . . . Chiang Kai-shek urges a higher morality and a greater Spartan ethic for China.

A	B	C	D	E
Includes developments that affect more than one world region, international organizations, and important meetings of world leaders.	*Includes all domestic and regional developments in Europe, including the Soviet Union.*	*Includes all domestic and regional developments in Africa and the Middle East.*	*Includes all domestic and regional developments in Latin America, the Caribbean, and Canada.*	*Includes all domestic and regional developments in Asian and Pacific nations (and colonies).*

U.S. Politics & Social Issues	U.S. Foreign Policy & Defense	Economics & Great Depression	Science, Technology & Nature	Culture, Leisure & Lifestyle	
Immigration through Ellis Island is down to 25 per day from its heyday high of 5,000.		The Civilian Conservation Corps (CCC) announces plans to accept war veterans without regard to previous CCC service. Nonveterans are allowed only a one-year term.	Kansas farmers explore the possibilities for irrigation as the drought continues. . . . University of Michigan researchers attach an electric eye to a camera to allow photographing traffic conditions automatically rather than manually.		Jul. 7
The head of the East Side Mission says New York City's model home program is a failure because it prices previous tenants out of new property or, by subsidizing rent, leaves them in old tenements. A new slum policy is called for. . . . A United Jewish Appeal drive to raise money for German Jews raises $1.5 million in pledges from 44 states.				Babe Ruth hits his 699th career home run. . . . Germany's Hans Sievert sets a world decathlon record of 8,709 points, beating the old mark set by Kansan Jim Bausch in the 1932 Olympics.	Jul. 8
An African-American man is lynched on the courthouse lawn by a crowd of 300 in Bastrop, La. . . . The convictions in the infamous murder case underway in Scottsboro, Ala., are appealed to the state supreme court; the executions are stayed. . . . Charles Ponzi is set to be deported. Ponzi defrauded investors out of millions in the 1920s. . . . The NAACP Board of Directors receives "with regret" the resignation of W.E.B. Du Bois as editor of Crisis. . . . An agricultural union strike in its fourth week in New Jersey turns violent. The sheriff wants martial law; the governor refuses. Dozens are arrested.		AAA wheat production is cut 15 percent, and the milling tax is retained. . . . The previous week's reported business failures are the lowest since 1920. . . . In East Chicago and Gary, Ind., 43,000 steel workers return to work, working three or four days a week to share jobs and prevent layoffs. Steel is at 42 percent of capacity.	The first flight of a night sleeper plane carries a dozen passengers from New York to Chicago in just over six hours.	Carl Hubbell starts against Vernon "Lefty" Gomez in the All-Star Game. The American League wins 9–7.	Jul. 9
The West Coast dock strike is quiet as negotiations continue under the guidance of Secretary of Labor Frances Perkins. . . . Republic Steel refuses to renew its contract with the union, citing the "radical" element.	The Senate's Nye Committee opens a New York office. The committee is mandated to investigate profiteering in the arms and munitions industries in the World War.	Hudson Motors' output is reported as nearly triple the previous year's. . . . The wheat crop is forecast to be the smallest since 1893 at 483 million bushels.	General Electric engineers create a 250,000 amp flash with a 30 million kilowatt discharge, the largest voltage to date. . . . New York orders a study of safety measures to reduce infection from telephones.	Chicago drunken driving accidents are up 300 percent.	Jul. 10
Huey Long ends Louisiana's poll tax. . . . Shippers in the dock strike on the West Coast agree to arbitration. . . . Mississippi "drys" fight off a "wet" attempt to repeal the state's decades-old Prohibition law.	The U.S. Marines are ordered to depart from Haiti by August 15. The Haitian Guard will assume their functions. . . . The Navy reports that plans are ready for construction of 35,000-ton ships if they are authorized.		Illinois tornadoes injure scores and cause $1 million in damage.		Jul. 11
Charles Ponzi attempts to have his conviction overturned so he will not be deported. . . . Three are arrested in Newark, N.J., at a protest against a department store allegedly selling Nazi goods. . . . American Communists deny that they receive instructions from the Soviet Union.		Secretary of the Interior Harold Ickes authorizes $57 million in Public Works Administration funds for flood control and irrigation projects. . . . A federal judge in Baltimore overturns the NRA oil code, ruling that the interstate commerce clause does not apply to gas stations operating within a single state, even if an owner has stations in more than one state.	A Soviet land and water auto carries 25 passengers in soft seats. . . . Fire is raging out of control in Mesa Verde National Forest in Colorado. . . . Prof. Emmanuel Carvallo says Einstein's theory of relativity is false.	Shirley Temple's father demands a $2,500 weekly salary for the child star.	Jul. 12
A relief riot in Ohio results in two deaths after a gun battle. Officials blame radicals. . . . Striking dockworkers on the West Coast waver over arbitration. Hundreds leave San Francisco, restaurants begin rationing food, and taxi drivers join the walkout.		The Grand Coulee Dam contracts are let for $30 million.	Prof. Albert Einstein counters Carvallo's criticism, citing flaws in the Italian's experiments.	Babe Ruth hits career home run number 700.	Jul. 13
Six San Francisco Bay area cities are on emergency alert in preparation for a general strike.		The Alabama Public Service Commission claims the authority to regulate the Tennessee Valley Authority. The ruling denies the claims of a coal company, an ice company, and other companies that TVA had no right to serve as a utility.	Congress provides $1 million to survey the Pan-American Road from the Argentine to Alaska. . . . Turntables on seaplane ramps on New York's East River are proposed to speed turnaround for commuter and private planes.		Jul. 14

F	G	H	I	J
Includes elections, federal-state relations, civil rights and liberties, crime, the judiciary, education, healthcare, poverty, urban affairs, and population.	Includes formation and debate of U.S. foreign and defense policies, veterans affairs, and defense spending. (Relations with specific foreign countries are usually found under the region concerned.)	Includes business, labor, agriculture, taxation, transportation, consumer affairs, monetary and fiscal policy, natural resources, pollution, and accidents.	Includes worldwide scientific, medical, and technological developments, natural phenomena, U.S. weather, and natural disasters.	Includes the arts, religion, scholarship, communications media, sports, entertainment, fashions, fads, and social life.

	World Affairs	Europe	Africa & The Middle East	The Americas	Asia & The Pacific
Jul. 15	Japan asks to postpone the naval congress. The United States and Britain are in discussions through the end of July.			Guatemala prepares to offer Jewish refugees land and citizenship. . . . Clashes occur between Conservatives and backers of the Argentine president deposed in February. In the San Juan province, three are killed and 40 wounded. . . . Brazil's new constitution restricts immigration, establishes the eight-hour workday, and authorizes nationalization of banks and industries.	
Jul. 16		Hungary dissolves its Nazi party. . . . Poland opposes the Eastern Locarno mutual assistance plan for central and northern Europe proposed by France, fearing it might be caught in the middle. Besides, Poland already has nonaggression pacts with Germany and Russia. . . . The Eugenics Court in Essen, Germany, has sterilized 190 people since the beginning of the year.		Vancouver longshoremen support the general strike on the West Coast by refusing to load American ships. . . . In Mexico, the rebels under Gen. Felix Lozano surrender, but Lozano is nowhere to be found.	
Jul. 17		Floods in Poland kill hundreds and maroon thousands on trains. . . . In Yugoslavia, lightning kills 30. . . . Brown Shirts are reappearing in Germany.		Getulio Vargas is elected the first Brazilian president under the new constitution. He seized power in a 1930 rebellion. . . . Lack of rain in Canada continues to damage crops.	
Jul. 18		Germany accuses Romanians of barring Nazi propaganda. . . . France begins a recruiting drive for an unlimited number of new men for its army.		Nicaragua begins exporting coffee to China. . . . Peru opens its tungsten fields to company and individual claims.	Heavy fighting is reported in the Fukien province between Communist rebels and the Chinese government's forces.
Jul. 19		Bombings continue to occur in Austria. . . . Prussia bans the works of the American author Upton Sinclair, whose books were among those burned in Hermann Goering's 1933 bonfire. . . . Czechoslovakia is becoming overwhelmed by refugees—Germans, Hungarians, Ukrainians, and Poles—from the various failed leftist and rightist uprisings in neighboring countries. . . . Germany increases potato imports. . . . The secret treason court in Germany is holding 2,000 Brown Shirts. Roehm is accused of having formed a private army of 100,000. . . . Police in the Saar raid a German Labor Front (Nazi) office.		The Bolivians, freshly supplied with arms, prepare to resume the fighting in Chaco. . . . Severe earthquakes rock Panama.	Maurice Wilson of Britain dies in an unsuccessful solo attempt to scale Mt. Everest in Tibet.
Jul. 20	The world cotton crop is expected to exceed that of the United States.	France praises the British decision to increase its air force, regarding it as a positive for mutual security. The rumor is that Britain and France have made a secret pact against Germany. . . . Germany seizes the offices of the *Times of London*, *Le Temps*, and other newspapers.	In adjustments of the Italian boundaries in Cyrenaica, Britain and Egypt agree to give Italy part of the Anglo-Egyptian Sudan, and France gives Italy a part of the Sahara Desert that controls the caravan route. . . . With the opening of the Mosul-Tripoli Pipeline, oil from Iraq now flows to Tripoli, Syria (Lebanon).	Chile reports its cost of living is up 2 percent, and increases are occurring in railroad traffic, retail sales, and mining. . . . The Canadian crop forecast is improved due to much-needed rain. . . . Cuba ends its tourist tax because it hampered tourism rather than stimulating it, as intended.	In China, the Harbin railroad reopens after repairs to damage caused by the recent floods.
Jul. 21	The British plan to increase its air force by 60 percent is seen as a sign that Britain is worried about security following the announcement of a major increase in the German air forces. The other world powers are concerned, fearing an arms race. . . . Germany is exploring trade links with Argentina and other South American nations.	Austria captures the bombers who dynamited a truck, but terrorists remain active in the Tyrol. . . . The Baieruth Wagner Festival is dominated by Nazis. . . . The drought puts Hitler into a dilemma—whether to raise prices, which will alienate consumers, or to maintain prices, which will ruin farmers. . . . Polish flooding kills 200 rural farmers and overwhelms Warsaw. . . . Hungary shuts down an anti-Nazi newspaper.		Paraguay announces that it has stopped a counter offensive at Fort Ballivian. . . . Mediation begins to find a resolution to the Chaco War.	
Jul. 22		German steel production and machinery orders are up. Germany restricts imports of manufactured goods. . . . Polish flooding continues, with 60,000 now homeless and the crest expected in Warsaw today.		Paraguay accuses Standard Oil of aiding Bolivia in the Chaco War.	To prevent smuggling, China bans the export of silver. . . . A typhoon strikes Nanking.

A	B	C	D	E
Includes developments that affect more than one world region, international organizations, and important meetings of world leaders.	Includes all domestic and regional developments in Europe, including the Soviet Union.	Includes all domestic and regional developments in Africa and the Middle East.	Includes all domestic and regional developments in Latin America, the Caribbean, and Canada.	Includes all domestic and regional developments in Asian and Pacific nations (and colonies).

U.S. Politics & Social Issues	U.S. Foreign Policy & Defense	Economics & Great Depression	Science, Technology & Nature	Culture, Leisure & Lifestyle	
		The federal government announces plans to lease idle plants for canning of meat, fish, and fruit on the model of Texas, which has 19 already running.			Jul. 15
The general strike on the West Coast results in food lines and armed escorts for trucks in the Bay area. . . . Workers in two Alabama mills walk out in anticipation of the upcoming statewide textile strike. . . . Paper mill workers strike for a higher wage in Michigan. . . . Teamsters strike in Minneapolis.	The United States firmly refuses to consider linking German trade with reparations.		President Franklin Roosevelt establishes the National Power Policy Commission to develop data to create support for ratification of the St. Lawrence seaway treaty.	Louis F. Gottschalk, light opera composer, dies of a stroke at age 70. . . . A license clerk's refusal to grant a marriage license to a Siamese twin is upheld by the courts.	Jul. 16
		Cotton prices continue to rise as the drought continues to stoke fears of a shortage.	In Liverpool, England, a record 46-foot-diameter tunnel under the Mersey River opens to vehicular traffic.	The cancer mortality rate is reported to have risen in 1933 from 122.7 to 124.7 per `100,000. . . . President Roosevelt's setter, Winks, is buried in a dog cemetery at Silver Springs, Md. . . . A Romanian woman gives birth to sextuplets, overshadowing the 50-day-old Dionne quintuplets.	Jul. 17
Norman Thomas of the American Socialist Party expresses his support for the West Coast strikers, but the strike appears to be failing.		Drought persists in the west. Cattle are shot. Cities experience water shortages. Crops are struggling. Industries slow as relief rolls grow. . . . The NRA changes its maximum underbid to 10 percent.	California roses shipped in airtight containers arrive at the East Coast in perfect condition. . . . Langley Field, Va., plans a wind tunnel capable of testing speeds up to 500 miles per hour.	The Dionne quintuplets are the first in medical history to live 50 days. . . . Dr. Brodie takes a third dose of polio vaccine. . . . Owens Illinois glass company enjoys a record year thanks to the manufacture of beer bottles.	Jul. 18
The end of the West Coast strike brings relief to San Franciscans. . . . Strikes are conservatively estimated to have cost 150,000 workdays and $50 million in lost wages since January 1.	Former secretary of war Newton Baker issues a report saying that a unified air force would be a mistake but that more planes are needed. The U.S. totals are third in the world, behind Russia and France. In quality the U.S. fleet is below Japan and equal to Britain.	Jobs and payrolls are reported to have dropped in June, the first decline in 1934.		Reportedly, 110 movie stars have larger annual salaries than the President of the United States.	Jul. 19
The Minneapolis strike turns violent as police shoot 50. . . . The Portland, Ore., strike is broken when police use tear gas against 2,000 strikers.		The U.S. Postal Service reports a surplus of $5 million in June, its first surplus since 1919.		When violinist Mischa Elman declines to give an encore in Rio, the crowd riots and drags him back onto the stage.	Jul. 20
The NAACP urges President Franklin Roosevelt to push for enactment of a national anti-lynching law, following a Mississippi lynching yesterday that was the nation's 10th of the year. . . . Prohibitionists announce they intend to fight to preserve dry laws in the 19 states that still have them.		While 1,020 banks have reopened this year, 2,291 remain closed under the Bank Holiday order. . . . A challenge to the government's imposition of rules not agreed to by the industry under the NRA steel code is watched with interest by those subject to other NRA codes. . . . AAA targets are exceeded because of draught and other natural forces.	Italy and Britain are testing devices to allow escape from submarines.	All Mormon men in Utah are growing beards in honor of Brigham Young.	Jul. 21
A vote on arbitration by strikers is ordered in Seattle as the 70-day strike ends. . . . Portland strikers begin voting on arbitration. . . . The 17th triennial convention of the National Association for the Deaf opens with 2,000 attendees, and receives messages from the New York Governor and U.S. President.	Plans are announced to increase the Army's inventory of planes by 2,320. There will be no separate air force.			Federal agents kill gangster John Dillinger in Chicago. The informant's reward is $15,000.	Jul. 22

F	G	H	I	J
Includes elections, federal-state relations, civil rights and liberties, crime, the judiciary, education, healthcare, poverty, urban affairs, and population.	Includes formation and debate of U.S. foreign and defense policies, veterans affairs, and defense spending. (Relations with specific foreign countries are usually found under the region concerned.)	Includes business, labor, agriculture, taxation, transportation, consumer affairs, monetary and fiscal policy, natural resources, pollution, and accidents.	Includes worldwide scientific, medical, and technological developments, natural phenomena, U.S. weather, and natural disasters.	Includes the arts, religion, scholarship, communications media, sports, entertainment, fashions, fads, and social life.

	World Affairs	Europe	Africa & The Middle East	The Americas	Asia & The Pacific
Jul. 23		Flooding in Poland has taken 240 lives, and typhoid is reported. . . . Germany continues to have destabilizing problems in the Saar and on the border with Austria. It also imposes economic restrictions because it feels itself under blockade, as in the World War.	Chile and South Africa are preparing to begin trading with one another. This will be the first trade link in history between the west coast of South America and Africa.	Mexico establishes state oversight of the prices of gasoline and other commodities in an effort to control prices. Also subject to price control are beans, maize, cotton goods, and other consumer items.	
Jul. 24	The exodus of Jews from Germany has reached 70,000. . . . Germany's sterilization laws apply to foreigners, both temporary and resident.	Germany regards the attempted assassination of a police chief in the Saar as a bad sign for the upcoming Saar plebiscite. . . . Austria hangs a Czech terrorist after a hasty trial. Austria also guards the home of Chancellor Engelbert Dollfuss while making wholesale arrests. . . . England's war games have revealed vulnerabilities, as planes are able to hit seven key targets in London. Rains hamper night flying and radio reception. . . . Germany cuts its stormtroopers to 200,000, with 2.3 million in reserve.		In Trinidad, 1,000 unemployed sugarcane workers riot, injuring two farm employees and five policemen. . . . Cuban labor difficulties now include a strike of 1,000 telephone workers in protest of the rehiring of 300 fired for sabotage.	Japan claims that its mandate over the South Sea islands will continue after Japan leaves the League of Nations because the mandate came under the Treaty of Versailles, not the League Covenant. . . . Japan presses Russia to finalize the agreement with Manchukuo over the Chinese Eastern Railway.
Jul. 25	Nazis kill Austrian Chancellor Engelbert Dollfuss. Austria is mostly quiet and is under martial law, with 147 rebels apprehended. Kurt Schussnigg replaces Dollfuss as Chancellor. France and Britain insist that Austria's independence must be preserved. Italy is prepared to intervene, and German troops are rumored to be on the way to the border as Germany says that Austria's crisis is internal and outsiders should stay out.	Forest fires in France put the entire Mediterranean fleet on standby. . . . Adolf Hitler's guards are to wear black shirts as the Brown Shirts are downgraded. . . . Ukrainian nationalists kill a Polish professor.			
Jul. 26	Austrians continue suppressing the rebellion, and many Nazis are fleeing to Yugoslavia. . . . Germans fear war. The government denies involvement in the Austrian putsch, but Austria is skeptical. . . . Italian Premier Benito Mussolini orders the Italian air force to the border of Austria, where the 48,000-man army is already gathering.	Albania alleges that Italy is plotting to invade. . . . Officials claim that the Ukrainian harvest is greater on the collective farms than on those of individuals.			The Chinese drought is endangering millions of peasants, so the government is preparing a relief program.
Jul. 27	Austria appears to be stabilizing, and the international community is beginning to regard the crisis as having passed. . . . The Italian force at the Austrian border is now 100,000, and includes tanks and planes. . . . Germany shifts Austrian Nazis to Bavaria to keep them from crossing into Austria.		An expedition from the University of Chicago has uncovered a temple in Iraq that dates to 700 B.C.E.	Standard Oil of New Jersey denies Paraguay's charge that it aided Bolivia in the Chaco War. . . . The first contingent of U.S. Marines is leaving Haiti. All are scheduled to be gone by mid-August.	
Jul. 28	Italy and France will not accept the royalist plan to allow the return of the Hapsburg monarchy to Austria. There are concerns that Prince Otto is weak, but of greater concern is the risk of an attempt to reestablish Austria-Hungary at the expense of the Little Entente.	French socialists and Communists agree to a mutual aid pact against the Nazis. . . . Polish diplomats are seeking to end the 14-year dispute with Lithuania. . . . Poland dislikes the Eastern Locarno pact because it might upset treaties already in place.	South Africa's trade commissioner says that his country has established trade with Canada, and will begin shipping 100,000 cases of oranges each year. . . . Marshal Louis Lyautey is lying in state in France. The Sultan of Morocco pays his respects to the "maker of Morocco."	Chile announces plans to establish air service to the southern tip of South America. . . . Brazil is establishing new banking standards. . . . Bolivia is preparing to renew the offensive at Fort Ballivian against Paraguay.	The Japanese Emperor's brother's goodwill visit to Manchukuo receives negative reactions from the local people. . . . The Philippines begins trade with Japan, although their preference is for trade with the United States. . . . The Autonomous Government of Inner Mongolia is setting up its new capital in a monastery, and Prince Teh is planning to create an army.
Jul. 29		German industry is operating at 59.6 percent of capacity. . . . Stock markets in Germany, Italy, France, and Holland are rising after the easing of the Austrian crisis. . . . Germany's eugenics program is providing free houses for those who produce four faultless children in 10 years. . . . Britain's fascist, Leonard Mosley, gives credit to fascism for the prevention of war over Austria. . . . German businessmen are anticipating that the Austrian affair means the end of any hope for *anschluss*, a joining of the two countries.			A Japanese business mission is due in San Francisco this week. This is the fifth annual trade visit.

A	B	C	D	E
Includes developments that affect more than one world region, international organizations, and important meetings of world leaders.	Includes all domestic and regional developments in Europe, including the Soviet Union.	Includes all domestic and regional developments in Africa and the Middle East.	Includes all domestic and regional developments in Latin America, the Caribbean, and Canada.	Includes all domestic and regional developments in Asian and Pacific nations (and colonies).

U.S. Politics & Social Issues	U.S. Foreign Policy & Defense	Economics & Great Depression	Science, Technology & Nature	Culture, Leisure & Lifestyle	
Rains hit Texas; cotton prices rebound. . . . Heat-related deaths in the Midwest climb to 507 as temperatures hit 108°F in St Louis and 106°F in Minneapolis. Illinois, Missouri, and Nebraska are hardest hit. Temperatures are over 100°F as far south as Texas. . . . A manhunt for "Baby Face" Nelson begins in Detroit.	Brig. Gen. Billy Mitchell claims that the rest of the world has a 15-year lead on U.S. aviation.	Business purchasing agents are reportedly confused about pricing under the NRA codes, and business is down as a result. . . . Weekly business failures are up again at 234 nationally.		Dizzy Dean of the St. Louis Cardinals wins his 10th game in a row, 18th of the year. . . . Endeavor sets sail for England and the America's Cup contest. . . . The U.S. tennis doubles team beats Australia and remains in the hunt for the Davis Cup.	Jul. 23
Oklahoma cattle are dying by the thousands due to the heat and drought. . . . The Arkansas River is dry due to the drought. Heat-related deaths have reached 700.	U.S. Emergency Relief Coordinator Harry Hopkins meets with Italian Premier Benito Mussolini and Pope Pius XI after examining Italian relief efforts.	Eddie Cantor of the American Federation of Actors and other New York actors ask Mayor Fiorello LaGuardia to expand Civilian Works Administration (CWA) coverage to include vaudeville and circus performers and to add more productions. . . . Under the NRA code, cigar manufacturers are losing $1 per 1,000 cigars.	Admiral Byrd is stranded in a blizzard at his Antarctic base at Little America, and a relief column is turned back by the storm.	The American rodeo is back from London after a disappointing reception.	Jul. 24
West Coast dock workers agree to arbitration 4 to 1, and work will resume on Monday. . . . A tropical storm off the Texas coast causes uncertainty in the cotton market. . . . Heat-related deaths exceed 1,200, with over 300 in Missouri alone. . . . A three-inch rain helps alleviate the situation in Kansas.		Drought relief efforts include plans to open eastern meat packing plants and to provide $10 million in Reconstruction Finance Corporation (RFC) loans to tanners. . . . General Motors reports profits are up 50 percent, as are sales—three-quarters of a million vehicles at $500 million.	The Byrd relief column arrives at Little America.	Catholic Archbishop MacNicholas says Catholics oppose censorship, preferring voluntary responses to aroused public opinion. Protestants deny that they want censorship. Rather they want the association's censor to do his job. . . . America defeats Australia in the Davis Cup doubles in a stirring comeback.	Jul. 25
The Texas Democratic Committee bars Mexican-Americans from voting, classifying Mexicans as nonwhite. . . . Texans kill 61,000 cattle to end their suffering from the drought. . . . The Bureau of Investigation establishes a list of 6,000 wanted criminals. The bureau claims a 93 percent conviction rate. . . . Martial law is declared in Minneapolis as labor unrest continues. . . . Rain and breeze help to ease the heat wave, but deaths are at 1,361.		Foreign news is causing the stock and grain markets to decline. . . . The NRA charges that the four Schecter brothers are selling sick chickens. Indictments are handed down. . . . The federal government is prepared to buy 4 million head of cattle when the processing plants are opened. . . . The New York Stock Exchange lays off 38 because trading is in a slump.		Ontario prohibits the exhibition of the Dionne quintuplets as a "vaudeville show."	Jul. 26
Midwest deaths are at 1,429 despite the rains. The high temperature in California is 122°F. . . . The level of the Mississippi River at St. Louis is reported at zero.	Secretary of State Cordell Hull agrees to allow American merchants to sell a final $615,000 worth of goods to Bolivia but orders deliveries to the Chaco War participants cut off after that—and no planes will be delivered.				Jul. 27
African Americans vote in El Paso, Texas. . . . The Nevada drought is hitting cattle and sheep producers hard. Relief rolls are growing. . . . Martial law is in effect at the "model" community of the Kohler Company in Wisconsin after a strike turns deadly, killing two and wounding 40.		The roll of those receiving drought relief is at 3.2 million.	A Stanford University researcher has developed a method of improving students' reading speed by photographing them and pointing out how they stray. An electric pacer is also expected to enhance reading skills.		Jul. 28
All ports are peaceful, and the proposed Great Lakes tugmen's sympathy work-slowdown is cancelled.	Japan objects to President Franklin Roosevelt's plans to strengthen the Navy, and praises the U.S. Army and Navy in an address in Hawaii. Japan still intends to send Admiral Yamamoto to the United States for naval talks. . . . Roosevelt orders the trade bank to extend loans to all nations except Russia. Negotiations with Russia over old loans are continuing.	Secretary of Agriculture Henry Wallace announces that AAA cuts will continue in 1935 as planned regardless of the conditions in 1934.			Jul. 29

F	G	H	I	J
Includes elections, federal-state relations, civil rights and liberties, crime, the judiciary, education, healthcare, poverty, urban affairs, and population.	Includes formation and debate of U.S. foreign and defense policies, veterans affairs, and defense spending. (Relations with specific foreign countries are usually found under the region concerned.)	Includes business, labor, agriculture, taxation, transportation, consumer affairs, monetary and fiscal policy, natural resources, pollution, and accidents.	Includes worldwide scientific, medical, and technological developments, natural phenomena, U.S. weather, and natural disasters.	Includes the arts, religion, scholarship, communications media, sports, entertainment, fashions, fads, and social life.

	World Affairs	Europe	Africa & The Middle East	The Americas	Asia & The Pacific
Jul. 30	Irish Free State President Eamon de Valera declines to attend the 25th jubilee of the King of England, but other commonwealth leaders will be there next May.	British Prime Minister Baldwin survives a vote of censure over his announced intent to enlarge the air force over five years. Winston Churchill criticizes the plan as too slow in light of Germany's air build-up. . . . Italian forces are massed along the Yugoslavian border. Yugoslavia warns Italy not to interfere in Austria. . . . Britain and Italy are discussing 35,000-ton warships in London.		Paraguay protests the U.S. decision to allow Bolivia to buy over $600,000 worth of military equipment.	Australian fliers have discovered a "lost" civilization of 200,000 people on 5,000 square miles in New Guinea. . . . Russia rejects the Japanese offer on Manchukuo's Chinese Eastern Railway. Japan breaks off talks.
Jul. 31		Estonia, Latvia, and Lithuania are won over to the concept of the Eastern Locarno pact. . . . Britain is celebrating the centenary of the emancipation of its slaves. . . . German President Paul von Hindenburg has a stroke and is reported to be gravely ill. . . . Italy backs off its diplomatic attacks on Germany amid concerns that the loss of Hindenburg might loosen restraints on Hitler.		Canadian Prime Minister Bennett says that the provinces will have to pick up a greater share of relief because the federal government is cutting its share. . . . Argentina lifts its restriction on remittances overseas. . . . Chile fears an epidemic of typhus.	Japan is seeking expanded trade with the East Indies and backs off its assertions that it wants naval parity at the 1935 naval conference.
Aug. 1		German President Paul von Hindenburg is dead at age 86. . . . Adolf Hitler consults his cabinet amid rumors that he is to take the presidency as well as the chancellorship. . . . Poland reports that the recent floods have left 50,000 families destitute. . . . Britain has requested airfields in Europe, but Belgium is skeptical. . . . Austria's government seeks support from the socialists against the Nazis. . . . Germany's Brown Shirts begin a 30 day "vacation."	Ibn Saud, King of the Hejaz, and Ibn Yahya, King of the Yemenis, have agreed to territorial realignments and will not support opposition groups in each other's territory in accordance with the concept of Hilm, Muslim Arab unity.	Paraguay reports that it has turned back the Bolivians' attack on Fort Galpan. . . . Chile announces that it will spend $20 million on work relief.	Swiss Prof. Alfred Metraux is beginning six months of research to find the origins of the stone figures on Easter Island, the Chilean possession in the South Pacific.
Aug. 2	The merchant marines of Russia, Greece, and Finland are reported as the only fleets to have grown in 1933. The world's total decreases.	As the world mourns German President Paul von Hindenburg, European governments worry about the future with Adolf Hitler unchecked. Italy is calm at the prospect.		A hurricane strikes Nicaragua. . . . Traffic through the Panama Canal is up 4 percent in July over June.	Kidnappings in Fengtien province, Manchukuo, during June total 2,000, out of over 3,500 bandit incidents due to the flooding. The dead include 66 soldiers, 200 civilians, and 700 bandits.
Aug. 3		France reports unemployment is near 1 million.	The estate of Sultan Ahmed Kadjar, Shah of Iran until deposed in 1925, has a value of $2.7 million. Two of his 10 wives receive nothing.	Bolivia claims to have halted the renewed Paraguayan offensive in Chaco.	Manila businessmen want changes to the Tydings-McDuffie Independence Act to allow free trade with the United States to continue after independence.
Aug. 4	The Women's International Conference Against War and Fascism opens its meeting in Paris. Twenty-seven women represent North America. The conference demands immediate emancipation for women.	Adolf Hitler abolishes the presidency and becomes Reichsfuhrer.	The Nazi turmoil is generating a large influx of Zionists in Palestine, destabilizing the area.	Bolivia objects to the League embargo, and its Cabinet quits. . . . The drought has created a water shortage on the U.S.-Mexican border, generating concern that it might spark violence. Mexico's Foreign Minister says there will be an amicable settlement.	In Australia, the Communist Party is declining and heading underground due to government efforts, including deportations. Australia is contemplating outlawing the party. . . . The Chinese army crushes a rebel army in Fukien province.
Aug. 5	The World Baptist Convention, meeting in Berlin, hears the request by an African American for universal racial equality, with India supporting the idea and China and Japan expected to agree.	Basque mayors are defiant, ordering the election of a defense commission despite orders not to from the Spanish government. . . . Croats are suspected of being behind the bombings in Zagreb, Yugoslavia. . . . Germany and Italy are suspected of supporting the effort of Archduke Otto to reestablish Hapsburg rule in Austria. . . . Russia is worried about the war threats of Germany in the west and Japan in the east.		Argentina's subsidized beef industry is preparing to provide Italy's army with 10,000 tons of meat under a new trade pact. . . . Argentine grain prices are the highest in three years because of the U.S. drought. . . . Puerto Ricans are prepared to protest the 27 percent cut in their sugar quota.	Japan offers to accept 50,000 German Jews as settlers in Manchukuo.

A	B	C	D	E
Includes developments that affect more than one world region, international organizations, and important meetings of world leaders.	Includes all domestic and regional developments in Europe, including the Soviet Union.	Includes all domestic and regional developments in Africa and the Middle East.	Includes all domestic and regional developments in Latin America, the Caribbean, and Canada.	Includes all domestic and regional developments in Asian and Pacific nations (and colonies).

U.S. Politics & Social Issues	U.S. Foreign Policy & Defense	Economics & Great Depression	Science, Technology & Nature	Culture, Leisure & Lifestyle	
Martial law is in effect in New Orleans after Governor Allen says that there is fraud in voter registration. The dispute is between the political forces of Mayor Walmsley and Senator Long.	Secretary of State Cordell Hull, on behalf of the Pan American Union, calls for an end to the Chaco War.	Nationally, business failures are down at 214 for the week.	Marconi demonstrates a device that allows ships to navigate through fog by means of short-wave signals.		Jul. 30
		A federal judge in Chicago rules in the case of Irma Hatters that the NRA codes are not applicable to intrastate commerce.... Samuel Insull requests a separate trial from the other 16 defendants in his mail fraud case because his health is poor and he may not survive a six-month trial. Also, the other defendants will complicate and prejudice his case.	Dr. J.A. Anderson of the Mt. Wilson Observatory reports that space is not empty but rather is full of radiation and gases.	The national balloon races are under way, with the Army balloon off first. The winner will represent the United States in international competition in September. . . . Marie Dressler's California funeral is attended by thousands. Jeanette McDonald sings. The actress died after a lingering illness.	Jul. 31
Golford Clobridge, the disabled war veteran who sent a ransom note to the Lindberghs after the kidnapping of their baby, is once again in trouble for sending a ransom note and threatening a kidnapping.	Secretary of War Claude Swanson proposes an across-the-board reduction in navies within the guidelines of the 5-5-3 ratio.	The AAA allows increased planting, but only for pasturage. The cotton restrictions under the Bankhead Act remain in effect, and the restriction on feeder pigs is lifted. . . . Unemployment is still over 10 million, and the AFL says the government might have to take over business.... New Jersey blocks the importation of African-American farm workers, fearing that they will increase the relief burden and cause sanitation problems.	In tests of the "air train," a plane tows three gliders carrying unofficial mail in a practice run before the run from Brooklyn to Washington, D.C.... A giant Sikorsky seaplane sets a record by averaging over 150 miles per hour on a course of 1,200 miles. . . . The Lindbergh Line begins overnight air service from Newark, N.J., to the West Coast.	Three balloons are already out of the American balloon race. . . . William Grady, New York City's superintendent of schools, decries the emphasis on history in schools, preferring current events.	Aug. 1
In New Orleans, despite a court order to disarm, Governor Huey Long's forces remain on the streets in front of the voter registry. Mayor Walmsley's forces are also on the streets and armed....The Minneapolis Teamsters' strike continues, with owners seeking a settlement but strikers balking. . . . Attorney General Homer Cummings rules that under the Equal Nationality Act of May 24, a child born overseas to one American parent is a citizen, but must reside in the United States for at least five years prior to his/her 18th birthday and take a loyalty oath by age 21.5 or lose the right to U.S. citizenship.	Maj. Gen. Benjamin Foulois says that the purchase of 1,000 planes in 1936 will get the Army to the standard of 2,350 recommended by Secretary of War Newton Baker. The War Department has already requested bids on 450 planes in 1934–35. . . . Japan says that Swanson's proposal for reductions within the 5-5-3 ratio is a further insult.		Adverse headwinds force the sky train to land in Philadelphia due to lack of fuel. The effort will continue tomorrow. . . . TWA's first overnight coast-to-coast flight is a success.	The Army and Navy balloons are in a virtual dead heat for first place....J.P. Morgan's yacht, Corsair, is back in Long Island after setting a round-trip record of 20 days to England. . . . Forty-five western polo ponies are traveling east on a fast, air-conditioned train for upcoming matches.	Aug. 2
The Aluminum Company of America, citing wages superior to the community standard, rejects the request of the aluminum workers' union for a closed shop.... In Kansas, corn crumbles at the touch after weeks of drought. . . . Minneapolis truckers vote to continue the strike.	Today is the 144th anniversary of the Coast Guard.	July raw material exports are reported as up by $9 million, with retail sales increased 5–7 percent.	Despite rain and wind, the air train arrives at the White House carrying 4,000 letters.... Midwestern hail and wind storms kill 15. A flood strikes New Jersey, causing $1 million in damages.		Aug. 3
		The Federal Emergency Relief Agency is asking for $3 million to take care of Oklahoma's needy in September. Welfare recipients in the west top 800,000.... The Farm Administration will buy 5 million more cattle and 2–5 million sheep and goats.	After examining 200,000 sets, Dr. Heinrich Poll reports that fingerprints may provide clues to health. Reportedly, sufferers of a given illness have the same fingerprint patterns.	The British Empire track and field games open in London to a crowd of 40,000.	Aug. 4
	Army planes have begun mapping Alaska.		The world's oldest ear of corn, kept by the Smithsonian for two decades, proves to be a fake....A new effort to reach Admiral Byrd is under way, and the Antarctic expedition and the base are in radio contact.		Aug. 5

F	G	H	I	J
Includes elections, federal-state relations, civil rights and liberties, crime, the judiciary, education, healthcare, poverty, urban affairs, and population.	Includes formation and debate of U.S. foreign and defense policies, veterans affairs, and defense spending. (Relations with specific foreign countries are usually found under the region concerned.)	Includes business, labor, agriculture, taxation, transportation, consumer affairs, monetary and fiscal policy, natural resources, pollution, and accidents.	Includes worldwide scientific, medical, and technological developments, natural phenomena, U.S. weather, and natural disasters.	Includes the arts, religion, scholarship, communications media, sports, entertainment, fashions, fads, and social life.

	World Affairs	Europe	Africa & The Middle East	The Americas	Asia & The Pacific
Aug. 6	June exports are reported to have increased nearly everywhere in the world.		Arabs and Jews clash in Algeria after a Jewish soldier intrudes on a mosque in Constantine. One hundred are dead and 300 injured, and the governor declares martial law.	Cuba arrests three Americans suspected of smuggling arms. . . . Chile withdraws its ambassador to Paraguay after Paraguay attacks Chilean aid to Bolivia, which Chile says is a 1904 treaty obligation.	
Aug. 7	The World Baptist Convention condemns gambling and offensive movies, but praises Adolf Hitler as a model for temperance.	Archduke Otto is in Italy trying to get Mussolini's assistance. Italians are annoyed that he is aggravating the situation in Austria.	In Algeria, Constantine is quiet after the arrest of 80 Arabs. France expresses its shock, but the underlying cause is attributed to Muslim economic hardship.	Argentina, Brazil, and Uruguay urge Chile not to break relations with Paraguay, and they also ask Paraguay for flexibility. . . . Brazil is receiving Jewish exiles. . . . The first flight of the air express service linking 30 countries carries one ton of cargo. . . . Peru enforces a 1932 law requiring all businesses to employ at least 80 percent native workers. . . . In a straw vote, Puerto Rico votes 3–1 for independence.	Mohandas Gandhi begins a seven-day fast to atone for the attack of his followers on Pundit Lal Nath, an opponent of Gandhi's campaign against Untouchability.
Aug. 8				Canadian wheat exports are down to 2.2 million bushels from last year's 2.7 million. . . . Cuba takes over the American-owned telephone company in an effort to resolve the labor dispute with its operators. . . . The United States offers to mediate the Chile-Paraguay dispute.	China's famine spreads across 11 provinces. . . . Japan's navy seeks a $67 million increase, but the army wants a $35 million cut.
Aug. 9		In Baden, Germany, officials warn that ridicule of the sterilized will not be tolerated. . . . The Protestant Bishop of Germany takes dictatorial powers over the church and orders an oath of allegiance to Adolf Hitler.	South African exports are imperiled by a shortage of grain. The 15,000 farmers in Transvaal and the Orange Free State stand to lose $1 million. . . . Arrests in Algeria now total 144, but the peace is holding under martial law.	Mexico expects to benefit from U.S. silver policy. Canada expects the rise in silver prices to help its Asian trade.	Shanghai drivers are on strike and 100 have been arrested for slashing the tires of nonstrikers' rickshaws and for other violence. . . . Half a million people are starving in the Chinese drought. Temperatures reach 120°F while floods plague south China and the central government claims helplessness.
Aug. 10	Avery Brundage, president of the U.S. Olympic Association, is in Berlin, expected to approve the participation of the United States in the 1936 Olympic Games after finding that the issue of Jewish participation is moot. Great Britain is the final major nation that has not accepted the invitation.			After some of the lowest wheat yields on record, the Canadian government is considering relocating thousands of farmers from the drought-stricken provinces. . . . Puerto Rico's sugar industry is idle, with only 2 percent working in the fields.	Chinese are engaging in food riots. . . . Manchukuo backs off nationalization of its oil industry and allows foreign participation. . . . Russia asks Japan to encourage Manchukuo to accept the Eastern Chinese Railway deal.
Aug. 11	World gold production is up over the past six months due to increases in U.S. and Soviet mines.	France deports 200, including striking Polish miners and their families.	European troops patrol the streets in Algeria to preclude additional rioting.	South American Bishops call on Bolivia to maintain peace in Chaco. . . . Bolivia denies it receives aid from Standard Oil. . . . To calm relations with Paraguay, Chile is preparing a constitutional ban on foreign military aid.	Russian newspapers blame the Japanese for allowing the degradation of the Eastern Chinese Railway and for the banditry and terrorism along its route. War tensions between Russia and Japan are growing.
Aug. 12		German Protestant pastors preach against last week's decision by the Bishop to require a loyalty oath to Adolf Hitler. Some are arrested. . . . Spain arrests 47 Basque mayors for allowing the election of a defense commission despite the national ban.		Argentine trade is up 25 percent, bankruptcies are down, and the peso is stronger.	
Aug. 13	German newspapers laud President Franklin Roosevelt as a Hitler disciple, citing their similar policies.	Germany sends 15,000 Austrian Nazis to labor camps. . . . Raw material shortages continue to plague Germany.		Peru reports a surplus of 15.76 million soles and a 111 million sol budget. The budget is up 20 million over 1931 and 1932, years in which Peru paid nothing on its debt service.	At Wenchow, a Chinese treaty port, the local Kuomintang bars the importation of foreign goods in the first anti-foreign action since the Japanese took Mukden in 1931. . . . The delegation from Manchukuo breaks off negotiations over the Eastern Chinese Railway.
Aug. 14	Germany announces that on September 1 airmail service to and from South America will be weekly instead of semi-monthly. The service will depend on completion of the second floating base, a rebuilt ocean liner.	Dutch merchants who buy German goods must pay the Dutch government, which will pay Dutch exporters before sending the balance to Germany. The Netherlands is trying to fix the problem of slow payment by Germany. . . . Poland arrests the French owners of two mills. . . . Bulgaria seizes a Macedonian newspaper as part of its continuing fight with the dissident minority. . . . The Saar Board asks for an outside force of 2,000 men until the plebiscite is over next week.		Colombian oil workers, shoemakers, and taxi drivers are on strike. Seventeen are dead in riots. . . . Chile recalls its ambassador to Paraguay as the United States, Brazil, and Argentina continue efforts to resolve the dispute. . . . In the first kidnapping in Canadian history, the brewer J.S. Labatt is taken for $15,000 ransom. . . . Cuba, reorganizing its economy, declares a moratorium on industry debts until 1936.	Chinese Communists and nationalists are fighting in Foochow.

A	B	C	D	E
Includes developments that affect more than one world region, international organizations, and important meetings of world leaders.	*Includes all domestic and regional developments in Europe, including the Soviet Union.*	*Includes all domestic and regional developments in Africa and the Middle East.*	*Includes all domestic and regional developments in Latin America, the Caribbean, and Canada.*	*Includes all domestic and regional developments in Asian and Pacific nations (and colonies).*

U.S. Politics & Social Issues	U.S. Foreign Policy & Defense	Economics & Great Depression	Science, Technology & Nature	Culture, Leisure & Lifestyle	
The League of Struggle for Indian Rights of North America calls for the release of the Scottsboro prisoners and decries the Wheeler-Howard Indian Self-Rule Bill as a whitewash of abuses of Indians.	The War Department wants an additional 165,000 men and 14,000 officers.	The CCC has 360,000 enrollees, and 315,000 families are receiving remittances. . . . The cost of the drought is now $5 billion, with 27 million people in 60 percent of the country affected. . . . Forty-eight planned farm communities are being built around the country as homesteads. . . . Bucks County, Pa., puts 1,500 farms up for sale despite a farmer protest parade and a request by Governor Pinchot to delay the sale.		New York's Women's Metropolitan Golf Association bans women from wearing shorts on golf courses.	Aug. 6
In San Diego, Calif., Nazi sympathizers are implicated in a plot to steal arms from the military. . . . Governor Huey Long gets a court ruling allowing him to keep the Louisiana voter registration lists, and a court hearing on his use of militias is set for three days hence.		The AAA mails relief checks totaling over $34.6 million. . . . A plan to reorganize the Insull companies has tentative approval by a federal judge. . . . Only 66 national banks remain closed, and 55 of them have approved reorganization plans. . . . Oil output, at 2.45 million barrels a week, is only 2,000 barrels over quota.	The temperature in Kansas hits 117°F.	Dizzy Dean wins his 20th baseball game of the season. . . . Police have to control crowds outside a New York stadium after 17,000 ballet fans fill the stadium and 10,000 additional ticket-seekers mill around outside.	Aug. 7
A Nazi camp for boys is opened near Princeton, N.J.		General Motors reports its best July since 1929, and Plymouth's numbers are also positive. . . . The estimate of a 9.1 million-bale cotton crop lifts cotton prices almost $2.50 a bale.	The Barosaurus, a new dinosaur discovered in Wyoming, is estimated to be 125 million years old. . . . The Byrd relief expedition loses its tractor but gets another and resumes the effort.	The Eisteddfod Welsh choral competition draws 15,000.	Aug. 8
		President Franklin Roosevelt nationalizes silver at 50.01 cents per ounce. Under new rules, citizens must turn in their bulk silver but can keep their fabricated items, such as spoons, jewelry, and coins.		FERA has a plan to provide a CWA-like white-collar relief program for writers, musicians, artists, and playwrights. Unlike the CWA, criticized as a make-work program, this program would expect the recipients to actually produce work.	Aug. 9
Aluminum workers vote for a strike against the Mellon-owned Aluminum Company of America. William Green of the AFL deplores the company's position. . . . New Orleans civic leaders want a mediator.	The U.S.-Soviet debt talks are at a critical stage, with most of the small issues resolved.	Following its sale of Eastern Airlines because of restrictions on airmail contracts to manufacturer-owned airlines, General Motors rids itself of other airlines. North American, TWA, and Western Air Express are expected to merge into an airmail company.		The movie industry's Hays office begins to censor fan magazines. . . . Babe Ruth announces that he will retire as a regular player at the end of this season and try to become a manager.	Aug. 10
The New School for Social Research hires six more émigré German Jewish scholars. . . . The Anti-Nazi League to Champion Human Rights asks Jewish athletes to boycott the 1936 Olympics.	Secretary of State Cordell Hull threatens to terminate the $500 million debt talks if the Soviets do not stop delaying.	Farm Administration cattle purchases to date total 2.63 million head.	Dr. William Beebe sets a bathysphere record of 2,510 feet off the coast of Bermuda.		Aug. 11
Republic Steel agrees to renew its union contract in the first success of the Steel Board's National Mediation Group.		The AAA plans to allow planting of 10 million additional acres in 1935 to offset the drought. The AAA is also implementing a publicity campaign and license controls to cut down on price gouging.	The Byrd relief party, on its third attempt, reaches the Admiral and finds him thin and weak but in good spirit.	Babe Ruth fails to hit a home run but receives a standing ovation in his final appearance at Boston.	Aug. 12
The federal government calls a conciliator to Washington, D.C., in preparation for mediation of the aluminum strike that affects six plants. . . . Outside Goshen, N.Y., three farmers who beat a federal agent are in jail for violating the Dillinger Law, which prohibits impeding a federal officer. . . . Two African Americans are lynched in Mississippi.		The NRA approves the pretzel code. . . . Republic Steel reports record earnings of $864,000 for the second quarter of 1934. . . . A seat on the New York Stock Exchange costs $95,000.	A 15,000-ton rockslide cuts a 250-foot section of the Canadian side of Niagara Falls, altering the shape of the falls. . . . In New Jersey, agricultural researchers are killing crop pests with radio waves. . . . Scientists are exploring the interior of Mt. Vesuvius.		Aug. 13
The Louisiana legislature opens its special session intended to assert state power over the mayor of New Orleans in the voter registration records dispute. . . . Philadelphia arrests six anti-Nazi demonstrators.	The United States sends France $1 million in gold, the first export of gold since April 1933. . . . The Navy opens bids on 24 new ships; the PWA will pay part of the cost. . . . The U.S. flag is furled in Haiti as the Marines prepare to depart.	The TVA is selling 100 percent of its output and plans two more dams.	Maximilian Weil demonstrates the audio projector, which allows sound to reach the human ear from a wide range rather than the narrow range allowed by standard radios.	Mary Pickford says she will meet with Douglas Fairbanks but is not optimistic they can resolve their estrangement. . . . The Dionne quintuplets weigh a combined 25.5 pounds.	Aug. 14

F	G	H	I	J
Includes elections, federal-state relations, civil rights and liberties, crime, the judiciary, education, healthcare, poverty, urban affairs, and population.	Includes formation and debate of U.S. foreign and defense policies, veterans affairs, and defense spending. (Relations with specific foreign countries are usually found under the region concerned.)	Includes business, labor, agriculture, taxation, transportation, consumer affairs, monetary and fiscal policy, natural resources, pollution, and accidents.	Includes worldwide scientific, medical, and technological developments, natural phenomena, U.S. weather, and natural disasters.	Includes the arts, religion, scholarship, communications media, sports, entertainment, fashions, fads, and social life.

	World Affairs	Europe	Africa & The Middle East	The Americas	Asia & The Pacific
Aug. 15		Belgium begins reform of its credit system.	The first oil from Mosul, Iraq, shipped from Tripoli, Libya, arrives in Le Havre, France.	Mexican students complain that they were refused service in restaurants in two Texas cities. . . . Paraguay reports it has taken Fort Piculba, 136 miles from Fort Ballivian.	
Aug. 16	The United States warns other wheat producers that it will end its restrictions unless they enforce theirs.	After five years of privation and shortages, the collectivization of Russian agriculture seems to be producing favorable results. . . . France raises import duties 4 percent, principally on autos and oil. . . . Italy's army is withdrawing from the border with Austria now that stability is returned.		A dispute between Mexican and Cuban fishermen in Veracruz leads to five deaths. . . . Reamortization of $16 million in Dominican debt is seen by creditors as a positive sign.	
Aug. 17	Britain and Japan deny rumors that they have signed a secret agreement restoring the defunct 1922 treaty and giving British recognition of Manchukuo in return for British hegemony in central Asia.	Germany protests unfair newspaper coverage in the Saar.		Kidnapped Canadian J.S. Labatt is free; authorities suspect that a ransom of $50,000 was paid.	
Aug. 18	The Women's Consultative Committee begins a worldwide drive for equal status for women based on the Montevideo agreement.	Germany is holding a plebiscite on Adolf Hitler, and Germans are unhappy with the purge as well as Nazi interference with the churches. The Nazis equate a vote against them with treason. . . . Irish farmers are suffering from the loss of British markets due to the dispute with Irish nationalists.			Japan denies that its efforts to encourage the Philippines to practice free trade are an interference with Filipino internal affairs. Manuel Quezon heads a new political party, the Nationalist Democratic Party, devoted to independence for the Philippines.
Aug. 19		Germans elect Adolf Hitler as their dictator by a 9–1 margin. France and Britain are cheered by the "no" vote in the German plebiscite. Some expect a German monarchy. . . . With rioting in Dublin, the Irish Blue Shirts vote to pay no British land taxes while their dispute continues.	Rabbi Israel Goldstein of the Jewish National Fund tells the Junior Hadassah that 90 percent of Jewish immigrants are headed to the cities, and Palestine needs more farmers, not an urban ghetto.	Paraguay has taken 57 positions from Bolivia, including a vital road intersection. Ballivian is reportedly running short of water.	
Aug. 20	The United States joins the International Labor Organization. . . . Despite long meetings between the Argentine and U.S. delegations, the international wheat accords are still pending.	Poland seizes radicals to prevent anti-Jewish attacks.		A measles epidemic in Arequipa, Peru, closes schools as it kills eight children per day. . . . President Franklin Roosevelt's decision to lift tariff restrictions on drought-feed alarms Canadian farmers, who need the feed themselves.	The arrest of three Russian employees of the Chinese Eastern Railway exacerbates tensions between Russia, Manchukuo, and Japan.
Aug. 21		France encourages all qualified citizens living in France to vote in the Saar plebiscite. . . . Spain is nearing a crisis, with eight sailors charged with plotting to kill the base commander at Cartagena, and Catalans supporting the Basques.		The first flight over the Andes is by a Sikorsky amphibian plane owned by Pan American-Grace Airways. It inaugurates air service between Chile and Uruguay. . . . Paraguay takes a major Bolivian army unit and breaches Bolivia's defenses. . . . Canada's pulp and paper industry declined over 9 percent in 1933.	China's flood and drought losses are set at $1 billion, and the impact is felt over two-thirds of the country.
Aug. 22		German auto production is up 90 percent over last year. . . . German socialists begin a massive strike, and Germany arrests five Communists. . . . Spain arrests 30 Communists in the Cartagena plot.		Col. Fulgencio Batista crushes a plot by Cuban army officers who once helped him to power and laments the betrayal of trust by his former friends. . . . Mexican Gold Shirts criticize Bernard Deutsch, head of the New York Board of Alderman, for his criticism of the anti-Semitic group, claiming he is interfering with Mexico's internal affairs.	
Aug. 23		Britain attempts to negotiate a settlement to the Irish agricultural strike as the strikers near a split between De Valera and those Blue Shirts who support violence.	South Africa agrees to pay the final £7.9 million of its £8.5 million war debt to Britain.	Puerto Rico drops English for Spanish as its language of instruction in public schools.	Russia demands that Japan and Manchukuo stop their aggression, free the Russian railroad men, and stop lying about Russian interference with the East China Railway.
Aug. 24	The U.S. dollar's rise against other currencies is not sufficient to stop the shipment of $7 million in gold to Europe in two days.	After military maneuvers, Italian Premier Benito Mussolini tells his military to prepare for war. . . . Germany's 10 commandments for marriage stress eugenics and racial purity and reject non-European mates. Germany bans the Freemasons for their "Semitism." . . . The pound hits a record low against the franc.		Argentina's trade balance on July 31 is 30 percent above that of the previous year. . . . Venezuela discounts the Bolivar for oil companies, saving the companies $23 million a year.	

A	B	C	D	E
Includes developments that affect more than one world region, international organizations, and important meetings of world leaders.	Includes all domestic and regional developments in Europe, including the Soviet Union.	Includes all domestic and regional developments in Africa and the Middle East.	Includes all domestic and regional developments in Latin America, the Caribbean, and Canada.	Includes all domestic and regional developments in Asian and Pacific nations (and colonies).

U.S. Politics & Social Issues	U.S. Foreign Policy & Defense	Economics & Great Depression	Science, Technology & Nature	Culture, Leisure & Lifestyle	
	The last U.S. Marines are gone from Haiti after 19 years. President Stenio Vincent thanks President Franklin Roosevelt for being a "Good Neighbor."	Postmaster General James Farley says the results of the primary election are a vindication of the New Deal. . . . Work relief in the drought areas covers 750,000 people.	Dr. William Beebe's new bathysphere record is more than 3,000 feet below water.	Dizzy Dean is suspended for not appearing at an exhibition game.	Aug. 15
Governor Huey Long's legislature passes 27 bills, many literally pulled out of his hat, to punish New Orleans.	The War Department announces that it will be returning the remains of 14 men killed in the 1918–19 Archangel Campaign. Seventy-five were previously brought back.	The locomotive business is the best it has been in three years, but the six-month loss is $1.2 million; interest in streamlined trains is a hopeful sign.	The 19-ton Brazilian Clipper flies from Miami to Puerto Rico via Haiti, keeping contact through radio. . . . A German veterinarian, R. von Ostertag, says pasteurized milk is just a temporary fad and will give way to use of whole raw milk from healthy cows.		Aug. 16
Hiram Evans, head of the Ku Klux Klan, calls for Louisiana Governor Huey Long's defeat. Long tells Evans to stay out of his state.	The Nye Committee is beginning to examine the DuPont records in its investigation of World War munitions profiteering.	The Agriculture Department says the wheat crop is so short that there will be no exports this year.	Dr. Kolmer says his infantile paralysis vaccine works on children.	Evangeline Booth, commander of the American Salvation Army, says she will take over the world organization if asked at the upcoming convention.	Aug. 17
The Methodist Board says that arrests for drunkenness are up 31.68 percent for the first quarter of this year. . . . Attorney General Homer Cummings, after inspecting the facility, approves Alcatraz as a prison for incorrigibles. . . . The American Federation of Labor begins to purge Communists.		Despite the drought, 1934 farm income is up $1 billion at nearly $6 billion, thanks to federal assistance and higher prices. . . . Philadelphia banks want postal savings to end, considering it unfair competition.	The Brazilian Clipper reaches Brazil.		Aug. 18
Speaker of the House Homer T. Rainey is dead.		Hog prices are at a three-year high.	W.L. Aycock of Harvard University says that nature immunizes most people, and only one in a thousand benefits from an infantile paralysis vaccination. . . . Mt. Wilson observations show Pluto to be one-tenth of Earth's size.	Helen Jacobs is victorious in the U.S. Tennis Open and refuses an offer of $25,000 to turn pro.	Aug. 19
The Georgia State Supreme Court grants a new hearing to Angelo Herndon, the African-American Communist convicted of inciting insurrection by distributing Communist literature. . . . The court denies Insull's request that he be tried separately from his 16 co-defendants.	Ten Army bombers return from a 10,000-mile round-trip flight to Alaska. Commanded by Lt. Col. H. H. Arnold, the planes left on July 19.	Hawaii accepts the sugar quota established by Secretary of Agriculture Henry Wallace.	It is reported that x-rays lower blood pressure by reducing glandular activity.	Baseball Commissioner "Kenesaw Mountain" Landis reinstates Dizzy Dean, but Dean has to pay $486, including the price of two uniforms he destroyed. . . . Harlem's "wishing tree" is now hundreds of souvenirs after being cut down to allow the widening of Seventh Avenue.	Aug. 20
In North Carolina, William D. Pelley, the founder of the Silver Shirts, an American Nazi organization, and three of his aides are indicted for stock fraud. . . . A Wheeling, W.Va., assistant manager admits that he illegally assisted the company union's petition drive by offering to pay petition circulators. . . . After five weeks, the Teamsters' strike in Minneapolis is over, settled by arbitration.	In the event of war, the U.S. tin supply will last only two months, reports the State Department.	The White House announces that all New Deal agencies will be coordinated to close the gap between NRA and AAA prices and to speed the recovery. . . . Hogs are at $6.95, almost double their price three months ago. Other livestock is either steady or up. . . . National business failures are down to 108 for the week.			Aug. 21
Al Capone and 42 others are now residents of Alcatraz Prison. . . . Al Smith and John W. Davis are among the board members of the American Liberty League, a bipartisan group formed to keep the New Deal from threatening freedom, the Constitution, and property rights. . . . Secretary of the Interior Harold Ickes suspends seven teachers at Indian schools for giving humiliating punishments.	The Navy awards $53 million in contracts for 24 warships. Plans are to add another 19.	The RFC makes $250 million available for cotton loans to maintain the price of cotton at 12 cents a bale.	The fourth annual Fisher Body prizes for automotive design by high school students give $53,000 to 24 boys.	The Mexican Army polo team is en route to the United States for competition with the U.S. Army team.	Aug. 22
Sam Rayburn of Texas enters the race for Speaker of the House.		The AAA announces that its $102 million wheat plan will allow a 5 percent increase in production in 1935. . . . PWA power grants other than the $75 million to the TVA total $192 million. Projects include dams at Bonneville, Grand Coulee, Boulder, Fort Peck, and Casper-Alcova.			Aug. 23
President Franklin Roosevelt scorns the Liberty League as lovers of property who forget the commandment to "love thy neighbor."	Maj. Gen. Benjamin Foulois, head of the Army Air Corps, asks Congress to delay his dismissal until he has a chance to read the reasons for its recommendation.	Hog prices are at a four-year high. . . . July economic statistics show a decline in industrial output led by steel and a drop in employment, but bank reserves and farm prices rose. . . . The U.S.-Cuba trade agreement gives Cuba favorable terms for sugar, rum, and cigars while the United States gets cuts on tariffs on agricultural products and automobiles. . . . Russia's need for credits stymies U.S.-Russia trade talks.		In his first outing since his suspension, Dizzy Dean wins his 22nd game by shutting out the New York Giants. . . . Max Schmeling begins preparations for his bout with Walter Neusel for the German heavyweight championship, the first step to regaining his world championship.	Aug. 24

F	G	H	I	J
Includes elections, federal-state relations, civil rights and liberties, crime, the judiciary, education, healthcare, poverty, urban affairs, and population.	*Includes formation and debate of U.S. foreign and defense policies, veterans affairs, and defense spending. (Relations with specific foreign countries are usually found under the region concerned.)*	*Includes business, labor, agriculture, taxation, transportation, consumer affairs, monetary and fiscal policy, natural resources, pollution, and accidents.*	*Includes worldwide scientific, medical, and technological developments, natural phenomena, U.S. weather, and natural disasters.*	*Includes the arts, religion, scholarship, communications media, sports, entertainment, fashions, fads, and social life.*

	World Affairs	Europe	Africa & The Middle East	The Americas	Asia & The Pacific
Aug. 25	Germany's Hjalmar Schacht, minister of economics and head of the Reichsbank, says that Germany will not pay interest owed on its Dawes and Young loans and that Germany probably cannot honor its arrangements with England and France either.	Bulgarian school reform will emphasize preparation for life rather than intellectual development. . . . Germany expels Dorothy Thompson, wife of Sinclair Lewis, under the law barring foreigners from speaking disrespectfully of German officials. . . . Hitler speaks to 500,000 Germans and asks the return of the Saar to the Reich.		Brazil's president creates a "brain trust" modeled on that of Franklin Roosevelt. . . . Canada reports gold tonnage is up 11 percent for the year, and the value of that gold is up 35 percent. . . . Mexican hunger strikers who have been singing on the radio for 100 hours quit their strike after the station pays higher wages. . . . Nicaraguan guardsmen kill Sandino Gen. Tomas Blandon after he refuses to lay down his arms.	Sixty pirates join the Shantung province's army. These pirates provoked an incident with Britain by seizing a British steamer a few months back, and their option is the army or a death sentence. . . . Indians upset with Gandhi split his party and endanger constitutional reform. . . . New Zealand women have the option of remaining New Zealanders when they marry foreigners. Previously, they lost British citizenship, taking the citizenship of their husbands.
Aug. 26		France estimates that French people are still hoarding between $390 million and $431 million in gold. . . . As Adolf Hitler campaigns in the Saar, 70,000 pledge to vote against him. . . . Poland denies it has a secret treaty obligation to aid Germany in the event of war.	Construction nearby threatens Istanbul's Santa Sophia mosque. . . . Persia seeks China's seat on the League council as Far Eastern representative.	Canadian newsprint exports are up $1 million over 1933's total. . . . Paraguay's assault in the Chaco continues to gain ground.	
Aug. 27	Recent shipments of gold have raised the price of the dollar and stopped the outflow of gold.	Finland plans to argue before the IAAF that each nation has the right to determine its athletes' amateur status. Finns hope to reinstate the amateur status of Paavo Nurmi. . . . Northern Ireland bans the Blue Shirts. . . . Joseph Goebbels prepares Germans for a hard winter by declaring hunger a virtue.	Zionist leader, Louis Lipsky of the American Palestine Campaign, says Europe is forcing Jews out and Palestine should prepare to receive a mass exodus.	Guatemala, El Salvador, and Honduras agree to settle their common borders. . . . Brazilian bakers and factory workers strike.	Japan blames the Third International for the railway conflict; Russia accuses Japanese of provocations, rather than Manchukuoans. . . . Java expels a Japanese writer accused of writing against the Dutch East Indies government.
Aug. 28	European armies are preparing for a fast war, with the Italians declaring trench warfare obsolete, the British buying fast tanks, and the French investing in fast planes. . . . Japan threatens to abrogate the naval treaty unless the other powers agree to parity.	Heimwehr clashes in Austria, although contained, raise concerns over a new Nazi rising. . . . The IAAF refuses to lift the ban on Nurmi's competing in international events, including the Olympics.		Costa Rican banana workers end their strike, agreeing to an eight-hour day at 15 cents an hour.	Chinese silver worth $450,000 is in the United States for refining before heading to Britain.
Aug. 29		Austria prepares for a putsch.		Brazilian strikes go to arbitration.	
Aug. 30	Britain, France, and Italy back Russia's admission to the League of Nations, virtually assuring victory. . . . Britain seeks agreement on a world reduction in merchant tonnage; the United States sees it as a thrust at the U.S. merchant marine.	To make industrial jobs for married men, Germany is sending bachelors under 25 to the farms.	Persia denies reports that Standard Oil is sovereign over Bahrain Island, noting that the issue has not been to the League yet.	Chile becomes the first Latin American nation to ratify the women's equality agreement. . . . Canada's wheat crop is forecast to be up 14 million bushels at 265 million bushels.	Japan tries to block the U.S.-Philippines trade pact as discriminatory against Japan.
Aug. 31	The Little Entente backs Russia's admission into the League of Nations. . . . The British pound is at its lowest level since February.	British labor goes on record in opposition to fascism and Nazism. . . . German film production is down; filmmakers try to avoid censorship by setting their films in the 19th century. . . . Direct phone service begins between Paris and Moscow. . . . Austria breaks up a rally of Socialists, closes the Nazi-friendly German Club, and takes a German Krupp official into custody.		Paraguay agrees to arbitration, but the fighting continues. . . . Stevedores in Rio get a 28 percent pay raise. . . . A storm in the Gulf of Mexico keeps ships in harbor at Tampico, Mexico.	
Sept. 1		Bulgaria warns its leftist rebels that they face prison terms of up to 10 years.	Anti-Jewish Arab youth are patrolling to prevent the smuggling of Jews into Palestine. The activity delays implementation of limited self-rule for Palestine.	The Argentine wheat crop is coming in at nearly 30 million bushels above estimate. . . . A gold rush is under way in Brazil.	Scientists determine that the craters of central Australia are due to meteors.
Sept. 2	China asks Britain to cancel its trade meeting with Manchukuo and come to China instead.	In what appears to be a united front against Nazism, Estonia, Lithuania, and Latvia sign a treaty joining their foreign policies, leading to Polish worries that its efforts to establish better relations with Lithuania will be hampered.			The Manila constitutional convention defeats giving women the right to vote.
Sept. 3	The dollar holds steady in French trading because it is at parity with gold; the British pound continues to decline.	Austria arrests 120 Communists and affirms that there is no interest in a Hapsburg restoration. Austrian Chancellor Schuschnigg says he will free the rebels if they behave.		The Paraguayan drive in the Chaco War is approaching Standard Oil's fields. . . . Archaeologists unearth a pre-Incan village in Bolivia. . . . Martial law returns to Cuba, this time because students are rioting. . . . Uruguay bans imports from countries that do not buy Uruguayan products.	To scatter pirate bands before they begin harassing coastal shipping, Chinese gunboats join land forces in pursuit of the pirates.

A	B	C	D	E
Includes developments that affect more than one world region, international organizations, and important meetings of world leaders.	Includes all domestic and regional developments in Europe, including the Soviet Union.	Includes all domestic and regional developments in Africa and the Middle East.	Includes all domestic and regional developments in Latin America, the Caribbean, and Canada.	Includes all domestic and regional developments in Asian and Pacific nations (and colonies).

U.S. Politics & Social Issues	U.S. Foreign Policy & Defense	Economics & Great Depression	Science, Technology & Nature	Culture, Leisure & Lifestyle	
New Orleans civic leaders organize to prevent Governor Huey Long from abusing the electoral process. Meanwhile, a federal jury is investigating Long's income.			John Grierson of Britain flies across Greenland despite radio and engine trouble. . . . Greece reports that golden axes and other archaeological treasures from the 16th century B.C.E. have been stolen from a newly discovered site.		Aug. 25
Fifty fascist Star Shirts are arrested in New Jersey for causing disorder. . . . A survey reveals that 25 percent of Manhattan's homes lack adequate sanitation.		Cotton farmers in 17 states receive $38 million in support. . . . Studebaker's receivers report the auto company had a small profit in the last quarter.	The colds among Admiral Byrd's men in the "germless" Antarctic are blamed on germs in their clothes. . . . Pomona scientists using a camera capture the spectrum of the Perseid meteor shower.	Two bicycle teams set a new mark by riding across the United States in less than eight days. . . . Arturo Toscanini conducts and Lotte Lehmann performs as a soloist in Strasbourg to highly enthusiastic audiences. . . . The U.S. rifle team wins the Dewar Trophy, beating Britain and setting a world mark.	Aug. 26
Three thousand Polish and African Americans engage in a race riot at Niagara Falls.		The NRA codes are consolidated into 22 groups. A New York federal court rules that flight from the NRA, or leaving a state to avoid NRA coverage, is illegal. Chicago begins paying its teachers $26 million it owes in back pay.	In French Indo-China, Dr. Georges H. Montel says he has made contagious leprosy cases uncontagious. . . . The University of Minnesota begins an experiment with cast-iron paving in Minneapolis.	Babe Ruth's pinch-hit double earns the Yankees a 3–2 win over the White Sox.	Aug. 27
Upton Sinclair, socialist author, has a 3–1 majority over Woodrow Wilson's propagandist, George Creel, in the race for the Democratic Senatorial nomination.	Senator Gerald Nye's committee has a witness list of 100 munitions makers and suppliers.	A seat on the Cotton Exchange is up $250 at $18,250. . . . Customs receipts are up 25 percent at $314 million for the year. Food prices are the highest since 1931 but are still 30 percent below 1926 costs. . . . With 26 percent of its population on relief, New York City leads other cities by far.			Aug. 28
National and state Democrats are not sure they will back Upton Sinclair in the Senate race. President Franklin Roosevelt says he stays out of local races.	Nye wants government control of the munitions industry.	Judge Marcus B. Campbell rules that the NIRA has changed anti-trust law, and 41 of the 60 findings against the A.L.A. Schechter Poultry Corporation are valid.		Detroit's Lynwood "Schoolboy" Rowe loses to the Philadelphia Athletics in his attempt to win a record 17th straight ballgame.	Aug. 29
	Secretary of War Newton Baker refuses to fire Maj. Gen. Benjamin Foulois, head of the Army Air Corps.	Cotton prices fall in anticipation of a national textile strike set for September 1. . . . Thirty days of rising hog prices come to an end. . . . Henry Ford is building his own $1.275 million steel mill.			Aug. 30
Police break up a protest by 1,500 people in Harlem against discrimination by a local employer. Two are charged with incitement to riot and malicious mischief. . . . The American Legion commander calls for the elimination of Communism, revived patriotism, and a strong defense. . . . Governor Huey Long's troops take charge of the streets of New Orleans.	The head of the Navy League backs President Roosevelt's position that a strong merchant marine is vital in wartime.	The textile strike of 650,000 workers begins violently in Georgia and expands to cover woolen workers, with silk workers sympathetic.	London is experimenting with helicopters for traffic control. . . . France is trying to synthesize oil from coal.	Dizzy Dean wins his 23rd game, and the Cardinals tie the Cubs for second place. . . . After months of trials, Rainbow edges Yankee by a second to defend the America's Cup against the British Endeavour. . . . The Chicago Bears and the College All-Stars play to a scoreless tie.	Aug. 31
	The Army contracts for 2,000 autos at a total of $1 million.	Kansas farmers are using deep plowing to reduce erosion from the wind.	Airline safety for the first half of 1934 is improved over the first half of 1933, with 27 mishaps rather than 48 and an average of one accident every 800,000 miles flown. . . . The Cartier Bridge over the St. Lawrence River opens. . . . Four Soviet scientists are rescued after being stranded in the Arctic for two years.		Sept. 1
A meeting of 1,000 unionists in Charlotte, S.C., turns into a prayer meeting as the textile strike looms. . . . Jewish war veterans ask for a boycott of the Olympics and a stop to U.S. loans to Germany.	The president of Electric Boat is the first witness in the Senate munitions hearings.	The first heavy rain since May marks the end of drought in Arkansas.		Five American and five foreign crews compete in the Hudson River lifeboat races. . . . Russ Columbo, the popular singer, dies in a pistol accident.	Sept. 2
Herbert Hoover calls the New Deal an enemy to human liberty. . . . William Green of the AFL calls for a 30-hour workweek under the NRA. . . . Upton Sinclair explains his End Poverty in California Plan to President Franklin Roosevelt. . . . Twenty-one percent of textile workers are on strike.		The Fuel Code group resigns en masse, citing the dilatory tactics of the NRA regarding coal.		On the fourth ballot, Evangeline Booth becomes the first American and first woman to head the Salvation Army. . . . Babe Ruth hits his 21st home run and Jimmy Foxx of the Philadelphia Athletics hits his 40th as the Yankees close their home season. . . . An Italian crew wins the lifeboat races handily.	Sept. 3

F	G	H	I	J
Includes elections, federal-state relations, civil rights and liberties, crime, the judiciary, education, healthcare, poverty, urban affairs, and population.	Includes formation and debate of U.S. foreign and defense policies, veterans affairs, and defense spending. (Relations with specific foreign countries are usually found under the region concerned.)	Includes business, labor, agriculture, taxation, transportation, consumer affairs, monetary and fiscal policy, natural resources, pollution, and accidents.	Includes worldwide scientific, medical, and technological developments, natural phenomena, U.S. weather, and natural disasters.	Includes the arts, religion, scholarship, communications media, sports, entertainment, fashions, fads, and social life.

	World Affairs	Europe	Africa & The Middle East	The Americas	Asia & The Pacific
Sept. 4	Russia backs Turkey's desire to refortify the Straits of the Dardanelles. . . . With governmental support, the British pound rises sharply.	In an anti-Nazi move, British unions ask the government to ban civilian organizations from acquiring arms and drilling. . . . France offers the Saar equality and the French stake in its mines if it votes in France's favor. . . . A crowd of 100,000 welcomes Adolf Hitler at the opening session of the Nuremburg rally. . . . Germany begins a campaign to remove non-Aryan pastors.		Gen. Juan Escamilla, a Mexican fighting in the Nicaraguan Guard against the Sandinistas, is not dead as earlier reported. . . . Peru protests a 15 percent rate hike on a British-owned railroad. . . . Meeting in San Juan, the American Legion calls for statehood for Puerto Rico.	Encouraged by Prince Fumimoro Konoe, Japan is opening a library in New York City to promote better understanding of Japan by Americans. . . . In Tokyo, 11,000 transport workers strike against pay cuts.
Sept. 5	Colombia protests the Italian embargo of its coffee. . . . The dollar is above its gold point, the franc is falling, and governmental support fails to sustain the pound.	Adolf Hitler proclaims the 1,000-year Reich.	Persia will withdraw its claim to the nonpermanent Far Eastern seat on the League Council and support Turkey's bid against China.	Fifteen bomb explosions in Havana lead Cuba to draft a tighter antiterrorism law. . . . Canadian textile unions and manufacturers are expecting fallout from the strike in the United States.	Russia and Manchukuo sign a frontier agreement, but Russo-Japanese tensions remain because of Japanese slowness to apologize for the kidnapping of Russian citizens and Russia's belief that Japan will take the Eastern Chinese Railway by force.
Sept. 6	Colombia restricts Italian goods in retaliation for the coffee embargo. . . . World oil output is up 7.7 percent, to 733 million barrels for July.	The Irish Free State reports a record trade deficit of $95 million and a 50 percent trade decrease in four years, primarily due to the conflict with Britain.		Bolivia's demand for a port on the Paraguay River before arbitration hampers the pursuit of peace in Chaco.	Australia and New Zealand restrict trade between each other in foreign ships. . . . A Japanese plane completes the first commercial flight between Japan and China since the beginning of Sino-Japanese difficulties.
Sept. 7		The British take offense to U.S. reports linking King George to the munitions controversy, but liberals consider an investigation of their own into the industry. . . . France and Italy prepare to sign a defense treaty against Hitler. . . . Czechoslovakia denies that President Thomas Masaryk is ill. . . . Russia's cities are suffering a food shortage because of poor distribution systems. . . . Sixty percent of Basque mayors quit, and threats of a leftist general strike and Catholic opposition to the government destabilize it.		Paraguay encourages the Santa Cruz area to secede from Bolivia. . . . Argentina bars discussion of tariffs at the Pan-American meetings. . . . Paraguay indicates that it will ask the Nye Committee to investigate the wearing of American uniforms by Bolivians.	Shanghai postal workers agree to arbitration and end their strike.
Sept. 8		Catalans crush anarcho-syndicalists in Spain. . . . Adolf Hitler says feminism is a Jewish product and women should be mothers. . . . Italians agree with Premier Benito Mussolini that a high birthrate equals a strong nation.	Italy prepares for an Ethiopian attack on Abyssinia and watches Japanese penetration of Africa warily.	Colombians are striking, while peasants take the land they work from their landlords. Inflation is high. . . . Mexican graphics arts workers go on strike in support of the U.S. textile walkout.	A typhoon strikes Japan.
Sept. 9		The six Balkan nations postpone their Balkan Conference because of disagreements. . . . Ireland bans foreign ownership of industry. . . . The League of Nations reports that Austria's economy is improving. . . . Five thousand Nazi Black Shirts and 5,000 British Communists rally peacefully near to each other in Hyde Park, as 7,000 police and 140,000 curious onlookers watch. . . . Russian gold helps to stem the drain on the Reichsbank. . . . The Spanish strike ends as Catholics expect to join the government.	Japan denies that Italy has any reason for sending additional troops to Africa because of fears that Japan might enter Italy's colonies in Africa, particularly Abyssinia. Japanese exports to Africa in the first seven months of 1934 were $31 million, up from $22 million for the same period in 1933. . . . Earthquakes rock Algeria.	Argentina sets up a commission to examine meatpacking profits. . . . The Pan-American Conference on Education opens in Chile with only Paraguay absent. . . . Paraguay renews its offensive in Chaco. . . . Scores are injured in protests involving 30,000 people against the government's closing of some Catholic churches in Mexico.	
Sept. 10		Germany rejects Eastern Locarno unless it allows German rearmament. Yugoslavs demonstrate against Italy as Italo Balbo, governor of Algiers, tours Dalmatia.		Cuba blames the *Morro Castle* blaze on Communists.	
Sept. 11	Australia blocks Russian entry into the League.	Czechoslovakia acknowledges that Masaryk is sick but denies that his facilities are impaired. . . . German Nazis kidnap an Austrian commander. . . . The German government takes control of all foreign trade. . . . Spain seizes an arms cargo and arrests socialist officials in Oviedo.		Failure of the Cuzco wheat crop produces a food shortage in Peru. . . . The Canadian wheat crop is 277 million bushels, up from 269 million in 1933. . . . Costa Rica accuses Nicaraguan vandals of looting the banana crop during the Costa Rican strike.	Japan is exploring ways to institute trade reprisals against Italy, Germany, and Portugal for their restrictions on Japanese goods. . . . Chinese bankers are worried about the outflow of silver from China.

A	B	C	D	E
Includes developments that affect more than one world region, international organizations, and important meetings of world leaders.	Includes all domestic and regional developments in Europe, including the Soviet Union.	Includes all domestic and regional developments in Africa and the Middle East.	Includes all domestic and regional developments in Latin America, the Caribbean, and Canada.	Includes all domestic and regional developments in Asian and Pacific nations (and colonies).

U.S. Politics & Social Issues	U.S. Foreign Policy & Defense	Economics & Great Depression	Science, Technology & Nature	Culture, Leisure & Lifestyle	
A strike of left-wing fur workers results in union recognition and a 25-hour week after the owners are unable to get AFL replacements. . . . Senator William G. McAdoo of California says that EPIC would cost the state $300 million. California's record budget is only $216 million. . . . A federal court bars Louisiana Governor Huey Long from altering New Orleans voter rolls and the use of state police on election day.	The Nye hearings disclose that American and British companies split submarine sales during World War I. Also, businesses gave German firms patent information that aided the development of the U-boat. . . . The reciprocal trade agreement with Belgium is the first with a European nation.	The fur trade joins the NRA.	The Byrd Antarctic expedition discovers that the Ross Sea is open, not ice-bound as long believed. . . . Plans to control erosion at Niagara Falls are dismissed as tampering with nature.	A world convention of philosophers in Prague is split over the issue of democracy.	Sept. 4
Police break up a crowd of about 5,000 African Americans attending an open-air meeting of the Young Liberators to urge a local lunchroom to hire African-American help. . . . Buses will replace trolleys on nine New York lines.		Oil and gasoline production for the previous week are below quotas.	The Byrd team is exploring the night sky and auroras. . . . Sir James Jeans opens a meeting of British scientists by declaring that, according to the new physics, the only reality is in the mind, but the new physics reestablishes free will. Newtonian physics is dead. . . . Aviator Wiley Post uses a pressurized rubber suit and reaches 40,000 feet.	The Mexican Army team beats the U.S. Army 9–2 to start the polo matches.	Sept. 5
Ten die in violence related to the textile strike. . . . Garment workers are called to strike on October 1. . . . Repeal of Prohibition has reduced the federal prison population from 18,636 to 15,433.	Again, the U.S.-Soviet trade talks reach impasse over the problem of lending the Russians an amount equal to the Russian debt.	Auburn, Hupp, Graham-Paige, Reo, and Pierce Arrow plan to merge to compete with Ford and General Motors. . . . Two Fisher brothers retire from General Motors, but four others remain. The family owns 35 percent of GM.	Dr. William Beebe adds a tail and fins to his bathysphere so he can explore the ocean floor off the coast of Bermuda. . . . Lord Raglan predicts that American blacks and whites will blend into one race.		Sept. 6
Mayor Fiorello LaGuardia says that Harlem "hot spots" are a tourist attraction, not typical of African-American life in New York. . . U.S. Methodists establish a committee to reunite their three groups by 1944. . . . A radio preacher is indicted on mail fraud charges for claiming psychic powers.	The Nye Committee reveals that King George of England interfered in a U.S.-Polish business deal and that aides to President Calvin Coolidge revealed U.S. gun secrets to increase foreign sales.	A court rules that dry-era alcohol is still subject to federal tax, regardless of fines paid. . . . Harry Hopkins acts to tighten FERA relief rolls to those actually in need, and works to control a glut of wool and hides due to drought relief. . . . President Franklin Roosevelt backs retention of the collective bargaining provision in the NRA codes.	German pilots lead the air race in Orly, France.		Sept. 7
Off New Jersey, the luxury liner Morro Castle catches fire, with 182 dead or missing and 375 survivors. . . . Louisiana Governor Huey Long and the New Orleans mayor declare a truce for Tuesday's election. . . . A mob in Princess Anne, Md., overwhelms the police and forces the African-American population to flee.		Now that Chicago has paid its teachers, the students return to school. . . . The United States is negotiating five reciprocal trade agreements with Latin American countries and plans four more.	People on the Great Plains are skeptical of the value of President Franklin Roosevelt's proposed $75 million shelterbelt project.	During the final regatta of the season, five yachts capsize.	Sept. 8
A Tennessee jury convicts eight white men of voluntary manslaughter in the death of a black man. . . . In New Jersey, 125,000 curiosity seekers view the burning hulk of the Morro Castle just off shore.	The Nye Committee turns its attention to airplanes and gunpowder.	AAA payments are $1 million a day. . . . The projected corn crop is 1.5 billion bushels, far below the average of 2.5 billion bushels. . . . Hog prices are down with demand.	M.I.T. researchers produce an explosive war gas.	The America's Cup races begin with both yachts carrying full sail in windy conditions and stormy seas. . . . A crowd of 20,000 watches the Black Yankees fall to the Chicago Giants in a Negro League baseball game.	Sept. 9
New Jersey sightseers pay $2,800 a day to see the Morro Castle hulk. . . . The textile strike begins to affect upholstery workers. . . . Federal mediators meet with textile owners as troops patrol New England mills. Some strikers return to work in the south.	The Navy approves a 500-plane program for 1936. . . . The Marines lower the recruitment age from 35 to 25.	Ford and Oldsmobile resume assembling cars, raising the auto index for the week. . . . Business failures, at 174, are the lowest since 1920. . . . At $78,000, a New York Stock Exchange seat is the cheapest since 1932. . . . The federal government is short $2 billion in its retirement account because of so many forced retirements.	Dr. E.F. Carpenter of Arizona discovers his second supergalaxy, the 20th found to date. . . . The American Chemical Society learns that Dr. Aristid von Grosse of Chicago has isolated protactinium, an extremely radioactive element that degenerates to actinium. . . . Naval Observatory astronomers report that Washington and San Diego are 40 feet farther apart than they were in 1926.	Princeton, University of Pennsylvania, Rutgers, Yale, and Lafayette form a 150-pound football league.	Sept. 10
Rhode Island textile strikers break through the militia's line in an effort to burn a Saylesville textile mill.	The Nye Committee's revelations of world involvement in munitions deals lead Secretary of State Cordell Hull to express support for the committee's work.	The FDIC insures 50 million accounts worth $35 billion.	Pittsburgh chemists report that a quinine derivative in tablet form reportedly helps in the treatment of pneumonia. . . . A Harvard astronomer rediscovers the planet Hidalgo, last seen in 1925.	The Mexican Army polo team beats the U.S. Army team 14–12 on a soggy field.	Sept. 11

F	G	H	I	J
Includes elections, federal-state relations, civil rights and liberties, crime, the judiciary, education, healthcare, poverty, urban affairs, and population.	Includes formation and debate of U.S. foreign and defense policies, veterans affairs, and defense spending. (Relations with specific foreign countries are usually found under the region concerned.)	Includes business, labor, agriculture, taxation, transportation, consumer affairs, monetary and fiscal policy, natural resources, pollution, and accidents.	Includes worldwide scientific, medical, and technological developments, natural phenomena, U.S. weather, and natural disasters.	Includes the arts, religion, scholarship, communications media, sports, entertainment, fashions, fads, and social life.

	World Affairs	Europe	Africa & The Middle East	The Americas	Asia & The Pacific
Sept. 12		British labor and liberals want an inquiry similar to the Nye Committee. . . . As a sign of lessened friction caused by border incidents, Hungary and Yugoslavia sign a trade agreement.		Cubans begin to notice that the decree suspending constitutional guarantees expired last week. . . . Mexico denies that its officials were involved in the munitions deals. . . . El Salvador denies rumors that it plans to annex to Mexico.	Japan asks Russia for a peace zone of 25 miles on either side of the Manchukuoan border.
Sept. 13	Poland's rejection of the treaty on minorities, with its provisions for international oversight, shocks the League members, who regard it as a blow to the concept of the League itself.	Macedonian separatist Ivan Mikhailoff flees Bulgaria for Turkey with gendarmes in hot pursuit.		Bolivia takes Paraguayan supplies as Argentina tightens air patrols over Indians on its border. . . . An explosion in Managua leads to martial law in Nicaragua. . . . Guatemala discovers plans for a rebellion.	A draft plan to reform the administration of Manchukuo gives the military greater authority. . . . Russia's reaction to the Japanese peace zone proposal is negative; it would require expensive border forts for Russia while it would cost Japan nothing.
Sept. 14	Japan thanks El Salvador for recognizing Manchukuo. . . . Britain, France, and Italy warn Poland about treaty obligations.	Austria agrees to allow the Hapsburg pretender and family to visit as private citizens for Christmas. . . . A British poll finds that 87.9 percent oppose foreign entanglements. . . . Germany bans gold rings. Germany admits that Rudolf Hess ruled on August 16 that party members could not associate with Jews.	Hubert Julian of New York, the "world's greatest Negro aviator," announces in Paris that he will fly Emperor Haile Selassie's plane from New York to Addis Ababa.	Argentina shuts down Standard Oil's radio transmitter near the Bolivian border as a violation of postal regulations. . . . British Columbia's Premier William A.C. Bennett asks the provinces to meet to develop social programs under a Canadian New Deal.	Siam's Cabinet resigns in a dispute over the rubber tariff. . . . China reports that smuggling costs Kwangtung $3 million a month. . . . U.S. cutters chase a Japanese fishing vessel, the *Hayun Maru*, whose crew reportedly attacked Filipino officers.
Sept. 15	Thirty countries invite Russia into the League of Nations.	The Reichsmark, at 40.55 cents, is at a 10-month high. The gain is attributed to German import controls. . . . The Balkan states propose a treaty among all nations on the Mediterranean Sea. . . . Britain is preparing for a significant exodus to the dominions. . . . Macedonian revolutionary Ivan Mikhailoff is in Turkey, which refuses to return him to Bulgaria.	King Fuad of Egypt has shifted from a pro-British stance to the anti-British nationalist Wafd, leaving a void that Palestinian Jews can use to demand imperial preference and greater influence in the empire.	Argentina claims that Bolivia agreed to arbitration in a 1932 treaty. . . . Banana cutting resumes in Costa Rica under military protection after the deportation of 18 Nicaraguans.	
Sept. 16		Joseph Goebbels promises that there will be food for all Germans this winter. . . . Poland's Foreign Minister says Poland will guarantee Jewish rights. . . . Dublin printers are in the eighth week of their strike. . . . A dozen Rhone Valley mayors threaten to resign if Paris does not aid the idle.	A breakdown in Cairo's drainage system causes floods and privation.	Bolivia and Paraguay attack Argentina's breach of confidentiality in its report on Chaco. . . . Canada partially lifts its embargo on hay shipments to the United States. . . . Peru reports customs duties up 61 percent over six months.	The Australian Communist vote is triple that of 1931, but they gain no seats and the current government retains power.
Sept. 17	Turkey replaces China as a nonpermanent member of the League Council. Spain and Chile are also members. The League votes 38–7 to admit Russia.	Russia dismisses the League's powers and says it will rely on the Red Army.	Cardinal Fumasoni-Biondi, head of Roman Catholic missions, asks Catholics to work to free the world's 6 million slaves, many in Ethiopia, Liberia, and many Muslim countries. Arabia buys 2,000 African slaves a year. . . . The expedition financed by Mrs. Oscar Straus returns to the United States with tropical birds and recordings of tribal music.	Argentina withdraws as mediator in the Chaco War, leaving it to the League, while Bolivia advances and Paraguay resolves its disagreement with Chile. . . . In a drought relief measure, British Guiana plans to grow 3,000 acres of irrigated rice. . . . Machine-gunners guard the Cuban presidential palace in expectation of an uprising.	Manchurian bandits kill 14 and injure 15 in an attack on a bus. . . . Police jail 22 radicals and fire on a mob of strikers trying to enter a cigar factory, killing three and wounding 19.
Sept. 18		Britain acknowledges that its firms are selling airplane engines to Germany and says the business is perfectly legal. . . . Italy says it will train eight-year-old boys for war and extend the post-active duty obligation to 10 years. . . . All Italian farming will be under central control.		Thirty-five bombs, blamed on student strikers, explode in Havana overnight. . . . Para, Brazil, finds business hamstrung by a strike of 40,000 workers.	China observes "Humiliation Day," and Japan mourns its dead on the third anniversary of the Mukden Incident.
Sept. 19	Irish Free State President Eamon De Valera calls on the League to send forces to end the Chaco War. France and Britain denounce the war.	Germany and Britain begin commercial negotiations. . . . Germany arrests a Bishop who resists the state merger of Protestants and Catholics. . . . Arson is suspected in the fire at Adolf Hitler's *Voelkischer Beobachter*. . . . The Netherlands announces a 93 million guilder cut to balance its budget. . . . In return for arms loans, Albania agrees to let Italian officers into its army and 10,000 Italian colonists into its Mushakia Valley.		Argentina denies foreigners writs of habeas corpus in deportation hearings.	

A	B	C	D	E
Includes developments that affect more than one world region, international organizations, and important meetings of world leaders.	Includes all domestic and regional developments in Europe, including the Soviet Union.	Includes all domestic and regional developments in Africa and the Middle East.	Includes all domestic and regional developments in Latin America, the Caribbean, and Canada.	Includes all domestic and regional developments in Asian and Pacific nations (and colonies).

U.S. Politics & Social Issues	U.S. Foreign Policy & Defense	Economics & Great Depression	Science, Technology & Nature	Culture, Leisure & Lifestyle	
The Louisiana National Guard begins withdrawing from New Orleans, opening the city again to its underworld. . . . Nine states hold primaries.	Secretary of State Cordell Hull blames German trade restrictions for increasing world unemployment. . . . Nye clarifies his statements on King George's involvement in munitions deals and pacifies British opinion. . . . The DuPont chemical company made $1.25 billion in profit from the war, declaring a 100 percent dividend in 1916.	Despite tariffs, foreign grains are coming into the United States in quantities sufficient to lower U.S. prices. . . . Hog prices rise 5–10 cents, the first increase in two weeks.	University of Pittsburgh researchers report that phosphotase, an enzyme in the kidneys, helps to fight cancer.		Sept. 12
Donations to the Jewish National Fund of America are up 42 percent over the past 11 months. . . . Treasury Secretary Henry Morgenthau says employees can contribute to and work for campaigns—but only on their own time. . . . President Roosevelt speaks at the Human Needs Conference, seeking private help for the 8 million needy not covered by federal programs.	The Nye Committee reveals that DuPont attempted to influence high-level government officials to drop the munitions embargo, and that American and British firms divided the chemical business.	South Carolina begins clearing the way for the Saluda Dam project in anticipation of the administration's rejection of the Duke Power objection.		The Yankees' Lefty Gomez ties Dizzy Dean with 25 victories. . . . Ford Motor Company pays $100,000 for the first-ever broadcast rights for the World Series.	Sept. 13
Georgia's governor orders troops to the mills to protect workers, and he outlaws strikers' flying squads. . . . The easing of violence in Rhode Island allows the governor to back off his call for federal troops.		Hogs gain 10 cents; cattle prices are steady. . . . Railway executive compensation is down 34 percent from 1929. . . . Railroad chiefs criticize ICC barge rates and the war department's management of inland waterways.		*Endeavour* is a 6–5 favorite to take the America's Cup as races begin.	Sept. 14
Upton Sinclair drops his plans for old-age pensions, communal farms, and state factories. . . . Tax officials charge that Andrew Mellon manipulated his family to avoid $3 million in taxes.	The Army dead from the 1919 Archangel expedition arrive in New York. . . . The Nye Committee reveals Germany is smuggling planes in parts from the United States, Great Britain, and Sweden.	The Federal Subsistence Homesteads Corporation reports that 177 of 463 planned homesteads are currently occupied. . . . Bankers are reluctant to lend money to Puerto Rican sugar growers because the quota is so indefinite; workers remain idle. . . . America First, Inc., calls on President Roosevelt to fire his "Red" NRA chiefs. . . . A Senate committee calls for reform of the "archaic" banking system.	A Danish scientist reports that the sun generates the Northern Lights and the magnetic pole attracts them. . . . New York, New Jersey, and Connecticut begin removing trees blighted with Dutch Elm disease.	Ralph Metcalfe ties the world 100-meter mark of 10.3 seconds in an American-Japanese competition. . . . The Germans encourage U.S. Olympic Committee president Avery Brundage to commit the United States to the Olympics. Brundage is noncommittal. . . . *Rainbow* has a mile lead at half a mile from the finish when the winds die, resulting in the cancellation of the first race of the America's Cup.	Sept. 15
	Germany asks the United States for a reciprocity agreement. Secretary of State Cordell Hull is cool to the idea.		Philadelphia scientists announce a five-year plan to explore the atmosphere and sea for the cause of hay fever. . . . Scientists at Cold Spring Harbor announce that they have a genetics Rosetta Stone, a yeast fly gene large enough to reveal individual chromosomes.		Sept. 16
The American Civil Liberties Union charges that America First's attacks on the patriotism of New Deal members of the ACLU are slanderous. . . . The Mississippi primary race between incumbent Hubert Stephens and former governor Theodore Bilbo is seen as a test of the New Deal against the tactics of Huey Long. . . . The Carnegie Foundation charges that 49 Pennsylvania institutions are diploma mills, no better than high schools.	Argentina asks for reparations from the United States for those named by the Nye Committee as implicated in the munitions trade. . . . The Nye Committee reveals that Germany is buying warplanes from the United States, but United Aircraft officials claim the planes are for commercial use only.	Thirty-eight national banks are cleared to reopen. . . . Steel output is up 1.4 points to 22.3 percent.	David Sarnoff says that tiny radio waves that allow faster transmission of pictures will speed the development of television.	*Endeavour* bests *Rainbow* in only the fourth individual race won by a challenger in America's Cup history. . . . Actress Ruth Chatterton asks for a divorce on the grounds that her husband was "surly."	Sept. 17
Bilbo beats Stephens in a close battle in the Mississippi primary. . . . Mayor Walmsley orders New Orleans police to clean up vice. . . . In Wisconsin, the Democrat vote totals are greater than those of the Progressives or the Republicans.	Secretary of State Cordell Hull says that boycotts are counter-productive because they lead to retaliation.	Three companies get $29 million of the estimated total $63 million in contracts for the Grand Coulee Dam. . . . Secretary of the Interior Harold Ickes tells the House of Representatives that the United States needs an oil conservation policy.	The British Transportation Minister wants to install 20,000 Belisha Beacons, amber reflectors mounted on posts, at 10,000 crosswalks for traffic safety in London.	*Endeavour* leads from start to finish and wins race two of the America's Cup. . . . Seventy-year-old J. Franklin Jameson, former editor of the *American Historical Review* and historian responsible for the *Dictionary of American Biography*, is named Historian of Historians.	Sept. 18
Bayer agrees to a federal order to end its advertising claim that it is the "only genuine aspirin."		A Maryland federal judge rules the farm bankruptcy moratorium unconstitutional.	The New York Radio Show features home all-wave radios capable of picking up broadcasts from throughout the world. . . . The Byrd Antarctic expedition has freed a large plane from the snow that was left by the expedition five years earlier.	A revamped Army polo team beats the Mexican team 11–6. . . . The East-West polo matches are underway with the East taking the first game.	Sept. 19

F	G	H	I	J
Includes elections, federal-state relations, civil rights and liberties, crime, the judiciary, education, healthcare, poverty, urban affairs, and population.	Includes formation and debate of U.S. foreign and defense policies, veterans affairs, and defense spending. (Relations with specific foreign countries are usually found under the region concerned.)	Includes business, labor, agriculture, taxation, transportation, consumer affairs, monetary and fiscal policy, natural resources, pollution, and accidents.	Includes worldwide scientific, medical, and technological developments, natural phenomena, U.S. weather, and natural disasters.	Includes the arts, religion, scholarship, communications media, sports, entertainment, fashions, fads, and social life.

	World Affairs	Europe	Africa & The Middle East	The Americas	Asia & The Pacific
Sept. 20	Japan sees the planned U.S. maneuvers in Alaska as targeting Japan.	Russia reports that steel, coal, and chemical production are down, and spoilage is rising.		Jamaica and Cuba announce plans to take censuses. . . . The Para, Brazil, strike ends. . . . David Meisner, suspect in the Labatt kidnapping, surrenders and claims he has an alibi.	Manila cigar makers return to work. . . . In Java, the eruption of Merapi forces evacuation of nearby villages.
Sept. 21				Five die and 160 are arrested in strikes Brazil. . . . An Argentine socialist deputy warns that the Bolivian oil field extends to Argentina and conflict is likely because Argentina never ratified the treaty defining the border.	A typhoon in Japan kills 1,500, injures 5,000, and leaves 200,000 homeless, primarily in Osaka and Kyoto.
Sept. 22	Britain praises Eamon De Valera's opposition on moral grounds to Russia's entry into the League. . . . Russia's Maxim Litvinoff asks the League to put women's rights on the agenda.	France's army switches its uniforms from blue to khaki. . . . One hundred miners are trapped in a coal mine explosion in Wales.		Sales of most South American bonds are up 1–7 points.	Manchukuo indicates that it will return $100 million in property to refugees who take an oath of allegiance. . . . Farm reform in Kashmir includes scientific agriculture, a rational distribution scheme, and eradication of rats.
Sept. 23	Foreign Minister Louis Barthou of France heads for League meetings in Geneva hoping for a European Peace Plan to replace his failed Eastern Locarno. . . . The eighth annual meeting of the Women's International League for Peace and Freedom concludes with calls for peace and protection of minorities.	The number of dead from the Welsh mine explosion reaches 261.	The United States announces it will help Liberia improve economic and social conditions after the League abandoned it in January.		Japanese typhoon deaths now top 2,000, with over 13,000 injured. . . . Japan and Russia are close to a settlement of the Chinese Eastern Railway negotiations.
Sept. 24	The League of Nations is short 37.4 million francs; 45 nations are in arrears on their 1934 dues.	England and Germany establish a trade agreement.		Argentine trade is up 23 percent in the first eight months of the year. . . . Bolivia claims it has killed 1,400 at Algodonal.	Western Australia petitions the King of England for separation from the Commonwealth. . . . The crew of the Harun Maru is taken in Formosa.
Sept. 25	The League of Nations abandons disarmament in favor of mutual security agreements.	President Masaryk of Czechoslovakia is in improved health. . . . Austrian Nazis continue to flee to Yugoslavia.		Cuban sugar exports are rising. . . . Guatemalan troops are in revolt.	China and Japan reach agreement on the sale of the Chinese Eastern Railway, giving Japan economic, military, and political control of its 4,000 miles.
Sept. 26	The League of Nations intends campaigns against slavery and vice.	In preparation for the visit of King Alexander and Queen Marie of Yugoslavia, Bulgaria rounds up 10,000 Macedonian, Croat, Serbian, and Montenegran opponents of the king.	The League of Nations admits Afghanistan.	Quakes kill 50 and injure 400 in Jalisco, Mexico. The state's mining industry is severely damaged. . . . The Argentine peso falls sharply. . . . Police shoot two in Yucatan who protest restrictions on the Catholic Church.	A Tokyo-Manila phone link opens.
Sept. 27	The dollar is up, but other gold bloc currencies are down. . . . The League ends its session without considering the Litvinoff plan for a permanent disarmament council or acting on the Saar.	France, Britain, and Italy reaffirm the need for Austrian independence. . . . Russian taxes on private farms are intended to force private farmers into collectives.		The Pan-American arbitration agency begins operation. . . . Argentina estimates its year-end deficit at 60 million pesos. . . . British Guiana overwhelms Barbados by 396 runs to advance to the British West Indian finals against Trinidad in cricket. . . . Costa Rican students protest the executions of rebels in Guatemala.	
Sept. 28	Argentina and Germany sign a trade agreement. . . . Ecuador enters the League. . . . Gold bloc currencies are down sharply as London silver reaches a record high.	German emissaries in Rome attempt to reestablish cordial German-Italian relations. . . . France is perturbed with Poland, blaming Poland for the defeat of Eastern Locarno. . . . The Dublin newspaper strike is ended.	Twenty-thousand Assyrians will leave Iraq for Nigeria in French West Africa and British Guiana at the invitation of Britain and France.	Bolivia takes three Paraguayan positions. . . . Four escapees from Devil's Island arrive in Trinidad after days in a leaky boat. . . . Canadian business volume is up 23.6 percent through August. . . . A hurricane strikes Brazil, ending an eight-month drought.	China claims that U.S. silver policy is harmful.

A	B	C	D	E
Includes developments that affect more than one world region, international organizations, and important meetings of world leaders.	*Includes all domestic and regional developments in Europe, including the Soviet Union.*	*Includes all domestic and regional developments in Africa and the Middle East.*	*Includes all domestic and regional developments in Latin America, the Caribbean, and Canada.*	*Includes all domestic and regional developments in Asian and Pacific nations (and colonies).*

U.S. Politics & Social Issues	U.S. Foreign Policy & Defense	Economics & Great Depression	Science, Technology & Nature	Culture, Leisure & Lifestyle	
Bruno Richard Hauptmann, the Lindbergh kidnapper, is arrested in New York. . . . The Farm Holiday Association downplays the strike in favor of the right to organize. . . . A plot to dynamite the Houston, Texas, docks fails 41 minutes before the dynamite is set to explode.	Germany and France defend their aircraft and munitions deals; Britain denies that its diplomats were involved. . . . Russia and the United States agree to resume debt talks.	The court prohibits CWA assistance to a public light plant.	A camera with a constant speed motor allows examination of every detail of a work process.	*Rainbow* wins the third race of the America's Cup meet.	Sept. 20
	Secretary of State Cordell Hull clears the air with Argentina over the arms-dealing allegations. . . . Chile prohibits airplane deals with the United States. . . . The Nye Committee recesses until after the elections. . . . Discussions of the Russian debt resume.	Controller General McCarl halts President Roosevelt's $15 million tree-planting scheme because it is not immediate relief.		Paul Dean pitches the first National League no-hit game since 1929, but walks one and misses throwing only the seventh perfect game in history.	Sept. 21
Fire in a California Filipino labor camp is linked to a labor dispute in the lettuce fields. . . . The textile strike is over. . . . The Bureau of Narcotics reports an increase in trafficking of opium, heroin, and morphine and a decline of trafficking in cocaine.		The federal government stops funding for state fuel aid. . . . A federal judge rules that the oil code's limit on the number of oil wells is unconstitutional.	Astronomers report that the Milky Way is smaller than previously thought.	Baseball writers vote Dizzy Dean an all-star, but Babe Ruth fails to get a single vote.	Sept. 22
			Lack of vitamin A in the eye's pigment is found to cause night blindness.	Football player Bronco Nagurski stars in the Bears' win over the Packers before a crowd of 13,500.	Sept. 23
The courts receive the Insull company restructuring plan. . . . The Democrats propose that federal employees give $10 per $1,000 of pay to erase the party debt; party leader Henry Wallace says it must be voluntary.	Senator Nye suggests a ban on profits from sales of war materiel.	The Federal Debt Coordinator says that economic upswing has definitely arrived. . . . Jesse Jones of the RFC urges that the new railway board include government and citizen participation so that the government will not have to take it over.	J.E. Williamson announces plans to hunt the Loch Ness monster from a submarine.	In Babe Ruth's final home game, the Yankees lose, and the Tigers win their first American League title since 1909. . . . *Rainbow* wins its third in a row. For the first time, the America's Cup will require a sixth race.	Sept. 24
Garment workers repudiate Charles Zimmerman's call for a national walkout, saying he speaks only for himself.	Italy asks the United States to begin trade talks.	Gen. Hugh Johnson resigns as head of the NRA, calling the job superfluous now that Roosevelt is reorganizing the agency.		The Westbury Horticultural Society and New York Garden Club open a three-day flower show. . . . East downs West 14–13 and takes the polo series before a crowd of 17,000. . . . *Rainbow* wins the America's Cup. . . . Lou Gehrig hits home run 48 in his 1,500th consecutive game.	Sept. 25
	Secretary of the Navy Claude Swanson approves an extended cruise of the Pacific by the U.S. Asiatic Fleet under Chester Nimitz and a shakedown cruise through the West Indies and South America by the cruiser *Tuscaloosa*. . . . Under the Roosevelt-Litvinoff Pact, the United States begins suing to collect $25 million Russian debt.	President Roosevelt establishes a new textile board whose first order of business is investigating discrimination in rehiring strikers.	A Columbia University chemist determines that Rhenium is effective in electroplating. . . . The liner formerly known as 534, the *Queen Mary* (named by the queen for herself), is launched. . . . M.I.T. scientists create the thermocouple to measure the heat and cold of sound.	The United States accepts its invitation to the 1936 Olympics. . . . Plans are complete for broadcasting the World Series. . . . The Army's 12–8 victory over Mexico clinches the polo series.	Sept. 26
The AFL's building trades meeting, representing 1.5 million members, refuses to seat representatives of the 400,000 carpenters, electricians, and bricklayers lest the "triple alliance" take over the building trades federation. . . . Fifty thousand youth join a Catholic Legion of Decency march for clean movies in Chicago. . . . Two hundred pigeons fail to return home in an Ohio race.		Edward Corsi, home relief director for New York's welfare department, encourages expansion of the program to 3,000 New York area residents. Four acres provide 100 50-square-foot plots that produce $25 worth of vegetables each. . . . Fifty-eight railroads report net income is down 32.2 percent due to higher costs and wages. . . . The B&O, New York Central, and Lehigh Valley railroads are indicted for providing illegal concessions to shippers. . . . Wall Street applauds the requirement for 25 to 45 percent margin on loans.	Scientists report that uranium and thorium increase the penetrating power of x-rays.	The St. Louis Cardinals are within a half game of the New York Giants in the pennant race. . . . Germany hails the U.S. Olympics decision, while Jewish groups protest.	Sept. 27
The building trades reject AFL leader William Green's plea to take in the triple alliance. . . . Green foresees a five-day week and six-hour day.	To advance motorization of the field artillery, the War Department lets $1.5 million in contracts to five companies for 849 trucks and trailers.	Tennessee stockholders ask the courts to halt TVA plans to buy the Tennessee Public Service Commission power utility with PWA money. . . . Production of cigars costing five cents or less is up markedly, but production of expensive cigars is down. . . . The SEC approves the rules of 24 exchanges.	The Brussels Observatory finds seven asteroids and names one Albert. . . . Admiral Byrd begins the Antarctic survey.		Sept. 28

F	G	H	I	J
Includes elections, federal-state relations, civil rights and liberties, crime, the judiciary, education, healthcare, poverty, urban affairs, and population.	Includes formation and debate of U.S. foreign and defense policies, veterans affairs, and defense spending. (Relations with specific foreign countries are usually found under the region concerned.)	Includes business, labor, agriculture, taxation, transportation, consumer affairs, monetary and fiscal policy, natural resources, pollution, and accidents.	Includes worldwide scientific, medical, and technological developments, natural phenomena, U.S. weather, and natural disasters.	Includes the arts, religion, scholarship, communications media, sports, entertainment, fashions, fads, and social life.

	World Affairs	Europe	Africa & The Middle East	The Americas	Asia & The Pacific
Sept. 29	Argentina, Brazil, Peru, and Chile, no longer upset at the Nye revelations, begin their own investigations.	The French government is back in session amid rumors of a Cabinet crisis and right-left divisions. . . . The Soviet plant at Kramatorks, the largest in the world, is unveiled.	Amid reports that each is making warlike moves, Italy and Ethiopia reaffirm their friendship and the treaty of 1928.	Canadian polls show a shift to the liberals.	China denies that it will embargo silver.
Sept. 30	Germany is not meeting debt obligations, complain the Netherlands and other nations. A trade policy group attributes Germany's debt problems to the purchase of imports for rearming. . . . Britain opposes a gold bloc trading community on the grounds that it will prolong the depression.	Catalans increase defiance of the weak Spanish government. . . . Adolf Hitler reacts angrily to papal nuncio Cardinal Pacelli's assertions that Germany is not living up to its Concordat with the church in Rome. Negotiations over the Concordat have been off and on since May.		Cuban troops fire on students as taxi drivers prepare to walk out again.	A typhoon drenches Luzon.
Oct. 1			Charles Nicolle of France reports success in inoculating 5,000 with the Laigret-Sellards yellow fever serum in Tunis and French West Africa.	A successful Bolivian counter-offensive leads Bolivia to refuse any truce that lacks a settlement of the Chaco dispute. . . . Cuba suspends civil liberties and imposes military rule in two provinces where Communists are a persistent problem.	Leaders of Japan's army ask the government to impose socialism to end agrarian unrest and reduce class differences. The army lists the United States, China, and Russia as potential enemies.
Oct. 2	Germany is reported to have renewed interest in League membership now that Russia has joined. . . . World wheat prices are down.	Germany and Hungary agree on trade, but the Dutch refuse to accept a pact while Germany still owes them 100 million guilders. . . . France restricts export of scrap metal. . . . Alejandro Lerroux is forming a Spanish center-right Cabinet excluding leftists but including Catholics and Catalans. Lerroux has headed three previous Cabinets in the past year. . . . British labor defeats socialization resolutions.		Troops are fighting rebels in Morelos province, Mexico. . . . Cuban taxi drivers prepare to strike yet again.	The Japanese Minister of War disavows the army pamphlet calling for socialism. . . . Western Australia's government reports a deficit.
Oct. 3	A Canadian wheat pool and the French government are allegedly dumping wheat, causing the price to tumble.	The Estonian parliament is suspended because it opposes the Cabinet, which has been ruling through martial law for six months in an effort to control Nazis, fascists, and Communists. . . . Spain is bracing for a general strike by 1 million excluded labor leftists.		Santiago, Cuba, is the site of 20 bomb blasts as the army takes over the city and the navy takes over Cienfuegos. . . . Mexico uses tear gas to oust students and parents as it takes over a Catholic school.	Formosa exonerates the crew of the fishing vessel *Haiun Maru*. The fishermen were charged with attacking Filipino sailors. . . . The Philippines may pursue extradition.
Oct. 4		The Dutch report a plot by U.S. sailors to smuggle German aliens into the United States. . . . Three are dead in the Madrid strike.	George Vanderbilt, leader of a scientific expedition to Uganda and the Belgian Congo, having escaped the crocodiles, is ill from an insect bite and hospitalized in Nairobi, British East Africa.	Three die in the takeover of a Mexican church. . . . The wires to Santiago, Cuba, are cut and the city is isolated.	The Red Cross is among the relief agencies helping the 100,000 victims of a Japanese typhoon. . . . Russia agrees to accept 170 million yen for the Chinese Eastern Railway.
Oct. 5		Otto, the Hapsburg pretender, announces that he will return to the family estates just as soon as Austria opens its borders to him. . . . Germany bars the importation of foreign watches, orders the home manufacture of gasoline, and informs professors that they must have views compatible with Nazism if they want to keep their jobs. . . . Russia restores political rights of former clergy and czarist officials. . . . Spain imposes martial law and uses planes in an attempt to restore order as 85 die.	Abyssinians attempt to purchase arms from Denmark. . . . Algerian wine producers refuse to deal with the municipal government or wine houses because France has failed to alleviate the depression.		Australian trade is up over 1933, and has improved in New Zealand. Japanese trade figures are down due to a seasonal slump.
Oct. 6		Gen. Lieuytan of the Belgian general staff recommends withdrawal from the forts on the Liege and Meuse along with other defense cutbacks. . . . Catalonia secedes. . . . Italian Premier Benito Mussolini warns the Yugoslavian press to stop calling Italians cowards. . . . Poland prepares to parcel large estates and give farmers price supports.		Cuban customs receipts are expected to reach $30 million for the year, up from an early estimate of $18 million. . . . Paraguay refuses to consider any settlement that gives Bolivia anything. With the League unable to establish a Chaco peace, American nations are preparing to resume the initiative.	
	A *Includes developments that affect more than one world region, international organizations, and important meetings of world leaders.*	**B** *Includes all domestic and regional developments in Europe, including the Soviet Union.*	**C** *Includes all domestic and regional developments in Africa and the Middle East.*	**D** *Includes all domestic and regional developments in Latin America, the Caribbean, and Canada.*	**E** *Includes all domestic and regional developments in Asian and Pacific nations (and colonies).*

U.S. Politics & Social Issues	U.S. Foreign Policy & Defense	Economics & Great Depression	Science, Technology & Nature	Culture, Leisure & Lifestyle	
The FCC begins hearings to determine whether or not educational and religious entities should have a percentage of the airwaves. . . . President Roosevelt's Committee on Economic Security recommends a contributory pension system for the nation's 6.6 million people over age 66. Employer, employee, and the government would contribute. None of the 28 state old-age pension systems is contributory.	Senator Nye goes on the lecture circuit to talk about the munitions business and war.	Secretary of the Interior Harold Ickes, in Atlanta, attacks slums as breeders of political machines as he razes a building to start his slum clearance program. Chicago Democratic Party leaders oppose the plan. . . . Upton Sinclair upsets business by proposing a $300 million property tax. California Democrats distance themselves from their candidate.			**Sept. 29**
Fifty-three economists sign a statement urging the election of gold standard advocates to Congress to head off inflation.		The season's halibut catch is 24 million pounds. . . . Roosevelt asks for an industrial truce to give the NRA time to work.	Yonkers and Poughkeepsie announce that they will equip their police cars with radios.	Army sweeps the polo series with Mexico, winning 14–4. . . . Dizzy Dean wins his 30th ballgame by shutting out the Reds as the Cardinals win the pennant by two games and prepare to face the Tigers. Babe Ruth's final game is a loss to the Washington Senators.	**Sept. 30**
President Franklin Roosevelt proclaims October 12 of each year to be Columbus Day. . . . Roosevelt's Sunday night fireside-chat call for industrial peace brings a favorable response from the National Association of Manufacturers, which calls for preservation of the status quo for the duration of the depression on the World War model. The AFL's William Green applauds Roosevelt's stance on collective bargaining. . . . Twenty-eight ship lines avert a strike by recognizing the seamen's union.	The United States and Brazil open trade talks to reverse the trade decline of $79 million over four years.	Business failures for the week are up to 203. . . . SEC rules cover margin accounts. . . . Congressman Wright Patman of Texas demands immediate payment of the World War soldiers' bonus. . . . A West Virginia judge invalidates the NRA.			**Oct. 1**
The nomination of Upton Sinclair is reportedly causing capital flight from California. . . . Fundamentalist Baptists in the Interstate Evangelistic Association charge the Federal Council of Churches of Christ with promoting indecent literature and subversion and call on conservative Christians to leave the Federal Council. . . . Jury selection begins in the Insull trial.	The Army air force restructures into a regional arrangement and reduces the power of Maj. Gen. Benjamin Foulois.		The Smithsonian reports that death stars emit deadly blue rays that the earth's atmosphere blocks. . . . A new process for radio facsimiles speeds transmission time for a letter to eight minutes.		**Oct. 2**
AFL president William Green asks the government to ban company unions. . . . The Interstate Evangelistic Association resolves against pacifism and Russia. . . . The *President Harding* sails with 130 deportees, including 90 leaving at their own request, some with American-born children. Twelve are criminals and the others are "undesirables." . . . Samuel Leibowitz threatens to withdraw from the defense of the Scottsboro boys unless all Communists are removed.	Eddie Rickenbacker proposes a dirigible airline between the United States and Japan to promote peace, countering Billy Mitchell's contention that the United States should be arming against Japan. . . . China formally protests to Secretary of State Cordell Hull that the U.S. silver policy is deflating Chinese currency. . . . Senator Nye calls for a 98 percent tax on war incomes and a federal monopoly on munitions manufacture.		France reports successful tests of deadly light rays, the "searchlight of war."	Dizzy Dean and Ducky Medwick lead the Cardinals to a game one 8–3 win over the Tigers in the World Series.	**Oct. 3**
An Alabama appeals court refuses to overturn the death sentences for two of the Scottsboro Boys. Execution is set for December, but a federal appeal is expected.			Enrico Fermi reports that a neutron pierces the nucleus of an atom in one thousand million-million-millionths of a second. . . . A new process creates x-rays from mercury.	Detroit takes game two of the Word Series in 12 innings, 3–2. . . . The Aga Khan's Umidwar wins the Jockey Cup Stakes.	**Oct. 4**
The NAACP calls on the AFL to end segregation and discrimination in the treatment of black workers.		Air mail poundage for July is 682,520. For August it is 773,050. Both numbers are up from 1933. . . . Labor Secretary Frances Perkins tells the AFL that there will be no compulsory arbitration of labor disputes.		Dizzy Dean beats the Tigers 4–1. . . . In football, Duquesne beats Ashland 99–0. . . . The Mutual Radio Network is formed.	**Oct. 5**
Lutherans call American movies immoral.	The Army announces plans to test all pilots with 15 or more years of experience to weed out "armchair pilots" and give younger men a chance.	Americans are still holding onto $140 million in gold notes.	U.S. delegates returned from the Highway Congress report that Germany is planning to build high-speed roads and pay for them with tolls only.		**Oct. 6**

F	G	H	I	J
Includes elections, federal-state relations, civil rights and liberties, crime, the judiciary, education, healthcare, poverty, urban affairs, and population.	*Includes formation and debate of U.S. foreign and defense policies, veterans affairs, and defense spending. (Relations with specific foreign countries are usually found under the region concerned.)*	*Includes business, labor, agriculture, taxation, transportation, consumer affairs, monetary and fiscal policy, natural resources, pollution, and accidents.*	*Includes worldwide scientific, medical, and technological developments, natural phenomena, U.S. weather, and natural disasters.*	*Includes the arts, religion, scholarship, communications media, sports, entertainment, fashions, fads, and social life.*

	World Affairs	Europe	Africa & The Middle East	The Americas	Asia & The Pacific
Oct. 7	Catholics by the thousands are in Buenos Aires for the World Eucharistic Council. The army will keep order as leftists threaten the meetings.	Because the War Minister opposes Lieuytan's economy measures, Belgium faces a Cabinet crisis unless one or the other resigns. . . . Italian Premier Benito Mussolini visits Gabriele D'Annunzio and ends their estrangement. . . . The revolt in Spain collapses. Catalonia surrenders. Casualties include 500 dead, 1,100 wounded, and 5,000 arrested.	British Jews ask for increased immigration to Palestine to ease the labor shortage there.	Six die in Sao Paolo rioting.	Admiral Yamamoto, in the United States en route to the London naval conference, is close-mouthed about his plans.
Oct. 8	The World Bank reports that the move to devalue currencies has subsided and the gold bloc countries are standing firm in favor of the gold standard.	Madrid violence resumes with the burnings of a priest and two guardsmen, 52 soldiers killed in a truck bombing, 20 insurgents dead in a failed attempt on a radio station, and the bombing of an orphanage. . . . Germans now have to carry cards identifying their race.		Sao Paolo leftists kill eight and wound 36 fascists.	Admiral Yamamoto calls for major naval reductions and parity for the Japanese with the world's navies.
Oct. 9		A Croat assassinates King Alexander of Yugoslavia and French Foreign Minister Louis Barthou in Marseilles, France, creating border tensions between Yugoslavia and Italy and Hungary.	The New York Department of Hospitals announces that it is sending an ambulance to Hadassah Rothschild Hospital in Jerusalem to replace oxcarts, donkeys, and mules. . . . British police raid Nazi offices in Southwest Africa, the former German colony administered by British South Africa.	Nicaraguan liberals win. . . . Peruvian sugar growers are facing low prices, high taxes, and loss of markets.	
Oct. 10	The World Eucharistic Council at Buenos Aires opens with 500,000 attending. . . . The League hears from groups in the Saar that a Nazi coup will occur after the plebiscite.	Italy seeks a treaty with Yugoslavia and one with France to ease tensions. . . . Britain expresses concern that the crisis might generate a general war in the Adriatic region.	Mohammed Zahir Shah, ascended to the Afghan throne on the assassination of his father last November, has an heir—Shahzada Ahmad Shah Khan.	The Nicaraguan congress closes peacefully.	Australia's ruling party fails to establish a coalition and begins single-party rule. . . . Russia protests that Japan is allowing authorities in Manchukuo to arrest Russian railway employees.
Oct. 11		Peter is proclaimed King of Yugoslavia and his regents are named.		Mexico insists that it will persist with socialist anti-Catholic education despite opposition. . . . In Chile, a 30,000-man "civil army" of militiamen parades over the objections of the regular forces.	
Oct. 12	Japan and El Salvador are working on a coffee deal.	Germany agrees to pay 75 percent of the interest due on Dawes bonds. . . . In Poland, coal, iron, petroleum, and zinc production are reported up. . . . Dissident Protestants march in Munich and mock Hitler.		Mexican authorities use tear gas and fire hoses to put down protests against secular schools.	
Oct. 13	The Hebrew Sheltering and Immigrant Aid Society reports that of the 5,048 aliens arriving in the United States in the first seven months of the year, over half are refugee German Jews.	Yugoslavia declines to hold the annual unofficial meeting of the Balkan states. Friction with Bulgaria is rumored. . . . Tens of thousands line the streets as the boy King Peter returns to Yugoslavia. . . . Adolf Hitler warns Germans to help the needy or face public pillorying. . . . Spanish socialists have lost control in Asturias.		Nicaragua holds a priest and nun alleged to be Communists.	In India on the frontier near Chitral, British planes bomb the forces of the Fakir of Alingar after the Fakir's tribal forces snipe at a British column.

A	B	C	D	E
Includes developments that affect more than one world region, international organizations, and important meetings of world leaders.	Includes all domestic and regional developments in Europe, including the Soviet Union.	Includes all domestic and regional developments in Africa and the Middle East.	Includes all domestic and regional developments in Latin America, the Caribbean, and Canada.	Includes all domestic and regional developments in Asian and Pacific nations (and colonies).

U.S. Politics & Social Issues	U.S. Foreign Policy & Defense	Economics & Great Depression	Science, Technology & Nature	Culture, Leisure & Lifestyle	
The International Poe Society is formed in Philadelphia on the 85th anniversary of Poe's death. . . . Ponzi is finally deported to Italy.		With the 15 reopened in September, 377 national banks have reopened in 1934 to date. . . . Government chemists report that wine can be made from surplus citrus fruit for 32 cents a gallon.	Corning finishes the 200-inch lens it will use as the test before creating the one actually intended for the world's largest telescope.	The Tigers beat Dizzy Dean 3–1 to tie the series.	Oct. 7
The AFL votes to support the 30-hour week without a wage reduction. . . . A grand jury indicts Bruno Richard Hauptmann in the Lindbergh kidnapping/murder . . . . In protest of attendance of African Americans at their school, over 1,700 Morgan Park High School (Chicago) students walk out. . . . In Harlem, Abdel Hamid, the black Sufi, is brought up on charges of inciting a race war against the Jews.		The cotton crop, at an estimated 9.44 million bales, is the lowest since 1921. . . . Farm buying power is up 44 percent over 1933. . . . The Supreme Court agrees to hear cases on suspension of the gold standard and imposition of the oil industry code.	Resolving litigation dating to 1922, the Supreme Court rules that Lee DeForest retains the patent to the feedback circuit integral to the radio receiver after a failed challenge by Edwin H. Armstrong. . . . Hawaii begins inter-island airmail service.		Oct. 8
A raid of a warehouse that supplies back number shops, instigated by John Sumner's New York Society for the Suppression of Vice, captures 11,774 copies of Real Boudoir Tales, Real Temptation Tales, Real Forbidden Sweets, and Real French Capers.		The electric industry asks an increase of its code workweek from 36 to 40 hours. . . . The government buys a million acres of worn-out farmland in the midwest, southeast, and western United States. The families relocate.	Pratt and Whitney unveils a new air-cooled, self-lubricating, gear-drive engine capable of 550 horsepower.	Dizzy Dean and the Cardinals rout the Tigers 11–0, and Tiger fans riot. . . . John Roosevelt chases and captures a news photographer taking pictures of Franklin Roosevelt, Jr., dressed as a bride for his Harvard initiation.	Oct. 9
At the Insull trial in Chicago, testimony reveals that stocks bought for $16 million were marked up to $45 million on the books. . . . Italian and anti-fascist students confront one another at New York University. . . . Methodists, at their sesquicentennial, talk of unifying their three branches and restoring lay involvement. . . . The Scottsboro defendants and their families want an end to Communist aid. Black churches agree to take on the burden.	Admiral Yamamoto says that Japan will abrogate the naval treaty, but not at the talks. Foreign Minister Saito is going to present a peace plan to the United States if the naval talks fail.	David Lilienthal of the TVA says it is exempt from state jurisdiction. . . . Women's wages are lower than men's in 120 codes.		The Wanamaker exhibit in New York City includes a farmhouse scene by a New Britain, Conn., electrician with no formal training. The show rejected works by several New Britain professionals. . . . Will Hays says the public backs clean films and is increasingly interested in the classics, history, and biography. . . . Jack Dempsey announces plans to build a $250,000 restaurant near Madison Square Garden.	Oct. 10
Pretty Boy Floyd avoids a trap in Iowa, blasting his way out, and escapes to Minnesota, where a federal and state manhunt is under way. . . . Harlem's Abdel Hamid is not guilty of anti-Jewish statements. . . . The Insull defendants blame the 1929 crash for bringing down a sound company. . . . Completion of the scaffolding around the 550-foot Washington Monument will allow the cleaning and repair of the structure's mortar. This is the highest continuous scaffolding erected to date. . . . The AFL votes to implement "vertical" unionism in industry, trying to unionize the whole industry rather than each individual craft.		Father Charles Coughlin, the radio priest, reveals that President Roosevelt is interested in his idea of allocating jobs to universities for their graduates. . . . Interior Secretary Harold Ickes and Attorney General Homer Cummings indicate that they will prosecute east Texas oilmen who persist in bringing in "hot" oil, 125,000 barrels over quota each day. . . . Radio broadcasters await the federal decision on what constitutes "profanity."	Prof. L. Ruzicka reports in Nature that he and his team have created an artificial male sex hormone.	Italian fencers beat the United States 18–9. . . . Plans are final for Babe Ruth to manage a team of all-stars on a tour of Hawaii, Japan, the Philippines, and China.	Oct. 11
An Illinois court allows the Socialist Party a ballot spot. . . . A Catholic review group reports it has been favorable to 90 percent of the movies it has examined since July. . . . Pretty Boy Floyd is reportedly in Missouri, where an airplane joins the hunt. . . . New York police take clubs to socialists protesting the fascist games at Yankee Stadium. . . . The Scottsboro case is before the Supreme Court.	The newly established Export Bank makes its first sale, $1 million in Kentucky tobacco, to a Spanish firm.	Roosevelt appoints 11 committees to study social insurance.		Madison Square Garden is arranging a bout for Max Schmeling with an opponent to be named later.	Oct. 12
In Akron, Ohio, the General Conference of the Evangelical Church condemns the current economic system and its concentration of wealth. . . . Methodists vote to reunify and back Prohibition.	Germany rejects the U.S. proposal for a trade treaty that eliminates the most-favored-nation clause. The United States is unhappy with the German proposal to pay only 75 percent of interest owed to bondholders.	Federal judges in Louisiana and Arkansas uphold the lumber code.	An experiment in the Dutch East Indies with a plague serum is reported to be so successful that the serum will be tried on a larger population. . . . Fliers from 50 nations are gathered in England for the race to Australia.	American artist Childe Hassam says that American art is freeing itself of the European influence and enjoying a renaissance. . . . Douglas S. Freeman's biography of Robert E. Lee receives favorable reviews as the definitive biography.	Oct. 13

F	G	H	I	J
Includes elections, federal-state relations, civil rights and liberties, crime, the judiciary, education, healthcare, poverty, urban affairs, and population.	Includes formation and debate of U.S. foreign and defense policies, veterans affairs, and defense spending. (Relations with specific foreign countries are usually found under the region concerned.)	Includes business, labor, agriculture, taxation, transportation, consumer affairs, monetary and fiscal policy, natural resources, pollution, and accidents.	Includes worldwide scientific, medical, and technological developments, natural phenomena, U.S. weather, and natural disasters.	Includes the arts, religion, scholarship, communications media, sports, entertainment, fashions, fads, and social life.

	World Affairs	Europe	Africa & The Middle East	The Americas	Asia & The Pacific
Oct. 14	Albert Einstein supports the International Student Service campaign to aid German university refugees under the auspices of the League of Nations High Commissioner for German Refugees. . . . The Pope blesses the million people gathered for the finale of the Buenos Aires Ecumenical Council.	Bavarian pastors reject rule of the church by the Nazis. . . . Both unemployment and factory output are down in Germany. . . . The Belgian army chief of staff, Nuyten, is forced to retire. . . . In Hungary, 1,156 miners are engaging in a suicide strike and refusing to leave the mines.	In a slap to Adolf Hitler, Hadassah appoints refugee scientists from Germany as the head of its new hospital and head of research in Palestine. . . . British Jews are buying more land in Palestine, but the colonial office refuses to reveal the location because of unsettled conditions. . . . Gold output is down in the Transvaal.	Canadian exports, particularly to the United States, are up for the year.	Japanese trade is better than 1929 after a devaluation of the yen. Imports from the United States are up 50 million yen over six months, but exports are down.
Oct. 15	The League's Chaco committee convokes the League Assembly for November 20. Bolivia wants a police presence before the truce. . . . The Chinese tax increase raises the prices of silver in London and elsewhere.	Moscow subway's first test run is hailed by commuters hampered by above-ground transportation. With 70,000 men and women working to complete the line, opening in January is expected. . . . Hungary's suicide miners win after five days. They will have more work at higher wages.	Hadassah calls for more settlement of Palestine and the opening of Trans-Jordan to Jewish settlement.		Japanese Admiral Suyegetsu assures his government that the navy is ready for a race with the powers if the London talks fail. . . . The Manila typhoon is the worst since 1920.
Oct. 16	A rise in sterling prices drops the value of the dollar and prices on the Chinese exchange, already adversely affected by the Chinese silver tax.	The Hungarian miners claim they were duped; the owners claim the miners faked their hunger strike, having ample food the whole time. . . . King Leopold of Belgium opens a canal between Antwerp and Liege on the frontier with the Netherlands. The canal is expected to be a barrier that will help in Dutch defense. . . . In Spain, government forces kill 600 rebels, martial law is established in the north, rebels in Asturias ambush a government column, and the government votes 5 million pesetas for disabled soldiers' pensions.		Canadian gold output is the greatest since June 1932. . . . A hurricane in Baja California does extensive damage but takes no lives. . . . The first of Argentina's new wheat crop sells for 80.75 cents a bushel while wheat on the spot market goes for 58.5 cents.	Australia is seeking trade agreements to end the slump in its exports.
Oct. 17	Chile buys £100,000 worth of British planes for training and aerial photography.	Registrations for the Saar vote are at least 100,000 too high at 500,000. France may seek a delay of the plebiscite until the rolls are purged.	Sir Charles Marston says he has unearthed a ewer that shows Israelite script predating that of Phoenicia.	The Cienfuegos, Cuba, Woolworth store is damaged by a bomb blast.	Japanese troops enforce military control of Manchuria to silence opposition.
Oct. 18	Italian police arrest two leaders of the Yugoslavian assassination plot based in Hungary. . . . Sterling rises and the English, U.S., and Chinese silver markets decline. . . . The gold bloc meeting at Brussels calls for increased trade.	Irish farmers tear up rails and block roads in tax protests.	German exports to Palestine decrease because Germany is releasing Jewish assets only for use in Germany. Palestine will export Jaffa oranges to Germany. . . . Italian fliers are en route to Aden, southern Arabia, seeking a seaplane distance record.	Peru delays action on reinstitution of a national airline. . . . Mexican President Rodriguez warns dissenters that he will use troops to enforce his socialization of the schools.	
Oct. 19	The Little and Balkan Ententes ask all nations to help in stopping assassinations. . . . Japan seeks a nonaggression pact with Britain and the United States. . . . Lisbon to South America air service begins.	Schismatic German churches declare themselves independent and refuse to pay Nazi taxes. . . . Ireland prohibits importation of complete autos, but American makers with plants there are exempt. . . . Italy begins work on two 35,000-ton warships.	Algerian mayors cut ties with the French government in protest of export problems. . . . The Italian team flies 2,561 miles from Monfalcone, Italy, to Massaua, North Africa, in 26.5 hours.	Alberta establishes wage and price controls. . . . Brazil begins searching for 10 Yugoslavian terrorists. . . . Argentina calls for the United States to assist in establishing world free trade. . . . Mexico's congress votes to unseat Mexican Bishops because they resisted socialization of the schools.	
Oct. 20	The seven gold bloc nations reaffirm the existing parities and their intent to institute bilateral trade negotiations expected to increase trade by 10 percent.			Former president Marcelo Alvear is welcomed back to Argentina by 100,000.	Chiang Kai-shek orders provincial governors to report to the central government on their efforts to quell the opium problem.

A	B	C	D	E
Includes developments that affect more than one world region, international organizations, and important meetings of world leaders.	*Includes all domestic and regional developments in Europe, including the Soviet Union.*	*Includes all domestic and regional developments in Africa and the Middle East.*	*Includes all domestic and regional developments in Latin America, the Caribbean, and Canada.*	*Includes all domestic and regional developments in Asian and Pacific nations (and colonies).*

U.S. Politics & Social Issues	U.S. Foreign Policy & Defense	Economics & Great Depression	Science, Technology & Nature	Culture, Leisure & Lifestyle	
The 21-station American Broadcasting System begins operations. . . . America First alleges that the new credit unions are a "tax spy" ploy by the federal government. . . . Harlem's population is 204,000, up from 83,000 in 1920.	China levies a 10 percent tax on silver exports, leading to a protest by Secretary of State Cordell Hull, who notes that purchases are mandatory. . . . The American Legion commander announces that his organization will push for a universal draft and an end to war profiteering.	Cotton prices are up but exports remain slow. . . . Corn is down 60 percent from a year ago, and the year's crop is off 600,000 bushels from last year's 2 million.		Best sellers include *Lust for Life* and *Goodbye, Mr. Chips*, as well as Herbert Hoover's *Farewell to Liberty* and Ike Hoover's *Forty-two Years in the White House*.	Oct. 14
The Supreme Court declines to hear Al Capone's request for a habeas corpus hearing. . . . A report to the Episcopal Bishops reiterates support for divorce in some cases, allows occasional waiver of the three-day waiting rule for marriage, and takes a hesitant step toward supporting birth control, in part for eugenic reasons. . . . J.E. Seagram and Sons begins a temperance campaign. . . . Bruno Hauptmann fights extradition to New Jersey. . . . General Motors' Alfred Sloan sends 130,000 employees a pamphlet outlining grievance procedures, but denies that labor is running GM. . . . Treasury Secretary Henry Morgenthau supports wiretapping in the fight against narcotics.		In a case brought by TWA, the Supreme Court upholds Postmaster General James Farley's cancellation of airmail contracts as an action on behalf of the United States. . . . The presidential committee on social insurance agrees to include the unemployed and to take the British approach of incremental implementation. . . . Former NRA chief Hugh Johnson says the 30-hour week would be disastrous. . . . President Roosevelt says he will let industries regulate themselves.	The annual Business Machine Show, with attendance up 40 percent, features typewriters capable of 15 percent greater speed.	After the first day's play, the English lead the Americans by over 5,000 points in the Schwab Trophy bridge match. The Maharajah and Maharani of Baroda are the only kibitzers.	Oct. 15
The Episcopal Council waives the three-day-wait rule and adds four women members. . . . Hauptmann's extradition is ordered but stayed pending appeal.	The United States and Japanese contingents reach London for the naval talks. . . . China threatens to go on the gold standard, and Secretary of State Cordell Hull indicates that there might be room for trading of gold for silver.	Corn prices, because of the short crop, are up, and other grain prices rise too. The grain increases help cotton prices, already rising on rumors of inflation and readjustment of the program quotas. . . . Farmers vote 2–1 to continue the corn-hog plan. . . . President Roosevelt suggests a national TVA, a water-land use plan. . . . Weekly oil production is 95,000 barrels over quota.	Surgeons transplant a thyroid and parathyroid successfully. . . . Admiral Byrd speaks on radio for the first time since his isolation in March.	To develop an opponent for heavyweight champion Max Baer, the New York boxing commission sets up a round-robin of 15-round bouts by the contenders—Art Lasky, Max Schmeling, Steve Hamas, and Primo Carnera. . . . With 78 points out of a possible 80, Dizzy Dean is the league's most valuable player.	Oct. 16
Justice Department officials tout their 74 convictions in 31 kidnapping cases under the 1932 Lindbergh law.	At the hearings of the aviation commission, a witness says that the Pacific Northwest is unprotected. . . . Secretary Hull criticizes those nations that pad tariffs and notes that reciprocity will improve world trade.	The government asks the Supreme Court for an early ruling on the legitimacy of its suspension of the gold standard. . . . The NRA announces that it will publicize willful violators of the codes.	The final lineup for the 11,300-mile England to Australia commercial airplane race includes 21 planes, three of them American. First prize is $75,000 and aviation supremacy.	The American bridge-playing team is only 3,000 points behind, but American Ely Culbertson is criticized as dictatorial in interpreting the rules.	Oct. 17
California attempts to purge 24,000 "idle" from the rolls as voting begins in the Sinclair race. . . . Witnesses testify that providing education time on radio would be a waste because disinterested listeners would tune out. . . . The new Liberal Party begins its campaign to oust Tammany.		A *Literary Digest* poll of 65,000 shows an 18 percent decline in support for the New Deal and 17 states in opposition. . . . Secretary of the Interior Harold Ickes says that PWA housing needs total $2 billion.	American surgeons at Harvard hear and photograph electricity in the human brain.	The Americans lead the bridge tournament by 990 points. . . . Mickey Cochrane, Tigers player-manager, is the league's most valuable player.	Oct. 18
His appeal rejected, Hauptmann is taken to New Jersey. . . . The head of the Lutheran mission board says Lutherans are robbing God by paying only 75 cents per capita for missions.	Igor Sikorsky and Frank Hawks tell Congress that the United States is vulnerable to foreign bombers; other witnesses call for protection of Alaska and Hawaii and larger bombers.	A federal judge rules that the AAA cannot regulate milk sold solely in Iowa because the interstate effect is "remote." . . . The employment index for August stands at 75.8, down from 80 last year. . . . The Petroleum Board begins requiring paper certificates before oil can ship—this is an attempt to stem east Texas hot oil. . . . President Roosevelt tells veterans that they will get no bonus until the unemployed are tended to.		The American bridge players win the Schwab Trophy by 3,600 points after 300 hands. . . . England's Jockey Club makes the Aga Khan an honorary member.	Oct. 19
California bars Admiral Byrd from voting by radio. . . . Episcopal Bishops vote 44–38 to support dissemination of birth control information, but only by medical doctors. . . . State officials generally agree that being on relief will not disqualify voters. . . . Norman Thomas says that the major parties ignore the issues; he wants an active party and a peaceful revolution. . . . Friends of the New Germany, an American Nazi group, meet in New Jersey after being rebuffed elsewhere. . . . The Scottsboro defendants rid themselves of the Communists.		Grain markets remain down on slow foreign sales.	Scientists report that the eye integrates short bursts of light. . . . Princeton has finished installation of its electrically controlled 23-inch telescope on a movable floor.	President Franklin Roosevelt visits Colonial Williamsburg, newly restored by John D. Rockefeller, Jr., and colonial dames strew his path with rose petals.	Oct. 20

F	G	H	I	J
Includes elections, federal-state relations, civil rights and liberties, crime, the judiciary, education, healthcare, poverty, urban affairs, and population.	*Includes formation and debate of U.S. foreign and defense policies, veterans affairs, and defense spending. (Relations with specific foreign countries are usually found under the region concerned.)*	*Includes business, labor, agriculture, taxation, transportation, consumer affairs, monetary and fiscal policy, natural resources, pollution, and accidents.*	*Includes worldwide scientific, medical, and technological developments, natural phenomena, U.S. weather, and natural disasters.*	*Includes the arts, religion, scholarship, communications media, sports, entertainment, fashions, fads, and social life.*

	World Affairs	Europe	Africa & The Middle East	The Americas	Asia & The Pacific
Oct. 21	Sixty-eight nations participate in the World Agriculture Institute in Rome, including the United States after a six-year absence.	German Protestants continue to defy Adolf Hitler and select their own Bishops. . . . The Yugoslav regents ask the current government to remain in place. . . . Hermann Goering denies rumors that he has fallen out with Hitler and that he has been shot.	Italy's King Victor Emmanuel is en route to Somaliland to inspect coastal fortifications.	Montreal opens its silver exchange. . . . Peru authorizes money for a monument to Daniel Carrion, father of Peruvian medicine.	
Oct. 22	The Japanese envoy to Berlin says that he agrees with the German view that bilateral treaties have merit. . . . Germany wants to buy more Brazilian hides, coffee, and cocoa, but Brazil is unresponsive. . . . The world farm body offers technical assistance with trade and starts examining the possibility of a planned world economy.	Aides of former Greek premier Venizelos capture the assailants the police had been unable to locate for 10 months. . . . Belgium denies that it is on the verge of financial collapse. . . . Berlin begins a bomb shelter building program that will provide shelter for every household and jobs for many.	In an attempt to ease Algerian unrest, French Minister of Colonies Louis Rollin broadcasts a radio appeal to all the French colonies for closer economic ties. Rollin promises to call an all-empire economic conference quickly.	Cubans raid the Spanish Consulate at Camaguey. . . . Colima becomes the fourth Mexican state without churches after the governor closes them and expels the priests.	The constitutional convention in the Philippines votes for a unicameral legislature.
Oct. 23	Japan demands an end to naval inequality.	German Opel workers go on half time, working alternate weeks. . . . Hungary is upset that Yugoslavia is portraying its government as linked with terrorists.	Selection is complete of the 25 American Jews on the team for the Maccabiah Games, expected to draw 5,000 athletes from 38 nations to Palestine in April 1935.	Guerrero gives priests 72 hours to leave and becomes the fifth Mexican state to ban the Catholic Church.	
Oct. 24	Britain supports the Japanese call for parity, but the United States wants security guarantees in any agreement. . . . Turkey, Greece, and Palestine bar a vessel carrying 318 Czech and Polish Jews looking for a new home.	Russian grain production is 60 million bushels above the 1933 crop. . . . Austria seizes a press of the outlawed Socialists.	Persia holds two American fliers forced to land there during the great race.	Extreme cold and snow damage Chilean crops.	Manchukuo's plan to establish a state oil monopoly is thwarted by the United States and Britain, but a state tobacco monopoly is expected.
Oct. 25		Germany and Poland exchange ambassadors. The French see their influence in Poland waning. . . . Germany wants an oil monopoly; Royal Dutch and Shell do not like the terms.		Cuba sets a minimum price for sugar sold to the United States. . . . Colima and Chihuahua bar Catholic priests, and in a shootout between federal forces and police, each mistaking the other for insurgents, several die.	Japan tells the United States and Britain to talk to China about Manchukuo's oil monopoly if they insist on considering Manchukuo part of China. . . . Troop activity along the border and a new Japanese map are signs that Manchukuo is preparing to annex Chahar, Mongolia. . . . New Zealand announces it plans a three-person commission to control agriculture.
Oct. 26	Manchukuo orders $40 million of British rails and steel in a move seen as a Japanese effort to shore up support for naval parity, which Japan wants immediately rather than at the 1935 conference.	Diphtheria and scarlet fever epidemics affect east Prussia. . . . Germany lifts its ban on student dueling societies.		Argentina raises wool prices to support producers regardless of loss of foreign sales. . . . A Peruvian dock strike fails. . . . Catholics in Michoacan kill eight soldiers and seven civilians.	King Prajadhipok of Siam threatens to abdicate after the legislature reduces his powers.
Oct. 27		France begins compiling a list of vehicles so it can requisition them in wartime. . . . Another 19 rebels die in Spain.		Six are injured in Cuban bombings. . . . Mexico seizes a U.S. fisherman illegally in Mexican waters. . . . Ontario's gold output is at $52 million for nine months, up from $37 million during the same period in 1933.	The Philippines, tired of waiting for the United States, imposes a tariff on itself.
Oct. 28		Smaller crowds for the talks of Oswald Mosley indicate the decline of British fascism. . . . Italy celebrates the 1922 march on Rome; Premier Benito Mussolini gives prizes to families who have been on their farms for a long time. . . . Irate Irish farmers egg police and seize their property. . . . Turkey seizes Mikhailoff in Bulgaria. . . . The cost of the Asturias rising is set at $300 million pesetas. . . . Members of the African Legion from Morocco are blamed for the deaths at Oviedo.	The head of the American University at Cairo University sees new opportunity for Americans to provide Christian service in helping Egypt develop as a modern state.	Mexico allows an anti-church march but bans pro-church marches. . . . Snipers fire on a Cuban political rally.	As India's socialists gain in strength, Gandhi resigns his post in the Indian Congress to aid village industries. . . . The Siamese government is negotiating with the King over conditions for his return.

A	B	C	D	E
Includes developments that affect more than one world region, international organizations, and important meetings of world leaders.	Includes all domestic and regional developments in Europe, including the Soviet Union.	Includes all domestic and regional developments in Africa and the Middle East.	Includes all domestic and regional developments in Latin America, the Caribbean, and Canada.	Includes all domestic and regional developments in Asian and Pacific nations (and colonies).

U.S. Politics & Social Issues	U.S. Foreign Policy & Defense	Economics & Great Depression	Science, Technology & Nature	Culture, Leisure & Lifestyle	
Norman Vincent Peale blames the current situation on "moral poverty." . . . The Institute of Social and Religious Research, funded by John D. Rockefeller, Jr., in 1921 to explore interdenominational cooperation, closes its doors.	The London naval conference opens with Japan asking parity but possibly at a reduced level for all.	After weeks of confusion and tinkering, the Federal Reserve explains its rules on margin trading.	Off Ostend, Belgium, a Swiss scientist demonstrates his machine for capturing wave energy and converting it to electricity.	The life of 10-year-old Gloria Vanderbilt, subject of a bitter custody battle, is threatened, and the police provide protection to her mother. . . . At the opening of the Museum of Irish Art, calls are made for a permanent Irish cultural center.	Oct. 21
Upton Sinclair's opponents are accusing him of being anti-church, and try to get Hollywood stars to contribute by claiming that Sinclair wants state control of the movie business. . . . Anthracite coal miners decline to strike for recognition of their union, instead asking President Roosevelt to intervene on their behalf. . . . President Roosevelt makes an appeal for all to support the 1934 Mobilization for Human Needs drive.		Secretary of the Interior Harold Ickes sends a representative of his petroleum agency to New Jersey to stop the gas war from spreading and to keep gasoline prices from dropping further. The lowest price reported is 7 cents a gallon. . . . Automobile output is up, particularly Chevrolet and Studebaker.	C.W.A. Scott and T. Campbell Black of Britain win the race to Australia in 71 hours; two racers die.	The King of England opens a library at Cambridge supported by $1.25 million in Rockefeller funds.	Oct. 22
A Missouri tornado wrecks a CCC camp, killing two. . . . Joe Tumulty calls on California Democrats to vote against Upton Sinclair, the party's gubernatorial nominee.	Maj. Gen. William Hase, chief of the Army coast artillery says he needs $33 million for anti-aircraft weapons to protect the United States, Hawaii, the Philippines, and Panama.	FERA allots $1 million to the states for rural health programs.			Oct. 23
Actor Rafael Lopez de Onata, denied a California license to marry Ellen McAdoo since federal law prohibits Filipinos from marrying Caucasians, says he will prove he is Spanish. . . . Bruno Hauptmann's trial is set for January 2. . . . The United Lutherans vote a war on liquor but table the question of allowing women delegates.	The Army announces it will buy 170 more trucks. . . . The U.S. balance of trade for the first six months of the year is $173 million. . . . U.S. gold purchases from abroad are $920 million.	A Washington, D.C., court rules the Railway Pension Act unconstitutional.	Three British researchers report they have a flu serum.	Gloria Vanderbilt tells the judge in her custody case that she wants to stay with her aunt.	Oct. 24
Father Coughlin presents the first talk of his radio season on 28 stations. . . . Senator William G. McAdoo threatens to cut off his daughter's $10,000 annuity and prosecute Onata if the two elope and marry. . . . By 987–183, the American Legion votes for the bonus. . . . A St. Louis newspaper reports it has a letter by Postmaster General James Farley endorsing Sinclair; Farley is mum. . . . New Jersey and New York silk workers, 25,000 strong, go on strike.		The Department of Justice dedicates its new $11 million building. . . . Cotton ginning is at its slowest rate since 1923. . . . Federal and Texas officials begin the drive against hot oil. . . . The administration estimates the veterans' bonus to cost $2.5 billion and will veto any such legislation.	A streamlined train takes 14.5 hours off the old record and sets a mark of 57 hours from Los Angeles to New York. At 4 cents a gallon, fuel costs less than $80. . . . G.R. Minot, W.P. Murphy, and G.H. Whipple share the Nobel Prize for Medicine after finding a cure for liver anemia.	Defending horseshoe champion Ted Allen sets a new consecutive double ringer mark with 13.	Oct. 25
George Creel repudiates Sinclair, the Farley letter is dismissed as a mistake, and President Roosevelt appears hostile to Sinclair too. . . . Attorney General Homer Cummings vetoes a proposed film on the life of G-man Melvin Purvis. . . . McAdoo is home, and there will be no elopement.	The U.S. objections to the Manchukuoan oil monopoly are seen as a hindrance to successful negotiations of the naval issue with Japan.		A Johns Hopkins researcher says that a little magnesium in the diet will cure grouchiness. . . . British air gunners now will have turrets to block the wind and not block their fire.		Oct. 26
A&P grocers abandon Cleveland after strikes. . . . Billy Sunday, old-time tent revivalist, says radio is a natural venue for preachers—it just takes personality and the ability to entertain. . . . Nineteen years after replacing Booker T. Washington, Dr. Robert R. Moton resigns as head of Tuskegee Institute. . . . After a lynching in Florida, southerners ask Roosevelt to use the federal kidnapping law to prosecute such cases.	Assistant Secretary of the Navy Henry Roosevelt, acting Chief of Naval Operations Rear Admiral Richard Taussig, and other Navy Day speakers call for a buildup of the Navy to treaty limits. . . . The Navy lays the keels of two ships at Mare Island and another at Bremerton.	The coal group will continue under the code even after the NRA expires. . . . The FHA agrees to cover refrigerators under its loan program. The Yeiba-Chai Navajo healing dance and sand painting are again part of Navajo life due to the Indian New Deal.	*Physical Education, Health,* and *Recreation Digest* debuts as a monthly, featuring health information.		Oct. 27
The Oklahoma burial of Pretty Boy Floyd attracts 20,000. . . . Father Coughlin calls the Liberty League a tool of the bankers. . . . The Cleveland strike of A&P grocery workers spreads to Milwaukee and Kroger's.				Ted Allen retains his title, although a near riot occurs when the horseshoe tournament prize money is not forthcoming.	Oct. 28

F	G	H	I	J
Includes elections, federal-state relations, civil rights and liberties, crime, the judiciary, education, healthcare, poverty, urban affairs, and population.	*Includes formation and debate of U.S. foreign and defense policies, veterans affairs, and defense spending. (Relations with specific foreign countries are usually found under the region concerned.)*	*Includes business, labor, agriculture, taxation, transportation, consumer affairs, monetary and fiscal policy, natural resources, pollution, and accidents.*	*Includes worldwide scientific, medical, and technological developments, natural phenomena, U.S. weather, and natural disasters.*	*Includes the arts, religion, scholarship, communications media, sports, entertainment, fashions, fads, and social life.*

	World Affairs	Europe	Africa & The Middle East	The Americas	Asia & The Pacific
Oct. 29	The gold bloc's currencies are weaker while England, Canada, and Japan see their currencies rise.... Germany's Hjalmar Schacht says that Germany cannot pay its debts, and countries that want to clear debts must take German goods.	Bulgaria, Romania, Greece, and Yugoslavia prepare an entente.... France announces it will mint a 100-franc gold coin but not release it immediately to thwart hoarders.... Stormtroopers with any Jewish blood must resign.... A Czech court rules that the name Hitler is slanderous.	Cape Town outlaws Nazis.	Mexico's Catholics rush to confirm babies before the church closes down. ... Colombia declares it will cut the gold content of the peso by 48.94 percent.... Cuba changes its Cabinet but retains the same policies.	
Oct. 30	The guilder joins the franc and belga under the gold point.	Belgium announces a balanced budget in hopes of avoiding a currency collapse.... Marshal Philippe Petain declares the French army ready to act in the Saar if necessary.... Germany accepts independent churches.... A hunger strike by miners begins underground in Katowice, Poland.... Poland sets a military service obligation for all between 17 and 60 and alternative service for both sexes.		Argentina begins subsidizing meat exports.... Mexico rules that homes where worship occurs can be seized. ... Peru breaks the stevedores strike.	
Oct. 31		An estimate places Germany's war-making capability on a par with that of 1914.	The New York-based Palestine Economic Corporation has assets of $3.3 million, is paying dividends, and is preparing to establish a structure to relocate refugees to Palestine.	The Mexican state of Aguascalientes expels all but five priests.	Military exercises at Nanking are testing and improving the city's defenses. ... Manuel Quezon is recovering from surgery.
Nov. 1	Germany and England announce that Germany will pay full interest to English debt-holders, provoking U.S. charges of discrimination because Germany has offered only 75 percent to American debt-holders.	Two state officials are on trial in Estonia for selling two warships to Peru.... Russia sends 12,000 from the Finnish border to Siberia as Soviet enemies.		Bombings in Cuba include the British Consulate in Cienfuegos.	
Nov. 2		Germany prohibits Nazi gatherings within 25 miles of the Saar border.... Hungary captures two Communist leaders; one commits suicide.... Fresh off a series of successes in borough races, the British Labor Party looks forward to the national elections.	Ivory dolls are discovered near the pyramid of Lisht that date from 2000 B.C.E. The dolls are unique in that they wear expressions.	Two more Mexican states ban unlicensed priests.	
Nov. 3	In control of most of disputed Chaco, Paraguay notifies the League that it will accept the armistice and send delegates to the peace conference.... To force U.S. trade, Germany cancels its plan to make partial cash payments of its debt to the United States.	The Nazis proscribe Prince Max von Hohenlohe, socialist Martin Ploetl, and 26 others.		Argentina's government proposes to Congress legislation to implement a homestead plan for its homeless as well as foreigners. The plan strongly resembles the New Deal's programs for relocation and urban garden plots. ... President Getulio Vargas reports that Brazil's budget deficit is 522,000 contos.	The ruling United Australia Party of Joseph Lyons, having invited the County Party of Earle Page into a coalition, is having difficulty allocating portfolios and forming a Cabinet.
Nov. 4		Britain and Russia settle a dispute over gold fields.	The Egyptian Cabinet resigns, citing the King's illness and British opposition.... In Syria the French High Commissioner suspends parliament and takes near-dictatorial powers because of economic problems and nationalism.... King Victor Emmanuel reviews Italian and Somali troops in Italian Somaliland.	Mexico fires 48 who broke their loyalty oaths by not marching in an anti-Catholic parade.	Japan declares it will not budge on the Manchukuo oil monopoly and claims an Anglo-American plot to force an open door.
Nov. 5	Nobubumi Ito denies, when asked by the League, that Japan is fortifying mandate islands it took over from Germany. The islands surround U.S.-controlled Guam.	Russia implements its "hostage decree" by arresting the relatives of a fugitive.... Germany pledges not to invade the Saar; Britain indicates it will not send troops to the region.... The compromise between German independent and state churches collapses.		Canadian nickel and copper outputs are up from last year. Income is up but exports are down.... Peruvian sugar growers petition congress to support and thereby save their industry.	

A	B	C	D	E
Includes developments that affect more than one world region, international organizations, and important meetings of world leaders.	*Includes all domestic and regional developments in Europe, including the Soviet Union.*	*Includes all domestic and regional developments in Africa and the Middle East.*	*Includes all domestic and regional developments in Latin America, the Caribbean, and Canada.*	*Includes all domestic and regional developments in Asian and Pacific nations (and colonies).*

U.S. Politics & Social Issues	U.S. Foreign Policy & Defense	Economics & Great Depression	Science, Technology & Nature	Culture, Leisure & Lifestyle	
Chicago plans to hire the 40,000 soon to be idled by the closing of the World's Fair. . . . A federal arbitrator is in Cleveland.	Treasury Secretary Henry Morgenthau is purchasing silver directly from Mexico. . . . The United States and Japan have no basis for agreement and the talks are about broken.	With hot oil restricted, independent gasoline prices rise 5 to 10.4 cents a gallon. . . . Business failures are up at 225 nationally for the week. . . . The employment insurance bill will include a payroll tax. . . . The PWA requests $12 billion for five years.	The plan to provide dirigible service to Asia and Europe gets governmental approval and a promise of aid.	The Cardinals' World Series share is $5,389, and the Tigers get $3,354 apiece.	Oct. 29
Brooklyn opens an adolescent court to separate deserving offenders 16–18 from adults and the children's court. . . . Bombs strike Arizona farms owned by Indians and Japanese. . . . Police battle relief strikers in Albany and Denver. . . . The Cleveland strike ends as both sides agree to arbitration.	The Japanese back down and the talks continue.	Col. Theodore Roosevelt charges that the NRA and AAA are making their own laws and that Postmaster General James Farley is creating his own Tammany Hall in Washington, D.C. . . . Wendell Willkie of the Commonwealth and Southern power company alleges that TVA's rate computations are rigged.	In Moscow an artificial heart revives a man dead three hours—for two minutes. . . . A book by J. Gordon Hayes claims that Peary's claim to have reached the North Pole is bogus.	The annual toy show reveals that Christmas toys—trains and scooters, even baby walkers—will be streamlined.	Oct. 30
Attendance at the final day of the Chicago World's Fair is 362,553. . . . Sears, Roebuck establishes its own home loan finance corporation. . . . After failing to get charges dropped against all but himself and his son, Samuel Insull begins his defense. . . . Supreme Court Justice Samuel Rosenman rules that blacks in Harlem have no right to picket a white-owned shoe store because picketing is for labor disputes, not racial ones.		Iowa pays its first old-age pensions. . . . An Alabama court invalidates the NIRA. . . . A Nashville judge halts the TVA's purchase of a public utility.	Peary's personal aide on his North Pole trek, Matthew Henson, says that Hayes is wrong. . . . The Academy of Physical Medicine hears a report that radio waves help a hangover by relaxing the stomach walls.	The Dionne sisters are baptized.	Oct. 31
Theodore Bilbo of Mississippi says he ran for the U.S. Senate to get a parking place. . . . Albany agrees to allow the hunger marchers if they remain orderly. . . . Colorado refuses to allow a relief strike.	The Army picks 10 pursuit plane pilots and four alternates for the Mitchell speed race set for November 17.	American wheat prices are up on the announcement that Canada will peg its wheat prices. . . . President Roosevelt orders a 5 percent rate for home loans. . . . Akron tire makers set a 17 percent national price increase, with some local increases reaching 75 percent.	A plane in Peru lifts 4,300 pounds of cargo 16,000 feet over the Andes, providing a total of 735 tons to a mining operation.	The French and Irish Free State teams are at Madison Square Garden to compete for the International Military Challenge Trophy. . . . Among the 20,000 people at the farewell to Evangeline Booth is Helen Keller. . . . Babe Ruth is offered $35,000 to play for the House of David.	Nov. 1
Daniel W. MacCormack, Commissioner of Immigration and Naturalization, tells a Yale audience that U.S. deportation law is as unjust as that of czarist Russia. . . . Rival coal mine unions fight in the anthracite region for the right to organize miners. . . . Seven unions accept the A&P terms.	England has moved to the U.S. position due to the issue of Manchukuo's oil monopoly. Without an ally, Japan is adamant that it will not compromise or offer an alternative.	Glenn Martin staves off bankruptcy for his aircraft company through a $1.5 million RFC loan. . . . A federal judge backs a PWA power plant in Missouri. . . . Greenville, S.C., wins the right to build a publicly owned power plant despite Duke Power's protest. . . . Knoxville, Tenn., gets a PWA loan to build its plant after the TVA surrenders to the private utility opposing TVA involvement.		There will be no radio diction prize this year because there are no distinguished candidates. . . . The Seventh Regiment's ball takes the theme, "On the Banks of the Congo." . . . Babe Ruth receives a hero's welcome from 100,000 in Tokyo, where he and an all-star team will play baseball.	Nov. 2
The governor of Arizona asks the federal government for agents to stop the violence against Japanese farmers. . . . The UMWA prevails in the anthracite strike, keeping the mines open until the opposing union concedes. . . . Dr. Ernest Gruening is head of the newly created Division of Territories and Island Possessions. . . . An Atlanta interracial committee says that African Americans oppose advocates of violence and revolution.		A welfare study reports that a family of five can eat on $8.17 a week. . . . The $1.5 million Arkansas model farming community on bottomland at Dyess has 15 families relocated from the hills and other depleted lands, with 200 families expected by January 1. . . . Agnes Regan of the National Council of Catholic Women asks the National Catholic Federation of Nurses to oppose birth control.	The director of the Pennsylvania bureau of mental health reports that feeblemindedness is not a disease but a deficiency in mental ability and that with proper training 90 percent of mental defectives can function in society.	Paul Wittgenstein, the one-armed Viennese pianist, is on tour in the U.S. . . . Paris fashions emphasize straight lines, a Russian look, and black for town wear.	Nov. 3
Declaring the two political parties have failed, Father Coughlin calls for two new parties. . . . Eighteen smuggled Chinese are found in a New Jersey cellar. . . . Socialist leader Norman Thomas attacks the New Deal and warns that the United States risks fascism.		The NRA litigation department reports that it prevails in 90 percent of its cases, attributing its success to the Schechter victory. . . . Savings insurance up to $5,000 covers 111 savings and loans in 27 states.		The National Steeplechase and Hunt Association rules that, because he endorsed cigarettes, Crawford Burton is no longer an amateur rider. . . . The Detroit Lions are scored on for the first time in the season but win their eighth game in a row. The Chicago Bears are also 8–0. . . . The U.S. all-star team including Babe Ruth whips a Japanese team 17–1 before 65,000 spectators in Tokyo.	Nov. 4
The U.S. Supreme Court rules that Huey Long can be sued for libel for a Senate speech. Justice Brandeis for a unanimous court says that Congressional immunity is only from arrest.	In a collision with another destroyer off the Mexican coast, the Mcfarland is damaged and a plane destroyed.	The Supreme Court rules that milk price controls are legal.		City College of New York freshmen IQ scores are the highest of 203 colleges in the United States. . . . The Cincinnati Pros of the National Football League are sold to a St. Louis group. They will finish the season as the St. Louis Gunners.	Nov. 5

F	G	H	I	J
Includes elections, federal-state relations, civil rights and liberties, crime, the judiciary, education, healthcare, poverty, urban affairs, and population.	Includes formation and debate of U.S. foreign and defense policies, veterans affairs, and defense spending. (Relations with specific foreign countries are usually found under the region concerned.)	Includes business, labor, agriculture, taxation, transportation, consumer affairs, monetary and fiscal policy, natural resources, pollution, and accidents.	Includes worldwide scientific, medical, and technological developments, natural phenomena, U.S. weather, and natural disasters.	Includes the arts, religion, scholarship, communications media, sports, entertainment, fashions, fads, and social life.

	World Affairs	Europe	Africa & The Middle East	The Americas	Asia & The Pacific
Nov. 6		Foreign Minister Eduard Benes of Czechoslovakia says that any attempt by Austria to restore the Hapsburgs would meet with strong resistance from Czechoslovakia and the Little Entente. . . . A Moscow parade marks the 17th anniversary of the Bolshevik Revolution. . . . Spanish Premier Alejandro Lerroux gets a vote of confidence that he requests after a strike is held in protest of executions of rebel leaders ordered by court-martial. . . . Labor wins Scottish city elections.		Brazil seizes Communists. . . . A dust storm in Alberta turns day to night. . . . Queretero, in Mexico, has only one priest under the new law specifying one priest for every 200,000 persons. . . . Nova Scotia's Presbyterians protest use of a "pagan" schoolbook that refers to the brute origins of man.	
Nov. 7	France has lost 335 million francs in gold in five days due to the Cabinet crisis and the U.S. elections. The United States has gained $20 million of the French gold. . . . Japan is adamant on parity. England is wavering and might agree to parity if Japan yields on the large ships.	Italian teachers begin wearing uniforms. . . . Italy sentences two anti-fascist Jews for seditious propaganda. . . . Poland reaffirms its alliance with France. . . . Germany protests that France's proposed use of troops in the Saar violates the Locarno agreement.		Chile is in an uproar after its prelate charges a legislator with blasphemy.	Four League engineers are in China to oversee reconstruction.
Nov. 8	Fourteen countries are invited to a London meeting to establish a boycott of Germany. . . . Chile orders its envoy to Rome to participate in the League meetings on Chaco.	Ireland cuts imports of completed cars, virtually ending import of British vehicles. . . . As rioting occurs and the old premier decries radical betrayal, Pierre-Etienne Flandin forms a new French Cabinet.	Victor Emmanuel dedicates a new fort on the Abyssinian frontier with Ethiopia.	Brokers sue Peru for $50,000 because the prospectus for its bonds failed to disclose its insolvency. . . . Mexico's Archbishop declares that the new anti-Catholic laws violate the constitution and threaten all religion.	Baiko Onoye, Japanese female impersonator and advocate of dance theater, is dead at age 64. . . . To establish soviets in Szechwan, 40,000 Chinese Communists are on the march. . . . Manchuria announces plans to pursue coal liquefaction.
Nov. 9	The League reports that 10,000 spies in the Saar are terrorizing residents. German radio stations are attempting to intimidate Saar voters.	The franc rises and the French gold drain ends as Flandin's quick formation of a Cabinet forestalls opposition and rioting. . . . Fritz von Papen, German Ambassador to Austria, says that Germany wants a soul union with the 31 million Germans outside its borders but denies he wants *anschluss*. . . . Fights between university monarchists and socialists in Madrid lead to four wounded.	Gulf Oil sells its holdings in Iraq to Standard Oil of New Jersey and Socony-Vacuum, giving them 23.75 percent of the Iraq Petroleum Company, which controls 89,000 square miles of Iraq.	A Mexican levy of 4 percent on money sent out of the country is slowing orders as intended. . . . Five thousand Bahamians greet the black fliers, Dr. Albert Forsythe and Alfred Anderson, on their goodwill tour of Latin America. Next stop—Havana. . . . Argentina imposes a 5 percent tariff on dividends and profits sent abroad. . . . Fighting resumes on three fronts in Chaco.	
Nov. 10	German newspapers report that Japanese dolls with yellow faces are replacing German dolls with white ones in the Asian and African markets, further weakening the German toy industry that has not recovered from competition from American makers of mechanical toys during the World War.	Adolf Hitler sends feelers to Britain on the return of Germany to the League and the end of Versailles restrictions.	Persian Prime Minister Mirza Muhammad Ali Khan Farrughi says Columbia University's recognition of the 100th birthday of Persia's national poet, Firdausi, will strengthen Persian-American friendship.	In El Salvador the church says it will excommunicate those who divorce and remarry. . . . In Argentina the Eucharistic Congress is credited with making masculine Christianity again respectable; men are returning to church.	Convicts in Kwangtung want to be released from jail to save the province money.
Nov. 11	It is Armistice Day, and throughout the world ministers pray for peace while national leaders pay tribute to the war's dead. In Paris, riots occur.	France says it is not concerned about the outflow of gold and actually wants to unload some of its excess. . . . Germans from Metz honor their former enemies at the Paris tomb. . . . German pay is down and food costs up 200–300 percent over last year. . . . The Nazis are to sterilize all the weak-minded, including those even slightly below normal.	Victor Emmanuel celebrates his birthday while continuing his African inspection tour.	The ninth Pan-American Sanitary Conference opens at Buenos Aires with delegates from 19 countries and 38 agenda topics, including how to reduce the spread of disease from airplanes. . . . Bolivia claims that the Paraguayans are retreating in northwest Chaco. . . . Ecuador's president refuses a congressional call for his resignation. . . . Forsythe and Anderson land in Cuba.	The Australian shrine to its war dead at Melbourne is opened by the Duke of Gloucester before 300,000 spectators. Rudyard Kipling reads an ode he composed for the occasion.
Nov. 12	The League asks Brazil and the United States to intervene in the Chaco War. . . . France is worried by reports that Germany has the capability of building 900 planes a month. . . . Belgium, France, and Italy are near agreement on an air pact against Germany.	Belgium's Cabinet resigns in a move to stabilize the belga. . . . The Estonian veterans' leader whose coup failed is at large again and expected to rally fascist support. . . . The emigrant station at Hamburg is closed. . . . Six are arrested in Warsaw for drugging race horses.	Tewfik Nessim Pasha is Egypt's new premier. . . . South Africa's Jan Christiaan Smuts asks Britain to seek amity with Japan but link its future to the United States.	Bolivia retakes three positions as Paraguay retreats. . . . Forsythe and Anderson are in Jamaica.	

A	B	C	D	E
Includes developments that affect more than one world region, international organizations, and important meetings of world leaders.	*Includes all domestic and regional developments in Europe, including the Soviet Union.*	*Includes all domestic and regional developments in Africa and the Middle East.*	*Includes all domestic and regional developments in Latin America, the Caribbean, and Canada.*	*Includes all domestic and regional developments in Asian and Pacific nations (and colonies).*

U.S. Politics & Social Issues	U.S. Foreign Policy & Defense	Economics & Great Depression	Science, Technology & Nature	Culture, Leisure & Lifestyle	
In what is regarded as a referendum on the New Deal, Democrats win in a landslide, gaining 10 Senate seats and a majority of two-thirds of both houses. . . . Californians reject EPIC and Upton Sinclair, who charges fraud and vows to initiate a recall of the Republican. . . . Five states repeal Prohibition. . . . The Labor Board orders textile strikers rehired. . . . Governor Huey Long says Louisiana should secede and "join Mexico or something." . . . In Minnesota Governor Floyd Olson and the Farmer Labor Party win handily.	Admiral H.I. Cone says that Japan has a secret navy consisting of merchant vessels easily converted to auxiliary cruisers and 18-knot tankers unregistered with Lloyds. The United States has no cargo vessels of comparable speeds.	The New Jersey coal code office shuts down after price fixing and lax enforcement destroy its ability to function. Local boards will take over. . . . At 2.28 million barrels, oil production is within quota.		Military riding teams from Canada, Chile, France, the Irish Free State, and the United States open the National Horse Show with a parade.	Nov. 6
All-black Boley, Okla., votes Democratic for the first time in its history. Even the sole African-American candidate, a Republican, loses the Boley vote.	Newton Baker says the United States should have a modified presence at the League, voting only on matters of peace.		France is building an 80-passenger flying boat in South America.	Almost 100 works of illustrator Charles Dana Gibson are on display at the American Academy of Arts and Letters.	Nov. 7
Chicago's fair management says it has the money to pay all of its debts. . . . Nebraska's legislature prepares to transition from a bicameral to a unicameral body.	American auto makers back Secretary Hull's refusal to accept barter, quotas, and other trade restrictions.	The AAA imposes a 25 percent reduction in cotton acreage for the coming year and seeks authority to export cotton to Germany to cut the surplus. . . . A court in San Francisco upholds NRA power to fix used car prices.	Eddie Rickenbacker flies a commercial transport coast to coast in 12 hours, cutting an hour from his previous record.	Walter Gay and Walter Lippman are chosen to replace two members of the 50-member American Academy of Arts and Letters, Charles Adams Platt and Paul Shorey, who died. . . . Ford Frick is elected president of the National Baseball League. . . . Italian Luigi Pirandello wins the Nobel Prize for Literature.	Nov. 8
General Motors leads the other auto makers in a switch to introducing new models through the year instead of all at one time. . . . A Louisiana jury clears aides of Governor Huey Long of buying votes. . . . The current offer to settle the silk workers' strike is a 36-hour week at higher pay. . . . Studebaker is preparing to give the bankruptcy court a restructuring plan that would give White Motors to its creditors, raise $5.5 million, and eliminate its funded debt.	The United States protests the detention of American fliers in Persia during the Great Race to Australia, claiming all contestants had overflight privileges.	Corn prices are the highest since September. . . . Cotton is up on strong export demand.	Britain begins surveying a route from Canada to Australia with only two stops. . . . A device that regulates propeller pitch and speed provides for safer flight. . . . "Tour-ways," a system of broad, landscaped roads linking cities and national parks, is proposed for the United States.	Gas in their small furnished room takes the lives of Ellen McCarthy, 1933's "Apple Annie," and her husband in a movie publicity stunt that clothed her in gown and fur and pampered her at the Waldorf for one day. . . . Nine of the 250 German children to be educated in the United States have arrived.	Nov. 9
Huey Long calls a debt moratorium and a special session of the legislature to come up with a two-year plan. . . . After intervention by Senators Harry Byrd and Carter Glass and threats for War Department involvement, the New Chamberlin Hotel at Old Point Comfort, Va., ends its exclusion of Jewish guests. . . . New York Justice Samuel Levy calls for the sterilization of unfit parents whose children are delinquent. . . . A student anti-war meeting is disrupted by a Maryland student, charging it is Communistic.		The NRA and canners disagree, with the canners wanting labels to be descriptive and the NRA preferring labels to address quality.	The Pennsylvania Railroad is investing $15 million in 57 electric engines capable of speeds up to 90 miles per hour.	A questionnaire reveals that Vassar faculty are more liberal than their students.	Nov. 10
Governor B.B. Moeur of Arizona has the National Guard on standby to back up his demand for half of the power generated by the Parker Dam on the Colorado River when it is finished.		Secretary Harold Ickes says that the PWA helps 2 million workers and 7 million people in all. . . . Corn traders are bullish on reports of shortages. Cotton prices are up in the south. . . . The Cotton Garment Code Authority wants an end to the use of the blue eagle on convict-made clothing.		A gala night at the horse show includes the victory of an American in the first military event, with an Irishman second. . . . The St. Louis Gunners shut out the Pittsburgh Pirates 6–0. . . . Martha Graham performs four new dances.	Nov. 11
Senator Nye calls for a tax of 98 percent on all incomes over $10,000 during time of war. . . . Christmas club holdings of $369.8 million by 7.5 million people are a 6 percent increase over last year.		An Oklahoma City court rules the NRA code on used cars unconstitutional, directly contradicting an earlier ruling in San Francisco. . . . The treasury lifts foreign exchange curbs, except on gold. . . . President Roosevelt gets a report that the St. Lawrence project could halve power costs.	An airliner in Peru sets an altitude record of five miles.		Nov. 12

F	G	H	I	J
Includes elections, federal-state relations, civil rights and liberties, crime, the judiciary, education, healthcare, poverty, urban affairs, and population.	*Includes formation and debate of U.S. foreign and defense policies, veterans affairs, and defense spending. (Relations with specific foreign countries are usually found under the region concerned.)*	*Includes business, labor, agriculture, taxation, transportation, consumer affairs, monetary and fiscal policy, natural resources, pollution, and accidents.*	*Includes worldwide scientific, medical, and technological developments, natural phenomena, U.S. weather, and natural disasters.*	*Includes the arts, religion, scholarship, communications media, sports, entertainment, fashions, fads, and social life.*

	World Affairs	Europe	Africa & The Middle East	The Americas	Asia & The Pacific
Nov. 13	Paraguay asks the League to help end the war. . . . The fall of the Belgian Cabinet causes declines in gold bloc currencies and strengthening of the U.S. dollar.	Chancellor Schuschnigg declares that Austria has the right to any form of government it wants, including monarchy. . . . Eamon De Valera's Fianna Fail begins its annual meeting with a report of increased membership and money. . . . Flandin gets parliamentary support for expanding free trade. . . . Chancellor Joachim von Ribbentrop tells British Foreign Secretary John Simon that Germany is rearming for defense but has no intention of abandoning the Versailles agreements.		Bolivia secures oil fields in the conflict.	Manchukuo nationalizes foreign oil—taking control of import, export, and manufacturing—and sets up a board to determine compensation to former owners.
Nov. 14	A world wheat conference opens.	Czechoslovakia announces plans to fortify border towns and institute military training. . . . Germany retains priests proscribed by the Vatican for supporting sterilization. . . . Romania detains 5,000 in its pursuit of terrorists.	New York Zionists announce plans to recruit 75,000 to support a Jewish homeland in Palestine.		
Nov. 15	The League is exploring ways to cut down on use of falsified passports, particularly by narcotics smugglers.	The British House of Lords restricts sweepstakes in an effort to limit flows of money out of the country and bars printing of sweepstake results in newspapers. . . . Yugoslavia expels Hungarians for complicity in the death of Alexander. . . . Britain holds Mosley and three other fascists for rioting.	Now complete, the Nessim Cabinet in Egypt is regarded as weak, save for the minister of finance.	Leftists depart the Chilean congress. . . . Mexico pursues indictments of prelates, including two in the United States. . . . Paraguay renews its offensive against Fort Ballivian to counter Bolivian successes in the north.	French in China worry over Communists nearing their sphere of influence. . . . Japan offers to mediate in Manchukuo to ensure that all foreigners get equal treatment.
Nov. 16	Officials in Paris deny rumors that the United States and Britain are planning to intervene to stabilize the gold bloc currencies. . . . The United States declines participation in the League effort to bring peace to Chaco.	Yugoslav nationalist students in Zagreb demonstrate against Croat professors. . . . Italy says it will enroll infants in military training corps. . . . Belgium's King Leopold rejects a Cabinet too closely tied to big bankers.	A shipment of 100,000 Palestinian oranges with Adolf Hitler's picture on the wrapper goes to London by mistake and gets a jeering reception.	Paraguay takes a divisional staff near Ballivian while Bolivia uses air power in the north. Bolivia rejects a proposed truce. . . . Canadian trade continues to improve. . . . The U.S. Catholic Bishops protest tyrannical Mexican laws. One hundred and eight Cuban political prisoners begin a hunger strike to protest their lack of trials.	
Nov. 17	The United States lends $25 million to Belgium, easing pressure on the belga.	Greece demands that Albania stop abusing Greeks. Macedonian irregulars threaten to invade.	A riot in Abyssinia leads to attacks on the Italian Consulate at Gondar and Italian demands for punishment of the guilty.	Brazilian cotton exports are up, maybe enough to compete with the United States.	The U.S. legation in Nanking protests the Chinese requirement that all members of the press register.
Nov. 18	The League demands an immediate truce in Chaco. . . . France indicates that it will block any Yugoslav move to bring the assassination investigation before the League.	Austria is optimistic that Italy wants to establish an alliance while Germany is beset by internal problems. . . . After Russia cuts orders, Germany reverses its anti-Russian position and offers a long-term credit.	Egypt halts public demonstrations in support of the new regime, fearing violence. . . . Italy sends troops to Eritrea and Italian Somaliland and demands Abyssinian reparations.	Costa Ricans protest a proposed law to outlaw criticism of foreigners. . . . After the fall of Ballivian, Paraguayan troops surge toward the Argentine border, where Argentine troops are mobilized to intern soldiers of both belligerents. . . . The two black fliers on a goodwill tour of Latin America damage their plane, the *Booker T. Washington*, in the Dominican Republic.	Japan suffers a Cabinet crisis, local officials resign, and one tries suicide because a wrong turn led to the Emperor's arriving at an affair early.
Nov. 19	The franc leads a rise in gold currencies that slows the inflow of gold to the United States. . . . Paraguay rejects the League peace plan.	According to the American Jewish Joint Defense Committee, anti-Semitism has been rising in eastern and central Europe, particularly Poland and Romania, since 1933 and Nazi propaganda is to blame. . . . Austria and Italy establish friendly relations. . . . Belgium's King approves the new Cabinet.		Brazil rejects issue of paper money to cover its debts, preferring an internal loan.	Japan's home minister apologizes, easing the crisis. . . . China claims to have reduced the red force in Kiangsi from 100,000 to 10,000 in a year.
Nov. 20	Belgium denies that it received $25 million from the United States.	Nuremburg Nazis close a large Jewish department store as they begin their drive against Jewish businesses. . . . The French Cabinet approves restrictions on political demonstrations and the arming of political groups. . . . Russia sentences five kulaks to death for hindering the cotton crop.		Argentina begins a campaign to halt the chewing of coca leaves. . . . Bolivia recaptures Picuiba in the north. . . . Trinidad's exports increase. . . . Former trade minister Harry Stevens, recently ousted from the Cabinet for his criticism of Canadian business policy, calls for a Canadian "New Deal" as a rallying point for Conservatives.	The Soviet sale of the Eastern China Railroad hits a snag when Russia rejects an American arbitrator. . . . Japan launches the heavily armed 8,500-ton cruiser *Suzuya* and lays the keel of a 10,000-ton aircraft carrier. The *Suzuya* is third of her class, and three more are planned. . . . Admiral Yamamoto says that Japan will not limit types, but Minister Saito supports navy limitation.

A	B	C	D	E
Includes developments that affect more than one world region, international organizations, and important meetings of world leaders.	*Includes all domestic and regional developments in Europe, including the Soviet Union.*	*Includes all domestic and regional developments in Africa and the Middle East.*	*Includes all domestic and regional developments in Latin America, the Caribbean, and Canada.*	*Includes all domestic and regional developments in Asian and Pacific nations (and colonies).*

U.S. Politics & Social Issues	U.S. Foreign Policy & Defense	Economics & Great Depression	Science, Technology & Nature	Culture, Leisure & Lifestyle	
With the Arizona National Guard in position, the federal government ceases work on the Parker Dam until a compromise can be reached.... City College expels 21 students for rioting during anti-fascist protests.	The U.S. proposal that all munitions imports, exports, and manufacture be licensed receives a favorable international response. . . . After Prime Minister Ramsay MacDonald blocks parliamentary efforts to open discussion of the debt to the United States, the United States indicates it will send Britain reminders that the debt is outstanding.	The HOLC shuts off applications for loans because current applications will exhaust its remaining $1.2 billion. . . . Rabbi Steven Wise asks President Roosevelt to prevent the AAA from sending cotton to Germany because it will hamper the Jewish boycott of Germany.	Rickenbacker sets a record of under 15 hours for a round-trip from Newark to Miami with passengers.	The French team takes the final prize of the horse show as it closes. . . . Babe Ruth's all-star team wins a shutout in Toyama.	Nov. 13
CCNY alumni call for the resignation of the president over the expulsions.	Britain and the United States resume naval talks to determine their course if Japan abandons treaty limits. . . . The United States resumes efforts to collect $1.1 million owed by the Soviet Union. . . . President Roosevelt reappoints Douglas MacArthur as Army Chief of Staff.	Oldsmobile announces plans to spend $2.5 million to double plant capacity. . . . President Franklin Roosevelt says the time is not right for broad social insurance. He wants only employment insurance.	A Dutch submarine begins a 25,000-mile trip to the East Indies by way of South America and Africa to explore the ocean floor.	Lew Ayres and Ginger Rogers marry. . . . The judge in the Gloria Vanderbilt custody trial says he will give her a new life.	Nov. 14
Five hundred protest the CCNY expulsions.	Britain proposes improved Japanese status under the 5-5-3 ratio, with increases in British cruisers, U.S. aircraft carriers, and Japanese submarines.	Labor Secretary Frances Perkins predicts that old-age pensions will be part of the social insurance legislation. . . . Oil men ignore Secretary Harold Ickes and establish their own organization to allocate oil.	Columbia scientist Harold Urey receives the Nobel Prize in Chemistry for his discovery of heavy water.	The child Gloria Vanderbilt is in the custody of Mrs. Harry Payne Whitney, her aunt, temporarily until the judge feels that a transfer to Mrs. Gloria Morgan Vanderbilt, her mother, can occur smoothly.... Ignoring a petition by 837 undergraduates, Princeton restates its opposition to post-season football.	Nov. 15
The Catholic Bishops order the establishment in every parish of a legion of decency and renewal of the fight against letting the movie industry set its own decency standards. . . . Louisiana passes a debt moratorium and 43 other laws in a speedy session overseen by Governor Huey Long.... As the Insull trial continues, stockholders in his failed company reject a sale offer. . . . The Women's Party convention opens with an announcement that it will pursue an equal rights amendment.	American naval architects call for the Navy to build battle cruisers. . . . Japan says it will reject the British plan but is willing to negotiate on submarines and carriers.	Secretary Harold Ickes says that the PWA could provide work for 11.5 million men who need it if it had $5 billion. . . . Renewed Tennessee litigation stalls the TVA effort to expand. . . . Taking a break from his tour of the TVA projects, President Roosevelt dedicates a monument to the frontiersmen at Harrodsburg, Ky.		Alice Hargreaves, the inspiration for *Alice in Wonderland*, is dead. . . . The crowd boos the official scorers as Bob Olin upsets "Slapsie" Maxie Rosenbloom for the light heavyweight title. . . . The Vanderbilt judge further clarifies that the child will spend weekends with her mother until they reestablish affection. Otherwise, the child is with her aunt.	Nov. 16
Insull's trial goes to the jury. . . . The strike of 25,000 silk workers continues with 8,000 more due out. . . . The CCNY student military organization backs the expulsions.	Capt. Fred Nelson wins the Army's premier flying contest, the Mitchell Trophy race, with an average speed over 216 miles per hour, well above the previous mark of 175. In fact, all entrants exceeded 175 miles per hour. . . . A private group organizes to work toward establishment of 100 frontier bases to protect the United States.	The PWA suspends $2.5 million for New Orleans pending determination of the impact of Governor Huey Long's 44 new laws. A New Orleans cigar store chain shuts down because of the tax increase.	The rail association orders that all railroad cars have air brakes by 1945. . . . Germany is using a "robot" pilot on long flights.	The recently revived *Police Gazette* files for bankruptcy.	Nov. 17
In his radio broadcast, Father Coughlin calls for 5 million people to join his Social Justice Union and force Congress to pass fair laws.	Lammot Dupont of E.I. Dupont Nemours writes Senator Nye that he supports controls on war profits but opposes government control of the industry.	Attorney General Homer Cummings makes his first-ever appearance before the Supreme Court in defense of the U.S. withdrawal from the gold standard.... Roosevelt calls for a child labor law to safeguard NRA gains.	Members of the Byrd expedition are trapped between crevasses.	Detroit wins its 10th straight, outgunning the St Louis Gunners, 40–7. . . . Chicago beats the New York Giants, 10–9, to match Detroit's winning streak. Chicago also has a streak of 29 straight exhibition and league victories.	Nov. 18
	Japan offers a 5-4-4 plan that gives it parity with the United States and an edge over England.	The Supreme Court promises a ruling on the gold issue for January 8. . . . President Roosevelt receives the proposed gasoline code.	Dr. Harlow Shapley of the Harvard Observatory reports the discovery of a twin star with a 30-day eclipse. . . . Byrd's men begin a cautious withdrawal from the dangerous ice.		Nov. 19
CCNY students and police clash. . . . Retired Marine Maj. Gen. Butler tells the House Committee on Un-American Activities that he was offered command of a fascist army of 500,000 seeking to overthrow the government. . . . Methodist churches are being sold for debt; 400 are reported in distress.	The United States submits proposals for arms trade controls to the League, which sends them to committee.		Discovery of a large plateau seems to confirm Byrd's theory of a link between Antarctica and the Andes.	The new White House china set of 1,000 pieces costs $9,301.	Nov. 20

F	G	H	I	J
Includes elections, federal-state relations, civil rights and liberties, crime, the judiciary, education, healthcare, poverty, urban affairs, and population.	*Includes formation and debate of U.S. foreign and defense policies, veterans affairs, and defense spending. (Relations with specific foreign countries are usually found under the region concerned.)*	*Includes business, labor, agriculture, taxation, transportation, consumer affairs, monetary and fiscal policy, natural resources, pollution, and accidents.*	*Includes worldwide scientific, medical, and technological developments, natural phenomena, U.S. weather, and natural disasters.*	*Includes the arts, religion, scholarship, communications media, sports, entertainment, fashions, fads, and social life.*

	World Affairs	Europe	Africa & The Middle East	The Americas	Asia & The Pacific
Nov. 21	Italy plans to eliminate the United States from the Chinese aircraft market.	Britain's lords criticize the Cabinet for letting Dutch planes fly to the East Indies faster than British planes. . . . Germany's established church is losing membership to the independent bodies.	The 318 Polish immigrants who left Greece for Palestine six weeks ago but were refused entry will land in Romania before returning to Poland.	Bolivia changes ministers of war, national defense, and government. . . . Brazil denies that Britain has offered old warships for cotton.	Britain releases a constitution that will give India self-rule as a federation of states. . . . Japan's military warns China to quit stalling on complying with the Tangku truce, but Japanese diplomats praise Chinese cooperation.
Nov. 22	Argentina breaks from the big four wheat restriction agreement and France asks a quota of its own. . . . The Little Entente charges Hungary before the League with complicity in Alexander's assassination.	Germany decries a Saar ban on officials engaging in politics as a muzzling of their rights. . . . Britain announces that it will hold its own armaments inquiry.	Tel Aviv institutes rent controls.	Brazil places an order for arms with Sweden.	Japan passes a record arms budget of 1 billion yen. . . . Seen as a test of the Cabinet's stability in London, the draft constitution is an outrage to Indian nationalists.
Nov. 23	The League modifies its Chaco peace plan at Paraguay's request to require demobilization rather than a neutral zone.	Security is heavy in Greece at the trial of the 14 accused of attempting to assassinate former premier Eleutherio Venizelos. . . . Russia sends to Bulgaria its first ambassador in 19 years.	Dr. John R. Mott of the International Missionary Council asks Methodists to set up three normal schools in the Belgian Congo for training native teachers.	Cuba raids a radical labor office.	After Britain and the United States reaffirm that capital ship tonnage should remain at the agreed ratio of 5:5:3, Japanese Ambassador Saito states Japan must withdraw from the unequal agreement.
Nov. 24	The League unanimously approves the Chaco peace plan, with Bolivia and Paraguay not voting. Brazil and the United States are invited to participate.	Bulgaria establishes a state oil monopoly.	Representatives of the Central Bureau for the Settlement of German Jews in Palestine report that Palestine can handle at least 40,000 immigrants annually.	Bombs explode in Havana, and marines take charge in Cienfuegos. . . . The Pan-American eugenics conference opens in Buenos Aires with a report on how the United States deals with its defectives.	China eases press censorship.
Nov. 25	The Nazi boycott group, meeting in London, claims that 510 items formerly imported from Germany are now made domestically.	Austria concentrates forces at the Yugoslav border, and Yugoslavia cancels military leaves. . . . France expels 20 German nudists on suspicion of espionage.	Ghazi Mustapha Kemal receives the name Ataturk (chief Turk) as Turks begin acquiring family names. . . . The Foreign Policy Association calls for U.S. action on Liberian reconstruction.	Chihuahua, Mexico, closes Mormon churches. . . . The eugenics conference supports aid to parents and an experiment with sex education in schools.	The Philippines balances its budget through economy measures.
Nov. 26	Germany says it can pay only one-sixth of the Young bond debt due on December 1.	In the face of a price increase by butchers, the Irish Free State begins distribution of free meat to the destitute. . . . Germany bans atheists. . . . Romania bans Communist groups.	Syria accepts Jews who have the capital to hire workers.	In the Chaco area, planes believed to be Bolivian fire on a Brazilian ship, leading Brazil to send naval aircraft to the area. . . . Peru blocks the seizure of an armory and crushes the Huancayo revolt. . . . U.S. Protestant, Catholic, and Jewish leaders call on Mexico to allow free worship.	Japan denies that it plans to flood Manchuria with narcotics. . . . Japan's finance minister resigns after failing to reduce the defense budget.
Nov. 27	Japan asks France and Italy to join it in withdrawing from the naval treaty.	Six hundred crippled veterans seeking a pension block Paris traffic. . . . Premier Flandin proposes a French New Deal. . . . Christmas leaves are cancelled for the military and police because the Reichswehr and SS are feuding. . . . France votes a $732 million defense budget.	Abyssinia pays reparations and gives military honors to the Italian flag. . . . The 318 immigrants who tried to settle in Palestine are home in Poland. . . . Turkey bans religious garb except at religious gatherings.	Canada's new currency features royalty and former prime ministers.	
Nov. 28	Japan proposes overall naval reductions, but France and Italy are cool to the idea.	Austria's fascist constitution goes into effect. . . . France raises tariffs 40 to 100 percent. . . . Danzig elects a Nazi who promises to maintain positive relations with Poland.		Bolivia apologizes to Brazil for its attack. . . . Cuban squatters set up an agrarian socialist government. . . . Peruvian officers reaffirm their loyalty. . . . A coup ousts the Bolivian president.	
Nov. 29	The naval talks are on hold because of the royal wedding and American Thanksgiving.	The Austrian fascist Heimwehr party begins a newspaper campaign of strong attacks against the clericals, its coalition partner. . . . Greece protests the Turkish ban on clerical garb.		Bolivia's forces are in full-scale retreat. . . . The new Mexican President, Lázaro Cárdenas, is expected to appoint a Catholic to his Cabinet.	Chinese Communists near Wuchow. . . . The fourth typhoon in six weeks strikes the Philippines.
Nov. 30		Britain announces it will subsidize freight shipping and that it opposes the low-cost passenger line that will compete with its subsidized lines. . . . Czechoslovakia eases its ban on U.S. films.	King Fuad abolishes the Egyptian constitution and parliament.	Cuba abolishes liberal, popular, and conservative parties.	Although the Nationalists win elections in India, the viceroy's appointees outnumber them and retain control of parliament.
Dec. 1	France declines to join Japan in withdrawing from the naval treaty.	Following the American example, Britain begins naming ships for cities. . . . Bulgaria kills five Turkish Muslims in Greece.	An explosion in a Beirut customs house shed kills 13. . . . The Muslim Supreme Council in Jerusalem tells fathers to lower their bride prices or find their daughters replaced by brides from Cyprus, where the price is lower.	Brazilian police break up crowds of students demonstrating for an end to examinations.	An Australian government survey shows that the aborigines are dying out. . . . Manchukuo creates 10 new provinces.

A	B	C	D	E
Includes developments that affect more than one world region, international organizations, and important meetings of world leaders.	*Includes all domestic and regional developments in Europe, including the Soviet Union.*	*Includes all domestic and regional developments in Africa and the Middle East.*	*Includes all domestic and regional developments in Latin America, the Caribbean, and Canada.*	*Includes all domestic and regional developments in Asian and Pacific nations (and colonies).*

U.S. Politics & Social Issues	U.S. Foreign Policy & Defense	Economics & Great Depression	Science, Technology & Nature	Culture, Leisure & Lifestyle	
The Liberty League denies that it asked Smedley Butler to lead a coup.	Senators William Borah and Gerald Nye praise former minister Saito for his anti-jingoism and support for naval restrictions. . . . Six new submarines under construction will be named for fish.	Steel mills are at 28.5 percent of capacity, the highest since June. . . . Detroit completes its $278 million debt refunding. . . . The Treasury Department busts a counterfeiting ring that passed $2 million in 18 months.	A scientist demonstrates that the brain glows in the dark. . . . Amelia Earhart receives a plane radio permit, normally issued for major flights, but her husband denies plans for a big trip.	A young baseball player, Joe DiMaggio, moves from the San Francisco Seals to the New York Yankees. . . . Columbia's fraternity men's grades meet the college average for the first time in "many" years. . . . Gloria Vanderbilt gets a good home as the judge awards custody to her aunt.	Nov. 21
A rally of 2,000 at CCNY asks for a truce and reinstatements. . . . In closing arguments, Insull's attorney asks the jury to blame it all on the crazy times. . . . The HUAC hears that Communists are active in the fur industry. . . . Columbia students vote for pacifism.	The United States notifies 12 nations that installments on their war loans are due on December 15. Only Finland is expected to pay. . . . Secretary Cordell Hull reiterates the U.S. commitment to a most-favored-nation approach.	The National Grange asks President Franklin Roosevelt to fix a gold price fair to commodities and to provide work for those on relief.		The American Association and International League are unable to agree, so the Little World Series is called off.	Nov. 22
Long says Louisiana does not need the PWA. . . . The American Legion reiterates that the veterans' bonus is its first priority. NYU students open an anti-war conference.	Secretary Cordell Hull praises the British stance as the naval talks end.	The Labor Board orders Danbury Hatters to deal with the union. . . . Kelvinator's earnings are $1.2 million for the year, up half a million from last year.	Dr. W. Gardner Lynn of Johns Hopkins donates to the Smithsonian a 60-million-year-old vertebra from a 25-foot snake.	President James Rowland Angell of Yale says that universities that put sports above academics betray their trust.	Nov. 23
A jury acquits Insull and his 16 co-defendants of all counts after two hours of deliberation.		The NRA hires a head of public relations, W. Averill Harriman, who immediately overturns Johnson-era restrictions on press access to agency chiefs. . . . President Roosevelt orders a study of employment in the auto industry.	A Harvard report indicates that radio educates poorly.		Nov. 24
	Japan tells the United States it will terminate the naval pact, maybe as early as December 10.	The FERA buys land in 20 states for 50 rural-industrial communities. . . . New Deal lending to businesses reaches almost $7 billion. . . . The NRA backs a 40-hour week although labor wants less.	The Canadian sea serpent is reported to be similar to an extinct sea cow. . . . Smithsonian experts refute the theory that a Nebraska skull is that of a Neanderthaler.	Chicago wins its 11th straight to take the league lead as the Packers shut out the Lions 3–0. . . . German conductor Wilhelm Fuertwangler denies that Paul Hindemuth is Jewish and criticizes Nazi fanatics.	Nov. 25
The editor and five staff members of the Louisiana State University student newspaper quit, alleging Governor Huey Long censors them. . . . National business failures for the week are 229.	Secretary of War Dern says that the United States needs navigable inland waters for national defense.	Denying that its programs conflict with housing programs, the PWA presses on with plans to spend millions.		The start-up Red Star Line announces it will offer $50 fares for tourist class between the United States and Europe.	Nov. 26
Baby Face Nelson kills two federal agents in Illinois. . . . John Collier of the Bureau of Indian Affairs reports that 55 reservations have voted for the Indian Bill of Rights. . . . An Alabama grand jury indicts three Scottsboro lawyers for trying to bribe the state's star witness.	Rep. Carl Vinson, chair of the House Naval Affairs Committee, says he will have Congress fund five ships for every three that Japan builds. . . . Secretary Cordell Hull denies that the United States and Britain are working on a joint Pacific security pact.	The AAA cotton reduction plan for 1935 calls for a 25 percent decrease, less than 1934's 40 percent cut. Growers will receive $95 million. . . . Actors Equity reports that actors are treated fairly by the CCC.		Scalpers are asking $75 for Army-Navy tickets after demand exceeds supply by 40,000. . . . Fordham debaters defeat Oxford on military training. . . . A fire in G.P. Putnam's home destroys Washington Irving's desk.	Nov. 27
Christmas seals to fight tuberculosis go on sale. . . . Nelson is found dead from officers' bullets. . . . Dutch Schultz surrenders.		PWA engineers agree to examine a Puerto Rican slum clearance plan. . . . Major companies agree to a 23-state oil marketing plan that goes to Washington for approval.			Nov. 28
The AFL's William Green says unemployment, although down, is still 500,000 higher than a year ago, showing the need for relief. . . . The Macy's Thanksgiving Day Parade features Mickey and Minnie Mouse and Santa Claus.		President Franklin Roosevelt presides over a Thanksgiving dinner for 600 child patients in Warm Springs, Ga. . . . Two more Japanese homes are bombed in Arizona's land war.	Listeners through the British Empire and in the United States listen to the royal wedding on the radio.	A million spectators line the streets for the wedding procession as George Edward Alexander Edmund, the Duke of Kent, fourth son of King George and Queen Mary, marries Princess Marina of the former Greek royal house. . . . Gloria Vanderbilt invites eight invalids to her party.	Nov. 29
Leaders of both sides in the silk strike agree to terms.		A thousand treasury agents due to be laid off in an economy measure may remain as unpaid workers in the fight against bootlegging.	Pan Am and Martin unveil the giant clipper intended to carry passengers and mail to the Pacific.		Nov. 30
Senator William Borah tells Republicans to abandon the old guard and become liberal.		In a dispute between the Doll and Toy Workers and Ralph A. Freundlich, Inc., Justice William H. Black upholds the closed shop under section 7a of the NIRA.		Eddie Cantor sails for Italy in hope of meeting Mussolini. . . . An international field of 15 teams begins the six-day bicycle race at Madison Square Garden. . . . The Ruth all stars end their tour of Japan undefeated.	Dec. 1

F	**G**	**H**	**I**	**J**
Includes elections, federal-state relations, civil rights and liberties, crime, the judiciary, education, healthcare, poverty, urban affairs, and population.	Includes formation and debate of U.S. foreign and defense policies, veterans affairs, and defense spending. (Relations with specific foreign countries are usually found under the region concerned.)	Includes business, labor, agriculture, taxation, transportation, consumer affairs, monetary and fiscal policy, natural resources, pollution, and accidents.	Includes worldwide scientific, medical, and technological developments, natural phenomena, U.S. weather, and natural disasters.	Includes the arts, religion, scholarship, communications media, sports, entertainment, fashions, fads, and social life.

	World Affairs	Europe	Africa & The Middle East	The Americas	Asia & The Pacific
Dec. 2		Austria bans unfavorable reporting on Germany. . . . British-supported German film output is halted by attacks from Joseph Goebbels.	U.S. financiers offer to invest up to $2 million in Arabia.	Paraguay's offensive continues in Chaco. . . . Railway strikes in Cuba hamper sugar production.	
Dec. 3	Austria conducts air war games in violation of the terms of the World War I peace treaty. . . . A Dutch credit of $100 million guilders helps to stabilize the belga, and $20 million in Dutch gold arrives in the United States. . . . Italy rejects the Japanese proposal for withdrawal from the naval treaty.	France and the empire open trade talks. France and Germany sign a Saar accord.		Thirty percent of Mexican students are absent from the state schools in a Catholic protest. . . . Representatives of Paraguay and Bolivia meet in Washington.	
Dec. 4		Eamon DeValera's party gains seven Senate seats to bring its total to 29, with 31 in opposition. . . . Stanley Baldwin's government stands after a conservative attempt to weaken the India bill fails. . . . Russia is sending submarines by train to Vladivostok and increasing its eastern air defenses.		A Honduran earthquake levels three towns.	The Chinese government tells foreign investors that it will not guarantee their loans to Kwangtung province.
Dec. 5	Britain will send troops to the League's Saar Army, as will Italy and Czechoslovakia. France will not.	Stocks are off in Germany after Hjalmar Schacht's decree that all loans must clear through the government and maximum interest is six percent. . . . Germany bans Salvation Army street bands.	Palestine has deported 627 Jews this year.	The low death toll in the Honduran quake is attributed to early warning.	
Dec. 6	Former Japanese prime minister Saito says that he sees no arms race before 1942.	France and Russia agree not to negotiate Eastern Locarno separately. Both want Germany in Eastern Locarno and the League. . . . Germany agrees to a League army excluding France in the Saar. . . . Exiles from Yugoslavia are entering Hungary, including a contingent of Serb soldiers. . . . Spanish Carlists and Alfonists press for a corporate state on the Italian model.		Panama gives its president extraordinary fiscal powers. . . . As Paraguay drives in the north, reports are that a Bolivian general popular with the Indians has staged a rebellion.	
Dec. 7	The major powers combine to end talk of war between Yugoslavia and Hungary. . . . The United States agrees to join the group overseeing the Chaco truce but will not take a seat in the League body at Geneva.	The Hungarian-Yugoslav border is tense as refugees flood into Hungary. . . . Yugoslavia agrees to ease its expulsion approach and denies that it has increased its border army. . . . Russia takes 12 White Russian plotters into custody.	The second Abyssinian attack in two months provokes an Italian protest.	A statue of Pizarro created for the 400th anniversary of Peru leaves New York. . . . Honduran quakes level 11 towns and leave 30,000 homeless.	
Dec. 8	Japan accuses Arizona officials of bad faith in the handling of the Arizona farm bombings.	Joseph Goebbels, Hermann Goering, and other Nazi leaders stand on street corners with tin boxes collecting winter relief for Germany's poor. Hjalmar Schacht collects the most because he solicits the stock market.	Abyssinia charges that Italian forces from Somaliland have penetrated 75 miles from the border. Italy denies the claim and says it will demand reparations.	Bolivia calls up additional reserves. . . . In what seems an opening of the election campaign against the Liberals, Canadian Prime Minister Bennett says that Canada will be better served by the Ottawa accords with the empire than by reciprocity with the United States. . . . A progress report states that Henry Ford's 3.7-million-acre Fordlandia, in the Brazilian jungle, has 7 million rubber trees growing.	Australia's Prime Minister announces that his country will further back away from protectionism, citing 68,000 new jobs since abandoning the economic nationalism of the preceding administration. . . . Chinese efforts to counter U.S. silver policy are failing as deflation gains momentum.
Dec. 9		Hungary reacts skeptically to Yugoslavia's ending of expulsions. . . . Bulgaria holds 23 Communists and is preparing courts-martial for 20 others for propagandizing in the army. . . . Eamon De Valera amends the draft Irish citizenship bill to strike British nationality. . . . Austria frees 2,500 Nazi detainees.	Jewish groups begin a drive to raise $25,000 for purchase of land in Palestine.	Bolivia mobilizes all manpower, with men from 31 to 49 serving as auxiliary support. . . . As part of a six-year agrarian reform plan, Mexico promises $5.5 million to its farmers on January 1 for purchase of communal acres and purchase of machinery to allow farmers independence from landowners.	Japan proposes a dirigible line to use German airships and link Asia and the United States. . . . Gen. Jiro Minami becomes Japanese ambassador to Manchukuo and head of Japanese forces in Manchukuo, therefore de facto ruler of Manchukuo.

A	B	C	D	E
Includes developments that affect more than one world region, international organizations, and important meetings of world leaders.	Includes all domestic and regional developments in Europe, including the Soviet Union.	Includes all domestic and regional developments in Africa and the Middle East.	Includes all domestic and regional developments in Latin America, the Caribbean, and Canada.	Includes all domestic and regional developments in Asian and Pacific nations (and colonies).

U.S. Politics & Social Issues	U.S. Foreign Policy & Defense	Economics & Great Depression	Science, Technology & Nature	Culture, Leisure & Lifestyle	
The Socialist Party's executive committee agrees in principle to a united front with the Communists. . . . The Steuben Society criticizes the Friends of New Germany.	A new eight-ton war tank attains top speeds of 60 miles per hour, and cruises at 30. The Army makes plans to purchase some.		The Corning 200-inch lens is finished.	The Bears beat Detroit to win their 13th straight. . . . The White House modernization, with a new presidential office in an enlarged wing, is complete. . . . New York Mayor Fiorello LaGuardia accompanies former governor Al Smith as the first visitors to the new Central Park Zoo.	Dec. 2
The Supreme Court rules that land-grant schools can require military training with no religious exemption. . . . The ship line and two officers are indicted in the *Morro Castle* disaster. . . . Silk workers return to the job.		The head of the Postal Telegraph Company recommends that Congress merge the telegraph companies because competition hurts all of them.	Dr. George Cowgill of Yale sets the daily requirement of vitamin B for good health and to ward off beriberi based on weight and metabolism. . . . Wiley Post sets an altitude record of 48,000 feet over Oklahoma.	The New York Giants set shares for 23 players and coaches for this week's championship game with the Bears.	Dec. 3
Responding to comment from 22,000 customers, grocery chains agree to put the AAA's "quality" labels on canned foods. . . . A poll shows that 45 Senators oppose the veterans' bonus.	U.S. foreign trade was up $13 million in October over the previous year. Japan replaced Canada as the second best customer, with Britain remaining first.	Western Union is cool to the idea of merger, but David Sarnoff of Radio Corporation of America supports it, as does the head of American Telephone and Telegraph.		Columbia announces it will raise tuition to $400 a year starting next year. . . . Furtwaengler resigns all his German posts in the flap over his defense of Hindemith. . . . Red Grange announces that he will retire from playing and seek a coaching job.	Dec. 4
Four Ohio utilities get the okay to buy four former Insull companies. . . . President Franklin Roosevelt begins his return from Warm Springs. En route, he becomes honorary chair of the blind foundation.	The Nye Committee hears testimony that the arms makers ignored trade restrictions and an embargo in rearming Germany and sending munitions to Manchuria.	Cunard ship lines agrees to serve as ticket agent for Imperial Airways, allowing easier booking of travel to Europe and Africa. . . . The ICC cuts freight rates for western farmers, costing the roads $6 million in revenue. . . . Steel output is up for the seventh straight week. . . . American toymakers ask NRA protection from Japanese goods.	Niagara Falls loses another 200 tons in a nighttime rock fall.	Ruth homers three times against a Shanghai team.	Dec. 5
Two Louisiana legislators, supporters of Governor Huey Long, are indicted for tax evasion. . . . Long ousts the state Democratic chairman and takes the office for himself.	Senator Nye claims that munitions makers are trying to provoke an arms race with Japan.	Industry leaders ask for an extension of the NRA for another year with increased freedom for business.	Dr. Edward Jackson of the University of Colorado reports to the National Society for the Prevention of Blindness that proper diet can reduce the risk of blindness in old age. . . . A commission reports that Niagara's table rock is safe.		Dec. 6
A draft Auto Labor Board provides that workers can choose any bargaining agent they want. . . . Norman Thomas says there will be no merger of Communists and Socialists. . . . Henry Wallace calls on the wealthy to abandon their "Bourbonism" and start contributing to society. . . . Huey Long appoints himself counsel for the Louisiana group investigating utility rates.	Britain reiterates its support for smaller warships, an issue on which Britain and the United States disagree, but also agrees with the United States that failure of the Washington Accords will destabilize the Pacific. . . . The telephone line between the Secretary of State and Japan's Foreign Minister is inaugurated.	November Chevrolet sales of 50,896 are the greatest since 1926. . . . A coalition of trade and civic groups announces that it will fight the St. Lawrence power development project. . . . The FERA acknowledges that some on its rolls do not need aid.	A Swiss laboratory reveals it has a method for making androsterone from cholesterol, a much faster and cheaper process than the current method. . . . Wiley Post claims another altitude record, over 50,000 feet.	As the Amateur Athletic Union convention meets, opposition to sending a contingent to the 1936 Olympics increases. . . . The owner of the Boston Braves wants to convert his baseball park to a dog racing track and move to the Red Sox's field.	Dec. 7
The AFL rejects the Auto Labor Board plan as proportionate representation and calls for majority vote to determine representation. . . . Archbishop John McNicholas of Cincinnati asks all 22 million American Catholics to boycott movies. . . . Fearing undesirable population shifts, San Franciscans try to block construction of two new bridges. . . . Kentucky calls out the military to help mine officials besieged in Harlan. . . . Nationwide anti-drug raids capture 560.	Rear Admiral Ernest R. King, chief of naval aviation, reports that the United States needs a stronger dirigible fleet and 1,910 new planes by 1940 or 1942.	Cotton ginned to December 1 exceeds 9 million bales.	A party of the Byrd expedition reports that Antarctica seems to have dormant volcanic peaks. . . . Publishers view a linotype that sets type electronically. . . . Forsythe and Anderson, their ship repaired, reach Santo Domingo.	Arthur Conan Doyle's widow says she is in constant communication with the late author. . . . The AAU supports Brundage and sidetracks the issue of the 1936 Olympics. . . . The French team wins the six-day bicycle race.	Dec. 8
Father Coughlin attacks Cardinal O'Connell for being silent on social issues. . . . The total in the narcotics raids rises to 765. . . . An effigy of the Louisiana State University president is found near the Huey P. Long Fieldhouse.			An M.I.T. stratosphere test balloon reaches 65,000 feet.	The AAU decides to keep the Olympic issue open and watch Germany's treatment of Jews. . . . The New York Giants beat the Chicago Bears, 30–13, ending the Bears' streak and taking the league title.	Dec. 9

F	G	H	I	J
Includes elections, federal-state relations, civil rights and liberties, crime, the judiciary, education, healthcare, poverty, urban affairs, and population.	*Includes formation and debate of U.S. foreign and defense policies, veterans affairs, and defense spending. (Relations with specific foreign countries are usually found under the region concerned.)*	*Includes business, labor, agriculture, taxation, transportation, consumer affairs, monetary and fiscal policy, natural resources, pollution, and accidents.*	*Includes worldwide scientific, medical, and technological developments, natural phenomena, U.S. weather, and natural disasters.*	*Includes the arts, religion, scholarship, communications media, sports, entertainment, fashions, fads, and social life.*

	World Affairs	Europe	Africa & The Middle East	The Americas	Asia & The Pacific
Dec. 10	Defusing the Balkan crisis, the League orders Hungary to prosecute plotters against Yugoslavia. . . . France proposes a five-member world court to try terrorism cases. . . . Britain and France announce that they will not pay the war debts coming due.	An impeachment court finds the former Estonian defense minister and the former army chief of staff not guilty of selling destroyers to Peru. . . . Thirty-seven more arrests bring the total number of "plotters" and "saboteurs" against the Soviet Union to 120. . . . Debate begins in the Commons on the Indian constitution.	The Palestinian government announces that it will transmit telegrams in Hebrew.	Chile's government announces that it will expand production of sulfur. . . . Cuba drops 28 from the army for conspiring against the government. . . . Bolivia accepts the Chaco peace plan but continues to mobilize as Paraguay presses its assault in hopes of winning victory before the truce.	Australia inaugurates air mail service to England. . . . The Nationalist Executive Council hears positive reports of the successful campaign against the Communists.
Dec. 11	The World Bank directors end their meeting with concern over gold flows but general optimism about the world economy.	Italy indicates that it will default on its debt payment.	The Hague rules against Britain in the case of Oscar Chinn, who claims that Belgian rules in the Congo River trade hamper his business.	In Nuevo Leon, protected by the local government, church activity goes on as normal despite the federal law. . . . Canada charges the Bronfman brothers, owners of Seagrams Distilling, with $5 million in tax fraud.	Japan's Cabinet deliberates withdrawal from the naval agreement, assuming that it will not produce an arms race.
Dec. 12		Belgium asks France to support the belga. . . . British officers head to the Saar to assume command. . . . The Commons votes 410–127 to support the government's India bill. . . . Greece entry law now provides visas for Jews on the same basis as others.		A general strike begins in Tampico, Mexico. . . . McKenzie King urges Canada to lead the empire in calling for a British investigation of arms dealing.	King Prajadhipok meets with the Siamese and sets terms for his return. . . . A north-south split is forming in China after failure of a million man nationalist army to take 60,000 Communists.
Dec. 13		Austria permits publication of a Nazi newspaper, which attacks Jews in its first issue. . . . Belgium indicates it will not pay its U.S. debt. . . . Lithuania charges 126 Nazis with plotting to seize Memel for Germany. . . . France's loan to Belgium helps stabilize the Belgian currency. . . . Hungary welcomes the chancellor and foreign minister of Austria.		Cuba suspends habeas corpus. . . . The black goodwill fliers reach Trinidad.	
Dec. 14	After Austen Chamberlain protests that it might convert the League into an aggressor force, the League postpones for six months the examination of a proposal for a League air police force.	Streicher calls for more stringent anti-Jewish laws and the death penalty in Germany, citing new racial discoveries. . . . Germany launches the 18,000-ton *Scharnhorst*, the first big ship of the Nazi era.	Abyssinia reports its clash with Italy to the League. Italy demands reparations, citing 140 lost soldiers. . . . Claiming it signed under duress, Persia protests Iraq's accusations in the League that Persia violated a 1913 accord defining their border.	Expressions of mourning pour into Peru after Peru's former poet laureate Jose Santos Chocano is murdered. . . . The crash of the goodwill fliers on takeoff from Trinidad effectively ends their tour.	A Japanese naval attaché says that technical progress has made Japan unsafe under 5-5-3 and that it is inexplicable that the United States. will not reduce tonnage in the interest of economy.
Dec. 15	The League is fearful that the clash in Abyssinia might provide Italy with an excuse to bypass the League and bring on a full-scale war. . . . The Pope orders Catholic clergy to be neutral on the Saar.	Two Austrians are killed on the German border. Both Germany and Austria downplay the incident. . . . Dummies in Italian store windows wear gas masks.	Abyssinia claims that Italians attacked a surveying party 60 miles from the border. . . . A Turkish quake destroys eight villages.	Cuba's Batista tells his foes he is too strong for them to stage a successful rising. . . . Brazil reports six cases of bubonic plague. . . . Canadian leaders oppose development of the St. Lawrence because of the current power surplus and the potential to damage Canada's railroads.	Needing tourist income, Japan begins efforts to curb overzealous, spy-phobic enforcement of laws against foreigners. . . . A malaria epidemic in Ceylon has affected 500,000 so far.
Dec. 16	Chile's Finance Minister orders more domestic purchasing as the trade deficit with Japan grows.	Because of a tight allowance, King Boris of Romania is considering the sale of one or two of the royal elephants. . . . Four thousand would-be German Olympic athletes take the oath in unison.	Mussolini rejects League mediation of the clash with Abyssinia.	Colombia's Cabinet resigns. . . . Lázaro Cárdenas decrees that Mexicans will have preference in all concessions and government jobs.	Three U.S. Marines are injured as a 700-man contingent leaves Singapore, leaving a handful behind.
Dec. 17		Russian executions of "left deviationist" followers of Zinoviev in the Ukraine reach 103. . . . Germany captures 600 in a drive to clean up bars and public baths.	Britain pressures Italy and Abyssinia to resolve their differences peacefully. . . . The Palestine Foundation Fund reports it has received a $2.5 million loan from British sources.	Iceland repeals prohibition.	Western Australia presents its secession petition to Parliament.
	A Includes developments that affect more than one world region, international organizations, and important meetings of world leaders.	**B** Includes all domestic and regional developments in Europe, including the Soviet Union.	**C** Includes all domestic and regional developments in Africa and the Middle East.	**D** Includes all domestic and regional developments in Latin America, the Caribbean, and Canada.	**E** Includes all domestic and regional developments in Asian and Pacific nations (and colonies).

U.S. Politics & Social Issues	U.S. Foreign Policy & Defense	Economics & Great Depression	Science, Technology & Nature	Culture, Leisure & Lifestyle	
In the appeal of Scottsboro convict Clarence Norris to the Supreme Court, Alabama denies it systematically excludes African Americans from juries. . . . The National Consumers League rejects proposals for industry self-policing and calls for the abolition of home work, which is expanding despite wages as low as $12.50 a year. . . . A federal inquiry blames the sheriff and unfit officers for the labor disturbances in Harlan County.	President Franklin Roosevelt and Secretary of State Cordell Hull tell a Nashville conference that the world needs free trade and reciprocity to bring about recovery.	The Supreme Court hears arguments for and against the constitutionality of the oil and used car codes.	Dr. Theobald Smith of the Rockefeller Foundation dies. Smith is credited with finding the cure for turkey fever, discovering the tick that causes cattle fever, and instituting the first studies of the link between vitamins and health.	Mayor Fiorello LaGuardia is on hand as Jack Dempsey throws in his gloves and lays the cornerstone of his new restaurant. . . . A photo exhibition by Alfred Steiglitz spans 50 years. . . . Babe Ruth's all-star team ends its Far Eastern tour with a win over a Filipino team.	Dec. 10
A hotel fire in Lansing, Mich., claims at least 15 lives, including several legislators. . . . Congressman Wright Patman of Texas announces that he will introduce legislation to protect incompetent veterans from unscrupulous trustees and negligent banks. . . . J. Edgar Hoover calls for quick punishment and the end of political interference in the crime war.	The Nye Committee hears testimony that the Army and Navy supported sales of powder to Japan in expectation that it would give an opportunity for Du Pont to collect military data.		Byrd announces that his team will leave Little America in late January. . . . The Byrd team reports that it found coal and fossils at the head of the Thorne glacier, 212 miles from the pole.		Dec. 11
AFL president William Green drafts a 30-hour bill, supports the extension of the NRA, asks an end to federal pay cuts and support for employment insurance, and opposes company union. . . . Sam Rayburn quits the race for the House Speakership. . . . The Chamber of Commerce calls for laws barring Communists.	The Nye Committee moves to the chemical industry and hears that Du Pont used Senator Boies Penrose to get an embargo on foreign dyes.	President Roosevelt appoints a prison industries board and requires federal purchase of prison goods.	The Wiley Post record is denied after findings that he reached only 48,000 feet.	Max Baer proposes to fight Lasky and Hamas on the same night, contending that the double title fight would draw $1 million. . . . The National League approves a test of night games.	Dec. 12
	The Nye Committee reports that some companies had wartime profits of 800 percent, and the war created 181 million-dollar incomes.	Unions leave the federal auto board. . . . Chrysler reports $75 million in 1935 orders. . . . The SEC approves rate reductions for southern Atlantic ports to make them more competitive with northern ports.		Hamas's manager accepts Baer's offer. . . . Yale's president warns that increasing inheritance and income taxes will harm universities.	Dec. 13
The number of Huey Long supporters now indicted for tax evasion is eight. . . . The largest Christmas mail shipment since 1929, nearly a million pounds, sails for Europe. . . . Work begins on a new channel and construction of port facilities that will make Brownsville, Tex., a gulf port.	The United States okays the Japanese request that military language officers lose their diplomatic immunity. . . . Du Pont refutes charges that it made a profit of over 39,000 percent on a wartime project.	Cotton growers vote 9–1 to renew the Bankhead restrictions for 1935; California and Oklahoma fail to get the necessary two-thirds approval. . . . President Franklin Roosevelt's plan for state job insurance with federal backing gets approval from business groups.	Dr. C.B. Bridges reports that scientists are able to identify chromosomes by their stripes, the first step in isolating genes. . . . Pratt & Whitney announces a new airplane engine capable of 750 horsepower at 7,000 feet, the most powerful available. . . . T.A. Watson, first man to hear a voice over a telephone, is dead.	The number of college freshmen is up 5 percent. . . . Heavyweight Joe Louis beats Lee Ramage by TKO in eight rounds in Chicago.	Dec. 14
Although the legislature has passed 318 laws already, Louisiana Governor Huey Long calls another special session to increase his powers.	Iron exporters are gearing up for a fight in Congress to retain their scrap metal trade, which critics claim is helping Japan to arm.	Roger H. Whiteford takes the post of general counsel for the FHA, becoming the first dollar-a-year man in the Roosevelt administration.	Experts see the United States on the verge of a climate shift and a return to old-fashioned winters.		Dec. 15
Father Coughlin alleges that the U.S. Army, Navy, and State Department colluded in the sale of a secret powder-making process to Japan. . . . Jews, Protestants, and Catholics unite in protest of Mexico's anti-church stance. . . . Dr. Harold Rypins reports that despite reports that universities discriminate against Jews, in fact Jews are 17 percent of medical students, twice their share of the population. . . . William Green pushes unions to support child labor legislation in 1935. . . . Troops head to Rowan County, Ky, to prevent a riot.	Secretary Dern's annual report calls for an increase of the Army by 52,000, to 14,000 officers and 165,000 men, and the addition of 600 airplanes.	Shipments of stocker and feeder cattle to the grain belt are the lowest in 16 years.		Clara Bow gives birth to a son.	Dec. 16
Two Harvard students head for Louisiana to form the "Grey Shirts."	Chemical, watch, and clock industries oppose reciprocity with Switzerland, citing national security. . . . Secretary of State Cordell Hull promises to issue the U.S. definition of neutrality and its probable behavior in the event of war.	The week's business failures total 231. . . . Cotton prices are down on federal selling.	Eight thousand planes fly over Dayton in honor of the anniversary of the flight at Kitty Hawk.	The Vanderbilt custody case appeal is delayed until May 1.	Dec. 17

F	G	H	I	J
Includes elections, federal-state relations, civil rights and liberties, crime, the judiciary, education, healthcare, poverty, urban affairs, and population.	Includes formation and debate of U.S. foreign and defense policies, veterans affairs, and defense spending. (Relations with specific foreign countries are usually found under the region concerned.)	Includes business, labor, agriculture, taxation, transportation, consumer affairs, monetary and fiscal policy, natural resources, pollution, and accidents.	Includes worldwide scientific, medical, and technological developments, natural phenomena, U.S. weather, and natural disasters.	Includes the arts, religion, scholarship, communications media, sports, entertainment, fashions, fads, and social life.

	World Affairs	Europe	Africa & The Middle East	The Americas	Asia & The Pacific
Dec. 18	In the presence of the Emperor, the Japanese High Council votes to withdraw from the 1922 naval pact but to delay implementation so it will not appear linked to the failed London talks.	Germany denies reports that someone took a shot at Adolf Hitler. . . . Britain deplores the spread of American-style use of weapons in crime. . . . France rejects nationalization of the arms industry and votes an 800 million franc increase in defense spending. . . . Germany admits it intervened in Memel, but only to stop a fight and not to interfere with Lithuanian affairs.		Paraguay rejects the League truce and a prisoner exchange, claiming it has more prisoners than Bolivia has remaining soldiers. . . . Ecuador closes the Quito university and expels student strike leaders.	The British House of Lords approves the India plan 239–62.
Dec. 19	Argentina's Foreign Minister reports that 30 nations, including all 21 American nations, have ratified the Argentine Anti-War Pact. . . . The League explores the possibility of giving Paraguay more time to respond to the Chaco truce plan.	British doctors join the Trades Union Congress. . . . The Saar Plebiscite Commission sets a Christmas truce for December 23–27. . . . Estonia is the last to notify the United States that it will default on its debt payment. . . . Britain executes a woman poisoner, its first execution in eight years.	Abyssinia alleges that the Italians were aggressors.		Americans in China are encouraged to leave Anwhei province for safety from the Communists.
Dec. 20	Britain and Argentina agree to investigate the meat packing trade. Four U.S. firms are involved.	Spain's executioner is on strike. . . . The French government talks with bankers and industrialists about how to aid the insolvent Citroen motors. . . . Serbian radicals break off talks on joining the Yugoslav Cabinet after they cannot get the posts they want.		Air travel to the Caribbean is reported as heavy.	The British Barnby Mission criticizes the state oil monopoly but also sees business opportunities and asks for aid to Manchukuo.
Dec. 21		Austrian raids capture Nazis and arms caches as the Nazis attempt to reform an army. . . . Ramsay MacDonald announces the formation of a British commission to investigate arms dealing. . . . Citroen enters receivership. . . . Italy's 94 most prolific mothers are honored by Mussolini.	Seven die in the crash of a Dutch airliner in the Syrian desert.	Canadian relief is down 50,000 at 1.15 million. The all-time high was 1.59 million in April 1933.	The Aga Khan approves of the India bill and promises to work for it in India. . . . Although Britain is cool to the Barnby report, Japan sees it as a sign of improving relations. . . . Although the governments of Nanking and Canton disagree, their military chiefs agree to work together.
Dec. 22	A League commission reports favorably on the Rupununi district of British Guiana as the place to resettle 30,000 Iraqi Assyrians.	Adolf Hitler replaces the old Prussian heraldic emblem with a new eagle that holds in its claws a sword and lightning bolts and has a swastika on its chest.	Arab-Jewish clashes in Palestine injure two Jews.		
Dec. 23	Flandin says stability requires not devaluation of the franc but development of a tie between the pound and the dollar.	Austria amnesties 90 Socialists and 80 Nazis. . . . Germany denies smuggling American aircraft.	According to Addis Ababa, Italy invades Abyssinia.	Argentina proposes an international merchant marine, with two ships of each nation having free access to all ports.	As the malaria epidemic worsens in Ceylon, talk turns to famine in 1935. . . . China is using a workforce of 3,000 in building a big air base and port at Haichow, near the Japanese sphere of influence. . . . Aguinaldo asks earlier independence for the Philippines. . . . Russia denies and Japan downplays a reported Russian intrusion into Manchuria.
Dec. 24		Albania denies Greek reports of a rising against King Zog.	Italy denies invading Abyssinia, claiming the incident is just another in a long series.	The new Bolivian air contract provides La Paz to New York service in three days.	Australian airmail arrives in London three minutes ahead of schedule after 12 days en route.
Dec. 25			Abyssinia claims Italy has occupied Afdub and has begun building a road.		The Emperor opens the Japanese Diet.
Dec. 26	Chile and Germany sign a commercial treaty. . . . A report that oil is the cause of the Italian-Abyssinian conflict worries the League because oil is the cause of the Chaco War.	Belgium reduces state salaries and pensions by 5 percent. . . . Russia and Romania sign an agreement restoring telephone communication.		Canada reports 1934 imports from the United States were 2.5 times those from Britain. . . . President Harmadio Arias signs the Panama tariff law, which includes the largest free list in the country's history.	China denies it intends to devalue its currency. . . . Siam sentences Gen. Phya Devahastin to two years for fomenting unrest.
Dec. 27	German-Turkish trade is reported as doubled over the past 9 months.	Yugoslavia's four fascist groups unite into a "People's Movement." . . . The Irish Free State establishes a licensing system in preparation for restricting purchases of British coal.		Brazil starts its "New Deal" by authorizing bonds for relief and farm rehabilitation.	Statements of Manuel Quezon and others in the Philippines seem to indicate a shift away from independence and toward dominion status.

A	B	C	D	E
Includes developments that affect more than one world region, international organizations, and important meetings of world leaders.	*Includes all domestic and regional developments in Europe, including the Soviet Union.*	*Includes all domestic and regional developments in Africa and the Middle East.*	*Includes all domestic and regional developments in Latin America, the Caribbean, and Canada.*	*Includes all domestic and regional developments in Asian and Pacific nations (and colonies).*

U.S. Politics & Social Issues	U.S. Foreign Policy & Defense	Economics & Great Depression	Science, Technology & Nature	Culture, Leisure & Lifestyle	
The Louisiana legislature is reportedly enacting Huey Long's bills at a rate of one every three minutes.	The War Department offers 1,600 engineering projects at a cost of $8 billion for recovery spending.	Oil for the week is 2.4 million barrels, 80,000 barrels over quota. . . . National Christmas sales are up 16 percent, with a range of 2–20 percent. . . . Proctor and Gamble gives its employees 4 percent bonuses as part of its profit-sharing program.	Father Julius Nieuwland of Notre Dame is announced as the winner of the Nichols Medal of the American Chemical Society for his work with unsaturated hydrocarbons, which enabled the creation of artificial rubber.	The Knickerbocker Greys, 125 boys from age 8 to 16, perform their annual Christmas Review before 2,500.	Dec. 18
In Shelbyville, Tenn., troops kill two in a lynch mob, spirit their black target away, then have to withdraw, leaving the town in the hands of rioters. . . . U.S. Nazis begin purging their membership.	The League applauds the U.S. decision to cede certain rights of its ships in the event of war, which will allow more effective blockades. . . . The U.S. war plan includes an army of 2 million.	Cadillac reports sales up 50 percent.	A Yale pathologist reports he has isolated the bacterium that causes brain inflammation.	The Yankees sell Sam Byrd, once thought to be the new Babe Ruth, to the Cincinnati Reds. . . . Pianist Hephzibah Menuhin, age 14, makes her recital debut with her 17-year-old brother Yehudi, the world-class violinist. . . . Paul Robeson announces that he has learned the language and will visit Russia.	Dec. 19
With 600 troops in place, Shelbyville is quiet. A mass meeting calls for vigilantes to preserve order.	The United States and Britain are optimistic that they will have a naval accord even without Japan. . . . Henry Ford praises the Nye Committee and says that he learned from his 1915 Peace Ship effort that war is for profit.	The NRA charges Anheuser-Busch with setting up chain stores by providing free bar equipment. . . . John L. Lewis threatens labor action unless the NRA puts a stop to chiseling and cutthroat competition in soft coal. . . . Northern ports assail the SEC ruling for lower southern rates as discriminatory.	W.R. Whitney wins the Edison Medal for "pioneering inventions.". . . A giant 52-passenger flying boat passes its first test.		Dec. 20
A Chicago jury finds Martin Insull, brother of magnate Samuel Insull, not guilty of embezzlement from his brother's operations. . . . Senator William Borah asks young Republicans to form their own committee and hold their own convention; others propose humanizing rather than liberalizing the party. . . . California's Dr. Francis Townsend is in New York to talk about his monthly pension plan.	The Army opposes nationalization of munitions plants in time of war. . . . The United States takes Austria off the debt default list, allowing the sale of Austrian securities in the United States.		Coast Guard Commander E. F. Stone sets an amphibian speed record of 191.76 miles per hour.	Asadata Dafor's African drama, Kykunkor, originally performed in the spring, reopens in New York.	Dec. 21
Thirteen Senators and 110 Congressmen are feeling the effect of the Norris lame-duck amendment, which moved the end of Congress from March 4 to January 3. Those not reelected lose two months' pay, and newcomers are having trouble finding office space. . . . Florida's transit camps are full and the governor wants border patrol aid in keeping employment-seekers out of the state.		Labor Secretary Frances Perkins says that the states must act soon on employment insurance and says not to expect large federal pensions. . . . The linen group leads opposition to the importation of low-cost Russian goods.	Harvard scientists report that germs from coughs stay in the air for hours, not minutes as previously thought.	Too ill to train, Argentine heavyweight Luis Angel Firpo, the "wild bull of the pampas," gives up his comeback.	Dec. 22
Rabbi Stephen Wise warns that the campaign for decency in the movies might turn anti-Jewish. . . . Educators want Congress to investigate William R. Hearst's attempt to foment a "Red scare." . . . Forty-four House members hire aides with their last names.	A year-end report on the National Guard reports that morale is high but the need exists for more training and equipment.	The year-end estimate is that 19 million people got relief and 6.5 million were on the federal payroll in 1934.	A Cape Cod ground station and a plane over Persia exchange greetings, setting a distance record.	Back at Broadway's Trans-Lux Theater is Walt Disney's Silly Symphony, The Three Little Pigs, that at its early 1933 debut caused patrons to storm the box office.	Dec. 23
	The Army lets a contract with Boeing for 71 more airplanes, bringing the six-month total to 312.	The United States has 24,952,007 cars, a 4.6 increase in the year, the first increase since 1930. . . . Hawaiian sugar growers accept AAA quotas. . . . A report shows that in 1933–34, 45 states fed 290,000 students free lunches.		Elsie Janis hosts a party for immigrants at Ellis Island. . . . President Roosevelt lights the Washington, D.C., community Christmas tree and reads Dickens's A Christmas Carol.	Dec. 24
			A French pilot sets a land plane speed record of 312 miles per hour.		Dec. 25
A Chicago railroad provides a smoking car for women.	The Army centralizes its air forces under one command.	President Roosevelt supports a private industry plan to buy appliances in bulk and sell them on credit. . . . Weekly oil output is within quota.			Dec. 26
A locomotive explosion on a Powellton, W.Va., train carrying 300 miners kills 16.	The Army is considering enlisting men from the CCC if the CCC's rolls increase as expected in the winter. . . . The United States and Britain protest Japanese requirements that their companies provide large oil storage facilities in Manchukuo.	A Kansas City judge rules that NRA code price fixing is unconstitutional. . . . New federal policy requires local agencies to handle unemployables on home relief.	Scientists meeting at Pittsburgh hear that there are two new vaccines against paralysis and one against encephalitis.	Sergei Rachmaninoff introduces his "Rhapsody on a Theme of Paganini."	Dec. 27
F Includes elections, federal-state relations, civil rights and liberties, crime, the judiciary, education, healthcare, poverty, urban affairs, and population.	**G** Includes formation and debate of U.S. foreign and defense policies, veterans affairs, and defense spending. (Relations with specific foreign countries are usually found under the region concerned.)	**H** Includes business, labor, agriculture, taxation, transportation, consumer affairs, monetary and fiscal policy, natural resources, pollution, and accidents.	**I** Includes worldwide scientific, medical, and technological developments, natural phenomena, U.S. weather, and natural disasters.	**J** Includes the arts, religion, scholarship, communications media, sports, entertainment, fashions, fads, and social life.	

	World Affairs	Europe	Africa & The Middle East	The Americas	Asia & The Pacific
Dec. 28	The Americans leave London, and Britain and Japan discontinue naval talks as pointless. . . . A German delegation arrives in Peru to explore trade agreements.	Albanian troops are in the north attempting to put down a rebellion. . . . Premier Flandin lowers the price of bread 25 centimes.	Italy continues building military roads in Abyssinia as fighting occurs in Gerlogubi.	The Chaco fighting involves 80,000 men, as Bolivia calls up draftees up to age 49.	
Dec. 29		The Reich Air League annual report claims 5 million members and 1.8 million officers. . . . German flax purchases cause prices to rise in Ireland and Belgium.	South Africa's Jan Christiaan Smuts asks Gandhi to help the British by conciliating between them and Indian nationalists.	Canada's marine minister calls for a requirement that all ships have radios.	Japan abrogates the naval treaty. . . . Japan's annual trade deficit is 92 million yen.
Dec. 30		Albania goes under martial law and asks Italian assistance. . . . A spokesman for the Hapsburgs says they want to rule all the Little Entente. . . . At Blieskastel in the Saar, an anti-Nazi meeting is broken up by Nazis and a riot ensues. . . . Vandals in Zells, Austria, break into a Catholic church and deface it, replacing crucifixes with swastikas.	The Sheikh of Kuwait, subsidized by the British government, grants an oil concession to an Anglo-American group.	Mexican "Red Shirt" attacks on Catholics kill six and injure 30. . . . Brazil establishes a security council to reform defense—after it ends the mail strike.	
Dec. 31	Dr. Nicholas Murray Butler, president of Columbia and the Carnegie Endowment for International Peace, says that Japan cannot gain equality through an arms race but rather through reduction and an international police force. . . . Germany agrees to buy $12 million in wool and South Africa agrees to buy the same amount of German goods.	The Pope gives Marquis Camillo Serafini dictatorial powers for six months to reform the Vatican's non-religious activities. . . . Germany decrees conscript labor. . . . Unable to publish under tight Nazi control, the *Augsburger Abendzeitung* ends publication after 325 years. . . . Catholics ask the League to impose martial law after Nazi disturbances in the Saar.	Persia announces that as of its New Year's Day, March 22, it will be Iran.	The action at Iribobo has cost Bolivia 800 dead and 2,000 captured. . . . Brazilians begin receiving mail as the strike appears to be broken. . . . Mexico captures 62 "Reds" responsible for attacks on Catholics.	Canton awards a Cleveland firm the contract to build a steel mill. . . . Australia's women lose to England in cricket.

A	B	C	D	E
Includes developments that affect more than one world region, international organizations, and important meetings of world leaders.	*Includes all domestic and regional developments in Europe, including the Soviet Union.*	*Includes all domestic and regional developments in Africa and the Middle East.*	*Includes all domestic and regional developments in Latin America, the Caribbean, and Canada.*	*Includes all domestic and regional developments in Asian and Pacific nations (and colonies).*

U.S. Politics & Social Issues	U.S. Foreign Policy & Defense	Economics & Great Depression	Science, Technology & Nature	Culture, Leisure & Lifestyle	
Republican Senator Arthur Vandenberg of Michigan introduces legislation to bar the Postmaster General from holding political jobs and to put the Post Office under civil service.	The House Military Affairs Committee reports that collusion between Army and War Department officials and contractors cost $7 million, and reiterates that Gen. Benjamin Foulois acted improperly in spending $7.5 million in PWA funds for military planes.		Einstein presents a modified basis for his mass-energy theory to a Pittsburgh audience, removing the Maxwell field equation.	A Philadelphia boy's rubber-band-driven model airplane sets a record by flying 11 minutes. . . . The NCAA adopts a fair practices code that addresses subsidies and recruiting.	Dec. 28
The NAACP petitions President Franklin Roosevelt to endorse the Costigan-Wagner anti-lynching legislation. . . . The year's total is 15 lynchings and 74 lynchings prevented by police. . . . The HUAC hears testimony of a Communist plot to kidnap the President and make the United States a Communist state, as well as testimony about a fascist effort, backed by $750 million, to take over the government.	Secretary Cordell Hull reaffirms that U.S. and British naval policy are in agreement.			Douglas Fairbanks, headed for Italy, is silent on speculation that Mary Pickford will pursue a divorce.	Dec. 29
Twelve building unions leave the AFL. . . . The prosecution finalizes preparations for the Bruno Hauptmann trial. . . . The pedestrian fare on the George Washington Bridge is reduced from 10 cents to 5 cents.		Top hogs are up $1.20 in 13 days. . . . Youngstown Steel's output is 50 percent.	An oil-powered train speeds from Chicago to Minneapolis in 400 minutes.	Bucknell is favored to beat Miami in a wide-open Orange Bowl.	Dec. 30
Laredo, Tex., authorities seize 2,000 rounds of ammunition intended for Mexican insurgents in Nuevo Laredo. . . . President Franklin Roosevelt issues a letter saying that veterans do not need the bonus now and that it will not aid recovery.	Chargé d'Affaires Boris Skvirsky tells Secretary Cordell Hull that Russia is prepared to reopen debt talks.	A proposed plan to electrify three southern states would pay for electricity through egg sales. The eggs of five hens would light a farmhouse. . . . An exchange seat sells for $100,000, up $5,000.	The Byrd Antarctic expedition reports it has discovered a rich vein of quartz.	New York's theater guild is negotiating with London to get John Gielgud's highly acclaimed standard-raising Hamlet. . . . The crowd for the toss-up Rose Bowl between Alabama and Stanford is expected to be 85,000. . . . In basketball, Wisconsin beats Michigan in overtime, 23–21.	Dec. 31

F	G	H	I	J
Includes elections, federal-state relations, civil rights and liberties, crime, the judiciary, education, healthcare, poverty, urban affairs, and population.	Includes formation and debate of U.S. foreign and defense policies, veterans affairs, and defense spending. (Relations with specific foreign countries are usually found under the region concerned.)	Includes business, labor, agriculture, taxation, transportation, consumer affairs, monetary and fiscal policy, natural resources, pollution, and accidents.	Includes worldwide scientific, medical, and technological developments, natural phenomena, U.S. weather, and natural disasters.	Includes the arts, religion, scholarship, communications media, sports, entertainment, fashions, fads, and social life.

1935

A massive dust storm rolls into Stratford, Texas, on April 18, 1935.

	World Affairs	Europe	Africa & The Middle East	The Americas	Asia & The Pacific
Jan.	The League of Nations lifts its embargo against Bolivia and Paraguay, which was imposed because of the Chaco War.	The French give the Italians a free hand in Ethiopia in Franco-Italian agreements. . . . Soviets announce the conviction of Gregory Zinoviev and Lev Kamenev, as well as the execution of 117 dissidents, signaling the beginning of purges. . . . The Saarland votes to pass from French control to German control.	Ethiopia appeals to the League for support against Italy, but is rejected. . . . Lower Zambezi Bridge is opened, connecting Nyasaland with the coast of Mozambique. . . . A pipeline is opened connecting the Mosul region of Iraq with the Mediterranean coast at Haifa in Palestine.	Newfoundland lifts tariffs on most goods. . . . President Franklin Roosevelt reiterates his Good Neighbor Policy toward Latin America, announced in his 1933 inaugural address. The policy is intended to reflect a change from earlier policies resulting in U.S. military intervention.	
Feb.			Italy reports a border clash with Ethiopia and sends troops to Africa.	The U.S. Senate begins investigation into rumors of repression of the Catholic Church in Mexico.	Britain offers Dominion status to India. . . . The Philippines adopts a new constitution, establishing itself as a commonwealth.
Mar.		The Saarland is formally turned over to Germany. . . . Lithuania tries 126 Nazis for criminal activity in Memel; Hitler responds with threats. Memel, largely populated with Germans, was administered after World War I as a French mandate, then seized by Lithuania in 1924.	Turkey elects Mustapha Kemal as president.		Japan removes its delegates from the League of Nations, formally resigning from the organization.
Apr.		Poland adopts a more authoritarian constitution.	Spain reorganizes its government of African colonies, providing separate rule for Fernando Po.		Earthquakes strike in Iran and Formosa almost simultaneously, with high casualties in Formosa.
May		King George V celebrates the 25th anniversary of his reign in Britain.			Pan-American Airways starts construction of a landing strip on Wake Island.
Jun.			Ethiopia requests League of Nations observers as border clashes continue with Italian forces.	In Uruguay, an assassination attempt on President Gabriel Terra fails. . . . The Cabinet of President Lázaro Cárdenas of Mexico resigns in order to allow him to replace members with men of his own choice.	Tensions mount between Japanese and Chinese on the border between Manchukuo and northern Chinese provinces.
Jul.	In the Soviet Union, the Third International (Comintern) calls on Communists throughout the world to support rearmament in democracies in order to oppose fascism.			A peace conference regarding the Chaco War convenes in Buenos Aires; the conference produces a peace treaty between Paraguay and Bolivia.	China ratifies an agreement to withdraw troops from northwestern provinces.
Aug.			Ethiopia sends troops to the frontier with Italian Somaliland as border incidents increase.		Colombia bans the export of silver.
Sept.		The Nazi Party holds its annual meeting in Nuremberg. The Nuremberg laws stripping Jews of citizenship are announced.	Tensions increase between Italy and Ethiopia.	The peace conference continues to resolve the Chaco War. . . . President Lázaro Cárdenas of Mexico proposes broader access to higher education.	
Oct.	The League of Nations adopts a resolution calling for an international arms embargo against Italy as a consequence of the invasion of Ethiopia.	A military coup ousts the government and demands a recall of King George II in Greece.	Italian aircraft bomb Ethiopian cities and Italian troops invade the country.		
	A Includes developments that affect more than one world region, international organizations, and important meetings of world leaders.	**B** Includes all domestic and regional developments in Europe, including the Soviet Union.	**C** Includes all domestic and regional developments in Africa and the Middle East.	**D** Includes all domestic and regional developments in Latin America, the Caribbean, and Canada.	**E** Includes all domestic and regional developments in Asian and Pacific nations (and colonies).

U.S. Politics & Social Issues	U.S. Foreign Policy & Defense	Economics & Great Depression	Science, Technology & Nature	Culture, Leisure & Lifestyle	
	The U.S. Senate rejects membership in the World Court.	The second phase of the New Deal is launched, with more emphasis on reform than on relief and recovery.	Technicolor is introduced.	The Lindbergh kidnapping trial begins.	Jan.
					Feb.
		Dust bowl conditions worsen; Secretary of Agriculture Henry Wallace warns of the impact on food prices.		The Czech film *Ecstasy* is impounded because of a nude scene with Hedy Lamarr. . . . The movie *Gold Diggers of 1935* is released.	Mar.
The Emergency Relief Appropriation Act is passed, establishing new agencies. Among them is the Works Progress Administration; Harry Hopkins is appointed as administrator. . . . The Soil Conservation Service is established as a permanent unit of the Agriculture Department.					Apr.
The Supreme Court invalidates the NRA in the Schechter Case. . . . The Resettlement Administration (RA) is established within the Agriculture Department, with Rexford Tugwell, Undersecretary of the department, as the administrator. . . . The Rural Electrification Administration (REA) is established by executive order.	The House of Representatives votes to override the veto by President Franklin Roosevelt of the Patman Bonus Bill, but the U.S. Senate upholds the veto. The bill would have granted World War I veterans payment of a bonus this year, due in 1945.			Amelia Earhart sets a new record for the flight time from Mexico City to Newark, N.J.	May
	The United States improves relations with Liberia, restoring diplomatic representation that had been cut off since 1930.	The National Youth Administration (NYA) is established by President Franklin Roosevelt under executive order; he appoints Aubrey Williams as director. The agency is directed to assist in the employment of needy students.			Jun.
	The United States and Soviet Union sign a trade agreement.	The Wagner-Connery Act (the National Labor Relations Act) establishes the National Labor Relations Board.			Jul.
Newspaper publisher William Randolph Hearst announces the formation of a third party, based on conservative Democrats, to oppose Roosevelt.	President Roosevelt signs the U.S. Neutrality Law of 1935 that allows the United States to embargo weapons, but not strategic materials, to both sides during an international conflict.	The Social Security Act is passed. . . . The Banking Act of 1935 is passed, changing administration of the Federal Reserve System. . . . The Public Utility Holding Company Act is passed. . . . The Guffey-Snyder Coal Stabilization Act is passed, regarded as a "Little NRA" for the coal industry. . . . The Revenue Act of 1935 imposes a high income tax on the wealthy and becomes known as the "Wealth Tax Act." . . . A federal court rules that the PWA can make loans to municipalities and states for the construction of publicly owned power plants.		Will Rogers is killed in an airplane crash in Alaska.	Aug.
Senator Huey Long is shot by an assassin on the steps of the Louisiana legislature; Long dies the next day.		Shooting erupts at a strike at a textile mill in Pelzer, S.C.			Sept.
President Franklin Roosevelt officially opens the Boulder Dam in Nevada.				George Gershwin's *Porgy and Bess* opens on Broadway. . . Dutch Schultz, a notorious bootlegger, is shot and killed in New Jersey by rival gang members.	Oct.

F	G	H	I	J
Includes elections, federal-state relations, civil rights and liberties, crime, the judiciary, education, healthcare, poverty, urban affairs, and population.	Includes formation and debate of U.S. foreign and defense policies, veterans affairs, and defense spending. (Relations with specific foreign countries are usually found under the region concerned.)	Includes business, labor, agriculture, taxation, transportation, consumer affairs, monetary and fiscal policy, natural resources, pollution, and accidents.	Includes worldwide scientific, medical, and technological developments, natural phenomena, U.S. weather, and natural disasters.	Includes the arts, religion, scholarship, communications media, sports, entertainment, fashions, fads, and social life.

	World Affairs	Europe	Africa & The Middle East	The Americas	Asia & The Pacific
Nov.		Germany announces the forcible closure of Protestant churches and seminaries. . . . The Labor government is voted out in Britain. . . . George II is restored as King of Greece.		The peace treaty between Paraguay and Bolivia is announced, formally ending the Chaco War. . . . Brazil announces it will not join in League of Nations sanctions against Italy, raising fears the Vargas regime may be more pro-fascist than others in the region.	The status of the Philippines is officially changed from territory to commonwealth of the United States.
Dec.	An international conference convenes in London to discuss naval arms limitations.	Czechoslovakia elects Eduard Benes as prime minister.		Uruguay severs diplomatic relations with the Soviet Union.	

A	B	C	D	E
Includes developments that affect more than one world region, international organizations, and important meetings of world leaders.	*Includes all domestic and regional developments in Europe, including the Soviet Union.*	*Includes all domestic and regional developments in Africa and the Middle East.*	*Includes all domestic and regional developments in Latin America, the Caribbean, and Canada.*	*Includes all domestic and regional developments in Asian and Pacific nations (and colonies).*

U.S. Politics & Social Issues	U.S. Foreign Policy & Defense	Economics & Great Depression	Science, Technology & Nature	Culture, Leisure & Lifestyle	
			A manned U.S. Army balloon reaches an altitude of 14 miles, setting a record.		Nov.
The National Association of Manufacturers urges members to oppose President Franklin Roosevelt's reelection.	The United States urges other nations attending the London Naval Disarmament Conference to endorse an across-the-board slash of 20 percent in naval armaments.	The president of the New York Stock Exchange notes that about one-half of the nation's banks that were open in 1929 have failed.	The DuPont company wins an award for a mass production method for a type of synthetic rubber.	A press poll declares Helen Moody, winner of the tennis championship at Wimbledon this year, as woman athlete of the year.	Dec.

F	**G**	**H**	**I**	**J**
Includes elections, federal-state relations, civil rights and liberties, crime, the judiciary, education, healthcare, poverty, urban affairs, and population.	*Includes formation and debate of U.S. foreign and defense policies, veterans affairs, and defense spending. (Relations with specific foreign countries are usually found under the region concerned.)*	*Includes business, labor, agriculture, taxation, transportation, consumer affairs, monetary and fiscal policy, natural resources, pollution, and accidents.*	*Includes worldwide scientific, medical, and technological developments, natural phenomena, U.S. weather, and natural disasters.*	*Includes the arts, religion, scholarship, communications media, sports, entertainment, fashions, fads, and social life.*

	World Affairs	Europe	Africa & The Middle East	The Americas	Asia & The Pacific
Jan. 1	U.S. and British journalists in Europe confer in Vienna after Nazi representatives arrest members of their organization for spying.	The Nazi government, as an act of good will, releases Elsa Sittell, a U.S. girl imprisoned in Berlin for insulting Adolf Hitler. . . . Lord Mayor of Dublin Alfred Byrne forecasts improvements in the city's modernization efforts, especially in its water and power systems.	The government of South Africa and Germany's Third Reich sign a trade pact, proving a long-suspected alliance between the countries.	Citing a "good neighbor policy," President Franklin Roosevelt praises profound positive changes in the relationship between the United States and Latin America. . . . Newfoundland announces that it has lowered import tariffs on almost all imported goods.	The president of Columbia University, Nicholas Murray Butler, warns Japan that its hopes of naval equality are an "impossibility."
Jan. 2	Pierre Laval, the French foreign minister, flies to Rome to discuss the French-Austrian Pact as tensions grow after diplomatic breakdowns. . . . According to W.E. Beatty, president of the Canadian Pacific Railway, Canada's financial recovery is "steady," though not "spectacular."				
Jan. 3	A new financial governor in France, Jean Tannery, is installed in the hope that he can work with his peers in other countries to help turn around Europe's unhealthy economy.	In Berlin, Nazi leaders demonstrate a call for national unity within Europe in an attempt to maintain their reputation. . . . Citing successes in America, British Prime Minister Ramsay MacDonald pushes for steady work and shorter hours to overcome England's current unemployment problem.	Ethiopia appeals to the League of Nations for assistance regarding its dispute with Italy.		
Jan. 4	James McDonald receives the 1934 American Hebrew Medal from the League of Nations for his promotion of Christian-Jewish alliances throughout the world. . . . General Booth, founder of the Salvation Army, tells a London audience that he believes Yugoslavia, once a country under a despot, is making real advances toward political reform.	Maxim Litvinoff, Russian commissioner for foreign affairs, emphasizes the necessity of a European pact to ensure peace "not only in Eastern Europe but in all of Europe." . . . Italian Premier Benito Mussolini and French statesman Pierre Laval open talks to end Franco-Italian animosities.	The British open a major oil pipeline from the Mosul region in Iraq to the Mediterranean port of Haifa.		
Jan. 5	The Russian government executes 117 dissidents; political analysts deem it a sign of a newer, harsher Russia. . . . The British shipping lines Cunard and White Star merge, naming Liverpool as their base headquarters.				Briton Sir Maurice Hinkey urges his country to beware Japan's intentions on its holdings in the Pacific. He urges tighter defense of British territories there.
Jan. 6		According to the Russian newspaper *Izvestia*, Russia urges Poland to join the Franco-Soviet project, which is part of the eastern European Locarno Pact. . . . France and Italy pledge their friendship in a ceremony attended by Italian Premier Benito Mussolini and French Minister Pierre Laval.		Due to recent revenue and tariff restructuring, Panama will soon be offering free trade between itself and the United States. The accord, viewed positively by both parties, is expected to be signed within days.	Japan withdraws from the Navy Ratio Treaty, upset with the U.S. view that it should not build up its current navy. Japanese Ambassador Saito and U.S. Rear Admiral Henry Pratt meet at the Hotel Astor in an attempt to ease tensions.
Jan. 7		Benito Mussolini, premier of Italy, cosigns a communication with French Minister Pierre Laval, asking that Germany refrain from illegal arming without the consent of the League of Nations. The agreement includes provisions formally ceding territory from French Djibouti to Italian Eritrea, and provides other concessions to Italy in exchange for Italian support regarding Germany.	Turkey is growing apprehensive of the surrounding political scene, says its diplomatic corps. The country will take a watch-and-wait stance on most issues affecting its future and its relationships with other countries.		
Jan. 8	In Dublin, Ireland, Bishop Jeremiah Kinane condemns both Communist organizations and the Irish Republican Army for interfering with the world's peace.	Britain expresses its hope that a shaky relationship between France and Germany can be mended. It fears the spreading of ill will across Europe if hard feelings are not corrected soon.	In a sign of harmony between itself and Italy, France cedes 440,000 square miles of its African holdings to Italy, on the Djibouti-Eritrea border.		
Jan. 9		Free Ireland is reeling after two years of trade wars with Britain; exports have fallen more than 50 percent compared with 1930 figures; imports have dropped by one-third. . . . Britain strongly urges Germany against its aggressiveness to arm and warns it to respect the arms agreements already established between other countries.		Brazil seeks to suspend its debt to the United States in the wake of its shaky export trade; a financial commission leaves Rio de Janeiro for Washington for formal talks.	

A	B	C	D	E
Includes developments that affect more than one world region, international organizations, and important meetings of world leaders.	*Includes all domestic and regional developments in Europe, including the Soviet Union.*	*Includes all domestic and regional developments in Africa and the Middle East.*	*Includes all domestic and regional developments in Latin America, the Caribbean, and Canada.*	*Includes all domestic and regional developments in Asian and Pacific nations (and colonies).*

U.S. Politics & Social Issues	U.S. Foreign Policy & Defense	Economics & Great Depression	Science, Technology & Nature	Culture, Leisure & Lifestyle	
Henry Harriman, president of the U.S. Chamber of Commerce, cites "steady recovery" as a watch-phrase for 1935's economy.		In a boost to America's financial status, Secretary of State Cordell Hull announces the Russian Premier's commitment to reopening negotiations that will lead to Russia paying off its debts to the United States.		The London Times—known as "The Thunderer"—celebrates its 150th anniversary. . . . Flemington, N.J., expects a huge media turnout for the trial of Bruno Hauptmann, alleged murderer of Charles Lindbergh's infant son.	Jan. 1
President Franklin Roosevelt warns Louisiana Senator Huey Long to correct some malfunctions in his state's government and promises to hold back loans for public works until those wrongs are addressed.		New York City begins 1935 with 325,000 families on relief, with more than 1,300 new families applying for relief. These figures starkly indicate no easing in the Depression.		The thoroughbred, Alger's Azucar, wins $5,000 added stake, shattering track records at the Santa Anita Race Track in California.	Jan. 2
The second legislative phase of the New Deal begins with the convening of the 74th Congress; its target is unemployment.				Governor-elect of New Jersey Harold G. Hoffman suggests needed changes to the National Crime Conference to meet in March 1935, in his state's capital. Current policies, he feels, do not adequately fight crime.	Jan. 3
The 1935 Congress prepares to address financial issues first and foremost, while other issues will be postponed, say Wall Street watchers. . . . Senator Connery of Massachusetts proposes a 30-hour workweek as a means to battle the poor economy. Rivals assail the impracticality of his plan.		President Franklin Roosevelt tells Congress that they must "quit this business of relief" and proposes 3.5 million jobs on public works projects to get the unemployed people of America back in the market.		The International Nudists Conference attacks New York Governor Alfred E. Smith's "inconsistencies" in his stand against nudism. They cite their freedom for free expression found in the Constitution.	Jan. 4
President Roosevelt's latest fireside chats show a trend toward a conservative, rather than liberal, direction. . . . Aviator Charles Lindbergh, after hearing testimony, publicly names Bruno Hauptmann as the murderer of his infant son on March 1, 1932.	The Congress promises to make the nation's tin shortage a topic for debate in the coming session; in the event of war, it says, tin would prove to be a priceless commodity.	U.S. foreign trade power increased during the first 11 months of 1934, according to a government report; figures show a $480,375 jump for the same months of 1933.	Aviatrix Elly Beinhorn lands in New York City after flying solo from Central America.		Jan. 5
As he had promised the public, President Franklin Roosevelt turns his attention to Social Security. His changes, he says, will set a pattern for further development in the country's economy.	King George of England celebrates his 25th anniversary as British monarch. . . . For the second time in his presidency, Franklin Roosevelt chooses to deliver his annual address before Congress, a ritual not followed since President John Adams.	Sales returns for the American motor industry show a startling increase in car sales outside the United States. Sales reached 435,000—up from 242,445 the same period a year earlier.	Scientists admit that the latest aid for battling cancer—radioactive sodium—is far too costly for the average patient to afford.	Eleanor Roosevelt is named chairwoman of the Cosmopolitan Opera's fall season in Washington. . . . The ocean liner, Havana, which was bound for Veracruz from New York, slams into a Bahamian reef during a storm; miraculously, all but one person are saved.	Jan. 6
Citing the "Give to Caesar what is Caesar's and to God what is God's" axiom, the Rev. John McComb of Baltimore issues a statement that upholds the church's support of capitalism. He asks members of his church to support the government.	The founder of the League of Nations Association, Hamilton Holt, urges President Franklin Roosevelt to consider his influence in leading the United States into both the World Court and the League of Nations at this politically sensitive juncture.				Jan. 7
Dr. Louis Wright, new chairman of the NAACP, vows to battle "widespread color discrimination under the New Deal."		A squabble between the mayor of the city of New Orleans and Louisiana Governor Huey Long erupts into scandal. Long has slapped the city with a technical bankruptcy, thus tying up the city's funds for improvement. President Franklin Roosevelt promises to intervene.			Jan. 8
The war against crime has been effective over the last year, according to Attorney General Homer Cummings. The Department of Justice has arrested more kidnappers and other urban gangsters than in the previous period of 1933–34.					Jan. 9

F	G	H	I	J
Includes elections, federal-state relations, civil rights and liberties, crime, the judiciary, education, healthcare, poverty, urban affairs, and population.	Includes formation and debate of U.S. foreign and defense policies, veterans affairs, and defense spending. (Relations with specific foreign countries are usually found under the region concerned.)	Includes business, labor, agriculture, taxation, transportation, consumer affairs, monetary and fiscal policy, natural resources, pollution, and accidents.	Includes worldwide scientific, medical, and technological developments, natural phenomena, U.S. weather, and natural disasters.	Includes the arts, religion, scholarship, communications media, sports, entertainment, fashions, fads, and social life.

	World Affairs	Europe	Africa & The Middle East	The Americas	Asia & The Pacific
Jan. 10		Pierre Laval, French foreign minister, submits his plans on diplomacy to the League Council. He hopes to meet with British Foreign Secretary Sir John Simon to begin a round of talks with the Continental powers. . . . Germany announces that it is temporarily leaving the bargaining table of the League of Nations.	Executives of African copper mines meet in London to discuss and develop a mining output plan.		
Jan. 11	The U.S. Department of Commerce reports that Britain's trade and industry both slackened in late 1934, due to a seasonal influence as well as a stall in the rate of recovery.	From Vienna, the Austrian Embassy expresses relief over the recent peace accord signed between Italy and France.	After Abyssinia expressed doubts about Italy's political intentions in the area, Premier Benito Mussolini reassures Abyssinia that it plans no aggression toward it.		
Jan. 12	Speaking to the International Coalition, Italian Premier Benito Mussolini calls the suggestion of peace "an illusion." He claims that permanent peace is neither possible nor desirable.	European royalty and its wealthy turn out in droves to meet Infanta Beatriz and Prince Alessandro Torlonia today in Rome at their pre-nuptial reception.			
Jan. 13	The immigration of refugees into London from across Europe is adding to the city's financial and population problems.	A plebiscite held in the Saar region overwhelmingly supports reunification of the Saar with Germany. . . . Russia exiles two of its veteran leaders for opposing the Communist Party's programs.			A representative from the U.S. Navy says that Japan's navy surpasses the U.S. fleet. Japan's navy is larger, better manned, has more advanced battleships, and possesses shipbuilding capacities greater than any other nation.
Jan. 14		Germany claims that it has the right to arm as does any other nation.	The first bridge to span Africa's Zambesi River opens. The bridge is 12,000 feet long. It links Nyasaland to the east African coast at Beira in Mozambique.		
Jan. 15		Britain promises to support France in the event of German aggression, adding that Europe can no longer rely on isolationist policies. . . . Nazi representatives begin handing out Reich propaganda on the streets of Vienna, Austria.	A 1,150-mile oil pipeline from the Mosul petroleum fields to the Mediterranean coast is formally opened. Attending the opening ceremonies are King Ghazi of Iraq and Sir John Cadman, chairman of the British-controlled Iraq Petroleum Company.		
Jan. 16		In the Soviet Union, Grigori Zinoviev, Leo Kamenev, and other former leaders are found guilty of conspiracy and treason, receiving 5–10 year prison terms.		The League of Nations lifts its embargo on Bolivia and Paraguay imposed during the Chaco War.	
Jan. 17					Japanese Vice Admiral Isoroku Yamamoto announces that he plans to visit the United States after his meeting with the British navy. His purpose, he claims, is to create peace channels with Washington, D.C.
Jan. 18		German government spokesman Dr. Alfred Rosenberg tells foreign diplomats and reporters that Chancellor Hitler's drive to rearm Germany means nothing harmful—that it is nothing more than the country's expression of "peace with equality."			In Tokyo, Foreign Minister Koki Hirota tells the Japanese people that Japan's policy in foreign affairs is to remain a "non-menace" to the rest of the world—that whatever plans Japan has, it will meet them peaceably.
Jan. 19				Brazilian President Getulio Vargas asks his ministers for special powers to ban subversive newspapers and labor strikes as a means to crush radicalism in his country.	

A	B	C	D	E
Includes developments that affect more than one world region, international organizations, and important meetings of world leaders.	Includes all domestic and regional developments in Europe, including the Soviet Union.	Includes all domestic and regional developments in Africa and the Middle East.	Includes all domestic and regional developments in Latin America, the Caribbean, and Canada.	Includes all domestic and regional developments in Asian and Pacific nations (and colonies).

U.S. Politics & Social Issues	U.S. Foreign Policy & Defense	Economics & Great Depression	Science, Technology & Nature	Culture, Leisure & Lifestyle	
As reported by the Association of Southern Women for the Prevention of Lynching, who gathered this week in Atlanta, more than 50 lynchings were prevented in 1934 with 50 percent less victims of mob violence.		The National Resources Board, which is holding its annual Land Planning Committee, asks President Franklin Roosevelt for a broad and permanent policy governing the integration of farm and industrial employment by establishing homes for nonagricultural workers where they can produce their own living.			Jan. 10
Henry W. Taft, newly announced chairman of the United Parents' Organization, declares juvenile delinquency a national problem.		During the last 12 months, more than 30,000 professional men and women were placed in jobs of a "white collar" variety, says William Hodson of the Public Works and Emergency Relief Bureau.			Jan. 11
		Great Britain and the Irish Free State come to an understanding on cattle and coal trade rights after nearly 24 months of negotiations.			Jan. 12
German refugees fleeing Nazi Germany are given aid in the United States. Nearly 7,000 professional and academic families are housed across the country.			Chicago lawmakers insist that the new polygraph (lie detector) machine is the best way to catch criminals. The device, perfected by Dr. Leonard Keeler of the Scientific Crime Detection Laboratory at Northwestern University, has proven invaluable in trapping many prevaricators, say Chicago police.	Bruno Richard Hauptmann, on trial in Flemington, N.Y., for the murder of Charles Lindbergh's child, demands to be put on the stand.	Jan. 13
	President of Columbia University Nicholas Murray Butler presents his own five-point plan to end the Depression and attain world peace. The detailed program includes revisions of tariffs, World Court participation, and total U.S. disarmament.	New York Rabbi Samuel Goldenson emphasizes that America's economic reform movements must be for more than mere profit. "We must . . . reintroduce into economic endeavor the motive of usefulness to mankind," he says.		The funeral for opera singer Marcella Sembrich is held in New York City.	Jan. 14
		Members of the National Retail Dry Goods Association express their dissatisfaction over the New Deal at their convention. They want less wasteful spending and less government restriction.			Jan. 15
	Members of the Senate oppose President Franklin Roosevelt's desire to join the World Court. . . . The Senate rejects the treaty that would allow the United States to join the Court by a vote of 52–35.	The auto industry faces greater federal control if it does not start paying more attention to its priorities, claims Donald Richberg, executive director of the National Emergency Council. The industry, he says, must put more focus on production, distribution, and employment. . . . Republican House Rep. Bertrand Snell accuses the Roosevelt administration of using its public works policies as a political weapon to reward its allies and chastise its foes. Snell asks for an "honestly balanced budget."		An American League meeting in Chicago urges birth control for families on relief; member doctors are prepared to offer medical advice to interested families.	Jan. 16
			Australian scientist Sir Douglas Mawson predicts Antarctica to be the next "playground" for the wealthy.	As a whole, the southern states are insulted by comments made by modernist painter Thomas Benton. He appraises the quality of a series of Civil War murals painted in Richmond, Va., as no better than that of hastily done "sign paintings."	Jan. 17
	The American Federation of Labor and its affiliated unions agree to boycott products from Germany. Federation spokesperson Dr. Harry Lee—once a counsel to Berlin—seeks $250,000 to fund the campaign.			The National Lutheran Council urges its 200 million members to avoid Hollywood films that suggest immoral themes and portray "morally offensive" situations.	Jan. 18
		It appears that Congress may pass both President Roosevelt's Social Security plan and his latest work relief program, which would put 3.5 million people back to work and another 1.5 million on local care.	Tycoon Alfred Whitehall proves the efficiency of today's undersea cable systems by phoning his wife aboard the Canadian liner Empress of Britain from Chicago.	Fourteen nations have entered the upcoming Davis Cup tournament, sponsored by the British Lawn Tennis Association. It is one of the largest participations in years.	Jan. 19

F	G	H	I	J
Includes elections, federal-state relations, civil rights and liberties, crime, the judiciary, education, healthcare, poverty, urban affairs, and population.	Includes formation and debate of U.S. foreign and defense policies, veterans affairs, and defense spending. (Relations with specific foreign countries are usually found under the region concerned.)	Includes business, labor, agriculture, taxation, transportation, consumer affairs, monetary and fiscal policy, natural resources, pollution, and accidents.	Includes worldwide scientific, medical, and technological developments, natural phenomena, U.S. weather, and natural disasters.	Includes the arts, religion, scholarship, communications media, sports, entertainment, fashions, fads, and social life.

	World Affairs	Europe	Africa & The Middle East	The Americas	Asia & The Pacific
Jan. 20		Germany plans to introduce conscription for all men 20 years of age and older.		Credit conditions in the 21 countries of Latin America vastly improved in the last quarter of 1934, says William S. Swingle, head of the National Association of Credit Men.	
Jan. 21	Adolf Hitler asks the powers of the world to assent to German rearmament, although it is contrary to the Treaty of Versailles.	Moscow remembers Vladimir Ilich Lenin, who died 11 years ago. To mark the anniversary of his death, citizens dress in black.			Fears of war between China and Japan grow as Japanese fighter planes patrol over the borders of the Manchukuo and Chahar provinces.
Jan. 22		Britain suggests to Germany that it join the nonaggression pact that France, Italy, and Austria have co-authored. Germany states that it is in no hurry to negotiate.			The Philippines grow nervous following Japan's denunciation of the recent Washington Naval Treaty. If ties are severed between the United States and Japan, says Philippine Commissioner Pedro Guevara, the islands will be geographically menaced by what they see as an openly hostile Japan.
Jan. 23					Tokyo reports that Emperor Hirohito is not closed to the possibility of discussing a peace plan with Britain over territorial holdings in the Pacific Ocean.
Jan. 24				Brazil's Minister of Finance Arthur de Souza Costa and his assistants disembark the SS *Western Prince* in New York. They plan a visit to Washington, D.C., to discuss trade enhancements with the United States.	The United States opts to stay out of the dispute between Japan and China in the Chahar border area. Washington does not see, at this point, a long-lasting situation.
Jan. 25		Reports from Germany indicate that airplane production has accelerated to a wartime pace. . . . Germany has reorganized into 20 provinces, which promise easier maintenance of the administration, says Minister of Interior Wilhelm Frick.			Border skirmishes between China and Japan result in hundreds of casualties.
Jan. 26		Lord Allen of England visits Germany to discuss the arms question. On his schedule are interviews with the Third Reich's propaganda chief, Dr. Joseph Goebbels, Prussian Premier Hermann Wilhelm Goering, and German Foreign Minister Baron von Neurath. . . . Adolf Hitler reassures Poland that Germany holds no animosity toward them. This comes on the anniversary of the Amity Pact.		The Rockefeller Foundation warns that Cuba is headed toward upheaval and dictatorship.	
Jan. 27	World trade will only prosper if European business leaders work together to effect recovery, says Thomas Watson, president of Business Machines Corporation.			A long-awaited single highway from southern Texas to Mexico City nears completion. It will be the first stretch of road connecting Mexico City to the U.S. border. . . . In Buenos Aires, a Nazi group attempts to burn a theater where people are watching an anti-Nazi feature. No one is hurt.	Japanese troops march into Jehol on the Mongolian frontier, driving back 4,000 Chinese soldiers.
Jan. 28	Eleanor Roosevelt, in a radio address to the American people, urges support of the World Court, which, she stresses, is the greatest advocate of world peace.	Soviet Premier Vyacheslaff Molotov claims the Soviet Union is strong enough to withstand any attacks from East or West. . . . José Antonio Sánchez Guerra, former premier of Spain, is buried in Madrid.		Revolt erupts in Uruguay against dictator Gabriel Terra.	
Jan. 29		Berlin reports that Germans are reproducing faster than any people around the globe.			Japan's minister to Nanking, Akira Ariyoshi, and Chinese Gen. Chiang Kai-shek hold peace talks.
Jan. 30					Japanese Admiral Mineo Osumi states that Japan will find the funds to construct an even larger fleet, even if the people are "reduced to eating rice gruel."

A	B	C	D	E
Includes developments that affect more than one world region, international organizations, and important meetings of world leaders.	Includes all domestic and regional developments in Europe, including the Soviet Union.	Includes all domestic and regional developments in Africa and the Middle East.	Includes all domestic and regional developments in Latin America, the Caribbean, and Canada.	Includes all domestic and regional developments in Asian and Pacific nations (and colonies).

U.S. Politics & Social Issues	U.S. Foreign Policy & Defense	Economics & Great Depression	Science, Technology & Nature	Culture, Leisure & Lifestyle	
The country again takes a look at its three latest territorial acquisitions—Alaska, Hawaii, and Puerto Rico—for possible entry as states into the Union. Most desirable is Alaska with its wide array of natural resources.			The *Detroit News* successfully puts to the test a new airplane equipped with a camera in its wing to take dramatic journalism photos previously unthinkable. A photographer and writer are on board, as well as a supply of processing equipment for immediate reporting.	Comparing the sizes of female classes since 1925, dean of Holyoke College, Dr. Woolley, concludes that more women are attending college than ever. As far as she is concerned, the idea of higher education is becoming affixed in the mind of the young American female.	Jan. 20
			British anthropologist Sir Arthur Keith explains that, with each new discovery, the origin of humankind is being rewritten. Current theories state that "cousin peoples," across the world from each other, underwent parallel but independent evolution.		Jan. 21
			Lincoln Ellsworth and the members of his Transatlantic Flight Expedition, studying the Antarctic, return home after three months of study.	After the U.S. Senate asks the Federal Communications Commission to consider setting aside a certain ratio of time each week to broadcast religious, educational, and labor programs, the FCC responds that it sees no reason to legitimize a percentage of airspace for any particular entity.	Jan. 22
		Dr. John Madden, dean of the College of Business Administration and president of the Alexander Hamilton Institute, predicts 1935 will be a good year for retailers but a bad one for manufacturers.	The National Forest Reservation Commission announces the creation of 20 new national forests in 19 states. The project involves the setting aside of 457,461 acres of land.	A fresco painted in New York by artist Conrad Albrizio and entitled "The New Deal" is a salute to President Franklin Roosevelt. It depicts "FDR" as a man of the people, clad in denim overalls and poised for work.	Jan. 23
			Philadelphia faces the fourth worst snowstorm on record.		Jan. 24
The Building Trades Employers Association questions the effectiveness of President Roosevelt's Public Works Administration program. Their chief concern is redundancy.		The unemployment compensation plan as proposed by the Roosevelt administration is reviewed by the Senate Finance Committee. They suggest extensive changes. . . . The Senate intends to pass the $4.9 billion relief bill, which was approved by the House yesterday.	A vaccine developed to battle infantile paralysis and capable of immunizing patients for five months is introduced by the government in New York's Bureau of Laboratories.	Warner Bros. announces that the novel *Captain Blood*, by Rafael Sabatini, will be made into a motion picture. Warner Bros. is scouting for a new star to play the title role.	Jan. 25
					Jan. 26
			Short-wave radio proves to be the best communications system in much of Africa. Explorers and cargo pilots relate that because of the difficult conditions and bad weather, long and medium-wave transmission is not very effective.	A new three-color process has been patented by the Massachusetts Institute of Technology, and is scheduled to make its debut in the movie *The World Outside*, which will star Ann Harding.	Jan. 27
For the second year in a row, Davenport, Iowa, leads the nation in suicides—40.3 suicides per 100,000 people. . . . Medical officers representing the states of Delaware, Maryland, Massachusetts, New Hampshire, New Jersey, New York, Pennsylvania, and West Virginia co-author a program aimed at care provision for lower-income families.				MGM's *David Copperfield*, starring Freddie Bartholomew, opens in U.S. theaters.	Jan. 28
The U.S. Senate rejects a treaty to allow the United States to join the World Court.	The U.S. Navy says it is open to discussing armament reduction according to the policy guidelines of the recent Washington Treaty.	Republicans attempting to stall the Roosevelt relief bill by opening it to public scrutiny are defeated in the Senate by a majority vote.			Jan. 29
					Jan. 30

F	G	H	I	J
Includes elections, federal-state relations, civil rights and liberties, crime, the judiciary, education, healthcare, poverty, urban affairs, and population.	*Includes formation and debate of U.S. foreign and defense policies, veterans affairs, and defense spending. (Relations with specific foreign countries are usually found under the region concerned.)*	*Includes business, labor, agriculture, taxation, transportation, consumer affairs, monetary and fiscal policy, natural resources, pollution, and accidents.*	*Includes worldwide scientific, medical, and technological developments, natural phenomena, U.S. weather, and natural disasters.*	*Includes the arts, religion, scholarship, communications media, sports, entertainment, fashions, fads, and social life.*

	World Affairs	Europe	Africa & The Middle East	The Americas	Asia & The Pacific
Jan. 31					Japanese forces stun and defeat a Chinese-Mongolian army outside Kalkha Miao on the Manchukuoan border.
Feb. 1		France declares it does not approve of German rearmament. . . . A Vienna newspaper reports that there have been 38,000 political arrests under Nazi-led Vienna in only 22 months.		The U.S. Senate begins to investigate rumors of religious persecution in Mexico. The Foreign Relations Committee is spearheading the investigation.	The Naval Pact dissolves. Senator William G. McAdoo of California says the United States should start to build up its navy in case of trouble from Japan, whom he labels as an aggressor. . . . Japan declares to China that it must accept the offered peace terms or be annihilated.
Feb. 2		The Irish Free State version of the New Deal is based closely on that of the United States, states Industry and Commerce Commissioner Sean Lemass.			Japanese and Chinese ambassadors meet together in Nanking.
Feb. 3		Britain and France invite Germany to discuss disarmament and security in Europe.	In Tel Aviv, economist Moshe Smilansky tells members of the convened Palestine Jewish Farmers Federation that they should deal only with Jewish labor and avoid Arab influence.		
Feb. 4				South America suffers through a heat wave, with temperatures exceeding 100°F.	
Feb. 5		Italy presses for a trade pact with the United States. Italian Ambassador Augusto Rosso professes that Italy's trade revenue will fall without the partnership of the United States.		Brazil and the United States agree on a trade treaty, signed by Brazil's Ambassador Oswald Aranha and Washington's Secretary of State Cordell Hull.	
Feb. 6					War is unlikely between Japan and Russia, despite their animosities. Both are not ready for war, declares the Earl of Lytton, speaking to the European and Far Eastern Politics Association.
Feb. 7		Josef Stalin reenters politics, winning a seat in the Presidium of the Soviet Central Executive Committee.			
Feb. 8					Trouble is brewing in the Pacific, concludes statesman Gen. Jan Christiaan Smuts. Speaking before the South African Institute of National Affairs, he advises the United States and Britain to unite their forces immediately.
Feb. 9		The son of former Kaiser Wilhelm of Germany announces to a Nazi-sympathetic crowd in Budapest, Hungary, that he is proud to be a member of the Nazi party.			Manchukuo, where Japanese and Chinese troops have recently clashed, remains dependent on Japan for its safety, says Japanese Ambassador Saito to a Chicago foreign relations society.
Feb. 10		Germany reports a rise in unemployment, contrary to previous statements by Adolf Hitler. January 1935 figures indicate nearly 3 million out of work.			Because of tensions with Japan, China constructs a modern air force base near the city of Loyang.

A	B	C	D	E
Includes developments that affect more than one world region, international organizations, and important meetings of world leaders.	Includes all domestic and regional developments in Europe, including the Soviet Union.	Includes all domestic and regional developments in Africa and the Middle East.	Includes all domestic and regional developments in Latin America, the Caribbean, and Canada.	Includes all domestic and regional developments in Asian and Pacific nations (and colonies).

U.S. Politics & Social Issues	U.S. Foreign Policy & Defense	Economics & Great Depression	Science, Technology & Nature	Culture, Leisure & Lifestyle	
President Roosevelt celebrates his 53rd birthday in Washington; around the country private and public organizations hold balls and dances in commemoration, many of whose proceeds will benefit charity.		The United States tells the International Labor Office in Geneva, Switzerland, that it is considering a 40-hour workweek, a strategy that could effectively reduce unemployment domestically.	Columbia University announces that one of its research associates, Robert Williams, has discovered the chemical structure of vitamin B. The finding promises to yield important medical and nutritional data.	A recent furor over the press supposedly giving too much space to the Lindbergh baby murder trial takes on a new angle when Columbia University's Dean of Journalism, Carl W. Ackerman, defends newspaper coverage. It is the duty of journalists, he says, to be where the news is being made—and the trial is definitely one meriting public attention.	Jan. 31
				The Legion of Decency's rating of movies begins, published in the current edition of the *Catholic News*. To Hollywood's relief, the list approves all of the newest movies.	Feb. 1
		Congress proposes, as part of President Roosevelt's security plan, to lend additional financial support to those states that cannot meet the plan's full commitment to the elderly poor.	Britain is on the verge of introducing television to the public, a move that aggravates American technicians who had been boasting that they were pioneering the latest technology.	The United States team will open the 1935 Davis Cup tournament, paired against a team from China. The event will take place in London.	Feb. 2
	Three major shipbuilders and certain U.S. naval representatives appear before the Senate Munitions Committee to answer suspicions of collusion in the awarding of contracts. Homer Ferguson, whose company is questioned, calls the charges ridiculous.	According to latest figures, America has regained the bulk of the competitive table glassware industry from foreign manufacturers. For some time, Japan has dominated the market.	Explorer Wynant Davis Hubbard promises to broadcast live directly from the jungle on his next safari.		Feb. 3
Thomas E. Maloy, a business agent in Chicago's Moving Pictures Operating Union, is found shot dead on a central Chicago avenue.		The finance and currency committee of the Chamber of Commerce of New York recommends that a panel be created by Congress to study banking and monetary reform across the United States.			Feb. 4
		According to Lloyd's of London, the world's central shipping countries launched almost 968,000 tons of merchant vessels in 1934, nearly doubling the total tonnage of 1933. It was the first noticeable gain in five years.			Feb. 5
	Because of Russia's inability to negotiate and its nonpayment of debts to the United States, the latter ceases its consular relationship with Moscow. For now, plans to build an embassy in Russia are dropped.	The U.S. Commerce Department states that, in all aspects, the nation experienced a memorable upbeat trading year of 1934; all overseas nations purchased its goods.			Feb. 6
		Railroads facing bankruptcy are offered relief by the Reconstruction Finance Corporation, which promises to buy their bonds and cut service fees.	The U.S. Navy plans to utilize fingerprinting procedures invented by Erasmus Mead, a New York physician who found 500 fingerprints on the ladder alleged to have been used by the killer of Charles Lindbergh's son—fingerprints undetected by the New Jersey Police Department.	Frank Greges, who makes $1 a day, is celebrated by Wall Street for returning a wallet that he found containing $45,000 from a securities exchange. The firm owning the money awards him a full-time job as a reward.	Feb. 7
Members of the U.S. Senate's Territories and Insular Affairs Committee report that the Philippine Islands are on the verge of falling to rebels. The committee fears that Japan will take over the islands.		A sale of four U.S. locomotives to Brazil is made possible by the Second Export-Import Bank. It is part of the recent trading pact signed between the two countries.			Feb. 8
Admiral Cary Grayson, once President Woodrow Wilson's personal physician, is named head of the Red Cross by President Franklin Roosevelt.	The U.S. military meets with government officials to propose strengthening the coastal defenses of Hawaii. The Army proposes an air base at the cost of $11 million.		A four-mile tunnel is blasted through the Rocky Mountains to allow for water diversion. It will ease the overflow of drainage caused by the melting of mountain snow in the springtime.	A tornado strikes Grapeland, Tex., leaving many homeless and several dead. Seventy people are critically injured. . . . The International Roman Catholic Alumnae issues a statement to all of its churches to help combat the spread of Communism in the cities. The Alumnae asks that pastors make this message the Homily at their next Mass.	Feb. 9
		Thanks to the New Deal, which has funded improvements to America's zoos, each of the 130 zoos across the United States reports increased business.	In Cairo, Egypt, Prof. Selim Hassam, an archaeologist, claims to have determined the age of the Sphinx at Gaza. He estimates it was built during the reign of Pharaoh Chephren of the 4th Dynasty—circa 2520 B.C.E.	The Central Agency, which governs the content of American radio, begins a campaign to keep children's radio free of subject matter that might frighten them. The campaign is a result of parents' fears that programs feature too much violence and an abundance of scary stories and characters.	Feb. 10

F	G	H	I	J
Includes elections, federal-state relations, civil rights and liberties, crime, the judiciary, education, healthcare, poverty, urban affairs, and population.	*Includes formation and debate of U.S. foreign and defense policies, veterans affairs, and defense spending. (Relations with specific foreign countries are usually found under the region concerned.)*	*Includes business, labor, agriculture, taxation, transportation, consumer affairs, monetary and fiscal policy, natural resources, pollution, and accidents.*	*Includes worldwide scientific, medical, and technological developments, natural phenomena, U.S. weather, and natural disasters.*	*Includes the arts, religion, scholarship, communications media, sports, entertainment, fashions, fads, and social life.*

	World Affairs	Europe	Africa & The Middle East	The Americas	Asia & The Pacific
Feb. 11		Tax receipts show that Germany has experienced an upswing in its economy—the first in years.	The United Jewish Appeal begins a fundraising campaign to raise $3.2 million for a new state in Palestine, mostly for Jews evicted from Germany. Assisting the drive are the American Jewish Joint Distribution Committee and the American Palestine Campaign.		
Feb. 12			An Italian force of 35,000 clashes with natives in Abyssinia. Premier Benito Mussolini dispatches airplanes and naval equipment to retaliate.		
Feb. 13					
Feb. 14		Germany chooses to take part in the western European air convention, but continues to abstain from the Eastern Security pact binding most other European nations.			Intent on colonizing in South America, members of the Tokyo Foreign Office meet with a Paraguayan committee in the city of Asunción.
Feb. 15		The French suffragette movement gains momentum as women demand to be allowed to vote in the upcoming municipal elections in May. In Paris, thousands of women turn out to protest on the Champs-Élysées.			
Feb. 16				Hawaii's 140,000-plus Japanese residents prepare to celebrate the 50th anniversary of their first immigration to the island.	
Feb. 17				According to the U.S. Chamber of Commerce, Argentina tripled its exports to the United States in January, compared to January 1934, from $2.3 million to $7 million.	Three U.S. businessmen accuse Japanese police in the town of Osaka of manhandling them for no reason. One of the men files a complaint with the U.S. Consulate in Kobe.
Feb. 18		Two women, Benita von Berg and Renata von Natzner, are beheaded in Berlin for spying. Adolf Hitler states that they were passing state secrets and were rightly tried by the People's Court.		Archbishop Michael J. Curley of Baltimore demands from the State Department that inquiries be made into the allegations that Mexicans are being refused the right to practice their religion by their government.	
Feb. 19	Dr. Alvin A. Johnson, director of the New School for Social Research, is leading a "University in Exile" campaign. His strategy is to help scholars escaping Nazi Germany continue their education here in the United States and abroad in free territories.	Nazis in Düsseldorf, Germany, shut down the Roman Catholic Workers Society and confiscate its treasury, claiming that its members were anti-government.			Japan simultaneously holds peace talks with Russia and China.
Feb. 20					
Feb. 21		Since France returned the Saar Valley to Germany last month, around 10,000 refugees have fled the area, many heading to the United States or Britain. . . . James G. McDonald, High Commissioner for Refugees, announces his plan for deployment. He is engaged in talks with several South American countries that might be open to receiving refugees from Europe.	Four thousand Italian troops are sent to Ethiopia.	Cuban students in Havana refuse to attend classes until the current military rule ends and freedom is restored. . . . Peru's Minister of Affairs announces that Roman Catholicism, the national religion of the country, will be taught in all of its schools.	With an announcement from China's Premier, Wang Ching-Wei, it appears that China and Japan may be close to an understanding. "A rational solution of (our) fundamental issues will be obtained," Premier Wang promises.

A	B	C	D	E
Includes developments that affect more than one world region, international organizations, and important meetings of world leaders.	Includes all domestic and regional developments in Europe, including the Soviet Union.	Includes all domestic and regional developments in Africa and the Middle East.	Includes all domestic and regional developments in Latin America, the Caribbean, and Canada.	Includes all domestic and regional developments in Asian and Pacific nations (and colonies).

U.S. Politics & Social Issues	U.S. Foreign Policy & Defense	Economics & Great Depression	Science, Technology & Nature	Culture, Leisure & Lifestyle	
			Archaeologists announce the discovery of the ruins of the oldest city yet known, Tepe Gawra in Mesopotamia. It is thought to be 5,700 years old.		Feb. 11
		Congress continues to debate the $4.9 billion relief bill. About 2.2 million people have been employed through work programs.			Feb. 12
	California state representatives are concerned over the 25,000 Japanese living in the state. They ask the House Military Affairs Committee for an increase in California's National Guard troops.			A jury finds Bruno Richard Hauptmann guilty in the murder of Charles Lindbergh's son in 1932. Outside the Flemington, N.J., courthouse, a crowd of 6,000 applauds the verdict.	Feb. 13
Utah's Senator Elbert Thomas proposes a student exchange program between the United States and Japan, in order to promote "necessary understanding."				Scottish novelist Archibald Joseph Cronin claims in an interview that new British authors lack the talent to keep their works lively and fresh. Their ideas, he says, reek of staleness and their prose has lost its color.	Feb. 14
				Actor Douglas Fairbanks, Sr., leaves London for a trip around the world with his new bride, Lady Sylvia Ashley.	Feb. 15
		With his $4.9 billion relief bill stalled in Congress, President Franklin Roosevelt reminds the public that, once passed, it will provide work for 3.5 million families.		The 115th anniversary of Susan B. Anthony's birth is celebrated throughout the country, especially by women's rights advocates.	Feb. 16
Edwin Witte, President Roosevelt's Executive Director on Economic Security, predicts that by 1970 there will be 15 million people age 65 and older and by the year 2000, 19 million. He is concerned over the state of "planned security" by that time. . . . J. Edgar Hoover, Director of the FBI, tells Congress that his organization requires more freedom to fight crime.		Oscar Johnston, cotton expert and representative of the U.S. Agriculture Department, sails for Europe to make possible arrangements to sell American cotton overseas. A trade agreement would greatly boost the falling domestic cotton trade.	The American Association of University Women gives 10 Science Fellowships to female graduate students around the world for their contributions to research.	Warner Bros. Midsummer Night's Dream, directed by Max Reinhardt and starring James Cagney and Olivia DeHavilland, opens in theaters across the country. . . . Thirty-one convicts escape from the State Correctional Center in Granite, Okla., killing one guard. Five are recaptured immediately.	Feb. 17
				Some 60 original Currier & Ives lithographs are stolen from a private dealer in New Haven, Conn. Though worth millions, detectives think the pictures were not stolen for ransom. . . . Cuban José Capablanca wins the third round of the Russian Chess Masters' Tournament in Moscow.	Feb. 18
		The U.S. Chamber of Commerce requests that the relief bill be reduced from $4.9 billion to $2.9 billion. The White House states that the request is ridiculous.		Due to the request of the major leagues, the Public Works Administration is considering the construction of 500 new neighborhood baseball parks across the United States.	Feb. 19
				Sociologist Dr. Ira S. Wilde says that American readers pay more attention to news events involving Caucasian figures than they do to items about African Americans. . . . The New York Yankees re-sign Lou Gehrig for a one-year contract worth $30,000. Now that Babe Ruth has announced that he is leaving the Yankees, Gehrig's is the highest salary paid to a New York sportsman.	Feb. 20
Victor A. Christgau resigns his position as chief aide of the Agricultural Adjustment Administration amid rumors that Rexford Tugwell, the Undersecretary of Agriculture, will soon resign.	With the U.S. armed forces considering the use of dirigibles, Secretary of the Navy Claude Swanson orders the Science Advisory Board to study the practical use of this type of aircraft during both peace and wartime.	President Franklin Roosevelt asks Congress to extend his National Industrial Recovery Act for another two years.	James MacNaughton, president and general manager of the Calumet and Hecla Consolidated Copper Mines in Calumet, Mich., wins the William Saunders Medal for distinguished achievement in mining.	Vassar College revises its curriculum to better suit both faculty and students. Changes include an enhanced "tutorial guidance" program, a final all-inclusive examination for seniors, and a reduction from five to four courses per annum.	Feb. 21

F	G	H	I	J
Includes elections, federal-state relations, civil rights and liberties, crime, the judiciary, education, healthcare, poverty, urban affairs, and population.	Includes formation and debate of U.S. foreign and defense policies, veterans affairs, and defense spending. (Relations with specific foreign countries are usually found under the region concerned.)	Includes business, labor, agriculture, taxation, transportation, consumer affairs, monetary and fiscal policy, natural resources, pollution, and accidents.	Includes worldwide scientific, medical, and technological developments, natural phenomena, U.S. weather, and natural disasters.	Includes the arts, religion, scholarship, communications media, sports, entertainment, fashions, fads, and social life.

	World Affairs	Europe	Africa & The Middle East	The Americas	Asia & The Pacific
Feb. 22	Vying with Finland and Italy for the 1940 Olympics, Tokyo says it will build a 150,000-seat stadium if it were made host. Finland's committee is slated to meet next week in Oslo and promises to outdo anything that Japan can offer.	Adolf Hitler authorizes Finance Minister Count Lutz von Krosigk with the power to demand between 750 million and 1 billion marks worth of loans from banks, businesses, and private individuals.			An assassin stabs Tokyo publisher Matsytaro Shoriki because he helped sponsor American baseball player Babe Ruth's tour of the Orient. . . . A Chinese judge of the World Court denies any alliance with Japan or that China plans to leave the League of Nations.
Feb. 23		In Yugoslavia, rioting breaks out on the streets of Belgrade after an extremist group disseminates literature to the peasants in the Brod district. Minister of Interior Veba Popoviech explains that the police used force as a last resort.	Italy dispatches more troops to Italian Somaliland in preparation for attacks on Ethiopia.	Paraguay threatens to leave the League of Nations due to tensions with Bolivia, despite fellow members' pleas to find a peaceable solution.	The American tanker Elizabeth Kellogg is detained and its crew questioned after it accidentally runs aground near Tokyo; after several hours of questioning the captain and his men are released. . . . An assassin kills Siam's Defense Minister Luang Bipul Songgram.
Feb. 24		The Red Army of Russia celebrates its 17th anniversary. . . . A plebiscite in Switzerland approves an extension of the period of military training.		A representative from El Salvador says that his country has not allowed Japan access to the country, and that all such rumors are false.	
Feb. 25	Paraguay announces that it is withdrawing from the League of Nations.	Russia claims that Germany's efforts to rebuild its main road are for the purpose of building the infrastructure necessary for moving material in wartime.			The Soviets, who have been watching the state of affairs between Japan and China, say they are convinced that Japan is attempting to set up an economic dictatorship over China.
Feb. 26		The British ministry receives a visit from Austrian diplomats—including Austrian Chancellor Kurt Schuschnigg and Foreign Minister Baron Egon Berger-Waldenegg—who wish to discuss Austrian involvement in the peace pacts.			
Feb. 27					
Feb. 28					Japan denies trying to isolate the Chinese for economic purposes. Eiji Amau from the Foreign Office calls the charges "absurd and baseless."
Mar. 1		In Berlin, more than 500,000 wave banners bearing the Nazi swastika, the new emblem of the Third Reich. . . . Anti-royalist Greeks launch an abortive rebellion.	Turkey elects Mustapha Kemal Ataturk president.		The U.S. Navy has been asked by the House Patents Committee to ban all Japanese sailors from its vessels.
Mar. 2		Britain adopts a new air defense system, based on the protection of its main cities by air attack, as part of a broader plan of modernization of defenses.		Cuban industry is threatened by the closing of its manganese mines, due to economic troubles.	The Department of Commerce states that Japan was the leading buyer of America's tin plates last year (some 39,863 tons), as well as the buyer of 63 percent of all scrap iron and steel exported from the United States.

A	B	C	D	E
Includes developments that affect more than one world region, international organizations, and important meetings of world leaders.	Includes all domestic and regional developments in Europe, including the Soviet Union.	Includes all domestic and regional developments in Africa and the Middle East.	Includes all domestic and regional developments in Latin America, the Caribbean, and Canada.	Includes all domestic and regional developments in Asian and Pacific nations (and colonies).

U.S. Politics & Social Issues	U.S. Foreign Policy & Defense	Economics & Great Depression	Science, Technology & Nature	Culture, Leisure & Lifestyle	
First Lady Eleanor Roosevelt, in addressing the American Council of Guidance and Personnel, stresses the importance of education for today's youth. She advises teachers to instill not only a good set of morals but an enlivened community spirit, as well.		Liquidation of Britain's largest wool merchant, Francis Willey & Co., puts 10,000 people in Britain, Poland, and the United States out of work. . . . The Senate forces recommittal of President Roosevelt's $4.9 billion relief resolution by returning it to the Appropriations Committee for further consideration.		The Augusta, Ga., National Golf Club announces its second annual tournament, to take place in April. Taking part in the event will be golfer Bobby Jones and 137 other invitees from six nations.	Feb. 22
Father John F. O'Hara, president of Notre Dame University, along with the Rev. James Donahue and Rev. Casimir Sytucsko of the Congregation of the Holy Cross, leave for a scholastic tour of France, Belgium, and Italy to study medieval philosophy.			The ruins of Christopher Columbus's first fort in North America are discovered near Mont St. Michel, Haiti, by explorer Maurice Ries.		Feb. 23
			A team of scientists associated with Cornell University has created an apparatus for separating the components of the more penetrating types of x-rays into their individual wavelengths. The 14-year project was directed by Prof. F.K. Richtmyer. . . . Germany builds several railroad locomotives that exceed the speed of 100 miles per hour, surpassing the record of England's Flying Scotsman. . . . Transatlantic air travel will be a regular service in the not-too-distant future, says Baron Amaury de La Grange of the French Air Ministry, who is in the United States on a diplomatic mission.		Feb. 24
It is revealed that, when the child of Charles Lindbergh first disappeared in 1932, Al Capone offered the assistance of the Chicago mob to locate the boy and his kidnapper. The offer was refused.		William A. Kallman, chairman of the New York State Petroleum Industries Committee, announces that the state has collected $4.6 billion since the first gasoline tax was imposed in 1919.	A scientific expedition comprised of archaeologists and geologists from Yale University announces that it will travel to India to seek evidence supporting theories on the evolution of human beings.	Awards are presented to the most professional (and family-oriented) programs on the air by the Women's National Radio Committee. The league was created in late 1934 to recognize high scholastic and moral achievement on the airwaves.	Feb. 25
The House Ways and Means Committee predicts a $50 billion reserve fund by the year 1980; from that, the government could take tax-exempt securities from the market to pay annuities to persons 65 and older. . . . In Chicago, Edward J. Kelly is reelected as mayor.		Fifteen thousand people gather in New York's Madison Square Garden to protest Secretary of State Cordell Hull's recent suspension of debt negotiations with the Soviet Union.			Feb. 26
The U.S. government charges Andrew W. Mellon, one-time secretary of the treasury, with giving preferential treatment to his family-owned banks while in that position.			Sir Philip Sassoon of the British House of Commons calls upon a group of scientists to help prepare Britain in the event of air attacks from the Continent.	Babe Ruth becomes a player as well as an executive of the Boston Braves. Rumors suggest he might assume manager Bill McKechnie's job next year. . . . At the Academy Awards, Claudette Colbert wins as Best Actress and Frank Capra takes the Best Director award for It Happened One Night.	Feb. 27
		The United States and Japan hold another series of reciprocal trade talks.	In Washington, D.C., plans are being made to build the new Federal Reserve Board structure. The architect will depart from the usual columns-and-marble classicism of the capital city.	Actress Helen Hayes quits movies to devote her art to legitimate theater and her free time to her family. She has appeared in such popular films as The White Sisters and A Farewell to Arms, with Gary Cooper.	Feb. 28
It is learned today that a group of Republicans, led by New York State Chairman Melvin C. Eaton, are planning to attack President Roosevelt's New Deal policy by detailing exactly where it has failed the American people.		President Roosevelt buys six new U.S. Treasury "baby bonds" worth $113 from a Treasury executive. One bond is for himself, another for his five grandchildren. His aim is to show the United States the usefulness of bonds.			Mar. 1
A sharp rise in the murder rate is seen in the statistics gathered by the Metropolitan Life Insurance Company. Last year, 11,000 people were murdered. Over the last five years, eight times the number of African-American men than Caucasians were murdered, with more deaths tallied in the southern than in the northern states.	Speaking in Chicago, Raymond Leslie Buell declares that this is the closest the United States has come to the threshold of war since 1917, blaming Roosevelt's policies. Buell heads the Foreign Policy Association.	Pointing out the rising price of groceries, Agriculture Secretary Henry Wallace estimates that the American household, during the first half of 1935, will pay 11 percent more for food than it did six months earlier. Much of this is blamed on the shortage of produce caused by drought.	If the newest freshman class at Hunter College is a barometer of other colleges and universities, student interest in the sciences has increased; a semi-annual survey of 857 students indicates that most are pursuing specialization in one of the sciences.	In New York City, Police Commissioner Lewis Valentine charges Capt. George M. Renselaer with purposely destroying evidence pointing to the guilt of Henry Miro, a worker for Arthur Flegenheimer, alias Dutch Schultz.	Mar. 2

F	G	H	I	J
Includes elections, federal-state relations, civil rights and liberties, crime, the judiciary, education, healthcare, poverty, urban affairs, and population.	Includes formation and debate of U.S. foreign and defense policies, veterans affairs, and defense spending. (Relations with specific foreign countries are usually found under the region concerned.)	Includes business, labor, agriculture, taxation, transportation, consumer affairs, monetary and fiscal policy, natural resources, pollution, and accidents.	Includes worldwide scientific, medical, and technological developments, natural phenomena, U.S. weather, and natural disasters.	Includes the arts, religion, scholarship, communications media, sports, entertainment, fashions, fads, and social life.

	World Affairs	Europe	Africa & The Middle East	The Americas	Asia & The Pacific
Mar. 3		Near the island of Hydra, nine Greek airplanes attack five vessels taken by insurgent forces, while in Athens 10 rebels die in a gunfight with government forces.	Search parties fail to locate any sign of an airplane believed to have gone down in Africa's Congo jungles. Aboard the craft were Lady Young, wife of Governor General Edouard Renard of French Equatorial Africa; her personal physician, Dr. J. Kerby; and five French companions.	Politicians in Washington aim to turn the Virgin Islands into a useful commodity-producing area. According to George H. Ivins, director of education, a vocational school has been established in St. Croix to teach islanders agriculture, arts and crafts, and the manufacturing of local products such as rum and bay rum.	With word of Japan trying to force China into a trade agreement, the United States and Britain consider a plan to aid China's economic plight so that it is not dependent upon Japan. Japan argues that it is not attempting any coercion of China.
Mar. 4		Britain begins preparations in case of war. All peace policies, it claims, have failed or are stalled in the League of Nations.		The Sixth Scientific Congress, sponsored by the Pan-American Conference and which convenes top physicians, surgeons, and healthcare professionals from across the Western Hemisphere, has been scheduled for the summer. It will take place aboard a cruise ship touring Brazil and the West Indies.	
Mar. 5		Acknowledging that Russia's doctors are "forgotten" heroes and much deserving of the country's thanks, Josef Stalin signs a decree increasing the public health budget to finance the Soviet Union's medical personnel.	Lady Young and her physician, along with several others who disappeared over Africa last week, are found. They have made their way on foot through the jungle after a forced landing in the Congo.	Relations between former allies Argentina and Chile begin to take hostile overtones.	Prince Ananda, 11 years old, inherits the throne of Siam on the death of his uncle, King Prajadhipok. Ananda has been living and studying in Switzerland and will soon return to Bangkok for coronation.
Mar. 6		Adolf Hitler postpones peace talks with British Minister Sir John Simon. Poland, which had also been slated on Sir John's list of European visitations, grows irritated. Warsaw blames Hitler for being purposely evasive at a time when peace parleys are gravely important.	Problems over territory might be settled between Italy and Ethiopia with the announcement of a peace agreement between the two, signed at Addis Ababa. A neutral ground is established at the Italian Somaliland-Ethiopian frontier.		
Mar. 7		Bulgaria testifies to the League of Nations Secretary-General Joseph Avenol that Turkey, a long-time rival, is threatening it. Six Turkish divisions have installed themselves on the border.			
Mar. 8		Italy mobilizes 1,000 fliers to leave Naples for the African continent today. Trains carrying troops from Florence pass in and out of Naples throughout the day.			
Mar. 9		Lithuania tries 126 members of the Nazi party for criminal activities committed in the town of Memel. Now, with the trial concluding with guilty verdicts, it appears that the Nazis may be executed or imprisoned for long terms. Germany hints at violent retaliation.			A U.S Department of Commerce survey shows Japanese trade gaining 31 percent over the same period in 1934.
Mar. 10	The United States is determined to construct a Pan-American air flight center, adding facilities and landing strips throughout the outer islands. The city of New York is already considered the major "aeroport" of America. . . . The United States and Britain announce plans to use the Azores for commercial airstrips, once transatlantic flight services begin full business in a few years.	In Yugoslavia, the Serbs celebrate the 700th anniversary of the founding of the Orthodox Church by St. Sava.			Fireworks, skyrockets, and banners color the streets of Manchukuo as citizens celebrate "Army Day" and Japan's victory over Russia at Mukden in 1905. . . . While outside forces have shown a reluctance to see Emperor Hirohito as "divine," Japan's House of Peers rushes to his defense, arguing that their emperor is a "super individual human being."
Mar. 11		A journalist who escaped Greece through the Yugoslavian frontier claims that the present administration is forcefully holding journalists and diplomats from other countries. The U.S. Senate investigates.		The Bank of Canada is officially opened, making it the central bank of the dominion.	

A	B	C	D	E
Includes developments that affect more than one world region, international organizations, and important meetings of world leaders.	Includes all domestic and regional developments in Europe, including the Soviet Union.	Includes all domestic and regional developments in Africa and the Middle East.	Includes all domestic and regional developments in Latin America, the Caribbean, and Canada.	Includes all domestic and regional developments in Asian and Pacific nations (and colonies).

U.S. Politics & Social Issues	U.S. Foreign Policy & Defense	Economics & Great Depression	Science, Technology & Nature	Culture, Leisure & Lifestyle	
	Herbert Agar, political author and former attaché of the American Embassy in London, urges the United States to consider isolation, based primarily upon economic nationalism, as a way to bypass exterior troubles. His comments come at a meeting of the Foreign Policy Association.	The United States shows an eight-month deficit of $2.3 billion in the Treasury's latest report covering the fiscal year—a deficit less than that of the previous year.	Scientists find and study a rare group of people in the Canary Islands who do not talk, but communicate through whistling. . . . Germany's broadcasting technology is the most powerful in the world—and getting stronger, say experts. By year's end it is expected to have seven 100-kilowatt radio stations and one 120-watt long-wave station.	The National Committee for Religion and Welfare Recovery, whose aim is the uplifting of all things ethical and moral in the United States, issues a statement, via Chairman Walter Heald, calling for a "program and a calendar for religion and welfare recovery for 1935." . . . The Wisconsin legislature is investigating the University of Wisconsin to determine the school's ethical standards. Atheism, agnosticism, and Communism are alleged to have been taught in its classrooms.	Mar. 3
					Mar. 4
		One of the nation's oldest railroads, the Baltimore & Ohio, applies for permission to extend a $7 million loan with the Reconstruction Finance Corporation for another five years. At the same time, it seeks another loan of $5 million from the RFC for maintenance.			Mar. 5
Former Associate Justice of the Supreme Court Oliver Wendell Homes dies of bronchial pneumonia at the age of 93.				The Czechoslovakian film, *Ecstasy*, starring Hedy Lamarr, is scheduled to appear in some American theaters—but U.S. Attorney Martin Conboy seeks to ban it because of a controversial scene in which Lamarr swims nude in a wooded glen. Meanwhile, all copies of the film sit in customs offices, without public release dates.	Mar. 6
Historian James Truslow Adams, blaming "the extremely reckless spending program" of the Roosevelt administration, urges the federal government to balance the budget and to forestall inflation by stabilizing the currency with no further devaluation.		The New Deal is a failure, according to Louisiana Governor Huey Long. Long calls on the President to "admit the facts" to the American people and explain where his New Deal failed.			Mar. 7
	Voting 68–15, the U.S. Senate approves $400 million for the War Department to increase its standing army from 118,750 men to 165,000.				Mar. 8
		Washington announces that $150 million is spent on relief every month.	The National Geographic Society reports discovering an enormous glacier in Canada, descending from the peak of Mount Hubbard (Alsek Valley, the Yukon) to a previously unrecorded mountain range running between Mount Hubbard and Mount Luciana of the St. Elias Range.		Mar. 9
Foreseeing the return of Prohibition, Philadelphia's Dr. Clarence True Wilson, general secretary of the Methodist Board of Temperance, Prohibition and Public Morals, sees a need for the restoration of a "dry" nation. But, he cautions, 40 states must ratify an amendment to the Constitution this time around.		Forecaster Robert E. Simon lays much hope in the building trades to be a driving force in restoring the U.S. economy. He believes a building boom is forthcoming, he tells the Eastern Savings Conference of the American Banking Association.	An "odorless" variety of cabbage, one that does not emanate a strong smell while cooking, has been bred at Cornell University's Department of Plant Breeding. Whether or not its flavor equals that of natural cabbage remains to be seen.	Protestants in Nazi Saxony are no longer allowed to practice or demonstrate their religion in a church, public meeting hall, or other public arena. The Nazi governor's declaration is compared to those of the pagan Roman emperors who drove the Christians into the catacombs.	Mar. 10
	The Church of Christ in the United States decries that the U.S. Navy has begun maneuvers in the Pacific; 198 church leaders from across the country sign a petition labeling that action as an acceptance of war before the fact.		Silver has been changed metallurgically into cadmium in an experiment at the Massachusetts Institute of Technology. The crowd invited to watch the procedure calls the results a "miracle."	German boxer Max Schmeling knocks out Steve Hamas in a well-awaited fight in Hamburg, Germany. Schmeling was expected to win, but many thought the bout would at least carry to a 12-round decision. Hamas falls in the ninth.	Mar. 11

F	G	H	I	J
Includes elections, federal-state relations, civil rights and liberties, crime, the judiciary, education, healthcare, poverty, urban affairs, and population.	*Includes formation and debate of U.S. foreign and defense policies, veterans affairs, and defense spending. (Relations with specific foreign countries are usually found under the region concerned.)*	*Includes business, labor, agriculture, taxation, transportation, consumer affairs, monetary and fiscal policy, natural resources, pollution, and accidents.*	*Includes worldwide scientific, medical, and technological developments, natural phenomena, U.S. weather, and natural disasters.*	*Includes the arts, religion, scholarship, communications media, sports, entertainment, fashions, fads, and social life.*

	World Affairs	Europe	Africa & The Middle East	The Americas	Asia & The Pacific
Mar. 12	It is decided today that Dutch financier Dr. L.J.A. Trip would succeed Leon Fraser as president of the Bank of International Settlements (the World Bank), starting May 14, immediately after the annual General Meeting.				The Chinese government sells its Eastern Railway to Russia as part of a larger trade pact; the deal was co-signed by Chinese Minister Ting Shi-Yuan and the Soviet's Ambassador, Constantin Yureneff.
Mar. 13		British Foreign Secretary Sir John Simon has made arrangements to fly to Berlin on March 24 to meet with Adolf Hitler. On his way back, he will meet with the minister of Poland. Anthony Eden, the Lord Privy Seal, will accompany him. . . . U.S. Secretary of the Navy Claude Swanson admits that there remains very little hope for a naval agreement among world powers.			Japanese Ambassador to the United States Hiroso Saito insists that the Western world remove its current and excessive trade barriers for the good of international trade. Not only is commerce suffering, he states, but so are international relationships. . . . W. Cameron Forbes, former U.S. Ambassador to Tokyo, visits with respective trade consultants in China and Japan in order to enhance trade with the Orient.
Mar. 14		Poland announces that upcoming elections in Danzig will give voters a wide variety of choices, some of which are anti-Nazi tickets. This suggests a cooling of the relationship between Poland and Germany. . . . The Soviet Union vows to increase its arsenal if Great Britain, in its talks with Germany, does not counter Germany's latest move to rebuild its forces.		Fifty-eight race cars representing many countries speed out of Buenos Aires, opening a race between Argentina and Chile. The route—2,786 miles—is dangerous, cutting through steep mountain passes.	
Mar. 15				Doctors are urgently needed in Brazil where a plague of influenza is breaking out. A call to other Latin American nations and to the United States is being answered as hospital tents begin appearing on the hillsides outside the affected hamlets.	The U.S. announcement of a Pacific airline and the related building of required airfields along a successive stretch of islands—Guam, Midway, and the Wake Islands—worries Japan. U.S. Secretary of the Navy Claude Swanson responds that the fields do serve a double purpose: as commercial bases and as fortifications against unfriendly forces.
Mar. 16		Count Viola di Compalto brings word to Prince Paul of Yugoslavia that Premier Benito Mussolini is willing to renew relations between the countries. . . . The German government officially announces that it will disregard the disarmament clauses of the Treaty of Versailles. Of all the world's armies, Germany's is expected to be the largest now that it has begun conscription.			
Mar. 17		Adolf Hitler suggests a commercial air base in Ireland. Both Ireland and Britain plan to fight it.	An American team of 14 Olympians leaves today on the liner *Conte di Savoia* for Tel Aviv for the Jewish Olympics.	It is learned that Nazi propagandists from Germany are now in South America, locating all German immigrants to persuade them to become party members.	
Mar. 18		Germany tests its cities' vulnerability to air attack by darkening Berlin while its own fighter planes soar over.			
Mar. 19					Rumors circulate that Japan has sought a secret alliance with Nazi Germany. When confronted, the Ambassador of Japan denies both Nazi ties and dangerous intentions.

A	B	C	D	E
Includes developments that affect more than one world region, international organizations, and important meetings of world leaders.	Includes all domestic and regional developments in Europe, including the Soviet Union.	Includes all domestic and regional developments in Africa and the Middle East.	Includes all domestic and regional developments in Latin America, the Caribbean, and Canada.	Includes all domestic and regional developments in Asian and Pacific nations (and colonies).

U.S. Politics & Social Issues	U.S. Foreign Policy & Defense	Economics & Great Depression	Science, Technology & Nature	Culture, Leisure & Lifestyle	
				The Mae West "look" is passé, say today's fashion moguls—and the sleek, less-buxom, more svelte appearance is in vogue. The classy woman must remain less than 100 pounds, be naturally pert, and insinuate that glide-on-air quality. Actress Myrna Loy suggests the new trend.	Mar. 12
		General Motors announces that the auto manufacturer's overseas sales increased 98 percent over the same period last year.		Five of Europe's top skaters arrive in New York to start their American tour. They are Maxi Herber, Vivi-Ann Hulten, Idi Papez, Ernst Baier, and Karl Zwack.	Mar. 13
				The musical Gold Diggers of 1935, starring Dick Powell and Gloria Stuart, opens in American movie houses. . . . The National Council of Jewish Women at its annual convention in New Orleans opposes compulsory military training currently being conducted in some high schools, colleges, and universities in the United States. They also push President Roosevelt to sign legislation putting an embargo on munitions and arms.	Mar. 14
Taxation must be applied to providing employment to those currently out of work, Governor of the Federal Reserve Board Mariner S. Eccles tells the House Banking and Currency Committee.		Washington calls for the redemption of the First U.S. Liberty Loan Bonds by June 15, 1935, worth $1.9 billion. Secretary of the Treasury Henry Morgenthau adds that holders will have the opportunity to exchange them for other government obligations.		Pope Pius XI, observing the trouble in Germany and throughout Europe, reminds all Catholics to participate in politics where the common good is concerned.	Mar. 15
			Through electrolysis, a new type of "heavy water"—tritium—has been produced at Princeton University by boiling down 75 tons of ordinary water. Chemistry professor Hugh S. Taylor led the project under the auspices of the university's Electrochemical Society.	Columbia University's Scholastic Press Association calls this era a progressive age for journalism, citing the public's interest in and dependency on newspapers and publishing houses for information, as well as a new brand of reporting that is moving today's journalist.	Mar. 16
President Franklin Roosevelt officially opens National Business Women's Week at a celebration given by the National Federation of Business and Professional Women in Washington, D.C. . . . More than 400 political delegates, sociologists, and celebrities, many of them known for their philanthropic work, convene in Florida for a conference on social work.	Money is appropriated by Congress to build defense bases on Pacific islands belonging to the United States. Admiral Stirling of the Navy explains that these sites will serve as outlying defense positions should the United States find itself threatened.	Texas is leading the south and southwest in a sudden—if not unexpected—building surge. Building permits have increased throughout the 40 largest cities—174 percent more in January and 312 percent more in February.	Five American yachtsmen sign up to participate in the 3,050-mile race from Newport, R.I., to Oslo, Norway. At race's end, Norwegian King Haakon VII will present the Winners Cup.	The Knights of Columbus open their annual membership drive across the United States. They expect 50,000 new Catholic laypersons and 2,000 new councils to spring up in the cities and towns of the United States. . . . Lord Mayor Alfred Byrne of Dublin is touring the United States for St. Patrick's Day. In New York, he hands out shamrocks to Mayor Fiorello LaGuardia and the delegates of the St. Patrick's Day Parade committee. The shamrocks were grown in Free Ireland.	Mar. 17
			Massachusetts Institute of Technology president Dr. Karl T. Compton tells a Yale University audience that he rues the fact that other countries—and not the United States—have done so much scientifically to make social, economic, and physical improvements, such as conquering disease. He suggests a keener focus in the United States on what must be done—scientifically, and not politically.		Mar. 18
Illinois, Indiana, Iowa, Ohio, and Kansas are the current focus of the Republican Party, says Kansas's national committee chairman John D.M. Hamilton.	Key Pittman, chairman of the Senate Foreign Relations Committee, tells the United States to cease all monetary pacts with Europeans until matters turn more settled overseas.	The New Orleans press states that cotton is off 44 to 58 points in an active market.		In Los Angeles, Judge Ben Lindsey decries the state of marriage today, saying that "free love, domestic chaos, and sexual anarchy" are dooming the institution.	Mar. 19

F	G	H	I	J
Includes elections, federal-state relations, civil rights and liberties, crime, the judiciary, education, healthcare, poverty, urban affairs, and population.	Includes formation and debate of U.S. foreign and defense policies, veterans affairs, and defense spending. (Relations with specific foreign countries are usually found under the region concerned.)	Includes business, labor, agriculture, taxation, transportation, consumer affairs, monetary and fiscal policy, natural resources, pollution, and accidents.	Includes worldwide scientific, medical, and technological developments, natural phenomena, U.S. weather, and natural disasters.	Includes the arts, religion, scholarship, communications media, sports, entertainment, fashions, fads, and social life.

	World Affairs	Europe	Africa & The Middle East	The Americas	Asia & The Pacific
Mar. 20					
Mar. 21		Germany arrests Johann Schaeffer, editor of the Nazi-leaning newspaper *Koelnische Zeitung*, after he refuses to make subscriptions to the paper mandatory—as prescribed by law.		Brazilian coffee growers react angrily to a new tax on coffee beans.	
Mar. 22		The French and Italians display increasingly cordial ties, now that Britain has taken a singular path of dealing with Hitler's politics. The French Chamber of Deputies votes 555–9 for ratification of Rome's peace policy.			
Mar. 23		Italy's Benito Mussolini calls for a resurgence of his country's armed forces. . . . When war comes it will be a world war, prophesies Alexander A. Troyanovsky, Russian Ambassador to the United States. He presses the United States to be ready for it, as the Soviet Union is prepared.			The Soviet Union sells its interest in the Chinese Eastern Railway in Manchukuo, helping to reduce tensions between Russia and Japan. . . . The Shanghai press claims that, while the world is kept busy watching the drama of conflict unfold in Europe, no one notices Japan taking the advantage.
Mar. 24		Germany breaks the Treaty of Versailles naval regulations by introducing 400,000 tons of naval warships—including submarines—into the seas, surpassing the 150,000 legal tonnage stated by the treaty.		An urgent request from the United States—signed by Federal Judge George Anderson, Bishop Francis J. McConnell, and Prof. James Shotwell of Columbia University—is delivered to Cuban dictator Carlos Mendita to spare the lives of 800 Cuban civilians being held for disturbances on the island. . . . Brazil toughens its stance on immigration, which has gone unchecked lately. Setting a limitation, only 126 Americans will be allowed to settle there this year.	The life of Kitokuro Ikki, president of Japan's Privy Council, is saved by police who catch a dagger-wielding assassin before he is able to enter Ikki's residence. No motive is known.
Mar. 25	British National Socialists by the thousands convene at London's Albert Hall to hear anti-Semitic speaker Oswald Mosley. Mosley heads the British Union of Fascists. . . . Catholic Monsignor Arthur Hinsley is appointed the new Archbishop of Westminster, England, by Pope Pius XI. He succeeds Francis Cardinal Bourne.	Rumors circulate that nearly 200,000 "dark" Germans have been sterilized to prevent them from reproducing in an attempt to create a race of blonde, blue-eyed people.		Local businessmen have pledged subscriptions worth $50,000 to initiate a bank on the Virgin Islands, in the city of St. Thomas. The institution is expected to open in May or June 1935.	Lured by its prospects of oil and other natural resources, Japan offers to purchase the northern half of Sakhalin Island from the Russians.
Mar. 26		Poland backs off from its alliance with war-minded Germany, refusing to go along with German conscription. . . . In Lithuania, the death sentences of Nazi conspirators are commuted.			
Mar. 27	Japan quits the League of Nations. Former delegate Uchiro Yokoyama asserts that despite disagreements with the League's policies, Japan promises to continue aiding the League on nonpolitical issues.				
Mar. 28				By an order signed today by King George of England, John Buchanan is appointed as Governor General of Canada.	Japan urges Ecuador to increase its cotton output. An official pact is expected to be announced shortly.

A	B	C	D	E
Includes developments that affect more than one world region, international organizations, and important meetings of world leaders.	Includes all domestic and regional developments in Europe, including the Soviet Union.	Includes all domestic and regional developments in Africa and the Middle East.	Includes all domestic and regional developments in Latin America, the Caribbean, and Canada.	Includes all domestic and regional developments in Asian and Pacific nations (and colonies).

U.S. Politics & Social Issues	U.S. Foreign Policy & Defense	Economics & Great Depression	Science, Technology & Nature	Culture, Leisure & Lifestyle	
	Ray Atherton, American Chargé d'Affaires, joins London's Sir John Simon in talks in Washington concerning the situation in Europe.	Agriculture Secretary Henry Wallace removes all restrictions on the planting of spring wheat in order to protect against the effects of a possible drought similar to that in the lower Midwest in 1934. Farmers, this year, are required to sign agreements to offset 1935 increases with corresponding reductions next year.		Conductor Werner Janssen appears at Carnegie Hall to celebrate the 250th birthday of composer Johann Sebastian Bach.	Mar. 20
The Democratic political organization is eyeing Atlantic City, N.J., as the site of its 1936 presidential campaign convention. The body handling the Atlantic City proposal is reportedly about to submit a bid of $150,000— a third of that amount comes from a private, unnamed New Jersey citizen.		Saying that the United States has grown from a "Little Orphan Annie" to a "Very Live Young Lady," President Roosevelt promotes a two-year extension of his NRA policy.		The committee responsible for financing the 1933–34 World's Fair in Chicago has paid off its debt of $702,171. Observers have called the fair one of the best in history.	Mar. 21
				Currently, the most "virile" writing comes out of the United States, says Alfred A. Knopf, international publisher. Mr. Knopf has just spent more than two months in Europe studying the styles of novelists and journalists overseas.	Mar. 22
Edmund L. Dolan, who once served as city treasurer under former Boston mayor James M. Curley, is being investigated for possible wrongdoings during his tenure in office. Curley, now the governor of Massachusetts, calls the charges an attempt to discredit the political party itself as the 1936 presidential campaign draws near.		Secretary of State Cordell Hull tells radio listeners that he promotes a reciprocal treaty on trade, so that the United States, now one of the trading giants, does not fall behind in the months ahead.			Mar. 23
				The National League of Pen-Women gathers in Coral Gables, Fla., representing female authors and journalists from all 50 states. . . . Congress approves a $2.1 million appropriation to build the Alaska-Yukon link of the Pan-American Highway to stretch from the north Oregon highways to Vancouver to Fairbanks, Alaska.	Mar. 24
					Mar. 25
		With the succession of wind storms battering the Midwest, Col. Lawrence Westbrook, Assistant Federal Emergency Relief Administrator, promises one of the hardest-hit states, Kansas, a $1 million "dust fund" to help with plowing wind barriers to prevent drifting of soil. The fund is the result of cooperation between federal and state boards coordinated by the governor of Kansas, Alf Landon.		Warden Lewis E. Lawes, current officiate of Sing Sing Prison, is honored for 30 years of service in the penal system at a testimonial dinner attended by 500 men and women in business and politics.	Mar. 26
		The Consumer Goods Industry suggests to Chairman Harrison of the Senate Finance Committee a resolution demanding that Congressional action be taken to extend the National Recovery Act.	RCA's president, David Sarnoff, receives France's Cross of the Legion of Honor for his work in making the radio a useful entity of mankind.		Mar. 27
President and Mrs. Roosevelt host a ball for officer ranks from the Army, Navy, and Marines and their spouses at the White House.	Representing President Roosevelt's committee to study war control, Bernard M. Baruch tells the Senate Munitions Committee that he fears a world war could "burn up" the globe's remaining natural resources.				Mar. 28

F	G	H	I	J
Includes elections, federal-state relations, civil rights and liberties, crime, the judiciary, education, healthcare, poverty, urban affairs, and population.	Includes formation and debate of U.S. foreign and defense policies, veterans affairs, and defense spending. (Relations with specific foreign countries are usually found under the region concerned.)	Includes business, labor, agriculture, taxation, transportation, consumer affairs, monetary and fiscal policy, natural resources, pollution, and accidents.	Includes worldwide scientific, medical, and technological developments, natural phenomena, U.S. weather, and natural disasters.	Includes the arts, religion, scholarship, communications media, sports, entertainment, fashions, fads, and social life.

	World Affairs	Europe	Africa & The Middle East	The Americas	Asia & The Pacific
Mar. 29	Three weeks of negotiations have finally produced a deal between members of the International Copper Union, says conference chairman Cornelius F. Kelley. Copper will be produced—on a limited basis—outside the United States as a means of establishing an ongoing and even trade among foreign markets.	Britain's Anthony Eden becomes the first British emissary to be received by Josef Stalin.	Premier Benito Mussolini of Italy appoints Gen. Emilio Debono, former Minister of Colonies, as High Commissioner for the Italian East African Colonies.	At Cabana Fortress, Cuba, rebel Manuel Fonseca is sentenced to death by a military court-martial after a tribunal found him guilty of possessing firearms. The verdict stuns the island, which never expected such a severe punishment.	
Mar. 30				Brazilian Marcos Souza Dantas takes the Integralista (Fascist) oath. Souza is the former director of the Bank of Brazil and president of the National Coffee Council.	Japan rejects British and American protests against the Manchukuo oil monopoly.
Mar. 31				Colombia finds itself dangerously short of teachers—but swamped with lawyers—according to the magazine *Education*, published in Bogotá.	
Apr. 1		Meeting in Moscow this week, British Lord Privy Anthony Eden and Ambassador Maxim Litvinoff agree to write a working plan for common international policies. . . . Eighty thousand dollars has been set aside by Germany to promote its foreign trade with other countries; in turn, funds generated from that trade will be used to build the new army.	Britain complains that Italy's harassment of Ethiopia is unfair; Britain gave that country its independence in 1906, proclaiming it the only "free" African nation.		Britain establishes the Reserve Bank of India as the central banking institution.
Apr. 2	Pope Pius XI warns the world that a global war would be "an enormous crime."	Lord Anthony Eden of Britain arrives in Warsaw to converse with Polish officials. . . . France's Chamber of Deputies votes to strengthen its air power and, at the same time, make its air service a separate entity from the navy.			The Chinese government, halfway through its agreement with the RFC to buy $50 million worth of cotton and wheat from the United States, backs out of the deal without explanation.
Apr. 3		American lawyer, civic leader, and defender of Jewish rights, Samuel Untermyer, calls upon the League of Nations to impose economic sanctions against Germany. . . . Germany is invited to attend naval peace talks organized by Britain.		The Catholic Church protests a new bill in Puerto Rico recommending the use of birth control, arguing that overpopulation is not the cause of the island's problems. The Church points to education, religion, and an improved economy as hopes for needy families.	
Apr. 4		According to Britain's Foreign Secretary Sir John Simon, Adolf Hitler admitted to him that the size of Germany's air force equals that of England's. . . . Britain's Lord Privy Seal Anthony Eden cannot convince Poland to join in a defensive pact. . . . The Irish Free State begins to pay back a $5.2 million debt owed to the United States incurred during its struggle for freedom from Great Britain.			Admiral Frank B. Upham, the U.S. Navy's commander in chief of the Asiatic fleet, makes a goodwill visit to Yokohama, Japan, with his personal flagship, the *Augusta*. The visit coincides with the opening of sea maneuvers in the northeast Pacific.
Apr. 5	Almost $80,000 has been donated to the "Exile University," an organization established to help German scholars who have fled their country.				A U.S. Trade Mission, led by former ambassador to Japan W. Cameron Forbes, arrives in Tokyo.
Apr. 6					
Apr. 7			As 10,000 Ethiopians rally to meet the invading Italians, their King, Haile Selassie, denies he is worried about the outcome. The battle will pit shields, black powder rifles, and scimitars against tanks and machine guns.	Sixty people are hurt during a riot in Belem, Brazil, between soldiers and dissidents. . . . The Canadian House of Commons discusses the subject of neutrality in the face of a world war; their preference is to follow the U.S. lead: to respect the Monroe Doctrine and avoid harm's way.	Japanese Ambassador Hirosi Saito tells the Alumni Council in Washington, D.C., that he does not foresee the possibility of war, despite the world's "perplexing problems." Instead, he sees a productive future for everyone.

A	B	C	D	E
Includes developments that affect more than one world region, international organizations, and important meetings of world leaders.	*Includes all domestic and regional developments in Europe, including the Soviet Union.*	*Includes all domestic and regional developments in Africa and the Middle East.*	*Includes all domestic and regional developments in Latin America, the Caribbean, and Canada.*	*Includes all domestic and regional developments in Asian and Pacific nations (and colonies).*

U.S. Politics & Social Issues	U.S. Foreign Policy & Defense	Economics & Great Depression	Science, Technology & Nature	Culture, Leisure & Lifestyle	
					Mar. 29
	North Dakota Senator Gerald Nye attests that at this point, the United States has no intention of joining the conflict brewing overseas. His President, he says, "has voiced a determination to keep America out of another war at all costs."	The Roosevelt administration enters a series of talks between bituminous coal and mine workers and their representing unions to soothe difficulties between the two. The administration asks for a truce through mid-June.			Mar. 30
	The American Academy of Political and Social Science in Philadelphia plans to have a weekend debate, arguing the values of democracy over fascism and socialism.	Colorado, Kansas, Missouri, Nebraska, Oklahoma, and Texas have been hit so hard this last month with dust storms that the wheat crop is all but lost.		Eleanor Roosevelt asks for the country's support to help wipe out tuberculosis.	Mar. 31
The Republican Party believes that the Midwest middle-class will vote Republican in the next election.	The House of Representatives votes down a bill to grant the U.S. Army $405 million for modernization. Despite troubles in Europe, many claim there are more urgent needs.	Goodyear Rubber Company employees vote to strike.	The nation's current power capacity would not be enough to sustain the United States during wartime, asserts the Federal Power Commission. It recommends the construction of additional power plants with the capacity of 4 million kilowatts.		Apr. 1
		Myron C. Taylor, chairman of U.S. Steel, tells stockholders that he is happy to see the resurgence of the U.S. economy and hopes that it will put to an end the many "quack" economic cures presented by various critics over the last few years.			Apr. 2
		President Roosevelt's redrafted social and economic security bill enters the Ways and Means Committee for further scrutiny.... For the first time since March 1933, the Treasury reports a surplus.			Apr. 3
		Nearly all of the 20,000 employees laid off from the Railway Express Agency at the beginning of the Depression are back on the job, according to its president, L.O. Head.		The National Association of Penmanship Teachers blames laziness—not the typewriter, as some suggest—on students' poor handwriting habits.	Apr. 4
A jury finds four people guilty of conspiring to hide bandit Lester Gillis, better known as "Baby Face Nelson," who was killed by FBI agents near Chicago in September 1934.		Congress passes the $4.9 billion Relief Bill.			Apr. 5
		Secretary of State Cordell Hull advises Europe in a radio address to "adopt a sound, comprehensive economic program, both domestic and international," and avoid war. Instead of war, he offers, "Lay a solid foundation on which to rebuild a stable peace and political structures."	St. John's Guild of Camden, N.J., launches a floating hospital with 1,500 beds—the first of its kind.	The Federal Bureau of Investigation arrests former member of the Bonnie & Clyde gang Raymond Hamilton in Dallas. When taken, he was masquerading as a country preacher.	Apr. 6
Postmaster General James A. Farley, chair of the Democratic Party, upholds the New Deal, despite the Republicans' opposition, because none of them have "offered a better alternative."	College students across the nation plan to stage campus protests against possible military involvement in Europe.	A strike against shipping companies on the West Coast curtails all of the U.S. trade in the Pacific Ocean. The Federal Mediation Board intervenes to reach an agreement of seamen and officers to get the Pacific shipping fleet sailing again.	Britain's Cunard ship lines will dismantle the old liner *Mauritania*, sister ship of the *Lusitania*.	Thoroughbred Good Harvest takes the Rowe Handicap, a preliminary race of the Kentucky Derby, in Bowie, Md.... Two veteran teachers of history and political science in a Muskegon, Mich., school are fired by the state Board of Education for professing liberal teachings. The teachers promise to fight all allegations.	Apr. 7

F	G	H	I	J
Includes elections, federal-state relations, civil rights and liberties, crime, the judiciary, education, healthcare, poverty, urban affairs, and population.	Includes formation and debate of U.S. foreign and defense policies, veterans affairs, and defense spending. (Relations with specific foreign countries are usually found under the region concerned.)	Includes business, labor, agriculture, taxation, transportation, consumer affairs, monetary and fiscal policy, natural resources, pollution, and accidents.	Includes worldwide scientific, medical, and technological developments, natural phenomena, U.S. weather, and natural disasters.	Includes the arts, religion, scholarship, communications media, sports, entertainment, fashions, fads, and social life.

	World Affairs	Europe	Africa & The Middle East	The Americas	Asia & The Pacific
Apr. 8		The United States learns that Germany has begun to place all political prisoners into work camps while under "protective custody." According to Dr. Wilhelm Frick, German Minister of the Interior, all prisoners are told why they have been arrested. . . . Czechoslovakia's Foreign Minister Eduard Benes reports that his country stands behind the British-French-Italian peace movement and believes that, if they continue to seek the alliance of other countries, war will be avoided.			
Apr. 9					
Apr. 10					The Japanese Emperor bans two books that have been a staple of civic government education for more than 30 years, *Essentials of Consultation Law* and *A Course in Constitutional Law*.
Apr. 11		Turkey, Czechoslovakia, Yugoslavia, and Romania give their support to the peace alliance of Britain, Italy, Russia, and France. This earns the newest four signatories the moniker of "the Little Entente."		After the release of Eutimo Falla Gutierrez Bonet, called the "richest man in Cuba" by kidnappers who collected a $300,000 ransom, police begin seeking suspects.	Japanese trade officials and private businessmen propose a trade agreement among Japanese, American, and Latin American countries.
Apr. 12			The 12th Congress of the International Woman Suffrage Alliance opens in Istanbul, Turkey. Some 300 delegates representing 35 countries take part in the sessions.	Peru seizes four converted bombers belonging to the New Orleans-Tampa-Tampico Air Lines and, until reassured that these planes are being used only for commercial purposes by the airlines, will not release the crafts. U.S. Ambassador Fred Dearing intervenes.	
Apr. 13		In Berlin, Germans celebrate the 70th birthday of Erich Ludendorff, a general of the World War. He is an avid supporter of the Nazi movement.			According to the U.S. Department of Commerce, Japan's exports rose 26 percent in March and its imports increased by 12 percent over 1934 figures.
Apr. 14		A conference in Stresa, Italy, between Britain, France, and Italy concludes without any concrete plan to restrain Germany.		Bermudans celebrate the birthday of their patron saint, St. George. . . . Assistant Secretary of State Sumner Welles uses the U.S. trade pact with Cuba as an example of an amiable trading partnership coming from the U.S. "good neighbor" policy.	Japan threatens to ban cotton imports from the United States if a ban is not issued on Latin American goods from rebel countries. Japan has a large investment in South America.
Apr. 15				Curaçao in the West Indies celebrates its 300th anniversary under Dutch rule.	
Apr. 16			The Spanish reorganize their African colonies, establishing a separate administration for the island of Fernando Po.	Dr. Ramon Grau y San Martin, former president of Cuba, warns that the island is about to explode with revolution.	

A	B	C	D	E
Includes developments that affect more than one world region, international organizations, and important meetings of world leaders.	*Includes all domestic and regional developments in Europe, including the Soviet Union.*	*Includes all domestic and regional developments in Africa and the Middle East.*	*Includes all domestic and regional developments in Latin America, the Caribbean, and Canada.*	*Includes all domestic and regional developments in Asian and Pacific nations (and colonies).*

U.S. Politics & Social Issues	U.S. Foreign Policy & Defense	Economics & Great Depression	Science, Technology & Nature	Culture, Leisure & Lifestyle	
		President Roosevelt signs into law the Emergency Relief Appropriation Act, which allows the establishment of several new agencies, including the Works Progress Administration (WPA).		Small- to mid-size movie production companies demand that the Motion Picture Industry Code be rewritten because its current terminology, in effect, eliminates the lesser, independent producers while allowing the largest producers—such as MGM, Universal, and 20th Century Fox—to prosper.	Apr. 8
President Roosevelt signs the $4.9 billion Relief Bill into law.		Charles R. Gay, senior partner in the accounting firm, Whitehouse & Co. is selected to head the New York Stock Exchange. . . . Charles M. Schwab sees U.S. industrial development climbing "onward and upward." The chairman of Bethlehem Steel, speaking at its stockholder meeting, states that the United States will always be the leading industrial country.		*New York Times* publisher Adolph S. Ochs dies at age 77.	Apr. 9
		A committee is investigating allegations that $750,000 may have been used to hire men outside of relief programs to work in New York's Park Department, which is against NRA rules. Park Commissioner Robert Moses denies the allegations.	Four Nobel Prize recipients—George Minot, Walter Murphy, Harold Urey, and George Whipple—celebrate the 101st anniversary of Alfred Nobel's birth, for whom the award is named and who, as the four winners say, inspired so much scientific research.		Apr. 10
				Hannes Schroll, an amateur Austrian skier, wins the U.S. downhill championship at the international event held in Rainier National Park, Wash.	Apr. 11
				Madison Square Garden's promoter, James Johnston, announces that he has selected boxer Jimmy Braddock as the contender to face heavyweight champion Max Baer in early June.	Apr. 12
President Roosevelt participates in a comedic skit at the Gridiron Correspondents' Group Meeting in Washington, D.C., before giving a speech to honor the group's 50 years of service.				Lenore Kight of Homestead, Pa., wins the 220-yard freestyle at the Women's National Indoor Swimming Championship in Chicago. . . . All 33 branches of the American Council of the World Alliance for International Peace attend the national meeting in New York. The agenda is peace through prayer.	Apr. 13
The Kerr-Smith Act, which attempted to control tobacco production, is ruled unconstitutional by a federal judge in Lexington, Ky. The act imposed a 25-percent sales tax on tobacco crops without approval from the Agricultural Board. . . . Former president Herbert Hoover begins an automobile tour from New York to California to promote the Republican vote in the upcoming 1936 presidential elections.	Congress votes the War Department $60,000 for the expenses of military attachés assigned to monitoring the situation in Europe.	As the Senate considers whether to extend the National Recovery Act, a group of small business owners pleads for extension of the bill, which they term a "savior."	Union Castle shipbuilders of Belfast announce that two of their 25,000-ton passenger liners being built in the Harland & Wolff yards will be equipped with solar-time synchronized clocks, the newest energy clocks, replacing old-fashioned clocks. Upon construction, the ships will be used for South African commerce.	Extra-curricular activities in schools are a waste of educational time unless they are tied in with the agenda and objectives of the institutions, says Roscoe L. West, president of the New Jersey State Teachers College. His audience is the Eastern States Teachers Association.	Apr. 14
				Collector Richard Gimbel unearths an old Philadelphia newspaper that ran several stories by Charles Dickens, written in 1834—before he became famous with *Oliver Twist* and *A Christmas Carol*. The find changes the belief that Dickens was only printed in the United States after he became famous.	Apr. 15
		The western states continue to experience a severe drought. . . . New England textile manufacturers decry the tax on the processing of cotton.		Former New York Yankee slugger Babe Ruth, now with the Boston Braves but expected to coach the team next year, plays his final opening game as a player. Some 50,000 spectators—including the governor of Massachusetts—are on hand.	Apr. 16

F	G	H	I	J
Includes elections, federal-state relations, civil rights and liberties, crime, the judiciary, education, healthcare, poverty, urban affairs, and population.	Includes formation and debate of U.S. foreign and defense policies, veterans affairs, and defense spending. (Relations with specific foreign countries are usually found under the region concerned.)	Includes business, labor, agriculture, taxation, transportation, consumer affairs, monetary and fiscal policy, natural resources, pollution, and accidents.	Includes worldwide scientific, medical, and technological developments, natural phenomena, U.S. weather, and natural disasters.	Includes the arts, religion, scholarship, communications media, sports, entertainment, fashions, fads, and social life.

	World Affairs	Europe	Africa & The Middle East	The Americas	Asia & The Pacific
Apr. 17		Following the recommendation from the recent Stresa Conference, the League of Nations condemns Germany for its aggressive policies. The League states that Germany has "failed in the duty which lies on all the members of the international community" to live up to its obligation of peace.			
Apr. 18			Italy's campaign in Ethiopia has cost $31 million to date.		
Apr. 19		In polls in the Netherlands, the Nazi party wins only 264,000 votes out of 3,320,000—not even 8 percent. . . . Father Doberstein of East Prussia is taken into custody for criticizing Joseph Goebbels, Nazi propaganda minister.		Argentineans are angry over a proposed import tax and, according to the newspaper *La Prensa*, they plan to demonstrate.	American clergy, travelers, and newspapermen caught in Chengtu, the Szechwan provincial capital and center of the west Chinese missions, are rescued by plane and brought to Shanghai as news of an attacking Communist army brings panic.
Apr. 20		Germans celebrate Adolf Hitler's 46th birthday.			
Apr. 21	Albert Einstein urges Americans not to support organizations whose activities prevent amiable relationships between the Jews and Arabs in Palestine.	Of all the countries of the world pushing to return to their former economic status—including the United States—Britain leads with 80 percent of its prosperity restored, announces Chancellor of the Exchequer Neville Chamberlain.			According to Dr. Lo Chia-lun, chancellor of National Central University in Nanking, China has increased the number of grade school pupils from 2.8 million in 1912 to a current 11.7 million. He points to better schools, better teachers, and an improved educational system. . . . The Viceroy of India, Lord Willingdon, ends his rule. The press speculates on his successor.
Apr. 22	Attendees of the Congress of the International Alliance of Women for Suffrage and Equal Citizenship—including U.S. representative Josephine Schain—discuss the role of today's female in maintaining peace around the world.	In Dublin, Irish President Eamon de Valera celebrates the 19th anniversary of the Easter Uprising, when freedom fighters took over the city in an unsuccessful attempt at ousting Great Britain.		Nicaragua plans to modernize its commerce this year with the addition of two railroads that will carry both people and freight throughout the country. The construction deadline is the end of the year.	China's National Health Administration begins a new program to sustain the health of its citizens across the country. Under the direction of Dr. J. Heng Liu, appointed health workers will begin monitoring the health of residents in rural hamlets. . . . Earthquakes hit both the island of Formosa and Iran simultaneously. The quake in Iran kills 600, while in Formosa 3,000 die, 11,000 are injured, and 20,000 houses are destroyed. Scientists say the tremors are related.
Apr. 23				Mexican bandits shoot two people during a bank robbery; they steal 250,000 pesos.	To thwart any trespassing by Japanese in Manchukuo, a huge Russian force assembles along the border of Siberia. The army is comprised of 200,000 men, 600 airplanes, and 600 tanks. The threat of invasion has been growing since relations between the two countries were broken off.
Apr. 24		Russia refuses to let one of its nuclear scientists, Prof. Peter Kapitza, return to England to finish a research project that he had begun with the Royal Society of Mond Laboratory, Cambridge. Britain's Lord Rutherford pleads for his participation, but Russia refuses. . . . Poland adopts a new, more authoritarian constitution, reducing the power of the Sejm, the legislative body.			

A	B	C	D	E
Includes developments that affect more than one world region, international organizations, and important meetings of world leaders.	Includes all domestic and regional developments in Europe, including the Soviet Union.	Includes all domestic and regional developments in Africa and the Middle East.	Includes all domestic and regional developments in Latin America, the Caribbean, and Canada.	Includes all domestic and regional developments in Asian and Pacific nations (and colonies).

U.S. Politics & Social Issues	U.S. Foreign Policy & Defense	Economics & Great Depression	Science, Technology & Nature	Culture, Leisure & Lifestyle	
		General Electric reports a profit increase over 1934—$5.4 million net for the first quarter, over $4.6 million for the same quarter last year.		*Mississippi*, a musical starring Joan Bennett and Bing Crosby, opens in theaters this weekend. . . . Russian aviation pioneer Igor Sikorsky tells the Motion Picture Association that he predicts, in the near future, flying "boats" that will carry 100 passengers across the Atlantic in 24 hours.	Apr. 17
The Republican Party begins to plan a campaign strategy for 1936 with a series of conferences in Washington, D.C.		Daily oil consumption in the United States for the week of April 8–15 was 2.6 million barrels, up slightly from the previous week. According to the Petroleum Institute, Oklahoma leads in oil production.	Admiral Richard Byrd's plane returns to Washington, D.C., after his second Antarctic expedition. On hand to meet him are a number of delegates, including President Franklin Roosevelt.	Helene Mayer of Los Angeles takes first place at the U.S. Fencing Nationals, sponsored by the Fencers' Club in New York City. . . . When cornered by prosecutors during his trial for racketeering, Dutch Schultz admits he is the holder of a $1.6 million bank account.	Apr. 18
		"A vast majority" of U.S. trade and industry members are hoping for an extension of the NRA wage and hour commitments, says Donald R. Richberg, chairman of the National Industrial Recovery Board. . . . Alf Landon, Republican governor of Kansas, calls the most recent bout of dust storms in his state an "appalling catastrophe." He questions why the Roosevelt administration is not moving quicker to provide aid.		An entourage of professional Japanese golfers begins a tour of U.S. golf courses, starting with those on the West Coast.	Apr. 19
		President Roosevelt orders an investigation into disputes between textile producers in the south and New England.	In an American Philosophical Society experiment, certain hormones are used to tame the natural desire to kill in wild rats; after injection, the rats are filmed mothering young pigeons. . . . Amelia Earhart attempts to be the first woman to fly from California to Mexico City, nonstop—some 1,800 miles. She leaves San Francisco at 9:55 p.m.	About 500,000 runners participate in the 38th Boston Marathon; 27-year-old Johnny Kelley from Massachusetts wins the race, just ahead of the expected winner, Pat Dingle of Maryland.	Apr. 20
The Illinois Senators investigate charges of Communist teachings in certain Chicago-area schools. The scandal has grown to such an extent that Charles R. Walgreen, the drugstore magnate, pulls his niece, Lucille Norton, from the University of Chicago.			Celebrating the 300th anniversary of chemistry in the United States, some 10,000 chemists and industrialists gather in New York for several days of meetings hosted by the American Chemical Society. John Winthrop, Jr., first colonial governor of Connecticut, founded the association in 1635.	The Chamber of Commerce of Chattanooga, Tenn., announces it will host this year's National Folk Festival, which will demonstrate authentic mountain music from Tennessee and throughout the American south. Auditions for singers, musicians, and dancers are being held.	Apr. 21
The vice president of the Southern Tenant Farmer's Union, E.B. McKinney, arrives in Chicago a day late for a conference of the Socialist Party. He says he was kidnapped by—but escaped from—a group of vigilantes in his home state of Tennessee.		Despite the harmful effects of dust storms on the wheatfields of the midwestern United States, a spring crop ample enough to meet the needs of the country is predicted.		A pageant and carnival in San Antonio, Tex., kicks off today in remembrance of the battle of the Alamo and the subsequent routing of Santa Anna's forces by Sam Houston at San Jacinto, 99 years ago this month.	Apr. 22
	Tin and other strategic materials should not be traded to other countries, states the House Foreign Affairs subcommittee, which spent the last 12 months investigating international use of aluminum, tins, and other metals by foreign nations. The United States faces a handicap, says the committee, if caught short of these supplies.			Actress Mae West, whose motto has been "I never met a man I wanted to marry," faces a minor scandal. A reporter has uncovered that in 1928 she did indeed marry a man named Frank Wallace, who died two years ago.	Apr. 23
	The U.S. War Department selects 52,000 troops to take part in Army maneuvers on the East Coast in August. . . . A new bill is presented in the House asking legislators to approve $458,000 for refurbishment of the Navy.	General Foods Corporation experienced a first quarter slightly lower than that of 1934—a net profit of $3.4 million, as compared to $3.7 million—but shareholders consider the trend normal in light of the economy. . . . Decline in world trading is the smallest of any year since the Depression began in 1929, according to the League of Nations.	Father Julius A. Nieuwland, professor of organic chemistry at Notre Dame University in South Bend, Ind., is acknowledged by the American Chemical Society for his advancements in the field of synthetic rubber. . . . President Roosevelt greets members of the National Academy of Sciences in Washington, D.C., applauding their outstanding contributions over many years.		Apr. 24

F	G	H	I	J
Includes elections, federal-state relations, civil rights and liberties, crime, the judiciary, education, healthcare, poverty, urban affairs, and population.	*Includes formation and debate of U.S. foreign and defense policies, veterans affairs, and defense spending. (Relations with specific foreign countries are usually found under the region concerned.)*	*Includes business, labor, agriculture, taxation, transportation, consumer affairs, monetary and fiscal policy, natural resources, pollution, and accidents.*	*Includes worldwide scientific, medical, and technological developments, natural phenomena, U.S. weather, and natural disasters.*	*Includes the arts, religion, scholarship, communications media, sports, entertainment, fashions, fads, and social life.*

	World Affairs	Europe	Africa & The Middle East	The Americas	Asia & The Pacific
Apr. 25		The Nazi party decides to place the Nazi logo—the swastika—above the German national emblem on the nation's flag.		A Central Bank of Argentina is proposed by 50 Argentine bank representatives, who also name a board of directors. This financial institution would be located in Buenos Aires. . . . Republicans and Democrats agree to petition the Federal Communications Commission to strip a Mexico City radio station of its license for running programs with sexually suggestive dialogue.	Japan and Australia consider a trade pact.
Apr. 26					
Apr. 27		Saying that he has "revealed himself" in the form of Man, the Germanic Pagan Faith Movement calls German Chancellor Adolf Hitler a "god."		Nearly 20,000 Mexican laborers are hard at work constructing a modern thoroughfare through dry brush country below the Rio Grande River to Mexico City, says Department of National Highways chief, José Gonzales. Another 8,000 Americans build the road north of the river to Laredo, Tex. . . . Victor Humphrey, a Nassau Island youth accused of murdering a German swimming pool manager, is exonerated.	
Apr. 28		Cardinal Pacelli, the Pope's Secretary of State in Rome, warns Nazis in the town of Lourdes, France, to cease in their racial bigotry, which is "contrary to the Christian faith." Lourdes is the town where the Blessed Virgin appeared to young Bernadette Soubirous in 1858. . . . Adolf Hitler promises to reward his people for their loyalty by increasing wages for "just" work.	Lord Hyde, the 29-year-old son of the governor of South Africa, the Earl of Clarendon, is accidentally shot by a fellow member of his hunting party.	Secretary of State Cordell Hull sends six delegates to take part in the upcoming Pan-American Trading Conference in Buenos Aires. The meeting is expected to lay the groundwork for future trade relationships between South and North America. . . . The Canadian government says it foresees the rise of socialism in the world—and in Canada.	
Apr. 29		Jews and other "enemies of the people" living in Germany will never again be considered German citizens, proclaims Germany's Minister of the Interior Wilhelm Frick. . . . Yugoslavia's Consul General Radoye Yankovitch denies he is running a dictatorship—even though 50 of his opposition candidates for the upcoming May 5 elections have been arrested and thrown in prison.			
Apr. 30					Japanese Emperor Hirohito turns 34.
May 1		German Air Minister Hermann Goering boasts to a roomful of national correspondents that Germany's air power is second to none, although he does not give any figures.		In Havana, the four opposition parties of Cuba agree to hold a general election in November under a modified, more conservative type of government in an effort to end the disputes among the factions.	Japan considers ending trade with the British-Canadian Ottawa Pact in protest against heavy import restrictions until rules are modified. . . . India announces improvements in its agriculture sector as a $200-million rural development program goes into effect. Roughly 80 percent of India's population makes its living from agriculture.

A	B	C	D	E
Includes developments that affect more than one world region, international organizations, and important meetings of world leaders.	Includes all domestic and regional developments in Europe, including the Soviet Union.	Includes all domestic and regional developments in Africa and the Middle East.	Includes all domestic and regional developments in Latin America, the Caribbean, and Canada.	Includes all domestic and regional developments in Asian and Pacific nations (and colonies).

U.S. Politics & Social Issues	U.S. Foreign Policy & Defense	Economics & Great Depression	Science, Technology & Nature	Culture, Leisure & Lifestyle	
Dr. John W. Studebaker, commissioner for the U.S. Education Department, proposes 10,000 open forums to take place around the nation over the next decade, forums that will give educators, lawmakers, sociologists, scientists, and bankers the opportunity to discuss current issues—be they economic, social, or political. Forums would be held under the auspices of the separate states' education departments.		With the signing of the Relief Bill, President Roosevelt promotes the strengthening of the Civilian Conservation Corps, which employs men to build forest trails, construct roadbeds, clean swamps, and perform many other tasks that will enhance the U.S. landscape.		A U.S. mail truck in Warren, Ohio, is robbed by a trio of bandits who steal not only the truck, but also the $72,000 that was inside. Local and federal law enforcement agencies promise quick recovery of the money.	Apr. 25
		A plan to extend the National Recovery Act for 10 months—giving the Senate time to review and revise the Act—is given to President Roosevelt by the Senate Finance Committee Chairman, who formally presents the proposal to the White House.		With almost 700 consumers ill with food poisoning after snacking on éclairs and cream puffs from a White Plains, N.Y., bakery, authorities trace the eggs used to make the pastries back to a Missouri provider and a Chicago freighter. If negligent handling is proven, a federal indictment may be forthcoming. . . . The National Federation of Music Clubs asks President Roosevelt to enact legislation that would "make America first in the Arts."	Apr. 26
The American agricultural program under President Roosevelt is a disaster with all of its midwest farmlands mortgaged for survival, according to Louisiana Governor Huey Long, stumping for the Democratic Party in Des Moines, Iowa. He says the $262 billion debt will never be paid.		The government begins taking applications from people wanting to enroll in one of several relief work programs, now that the Relief Bill has been made law. . . . President Roosevelt signs into law the Soil Conservation Act, making the Soil Conservation Services a permanent part of the Department of Agriculture.			Apr. 27
During a radio speech, President Roosevelt assumes personal responsibility for every dollar spent of the $4.9-billion relief fund. . . . Greek archaeologist Apostoloe Arvanitopolous claims that the ancient statue of athlete Diadoumenos now on view at the Metropolitan Museum of Art in New York was not a gift of the Italian government, as the United States believes, but was illegally smuggled out of Athens.		March 1935 exports fall below those of the prior year by $6 million. The Department of Commerce investigates the reason. . . . The New Deal is helping relocate 45,000 people from Missouri's Ozark Mountains to more fertile areas.	While floods ravage the Yellow River region, affecting the lives of 10,000 people, famine strikes the basin of the Yangtze River. No adequate form of relief is in sight, the Chinese national government admits.	Shirley Temple gains fame in Berlin; her film Baby Takes a Bow has been dubbed for German audiences.	Apr. 28
		The national director of the Emergency Relief Bureau says that one of the economically hardest-hit sectors in New York City is the African-American district of Harlem. The government needs to direct relief to this area, says relief boss Oswald W. Knauth.	The American Telephone & Telegraph Company celebrates its 50th Anniversary, having been founded in 1885 after the invention of the phone by Alexander Graham Bell. . . . An Army balloon ascends a record 26,000 feet for four hours over the little town of Boos, Ill., in a military test to observe substratospheric phenomena.	Philadelphia hosts the American College of Physicians' annual meeting, bringing 5,000 physicians from throughout North America.	Apr. 29
	The United States should avoid taking part in any war, says the Parent-Teachers' Association (PTA) guest speaker, Representative Lee of Oklahoma, at the annual meeting in Miami.			RKO Radio Pictures announces it has bought the screen rights to Sean O'Casey's play The Plough and the Stars. The movie will be directed by John Ford and will star Barbara Stanwyck and Barry Fitzgerald.	Apr. 30
At its congress in Miami, the National Congress of Parents and Teachers hears Chicago PTA director Joseph Armtan suggest closer cooperation between social agencies to improve character education for the young. . . . President Roosevelt complains to the Congress about its slowness in advancing any of his New Deal measures since the start of the year.	Suggesting that subversives are at work in the United States, Aldermanic President Bernard Deutsch calls for militant action against "those who would destroy American tradition and ideals."	Percival E. Foerderer, chairman of the Tanners Council of America, urges shoe companies and associated enterprises to campaign for more shoe sales. One more pair for every person in America would bring a gain of 35 percent to the tanning industry. . . . The Resettlement Administration is established in the Agriculture Department, under the direction of Undersecretary Rexford G. Tugwell.			May 1

F	G	H	I	J
Includes elections, federal-state relations, civil rights and liberties, crime, the judiciary, education, healthcare, poverty, urban affairs, and population.	Includes formation and debate of U.S. foreign and defense policies, veterans affairs, and defense spending. (Relations with specific foreign countries are usually found under the region concerned.)	Includes business, labor, agriculture, taxation, transportation, consumer affairs, monetary and fiscal policy, natural resources, pollution, and accidents.	Includes worldwide scientific, medical, and technological developments, natural phenomena, U.S. weather, and natural disasters.	Includes the arts, religion, scholarship, communications media, sports, entertainment, fashions, fads, and social life.

	World Affairs	Europe	Africa & The Middle East	The Americas	Asia & The Pacific
May 2		A blizzard dumps 20 inches of snow across Poland. It is one of the worst snowstorms in recent history in the region. . . . The French and Russians negotiate a five-year alliance pledging to come to the aid of the other in the event of an unprovoked attack; the agreement is seen as a response to the German announcement of rearmament.		Cuban police have arrested six Spaniards who, they say, are architects of terrorist plots in and around Cuba, including the burning of the ship *Morro Castle*.	Pan-American Airlines puts a construction crew on Wake Island in the Pacific Ocean to create a landing strip for its island-to-island air service.
May 3	An international penal court is not approved by the League of Nations because of Italy's rejection of the idea. Italy does not think the League should be used as a body of punishment.	A Russian-speaking woman named Anastasia Tschaikowsky files papers in New York claiming she is actually the daughter of the late Czar Nikolai Romanov, the deposed monarch of Russia, and is therefore eligible for a share of his estate.			Japanese officials in Formosa detain three men—one of them a former American naval officer—for spying. The men's defense is that they are three adventurers who sailed into Formosa for holidays.
May 4		The percentage of Italians that disapprove of war against Ethiopia has declined, thanks to what experts say is a well-organized Italian propaganda machine. . . . Berlin and Poland swap captured spies; one of them is Poland's George Sosnowski, whom the Nazi secret police call "one of the most dangerous spies in Europe."			Japan's Foreign Office announces that its country will establish a worldwide news agency to avoid dependency on non-Japanese sources. . . . Japan seeks to buy from Brazil a larger supply of cotton than what they are already purchasing, in effect cutting into the percentage of cotton now being sold to America. The Japanese envoy and Brazil's ministers meet today in Rio de Janeiro.
May 5		London prepares for the 25th anniversary of the coronation of George V. A total of 14,000 troops and 12,000 constables will line the procession route from St. Paul's Cathedral to Buckingham Palace.		Panama passes legislation that limits the number of foreigners running retail businesses and that limits foreign residents.	
May 6		King George V celebrates his Jubilee today, having ascended to the British throne in 1910.			
May 7	Rudyard Kipling, known for his works *Gunga Din* and *Captains Courageous*, denounces the "religion of war" across the sphere. He reminds his London radio audience that they should beware of Germany, which is "well-planned" for war.	The British press improves its transmittal time of news items to America's city desks by installing telegraphic typewriters in American pressrooms, operated remotely by Associated Press staff in London.			
May 8			Italy and Ethiopia temporarily cease hostilities to discuss a possible resolution to their border dispute.		In Manila, government authorities have arrested 500 Sakdalista rebels who have been fighting around the Philippines for many months.
May 9		It is now a treasonous offense to slander any member of the Nazi party or a Nazi institution, states Dr. Fran Guertner, German Minister of Justice. . . . Premier Alejandro Lerroux of Spain announces that his country has reworked its agenda to concentrate on the most pressing topics affecting not only Spain, but the world—unemployment, national defense, and agricultural reform.			Vermont Senator Ernest Gibson warns the United States not to be too hasty in giving the Philippines too much independence. He claims that once the Americans pull out, Japan will move in. Currently, the Philippines are a commonwealth with their own president, Manuel Quezon y Molina.
May 10				Secretary of State Cordell Hull convinces Bolivia and Paraguay to begin peace talks concerning the Chaco dispute.	Tokyo learns that the Russians are building a naval base in Siberia's Possiet Bay, near Japanese territory.

A	B	C	D	E
Includes developments that affect more than one world region, international organizations, and important meetings of world leaders.	*Includes all domestic and regional developments in Europe, including the Soviet Union.*	*Includes all domestic and regional developments in Africa and the Middle East.*	*Includes all domestic and regional developments in Latin America, the Caribbean, and Canada.*	*Includes all domestic and regional developments in Asian and Pacific nations (and colonies).*

U.S. Politics & Social Issues	U.S. Foreign Policy & Defense	Economics & Great Depression	Science, Technology & Nature	Culture, Leisure & Lifestyle	
Republicans from six states convene in Boston to set campaign strategies for the 1936 presidential campaign. This is the first of five such conferences slated for this year.		Shell Oil Corporation releases its latest financial figures. While it lost $1 million in 1934, it was a great improvement over the $5.3 million lost in 1933.	Scientists have discovered that mothers' natural milk contains certain chemicals that protect the child's body from disease. Among these diseases, according to the American College of Physicians, are infantile paralysis, scarlet fever, and diphtheria.	Award-winning playwright Noel Coward makes his acting debut in Paramount's *The Scoundrel*, released today.	May 2
Campaigning intensifies as the presidential election nears. Republicans dissect President Roosevelt's New Deal policy to show where it is heading America in the wrong direction.	The U.S. Navy conducts maneuvers in the South Pacific.	The National Industry Recovery Board and the Newspaper Code announce that a basic minimum wage is established for reporters, editors, and other essential jobs in newspaper publishing.	Tornadoes strike Arkansas, Kentucky, Mississippi, Tennessee, and Texas, killing 16 people and injuring 100. Many homes are ruined and many areas are without electricity.	Fifty-eight drivers enroll for a 500-mile race to be called the "Indianapolis Classic," scheduled for May 30. The 33 fastest cars will start.	May 3
		Former budget director Lewis Douglas, who resigned in September, blasts the present administration's federal spending in front of the Banker's Club meeting in New York. Such government intervention, he says, spoils a free-flowing capitalistic system.	The State of Arizona wins its fight against Colorado over the issue of a dam—the Colorado River-Parker Dam—when the Supreme Court agrees that such a major work cannot be built without the approval of both states. . . . Albert Einstein, who stated the theory of quantum mechanics, now says that even though the theory is correct, it is not complete.	The thoroughbred Omaha wins the 61st Kentucky Derby in Louisville. The favorite, Roman Soldier, comes in second.	May 4
According to a government report, the number of workers in unions is 6.7 million. A report from the Twentieth Century Fund states that "union organization in the United States has penetrated…every industry and geographic area…"			Harvard University's president James Bryant Conant explains that the school is implementing a new Doctorate of Philosophy degree designed specifically for teachers in the fields of history of science and learning.		May 5
	Governor Alfred E. Smith of New York calls upon all Americans in a radio address to help support the United Jewish Appeal against Hitler.	President Roosevelt selects Harry Hopkins to serve as administrator of the Works Progress Administration.		Members of the Women's International League for Peace and Freedom vote to participate in an anti-war movement across the world; specifics are not yet established, but the purpose is to make the world aware of the uselessness of war.	May 6
			Television will get its first field test when the Radio Corporation of America installs a working set outside the laboratory for monitoring, at a cost of $1 million.		May 7
President Roosevelt signs an executive order to create three new relief divisions: (1) Division of Applications and Information (to handle relief work program enrollment), (2) Advisory Committee on Allotments (to dole out relief work), and (3) the Works Progress Administration (to monitor progress).		The Radio Corporation of America shows a gain in the first quarter of 1935; profit is $1.6 million.	Influenza has broken out in Alaska. One doctor, H.W. Greist, and two nurses who are battling the disease at Point Barrow ask American medics for help in stopping the disease from spreading.		May 8
In a letter to the convention of the National Committee for Religion and Welfare Recovery, President Roosevelt reminds attendees that "if permanent economic prosperity is given safeguards, the business, social and religious life of our people must be coordinated."			Amelia Earhart sets a record by flying from the airport at Mexico City to Newark, N.J., in 14 hours and 18 minutes.	Bank robber, kidnapper, and gunman Ray Hamilton, who had previously escaped from prison, is hanged in Texas. Hamilton was once a member of the Bonnie and Clyde gang.	May 9
				St. Bernard, the thoroughbred that many thought would win this year's Kentucky Derby, wins instead the Perryville Purse today at Churchill Downs. . . . The American Law Institute decides to write a new set of laws for the administration of criminal justice, "more nearly suited to modern social and economic conditions."	May 10

F	G	H	I	J
Includes elections, federal-state relations, civil rights and liberties, crime, the judiciary, education, healthcare, poverty, urban affairs, and population.	*Includes formation and debate of U.S. foreign and defense policies, veterans affairs, and defense spending. (Relations with specific foreign countries are usually found under the region concerned.)*	*Includes business, labor, agriculture, taxation, transportation, consumer affairs, monetary and fiscal policy, natural resources, pollution, and accidents.*	*Includes worldwide scientific, medical, and technological developments, natural phenomena, U.S. weather, and natural disasters.*	*Includes the arts, religion, scholarship, communications media, sports, entertainment, fashions, fads, and social life.*

	World Affairs	Europe	Africa & The Middle East	The Americas	Asia & The Pacific
May 11		Danish newspapers report that German military forces are moving into the northern Schleswig region on the Baltic Sea.			
May 12		Germany announces plans to raise 1 billion marks for export promotion. Economic Director Hjalmar Schacht states that this will "mobilize (our) industry…on a scale hitherto unprecedented."	If a portion of South African mines return to Germany, which claims it owns them, the Germans would be in a position to monopolize the country's gold reserves, according to Sir Abe Bailey, a mine owner testifying in London.		
May 13		Adolf Hitler promises to respond to the League of Nations after receiving word of their latest censure of his rearmament. He says he will explain his actions, but at the same time reaffirm his commitment to Germany first.			Siam denies any association with the Japanese government, although members of the League of Nations have noticed some trade activity.
May 14			F.G. Carnochan, an ethnologist and explorer who has just returned to America from Africa after 15 years of research, describes to magazines the strange customs he encountered, particularly of one tribe with a rare form of "sleeping sickness."		Voters ratify the new Philippine constitution which provides for commonwealth status and local rule by Filipinos.
May 15		King Christian of Denmark ribboncuts his country's new $8-million technological wonder, the Little Belt Bridge, which connects the island of Fuenen with Jutland.			Japan offers to buy the Portuguese-held city of Macao in southern China.
May 16		The Soviet Union and Czechoslovakia sign a Mutual Assistance Pact. . . . German Nazis parade through Berlin. During the event, Jews are thrown from their shops in the middle of the workday.		In Lima, Peru, Dr. Antonio Quesada, managing editor of the newspaper *Comercio*, and his wife are slain by a 21-year-old student dissident.	
May 17		The Graphia Publishing Company in Carlsbad, Czechoslovakia, is raided by secret police after it is learned that it is printing copies of a humor book, *Deutsche Flusterwitze (German Whispered Jokes)*, ridiculing the Third Reich.			Educator and diplomat Jacob Gold Schurman tells the International Association of Torch Clubs, in Utica, N.Y., "The Asiatic policy of Japan is a menace to the world (that) challenges other nations."
May 18		Citizens of Stockholm, Sweden, do not turn out to greet visiting Nazi Reichsdeputie Rudolf Hess. The Berlin press claims the turnout was very large.			

A	B	C	D	E
Includes developments that affect more than one world region, international organizations, and important meetings of world leaders.	Includes all domestic and regional developments in Europe, including the Soviet Union.	Includes all domestic and regional developments in Africa and the Middle East.	Includes all domestic and regional developments in Latin America, the Caribbean, and Canada.	Includes all domestic and regional developments in Asian and Pacific nations (and colonies).

U.S. Politics & Social Issues	U.S. Foreign Policy & Defense	Economics & Great Depression	Science, Technology & Nature	Culture, Leisure & Lifestyle	
A federally funded National Crime Institute is being developed, as well as a central radio station for broadcasting police news, in an effort to curb crime in all states. The institute will teach law authorities and policemen the newest technology for stopping various crimes and apprehending criminals.		By executive order, President Roosevelt establishes the Rural Electrification Administration to finance cooperatives to distribute electric power.	Antarctic explorer Richard Byrd speaks to the National Geographic Society. He describes his adventures and findings, including how an echo-sensitive machine he used revealed ice floes of 1.5 miles in thickness.		May 11
Will Rogers congratulates King George V of England on his Jubilee and suggests that "maybe we could make some arrangements" to talk about reuniting after the "big split" of 1776.			New theories are being produced about cosmic rays, the latest coming from Drs. W. Baade and F. Zwicky of the California Institute of Technology. These rays, they say, were emitted from stars that exploded. . . . Vitamin A is good for adults, too, not just children, asserts the American Chemical Society. In fact, a diet of Grade A milk, fresh fruits, and vegetables is more important for an adult than for a child.	The art magazine American Mercury is ordered by Supreme Court Justice Jeremiah T. Mahoney to rehire three people it laid off illegally for striking; Section 7A of the National Industrial Recovery Act and the Graphic Arts Code sanction their strike.	May 12
	Two Navy men are killed during maneuvers off Hawaii, near Pearl Harbor. One is killed in a plane crash, and the other is killed during a collision of two warships. Altogether 40 ships participated in the maneuvers that resulted in the injury of five other men.	A review of the Veterans' Bureau shows that it pays $68 million yearly for salaries for 27,000 employees. . . . Almost 4,000 men begin a strike at the New York Shipbuilding Company, demanding a 15 percent wage increase and improved working conditions. The strike halts construction of seven naval vessels and an oil tanker.		Millionaire Alfred I. DuPont dies, leaving as principal heirs to his fortune the crippled and aged of the United States. The financier leaves his estate in Wilmington, Del., as well as $1 million to establish a special fund. . . . The U.S. tennis team sweeps the Chinese team in the Davis Cup semifinals.	May 13
		Federal and state revenues for liquor sales and liquor licenses in 1934 amounted to $490.6 million, states Dr. James M. Moran, administrator of the Distilled Spirits Institute and National Distillers Products Corporation.	The ancient city of Lachish, once believed to have been mythical, may have existed, according to archaeologist Sir Charles Marston, who found scrolls at Tell Duweir, 25 miles south of Jerusalem, that refer to a town by that name.	Col. Thomas E. Lawrence—once the famous "Lawrence of Arabia"—lies dying in a hospital in Dorset, England, after he crashes his motorcycle trying to avoid hitting a child.	May 14
				The gangster drama G-Men opens in theatres across America. It stars James Cagney and Robert Armstrong.	May 15
Lawyers, bankers, and public officials from across the country comprising the National Municipal League are formulating a better way to collect real estate taxes, a problem that some parts of the country find complex and time consuming.		The Industry and Business Committee for NRA Extension is demanding "an improved, enforceable and efficiently administered NRA" to replace the 10-month "test" extension now being considered by Congress. . . . Farmers from 34 states and Puerto Rico gather in Washington, D.C., to adopt a resolution demanding continuation of the Agricultural Adjustment Act.		College athletes at the University of Wisconsin upset by the presence of three liberal leaders there to convene the League for Industrial Democracy committee toss the trio into Lake Mundota. . . . A group of governmental officials, broadcasters, educators, and radio station authorities convene to discuss on-air free speech with the Federal Communications Commission.	May 16
Eleanor Roosevelt opens a meeting at the White House focused on the curbing of crime in the United States. The result is the creation of a social education program to "mobilize" community forces against criminal elements in small towns and cities.		The Advisory Committee on Allotments, part of President Roosevelt's recently passed Relief Bill, begins amassing thousands of applications and approving projects to get the unemployed on payrolls. . . . President Roosevelt signs a seven-point program for a two-year extension of the National Recovery Act.	Dr. Stephen J. Maher, associated with the Connecticut Tuberculosis Commission, claims he has discovered a cure for certain types of asthma. Oral applications of avian tubercle bacillus have worked on several people suffering from the disease where "all kinds of injections" have not helped before. . . . A clock made for Pharaoh Tutankhamen, whose tomb was discovered in 1922, is described by Prof. James Breasted of the University of Chicago. The clock is from 1300 B.C.E.	The Boy Scouts of America National Convention in Chicago receives a personal letter from President Roosevelt that praises a "splendid record of achievement." . . . Artist Michael Califona, who has produced a series of anti-Nazi paintings, is beaten while his pictures are slashed in his New York City studio. The assailants are unknown.	May 17
		Howard Heinz, president of Heinz Ketchup and a political activist, predicts an end to the NRA. The NRA, he says, strays too far from the fundamentals of American commerce.		Gangster Dutch Schultz's lawyers—J. Richard Davis and Terence J. McManus—argue to keep his personal bank accounts out of court during his trial for racketeering. . . . Jesse Owens, a young sprinter from Ohio State University, makes headlines at the Quadrangle Meet at Northwestern's Dyche Stadium, Evanston, Ill. Owens breaks three world records and matches a fourth.	May 18

F	G	H	I	J
Includes elections, federal-state relations, civil rights and liberties, crime, the judiciary, education, healthcare, poverty, urban affairs, and population.	Includes formation and debate of U.S. foreign and defense policies, veterans affairs, and defense spending. (Relations with specific foreign countries are usually found under the region concerned.)	Includes business, labor, agriculture, taxation, transportation, consumer affairs, monetary and fiscal policy, natural resources, pollution, and accidents.	Includes worldwide scientific, medical, and technological developments, natural phenomena, U.S. weather, and natural disasters.	Includes the arts, religion, scholarship, communications media, sports, entertainment, fashions, fads, and social life.

	World Affairs	Europe	Africa & The Middle East	The Americas	Asia & The Pacific
May 19	Evangeline Cory Booth, daughter of the founder of the Salvation Army, is on a world tour to spread the word of her organization's goodwill. In San Pedro, Calif., she tells a large audience that the youth of today are needed more than ever to make a positive difference in the world.	A Jewish social/business club in Hamburg, Germany, makes a mistake by calling itself a "citizens' club." The club is quickly closed by the police.			No trace remains of Father Bush, a Catholic priest who disappeared suddenly from Kaiping, China. Two hundred soldiers have been searching the Kwantung province without result. Father Bush was the rector at a nearby Maryknoll mission.
May 20		The first leg of a proposed 4,000-mile road through Germany opens. Adolf Hitler, accompanied by officials, drives in an open car between the initial destinations of Frankfurt and Darmstadt. . . . The Nazi Party places first in general elections in the German parts of Czechoslovakia. While the Sudeten Party expected good results, they did not expect to take more votes than any other party; the party becomes the second largest in the nation.			
May 21			Ethiopian King Haile Selassie begs the League of Nations for assistance as Italian Premier Benito Mussolini refuses to cease hostilities in their border dispute. The League promises involvement.		
May 22		In Wuertemberg, Germany, civil employees are instructed to remove their children from Catholic and Protestant schools and to keep them out of any religious organizations. Instead, they are told to enroll them into the Nazi youth groups.	Despite the League of Nations pleas, Italian Premier Benito Mussolini prepares to invade Ethiopia. Talks between the Italian emissary Baron Pompeo Aloisi, Britain's Anthony Eden, and France's Rene Massigli produce no results.	President Getulio Vargas of Brazil visits Buenos Aires to confer with Argentine President Agustin P. Justo over matters of relationship and materials trading between the countries.	
May 23					
May 24					
May 25					
May 26		France announces it is increasing the size of its armed forces. It is lowering the draft age from 21 to 20. Because of the growing tensions in Europe, the French parliament will almost certainly approve these measures.			President Quezon y Molina of the Philippines ratifies the new constitution, giving the country the power to govern itself under U.S. auspices. Quezon promises a good relationship between the Philippines and the United States.
May 27					Japan does not approve of the recent U.S. naval maneuvers in the Pacific. It expresses its displeasure in a pamphlet, released in Tokyo, calling this a "dangerous sign."

A	B	C	D	E
Includes developments that affect more than one world region, international organizations, and important meetings of world leaders.	Includes all domestic and regional developments in Europe, including the Soviet Union.	Includes all domestic and regional developments in Africa and the Middle East.	Includes all domestic and regional developments in Latin America, the Caribbean, and Canada.	Includes all domestic and regional developments in Asian and Pacific nations (and colonies).

U.S. Politics & Social Issues	U.S. Foreign Policy & Defense	Economics & Great Depression	Science, Technology & Nature	Culture, Leisure & Lifestyle	
		In a poll of 228 newspapers in 30 states—representing a circulation of nearly 3 million people—editors come out evenly divided on President Roosevelt's New Deal. Some 114 newspapers oppose it; 70 support it; 44 approve in part.	The U.S. government proposes to bring electricity to America's rural areas, many still using lantern light and coal. A federal committee will study the plan, which has been given a $100 million budget. . . . Refrigerator sales have increased 70 percent while prices have declined nearly 10 percent, reports the National Electrical Manufacturers Association.	Actress Grace Moore is awarded a fellowship of the Society of Arts and Sciences for "conspicuous achievement in raising the standard of cinema entertainment." This award has also been awarded to Thomas Alva Edison and John Philip Sousa.	May 19
Kiwanis Clubs in San Antonio, Tex., hear Gen. John F. O'Ryan say that the American public needs to have more interest and involvement in governmental affairs to end political corruption, a growing problem in the United States.			The Board of Education's James Marshall claims that sound film, which came to the public six years ago, is one of the greatest tools of education, if used correctly. Movies could be produced to teach students everything from the alphabet to politics to chemistry.		May 20
			A burial cave is discovered in Mizpah, Palestine. Prof. William Bade says it is identical to the one described in the interment of Sarah by Abraham in the Old Testament.	According to the General Motors president of research, Charles F. Kettering, science and scientists in the United States are as much as 25 years behind the times.	May 21
	The House of Representatives votes 322–98 to override President Roosevelt's veto of the Patman Bonus Bill which would immediately pay the bonus to World War veterans, not scheduled until 1945.				May 22
	The Senate sustains President Roosevelt's veto of the Patman Bonus Bill.	Economic recovery is on the way, despite a number of problems still facing business, claims Dr. Neil Carothers, director of the College of Business Administration of Lehigh University, speaking at the National Association of Purchasing Agents' 20th anniversary meeting in New York City.		The first major league baseball evening game occurs tonight when President Roosevelt throws the switch from the White House to light Crosley Field, home of the Philadelphia Phillies, 600 miles away. Under the illumination, the Phillies take on the Boston Braves. . . . The chairman of the Federal Alcohol Control Administration, Frank Choate, urges lawmakers to enforce liquor codes to prevent abuses of liquor, fearing such abuses will rise in the United States.	May 23
The American electoral and judicial systems require an overhaul, according to the American Academy of Political and Social Science, which calls the systems "antiquated." What the country needs, it says, is a more attentive procedure allowing voters to better control who is elected to run the government.				Plans have been presented to the Legitimate Theatre Code Authority to create a "national theatre organization" whose goals would be to aid productions with federal funding, revive traveling groups, and relieve unemployment in the industry. Heading the project is Frank Gilmore, president of the Actors Theatre Guild. . . . *The Girl From 10th Avenue*, a comedy from Warner Bros. First National starring Bette Davis and Ian Hunter, appears in theaters today.	May 24
Vice President John Nance Garner officially announces he will run again in 1936. . . . The German language professor at New Jersey College for Women, Dr. Friederich Johannes Hauptman, is caught writing letters to Germany's Propaganda Minister Joseph Goebbels, requesting literature to send "all over the United States."	W. Starling Burgess, who has designed yachts for America's Cup races, is turning his attention to defense: the design of a speedboat to be used by the U.S. Navy as a submarine chaser.			Pope Pius XI denounces Germany's purported experiments with sterilization.	May 25
There will be no third party in this election campaign, as the Milwaukee Progressive Party bows out of the race. Its leaders decide to build a stronger presence across the country before tackling the established political parties. They plan to field candidates in 1940.		A group of 1,500 nonunion miners in Picher, Okla., destroy a union headquarters. The National Guard is summoned by Governor Marland to prevent further violence.			May 26
	The general assembly of the Presbyterian front, based in Cincinnati, Ohio, urges the denomination to fight liquor, child labor, and the menace of war. The boards of Christian Education and the National Missions are supporting the call.	The Supreme Court rules that the National Recovery Act is unconstitutional.		Amelia Earhart receives an honorary Doctor of Public Service degree from Georgia University in Atlanta.	May 27

F	G	H	I	J
Includes elections, federal-state relations, civil rights and liberties, crime, the judiciary, education, healthcare, poverty, urban affairs, and population.	*Includes formation and debate of U.S. foreign and defense policies, veterans affairs, and defense spending. (Relations with specific foreign countries are usually found under the region concerned.)*	*Includes business, labor, agriculture, taxation, transportation, consumer affairs, monetary and fiscal policy, natural resources, pollution, and accidents.*	*Includes worldwide scientific, medical, and technological developments, natural phenomena, U.S. weather, and natural disasters.*	*Includes the arts, religion, scholarship, communications media, sports, entertainment, fashions, fads, and social life.*

	World Affairs	Europe	Africa & The Middle East	The Americas	Asia & The Pacific
May 28		Hungarian Premier Julius Goemboes suggests that parliament consider conscription and the expansion of the country's air forces.		Two people are killed in election violence in Colombia. The Liberal Party wins 105 of the 118 seats in the Lower House.	
May 29					Vice Admiral Sadakichi Takahashi of the Japanese Imperial Fleet holds a ceremony honoring Admiral Heihachiro Togo's defeat of Russian forces in 1906.
May 30					Japan claims to have been insulted by China. Japan threatens to march on the Peiping-Tientsin area with a huge force.
May 31		Rumors circulate that despite Adolf Hitler's claims, Germany is experiencing an economic depression. Wages are at their lowest and production is down.			Chinese Ambassador Chang Tso-pin visits Japanese Foreign Minister Koki Hirota to report that two of Japan's demands will be met—the ousting of an aggressive anti-Japanese governor and the disbanding of all anti-Japanese groups. . . . More than 20,000 people die in an earthquake that strikes India's Baluchistan Valley.
Jun. 1	The Jews are not a race, emphasizes Dr. Cyrus Adler, who presides over the Jewish Theological Seminary of America. In addressing commencement exercises, he says it is each Jew's commitment to explain to the rest of the world that being Jewish means practicing one's faith, not one's politics.	Great Britain insists on parity in an air agreement, which may result through its talks with Nazi Germany, according to Lord Privy Seal Anthony Eden. . . . Crime has dropped 50 percent in Germany due to the work of its secret police agency that sends habitual criminals off to "training camps."			Victor Hoo, Chinese delegate to the League of Nations Opium Advisory Committee, says that 263 persons were executed in his country for illicit manufacturing or selling of narcotics. Many sellers were also transporters of the substances.
Jun. 2		The Borsig Locomotive Works in Berlin sends its latest product—a locomotive capable of reaching 109 miles per hour—to Germany's National Railroad Company. . . . Observers report that Russia continues to face economic hardships—low wages but a high cost of living.		Gabriel Terra, president of Uruguay, is wounded in an assassination attempt while entertaining the president of Brazil at a local racetrack.	
Jun. 3		Croats boycott the Yugoslav parliament.	Italy and Ethiopia skirmish in the Eritrea and Somaliland border regions.		
Jun. 4		The highest court in Germany rules that the intelligence constabulary of the Third Reich must answer to no one except the military high command and Adolf Hitler.			Leaving the Philippines to their own government might be a serious mistake, warns Judge John W. Haussermann, president of the Benquet Consolidated Mining Company. He fears that Japan wants to claim the islands' mineral wealth.
Jun. 5		Editors of certain German magazines and newspapers who defended members of the Catholic Church recently accused of smuggling money out of Germany have their publishing licenses revoked.	Britain accuses Italy of imperialism in Ethiopia.		
Jun. 6			More Italian troops are dispatched for Ethiopia.		

A	B	C	D	E
Includes developments that affect more than one world region, international organizations, and important meetings of world leaders.	Includes all domestic and regional developments in Europe, including the Soviet Union.	Includes all domestic and regional developments in Africa and the Middle East.	Includes all domestic and regional developments in Latin America, the Caribbean, and Canada.	Includes all domestic and regional developments in Asian and Pacific nations (and colonies).

U.S. Politics & Social Issues	U.S. Foreign Policy & Defense	Economics & Great Depression	Science, Technology & Nature	Culture, Leisure & Lifestyle	
President Roosevelt signs a $1.75 billion home loan bill.		Talks between the clothing industry sector and its garment unions yield no results. Workers are warned to expect a strike if the situation is not resolved.		The National Broadcasting Corporation's Merlin Aylesworth submits to the advisory board recommendations regarding realigned priorities of free speech and the elimination of propaganda on the airwaves.	May 28
	An Army bomber carrying two aviators and a pair of cameramen crashes in Sequoia National Park in California. All aboard are killed.	Railroads have an opportunity to compete with other modes of transportation—and win, claims J.J. Pelley, president of American Railroads. Now that the economy is improving, the rail lines have more power than ever to help bring the economy of travel back to prosperity.	The science of colored film has come such a far way that movie producers say it will be used more and more over the next several years in major motion pictures. The Technicolor process has made it possible for Hollywood to produce color films at a lower cost.		May 29
			Torrential rains cause flooding in the Rocky Mountains, near Colorado Springs, where three people are drowned, seven are reported missing, and major roads are washed away.... Double-engine airplanes are recommended for safety by aircraft industrialist Donald Douglas, who tells the Royal Aeronautical Society in London that the planes are also easier to maneuver and overall are more reliable.	President Roosevelt applauds San Diego's World's Fair—the California Pacific International Exposition. Its theme, he says, underscores "the courage and confidence (of) our future."	May 30
				Twentieth Century Fox announces it plans to release 164 feature films and 110 short subjects during the 1935-36 season.... In New York, an overzealous opera singer, in what is supposed to be a choreographed fight scene in *Cavalleria Rusticana*, bites a fellow performer's cheek, drawing so much blood that a doctor is summoned.	May 31
American industrialist Owen D. Young tells a Purdue University audience of bankers and businessmen that modern housing is the newest industry through which to revive employment.		Eighty-seven percent of the farmers polled in U.S. wheat-producing areas want to see a continuation of the U.S. agricultural adjustment administration program for the commodity.	Twenty-two people are dead after flooding across Colorado, Nebraska, and Wyoming. The waters of the Missouri River, already swollen, are expected to rise even higher.... The maiden voyage of the French liner *Normandie* experiences mechanical troubles that delay the trip by a half day.	Lieutenant Governor William Bray of New York commutes to life imprisonment the death sentence of Frank Kiekart, one of seven bank robbers who shot two men in a hold up in 1924. Kiekart was to be executed next week.	Jun. 1
William Green, president of the American Federation of Labor, sees the Supreme Court's recent anti-NRA ruling as a blow to economic advancement and social justice. He calls for a special meeting of AFL chiefs to propose a plan of action against potential wage cuts.		Mary Hughes, former head of an NRA-associated group, calls for women to patronize merchants who have voluntarily chosen to continue those NRA codes—pricing options—adopted by the Roosevelt administration before the Supreme Court's decision to ban all such future codes last month.	About 250 are reported dead as tornados and flooding strike Nebraska.	Some 350 U.S. teachers will study at the University of Moscow as part of the Anglo-American division, says Dr. George S. Counts, Columbia University's professor of education.	Jun. 2
			Godfrey Cabot, vice president of the Fédération Aéronautique Internationale, offers a $10,000 prize for a device to overcome poor visibility due to fog while flying.	Babe Ruth quits after only three months with the Baltimore Braves; rumors claim a disagreement with management. In 20 years as a regular player, he has set 76 baseball records.	Jun. 3
District Attorney William C. Dodge and lawyer Harold H. Corbin say they will investigate and collect evidence against wrongdoers involved in the growing problem of racketeering in New York City.		President Roosevelt takes steps to move forward after the Supreme Court's declaration that the NRA is unconstitutional. A series of conferences results in the agreement that the NRA may be redesigned. A "stop-gap" program resumes the plan for another nine months—stripped of the powers that the Supreme Court disallowed—giving the administration time to create a suitable replacement.			Jun. 4
Officials of the American Newspaper Guild vote for an industrial union for newspapers. It will be an inclusive union open to different groups, they say, covering business and promotion employees, editors, and clerical and circulation staff.		Although the NRA was ruled unconstitutional, many industries support the wage and hour standards set under its authority, according to a national survey.			Jun. 5
New York Senator Royal S. Copeland, who is also a physician, tells the American Institute of Homeopathy that science and medicine have done very little in the last half century in the way of treating diseases known to affect the middle-aged.					Jun. 6

F	G	H	I	J
Includes elections, federal-state relations, civil rights and liberties, crime, the judiciary, education, healthcare, poverty, urban affairs, and population.	Includes formation and debate of U.S. foreign and defense policies, veterans affairs, and defense spending. (Relations with specific foreign countries are usually found under the region concerned.)	Includes business, labor, agriculture, taxation, transportation, consumer affairs, monetary and fiscal policy, natural resources, pollution, and accidents.	Includes worldwide scientific, medical, and technological developments, natural phenomena, U.S. weather, and natural disasters.	Includes the arts, religion, scholarship, communications media, sports, entertainment, fashions, fads, and social life.

	World Affairs	Europe	Africa & The Middle East	The Americas	Asia & The Pacific
Jun. 7		German Air Minister Hermann Goering is believed to be trying to set up an anti-Soviet bloc in Europe, but Yugoslavia reportedly refuses to participate on the grounds that the Nazi regime is not stable.		Argentina officially opens the Central Bank in Buenos Aires. . . . Former governor Theodore Roosevelt, Jr., begins a goodwill tour in Puerto Rico.	The Chinese remove another government official who has offended Japan, Manchurian general and current governor of Hopei province Yu Hsueh-chung.
Jun. 8		British sociologists, economists, and social scientists studying the present crises in Europe predict a long and arduous struggle ahead for those countries involved. They foresee a decade of unrest, of political upheaval, and economic indecision.		In Mexico, kidnappers release Antonio San Miguel, president of the Guantanamo & Western Railway, without collecting the $286,000 ransom they demanded.	
Jun. 9		The latest European country to join the race for aviation power is Switzerland, which announces plans to promote intercontinental transport service and sports flying.		With a new Laredo-to-Mexico City highway in place, an American tourist boom is in the making. Observers tell of an ongoing stream of motorists all along the 750-plus miles.	It is announced that Japanese forces have amassed north of the Great Wall, perhaps preparing for an invasion of China. . . . Military representatives from China and Japan meet in Peiping. The Chinese agree to withdraw troops from five northern provinces.
Jun. 10					An old airbase on Guam is being repaired for new Pan-American commercial service.
Jun. 11	U.S. Secretary of State Cordell Hull urges peace as a world policy. He tells the graduating class of the Pennsylvania Military College in Chester, Pa., that "a vicious circle of great and even greater armaments…can only lead to impoverishment and economic suicide."			Havana papers report that rebellion ends today in Cuba after many months with the reinstatement of the Constitution of 1901, which allows for both general election and the female vote.	
Jun. 12				A ceasefire is announced between Bolivia and Paraguay. They have fought over the Chaco region for three years, with an estimated 100,000 lives lost; a peace conference is planned to convene in July in Buenos Aires.	
Jun. 13		The Westphalian and Anhalt Explosive Works in Reinsdorf, Germany, explodes. An estimated 52 people are dead.			Peace talks in Peiping between ambassadors of China and Japan fail; the Chinese refuse to accept Japanese demands because, they say, the demands diminish China to nothing but a "Japanese protectorate."
Jun. 14					

A	B	C	D	E
Includes developments that affect more than one world region, international organizations, and important meetings of world leaders.	Includes all domestic and regional developments in Europe, including the Soviet Union.	Includes all domestic and regional developments in Africa and the Middle East.	Includes all domestic and regional developments in Latin America, the Caribbean, and Canada.	Includes all domestic and regional developments in Asian and Pacific nations (and colonies).

U.S. Politics & Social Issues	U.S. Foreign Policy & Defense	Economics & Great Depression	Science, Technology & Nature	Culture, Leisure & Lifestyle	
		The "stop-gap" NRA is rushed through the House today and passed on a vote of 264–121. President Roosevelt aims to revive the $4.9 billion program.	Doctors attending today's meeting of the American Society of Clinical Pathologists learn that liver extract has been discovered as a remedy for agranulocytosis, a disease that destroys blood cells. Until now, such extract was known only as a preventative of pernicious anemia.	Jesse Owens breaks another world record for speed at Milwaukee's Central Intercollegiate Conference track and field championship.	Jun. 7
Graduates of New York University hear activist Dr. Emanuel D. Friedman stress the importance of guarding the spirit of tolerance and liberty in America.		A federal survey indicates a gain of 12 percent in farm output over last year, according to the Bureau of Agriculture.	To combat crime effectively, U.S. authorities need to look closer at scientific techniques ignored in America, according to Sanford Bates, director of prisons for the Department of Justice.	Actor John Barrymore sails his yacht back from Havana to Hollywood, where reporters inquire about his divorce from actress Dolores Costello. Barrymore admits he has offered her a settlement of property as well as $75,000 in cash.	Jun. 8
West Point Chaplain Roscoe T. Foust reminds graduating cadets to "keep open minds" in a "frightening world," in which doors of opportunity are closing where they should be kept open for hope and prosperity.				American Telephone & Telegraph has created a special cable that it claims will effectively link television studios to transmitters for long-term reception. The cable—and television technology itself—will be tested outside the lab at Radio City Music Hall. . . . John Barrymore accuses Dolores Costello of once keeping him "captive" on his own yacht so he would not meet with other women.	Jun. 9
	Illinois Senator J. Hamilton Lewis suggests that the United States serve as the mediator between arguing countries overseas. By playing arbiter, he believes that the United States might be the peacekeeper of the world.				Jun. 10
The National Dress Manufacturers Association announces that it has formed agencies and committees "necessary to insure complete observance of established business standards."		Good harvests are predicted for 1935. By all indications, the grain- and wheat-producing states are showing improvement over 1934.			Jun. 11
Several governors express their disapproval of President Roosevelt's tendency to increase the power of the federal government while depriving individual states of certain powers. Leading the outcry is Governor Paul V. McNutt of Indiana. . . . Some 11 million homes across the United States have been classified "slum class" by a Public Works Administration report. The number constitutes a national emergency, but the only real solution to the problem, says the report, would be corrective programs in which both federal and state authorities cooperate.		The number of industries choosing to keep the old NRA rules of wage and pricing continues to grow. The latest industries to make the choice are the luggage and leather goods manufacturers, the leather garment industry, and manufacturers of shoe laces.	An exhibit at the American and Canadian Health Convention reveals the discovery of a "black light" used under exploratory conditions that allows surgeons to locate heart disease undetectable by previous means.	Warner Bros. First National and Cosmopolitan Pictures announce they will make 60 feature films this year—among them *Anthony Adverse*, *The Charge of the Light Brigade*, and *The Story of Louis Pasteur*.	Jun. 12
Louisiana Senator Huey Long carries a filibuster in Congress throughout the night to make sure his complaints against the Roosevelt administration's "skeletonized" version of the National Recovery Act are heard. . . . An African-American theater employee charges the Motion Pictures Union with discrimination. Granville Dick asks for an investigation to show how all jobs are going to whites.			*Becky Sharp*, the world's first mainstream movie shot in Technicolor, opens at Radio City Music Hall, but the response is not all positive. One viewer comments that the screen resembles, "boiled salmon dipped in mayonnaise." . . . Pilot Eddie Rickenbacker retraces the flight Charles Hamilton made from New York to Philadelphia 25 years ago. Hamilton did it in one day; Rickenbacker does it in one hour.	On the heels of competitor Warner Bros. announcement yesterday, Paramount reports that it will shoot 65 movies in 1935. These include *Peter Ibbetson* and Cecil B. DeMille's *The Crusades*.	Jun. 13
The House votes 336–31 to renew the National Recovery Act in a new version, bare of the industrial code provisions that the Supreme Court found objectionable.		The Firestone Tire and Rubber Company and its subsidiaries end six months with an increase in profit, up 40 cents a share from six cents last year. . . . Bankrupt, the Postal Telegraph and Cable Company requests the right to reorganize. Under its current structure, it was unable to meet its obligation of $1.3 million due July 1.	Thirteen people are dead, many missing, and an estimated $1 million of crops destroyed after a flood hits central Texas.	Awareness of Jewish issues and Jewish education have recently progressed in the United States, according to statistics presented today at the opening of the annual meeting of the combination National Association of Jewish Center Executives and National Council for Jewish Education.	Jun. 14

F	G	H	I	J
Includes elections, federal-state relations, civil rights and liberties, crime, the judiciary, education, healthcare, poverty, urban affairs, and population.	*Includes formation and debate of U.S. foreign and defense policies, veterans affairs, and defense spending. (Relations with specific foreign countries are usually found under the region concerned.)*	*Includes business, labor, agriculture, taxation, transportation, consumer affairs, monetary and fiscal policy, natural resources, pollution, and accidents.*	*Includes worldwide scientific, medical, and technological developments, natural phenomena, U.S. weather, and natural disasters.*	*Includes the arts, religion, scholarship, communications media, sports, entertainment, fashions, fads, and social life.*

	World Affairs	Europe	Africa & The Middle East	The Americas	Asia & The Pacific
Jun. 15				Mexican President Lázaro Cárdenas's Cabinet resigns suddenly.	
Jun. 16					Japanese forces hold training exercises in the streets of Tientsin, China. Japan explains it as a "defense drill." . . . The Russian press theorizes that Japan, as it moves through northern China, is actually contemplating a new empire through Inner China and Mongolia.
Jun. 17			Explorer Mary L. Jobe Akeley sets sail on the *Berengeria* for South Africa to conduct ethnological studies of the Zulu.	In the Mexican elections, President Lázaro Cárdenas wins over Plutarco Elias Calles. Calles announces he is leaving public life while Cárdenas appoints a new Cabinet to replace the one that recently resigned. . . . Fifteen hundred Catholics stage a demonstration for religious liberty in Mexico City while 4,000 Rotarians are in town for a convention.	A school in Tokyo is training young girls—all daughters of either active or retired officers—to be "soldiers' brides." A class of 247 girls opens the school's first session.
Jun. 18		Berlin and London agree on a naval treaty; Germany is allowed to build a navy of a size approximate to that of Britain. The French call the agreement a disastrous move.			
Jun. 19		Germany pauses in its workday to remember the 60 workers killed in the Reinsdorf ammunition plant explosion last week.			British Foreign Secretary Sir Samuel Hoare, in dialogue with the House of Commons, says that Britain is keeping in close contact with the United States regarding the tensions between China and Japan.
Jun. 20			Ethiopia requests that the League of Nations send an official observer to the frontier region to see for itself that Italy—and not Ethiopia—is the aggressive party in the ongoing conflict on the Somaliland border.		Many Chinese begin to flee the Chahar province, which is being threatened by Japanese forces. . . . Japanese stock markets have stalled. Economists announce that they are uncertain what is causing the troubles.
Jun. 21		Britain invites the Soviet government to open talks on naval armaments.			
Jun. 22		The French airplane *Southern Cross* leaves Cherbourg, France, for Konarky, Africa, in an attempt to break the nonstop distance record. Aboard the *Southern Cross* is a crew of six men and 3,170 gallons of fuel.			
Jun. 23				International trade organizations are claiming that Germany is cheating Latin American countries. They are seeking to investigate and prosecute all perpetrators.	
Jun. 24				Colombia states that it will no longer purchase goods from Japan, unless Japan reciprocates. . . . Latin American movie star Carlos Gardel, pilot Ernesto Samper, and 15 passengers die when their plane collides with another at Olaya Herrera airport, 200 miles northwest of Bogotá.	Kanju Kato, chairman of the General Council of Trade Unions of Japan, asks the military leaders to proceed with caution in China in order not to anger other countries.

A	B	C	D	E
Includes developments that affect more than one world region, international organizations, and important meetings of world leaders.	Includes all domestic and regional developments in Europe, including the Soviet Union.	Includes all domestic and regional developments in Africa and the Middle East.	Includes all domestic and regional developments in Latin America, the Caribbean, and Canada.	Includes all domestic and regional developments in Asian and Pacific nations (and colonies).

U.S. Politics & Social Issues	U.S. Foreign Policy & Defense	Economics & Great Depression	Science, Technology & Nature	Culture, Leisure & Lifestyle	
President Roosevelt fires Assistant Secretary of Commerce Ewing J. Mitchell and replaces him with John Monroe Johnson. Mitchell and the President had argued over decisions in the Commerce Bureau.		Secretary of the Interior Harold Ickes reports that employment in America has been given to about 4 million people under the Public Works Administration program. . . . The state militia is summoned after the streetcar workers' strike in Omaha, Nebr., turns violent. The governor establishes martial law.		The U.S. government announces that 26 original paintings by members of the Civilian Conservation Corps have been selected to hang in the White House.	Jun. 15
Dr. Tracy F. Tyler of the National Committee on Education by Radio tells the Detroit Federation of Women's Clubs that it is essential for their children's upbringing to be careful in selecting what they may listen to on the radio.		Striking streetcar employees are ordered by Nebraska Governor R.L. Cochran to cease their disturbances. . . . The manpower of the Civilian Conservation Corps is growing from 353,000 people to about 600,000.	Russian biologist Peter Lasareff of the Soviet Academy of Science believes that, with the proper care, humans could live to be 150 years old. He has succeeded in prolonging the lives of certain freshwater crustaceans by four times the normal through use of Roentgen rays.		Jun. 16
Yale graduates hear the university's president describe the brutality that is rampant in Russia; he warns students making their way in the world against the onslaught of spreading fascism and Communism.		According to Elinore Herrick of the executive board, during its 19 months of operation, the NRA Regional Labor Board has settled 557 strikes and prevented another 210. The strikes have involved nearly 176,000 people.		Golfer Johnny Revolta wins the Western Open championship in South Bend, Ind.	Jun. 17
	Political science professor Philips Bradley of Amherst College, testifying before the House Committee on Foreign Affairs, states that the United States needs to enact a hard policy of neutrality before it is swept into another war.	Arbitrators are called in to settle the streetcar strike between the Omaha & Council Bluffs Street Railway Company and its union employees.			Jun. 18
		The Roosevelt administration solicits opinions and suggestions from business and industry as to what steps are necessary to provide an NRA-like program that would remain within the limitation set by the Supreme Court.		The film Nell Gwynn, starring Sir Cedric Hardwicke and Anna Neagle, opens in theaters. The film had encountered difficulty passing through censors because of its adult themes. . . . Executives of RKO Radio Pictures, meeting in Chicago, announce they will produce 48 feature films during the 1935–36 season.	Jun. 19
		The House of Representatives passes the Wagner-Connery Labor Dispute Bill, which reinstates Section 7a of the NRA, which the Supreme Court had earlier invalidated. The bill establishes a National Labor Relations Board to handle disputes and to guarantee the right of workers to organize.		The Summit Hotel Company of Uniontown, Pa., is suing singer and entertainer Al Jolson after the inn claims he poked fun at it on a national radio show. The suit is for $100,000 in damages. . . . Actress Lily Damita marries actor Errol Flynn in a ceremony in Yuma, Ariz.	Jun. 20
Kansas is reevaluating its prison system. Last week's revolt in the state penitentiary in Lansing resulted in 348 convicts barricading themselves in a mine shaft for 48 hours.		President Roosevelt announces that federal projects begun under the Public Works Administration would be continued under the work relief program.	The Rockefeller Institute for Medical Research announces the creation of an "artificial heart" and "man-made" bloodstream, which now enable surgeons to keep vital organs functioning outside the body. The device is the creation of French scientist Alexis Carrel and American Charles Lindbergh.	The ruling committee of the Lutheran Synod in New York condemns divorce. At the same time, it banishes any activities such as bazaars, games of chance, dances or raffles, even for the purpose of raising church funds.	Jun. 21
The National Women's Party, meeting in Atlantic City, N.J., demands "equal rights with men." . . . The president of the International Association of Police Chiefs, Arthur J. Kavanaugh, proposes a plan for a crime and accident bureau that will "strike at the roots of crime."	General Motors president Alfred P. Sloan, Jr., sends a letter and check for $1,000 as "sympathetic support" for the Women's International Organization's disarmament committee.	The Federal Reserve Board announces that national income has been greater this spring than at any other time since 1931.	A group of mountain climbers from the Sierra Club leave Oakland, Calif., headed for Canada where they plan to scale Mount Waddington. The mountain has never been scaled.		Jun. 22
The Northern Baptist Convention condemns scenes of alcohol use in motion pictures.		The Bureau of Labor Statistics reports an increase in new building construction and repairs through the month of May.	Dr. M.H. Nathanson devises a method for treating heart problems by temporarily stopping the heart. His theories and diagnoses are presented to a conference of scientists gathered in Minneapolis.		Jun. 23
	The Senate Munitions Committee recommends a bill to "prevent collusion in the making of contracts for the construction of naval vessels in private shipyards, and to safeguard military secrets."	Rioting breaks out in Tacoma, Wash., between 5,000 striking lumbermen and nonunion "scabs" entering the workplace. National Guardsmen move in to stop the violence.		Jack L. Warner, of Warner Bros., announces that he has hired playwright Marc Connelly to write a screenplay for his popular play The Green Pastures. . . . The National Knitted Outerwear Association warns retailers against fraudulently pricing garments. The Association has recorded many examples of misleading advertisements.	Jun. 24

F	G	H	I	J
Includes elections, federal-state relations, civil rights and liberties, crime, the judiciary, education, healthcare, poverty, urban affairs, and population.	Includes formation and debate of U.S. foreign and defense policies, veterans affairs, and defense spending. (Relations with specific foreign countries are usually found under the region concerned.)	Includes business, labor, agriculture, taxation, transportation, consumer affairs, monetary and fiscal policy, natural resources, pollution, and accidents.	Includes worldwide scientific, medical, and technological developments, natural phenomena, U.S. weather, and natural disasters.	Includes the arts, religion, scholarship, communications media, sports, entertainment, fashions, fads, and social life.

	World Affairs	Europe	Africa & The Middle East	The Americas	Asia & The Pacific
Jun. 25		Germany promises Great Britain to never again use its submarines against an unsuspecting nation. The case of the sinking of the *Lusitania*, for instance, where a private liner was torpedoed, will never be repeated. Many in the British House of Commons rejoice; others remain skeptical.			Japanese Finance Minister Korekiyo Takahashi argues that unnecessary expenses be cut in order to help build up the army and navy.
Jun. 26					
Jun. 27				Argentine exports to the United States doubled the first five months of this year over the same period last year.	
Jun. 28		Winston Churchill of England suggests a national defense loan to help rebuild Britain's navy. Supporting him is Sir Bolton Eyres-Monsell, First Lord of the Admiralty, who also believes that a large navy is key to Britain's defense.			
Jun. 29	According to League of Nations statistics, the global death rate declined in 1934.	Citing Germany's ill treatment of Jews as an "insane European antagonism," political activist Dr. Sidney Tedesche tells a conference of Rabbis in Chicago that "Israel is the phalanx against which the ranks of medievalism and hatred break."			Japan announces that it will deploy more soldiers to Manchukuo to guard the border. It claims the border is threatened by a 200,000-man Russian force that is assembled there.
Jun. 30				President Rafael L. Trujillo signs a bill issued by the Dominican Senate to allow political refugees to return to the Dominican Republic without harassment. This includes six recent evacuees, among them former president Rafael Estrella Urena. . . . Latin America, says Dr. Samuel Guy Inman from the High Commission of German Refugees, is becoming a haven for German refugees.	Severe flooding in the southwest of Japan kills 43 people. Eighteen people are missing and damage is estimated at 40 million yen.
Jul. 1		At the first gathering of Britain's new Council for Action for Peace and Reconstruction, both the Labor and Liberal parties express their concern for Italy's aggression in Ethiopia. . . . Under the Nazi regime, all women fall under the title of "hausfrau"—housewife—and are expected to tend a home and bear children for Germany.			
Jul. 2		In a Paris ceremony, France names Walter S. Adams of the Mount Wilson Observatory in California as a correspondent of the French Academy of Sciences. . . . Progressive British parliamentarian David Lloyd George attacks his country's rearmament plans, saying that he senses more war paranoia than he did in 1914.		Clifford Odets, author of the play *Waiting for Lefty*, and 15 others with Communist Party connections are detained in Havana. There to investigate the social and labor unrest, the Cuban government does not approve their visit.	
Jul. 3		In Germany, some 12,000 postal workers are fired from their jobs and replaced by Nazi party members.			A Japanese steamer, the *Midori Maru*, sinks with 104 passengers in Japan's Inland Sea after striking a freighter. There are 147 survivors rescued by emergency craft from the water.
Jul. 4		Milan Stoyadinovitch, the new Yugoslavian premier, promises to continue his predecessor's foreign policy of maintaining good relationships with neighbors in Europe.		All telegraph lines and wireless communications out of Buenos Aires go silent for a moment today in honor of the inventor of the telegraph, Samuel F.B. Morse. A statue in honor of him is dedicated at the central post office.	

A	B	C	D	E
Includes developments that affect more than one world region, international organizations, and important meetings of world leaders.	*Includes all domestic and regional developments in Europe, including the Soviet Union.*	*Includes all domestic and regional developments in Africa and the Middle East.*	*Includes all domestic and regional developments in Latin America, the Caribbean, and Canada.*	*Includes all domestic and regional developments in Asian and Pacific nations (and colonies).*

U.S. Politics & Social Issues	U.S. Foreign Policy & Defense	Economics & Great Depression	Science, Technology & Nature	Culture, Leisure & Lifestyle	
			Metropolitan Life Insurance vice president Dr. Louis I. Dublin predicts that tuberculosis will be completely eradicated by 1985.		Jun. 25
At a dinner honoring his services to the United Jewish Appeal, Albert Einstein promotes the building of Jewish settlements in Palestine.		The number of unemployed rose 9 percent in May to 9.7 million. . . . President Roosevelt directs $50 million to establish the National Youth Administration under the direction of Aubrey Williams.			Jun. 26
		After eight weeks of strike, 2,700 lumbermen and loggers in Seattle return to work. The National Guard is on watch to prevent violence.		A federal jury deems the Czechoslovakian film *Ecstasy* objectionable because of a brief nude scene. The film will not be shown in the United States.	Jun. 27
America's gangster movies are criticized by British film censor Edward Shortt at the Cinematography Association in Cardiff, Wales. Shortt points to them as a root of social problems in the United States.			Weather experts testify to the American Association for the Advancement of Science that they believe the dust storms that have been plaguing the West and Midwest do not originate on land, but rather in the Pacific Ocean.		Jun. 28
The Interstate Conference on Labor Compacts, meeting in New Jersey, adopts improved child labor and minimum wage laws for 16 states. The proposals must now be ratified by the individual state legislatures and approved by Congress.		President Roosevelt's intercessions are responsible for helping to avoid a strike by 400,000 employees against the United Mine Workers.		The Wagner-McLaughlin bill is passed, creating the American National Theatre and Academy.	Jun. 29
Former attorney general Thomas E. Dewey is selected by Governor Herbert Lehman of New York to serve as Special Prosecutor to investigate vice, rackets, and other crimes in New York County. . . . Rep. Thomas Amlie of Wisconsin asks the AFL to take the side of the Progressives in the Senate, who want to see the creation of a third political party.	Both Army and Navy recruiting stations announce that they will be open tomorrow all day for enlistment. They seek 60,000 new recruits each.	The fiscal year ends today with the government having spent a record $8.2 billion—most of it between January and June of this year.			Jun. 30
Republicans state that they would like the adjournment of Congress rescheduled for November 18, with a new session devoted to examining the long- and short-term effects of President Roosevelt's programs.		President Roosevelt signs an order temporarily continuing the work of the labor boards established under the NRA. . . . President Roosevelt directs $316.3 million for the employment of 169,000 people.	The federal government considers setting aside ancient ruins in Arizona for research by geologists, scientists, and archaeologists. . . . The Key brothers finally land their airplane in Meridian, Miss., after a month in the air. They have broken all endurance-flying records.	Columbia Pictures announces the production of 52 motion pictures for the 1935–36 season. . . . George Watson and Leverett G. Gross, former New Jersey bank officers, fight the U.S. Marshal's Office over the "indignity" of being fingerprinted after being accused of mail fraud.	Jul. 1
Willard E. Givens, secretary of the National Education Association, promises attendees at the Denver-area NEA convention that a bill is forthcoming in the Senate that focuses on enhancing children's scholastic opportunities. If passed, the federal government will pay at least a quarter of the nation's public school costs.		The Longshoremen's Association in Louisiana threatens to halt merchant shipping on Lake Charles if nonunion longshoremen are hired. . . . The AFL announces that the Brotherhood of Sleeping Car Porters finally has its own union, winning a decade-long fight against the Pullman Company for recognition.			Jul. 2
		Postmaster General James Farley endorses a 40-hour workweek for all postal workers; the plan must be approved by the Senate.		The Merchants National Bank of Dunkirk, N.Y., is robbed by men carrying machine guns; no one is injured, but the men escape with $21,000.	Jul. 3
John D.M. Hamilton, Republican National Committee member from Kansas, tells the Convention of Republican Women, "You can't win a war being nice." He urges the 1936 campaign be based on the same "vicious, dirty, low propaganda" that he accuses the Democrats of using. . . . The new prosecutor for New York City, Thomas E. Dewey, meets with Governor Herbert Lehman to explain the strategy of his all-out war on murder, racketeering, and all professional crime in the metropolis.				In Philadelphia, Dr. Dahlberg of the International Christian Endeavor Society promotes marriage "lessons" before matrimony. He believes premarriage counseling will slow the divorce rate in the nation.	Jul. 4

F	G	H	I	J
Includes elections, federal-state relations, civil rights and liberties, crime, the judiciary, education, healthcare, poverty, urban affairs, and population.	*Includes formation and debate of U.S. foreign and defense policies, veterans affairs, and defense spending. (Relations with specific foreign countries are usually found under the region concerned.)*	*Includes business, labor, agriculture, taxation, transportation, consumer affairs, monetary and fiscal policy, natural resources, pollution, and accidents.*	*Includes worldwide scientific, medical, and technological developments, natural phenomena, U.S. weather, and natural disasters.*	*Includes the arts, religion, scholarship, communications media, sports, entertainment, fashions, fads, and social life.*

	World Affairs	Europe	Africa & The Middle East	The Americas	Asia & The Pacific
Jul. 5			Ethiopia asks the United States to intervene in its conflict with Italy. The United States makes no firm commitment.		
Jul. 6		Britain announces that the number of people in its workforce is the highest it has been since the World War.	Italian Premier Benito Mussolini makes a surprise visit to Salerno to review troops before they depart for Ethiopia.		The Japanese and Soviets agree to form a commission to peacefully settle their Siberian-Manchurian border disputes. . . . China officially ratifies the Ho-Umezu Agreement in which they agree to withdraw troops from northeastern provinces.
Jul. 7		Reports from Europe indicate that the Catholic Church is experiencing increasing persecution by German authorities.	Ethiopia reminds the League of Nations that Italy signed the 1928 Kellogg-Briand Pact that denounced war. The League takes no action.		Japan announces that it has no interest in the Philippines beyond establishing trade ties.
Jul. 8					Chinese-born Pearl S. Buck, author of *A House Divided* and *The Good Earth*, notes similarities between Americans and the Chinese. Both are emotionally similar and, she writes, "(we) should understand each other because we are extraordinarily alike."
Jul. 9		The Bank for International Settlements warns Italy that a war with Ethiopia at this time could ruin it financially.			
Jul. 10		Polish President Ignaz Moscicki dissolves parliament in order to prepare for the new Sejm and Senate.			Japan announces that the Empress is expecting a child in November.
Jul. 11			U.S. Secretary of State Cordell Hull pushes peace talks for Italy and Ethiopia to the League of Nations. The League thanks Hull for his peacemaking efforts.		As Japan moves its army toward the Mongolian frontier, it is warned by Russia not to cross over into Russian-owned Mongolia.
Jul. 12				The latest figures from the U.S. Commerce Department indicate that, although the dollar value of U.S. exports rose in May, trade with South America declined at the same time. . . . Canada's new Reconstruction Party is launched today by its chairman, Harry M. Stevens.	
Jul. 13		When the Nazi party threatens his Jewish librettist, the president of the Reich Music Chamber Richard Strauss resigns his post in Berlin, according to a government announcement.			
Jul. 14		Germany's Sunday morning radio shows managed by Nazi spokesmen hint that Hitler is heaven's messenger.		Finding that the duties of law enforcement in Panama have been disregarded by the chief of police, President Harmodio Arias fires him and assumes personal charge of the nation's constabulary.	Japan announces that its exports have doubled and the unemployment rate is down to a half of one percent.
Jul. 15	The National Industrial Conference announces that global production increased in May.			Spruille Braden, the U.S. delegate to the Pan-American commercial conference in Buenos Aires, praises President Roosevelt's policy of good relations with South America. His remarks come during a conversation with local press about foreign policy.	
Jul. 16		Former Greek premier and current head of Greece's opposition party Alexander Papanastasiou arrives in America on the liner *Majestic*. He hopes to raise support from the 700,000 Greeks living in America.			

A	B	C	D	E
Includes developments that affect more than one world region, international organizations, and important meetings of world leaders.	Includes all domestic and regional developments in Europe, including the Soviet Union.	Includes all domestic and regional developments in Africa and the Middle East.	Includes all domestic and regional developments in Latin America, the Caribbean, and Canada.	Includes all domestic and regional developments in Asian and Pacific nations (and colonies).

U.S. Politics & Social Issues	U.S. Foreign Policy & Defense	Economics & Great Depression	Science, Technology & Nature	Culture, Leisure & Lifestyle	
		According to economists Dr. David I. Saposs and Col. Harvey Breckenridge, President Roosevelt's New Deal is a failure. They predict not only another depression, but also a war with Europe.		*Escapade*, a new release from MGM starring William Powell and Luise Rainer, opens in theaters.	Jul. 5
					Jul. 6
				Mary Pickford, actress during the silent era of the early 1920s, announces that she has been hired by United Artists to produce two films for the 1935–36 season.	Jul. 7
The 13th annual convention of the National Association of Broadcasters, opening today, will examine copyright laws and the barring of objectionable on-air programming.		Eighty-five banks have been liquidated since October 31, 1934, according to the Controller of Currency, J.F.T. O'Connor. The last 20 were liquidated in June. . . . The National Gypsum Company and the Universal Gypsum and Lime Company consider a possible merger.		America's top 15 swimmers and divers arrive in Tokyo to start training under Robert Kiphuth, Yale University's coach. The Japanese and Americans will soon have a three-day meet.	Jul. 8
Worried that African-American workers might join Communist unions, the AFL urges labor unions to represent black employees.		Food, coal, and clothing prices went down in June, balancing an increase in rents and sundries, according to the National Industrial Conference Board.		Pressed by prosecutor Thomas E. Dewey, New York detective divisions reorganize. The city, with the assistance of Mayor Fiorello LaGuardia, initiates a new investigative bureau.	Jul. 9
			Three hundred astronomers from 25 nations gather in Paris to participate in the International Astronomical Union.	Floods devastate parts of Chemung County, N.Y.	Jul. 10
				American nude dancer Joan Warner, performing in Paris, is slated to dance before a French court to prove that her act is not obscene, but "absolutely chaste."	Jul. 11
The President's eldest son, James Roosevelt, joins the board of the National Grain Yeast Corporation.		Joseph P. Ryan is elected the president of the Longshoremen's Union, based in New York. . . . Kentucky receives $15 million from the federal government's Agricultural Adjustment Administration to help farms in the state.	Capiapo, Chile, is struck by a series of earthquakes. Professional seismologists learn that a Greenwich Village mathematics teacher had predicted the tremors a week ago.		Jul. 12
Women do not, nor will they ever, have an interest in running for president of the United States, claims Celine MacDonald Brown, president of the National Federation of Business and Professional Women.	A new service command unit, managed by Maj. Gen. Hugh A. Drum of the U.S. Army's Hawaiian Department, has been established to coordinate military and civilian activities should Hawaii ever be blocked from the mainland by an enemy force.	The United States and Russia sign a trade agreement.			Jul. 13
For the benefit of the consumer and the reputation of the retailer, honest advertising is needed in this country, says Paul E. Murphy, chairman of sales promotion for the National Retail Dry Goods Association.	U.S. Secretary of State Cordell Hull meets with Italian Ambassador Augusto Russo concerning the situation in Ethiopia. He reminds Italy that it did sign the Kellogg-Briand peace pact of 1928.			Chicago announces that crime has fallen by 20 percent in the last six months.	Jul. 14
Fifteen thousand members of the National Federation of Business and Professional Women's Clubs arrive in Seattle for the organization's biennial celebration.		The Public Works Administration cannot legally claim land to build low-cost housing for the poor, proclaims the Sixth District U.S. Court of Appeals in Cincinnati. . . . Packard Motor Car Company President Alvan McCauley announces that his company earned a profit of about $1.4 million during the second quarter.		Fay Wray, star of *King Kong*, leaves on the luxury liner *Europa* for England. She has been cast in the starring role of a Gaumont-British comedy, *His Majesty's Pajamas*. . . . The state park at Niagara Falls celebrates its 50th anniversary, with New York Governor Herbert Lehman dedicating the newly completed Grand Island bridges.	Jul. 15
Women are beginning to take some of the very important jobs in this country, proving their ability in a man's world, say the speakers at the National Federation of Business and Professional Women's Club meeting in Seattle.	The House Military Committee petitions Congress to fund $440 million to strengthen the U.S. Army Air Corps.	The "Toledo Labor Plan"—the Department of Labor's program to adjudicate labor disputes—is attacked by William Green, president of the AFL, as "impractical."	A five-hour and 28-minute eclipse of the moon—the longest in history—is viewable to half the population of the world.	The New York Yankees' manager Joe McCarthy signs for another two years under club owner Col. Jacob Ruppert for a salary of $35,000. . . . Warner Bros. releases *Alibi Ike* today, based on author Ring Lardner's popular baseball story.	Jul. 16

F	G	H	I	J
Includes elections, federal-state relations, civil rights and liberties, crime, the judiciary, education, healthcare, poverty, urban affairs, and population.	Includes formation and debate of U.S. foreign and defense policies, veterans affairs, and defense spending. (Relations with specific foreign countries are usually found under the region concerned.)	Includes business, labor, agriculture, taxation, transportation, consumer affairs, monetary and fiscal policy, natural resources, pollution, and accidents.	Includes worldwide scientific, medical, and technological developments, natural phenomena, U.S. weather, and natural disasters.	Includes the arts, religion, scholarship, communications media, sports, entertainment, fashions, fads, and social life.

	World Affairs	Europe	Africa & The Middle East	The Americas	Asia & The Pacific
Jul. 17		Italy seeks financial aid to fund its war against Ethiopia, states Luigi Criscuolo, investment banker. . . . Ignoring criticism, Nazis continue to promote their sterilization program, designed to create a select race of humans, while reducing "inferior" types.		James G. McDonald, who is overseeing the housing of refugees from Germany, announces that the effort has found funding of $10 million.	W. Cameron Forbes, chairman of the Chinese-American Economic Mission to the United States, believes that there is a great relationship and financial potential in a trade agreement with China.
Jul. 18			The National Peace Conference pushes the Roosevelt administration to help mediate the escalating Italian-Ethiopian conflict.		Japan claims it has a right to invade China, citing the 1933 Tangku Truce, which it claims allows Japan to "establish not only civil aviation in China, but also several other enterprises such as radio, telegraphs (and) railroads."
Jul. 19		Germany selects Count Wolf von Helldorf as its Police President of Berlin. . . . One thousand Parisian demonstrators picket outside the Place de l'Opera against French Premier Pierre Laval's national pay cuts, which are designed to ease economic burdens. Police say the crowd remains peaceful.			Ambassador Yotaro Sugimura of Japan informs Italian Premier Benito Mussolini that Japan will not interfere in the Italo-Ethiopian war.
Jul. 20			Haile Selassie of Ethiopia demands to know why the League of Nations has not done more on his country's behalf in face of Italian aggression.	Argentina announces that it intends to curb outgoing news by putting foreign news agencies and correspondents under a heavy cash bond. National editorials denounce the government's latest attempts at censorship.	Japan levies a 50 percent tax on Canadian imports. Canada calls the tax a violation of the 1913 Anglo-Japanese trade treaty, which outlawed such legislation.
Jul. 21				The new highway from Laredo, Tex., to Mexico City has increased the number of tourists to Mexico coming from the United States.	
Jul. 22		Russia attempts a flight from Moscow to San Francisco via the North Pole. Russia considers regular air service on the "polar route," if all goes well.			Soldiers representing the "Progressive" faction—including officers—are removed from the Japanese armed forces.
Jul. 23					
Jul. 24		Foreign correspondents tell of abuse by the Nazi government; the German press tries to suppress all negative articles, i.e., religious prejudices, "atrocity stories," and economic downtrends.		Cuba's National Renovation Party decrees that any revolutionary will be excluded from the upcoming general elections.	
Jul. 25		The number of female workers in Germany falls from 37.2 to 31.9 percent, according to the German Labor Office. For some time, the Nazi party has sought to reduce the number of women in the workforce.	Italian Premier Benito Mussolini wires Joseph Avenol, the League of Nations Secretary-General, to offer a contingency plan for Ethiopia after the League pleads once again for harmony.	In Argentina, two arguing politicians—Finance Minister Federico Pinedo and National Senator Leandro de la Torre—agree to a duel. Formalities aside, they both fire into the air.	Japan apologizes to the United States for an incident that occurred last week, when a Japanese gunboat accidentally opened fire on a missionary school at Yochow in the Hunan province. No one was injured.
Jul. 26	It is announced that the 1936 Olympic Games will be hosted in Berlin, Germany.			Chihuahua citizens assemble outside Mexico's National Revolutionary Party headquarters to protest Governor Rodrigo Quevedo's anti-agrarian administration.	
Jul. 27				A special body of experts representing the American Committee on the Rights of Religious Minorities plans a seminar to examine the interracial conditions and church-state animosities in Mexico. The first meeting is slated for Williamstown, Mass.	

A	B	C	D	E
Includes developments that affect more than one world region, international organizations, and important meetings of world leaders.	Includes all domestic and regional developments in Europe, including the Soviet Union.	Includes all domestic and regional developments in Africa and the Middle East.	Includes all domestic and regional developments in Latin America, the Caribbean, and Canada.	Includes all domestic and regional developments in Asian and Pacific nations (and colonies).

U.S. Politics & Social Issues	U.S. Foreign Policy & Defense	Economics & Great Depression	Science, Technology & Nature	Culture, Leisure & Lifestyle	
	The National Federation of Business and Professional Women denounces recent legislation approving increases in armaments.	The Tennessee Valley Authority, created by the Roosevelt administration to generate water/electric power in the state of Tennessee, is empowered by the federal Fifth Court of Appeals to sell in competition with private utilities all surplus power generated by its hydroelectric plants.	The Massachusetts Institute of Technology announces that is has developed spectroscopic methods to detect sulfur and selenium.		Jul. 17
		The National Biscuit Company announces a net profit of $2.4 million for the second quarter of 1934.		Mayor Edward J. Kelly of Chicago wants to initiate plans for a permanent fairground at Burnham Park, the site of the Chicago World's Fair of 1933. Neighborhood and religious groups protest.	Jul. 18
The U.S. government announces that Americans cannot enlist to fight for or against a foreign power while residing in the United States. Punishment is a fine of $1,000 and three years in prison.	The government has agreed to allocate more than $5 million toward the building of new U.S. Coast Guard patrol boats.	Randolph Bryant of the Federal District Court in Sherman, Tex., grants a restraining order against the collection of taxes levied on cotton gins. He calls the law "unconstitutional." . . . About 400 strikers and nonstrikers in Iowa clash at Sioux Falls' Morrell Packing Plant. The strikers seek higher wages.			Jul. 19
In New Haven, Conn., President Franklin Roosevelt meets with a group of disabled veterans, calling them a "living example of the sacrifices made by our citizens" in World War I. He pledges financial support for America's veterans.					Jul. 20
			In Ukraine, a young boy constructs a tiny motor that weighs less than one-sixteenth of an ounce. Scientists call the achievement a technological wonder.	The face of Theodore Roosevelt will be carved on Mount Rushmore in the Black Hills of South Dakota, says National Memorial Superintendent W.S. Tallman.	Jul. 21
The tax plan offered by the Roosevelt administration is deemed unfair by the National Industrial Conference Board, which says the plan does not just raise revenue but personally and socially attacks "bigness"—large conglomerates and major businesses.	The House Military Committee meets to agree on pressing President Roosevelt to commit $40 million toward the building of 800 new aircraft.				Jul. 22
				Memorial services are conducted at Grant's Tomb in New York City to remember the Civil War general who died 50 years ago today.	Jul. 23
Senator William H. King of Utah proposes a board to investigate Nazi persecution against Jews and Catholics, as a prelude to severing diplomatic ties with Germany.					Jul. 24
Arkansas Senator Joseph T. Robinson tells constituents in Forrest City that he has no use for Democrats who discredit President Roosevelt for no other reason except to "seize control of the government."			North Pole explorer Sir Hubert Wilkins is joining the National Geographic Society in South America for an expedition to the Antarctic. . . . Aviation experts converge on Akron, Ohio, for a two-day seminar on lighter-than-air flight.		Jul. 25
President Roosevelt offers 151 aliens in federal prisons their release on the condition that they accept deportation. . . . Mo Weinberg and Moe Margolese, associates of gangster Dutch Schultz, testify at his trial for racketeering but, as expected, reveal nothing substantial.			A national parkway is urged from the Blue Ridge Mountains of the southeast to Vermont's Green Mountains. The Senate says it will be a tribute to the country's scenery.		Jul. 26
		Congress prepares to introduce a new bill aimed at establishing labor standards for the textile industry. The bill, sponsored by Rep. Henry Ellenbogen of Pennsylvania, is backed by the United Textile Workers.			Jul. 27

F	G	H	I	J
Includes elections, federal-state relations, civil rights and liberties, crime, the judiciary, education, healthcare, poverty, urban affairs, and population.	*Includes formation and debate of U.S. foreign and defense policies, veterans affairs, and defense spending. (Relations with specific foreign countries are usually found under the region concerned.)*	*Includes business, labor, agriculture, taxation, transportation, consumer affairs, monetary and fiscal policy, natural resources, pollution, and accidents.*	*Includes worldwide scientific, medical, and technological developments, natural phenomena, U.S. weather, and natural disasters.*	*Includes the arts, religion, scholarship, communications media, sports, entertainment, fashions, fads, and social life.*

	World Affairs	Europe	Africa & The Middle East	The Americas	Asia & The Pacific
Jul. 28					Japan's claims that the Truce of Tangku in 1933 gives it access to China's commerce are denied by China.
Jul. 29				U.S. President Franklin Roosevelt receives a formal thank you from the National Cane Planters Association of Cuba, lauding his relationship-building efforts and commercial support.	
Jul. 30			Lord Arthur Upham returns to London with evidence of the Persian origin of Gothic architecture.		
Jul. 31		The Gross Glockner Road, connecting Italy and Germany through the Austrian Alps, is completed today. Its official opening by Austrian authorities will be August 3.	Yemen, which sits on the east shore of the Red Sea, flatly refuses to assist Italy in attacking its neighbor, Ethiopia. Premier Benito Mussolini had wanted to use Yemeni laborers to help his soldiers lay a road through Eritrea for the purpose of marching his forces into Ethiopia. Zaidi Imam Yahya, Yemen's ruler, admits his sympathies rest with the Ethiopians.		Yosuke Matsuoka, Japan's former representative to the League of Nations, is appointed president of the South Manchurian Railway, a prominent position in Japanese business. . . . Japan forbids sales of three American books: *Japan in Crisis, The Challenge Behind the Face of Japan,* and *The Far East Front.* The Japanese home office considers them inflammatory.
Aug. 1		Newspapers in Nuremberg, Germany, print an interview in which a Columbia University professor, Peter W. Dykema, praises the Hitler regime.		In Bogotá, the export of silver is banned, as Colombia seeks to stockpile the metal; other materials will replace silver notes and coins.	
Aug. 2		The German liner *Bremen* arrives in New York without incident, unlike the riot that met it last time when angry Americans tore its Nazi swastika from the mast. Of that incident, Acting Secretary of State William Phillips tells Germany that it was "in no way due to neglect on the part of the American authorities."			British Parliament passes the Government of India Act that separates Burma and Aden from Indian government and establishes a plan for an All-India Federation of native states and British-ruled provinces. The plan will go into effect in April 1937.
Aug. 3					Japanese Emperor Hirohito reviews his royal fleet of 60 warships as they sail out to sea for naval maneuvers in the northwest Pacific.
Aug. 4		Dublin opens the annual Irish Horse Show.		The world's tallest waterfall, which drops more than 1,000 feet, is discovered by a Costa Rican pilot flying over the Chirripo Mountains.	Maoris in New Zealand threaten revolt if others on the island do not soon recognize their tribal king. . . . Governor-General Frank Murphy completes two years as the chief executive of the Philippines. He has helped pass the draft of the Philippine constitution.
Aug. 5		French Ministers Edouard Herriot and Henri Maupoil urge France to prepare for war in light of Hitler's aggressive policies.			

A	B	C	D	E
Includes developments that affect more than one world region, international organizations, and important meetings of world leaders.	*Includes all domestic and regional developments in Europe, including the Soviet Union.*	*Includes all domestic and regional developments in Africa and the Middle East.*	*Includes all domestic and regional developments in Latin America, the Caribbean, and Canada.*	*Includes all domestic and regional developments in Asian and Pacific nations (and colonies).*

U.S. Politics & Social Issues	U.S. Foreign Policy & Defense	Economics & Great Depression	Science, Technology & Nature	Culture, Leisure & Lifestyle	
An independent school of law enforcement, created by Indiana State University, is described to lawmakers from across America. Its curriculum underscores crime prevention, personnel training, and criminal law administration in cooperation with public officials and national bureaus.			Archaeologists at the University of Chicago decipher hieroglyphic carvings from an Egyptian temple dated to 1200 B.C.E. The writing narrates the triumphs of Ramses III. . . . The development of a new kind of classroom-specific textbook that illustrates social and economic changes in society is announced by its publisher, the Society for Curriculum Study, an organization of teachers and education specialists.		Jul. 28
		Robert Wood Johnson, president of the Johnson & Johnson company, urges American industrialists to work together to create a workday "short enough to re-employ those unable to find work" with "minimum wages high enough for people to buy what they produce."		Hawaiian Airlines and Pan-American Airlines merge.	Jul. 29
		The spring wheat crop in the United States and Canada, which for a while promised abundance, has declined over the last month, says the Chicago Board of Trade.		The Rev. James McDonnell of New York's St. Patrick's Cathedral warns in a sermon to beware political demagogues and dictators.	Jul. 30
The Catholic publication, The Commonwealth, asks Catholics to boycott the 1936 Olympics in Berlin over that country's treatment of not only Roman Catholics, but also Jews. . . . A mob of Caucasians and African Americans breaks into the Louisburg, N.C., jail and lynches a prisoner. The African-American victim was being held in connection with an axe murder.	Many in the government have raised the question of tightening defenses in the Pacific, but President Roosevelt and Secretary of the Navy Claude A. Swanson respond that they feel no urgency for such defenses now. Swanson says that if and when the current Washington Naval Treaty dissolves, a plan of fortification will then be "inevitably considered."	President Roosevelt signs the Army Promotion Bill, giving full benefits to veterans of the Spanish-American War of 1898.		A French court fines American Joan Warner and bans her nude dance from Parisian nightclubs, even though she just "gives an impression" that she is naked. . . . Creek Indian and art instructor from the University of Oklahoma, Ace Blue Eagle, boards the Normandie on his way to England, where he will teach art at Oxford University. His native dress stirs curiosity on the deck of the liner.	Jul. 31
The Justice Department states that there have been 5,000 small-town bank robberies so far this decade.	The Army holds maneuvers. With 36,000 men, it is the largest concentration of troops ever during peacetime.	Some 34 representatives from business, labor, agriculture, and education are called by President Roosevelt to make up his Committee on Youth. They will serve as an advisory group on how best to allocate the $50 million youth fund. . . . The Republican Party is experiencing a rift between its eastern faction, which attacks Roosevelt's Agricultural Adjustment Administration program, and the midwest faction, which supports the AAA's attempts at wheat surplus control.			Aug. 1
Dutch Schultz, who had been on trial for income tax evasion in New York, is acquitted; the jury could not find the proof to convict him. Now he dares Mayor Fiorello LaGuardia of New York City, who threatened to keep him out of the city, to stop his return.		A drop in food prices occurs because of a good crop. For the last six months, food prices have been rising.	At the International Neurological Congress in London, a representative from the Mayo Clinic of Rochester, Minn., announces a new surgical procedure to cure Raynaud's Disease and other disorders of the blood vessels.	Avery Brundage, who heads the American Olympics Committee, asks Americans not to boycott the 1936 Berlin Olympics because of Germany's actions; he underlines the spirit of goodwill that is being shown by all other participants.	Aug. 2
Twenty-five masked men in California overpower county policemen and drag 24-year-old C.L. Johnson from the courthouse and lynch him. Johnson had been the alleged killer of a local police chief, F.R. Dew. . . . Midget bank robber Henry Fernekes escapes from Joliet State Penitentiary in Illinois.					Aug. 3
Caucasians and African Americans in separate demonstrations rally against war in the Harlem district of New York City.	Dr. Ivan Lee Holt, president of the committee of the Federal Council of Churches of Christ in America, wants an embargo placed on all war-related materials in an attempt to curb the spirit of war in the country. He also asks for a ban on loans and credits to other nations involved in a war.	At least $70 million will be raised this year through private philanthropies, according to a bulletin released by Community Chests and Councils, Inc., which represents community chests in 417 U.S. cities. The council's leader, however, expresses regret over Roosevelt's tax on gift-giving, which he calls a blow to private charities.		A national park will be built at King's Mountain, S.C., to commemorate the rout of a British force during the American Revolution.	Aug. 4
					Aug. 5

F	G	H	I	J
Includes elections, federal-state relations, civil rights and liberties, crime, the judiciary, education, healthcare, poverty, urban affairs, and population.	Includes formation and debate of U.S. foreign and defense policies, veterans affairs, and defense spending. (Relations with specific foreign countries are usually found under the region concerned.)	Includes business, labor, agriculture, taxation, transportation, consumer affairs, monetary and fiscal policy, natural resources, pollution, and accidents.	Includes worldwide scientific, medical, and technological developments, natural phenomena, U.S. weather, and natural disasters.	Includes the arts, religion, scholarship, communications media, sports, entertainment, fashions, fads, and social life.

	World Affairs	Europe	Africa & The Middle East	The Americas	Asia & The Pacific
Aug. 6				Plutarco Elias Calles wins the governorship of the State of Nuevo Leon, Mexico. Runner-up Fortunato Zuazua charges that Calles's father, a former Mexican president, rigged the vote in his son's favor.	
Aug. 7	Over the last year, members of the world trading community made some poor decisions, says U.S. Secretary of State Cordell Hull. The result was damage to international trade to the extent of $20–25 billion.	Some 1,500 youths of German descent, representing 50 countries, gather in Nuremberg to pledge to spread the Nazi message across the world.	Ethiopian Emperor Haile Selassie announces the establishment of the Red Cross in his country. While many say it is in preparation for a war with Italy, Selassie responds that the Red Cross is important to have on one's side even during peacetime.		
Aug. 8		A violent strike of French shipping lines in protest of President Pierre Laval's pay cuts postpones the sailing of outgoing vessels. . . . A riot in Toulon, France, which exploded in anger at the government's wage cuts, leaves five dead and 200 wounded.	Rumors suggest that Ethiopia is trying to purchase arms from Japan. Attempts to buy guns from Western countries have failed.	Chile and Bolivia are in talks over allowing Bolivia, which is landlocked, access to the sea so that it may export its oil.	A Japanese Embassy spokesman denies having threatened China during a broadcast; his references to forthcoming "policy changes," he says, were general and not meant to sound aggressive.
Aug. 9					
Aug. 10			India denounces Italy's aggression against Ethiopia. Newspapers describe it as typical European expansionism.		
Aug. 11				Twenty-one delegates from Havana, Cuba, headed by the president of the Cuban Social and Economic Union, Jose Manuel Casanova, arrive in Washington, D.C. They plan to meet with U.S. representatives for reviews on Cuba's industry, agriculture, commerce, and labor.	The fact that China is not flinching in the face of Japanese aggression is a sign of China's strength and confidence, says philosopher Dr. Hu Shih.
Aug. 12					
Aug. 13		Claiming "spontaneous support" of the entire German peoples, the Nazi party accelerates its anti-Semitic drive with the press and radio forced into the campaign.		Air France announces the first transatlantic passenger service—from Paris to Buenos Aires—to begin January 1936.	
Aug. 14			Ethiopian Emperor Haile Selassie dispatches 60,000 men to the eastern border to meet the growing Italian forces.		
Aug. 15					
Aug. 16		From New York, political analyst Dr. Goldberg urges more Jews to make their exodus from Poland—immediately. Economic conditions there could push the Nazis into making some desperate actions against them, he warns.	The United States is for peace in Africa, says a telegram from the U.S. State Department, responding to an inquiry from Mrs. Arthur Brin of the National Council of Jewish Women. The wire remarked that the Ethiopia-Italy dispute rests "squarely upon the principles declared in the Pact of Paris."	After public disorder throughout Buenos Aires, former president Marcelo Alvear denies that the Radical Party, with whom he is associated, incited the trouble.	

A	B	C	D	E
Includes developments that affect more than one world region, international organizations, and important meetings of world leaders.	Includes all domestic and regional developments in Europe, including the Soviet Union.	Includes all domestic and regional developments in Africa and the Middle East.	Includes all domestic and regional developments in Latin America, the Caribbean, and Canada.	Includes all domestic and regional developments in Asian and Pacific nations (and colonies).

U.S. Politics & Social Issues	U.S. Foreign Policy & Defense	Economics & Great Depression	Science, Technology & Nature	Culture, Leisure & Lifestyle	
Convened war veterans—decorated members of the American Legion of Valor—lambaste the so-called "academic freedom" resolution of the National Education Association as a too-liberal direction for the U.S. education system to be heading. They fear that America's youth will be taught un-American principles.		The Interstate Commerce Commission this week begins to examine a plan for the reorganization of one of the more well-known railways, the Chicago, Milwaukee, St. Paul & Pacific.			Aug. 6
The Republicans hope to field Charles Lindbergh as a candidate in the 1936 elections. In a poll of 5,000 Republican leaders, Lindbergh seems like a viable candidate—but Lindbergh himself has not yet agreed.		In Washington, Rep. Ellenbogen of Pennsylvania introduces a bill to create a seven-person commission to regulate business, protect the consumer, and license textile plants.	Yosemite Park rangers in California save the lives of two climbers stuck on a 2,000-foot precipice. The rescue is hailed as one of the most dangerous in West Coast history.		Aug. 7
			Rocky Mountain National Park is threatened with the discovery of the Black Hills beetle, a danger to woodlands. This pest has already damaged thousands of acres in Yellowstone and Grand Teton in Wyoming and three government forests in Colorado.		Aug. 8
The Roman Catholic Church is considering the canonization of a black missionary, the Blessed Martin de Porres, who lived in Peru during the 17th century and devoted his life to the poor and sick.			Flooding in Ohio causes damage estimated at $5 million.	David Selznick announces that his newest film will be a screen version of Frances Burnett's *Little Lord Fauntleroy*. It will star Freddie Bartholomew and W.C. Fields.	Aug. 9
Archbishop John Gregory Murray bans birth control in the St. Paul, Minn., Archdiocese. He also cautions Catholics against taking part in or joining any endeavor that they know supports the birth control movement.		With certain Works Progress Administration enrollees asking for higher pay, the AFL offers to mediate a settlement.		Congress declares that a committee protecting the nation's historic sites will be created. The preservation of buildings and particular landmarks will be a national priority.	Aug. 10
Chicago newspaper publisher Col. Frank Knox, who is considered by a large part of the Republican Party to be a good candidate for the 1936 race, speaks tonight at New York State College. Observers see the event as Knox's commitment to his campaign. . . . Attorney General Homer Cummings proposes opening Rat Island off the coast of Alaska as a penal colony—with no bars because it is surrounded by sea—where the prisoners fend for themselves.		An independent demographic study by General Mills of 100 large U.S. companies representing two dozen different industries shows that they are owned, in total, by 4.7 million shareholders, who own an average 114 shares each.	A French ship, the *Ampere*, discovers a submerged peak in the Atlantic. Because it is the location where some believe Atlantis to have been located, many eagerly set out to examine the discovery.		Aug. 11
Joining the prosecution team of Thomas E. Dewey in New York is Jacob Rosenblum, the District Attorney who ran the case against Dutch Schultz.		National income has risen 11 percent over 1933, according to the Bureau of Economic Research of the Department of Commerce.			Aug. 12
Huey Long, senator and former governor of Louisiana, announces his intention to run for president; he has no aim but to "beat Roosevelt."					Aug. 13
		The Social Security Act is signed into law, establishing a nationwide system of unemployment compensation, old-age insurance, and aid to destitute children.		*Call of the Wild*, a Darryl F. Zanuck production starring Clark Gable and Loretta Young, opens in theaters.	Aug. 14
Col. Theodore Roosevelt, Jr., claims that President Roosevelt's agricultural policies have forced U.S. textile companies to move to Brazil where the cost of cotton is cheaper.	Both the Armory Board and the National Guard and Naval Militia seek small budgetary operating increases for the coming year. They meet today with Budget Director Rufus E. McGahen.	The Senate passes the $250 million Tax Bill, much to the consternation of the Democrats. It passes by a vote of 57–22.		The giant sequoia is selected as the National Tree of America, according to the National Life Conservation Society. . . . Will Rogers and Wiley Post are killed when their airplane crashes at Point Barrow, Alaska.	Aug. 15
	American Legionnaires at their state convention in Pennsylvania hear Governor George H. Earle warn them to ignore anti-Communist sentiment and just "follow the path of liberalism." He added, "(We must) block the attempt of organized wealth (designed to) deliver us into fascism and dictatorship."			With Virginia Van Wie having decided not to defend her title this year, 94 other contestants qualify for the U.S. women's amateur golf championship. The event will be held at the Interlachen Country Club in Hopkins, Minn. . . . The Baseball Museum in Cooperstown, N.Y., announces plans to open a Hall of Fame, devoted to major league stars.	Aug. 16

F	G	H	I	J
Includes elections, federal-state relations, civil rights and liberties, crime, the judiciary, education, healthcare, poverty, urban affairs, and population.	*Includes formation and debate of U.S. foreign and defense policies, veterans affairs, and defense spending. (Relations with specific foreign countries are usually found under the region concerned.)*	*Includes business, labor, agriculture, taxation, transportation, consumer affairs, monetary and fiscal policy, natural resources, pollution, and accidents.*	*Includes worldwide scientific, medical, and technological developments, natural phenomena, U.S. weather, and natural disasters.*	*Includes the arts, religion, scholarship, communications media, sports, entertainment, fashions, fads, and social life.*

	World Affairs	Europe	Africa & The Middle East	The Americas	Asia & The Pacific
Aug. 17					
Aug. 18		London announces that since 1933 its number of unemployed has fallen from 3 million to 2 million.			The Japanese, according to the American Trade Commissioner, have replaced the Chinese as the major retail merchandisers doing business with the Philippine Islands. It is estimated that Japan currently holds 35 percent of the islands' business.
Aug. 19	According to Rev. John Kent of Glasgow, Scotland, the world's trade war is very much to blame for the crises in the world today.	In Germany, Dr. Franz Guertner, minister of justice, proclaims that the laws instituted by the Third Reich and practiced by the Nazi government will always prevail over any other law penned by God or man.			
Aug. 20		At the conclusion of the Third Internationale in Moscow, all Communist parties around the world are called on to support democratic governments in opposition to fascism.	Ethiopian Emperor Haile Selassie, in managing the defenses of his country against a threatening Italy, announces that men from impoverished families will not be drafted into the army.		U.S. Vice President John Nance Garner will participate in ceremonies in Manila, which are a prologue to the inauguration of the new Commonwealth Government of the Philippines in October.
Aug. 21			The League of Nations develops a nondenominational, nonpartisan group—the American Committee on the Ethiopian Crisis—to avert a war between Ethiopia and Italy.	The recent Chaco Peace Conference between Bolivia and Paraguay—which America helped to convene—is crumbling, report local newspapers.	
Aug. 22					In answer to a British request for a naval treaty, Japan replies it will be interested in negotiating only if parity is offered.
Aug. 23		Germany's Food and Agriculture Minister, Rickard-Walther Darre, takes on the responsibility of Price Commissar. His first order is to freeze food prices, which have been rising rapidly.	To prevent a war, Ethiopian Emperor Haile Selassie offers the long-contested province of Aussa to Italy. Premier Benito Mussolini does not respond.		
Aug. 24					
Aug. 25	At the World Zionist Congress in Lucerne, Switzerland, German delegate Kurt Blumenfield presses for a world campaign to help the Jews in anti-Semitic countries to fight back against persecution. While the world right now focuses on the systematic persecution of Jews in Germany, the same thing is happening, he adds, in Iran, Iraq, and Afghanistan.				Lt. Col. John Hamilton Jouett, who has spent the last three years establishing the Central Aviation School in Shienchaio, China, praises China's air force and believes that, within a short time, China will be a first-class air power. . . . The Marquess of Linlithgow is appointed the new Viceroy of India, representing King George V of England.
Aug. 26		Private automobiles in Magdeburg, Germany, display "No Jews" signs provided by a local company with Nazi affiliations.			

A	B	C	D	E
Includes developments that affect more than one world region, international organizations, and important meetings of world leaders.	Includes all domestic and regional developments in Europe, including the Soviet Union.	Includes all domestic and regional developments in Africa and the Middle East.	Includes all domestic and regional developments in Latin America, the Caribbean, and Canada.	Includes all domestic and regional developments in Asian and Pacific nations (and colonies).

U.S. Politics & Social Issues	U.S. Foreign Policy & Defense	Economics & Great Depression	Science, Technology & Nature	Culture, Leisure & Lifestyle	
Senator William Borah of Idaho, considered by many Republicans as a candidate for the upcoming 1936 presidential elections, is preparing pre-primary visits to several cities.	The House of Representatives introduces the Neutrality Bill, designed to keep the nation neutral in event of foreign wars. Chairman S.D. McReynolds introduces the bill.	The Federal Reserve Board announces that the amount of money in circulation has increased by $140 million so far this year.			Aug. 17
Kansas City completes an auditorium large enough to seat 20,000 people and with an "air-cooled" system. The WPA project cost $6.5 million. Both the Democrats and Republicans eye it for their upcoming national conventions.				The Whitman Cup for tennis goes to the United States for the fifth consecutive year.	Aug. 18
A series of interviews with more than 100 witnesses who knew Rutgers University professor Lienhard Bergel—accused of spreading Nazi propaganda in America—concludes with the opinion that he bears "a feeling of authority because of his Aryan blood."		Unless the federal budget is balanced, warns Louis K. Comstock of the Merchants Association of New York, the United States will meet with disaster.	At its general session in San Francisco, the American Chemical Society explains its find of a powerful new male sex hormone previously unknown to research.		Aug. 19
		In Denver, the 10th Circuit Court of Appeals rules that the federal government can make loans and grants to municipalities and states under the Public Works Administration for construction of publicly owned power plants.			Aug. 20
				The American Wildlife Institute donates $150,000 toward the government's proposed series of game-management courses to be taught at certain colleges in the United States. A sum of $900,000 has already been budgeted toward the development of these courses.	Aug. 21
The New York State Liquor Authority complains that other states—most notably Michigan, Ohio, and Pennsylvania—are "dumping" unsold shipments of liquor into New York City. Edward P. Mulrooney of the Liquor Authority promises to deal with the problem.					Aug. 22
The Omnibus Banking Bill is signed by President Roosevelt. The bill—very unpopular with Democrats—creates a program of credit control by the government. . . . The Banking Act of 1935 is signed into law, changing the administration of the Federal Reserve System from the Federal Reserve Board to the Board of Governors of the Federal Reserve System and establishing an Open Market Committee.		President Roosevelt names J.D. Ross as a member of the Securities and Exchange Commission. Ross is an advocate of public ownership of utilities and superintendent of a municipal power development.			Aug. 23
The last existing 198 members of the Cayuga Indian nation begin dialogue with U.S. representatives, seeking their own reservation near Cayuga Lake, N.Y., and changes to agreements they made with the government when George Washington was in office.					Aug. 24
	The Army admits that recent maneuvers have revealed inadequacies in training and equipment.	Republican Senator Lester Dickinson of Iowa claims there is much antagonism against President Roosevelt's New Deal reform in the Corn Belt. He declares that, come election time, farmers are going to vote Republican.		A "humidity control" system is being installed in Carnegie Hall in New York. Actual refrigeration will not be included in the improvement, since the system is designed strictly for the cooler months.	Aug. 25
		General business conditions in the United States improved in 1934, according to the World Economic Review of the Department of Congress. On the negative side, unemployment remains widespread.		The 16th Annual Convention of the National Association of Negro Musicians is held in New York City.	Aug. 26

F	G	H	I	J
Includes elections, federal-state relations, civil rights and liberties, crime, the judiciary, education, healthcare, poverty, urban affairs, and population.	Includes formation and debate of U.S. foreign and defense policies, veterans affairs, and defense spending. (Relations with specific foreign countries are usually found under the region concerned.)	Includes business, labor, agriculture, taxation, transportation, consumer affairs, monetary and fiscal policy, natural resources, pollution, and accidents.	Includes worldwide scientific, medical, and technological developments, natural phenomena, U.S. weather, and natural disasters.	Includes the arts, religion, scholarship, communications media, sports, entertainment, fashions, fads, and social life.

	World Affairs	Europe	Africa & The Middle East	The Americas	Asia & The Pacific
Aug. 27			As Italian troops move closer to Addis Ababa, Ethiopia begins to evacuate noncombatants.		
Aug. 28	The World Population Congress, this year meeting in Berlin, opens with a Nazi speaker praising the people of Germany, followed by a prayer of thanksgiving that Providence chose to give Adolf Hitler to Germany. Meanwhile, America shuns this year's Congress because of its location.	Finland increases its defense budget for 1936. It joins with other Scandinavian countries in the attempt to form a neutral bloc.	Japan delivers a six-month supply of weapons and munitions to Ethiopia. It appears that Japan's earlier promises to Italy to remain strictly neutral are no longer valid.		
Aug. 29		The French promise to stand by all recommendations offered by the League of Nations on the Ethiopian situation and hope that Britain will do the same.			
Aug. 30					
Aug. 31					
Sept. 1		Germany's top economics scholar, Dr. Hjalmar Schacht, openly criticizes Germany's current social situation.	Cornelius de Villers of Stellenbosch University in South Africa warns that once a war starts between Italy and Africa, another will follow—a "conflagration" between white and black races in Africa.	Mexican President Lázaro Cárdenas proclaims to the Senate that working women should be given the right to vote and other privileges thus far denied them.	Japan proposes to Russia that both countries peacefully share the border in dispute at Manchukuo. Russia hears the proposal, but does not respond immediately.
Sept. 2					
Sept. 3			John Martin, the nine-year-old son of the Ethiopian envoy to London, interrupts his father's plea to the Nile Society for international help against the invading Italians by climbing on the table, shouting, "Give us guns and we'll fight!" . . . The League of Nations Arbitration Tribunal investigating the dispute between Italy and Ethiopia says neither side is to blame.	Liberal leader Mackenzie King assails Canada's Prime Minister R.B. Bennett in front a St. John, New Brunswick, audience. He accuses him of using the forum of the Canadian government to create his own national government.	

A	B	C	D	E
Includes developments that affect more than one world region, international organizations, and important meetings of world leaders.	Includes all domestic and regional developments in Europe, including the Soviet Union.	Includes all domestic and regional developments in Africa and the Middle East.	Includes all domestic and regional developments in Latin America, the Caribbean, and Canada.	Includes all domestic and regional developments in Asian and Pacific nations (and colonies).

U.S. Politics & Social Issues	U.S. Foreign Policy & Defense	Economics & Great Depression	Science, Technology & Nature	Culture, Leisure & Lifestyle	
Liquor companies should decrease the price of alcohol to the same as soda pop to increase national consumption, says Louise Gross, chairperson of the Women's Moderation Union. She campaigns for the rights of women to drink at public bars. . . . The AFL proposes a charter to the International Automobile Workers Union, asking union delegates to recruit a quarter of a million new members for the motorcar industry.		As the government considers forcing the price of silver up from 66 cents to $1.29 per ounce, which is allowable under the Silver Purchase Act of 1934, jewelers in turn complain that this move will injure the sterling business. . . . Six banks in South Dakota merge to form the state's largest bank, with deposits of $7.5 million. The institution is located in Sioux Falls.			Aug. 27
James A. Moffett resigns as Federal Housing Administrator, effective September 1. The news is a surprise to most of official Washington. The President reluctantly accepts his resignation.			A scientist from the British National Committee for Radio Telegraphy discovers a heat band circling the earth, never before detected. Prof. Edward Victor Appleton claims the upper stratosphere "girdle" is a temperature of 1,000°F or more.		Aug. 28
Newspaper magnate William Randolph Hearst announces his decision to start a third political party of conservative Democrats. He asks Senator Al Smith, who ran unsuccessfully in 1928, to be his candidate for 1936.		Some 4,500 workers vote to strike against the Wabash Railway Company. They demand higher wages and better working conditions.			Aug. 29
A German publication writes a feature story on racial hatred in America, telling of lynchings of African Americans and other examples of violence.		The Revenue Act of 1935, known as the Wealth Tax Act, increases the income tax rates on high incomes, with the highest bracket at 75 percent. . . . A new record of oil consumption is met, says the Standard Oil Company publication, *The Lamp.* Domestic consumption and export demand for crude oil during the first six months of 1935 is 518.3 million barrels, an increase of 14 million over the same time last year.	The Naval Observatory in Washington, D.C., is considered the most accurate timekeeper on the globe. According to Capt. J.N. Hellweg, superintendent of the Arlington radio station, the time that is continuously broadcast by the observatory is accurate within one-thousandth of a second.		Aug. 30
	President Roosevelt signs the Neutrality Act of 1935 which allows embargoes on arms, but not strategic materials during war. . . . Secretary of State Cordell Hull firmly iterates a "hands-off" policy to any American businessman thinking about investing abroad; if they do, it is their prerogative, but the United States cannot and will not offer protection. The new neutrality law will state that Americans traveling on belligerent ships do so at their own risk.	A strike by Wabash Railway trainmen is averted by the National Mediation Board.		Jewish war veterans meeting in Saratoga Springs, Fla., encourage the Amateur Athletic Union to keep away from participating in the Berlin Olympics next year. The reason is the desecration of Jewish laws in Germany and the persecution of the Jewish people.	Aug. 31
Police detail increases from 200 to 300 officers per day as the Ladies Apparel Shipping Clerks strike intensifies; currently, 15,000 strikers are out, many picketing on busy thoroughfares. . . . Many card-carrying members of the International Seaman's Union are booted from the union for associating with radical political leaders in California. The radicals want to involve the union in a strike to cripple the ports in the near future.	By observing recent Army maneuvers, the National Broadcasting Company learns that the present radio equipment could transmit intelligible signals through short-wave relay despite battlefield static.	The National Industrial Board announces that despite all efforts the number of unemployed has risen 2.7 percent. . . . The Federal Deposit Insurance Corporation reports a six-month rise in the number of savings accounts in the nation. Reports from 14,173 banks show a gain of $1.3 billion. This does not include Christmas savings or other temporary accounts.		The National Constitution Day Committee proposes September 17 for honoring the Constitution of the United States. Celebrations will take place in Boston, Washington, D.C., and other major cities. . . . Three people die when the Western Air Express plane they are in crashes in thick fog just outside Burbank, Calif.	Sept. 1
The Republican Party derides the Democratic patronage machine, calling all federal representatives "political appointees." . . . Dr. Gustav A. Mueller, Germany's Acting Consul assigned to New York, scorns the owners of various New York City nightspots who refused to allow a Nazi organization to display the swastika flag last night.		Violence erupts at the Pelzer Manufacturing Company in South Carolina. What began as a demonstration ends in bloodshed when gunmen open fire on workers trying to pass the picket line—killing one woman and injuring 22 others.	Harold Neumann wins the Thompson Trophy at the National Air Races in Cleveland for flying his plane at a speed of 220 miles per hour.		Sept. 2
				Robert C. Nelson is apprehended by federal agents, accused of robbing Margaret Hawksworth Bell of Florida of $185,000 worth of jewels.	Sept. 3

F	G	H	I	J
Includes elections, federal-state relations, civil rights and liberties, crime, the judiciary, education, healthcare, poverty, urban affairs, and population.	*Includes formation and debate of U.S. foreign and defense policies, veterans affairs, and defense spending. (Relations with specific foreign countries are usually found under the region concerned.)*	*Includes business, labor, agriculture, taxation, transportation, consumer affairs, monetary and fiscal policy, natural resources, pollution, and accidents.*	*Includes worldwide scientific, medical, and technological developments, natural phenomena, U.S. weather, and natural disasters.*	*Includes the arts, religion, scholarship, communications media, sports, entertainment, fashions, fads, and social life.*

	World Affairs	Europe	Africa & The Middle East	The Americas	Asia & The Pacific
Sept. 4					
Sept. 5			Haile Selassie of Ethiopia forbids public anti-Italian talk. He has the editor of the *Voice of Ethiopia*, Kidane Miriam Takle, arrested for printing anti-Italian editorials.		Japan receives a warning from Canadian Prime Minister Richard Bennett concerning the 50 percent tax on Canadian imports. According to Bennett, the tax goes against the Trade Agreement of 1933. Unless it is removed, he says, all other agreements between the countries are ended.
Sept. 6	Waging her own "world war against sin," Gen. Evangeline Booth, daughter of the founder of the Salvation Army, states her "manifesto" to 99 nations today. She has helped lead her organization for more than 25 years.	France admits that its collective peace efforts, for which it has worked so hard with other countries, cannot be considered a success as long as Italy shows aggressiveness toward Ethiopia. . . . In Geneva, the countries of Scandinavia declare that their 12 million citizens support the League of Nations and that they hope and pray for an avoidance of war.		Easing the Commonwealth's anxieties, Canadian Prime Minister Richard Bennett says, "We will not be embroiled in any foreign quarrel where the rights of Canadians are not involved."	
Sept. 7		Germany protests America's release of five perpetrators who allegedly tore up a flag bearing the Nazi swastika on the liner *Bremen* in New York.			
Sept. 8	Premier Benito Mussolini's representative, Salvador de Madariaga, informs the League of Nations that Italy will consider peace negotiations on the Ethiopian situation.				
Sept. 9	The 16th Assembly of the League of Nations opens, with talk focusing on such topics as the German refugee problem and the role of women in world society. The subject of the Italo-Ethiopian War is not addressed. . . . The president of Columbia University, Dr. Nicholas Butler Murray, diagnoses the condition of the world as extremely serious. Its ailment, he says, is human faithlessness, which, he predicts, will lead to a world war. He makes his remarks to the Carnegie Endowment for International Peace.				
Sept. 10		The sixth Nazi Party Conference opens in Nuremberg. Adolf Hitler accepts the keys to the city from town officials.			Japan vows to battle Communism, which it "will not tolerate," in any part of eastern Asia.
Sept. 11		The editor of the newspaper, *Friends of New Germany*, Walter Kappe, asserts that Nazism will be spread throughout the world; in particular, he cites a plan to establish the "complete principles of National Socialism" in the United States.		Details of a plot to overthrow Panama's President, Harmodio Arias, are discovered. Former police captain Homero Ayala, who engineered the plot, stole arms from the local U.S. Army base at Corozal; a U.S. Marine helped him for $1,000. Both men are arraigned at the Magistrate's Court at Balboa.	
Sept. 12	Sir Samuel Hoare, British foreign secretary, expresses his hope for peace between Italy and Ethiopia. He is anxious for a settlement that will do "justice to Ethiopia's national rights and Italy's claims for expansion."	Britain's naval power is greater than in any period of its history, asserts naval authority Hector Bywater in the *Daily Telegraph*. It continues to grow as more cruisers and destroyers are being built and as 5,000 more men are added to the existing force.		Gunfire breaks out in the Mexican Chamber of Deputies in Mexico City when a discussion over legislation becomes overheated. Manuel Martinez Valadez, deputy for the state of Jalisco, is killed and three others are wounded.	
Sept. 13					

A	B	C	D	E
Includes developments that affect more than one world region, international organizations, and important meetings of world leaders.	*Includes all domestic and regional developments in Europe, including the Soviet Union.*	*Includes all domestic and regional developments in Africa and the Middle East.*	*Includes all domestic and regional developments in Latin America, the Caribbean, and Canada.*	*Includes all domestic and regional developments in Asian and Pacific nations (and colonies).*

U.S. Politics & Social Issues	U.S. Foreign Policy & Defense	Economics & Great Depression	Science, Technology & Nature	Culture, Leisure & Lifestyle	
The Girl Scouts of America name Constance Rittenhouse as National Director, replacing the outgoing Josephine Schain. Rittenhouse vows to take on her responsibilities immediately.		In a radio address from his private residence in Hyde Park, N.Y., President Roosevelt declares that America is on the road to recovery.	Nearly 200 people are killed and thousands of homes destroyed as a hurricane hits Florida.	Hal Roach Studios announces several major projects in the works, among them the movie *The Bohemian Girl*, with Stan Laurel and Oliver Hardy.	Sept. 4
The Winchester Star of Virginia, usually a Republican-leaning newspaper, concedes that President Roosevelt will receive the support of the Virginia delegation and thus will be renominated.	The United States must "help save Ethiopia," says the Rev. Dr. L.K. Williams of the Chicago Baptist Church, speaking in New York. He tells the 2,000 attendees at the Negro Baptist Convention in the Bronx Coliseum that it is America's duty to use its influence to preserve peace.	The last week of August ended with more businesses failing than the week prior, according to Dun & Bradstreet, Inc. On the other hand, the same week showed less insolvency in manufacturing. . . . President Franklin Roosevelt vetoes the Grazing Bill that, he claims, discourages conservation plans for the nation.	Dr. Verne Lyon tells the American Psychology Association in Ann Arbor, Mich., that lie detectors indicate a suspect's "painful complexes" as well as his untruths. He has noted this in more than 100 cases he has monitored while doing polygraphs for the Chicago Police Department.		Sept. 5
Mayor Fiorello LaGuardia of New York promises African Americans in the city that discrimination will be dealt with harshly. He speaks to 5,000 men and women assembled at the Bronx Coliseum.					Sept. 6
			A Berlin chemist, Dr. Gustav Herst, produces heavy neon in his lab in the Siemens Engineering Works.		Sept. 7
An assassin shoots former Louisiana governor Huey Long as he is leaving the Capitol building in Baton Rouge. He had just finished meeting with the House of Representatives. Long's bodyguards kill the assassin, a local doctor.		The eight-week strike at the Pelzer Manufacturing Plant cotton mills ends with an agreement between the shops and the United Textile Workers of America.	News comes that auto makers are advancing the process of producing types of sheet metals and plated steel immune to corrosion and rust—something that the industry has been researching for some time.		Sept. 8
In a speech at Drew University in New Jersey, Dean Lynn Hough blames the breakdown of Prohibition, "that noble experiment," on America's inherent dislike for authority—the same attitude, she says, that drove the colonists to break with England.	The Navy announces that 23 ships—including an aircraft carrier and a 10,000-ton cruiser—will be constructed at several yards, both private and government-owned.				Sept. 9
Senator Huey Long of Louisiana dies after being shot in the stomach two days ago. He was 42 years old.		The National Labor Relations Board steps into the dispute between dockworkers in New Orleans, La., and the International Longshoremen's Association, with the AFL helping to mediate.	C.C. Hurst, a British scientist, proposes that cosmic rays may be responsible for certain aspects of evolution. He suggests that the rays mutated genes and chromosomes resulting in important cellular changes.	New York's Municipal Art Commission approves a statue of the war hero, "Fighting" Father Duffy, to be placed in a prominent part of Times Square. The priest was a World War hero and a humanitarian.	Sept. 10
Radio broadcasters and city newspapers are to blame for promoting not only the use of alcohol, but violence and immorality, states the Women's Christian Temperance Union.	Statesmanship is breaking down so badly that international relationships have reached the lowest ebb since 1914, U.S. Secretary of State Cordell Hull tells visiting foreign students in Washington, D.C. The body of students represents the Confederation Internationale des Étudiants.	Washington economists say the nation produced $3.3 billion in internal revenue from 1934–35. It is the greatest amount recovered in 14 years. . . . Tonight, President Roosevelt holds a series of conferences in his Hyde Park estate to review the completion of the $4 billion relief program and to study work relief disputes.			Sept. 11
				A Texan, Wilmer Lee Allison, Jr., wins the U.S. tennis championship. At 31 years old, he is the oldest player to win the championship for the first time.	Sept. 12
Eleven ships' radio operators—members of the American Radio Telegraphists Union—go on strike. But, while they picket on the New York dock, their ships pull away from the wharf with substitute operators.		Worried that a proposed increase in intercoastal shipping rates will add an approximate $1 million per year to chain stores' and wholesalers' costs, representatives of those concerns file an official protest with the Shipping Board Bureau of the Department of Commerce.	Closer cooperation is needed between lovers of wildlife and forestry experts to regain a full tribute to nature here in the United States, says Conservation Commissioner Lithgow Osborne at a dinner of the American Forestry Association, attended by 700 people.	The U.S. Arts Relief Fund sends out letters to 18,500 writers—members of the Authors League of America—describing a new program aimed at giving funds to needy authors and playwrights.	Sept. 13

F	G	H	I	J
Includes elections, federal-state relations, civil rights and liberties, crime, the judiciary, education, healthcare, poverty, urban affairs, and population.	*Includes formation and debate of U.S. foreign and defense policies, veterans affairs, and defense spending. (Relations with specific foreign countries are usually found under the region concerned.)*	*Includes business, labor, agriculture, taxation, transportation, consumer affairs, monetary and fiscal policy, natural resources, pollution, and accidents.*	*Includes worldwide scientific, medical, and technological developments, natural phenomena, U.S. weather, and natural disasters.*	*Includes the arts, religion, scholarship, communications media, sports, entertainment, fashions, fads, and social life.*

	World Affairs	Europe	Africa & The Middle East	The Americas	Asia & The Pacific
Sept. 14		Former King George of Greece turns down the Greek Royalists' pleas for him to reassume the throne. Through an emissary in Athens, he stresses that he would prefer his return to be the choice of the whole country, not just a few. If the situation changes, he will consider returning.			
Sept. 15		The Third Reich officially adopts the swastika as Germany's national emblem.... The German government announces the Nuremberg Laws that deprive Jews of citizenship and prohibit intermarriage between Jews and Gentiles.		A border clash erupts between El Salvador and Guatemala.	
Sept. 16					
Sept. 17		Adolf Hitler suddenly orders the Nazi Party to desist from "individual action" against the Jews. This positive—but uncharacteristic—action draws suspicion. Some wonder if it is an attempt to remove the boycotts that have hurt the Third Reich's trading power.		Mexico celebrates its 125th anniversary of independence.	For the first time, the Philippine Islands—now a commonwealth of the United States—run their own election for their president. But the winning candidate, Manuel L. Quezon, afterward tells of an election night fraught with death threats and voting irregularities.
Sept. 18		Jewish businessmen are informed that members of the Nazi Union are collecting funds to purchase their shops.		Argentina and Bolivia dispute the ownership of 2,700 square miles of land in the Jujuy province. Meetings are held to reach an agreement.	
Sept. 19		Greece prepares to conduct a plebiscite to decide whether or not the people want a national or monarchial government.... In Germany, school curricula change today; now each child will devote one full day of the week to either the Hitler Youth program or to studying the history of Nazism.			Douglas MacArthur, retiring Chief of the General Staff of the U.S. Army, is given the responsibility of organizing defenses and building up an army in the new Commonwealth Government of the Philippines.
Sept. 20		The League for Germanism Abroad, a Nazi administrative branch, issues an appeal to all Third Reich citizens to hand in lists of addresses of their German-born friends and relatives living abroad so that Nazi propaganda may be mailed out to them.			According to Japanese Ambassador Hirosi Saito, Japan and the U.S. State Department reach an agreement limiting exports of Japanese textiles to the Philippines Commonwealth.
Sept. 21	The Italian cabinet rejects the League of Nations' latest peace offering.	The French Senate approves an increase in the defense budget in view of the Italo-Ethiopian conflict and Adolf Hitler's aggressive policies.			
Sept. 22		A general budget for 1936 is approved by the French Council of Ministers; its aim is to reduce expenditures by 20 percent, as compared to 1935. President Pierre Laval promises his people that deflation will restore finances.... Author Frank H. Simonds, in his article in the magazine *Current History*, calls Germany the real threat of war.			Defeated Filipino presidential candidate Emilio Aguinaldo sends a letter to President Roosevelt, accusing President Quezon's party of voting fraud.

A	B	C	D	E
Includes developments that affect more than one world region, international organizations, and important meetings of world leaders.	*Includes all domestic and regional developments in Europe, including the Soviet Union.*	*Includes all domestic and regional developments in Africa and the Middle East.*	*Includes all domestic and regional developments in Latin America, the Caribbean, and Canada.*	*Includes all domestic and regional developments in Asian and Pacific nations (and colonies).*

U.S. Politics & Social Issues	U.S. Foreign Policy & Defense	Economics & Great Depression	Science, Technology & Nature	Culture, Leisure & Lifestyle	
The repeal of the Prohibition Act of the 1920s did not end illegal liquor manufacturing, according to the Treasury Department. The Alcohol Tax Unit says that moonshiners continue to operate. During the last fiscal year, the Treasury found and demolished 16,988 illegal stills. . . . The late Senator Huey Long's pastor, the Rev. Gerald L.K. Smith, addresses 10,000 Louisianans in Alexandria urging a campaign for the Share Our Wealth program for redistribution of the country's wealth, a program the senator had begun before he was shot on September 8.		President Roosevelt reassigns 2.4 million jobless persons from the Public Works Administration to the Works Progress Administration after he learns the former will not be fully operational until spring of next year.			Sept. 14
		The companies able to offer more consistent employment—and where the most increase in employment occurs—are those that are mechanized, says Herman H. Lind of the National Machine Tool Builders Association.	With all instruments covered, pilot Ray Brown flies his Lockheed Vega from Roosevelt Field, Long Island, to Albany, N.Y., where he lands safely. The entire trip was navigated solely by radio.		Sept. 15
In a Baton Rouge, La., courtroom, during an inquest into the assassination of Senator Huey Long, certain associates of Long suggest the Roosevelt administration is to blame.	Representatives of the Dai Nippon Zaigo-Gunjin-Kai, the Japanese veterans association, pledge their loyalty to the United States in a national meeting in New Orleans.			The South Atlantic Association of the Amateur Athletic Union votes unanimously to boycott the upcoming Berlin Olympics. It recommends that the National America Athletic Union do likewise. . . . The National Boxing Association names the current three top heavyweights in America: James Braddock, Max Baer, and Joe Louis.	Sept. 16
With the widow of President Theodore Roosevelt—fifth cousin of the current President Roosevelt—leading the way, Republican women from 20 states collect in New York to defend "the liberty that we stand in terror of losing" if Roosevelt remains in office.	Americans can trust President Roosevelt to keep the country safe in the event of war, says Lt. George Ijams, commander in chief of the Military Order of the World War. From Baltimore, he assures the public that the President totally understands the necessity for adequate defense.				Sept. 17
James A. Emery, chief counsel of the National Association of Manufacturers, assails the New Deal and warns that the President will only insinuate more government control—"perhaps more extreme than any yet suggested."				President H.H. Curtice of the Buick Motor Company announces price reductions on all 1936 models; reductions range from $40 to $385.	Sept. 18
The University of Virginia makes a decision to "refuse respectfully" an entrance application from an African American. Alice C. Jackson sought admission into the college's School of Romance Languages.	In an effort to save tin—a commodity that would prove valuable for the making of war machinery—the Glass Container Association of America announces it will introduce glass beer bottles to replace the present widespread use of cans. . . . The National Munitions Control Board and Secretary of State Cordell Hull meet to discuss the country's self-defense plans in case of attack. It is a meeting ordered by President Roosevelt.		Mastodon bones have been uncovered in Indiana, according to Dr. Walter Granger, fossil curator of the American Museum of Natural History.	The 48 states will be given an option shortly to decide on whether or not they want to legalize a lottery in their state. Lotteries may only be legal if conducted under the auspices of—and beneficial to—charitable institutions, such as hospitals or schools.	Sept. 19
The deadline nears for an agreement between the United Mine Workers and bituminous coal operators. Talks have been going on since February, making this the longest collective bargaining period in American trade-union history. The contract is set to expire at midnight in two days.	Postmaster General James A. Farley willingly accepts the Republicans' challenge to make the New Deal the campaign issue.	U.S. Chamber of Commerce board members submit a referendum to 1,500 member organizations—representing some 750,000 individual businessmen—asking for the distribution of a poll asking their honest opinions of New Deal legislation under President Roosevelt.	The American Association for the Advancement of Science claims that air treated with ultraviolet light becomes germ free.		Sept. 20
Chairman Joseph P. Kennedy of the Securities and Exchange Commission resigns from his position. . . . The University of Wisconsin is once again suspected of professing Communism. A state senate committee claims that "Communistic teachings (are) encouraged."		Renewed wage contracts are signed by a pair of steamship lines—the Oriole and Yankee companies—with the American Radio Telegraphists Association allowing increased pay to radio operators.			Sept. 21
When asked by the Republican Party to be a presidential candidate in 1936, Henry Ford declines. He states, "I do not believe the political campaign of next year will have any appreciable effect on business."		Opening the country's annual Mobilization for Human Needs Conference in Washington, D.C., President Roosevelt delivers an address on charitable giving. The aim of the two-day conference is to raise private charity funds for the coming winter.		H.G. Wells is collaborating with Hollywood writers on cinematic versions of some of his novels.	Sept. 22

F	G	H	I	J
Includes elections, federal-state relations, civil rights and liberties, crime, the judiciary, education, healthcare, poverty, urban affairs, and population.	Includes formation and debate of U.S. foreign and defense policies, veterans affairs, and defense spending. (Relations with specific foreign countries are usually found under the region concerned.)	Includes business, labor, agriculture, taxation, transportation, consumer affairs, monetary and fiscal policy, natural resources, pollution, and accidents.	Includes worldwide scientific, medical, and technological developments, natural phenomena, U.S. weather, and natural disasters.	Includes the arts, religion, scholarship, communications media, sports, entertainment, fashions, fads, and social life.

	World Affairs	Europe	Africa & The Middle East	The Americas	Asia & The Pacific
Sept. 23			Emperor Haile Selassie's army has grown to 1.7 million men in preparation for a possible Italian invasion.		
Sept. 24					
Sept. 25		As far as diplomat Frank B. Kellogg is concerned, war in Europe is "inconceivable." Kellogg is the former secretary of state and framer of the Kellogg-Briand Peace Pact.			Admiral Isamu Takesita, on a visit to America, declares that Japan and America share the desire to halt the spread of Communism.
Sept. 26			Egypt, having allied itself with Ethiopia, prepares to incarcerate all Italian soldiers taken in a shooting war. Details for detention are sparse and kept secret by Egypt's Public Security Department. . . . Once again, Ethiopia's Haile Selassie asks America for support against Italy.		
Sept. 27		Former mayor of New York George B. McClellan returns from a trip abroad and surprises many by defending Premier Mussolini's aggressive policies. He says Italy's two greatest accusers, the United States and Britain, are both in no position to judge.			The League of Nations debates China's request for a seat on the Council. Since Japan withdrew recently, there is no representation from the Far East.
Sept. 28		Germany issues a call for 20- and 21-year-old males to appear in any one of certain "garrison towns" for formal military training.		President Lázaro Cárdenas of Mexico tells his congress that he wants to see the establishment of higher learning revitalized—not available solely to the elite, but made available to the masses.	
Sept. 29		In Lithuania, the vote for local government in Memel returns 24 German delegates and only five Lithuanians.		A peace conference suggests that Paraguay and Bolivia release their prisoners of war as a means of ending the long-standing Chaco conflict.	
Sept. 30		Hungarian Premier Julius Goemboes makes a state visit to Berlin.			
Oct. 1		Dutch athletes decide to boycott the upcoming Olympics set in Berlin. . . . Anastasia Tschaikowsky, who claims she is the heiress of the Russian Czar Nicholas, is denied any part of the estate in a court ruling.			
Oct. 2					Japan refuses to hold naval talks with Britain. Japan states that it will not be limited in its sea power.
Oct. 3			Italian planes bomb the Ethiopian town of Adowa, which was the scene of an Italian defeat by Ethiopian tribesmen in the late 1800s. Ethiopia mobilizes its frontier forces. Emperor Selassie asks for "one heart" to repulse the invaders. According to the Emperor, 50,000 Italians have crossed the border.		Japanese warships converge at Swatow and Hankow, China.

A	B	C	D	E
Includes developments that affect more than one world region, international organizations, and important meetings of world leaders.	Includes all domestic and regional developments in Europe, including the Soviet Union.	Includes all domestic and regional developments in Africa and the Middle East.	Includes all domestic and regional developments in Latin America, the Caribbean, and Canada.	Includes all domestic and regional developments in Asian and Pacific nations (and colonies).

U.S. Politics & Social Issues	U.S. Foreign Policy & Defense	Economics & Great Depression	Science, Technology & Nature	Culture, Leisure & Lifestyle	
	Gen. Douglas MacArthur foresees America's Army transformed into a machine-gun rapid fighting force over the next five years. Its efficiency and striking power will be immense, he says.	More than 400,000 bituminous coal miners begin a strike in the Appalachians. The workers demand a raise in pay.	Soviet archaeologists find traces of a once well-populated settlement on the tundra of the Yamal Peninsula, near the Arctic Circle. The civilization that lived there, they say, seems to have been culturally developed. The expedition was funded by the Institute of Anthropology and Ethnography of the Soviet Academy of Sciences.		Sept. 23
	The National Munitions Board meets today to consider what is termed "munitions and implements of war" under the Neutrality Act. Chairing the session is the newly developed State Department Arms and Munitions Control Office.	Unless the current administration cuts expenses and curbs dangerous credit expansion, "the stage is set for a price rise surpassing that of the war years," explains Melvin T. Cooper, Harvard professor of marketing. He tells his audience, the Boston Conference on Retail Distribution, that such a scenario could result in a "disastrous wild boom."			Sept. 24
Seven thousand people gather in Madison Square Garden to protest Italian aggression in Ethiopia.		Former budget director Lewis W. Douglas calls the Roosevelt administration's spending program "irresponsible." Speaking to the American Mining meeting in Chicago, he claims that the present policy is destroying the currency and driving the middle class to "crucifixion."			Sept. 25
		Banker and economist Charles G. Dawes presents a method of determining when the Depression will end. He predicts December 12 will be the date.			Sept. 26
		Standard Gas files for bankruptcy after it is unable to refund $24.6 million worth of gold notes. It blames its state on "conditions in the money market."		The Chicago Cubs win their 14th National League pennant, a record unequaled by any other team in any league. They beat the St. Louis Cardinals, extending their winning streak to 21 games.	Sept. 27
			Borden's Farm Products Company announces a "silencing program" to take effect on early morning milk deliveries. Horses will be shod with rubber, and pneumatic tires with ball-bearing gears will replace the old-fashioned axle type.		Sept. 28
FBI chief J. Edgar Hoover tells the American people that his organization is stepping up its campaign against criminal rackets. The program is in conjunction with the Justice Department.				The American Automobile Association releases statistics that show 37 million people took vacations by motor car this year in 11 million automobiles. That figure is a gain of 15 percent over 1934.	Sept. 29
				The U.S. Safety Council reports that traffic fatalities are on the increase this year.	Sept. 30
		Christening the new Boulder Canyon Dam on the Colorado River in Nevada, President Roosevelt calls it a "splendid symbol" of what can be accomplished with New Deal work programs.			Oct. 1
	From the deck of the cruiser *Houston*, President Roosevelt watches the largest naval maneuvers in history, involving 129 ships.			The World Series opens with the Detroit Tigers facing the Chicago Cubs.	Oct. 2
				While deaths from typhoid and paratyphoid fever decreased by 3.4 percent in 1934, deaths from measles and whooping cough increased.	Oct. 3

F	G	H	I	J
Includes elections, federal-state relations, civil rights and liberties, crime, the judiciary, education, healthcare, poverty, urban affairs, and population.	Includes formation and debate of U.S. foreign and defense policies, veterans affairs, and defense spending. (Relations with specific foreign countries are usually found under the region concerned.)	Includes business, labor, agriculture, taxation, transportation, consumer affairs, monetary and fiscal policy, natural resources, pollution, and accidents.	Includes worldwide scientific, medical, and technological developments, natural phenomena, U.S. weather, and natural disasters.	Includes the arts, religion, scholarship, communications media, sports, entertainment, fashions, fads, and social life.

	World Affairs	Europe	Africa & The Middle East	The Americas	Asia & The Pacific
Oct. 4					
Oct. 5			Telegrams from Addis Ababa in Ethiopia confirm that Italian aircraft continue to bomb the country.	Guatemala and Japan reach a trade agreement. Japan promises to buy goods from Guatemala if it waives tariff surcharges.	
Oct. 6				A convention of teachers living and working in Cautia, Mexico, demands that the government take action to protect their lives after the murder of two teachers in the vicinity. Victims were professors Silvestre Gonzales and Gilberto Mendes, both found mutilated.	
Oct. 7			Envoys inform the Italian government that two particular towns in Ethiopia should not be bombed by air, since they contain a great number of foreigners. One is Addis Ababa, the other is Diredawa.... The League of Nations declares Italy the aggressor in the conflict.	Mexican demonstrators tear a Nazi flag from a German sympathizer's building in Mexico City. It is done in retaliation for the Third Reich's treatment of religion.	
Oct. 8					
Oct. 9	The League of Nations discusses non-military sanctions against Italy. Leading the dialogue are Britain and France.		British ships in the Mediterranean unload soldiers to the River Tana area to discourage Italian forces, which are cutting through Africa and nearing the British colony of Kenya. Britain affirms this deployment of ships is no sign of war, just a prevention of it.		
Oct. 10	The world's psychiatrists, despite their national backgrounds, agree that war is "insanity." Nearly 340 medical experts—representing 30 countries—meet in The Hague, Netherlands, to sign a pact against military conflict and the "psychosis" of war.	With the help of the Greek military, the royal party in Greece conducts a coup removing Premier Panayoti and his republicans to reestablish a monarchy. Marshal Kondylis remains Regent until the arrival of George II, waiting in London.	Many Italian troops in Ethiopia find the real enemy is the lack of water. The papers describe one force, Gen. Rodolfo Graziani's army, moving through the Ogaden province—existing well to well.	Under arbitration by presidents of six countries in the Americas, a new border is set between Paraguay and Bolivia. The agreement assigns most of the disputed Chaco territory to Paraguay, but provides Bolivia with an outlet to the sea via the Paraguay River.	
Oct. 11			The League of Nations proposes an embargo against Italy. Fifty-one countries sign and two, Austria and Hungary, abstain. The verdict reads: "The Italian government has resorted to war in disregard to...the League's covenant."		
Oct. 12				South America's trading relationships with Japan and Germany start fading, due to improved economic conditions. As a result, South America is now buying more from the United States, says R.C. Thompson, export manager of the Prest-O-Lite Battery Company. . . . Some South American countries refuse to agree to the League of Nations sanctions against Italy.	Japanese ships remain in Swatow Harbor, China. On shore, Chinese troops entrench along a front of 50 miles, from Swatow to Ungking.

A	B	C	D	E
Includes developments that affect more than one world region, international organizations, and important meetings of world leaders.	*Includes all domestic and regional developments in Europe, including the Soviet Union.*	*Includes all domestic and regional developments in Africa and the Middle East.*	*Includes all domestic and regional developments in Latin America, the Caribbean, and Canada.*	*Includes all domestic and regional developments in Asian and Pacific nations (and colonies).*

U.S. Politics & Social Issues	U.S. Foreign Policy & Defense	Economics & Great Depression	Science, Technology & Nature	Culture, Leisure & Lifestyle	
A Congressional party arrives in Honolulu for a two-week visit, which will be spent conducting open forums and private sessions throughout the Hawaiian Islands—all for the cause of deciding whether or not to recommend statehood. . . . Frank D. Whipp, warden of Joliet-Stateville Prison in Joliet, Ill., tenders his resignation one minute before a condemned man is to be electrocuted. Having officiated at five previous executions, he cannot bear another.	President Roosevelt names Newton D. Baker, former Secretary of War, as chairman of a committee to lead a "unified action" toward peace. He is to coordinate the various peace organizations in the country.	The cost of living has risen over last year, according to the Department of Labor.		Chicago's City Council is considering amending its clock-time so that it will be placed on daylight savings time all year round. Benefits would be many, among them that it will then be in the same time zone as the principal economic cities of the east, such as New York City.	Oct. 4
Alf Landon, governor of Kansas and a potential presidential candidate, opens the Republicans' "Spirit of '36" convention. He indicts the New Deal for its "careless" spending.			Scientists see many uses for stainless steel. The metal, hailed as the "wonder" of the ages, promises a new era in homemaking, described in the pamphlet released today by the Chemical Foundation, Inc.		Oct. 5
Federal agents bust a gang of narcotics dealers in New Orleans, seizing $75,600 worth of heroin. The 13 men taken into custody on the Harrison Act are believed to have been responsible for drug trafficking throughout the entire south.	The U.S. Naval Academy celebrates its 90th anniversary.				Oct. 6
Senator William E. Borah, one of the Republican Party's possible candidates for president, warns citizens of Boise, Idaho, that the United States must guard against the "subtle ways" of subversives, anarchists, and propagandists.		The nation's leading packers plead innocent to blanket charges of price fixing, sales apportionment, and competitive unfairness in the states of Alabama, Arkansas, Mississippi, Tennessee, and Texas. The Department of Agriculture's Secretary Henry Wallace hears the initial inquiries on the allegations today.		The Detroit Tigers beat the Chicago Cubs to win the World Series, four games to two.	Oct. 7
The American Arbitration Association forms a council to provide greater use of arbitration in insurance disputes. It promises to be a useful tool to both the industry and its clients.		President Roosevelt authorizes WPA projects in the amount of $1.9 billion, but estimators predict the actual amount approved will be more in the neighborhood of $1.1 billion.			Oct. 8
		The nation will be out of the Depression within six months, says Roger W. Babson, statistician and economist. He warns, however, that the upswing will bring a declining standard of living.			Oct. 9
Gangster Dutch Schultz, recently acquitted of tax evasion in New York, is rearrested on 11 charges of racketeering.		The Works Progress Administration is starting a $27 million program to relieve out-of-work actors, musicians, sculptors and other artists. . . . Because the New Deal reforms "fall short of going to the root of the problem," economist Ogden L. Mills suggests further banking structure reform. Mills, who was the secretary of the treasury under Herbert Hoover, fears a danger of economic collapse if things go unchanged.		George Gershwin's newest musical, Porgy and Bess, opens at the Alvin Theater in New York. Though fascinated with its musical score, critics are unsure whether to refer to it as a folk opera or musical drama.	Oct. 10
	Idaho Senator James P. Pope acknowledges in a newspaper article that the countries of Europe against war are hoping America joins in on a proposed trade embargo against Italy for its aggression in Ethiopia.				Oct. 11
An interstate anti-crime meeting in Trenton, N.J., adopts a resolution to endorse a nationwide fingerprinting program. It proposes that each state will have is own bureau of criminal identification and criminal intelligence department. Movies of police techniques will keep all member agencies informed of the latest techniques.	A group of New York-based exporters, shippers, manufacturers, and other concerns involved in overseas trade are planning to meet for the purpose of mapping out a trade program with friendly countries in the event of war. However, they ask President Roosevelt and Secretary of State Cordell Hull to reveal their neutrality plans, which so far have not been fully described to the American public.		Instances of radio-signal interference mystify scientists worldwide. Some attest that the high-frequency disturbances are caused by an unexplainable cosmic phenomenon. . . . Mrs. J. Norman Henry and daughter Josephine arrive home after a 1,200-mile journey on horseback from Philadelphia through British Columbia, where they collected 600 plant specimens for the Academy of Natural Sciences and other museums around the world.		Oct. 12

F	G	H	I	J
Includes elections, federal-state relations, civil rights and liberties, crime, the judiciary, education, healthcare, poverty, urban affairs, and population.	Includes formation and debate of U.S. foreign and defense policies, veterans affairs, and defense spending. (Relations with specific foreign countries are usually found under the region concerned.)	Includes business, labor, agriculture, taxation, transportation, consumer affairs, monetary and fiscal policy, natural resources, pollution, and accidents.	Includes worldwide scientific, medical, and technological developments, natural phenomena, U.S. weather, and natural disasters.	Includes the arts, religion, scholarship, communications media, sports, entertainment, fashions, fads, and social life.

	World Affairs	Europe	Africa & The Middle East	The Americas	Asia & The Pacific
Oct. 13					Japanese Special Foreign Office Representative Goro Morishima denies any aggressive policy toward China. He is in Shanghai to meet with fellow Japanese officials there to present Tokyo's perspective on the situation.
Oct. 14			Reports from Addis Ababa reveal that Ethiopian tribal chiefs are following their own private war strategies against the Italians, paying little attention to Emperor Haile Selassie's commands.		
Oct. 15	All materials used for war will be cut off from Italy, the League of Nations decides. The members of the economic sanction committee control production of most of those materials. The purpose of sanction is to prevent Italy from obtaining supplies to sustain a war against Ethiopia.		Mankale, Ethiopia, falls to the Italians.		George H. Dern, U.S. Secretary of War, and Edwin L. Neville, his Chargé d'Affaires, meet with Japanese Emperor Hirohito. The nature of the talk is secretive, but afterward Dern expresses to an Imperial audience that "President Roosevelt's good-neighbor policy is in force (regarding) Japan and other countries of the Far East."
Oct. 16		Two songwriters in Russia are sentenced to death for composing a song about "the downfall of the Soviet Union." The wandering minstrels had toured Kiev pastures, singing this song to anyone who would listen. . . . Lloyd's Register of Shipping says that Germany is the only country in the world whose shipbuilding efforts continue full-time.			
Oct. 17		The Ford Motor Company in Detroit, Mich., stops all shipments of vehicles to Italian Africa. . . . Italy accuses Britain of aggression for protecting its own territories in the Mediterranean. Italian press theorizes that Britain's real goal is Mussolini's downfall.			
Oct. 18		Paris is ready to stand by its pact to defend Britain in the event of war.			An article by British writer Oscar Parkes in the November issue of Scientific American comments that of all the navies in the world, Japan's ships show, "ton for ton," more useful design and practical, "all-round value than those of any other country."
Oct. 19		Italy agrees to withdraw some of its forces from Libya and pull back from the Egyptian border where England has interests. Britain thanks France for helping work out an agreement, even though it is not the full retreat desired.			The Cantonese, having lost northern China to the Japanese, express hope that the United States will intervene before southern China is lost too.
Oct. 20		Italy has been purchasing four different classes of products from the United States that are basic munitions supplies, says the U.S. Department of Commerce. Total exports have amounted to $4 million per year.			

A	B	C	D	E
Includes developments that affect more than one world region, international organizations, and important meetings of world leaders.	Includes all domestic and regional developments in Europe, including the Soviet Union.	Includes all domestic and regional developments in Africa and the Middle East.	Includes all domestic and regional developments in Latin America, the Caribbean, and Canada.	Includes all domestic and regional developments in Asian and Pacific nations (and colonies).

U.S. Politics & Social Issues	U.S. Foreign Policy & Defense	Economics & Great Depression	Science, Technology & Nature	Culture, Leisure & Lifestyle	
		Current food prices may have risen slightly, announces L.H. Bean, economic adviser for the Agricultural Adjustment Administration, but factory wages have increased.	To celebrate Air Navigation Week, United Airlines plans to fly one of its passenger planes from San Francisco, Calif., to Newark, N.J., overnight. They will follow the established air path designated by the U.S. Department of Commerce.		Oct. 13
					Oct. 14
First Lady Eleanor Roosevelt opens the Forum on Current Problems, which draws women from across the 48 states, as well as from foreign countries, to New York City. She speaks on "The American Woman's Place in the World Today."		According to the Bureau of Mines, Department of the Interior, stocks of domestic and foreign crude petroleum totaled 304.6 million barrels through the week of October 5; this is a decline of 455,000 barrels from the previous week, and indicative of the fluctuating production of the oil industry. . . . In September, new construction rose 134 percent over the same month in 1934.			Oct. 15
The Federal Trade Commission alleges that the California Packing Corporation, based in San Francisco, attempted to achieve a monopoly in interstate, coastal, and foreign trade.		In New York, Governor George Earle of Pennsylvania and former treasury secretary Ogden Mills debate the question of amending the Constitution to give the government more economic control. Their audience is 2,500 women delegates of the Herald Tribune Forum on Current Problems.		Pan-American's new *China Clipper* flying boat, which eclipses all cargo-carrying airplanes to date, flies two test circuits between Baltimore and New York City with press aboard.	Oct. 16
Republican Henry Breckenridge calls the Roosevelt administration "the first in all recorded history to go into partnership with drought to manufacture famine and call it a new deal." . . . Americans need to be more tolerant of other races and cultures: that is the theme of the speech by Dr. A.V. Kidder of the Carnegie Institute, which he presented to the Pan American Union today.	President Roosevelt emphasizes America's neutrality. He asks the country for patience and support to back up the government's policy. He believes it is for the best to keep out of foreign troubles.			The Golden Gate Bridge and its sister bridge spanning San Francisco Bay near completion.	Oct. 17
The American Federation of Labor's 55th Convention is spent in debate over the practicality of craft unionism (the belief that a union should be organized around its members' skills) and industrial unionism (that a union should be structured on an industry-wide basis).					Oct. 18
Al Capone, who was charged with income tax evasion and began an 11-year prison term in 1933, is given a further fine of $120,000. . . . Members of the Woman's Christian Temperance Union seek to make the nation's capital, the District of Columbia, "dry." Some 500 delegates sign the petition for such legislation at a Rochester, N.Y., convention.	After surveying American ships, the National Council of American Shipbuilders is amazed that many are still being employed; it states 90 percent of them are out of date. Council President H. Gerrish Smith says they are "rapidly approaching obsolescence."		The Rev. T. Emmett Reynolds, a Catholic priest, discovers remains of what is proposed as "the earliest mammal" in the San Juan Basin of New Mexico.		Oct. 19
The International Ladies Garment Workers Union declares that over the next year it will spend $100,000 on an employee education program. It is a broad program aimed at increasing the number of students taking basic training, applicable to their possible promotion. . . . The case against Bruno Hauptmann, already on death row for the kidnapping and murder of Charles Lindbergh's infant son, continues to grow. New Jersey prosecutors announce that nails in the ladder used to enter the Lindbergh home are found in a keg in Hauptmann's old home.		With the resignation of Gen. Hugh S. Johnson as the head of the NRA, Victor F. Ridder will now be responsible for keeping 220,000 relief workers employed.	Two doctors with the Rockefeller Institute announce that they have identified the influenza virus, up until now unidentifiable through a microscope.	The Detroit Tigers' Hank Greenberg wins this year's most valuable player award for the American League.	Oct. 20

F	**G**	**H**	**I**	**J**
Includes elections, federal-state relations, civil rights and liberties, crime, the judiciary, education, healthcare, poverty, urban affairs, and population.	*Includes formation and debate of U.S. foreign and defense policies, veterans affairs, and defense spending. (Relations with specific foreign countries are usually found under the region concerned.)*	*Includes business, labor, agriculture, taxation, transportation, consumer affairs, monetary and fiscal policy, natural resources, pollution, and accidents.*	*Includes worldwide scientific, medical, and technological developments, natural phenomena, U.S. weather, and natural disasters.*	*Includes the arts, religion, scholarship, communications media, sports, entertainment, fashions, fads, and social life.*

	World Affairs	Europe	Africa & The Middle East	The Americas	Asia & The Pacific
Oct. 21					
Oct. 22	The League of Nations in Geneva, Switzerland, awaits the U.S. decision on proposed sanctions against Italy.		Ethiopia's Haile Selassie denies rumors that Italian forces have been employing poisonous gases and dum-dum bullets on his country's people.	Argentina becomes the newest member of the World Court, with formal induction ceremonies being held today.	
Oct. 23		Spain's Foreign Ministry warns Paramount Pictures' head office that if the movie called *The Devil is a Woman*, starring Marlene Dietrich and Cesar Romero, is not removed from theaters, Spain will ban all Paramount productions. The movie negatively portrays Spanish policemen.			Japan announces that it might participate in the upcoming London Naval Conference.
Oct. 24		Italian Premier Benito Mussolini places all media outlets under state control.	Italy withdraws from Libyan soil, a conciliatory action that Italian Premier Mussolini hopes will appease the British.		
Oct. 25		The German government announces that the names of all Jewish soldiers who fell in battle during the World War will be removed from all war monuments.			Japan and China continue to skirmish on the Mongolian-Manchurian border.
Oct. 26					
Oct. 27		Word comes from Paris that France's Air Ministry is keeping its naval base at Berre on the Mediterranean.	Observers report that Haile Selassie's army continues to fight despite being outmanned and outgunned by Italian forces.	"Social education" in Mexico—though opposed by the dominant Catholic Church—has the support of the population as shown by attendance figures, states Minister Rafael Molina Betancourt.	
Oct. 28		England's Prime Minister Stanley Baldwin broadcasts a correction to a controversial statement he made a few days earlier, which had led many to believe that Britain was establishing a naval blockade around Italy.			
Oct. 29		Premier Benito Mussolini of Italy celebrates the 14th anniversary of his rule.			Japan, which withdrew from the League of Nations several weeks ago, now argues that it still has the same mandating rights as a League member.
Oct. 30		Women in Italy are going door to door gathering signatures and comments to send to the League of Nations in protest of the trade embargo imposed on Italy.			
Oct. 31		In a speech at the University of Rome, Benito Mussolini states that Italy shall not buckle under the League of Nations sanctions. . . . The League of Nations Coordination Committee prepares to impose tougher sanctions against Italy if it does not exit Ethiopia.		The Dominican Republic unveils its first phone system today; Secretary of State Cordell Hull makes the first call from Washington, D.C.	

A	B	C	D	E
Includes developments that affect more than one world region, international organizations, and important meetings of world leaders.	*Includes all domestic and regional developments in Europe, including the Soviet Union.*	*Includes all domestic and regional developments in Africa and the Middle East.*	*Includes all domestic and regional developments in Latin America, the Caribbean, and Canada.*	*Includes all domestic and regional developments in Asian and Pacific nations (and colonies).*

U.S. Politics & Social Issues	U.S. Foreign Policy & Defense	Economics & Great Depression	Science, Technology & Nature	Culture, Leisure & Lifestyle	
Some 450 members of the Cenacle Giuditta Guild, an organization of young women of Catholic-Italian descent, meet in New York to urge action against anti-Catholic teachings. . . . An irate Jeremiah T. Mahoney, former New York Supreme Court justice, demands that the United States boycott the Berlin Olympics.		"There is an earnest desire to continue the fundamental principles involved in the National Industrial Recovery Act," writes Commerce Secretary Daniel C. Roper in a newspaper article which supports wide business approval of the NRA.	General Electric Laboratories in Schenectady, N.Y., hosts a day of research education for corporate and financial executives. Under the auspices of the National Research Council, it demonstrates scientific advances that have been made during the Depression.		Oct. 21
			The Rockefeller Institute of America gives $60,000 to London's National Hospital, the world's leading center for research and treatment of nervous diseases.	National Boxing Association featherweight Freddie Miller retains his title in a decision over Vernon Cormier.	Oct. 22
Dutch Schultz is shot in a New Jersey diner along with four of his cohorts. Schultz is in grave condition with bullet wounds to his stomach.	Isolationist Senator Gerald Nye from South Dakota, orating in Atlantic City, questions President Roosevelt's neutrality policy. He wants to know why a group of Civilian Conservation Corpsmen is upgrading the water supply and roads for Camp Pike, a central military establishment in Arkansas.				Oct. 23
Dutch Schultz dies in a New York hospital. . . . The International Labor Office in Geneva opts to put on its June conference agenda a debate on a 40-hour week for the textile industry. Many in the Roosevelt administration support the move.	U.S. isolation is a "dead hope," according to Prof. Arthur Newell, holder of the first Bryce Fellowship for promoting Anglo-American understanding. Neutrality is not possible in these times, he tells the American Chamber of Commerce meeting in London.	The tin industry's output increases by almost 15 percent this year; world consumption is 90,910 tons since December 1934.			Oct. 24
	Prime Minister of Nova Scotia Angus Lewis MacDonald, speaking today in Canada, reminds the United States and his own country they both have a duty—and an opportunity—to resist and defeat dictatorial powers in the world.	The Works Progress Administration hires an advisory committee comprised of well-known musicians to help provide jobs for artists. Hired musicians will get $75 to $94 per month.			Oct. 25
	President Roosevelt states there is a need to keep on par with the other nations' defenses. He asks for a Navy "commensurate with the country's needs, interests, and responsibilities."			America has won more aviation honors than any other country. Unofficial records released today indicate that the United States leads with 47 records, with France holding 38.	Oct. 26
		Chemical makers are among the busiest of U.S. industries, demonstrating an increase in production over the recent year. According to executives in domestic companies, chemical corporations plan some $50 million in improvements over the next several months.			Oct. 27
		Editors of the economic magazine Guaranty Survey see the immediate economic outlook in the United States as "fairly favorable." They cite this year's continuing stability.			Oct. 28
		The government retracts its threat to the 3,500 employees of the Emergency Relief Board who staged a walkout last week to protest recent layoffs in the organization. At first, they were informed that they may lose their seniority rights; now they are told that the government is reconsidering the move.	Thousands of doctors, surgeons, and health workers from across the United States and Canada gather for the five-day American College of Surgeons Clinical Congress in San Francisco.		Oct. 29
		President Roosevelt announces that current industrial production is at 90 percent of what it was before the Depression, but, in contrast, employment is only at 82 percent.			Oct. 30
Two suspects are detained for questioning in the murder of Dutch Schultz and his cohorts at the Chop House diner in New Jersey.		The one millionth auto produced by the Ford Motor Company this year rolls off the assembly line.	A Boeing B-17 crashes when its engines fail after takeoff. One crewman is killed and four others are injured. An official inquiry into the accident is opened.		Oct. 31

F	G	H	I	J
Includes elections, federal-state relations, civil rights and liberties, crime, the judiciary, education, healthcare, poverty, urban affairs, and population.	Includes formation and debate of U.S. foreign and defense policies, veterans affairs, and defense spending. (Relations with specific foreign countries are usually found under the region concerned.)	Includes business, labor, agriculture, taxation, transportation, consumer affairs, monetary and fiscal policy, natural resources, pollution, and accidents.	Includes worldwide scientific, medical, and technological developments, natural phenomena, U.S. weather, and natural disasters.	Includes the arts, religion, scholarship, communications media, sports, entertainment, fashions, fads, and social life.

	World Affairs	Europe	Africa & The Middle East	The Americas	Asia & The Pacific
Nov. 1				Mediators claim that a peace agreement has finally been reached in the Chaco area between Paraguay and Bolivia. Many in both governments predict more fighting to come.	Premier Wang Ching-wei and three Chinese officials are shot in Nanking by an assassin who himself is killed by government bodyguards. The nationalist leaders were on hand to discuss the latest Japanese demands for non-Japanese activities in northern China.
Nov. 2	The League of Nations sanctions committee states that Italy has until November 18 to withdraw from Ethiopia or face stiff sanctions.				British economists are concerned over millions of pounds invested in China's railroads and other enterprises. The Bank of England appoints a bargaining committee to keep an eye on those investments.
Nov. 3	According to Dr. Nicholas Murray Butler of the Carnegie Endowment for International Peace, the world is experiencing a conflict between economic aspirations and political principles.	Almost 98 percent of the Greek population votes for the restoration of the monarch, King George II. He had said that he did not want the kingdom if the people did not wish a monarchy. Observers doubt the legitimacy of the plebiscite.			Japan presses for the five provinces of northern China, which it currently occupies, to pull away from China to become a separate entity, allied with Manchukuo.
Nov. 4				Chile announces today the opening of its airmail service, which will carry cargo back and forth between Santiago and Magallanes on the Straits of Magellan. . . . Ottawa, Canada, welcomes the capital's newest governor general, John Buchan, Baron Tweedsmuir, and his wife, Lady Tweedsmuir.	After China announces it is dropping silver as a currency and is distributing paper money instead, Japan expresses its distrust of the national monetary reorganization. Japan suggests that Britain has urged China to do this to upset the Japanese economy.
Nov. 5	Ethiopian Emperor Haile Selassie announces to the League of Nations that he is willing to discuss a peace settlement with Italy.				
Nov. 6					
Nov. 7	In a radio broadcast, Emperor Haile Selassie of Ethiopia begs the United States to back the sanction against Italy. In his speech, he thanks the many Americans who have sent letters of support.				
Nov. 8			Prof. Hugo Bergmann, a noted librarian and philosopher, is named rector of the Hebrew University of Jerusalem by the college senate.	Brazil refuses to support the sanctions against Italy proposed by the League of Nations.	
Nov. 9		According to Finance Minister Marcel Regnier of France, his country's economic and financial situation is "encouraging, without being optimistic."		Canada's Premier W.L. Mackenzie King and U.S. President Franklin Roosevelt agree to a reciprocal trade agreement.	Thirty thousand Japanese soldiers participate in war maneuvers. Observers worry this is an overture to Japan's invasion of southern China.
Nov. 10					

A	B	C	D	E
Includes developments that affect more than one world region, international organizations, and important meetings of world leaders.	*Includes all domestic and regional developments in Europe, including the Soviet Union.*	*Includes all domestic and regional developments in Africa and the Middle East.*	*Includes all domestic and regional developments in Latin America, the Caribbean, and Canada.*	*Includes all domestic and regional developments in Asian and Pacific nations (and colonies).*

U.S. Politics & Social Issues	U.S. Foreign Policy & Defense	Economics & Great Depression	Science, Technology & Nature	Culture, Leisure & Lifestyle	
The University of California's president, Robert Sproul, reminds the American College of Surgeons at their meeting in San Francisco that medicine and medicinal services should be equalized in the United States.				Cincinnati University is given songwriter Stephen Foster's memorabilia by the Foster estate to exhibit.	Nov. 1
		Should the Works Progress Administration not meet its goal of 396,000 people returned to work in New York, the state's Temporary Emergency Relief Administrator promises to meet with federal administrators to get the excess unemployed on other work projects.			Nov. 2
Democrats seem to be holding tightly onto most of America, with the Republicans making some headway, reports the Democratic Party Organization. Hope for third-party success in the Electoral College looks like an impossibility.				The American Automobile Association estimates that by the end of the year 11 million cars will have carried 37 million Americans across 400 million miles.	Nov. 3
			A hurricane strikes Florida. Three are dead, and 64 are injured.	The 1815 battlefield of Chalmette, where Andrew Jackson defeated the British along the Mississippi in New Orleans, will become a national park, according to a statement from Washington.	Nov. 4
The city of Cleveland ousts Democratic Mayor Ray Miller for Republican Harold H. Burton. The Republicans rejoice, comparing it to a Republican victory in the presidential elections in 1936.		Guests of the American Automobile Association's export committee, nearly 200 foreign consuls, tour the annual automobile show in New York. The association says it expects to build 4 million cars in the United States next year.			Nov. 5
Philadelphia's Democratic Mayor Kelly concedes to his Republican challenger, who won by 47,500 votes.		The price of world cotton gains 11 percent. The Washington Bureau forecasts a crop of 26.3 million bales by year's end.			Nov. 6
	Admiral William H. Standley defends President Roosevelt's naval policy against pacifist groups in the nation. His speech attacks "all subversive influences tending to destroy the national defense."	The rayon industry foresees an output of more than one billion pounds by the end of December 1935.		Author James Hilton (Goodbye Mr. Chips, Lost Horizon) arrives in the United States to begin his next novel. He tells reporters he is surprised by the popularity of his works.	Nov. 7
			The geophone, a new device for exploring the ocean floor, adds much possibility to projects initiated by scientists and oceanographers to study the earth's contour. Reading the shape of the ocean floor through scans, the machine helps researchers immensely, explains Prof. Richard Field of Princeton University.		Nov. 8
In a frank address to 400 Democrats in New Haven, Conn., Postmaster General James A. Farley alleges that many Connecticut businesses—all part of an organized effort—are trying to coerce their employees into voting against the New Deal and President Roosevelt.	President Roosevelt, on the 17th anniversary of the armistice that ended the World War, asks the world to join the United States in banning all future wars.	In a speech to 5,000 New Jersey teachers, the president of Rutgers University, Dr. Robert C. Clothier, opposes the Roosevelt administration's economic policies, which he refers to as "visions—beautiful but wholly without substance."			Nov. 9
Mrs. Daniel O'Day pushes a referendum that, if passed, would shift the power of declaring war away from the President to American citizens. O'Day is a representative-at-large from New York. . . . The American Legion central office dismisses its legislative officer of 14 years, Edward McIlheney Lewis, because of his objection to a national Legion drive to reclaim pensions for veterans' widows. William Barnes is named to succeed him.	Nobel Laureate and Columbia University president Nicholas Murray Butler asks for the United States to assume the leadership in the world's quest for peace. Dr. Butler is one of the framers of the Kellogg-Briand Peace Pact.	The National Youth Administration's executive director, Aubrey Williams, announces a plan to give $1.6 million in aid monthly to 104,501 needy undergraduates in 1,602 colleges and to 4,500 graduate students in 177 colleges.			Nov. 10

F	G	H	I	J
Includes elections, federal-state relations, civil rights and liberties, crime, the judiciary, education, healthcare, poverty, urban affairs, and population.	Includes formation and debate of U.S. foreign and defense policies, veterans affairs, and defense spending. (Relations with specific foreign countries are usually found under the region concerned.)	Includes business, labor, agriculture, taxation, transportation, consumer affairs, monetary and fiscal policy, natural resources, pollution, and accidents.	Includes worldwide scientific, medical, and technological developments, natural phenomena, U.S. weather, and natural disasters.	Includes the arts, religion, scholarship, communications media, sports, entertainment, fashions, fads, and social life.

	World Affairs	Europe	Africa & The Middle East	The Americas	Asia & The Pacific
Nov. 11					
Nov. 12				Mexico's airline, Aerovias Centrales, ceases flights until it can, by government order, hire only Mexican pilots.	
Nov. 13		The Nazi press releases a story coming from Frankfurt-am-Main, which states that some Aryan youths, unable to find employment elsewhere, were forced to serve as "kitchen maids" for certain Jewish households.	Cairo, Egypt, becomes the scene of anti-British rioting staged by thousands of students who regard this day, "National Independence Day," a sham as long as Egypt remains a colony of Great Britain.		Tokyo informs the press that it has rounded up 88 members of a secret terrorist group whom they refer to as an "anarchist Communist party."
Nov. 14		Greek monarch George II, who has been in exile in London for 11 years, leaves Britain today for his homeland. Through the help of royalists in his country, he has regained the throne.			
Nov. 15		Conservatives in England hold onto the government for another five years. They took 70 percent of the 31 million votes cast today.		A new Reciprocal Trade Agreement between the United States and Canada will lower some import fees on liquor crossing the border from Canada. Protests are expected.	President Roosevelt formally signs a certificate giving the Philippine Islands their freedom as a Commonwealth; the proclamation also recognizes Philippine leaders as those elected in a free ballot in September.
Nov. 16	Martin Wronsky, director of Deutsche Lufthansa Airlines, says he is confused by the competition rampant among countries vying for the North Atlantic airmail service; rather, he urges international cooperation.	Berlin decrees a new law forbidding Germans to marry into Jewish families.	Cairo's streets erupt with student riots when anti-British demonstrations take place outside the Higher School of Arabic and Religious Studies.	Cuba's Army Intelligence Unit alleges a plot to poison Havana City aqueducts and detains Andres Rey Rodriguez, a Spaniard, as one of the conspirators.	
Nov. 17	Premier Benito Mussolini announces that Italy will resist sanctions imposed by 51 countries belonging to the League of Nations.				
Nov. 18	Italy refuses to withdraw from Ethiopia by the deadline set by the League of Nations.			Panama initiates a public works administration to deal with its unemployment.... Seeing the new reciprocal trade agreement with Canada as "injurious" to the United States, the agricultural-minded National Grange in California calls upon the Roosevelt administration to rescind the agreement.	
Nov. 19		Learning the outcome of the recent British parliamentarian elections, Germany announces a campaign against the inclusion of Cabinet member Winston Churchill, who is noted for his dramatic anti-Nazi position.		Argentina is paying its old debts, according to Minister of Finance Dr. Federico Pinedo. He claims the country's cash status is solid and that obligations to creditors are being discharged "faithfully and promptly."	Philippine President Manuel Quezon announces a conscription plan, providing 500,000 reservists to defend the islands.
Nov. 20	World production rose sharply throughout the month of September, but not without prices rising along with it—notably in international foodstuffs and raw materials—according to the National Industrial Conference Board.	Angry coal miners in Britain vote 409,000–29,000 to strike against unfair wages and practices. The walkout is not immediate but threatened soon should the situation not improve.	The first shipment of medical supplies and equipment reaches Ethiopian war zones from Red Cross distributors.		
	A Includes developments that affect more than one world region, international organizations, and important meetings of world leaders.	**B** Includes all domestic and regional developments in Europe, including the Soviet Union.	**C** Includes all domestic and regional developments in Africa and the Middle East.	**D** Includes all domestic and regional developments in Latin America, the Caribbean, and Canada.	**E** Includes all domestic and regional developments in Asian and Pacific nations (and colonies).

U.S. Politics & Social Issues	U.S. Foreign Policy & Defense	Economics & Great Depression	Science, Technology & Nature	Culture, Leisure & Lifestyle	
Labor and fraternal organizations across the country pledge their aid to Jews escaping Nazi Germany.	Gen. John J. Pershing, U.S. Commander of all American Forces during the Word War, speaking on a special NBC Radio broadcast, says that he believes all American youths should be indoctrinated in the ways of world peace, fair competition, and good sportsmanship.			President Roosevelt opens the annual Red Cross Roll Call by stressing the "utmost importance" of the organization as a national relief agency.	Nov. 11
One of the most outspoken opponents of the anti-sedition law—which requires all teachers to take a special oath of allegiance to the Constitution—is Bernard S. Deutsch, New York's president of the Board of Aldermen. He tells the World Alliance for International Friendship that such a law is an insult to American ideals.		Efficient shipping is the key to efficient trade, remarks Major E.M. Markham, engineer chief for the War Department.	Two Army pilots fly a balloon to an altitude of 74,000 feet, or 14 miles. The balloon is the first ever to reach such a height.		Nov. 12
Attendees at the American Bankers Association meeting in New Orleans, after declaring that the federal budget sorely needs to be balanced, elect Salt Lake City banker Orval W. Adams as a second vice president of their organization.			Soviet Russia is buying Cambridge University's giant generator of magnetic fields and related equipment installed in the Mond Laboratory.	A rash of football-related deaths and accidents this year are blamed on lack of professional supervision and medical care. Professionals cite the need for stricter regulations.	Nov. 13
Father Richard J. Quinlan, supervisor of schools for the Archdiocese of Boston, tells educators and parents at the National Educational Association conference that children's "school life" should not be made too easy.		Wool consumption has risen 254 percent this month over November 1934, for a total of 29 million pounds.			Nov. 14
Georgia National Guardsmen prevent the lynching of John Henry Sloan in the town of Moultrie. Sloan is accused of slaying a white man. . . . According to polls, many Kansas Democrats are switching party allegiance to back their governor, Republican Alf M. Landon, as candidate for president in 1936. His strength lies in the fact that Kansas has remained economically sound during other states' rough years.	Retired Rear Admiral George H. Rock pushes President Roosevelt's program to federally aid the merchant marine organization. Rock, president of the Society of Naval Architects and Marine Engineers, calls the merchant marine a part of America's defenses.	The only way to avoid oncoming inflation is to balance the budget, advises Lewis W. Douglas, former budget director.			Nov. 15
	Illustrating his thoughts on the defense of America, Brig. Gen. Charles H. Sherrill points to the key elements of foreign policy contained in the Monroe Doctrine. Sherrill is a member of the 1936 Olympic Committee.	Answering the Republicans whose prescription for a better economy is a "balanced budget," Arthur E. Morgan, Tennessee Valley Authority chairman, says that the federal government's first responsibility is providing its citizens with employment—and bearing the brunt of the cost.			Nov. 16
To emphasize the impact of racketeering on legitimate businesses, FBI Director J. Edgar Hoover points to the late Dutch Schultz's illegal income—an estimated $827,253 in six weeks, which comes to $6 million per year. Hoover calls such numbers the "leech of racketeering."		A report released by the Department of Commerce states that U.S. production, including agriculture, sank to $26 billion between 1930 and 1934. . . . Republican National Committee Chairman Henry P. Fletcher scoffs at the notion that President Roosevelt's policies have been the cure-all of the U.S. economy. He plans to "tell the facts based on the record."		The United States announces the laying of a series of hard-surfaced highways to extend along the south, from the Atlantic to the Pacific coasts. . . . The National Roadside Council is fighting to improve the aesthetics of America's highways by demolishing ugly, dilapidated roadsigns on major thoroughfares and country byways.	Nov. 17
Members of the merchant marine meet today in New York to discuss the possibility of moving from under the auspices of the Post Office Department to that of either the Commerce or Navy departments. The move would include some 1,500 leading steamship operators.	At a dinner honoring assorted delegations to the Philippine Islands, Senator William King of Utah pledges U.S. assistance in any attacks by foreign powers on the Philippines.	The Agricultural Adjustment Administration announces that $204.5 million has been spent on farm surpluses and, of that, $187.5 million has been recovered in cash or in commodities distributed to the unemployed.	Scientists discover "dynamos" in the top layers of the human brain, within the area considered the seat of highest intelligence. This discovery is announced at the National Academy of Science seminar in Charlottesville, Va.	A 64-page pamphlet published by the Committee on Fair Play in Sports explains the reasons why America should not participate in the upcoming Berlin Olympics.	Nov. 18
Women are being asked to purchase only clothing bearing the "consumer protection label" that indicates they have been manufactured under fair wage and hour standards. Running the campaign is the Coat and Suit Industry Recovery Board.		The Rev. H.E. Woolever, editor of the national Methodist press, calls upon the administration to send missionaries to the various Civilian Conservation Corps camps around the nation to curb the "drinking, gambling and other vices."		Culturally, America remains stagnant at "high school level," according to Dr. Arthur E. Morgan, president of Antioch College and president of the Tennessee Valley Authority. He blames the educational methods of the nation's colleges and universities.	Nov. 19
The Republican National Committee, run by Henry Fletcher, appoints 16 of the most vocal foes of Roosevelt's New Deal to raise funds for the oncoming Republican presidential campaign. Making up the list are prominent lawyers and industrialists.		Dun & Bradstreet, Inc., reports that the number of retail-business failures in the United States continues to decline.		Beach erosion has become critical in New Jersey, enough to warrant the attention of President Roosevelt and the National Emergency Council.	Nov. 20

F	G	H	I	J
Includes elections, federal-state relations, civil rights and liberties, crime, the judiciary, education, healthcare, poverty, urban affairs, and population.	*Includes formation and debate of U.S. foreign and defense policies, veterans affairs, and defense spending. (Relations with specific foreign countries are usually found under the region concerned.)*	*Includes business, labor, agriculture, taxation, transportation, consumer affairs, monetary and fiscal policy, natural resources, pollution, and accidents.*	*Includes worldwide scientific, medical, and technological developments, natural phenomena, U.S. weather, and natural disasters.*	*Includes the arts, religion, scholarship, communications media, sports, entertainment, fashions, fads, and social life.*

	World Affairs	Europe	Africa & The Middle East	The Americas	Asia & The Pacific
Nov. 21		Soviet Russia is nearly 100 percent Communistic, says Josef Stalin at the Stakhanoffite Conference in Moscow. He warns that anyone trying to interfere with the process leading from Socialism to Communism will be dealt with severely.			
Nov. 22		As a sign of resistance to the trade embargo, Italian Premier Benito Mussolini donates a bust of himself to be melted down for much-needed scrap metal.			China threatens war against Japan if the northern provinces secede. More than 100,000 Chinese troops wait along the Peiping-Hankow border.
Nov. 23	Tolerance and respect for human liberty are the main ingredients needed to safeguard against evil in the world, claims Dr. Everett R. Clinchy, director of the National Conference of Jews and Christians.	A circular disseminated by Archbishop Kaila of Finland urges prayer as the only means of calming the beast of war stirring in Ethiopia. Peace, he writes, is seriously threatened as a result of human sinfulness.	Ethiopian troops retake the towns of Anele and Gabradarre.		
Nov. 24		Germany announces that 80 percent of its Olympic "village" in Berlin is now complete, with 2,000 men working around the clock to complete the site.			
Nov. 25				A period of 60 days of martial law is proclaimed in Brazil by President Getulio Vargas after rebels attack the states of Pernambuco and Rio Grande do Norte.	
Nov. 26		Walter Schulze-Wechsungen, the Nazi party's propaganda chief for the bureaus of Berlin, Brandenburg, and Kurkmark, faces questioning on fiscal irregularities. He is relieved of his duties.			A large section of the eastern Hopei province in northern China proclaims its independence from China. It is designated the East Hopei Autonomous Council. The commissioner of the area says he will "work with Japan" while Japanese militias maintain order in the region.
Nov. 27					
Nov. 28				Brazilian forces quash revolts in Rio de Janeiro and elsewhere. About 138 people are killed and hundreds wounded.	New Zealand elections install a heavy percentage of Laborites, ousting many national government figures. The Labor Party takes 52 of 80 seats.
Nov. 29		Germany's Minister of the Interior Dr. Wilhelm Frick announces that all parents are expected to enroll their children in the Hitler Youth or some other Nazi organization. . . . Germany announces that all men from age 18–45 who are not already serving in the armed forces will enroll in the reserves.			

A	B	C	D	E
Includes developments that affect more than one world region, international organizations, and important meetings of world leaders.	Includes all domestic and regional developments in Europe, including the Soviet Union.	Includes all domestic and regional developments in Africa and the Middle East.	Includes all domestic and regional developments in Latin America, the Caribbean, and Canada.	Includes all domestic and regional developments in Asian and Pacific nations (and colonies).

U.S. Politics & Social Issues	U.S. Foreign Policy & Defense	Economics & Great Depression	Science, Technology & Nature	Culture, Leisure & Lifestyle	
Members of the Atlas Bag and Burlap Company in Brooklyn, N.Y., claim they were coerced into joining a union while, at the same time, discouraged from associating with the United Textile Workers.					Nov. 21
From Indianapolis, Chairman of the National Labor Relations Board Francis Beverley Biddle appeals to the "conscience of America" to assist 500,000 children in the United States and Canada who are in "serious need" of care and protection. He speaks to the Child Welfare League, a federation of 160 units spread throughout Canada and the United States.		President Roosevelt is trying to shift the blame elsewhere for the failures of his work-relief programs, the Republican Party accuses. He created a "mass of ludicrous projects initiated by the Works Progress Administration," they say.			Nov. 22
Upon hearing that the Republican Party may name former president Herbert Hoover to run against President Roosevelt, Postmaster General Farley quips, "You cannot beat somebody with nobody—and the Republican Party has nobody."		The Committee of Economic Recovery, Inc.—comprised of businessmen from across America—submits a plan to President Roosevelt for the construction of homes throughout the nation for 10 years with private capital handling most of the construction. The framers believe such a plan can hasten industry recovery.			Nov. 23
Carrie Chapman Catt, founder and honorary president of the League of Women Voters, schedules a Conference on the Cause and Cure of War to be held in Washington, D.C., in January.			The Radio Corporation of America and the National Broadcasting Corporation are working hard atop the Empire State Building to assemble the modern apparatus required to conduct an exhibition on television, scheduled for early 1936.		Nov. 24
According to the president of the United Licensed Officers Association, government-owned merchant vessels openly violate the country's navigation safety standards. Capt. John F. Milliken, therefore, suggests that Secretary of Commerce Daniel Roper "straighten out the government fleet" before disaster strikes.		The Democrats announce that nearly 250,000 jobless returned to work in private industry in October, earning $8.2 million in weekly payrolls.			Nov. 25
	The United States, by shipping gasoline to Italy, is prolonging the Ethiopian War, accuses Raymond Leslie Buell of the Foreign Policy Association.				Nov. 26
The Federal Bureau of Investigation reports that experiments with radio broadcasts around the country have proven very effective in rounding up wanted criminals. Because of the encouraging results, J. Edgar Hoover, the FBI director, proposes short-wave radio to update agents and provide bulletins.		A plan to relocate 1,000 southern farmers to a more prosperous climate is attacked by critics. The idea is a conception of Rexford G. Tugwell, head of the Resettlement Administration, a division of the U.S. Agriculture Department.		The last open-cockpit mail plane is removed from service in a ceremony in New York. Marines and opera singer Lily Pons participate in the festivities.	Nov. 27
		Industries enjoying government favors should give a little back by being required to adjust prices and production values to benefit the public "in the light of general welfare," Secretary of Agriculture Henry Wallace suggests. . . . Earnings for America's top 40 railroads rose 62 percent last month.			Nov. 28
President Roosevelt will not run again, predicts Melvin C. Eaton, chairman of the New York Republicans, stating, "That boy can't take it." . . . Chicago proclaims that all forms of major crime rates have plummeted, thanks to an ever-efficient police force and a now-honest criminal court system.				First Lady Eleanor Roosevelt's new children's book arrives at bookstands; it tells the tale of a young boy and girl visiting the capital.	Nov. 29

F	G	H	I	J
Includes elections, federal-state relations, civil rights and liberties, crime, the judiciary, education, healthcare, poverty, urban affairs, and population.	Includes formation and debate of U.S. foreign and defense policies, veterans affairs, and defense spending. (Relations with specific foreign countries are usually found under the region concerned.)	Includes business, labor, agriculture, taxation, transportation, consumer affairs, monetary and fiscal policy, natural resources, pollution, and accidents.	Includes worldwide scientific, medical, and technological developments, natural phenomena, U.S. weather, and natural disasters.	Includes the arts, religion, scholarship, communications media, sports, entertainment, fashions, fads, and social life.

	World Affairs	Europe	Africa & The Middle East	The Americas	Asia & The Pacific
Nov. 30				Mexico's President Lázaro Cárdenas appoints Edward Hay as Minister of Foreign Affairs. Hay was once the Minister of Communications and General Consul to Paris.	
Dec. 1	The International Broadcasting Union's semi-annual report states that one in 10 persons around the globe is a radio listener, which equates to an audience of 200 million people.	Italy's Premier Benito Mussolini announces 88 new war decrees—measures to be taken immediately to strengthen the military—including plans to become more aggressive in Ethiopia, where his troops are now engaged. . . . King George, newly reinstated on the throne of Greece, gives amnesty to 758 rebels imprisoned since March.	At their meeting in Cleveland, Ohio, members of the Zionist Women's Organization of America donate $75,000 toward the construction of the Rothschild Hadassah University Hospital in Palestine. The hospital, which will cost $700,000 in all, is a joint venture of Hadassah and the American-Jewish Physicians' Committee.		
Dec. 2		Italian Premier Benito Mussolini states that he shall never surrender to the pressure of the embargo—and that he would commit suicide first.			
Dec. 3					
Dec. 4					
Dec. 5	The League of Nations weighs the British suggestion of cutting Italy's communications with its own troops in Africa by means of naval power.				The English demand an explanation of Japan's conduct in China.
Dec. 6		British Foreign Secretary Sir Samuel Hoare says that the Ethiopian conflict cannot be resolved until Italy is given the chance to expand, whether it be in Africa or elsewhere.			
Dec. 7		France's Premier Pierre Laval and Britain's Foreign Secretary Sir Samuel Hoare meet at the Quai d'Orsay to "determine bases that might be proposed for a friendly settlement of the Italo-Ethiopia dispute."	An Italian aircraft bombs the town of Dessye in Ethiopia. Ethiopian Emperor Haile Selassie, who was in the village, escapes unharmed.	Puerto Rican trade has improved in 1935; Governor Blanton Winship's annual report credits foreign aid.	
Dec. 8		Washington announces that the Soviet Union has purchased $36.5 million worth of U.S. goods this year, more than double the amount of last year.			Gen. Chen Wu-fang, visiting the United States, says that China does not need foreign help to solve its problems.
Dec. 9		The Cabinet of Spanish Premier Joaquin Chapaprieta, resigns over a budget dispute.		A special task force meets in Canada's parliament today to begin tackling problems of rising unemployment, debt taxation, and needed revisions to the Commonwealth's constitution. The meeting is considered the most important legislative session since 1867.	Assemblyman Agaton Yaranon introduces what he feels is a necessary tax increase on the people of the Philippines—one that would make it possible to start a defense fund.
Dec. 10	The United States, Canada, Great Britain, and the Irish Free State agree on commercial aviation agreements between the four countries. . . . A peace proposal from France and England to end the strife between Italy and Ethiopia is ridiculed by various League of Nations members; they claim that because it gives half of Ethiopia to Italy it rewards aggression.				Roy W. Howard, chairman of Scripps-Howard newspapers, doubts that the Philippine Islands will ever be self-sufficient. He predicts that the U.S. Congress will have to permanently declare them a dependent Commonwealth rather than independent.

A	B	C	D	E
Includes developments that affect more than one world region, international organizations, and important meetings of world leaders.	*Includes all domestic and regional developments in Europe, including the Soviet Union.*	*Includes all domestic and regional developments in Africa and the Middle East.*	*Includes all domestic and regional developments in Latin America, the Caribbean, and Canada.*	*Includes all domestic and regional developments in Asian and Pacific nations (and colonies).*

U.S. Politics & Social Issues	U.S. Foreign Policy & Defense	Economics & Great Depression	Science, Technology & Nature	Culture, Leisure & Lifestyle	
According to a *Literary Digest* poll, 91,351 voters approve of President Roosevelt's policies, 115,736 do not. . . . Hundreds of members of the national Woman's Party gather in Columbus, Ohio, where a proposed equal rights amendment for women is topmost on the agenda.		Justice George H. Pratt, the secretary of the State Committee for Tax Limitations, berates the attendees at the State Conference of Mayors for their stand against limiting real estate taxes. Says Pratt, "Public officials are blind to economics."			Nov. 30
In Ohio, the National Woman's Party proposes that any laws discriminating against women or limiting their activities be withdrawn.	Calling for an increase in Navy personnel, Rear Admiral William D. Leahy, chief of the Bureau of Navigation, says that the entire force needs to be enlarged.	The Roosevelt administration announces that 3 million jobs were created in the last two years.	An archaeological dig in the ruins at Dura, near the Euphrates in Iraq, has unearthed an ancient synagogue. The excavation was conducted by teams from both Yale University and the French Academy of Inscriptions.		Dec. 1
		The Reconstruction Finance Corporation proposes a new rail system for the southwest.	President Roosevelt recommends a full-time science advisory board to make the most practical use of the nation's scientific resources. The President appoints Dr. Karl T. Compton, chairman of the American Association for the Advancement of Science, to lead the project.	A visiting Japanese emissary, Consul Gen. Renzo Sawada, gives a pair of memorial lanterns to the widow of Thomas Alva Edison in honor of her late husband's inventions.	Dec. 2
Mayor Fiorello LaGuardia of New York City urges a withdrawal from the 1936 Olympics in Germany.					Dec. 3
A slum-clearance project called New Houses, being piloted in New York by the government, is meeting with such success that President Roosevelt praises its results publicly. . . . An associate of the late senator Huey Long is indicted for tax evasion.		It is expected that President Roosevelt will recommend to Congress a $5 billion budget for the next year.			Dec. 4
Nelson Gaskill, former chairman of the Federal Trade Commission, explains that industry should go after a policy of "self rule," based on permissive legislation and not influenced and confined by bureaucracy.		General Motors Corporation's president, Alfred P. Sloan, Jr., tells the Congress of American Industry that the days of the Depression are history, to be replaced by "the healing influences of world economic recovery."		The Sigmund Romberg-Oscar Hammerstein musical *May Wine* opens on Broadway at the St. James Theater; it stars Laurence Schwab.	Dec. 5
More than three-quarters of trade and industrial groups do not want to see a return of the National Industrial Recovery Act, a Trade-Ways, Inc., survey reports.		Washington reports that the national debt is $30.5 billion, or the equivalent of every person living in the nation owing $240.	Scientists discover a brain fluid in human beings that is linked to high blood pressure.		Dec. 6
The Statistical Bulletin of the Metropolitan Life Insurance Company states that the United States has had a slight increase in the birth rate over last year. . . . Governor Eugene Talmadge of Georgia announces that he is considering running for president in 1936.		Speaking in Los Angeles to the California Banker's Association, president of the New York Stock Exchange Charles R. Gay reports that the Depression closed half of America's banks—30,000 in 1929, 15,000 now.	E.I. duPont de Nemours & Company wins the Chemical and Metallurgical Award for chemical engineering for mass-scale production of synthetic rubber.		Dec. 7
		The automobile industry continues to adhere to hours and wages set by the NRA, even though the Supreme Court invalidated the NRA six months ago.		Flooding in Houston, Tex., results in $1 million in damages.	Dec. 8
In what is considered to be his first speech for reelection, President Roosevelt speaks to 50,000 Georgians in Atlanta. He promotes his record of putting millions of Americans to work and promises more of a social and economic resurgence in the term ahead.	The United States asks for a 20 percent naval cut by all countries participating in a five-power naval conference in London. Japan and Britain are not convinced that such a cost would be best for their national security.			Journalist Walter Ligget, publisher of the *Midwest American*, is murdered by two unidentified assassins.	Dec. 9
		Some 175,000 new homes will be erected in 1936, Federal Housing Administrator Stewart MacDonald predicts.			Dec. 10

F	G	H	I	J
Includes elections, federal-state relations, civil rights and liberties, crime, the judiciary, education, healthcare, poverty, urban affairs, and population.	Includes formation and debate of U.S. foreign and defense policies, veterans affairs, and defense spending. (Relations with specific foreign countries are usually found under the region concerned.)	Includes business, labor, agriculture, taxation, transportation, consumer affairs, monetary and fiscal policy, natural resources, pollution, and accidents.	Includes worldwide scientific, medical, and technological developments, natural phenomena, U.S. weather, and natural disasters.	Includes the arts, religion, scholarship, communications media, sports, entertainment, fashions, fads, and social life.

	World Affairs	Europe	Africa & The Middle East	The Americas	Asia & The Pacific
Dec. 11		Nazi Finance Minister Lutz Schwerin von Krosigk warns his government against constructing too many monumental structures, because of the extreme expense. . . . Premier Benito Mussolini tells British and French envoys that he is studying their latest peace recommendations to end the war in Ethiopia.			
Dec. 12	At the London naval parley, Japan balks at the suggestion of a "common upper limit," which places a maximum on the quantity of ships allowed in fleets.			Because the toll-collection system at the Panama Canal is based on a complex tonnage chart, the canal's governor, Col. J.L. Schley, believes that as much as $3 million is being lost—or pocketed—by collectors. He recommends a simplified system.	
Dec. 13				Argentina's announcement that it will purchase all its growers' wheat stock at a current-rate price of 89.5 cents a bushel creates excitement on the stock market.	
Dec. 14					
Dec. 15					
Dec. 16	At the naval conference in London, Japanese representatives demand a navy as large as that of the United States or Britain. . . . World trade rose 2.5 percent, according to the National Industrial Board.				
Dec. 17				Brazil lifts the martial law that it declared two days ago.	
Dec. 18		Premier Benito Mussolini rejects the French-British peace proposal.		In explaining his country's wheat-trading strategy, Argentina's Minister of Agriculture, Luis Duhau, says that its intention was "not to create artificial price levels (but) simply to keep the farmer in business and secure for him a decent subsistence." . . . Brazil passes a law forbidding Communist party membership.	
Dec. 19			Lt. Col. Cyril Rocke denounces Ethiopia at New York's Athletic Club. In defending Italy, Rocke calls Ethiopia "most uncivilized." . . . The Ethiopians state that the French-British peace proposal offers too much to Italy.		Senator Key Pittman of Nevada, chairman of the U.S. Foreign Relations Committee, states that it is his belief that all of Japan's recent territorial moves in the Pacific are aimed at world domination.
Dec. 20	A professor from Harvard Law School, Manley Ottmer Hudson, is appointed to the World Court in Geneva. An author, attorney, and expert on the tribunal, Hudson succeeds the retiring Frank B. Kellogg. . . . The five-power naval conference in London recesses without results. The Japanese representative states that there will be no agreement short of parity.		Sir Samuel Hoare's speech in the House of Commons suggests his belief in an eventual independence for Egypt.		
Dec. 21		Czechoslovakia elects Dr. Eduard Benes as president; he succeeds his mentor, Dr. Thomas G. Masaryk.			

A	B	C	D	E
Includes developments that affect more than one world region, international organizations, and important meetings of world leaders.	Includes all domestic and regional developments in Europe, including the Soviet Union.	Includes all domestic and regional developments in Africa and the Middle East.	Includes all domestic and regional developments in Latin America, the Caribbean, and Canada.	Includes all domestic and regional developments in Asian and Pacific nations (and colonies).

U.S. Politics & Social Issues	U.S. Foreign Policy & Defense	Economics & Great Depression	Science, Technology & Nature	Culture, Leisure & Lifestyle	
		In Houston, Chase National Bank chairman Winthrop W. Aldrich condemns President Roosevelt's New Deal policies and foresees a mild economic revolution should they continue.... Including those on relief, there are still 11.7 million jobless people in the United States as of October 1935, announces the AFL.			Dec. 11
The mayor of Jersey City, Frank Hague, admonishes fellow Democrats for not rushing to their President's aid in the face of so much criticism from the Republican front.		The 25 biggest chain stores of the United States had collectively their biggest month of earnings in November this year, according to Hammons & Company's monthly compilation.		A reorganization of the Methodist religion—consolidating three sectors into one to create a single Methodist Church—is proposed by Rev. Harry Woolever, secretary of a joint commission representing all three branches. Once combined, the congregation would number more than 7 million.	Dec. 12
The National Association of Manufacturers urges industry to vote President Roosevelt out of office.... Preliminary figures indicate that Maine will go Republican in the 1936 presidential vote.	Russia, which owes the United States $30 million, will never pay, asserts Illinois Senator J. Hamilton Lewis.		Suspended animation, as a means to preserve humans for long periods of time, may become—according to Nobel physicist Dr. Alexis Carrel—"one of the realities of tomorrow."		Dec. 13
Take advantage of "the new trends in women's work" and help to create your own job is what Mrs. Chase Going Woodhouse, professor of economics at Connecticut College for Women, tells a roomful of women gathered at Hunter College, N.Y.				Football is not a commendable sport, proclaims Prof. Philip O. Badger, chairman of athletics for New York University. Its violent nature incites other bad habits, such as drinking.	Dec. 14
		Donald E. Montgomery of the Agricultural Adjustment Administration promises the Women's Conference Against the High Cost of Living that prices for food, particularly meats, will decrease by the summer.	A French aviator successfully pilots a flying boat over the Atlantic, from Paris to Southern Africa.	Detroit, which won the baseball World Series this year, now takes the football championship. The Detroit Lions top the New York Giants, 26–7.	Dec. 15
Herbert Hoover, speaking in St. Louis, demands that relief be removed from its centralized system and placed where it belongs, into a "voluntary spirit of human service."			Astronomer Henry Barton of Manhattan's Museum of Natural History suggests that the Star of Bethlehem, which guided the wise men to the Child Jesus, was actually a nova.	Sidney Kingsley's play *Dead End* opens on Broadway. . . . Pope Pius XI appoints 20 new Cardinals. Observers are surprised that he refrains from mentioning the war in Ethiopia.	Dec. 16
				A newspaper poll of sports correspondents chooses boxer Joe Louis as Top Athlete of 1935.	Dec. 17
A nationwide safe-driving campaign kicks off from the White House. Its focus is on preserving lives while state delegates are appointed to find out why the death toll on America's highways did not come down from last year.				Helen Wills Moody, winner of this year's Wimbledon championship, also won the nationwide press poll honor of Most Outstanding Woman Athlete of 1935.	Dec. 18
Kansas seems to be leaning toward President Roosevelt in early election polls. Roosevelt's farming programs have greatly helped farmers of the state.	Former ambassador to Turkey, Brig. Gen. Charles H. Sherrill, suggests that European countries may pay their debts to the United States by turning over their Caribbean colonies.			Professional sportsmen nationwide select the Detroit Tigers as the Most Valuable Sports Team of 1935. The Tigers won the major league baseball championship.	Dec. 19
Officials in Arizona and Utah are checking into rumors of a religious cult practicing polygamy in their states. Both states forbid the practice.		According to an announcement by the company, the 50,000 employees of the Standard Oil Company of New Jersey will soon be able to take advantage of a new thrift plan. The plan allows employees to supplement federal savings plans.			Dec. 20
A grand jury questions former heavyweight champion Jack Dempsey, now the owner of a popular New York restaurant, if he has ever been "shaken down" by the mob for protection. Dempsey is not a suspect, but the city rackets are; they have been known to go after popular eateries and other businesses.					Dec. 21

F	G	H	I	J
Includes elections, federal-state relations, civil rights and liberties, crime, the judiciary, education, healthcare, poverty, urban affairs, and population.	*Includes formation and debate of U.S. foreign and defense policies, veterans affairs, and defense spending. (Relations with specific foreign countries are usually found under the region concerned.)*	*Includes business, labor, agriculture, taxation, transportation, consumer affairs, monetary and fiscal policy, natural resources, pollution, and accidents.*	*Includes worldwide scientific, medical, and technological developments, natural phenomena, U.S. weather, and natural disasters.*	*Includes the arts, religion, scholarship, communications media, sports, entertainment, fashions, fads, and social life.*

	World Affairs	Europe	Africa & The Middle East	The Americas	Asia & The Pacific
Dec. 22		Anthony Eden has been named by London to succeed Sir Samuel Hoarse as British foreign minister. Eden is known to be anti-fascist.	A new Palestine Archaeological Museum is now open to the public. Director E.T. Richmond of the Palestine government's Department of Antiquities explains that the museum houses a rare collection of Jewish relics and tells the story of the Ten Civilizations of the Middle East.		
Dec. 23					Near Kure, Japan, the nation launches its newest aircraft carrier. Presiding over the occasion is Admiral of the Fleet, Prince Hiroyasu Fushimi.
Dec. 24					
Dec. 25		The National Union of Combatants, comprised of French war veterans, notifies President Pierre Laval that they stand against all future wars.			
Dec. 26					Japanese troops in China are on the alert after the Vice Minister of Railways for Tokyo, Tang Yu-jen, is assassinated in the French quarter of Shanghai.
Dec. 27				Mexican exports are up 17 percent and imports have increased 26 percent during the first nine months of this year. . . . Citing a rash of revolts, Uruguay severs ties with the Soviet Union.	
Dec. 28		Rumors claim that Germany is building a huge zeppelin named after former German president von Hindenburg.	High Commissioner Sir Arthur Grenfell Wauchope reports from Jerusalem that the Palestine Council is upset over the possible creation of a new governing board, worried that the local Arabs will try to assert their influence.		
Dec. 29		Pierre Laval, premier of France, narrowly wins reelection.			Japanese-Manchukuoan troops push farther into northern China, into the Chahar province, cutting access to Outer Mongolia.
Dec. 30	The High Commissioner for Refugees, James G. McDonald, resigns. He leaves behind a warning to the rest of the world: Beware Hitler.			Dictator Juan Vincente Gomez of Venezuela dies at age 78. During his reign he called himself *El Benemerito,* or "The Meritorious One."	
Dec. 31	Italian warplanes patrolling the Ethiopian border bomb a Swedish Red Cross ambulance. Anger is so intense in Stockholm that riots are feared.				

A	B	C	D	E
Includes developments that affect more than one world region, international organizations, and important meetings of world leaders.	Includes all domestic and regional developments in Europe, including the Soviet Union.	Includes all domestic and regional developments in Africa and the Middle East.	Includes all domestic and regional developments in Latin America, the Caribbean, and Canada.	Includes all domestic and regional developments in Asian and Pacific nations (and colonies).

U.S. Politics & Social Issues	U.S. Foreign Policy & Defense	Economics & Great Depression	Science, Technology & Nature	Culture, Leisure & Lifestyle	
Bruno Hauptmann, on New Jersey's death row, will participate in the Court of Pardons' final inquiry into the evidence presented against him. Even though the evidence is strong, Hauptmann swears his innocence in the murder of Charles Lindbergh's baby.		A Sherlock & Arnold, Inc., survey reports that sales of family automobiles increased in New York by 150 percent over the last month.		Radio stations vote for 1935's most memorable broadcasts. Some are the Joe Louis-Max Baer prizefight and the report of the U.S. Army's experimental stratosphere balloon, which carried two pilots 14 miles into the air.	Dec. 22
Cleveland wins the bid to host the Republican National Convention in 1936, winning out over Chicago and Kansas City.			After an epidemic of meningitis is found in Kiowa County, Okla., the state's health officer quarantines 30,000 residents in the affected area.	Charles Lindbergh and his family leave for England, where they have chosen to live. They cite pressure from the press and the safety of their second son as reasons for leaving the United States.	Dec. 23
		Current tax collections in the United States represent about 20 percent of the national income, according to the National Industrial Conference Board. Collections in 1935 have been, they say, a "substantially" larger percentage than in recent years, closer to the level of pre-Depression years.			Dec. 24
Given the success of President Roosevelt's Tennessee Valley Authority, which has brought employment and progress to the state, the Republicans decide not to direct their campaign attentions there.	Rep. George H. Tinkham of Massachusetts suggests that the United States abrogate the Kellogg-Briand Pact, which bans war as an instrument of national policy.			George White's *Scandals*, the popular Broadway theatrical revue that is constantly changing its show to lure new audiences, is the only show open on Christmas night.	Dec. 25
Philadelphia will host the Democratic Presidential Convention. Albert M. Greenfield, who chairs the town's Chamber of Commerce, reports that $80,000 of the expected $150,000 has been raised so far from businesses and private citizens.		Republicans accuse the Democrats of using New Deal funds to support their political machine.			Dec. 26
The National Guard is called by Governor Olson of Minnesota to prevent violence during a strike at the Strutwear Knitting Company factory following a riot.			Vitamin C in prescribed doses can prevent infantile paralysis, says the Society of American Bacteriologists.		Dec. 27
A plan by the Roosevelt administration calls for "12 little capitals" created across the country to facilitate cooperation between the federal government and the states.	The War Department states that recent maneuvers reveal that America suffers from a lack of working air bases, as well as an inadequate number of war planes.	The Farm Credit Administration reports that 6,400 farms have been seized by Federal Land Banks this year because of mortgage defaults. . . . According to Prof. Walter Kemmerer of Princeton University, the nation needs to slow down its rate of borrowing. He declares that the national public debt—some $30 billion —will double if the country is not careful.			Dec. 28
To date, the dressmakers' union, manufacturers, and wholesalers have been unable to agree on terms for a new agreement. A strike is threatened if an agreement is not reached by January 31.		A new workers' insurance bill, to be studied in the House next week, calls for an immediate appropriation of $5 million. Introducing the relief bill is Progressive Republican Senator Frazier of North Dakota.			Dec. 29
Presidential candidate Senator William E. Borah of Idaho announces a tour of the New York area in late January, when he plans to speak to the Kismet Temple in Brooklyn.		A recent report issued by the U.S. government states that of the $12.5 billion in taxable net income for 1934, only .001 percent of the returns were from annual family incomes of $1 million or more. Eighty-nine percent are under $5,000 annually.		*The Littlest Rebel*, starring Shirley Temple, opens in theaters. . . . Celebrated author and poet Rudyard Kipling turns 70 years old.	Dec. 30
For the first time in its 146 years of existence, the Supreme Court gets a press representative.					Dec. 31

F	G	H	I	J
Includes elections, federal-state relations, civil rights and liberties, crime, the judiciary, education, healthcare, poverty, urban affairs, and population.	*Includes formation and debate of U.S. foreign and defense policies, veterans affairs, and defense spending. (Relations with specific foreign countries are usually found under the region concerned.)*	*Includes business, labor, agriculture, taxation, transportation, consumer affairs, monetary and fiscal policy, natural resources, pollution, and accidents.*	*Includes worldwide scientific, medical, and technological developments, natural phenomena, U.S. weather, and natural disasters.*	*Includes the arts, religion, scholarship, communications media, sports, entertainment, fashions, fads, and social life.*